T4-AKQ-417

CHIEF CONTEMPORARY DRAMATISTS

TWENTY PLAYS FROM THE RECENT DRAMA
OF ENGLAND, IRELAND, AMERICA,
GERMANY, FRANCE, BELGIUM,
NORWAY, SWEDEN, AND RUSSIA

SELECTED AND EDITED BY

THOMAS H. DICKINSON

ASSOCIATE PROFESSOR OF ENGLISH
IN THE UNIVERSITY OF WISCONSIN

BOSTON NEW YORK CHICAGO SAN FRANCISCO
HOUGHTON MIFFLIN COMPANY
The Riverside Press Cambridge

SEVENTEENTH IMPRESSION

PRINTED IN THE U.S.A.

CONTENTS

INTRODUCTION

INTRODUCTION

THIS volume contains complete plays by Wilde, Pinero, Jones, Galsworthy, Barker, Yeats, Synge, Lady Gregory, Fitch, Moody, Thomas, MacKaye, Hauptmann, Sudermann, Brieux, Hervieu, Maeterlinck, Björnson, Strindberg, and Tchekhov. It has not been found possible to include plays by Barrie and Shaw, but as, in the opinion of the editor, they cannot be ignored in making a list of the chief contemporary dramatists, materials for the study of these writers have been included in the notes.

The term "Contemporary" as used in the title of this volume requires definition. The primary intention in the issuing of "Chief Contemporary Dramatists" has been to provide within reasonable compass a series of plays which would as nearly as possible represent the abiding achievements of the present dramatic era. Naturally there was required, if this representative character was to be secured, a better basis of choice than that provided by the accidental collocation of plays that may have got themselves written within a certain arbitrary period. Diligent study enforces the conviction that there is to be found in the drama of the last generation a unity that is little dependent upon the accidents of time, and finds expression in the living formula of the play itself. In other words, a dramatic movement of recent times has now so nearly reached a culmination that it provides its own basis for discrimination. This movement, roughly speaking, may be said to find its source in the work of Ibsen, and to be connected with him, either directly through the stress of his particular technique and interests, or indirectly through his renovating influence on the theater as a social and art instrument. There is here a unity that transcends that of dates. It remains to apply the principles of this unity to the selection of plays, and to find an acceptable term by which this unity may be denominated.

The term "Contemporary" is chosen to represent the unit underlying this era in the same way that the term "Elizabethan" is made to do service for the large mass of plays written during the reigns of Elizabeth, James, and Charles. This usage is to-day so well accepted that when one speaks of Elizabethan, he is known to refer not only to the years comprised in the reign of Elizabeth, but to the solid mass of historical connotation that attaches to that name. In the same way it is thought that the term "Contemporary" may serve as a convenient handle to denominate an era, not yet complete, though in all probability nearing maturity, in which there may be found all the signs of an inherent solidity. In the choice of plays there is a positive advantage in laying dependence upon the salient characteristics of a clearly defined movement rather than upon the chances of the output of a certain period. The characteristics by which the era of Ibsen is identified are mainly two: its adherence to the naturalistic tendency mellowed to the motives of the humanities; and, on the side of production and organization, a tendency toward the reorganization of the theater to a nearer alignment to the social terms of the age. These provide bases of inclusion and exclusion which make it possible to overlook many of the dilemmas of date. How serious these dilemmas are is seen in the fact that there are still being written excellent plays which belong to the time of Scribe; on the other hand, that there were written a generation ago plays which for subject-matter and technique attach themselves to the present period. That against the claims of chronology logic may be brought to bear to exclude the former, whereas the latter are admitted, will perhaps be granted. And this same logic may compel us to omit plays, now being written, which will be properly understood only in the light of the coming technique. Considerations of this kind would exclude Dumas *fils* and Augier, while they would admit Björnson and Strindberg who lived and wrote about the same time. They would admit Yeats and Synge, while excluding some very interesting newer playwrights of England and the Continent. In the work of Yeats, of Maeterlinck, of MacKaye, and of Tchekhov, is to be seen the tendency toward the newer movements of the theater that have followed and are opposed to naturalism. By considerations that have been suggested it has seemed best merely to suggest the dawn of these movements rather than to attempt prematurely to represent them.

Perhaps little complaint will be raised against the decision to omit Ibsen from the book. Ibsen has paid the price of the pioneer in aging more rapidly than some of his fellows. For this reason he is not, strictly speaking, a contemporary even in the broad sense in which that word is used in this book. Furthermore, though himself the source and exemplar of the movement, he cannot be represented by a single play. No fair view of Ibsen's place in the era would be presented in a collection which made Ibsen one of many. It is the editor's purpose, in omitting Ibsen from the book, only the more to emphasize his outstanding position in the drama of the age. Some will charge that there is an excess of serious plays in this book. It would, of course, have been possible to include many romantic and fanciful plays, but only at the expense of the surrender of principles. The way was closed to the inclusion of many plays of the lighter sort through the strongly marked characteristics of the era itself, which on the side of absolute achievement has been so fixed in type that few noteworthy plays have been written outside the type. These considerations, as well as the natural limitations upon the translation of verse plays, have made it necessary to exclude even those few verse dramatists who might justly claim a leading place among the playwrights of the time.

This is not the place for a discussion of the relative claims of writers and plays for inclusion in a book of Chief Contemporary Dramatists. Such a discussion can more appropriately follow rather than accompany an essay in choice such as the present. Though there are in this list many names which would receive almost unanimous approval, the editor is well aware that it is unlikely that his list would secure the unqualified assent of any expert. For support he can only refer back to the principles he has outlined and the known limitations upon perfection in matters of contemporary judgment. It is safe to say that no two lists made by different experts would ever be identical. With all the counsel that may be secured, and the editor has been free in requisition for advice and guidance, final responsibility comes back to an individual judgment, exercised within the limitations set by the compass of the book, the mandates of authors, and the terms of holders of copyrights. Some of these conditions it seems fair to indicate. In spite of the liberality of the conception from the publishers' point of view, the number of plays to be included was severely restricted. It is still the editor's belief that the state of dramatic art of the era under consideration can be substantially represented by twenty plays, though he is aware that on this point there are many who will take issue with him. Aside from the limitation of size, which is really a matter of principle rather than one of policy, there has been one respect in which the constitution of the book has somewhat bowed to expediency. Upon the presumption that the book is to serve English-speaking readers, the larger representation has been given to plays written in the English tongue. It may be noted that it has been found impracticable to include works of at least two playwrights who in other circumstances might have been represented; also that in a large number of cases, always indicated in the notes, the authors themselves selected the play to be included, and in some instances this selection amounted to a stipulation.

The editor has received assistance from so many men and women in America and abroad that it would be impossible to mention all. To the authors and their representatives, with whom correspondence has been held, acknowledgments are due for the uniform sympathy with which the project has been viewed from the first. To those who have generously given their assistance in the creation of this book the best courtesy he can render is to offer an anonymous gratitude that he may not seem to be seeking to share with others the burden of faults that belong only to the editor.

LADY WINDERMERE'S FAN

By OSCAR WILDE

DRAMATIS PERSONÆ

Lord Windermere

Lord Darlington

Lord Augustus Lorton

Mr. Cecil Graham

Mr. Dumby

Mr. Hopper

Parker, *butler*

Lady Windermere

The Duchess of Berwick

Lady Agatha Carlisle

Lady Plymdale

Lady Jedburgh

Lady Stutfield

Mrs. Cowper-Cowper

Mrs. Erlynne

Rosalie, *maid*

The Scenes of the Play

ACT I. Morning-Room in Lord Windermere's House

ACT II. Drawing-Room in Lord Windermere's House

ACT III. Lord Darlington's Rooms

ACT IV. Same as Act I

Time — The Present

Place — London

The action of the play takes place within twenty-four hours, beginning on a Tuesday afternoon at five o'clock, and ending the next day at 1.30 P.M.

LADY WINDERMERE'S FAN

ACT I

SCENE — *Morning-room of* LORD WINDER-MERE'S *house in Carlton House Terrace. Doors* C. *and* R. *Bureau with books and papers* R. *Sofa with small tea-table* L. *Window opening on to terrace* L. *Table* R.

LADY WINDERMERE *is at table* R. *Arranging roses in a blue bowl.*

[*Enter* PARKER.]

PARKER. Is your ladyship at home this afternoon?

LADY W. Yes — who has called?

PARKER. Lord Darlington, my lady.

LADY W. [*Hesitates for a moment.*] Show him up — and I 'm at home to any one who calls.

PARKER. Yes, my lady.   [*Exit* C.]

LADY W. It 's best for me to see him before to-night. I 'm glad he 's come.

[*Enter* PARKER C.]

PARKER. Lord Darlington.

[*Enter* LORD D. C. *Exit* PARKER.]

LORD D. How do you do, Lady Windermere?

LADY W. How do you do, Lord Darlington? No, I can't shake hands with you. My hands are all wet with these roses. Are n't they lovely? They came up from Selby this morning.

LORD D. They are quite perfect. [*Sees a fan lying on the table.*] And what a wonderful fan! May I look at it?

LADY W. Do. Pretty, is n't it! It 's got my name on it, and everything. I have only just seen it myself. It 's my husband's birth-day present to me. You know to-day is my birthday?

LORD D. No? Is it really?

LADY W. Yes; I 'm of age to-day. Quite an important day in my life, is n't it? That is why I am giving this party to-night. Do sit down.   [*Still arranging flowers.*]

LORD D. [*sitting down*]. I wish I had **known** it was your birthday, Lady Winder-

mere. I would have covered the whole street in front of your house with flowers to walk on. They are made for you.

[*A short pause.*]

LADY W. Lord Darlington, you annoyed me last night at the Foreign Office. I am afraid you are going to annoy me again.

LORD D. I, Lady Windermere?

[*Enter* PARKER *and* FOOTMAN C. *with tray and tea-things.*]

LADY W. Put it there, Parker. That will do. [*Wipes her hands with her pocket-hand-kerchief, goes to tea-table* L. *and sits down.*] Won't you come over, Lord Darlington?

[*Exit* PARKER C.]

LORD D. [*Takes chair and goes across* L. C.] I am quite miserable, Lady Windermere. You must tell me what I did.

[*Sits down at table* L.]

LADY W. Well, you kept paying me elaborate compliments the whole evening.

LORD D. [*smiling*]. Ah, nowadays we are all of us so hard up, that the only pleasant things to pay *are* compliments. They 're the only thing we *can* pay.

LADY W. [*shaking her head*]. No, I am talking very seriously. You must n't laugh, I am quite serious. I don't like compliments, and I don't see why a man should think he is pleasing a woman enormously when he says to her a whole heap of things that he does n't mean.

LORD D. Ah, but I did mean them.

[*Takes tea which she offers him.*]

LADY W. [*gravely*]. I hope not. I should be sorry to have to quarrel with you, Lord Darlington. I like you very much, you know that. But I should n't like you at all if I thought you were what most other men are. Believe me, you are better than most other men, and I sometimes think you pretend to be worse.

LORD D. We all have our little vanities, Lady Windermere.

LADY W. Why do you make that your special one?   [*Still seated at table* L.]

LORD D. [*still seated* L. C.]. Oh, nowadays so many conceited people go about Society pretending to be good, that I think it shows rather a sweet and modest disposition to pretend to be bad. Besides, there is this to be said. If you pretend to be good, the world takes you very seriously. If you pretend to be bad, it does n't. Such is the astounding stupidity of optimism.

LADY W. Don't you *want* the world to take you seriously then, Lord Darlington?

LORD D. No, not the world. Who are the people the world takes seriously? All the dull people one can think of, from the bishops down to the bores. I should like *you* to take me very seriously, Lady Windermere, *you* more than any one else in life.

LADY W. Why — why me?

LORD D. [*after a slight hesitation*]. Because I think we might be great friends. Let us be great friends. You may want a friend some day.

LADY W. Why do you say that?

LORD D. Oh! — we all want friends at times.

LADY W. I think we 're very good friends already, Lord Darlington. We can always remain so as long as you don't —

LORD D. Don't what?

LADY W. Don't spoil it by saying extravagant, silly things to me. You think I am a Puritan, I suppose? Well, I have something of the Puritan in me. I was brought up like that. I am glad of it. My mother died when I was a mere child. I lived always with Lady Julia, my father's eldest sister, you know. She was stern to me, but she taught me, what the world is forgetting, the difference that there is between what is right and what is wrong. *She* allowed of no compromise. *I* allow of none.

LORD D. My dear Lady Windermere!

LADY W. [*leaning back on the sofa*]. You look on me as being behind the age. — Well, I am ! I should be sorry to be on the same level as an age like this.

LORD D. You think the age very bad?

LADY W. Yes. Nowadays people seem to look on life as a speculation. It is not a speculation. It is a sacrament. Its ideal is Love. Its purification is sacrifice.

LORD D. [*smiling*]. Oh, anything is better than being sacrificed!

LADY W. [*leaning forward*]. Don't say that.

LORD D. I do say it. I feel it — I know it.

[*Enter* PARKER C.]

PARKER. The men want to know if they are to put the carpets on the terrace for to-night, my lady?

LADY W. You don't think it will rain, Lord Darlington, do you?

LORD D. I won't hear of its raining on your birthday!

LADY W. Tell them to do it at once, Parker.   [*Exit* PARKER C.]

LORD D. [*still seated*]. Do you think then — of course I am only putting an imaginary instance — do you think, that in the case of a young married couple, say about two years married, if the husband suddenly becomes the intimate friend of a woman of — well, more than doubtful character, is always calling upon her, lunching with her, and probably paying her bills — do you think that the wife should not console herself?

LADY W. [*frowning*]. Console herself?

LORD D. Yes, I think she should — I think she has the right.

LADY W. Because the husband is vile should the wife be vile also?

LORD D. Vileness is a terrible word, Lady Windermere.

LADY W. It is a terrible thing, Lord Darlington.

LORD D. Do you know I am afraid that good people do a great deal of harm in this world. Certainly the greatest harm they do is that they make badness of such extraordinary importance. It is absurd to divide people into good and bad. People are either charming or tedious. I take the side of the charming, and you, Lady Windermere, can't help belonging to them.

LADY W. Now, Lord Darlington. [*Rising and crossing* R., *front of him*.] Don't stir, I am merely going to finish my flowers.   [*Goes to table* R. C.]

LORD D. [*rising and moving chair*]. And I must say I think you are very hard on modern life, Lady Windermere. Of course there is much against it, I admit. Most women, for instance, nowadays, are rather mercenary.

LADY W. Don't talk about such people

LORD D. Well, then, setting mercenary people aside, who, of course, are dreadful, do you think seriously that women who have committed what the world calls a fault should never be forgiven?

LADY W. [*standing at table*]. I think they should never be forgiven.

LORD D. And me? Do you think that there should be the same laws for men as there are for women?

LADY W. Certainly!

LORD D. I think life too complex a thing to be settled by these hard and fast rules.

LADY W. If we had "these hard and fast rules," we should find life much more simple.

LORD D. You allow of no exceptions?

LADY W. None! .

LORD D. Ah, what a fascinating Puritan you are, Lady Windermere!

LADY W. The adjective was unnecessary, Lord Darlington.

LORD D. I couldn't help it. I can resist everything except temptation.

LADY W. You have the modern affectation of weakness.

LORD D. [*looking at her*]. It's only an affectation, Lady Windermere.

[*Enter* PARKER C.]

PARKER. The Duchess of Berwick and Lady Agatha Carlisle. [*Exit* PARKER C.]

[*Enter the* DUCHESS OF B. *and* LADY A. C. C.]

DUCHESS OF B. [*coming down* C. *and shaking hands*]. Dear Margaret, I am so pleased to see you. You remember Agatha, don't you? [*Crossing* L. C.] How do you do, Lord Darlington? I won't let you know my daughter, you are far too wicked.

LORD D. Don't say that, Duchess. As a wicked man I am a complete failure. Why, there are lots of people who say I have never really done anything wrong in the whole course of my life. Of course they only say it behind my back.

DUCHESS OF B. Isn't he dreadful? Agatha, this is Lord Darlington. Mind you don't believe a word he says. [LORD DARLINGTON *crosses* R. C.] No, no tea, thank you, dear. [*Crosses and sits on sofa.*] We have just had tea at Lady Markby's. Such bad tea, too. It was quite undrinkable. I wasn't at all surprised. Her own son-in-law supplies it. Agatha is looking forward so much to your ball to-night, dear Margaret.

LADY W. [*seated* L. C.] Oh, you mustn't think it is going to be a ball, Duchess. It is only a dance in honor of my birthday. A small and early.

LORD D. [*standing* L. C.]. Very small, very early, and very select, Duchess.

DUCHESS OF B. [*On sofa* L.] Of course it's going to be select. But we know *that*, dear Margaret, about *your* house. It is really one of the few houses in London where I can take Agatha, and where I feel perfectly secure about poor Berwick. I don't know what Society is coming to. The most dreadful people seem to go everywhere. They certainly come to my parties — the men get quite furious if one doesn't ask them. Really, some one should make a stand against it.

LADY W. *I* will, Duchess. I will have no one in my house about whom there is any scandal.

LORD D. [R. C.] Oh, don't say that, Lady Windermere. I should never be admitted! [*Sitting.*]

DUCHESS OF B. Oh, men don't matter. With women it is different. We're good. Some of us are, at least. But we are positively getting elbowed into the corner. Our husbands would really forget our existence if we didn't nag at them from time to time, just to remind them that we have a perfect legal right to do so.

LORD D. It's a curious thing, Duchess, about the game of marriage — a game, by the way, that is going out of fashion — the wives hold all the honors, and invariably lose the odd trick.

DUCHESS OF B. The odd trick? Is that the husband, Lord Darlington?

LORD D. It would be rather a good name for the modern husband.

DUCHESS OF B. Dear Lord Darlington, how thoroughly depraved you are!

LADY W. Lord Darlington is trivial.

LORD D. Ah, don't say that, Lady Windermere.

LADY W. Why do you *talk* so trivially about life, then?

LORD D. Because I think that life is far too important a thing ever to talk seriously about it. [*Moves up* C.]

DUCHESS OF B. What does he mean? Do, as a concession to my poor wits, Lord Darlington, just explain to me what you really mean?

LORD D. [*coming down back of table*].
I think I had better not, Duchess. Nowa-
days to be intelligible is to be found out.
Good-bye! [*Shakes hands with* DUCHESS.]
And now [*goes up stage*], Lady Windermere,
good-bye. I may come to-night, may n't I?
Do let me come.

LADY W. [*standing up stage with* LORD
D.]. Yes, certainly. But you are not to say
foolish, insincere things to people.

LORD D. [*smiling*]. Ah, you are beginning to reform me. It is a dangerous thing
to reform any one, Lady Windermere.
                              [*Bows, and exit* C.]

DUCHESS OF B. [*who has risen, goes* C.].
What a charming, wicked creature! I like
him so much. I 'm quite delighted he 's
gone! How sweet you 're looking! Where
do you get your gowns? And now I must
tell you how sorry I am for you, dear Margaret. [*Crosses to sofa and sits with* LADY
W.] Agatha, darling!

LADY A. Yes, mamma.   [*Rises.*]

DUCHESS OF B. Will you go and look
over the photograph album that I see there?

LADY A. Yes, mamma. [*Goes to table* L.]

DUCHESS OF B. Dear girl! She is so fond
of photographs of Switzerland. Such a pure
taste, I think. But I really am so sorry for
you, Margaret.

LADY W. [*smiling*]. Why, Duchess?

DUCHESS OF B. Oh, on account of that
horrid woman. She dresses so well, too,
which makes it much worse, sets such a
dreadful example. Augustus — you know
my disreputable brother — such a trial to
us all — well, Augustus is completely in-
fatuated about her. It is quite scandalous,
for she is absolutely inadmissible into society. Many a woman has a past, but I am
told that she has at least a dozen, and that
they all fit.

LADY W. Whom are you talking about,
Duchess?

DUCHESS OF B. About Mrs. Erlynne.

LADY W. Mrs. Erlynne? I never heard
of her, Duchess. And what *has* she to do
with me?

DUCHESS OF B. My poor child! Agatha, darling!

LADY A. Yes, mamma.

DUCHESS OF B. Will you go out on the
terrace and look at the sunset?

LADY A. Yes, mamma.

                    [*Exit through window* L.]

DUCHESS OF B. Sweet girl! So devoted
to sunsets! Shows such refinement of feeling, does it not? After all, there is nothing
like nature, is there?

LADY W. But what is it, Duchess? Why
do you talk to me about this person?

DUCHESS OF B. Don't you really know?
I assure you we 're all so distressed about
it. Only last night at dear Lady Fansen's
every one was saying how extraordinary it
was that, of all men in London, Windermere should behave in such a way.

LADY W. My husband — what has *he* to
do with any woman of that kind?

DUCHESS OF B. Ah, what indeed, dear?
That is the point. He goes to see her continually, and stops for hours at a time, and
while he is there she is not at home to any
one. Not that many ladies call on her, dear,
but she has a great many disreputable men
friends — my own brother in particular, as
I told you — and that is what makes it so
dreadful about Windermere. We looked
upon *him* as being such a model husband,
but I am afraid there is no doubt about it.
My dear nieces — you know the Saville
girls, don't you? — such nice domestic
creatures — plain, dreadfully plain, but so
good — well, they 're always at the window doing fancy work, and making ugly
things for the poor, which I think so useful
of them in these dreadful socialistic days,
and this terrible woman has taken a house
in Curzon Street, right opposite them —
such a respectable street, too. I don't know
what we 're coming to! And they tell me
that Windermere goes there four and five
times a week — they *see* him. They can't
help it — and although they never talk
scandal, they — well, of course — they remark on it to every one. And the worst
of it all is, that I have been told that this
woman has got a great deal of money out
of somebody, for it seems that she came to
London six months ago without anything at
all to speak of, and now she has this charming house in Mayfair, drives her pony in
the Park every afternoon, and all — well
all — since she has known poor dear Windermere.

LADY W. Oh, I can't believe it!

DUCHESS OF B. But it 's quite true, my
dear. The whole of London knows it. That
is why I felt it was better to come and talk
to you, and advise you to take Windermere

away at once to Homburg or to Aix where he 'll have something to amuse him, and where you can watch him all day long. I assure you, my dear, that on several occasions after I was first married I had to pretend to be very ill, and was obliged to drink the most unpleasant mineral waters, merely to get Berwick out of town. He was so extremely susceptible. Though I am bound to say he never gave away any large sums of money to anybody. He is far too high-principled for that.

LADY W. [*interrupting*]. Duchess, Duchess, it 's impossible ! [*Rising and crossing stage* C.] We are only married two years. Our child is but six months old.

[*Sits in chair* R. *of* L. *table.*]

DUCHESS OF B. Ah, the dear, pretty baby ! How is the little darling ? Is it a boy or a girl ? I hope a girl — Ah, no, I remember it 's a boy ! I 'm so sorry. Boys are so wicked. My boy is excessively immoral. You would n't believe at what hours he comes home. And he 's only left Oxford a few months — I really don't know what they teach them there.

LADY W. Are *all* men bad ?

DUCHESS OF B. Oh, all of them, my dear, all of them, without any exception. And they never grow any better. Men become old, but they never become good.

LADY W. Windermere and I married for love.

DUCHESS OF B. Yes, we begin like that. It was only Berwick's brutal and incessant threats of suicide that made me accept him at all, and before the year was out he was running after all kinds of petticoats, every color, every shape, every material. In fact, before the honeymoon was over, I caught him winking at my maid, a most pretty, respectable girl. I dismissed her at once without a character. — No, I remember I passed her on to my sister; poor dear Sir George is so short-sighted, I thought it would n't matter. But it did, though it was most unfortunate. [*Rises.*] And now, my dear child, I must go, as we are dining out. And mind you don't take this little aberration of Windermere's too much to heart. Just take him abroad, and he 'll come back to you all right.

LADY W. Come back to me ? [C.]

DUCHESS OF B. [L. C.] Yes, dear, these wicked women get our husbands away from

us, but they always come back, slightly damaged, of course. And don't make scenes, men hate them !

LADY W. It is very kind of you, Duchess, to come and tell me all this. But I can't believe that my husband is untrue to me.

DUCHESS OF B. Pretty child ! I was like that once. Now I know that all men are monsters. [LADY W. *rings bell.*] The only thing to do is to feed the wretches well. A good cook does wonders, and that I know you have. My dear Margaret, you are not going to cry ?

LADY W. You need n't be afraid, Duchess, I never cry.

DUCHESS OF B. That 's quite right, dear. Crying is the refuge of plain women, but the ruin of pretty ones. Agatha, darling !

LADY A. [*entering* L.]. Yes, mamma.

[*Stands back of table* L. C.]

DUCHESS OF B. Come and bid good-bye to Lady Windermere, and thank her for your charming visit. [*Coming down again.*] And by the way, I must thank you for sending a card to Mr. Hopper — he 's that rich young Australian people are taking such notice of just at present. His father made a great fortune by selling some kind of food in circular tins — most palatable, I believe, — I fancy it is the thing the servants always refuse to eat. But the son is quite interesting. I think he 's attracted by dear Agatha's clever talk. Of course, we should be very sorry to lose her, but I think that a mother who does n't part with a daughter every season has no real affection. We 're coming to-night, dear. [PARKER *opens* C. *doors.*] And remember my advice, take the poor fellow out of town at once, it is the only thing to do. Good-bye, once more; come, Agatha.

[*Exeunt* DUCHESS *and* LADY A. C.]

LADY W. How horrible! I understand now what Lord Darlington meant by the imaginary instance of the couple not two years married. Oh ! it can't be true — she spoke of enormous sums of money paid to this woman. I know where Arthur keeps his bank-book — in one of the drawers of that desk. I might find out by that. I *will* find out. [*Opens drawer.*] No, it is some hideous mistake. [*Rises and goes* C.] Some silly scandal ! He loves *me !* He loves *me !* But why should I not look ? I am his wife, I have a right to look ! [*Returns to bureau, takes out book and examines it, page by page, smiles and gives a sigh of relief.*] I knew it, there is not a word of truth in this stupid story. [*Puts book back in drawer. As she does so, starts and takes out another book.*] A second book — private — locked ! [*Tries to open it, but fails. Sees paper knife on bureau, and with it cuts cover from book: Begins to start at the first page.*] Mrs. Erlynne — £600 — Mrs. Erlynne — £700 — Mrs. Erlynne — £400. Oh ! it is true ! it is true ! How horrible !   [*Throws book on floor.*]

[*Enter* LORD W. C.]

LORD W. Well, dear, has the fan been sent home yet ? [*Going* R. C. *sees book.*] Margaret, you have cut open my bank book. You have no right to do such a thing !

LADY W. You think it wrong that you are found out, don't you ?

LORD W. I think it wrong that a wife should spy on her husband.

LADY W. I did not spy on you. I never knew of this woman's existence till half an hour ago. Some one who pitied me was kind enough to tell me what every one in London knows already — your daily visits to Curzon Street, your mad infatuation, the monstrous sums of money you squander on this infamous woman !   [*Crossing* L.]

LORD W. Margaret, don't talk like that of Mrs. Erlynne, you don't know how unjust it is !

LADY W. [*turning to him*]. You are very jealous of Mrs. Erlynne's honor. I wish you had been as jealous of mine.

LORD W. Your honor is untouched, Margaret. You don't think for a moment that — [*Puts book back into desk.*]

LADY W. I think that you spend your money strangely. That is all. Oh, don't imagine I mind about the money. As far as I am concerned, you may squander everything we have. But what I *do* mind is that you who have loved me, you who have taught me to love you, should pass from the love that is given to the love that is bought. Oh, it's horrible ! [*Sits on sofa.*] And it is I who feel degraded. *You* don't feel anything. I feel stained, utterly stained. You can't realize how hideous the last six months seem to me now — every kiss you have given me is tainted in my memory.

LORD W. [*crossing to her*]. Don't say that, Margaret, I never loved any one in the whole world but you.

LADY W. [*Rises.*] Who is this woman, then ? Why do you take a house for her ?

LORD W. I did not take a house for her.

LADY W. You gave her the money to do it, which is the same thing.

LORD W. Margaret, as far as I have known Mrs. Erlynne —

LADY W. Is there a Mr. Erlynne — or is he a myth ?

LORD W. Her husband died many years ago. She is alone in the world.

LADY W. No relations ?   [*A pause.*]

LORD W. None.

LADY W. Rather curious, is n't it ? [L.]

LORD W. [L. C.] Margaret, I was saying to you — and I beg you to listen to me — that as far as I have known Mrs. Erlynne, she has conducted herself well. If years ago —

LADY W. Oh ! [*Crossing* R. C.] I don't want details about her life.

LORD W. I am not going to give you any details about her life. I tell you simply this — Mrs. Erlynne was once honored, loved, respected. She was well born, she had a position — she lost everything — threw it away, if you like. That makes it all the more bitter. Misfortunes one can endure — they come from outside, they are accidents. But to suffer for one's own faults — ah ! there is the sting of life. It was twenty years ago, too. She was little more than a girl then. She had been a wife for even less time than you have.

LADY W. I am not interested in her — and — you should not mention this woman and me in the same breath. It is an error of taste.   [*Sitting* R. *at desk.*]

LORD W. Margaret, you could save this woman. She wants to get back into society, and she wants you to help her.

          [*Crossing to her.*]

LADY W. Me !

LORD W. Yes, you.

LADY W. How impertinent of her !

          [*A pause.*]

LORD W. Margaret, I came to ask you a great favor, and I still ask it of you, though you have discovered what I had intended you should never have known, that I have given Mrs. Erlynne a large sum of money. I want you to send her an invitation for our party to-night.   [*Standing* L. *of her.*]

LADY W. You are mad.   [*Rises.*]

LORD W. I entreat you. People may chatter about her, do chatter about her, of course, but they don't know anything definite against her. She has been to several houses — not to houses where you would go, I admit, but still to houses where women who are in what is called Society nowadays do go. That does not content her. She wants you to receive her once.

LADY W. As a triumph for her, I suppose.

LORD W. No; but because she knows that you are a good woman — and that if she comes here once she will have a chance of a happier, a surer life, than she has had. She will make no further effort to know you. Won't you help a woman who is trying to get back ?

LADY W. No! If a woman really repents, she never wishes to return to the society that has made or seen her ruin.

LORD W. I beg of you.

LADY W. [crossing to door R.]. I am going to dress for dinner, and don't mention the subject again this evening. Arthur [going to him C.], you fancy because I have no father or mother that I am alone in the world and you can treat me as you choose. You are wrong, I have friends, many friends.

LORD W. [L. C.] Margaret, you are talking foolishly, recklessly. I won't argue with you, but I insist upon your asking Mrs. Erlynne to-night.

LADY W. [R. C.] I shall do nothing of the kind. [Crossing L. C.]

LORD W. You refuse ? [C.]

LADY W. Absolutely !

LORD W. Ah, Margaret, do this for my sake ; it is her last chance.

LADY W. What has that to do with me ?

LORD W. How hard good women are !

LADY W. How weak bad men are !

LORD W. Margaret, none of us men may be good enough for the women we marry — that is quite true — but you don't imagine I would ever — oh, the suggestion is monstrous !

LADY W. Why should you be different from other men ? I am told that there is hardly a husband in London who does not waste his life over some shameful passion.

LORD W. I am not one of them.

LADY W. I am not sure of that.

LORD W. You are sure in your heart. But don't make chasm after chasm between us. God knows the last few minutes have

thrust us wide enough apart. Sit down and write the card.

LADY W. Nothing in the whole world would induce me.

LORD W. [crossing to the bureau]. Then I will.

[Rings electric bell, sits down and writes card.]

LADY W. You are going to invite this woman ? [Crossing to him.]

LORD W. Yes. [Pause.]

[Enter PARKER]

LORD W. Parker !

PARKER. Yes, my lord. [Comes down L. C.]

LORD W. Have this note sent to Mrs. Erlynne at No. 84A Curzon Street. [Crossing to L. C. and giving note to PARKER.] There is no answer. [Exit PARKER C.]

LADY W. Arthur, if that woman comes here, I shall insult her.

LORD W. Margaret, don't say that.

LADY W. I mean it.

LORD W. Child, if you did such a thing, there 's not a woman in London who would n't pity you.

LADY W. There is not a good woman in London who would not applaud me. We have been too lax. We must make an example. I propose to begin to-night. [Picking up fan.] Yes, you gave me this fan to-day; it was your birthday present. If that woman crosses my threshold, I shall strike her across the face with it.

LORD W. Margaret, you could n't do such a thing.

LADY W. You don't know me ! [Moves R.]

[Enter PARKER.]

LADY W. Parker !

PARKER. Yes, my lady.

LADY W. I shall dine in my own room. I don't want dinner, in fact. See that everything is ready by half-past ten. And, Parker, be sure you pronounce the names of the guests very distinctly to-night. Sometimes you speak so fast that I miss them. I am particularly anxious to hear the names quite clearly, so as to make no mistake. You understand, Parker ?

PARKER. Yes, my lady.

LADY W. That will do !

[Exit PARKER C.]

[Speaking to LORD W.] Arthur, if that woman comes here — I warn you —

LORD W. Margaret, you'll ruin us!

LADY W. Us! From this moment my life is separate from yours. But if you wish to avoid a public scandal, write at once to this woman, and tell her that I forbid her to come here!

LORD W. I will not — I cannot — she must come!

LADY W. Then I shall do exactly as I have said. [*Goes* R.] You leave me no choice. [*Exit* R.]

LORD W. [*calling after her*]. Margaret! Margaret! [*A pause.*] My God! What shall I do! I dare not tell her who this woman really is. The shame would kill her.

[*Sinks down into a chair and buries his face in his hands.*]

ACT II

SCENE — *Drawing-room in* LORD W.'s *house. Door* R. U. *opening into ballroom, where band is playing. Door* L. *through which guests are entering. Door* L. U. *opens on an illuminated terrace. Palms, flowers, and brilliant lights. Room crowded with guests.* LADY W. *is receiving them.*

DUCHESS OF B. [*up* C.]. So strange Lord Windermere is n't here. Mr. Hopper is very late, too. You have kept those five dances for him, Agatha! [*Comes down.*]

LADY A. Yes, mamma.

DUCHESS OF B. [*sitting on sofa*]. Just let me see your card. I 'm so glad Lady Windermere has revived cards.—They 're a mother's only safeguard. You dear simple little thing! [*Scratches out two names.*] No nice girl should ever waltz with such particularly younger sons! It looks so fast! The last two dances you must pass on the terrace with Mr. Hopper.

[*Enter* MR. DUMBY *and* LADY PLYMDALE *from the ballroom.*]

LADY A. Yes, mamma.

DUCHESS OF B. [*fanning herself*]. The air is so pleasant there.

PARKER. Mrs. Cowper-Cowper. Lady Stutfield. Sir James Royston. Mr. Guy Berkeley.

[*These people enter as announced.*]

DUMBY. Good-evening, Lady Stutfield. I suppose this will be the last ball of the season?

LADY S. I suppose so, Mr. Dumby. It 's been a delightful season, has n't it?

DUMBY. Quite delightful! Good-evening, Duchess. I suppose this will be the last ball of the season?

DUCHESS OF B. I suppose so, Mr. Dumby. It has been a very dull season, has n't it?

DUMBY. Dreadfully dull! Dreadfully dull!

MRS. C.-C. Good-evening, Mr. Dumby. I suppose this will be the last ball of the season?

DUMBY. Oh, I think not. There 'll probably be two more. [*Wanders back to* LADY P.]

PARKER. Mr. Rufford. Lady Jedburgh and Miss Graham. Mr. Hopper.

[*These people enter as announced.*]

HOPPER. How do you do, Lady Windermere? How do you do, Duchess?
[*Bows to* LADY A.]

DUCHESS OF B. Dear Mr. Hopper, how nice of you to come so early. We all know how you are run after in London.

HOPPER. Capital place, London! They are not nearly so exclusive in London as they are in Sydney.

DUCHESS OF B. Ah! we know your value, Mr. Hopper. We wish there were more like you. It would make life so much easier. Do you know, Mr. Hopper, dear Agatha and I are so much interested in Australia. It must be so pretty with all the dear little kangaroos flying about. Agatha has found it on the map. What a curious shape it is! Just like a large packing-case. However, it is a very young country, is n't it?

HOPPER. Was n't it made at the same time as the others, Duchess?

DUCHESS OF B. How clever you are, Mr. Hopper. You have a cleverness quite of your own. Now I must n't keep you.

HOPPER. But I should like to dance with Lady Agatha, Duchess.

DUCHESS OF B. Well, I *hope* she has a dance left. Have you got a dance left, Agatha?

LADY A. Yes, mamma.

DUCHESS OF B. The next one?

LADY A. Yes, mamma.

HOPPER. May I have the pleasure?
[LADY AGATHA *bows.*]

DUCHESS OF B. Mind you take great care of my little chatter-box, Mr. Hopper.
[LADY A. *and* MR. H. *pass into ball-room.*]

[*Enter* LORD W. C.]

LORD W. Margaret, I want to speak to you.

LADY W. In a moment.
[*The music stops.*]

PARKER. Lord Augustus Lorton.

[*Enter* LORD A.]

LORD A. Good-evening, Lady Windermere.

DUCHESS OF B. Sir James, will you take me into the ballroom? Augustus has been dining with us to-night. I really have had quite enough of dear Augustus for the moment.

[SIR JAMES R. *gives the* DUCHESS *his arm and escorts her into the ball-room.*]

PARKER. Mr. and Mrs. Arthur Bowden. Lord and Lady Paisley. Lord Darlington.

[*These people enter as announced.*]

LORD A. [*coming up to* LORD W.]. Want to speak to you particularly, dear boy. I'm worn to a shadow. Know I don't look it. None of us men do look what we really are. Demmed good thing, too. What I want to know is this. Who is she? Where does she come from? Why hasn't she got any demmed relations? Demmed nuisance, relations! But they make one so demmed respectable.

LORD W. You are talking of Mrs. Erlynne, I suppose? I only met her six months ago. Till then I never knew of her existence.

LORD A. You have seen a good deal of her since then.

LORD W. [*coldly*]. Yes, I have seen a good deal of her since then. I have just seen her.

LORD A. Egad! the women are very down on her. I have been dining with Arabella this evening! By Jove! you should have heard what she said about Mrs. Erlynne. She didn't leave a rag on her. . . . [*Aside.*] Berwick and I told her that did n't matter much, as the lady in question must have an extremely fine figure. You should have seen Arabella's expression! . . . But, look here, dear boy. I don't know what

to do about Mrs. Erlynne. Egad! I might be married to her; she treats me with such demmed indifference. She's deuced clever, too! She explains everything. Egad! She explains you. She has got any amount of explanation for you — and all of them different.

LORD W. No explanations are necessary about my friendship with Mrs. Erlynne.

LORD A. Hem! Well, look here, dear old fellow. Do you think she will ever get into this demmed thing called Society? Would you introduce her to your wife? No use beating about the confounded bush. Would you do that?

LORD W. Mrs. Erlynne is coming here to-night.

LORD A. Your wife has sent her a card?

LORD W. Mrs. Erlynne has received a card.

LORD A. Then she's all right, dear boy. But why did n't you tell me that before. It would have saved me a heap of worry and demmed misunderstandings!

[LADY A. *and* MR. H. *cross and exit on terrace* L. U. E.]

PARKER. Mr. Cecil Graham!

[*Enter* MR. CECIL G.]

CECIL G. [*Bows to* LADY W., *passes over and shakes hands with* LORD W.*]* Good-evening, Arthur. Why don't you ask me how I am? I like people to ask me how I am. It shows a widespread interest in my health. Now to-night I am not at all well. Been dining with my people. Wonder why it is one's people are always so tedious? My father would talk morality after dinner. I told him he was old enough to know better. But my experience is that as soon as people are old enough to know better, they don't know anything at all. Hullo, Tuppy! Hear you're going to be married again; thought you were tired of that game.

LORD A. You're excessively trivial, my dear boy, excessively trivial!

CECIL G. By the way, Tuppy, which is it? Have you been twice married and once divorced, or twice divorced and once married? I say, you've been twice divorced and once married. It seems so much more probable.

LORD A. I have a very bad memory. I really don't remember which.

[*Moves away* R.]

LADY P. Lord Windermere, I've something most particular to ask you.

LORD W. I am afraid — if you will excuse me — I must join my wife.

LADY P. Oh, you mustn't dream of such a thing. It's most dangerous nowadays for a husband to pay any attention to his wife in public. It always makes people think that he beats her when they're alone. The world has grown so suspicious of anything that looks like a happy married life. But I'll tell you what it is at supper.

[*Moves towards door of ballroom.*]

LORD W. [C.] Margaret, I *must* speak to you.

LADY W. Will you hold my fan for me, Lord Darlington? Thanks.

[*Comes down to him.*]

LORD W. [*crossing to her*]. Margaret, what you said before dinner was, of course, impossible?

LADY W. That woman is not coming here to-night!

LORD W. [R. C.] Mrs. Erlynne is coming here, and if you in any way annoy or wound her, you will bring shame and sorrow on us both. Remember that! Ah, Margaret! only trust me! A wife should trust her husband!

LADY W. [C.] London is full of women who trust their husbands. One can always recognize them. They look so thoroughly unhappy. I am not going to be one of them. [*Moves up.*] Lord Darlington, will you give me back my fan, please? Thanks . . . A useful thing, a fan, isn't it? . . . I want a friend to-night, Lord Darlington. I didn't know I would want one so soon.

LORD D. Lady Windermere! I knew the time would come some day; but why to-night!

LORD W. I *will* tell her. I must. It would be terrible if there were any scene. Margaret —

PARKER. Mrs. Erlynne.

[LORD W. *starts.* MRS. E. *enters, very beautifully dressed and very dignified.* LADY W. *clutches at her fan, then lets it drop on the floor. She bows coldly to* MRS. E., *who bows to her sweetly in turn, and sails into the room.*]

LORD D. You have dropped your fan, Lady Windermere.

[*Picks it up and hands it to her.*]

MRS. E. [C.] How do you do again, Lord Windermere? How charming your sweet wife looks! Quite a picture!

LORD W. [*in a low voice*]. It was terribly rash of you to come!

MRS. E. [*smiling*]. The wisest thing I ever did in my life. And, by the way, you must pay me a good deal of attention this evening. I am afraid of the women. You must introduce me to some of them. The men I can always manage. How do you do, Lord Augustus? You have quite neglected me lately. I have not seen you since yesterday. I am afraid you're faithless. Every one told me so.

LORD A. [R.] Now really, Mrs. Erlynne, allow me to explain.

MRS. E. [R. C.] No, dear Lord Augustus, you can't explain anything. It is your chief charm.

LORD A. Ah! if you find charms in me, Mrs. Erlynne — [*They converse together.* LORD W. *moves uneasily about the room watching* MRS. E.]

LORD D. [*To* LADY W.] How pale you are!

LADY W. Cowards are always pale.

LORD D. You look faint. Come out on the terrace.

LADY W. Yes. [*To* PARKER.] Parker, send my cloak out.

MRS. E. [*crossing to her*]. Lady Windermere, how beautifully your terrace is illuminated. Reminds me of Prince Doria's at Rome. [LADY W. *bows coldly, and goes off with* LORD D.] Oh, how do you do, Mr. Graham? Isn't that your aunt, Lady Jedburgh? I should so much like to know her.

CECIL G. [*after a moment's hesitation and embarrassment*]. Oh, certainly, if you wish it. Aunt Caroline, allow me to introduce Mrs. Erlynne.

MRS. E. So pleased to meet you, Lady Jedburgh. [*Sits beside her on the sofa.*] Your nephew and I are great friends. I am so much interested in his political career. I think he's sure to be a wonderful success. He thinks like a Tory, and talks like a Radical, and that's so important nowadays. He's such a brilliant talker, too. But we all know from whom he inherits that. Lord Allendale was saying to me only yesterday in the Park, that Mr. Graham talks almost as well as his aunt.

LADY J. [R.] Most kind of you to say

these charming things to me! [MRS. E. *smiles and continues conversation.*]

DUMBY. [*To* CECIL G.] Did you introduce Mrs. Erlynne to Lady Jedburgh.

CECIL G. Had to, my dear fellow. Couldn't help it. That woman can make one do anything she wants. How, I don't know.

DUMBY. Hope to goodness she won't speak to me! [*Saunters towards* LADY P.]

MRS. E. [c. *To* LADY J.] On Thursday? With great pleasure. [*Rises and speaks to* LORD W. *laughing.*] What a bore it is to have to be civil to these old dowagers. But they always insist on it.

LADY P. [*To* MR. D.] Who is that well-dressed woman talking to Windermere?

DUMBY. Haven't got the slightest idea. Looks like an *edition de luxe* of a wicked French novel, meant specially for the English market.

MRS. E. So that is poor Dumby with Lady Plymdale? I hear she is frightfully jealous of him. He doesn't seem anxious to speak to me to-night. I suppose he is afraid of her. Those straw-colored women have dreadful tempers. Do you know, I think I'll dance with you first, Windermere. [LORD W. *bites his lip and frowns.*] It will make Lord Augustus so jealous! Lord Augustus! [LORD A. *comes down.*] Lord Windermere insists on my dancing with him first, and, as it's his own house, I can't well refuse. You know I would much sooner dance with you.

LORD A. [*with a low bow*]. I wish I could think so, Mrs. Erlynne.

MRS. E. You know it far too well. I can fancy a person dancing through life with you and finding it charming.

LORD A. [*placing his hand on his white waistcoat*]. Oh, thank you, thank you. You are the most adorable of all ladies!

MRS. E. What a nice speech! So simple and so sincere! Just the sort of speech I like. Well, you shall hold my bouquet. [*Goes towards ballroom on* LORD W.'s *arm.*] Ah, Mr. Dumby, how are you? I am so sorry I have been out the last three times you have called. Come and lunch on Friday.

DUMBY [*with perfect nonchalance*]. Delighted.

[LADY P. *glares with indignation at* MR. D. LORD A. *follows* MRS. E. *and* LORD W. *into the ballroom holding bouquet.*]

LADY P. [*To* MR. D.] What an absolute brute you are! I never can believe a word you say! Why did you tell me you didn't know her? What do you mean by calling on her three times running? You are not to go to lunch there; of course you understand that?

DUMBY. My dear Laura, I wouldn't dream of going!

LADY P. You haven't told me her name yet. Who is she?

DUMBY. [*Coughs slightly and smooths his hair.*] She's a Mrs. Erlynne.

LADY P. *That* woman!

DUMBY. Yes, that is what every one calls her.

LADY P. How very interesting? How intensely interesting! I really must have a good stare at her. [*Goes to door of ballroom and looks in.*] I have heard the most shocking things about her. They say she is ruining poor Windermere. And Lady Windermere, who goes in for being so proper, invites her! How extremely amusing! It takes a thoroughly good woman to do a thoroughly stupid thing. You are to lunch there on Friday.

DUMBY. Why?

LADY P. Because I want you to take my husband with you. He has been so attentive lately, that he has become a perfect nuisance. Now, this woman is just the thing for him. He'll dance attendance upon her as long as she lets him, and won't bother me. I assure you, women of that kind are most useful. They form the basis of other people's marriages.

DUMBY. What a mystery you are!

LADY P. [*looking at him*]. I wish *you* were!

DUMBY. I am — to myself. I am the only person in the world I should like to know thoroughly; but I don't see any chance of it just at present.

[*They pass into the ballroom, and* LADY W. *and* LORD D. *enter from the terrace.*]

LADY W. Yes. Her coming here is monstrous, unbearable. I know now what you meant to-day at tea time. Why didn't you tell me right out? You should have!

LORD D. I couldn't! A man can't tell these things about another man! But if I had known he was going to make you ask her here to-night, I think I would have told you. That insult, at any rate, you would have been spared.

LADY W. I did not ask her. He insisted on her coming — against my entreaties — against my commands. Oh ! the house is tainted for me ! I feel that every woman here sneers at me as she dances by with my husband. What have I done to deserve this ? I gave him all my life. He took it — used it — spoiled it ! I am degraded in my own eyes ; and I lack courage — I am a coward ! [Sits down on sofa.]

LORD D. If I know you at all, I know that you can't live with a man who treats you like this ! What sort of life would you have with him ? You would feel that he was lying to you every moment of the day. You would feel that the look in his eyes was false, his voice false, his touch false, his passion false. He would come to you when he was weary of others ; you would have to comfort him. He would come to you when he was devoted to others; you would have to charm him. You would have to be to him the mask of his real life, the cloak to hide his secret.

LADY W. You are right — you are terribly right. But where am I to turn ? You said you would be my friend, Lord Darlington. — Tell me, what am I to do ? Be my friend now.

LORD D. Between men and women there is no friendship possible. There is passion, enmity, worship, love, but no friendship. I love you —

LADY W. No, no !   [Rises.]

LORD D. Yes, I love you ! You are more to me than anything in the whole world. What does your husband give you ? Nothing. Whatever is in him he gives to this wretched woman, whom he has thrust into your society, into your home, to shame you before every one. I offer you my life —

LADY W. Lord Darlington !

LORD D. My life — my whole life. Take it, and do with it what you will. . . . I love you — love you as I have never loved any living thing. From the moment I met you I loved you, loved you blindly, adoringly, madly ! You did not know it then — you know it now ! Leave this house to-night. I won't tell you that the world matters nothing, or the world's voice, or the voice of Society. They matter a good deal. They matter far too much. But there are moments when one has to choose between living one's own life, fully, entirely, completely — or dragging out some false, shallow, degrading existence that the world in its hypocrisy demands. You have that moment now. Choose ! Oh, my love, choose !

LADY W. [moving slowly away from him, and looking at him with startled eyes]. I have not the courage.

LORD D. [following her]. Yes ; you have the courage. There may be six months of pain, of disgrace even, but when you no longer bear his name, when you bear mine, all will be well. Margaret, my love, my wife that shall be some day — yes, my wife ! You know it ! What are you now ? This woman has the place that belongs by right to you. Oh ! go — go out of this house, with head erect, with a smile upon your lips, with courage in your eyes. All London will know why you did it ; and who will blame you ? No one. If they do, what matter. Wrong ? What is wrong ? It's wrong for a man to abandon his wife for a shameless woman. It is wrong for a wife to remain with a man who so dishonors her. You said once you would make no compromise with things. Make none now. Be brave ! Be yourself !

LADY W. I am afraid of being myself. Let me think ! Let me wait ! My husband may return to me.   [Sits down on sofa.]

LORD D. And you would take him back ! You are not what I thought you were. You are just the same as every other woman. You would stand anything rather than face the censure of a world whose praise you would despise. In a week you will be driving with this woman in the Park. She will be your constant guest — your dearest friend. You would endure anything rather than break with one blow this monstrous tie. You are right. You have no courage ; none.

LADY W. Ah, give me time to think. I cannot answer you now.

[Passes her hand nervously over her brow.]

LORD D. It must be now or not at all.

LADY W. [rising from the sofa]. Then not at all !   [A pause.]

LORD D. You break my heart !

LADY W. Mine is already broken.
                                [A pause.]

LORD D. To-morrow I leave England. This is the last time I shall ever look on you. You will never see me again. For one moment our lives met — our souls touched. They must never meet or touch again. Good-bye, Margaret.   [*Exit.*]

LADY W. How alone I am in life ! How terribly alone !

[*The music stops. Enter the* DUCHESS OF B. *and* LORD P. *laughing and talking. Other guests come on from ballroom.*]

DUCHESS OF B. Dear Margaret, I 've just been having such a delightful chat with Mrs. Erlynne. I am so sorry for what I said to you this afternoon about her. Of course, she must be all right if *you* invite her. A most attractive woman, and has such sensible views on life. Told me she entirely disapproved of people marrying more than once, so I feel quite safe about poor Augustus. Can't imagine why people speak against her. It's those horrid nieces of mine — the Saville girls — they 're always talking scandal. Still, I should go to Homburg, dear, I really should. She is just a little too attractive. But where is Agatha ? Oh, there she is. [LADY A. *and* MR. H. *enter from the terrace* L. U. E.] Mr. Hopper, I am very angry with you. You have taken Agatha out on the terrace, and she is so delicate.

HOPPER. [L. C.] Awfully sorry, Duchess. We went out for a moment and then got chatting together.

DUCHESS OF B. [C.] Ah, about dear Australia, I suppose ?

HOPPER. Yes.

DUCHESS OF B. Agatha, darling !
[*Beckons her over.*]

LADY A. Yes, mamma !

DUCHESS OF B. [*aside*]. Did Mr. Hopper definitely —

LADY A. Yes, mamma.

DUCHESS OF B. And what answer did you give him, dear child ?

LADY A. Yes, mamma.

DUCHESS OF·B. [*affectionately*]. My dear one ! You always say the right thing. Mr. Hopper ! James ! Agatha has told me everything. How cleverly you have both kept your secret.

HOPPER. You don't mind my taking Agatha off to Australia, then, Duchess ?

DUCHESS OF B. [*indignantly*]. To Australia ? Oh, don't mention that dreadful vulgar place.

HOPPER. But she said she 'd like to come with me.

DUCHESS OF B. [*severely*]. Did you say that, Agatha ?

LADY A. Yes, mamma.

DUCHESS OF B. Agatha, you say the most silly things possible. I think on the whole that Grosvenor Square would be a more healthy place to reside in. There are lots of vulgar people live in Grosvenor Square, but at any rate there are no horrid kangaroos crawling about. But we 'll talk about that to-morrow. James, you can take Agatha down. You 'll come to lunch, of course, James. At half past one instead of two. The Duke will wish to say a few words to you, I am sure.

HOPPER. I should like to have a chat with the Duke, Duchess. He has not said a single word to me yet.

DUCHESS OF B. I think you 'll find he will have a great deal to say to you to-morrow. [*Exit* LADY A. *with* MR. H.] And now good-night, Margaret. I 'm afraid it 's the old, old story, dear. Love — well, not love at first sight, but love at the end of the season, which is so much more satisfactory.

LADY W. Good-night, Duchess.

[*Exit the* DUCHESS OF B. *on* LORD P.'s *arm.*]

LADY P. My dear Margaret, what a handsome woman your husband has been dancing with ! I should be quite jealous if I were you ! Is she a great friend of yours ?

LADY W. No !

LADY P. Really ? Good-night, dear.
[*Looks at* MR. D. *and exit.*]

DUMBY. Awful manners young Hopper has !

CECIL G. Ah ! Hopper is one of Nature's gentlemen, the worst type of gentlemen I know.

DUMBY. Sensible woman, Lady Windermere. Lots of wives would have objected to Mrs. Erlynne coming. But Lady Windermere has that uncommon thing called common sense.

CECIL G. And Windermere knows that nothing looks so like innocence as an indiscretion.

DUMBY. Yes ; dear Windermere is becoming almost modern. Never thought he would.   [*Bows to* LADY W. *and exit.*]

LADY J. Good-night, Lady Windermere. What a fascinating woman Mrs. Erlynne is ! She is coming to lunch on Thursday,

won't you come too? I expect the Bishop
and dear Lady Merton.

LADY W. I am afraid I am engaged,
Lady Jedburgh.

LADY J. So sorry. Come, dear.

[*Exeunt* LADY J. *and* MISS G.]

[*Enter* MRS. E. *and* LORD W.]

MRS. E. Charming ball it has been!
Quite reminds me of old days. [*Sits on the
sofa.*] And I see that there are just as
many fools in society as there used to be.
So pleased to find that nothing has altered!
Except Margaret. She's grown quite pretty.
The last time I saw her — twenty years ago,
she was a fright in flannel. Positive fright,
I assure you. The dear Duchess! and that
sweet Lady Agatha! Just the type of girl
I like! Well, really, Windermere, if I am
to be the Duchess's sister-in-law —

LORD W. [*sitting* L. *of her*]. But are
you — ?

[*Exit* MR. CECIL G. *with rest of
guests.* LADY W. *watches with a
look of scorn and pain,* MRS. E.
*and her husband. They are uncon-
scious of her presence.*]

MRS. E. Oh yes! He's to call to-morrow
at twelve o'clock. He wanted to propose
to-night. In fact he did. He kept on proposing. Poor Augustus, you know how he
repeats himself. Such a bad habit! But I
told him I would n't give him an answer till
to-morrow. Of course I am going to take
him. And I dare say I'll make him an admirable wife, as wives go. And there is a
great deal of good in Lord Augustus. Fortunately it is all on the surface. Just where
good qualities should be. Of course you
must help me in this matter.

LORD W. I am not called on to encourage Lord Augustus, I suppose?

MRS. E. Oh, no! I do the encouraging.
But you will make me a handsome settlement, Windermere, won't you?

LORD W. [*frowning*]. Is that what you
want to talk to me about to-night?

MRS. E. Yes.

LORD W. [*with a gesture of impatience*].
I will not talk of it here.

MRS. E. [*laughing*]. Then we will talk
of it on the terrace. Even business should
have a picturesque background. Should it
not, Windermere? With a proper background women can do anything.

LORD W. Won't to-morrow do as well?

MRS. E. No; you see, to-morrow I am
going to accept him. And I think it would
be a good thing if I was able to tell him
that — well, what shall I say — £2000 a
year left me by a third cousin — or a second
husband — or some distant relative of that
kind. It would be an additional attraction,
would n't it? You have a delightful opportunity now of paying me a compliment,
Windermere. But you are not very clever
at paying compliments. I am afraid Margaret does n't encourage you in that excellent habit. It's a great mistake on her part.
When men give up saying what is charming, they give up thinking what is charming.
But seriously, what do you say to £2000?
£2500, I think. In modern life margin is
everything. Windermere, don't you think
the world an intensely amusing place? I
do!

[*Exit on terrace with* LORD W. *Music
strikes up in ballroom.*]

LADY W. To stay in this house any
longer is impossible. To-night a man who
loves me offered me his whole life. I refused it. It was foolish of me. I will offer
him mine now. I will give him mine. I will
go to him! [*Puts on cloak and goes to door,
then turns back. Sits down at table and writes
a letter, puts it into an envelope, and leaves it
on table.*] Arthur has never understood me.
When he reads this, he will. He may do as
he chooses now with his life. I have done
with mine as I think best, as I think right.
It is he who has broken the bond of marriage — not I. I only break its bondage.

[*Exit.*]

[PARKER *enters* L. *and crosses towards the ballroom* R. *Enter* MRS. E.]

MRS. E. Is Lady Windermere in the ballroom?

PARKER. Her ladyship has just gone
out.

MRS. E. Gone out? She's not on the
terrace?

PARKER. No, madam. Her ladyship has
just gone out of the house.

MRS. E. [*Starts and looks at the servant
with a puzzled expression on her face.*] Out
of the house?

PARKER. Yes, madam — her ladyship told
me she had left a letter for his lordship on
the table.

Mrs. E. A letter for Lord Windermere?

Parker. Yes, madam.

Mrs. E. Thank you. [*Exit* Parker. *The music in the ballroom stops.*] Gone out of her house! A letter addressed to her husband! [*Goes over to table and looks at letter. Takes it up and lays it down again with a shudder of fear.*] No, no! It would be impossible! Life doesn't repeat its tragedies like that! Oh, why does this horrible fancy come across me? Why do I remember now the one moment of my life I most wish to forget? Does life repeat its tragedies? [*Tears letter open and reads it, then sinks down into a chair with a gesture of anguish.*] Oh, how terrible! the same words that twenty years ago I wrote to her father! and how bitterly I have been punished for it! No; my punishment, my real punishment is to-night, is now! [*Still seated* R.]

[*Enter* Lord W. L. U. E.]

Lord W. Have you said good-night to my wife? [*Comes* C.]

Mrs. E. [*crushing letter in her hand*]. Yes.

Lord W. Where is she?

Mrs. E. She is very tired. She has gone to bed. She said she had a headache.

Lord W. I must go to her. You'll excuse me?

Mrs. E. [*rising hurriedly*]. Oh, no! It's nothing serious. She's only very tired, that is all. Besides, there are people still in the supper-room. She wants you to make her apologies to them. She said she didn't wish to be disturbed. [*Drops letter.*] She asked me to tell you.

Lord W. [*Picks up letter.*] You have dropped something.

Mrs. E. Oh, yes, thank you, that is mine. [*Puts out her hand to take it.*]

Lord W. [*still looking at letter*]. But it's my wife's handwriting, isn't it?

Mrs. E. [*Takes the letter quickly.*] Yes, it's — an address. Will you ask them to call my carriage, please?

Lord W. Certainly. [*Goes* L. *and exit.*]

Mrs. E. Thanks. What can I do? What can I do? I feel a passion awakening within me that I never felt before. What can it mean? The daughter must not be like the mother — that would be terrible. How can I save her? How can I save my child? A moment may ruin a life. Who knows that

better than I? Windermere must be got out of the house; that is absolutely necessary. [*Goes* L.] But how shall I do it? It must be done somehow. Ah!

[*Enter* Lord A. R. U. E. *carrying bouquet.*]

Lord A. Dear lady, I am in such suspense! May I not have an answer to my request?

Mrs. E. Lord Augustus, listen to me. You are to take Lord Windermere down to your club at once, and keep him there as long as possible. You understand?

Lord A. But you said you wished me to keep early hours!

Mrs. E. [*nervously*]. Do what I tell you. Do what I tell you.

Lord A. And my reward?

Mrs. E. Your reward? Your reward? Oh! ask me that to-morrow. But don't let Windermere out of your sight to-night. If you do I will never forgive you. I will never speak to you again. I'll have nothing to do with you. Remember you are to keep Windermere at your club, and don't let him come back to-night. [*Exit.*]

Lord A. Well, really, I might be her husband already. Positively I might.

[*Follows her in a bewildered manner.*]

ACT III

Scene — Lord Darlington's *rooms. A large sofa is in front of fireplace* R. *At the back of the stage a curtain is drawn across the window. Doors* L. *and* R. *Table* R. *with writing materials. Table* C. *with syphons, glasses, and Tantalus frame. Table* L. *with cigar and cigarette box. Lamps lit.*

Lady W. [*standing by the fireplace*]. Why doesn't he come? This waiting is horrible. He should be here. Why is he not here, to wake by passionate words some fire within me? I am cold — cold as a loveless thing. Arthur must have read my letter by this time. If he cared for me, he would have come after me, would have taken me back by force. But he doesn't care. He's entrammeled by this woman — fascinated by her — dominated by her. If a woman wants to hold a man, she has merely to appeal to what is worst in him. We make gods of men, and they leave us. Others make brutes of them and they fawn and are faithful. How hideous life is! . . .

Oh ! it was mad of me to come here, horribly mad. And yet which is the worst, I wonder, to be at the mercy of a man who loves one, or the wife of a man who in one's own house dishonors one ? What woman knows ? What woman in the whole world ? But will he love me always, this man to whom I am giving my life ? What do I bring him ? Lips that have lost the note of joy, eyes that are blighted by tears, chill hands and icy heart. I bring him nothing. I must go back — no ; I can't go back, my letter has put me in their power — Arthur would not take me back ! That fatal letter ! No ! Lord Darlington leaves England to-morrow. I will go with him — I have no choice. [*Sits down for a few moments. Then starts up and puts on her cloak.*] No, no ! I will go back, let Arthur do with me what he pleases. I can't wait here. It has been madness my coming. I must go at once. As for Lord Darlington — Oh ! here he is ! What shall I do ? What can I say to him ? Will he let me go away at all ? I have heard that men are brutal, horrible. . . . Oh ! [*Hides her face in her hands.*]

[*Enter* MRS. E. L.]

MRS. E. Lady Windermere ! [LADY W. *starts and looks up. Then recoils in contempt.*] Thank Heaven I am in time. You must go back to your husband's house immediately.

LADY W. Must ?

MRS. E. [*authoritatively*]. Yes, you must ! There is not a second to be lost. Lord Darlington may return at any moment.

LADY W. Don't come near me !

MRS. E. Oh ! you are on the brink of ruin ; you are on the brink of a hideous precipice. You must leave this place at once, my carriage is waiting at the corner of the street. You must come with me and drive straight home. [LADY W. *throws off her cloak and flings it on the sofa.*] What are you doing ?

LADY W. Mrs. Erlynne — if you had not come here, I would have gone back. But now that I see you, I feel that nothing in the whole world would induce me to live under the same roof as Lord Windermere. You fill me with horror. There is something about you that stirs the wildest rage within me. And I know why you are here. My husband sent you to lure me back that I might serve as a blind to whatever relations exist between you and him.

MRS. E. Oh ! You don't think that — you can't.

LADY W. Go back to my husband, Mrs. Erlynne. He belongs to you and not to me. I suppose he is afraid of a scandal. Men are such cowards. They outrage every law of the world, and are afraid of the world's tongue. But he had better prepare himself. He shall have a scandal. He shall have the worst scandal there has been in London for years. He shall see his name in every vile paper, mine on every hideous placard.

MRS. E. No — no —

LADY W. Yes ! he shall. Had he come himself, I admit I would have gone back to the life of degradation you and he had prepared for me — I was going back — but to stay himself at home, and to send you as his messenger — oh ! it was infamous — infamous.

MRS. E. [C.] Lady Windermere, you wrong me horribly — you wrong your husband horribly. He does n't know you are here — he thinks you are safe in your own house. He thinks you are asleep in your own room. He never read the mad letter you wrote to him !

LADY W. [R.] Never read it !

MRS. E. No — he knows nothing about it.

LADY W. How simple you think me ! [*Going to her.*] You are lying to me !

MRS. E. [*restraining herself*]. I am not. I am telling you the truth.

LADY W. If my husband did n't read my letter, how is it that you are here ? Who told you I had left the house you were shameless enough to enter ? Who told you where I had gone to ? My husband told you, and sent you to decoy me back. [*Crosses* L.]

MRS. E. [R.C.] Your husband has never seen the letter. I — saw it, I opened it. I — read it.

LADY W. [*turning to her*]. You opened a letter of mine to my husband ? You would n't dare !

MRS. E. Dare ! Oh ! to save you from the abyss into which you are falling, there is nothing in the world I would not dare, nothing in the whole world. Here is the letter. Your husband has never read it He never shall read it. [*Going to fire-*

place]. It should never have been written.   [*Tears it and throws it into the fire.*]

LADY W. [*with infinite contempt in her voice and look*]. How do I know that was my letter after all ? You seem to think the commonest device can take me in !

MRS. E. Oh ! why do you disbelieve everything I tell you ! What object do you think I have in coming here, except to save you from utter ruin, to save you from the consequence of a hideous mistake ? That letter that is burning now *was* your letter. I swear it to you !

LADY W. [*slowly*]. You took good care to burn it before I had examined it. I cannot trust you. You, whose whole life is a lie, how could you speak the truth about anything ?   [*Sits down.*]

MRS. E. [*hurriedly*]. Think as you like about me — say what you choose against me, but go back to the husband you love.

LADY W. [*sullenly*]. I do *not* love him !

MRS. E. You do, and you know that he loves you.

LADY W. He does not understand what love is. He understands it as little as you do — but I see what you want. It would be a great advantage for you to get me back. Dear Heaven ! what a life I would have then ! Living at the mercy of a woman who has neither mercy nor pity in her, a woman whom it is an infamy to meet, a degradation to know, a vile woman, a woman who comes between husband and wife !

MRS. E. [*with a gesture of despair*]. Lady Windermere, Lady Windermere, don't say such terrible things. You don't know how terrible they are, how terrible and how unjust. Listen, you must listen ! Only go back to your husband, and I promise you never to communicate with him again on any pretext — never to see him — never to have anything to do with his life or yours. The money that he gave me, he gave me not through love, but through hatred, not in worship, but in contempt. The hold I have over him —

LADY W. [*rising*]. Ah ! you admit you have a hold !

MRS. E. Yes, and I will tell you what it is. It is his love for you, Lady Windermere.

LADY W. You expect me to believe that ?

MRS. E. You must believe it ! It is true. It is his love for you that has made him

submit to — oh ! call it what you like, tyranny, threats, anything you choose. But it is his love for you. His desire to spare you — shame, yes, shame and disgrace.

LADY W. What do you mean ? You are insolent ! What have I to do with you ?

MRS. E. [*humbly*]. Nothing. I know it — but I tell you that your husband loves you — that you may never meet with such love again in your whole life — that such love you will never meet — and that if you throw it away, the day may come when you will starve for love and it will not be given to you, beg for love and it will be denied you — Oh ! Arthur loves you !

LADY W. Arthur ? And you tell me there is nothing between you ?

MRS. E. Lady Windermere, before Heaven your husband is guiltless of all offense towards you ! And I — I tell you that had it ever occurred to me that such a monstrous suspicion would have entered your mind, I would have died rather than have crossed your life or his — oh ! died, gladly died !   [*Moves away to sofa* R.]

LADY W. You talk as if you had a heart. Women like you have no hearts. Heart is not in you. You are bought and sold.
                                        [*Sits* L. C.]

MRS. E. [*Starts, with a gesture of pain. Then restrains herself, and comes over to where* LADY W. *is sitting. As she speaks, she stretches out her hands towards her, but does not dare to touch her.*] Believe what you choose about me. I am not worth a moment's sorrow. But don't spoil your beautiful young life on my account ! You don't know what may be in store for you, unless you leave this house at once. You don't know what it is to fall into the pit, to be despised, mocked, abandoned, sneered at — to be an outcast ! to find the door shut against one, to have to creep in by hideous byways, afraid every moment lest the mask should be stripped from one's face, and all the while to hear the laughter, the horrible laughter of the world, a thing more tragic than all the tears the world has ever shed. You don't know what it is. One pays for one's sin, and then one pays again, and all one's life one pays. You must never know that. — As for me, if suffering be an expiation, then at this moment I have expiated all my faults, whatever they have been ; for to-night you have made a heart in one who had it not, made it and broken it. — But let that pass. I may have wrecked my own life, but I will not let you wreck yours. You — why, you are a mere girl, you would be lost. You have n't got the kind of brains that enables a woman to get back. You have neither the wit nor the courage. You could n't stand dishonor. No! Go back, Lady Windermere, to the husband who loves you, whom you love. You have a child, Lady Windermere. Go back to that child who even now, in pain or in joy, may be calling to you. [LADY W. *rises.*] God gave you that child. He will require from you that you make his life fine, that you watch over him. What answer will you make to God if his life is ruined through you? Back to your house, Lady Windermere — your husband loves you. He has never swerved for a moment from the love he bears you. But even if he had a thousand loves, you must stay with your child. If he was harsh to you, you must stay with your child. If he ill-treated you, you must stay with your child. If he abandoned you, your place is with your child.

[LADY W. *bursts into tears and buries her face in her hands.*]

[*Rushing to her.*] Lady Windermere!

LADY W. [*holding out her hands to her, helplessly, as a child might do*]. Take me home. Take me home.

MRS. E. [*Is about to embrace her. Then restrains herself. There is a look of wonderful joy in her face.*] Come! Where is your cloak? [*Getting it from sofa.*] Here. Put it on. Come at once! [*They go to the door.*]

LADY W. Stop! Don't you hear voices?

MRS. E. No, no! There is no one!

LADY W. Yes, there is! Listen! Oh! that is my husband's voice! He is coming in! Save me! Oh, it 's some plot! You have sent for him!   [*Voices outside.*]

MRS. E. Silence! I am here to save you if I can. But I fear it is too late! There! [*Points to the curtain across the window.*] The first chance you have, slip out, if you ever get a chance!

LADY W. But you!

MRS. E. Oh! never mind me. I 'll face them.

[LADY W. *hides herself behind the curtain.*]

LORD A. [*outside*]. Nonsense, dear Windermere, you must not leave me!

MRS. E. Lord Augustus! Then it is I who am lost!

[*Hesitates for a moment, then looks round and sees door R., and exit through it.*]

[*Enter* LORD D., MR. A., LORD W., LORD A. L., *and* CECIL G.]

DUMBY. What a nuisance their turning us out of the club at this hour! It 's only two o'clock. [*Sinks into a chair.*] The lively part of the evening is only just beginning.
[*Yawns and closes his eyes.*]

LORD W. It is very good of you, Lord Darlington, allowing Augustus to force our company on you, but I 'm afraid I can't stay long.

LORD D. Really! I am so sorry! You 'll take a cigar, won't you?

LORD W. Thanks!   [*Sits down.*]

LORD A. [*To* LORD W.] My dear boy, you must not dream of going. I have a great deal to talk to you about, of demmed importance, too.
[*Sits down with him at* L. *table.*]

CECIL G. Oh! we all know what that is! Tuppy can't talk about anything but Mrs. Erlynne!

LORD W. Well, that is no business of yours, is it, Cecil?

CECIL G. None! That is why it interests me. My own business always bores me to death. I prefer other people's.

LORD D. Have something to drink, you fellows. Cecil, you 'll have a whiskey and soda?

CECIL G. Thanks. [*Goes to the table with* LORD D.] Mrs. Erlynne looked very handsome to-night, did n't she?

LORD D. I am not one of her admirers.

CECIL G. I use n't to be, but I am now. Why! she actually made me introduce her to poor dear Aunt Caroline. I believe she is going to lunch there.

LORD D. [*in surprise*]. No?

CECIL G. She is, really.

LORD D. Excuse me, you fellows. I 'm going away to-morrow. And I have to write a few letters.
[*Goes to writing table and sits down.*]

DUMBY. Clever woman, Mrs. Erlynne.

CECIL G. Hallo, Dumby! I thought you were asleep.

DUMBY. I am, I usually am!

LORD A. A very clever woman. Knows

perfectly well what a demmed fool I am — knows it as well as I do myself. [CECIL G. *comes towards him laughing.*] Ah! you may laugh, my boy, but it is a great thing to come across a woman who thoroughly understands one.

DUMBY G. It is an awfully dangerous thing. They always end by marrying one.

CECIL G. But I thought, Tuppy, you were never going to see her again. Yes! you told me so yesterday evening at the club. You said you'd heard —

[*Whispering to him.*]

LORD A. Oh, she's explained that.

CECIL G. And the Wiesbaden affair?

LORD A. She's explained that, too.

DUMBY. And her income, Tuppy? Has she explained that?

LORD A. [*in a very serious voice*]. She's going to explain that to-morrow.

[CECIL G. *goes back to* C. *table.*]

DUMBY. Awfully commercial, women nowadays. Our grandmothers threw their caps over the mills, of course, but, by Jove, their granddaughters only throw their caps over mills that can raise the wind for them.

LORD A. You want to make her out a wicked woman. She is not!

CECIL G. Oh! Wicked women bother one. Good women bore one. That is the only difference between them.

LORD D. [*puffing a cigar*]. Mrs. Erlynne has a future before her.

DUMBY. Mrs. Erlynne has a past before her.

LORD A. I prefer women with a past. They're always so demmed amusing to talk to.

CECIL G. Well, you'll have lots of topics of conversation with *her*, Tuppy.

[*Rising and going to him.*]

LORD A. You're getting annoying, dear boy; you're getting demmed annoying.

CECIL G. [*Puts his hands on his shoulders.*] Now, Tuppy, you've lost your figure and you've lost your character. Don't lose your temper; you have only got one.

LORD A. My dear boy, if I was n't the most good-natured man in London —

CECIL G. We'd treat you with more respect would n't we, Tuppy? [*Strolls away.*]

DUMBY. The youth of the present day are quite monstrous. They have absolutely no respect for dyed hair.

[LORD A. *looks round angrily.*]

CECIL G. Mrs. Erlynne has a very great respect for dear Tuppy.

DUMBY. Then Mrs. Erlynne sets an admirable example to the rest of her sex. It is perfectly brutal the way most women nowadays behave to men who are not their husbands.

LORD W. Dumby, you are ridiculous, and Cecil, you let your tongue run away with you. You must leave Mrs. Erlynne alone. You don't really know anything about her, and you're always talking scandal against her.

CECIL G. [*coming towards him* L. C.]. My dear Arthur, *I* never talk scandal. *I* only talk gossip.

LORD W. What is the difference between scandal and gossip?

CECIL G. Oh! gossip is charming! History is merely gossip. But scandal is gossip made tedious by morality. Now I never moralize. A man who moralizes is usually a hypocrite, and a woman who moralizes is invariably plain. There is nothing in the whole world so unbecoming to a woman as a Non-conformist conscience. And most women know it, I'm glad to say.

LORD A. Just my sentiments, dear boy just my sentiments.

CECIL G. Sorry to hear it, Tuppy; whenever people agree with me, I always feel I must be wrong.

LORD A. My dear boy, when I was your age —

CECIL G. But you never were, Tuppy, and you never will be. [*Goes up* C.] I say, Darlington, let us have some cards. You'll play, Arthur, won't you?

LORD W. No, thanks, Cecil.

DUMBY [*with a sigh*]. Good heavens! how marriage ruins a man! It's as demoralizing as cigarettes, and far more expensive.

CECIL G. You'll play, of course, Tuppy?

LORD A. [*pouring himself out a brandy and soda at table*]. Can't, dear boy. Promised Mrs. Erlynne never to play or drink again.

CECIL G. Now, my dear Tuppy, don't be led astray into the paths of virtue. Reformed, you would be perfectly tedious. That is the worst of women. They always want one to be good. And if we are good, when they meet us, they don't love us at all. They like to find us quite irretrievably bad, and to leave us quite unattractively good.

LORD D. [*rising from* R. *table, where he has been writing letters*]. They always do find us bad!

DUMBY. I don't think we are bad. I think we are all good except Tuppy.

LORD D. No, we are all in the gutter, but some of us are looking at the stars.
[*Sits down at* C. *table.*]

DUMBY. We are all in the gutter, but some of us are looking at the stars? Upon my word, you are very romantic to-night, Darlington.

CECIL G. Too romantic! You must be in love. Who is the girl?

LORD D. The woman I love is not free, or thinks she isn't. [*Glances instinctively at* LORD W. *while he speaks.*]

CECIL G. A married woman, then! Well, there's nothing in the world like the devotion of a married woman. It's a thing no married man knows anything about.

LORD D. Oh! she doesn't love me. She is a good woman. She is the only good woman I have ever met in my life.

CECIL G. The only good woman you have ever met in your life?

LORD D. Yes!

CECIL G. [*lighting a cigarette*]. Well, you are a lucky fellow! Why, I have met hundreds of good women. I never seem to meet any but good women. The world is perfectly packed with good women. To know them is a middle-class education.

LORD D. This woman has purity and innocence. She has everything we men have lost.

CECIL G. My dear fellow, what on earth should we men do going about with purity and innocence? A carefully thought-out buttonhole is much more effective.

DUMBY. She doesn't really love you then?

LORD D. No, she does not!

DUMBY. I congratulate you, my dear fellow. In this world there are only two tragedies. One is not getting what one wants, and the other is getting it. The last is much the worst, the last is a real tragedy! But I am interested to hear she does not love you. How long could you love a woman who did n't love you, Cecil?

CECIL G. A woman who did n't love me? Oh, all my life!

DUMBY. So could I. But it's so difficult to meet one.

LORD D. How can you be so conceited, Dumby?

DUMBY. I didn't say it as a matter of conceit. I said it as a matter of regret. I have been wildly, madly adored. I am sorry I have. It has been an immense nuisance. I should like to be allowed a little time to myself, now and then.

LORD A. [*looking round*]. Time to educate yourself, I suppose.

DUMBY. No, time to forget all I have learned. That is much more important, dear Tuppy.
[LORD A. *moves uneasily in his chair.*]

LORD D. What cynics you fellows are!

CECIL G. What is a cynic?
[*Sitting on the back of the sofa.*]

LORD D. A man who knows the price of everything, and the value of nothing.

CECIL G. And a sentimentalist, my dear Darlington, is a man who sees an absurd value in everything, and does n't know the market price of any single thing.

LORD D. You always amuse me, Cecil. You talk as if you were a man of experience.

CECIL G. I am.
[*Moves up to front of fireplace.*]

LORD D. You are far too young!

CECIL G. That is a great error. Experience is a question of instinct about life. I have got it. Tuppy has n't. Experience is the name Tuppy gives to his mistakes. That is all.
[LORD A. *looks round indignantly.*]

DUMBY. Experience is the name every one gives to their mistakes.

CECIL G. [*standing with his back to fireplace*]. One should n't commit any.
[*Sees* LADY W.'s *fan on sofa.*]

DUMBY. Life would be very dull without them.

CECIL G. Of course you are quite faithful to this woman you are in love with, Darlington, to this good woman?

LORD D. Cecil, if one really loves a woman, all other women in the world become absolutely meaningless to one. Love changes one — I am changed.

CECIL G. Dear me! How very interesting. Tuppy, I want to talk to you.
[LORD A. *takes no notice.*]

DUMBY. It's no use talking to Tuppy. You might as well talk to a brick wall.

CECIL G. But I like talking to a brick wall — it's the only thing in the world that never contradicts me! Tuppy!

LORD A. Well, what is it? What is it? [*Rising and going over to* CECIL G.]

CECIL G. Come over here. I want you particularly. [*Aside.*] Darlington has been moralizing and talking about the purity of love, and that sort of thing, and he has got some woman in his rooms all the time.

LORD A. No, really! really!

CECIL G. [*in a low voice*]. Yes, here is her fan. [*Points to the fan.*]

LORD A. [*chuckling*]. By Jove! By Jove!

LORD W. [*up by door*]. I am really off now, Lord Darlington. I am sorry you are leaving England so soon. Pray call on us when you come back! My wife and I will be charmed to see you!

LORD D. [*up stage with* LORD W.]. I am afraid I shall be away for many years. Good-night!

CECIL G. Arthur!

LORD W. What?

CECIL G. I want to speak to you for a moment. No, do come!

LORD W. [*putting on his coat*]. I can't — I'm off!

CECIL G. It is something very particular. It will interest you enormously.

LORD W. [*smiling*]. It is some of your nonsense, Cecil.

CECIL G. It isn't. It isn't really!

LORD A. [*going to him*]. My dear fellow, you mustn't go yet. I have a lot to talk to you about. And Cecil has something to show you.

LORD W. [*walking over*]. Well, what is it?

CECIL G. Darlington has got a woman here in his rooms. Here is her fan. Amusing, isn't it? [*A pause.*]

LORD W. Good God!

[*Seizes the fan* — DUMBY *rises.*]

CECIL G. What is the matter?

LORD W. Lord Darlington!

LORD D. [*turning round*]. Yes!

LORD W. What is my wife's fan doing here in your rooms? Hands off, Cecil. Don't touch me.

LORD D. Your wife's fan?

LORD W. Yes, here it is!

LORD D. [*walking towards him*]. I don't know!

LORD W. You must know. I demand an explanation. [*To* CECIL G.] Don't hold me, you fool.

LORD D. [*aside*]. She is here after all!

LORD W. Speak, sir! Why is my wife's fan here? Answer me, by God! I'll search your rooms, and if my wife's here, I'll — [*Moves.*]

LORD D. You shall not search my rooms. You have no right to do so. I forbid you.

LORD W. You scoundrel! I'll not leave your room till I have searched every corner of it! What moves behind that curtain? [*Rushes towards the curtain* C.]

MRS. E. [*Enters behind* R.] Lord Windermere!

LORD W. Mrs. Erlynne!

[*Every one starts and turns round.* LADY W. *slips out from behind the curtain and glides from the room* L.]

MRS. E. I am afraid I took your wife's fan in mistake for my own, when I was leaving your house to-night. I am so sorry.

[*Takes fan from him.* LORD W. *looks at her in contempt.* LORD D. *in mingled astonishment and anger.* LORD A. *turns away. The other men smile at each other.*]

ACT IV

SCENE — *Same as in Act I.*

LADY W. [*lying on sofa*]. How can I tell him? I can't tell him. It would kill me. I wonder what happened after I escaped from that horrible room. Perhaps she told them the true reason of her being there, and the real meaning of that — fatal fan of mine. Oh, if he knows — how can I look him in the face again? He would never forgive me. [*Touches bell.*] How securely one thinks one lives — out of reach of temptation, sin, folly. And then suddenly — Oh! Life is terrible. It rules us, we do not rule it.

[*Enter* ROSALIE R.]

ROSALIE. Did your ladyship ring for me?

LADY W. Yes. Have you found out at what time Lord Windermere came in last night?

ROSALIE. His lordship did not come in till five o'clock.

LADY W. Five o'clock! He knocked at my door this morning, did n't he?

ROSALIE. Yes, my lady — at half past nine. I told him your ladyship was not awake yet.

LADY W. Did he say anything?

ROSALIE. Something about your ladyship's fan. I did n't quite catch what his lordship said. Has the fan been lost, my lady? I can't find it, and Parker says it was not left in any of the rooms. He has looked in all of them and on the terrace as well.

LADY W. It does n't matter. Tell Parker not to trouble. That will do.

[*Exit* ROSALIE.]

LADY W. [*rising*]. She is sure to tell him. I can fancy a person doing a wonderful act of self-sacrifice, doing it spontaneously, recklessly, nobly — and afterwards finding out that it costs too much. Why should she hesitate between her ruin and mine? . . . How strange! I would have publicly disgraced her in my own house. She accepts public disgrace in the house of another to save me. . . . There is a bitter irony in things, a bitter irony in the way we talk of good and bad women. . . . Oh, what a lesson! and what a pity that in life we only get our lessons when they are of no use to us! For even if she does n't tell, I must. Oh! the shame of it, the shame of it. To tell it is to live through it all again. Actions are the first tragedy in life, words are the second. Words are perhaps the worst. Words are merciless. . . . Oh!

[*Starts as* LORD W. *enters.*]

LORD W. [*kisses her*]. Margaret — how pale you look!

LADY W. I slept very badly.

LORD W. [*sitting on sofa with her*]. I am so sorry. I came in dreadfully late, and I did n't like to wake you. You are crying, dear.

LADY W. Yes, I am crying, for I have something to tell you, Arthur.

LORD W. My dear child, you are not well. You 've been doing too much. Let us go away to the country. You 'll be all right at Selby. The season is almost over. There is no use staying on. Poor darling! We 'll go away to-day, if you like. [*Rises.*] We can easily catch the 4.30. I 'll send a wire to Fannen. [*Crosses and sits down at table to write a telegram.*]

LADY W. Yes; let us go away to-day. No; I can't go away to-day, Arthur. There is some one I must see before I leave town — some one who has been kind to me.

LORD W. [*rising and leaning over sofa*]. Kind to you?

LADY W. Far more than that. [*Rises and goes to him.*] I will tell you, Arthur, but only love me, love me as you used to love me.

LORD W. Used to? You are not thinking of that wretched woman who came here last night? [*Coming round and sitting* R. *of her.*] You don't still imagine — no, you could n't.

LADY W. I don't. I know now I was wrong and foolish.

LORD W. It was very good of you to receive her last night — but you are never to see her again.

LADY W. Why do you say that?

[*A pause.*]

LORD W. [*holding her hand*]. Margaret, I thought Mrs. Erlynne was a woman more sinned against than sinning, as the phrase goes. I thought she wanted to be good, to get back into a place that she had lost by a moment's folly, to lead again a decent life. I believed what she told me — I was mistaken in her. She is bad — as bad as a woman can be.

LADY W. Arthur, Arthur, don't talk so bitterly about any woman. I don't think now that people can be divided into the good and the bad, as though they were two separate races or creations. What are called good women may have terrible things in them, mad moods of recklessness, assertion, jealousy, sin. Bad women, as they are termed, may have in them sorrow, repentance, pity, sacrifice. And I don't think Mrs. Erlynne a bad woman — I know she 's not.

LORD W. My dear child, the woman's impossible. No matter what harm she tries to do us, you must never see her again. She is inadmissible anywhere.

LADY W. But I want to see her. I want her to come here.

LORD W. Never!

LADY W. She came here once as *your* guest. She must come now as *mine*. That is but fair.

LORD W. She should never have come here.

LADY W. [*rising*]. It is too late, Arthur, to say that now. [*Moves away.*]

LORD W. [*rising*]. Margaret, if you knew where Mrs. Erlynne went last night, after she left this house, you would not sit in the same room with her. It was absolutely shameless, the whole thing.

LADY W. Arthur, I can't bear it any longer. I must tell you. Last night —

[*Enter* PARKER *with a tray on which lie* LADY W.'s *fan and a card.*]

PARKER. Mrs. Erlynne has called to return your ladyship's fan which she took away by mistake last night. Mrs. Erlynne has written a message on the card.

LADY W. Oh, ask Mrs. Erlynne to be kind enough to come up. [*Reads card.*] Say I shall be very glad to see her. [*Exit* PARKER.] She wants to see me, Arthur.

LORD W. [*Takes card and looks at it.*] Margaret, I *beg* you not to. Let me see her first, at any rate. She's a very dangerous woman. She is the most dangerous woman I know. You don't realize what you're doing.

LADY W. It is right that I should see her.

LORD W. My child, you may be on the brink of a great sorrow. Don't go to meet it. It is absolutely necessary that I should see her before you do.

LADY W. Why should it be necessary?

[*Enter* PARKER.]

PARKER. Mrs. Erlynne.

[*Enter* MRS. E. *Exit* PARKER.]

MRS. E. How do you do, Lady Windermere? [*To* LORD W.] How do you do? Do you know, Lady Windermere, I am so sorry about your fan. I can't imagine how I made such a silly mistake. Most stupid of me. And as I was driving in your direction, I thought I would take the opportunity of returning your property in person, with many apologies for my carelessness, and of bidding you good-bye.

LADY W. Good-bye? [*Moves towards sofa with* MRS. E. *and sits down beside her.*] Are you going away, then, Mrs. Erlynne?

MRS. E. Yes; I am going to live abroad again. The English climate doesn't suit me. My — heart is affected here, and that I don't like. I prefer living in the south. London is too full of fogs and — and serious people, Lord Windermere. Whether the fogs produce the serious people or whether

the serious people produce the fogs, I don't know, but the whole thing rather gets on my nerves, and so I'm leaving this afternoon by the Club Train.

LADY W. This afternoon? But I wanted so much to come and see you.

MRS. E. How kind of you? But I am afraid I have to go.

LADY W. Shall I never see you again, Mrs. Erlynne?

MRS. E. I am afraid not. Our lives lie too far apart. But there is a little thing I would like you to do for me. I want a photograph of you, Lady Windermere — would you give me one? You don't know how gratified I should be.

LADY W. Oh, with pleasure. There is one on that table. I'll show it to you. [*Goes across to the table.*]

LORD W. [*coming up to* MRS. E. *and speaking in a low voice*]. It is monstrous your intruding yourself here after your conduct last night.

MRS. E. [*with an amused smile*]. My dear Windermere, manners before morals!

LADY W. [*returning*]. I'm afraid it is very flattering — I am not so pretty as that. [*Showing photograph.*]

MRS. E. You are much prettier. But haven't you got one of yourself with your little boy?

LADY W. *I have.* Would you prefer one of those?

MRS. E. Yes.

LADY W. I'll go and get it for you, if you'll excuse me for a moment. I have one upstairs.

MRS. E. So sorry, Lady Windermere, to give you so much trouble.

LADY W. [*Moves to door* R.] No trouble at all, Mrs. Erlynne.

MRS. E. Thanks so much. [*Exit* LADY W. R.] You seem rather out of temper this morning, Windermere. Why should you be? Margaret and I get on charmingly together.

LORD W. I can't bear to see you with her. Besides, you have not told me the truth, Mrs. Erlynne.

MRS. E. I have not told *her* the truth, you mean.

LORD W. [*standing* C.]. I sometimes wish you had. I should have been spared then the misery, the anxiety, the annoyance of the last six months. But rather than my

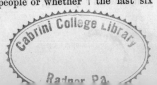

wife should know — that the mother whom she was taught to consider as dead, the mother whom she has mourned as dead, is living — a divorced woman going about under an assumed name, a bad woman preying upon life, as I know you now to be — rather than that, I was ready to supply you with money to pay bill after bill, extravagance after extravagance, to risk what occurred yesterday, the first quarrel I have ever had with my wife. You don't understand what that means to me. How could you? But I tell you that the only bitter words that ever came from those sweet lips of hers were on your account, and I hate to see you next her. You sully the innocence that is in her. [*Moves* L. C.] And then I used to think that with all your faults you were frank and honest. You are not.

MRS. E. Why do you say that?

LORD W. You made me get you an invitation to my wife's ball.

MRS. E. For my daughter's ball — yes.

LORD W. You came, and within an hour of your leaving the house, you are found in a man's rooms — you are disgraced before every one. [*Goes up stage* C.]

MRS. E. Yes.

LORD W. [*turning round on her*]. Therefore I have a right to look upon you as what you are — a worthless, vicious woman. I have the right to tell you never to enter this house, never to attempt to come near my wife —

MRS. E. [*coldly*]. My daughter, you mean.

LORD W. You have no right to claim her as your daughter. You left her, abandoned her, when she was but a child in the cradle, abandoned her for your lover, who abandoned you in turn.

MRS. E. [*rising*]. Do you count that to his credit, Lord Windermere — or to mine?

LORD W. To his, now that I know you.

MRS. E. Take care — you had better be careful.

LORD W. Oh, I am not going to mince words for you. I know you thoroughly.

MRS. E. [*looking steadily at him*]. I question that.

LORD W. I *do* know you. For twenty years of your life you lived without your child, without a thought of your child. One day you read in the papers that she had married a rich man. You saw your hideous

chance. You knew that to spare her the ignominy of learning that a woman like you was her mother, I would endure anything. You began your blackmailing.

MRS. E. [*shrugging her shoulders*]. Don't use ugly words, Windermere. They are vulgar. I saw my chance, it is true, and took it.

LORD W. Yes, you took it — and spoiled it all last night by being found out.

MRS. E. [*with a strange smile*]. You **are** quite right, I spoiled it all last night.

LORD W. And as for your blunder in taking my wife's fan from here, and then leaving it about in Darlington's rooms, it is unpardonable. I can't bear the sight of it now. I shall never let my wife use it again. The thing is soiled for me. You should have kept it, and not brought it back.

MRS. E. I think I *shall* keep it. [*Goes up.*] It's extremely pretty. [*Takes up fan.*] I shall ask Margaret to give it to me.

LORD W. I hope my wife will give it you.

MRS. E. Oh, I'm sure she will have no objection.

LORD W. I wish that at the same time she would give you a miniature she kisses every night before she prays — It's the miniature of a young, innocent-looking girl with beautiful dark hair.

MRS. E. Ah, yes, I remember. How long ago that seems! [*Goes to sofa and sits down.*] It was done before I was married. Dark hair and an innocent expression were the fashion then, Windermere! [*A pause.*]

LORD W. What do you mean by coming here this morning? What is your object?

[*Crossing* L. C. *and sitting.*]

MRS. E. [*with a note of irony in her voice*]. To bid good-bye to my dear daughter, of course. [LORD W. *bites his underlip in anger.* MRS. E. *looks at him, and her voice and manner become serious. In her accents as she talks there is a note of deep tragedy. For a moment she reveals herself.*] Oh, don't imagine I am going to have a pathetic scene with her, weep on her neck and tell her who I am, and all that kind of thing. I have no ambition to play the part of a mother. Only once in my life have I known a mother's feelings. That was last night. They were terrible — they made me suffer — they made me suffer too much. For twenty years, as you say, I have lived childless — I want to ive childless still. [*Hiding her feelings with a trivial laugh.*] Besides, my dear Windermere, how on earth could I pose as a mother with a grown-up daughter? Margaret is twenty-one, and I have never admitted that I am more than twenty-nine, or thirty at the most. Twenty-nine when there are pink shades, thirty when there are not. So you see what difficulties it would involve. No, as far as I am concerned, let your wife cherish the memory of this dead, stainless mother. Why should I interfere with her illusions? I find it hard enough to keep my own. I lost one illusion last night. I thought I had no heart. I find I have, and a heart does n't suit me, Windermere. Somehow it does n't go with modern dress. It makes one look old. [*Takes up hand-mirror from table and looks into it.*] And it spoils one's career at critical moments.

LORD W. You fill me with horror — with absolute horror.

MRS. E. [*rising*]. I suppose, Windermere, you would like me to retire into a convent or become a hospital nurse or something of that kind, as people do in silly modern novels. That is stupid of you, Arthur; in real life we don't do such things — not as long as we have any good looks left, at any rate. No — what consoles one nowadays is not repentance, but pleasure. Repentance is quite out of date. And, besides, if a woman really repents, she has to go to a bad dressmaker, otherwise no one believes in her. And nothing in the world would induce me to do that. No; I am going to pass entirely out of your two lives. My coming into them has been a mistake — I discovered that last night.

LORD W. A fatal mistake.

MRS. E. [*smiling*]. Almost fatal.

LORD W. I am sorry now I did not tell my wife the whole thing at once.

MRS. E. I regret my bad actions. You regret your good ones — that is the difference between us.

LORD W. I don't trust you. I *will* tell my wife. It 's better for her to know, and from me. It will cause her infinite pain — it will humiliate her terribly, but it 's right that she should know.

MRS. E. You propose to tell her?

LORD W. I am going to tell her.

MRS. E. [*going up to him*]. If you do, I will make my name so infamous that it will mar every moment of her life. It will ruin her and make her wretched. If you dare to tell her, there is no depth of degradation I will not sink to, no pit of shame I will not enter. You shall not tell her — I forbid you.

LORD W. Why?

MRS. E. [*after a pause*]. If I said to you that I cared for her, perhaps loved her even — you would sneer at me, would n't you?

LORD W. I should feel it was not true. A mother's love means devotion, unselfishness, sacrifice. What could you know of such things?

MRS. E. You are right. What could I know of such things? Don't let us talk any more about *it*, as for telling my daughter who I am, that I do not allow. It is my secret, it is not yours. If I make up my mind to tell her, and I think I will, I shall tell her before I leave this house — if not, I shall never tell her.

LORD W. [*angrily*]. Then let me beg of you to leave our house at once. I will make your excuses to Margaret.

[*Enter* LADY W. R. *She goes over to* MRS. E. *with the photograph in her hand.* LORD W. *moves to back of sofa, and anxiously watches* MRS. E. *as the scene progresses.*]

LADY W. I am so sorry, Mrs. Erlynne, to have kept you waiting. I could n't find the photograph anywhere. At last I discovered it in my husband's dressing-room — he had stolen it.

MRS. E. [*Takes the photograph from her and looks at it.*] I am not surprised — it is charming. [*Goes over to sofa with* LADY W. *and sits down beside her. Looks again at the photograph.*] And so that is your little boy! What is he called?

LADY W. Gerard, after my dear father.

MRS. E. [*laying the photograph down*]. Really?

LADY W. Yes. If it had been a girl, I would have called it after my mother. My mother had the same name as myself, Margaret.

MRS. E. My name is Margaret, too.

LADY W. Indeed!

MRS. E. Yes. [*Pause.*] You are devoted to your mother's memory, Lady Windermere, your husband tells me.

LADY W. We all have ideals in life. At

least we all should have. Mine is my mother.

MRS. E. Ideals are dangerous things. Realities are better. They wound, but they are better.

LADY W. [*shaking her head*]. If I lost my ideals, I should lose everything.

MRS. E. Everything?

LADY W. Yes. [*Pause.*]

MRS. E. Did your father often speak to you of your mother?

LADY W. No, it gave him too much pain. He told me how my mother had died a few months after I was born. His eyes filled with tears as he spoke. Then he begged me never to mention her name to him again. It made him suffer even to hear it. My father — my father really died of a broken heart. His was the most ruined life I know.

MRS. E. [*rising*]. I am afraid I must go now, Lady Windermere.

LADY W. [*rising*]. Oh no, don't.

MRS. E. I think I had better. My carriage must have come back by this time. I sent it to Lady Jedburgh's with a note.

LADY W. Arthur, would you mind seeing if Mrs. Erlynne's carriage has come back?

MRS. E. Pray don't trouble Lord Windermere, Lady Windermere.

LADY W. Yes, Arthur, do go, please. [LORD W. *hesitates for a moment, and looks at* MRS. E. *She remains quite impassive. He leaves the room.*]

[*To* MRS. E.] Oh, what am I to say to you? You saved me last night! [*Goes toward her.*]

MRS. E. Hush — don't speak of it.

LADY W. I must speak of it. I can't let you think that I am going to accept this sacrifice. I am not. It is too great. I am going to tell my husband everything. It is my duty.

MRS. E. It is not your duty — at least you have duties to others besides him. You say you owe me something?

LADY W. I owe you everything.

MRS. E. Then pay your debt by silence. That is the only way in which it can be paid. Don't spoil the one good thing I have done in my life by telling it to any one. Promise me that what passed last night will remain a secret between us. You must not bring misery into your husband's life. Why spoil his love? You

must not spoil it. Love is easily killed. Oh, how easily love is killed! Pledge me your word, Lady Windermere, that you will *never* tell him. I insist upon it.

LADY W. [*with bowed head*]. It is your will, not mine.

MRS. E. Yes, it is my will. And never forget your child — I like to think of you as a mother. I like you to think of yourself as one.

LADY W. [*looking up*]. I always will now. Only once in my life I have forgotten my own mother — that was last night. Oh, if I had remembered her, I should not have been so foolish, so wicked.

MRS. E. [*with a slight shudder*]. Hush, last night is quite over.

[*Enter* LORD W.]

LORD W. Your carriage has not come back yet, Mrs. Erlynne.

MRS. E. It makes no matter. I'll take a hansom. There is nothing in the world so respectable as a good Shrewsbury and Talbot. And now, dear Lady Windermere, I am afraid it is really good-bye. [*Moves up* C.] Oh, I remember. You'll think me absurd, but do you know, I've taken a great fancy to this fan that I was silly enough to run away with last night from your ball. Now, I wonder would you give it to me? Lord Windermere says you may. I know it is his present.

LADY W. Oh, certainly, if it will give you any pleasure. But it has my name on it. It has "Margaret" on it.

MRS. E. But we have the same Christian name.

LADY W. Oh, I forgot. Of course, do have it. What a wonderful chance our names being the same!

MRS. E. Quite wonderful. Thanks — it will always remind me of you.

[*Shakes hands with her.*]

[*Enter* PARKER.]

PARKER. Lord Augustus Lorton. Mrs. Erlynne's carriage has come.

[*Enter* LORD A.]

LORD A. Good-morning, dear boy. Good-morning, Lady Windermere. [*Sees* MRS. E.] Mrs. Erlynne!

MRS. E. How do you do, Lord Augustus? Are you quite well this morning?

LORD A. [*coldly*]. Quite well, thank you, Mrs. Erlynne.

Mrs. E. You don't look at all well, Lord Augustus. You stop up too late — it is so bad for you. You really should take more care of yourself. Good-bye, Lord Windermere. [*Goes towards door with a bow to* Lord A. *Suddenly smiles, and looks back at him.*] Lord Augustus ! Won't you see me to my carriage ? You might carry the fan.

Lord W. Allow me !

Mrs. E. No, I want Lord Augustus. I have a special message for the dear Duchess. Won't you carry the fan, Lord Augustus ?

Lord A. If you really desire it, Mrs. Erlynne.

Mrs. E. [*laughing*]. Of course I do. You 'll carry it so gracefully. You would carry off anything gracefully, dear Lord Augustus.

[*When she reaches the door she looks back for a moment at* Lady W. *Their eyes meet. Then she turns, and exit* c., *followed by* Lord A.]

Lady W. You will never speak against Mrs. Erlynne again, Arthur, will you ?

Lord W. [*gravely*]. She is better than one thought her.

Lady W. She is better than I am.

Lord W. [*smiling as he strokes her hair*]. Child, you and she belong to different worlds. Into your world evil has never entered.

Lady W. Don't say that, Arthur. There is the same world for all of us, and good and evil, sin and innocence, go through it hand in hand. To shut one's eyes to half of life that one may live securely is as though one blinded one's self that one might walk with more safety in a land of pit and precipice.

Lord W. [*Moves down with her.*] Darling, why do you say that ?

Lady W. [*Sits on sofa.*] Because I, who had shut my eyes to life, came to the brink And one who had separated us —

Lord W. We were never parted.

Lady W. We never must be again. Oh, Arthur, don't love me less, and I will trust you more. I will trust you absolutely. Let us go to Selby. In the Rose Garden at Selby, the roses are white and red.

[*Enter* Lord A.]

Lord A. Arthur, she has explained everything ! [Lady W. *looks horribly frightened.* Lord W. *starts.* Lord A. *takes* Lord W. *by the arm, and brings him to front of stage.*] My dear fellow, she has explained every demmed thing. We all wronged her immensely. It was entirely for my sake she went to Darlington's rooms — called first at the club. Fact is, wanted to put me out of suspense, and being told I had gone on, followed — naturally—frightened when she heard a lot of men coming in — retired to another room — I assure you, most gratifying to me, the whole thing. We all behaved brutally to her. She is just the woman for me. Suits me down to the ground. All the condition she makes is that we live out of England — a very good thing, too ! — Demmed clubs, demmed climate, demmed cooks, demmed everything ! Sick of it all.

Lady W. [*frightened*]. Has Mrs. Erlynne — ?

Lord A. [*advancing towards her with a bow*]. Yes, Lady Windermere, Mrs. Erlynne has done me the honor of accepting my hand.

Lord W. Well, you are certainly marrying a very clever woman.

Lady W. [*taking her husband's hand*]. Ah ! you 're marrying a very good woman.

THE SECOND MRS. TANQUERAY

A PLAY IN FOUR ACTS

By ARTHUR W. PINERO

PERSONS

AUBREY TANQUERAY

PAULA

ELLEAN

CAYLEY DRUMMLE

MRS. CORTELYON

CAPTAIN HUGH ARDALE

GORDON JAYNE, M.D.

FRANK MISQUITH, Q.C., M.P.

SIR GEORGE ORREYED, BART.

LADY ORREYED

MORSE

Time — The Present Day

The Scene of the First Act is laid at MR. TANQUERAY'S rooms, No. 2 x, The Albany, in the month of November; the occurrences of the succeeding Acts take place at his house, "Highercoombe," near Willowmere, Surrey, during the early part of the following year.

THE SECOND MRS. TANQUERAY

THE FIRST ACT

AUBREY TANQUERAY'S *chambers in the Albany — a richly and tastefully decorated room, elegantly and luxuriously furnished: on the right a large pair of doors opening into another room, on the left at the further end of the room a small door leading to a bed-chamber. A circular table is laid for a dinner for four persons, which has now reached the stage of dessert and coffee. Everything in the apartment suggests wealth and refinement. The fire is burning brightly.*

AUBREY TANQUERAY, MISQUITH, *and* JAYNE *are seated at the dinner table.* AUBREY *is forty-two, handsome, winning in manner, his speech and bearing retaining some of the qualities of young manhood.* MISQUITH *is about forty-seven, genial and portly.* JAYNE *is a year or two* MISQUITH'S *senior; soft-speaking and precise — in appearance a type of the prosperous town physician.* MORSE, AUBREY'S *servant, places a little cabinet of cigars and the spirit-lamp on the table beside* AUBREY, *and goes out.*

MISQUITH. Aubrey, it is a pleasant yet dreadful fact to contemplate, but it's nearly fifteen years since I first dined with you. You lodged in Piccadilly in those days, over a hat-shop. Jayne, I met you at that dinner, and Cayley Drummle.

JAYNE. Yes, yes. What a pity it is that Cayley is n't here to-night.

AUBREY. Confound the old gossip! His empty chair has been staring us in the face all through dinner. I ought to have told Morse to take it away.

MISQUITH. Odd, his sending no excuse.

AUBREY. I'll walk round to his lodgings later on and ask after him.

MISQUITH. I'll go with you.

JAYNE. So will I.

AUBREY [*opening the cigar-cabinet*]. Doctor, it's useless to tempt you, I know. Frank — [MISQUITH *and* AUBREY *smoke*.] I particularly wished Cayley Drummle to be one of us to-night. You two fellows and Cayley are my closest, my best friends —

MISQUITH. My dear Aubrey!

JAYNE. I rejoice to hear you say so.

AUBREY. And I wanted to see the three of you round this table. You can't guess the reason.

MISQUITH. You desired to give us a most excellent dinner.

JAYNE. Obviously.

AUBREY [*hesitatingly*]. Well — I — [*glancing at the clock*] — Cayley won't turn up now.

JAYNE. H'm, hardly.

AUBREY. Then you two shall hear it. Doctor, Frank, this is the last time we are to meet in these rooms.

JAYNE. The last time?

MISQUITH. You're going to leave the Albany?

AUBREY. Yes. You've heard me speak of a house I built in the country years ago, have n't you?

MISQUITH. In Surrey.

AUBREY. Well, when my wife died I cleared out of that house and let it. I think of trying the place again.

MISQUITH. But you'll go raving mad if ever you find yourself down there alone.

AUBREY. Ah, but I shan't be alone, and that's what I wanted to tell you. I'm going to be married.

JAYNE. Going to be married?

MISQUITH. Married?

AUBREY. Yes — to-morrow.

JAYNE. To-morrow?

MISQUITH. You take my breath away! My dear fellow, I — I — of course, I congratulate you.

JAYNE. And — and — so do I — heartily.

AUBREY. Thanks — thanks.

[*There is a moment or two of embarrassment.*]

MISQUITH. Er — ah — this is an excellent cigar.

JAYNE. Ah — um — your coffee is remarkable.

AUBREY. Look here; I dare say you two old friends think this treatment very strange, very unkind. So I want you to understand me. You know a marriage often cools friendships. What's the usual course of things? A man's engagement is given out, he is congratulated, complimented upon his choice; the church is filled with troops of friends, and he goes away happily to a chorus of good wishes. He comes back, sets up house in town or country, and thinks to resume the old associations, the old companionships. My dear Frank, my dear good doctor, it's very seldom that it can be done. Generally, a worm has begun to eat its way into those hearty, unreserved, pre-nuptial friendships; a damnable constraint sets in and acts like a wasting disease; and so, believe me, in nine cases out of ten a man's marriage severs for him more close ties than it forms.

MISQUITH. Well, my dear Aubrey, I earnestly hope —

AUBREY. I know what you're going to say, Frank. I hope so, too. In the meantime let's face dangers. I've reminded you of the *usual* course of things, but my marriage is n't even the conventional sort of marriage likely to satisfy society. Now, Cayley's a bachelor, but you two men have wives. By the bye, my love to Mrs. Misquith and to Mrs. Jayne when you get home — don't forget that. Well, your wives may not — like — the lady I 'm going to marry.

JAYNE. Aubrey, forgive me for suggesting that the lady you are going to marry may not like our wives — mine at least; I beg your pardon, Frank.

AUBREY. Quite so; then I must go the way my wife goes.

MISQUITH. Come, come, pray don't let us anticipate that either side will be called upon to make such a sacrifice.

AUBREY. Yes, yes, let us anticipate it. And let us make up our minds to have no slow bleeding to death of our friendship. We 'll end a pleasant chapter here to-night, and after to-night start afresh. When my wife and I settle down at Willowmere it 's possible that we shall all come together. But if this is n't to be, for Heaven's sake let us recognize that it is simply because it *can't* be, and not wear hypocritical faces and suffer and be wretched. Doctor, Frank — [*holding out his hands, one to* MISQUITH,

the other to JAYNE] — good luck to all of us!

MISQUITH. But — but — do I understand we are to ask nothing? Not even the lady's name, Aubrey?

AUBREY. The lady, my dear Frank, belongs to the next chapter, and in that her name is Mrs. Aubrey Tanqueray.

JAYNE [*raising his coffee-cup*]. Then, in an old-fashioned way, I propose a toast. Aubrey, Frank, I give you "The Next Chapter!"

[*They drink the toast, saying, "The Next Chapter!"*]

AUBREY. Doctor, find a comfortable chair; Frank, you too. As we 're going to turn out by and by, let me scribble a couple of notes now while I think of them.

MISQUITH *and* JAYNE. Certainly — yes, yes.

AUBREY. It might slip my memory when I get back.

[AUBREY *sits at a writing-table at the other end of the room, and writes.*]

JAYNE. [*To* MISQUITH *in a whisper.*] Frank — [MISQUITH *quietly leaves his chair, and sits nearer to* JAYNE.] What is all this? Simply a morbid crank of Aubrey's with regard to ante-nuptial acquaintances?

MISQUITH. H'm! Did you notice *one* expression he used?

JAYNE. Let me think —

MISQUITH. "My marriage is not even the conventional sort of marriage likely to satisfy society."

JAYNE. Bless me, yes! What does that suggest?

MISQUITH. That he has a particular rather than a general reason for anticipating estrangement from his friends, I 'm afraid.

JAYNE. A horrible *mésalliance!* A dairymaid who has given him a glass of milk during a day's hunting, or a little anæmic shopgirl! Frank, I 'm utterly wretched!

MISQUITH. My dear Jayne, speaking in absolute confidence, I have never been more profoundly depressed in my life.

[MORSE *enters.*]

MORSE [*announcing*]. Mr. Drummle.
[CAYLEY DRUMMLE *enters briskly. He is a neat little man of about five-and-forty, in manner bright, airy, debonair, but with an undercurrent of seriousness.* MORSE *retires.*]

DRUMMLE. I 'm in disgrace; nobody

realizes that more thoroughly than I do. Where 's my host ?

AUBREY [*who has risen*]. Cayley.

DRUMMLE [*shaking hands with him*]. Don't speak to me till I have tendered my explanation. A harsh word from anybody would unman me.

[MISQUITH *and* JAYNE *shake hands with* DRUMMLE.]

AUBREY. Have you dined ?

DRUMMLE. No — unless you call a bit of fish, a cutlet, and a pancake dining.

AUBREY. Cayley, this is disgraceful.

JAYNE. Fish, a cutlet, and a pancake will require a great deal of explanation.

MISQUITH. Especially the pancake. My dear friend, your case looks miserably weak.

DRUMMLE. Hear me ! hear me !

JAYNE. Now then !

MISQUITH. Come !

AUBREY. Well !

DRUMMLE. It so happens that to-night I was exceptionally early in dressing for dinner.

MISQUITH. For which dinner — the fish and cutlet ?

DRUMMLE. For *this* dinner, of course — really, Frank ! At a quarter to eight, in fact, I found myself trimming my nails, with ten minutes to spare. Just then enter my man with a note — would I hasten, as fast as cab could carry me, to old Lady Orreyed in Bruton Street ? — "sad trouble." Now, recollect, please, I had ten minutes on my hands, old Lady Orreyed was a very dear friend of my mother's, and was in some distress.

AUBREY. Cayley, come to the fish and cutlet !

MISQUITH *and* JAYNE. Yes, yes, and the pancake !

DRUMMLE. Upon my word ! Well, the scene in Bruton Street beggars description; the women servants looked scared, the men drunk; and there was poor old Lady Orreyed on the floor of her boudoir like Queen Bess among her pillows.

AUBREY. What 's the matter ?

DRUMMLE. [*To everybody.*] You know George Orreyed ?

MISQUITH. Yes.

JAYNE. I 've met him.

DRUMMLE. Well, he 's a thing of the past.

AUBREY. Not dead !

DRUMMLE. Certainly, in the worst sense He 's married Mabel Hervey.

MISQUITH. What !

DRUMMLE. It 's true — this morning. The poor mother showed me his letter — a dozen curt words, and some of those ill-spelt.

MISQUITH [*walking up to the fireplace*]. I 'm very sorry.

JAYNE. Pardon my ignorance — who *was* Mabel Hervey ?

DRUMMLE. You don't — ? Oh, of course not. Miss Hervey — Lady Orreyed, as she now is — was a lady who would have been, perhaps has been, described in the reports of the Police or the Divorce Court as an actress. Had she belonged to a lower stratum of our advanced civilization she would, in the event of judicial inquiry, have defined her calling with equal justification as that of a dressmaker. To do her justice, she is a type of a class which is immortal. Physically, by the strange caprice of creation, curiously beautiful ; mentally, she lacks even the strength of deliberate viciousness. Paint her portrait, it would symbolize a creature perfectly patrician ; lance a vein of her superbly-modelled arm, you would get the poorest *vin ordinaire !* Her affections, emotions, impulses, her very existence — a burlesque ! Flaxen, five-and-twenty, and feebly frolicsome ; anybody's, in less gentle society I should say everybody's, property ! That, doctor, was Miss Hervey who is the new Lady Orreyed. Dost thou like the picture ?

MISQUITH. Very good, Cayley ! Bravo !

AUBREY [*laying his hand on* DRUMMLE'S *shoulder*]. You 'd scarcely believe it, Jayne, but none of us really know anything about this lady, our gay young friend here, I suspect, least of all.

DRUMMLE. Aubrey, I applaud your chivalry.

AUBREY. And perhaps you 'll let me finish a couple of letters which Frank and Jayne have given me leave to write. [*Returning to the writing-table.*] Ring for what you want, like a good fellow !

[AUBREY *resumes his writing.*]

MISQUITH. [*To* DRUMMLE.] Still, the fish and the cutlet remain unexplained.

DRUMMLE. Oh, the poor old woman was so weak that I insisted upon her taking some food, and felt there was nothing for it but to sit down opposite her. The fool! the blackguard!

MISQUITH. Poor Orreyed! Well, he's gone under for a time.

DRUMMLE. For a time! My dear Frank, I tell you he has absolutely ceased to be. [AUBREY, *who has been writing busily, turns his head towards the speakers and listens. His lips are set, and there is a frown upon his face.*] For all practical purposes you may regard him as the late George Orreyed. To-morrow the very characteristics of his speech, as we remember them, will have become obsolete.

JAYNE. But surely, in the course of years, he and his wife will outlive —

DRUMMLE. No, no, doctor, don't try to upset one of my settled beliefs. You may dive into many waters, but there is *one* social Dead Sea — !

JAYNE. Perhaps you're right.

DRUMMLE. Right! Good God! I wish you could prove me otherwise! Why, for years I've been sitting, and watching and waiting.

MISQUITH. You're in form to-night, Cayley. May we ask where you've been in the habit of squandering your useful leisure?

DRUMMLE. Where? On the shore of that same sea.

MISQUITH. And, pray, what have you been waiting for?

DRUMMLE. For some of my best friends *to come up.* [AUBREY *utters a half-stifled exclamation of impatience ; then he hurriedly gathers up his papers from the writing-table. The three men turn to him.*] Eh?

AUBREY. Oh, I — I'll finish my letters in the other room if you'll excuse me for five minutes. Tell Cayley the news.

[*He goes out.*]

DRUMMLE [*hurrying to the door*]. My dear fellow, my jabbering has disturbed you! I'll never talk again as long as I live!

MISQUITH. Close the door, Cayley.

[DRUMMLE *shuts the door.*]

JAYNE. Cayley —

DRUMMLE [*advancing to the dinner table*]. A smoke, a smoke, or I perish!

[*Selects a cigar from the little cabinet.*]

JAYNE. Cayley, marriages are in the air.

DRUMMLE. Are they? Discover the bacillus, doctor, and destroy it.

JAYNE. I mean, among our friends.

DRUMMLE. Oh, Nugent Warrinder's en-

gagement to Lady Alice Tring. I've heard of that. They're not to be married till the spring.

JAYNE. Another marriage that concerns us a little takes place to-morrow.

DRUMMLE. Whose marriage?

JAYNE. Aubrey's.

DRUMMLE. Aub—! [*Looking towards* MISQUITH.] Is it a joke?

MISQUITH. No.

DRUMMLE [*looking from* MISQUITH *to* JAYNE]. To whom?

MISQUITH. He doesn't tell us.

JAYNE. We three were asked here to-night to receive the announcement. Aubrey has some theory that marriage is likely to alienate a man from his friends, and it seems to me he has taken the precaution to wish us good-bye.

MISQUITH. No, no.

JAYNE. Practically, surely.

DRUMMLE [*thoughtfully*]. Marriage in general, does he mean, or *this* marriage?

JAYNE. That's the point. Frank says —

MISQUITH. No, no, no ; I feared it suggested —

JAYNE. Well, well. [*To* DRUMMLE.] What do you think of it?

DRUMMLE [*after a slight pause*]. Is there a light there? [*Lighting his cigar.*] He — wraps the lady — in mystery — you say?

MISQUITH. Most modestly.

DRUMMLE. Aubrey's — not — a very — young man.

JAYNE. Forty-three.

DRUMMLE. Ah! *L'âge critique!*

MISQUITH. A dangerous age — yes, yes.

DRUMMLE. When you two fellows go home, do you mind leaving me behind here?

MISQUITH. Not at all.

JAYNE. By all means.

DRUMMLE. All right. [*Anxiously.*] Deuce take it, the man's second marriage mustn't be another mistake!

[*With his head bent he walks up to the fireplace.*]

JAYNE. You knew him in his short married life, Cayley. Terribly unsatisfactory, wasn't it?

DRUMMLE. Well — [*Looking at the door.*] I quite closed that door?

MISQUITH. Yes.

[*Settles himself on the sofa;* JAYNE *is seated in an arm-chair.*]

DRUMMLE [*smoking with his back to the*

nre]. He married a Miss Herriott; that was in the year eighteen — confound dates — twenty years ago. She was a lovely creature — by Jove, she was ; by religion a Roman Catholic. She was one of your cold sort, you know — all marble arms and black velvet. I remember her with painful distinctness as the only woman who ever made me nervous.

MISQUITH. Ha, ha !

DRUMMLE. He loved her — to distraction, as they say. Jupiter, how fervently that poor devil courted her ! But I don't believe she allowed him even to squeeze her fingers. She *was* an iceberg ! As for kissing, the mere contact would have given him chapped lips. However, he married her and took her away, the latter greatly to my relief.

JAYNE. Abroad, you mean ?

DRUMMLE. Eh? Yes. I imagine he gratified her by renting a villa in Lapland, but I don't know. After a while they returned, and then I saw how woefully Aubrey had miscalculated results.

JAYNE. Miscalculated — ?

DRUMMLE. He had reckoned, poor wretch, that in the early days of marriage she would thaw. But she did n't. I used to picture him closing his doors and making up the fire in the hope of seeing her features relax. Bless her, the thaw never set in ! I believe she kept a thermometer in her stays and always registered ten degrees below zero. However, in time a child came — a daughter.

JAYNE. Did n't that — ?

DRUMMLE. Not a bit of it ; it made matters worse. Frightened at her failure to stir up in him some sympathetic religious belief, she determined upon strong measures with regard to the child. He opposed her for a miserable year or so, but she wore him down, and the insensible little brat was placed in a convent, first in France, then in Ireland. Not long afterwards the mother died, strangely enough, of fever, the only warmth, I believe, that ever came to that woman's body.

MISQUITH. Don't, Cayley !

JAYNE. The child is living, we know.

DRUMMLE. Yes, if you choose to call it living. Miss Tanqueray — a young woman of nineteen now — is in the Loretto convent at Armagh. She professes to have found her true vocation in a religious life, and within a month or two will take final vows.

MISQUITH. He ought to have removed his daughter from the convent when the mother died.

DRUMMLE. Yes, yes, but absolutely at the end there was reconciliation between husband and wife, and she won his promise that the child should complete her conventual education. He reaped his reward. When he attempted to gain his girl's confidence and affection he was too late ; he found he was dealing with the spirit of the mother. You remember his visit to Ireland last month ?

JAYNE. Yes.

DRUMMLE. That was to wish his girl good-bye.

MISQUITH. Poor fellow !

DRUMMLE. He sent for me when he came back. I think he must have had a lingering hope that the girl would relent — would come to life, as it were — at the last moment, for, for an hour or so, in this room, he was terribly shaken. I'm sure he'd clung to that hope from the persistent way in which he kept breaking off in his talk to repeat one dismal word, as if he could n't realize his position without dinning this damned word into his head.

JAYNE. What word was that ?

DRUMMLE. Alone — alone.

[AUBREY *enters*.]

AUBREY. A thousand apologies !

DRUMMLE [*gayly*]. We are talking about you, my dear Aubrey.

[*During the telling of the story,* MISQUITH *has risen and gone to the fire, and* DRUMMLE *has thrown himself full-length on the sofa.* AUBREY *now joins* MISQUITH *and* JAYNE.]

AUBREY. Well, Cayley, are you surprised ?

DRUMMLE. Surp — ! I have n't been surprised for twenty years.

AUBREY. And you 're not angry with me?

DRUMMLE. Angry! [*Rising.*] Because you considerately withhold the name of a lady with whom it is now the object of my life to become acquainted ? My dear fellow, you pique my curiosity, you give zest to my existence ! And as for a wedding, who on earth wants to attend that familiar and probably draughty function ? Ugh ! My cigar 's out.

AUBREY. Let's talk about something else.

MISQUITH [*looking at his watch*]. Not to-night, Aubrey.

AUBREY. My dear Frank!

MISQUITH. I go up to Scotland to-morrow, and there are some little matters —

JAYNE. I am off too.

AUBREY. No, no.

JAYNE. I must : I have to give a look to a case in Clifford Street on my way home.

AUBREY [*going to the door*]. Well ! [MISQUITH *and* JAYNE *exchange looks with* DRUMMLE. *Opening the door and calling.*] Morse, hats and coats ! I shall write to you all next week from Genoa or Florence. Now, doctor, Frank, remember, my love to Mrs. Misquith and to Mrs. Jayne !

[MORSE *enters with hats and coats.*]

MISQUITH *and* JAYNE. Yes, yes — yes, yes.

AUBREY. And your young people !

[*As* MISQUITH *and* JAYNE *put on their coats there is the clatter of careless talk.*]

JAYNE. Cayley, I meet you at dinner on Sunday.

DRUMMLE. At the Stratfields'. That's very pleasant.

MISQUITH [*putting on his coat with* AUBREY's *aid*]. Ah-h !

AUBREY. What's wrong ?

MISQUITH. A twinge. Why didn't I go to Aix in August ?

JAYNE [*shaking hands with* DRUMMLE]. Good-night, Cayley.

DRUMMLE. Good-night, my dear doctor !

MISQUITH [*shaking hands with* DRUMMLE]. Cayley, are you in town for long ?

DRUMMLE. Dear friend, I'm nowhere for long. Good-night.

MISQUITH. Good-night.

[AUBREY, JAYNE, *and* MISQUITH *go out, followed by* MORSE; *the hum of talk is continued outside.*]

AUBREY. A cigar, Frank.

MISQUITH. No, thank you.

AUBREY. Going to walk, doctor ?

JAYNE. If Frank will.

MISQUITH. By all means.

AUBREY. It's a cold night.

[*The door is closed.* DRUMMLE *remains standing with his coat on his arm and his hat in his hand*]

DRUMMLE. [*To himself, thoughtfully.*] Now then ! What the devil ! —

[AUBREY *returns.*]

AUBREY [*eyeing* DRUMMLE *a little awkwardly*]. Well, Cayley ?

DRUMMLE. Well, Aubrey ?

[AUBREY *walks up to the fire and stands looking into it.*]

AUBREY. You're not going, old chap ?

DRUMMLE [*sitting*]. No.

AUBREY [*after a slight pause, with a forced laugh*]. Hah, Cayley, I never thought I should feel — shy — with you.

DRUMMLE. Why do you ?

AUBREY. Never mind.

DRUMMLE. Now, I can quite understand a man wishing to be married in the dark, as it were.

AUBREY. You can ?

DRUMMLE. In your place I should very likely adopt the same course.

AUBREY. You think so ?

DRUMMLE. And if I intended marrying a lady not prominently in society, as I presume you do — as I presume you do —

AUBREY. Well ?

DRUMMLE. As I presume you do, I'm not sure that *I* should tender her for preliminary dissection at afternoon tea-tables.

AUBREY. No ?

DRUMMLE. In fact, there is probably only one person — were I in your position to-night — with whom I should care to chat the matter over.

AUBREY. Who's that ?

DRUMMLE. Yourself, of course. [*Going to* AUBREY *and standing beside him.*] Of course, yourself, old friend.

AUBREY [*after a pause*]. I must seem a brute to you, Cayley. But there are some acts which are hard to explain, hard to defend —

DRUMMLE. To defend —

AUBREY. Some acts which one must trust to time to put right.

[DRUMMLE *watches him for a moment, then takes up his hat and coat.*]

DRUMMLE. Well, I'll be moving.

AUBREY. Cayley ! Confound you and your old friendship ! Do you think I forget it ? Put your coat down ! Why did you stay behind here ? Cayley, the lady I am going to marry is the lady — who is known as — Mrs. Jarman. [*There is a pause.*

DRUMMLE [*in a low voice*]. Mrs. Jarman! are you serious?

[*He walks up to the fireplace, where he leans upon the mantelpiece uttering something like a groan.*]

AUBREY. As you've got this out of me I give you leave to say all you care to say. Come, we'll be plain with each other. You know Mrs. Jarman?

DRUMMLE. I first met her at — what does it matter?

AUBREY. Yes, yes, everything! Come!

DRUMMLE. I met her at Homburg, two — three seasons ago.

AUBREY. Not as Mrs. Jarman?

DRUMMLE. No.

AUBREY. She was then — ?

DRUMMLE. Mrs. Dartry.

AUBREY. Yes. She has also seen you in London, she says.

DRUMMLE. Certainly.

AUBREY. In Alford Street. Go on.

DRUMMLE. Please!

AUBREY. I insist.

DRUMMLE [*with a slight shrug of the shoulders*]. Some time last year I was asked by a man to sup at his house, one night after the theater.

AUBREY. Mr. Selwyn Ethurst — a bachelor.

DRUMMLE. Yes.

AUBREY. You were surprised therefore to find Mr. Ethurst aided in his cursed hospitality by a lady.

DRUMMLE. I was unprepared.

AUBREY. The lady you had known as Mrs Dartry? [DRUMMLE *inclines his head silently.*] There is something of a yachting cruise in the Mediterranean, too, is there not?

DRUMMLE. I joined Peter Jarman's yacht at Marseilles, in the Spring, a month before he died.

AUBREY. Mrs. Jarman was on board?

DRUMMLE. She was a kind hostess.

AUBREY. And an old acquaintance?

DRUMMLE. Yes.

AUBREY. You have told your story.

DRUMMLE. With your assistance.

AUBREY. I have put you to the pain of telling it to show you that this is not the case of a blind man entrapped by an artful woman. Let me add that Mrs. Jarman has no legal right to that name; that she is simply Miss Ray — Miss Paula Ray.

DRUMMLE [*after a pause*]. I should like to express my regret, Aubrey, for the way in which I spoke of George Orreyed's marriage.

AUBREY. You mean you compare Lady Orreyed with Miss Ray? [DRUMMLE *is silent.*] Oh, of course! To you, Cayley, all women who have been roughly treated, and who dare to survive by borrowing a little of our philosophy, are alike. You see in the crowd of the ill-used only one pattern; you can't detect the shades of goodness, intelligence, even nobility there. Well, how should you? The crowd is dimly lighted! And, besides, yours is the way of the world.

DRUMMLE. My dear Aubrey, I *live* in the world.

AUBREY. The name we give our little parish of St. James's.

DRUMMLE [*laying a hand on* AUBREY'S *shoulder*]. And you are quite prepared, my friend, to forfeit the esteem of your little parish?

AUBREY. I avoid mortification by shifting from one parish to another. I give up Pall Mall for the Surrey hills; leave off varnishing my boots, and double the thickness of the soles.

DRUMMLE. And your skin — do you double the thickness of that also?

AUBREY. I know you think me a fool, Cayley — you needn't infer that I'm a coward into the bargain. No! I know what I'm doing, and I do it deliberately, defiantly. I'm alone: I injure no living soul by the step I'm going to take; and so you can't urge the one argument which might restrain me. Of course, I don't expect you to think compassionately, fairly even, of the woman whom I — whom I am drawn to —

DRUMMLE. My dear Aubrey, I assure you I consider Mrs. — Miss Jarman — Mrs. Ray — Miss Ray — delightful. But I confess there is a form of chivalry which I gravely distrust, especially in a man of — our age.

AUBREY. Thanks. I've heard you say that from forty till fifty a man is at heart either a stoic or a satyr.

DRUMMLE [*protestingly*]. Ah! now —

AUBREY. I am neither. I have a temperate, honorable affection for Mrs. Jarman. She has never met a man who has treated her well — I intend to treat her well. That's all. And in a few years, Cayley, if you've not quite forsaken me, I 'll prove to you that it 's possible to rear a life of happiness, of good repute, on a — miserable foundation.

DRUMMLE [*offering his hand*]. Do prove it!

AUBREY [*taking his hand*]. We have spoken too freely of — of Mrs. Jarman. I was excited — angry. Please forget it!

DRUMMLE. My dear Aubrey, when we next meet I shall remember nothing but my respect for the lady who bears your name.

[MORSE *enters, closing the door behind him carefully.*]

AUBREY. What is it?

MORSE [*hesitatingly*]. May I speak to you, sir? [*In an undertone.*] Mrs. Jarman, sir.

AUBREY [*softly to* MORSE]. Mrs. Jarman! Do you mean she is at the lodge in her carriage?

MORSE. No, sir — here. [AUBREY *looks towards* DRUMMLE, *perplexed.*] There 's a nice fire in your — in that room, sir.

[*Glancing in the direction of the door leading to the bedroom.*]

AUBREY [*between his teeth, angrily*]. Very well. [MORSE *retires.*]

DRUMMLE [*looking at his watch*]. A quarter to eleven — horrible! [*Taking up his hat and coat.*] Must get to bed — up late every night this week. [AUBREY *assists* DRUMMLE *with his coat.*] Thank you. Well, good-night, Aubrey. I feel I 've been doooed serious, quite out of keeping with myself; pray overlook it.

AUBREY [*kindly*]. Ah, Cayley!

DRUMMLE [*putting on a neck-handker-chief*]. And remember that, after all, I 'm merely a spectator in life; nothing more than a man at a play, in fact; only, like the old-fashioned play goer, I love to see certain characters happy and comfortable at the finish. You understand?

AUBREY. I think I do.

DRUMMLE. Then, for as long as you can, old friend, will you — keep a stall for me?

AUBREY. Yes, Cayley.

DRUMMLE [*gayly*]. Ah, ha! Good-night! [*Bustling to the door.*] Don't bother! I 'll let myself out! Good-night! God bless yer!

[*He goes out;* AUBREY *follows him.* MORSE *enters by the other door, carrying some unopened letters, which after a little consideration he places on the mantelpiece against the clock.* AUBREY *returns.*]

AUBREY. Yes?

MORSE. You had n't seen your letters that came by the nine o'clock post, sir; I 've put 'em where they 'll catch your eye by and by.

AUBREY. Thank you.

MORSE [*hesitatingly*]. Gunter's cook and waiter have gone, sir. Would you prefer me to go to bed?

AUBREY [*frowning*]. Certainly not.

MORSE. Very well, sir. [*He goes out.*]

AUBREY [*opening the upper door*]. Paula! Paula!

[PAULA *enters and throws her arms round his neck. She is a young woman of about twenty-seven: beautiful, fresh, innocent-looking. She is in superb evening dress.*]

PAULA. Dearest!

AUBREY. Why have you come here?

PAULA. Angry?

AUBREY. Yes — no. But it 's eleven o'clock.

PAULA [*laughing*]. I know.

AUBREY. What on earth will Morse think?

PAULA. Do you trouble yourself about what servants *think*?

AUBREY. Of course.

PAULA. Goose! They 're only machines made to wait upon people — and to give evidence in the Divorce Court. [*Looking round.*] Oh, indeed! A snug little dinner!

AUBREY. Three men.

PAULA [*suspiciously*]. Men?

AUBREY. Men.

PAULA [*penitently*]. Ah! [*Sitting at the table.*] I 'm so hungry.

AUBREY. Let me get you some game pie, or some —

PAULA. No, no, hungry for this. What beautiful fruit! I love fruit when it 's expensive. [*He clears a space on the table, places a plate before her, and helps her to fruit.*] I have n't dined, Aubrey dear.

AUBREY. My poor girl! Why?

PAULA. In the first place, I forgot to order any dinner, and my cook, who has always loathed me, thought he 'd pay me out before he departed.

AUBREY. The beast!

PAULA. That 's precisely what I —

AUBREY. No, Paula!

PAULA. What I told my maid to call him. What next will you think of me?

AUBREY. Forgive me. You must be starved.

PAULA [*eating fruit*]. I did n't care. As there was nothing to eat, I sat in my best frock, with my toes on the dining-room fender, and dreamt, oh, such a lovely dinner party.

AUBREY. Dear lonely little woman!

PAULA. It was perfect. I saw you at the end of a very long table, opposite me, and we exchanged sly glances now and again over the flowers. We were host and hostess, Aubrey, and had been married about five years.

AUBREY [*kissing her hand*]. Five years.

PAULA. And on each side of us was the nicest set imaginable — you know, dearest, the sort of men and women that can't be imitated.

AUBREY. Yes, yes. Eat some more fruit.

PAULA. But I have n't told you the best part of my dream.

AUBREY. Tell me.

PAULA. Well, although we had been married only such a few years, I seemed to know by the look on their faces that none of our guests had ever heard anything — anything — anything peculiar about the fascinating hostess.

AUBREY. That 's just how it will be, Paula. The world moves so quickly. That 's just how it will be.

PAULA [*with a little grimace*]. I wonder! [*Glancing at the fire.*] Ugh! Do throw another log on.

AUBREY [*mending the fire*]. There. But you must n't be here long.

PAULA. Hospitable wretch! I 've something important to tell you. No, stay where you are. [*Turning from him, her face averted.*] Look here, that was my dream, Aubrey; but the fire went out while I was dozing, and I woke up with a regular fit of the shivers. And the result of it all was that I ran upstairs and scribbled you a letter.

AUBREY. Dear baby!

PAULA. Remain where you are. [*Taking a letter from her pocket.*] This is it. I 've given you an account of myself, furnished you with a list of my adventures since I — you know. [*Weighing the letter in her hand.*] I wonder if it would go for a penny. Most of it you 're acquainted with; *I* 've told you a good deal, have n't I?

AUBREY. Oh, Paula!

PAULA. What I have n't told you I dare say you 've heard from others. But in case they 've omitted anything — the dears — it 's all here.

AUBREY. In Heaven's name, why must you talk like this to-night?

PAULA. It may save discussion by and by, don't you think? [*Holding out the letter.*] There you are.

AUBREY. No, dear, no.

PAULA. Take it. [*He takes the letter.*] Read it through after I 've gone, and then — read it again, and turn the matter over in your mind finally. And if, even at the very last moment, you feel you — ought n't to go to church with me, send a messenger to Pont Street, any time before eleven to-morrow, telling me that you 're afraid, and I — I 'll take the blow.

AUBREY. Why, what — what do you think I am?

PAULA. That 's it. It 's because I know you 're such a dear good fellow that I want to save you the chance of ever feeling sorry you married me. I really love you so much, Aubrey, that — to save you that, I 'd rather you treated me as — as the others have done.

AUBREY [*turning from her with a cry*]. Oh!

PAULA [*after a slight pause*]. I suppose I 've shocked you. I can't help it if I have.

[*She sits, with assumed languor and indifference. He turns to her, advances, and kneels by her.*]

AUBREY. My dearest, you don't understand me. I — I can't bear to hear you always talking about — what 's done with. I tell you I 'll never remember it; Paula, can't you dismiss it? Try. Darling, if we promise each other to forget, to forget, we 're bound to be happy. After all, it 's a mechanical matter; the moment a wretched thought enters your head, you quickly think of something bright — it depends on one's will. Shall I burn this, dear? [*Referring to the letter he holds in his hand.*] Let me, let me!

PAULA [*with a shrug of the shoulders*]. I don't suppose there 's much that 's new to you in it, — just as you like.

[*He goes to the fire and burns the letter.*]

AUBREY. There 's an end of it. [*Returning to her.*] What 's the matter?

PAULA [*rising coldly*]. Oh, nothing ! I 'll go and put my cloak on.

AUBREY [*detaining her*]. What *is* the matter ?

PAULA. Well, I think you might have said, "You 're very generous, Paula," or at least, "Thank you, dear," when I offered to set you free.

AUBREY [*catching her in his arms*]. Ah !

PAULA. Ah ! ah ! Ha ! ha ! It 's all very well, but you don't know what it cost me to make such an offer. I do so want to be married.

AUBREY. But you never imagined — ?

PAULA. Perhaps not. And yet I *did* think of what I 'd do at the end of our acquaintance if you had preferred to behave like the rest. [*Taking a flower from her bodice.*]

AUBREY. Hush !

PAULA. Oh, I forgot !

AUBREY. What would you have done when we parted ?

PAULA. Why, killed myself.

AUBREY. Paula, dear !

PAULA. It 's true. [*Putting the flower in his buttonhole.*] Do you know, I feel certain I should make away with myself if anything serious happened to me.

AUBREY. Anything serious ! What, has nothing ever been serious to you, Paula ?

PAULA. Not lately ; not since a long while ago. I made up my mind then to have done with taking things seriously. If I had n't, I — However, we won't talk about that.

AUBREY. But now, now, life will be different to you, won't it — quite different ? Eh, dear ?

PAULA. Oh, yes, now. Only, Aubrey, mind you keep me always happy.

AUBREY. I will try to.

PAULA. I know I could n't swallow a second big dose of misery. I know that if ever I felt wretched again — truly wretched — I should take a leaf out of Connie Tirlemont's book. You remember ? They found her — [*With a look of horror.*]

AUBREY. For God's sake, don't let your thoughts run on such things !

PAULA [*laughing*]. Ha, ha, how scared you look ! There, think of the time ! Dearest, what will my coachman say ? My cloak !

[*She runs off, gayly, by the upper door. AUBREY looks after her for a moment, then he walks up to the fire*

and stands warming his feet at the bars. As he does so he raises his head and observes the letters upon the mantelpiece. He takes one down quickly.*]

AUBREY. Ah ! Ellean ! [*Opening the letter and reading.*] "My dear father, — A great change has come over me. I believe my mother in Heaven has spoken to me, and counseled me to turn to you in your loneliness. At any rate, your words have reached my heart, and I no longer feel fitted for this solemn life. I am ready to take my place by you. Dear father, will you receive me ? — ELLEAN."

[*PAULA reënters, dressed in a handsome cloak. He stares at her as if he hardly realized her presence.*]

PAULA. What are you staring at ? Don't you admire my cloak ?

AUBREY. Yes.

PAULA. Could n't you wait till I 'd gone before reading your letters ?

AUBREY [*putting the letter away*]. I beg your pardon.

PAULA. Take me downstairs to the carriage. [*Slipping her arm through his.*] How I tease you ! To-morrow ! I 'm so happy ! [*They go out..*

THE SECOND ACT

A morning-room in AUBREY TANQUERAY'S *house, "Highercoombe," near Willowmere, Surrey — a bright and prettily furnished apartment of irregular shape, with double doors opening into a small hall at the back, another door on the left, and a large recessed window through which is obtained a view of extensive grounds. Everything about the room is charming and graceful. The fire is burning in the grate, and a small table is tastefully laid for breakfast. It is a morning in early spring, and the sun is streaming in through the window.*

AUBREY *and* PAULA *are seated at breakfast, and* AUBREY *is silently reading his letters. Two servants, a man and a woman, hand dishes and then retire. After a little while* AUBREY *puts his letters aside and looks across to the window.*

AUBREY. Sunshine ! Spring !

PAULA [*glancing at the clock*]. Exactly six minutes.

AUBREY. Six minutes ?

PAULA. Six minutes, Aubrey dear, since you made your last remark.

AUBREY. I beg your pardon : I was reading my letters. Have you seen Ellean this morning?

PAULA [*coldly*]. Your last observation but one was about Ellean.

AUBREY. Dearest, what shall I talk about?

PAULA. Ellean breakfasted two hours ago, Morgan tells me, and then went out walking with her dog.

AUBREY. She wraps up warmly, I hope; this sunshine is deceptive.

PAULA. I ran about the lawn last night, after dinner, in satin shoes. Were you anxious about me?

AUBREY. Certainly.

PAULA [*melting*]. Really.

AUBREY. You make me wretchedly anxious; you delight in doing incautious things. You are incurable.

PAULA. Ah, what a beast I am! [*Going to him and kissing him, then glancing at the letters by his side.*] A letter from Cayley?

AUBREY. He is staying very near here, with Mrs. —— Very near here.

PAULA. With the lady whose chimneys we have the honor of contemplating from our windows?

AUBREY. With Mrs. Cortelyon — Yes.

PAULA. Mrs. Cortelyon! The woman who might have set the example of calling on me when we first threw out roots in this deadly-lively soil! Deuce take Mrs. Cortelyon!

AUBREY. Hush! my dear girl!

PAULA [*returning to her seat*]. Oh, I know she's an old acquaintance of yours — and of the first Mrs. Tanqueray. And she joins the rest of 'em in slapping the second Mrs. Tanqueray in the face. However, I have my revenge — she's six-and-forty, and I wish nothing worse to happen to any woman.

AUBREY. Well, she's going to town, Cayley says here, and his visit's at an end. He's coming over this morning to call on you. Shall we ask him to transfer himself to us? Do say yes.

PAULA. Yes.

AUBREY [*gladly*]. Ah, ha! old Cayley.

PAULA [*coldly*]. He'll amuse *you*.

AUBREY. And you too.

PAULA. Because you find a companion, shall I be boisterously hilarious?

AUBREY. Come, come! He talks London, and you know you like that.

PAULA. London! London or Heaven! which is farther from me!

AUBREY. Paula!

PAULA. Oh! Oh, I am so bored, Aubrey!

AUBREY [*gathering up his letters and going to her, leaning over her shoulder*]. Baby, what can I do for you?

PAULA. I suppose, nothing. You have done all you can for me.

AUBREY. What do you mean?

PAULA. You have married me.

[*He walks away from her thoughtfully, to the writing table. As he places his letters on the table he sees an addressed letter, stamped for the post, lying on the blotting-book; he picks it up.*]

AUBREY [*in an altered tone*]. You've been writing this morning before breakfast?

PAULA [*looking at him quickly, then away again*]. Er — that letter.

AUBREY [*with the letter in his hand*]. To Lady Orreyed. Why?

PAULA. Why not? Mabel's an old friend of mine.

AUBREY. Are you — corresponding?

PAULA. I heard from her yesterday. They've just returned from the Riviera. She seems happy.

AUBREY [*sarcastically*]. That's good news.

PAULA. Why are you always so cutting about Mabel? She's a kind-hearted girl. Everything's altered; she even thinks of letting her hair go back to brown. She's Lady Orreyed. She's married to George. What's the matter with her?

AUBREY [*turning away*]. Oh!

PAULA. You drive me mad sometimes with the tone you take about things! Great goodness, if you come to that, George Orreyed's wife isn't a bit worse than yours! [*He faces her suddenly.*] I suppose I needn't have made that observation.

AUBREY. No, there was scarcely a necessity.

[*He throws the letter on to the table, and takes up the newspaper.*]

PAULA. I am very sorry.

AUBREY. All right, dear.

PAULA [*trifling with the letter*]. I — I'd better tell you what I've written. I meant to do so, of course. I — I've asked the Orreyeds to come and stay with us. [*He looks at her, and lets the paper fall to the ground in a helpless way.*] George was a great friend of Cayley's; I 'm sure *he* would be delighted to meet them here.

AUBREY [*laughing mirthlessly*]. Ha, ha, ha ! They say Orreyed has taken to tippling at dinner. Heavens above !

PAULA. Oh! I 've no patience with you ! You 'll kill me with this life ! [*She selects some flowers from a vase on the table, cuts and arranges them, and fastens them in her bodice.*] What is my existence, Sunday to Saturday ? In the morning, a drive down to the village, with the groom, to give my orders to the tradespeople. At lunch, you and Ellean. In the afternoon, a novel, the newspapers; if fine, another drive — *if* fine ! Tea — you and Ellean. Then two hours of dusk ; then dinner — you and Ellean. Then a game of Bésique, you and I, while Ellean reads a religious book in a dull corner. Then a yawn from me, another from you, a sigh from Ellean ; three figures suddenly rise — " Good-night, good-night, good-night!" [*Imitating a kiss.*] "God bless you ! " Ah!

AUBREY. Yes, yes, Paula — yes, dearest — that 's what it is *now.* But by and by, if people begin to come round us —

PAULA. Hah ! That 's where we 've made the mistake, my friend Aubrey ! [*Pointing to the window.*] Do you believe these people will *ever* come round us ? Your former crony, Mrs. Cortelyon ? Or the grim old vicar, or that wife of his whose huge nose is positively indecent ? Or the Ullathornes, or the Gollans, or Lady William Petres ? I know better ! And when the young ones gradually take the place of the old, there will still remain the sacred tradition that the dreadful person who lives at the top of the hill is never, under any circumstances, to be called upon ! And so we shall go on here, year in and year out, until the sap is run out of our lives, and we 're stale and dry and withered from sheer, solitary respectability. Upon my word, I wonder we did n't see that we should have been far happier if we 'd gone in for the devil-may-care, café-living sort of life in town ! After all, *I* have a set, and you might have joined it. It 's true, I did want, dearly, dearly, to be a married woman, but where 's the pride in being a married woman among married women who are — married ! If — [*Seeing*

that AUBREY'S *head has sunk into his hands.*] Aubrey ! My dear boy ! You 're not — crying ?

[*He looks up, with a flushed face. ELLEAN enters, dressed very simply for walking. She is a low-voiced, grave girl of about nineteen, with a face somewhat resembling a Madonna. Towards PAULA her manner is cold and distant.*]

AUBREY [*in an undertone*]. Ellean !

ELLEAN. Good-morning, papa. Good-morning, Paula.

[*PAULA puts her arms round ELLEAN and kisses her. ELLEAN makes little response.*]

PAULA. Good-morning. [*Brightly.*] We've been breakfasting this side of the house, to get the sun.

[*She sits at the piano and rattles at a gay melody. Seeing that PAULA'S back is turned to them, ELLEAN goes to AUBREY and kisses him; he returns the kiss almost furtively. As they separate, the servants re-enter, and proceed to carry out the breakfast table.*]

AUBREY. [*To ELLEAN.*] I guess where you 've been : there 's some gorse clinging to your frock.

ELLEAN [*removing a sprig of gorse from her skirt*]. Rover and I walked nearly as far as Black Moor. The poor fellow has a thorn in his pad ; I am going upstairs for my tweezers.

AUBREY. Ellean ! [*She returns to him.*] Paula is a little depressed — out of sorts. She complains that she has no companion.

ELLEAN. I am with Paula nearly all the day, papa.

AUBREY. Ah, but you 're such a little mouse. Paula likes cheerful people about her.

ELLEAN. I 'm afraid I am naturally rather silent ; and it 's so difficult to seem to be what one is not.

AUBREY. I don't wish that, Ellean.

ELLEAN. I will offer to go down to the village with Paula this morning — shall I ?

AUBREY [*touching her hand gently*]. Thank you — do.

ELLEAN. When I 've looked after Rover, I 'll come back to her.

[*She goes out; PAULA ceases playing, and turns on the music-stool, looking at AUBREY.*]

PAULA. Well, have you and Ellean had your little confidence?

AUBREY. Confidence?

PAULA. Do you think I could n't feel it, like a pain between my shoulders?

AUBREY. Ellean is coming back in a few minutes to be with you. [*Bending over her.*] Paula, Paula dear, is this how you keep your promise?

PAULA. Oh! [*Rising impatiently, and crossing swiftly to the settee, where she sits, moving restlessly.*] I *can't* keep my promise; I *am* jealous; it won't be smothered. I see you looking at her, watching her; your voice drops when you speak to her. I know how fond you are of that girl, Aubrey.

AUBREY. What would you have? I've no other home for her. She is my daughter.

PAULA. She is your saint. Saint Ellean!

AUBREY. You have often told me how good and sweet you think her.

PAULA. Good! — Yes! Do you imagine *that* makes me less jealous? [*Going to him and clinging to his arm.*] Aubrey, there are two sorts of affection — the love for a woman you respect, and the love for the woman you — love. She gets the first from you: I never can.

AUBREY. Hush, hush! you don't realize what you say.

PAULA. If Ellean cared for me only a little, it would be different. I should n't be jealous then. Why does n't she care for me?

AUBREY. She — she — she will, in time.

PAULA. You can't say that without stuttering.

AUBREY. Her disposition seems a little unresponsive; she resembles her mother in many ways; I can see it every day.

PAULA. She's marble. It's a shame. There's not the slightest excuse; for all she knows, I'm as much a saint as she — only married. Dearest, help me to win her over!

AUBREY. Help you?

PAULA. You can. Teach her that it is her duty to love me; she hangs on to every word you speak. I'm sure, Aubrey, that the love of a nice woman who believed me to be like herself would do me a world of good. You'd get the benefit of it as well as I. It would soothe me; it would make me less horribly restless; it would take this — this — mischievous feeling from me. [*Coaxingly.*] Aubrey!

AUBREY. Have patience; everything will come right.

PAULA. Yes, if you help me.

AUBREY. In the meantime you will tear up your letter to Lady Orreyed, won't you?

PAULA [*kissing his hand*]. Of course I will — anything!

AUBREY. Ah, thank you, dearest! [*Laughing.*] Why, good gracious! — ha, ha! — just imagine "Saint Ellean" and that woman side by side!

PAULA [*going back with a cry*]. Ah!

AUBREY. What?

PAULA [*passionately*]. It's Ellean you're considering, not me! It's all Ellean with you! Ellean! Ellean!

[ELLEAN *reënters.*]

ELLEAN. Did you call me, Paula? [*Clenching his hands,* AUBREY *turns away and goes out.*] Is papa angry?

PAULA. I drive him distracted, sometimes. There, I confess it!

ELLEAN. Do you? Oh, why do you!

PAULA. Because I — because I'm jealous.

ELLEAN. Jealous?

PAULA. Yes — of you. [ELLEAN *is silent.*] Well, what do you think of that?

ELLEAN. I knew it; I've seen it. It hurts me dreadfully. What do you wish me to do? Go away?

PAULA. Leave us! [*Beckoning her with a motion of the head.*] Look here! [ELLEAN *goes to* PAULA *slowly and unresponsively.*] You could cure me of my jealousy very easily. Why don't you — like me?

ELLEAN. What do you mean by — like you? I don't understand.

PAULA. Love me.

ELLEAN. Love is not a feeling that is under one's control. I shall alter as time goes on, perhaps. I did n't begin to love my father deeply till a few months ago, and then I obeyed my mother.

PAULA. Ah, yes, you dream things, don't you — see them in your sleep? You fancy your mother speaks to you?

ELLEAN. When you have lost your mother it is a comfort to believe that she is dead only to this life, that she still watches over her child. I do believe that of my mother.

PAULA. Well, and so you have n't been bidden to love *me?*

ELLEAN [*after a pause, almost inaudibly*]. No.

PAULA. Dreams are only a hash-up of one's day-thoughts, I suppose you know. Think intently of anything, and it's bound to come back to you at night. I don't cultivate dreams myself.

ELLEAN. Ah, I knew you would only sneer!

PAULA. I'm not sneering; I'm speaking the truth. I say that if you cared for me in the daytime I should soon make friends with those nightmares of yours. Ellean, why don't you try to look on me as your second mother? Of course there are not many years between us, but I'm ever so much older than you — in experience. I shall have no children of my own, I know that; it would be a real comfort to me if you would make me feel we belonged to each other. Won't you? Perhaps you think I'm odd — not nice. Well, the fact is I've two sides to my nature, and I've let the one almost smother the other. A few years ago I went through some trouble, and since then I haven't shed a tear. I believe if you put your arms around me just once I should run upstairs and have a good cry. There, I've talked to you as I've never talked to a woman in my life. Ellean, you seem to fear me. Don't! Kiss me!

[*With a cry, almost of despair,* ELLEAN *turns from* PAULA *and sinks on to the settee, covering her face with her hands.*]

PAULA [*indignantly*]. Oh! Why is it! How dare you treat me like this? What do you mean by it? What do you mean?

[*A* SERVANT *enters.*]

SERVANT. Mr. Drummle, ma'am.

[CAYLEY DRUMMLE, *in riding-dress, enters briskly. The* SERVANT *retires.*]

PAULA [*recovering herself*]. Well, Cayley!

DRUMMLE [*shaking hands with her cordially*]. How are you? [*Shaking hands with* ELLEAN, *who rises.*] I saw you in the distance an hour ago, in the gorse near Stapleton's.

ELLEAN. I didn't see you, Mr. Drummle.

DRUMMLE. My dear Ellean, it is my experience that no charming young lady of nineteen ever does see a man of forty-five. [*Laughing.*] Ha, Ha!

ELLEAN [*going to the door*]. Paula, papa wishes me to drive down to the village with you this morning. Do you care to take me?

PAULA [*coldly*]. Oh, by all means. Pray tell Watts to balance the cart for three.

[ELLEAN *goes out.*]

DRUMMLE. How's Aubrey?

PAULA. Very well — when Ellean's about the house.

DRUMMLE. And you? I need n't ask.

PAULA [*walking away to the window*]. Oh, a dog's life, my dear Cayley, mine.

DRUMMLE. Eh?

PAULA. Does n't that define a happy marriage? I'm sleek, well-kept, well-fed, never without a bone to gnaw and fresh straw to lie upon. [*Gazing out of the window.*] Oh, dear me!

DRUMMLE. H'm! Well, I heartily congratulate you on your kennel. The view from the terrace here is superb.

PAULA. Yes; I can see London.

DRUMMLE. London! Not quite so far, surely?

PAULA. *I* can. Also the Mediterranean, on a fine day. I wonder what Algiers looks like this morning from the sea! [*Impulsively.*] Oh, Cayley, do you remember those jolly times on board Peter Jarman's yacht when we lay off — ? [*Stopping suddenly, seeing* DRUMMLE *staring at her.*] Good gracious! What are we talking about!

[AUBREY *enters.*]

AUBREY. [*To* DRUMMLE.] Dear old chap! Has Paula asked you?

PAULA. Not yet.

AUBREY. We want you to come to us, now that you 're leaving Mrs. Cortelyon — at once, to-day. Stay a month, as long as you please — eh, Paula?

PAULA. As long as you can possibly endure it — do, Cayley.

DRUMMLE [*looking at* AUBREY]. Delighted. [*To* PAULA.] Charming of you to have me.

PAULA. My dear man, you 're a blessing. I must telegraph to London for more fish! A strange appetite to cater for! Something to do, to do, to do!

[*She goes out in a mood of almost childish delight.*]

DRUMMLE [*eyeing* AUBREY]. Well?

AUBREY [*with a wearied, anxious look*]. Well, Cayley?

DRUMMLE. How are you getting on?

AUBREY. My position does n't grow less difficult. I told you, when I met you last week, of this feverish, jealous attachment of Paula's for Ellean?

DRUMMLE. Yes. I hardly know why, but I came to the conclusion that you don't consider it an altogether fortunate attachment.

AUBREY. Ellean does n't respond to it.

DRUMMLE. These are early days. Ellean will warm towards your wife by and by.

AUBREY. Ah, but there's the question. Cayley!

DRUMMLE. What question?

AUBREY. The question which positively distracts me. Ellean is so different from — most women; I don't believe a purer creature exists out of heaven. And I — I ask myself, am I doing right in exposing her to the influence of poor Paula's light, careless nature?

DRUMMLE. My dear Aubrey!

AUBREY. That shocks you! So it does me. I assure you I long to urge my girl to break down the reserve which keeps her apart from Paula, but somehow I can't do it — well, I don't do it. How can I make you understand? But when you come to us you'll understand quickly enough. Cayley, there's hardly a subject you can broach on which poor Paula has n't some strange, out-of-the-way thought to give utterance to; some curious, warped notion. They are not mere worldly thoughts — unless, good God! they belong to the little hellish world which our blackguardism has created: no, her ideas have too little calculation in them to be called worldly. But it makes it the more dreadful that such thoughts should be ready, spontaneous; that expressing them has become a perfectly natural process; that her words, acts even, have almost lost their proper significance for her, and seem beyond her control. Ah, and the pain of listening to it all from the woman one loves, the woman one hoped to make happy and contented, who is really and truly a good woman, as it were, maimed! Well, this is my burden, and I should n't speak to you of it but for my anxiety about Ellean. Ellean! What is to be her future? It is in my hands; what am I to do? Cayley, when I remember how Ellean comes to me, from another world I always think, — when

I realize the charge that's laid on me, I find myself wishing, in a sort of terror, that my child were safe under the ground!

DRUMMLE. My dear Aubrey, are n't you making a mistake?

AUBREY. Very likely. What is it?

DRUMMLE. A mistake, not in regarding your Ellean as an angel, but in believing that, under any circumstances, it would be possible for her to go through life without getting her white robe — shall we say, a little dusty at the hem? Don't take me for a cynic. I am sure there are many women upon earth who are almost divinely innocent; but being on earth, they must send their robes to the laundry occasionally. Ah, and it's right that they should have to do so, for what can they learn from the checking of their little washing-bills but lessons of charity? Now I see but two courses open to you for the disposal of your angel.

AUBREY. Yes?

DRUMMLE. You must either restrict her to a paradise which is, like every earthly paradise, necessarily somewhat imperfect, or treat her as an ordinary flesh-and-blood young woman, and give her the advantages of that society to which she properly belongs.

AUBREY. Advantages?

DRUMMLE. My dear Aubrey, of all forms of innocence mere ignorance is the least admirable. Take my advice, let her walk and talk and suffer and be healed with the great crowd. Do it, and hope that she'll some day meet a good, honest fellow who'll make her life complete, happy, secure. Now you see what I'm driving at.

AUBREY. A sanguine programme, my dear Cayley! Oh, I'm not pooh-poohing it. Putting sentiment aside, of course I know that a fortunate marriage for Ellean would be the best — perhaps the only — solution of my difficulty. But you forget the danger of the course you suggest.

DRUMMLE. Danger?

AUBREY. If Ellean goes among men and women, how can she escape from learning, sooner or later, the history of — poor Paula's — old life?

DRUMMLE. H'm! You remember the episode of the Jeweler's Son in the Arabian Nights? Of course you don't. Well, if your daughter lives, she *can't* escape —

what you're afraid of. [AUBREY *gives a half-stifled exclamation of pain.*] And when she does hear the story, surely it would be better that she should have some knowledge of the world to help her to understand it.

AUBREY. To understand!

DRUMMLE. To understand, to — philosophize.

AUBREY. To philosophize?

DRUMMLE. Philosophy is toleration, and it is only one step from toleration to forgiveness.

AUBREY. You're right, Cayley; I believe you always are. Yes, yes. But, even if I had the courage to attempt to solve the problem of Ellean's future in this way, I — I 'm helpless.

DRUMMLE. How?

AUBREY. What means have I now of placing my daughter in the world I 've left?

DRUMMLE. Oh, some friend — some woman friend.

AUBREY. I have none; they 're gone.

DRUMMLE. You 're wrong there; I know one —

AUBREY [*listening*]. That 's Paula's cart. Let 's discuss this again.

DRUMMLE [*going up to the window and looking out*]. It is n't the dog-cart. [*Turning to* AUBREY.] I hope you 'll forgive me, old chap.

AUBREY. What for?

DRUMMLE Whose wheels do you think have been cutting ruts in your immaculate drive?

[*A* SERVANT *enters.*]

SERVANT. [*To* AUBREY.] Mrs. Cortelyon, sir.

AUBREY. Mrs. Cortelyon! [*After a short pause.*] Very well. [*The* SERVANT *withdraws.*] What on earth is the meaning of this?

DRUMMLE. Ahem! While I 've been our old friend's guest, Aubrey, we have very naturally talked a good deal about you and yours.

AUBREY. Indeed, have you?

DRUMMLE. Yes; and Alice Cortelyon has arrived at the conclusion that it would have been far kinder had she called on Mrs. Tanqueray long ago. She 's going abroad for Easter before settling down in London for the season, and I believe she has come over this morning to ask for Ellean's companionship.

AUBREY. Oh, I see! [*Frowning.*] Quite a friendly little conspiracy, my dear Cayley!

DRUMMLE. Conspiracy! Not at all, I assure you. [*Laughing.*] Ha, ha!

[ELLEAN *enters from the hall with* MRS. CORTELYON, *a handsome, good-humored, spirited woman of about forty-five.*]

ELLEAN. Papa —

MRS. CORTELYON. [*To* AUBREY, *shaking hands with him heartily.*] Well, Aubrey, how are you? I 've just been telling this great girl of yours that I knew her when she was a sad-faced, pale baby. How is Mrs. Tanqueray? I have been a bad neighbor, and I 'm here to beg forgiveness. Is she indoors?

AUBREY. She 's upstairs putting on a hat, I believe.

MRS. CORTELYON [*sitting comfortably*]. Ah! [*She looks round:* DRUMMLE *and* ELLEAN *are talking together in the hall.*] We used to be very frank with each other, Aubrey. I suppose the old footing is no longer possible, eh?

AUBREY. If so, I 'm not entirely to blame, Mrs. Cortelyon.

MRS. CORTELYON. Mrs. Cortelyon? H'm! No, I admit it. But you must make some little allowance for me, *Mr. Tanqueray.* Your first wife and I, as girls, were like two cherries on one stalk, and then I was the confidential friend of your married life. That post, perhaps, was n't altogether a sinecure. And now — well, when a woman gets to my age I suppose she 's a stupid, prejudiced, conventional creature. However, I 've got over it and — [*giving him her hand*] — I hope you 'll be enormously happy and let me be a friend once more.

AUBREY. Thank you, Alice.

MRS. CORTELYON. That 's right. I feel more cheerful than I 've done for weeks. But I suppose it would serve me right if the second Mrs. Tanqueray showed me the door. Do you think she will?

AUBREY [*listening*]. Here is my wife. [MRS CORTELYON *rises, and* PAULA *enters, dressed for driving; she stops abruptly on seeing* MRS. CORTELYON.] Paula, dear, Mrs. Cortelyon has called to see you.

[PAULA *starts, looks at* MRS. CORTELYON *irresolutely, then after a slight pause barely touches* MRS. CORTELYON'S *extended hand.*]

PAULA [*whose manner now alternates between deliberate insolence and assumed sweetness*]. Mrs. —— ? What name, Aubrey?

AUBREY. Mrs. Cortelyon.

PAULA. Cortelyon? Oh, yes. Cortelyon.

MRS. CORTELYON [*carefully guarding herself throughout against any expression of resentment*]. Aubrey ought to have told you that Alice Cortelyon and he are very old friends.

PAULA. Oh, very likely he has mentioned the circumstance. I have quite a wretched memory.

MRS. CORTELYON. You know we are neighbors, Mrs. Tanqueray.

PAULA. Neighbors? Are we really? Won't you sit down? [*They both sit.*] Neighbors! That 's most interesting!

MRS. CORTELYON. Very near neighbors. You can see my roof from your windows.

PAULA. I fancy I *have* observed a roof. But you have been away from home; you have only just returned.

MRS. CORTELYON. I? What makes you think that?

PAULA. Why, because it is two months since we came to Highercoombe, and I don't remember your having called.

MRS. CORTELYON. Your memory is now terribly accurate. No, I 've not been away from home, and it is to explain my neglect that I am here, rather unceremoniously, this morning.

PAULA. Oh, to explain — quite so. [*With mock solicitude.*] Ah, you 've been very ill; I ought to have seen that before.

MRS. CORTELYON. Ill!

PAULA. You look dreadfully pulled down. We poor women show illness so plainly in our faces, don't we?

AUBREY [*anxiously*]. Paula dear, Mrs. Cortelyon is the picture of health.

MRS. CORTELYON [*with some asperity*]. I have never *felt* better in my life.

PAULA [*looking around innocently*]. Have I said anything awkward? Aubrey, tell Mrs. Cortelyon how stupid and thoughtless I always am!

MRS. CORTELYON. [*To* DRUMMLE, *who is now standing close to her.*] Really, Cayley — ! [*He soothes her with a nod and smile and a motion of his finger to his lip.*] Mrs. Tanqueray, I am afraid my explanation will not be quite so satisfactory as either of those you have just helped me to.

You may have heard — but, if you have heard, you have doubtless forgotten — that twenty years ago, when your husband first lived here, I was a constant visitor at Highercoombe.

PAULA. Twenty years ago — fancy! I was a naughty little child then.

MRS. CORTELYON. Possibly. Well, at that time, and till the end of her life, my affections were centered upon the lady of this house.

PAULA. Were they? That was very sweet of you.

[ELLEAN *approaches* MRS. CORTELYON, *listening intently to her.*]

MRS. CORTELYON. I will say no more on that score, but I must add this: when, two months ago you came here, I realized, perhaps for the first time, that I was a middle-aged woman, and that it had become impossible for me to accept without some effort a breaking-in upon many tender associations. There, Mrs. Tanqueray, that is my confession. Will you try to understand it and pardon me?

PAULA [*watching* ELLEAN, — *sneeringly*]. Ellean dear, you appear to be very interested in Mrs. Cortelyon's reminiscences; I don't think I can do better than make you my mouthpiece — there is such sympathy between us. What do you say — can we bring ourselves to forgive Mrs. Cortelyon for neglecting us for two weary months?

MRS. CORTELYON. [*To* ELLEAN, *pleasantly.*] Well, Ellean? [*With a little cry of tenderness* ELLEAN *impulsively sits beside* MRS. CORTELYON *and takes her hand.*] My dear child!

PAULA [*in an undertone to* AUBREY]. Ellean is n't so very slow in taking to Mrs. Cortelyon!

MRS. CORTELYON. [*To* PAULA *and* AUBREY.] Come, this encourages me to broach my scheme. Mrs. Tanqueray, it strikes me that you two good people are just now excellent company for each other, while Ellean would perhaps be glad of a little peep into the world you are anxious to avoid. Now, I 'm going to Paris to-morrow for a week or two before settling down in Chester Square, so — don't gasp, both of you! — if this girl is willing, and you have made no other arrangements for her, will you let her come with me to Paris, and afterwards remain with me in town during the season?

[ELLEAN *utters an exclamation of surprise.*
PAULA *is silent.*] What do you say?

AUBREY. Paula — Paula dear. [*Hesitatingly.*] My dear Mrs. Cortelyon, this is wonderfully kind of you; I am really at a loss to — eh, Cayley?

DRUMMLE [*watching* PAULA *apprehensively*]. Kind! Now I must say I don't think so! I begged Alice to take *me* to Paris, and she declined! I am thrown over for Ellean! Ha! ha!

MRS. CORTELYON [*laughing*]. What nonsense you talk, Cayley!

[*The laughter dies out.* PAULA *remains quite still.*]

AUBREY. Paula dear.

PAULA [*slowly collecting herself*]. One moment. I — I don't quite — [*To* MRS. CORTELYON.] You propose that Ellean leaves Highercoombe almost at once, and remains with you some months?

MRS. CORTELYON. It would be a mercy to me. You can afford to be generous to a desolate old widow. Come, Mrs. Tanqueray, won't you spare her?

PAULA. Won't *I* spare her. [*Suspiciously.*] Have you mentioned your plan to Aubrey — before I came in?

MRS. CORTELYON. No; I had no opportunity.

PAULA. Nor to Ellean?

MRS. CORTELYON. Oh, no.

PAULA [*looking about her in suppressed excitement*]. This has n't been discussed at all, behind my back?

MRS. CORTELYON. My dear Mrs. Tanqueray!

PAULA. Ellean, let us hear your voice in the matter!

ELLEAN. I should like to go with Mrs. Cortelyon —

PAULA. Ah!

ELLEAN. That is, if — if —

PAULA. If — what?

ELLEAN [*looking towards* AUBREY, *appealingly*]. Papa!

PAULA [*in a hard voice*]. Oh, of course — I forgot. [*To* AUBREY.] My dear Aubrey, it rests with you, naturally, whether I am — to lose — Ellean.

AUBREY. Lose Ellean! [*Advancing to* PAULA.] There is no question of losing Ellean. You would see Ellean in town constantly when she returned from Paris; is n't that so, Mrs. Cortelyon?

MRS. CORTELYON. Certainly.

PAULA [*laughing softly*]. Oh, I did n't know I should be allowed that privilege.

MRS. CORTELYON. Privilege, my dear Mrs. Tanqueray!

PAULA. Ha, ha! that makes all the difference, does n't it?

AUBREY [*with assumed gayety*]. All the difference? I should think so! [*To* ELLEAN, *laying his hand upon her head tenderly.*] And you are quite certain you wish to see what the world is like on the other side of Black Moor!

ELLEAN. If you are willing, papa, I am quite certain.

AUBREY [*looking at* PAULA *irresolutely, then speaking with an effort*]. Then I — I am willing.

PAULA [*rising and striking the table lightly with her clenched hand*]. That decides it! [*There is a general movement. Excitedly to* MRS. CORTELYON, *who advances towards her.*] When do you want her?

MRS. CORTELYON. We go to town this afternoon at five o'clock, and sleep to-night at Bayliss's. There is barely time for her to make her preparations.

PAULA. I will undertake that she is ready.

MRS. CORTELYON. I've a great deal to scramble through at home too, as you may guess. Good-bye!

PAULA [*turning away*]. Mrs. Cortelyon is going.

[PAULA *stands looking out of the window, with her back to those in the room.*]

MRS. CORTELYON. [*To* DRUMMLE.] Cayley —

DRUMMLE. [*To her.*] Eh?

MRS. CORTELYON. I've gone through it, for the sake of Aubrey and his child, but I — I feel a hundred. Is that a mad-woman?

DRUMMLE. Of course; all jealous women are mad. [*He goes out with* AUBREY.]

MRS. CORTELYON [*hesitatingly, to* PAULA]. Good-bye, Mrs. Tanqueray.

[PAULA *inclines her head with the slightest possible movement, then resumes her former position.* ELLEAN *comes from the hall and takes* MRS. CORTELYON *out of the room. After a brief silence,* PAULA *turns with a fierce cry, and hurriedly takes off her coat and hat, and tosses them upon the settee.*]

PAULA. Who's that? Oh! Oh! Oh!

[*She drops into the chair as* AUBREY *returns; he stands looking at her.*]

AUBREY. I — you have altered your mind about going out.

PAULA. Yes. Please to ring the bell.

AUBREY [*touching the bell*]. You are angry about Mrs. Cortelyon and Ellean. Let me try to explain my reasons —

PAULA. Be careful what you say to me just now! I have never felt like this — except once — in my life. Be careful what you say to me!

[*A* SERVANT *enters.*]

PAULA [*rising*]. Is Watts at the door with the cart?

SERVANT. Yes, ma'am.

PAULA. Tell him to drive down to the post-office directly with this.

[*Picking up the letter which has been lying upon the table.*]

AUBREY. With that?

PAULA. Yes. My letter to Lady Orreyed.

[*Giving the letter to the* SERVANT, *who goes out.*]

AUBREY. Surely you don't wish me to countermand any order of yours to a servant. Call the man back — take the letter from him!

PAULA. I have not the slightest intention of doing so.

AUBREY. I must, then. [*Going to the door. She snatches up her hat and coat and follows him.*] What are you going to do?

PAULA. If you stop that letter, I walk out of the house.

[*He hesitates, then leaves the door.*]

AUBREY. I am right in believing that to be the letter inviting George Orreyed and his wife to stay here, am I not?

PAULA. Oh, yes — quite right.

AUBREY. Let it go; I'll write to him by and by.

PAULA [*facing him*]. You dare!

AUBREY. Hush, Paula!

PAULA. Insult me again and, upon my word, I'll go straight out of the house!

AUBREY. Insult you?

PAULA. Insult me! What else is it? My God! what else is it? What do you mean by taking Ellean from me?

AUBREY. Listen — !

PAULA. Listen to *me*! And how do you take her? You pack her off in the care of a woman who has deliberately held aloof from me, who's thrown mud at me! Yet this Cortelyon creature has only to put foot here once to be entrusted with the charge of the girl you know I dearly want to keep near me!

AUBREY. Paula dear! hear me — !

PAULA. Ah! of course, of course! I can't be so useful to your daughter as such people as this; and so I'm to be given the go-by for any town friend of yours who turns up and chooses to patronize us! Hah! Very well, at any rate, as you take Ellean from me you justify my looking for companions where I can most readily find 'em.

AUBREY. You wish me to fully appreciate your reason for sending that letter to Lady Orreyed?

PAULA. Precisely — I do.

AUBREY. And could you, after all, go back to associates of that order? It's not possible!

PAULA [*mockingly*]. What, not after the refining influence of these intensely respectable surroundings? [*Going to the door.*] We'll see!

AUBREY. Paula!

PAULA [*violently*]. We'll see!

[*She goes out. He stands still looking after her.*]

THE THIRD ACT

The drawing-room at "Highercoombe." Facing the spectator are two large French windows, sheltered by a verandah, leading into the garden; on the right is a door opening into a small hall. The fireplace, with a large mirror above it, is on the left-hand side of the room, and higher up in the same wall are double doors recessed. The room is richly furnished, and everything betokens taste and luxury. The windows are open, and there is moonlight in the garden.

LADY ORREYED, *a pretty, affected doll of a woman, with a mincing voice and flaxen hair, is sitting on the ottoman, her head resting against the drum, and her eyes closed.* PAULA, *looking pale, worn, and thoroughly unhappy, is sitting at a table. Both are in sumptuous dinner-gowns.*

LADY ORREYED [*opening her eyes*]. Well. I never! I dropped off! [*Feeling her hair.*] Just fancy! Where are the men?

PAULA [*icily*]. Outside, smoking.

[*A* Servant *enters with coffee, which he hands to* Lady Orreyed. Sir George Orreyed *comes in by the window. He is a man of about thirty-five, with a low forehead, a receding chin, a vacuous expression, and an ominous redness about the nose.*]

Lady Orreyed [*taking coffee*]. Here's Dodo.

Sir George. I say, the flies under the verandah make you swear. [*The* Servant *hands coffee to* Paula, *who declines it, then to* Sir George, *who takes a cup.*] Hi! wait a bit! [*He looks at the tray searchingly, then puts back his cup.*] Never mind. [*Quietly to* Lady Orreyed.] I say, they're dooced sparin' with their liqueur, ain't they?

[*The* Servant *goes out at window.*]

Paula. [*To* Sir George.] Won't you take coffee, George?

Sir George. No, thanks. It's gettin' near time for a whiskey and potass. [*Approaching* Paula, *regarding* Lady Orreyed *admiringly.*] I say, Birdie looks rippin' to-night, don't she?

Paula. Your wife?

Sir George. Yaas — Birdie.

Paula. Rippin'?

Sir George. Yaas.

Paula. Quite — quite rippin'.

[*He moves round to the settee.* Paula *watches him with distaste, then rises and walks away.* Sir George *falls asleep on the settee.*]

Lady Orreyed. Paula love, I fancied you and Aubrey were a little more friendly at dinner. You haven't made it up, have you?

Paula. We? Oh, no. We speak before others, that's all.

Lady Orreyed. And how long do you intend to carry on this game, dear?

Paula [*turning away impatiently*]. I really can't tell you.

Lady Orreyed. Sit down, old girl; don't be so fidgety. [Paula *sits on the upper seat of the ottoman, with her back to* Lady Orreyed.] Of course, it's my duty, as an old friend, to give you a good talking-to — [Paula *glares at her suddenly and fiercely*] — but really I've found one gets so many smacks in the face through interfering in matrimonial squabbles that I've determined to drop it.

Paula. I think you're wise.

Lady Orreyed. However, I must say

that I do wish you'd look at marriage in a more solemn light — just as I do, in fact. It is such a beautiful thing — marriage, and if people in our position don't respect it, and set a good example by living happily with their husbands, what can you expect from the middle classes? When did this sad state of affairs between you and Aubrey actually begin?

Paula. Actually, a fortnight and three days ago; I have n't calculated the minutes.

Lady Orreyed. A day or two before Dodo and I turned up — arrived.

Paula. Yes. One always remembers one thing by another; we left off speaking to each other the morning I wrote asking you to visit us.

Lady Orreyed. Lucky for you I was able to pop down, was n't it, dear?

Paula [*glaring at her again*]. Most fortunate.

Lady Orreyed. A serious split with your husband without a pal on the premises — I should say, without a friend in the house — would be most unpleasant.

Paula [*turning to her abruptly*]. This place must be horribly doleful for you and George just now. At least you ought to consider him before me. Why did n't you leave me to my difficulties?

Lady Orreyed. Oh, we 're quite comfortable, dear, thank you — both of us. George and me are so wrapped up in each other, it does n't matter where we are. I don't want to crow over you, old girl, but I 've got a perfect husband.

[Sir George *is now fast asleep, his head thrown back and his mouth open, looking hideous.*]

Paula [*glancing at* Sir George]. So you 've given me to understand.

Lady Orreyed. Not that we don't have our little differences. Why, we fell out only this very morning. You remember the diamond and ruby tiara Charley Prestwick gave poor dear Connie Tirlemont years ago, don't you?

Paula. No, I do not.

Lady Orreyed. No? Well, it 's in the market. Benjamin of Piccadilly has got it in his shop window, and I 've set my heart on it.

Paula. You consider it quite necessary?

Lady Orreyed. Yes; because what I say to Dodo is this — a lady of my station

must smother herself with hair ornaments.
It's different with you, love — people don't
look for so much blaze from you, but I've
got rank to keep up; have n't I ?

PAULA. Yes.

LADY ORREYED. Well, that was the
cause of the little set-to between I and
Dodo this morning. He broke two chairs,
he was in such a rage. I forgot they're
your chairs; do you mind ?

PAULA. No.

LADY ORREYED. You know, poor Dodo
can't lose his temper without smashing something; if it is n't a chair, it's a mirror; if it
is n't that, it's china — a bit of Dresden
for choice. Dear old pet ! he loves a bit of
Dresden when he's furious. He does n't
really throw things *at* me, dear; he simply
lifts them up and drops them, like a gentleman. I expect our room upstairs will look
rather wrecky before I get that tiara.

PAULA. Excuse the suggestion; perhaps
your husband can't afford it.

LADY ORREYED. Oh, how dreadfully
changed you are, Paula ! Dodo can always
mortgage something, or borrow of his ma.
What *is* coming to you !

PAULA. Ah !

[*She sits at the piano and touches the
keys.*]

LADY ORREYED. Oh, yes, do play !
That's the one thing I envy you for.

PAULA. What shall I play ?

LADY ORREYED. What was that heavenly piece you gave us last night, dear ?

PAULA. A bit of Schubert. Would you
like to hear it again ?

LADY ORREYED. You don't know any
comic songs, do you ?

PAULA. I'm afraid not.

LADY ORREYED. I leave it to you.

[PAULA *plays.* AUBREY *and* CAYLEY
DRUMMLE *appear outside the window; they look into the room.*]

AUBREY. [*To* DRUMMLE.] You can see
her face in that mirror. Poor girl, how ill
and wretched she looks.

DRUMMLE. When are the Orreyeds going ?

AUBREY [*entering the room*]. Heaven
knows !

DRUMMLE [*following* AUBREY]. But
you're entertaining them; what's it to do
with heaven ?

AUBREY. Do you know, Cayley, **that**

even the Orreyeds serve a useful purpose ?
My wife actually speaks to me before our
guests — think of that ! I've come to rejoice at the presence of the Orreyeds !

DRUMMLE. I dare say; we're taught
that beetles are sent for a benign end.

AUBREY. Cayley, talk to Paula again
to-night.

DRUMMLE. Certainly, if I get the chance.

AUBREY. Let's contrive it. George is
asleep ; perhaps I can get that doll out of
the way. [*As they advance into the room,*
PAULA *abruptly ceases playing and finds interest in a volume of music.* SIR GEORGE *is
now nodding and snoring apoplectically.*]
Lady Orreyed, whenever you feel inclined
for a game of billiards I'm at your service.

LADY ORREYED [*jumping up*]. Charmed,
I'm sure ! I really thought you had forgotten poor little me. Oh, look at Dodo !

AUBREY. No, no, don't wake him ; he's
tired.

LADY ORREYED. I must, he looks so
plain. [*Rousing* SIR GEORGE.] Dodo !
Dodo !

SIR GEORGE [*stupidly*]. 'Ullo !

LADY ORREYED. Dodo dear, you were
snoring.

SIR GEORGE. Oh, I say, you could 'a' told
me that by and by.

AUBREY. You want a cigar, George ;
come into the billiard-room. [*Giving his
arm to* LADY ORREYED.] Cayley, bring
Paula.

[AUBREY *and* LADY ORREYED *go out.*]

SIR GEORGE [*rising*]. Hey, what ! Billiard-room ! [*Looking at his watch.*] How
goes the — ? Phew ! 'Ullo, 'Ullo ! Whiskey and potass !

[*He goes rapidly after* AUBREY *and*
LADY ORREYED. PAULA *resumes
playing.*]

PAULA [*after a pause*]. Don't moon about
after me, Cayley; follow the others.

DRUMMLE. Thanks, by and by. [*Sitting.*]
That's pretty.

PAULA [*after another pause, still playing*].
I wish you would n't stare so.

DRUMMLE. Was I staring ? I'm sorry.
[*She plays a little longer, then stops suddenly,
rises, and goes to the window, where she stands
looking out.* DRUMMLE *moves from the ottoman to the settee.*] A lovely night.

PAULA [*startled*]. Oh ! [*Without turning*

to him.] Why do you hop about like a monkey?

DRUMMLE. Hot rooms play the deuce with the nerves. Now, it would have done you good to have walked in the garden with us after dinner and made merry. Why did n't you?

PAULA. You know why.

DRUMMLE. Ah, you 're thinking of the — difference between you and Aubrey?

PAULA. Yes, I *am* thinking of it.

DRUMMLE. Well, so am I. How long — ?

PAULA. Getting on for three weeks.

DRUMMLE. Bless me, it must be! And this would have been such a night to have healed it! Moonlight, the stars, the scent of flowers ; and yet enough darkness to enable a kind woman to rest her hand for an instant on the arm of a good fellow who loves her. Ah, ha! It 's a wonderful power, dear Mrs. Aubrey, the power of an offended woman! Only realize it! Just that one touch — the mere tips of her fingers — and, for herself and another, she changes the color of the whole world.

PAULA [*turning to him calmly*]. Cayley, my dear man, you talk exactly like a very romantic old lady.

[*She leaves the window and sits playing with the knick-knacks on the table.*]

DRUMMLE. [*To himself.*] H'm, that has n't done it! Well — ha, ha! — I accept the suggestion. An old woman, eh?

PAULA. Oh, I did n't intend —

DRUMMLE. But why not? I 've every qualification — well, almost. And I confess it would have given this withered bosom a throb of grandmotherly satisfaction if I could have seen you and Aubrey at peace before I take my leave to-morrow.

PAULA. To-morrow, Cayley!

DRUMMLE. I must.

PAULA. Oh, this house is becoming unendurable.

DRUMMLE. You 're very kind. But you 've got the Orreyeds.

PAULA [*fiercely*]. The Orreyeds! I — I hate the Orreyeds! I lie awake at night, hating them!

DRUMMLE. Pardon me, I 've understood that their visit is, in some degree, owing to — hem — your suggestion.

PAULA. Heavens! that does n't make me like them better. Somehow or another,

I — I 've outgrown these people. This woman — I used to think her "jolly!" — sickens me. I can't breathe when she 's near me : the whiff of her handkerchief turns me faint! And she patronizes me by the hour, until I — I feel my nails growing longer with every word she speaks!

DRUMMLE. My dear lady, why on earth don't you say all this to Aubrey?

PAULA. Oh, I 've been such an utter fool, Cayley!

DRUMMLE [*soothingly*]. Well, well, mention it to Aubrey!

PAULA. No, no, you don't understand. What do you think I 've done?

DRUMMLE. Done! What, *since* you invited the Orreyeds?

PAULA. Yes; I must tell you —

DRUMMLE. Perhaps you 'd better not.

PAULA. Look here! I 've intercepted some letters from Mrs. Cortelyon and Ellean to — him. [*Producing three unopened letters from the bodice of her dress.*] There are the accursed things! From Paris — two from the Cortelyon woman, the other from Ellean!

DRUMMLE. But why — why?

PAULA. I don't know. Yes, I do! I saw letters coming from Ellean to her father ; not a line to me — not a line. And one morning it happened I was downstairs before he was, and I spied this one lying with his heap on the breakfast table, and I slipped it into my pocket — out of malice. Cayley, pure deviltry! And a day or two afterwards I met Elwes the postman at the Lodge, and took the letters from him, and found these others amongst 'em. I felt simply fiendish when I saw them — fiendish! [*Returning the letters to her bodice.*] And now I carry them about with me, and they 're scorching me like a mustard plaster!

DRUMMLE. Oh, this accounts for Aubrey not hearing from Paris lately!

PAULA. That 's an ingenious conclusion to arrive at! Of course it does! [*With an hysterical laugh.*] Ha, ha!

DRUMMLE. Well, well! [*Laughing.*] Ha, ha, ha!

PAULA [*turning upon him*]. I suppose it *is* amusing!

DRUMMLE. I beg pardon.

PAULA. Heaven knows I 've little enough to brag about! I 'm a bad lot, but not in mean tricks of this sort. In all my life this is the most caddish thing I 've done. How am I to get rid of these letters — that 's what I want to know? How am I to get rid of them?

DRUMMLE. If I were you I should take Aubrey aside and put them into his hands as soon as possible.

PAULA. What! and tell him to his face that I —! No, thank you. I suppose *you* would n't like to —

DRUMMLE. No, no; I won't touch 'em!

PAULA. And you call yourself my friend?

DRUMMLE [*good-humoredly*]. No, I don't!

PAULA. Perhaps I 'll tie them together and give them to his man in the morning.

DRUMMLE. That won't avoid an explanation.

PAULA [*recklessly*]. Oh, then he must miss them —

DRUMMLE. And trace them.

PAULA [*throwing herself upon the ottoman*]. I don't care!

DRUMMLE. I know you don't; but let me send him to you now, may I?

PAULA. Now! What do you think a woman's made of? I could n't stand it, Cayley. I have n't slept for nights; and last night there was thunder, too! I believe I 've got the horrors.

DRUMMLE [*taking the little hand-mirror from the table*]. You 'll sleep well enough when you deliver those letters. Come, come, Mrs. Aubrey — a good night's rest! [*Holding the mirror before her face.*] It 's quite time.

[*She looks at herself for a moment, then snatches the mirror from him.*]

PAULA. You brute, Cayley, to show me that!

DRUMMLE. Then — may I? Be guided by a fr— a poor old woman! May I?

PAULA. You 'll kill me, amongst you!

DRUMMLE. What do you say?

PAULA [*after a pause*]. Very well. [*He nods his head and goes out rapidly. She looks after him for a moment, and calls "Cayley! Cayley!" Then she again produces the letters, deliberately, one by one, fingering them with aversion. Suddenly she starts, turning her head towards the door.*] Ah!

[AUBREY *enters quickly.*]

AUBREY. Paula!

PAULA [*handing him the letters, her face averted*]. There! [*He examines the letters, puzzled, and looks at her enquiringly.*] They are many days old. I stole them, I suppose to make you anxious and unhappy.

[*He looks at the letters again, then lays them aside on the table.*]

AUBREY [*gently*]. Paula, dear, it does n't matter.

PAULA [*after a short pause*]. Why — why do you take it like this?

AUBREY. What did you expect?

PAULA. Oh, but I suppose silent reproaches are really the severest. And then, naturally, you are itching to open your letters. [*She crosses the room as if to go.*]

AUBREY. Paula! [*She pauses.*] Surely, surely, it 's all over now?

PAULA. All over! [*Mockingly.*] Has my step-daughter returned then? When did she arrive? I have n't heard of it!

AUBREY. You can be very cruel.

PAULA. That word 's always on a man's lips; he uses it if his soup 's cold. [*With another movement as if to go.*] Need we —

AUBREY. I know I 've wounded you, Paula. But is n't there any way out of this?

PAULA. When does Ellean return? Tomorrow? Next week?

AUBREY [*wearily*]. Oh! Why should we grudge Ellean the little pleasure she is likely to find in Paris and in London?

PAULA. I grudge her nothing, if that 's a hit at me. But with that woman —?

AUBREY. It must be that woman or another. You know that at present we are unable to give Ellean the opportunity of — of —

PAULA. Of mixing with respectable people.

AUBREY. The opportunity of gaining friends, experience, ordinary knowledge of the world. If you are interested in Ellean, can't you see how useful Mrs. Cortelyon's good offices are?

PAULA. May I put one question? At the end of the London season, when Mrs. Cortelyon has done with Ellean, is it quite understood that the girl comes back to us? [AUBREY *is silent.*] Is it? Is it?

AUBREY. Let us wait till the end of the season —

PAULA. Oh! I knew it. You 're only fooling me; you put me off with any trash.

I believe you've sent Ellean away, not for the reasons you give, but because you don't consider me a decent companion for her, because you're afraid she might get a little of her innocence rubbed off in my company? Come, isn't that the truth? Be honest! Isn't that it?

AUBREY. Yes.

[*There is a moment's silence, on both sides.*]

PAULA [*with uplifted hands as if to strike him*]. Oh!

AUBREY [*taking her by the wrists*]. Sit down. Sit down. [*He puts her into a chair; she shakes herself free with a cry.*] Now listen to me. Fond as you are, Paula, of harking back to your past, there's one chapter of it you always let alone. I've never asked you to speak of it; you've never offered to speak of it. I mean the chapter that relates to the time when you were — like Ellean. [*She attempts to rise; he restrains her.*] No, no.

PAULA. I don't choose to talk about that time. I won't satisfy your curiosity.

AUBREY. My dear Paula, I have no curiosity — I know what you were at Ellean's age. I'll tell you. You hadn't a thought that wasn't a wholesome one, you hadn't an impulse that didn't tend towards good, you never harbored a notion you couldn't have gossiped about to a parcel of children. [*She makes another effort to rise: he lays his hand lightly on her shoulder.*] And this was a very few years back — there are days now when you look like a schoolgirl — but think of the difference between the two Paulas. You'll have to think hard, because after a cruel life, one's perceptions grow a thick skin. But, for God's sake, do think till you get these two images clearly in your mind, and then ask yourself what sort of a friend such a woman as you are to-day would have been for the girl of seven or eight years ago.

PAULA [*rising*]. How dare you? I could be almost as good a friend to Ellean as her own mother would have been had she lived. I know what you mean. How dare you?

AUBREY. You say that; very likely you believe it. But you're blind, Paula; you're blind. You! Every belief that a young, pure-minded girl holds sacred — that you once held sacred — you now make a target for a jest, a sneer, a paltry cynicism. I tell you, you're not mistress any longer of your

thoughts or your tongue. Why, how often, sitting between you and Ellean, have I seen her cheeks turn scarlet as you've rattled off some tale that belongs by right to the club or the smoking-room! Have you noticed the blush? If you have, has the cause of it ever struck you? And this is the girl you say you love, I admit that you *do* love, whose love you expect in return! Oh, Paula, I make the best, the only, excuse for you when I tell you you're blind!

PAULA. Ellean — Ellean blushes easily.

AUBREY. You blushed as easily a few years ago.

PAULA [*after a short pause*]. Well! have you finished your sermon?

AUBREY [*with a gesture of despair*]. Oh, Paula!

[*Going up to the window, and standing with his back to the room.*]

PAULA. [*To herself.*] A few — years ago! [*She walks slowly towards the door, then suddenly drops upon the ottoman in a paroxysm of weeping.*] O God! A few years ago!

AUBREY [*going to her*]. Paula!

PAULA [*sobbing*]. Oh, don't touch me!

AUBREY. Paula!

PAULA. Oh, go away from me! [*He goes back a few steps, and after a little while she becomes calmer and rises unsteadily; then in an altered tone.*] Look here —! [*He advances a step; she checks him with a quick gesture.*] Look here! Get rid of these people — Mabel and her husband — as soon as possible! I — I've done with them!

AUBREY [*in a whisper*]. Paula!

PAULA. And then — then — when the time comes for Ellean to leave Mrs. Cortelyon, give me — give me another chance! [*He advances again, but she shrinks away.*] No, no!

[*She goes out by the door on the right. He sinks onto the settee, covering his eyes with his hands. There is a brief silence, then a SERVANT enters.*]

SERVANT. Mrs. Cortelyon, sir, with Miss Ellean.

[AUBREY *rises to meet* MRS. CORTELYON, *who enters, followed by* ELLEAN, *both being in traveling dresses. The* SERVANT *withdraws.*]

MRS. CORTELYON [*shaking hands with* AUBREY]. Oh, my dear Aubrey!

AUBREY. Mrs. Cortelyon! [*Kissing* EL-LEAN.] Ellean dear!

ELLEAN. Papa, is all well at home?

MRS. CORTELYON. We're shockingly anxious.

AUBREY. Yes, yes, all's well. This is quite unexpected. [*To* MRS. CORTELYON.] You've found Paris insufferably hot?

MRS. CORTELYON. Insufferably hot! Paris is pleasant enough. We've had no letter from you!

AUBREY. I wrote to Ellean a week ago.

MRS. CORTELYON. Without alluding to the subject I had written to you upon.

AUBREY [*thinking*]. Ah, of course —

MRS. CORTELYON. And since then we've both written, and you've been absolutely silent. Oh, it's too bad!

AUBREY [*picking up the letters from the table*]. It isn't altogether my fault. Here are the letters —

ELLEAN. Papa!

MRS. CORTELYON. They're unopened.

AUBREY. An accident delayed their reaching me till this evening. I'm afraid this has upset you very much.

MRS. CORTELYON. Upset me!

ELLEAN [*in an undertone to* MRS. COR-TELYON]. Never mind. Not now, dear — not to-night.

AUBREY. Eh?

MRS. CORTELYON. [*To* ELLEAN, *aloud.*] Child, run away and take your things off. She doesn't look as if she'd journeyed from Paris to-day.

AUBREY. I've never seen her with such a color. [*Taking* ELLEAN'S *hands.*]

ELLEAN. [*To* AUBREY, *in a faint voice.*] Papa, Mrs. Cortelyon has been so very, very kind to me, but I — I have come home. [*She goes out.*]

AUBREY. Come home! [*To* MRS. COR-TELYON.] Ellean returns to us then?

MRS. CORTELYON. That's the very point I put to you in my letters, and you oblige me to travel from Paris to Willowmere on a warm day to settle it. I think perhaps it's right that Ellean should be with you just now, although I — My dear friend, circumstances are a little altered.

AUBREY. Alice, you're in some trouble.

MRS. CORTELYON. Well — yes, I *am* in trouble. You remember pretty little Mrs. Brereton who was once Caroline Ardale?

AUBREY. Quite well.

MRS. CORTELYON. She's a widow now, poor thing. She has the *entresol* of the house where we've been lodging in the Avenue de Friedland. Caroline's a dear chum of mine; she formed a great liking for Ellean.

AUBREY. I'm very glad.

MRS. CORTELYON. Yes, it's nice for her to meet her mother's friends. Er — that young Hugh Ardale the papers were full of some time ago — he's Caroline Brereton's brother, you know.

AUBREY. No, I didn't know. What did he do? I forget.

MRS. CORTELYON. Checked one of those horrid mutinies at some far-away station in India. Marched down with a handful of his men and a few faithful natives, and held the place until he was relieved. They gave him his company and a V.C. for it.

AUBREY. And he's Mrs. Brereton's brother?

MRS. CORTELYON. Yes. He's with his sister — *was*, rather — in Paris. He's home — invalided. Good gracious, Aubrey, why don't you help me out? Can't you guess what has occurred?

AUBREY. Alice!

MRS. CORTELYON. Young Ardale — Ellean!

AUBREY. An attachment?

MRS. CORTELYON. Yes, Aubrey. [*After a little pause.*] Well, I suppose I've got myself into sad disgrace. But really I didn't foresee anything of this kind. A serious, reserved child like Ellean, and a boyish, high-spirited soldier — it never struck me as being likely. [AUBREY *paces to and fro thoughtfully.*] I did all I could directly Captain Ardale spoke — wrote to you at once. Why on earth don't you receive your letters promptly, and when you do get them why can't you open them? I endured the anxiety till last night, and then made up my mind — home! Of course, it has worried me terribly. My head's bursting. Are there any salts about? [AU-BREY *fetches a bottle from the cabinet and hands it to her.*] We've had one of those hateful smooth crossings that won't let you be properly indisposed.

AUBREY. My dear Alice, I assure you I've no thought of blaming you.

MRS. CORTELYON. That statement always precedes a quarrel.

AUBREY. I don't know whether this is

the worst or the best luck. How will my wife regard it ? Is Captain Ardale a good fellow ?

MRS. CORTELYON. My dear Aubrey, you 'd better read up the accounts of his wonderful heroism. Face to face with death for a whole week; always with a smile and a cheering word for the poor helpless souls depending on him ! Of course it 's that that has stirred the depths of your child's nature. I 've watched her while we 've been dragging the story out of him, and if angels look different from Ellean at that moment, I don't desire to meet any, that 's all !

AUBREY. If you were in my position —? But you can't judge.

MRS. CORTELYON. Why, if I had a marriageable daughter of my own, and Captain Ardale proposed for her, naturally I should cry my eyes out all night — but I should thank Heaven in the morning.

AUBREY. You believe so thoroughly in him ?

MRS. CORTELYON. Do you think I should have only a headache at this minute if I did n't ! Look here, you 've got to see me down the lane; that 's the least you can do, my friend. Come into my house for a moment and shake hands with Hugh.

AUBREY. What, is he here ?

MRS. CORTELYON. He came through with us, to present himself formally to-morrow. Where are my gloves ? [AUBREY *fetches them from the ottoman.*] Make my apologies to Mrs. Tanqueray, please. She 's well, I hope ? [*Going towards the door.*] I can't feel sorry she has n't seen me in this condition.

[ELLEAN *enters.*]

ELLEAN. [*To* MRS. CORTELYON.] I 've been waiting to wish you good-night. I was afraid I 'd missed you.

MRS. CORTELYON. Good-night, Ellean.

ELLEAN [*in a low voice, embracing* MRS. CORTELYON]. I can't thank you. Dear Mrs. Cortelyon !

MRS. CORTELYON [*her arms round* EL-LEAN, *in a whisper to* AUBREY]. Speak a word to her.   [MRS. CORTELYON *goes out.*]

AUBREY. [*To* ELLEAN.] Ellean, I 'm going to see Mrs. Cortelyon home. Tell Paula where I am; explain, dear.

[*Going to the door.*]

ELLEAN [*her head drooping*]. Yes. [*Quickly.*] Father ! You are angry with me — disappointed ?

AUBREY. Angry ? No.

ELLEAN. Disappointed ?

AUBREY [*smiling and going to her and taking her hand*]. If so, it 's only because you 've shaken my belief in my discernment. I thought you took after your poor mother a little, Ellean; but there 's a look on your face to-night, dear, that I never saw on hers — never, never.

ELLEAN [*leaning her head on his shoulder*]. Perhaps I ought not to have gone away.

AUBREY. Hush ! You 're quite happy ?

ELLEAN. Yes.

AUBREY. That 's right. Then, as you are quite happy, there is something I particularly want you to do for me, Ellean.

ELLEAN. What is that ?

AUBREY. Be very gentle with Paula. Will you ?

ELLEAN. You think I have been unkind.

AUBREY [*kissing her upon the forehead*]. Be very gentle with Paula.

[*He goes out, and she stands looking after him; then, as she turns thoughtfully from the door, a rose is thrown through the window and falls at her feet. She picks up the flower wonderingly and goes to the window.*]

ELLEAN [*starting back*]. Hugh !

[HUGH ARDALE, *a handsome young man of about seven-and-twenty, with a boyish face and manner, appears outside the window.*]

HUGH. Nelly ! Nelly dear !

ELLEAN. What 's the matter ?

HUGH. Hush ! Nothing. It 's only fun. [*Laughing.*] Ha, ha, ha ! I 've found out that Mrs. Cortelyon's meadow runs up to your father's plantation; I 've come through a gap in the hedge.

ELLEAN. Why, Hugh ?

HUGH. I 'm miserable at The Warren : it 's so different from the Avenue de Friedland. Don't look like that ! Upon my word I meant just to peep at your home and go back, but I saw figures moving about here, and came nearer, hoping to get a glimpse of you. Was that your father ?

[*Entering the room.*]

ELLEAN. Yes.

HUGH. Is n't this fun ! A rabbit ran

across my foot while I was hiding behind that old yew.

ELLEAN. You must go away; it's not right for you to be here like this.

HUGH. But it's only fun, I tell you. You take everything so seriously. Do wish me good-night.

ELLEAN. We have said good-night.

HUGH. In the hall at The Warren, before Mrs. Cortelyon and a man-servant. Oh, it's so different from the Avenue de Friedland !

ELLEAN [giving him her hand hastily]. Good-night, Hugh !

HUGH. Is that all ? We might be the merest acquaintances.

[He momentarily embraces her, but she releases herself.]

ELLEAN. It's when you're like this that you make me feel utterly miserable. [Throwing the rose from her angrily.] Oh !

HUGH. I've offended you now, I suppose ?

ELLEAN. Yes.

HUGH. Forgive me, Nelly. Come into the garden for five minutes ; we'll stroll down to the plantation.

ELLEAN. No, no.

HUGH. For two minutes — to tell me you forgive me.

ELLEAN. I forgive you.

HUGH. Evidently. I shan't sleep a wink to-night after this. What a fool I am ! Come down to the plantation. Make it up with me.

ELLEAN. There is somebody coming into this room. Do you wish to be seen here ?

HUGH. I shall wait for you behind that yew-tree. You must speak to me. Nelly !

[He disappears. PAULA enters.]

PAULA. Ellean !

ELLEAN. You — you are very surprised to see me, Paula, of course.

PAULA. Why are you here ? Why aren't you with — your friend ?

ELLEAN. I've come home — if you'll have me. We left Paris this morning ; Mrs. Cortelyon brought me back. She was here a minute or two ago ; papa has just gone with her to The Warren. He asked me to tell you.

PAULA. There are some people staying with us that I'd rather you didn't meet. It was hardly worth your while to return for a few hours.

ELLEAN. A few hours ?

PAULA. Well, when do you go to London ?

ELLEAN. I don't think I go to London, after all.

PAULA [eagerly]. You — you've quarrelled with her ?

ELLEAN. No, no, no, not that ; but — Paula ! [In an altered tone.] Paula !

PAULA [startled]. Eh ! [ELLEAN goes deliberately to PAULA and kisses her.] Ellean !

ELLEAN. Kiss me.

PAULA. What — what's come to you ?

ELLEAN. I want to behave differently to you in the future. Is it too late ?

PAULA. Too — late ! [Impulsively kissing ELLEAN and crying.] No — no — no ! No — no !

ELLEAN. Paula, don't cry.

PAULA [wiping her eyes]. I'm a little shaky ; I haven't been sleeping. It's all right, — talk to me.

ELLEAN. There is something I want to tell you —

PAULA. Is there — is there ?

[They sit together on the ottoman, PAULA taking ELLEAN's hand.]

ELLEAN. Paula, in our house in the Avenue de Friedland, on the floor below us, there was a Mrs. Brereton. She used to be a friend of my mother's. Mrs. Cortelyon and I spent a great deal of our time with her.

PAULA [suspiciously]. Oh ! [Letting ELLEAN's hand fall.] Is this lady going to take you up in place of Mrs. Cortelyon ?

ELLEAN. No, no. Her brother is staying with her — was staying with her. Her brother — [Breaking off in confusion.]

PAULA. Well ?

ELLEAN [almost inaudibly]. Paula —

[She rises and walks away, PAULA following her.]

PAULA [taking hold of her]. You're not in love ! [ELLEAN looks at PAULA appealingly.] Oh, you in love ! You ! Oh, this is why you've come home ! Of course, you can make friends with me now ! You'll leave us for good soon, I suppose ; so it doesn't much matter being civil to me for a little while !

ELLEAN. Oh, Paula !

PAULA. Why, how you have deceived us — all of us ! We've taken you for a cold-blooded little saint. The fools you've made of us ! Saint Ellean, Saint Ellean !

ELLEAN. Ah, I might have known you'd only mock me !

PAULA [her tone changing]. Eh ?

ELLEAN. I — I can't talk to you. [*Sitting on the settee.*] You do nothing else but mock and sneer, nothing else.

PAULA. Ellean dear! Ellean! I did n't mean it. I'm so horribly jealous, it's a sort of curse on me. [*Kneeling beside* ELLEAN *and embracing her.*] My tongue runs away with me. I'm going to alter, I swear I am. I've made some good resolutions, and as God's above me, I'll keep them! If you are in love, if you do ever marry, that's no reason why we should n't be fond of each other. Come, you've kissed me of your own accord — you can't take it back. Now we're friends again, are n't we? Ellean, dear! I want to know everything, everything. Ellean, dear, Ellean!

ELLEAN. Paula, Hugh has done something that makes me very angry. He came with us from Paris to-day, to see papa. He is staying with Mrs. Cortelyon and — I ought to tell you —

PAULA. Yes, yes. What?

ELLEAN. He has found his way by The Warren meadow through the plantation up to this house. He is waiting to bid me good-night. [*Glancing towards the garden.*] He is — out there.

PAULA. Oh!

ELLEAN. What shall I do?

PAULA. Bring him in to see me! Will you?

ELLEAN. No, no.

PAULA. But I'm dying to know him. Oh, yes, you must. I shall meet him before Aubrey does. [*Excitedly running her hands over her hair.*] I'm so glad. [ELLEAN *goes out by the window.*] The mirror — mirror. What a fright I must look! [*Not finding the hand-glass on the table, she jumps onto the settee, and surveys herself in the mirror over the mantelpiece, then sits quietly down and waits.*] Ellean! Just fancy! Ellean!

[*After a pause* ELLEAN *enters by the window with* HUGH.]

ELLEAN. Paula, this is Captain Ardale — Mrs. Tanqueray.

    [PAULA *rises and turns, and she and* HUGH *stand staring blankly at each other for a moment or two; then* PAULA *advances and gives him her hand.*]

PAULA [*in a strange voice, but calmly*]. How do you do?

HUGH. How do you do?

PAULA. [*To* ELLEAN.] Mr. Ardale and I have met in London, Ellean. Er — Captain Ardale now?

HUGH. Yes.

ELLEAN. In London?

PAULA. They say the world's very small, don't they?

HUGH. Yes.

PAULA. Ellean, dear, I want to have a little talk about you to Mr. Ardale — Captain Ardale — alone. [*Putting her arms round* ELLEAN, *and leading her to the door.*] Come back in a little while. [ELLEAN *nods to* PAULA *with a smile and goes out, while* PAULA *stands watching her at the open door.*] In a little while — in a little — [*Closing the door and then taking a seat facing* HUGH.] Be quick! Mr. Tanqueray has only gone down to The Warren with Mrs. Cortelyon. What is to be done?

HUGH [*blankly*]. Done?

PAULA. Done — done. Something must be done.

HUGH. I understood that Mr. Tanqueray had married a Mrs. — Mrs. —

PAULA. Jarman?

HUGH. Yes.

PAULA. I'd been going by that name. You did n't follow my doings after we sep-arated.

HUGH. No.

PAULA [*sneeringly*]. No.

HUGH. I went out to India.

PAULA. What's to be done?

HUGH. Damn this chance!

PAULA. Oh, my God!

HUGH. Your husband does n't know, does he?

PAULA. That you and I — ?

HUGH. Yes.

PAULA. No. He knows about others.

HUGH. Not about me. How long were we — ?

PAULA. I don't remember, exactly.

HUGH. Do you — do you think it matters?

PAULA. His — his daughter. [*With a muttered exclamation he turns away, and sits with his head in his hands.*] What's to be done?

HUGH. I wish I could think.

PAULA. Oh! Oh! What happened to that flat of ours in Ethelbert Street?

HUGH. I let it.

PAULA. All that pretty furniture?

HUGH. Sold it.

PAULA. I came across the key of the escritoire the other day in an old purse! [*Suddenly realizing the horror and hopelessness of her position, and starting to her feet with an hysterical cry of rage.*] What am I maundering about?

HUGH. For God's sake, be quiet! Do let me think.

PAULA. This will send me mad! [*Suddenly turning and standing over him.*] You — you beast, to crop up in my life again like this!

HUGH. I always treated you fairly.

PAULA [*weakly*]. Oh! I beg your pardon — I know you did — I —

[*She sinks onto the settee crying hysterically.*]

HUGH. Hush!

PAULA. She kissed me to-night! I'd won her over! I've had such a fight to make her love me! And now — just as she's beginning to love me, to bring this on her!

HUGH. Hush, hush! Don't break down!

PAULA [*sobbing*]. You don't know! I — I have n't been getting on well in my marriage. It's been my fault. The life I used to lead spoilt me completely. But I'd made up my mind to turn over a new leaf from to-night. From to-night!

HUGH. Paula —

PAULA. Don't you call me that!

HUGH. Mrs. Tanqueray, there is no cause for you to despair in this way. It's all right, I tell you — it *shall* be all right.

PAULA [*shivering*]. What are we to do?

HUGH. Hold our tongues.

PAULA. Eh?   [*Staring vacantly.*]

HUGH. The chances are a hundred to one against any one ever turning up who knew us when we were together. Besides, no one would be such a brute as to split on us. If anybody did do such a thing we should have to lie! What are we upsetting ourselves like this for, when we've simply got to hold our tongues?

PAULA. You're as mad as I am.

HUGH. Can you think of a better plan?

PAULA. There's only one plan possible — let's come to our senses! — Mr. Tanqueray must be told.

HUGH. Your husband! What, and I lose Ellean! I lose Ellean!

PAULA. You've got to lose her.

HUGH. I won't lose her; I can't lose her!

PAULA. Did n't I read of your doing any number of brave things in India? Why, you seem to be an awful coward!

HUGH. That's another sort of pluck altogether; I have n't this sort of pluck.

PAULA. Oh, I don't ask *you* to tell Mr. Tanqueray. That's my job.

HUGH [*standing over her*]. You — you — you'd better! You —

PAULA [*rising*]. Don't bully me! I intend to.

HUGH [*taking hold of her; she wrenches herself free*]. Look here, Paula, I never treated you badly — you've owned it. Why should you want to pay me out like this? You don't know how I love Ellean!

PAULA. Yes, that's just what I *do* know.

HUGH. I say you don't! She's as good as my own mother. I've been downright honest with her, too. I told her, in Paris, that I'd been a bit wild at one time, and, after a damned wretched day, she promised to forgive me because of what I'd done since in India. She's behaved like an angel to me! Surely I ought n't to lose her, after all, just because I've been like other fellows! No; I have n't been half as rackety as a hundred men we could think of. Paula, don't pay me out for nothing; be fair to me, there's a good girl — be fair to me!

PAULA. Oh, I'm not considering you at all! I advise you not to stay here any longer: Mr. Tanqueray is sure to be back soon.

HUGH [*taking up his hat*]. What's the understanding between us, then? What have we arranged to do?

PAULA. I don't know what you're going to do; I've got to tell Mr. Tanqueray.

HUGH. By God, you shall do nothing of the sort!   [*Approaching her fiercely.*]

PAULA. You shocking coward!

HUGH. If you dare! [*Going up to the window.*] Mind! If you dare!

PAULA [*following him*]. Why, what would you do?

HUGH [*after a short pause, sullenly*]. Nothing. I'd shoot myself — that's nothing. Good-night.

PAULA. Good-night.

[*He disappears. She walks unsteadily to the ottoman, and sits; and as she does so her hand falls upon the little silver mirror, which she takes up staring at her own reflection.*]

THE FOURTH ACT

*The Drawing-room at "Highercoombe," the
same evening.*

PAULA *is still seated on the ottoman, looking
vacantly before her, with the little mirror in her
hand.* LADY ORREYED *enters.*

LADY ORREYED. There you are! You
never came into the billiard-room. Is n't it
maddening — Cayley Drummle gives me
sixty out of a hundred, and beats me. I
must be out of form, because I know I play
remarkably well for a lady. Only last
month — [PAULA *rises.*] Whatever is the
matter with you, old girl?

PAULA. Why?

LADY ORREYED [*staring*]. It 's the light,
I suppose. [PAULA *replaces the mirror on the
table.*] By Aubrey's bolting from the bil-
liard-table in that fashion I thought perhaps —

PAULA. Yes; it 's all right.

LADY ORREYED. You 've patched it up?
[PAULA *nods.*] Oh, I am jolly glad — ! I
mean —

PAULA. Yes, I know what you mean.
Thanks, Mabel.

LADY ORREYED [*kissing* PAULA]. Now
take my advice; for the future —

PAULA. Mabel, if I 've been disagreeable
to you while you 've been staying here, I
— I beg your pardon.

[*Walking away and sitting down.*]

LADY ORREYED. You disagreeable, my
dear? I have n't noticed it. Dodo and me
both consider you make a first-class hostess; but then you 've had such practice,
have n't you? [*Dropping on the ottoman and
gaping.*] Oh, talk about being sleepy — !

PAULA. Why don't you — !

LADY ORREYED. Why, dear, I must hang
about for Dodo. You may as well know it;
he 's in one of his moods.

PAULA [*under her breath*]. Oh — !

LADY ORREYED. Now, it 's not his fault;
it was deadly dull for him while we were
playing billiards. Cayley Drummle did ask
him to mark, but I stopped that; it 's so
easy to make a gentleman look like a bil-
liard-marker. This is just how it always is;
if poor old Dodo has nothing to do, he loses
count, as you may say.

PAULA. Hark!

[SIR GEORGE ORREYED *enters, walking slowly
and deliberately; he looks pale and watery-
eyed.*]

SIR GEORGE [*with mournful indistinctness*].
I 'm 'fraid we 've lef' you a grea' deal to
yourself to-night, Mrs. Tanqueray. At-
tra'tions of billiards. I apol'gise. I say,
where 's ol' Aubrey?

PAULA. My husband has been obliged to
go out to a neighbor's house.

SIR GEORGE. I want his advice on a rather
pressing matter connected with my family
— my family. [*Sitting.*] To-morrow will do
just as well.

LADY ORREYED. [*To* PAULA.] This is the
mood I hate so — driveling about his precious family.

SIR GEORGE. The fact is, Mrs. Tanqueray, I am not easy in my min' 'bout the way
I am treatin' my poor ol' mother.

LADY ORREYED. [*To* PAULA.] Do you
hear that? That 's *his* mother, but *my*
mother he won't so much as look at!

SIR GEORGE. I shall write to Bruton
Street firs' thing in the morning.

LADY ORREYED. [*To* PAULA.] Mamma
has stuck to me through everything — well,
you know!

SIR GEORGE. I 'll get ol' Aubrey to figure
out a letter. I 'll drop line to Uncle Fitz
too — dooced shame of the ol' feller to
chuck me over in this manner. [*Wiping his
eyes.*] All my family have chucked me over.

LADY ORREYED [*rising*]. Dodo!

SIR GEORGE. Jus' because I 've married
beneath me, to be chucked over! Aunt
Lydia, the General, Hooky Whitgrave,
Lady Sugnall — my own dear sister! — all
turn their backs on me. It 's more than I
can stan'!

LADY ORREYED [*approaching him with
dignity*]. Sir George, wish Mrs. Tanqueray
good-night at once, and come upstairs. Do
you hear me?

SIR GEORGE [*rising angrily*]. Wha— !

LADY ORREYED. Be quiet!

SIR GEORGE. You presoom to order me
about!

LADY ORREYED. You 're making an exhibition of yourself!

SIR GEORGE. Look 'ere — !

LADY ORREYED. Come along, I tell you!
[*He hesitates, utters a few inarticulate
sounds, then snatches up a fragile
ornament from the table, and is*

about to dash it on the ground.
LADY ORREYED *retreats, and*
PAULA *goes to him.*]

PAULA. George !

[*He replaces the ornament.*]

SIR GEORGE [*shaking* PAULA'S *hand*].
Good ni', Mrs. Tanqueray.

LADY ORREYED. [*To* PAULA.] Good-
night, darling. Wish Aubrey good-night
for me. Now, Dodo ? [*She goes out.*]

SIR GEORGE. [*To* PAULA.] I say, are you
goin' to sit up for ol' Aubrey ?

PAULA. Yes.

SIR GEORGE. Shall I keep you comp'ny ?

PAULA. No, thank you, George.

SIR GEORGE. Sure ?

PAULA. Yes, sure.

SIR GEORGE [*shaking hands*]. Good-night
again.

PAULA. Good-night.

[*She turns away. He goes out, steady-
ing himself carefully.* DRUMMLE
*appears outside the window, smok-
ing.*]

DRUMMLE [*looking into the room and seeing* PAULA]. My last cigar. Where's
Aubrey ?

PAULA. Gone down to The Warren to
see Mrs. Cortelyon home.

DRUMMLE [*entering the room*]. Eh ? Did
you say Mrs. Cortelyon ?

PAULA. Yes. She has brought Ellean
back.

DRUMMLE. Bless my soul ! Why ?

PAULA. I — I 'm too tired to tell you,
Cayley. If you stroll along the lane you 'll
meet Aubrey. Get the news from him.

DRUMMLE [*going up to the window*]. Yes,
yes. [*Returning to* PAULA.] I don't want to
bother you, only — the anxious old woman,
you know. Are you and Aubrey — ?

PAULA. Good friends again ?

DRUMMLE [*nodding*]. Um.

PAULA [*giving him her hand*]. Quite, Cayley, quite.

DRUMMLE [*retaining her hand*]. That 's
capital. As I 'm off so early to-morrow
morning, let me say now — thank you for
your hospitality.

[*He bends over her hand gallantly, then
goes out by the window.*]

PAULA. [*To herself.*] " Are you and Aubrey — ? " " Good friends again ? " " Yes."
" Quite, Cayley, quite."

[*There is a brief pause, then* AUBREY

*enters hurriedly, wearing a light
overcoat and carrying a cap.*]

AUBREY. Paula dear ! Have you seen
Ellean ?

PAULA. I found her here when I came
down.

AUBREY. She — she 's told you ?

PAULA. Yes, Aubrey.

AUBREY. It 's extraordinary, is n't it !
Not that somebody should fall in love with
Ellean, or that Ellean herself should fall
in love. All that 's natural enough and was
bound to happen, I suppose, sooner or later.
But this young fellow ! You know his history ?

PAULA. His history ?

AUBREY. You remember the papers were
full of his name a few months ago ?

PAULA. Oh, yes.

AUBREY. The man 's as brave as a lion,
there 's no doubt about that; and, at the
same time, he 's like a big good-natured
school-boy, Mrs. Cortelyon says. Have you
ever pictured the kind of man Ellean would
marry some day ?

PAULA. I can't say that I have.

AUBREY. A grave, sedate fellow I 've
thought about — hah ! She has fallen in
love with the way in which Ardale practically laid down his life to save those poor
people shut up in the Residency. [*Taking
off his coat.*] Well, I suppose if a man can
do that sort of thing, one ought to be content. And yet — [*Throwing his coat on the
settee.*] I should have met him to-night,
but he 'd gone out. Paula dear, tell me how
you look upon this business.

PAULA. Yes, I will — I must. To begin
with, I — I 've seen Mr. Ardale.

AUBREY. Captain Ardale ?

PAULA. Captain Ardale.

AUBREY. Seen him ?

PAULA. While you were away he came
up here, through our grounds, to try to get
a word with Ellean. I made her fetch him
in and present him to me.

AUBREY [*frowning*]. Does n't Captain
Ardale know there 's a lodge and a front
door to this place ? Never mind ! What is
your impression of him ?

PAULA. Aubrey, do you recollect my
bringing you a letter — a letter giving you
an account of myself — to the Albany late
one night — the nigh. before we got married ?

AUBREY. A letter?

PAULA. You burnt it; don't you know?

AUBREY. Yes; I know.

PAULA. His name was in that letter.

AUBREY [*going back from her slowly, and staring at her*]. I don't understand.

PAULA. Well — Ardale and I once kept house together. [*He remains silent, not moving.*] Why don't you strike me? Hit me in the face — I'd rather you did! Hurt me! hurt me!

AUBREY [*after a pause*]. What did you — and this man — say to each other — just now?

PAULA. I — hardly — know.

AUBREY. Think!

PAULA. The end of it all was that I — I told him I must inform you of — what had happened . . . he didn't want me to do that . . . I declared that I would . . . he dared me to. [*Breaking down.*] Let me alone! — oh!

AUBREY. Where was my daughter while this went on?

PAULA. I — I had sent her out of the room . . . that is all right.

AUBREY. Yes, yes — yes, yes.

[*He turns his head towards the door.*]

PAULA. Who's that?

[*A* SERVANT *enters with a letter.*]

SERVANT. The coachman has just run up with this from The Warren, sir. [AUBREY *takes the letter.*] It's for Mrs. Tanqueray, sir; there's no answer.

[*The* SERVANT *withdraws.* AUBREY *goes to* PAULA *and drops the letter into her lap; she opens it with uncertain hands.*]

PAULA [*reading it to herself*]. It's from — him. He's going away — or gone — I think. [*Rising in a weak way.*] What does it say? I never could make out his writing.

[*She gives the letter to* AUBREY, *and stands near him, looking at the letter over his shoulder as he reads.*]

AUBREY [*reading*]. "I shall be in Paris by to-morrow evening. Shall wait there, at Meurice's, for a week, ready to receive any communication you or your husband may address to me. Please invent some explanation to Ellean. Mrs. Tanqueray, for God's sake, do what you can for me."

[PAULA *and* AUBREY *speak in low voices, both still looking at the letter.*]

PAULA. Has he left The Warren, I wonder, already?

AUBREY. That doesn't matter.

PAULA. No; but I can picture him going quietly off. Very likely he's walking on to Bridgeford or Cottering to-night, to get the first train in the morning. A pleasant stroll for him.

AUBREY. We'll reckon he's gone, that's enough.

PAULA. That isn't to be answered in any way?

AUBREY. Silence will answer that.

PAULA. He'll soon recover his spirits, I know.

AUBREY. You know. [*Offering her the letter.*] You don't want this, I suppose?

PAULA. No.

AUBREY. It's done with — done with.

[*He tears the letter into small pieces. She has dropped the envelope; she searches for it, finds it, and gives it to him.*]

PAULA. Here!

AUBREY [*looking at the remnants of the letter*]. This is no good; I must burn it.

PAULA. Burn it in your room.

AUBREY. Yes.

PAULA. Put it in your pocket for now.

AUBREY. Yes.

[*He does so.* ELLEAN *enters, and they both turn, guiltily, and stare at her.*]

ELLEAN [*after a short silence, wonderingly*]. Papa —

AUBREY. What do you want, Ellean?

ELLEAN. I heard from Willis that you had come in; I only want to wish you goodnight. [PAULA *steals away, without looking back.*] What's the matter? Ah! Of course, Paula has told you about Captain Ardale?

AUBREY. Well?

ELLEAN. Have you and he met?

AUBREY. No.

ELLEAN. You are angry with him; so was I. But to-morrow when he calls and expresses his regret — to-morrow —

AUBREY. Ellean — Ellean!

ELLEAN. Yes, papa.

AUBREY. I — I can't let you see this man again. [*He walks away from her in a paroxysm of distress, then, after a moment or two, he returns to her and takes her to his arms.*] Ellean! my child!

ELLEAN [*releasing herself*]. What has happened, papa? What is it?

AUBREY [*thinking out his words deliberately*]. Something has occurred, something has come to my knowledge, in relation to Captain Ardale, which puts any further acquaintanceship between you two out of the question.

ELLEAN. Any further acquaintanceship . . . out of the question?

AUBREY. Yes.

[*Advancing to her quickly, but she shrinks from him.*]

ELLEAN. No, no — I am quite well. [*After a short pause.*] It's not an hour ago since Mrs. Cortelyon left you and me together here; you had nothing to urge against Captain Ardale then.

AUBREY. No.

ELLEAN. You don't know each other; you have n't even seen him this evening. Father!

AUBREY. I have told you he and I have not met.

ELLEAN. Mrs. Cortelyon could n't have spoken against him to you just now. No, no, no; she's too good a friend to both of us. Are n't you going to give me some explanation? You can't take this position towards me — towards Captain Ardale — without affording me the fullest explanation.

AUBREY. Ellean, there are circumstances connected with Captain Ardale's career which you had better remain ignorant of. It must be sufficient for you that I consider these circumstances render him unfit to be your husband.

ELLEAN. Father!

AUBREY. You must trust me, Ellean; you must try to understand the depth of my love for you and the — the agony it gives me to hurt you. You must trust me.

ELLEAN. I will, father; but you must trust me a little too. Circumstances connected with Captain Ardale's career?

AUBREY. Yes.

ELLEAN. When he presents himself here to-morrow, of course you will see him and let him defend himself?

AUBREY. Captain Ardale will not be here to-morrow.

ELLEAN. Not! You have stopped his coming here?

AUBREY. Indirectly — yes.

ELLEAN. But just now he was talking to me at that window! Nothing had taken place then! And since then nothing can

have — ! Oh! Why — you have heard something against him from Paula.

AUBREY. From — Paula!

ELLEAN. She knows him.

AUBREY. She has told you so?

ELLEAN. When I introduced Captain Ardale to her she said she had met him in London. Of course! It is Paula who has done this!

AUBREY [*in a hard voice*]. I — I hope you — you 'll refrain from rushing at conclusions. There 's nothing to be gained by trying to avoid the main point, which is that you must drive Captain Ardale out of your thoughts. Understand that! You 're able to obtain comfort from your religion, are n't you? I 'm glad to think that 's so. I talk to you in a harsh way, Ellean, but I feel your pain almost as acutely as you do. [*Going to the door.*] I — I can't say anything more to you to-night.

ELLEAN. Father! [*He pauses at the door.*] Father, I 'm obliged to ask you this; there 's no help for it — I 've no mother to go to. Does what you have heard about Captain Ardale concern the time when he led a wild, a dissolute life in London?

AUBREY [*returning to her slowly and staring at her*]. Explain yourself!

ELLEAN. He has been quite honest with me. One day — in Paris — he confessed to me — what a man's life is — what his life had been.

AUBREY [*under his breath*]. Oh!

ELLEAN. He offered to go away, not to approach me again.

AUBREY. And you — you accepted his view of what a man's life is?

ELLEAN. As far as *I* could forgive him, I forgave him.

AUBREY [*with a groan*]. Why, when was it you left us? It has n't taken you long to get your robe "just a little dusty at the hem!"

ELLEAN. What do you mean?

AUBREY. Hah! A few weeks ago my one great desire was to keep you ignorant of evil.

ELLEAN. Father, it is impossible to be ignorant of evil. Instinct, common instinct, teaches us what is good and bad. Surely I am none the worse for knowing what is wicked and detesting it!

AUBREY. Detesting it! Why, you love this fellow!

ELLEAN. Ah, you don't understand! I have simply judged Captain Ardale as we all pray to be judged. I have lived in imagination through that one week in India when he deliberately offered his life back to God to save those wretched, desperate people. In his whole career I see now nothing but that one week; those few hours bring him nearer the saints, I believe, than fifty uneventful years of mere blamelessness would have done! And so, father, if Paula has reported anything to Captain Ardale's discredit —

AUBREY. Paula —!

ELLEAN. It must be Paula; it can't be anybody else.

AUBREY. You — you'll please keep Paula out of the question. Finally, Ellean, understand me — I have made up my mind.

[Again going to the door.]

ELLEAN. But wait — listen! I have made up my mind also.

AUBREY. Ah! I recognize your mother in you now!

ELLEAN. You need not speak against my mother because you are angry with me!

AUBREY. I — I hardly know what I 'm saying to you. In the morning — in the morning —

[He goes out. She remains standing, and turns her head to listen. Then, after a moment's hesitation she goes softly to the window, and looks out under the veranda.]

ELLEAN [in a whisper]. Paula! Paula!

[PAULA appears outside the window and steps into the room; her face is white and drawn, her hair is a little disordered.]

PAULA [huskily]. Well?

ELLEAN. Have you been under the veranda all the while — listening?

PAULA. No — no.

ELLEAN. You have overheard us — I see you have. And it is you who have been speaking to my father against Captain Ardale. Is n't it? Paula, why don't you own it or deny it?

PAULA. Oh, I — I don't mind owning it; why should I?

ELLEAN. Ah! You seem to have been very, very eager to tell your tale.

PAULA. No, I was n't eager, Ellean. I 'd have given something not to have had to do it. I was n't eager.

ELLEAN. Not! Oh, I think you might safely have spared us all for a little while.

PAULA. But, Ellean, you forget I — I am your stepmother. It was my — my duty — to tell your father what I — what I knew —

ELLEAN. What you knew! Why, after all, what can you know? You can only speak from gossip, report, hearsay! How is it possible that you — ! [She stops abruptly. The two women stand staring at each other for a moment; then ELLEAN backs away from PAULA slowly.] Paula!

PAULA. What — what's the matter?

ELLEAN. You — you knew Captain Ardale in London!

PAULA. Why — what do you mean?

ELLEAN. Oh!

[She makes for the door, but PAULA catches her by the wrist.]

PAULA. You shall tell me what you mean!

ELLEAN. Ah! [Suddenly, looking fixedly into PAULA's face.] You know what I mean.

PAULA. You accuse me!

ELLEAN. It's in your face!

PAULA [hoarsely]. You — you think I 'm — that sort of creature, do you?

ELLEAN. Let me go!

PAULA. Answer me! You've always hated me! [Shaking her.] Out with it!

ELLEAN. You hurt me!

PAULA. You 've always hated me! You shall answer me!

ELLEAN. Well, then, I have always — always —

PAULA. What?

ELLEAN. I have always known what you were!

PAULA. Ah! Who — who told you?

ELLEAN. Nobody but yourself. From the first moment I saw you I knew you were altogether unlike the good women I 'd left; directly I saw you I knew what my father had done. You 've wondered why I 've turned from you! There — that's the reason! Oh, but this is a horrible way for the truth to come home to every one! Oh!

PAULA. It's a lie! It's all a lie! [Forcing ELLEAN down upon her knees.] You shall beg my pardon for it. [ELLEAN utters a loud shriek of terror.] Ellean, I'm a good woman! I swear I am! I've always been a good woman! You dare to say I've ever been anything else ! It 's a lie ! [*Throwing her off violently.*]

[AUBREY *reënters.*]

AUBREY. Paula ! [PAULA *staggers back as* AUBREY *advances. Raising* ELLEAN.] What 's this ? What 's this ?

ELLEAN [*faintly*]. Nothing. It — it 's my fault. Father, I — I don't wish to see Captain Ardale again.

[*She goes out,* AUBREY *slowly following her to the door.*]

PAULA. Aubrey, she — she guesses.

AUBREY. Guesses ?

PAULA. About me — and Ardale.

AUBREY. About you — and Ardale ?

PAULA. She says she suspected my character from the beginning . . . that 's why she 's always kept me at a distance . . . and now she sees through —

[*She falters; he helps her to the ottoman, where she sits.*]

AUBREY [*bending over her*]. Paula, you must have said something — admitted something —

PAULA. I don't think so. It — it 's in my face.

AUBREY. What ?

PAULA. She tells me so. She 's right ! I 'm tainted through and through; anybody can see it, anybody can find it out. You said much the same to me to-night.

AUBREY. If she has got this idea into her head we must drive it out, that 's all. We must take steps to — What shall we do ? We had better — better — What — what ? [*Sitting and staring before him.*]

PAULA. Ellean ! So meek, so demure ! You 've often said she reminded you of her mother. Yes, I know now what your first marriage was like.

AUBREY. We must drive this idea out of her head. We 'll do something. What shall we do ?

PAULA. She 's a regular woman, too. She could forgive *him* easily enough — but *me !* That 's just a woman !

AUBREY. What *can* we do ?

PAULA. Why, nothing ! She 'd have no difficulty in following up her suspicions. Suspicions ! You should have seen how she looked at me ! [*He buries his head in his hands. There is silence for a time, then she rises slowly, and goes and sits beside him.*] Aubrey.

AUBREY. Yes.

PAULA. I 'm very sorry.

[*Without meeting her eyes, he lays his hand on her arm for a moment.*]

AUBREY. Well, we must look things straight in the face. [*Glancing around.*] At any rate, we 've done with this.

PAULA. I suppose so. [*After a brief pause.*] Of course, she and I can't live under the same roof any more. You know she kissed me to-night, of her own accord.

AUBREY. I asked her to alter towards you.

PAULA. That was it, then.

AUBREY. I — I 'm sorry I sent her away.

PAULA. It was my fault ; I made it necessary.

AUBREY. Perhaps now she 'll propose to return to the convent — well, she must.

PAULA. Would you like to keep her with you and — and leave me ?

AUBREY. Paula — !

PAULA. You need n't be afraid I 'd go back to — what I was. I could n't.

AUBREY. S—sh, for God's sake ! We — you and I — we 'll get out of this place . . . what a fool I was to come here again !

PAULA. You lived here with your first wife !

AUBREY. We 'll get out of this place and go abroad again, and begin afresh.

PAULA. Begin afresh ?

AUBREY. There 's no reason why the future should n't be happy for us — no reason that I can see —

PAULA. Aubrey !

AUBREY. Yes.

PAULA. You 'll never forget this, you know.

AUBREY. This ?

PAULA. To-night, and everything that 's led up to it. Our coming here, Ellean, our quarrels — cat and dog ! — Mrs. Cortelyon, the Orreyeds, this man ! What an everlasting nightmare for you !

AUBREY. Oh, we can forget it, if we choose.

PAULA. That was always your cry. How *can* one do it !

AUBREY. We 'll make our calculations solely for the future, talk about the future, think about the future.

PAULA. I believe the future is only the past again, entered through another gate.

AUBREY. That 's an awful belief.

PAULA. To-night proves it. You must see now that, do what we will, go where we will, you'll be continually reminded of — what I was. I see it.

AUBREY. You're frightened to-night; meeting this man has frightened you. But that sort of thing is n't likely to recur. The world is n't quite so small as all that.

PAULA. Is n't it! The only great distances it contains are those we carry within ourselves — the distances that separate husbands and wives, for instance. And so it 'll be with us. You'll do your best — oh, I know that — you 're a good fellow. But circumstances will be too strong for you in the end, mark my words.

AUBREY. Paula — !

PAULA. Of course I 'm pretty now — I 'm pretty still — and a pretty woman, whatever else she may be, is always — well, endurable. But even now I notice that the lines of my face are getting deeper; so are the hollows about my eyes. Yes, my face is covered with little shadows that use n't to be there. Oh, I know I 'm "going off." I hate paint and dye and those messes, but by and by, I shall drift the way of the others; I shan't be able to help myself. And then, some day — perhaps very suddenly, under a queer, fantastic light at night or in the glare of the morning — that horrid, irresistible truth that physical repulsion forces on men and women will come to you, and you 'll sicken at me.

AUBREY. I — !

PAULA. You 'll see me then, at last, with other people's eyes; you 'll see me just as your daughter does now, as all wholesome folks see women like me. And I shall have no weapon to fight with — not one serviceable little bit of prettiness left me to defend myself with! A worn-out creature — broken up, very likely, some time before I ought to be — my hair bright, my eyes dull, my body too thin or too stout, my cheeks raddled and ruddled — a ghost, a wreck, a caricature, a candle that gutters, call such an end what you like! Oh, Aubrey, what shall I be able to say to you then? And this is the future you talk about! I know it — I know it! [*He is still sitting staring forward; she rocks herself to and fro as if in pain.*] Oh, Aubrey! Oh! Oh!

AUBREY. Paula — ! [*Trying to comfort her.*]

PAULA. Oh, and I wanted so much to sleep to-night! [*Laying her head upon his shoulder. From the distance, in the garden, there comes the sound of* DRUMMLE'S *voice; he is singing as he approaches the house.*] That's Cayley, coming back from The Warren. [*Starting up.*] He does n't know, evidently. I — I won't see him!

[*She goes out quickly.* DRUMMLE'S *voice comes nearer.* AUBREY *rouses himself and snatches up a book from table, making a pretence of reading. After a moment or two,* DRUMMLE *appears at the window and looks in.*]

DRUMMLE. Aha! my dear chap!

AUBREY. Cayley?

DRUMMLE [*coming into the room*]. I went down to The Warren after you.

AUBREY. Yes?

DRUMMLE. Missed you. Well — I 've been gossiping with Mrs. Cortelyon. Confound you, I 've heard the news!

AUBREY. What have you heard?

DRUMMLE. What have I heard! Why — Ellean and young Ardale! [*Looking at* AUBREY *keenly.*] My dear Aubrey! Alice is under the impression that you are inclined to look on the affair favorably.

AUBREY [*rising and advancing to* DRUMMLE]. You've not — met — Captain Ardale?

DRUMMLE. No. Why do you ask? By the by, I don't know that I need tell you — but it 's rather strange. He 's not at The Warren to-night.

AUBREY. No?

DRUMMLE. He left the house half an hour ago, to stroll about the lanes; just now a note came from him, a scribble in pencil, simply telling Alice that she would receive a letter from him to-morrow. What 's the matter? There 's nothing very wrong, is there? My dear chap, pray forgive me, if I 'm asking too much.

AUBREY. Cayley, you — you urged me to send her away!

DRUMMLE. Ellean! Yes, yes. But — but — by all accounts this is quite an eligible young fellow. Alice has been giving me the history —

AUBREY. Curse him! [*Hurling his book to the floor.*] Curse him! Yes, I do curse him — him and his class! Perhaps I curse myself, too, in doing it. He has only led "a man's life" — just as I, how many of us,

have done ! The misery he has brought on
me and mine it's likely enough we, in our
time, have helped to bring on others by this
leading " a man's life ! " But I do curse him
for all that. My God, *I've* nothing more
to fear — I've paid *my* fine ! And so I can
curse him in safety. Curse him ! Curse him !

DRUMMLE. In Heaven's name, tell me
what's happened ?

AUBREY [*gripping* DRUMMLE'S *arm*].
Paula ! Paula !

DRUMMLE. What ?

AUBREY. They met to-night here. They
— they — they're not strangers to each
other.

DRUMMLE. Aubrey !

AUBREY. Curse him ! My poor, wretched
wife ! My poor, wretched wife !

> [*The door opens and* ELLEAN *appears.
> The two men turn to her. There is a
> moment's silence.*]

ELLEAN. Father . . . father . . . !

AUBREY. Ellean ?

ELLEAN. I — I want you. [*He goes to
her.*] Father . . . go to Paula ! [*He looks
into her face, startled.*] Quickly — quickly !
[*He passes her to go out ; she seizes his arm,
with a cry.*] No, no ; don't go !

> [*He shakes her off and goes.* ELLEAN
> *staggers back towards* DRUMMLE.]

DRUMMLE [*to* ELLEAN]. What do you
mean ? What do you mean ?

ELLEAN. I — I went to her room — to
tell her I was sorry for something I had
said to her. And I *was* sorry — I *was* sorry.
I heard the fall. I — I've seen her. It's
horrible.

DRUMMLE. She — she has — !

ELLEAN. Killed — herself ? Yes — yes.
So everybody will say. But I know — I
helped to kill her. If I'd only been merciful !

> [*She faints upon the ottoman. He
> pauses for a moment irresolutely —
> then he goes to the door, opens it,
> and stands looking out.*]

MICHAEL AND HIS LOST ANGEL

A PLAY IN FIVE ACTS

By HENRY ARTHUR JONES

PERSONS REPRESENTED

The Reverend Michael Feversham

Sir Lyolf Feversham

Edward Lashmar (Father Hilary)

Andrew Gibbard

The Reverend Mark Docwray

Withycombe

Audrie Lesden

Rose Gibbard

Mrs. Cantelo

Fanny Clover

Villagers, Congregation, Choristers, Priests

ACT I. The Vicarage Parlor at Cleveheddon
(Four months pass)

ACT II. The Shrine on Saint Decuman's Island
(Two nights and a day pass)

ACT III. The Vicarage Parlor as in Act I
(A year passes)

ACT IV. The Minster Church at Cleveheddon
(Ten months pass)

ACT V. Reception Room of the Monastery of San
Salvatore at Majano, Italy

MICHAEL AND HIS LOST ANGEL

ACT I

SCENE — *The Vicarage parlor at Cleveheddon. An old-fashioned comfortable room in an old English house. A large window, with low broad sill, takes up nearly all the back of the stage, showing to the right a part of Cleveheddon Minster in ruins. To the left a stretch of West Country landscape. A door, right, leading to house. A fireplace, right. A door, left. Table with chairs, right. A portrait of MICHAEL'S mother hangs on wall at a height of about nine feet. It is a very striking painting of a lady about twenty-eight, very delicate and spirituelle. Time. — A fine spring morning. Discover at the window, looking off right, with face turned away from audience, and in an attitude of strained attention to something outside, ANDREW GIBBARD. Enter FANNY CLOVER, the vicarage servant, showing in the REVEREND MARK DOCWRAY, a middle-aged clergyman.*

FANNY. Mr. Feversham is over to the church, sir, but he 'll be back directly.

[*Exit.*]

MARK. Andrew —

[ANDREW *turns round, an odd, rather seedy, carelessly-dressed man, a little over forty, rather gaunt, longish hair, an intelligent face with something slightly sinister about it. He shows signs of great recent sorrow and distress.*]

MARK. Andrew, what is it ?

ANDREW. I 'd rather not tell you, Mr. Docwray.

MARK. Nothing has happened to Mr. Feversham?

ANDREW. No.

MARK. Come ! Come ! What 's the matter ?

ANDREW. My daughter —

MARK. What ails her ? Where is she ?

ANDREW. Over at the church.

MARK. What is she doing ?

ANDREW. Making a public confession.

MARK. Public confession — of what ?

ANDREW. You 'll be sure to hear all about it, so I may as well tell you myself.

Perhaps it was my fault, perhaps I neglected her. All my time is given to Mr. Feversham in the library here. While I was buried in my work, and sometimes staying here half the night with Mr. Feversham, a scoundrel ruined my girl. Of course my only thought was to hide it. Was I wrong ?

MARK. Go on. Tell me all.

ANDREW. Well, right or wrong, I sent her away to the other end of England. Her child only lived a few weeks. And I brought her back home thinking it was all hushed up.

MARK. But it became known ?

ANDREW. Yes. Little by little, things began to leak out. Well, you may blame me, if you like — I lied about it ; and the more lies I told, the more I had to tell to cover them. Mr. Feversham heard of it and questioned us. Like a fool I lied to him. It was n't like lying, it was like murdering the truth to tell lies to him. And she had to lie, too. Of course he believed us and defended us against everybody. And then we dared n't tell him the truth.

MARK. Go on. What else ?

ANDREW. There 's nothing else. It all had to come out at last.

MARK. What did Mr. Feversham do ?

ANDREW. He persuaded us that we could never be right with ourselves, or right with our neighbors, or right with our God, till we had unsaid all our lies, and undone our deceit. So we 've confessed it this morning.

MARK. In church ? In public ?

ANDREW. Yes. I would n't have minded it for myself. But was it necessary for her — for Rose ? Was it bound to be in public before all her companions, before all who had watched her grow up from a child ?

MARK. You may be sure Mr. Feversham would n't have urged it unless he had felt it to be right and necessary.

ANDREW. I would n't have done it for anybody else in the world. I feel almost as if I were quits with him for all his favors to me.

MARK. You mustn't speak like this. Remember all he has done for you.

ANDREW. Oh, I don't forget it. I don't forget that I was his scout's son, and that he educated me and made him his friend and companion and helper — there isn't a crumb I eat or a thread I wear that I don't owe to him. I don't forget it. But after this morning, I feel it isn't I who am in Mr. Feversham's debt — it's he who is in my debt.

[*A penitential hymn, with organ accompaniment, is sung in church outside.*]

ANDREW [*looking off*]. It's over. They're coming out.

MARK. Why aren't you there, in church, by her side?

ANDREW. I was. I went to church with her. I stood up first and answered all his questions, and then I stood aside, and it was her turn. I saw her step forward, and I noticed a little twitch of her lip like her mother used to have, and then — I couldn't bear it any longer — I came away. I know it was cowardly, but I couldn't stay. [*Looking off.*] Hark! They're coming! She's coming with the sister who is going to take her away.

MARK. Take her away?

ANDREW. Mr. Feversham thinks it better for her to be away from the gossip of the village, so he has found a home for her with some sisters in London. She's going straight off there. Perhaps it's best. I don't know.

[ROSE GIBBARD, *sobbing, with her face in her hands, passes the window from right to left, supported by an Anglican sister. The REVEREND MICHAEL FEVERSHAM follows them and passes window. A crowd of villagers come up to the window and look in. A moment or two later, ROSE GIBBARD enters left, supported by the sister. ROSE is a pretty, delicate girl of about twenty, with rather refined features and bearing.*]

ANDREW [*holding out his arms to her*]. Bear up, my dear. Don't cry! It breaks my heart to see you.

[*Enter the* REVEREND MICHAEL FEVERSHAM, *about forty; pale, strong, calm, ascetic, scholarly face, with much sweetness and spiritu-*

ality of expression; very dignified, gentle manners, calm, strong, persuasive voice, rarely raised above an ordinary speaking tone. His whole presence and bearing denote great strength of character, great dignity, great gentleness, and great self-control.

The villagers gather round the outside of the window and look in with mingled curiosity, rudeness, and respect. MICHAEL *goes up to left window, opens it. The villagers draw back a little.*]

MICHAEL [*speaking in a very calm voice*]. Those of you who are filled with idle foolish curiosity, come and look in. [*They fall back.*] Those of you who have been moved by the awful lesson of this morning, go to your homes, ponder it in your hearts, so that all your actions and all your thoughts from this time forth may be as open as the day, as clear as crystal, as white as snow.

[*They all go away gradually.* MICHAEL *comes away from the window, leaving it open, goes to* MARK.]

MICHAEL. Mark! [*Cordial handshake.*] You've come to stay, I hope?

MARK. A few days. You have a little business here?

[*Glancing at the group of* ROSE, ANDREW, *and* Sister.]

MICHAEL. It's nearly finished. Leave me with them for a few moments.

MARK. I'll get rid of the dust of my journey and come back to you.

[*Exit* MARK. MICHAEL *turns towards* ROSE *with great tenderness.*]

MICHAEL. Poor child!

[*She comes towards him with evident effort; the* Sister *brings a chair and she sinks into it, sobbing.*]

MICHAEL [*bending over her with great tenderness*]. I know what you have suffered this morning. I would willingly have borne it for you, but that would not have made reparation to those whom you have deceived, or given you peace in your own soul. [*She continues sobbing.*] Hush! Hush! All the bitterness is past! Look only to the future! Think of the happy newness and whiteness of your life from this moment! Think of the delight of waking in the morning and knowing that you have nothing to hide! Be sure you have done right to own your sin. There won't be a softer pillow in England to-night than the one your head rests upon. [*She becomes quieter.* MICHAEL *turns to the* Sister.] Watch over her very carefully. Keep her from brooding. Let her be occupied constantly with work. And write to me very often to tell me how she is. [*Turns to* ROSE.] The carriage is ready. It's time to say good-bye.

ROSE. Good-bye, sir. Thank you for all your kindness. I've been very wicked —

MICHAEL. Hush! That is all buried now.

ROSE. Good-bye, father.

> [*Throws her arms round* ANDREW'S *neck, clings to him, sobs convulsively for some moments in a paroxysm of grief.* MICHAEL *watches them for some moments.*]

MICHAEL. [*Intercepts, gently separates them.*] It's more than she can bear. Say good-bye, and let her go.

ANDREW [*breaking down*]. Good-bye, my dear! [*Kissing her.*] Good-bye — I — I — I —

> [*Tears himself away, goes up to window, stands back to audience.*]

MICHAEL. [*To* ROSE.] No more tears! Tears are for evil and sin, and yours are all past! Write to me and tell me how you get on, and how you like the work. It will bring you great peace — great peace. Why, you are comforted already — I think I see one of your old happy smiles coming. What do you think, sister, is n't that the beginning of a smile?

SISTER. Yes, sir. I think it is.

ROSE. Good-bye, sir — thank you for all your goodness. I — I —

> [*Beginning to sob again.*]

MICHAEL. No, no, you are forgetting. I must see a little smile before you go. Look, Andrew. [ANDREW *turns round.*] For your father's sake. When you have gone you will like him to remember that the last time he saw your face it wore a smile. That's brave! Good-bye! Good-bye!

> [*Rose with great effort forces a smile and goes off with the* SISTER. *A moment or two later she is seen to pass the window sobbing in the* Sister's *arms.*]

ANDREW. Look! Oh, sir, was it bound to be in public, before everybody who knew her?

MICHAEL. Believe me, Andrew, if my own sister, if my own child had been in your daughter's place, I would have counseled her to act as your daughter has done.

ANDREW. She 'll never hold up her head again.

MICHAEL. Would you rather that she held up her head in deceit and defiance, or that she held it down in grief and penitence? Think what you and she have endured this last year, the deceit, the agony, the shame, the guilt!

ANDREW. I can't think of anything except her standing up in the church. I shall never forget it.

MICHAEL. Tell me you know I would willingly have spared you and her if it had been possible.

ANDREW. Then it was n't possible?

MICHAEL. I have done to you this morning as I would wish to be done by if I had followed a course of continued deception.

ANDREW. Ah, sir, it 's easy for you to talk. You are n't likely to be tempted, so you are n't likely to fall.

MICHAEL. I trust not! I pray God to keep me. But if ever I did, I should think him my true friend who made me confess and rid my soul of my guilt. And you think me your true friend, don't you, Andrew? [*Holding out hand.*] Won't you shake hands with me?

> [ANDREW *takes* MICHAEL'S *hand reluctantly, shakes it half-heartedly; is going off at door.*]

MICHAEL. [*Calls.*] Andrew, it will be very lonely in your own house now your daughter has gone. Come and live with me here. There is the large visitors' room. Take it for your own, and make this your home. You will be nearer to our work, and you will be nearer to me, my friend.

> [MARK *enters.*]

MARK [*at door*]. Am I interrupting?

MICHAEL. No. Come in. My little talk with Andrew is finished. [*To* ANDREW.] Say you know I have done what is right and best for you and her.

ANDREW. You 've done what you thought was best for us, sir. I 've never doubted that. I can't see anything straight or clear this morning. [*Exit.*]

MARK. You 've had a painful business here?

MICHAEL. Terrible! But I was bound to go through with it. The whole village was talking of it. I believed in her innocence and defended her to the last. So when the truth came out I dare n't hush it up. I should have been accused of hiding sin in my own household. But that poor child! My heart bled for her! Don't let us speak any more of it. Tell me about yourself and the work in London.

MARK. You must come and join us there. [MICHAEL shakes his head.]

MICHAEL. I could n't live there. Every time I go up for a day or two I come back more and more sickened and frightened and disheartened. Besides, you forget my Eastern studies. They are my real work. I could n't pursue them in the hurry and fever of London.

MARK. How are you getting on with the Arabic translations?

MICHAEL. Slowly but surely. Andrew is invaluable to me. In spite of his bringing up, he has the true instincts of the scholar.

MARK. Well, you know best. But we want you in London. You'd soon raise the funds for restoring the Minster.

MICHAEL. [Shakes his head.] I can't go round with the hat.

MARK. How 's the work getting on?

MICHAEL. Very slowly. I'm afraid I shall never live to finish it. By the by, I received fifty pounds anonymously only yesterday.

MARK. Have you any idea where it came from?

MICHAEL. No. The Bank advised me that it had been paid to my credit by a reader of my "Hidden Life," who desired to remain anonymous.

MARK. The book is having an enormous influence. Nothing else is talked about. And it has gained you one very rich proselyte — this Mrs. Lesden. She 's living here, is n't she?

MICHAEL. Yes. Curious woman —

MARK. Have you seen much of her?

MICHAEL. I called, of course. I 've met her once or twice at dinner. She has called here three or four times, and wasted several good hours for me.

MARK. How wasted?

MICHAEL. Kept me from my work. I wish the woman would take herself back to London.

MARK. Why?

MICHAEL. Her frivolity and insincerity repel me. No — not insincerity. I recall

that. For she said one or two things that seemed to show a vein of true, deep feeling. But on the whole I dislike her — I think I dislike her very much.

MARK. Why?

MICHAEL. She comes regularly to church —

MARK. Surely there 's no very great harm in that —

MICHAEL. No; but I don't know whether she 's mocking, or criticizing, or worshiping; or whether she 's merely bored, and thinking that my surplice is not enough starched, or starched too much.

MARK. She 's very rich, and would be an immense help to our movement. I should try and cultivate her.

MICHAEL. I can't cultivate people. What do you think of her?

MARK. A very clever society woman, all the more clever that she was not born in society.

MICHAEL. What do you know of her?

MARK. Merely what I wrote you in my letter. That she was the only daughter of an Australian millionaire. Her great-grandfather, I believe, was an Australian convict. She was sent to England to be educated, went back to Australia, married, lost her husband and father, came back to England a widow, took a house in Mayfair, entertained largely, gave largely to charities, read your book, "The Hidden Life," came down to see the country round here, made up her mind to live here, and wanted an introduction to you — which I gave her.

[Enter FANNY, announcing SIR LYOLF FEVERSHAM, an English country gentleman, about sixty-five, a little old-fashioned in manners and dress. Exit FANNY.]

SIR LYOLF. Michael — Mr. Docwray! Glad to see you. You 're talking business, or rather religion, which is your business. Am I in the way?

MICHAEL. No, we 're not talking business. We 're discussing a woman.

SIR LYOLF. Are n't women nine tenths of a parson's business? [MICHAEL looks a little shocked.] Excuse me, my dear boy. [To MARK.] I quite believe in all Michael is doing. I accept all his new doctrines, I 'm prepared to go all lengths with him, on condition that I indulge the latent old Adam in me with an occasional mild joke at his expense. But [with great feeling] he knows how proud I am of him, and how thankful I am to God for having given me a son who is shaping religious thought throughout England to-day, and who [with a change to sly humor] will never be a bishop — not even an archdeacon — I don't believe he'll be so much as a rural dean. What about this woman you were discussing? I'll bet — [coughs himself up] — I should say, I'll wager — [MICHAEL looks shocked, SIR LYOLF shrugs his shoulders at MARK, proceeds in a firm voice] — without staking anything, I will wager I know who the lady is — Mrs. Lesden? Am I right?

MICHAEL. Yes.

SIR LYOLF. Well, I have n't heard your opinion of her. But I'll give you mine — without prejudice — [with emphasis] very queer lot.

MARK. Michael had just said she was a curious creature.

MICHAEL. I don't understand her.

SIR LYOLF. When you don't understand a woman, depend upon it there's something not quite right about her.

MICHAEL. She seems to have immense possibilities of good and evil.

SIR LYOLF. Nonsense. There are all sorts of men, but, believe me, there are only two sorts of women — good and bad.

MICHAEL. You can't divide women into two classes like that.

SIR LYOLF. But I do — sheep and goats. Sheep on the right hand — goats on the left.

MICHAEL [shaking his head]. Women's characters have greater subtlety than you suppose.

SIR LYOLF. Subtlety is the big cant word of our age. Depend upon it, there's nothing in subtlety. It either means hair-splitting or it means downright evil. The devil was the first subtle character we meet with in history.

MICHAEL. And he has still something to do with the shaping of character in this world.

SIR LYOLF. I don't doubt it. And I think he has very likely something to do with the shaping of Mrs. Lesden's.

MICHAEL. Has n't he something to do with the shaping of all our characters? Don't all our souls swing continually between heaven and hell?

SIR LYOLF. Well, the woman whose soul swings continually between heaven and hell is not the woman whom I would choose to sit at my fireside or take the head of my table. Though I don't say I would n't ask her to dinner occasionally. That reminds me, how long are you staying, Mr. Docwray?

MARK. Only till Friday.

SIR LYOLF. You'll dine with me to-morrow evening?

MARK. Delighted.

SIR LYOLF. You too, Michael. I'll ask the Standerwicks, and [suddenly] suppose I ask this lady?

MICHAEL. Mrs. Lesden? I would rather you did n't.

SIR LYOLF. Why not? If her soul is swinging between heaven and hell, it would only be kind of you to give it a jog towards heaven.

MICHAEL. Very well — ask her. But I would rather you did n't speak lightly of —

SIR LYOLF. Of her soul?

MICHAEL. Of any one's soul?

SIR LYOLF. I won't — even of a woman's. But I wish they would n't swing about. Women's souls ought n't to swing anywhere, except towards heaven. Ah, Michael, you must let me have my fling. Remember when I was a boy, religion was a very simple, easy-going affair. Parson — clerk — old three-decker pulpit — village choir. What a village choir! I suppose it was all wrong — but they were very comfortable old days.

MICHAEL. Religion is not simple — or easy-going.

SIR LYOLF. No. Subtlety again. I want a plain "yes" or "no," a plain black or white, a plain right or wrong, and none of our teachers or preachers is prepared to give it to me. Oh dear! This world has grown too subtle for me! I'll step over to Island House and ask Mrs. Lesden to dinner to-morrow.

MARK. I'll come with you and pay my respects to her. You don't mind, Michael?

MICHAEL. Not at all. I want to set Andrew to work at once to keep him from dwelling on his trouble.

SIR LYOLF. I did n't come to the church this morning. I felt it would be too painful. [Glancing up at portrait.] What would she have said about it?

MICHAEL. I think she approves what I have done.

SIR LYOLF. [*Looks at portrait, sighs, turns away.*] Come, Mr. Docwray. I can't say I like this Mrs. Lesden of yours — I wonder why I 'm going to ask her to dinner.
[*Exit.*]

MARK [*who has been looking intently at portrait*]. What a wonderful portrait that is of your mother ! It seems as if she were alive !

MICHAEL. She is.
[*Exit* MARK *after* SIR LYOLF.]

MICHAEL. [*Goes up steps, takes portrait into his hand.*] Yes, I have acted faithfully to my people, have I not ? Whisper to me that I have done right to restore to this wandering father and child the blessing of a transparent life, a life without secrecy and without guile ! Whisper to me that in this morning's work I have done what is well pleasing to my God, and to you.

[AUDRIE LESDEN, *about thirty, in a very fashionable morning dress, enters at back of window in the opposite direction to that in which* SIR LYOLF *and* MARK *have gone off. At first she seems to be watching them off. When she gets to the open window, she turns and sees* MICHAEL *with the portrait in his hand.* MICHAEL *very reverently kisses the portrait and places it on table; as he does so he sees her.*]

MICHAEL. Mrs. Lesden !

AUDRIE. Was n't that Sir Lyolf who just went out ?

MICHAEL. Yes. I 'll call him back —

AUDRIE. Please don't.

MICHAEL. But he wishes to speak to you.

AUDRIE. I don't wish to speak to him.

MICHAEL. Why not ?

AUDRIE. I wish to speak to you.

MICHAEL. About what ?

AUDRIE. About my soul, about your soul, and about other people's souls. [*Leaning a little in at the window. He remains silent, and reserved. All through the early part of the scene his demeanor is cold, constrained, and a little impatient. A pause.*] I know you make it a rule always to see people about their souls.

MICHAEL [*very coldly*]. If they are really in need of spiritual advice.

AUDRIE. I think I 'm in need of spiritual advice. [*A pause. He stands cold, irresponsive.*] Did you see me in church ?

MICHAEL. Yes.

AUDRIE. The whole thing was delightfully novel. [*He frowns.*] Do you mean to repeat this morning's scene ?

MICHAEL. Scene ?

AUDRIE. It was a "scene," you know. I felt terribly distressed for the poor girl. And yet I envied her ?

MICHAEL. Envied her ?

AUDRIE [*leaning a little more in at the window*]. You must allow she was the heroine of the occasion, though you were certainly very impressive yourself, and did your part very well. Still, after all, it 's the man who is to be hanged who is the central figure in the proceedings. And the poor little creature looked exquisitely pathetic and graceful, and so sweetly innocent — quite good enough to go to heaven right away, I thought. A Sunday-school teacher told me once that it is nearly always the good girls who are betrayed. Is that so ?

MICHAEL [*coldly*]. You came to speak to me about yourself.

AUDRIE. So I did. Do you know when I saw that girl standing there and looking so interesting, I felt I could n't mind making a public confession myself — if you thought it would benefit the parish — and if you would allow me to wear a special dress for the occasion ?

[MICHAEL *turns round quickly as if about to speak angrily to her, stops, remains silent.*]

AUDRIE [*musingly*]. I suppose one could n't confess in anything except black or white. It could n't be done in red and yellow — or blue. Pale grey might do. [*Pause.*] What do you think ?

[MICHAEL *does not reply.*]

AUDRIE [*leaning a little more in at the window, in a much lower and subtler tone*]. Don't you find it an exquisite pleasure to feel your sense of power over your people, especially over us poor women?

MICHAEL. When you come to me you are neither man nor woman — you are only a soul in sin and distress.

AUDRIE. Oh, no ! I won't be an "it." I insist on being a woman, though I don't mind *having* a soul — and in sin and distress, too. And I would save it — only I always think it 's such a selfish piece of business, saving one's soul, — don't you ? — so unkind to all one's neighbors ? [*He stands half-bored, half-angry. A little pause.*] Do you know what I was thinking in church this morning?

MICHAEL. No.

AUDRIE. I was comparing the delights of three different professions, — the soldier's, the doctor's, and the priest's. What a glorious joy it must be to ride to meet a man who is riding to kill you — *and to kill him!* But I'd rather be a doctor, and play with life and death. To have a man in your power, to see him lying tossing on his bed, and to think, "This may cure him, or it may kill him. Shall I risk it? At any rate, if he dies, I shall have learnt so much. I will risk it! And — he dies — No, he lives! I've saved him." Would n't you like to be a doctor?

MICHAEL. No.

AUDRIE. That's because you know what far greater joy it is to be a priest. [*He turns very angrily.*] To play with people's souls —

MICHAEL. Play!

AUDRIE. You do play with our souls, don't you? They're in your hands. To think, "This man, or, say, this woman, has an immortal soul. She is vain, silly, deceitful, foolish, perhaps wicked, perhaps horribly wicked. She'll lose her soul and be eternally lost. But if I were to struggle with her for it, rebuke her, teach her, plead with her, entreat her, guide her — who knows — she's not wholly bad — I might save her? Is she worth saving? The worse she is, the greater will be my reward and honor for having saved her. Shall I do it? This woman's soul is in my keeping! I can choose for her eternal life or eternal death. What shall I do? Shall I save her, or let her be lost?"

MICHAEL. [*Comes eagerly to the window.*] Do you mean that?

AUDRIE. Mean what?

MICHAEL. That your soul is in my keeping.

AUDRIE. Not at all. I meant nothing except that thoughts like these must constantly stray through a priest's mind. Don't they? [*Long pause.*] Why don't you speak?

MICHAEL [*cold, stern*]. I have nothing to say.   [*Pause.*]

AUDRIE [*taking out purse, takes out two notes*]. Oh! I was forgetting — I've brought you a little contribution for the restoration of your Minster.

[*Putting notes on window-sill. MI-CHAEL stands cold, angry.*]

AUDRIE. Won't you take it?

MICHAEL. Thank you. No.

AUDRIE. I think you're a little rude to me. I came as a heart-stricken penitent; you would n't accept me in that character. Then I came as a pious donor. You would n't accept me in that. You've kept me outside here — you have n't even asked me in.

MICHAEL [*very sternly*]. Come in! [*She looks up, uncertain as to his intentions. Same cold, stern voice.*] Please to come in. That way — the outer door is open.

[*She goes off, he goes to door left, opens it, she comes in.*]

MICHAEL. [*The moment she has entered closes door decisively, then turns round on her very sternly.*] What brings you to this village, to my church, to my house? Why are you here? Come to me as a penitent, and I will try to give you peace! Come to me as a woman of the world, and I will tell you "The friendship of the world is enmity with God. It always has been so, it always will be. The Church has no need of you, of your pretended devotions, of your gifts, of your presence at her services. Go your way back to the world, and leave her alone." But you come neither as a penitent, nor as a woman of the world. You come like — like some bad angel, to mock, and hint, and question, and suggest. How dare you play with sacred things? How dare you!

AUDRIE [*in a very low, quiet, amused voice*]. I do not think it seemly or becoming in a clergyman to give way to temper. If any one had asked me I should have said it was impossible in you.

[*He stands stern, cold, repellent.*]

[*Enter ANDREW.*]

MICHAEL. What is it, Andrew?

ANDREW. I thought you were disengaged. [*Going.*]

MICHAEL. So I am. I'll come to you at once.   [*Exit ANDREW.*]

MICHAEL. [*To AUDRIE.*] You are right. It is unseemly to give way to temper, and perhaps you won't think me rude if I guard myself against it in future by asking you not to call upon me until I can be of real service to you. Good-morning.

AUDRIE. Mr. Feversham, Mr. Feversham. [MICHAEL *turns.*] I've been very rude and troublesome. I beg your pardon. Please forgive me.

MICHAEL. Certainly. Pray say no more.

AUDRIE. I saw you kissing that portrait as I stood at the window. It is your mother?

MICHAEL. Yes.

AUDRIE. What a good woman she must have been! Don't think because I am bad —

MICHAEL. Are you bad?

AUDRIE. Did n't you say I was? I don't know whether I 'm bad or good, but I know that no woman longs to be good more than I do — sometimes.

MICHAEL. Do you indeed?

AUDRIE [impulsively]. Let me kiss that portrait!   [Leaning forward to do it.]

MICHAEL [peremptorily]. No.
                [Intercepts and stops her.]

AUDRIE. Why not?

MICHAEL. I 'd rather you did n't.

AUDRIE. You don't think I 'm good enough.

MICHAEL. I cannot allow you.

AUDRIE. Who painted it?

MICHAEL. A young Italian. My mother's brother is a Catholic priest, and at that time he was living at Rome. My mother went there for her health when I was three years old. This young Italian saw her and asked permission to paint her. She came home and died of consumption. Then my uncle sent this portrait to my father with the news that the young painter had also died of consumption.

AUDRIE. How strange! And you 've had it ever since?

MICHAEL. I was only a child when it came. I fell into the habit of saying my prayers before it. So when I first left home my father gave it to me; it has been with me ever since, at Eton, and Oxford, and in my different curacies.

AUDRIE. Won't you let me kiss it before I go?   [Leaning towards it.]

MICHAEL [preventing her]. I 'd rather you did not.

AUDRIE. Why not?

MICHAEL. I have a strange belief about that picture. I 'll hang it up.

AUDRIE [a little intercepting him]. No. Let me look at it. Let me hold it in my hands. I won't kiss it without your permission. [She takes it and looks at it intently.] Tell me — what is your strange belief about it?

MICHAEL. My mother was a deeply religious woman, and before my birth she consecrated me to this service as Hannah consecrated Samuel. When she was dying she said to me, "I 'm not leaving you. I shall watch over you every moment of your life. There 's not a word, or a deed, or a thought of yours but I shall know it. You won't see me, but I shall be very near you. Sometimes my hands will be upon your head, but you won't know it; sometimes my arms will be round you, but you won't feel them; sometimes my lips will be on your face, but you won't know that I have kissed you. Remember you are watched by the dead."

AUDRIE. And you believe that you are watched by the dead?

MICHAEL. Yes.

AUDRIE. And that she is with us now — in this room?

MICHAEL. Yes.

AUDRIE. She is your good angel.

MICHAEL. She is my good angel.

AUDRIE. I can understand why you did not wish me to kiss her.
                [MICHAEL makes a movement to take the picture.]

AUDRIE [Retains it.] No. Yes, I feel she must be in this room.

MICHAEL. Why?

AUDRIE. I was full of silly wicked thoughts when I came — she has taken them away.

MICHAEL. Ah, if I dared hope that you would really change!

AUDRIE. Perhaps I will. [Very imploringly.] Do let me kiss this sweet face.
                [Pause.]

MICHAEL. No — at least not now, not yet. Please give it back to me. [He takes it.] I 'll hang it up. [He takes it to steps.] Will you hold it for a moment?
                [She comes to steps, holds it while he mounts, gives it to him.]

AUDRIE. What a wonderful thought that is, that we are watched by the dead. It never occurred to me before. I wonder what a spirit is like? [He hangs up the picture.] Now she is quite out of my reach. [He comes down steps.] Won't you take that money for rebuilding the Minster! It 's there on the window-sill. [He goes and takes it.] Thank you.

MICHAEL. Thank you.

AUDRIE. Then I'm not to call again? Not even about my soul?

MICHAEL. I'm going over to the Island for some time, and shall only be back on Sundays.

AUDRIE. Saint Decuman's Island. You've built yourself a house over there, have n't you?

MICHAEL. The shrine was neglected and decayed. I restored it and built myself a couple of rooms round it. I've a few books, and just food and drink. I go over there sometimes for work and meditation.

AUDRIE. And yours is the only house on the island?

MICHAEL. Yes.

AUDRIE. Is n't it awfully lonely there?

MICHAEL [glancing at picture]. I'm never alone.

AUDRIE. No, you have your millions and millions of good and bad angels, besides hundreds of cheap excursionists.

MICHAEL. Yes, in the summer, but they only stay a few hours.

AUDRIE. I can see the smoke from your chimney quite plainly in the evening from my drawing-room windows. How far is it across?

MICHAEL. About four miles.

AUDRIE. I shall get Hannaford to row me over some day. Don't look alarmed. I won't come when you are there. I should frighten all your good angels away. [MICHAEL shows a little impatience.] You want to get rid of me. [Going, suddenly turns.] If I come to you as a penitent, you won't send me away?

MICHAEL. Not if I can be of service to you.

AUDRIE. I seem to have changed my nature since I came into this room.

MICHAEL. How?

AUDRIE. I don't know. I wonder how many natures I have and how often I can change them.

MICHAEL. I wish you would n't speak like that.

AUDRIE. I won't. [Very seriously.] You said just now that I was playing with sacred things. I am, or I was until you spoke about her. [With warning.] Don't let me play with your soul.

MICHAEL. I don't understand you.

AUDRIE. You may do me good, but I am far more likely to do you harm.

MICHAEL. How?

AUDRIE. I'm not nearly so good a woman as you are a man.

MICHAEL. But perhaps I may influence you for good.

AUDRIE. Do you think that you can have any influence on my soul without my having an equal influence on yours?

MICHAEL. Action and reaction are equal and opposite. You think that law prevails in the spiritual world as well as in the material world?

AUDRIE. I'm sure it does. So let me go.

MICHAEL [suddenly, with great feeling]. Oh, if I could save you!

AUDRIE. You can if you will. I would try so hard if you would only help me. But you don't believe that I can.

MICHAEL. What makes you say that?

AUDRIE. You called me a bad angel — and you don't think me good enough to kiss her. [Sidling up to the steps; he makes a deprecating movement to prevent her, but she takes no notice.] If you knew it would give me a splendid impulse to goodness, would you refuse me? [She watches him very closely; he watches her, half deprecating, half consenting; she goes up a step or two; he again makes a deprecating gesture, but does not stop her.] Can't you see what an awful effect it would have on me if you thought me worthy to be in the company of your good angel? It would be almost a sacrament! [Going up steps. He makes a stronger gesture of deprecation.] Ah, you think I'm not worthy —

MICHAEL. No, no —

AUDRIE [on top of steps, very seductively]. Do save me. I'm worth saving. [Whispers.] I may kiss her? I may? I may? [He does not reply. She very reverently kisses the picture on the wall, turns round, comes down slowly to him.] Your bad angel has kissed your good angel. [A mock curtsy to him.] [Exit softly. MICHAEL stands troubled.]

[Four months pass between Acts I and II.]

ACT II

SCENE — *The Shrine on Saint Decuman's Island in the Bristol Channel. A living-room built round the shrine of the Saint, a fine piece of decayed Decorated Gothic now in the back wall of the room. A large fireplace down right. A door above fireplace. A door left; two windows, one on each side of the shrine, show the sea with the horizon line and the sky above. A bookcase; a table; old oaken paneling, about seven feet high, all round the room, and above them whitewashed walls. Red brick floor. Everything very rude and simple, and yet tasteful, as if it had been done by the village mason and carpenter under* MICHAEL'S *direction. Time, a September evening. Discover* ANDREW GIBBARD *packing a portmanteau, and* EDWARD LASHMAR (FATHER HILARY), *a Catholic priest, about sixty, very dignified and refined. Enter* WITHYCOMBE, *an old boatman.*

WITHYCOMBE. Now, gentlemen, if yu're ready to start! If yu daunt come sune, us shall lose the tide down.

FATHER HILARY. I'm quite ready, Withycombe, as soon as I have said "Goodbye" to Mr. Feversham.

WITHYCOMBE. Mr. Feversham ain't coming along with us, then?

ANDREW. No, he stays on the island all the week, and you are to fetch him on Saturday morning.

WITHYCOMBE. Saturday morning. To-day's Wednesday. Right you are. Well and good. Saturday morning. Yu're coming on to Saint Margaret's along with us, Mr. Gibbard?

ANDREW. Yes — we can find some accommodation there for the night, can't we?

WITHYCOMBE. Well, I warn ye 'tis rough.

FATHER HILARY. Rougher than my Master had on his first coming here?

WITHYCOMBE. Well, I waun't say that, but so fur as I can judge, 'tis about as rough.

FATHER HILARY. Then it will do for me. Where is Mr. Feversham?

WITHYCOMBE. A few minutes agone he wor watching the excursion steamer back to Lowburnham.

FATHER HILARY. Will you find him and tell him that I am waiting to start?

WITHYCOMBE. Right you are, sir. Well and good.   *[Exit.]*

FATHER HILARY. Andrew — have you noticed any change in Mr. Feversham lately?

ANDREW. Change, Father?

FATHER HILARY. He seems so restless and disturbed, so unlike himself.

ANDREW. Does he?

FATHER HILARY. It's six years since I was in England. But he was always so calm and concentrated. Has he any trouble, do you know?

ANDREW. He hasn't spoken of any.

FATHER HILARY. No. But you're with him constantly. Surely you must have seen the difference in him.

ANDREW. Yes. He has changed.

FATHER HILARY. How long has he been like this?

ANDREW. The last four months.

FATHER HILARY. Do you know of any reason for it?

ANDREW. He's coming!

[Enter MICHAEL.]

MICHAEL. You're ready to start, Uncle Ned?

FATHER HILARY. Yes. You won't change your mind and come with us?

MICHAEL. No, I must stay here. [*Glancing at books, restlessly.*] I want to be alone. I couldn't be of any service to you over at Saint Margaret's?

FATHER HILARY. There is the legend that connects her with Saint Decuman — I suppose no more is to be learned of that than we already know?

MICHAEL. No. The fisher people only know what they have learned from the guide books.

ANDREW [*standing with portmanteau*]. Have you anything more to take to the boat, Father?

FATHER HILARY. No, that's all, Andrew.

ANDREW. Then I'll take it down and wait for you there.

[Exit ANDREW *with portmanteau.]*

FATHER HILARY. Then this is good-bye, Michael?

MICHAEL. Unless you'll stay over the Sunday at Cleveddon?

FATHER HILARY. No, I've done my work in England, and I must be back among my people. I wanted to see the shrines on these two sister islands again before I died

I shall leave Saint Margaret's to-morrow morning, get back to Cleveheddon, take the afternoon train up to London, and leave for Italy on Friday morning. You'll come and see me at Majano?

MICHAEL. When I can.

FATHER HILARY. This winter?

MICHAEL. No, not this winter. I shall be at work at once on the restorations now I've got all the money.

FATHER HILARY. Strange that it should all come so soon within two or three months.

MICHAEL. Yes, and from such different quarters of England — a thousand one day from Manchester — five hundred the next from some unheard-of village — and then the last great final gift last week.

FATHER HILARY. It looks as if it all came from one giver?

MICHAEL. Yes, I had thought of that.

FATHER HILARY. You don't know of any one?

MICHAEL. I've one or two suspicions. However, the great fact is that I have it all, and can set my architects to work.

FATHER HILARY. Michael — I was asking Andrew just now, there is something troubling you?

MICHAEL. No — no. What makes you think that?

FATHER HILARY. You are not yourself. [Pause.] Is it anything where I can be of help?

MICHAEL. There is nothing. [Pause.] There has been something. But it is past. [FATHER HILARY looks grave.] You need have no fear for me. [Holding out hand.]

FATHER HILARY. [Takes his hand, holds it for a long while, looks gravely at him.] If you should ever need a deeper peace than you can find within or around you, come to me in Italy.

MICHAEL. But I am at peace now. [Restlessly, pushing his hand through hair, then a little querulously.] I am at peace now. [FATHER HILARY shakes his head.] You think you can give me that deeper peace?

FATHER HILARY. I know I can.

MICHAEL. I may come to you some day. [WITHYCOMBE puts his head in at door.]

WITHYCOMBE. Now, sir, if yu plaise, we 'me losing the tide — us shan't get to Margaret's avore supper-time.

FATHER HILARY. I'm coming, Withycombe.

MICHAEL. Withycombe, you'll come and fetch me on Saturday morning.

WITHYCOMBE. Saturday morning, twelve o'clock sharp, I'm here. Right you are, Mr. Feversham. Well and good.   [Exit.]

FATHER HILARY. Good-bye.

MICHAEL. Good-bye, Uncle Ned.

[Very hearty hand-shake. Exit FATHER HILARY. MICHAEL goes to door, stands looking a few seconds, comes in, turns to his books.]

[Reënter FATHER HILARY.]

MICHAEL. What is it?

FATHER HILARY. I don't like leaving you. Come with me to-night to Margaret's. Shall I?

MICHAEL. Shall I? Perhaps it would be best — wait a minute.

WITHYCOMBE. [Voice heard off.] Now, Mr. Lashmar, if you plaise, sir — we 'me losing the tide.

MICHAEL. Don't wait, I'm safe here. Good-bye.

FATHER HILARY [slowly and regretfully]. Good-bye.

[Exit slowly. MICHAEL watches FATHER HILARY off; stays at door for some time, waves his hand, then closes door.]

MICHAEL. Now I shall be at peace! [Takes out letter from his pocket.] Her letter! I will not read it! [Puts it back in pocket, kneels and lights the fire.] Why did you come into my life? I did not seek you! You came unbidden, and before I was aware of it you had unlocked the holiest places of my heart. Your skirts have swept through all the gateways of my being. There is a fragrance of you in every cranny of me. You possess me! [Rises.] No! No! No! I will not yield to you! [Takes up book, seats himself at fire, reads a moment or two.] You are there in the fire! Your image plays in the shadows — Oh, my light and my fire, will you burn me up with love for you? [Rises, sighs.] I'm mad! [Pause, very resolutely.] I will be master of myself — I will be servant to none save my work and my God! [Seats himself resolutely, reads a moment or two, then drops book on knees.] The wind that blows round here may perhaps play round her brow, the very breath that met my lips as I stood at the door may meet hers on the shore yonder. [Rises, flings book on table, goes to window ; takes out letter again, holds it undecidedly.] Why should n't

I read it? Every stroke of it is graven on my heart. — [*Opens it.*] "Dear keeper of souls in this parish, I have thought so much of our talk last night. I'm inclined to think that I have a soul after all, but it is a most uncomfortable possession. I believe if some-one gave me an enormous impulse I might make a saint or a martyr, or anything that's divine. And I believe there is one man living who could give me that impulse." "One man living who could give me that impulse — " "But I hope he won't. Frankly, you may save me at too great cost to your-self. So trouble yourself no further about me. But if after this, you still think my wandering, dangling soul worth a moment of your ghostly care, come and lunch with me to-morrow, and I will give you the sweet plain butter-cakes that you love, on the old blue china. And that our salvation may not be too easy, I will tempt you with one sip of the ancient Johannisburg." And I went — yes, I went. "But for your own sake — I speak with all a woman's care for your earthly and heavenly welfare — I would rather you did not come. Let it be so. Let this be farewell. Perhaps our souls may salute each other in aimless vacancy hereafter, and I will smile as sweet a smile as I can without lips or cheeks to smile with, when I remember as I pass you in the shades that I saved you from your bad angel, Audrie Lesden. P.S. Be wise and let me go." I cannot! I cannot! Yet if I do not — what remains for me? Tor-ture, hopeless love, neglected duty, work cast aside and spoilt, all my life disordered and wrecked. Oh, if I could be wise — I will! I will tear out this last one dear sweet thought of her. [*Goes to fire, tears up the letter in little pieces, watches them burn.*] It's done! I've conquered! Now I shall be at peace.

[*Seats himself resolutely at table, reads. A little tap at the door; he shows surprise; the tap is repeated; he rises, goes to door, opens it. At that moment* AUDRIE's *face appears at the right-hand window for a moment. He looks out, stays there a moment or two, closes door, seats himself again at table, reads. The tap is repeated; he rises,* AUDRIE *appears at door, he shows a moment of intense delight which he quickly subdues.*]

AUDRIE. May I come in? [*Pause.*] You are busy — I'll go —

MICHAEL. No — [*She stops on threshold.*] Come in.

[*She enters. He stands motionless at table. Sunset without. It gradually grows darker.*]

MICHAEL. What brings you here?

AUDRIE. You did not expect me. You are n't accustomed to entertain angels un-awares — even bad ones.

MICHAEL [*his voice thick and a little hoarse*]. Your boat, your companions?

AUDRIE. I have no boat, and no compan-ions.

MICHAEL [*horrified, delighted*]. You're alone?

AUDRIE. Quite alone.

MICHAEL. How did you come here?

AUDRIE. By the simplest and most pro-saic means in the world. This morning I took the train to Lowburnham to do some shopping. As I was coming back to the sta-tion, a boy put this little handbill into my hand. [*Showing a little yellow handbill.*] Afternoon excursion to Saint Decuman's and Saint Margaret's Isles. I had an im-pulse — I obeyed it. I telegraphed to Cleve-heddon for a boat to meet me here at six — [*takes out watch*] — it only wants ten minutes — and took the excursion steamer. They all landed here for half an hour. I hid myself till after the steamer had gone. Then I came up here to your cottage. I heard some voices, so I hid again — who was here?

MICHAEL. Only my secretary and my uncle Ned.

AUDRIE. The Catholic priest. I saw a boat leaving — it was they?

MICHAEL. Yes.

AUDRIE. They're not coming back?

MICHAEL. No.

AUDRIE. You're annoyed with me for coming?

MICHAEL. No, but was n't it a little — imprudent?

AUDRIE. Oh, I must do mad things some-times, just to preserve my general balance of sanity. Besides, my boat will be here in ten minutes. [*Pause.*]

AUDRIE. How strange we should be here alone!

MICHAEL. The only two beings on this island — we two!

AUDRIE. And our two souls.

MICHAEL. I wish you would n't jest with sacred things.

AUDRIE. I won't. [*Suddenly, impulsively.*] I want to be good! Help me to be good! You think I 'm foolish and light and frivolous! Well, perhaps I am, but when I 'm with you I 'm capable of anything, anything — except being an ordinary, average, good woman.

MICHAEL. But is n't that all that is required of a woman?

AUDRIE. Perhaps. It 's rather a damnable heritage, is n't it? And I 'm not a barndoor fowl.

MICHAEL. What are you?

AUDRIE. Just what you like to make of me. Don't think I 'm flattering you. Don't think I 'm bold and unwomanly. I 'm only speaking the truth. You have changed me. I 'm ready to do anything, believe anything, suffer anything that you bid me! To-night I 'm on a pinnacle! I shall either be snatched up to the skies, or tumble into the abyss. Which will it be, I wonder?

MICHAEL [*after a struggle, in a calm voice*]. Neither, I trust. I hope you will take your boat back in ten minutes, have a good passage across, a comfortable dinner from your pretty blue china, and a sound night's rest. And to-morrow you will wake and forget this rather imprudent freak.

AUDRIE. Oh, you won't tread the clouds with me! Very well! Down to the earth we come. I can be as earthy as the very clay itself. But I thought you wanted me to be spiritual.

MICHAEL. I want you to be sincere, to be yourself.

AUDRIE. Very well. Tell me how. You are my ghostly father.

MICHAEL. No, you 've never allowed me to be a priest to you.

AUDRIE. I 've never allowed you?

MICHAEL. And I 've never dared.

AUDRIE. Why not?

MICHAEL. Because you 've never allowed me to forget that I am a man.

AUDRIE. Very well. Don't be a priest to me — at least not now. Tell me some one thing that you would wish me to do, and I 'll do it!

MICHAEL. In that letter you wrote me —

AUDRIE. Did you keep it?

MICHAEL. No, I destroyed it.

AUDRIE. Destroyed it!

MICHAEL. In that letter you said it would be better for us if we did not meet again —

AUDRIE. No. I said it would be better for *you* if we did not meet again.

MICHAEL. Better for me?

AUDRIE. Yes, and worse for me. I came here to-night to warn you —

MICHAEL. Against what?

AUDRIE. Myself. I 've done something that may endanger your peace for ever.

MICHAEL. What do you mean?

AUDRIE. Sometimes I laugh at it, sometimes I 'm frightened. I dare n't tell you what I 've done. I 'll go.

[*Goes to door, opens it.*]

MICHAEL. No. [*Stops her.*] Mrs. Lesden, what have you done against me? You don't mean your gifts to the Minster?

AUDRIE. My gifts — what gifts?

MICHAEL. During the last four months I 've constantly received large sums for the restoration of the Minster, and last week a very large sum was sent me, enough to carry out all the work just as I wished.

AUDRIE. Well?

MICHAEL. It was you who sent it all.

AUDRIE. I must see if my boatman has come.

MICHAEL [*stopping her*]. No. Why did you send the money — so many different sums from so many different places?

AUDRIE. Because that gave me dozens of pleasures instead of one, in sending it. And I thought it would give you dozens of pleasures instead of one, in receiving it.

MICHAEL. I knew it was you! How glad I am to owe it all to you! Words could n't tell you how grateful I am.

AUDRIE. And yet you would n't walk the clouds with me for a few minutes?

MICHAEL. You know that I would do anything in my power for your best, your heavenly welfare.

AUDRIE. I don't think I care much for my heavenly welfare just at this moment. You tumbled me off my pinnacle, and here I am stuck in the mud. [*Looking off at the open door.*] Look! That boat is half-way to Saint Margaret's.

MICHAEL. Yes, they sleep there to-night.

AUDRIE. What a queer-looking man your secretary is. Is he quite trustworthy?

MICHAEL. Quite. Why?

AUDRIE. I caught him looking at you in a very strange way a week or two back.

MICHAEL. He's devoted to me.

AUDRIE. I'm glad of that. How far is it to Saint Margaret's?

MICHAEL. Three miles.

AUDRIE. Do you believe the legend about Saint Decuman and Saint Margaret?

MICHAEL. That they loved each other?

AUDRIE. Yes, on separate islands, and never met.

MICHAEL. They denied themselves love here that they might gain heavenly happiness hereafter.

AUDRIE. Now that their hearts have been dust all these hundreds of years, what good is it to them that they denied themselves love?

MICHAEL. You think —

AUDRIE. I think a little love on this earth is worth a good many paradises hereafter. It's a cold world, hereafter. It chills me to the bone when I think of it! [*Shivers a little and comes away from the door.*] I'm getting a little cold.

MICHAEL [*placing chair*]. Sit by the fire. [*She sits near fire, which is blazing up; he goes and closes door.*]

AUDRIE [*putting on some logs*]. Do I know you well enough to make your fire for you?

MICHAEL. I hope so. [*She sits; he stands above her for some seconds, watching her keenly; a long pause.*]

AUDRIE. You were looking at me. What were you thinking of?

MICHAEL. I was wondering what memories are stored in that white forehead.

AUDRIE. Memories? [*Long sigh.*] A few bright ones, and many sad ones.

MICHAEL. Your past life was not happy?

AUDRIE [*with a little shudder of recollection*]. No. And yours? Tell me —

MICHAEL. What?

AUDRIE. Something about your past life, something you've never told to a living creature.

MICHAEL. When I was twenty —

AUDRIE. Stay — what were you like when you were twenty? [*Shuts her eyes, puts her hand over them.*] Now I can see you when you were twenty.

MICHAEL. Is there any one with me?

AUDRIE. No, I can't see her. What was she like? Fair or dark?

MICHAEL. Fair, with changing gray eyes

that could be serious or merry as she pleased, and fine clear features, and the sweetest provoking mouth —

AUDRIE. I hate her. Who was she?

MICHAEL. Miss Standerwick's niece. She stayed there all the summer that year.

AUDRIE. Was that a happy summer?

MICHAEL. The happiest I have ever known — till this.

AUDRIE. Ah!

MICHAEL. I used to go to evening church and follow them home, and wait outside till I could see the candle in her window. When it went out I used to walk home.

AUDRIE. Across those fields where we walked the other night?

MICHAEL. Yes.

AUDRIE. I'll never walk that way again. Go on.

MICHAEL. One night as I was waiting, she came out suddenly. I could n't speak for trembling. At last I found my tongue, and we talked about silly commonplace things. When she was going in I dared to breathe, "Give me one kiss." She did n't answer. I just touched her cheek with my lips, and I whispered, "Good-night, Nelly." She said, "Good-night, Mike."

AUDRIE. She called you Mike?

MICHAEL. I was called Mike when I was a boy.

AUDRIE. And your next meeting?

MICHAEL. She was called away early the next morning to her father's deathbed. Her mother went abroad. I never saw her again. Tell me something about your past life.

AUDRIE. Can you see me when I was eight? I was a pretty little brown maid, and I set all aflame the heart of a cherub aged ten, with strong fat legs and curly red hair. His sister was my dearest friend. He spent all his pocket-money in buying sugar-plums for me, and gave them to her to give to me. She ate them herself, and slandered me to him, for she said I was false. He kicked her on the nose, and was sent far — far away to school. This was the first tragedy of my life. Now tell me some more of your life. You have had other romances, darker, deeper ones?

MICHAEL. Nothing that I dare show. I have told you of the one love of my youth. And you — Have you had darker, deeper romances?

AUDRIE. I was unhappy without romance. I would show you all my heart, all my thoughts, all my life, if I could do it as one shows a picture, and let it speak for itself. I wonder if you'd condemn me —

MICHAEL. Condemn you!

AUDRIE. I don't think you would. You have never guessed —

MICHAEL. Guessed —

AUDRIE. What a world there is within one's self that one never dares speak of! I wish to hide nothing from you. I would have you know me through and through for just the woman that I am, just that and no other, because, don't you see — I don't want to cheat you of a farthing's-worth of esteem on false pretenses — I want you to like me, Audrie Lesden, and not some myth of your imagination. But if you were armed with all the tortures of hell for plucking the truth about myself from my lips, I should still hide myself from you. So, guess, guess, guess, grand inquisitor — what is here [tapping her forehead] and here [putting her hand on her heart]. You'll never guess one thousandth part of the truth!

MICHAEL. But tell me something in your past life that you have never told to another creature.

AUDRIE. I have two great secrets — one is about yourself, one is about another man.

MICHAEL. Myself? Another man?

AUDRIE. My husband.

MICHAEL. You said you had been unhappy.

AUDRIE. I married as thousands of girls do, carelessly, thoughtlessly. I was married for my money. No one had ever told me that love was sacred.

MICHAEL. Nobody ever does tell us that, till we hear it from our own hearts.

AUDRIE. I suppose it was my own fault. I was very well punished.

MICHAEL. How long were you married?

AUDRIE. Two years.

MICHAEL. And then your husband died?

AUDRIE. He went away from me. I never saw him again — alive. [Passionately.] And there's an end of him!

MICHAEL. I won't ask you what that secret is. I would wish you to keep it sacred. But your secret about myself? Surely I may ask that?

AUDRIE. I have sold you to the devil.

MICHAEL. What?

AUDRIE. I have sold myself, too.

MICHAEL. Still jesting?

AUDRIE. No, I did it in real, deep earnest.

MICHAEL. I don't understand you.

AUDRIE. Six months ago I was tired, gnawed to the very heart with ennui, and one hot restless night I happened to take up your book, "The Hidden Life." It came to me — oh, like a breath of the purest, freshest air in a fevered room. I thought I should like to know you. I got up early, took the first morning train down here, looked about the place, saw the Island House was to let, and rented it for three years.

MICHAEL. Well?

AUDRIE. I got Mr. Docwray to give me an introduction to you. You annoyed me, you were so cold and priestlike. Each time I saw you, you piqued and angered me more and more. I longed to get some power over you. At last one day after you had been so frozen and distant a little black imp jumped into my brain and whispered to me. I said to the devil, "Give this sculptured saint to me, and I'll give both our souls to you."

MICHAEL. But you did n't mean it?

AUDRIE. Yes. I said it with all my heart, and I bit my arm — look — [Showing her arm.] I made the teeth meet. There's the mark. If there is a devil, he heard me.

MICHAEL. And you think he has given me to you?

AUDRIE. The next time I saw you, you let me kiss your mother's portrait.

MICHAEL. Ah!

AUDRIE. But you don't really believe there is a devil? Why don't you speak? Why don't you laugh at me and tell me it's all nonsense? I have n't really given the devil power over your soul?

MICHAEL. No devil has any power over any soul of man until the man himself first gives him entrance and consent.

AUDRIE. And you have n't! Say you don't care for me.

MICHAEL. How can I say that?

AUDRIE. You must! I'm not strong enough to leave you of my own free will. I shall hang about you, worry you, tease you, tempt you, and at last, destroy you. Don't let me do it! Beat me away from you, insult me, do something to make me hate you! Make me leave you!

MICHAEL. When I love you with all my being?

AUDRIE. [*Shows great delight.*] And you dare go on? It's an awful delight to think that a man would dare to risk hell for one! There are n't many men who would dare lose this world for the woman they love — how many men are there that would dare to lose the other?

MICHAEL. We must lose this world, for I am vowed away from all earthly things. But why should we lose the other? Why should we not make our love the lever to raise our souls? You do love me?

AUDRIE. Love is hardly the word. It is more like — if a man could create a dog, and be her master, friend, father, and God, I think she would feel towards him something of what I feel towards you. You have first made me know what love is, what life is. You have changed me thoroughly — no, you have changed half of me thoroughly — one half is still worthless, silly, capricious, hollow, worldly, and bad — that's my old self. She is gradually withering up under your influence, that old Audrie Lesden. The other half is looking out of my eyes at you now! Look! do you see the new Audrie Lesden that is your daughter and your creature? Are n't you proud of her?

MICHAEL. I shall be proud of her when she is full grown and dares to leave me of her own free will, because she loves me, and because I am vowed to Heaven!

AUDRIE. Do I tempt you? I'll go. You love me. That's enough, or it should be enough. I'll get back to London to-morrow, and strangle the new Audrie. Then the old Audrie will come back again, and live the old weary, dry, empty life — and grow old and wrinkled and heartless and perhaps — rouged —

MICHAEL. Why do you tear me so? What do you want of me here or hereafter? Take it! It's yours —

AUDRIE. You dare go on — now you know?

MICHAEL. Yes.

AUDRIE. Ah! I thought it was only

women who dared hell for love. I won't take your sacrifice — I will leave you.

MICHAEL. You will? Yes, it must be so! My work, my vows — I cannot, may not taste of earthly love. Oh, it's cruel to dash the cup from my lips! [*Pause; then very calmly.*] You are right! I feel that we are choosing heaven or hell for both our souls this night! Help me to choose heaven for you, and I'll help you to choose heaven for me.

AUDRIE. Good-bye, my love, for ever. Be brave — and very cold to me, now. Be like marble — and death.

MICHAEL. [*Takes her hand; a very long pause; then speaks very calmly.*] It is victory, is n't it? We have conquered? I'll go down to the bay and see if your boat has come. [*By this time it is dark outside.*]

AUDRIE. Half past six. I shall have a cold, dark voyage.

MICHAEL. And it is just a little rough. But Hannaford is a careful boatman.

AUDRIE. It's not Hannaford who is coming for me. I telegraphed for Withycombe.

MICHAEL. [*Pause — very pale and cold.*] Withycombe? But you always employ Hannaford.

AUDRIE. Yes; and I did write out one telegram to him, and then I thought I should like to go back in the boat that always takes you. So I tore up the telegram to Hannaford, and telegraphed to Withycombe.

MICHAEL. Withycombe?

AUDRIE. Yes, what's the matter?

MICHAEL. He lives alone. When he goes out, he locks up his cottage. Your telegram will wait at the post office.

AUDRIE. Why?

MICHAEL. Withycombe has gone over to Saint Margaret's with Gibbard and my uncle. They stay there the night.

AUDRIE. Your own boat?

MICHAEL. I had it towed back last week, so that I could n't be tempted to come to you.

AUDRIE. Then —

MICHAEL. [*Looks at her.*] No boat will come to-night. [*Looks at her more intently.*] No boat will come to-night!

[*They stand looking at each other.*]

[*Two nights and a day — from Wednesday evening to Friday morning — pass between Acts II and III.*]

ACT III

SCENE — *The Vicarage parlor, as in first act. Morning. Enter* MICHAEL, *haggard, troubled, with self-absorbed expression, the expression of a man trying to realize that he has committed a great and irrevocable sin; he stands for some moments helpless, dreamy, as if unconscious of his whereabouts; then looks round; his eyes fall upon his mother's picture, he shudders a little, shows intense pain. At length he goes up the steps, takes the picture down, places it on the floor with its face against the wall, carefully avoiding all the while to look at it. He then moves to table in the same dreamy, helpless, self-absorbed state, sits, looks in front of him. Enter* ANDREW, *comes up behind him.*

MICHAEL. Oh, Andrew — Well?

ANDREW [*coming up to him*]. I want to consult you on that passage in the Arabic — if you can spare the time.

MICHAEL. Bring the manuscripts here. [MICHAEL *unconsciously looks at his hands.*] What are you looking at?

ANDREW. Nothing. Your hands are blistered?

MICHAEL. I did a little rowing — the other day. Bring the manuscripts. [AN-DREW *goes to door.*] Andrew — [ANDREW *stops*] — I was very restless — did you hear me stirring in the night?

ANDREW. Stirring?

MICHAEL. Yes, I could n't sleep. I got up about one and went out — walked about for some hours — it was nearly light when I came in again. Did you hear me?

ANDREW. [*Pauses, then answers.*] No.

[*Is about to go off at right door when* FANNY *enters left. He stops.*]

FANNY. Mrs. Lesden wishes to see you for a minute or two about one of her cottagers.

[ANDREW *watches* MICHAEL *keenly, but unobtrusively.*]

MICHAEL [*after a little start of surprise, in a tone of affected carelessness*]. Show her in.

[*Exit* ANDREW, *right. Exit* FANNY, *left.* MICHAEL *rises, shows great perturbation, walks about, watches the door for her entrance.*]

[*Reënter* FANNY, *left, showing in* AUDRIE.]

FANNY. Mrs. Lesden.

[*Exit* FANNY. MICHAEL *and* AUD-RIE *stand looking at each other for some seconds; then he goes to her,*

takes her hand, kisses it with great reverence, motions her to a chair; she sits. He holds out to her the palms of his hands with a rueful smile, shows they are much blistered as if with rowing.]

AUDRIE. Poor hands!

MICHAEL. I 'm not used to rowing. [*Pause.*]

AUDRIE. I did n't thank you.

MICHAEL. Thank me!

AUDRIE. [*Pause.*] Was n't it a terrible voyage, terrible and delightful? But we ought to have been drowned together!

MICHAEL. Oh, don't say that — in sin! To be lost in sin!

AUDRIE. I 'd rather be lost with you than saved with any one else.

MICHAEL. You must n't speak like this —

AUDRIE. It won't be right, you know, unless we are lost or saved together, will it?

MICHAEL. Hush! Hush! [*Pause.*]

AUDRIE. You 're sorry?

MICHAEL. No. And you?

AUDRIE. No. Is all safe, do you think?

MICHAEL. Yes, I believe so.

AUDRIE. Did n't that strange secretary of yours think it curious that you came back on Thursday instead of Saturday?

MICHAEL. No. I explained that when Withycombe brought me your telegram I thought it better to return at once in case you had started to come, and had been somehow lost.

AUDRIE. Let us go carefully through it all as it happened, to make sure. To-day is Friday. On Wednesday I telegraphed to Withycombe to be at the landing-place at Saint Decuman's with a boat at six o'clock in the evening to bring me back home from there.

MICHAEL. Yes.

AUDRIE. But being a strange creature and quite unaccountable for my actions, I changed my mind, and instead of coming to Saint Decuman's I went up to London, stayed there all day yesterday, and returned by the night mail, reaching home at seven this morning.

MICHAEL. Yes.

AUDRIE. Meantime Withycombe has gone to Saint Margaret's with your uncle, stays there Wednesday night and does not get my telegram till his return home yesterday afternoon. He consults my servants, who know nothing of my whereabouts, consults Mr. Gibbard, who advises him to go to Saint Decuman's and see if I am there. He reaches Saint Decuman's last evening. You are surprised when he shows you the telegram — you explain that I'm not there, that I have n't been there, that you 've seen nothing of me. [*Very tenderly.*] Dear, I felt so sorry for you when I heard you blundering and stammering through your tale to Withycombe.

MICHAEL. Why?

AUDRIE. I knew the pain and shame it caused you to say what was n't true. I wished I could have told all the lies for you.

MICHAEL. No, no. Is n't the truth dear to you?

AUDRIE. Not in comparison with you. Besides, I shall be let off my fibs and little sins very cheaply, much more cheaply than you 'll be, great serious person.

MICHAEL. You grieve me to the heart when you speak like this —

AUDRIE [*penitent*]. I won't! I won't! I 'll be very good and quite serious. Where were we? Well, you explain to Withycombe that I have never been to Saint Decuman's, and at the same time you also change your mind and return with him last evening instead of staying till Saturday.

MICHAEL. You 've seen Withycombe and told him you went to London?

AUDRIE. Yes.

MICHAEL. He suspects nothing?

AUDRIE. No, I made it all quite clear to him.

MICHAEL. And your servants?

AUDRIE. They 're used to my absences. They think nothing of it.

MICHAEL. Then all is safe. The matter will never be heard of again — except —

AUDRIE. Except?

MICHAEL. In our two hearts, and in the High Court where such cases are tried.

[*With an inclination of the head and finger towards heaven.*]

AUDRIE. Don't preach, and — don't regret.

MICHAEL. I won't — only how strange it all is!

AUDRIE. What?

MICHAEL [*in a quiet, calm voice throughout, smiling a little*]. How men try to make their religion square with their practice! I was hard, cruelly hard, on that poor little girl of Andrew's. I was sure it was for the good of her soul that she should stand up and confess in public. But now it comes to my own self, I make excuses; I hide, and cloak, and equivocate, and lie — what a hypocrite I am!

AUDRIE. Ah, you 're sorry!

MICHAEL. No, I 'm strangely happy and — dazed. I feel nothing, except my great joy, and a curious bitter amusement in tracing it all out.

AUDRIE. Tracing what out?

MICHAEL. The hundred little chances, accidents as we call them, that gave us to each other. Everything I did to avoid you threw me at your feet. I felt myself beginning to love you. I wrote urgently to Uncle Ned in Italy, thinking I 'd tell him and that he would save me. He came — I could n't tell him of you, but his coming kept Withycombe from getting your telegram. I went to Saint Decuman's to escape from you. You were moved to come to me. I sent away my own boat to put the sea between us, and so I imprisoned you with me. Six years ago I used all my influence to have the new lighthouse built on Saint Margaret's Isle instead of Saint Decuman's, so that I might keep Saint Decuman's lonely for myself and prayer. I kept it lonely for myself and *you*. It was what we call a chance I did n't go to Saint Margaret's with Andrew and my uncle. It was what we call a chance that you telegraphed to my boatman instead of your own. If any one thing had gone differently —

AUDRIE [*shaking her head*]. We could n't have missed each other in this world. It 's no use blaming chance or fate, or whatever it is.

MICHAEL. I blame nothing. I am too happy. Besides, Chance? Fate? I had the mastery of all these things. They could n't have conquered me if my own heart had n't first yielded. You must n't stay here. [*Turning towards her with great tenderness.*] Oh, I 'm glad that no stain rests upon you through me —

AUDRIE. Don't trouble about me. I have been thinking of you. Your character?

MICHAEL. My character! My character! My character!

AUDRIE. [*Glances up at the place where the portrait had hung.*] Where is she?

[*He points to the picture on the floor.*]

MICHAEL. I dare n't look at her. I must hide it until —

AUDRIE. Until?

MICHAEL. Until we have done what we can to atone for this.

AUDRIE. What?

MICHAEL. Repent, confess, submit to any penance that may be enjoined us. And then if and when it shall be permitted us — marriage.

AUDRIE. Marriage?

MICHAEL. Retirement from all who know us, and lifelong consecration of ourselves to poverty and good works, so that at the last we may perhaps win forgiveness for what we have done.

AUDRIE. Marriage?

[*Reënter* ANDREW *with manuscripts.*]

ANDREW. I beg pardon. I thought Mrs. Lesden had gone.

[*Puts manuscripts on table and is going off.*]

AUDRIE. I am just going, Mr. Gibbard.

ANDREW. [*Turns and speaks to her.*] I met a stranger on the beach yesterday evening. He inquired for you and the way to your house.

AUDRIE. Indeed.

ANDREW. He asked a great many questions about you.

AUDRIE. What questions?

ANDREW. How you lived in this quiet place, and who were your friends, and where you were yesterday.

AUDRIE. Did he give his name?

ANDREW. I did n't ask for it. I suppose he 's staying in the place. I saw him at the door of the George later in the evening.

AUDRIE. One of my London friends, I suppose. What did you reply to his questions?

ANDREW. I told him Mr. Feversham was one of your friends, but as I did n't know where you were yesterday, of course I could n't tell him, could I?

[*Looks at her, exit.*]

AUDRIE. Did you notice that?

MICHAEL. Notice what?

AUDRIE. The look that man gave me as he went out. Does he suspect us?

MICHAEL. Impossible.

AUDRIE. I feel sure he does. Send for him and question him at once. I 'll go.

[*Enter* FANNY *with a letter.*]

FANNY. For you, ma'am.

[*Gives letter to* AUDRIE, *who glances at it, shows a sharp, frightened surprise, instantly concealed, and then stands motionless.*]

The gentleman 's waiting for an answer.

AUDRIE [*in a very quiet, cold voice.*] I 'll come at once. [*Exit* FANNY.]

MICHAEL. What 's the matter?

AUDRIE. Nothing. Question that man. Find out if he knows anything. I 'll come back as soon as I can.

[*Exit, without opening letter.*]

MICHAEL. [*Follows her to door, closes it after her, then goes to right door, calls.*] Andrew.

[*Reënter* ANDREW.]

What is this passage you 're in difficulty about?

ANDREW. [*Comes to him with old manuscripts.*] What 's the matter?

MICHAEL. My head is dizzy this morning.

ANDREW. Did n't you say you could n't sleep?

MICHAEL. What time did you get back from Saint Margaret's yesterday?

ANDREW. About twelve.

MICHAEL. You saw my uncle off by the afternoon train?

ANDREW. Yes.

MICHAEL. And then? [ANDREW *does not reply.*] You were surprised to see me coming back with Withycombe instead of staying till Saturday?

ANDREW. No.

MICHAEL. Withycombe's message about the telegram a little disturbed me. [*A little pause, watching* ANDREW.] I thought perhaps Mrs. Lesden might have started to come to Saint Decuman's [*pause, still watching* ANDREW], and been lost on the way.

ANDREW. Did you?

MICHAEL. She is such a strange, flighty creature, that I should scarcely be surprised at anything she took it into her head to do.

ANDREW [*looking him full in the face*]. She went up to London, did n't she?

MICHAEL [*wincing a little*]. Yes.

ANDREW. And came back through the night by the mail?

MICHAEL. Yes. Why do you look at me like that?

ANDREW. I beg your pardon. Is there any other question you'd like to ask me?

MICHAEL. Question? About what?

ANDREW. About Mrs. Lesden — or anything that's troubling you.

MICHAEL. Troubling me? I'm not troubled about anything.

ANDREW. Oh! I thought perhaps you were. [Going.]

MICHAEL. Andrew. [ANDREW stops.] I've been thinking about — about Rose.

ANDREW. Have you?

MICHAEL. Perhaps I was wrong in urging her to confess.

ANDREW. It isn't much good thinking that now, is it?

MICHAEL. No, except to ask you to forgive me, and to say that you don't cherish any ill-feeling against me on that account.

ANDREW. I forgive you, and I don't cherish any ill-feeling against you on that or any account.

MICHAEL. I may trust you entirely, Andrew?

ANDREW. If you doubt it — try me.

MICHAEL. Try you?

ANDREW. Didn't I tell you to ask me any question you like?

MICHAEL. [Alarmed.] What do you mean? [Pause, looks at ANDREW.] Enough. I trust you absolutely — [looks at him] — in everything.

ANDREW. You may. [Is again going.]

MICHAEL. No, Andrew, nothing has occurred — I was afraid — it seemed so strange — this telegram business. What are you thinking about me?

ANDREW. Take care, sir. Don't betray yourself to anybody but me.

MICHAEL. Betray myself?

ANDREW. You're a worse bungler at lying than I was. Don't look like that, or other people will guess. Don't give way. You're safe. Nobody but me suspects anything. Your character is quite safe — her character is quite safe. They're both in my keeping.

MICHAEL. [Stares helplessly at him.] How did you know?

ANDREW. I've suspected for some time past —

MICHAEL. You were wrong. There was nothing to suspect. It was a chance, an accident — there was no intention to deceive. What made you guess?

ANDREW. When Withycombe brought the telegram to me I guessed something was wrong. I heard you go out in the middle of the night. I followed you down to the beach; I saw you put off; I waited for you to come back. I was on the top of the cliff just above you when you landed with her. I saw you come on here, and I watched her take the road to the station, and saw her come back to her home as if she had come in by the early morning train.

MICHAEL. What are you going to do?

ANDREW. Nothing. Don't I owe everything I am and everything I have in this world to you? I shall never breathe a word of what I know to a living soul.

MICHAEL. Thank you, Andrew. Thank you. And you'll be sure above all that she is safe —

ANDREW. As safe as if I were in the grave. You go your way, just the same as if I didn't know.

MICHAEL. Andrew.

ANDREW. [Comes back.] Sir —

MICHAEL [breaking down]. I was harsh and cruel to Rose. I punished her more than she deserved. I was a hard, self-righteous priest! I hadn't been tempted myself then. Send for her to come home again! Comfort her and give her the best place in your heart. Write at once. Let her come back to-morrow! Oh, what weak, wretched Pharisees we are! What masks of holiness we wear! What whited sepulchres we are! Send for her! Make up to her for all she has suffered! Let me ask her pardon! Oh, Andrew, have pity on me! Forgive me, forgive me!

[Bending his head in tears. ANDREW steals out of the room. A long pause. AUDRIE appears at window in the same place as in Act I, looks in, sees him, taps the window, he goes up to it.]

AUDRIE. Let me in. Quickly. I want to speak to you.

[He goes to door, opens it; a moment later she enters.]

MICHAEL. Well?

AUDRIE. Why didn't you take my warning? Why didn't you beat me, drive

me, hound me away from you as I told
you?

MICHAEL. What now?

AUDRIE. Say you 'll forgive me before I
tell you! No, don't forgive me!

MICHAEL. I don't understand you. Is
anything discovered?

AUDRIE. What does that matter? Oh,
don't hate me. If you say one unkind word
to me I shall kill myself. Read the letter
which came here to me just now.

[*He takes the letter wonderingly.*]

MICHAEL. Whom did it come from?

AUDRIE. My husband.

MICHAEL. Your husband? [*She nods.*]
Your husband! He is alive? [*She nods.*]

AUDRIE [*with a laugh*]. Did n't I tell
you I should ruin you body and soul? [*He
stands overwhelmed.*] Why do you stand
there? Why don't you do something?
[*Laughing at him.*] I say, ghostly father,
we make a pretty pair, you and I, don't we?
What shall we do? Confess in white sheets
and candles together, you and I? Why
don't you do something — [*Laughing at
him.*] And you stand there like a stone
saint. [*Comes up to him.*] Kill me and have
done with me!

MICHAEL. You said your husband died
after two years.

AUDRIE. I said I never saw him again
— alive. I thought then that I never
should.

MICHAEL. But — you believed he was
dead. You believed he was dead — [*She
does not reply.*] You did n't know the night
before last that your husband was living?

AUDRIE. Don't I tell you to kill me and
have done with it.

MICHAEL [*horrified*]. You knew he was
living?

AUDRIE [*very imploringly*]. I love you, I
love you. Say one word to me! Say one
word to me! Say you forgive me.

MICHAEL. I forgive you. [*Stands overwhelmed.*] Take this letter — [*Offering it.*]

AUDRIE. I did n't mean to do this. Do
make excuses for me. We lived unhappily
together. When I came into all my money
I bargained with him that we would never
see each other again. It was a fair bargain
— a contract. He went away to America
— I gave out he was dead. From that time
to this I have never had a thought of his
return. He was dead to me. He has no

right to come and spoil my life. Read that
letter from him.

MICHAEL. No — take it.

[*Gives the letter back.*]

AUDRIE. Tell me what to do.

MICHAEL. I am not fit to advise you.

AUDRIE. What can we do?

MICHAEL. I don't know. We 're in a
blind alley with our sin. There 's no way
out of this.

AUDRIE. I shall defy him.

MICHAEL. No.

AUDRIE. Yes. A bargain 's a bargain. I
shall go back and defy him. I 'll never see
him again. But then — what then? What
will you do?

MICHAEL. Don't think of me.

AUDRIE. Speak to me. Say one word.
Oh, it has been on the tip of my tongue so
many times to tell you all, but I could n't
bear to lose your love, so I deceived you.
[*He walks about perplexed. She goes to him
very gently and coaxingly.*] Say you are n't
sorry — say that deep down in your inmost
heart you are n't sorry for what is past!

MICHAEL. Sorry? No. God forgive me.
I 'm not sorry. I can't be sorry. I wish I
could.

AUDRIE [*coming to him*]. Ah, now I know
you love me! If you only dare be as bold
as I dare —

MICHAEL. Bold?

AUDRIE. We love each other. Our loves
and lives are in our own hands.

MICHAEL. [*Repulses her, braces himself
to stern resolve, very coldly and command-
ingly.*] Listen! These are perhaps the last
words I shall ever speak to you. The past
is past. There 's no way out of that. But
the future is in our power. Can't you see,
woman, that we are half-way down the
precipice? We 'll go no further. From this
moment we part; I toil back to repentance
and peace one way, you toil back another.
So far as God will give me grace I 'll never
think of you from this moment — I 'll spend
all my life in putting a gulf between you
and me. You do the same — ask only one
thing for yourself and me, that we may
forget each other.

AUDRIE. [*Looks at him, smiles, sighs, then
as she is going off.*] I was right about man's
love. You are all cowards. There 's not one
of you that does n't think first of his comfort, or his pocket, or his honor, or his skin,

or his soul, and second of the woman he thinks he loves. Forget you? [*A little laugh.*] Do you think that possible? Do you think I was jesting with you when I gave myself to you? Forget you? [*A little laugh.*] My memory is good for such trifles. Forget you?

MICHAEL [*with a wild revulsion*]. Oh, take me where you will! I have no guide but you! Heaven, hell, wherever you go, I shall follow. Be sure of that. But won't you be my better angel, now I've lost her: If you love me as you say, you can yet be the master influence of my life, you can yet save yourself through me, and me through you. Won't you make our love a monument for good? Dearest of all, I'm at your feet — I think you come from heaven, and I'm all obedience to you. You are my angel. Lead me — Lead me, not back to sin — Lead me towards heaven — You can even now!

AUDRIE. What do you wish me to do?

MICHAEL. Go back to your duty and to deep repentance. Have strength, dearest. These are not idle words — duty, purity, holiness. They mean something. Love is nothing without them. Have courage to tread the hard road. Leave me.

AUDRIE. If I leave you now, shall we meet one day — hereafter?

MICHAEL. Yes.

AUDRIE. You're sure? You do believe it?

MICHAEL. With all my heart.

AUDRIE. And you'll stay here and carry on your work, restore the Minster, and let me think that I'm helping you.

MICHAEL. I can't do that now.

AUDRIE. Yes.

MICHAEL. No.

AUDRIE. Yes.

MICHAEL. But with that money — your money!

AUDRIE. Many churches are built with sinners' money. Do this for me.

MICHAEL. If I dared — if it would come to good — You know how dear a hope it has been to me all my life through.

AUDRIE. Do it, because I ask it. You will?

MICHAEL. And you'll leave me, leave this place, because I ask it. You will?

AUDRIE. I love you. I obey you.

[*She comes to him.*]

MICHAEL. No, I daren't come near to you. You'll go?

[*He opens the door; she passes out; reënters.*]

AUDRIE. Listen to this. Whatever happens, I shall never belong to anybody but you. You understand? [MICHAEL *bows his head.*] I shall never belong to anybody but you, Mike.

[*She goes out again. He closes door, goes up to window. She passes. He watches her off, stays there some moments.*]

[*Reënter* ANDREW. MICHAEL *comes from window; the two men stand looking at each other.*]

ANDREW. You won't begin work this morning, I suppose?

MICHAEL [*firmly*]. Yes. [*Goes to table, motions* ANDREW *to one chair, seats himself opposite. They take up the manuscripts.*] Where is the place?

ANDREW. Fifty-first Psalm, verse three. [MICHAEL *winces, turns over the manuscript.*] Have you found it? What are you looking at?

MICHAEL. [*Gets up suddenly.*] I can't bear it.

ANDREW. Can't bear what?

[MICHAEL *stands looking at him with terror.*]

ANDREW. [*Rises, comes to him.*] Don't I tell you that all is safe. I shan't blab. Nobody shall ever know.

MICHAEL. But *you* know!

ANDREW. I shall never remind you of it.

MICHAEL. But you do, you do. Your presence reminds me.

ANDREW. Shall I leave you now and come again by and by.

MICHAEL [*with an effort*]. No, stay. [*Points to seat.* ANDREW *seats himself.*] You've sent for Rose to come home?

ANDREW. No.

MICHAEL. No?

ANDREW. I don't want to have her in this place where everybody knows about her.

MICHAEL. Won't you send for her, Andrew — to please me?

ANDREW. She's well enough where she is. [*Pointing to the manuscripts.*] Shall we go on?

MICHAEL. What ought I to do, Andrew?

ANDREW. Don't you know what you ought to do?

MICHAEL. What?

ANDREW. Mete out to yourself the same measure you meted to others.

MICHAEL. Confess — in public. I can't! I can't! I dare n't. I'm a coward, a weak, miserable coward! Don't judge me harshly, Andrew! Don't be hard on me!

[*Covering his face with his hands.*]

ANDREW. [*Cold, firm.*] Come, sir! shall we get on with our work? [*Reading manuscript.*] "For I acknowledge my transgressions, and my sin is ever before me."

[MICHAEL *uncovers his face and sits staring at* ANDREW, *who sits cold and grim on the other side of the table.*]

[*A year passes between Acts III and IV.*]

ACT IV

SCENE — *The Chancel of the Minster church of Saint Decuman at Cleveheddon, a beautiful building of Decorated Gothic architecture with signs of recent restoration. The altar and reredos, approached by steps, face the audience, who take up the same position towards it as spectators in the nave would do. Behind the altar a long vista of columns, arches, roof, and stained-glass windows. An organ is built in left wall of the chancel at a considerable height. On both sides of the chancel are handsome high carved oak stalls. A large open place in front of the altar steps is flanked on each side by the transepts, which run to right and left of spectators and are filled with chair seats so far as can be seen. A small door in the north wall of the left transept leads to the organ loft. The whole church is most lavishly decorated with banners, hangings, scrolls, and large frescoes, and is smothered with flowers as if in readiness for a church festival. Large brass candlesticks on altar with lighted candles. Time, about nine on an autumn night. An organ voluntary is being played as curtain rises. Enter* MICHAEL *from transept. He has aged much, is very pale and emaciated. The voluntary ceases and the organ boy, a lad about fifteen, comes from small door in wall of left transept.*

WALTER [*carelessly*]. Good-night, sir.

MICHAEL [*stopping him, puts his hand on the boy's head*]. Good-bye, Walter. [*Pause, still detaining him, with considerable feeling.*] Good-bye, my dear lad.

[*Sighs, moves away from him. The boy shows slight respectful surprise and exit along transept. The* OR-GANIST *with keys enters from the little door, looks round the church admiringly.*]

ORGANIST. Everything ready for the ceremony to-morrow?

MICHAEL. Yes, I think, everything.

ORGANIST. I was just putting the finishing touches to my music. How beautiful the church looks! You must be very proud and happy now your work is complete.

MICHAEL. Not quite complete. I've to put the finishing touches to my part — to-morrow.

[ANDREW *enters rather suddenly from transept.*]

ANDREW. Can I speak to you for a moment?

ORGANIST. Good-night. [*Going.*]

MICHAEL. [*Detains him.*] Thank you for all you have done for me, and for the church, and for her services. [*Shakes hands warmly. Exit the* ORGANIST *by transept.*] Well?

ANDREW. I thought you'd like to know — Mrs. Lesden has come back to Cleveheddon, and she has brought a lady friend with her.

MICHAEL. I know.

ANDREW. You've seen her? [MICHAEL *looks at him with great dignity.*] I beg your pardon.

MICHAEL. I've not seen her.

ANDREW. I beg your pardon. It's no business of mine. [*Going.*]

MICHAEL [*quietly*]. Yes, it is business of yours.

ANDREW. What do you mean?

MICHAEL. Have n't you made it the chief business of your life all this last year?

ANDREW. How? I've kept my word. I've never reminded you of it.

MICHAEL. You've never allowed me to forget it for a single moment. Every time you've spoken to me, or looked at me, or crossed the room, or passed the window, every time I've heard your step on the stairs, or your voice speaking to the servants, you've accused me. If you had been in my place I would have been very kind to you, Andrew.

ANDREW. How did you treat my girl?

MICHAEL. I did what I thought was best for her soul.

ANDREW. Then why don't you do what is best for your own soul?

MICHAEL. I shall.

[ANDREW *looks at* MICHAEL *in startled inquiry.*]

[*Enter by transept* DOCWRAY *and* SIR LYOLF. SIR LYOLF *is in evening dress under summer overcoat.* DOCWRAY *points out the decorations to* SIR LYOLF.]

ANDREW. Why have you sent for Rose to come back to Cleveheddon?

MICHAEL. I wish her to be present at the services to-morrow. She is almost due. Go to the station and meet her. Bring her to me here.

[SIR LYOLF *and* DOCWRAY *saunter up towards* MICHAEL *and* AN-DREW. ANDREW *stands perplexed.*]

MICHAEL [*firmly, to* ANDREW]. Bring her to me here.

[ANDREW *goes off through transept, turns to look at* MICHAEL *before he goes off.*]

SIR LYOLF. You did n't turn up at dinner?

MICHAEL. I was too busy.

SIR LYOLF. All prepared for to-morrow?

MICHAEL. Yes, I think.

SIR LYOLF. So it seems Mrs. Lesden has come down from town.

MICHAEL. So I understand.

SIR LYOLF. [MICHAEL *is listening intently.*] I thought we had seen the last of her when the long-lost husband returned and took her off to London. By the way, what has become of her husband?

MARK. He has gone back to South America. [MICHAEL *is listening intently.*]

SIR LYOLF. Gone back to South America?

MARK. He only stayed three weeks in England. It is said that she has pensioned him off — he is to keep to his hemisphere, and she is to keep to hers.

SIR LYOLF. I don't like it!

MARK. Don't like what?

SIR LYOLF. I don't like women who pension off their husbands to live in South America.

MICHAEL. Do you see much of her in town?

MARK. Not much. About every two months she sweeps into church in a whirl-wind of finery and perfume, gives me a ridiculously large sum for the offertory, makes some most irreverent joke, or else pretends to be deeply religious —

MICHAEL. Pretends?

MARK. What can it be but pretense? Look at her life this last year.

MICHAEL. What of it?

MARK. It has been one continual round of gayety and excitement except when she was ill.

MICHAEL. She has been ill?

MARK. Yes, and no wonder.

MICHAEL. Why?

MARK. She goes everywhere, gives the most extravagant parties, mixes with the fastest, emptiest, London set. And she has taken for her companion a silly, flighty little woman, Mrs. Cantelo.

SIR LYOLF. I don't like it! Why has she come back to Cleveheddon just now?

MARK. To be present at the dedication service to-morrow, I suppose.

SIR LYOLF. Michael —

MICHAEL. Well?

SIR LYOLF. You know that everybody is asking where all the money came from for these magnificent restorations?

MICHAEL. It was sent to me anonymously. The giver wishes to remain unknown.

SIR LYOLF. Yes! Yes! That's what you 've told us. But of course you know who it is?

MICHAEL. I must n't speak of it.

SIR LYOLF. Forgive me.

MICHAEL. Let's say no more. I'm glad you came here to-night. I've been very much perplexed by a confession that has been made to me recently. A priest — you know him, Mark — he is to be present to-morrow — a priest some time ago discovered one of his people in a course of lying and deception, and insisted upon a very severe penalty from the man. And now the priest tells me, that in order to save one very dear to him, he himself has lately been practising exactly the same course of lying and deception. He came to me for advice. I said, "You must pay exactly the same penalty that you demanded from your parishioner." But he objects — he says it will bring disgrace on his family, and disgrace on our cloth. He urged all manner of excuses, but I would n't listen to him. He wishes to be present at the dedication service to-morrow. I've refused him. Have I done right?

SIR LYOLF. Yes, I should say so.

MARK. Was it a just penalty?

MICHAEL. Yes, I believe so — the just, the only penalty, in my opinion. Have I done right?

MARK. Yes, certainly.

MICHAEL. I 'm glad you both think that. To-morrow before the dedication service begins, I shall stand where I 'm standing now and confess that I have been guilty of deadly sin and deceit. Then I shall go out from this place and never return.

[*They come away from him, staring at him in speechless surprise for some moments.*]

SIR LYOLF. But — Good Heaven! — what have you done?

MICHAEL [*after a long pause*]. Guess.

SIR LYOLF. But you won't proclaim yourself?

MICHAEL. Yes.

SIR LYOLF. But your career — your reputation — your opportunities of doing good —

MARK. Have you thought what this will mean to you, to us, to the church?

MICHAEL. I have thought of nothing else for many months past.

SIR LYOLF. Surely there must be some way to avoid a public declaration. [MICHAEL *shakes his head.*] You know I don't speak for myself. My day is nearly done, but you 're in the full vigor of life, with a great reputation to sustain and increase. Don't do this — for my sake, for your own sake, for the sake of Heaven, don't do it!

MICHAEL. I must.

MARK. What are the circumstances?

MICHAEL. I can't tell you. I would n't have told you so much except that I knew I might trust both of you never to hint or whisper anything against — against any but myself. If you should guess — as most likely you will — the name of my companion in sin, it will never cross your lips? I may ask that of you?

SIR LYOLF. You know you may.

MARK. Of course we shall say nothing.

SIR LYOLF. But — but —

[*Sits down overwhelmed.*]

MARK. Can't we talk this over further? Have you considered everything?

MICHAEL. Everything. I have known for many months that this must come. I have tried to palter and spare myself, but each time the conviction has returned with

greater and greater force, "You must do it there, and then, and in that way."

MARK. But you 've repented?

MICHAEL. Most deeply. I have fasted and prayed. I have worn a hair shirt close to my skin. But my sin remains. It is n't rooted out of my heart. I can't get rid of its image.

MARK. Its image?

MICHAEL [*in same calm, tranquil, matter-of-fact tone*]. I believe that every sin has its exact physical image. That just as man is the expression of the thought of God, so our own thoughts and desires and aims, both good and bad, have somewhere or other their exact material counterpart, their embodiment. The image of my sin is a reptile, a greyish-green reptile, with spikes, and cold eyes without lids. It 's more horrible than any creature that was ever seen. It comes and sits in my heart and watches me with those cold eyes that never shut, and never sleep, and never pity. At first it came only very seldom ; these last few months it has scarcely left me day or night, only at night it 's deadlier and more distorted and weighs more upon me. It 's not fancy. Mark, I know, I know, that if I do not get rid of my sin, my hell will be to have that thing sitting beside me for ever and ever, watching me with its cold eyes. But [*hopefully*] I shall be rid of it after to-morrow.

MARK. My poor fellow!

SIR LYOLF [*rising, coming back to* MICHAEL]. Michael, can't you postpone this? Can't it be at some other time? Not in the very hour which should be the proudest and happiest of your life?

MICHAEL. There is no other hour, no other way. [*Looks at them both, takes both their hands affectionately.*] Tell me [*very piteously*] that you neither of you love me the less, — or at least say that you love me a little still, after what I 've told you.

SIR LYOLF. Don't you know?

MARK. How can you ask that?

[ANDREW *and* ROSE *appear in the transept.*]

MICHAEL. [*To* ANDREW.] One moment, Andrew. [*To his father.*] I 've a word or two to say to Andrew.

SIR LYOLF. Come and stay the night with me and let us talk this over.

MICHAEL. No, I must be alone to-night. Good-night, dear Mark.

[MARK *wrings his hand.*]

SIR LYOLF. You are resolved to go through with this? It must be? [MICHAEL *bows his head.*] I can't be here to-morrow. I could n't face it. But [*with great affection*] I shan't be far away when you want me. [*Very warm handshake.*] Come, Mr. Docwray.

[*Exeunt* SIR LYOLF *and* DOCWRAY *by transept.*]

ANDREW [*bringing* ROSE *to* MICHAEL]. I 've brought her.

[ROSE *is in an Anglican sister's dress; she is very pale and her manner is subdued. She comes slowly and reverently to* MICHAEL, *and is going to bend to him. He takes her hands and raises her.*]

MICHAEL. No. You must n't bend to me. I 've sent for you, Rose, to ask your pardon?

ROSE. My pardon?

MICHAEL. I made you pass through a terrible ordeal last year. Will you forgive me?

ROSE. What should I forgive? You were right. You said it would bring me great peace. And so it has — great peace.

MICHAEL. And you would n't undo that morning's work?

ROSE. No. It seems I died that morning and left all my old life in a grave. This is quite a new life. I would n't change it.

MICHAEL. Andrew, do you hear that?

ANDREW. Yes.

MICHAEL. I was right, then? I was right? You are happy?

ROSE. Yes, I am happy — at least, I 'm peaceful, and peace is better than happiness, is n't it?

MICHAEL. Yes, peace is best! Peace is best! I shall find it too, some day. Andrew, she has forgiven me. Can't you forgive me? We may never see each other again on this side the grave. Don't let us part in anger!

ANDREW. Part?

MICHAEL. As soon as I can arrange my affairs I shall leave Cleveheddon.

ANDREW. But your work?

MICHAEL. My work is ended. I 'll see that you and Rose are sufficiently provided for.

[*Taking their hands, trying to join them;* ANDREW *holds aloof.*]

ANDREW. No. I can't take any favor from you.

MICHAEL. It 's no favor. I 've trained you to a special work which has unfitted you for everything else. It is my duty to provide for your old age.

ANDREW. I can't take any favor from you.

MICHAEL. Old comrade [*leaning on* ANDREW'S *shoulder;* ANDREW *draws away*], old comrade [*draws* ANDREW *to him*], we had many happy days together in the summer of our life. Now the autumn has come, now the winter is coming, I 'm setting out on a cold, dark journey. Won't you light a little flame in our old lamp of friendship to cheer me on my way? You 'll take my gift — you 'll take it, and make a home for her?

ANDREW. [*Bursts out.*] You 'll break my heart with your kindness! I don't deserve it! I was a half-bred, starving dog. You took me in, and, like the hound I am, I turned and bit the hand that fed me. Let me be! Let me be!

MICHAEL. Rose, speak to him.

ROSE. Father, you are grieving Mr. Feversham.

ANDREW. I 'll do whatever you tell me. But don't forgive me.

MICHAEL. Take him home, Rose. I parted you. Let me think I have restored you to each other.   [*Joining them.*]

ANDREW. [*To* MICHAEL.] I can't say anything to-night. I never was good enough to black your shoes. I can't thank you. I can't speak. Good-night. Come, Rose!

[MICHAEL *shakes* ROSE'S *hand very tenderly. Exeunt* ROSE *and* ANDREW *by transept.* MICHAEL *watches them off, goes to altar.*]

MICHAEL [*alone*]. One thing more and all is done. [*Looking round the church.*] And I must give you up! Never enter your doors, never lead my people through you in chariots of fire, never make you the very presence-chamber of God to my soul and their souls who were committed to me! Oh, if I had been worthy!

[*A little pause. A woman's laugh is heard in the transept opposite to that by which* ANDREW *and* ROSE *have gone off.* MICHAEL *withdraws to the side of chancel, where he is seen by the audience, during the following scene, but is hidden from* AUDRIE *and* MRS. CANTELO.]

[AUDRIE *enters from transept in magnificent evening dress, cloak, and jewelry, and carrying a large basket of roses. Her features are much paler and sharpened, and she shows a constant restlessness and excitement.*]

AUDRIE. [*Looks round, calls out.*] Somebody is here ? [*Pause, calls out.*] Somebody is here ? No ? [*Speaks down transept.*] You may come in, Milly.

[MILLY CANTELO, *a fashionable little woman, enters at transept, looking admiringly round the church.*]

AUDRIE. There's nobody here except [*raising her voice*] a stone saint [*pointing up to carved figure*], and he can't hear, because he has only stone ears, and he can't feel, because he has only a stone heart.

[MICHAEL *shows intense feeling.*]

MILLY [*looking round*]. Isn't it gorgeous ?

AUDRIE. H'm — yes — [*Raises her voice.*] I can't bear that stone saint. Look how hard and lifeless he is. In a well-regulated world there would be no room for angels or devils, or stone saints, or any such griffins.

MILLY. Audrie, you are queer to-night. You'll be ill again.

AUDRIE. I hope so.

MILLY. What's the matter with you ?

AUDRIE. Life's the matter with me, I think. I've got it badly, and I don't know how to cure myself.

MILLY. I wish you would n't talk nonsense, and run about on silly errands in the dark.

AUDRIE. I won't for long. When my head is tightly bandaged in a white cloth, I can't talk any more nonsense, can I ? And when my feet are comfortably tucked up in my final nightgown I can't run after stone saints in the dark, can I ?

MILLY. Oh, you give me the creeps. I can't imagine why you wanted to come out to-night.

AUDRIE. To decorate the church.

MILLY. Don't you think it's decorated enough ?

AUDRIE [*looking*]. No, it wants a few more touches. I must just titivate a cherub's nose, or hang a garland on an apostle's toe, just to show my deep, deep devotion —

MILLY. Your deep, deep devotion.

AUDRIE. My deep, deep love, my deep, deep worship, my deep, deep remembrance.

MILLY. Of what ?

AUDRIE. The church, of course.

MILLY. What a heap of money all this must have cost ! Who gave it all ?

AUDRIE. I gave two hundred pounds when I lived here last year.

MILLY. I wonder who gave all the rest ?

AUDRIE. I wonder !

MILLY. Mr. Feversham must have some very devoted friends.

AUDRIE. So it seems.

MILLY. Did you know him very well when you lived here ?

AUDRIE. Not very well.

MILLY. What sort of a man is he ?

AUDRIE. Oh, a very cold, distant man — a good deal of the priest about him, and as much feeling as that stone figure up there.

MILLY. You did n't like him ?

AUDRIE. Oh, I liked him well enough. But I don't think he cared much for me. I dare say he has forgotten all about me by this time. Milly — [*Bursts into tears.*]

MILLY. What is it ?

AUDRIE. I'm not well to-night. I ought n't to have come here. Milly — I never forget anybody. If I had once loved you I should love you for ever. If you were wicked, or unfortunate, or unfaithful, it would make no difference to me. Kiss me, Milly — say you believe me.

MILLY. You know I do, darling.

AUDRIE [*very passionately*]. I can be constant, Milly — I can ! Constant in my friendship, constant in my love ! Oh, Milly, I'm the most wretched woman in the world !

MILLY. You're hysterical, dear.

AUDRIE. No, I'm forsaken. Nobody loves me ! [*Sobbing. Gesture from* MICHAEL.]

MILLY. Poor Audrie !

AUDRIE. Let me be a few minutes by myself. I want to be quite alone. Go home and wait for me there.

MILLY. I don't like leaving you.

AUDRIE [*getting her off at transept*]. Yes — go, dear. I shall be better soon. Do leave me.

MILLY. You won't be long ?

AUDRIE. No — I'll come soon.

[*Accompanying her along transept. Exit* MILLY *by transept.* AUDRIE *stands listening.* MICHAEL *comes forward a step or two.*]

AUDRIE. [*In the transept.*] Are you there ?

[*He comes forward; she goes towards*

him; they stand for a moment or two looking at each other.]

AUDRIE. Are you deaf? I thought it was only your memory that was gone.

MICHAEL. Why have you come here?

AUDRIE. May n't I come into my own church? And such a sinner as I am?

MICHAEL. Forgive me. You know how welcome I would make you — if I dared.

AUDRIE. Then you don't dare? Then I 'm not welcome?

MICHAEL [*troubled.*] Yes! Yes! Very welcome! The Church owes much to you.

AUDRIE. I think she does, for she has robbed me of your love. Why have you sent back all my letters unopened?

MICHAEL. Can't you guess what it cost me to return them? [*Pause.*] What have you been doing all this last year?

AUDRIE. Doing? Eating my heart. Racing through my life to get to the end of it. Skipping and chattering from Hyde Park Corner to the Inferno by a new short cut. What have you been doing?

MICHAEL. Trying to repent and to forget.

AUDRIE Ah, well — I have n't been wasting my time quite so foolishly as you after all.

MICHAEL. Will you never be serious?

AUDRIE. Yes — soon.

MICHAEL. You 've been ill?

AUDRIE. Oh, my dear spiritual doctor, you don't know how ill I 've been. I get up every morning without hope, I drag through the day without hope, I go to this thing and that, to this party, to that reception, to the theater, to church, to a pigeon-shooting match, to the park, to Ascot, to Henley — here, there, everywhere, all without hope.

MICHAEL. What is it you want?

AUDRIE. I want to live again! I 've never lived but those few months when we were learning to love each other! I want to feel that fierce breeze on my cheek that blew us together! Do you remember when we stood on the cliff hand in hand? And we shrieked and laughed down the wind like mad children? Do you remember?

MICHAEL. No.

AUDRIÉ. No? Nor the wonderful pale sunrise, with the lemon and green lakes of light, and then the path of diamonds all across the sea? Don't you remember?

MICHAEL. No.

AUDRIE. How strange you don't remember! Oh, my God, if I could forget!

MICHAEL [*apart from her*]. Oh, my God, if I could forget! [*A long pause. He comes to her.*] I have one awful thought — I am bound to you — There is but one of us — I never felt it more than at this moment — And yet the awful thought comes to me — if by any decree we should be put asunder hereafter — if we should be parted then!

AUDRIE. Don't you dread being parted now — now this moment? Don't you dread being unhappy here — here on this earth?

MICHAEL. I will not think of that. I have vowed!

AUDRIE. You don't love me! You don't love me! You don't love me!

MICHAEL. If I had ten thousand worlds I 'd sell them all and buy your soul. But I will keep the vow I have vowed. You are the holiest thing on earth to me. I will keep you white and stainless from me.

AUDRIE. You 'll never forget me.

MICHAEL. I have forgotten you.

AUDRIE. You 'll never forget me.

MICHAEL [*in the same cold tone, going up the altar steps*]. I have forgotten you.

[*Stands with his back to her for a few moments.*]

AUDRIE [*with a gesture of resignation*]. You 'll let me put a bunch or two of flowers about the church before I go?

MICHAEL. If I asked you not —

AUDRIE. I should obey you.

MICHAEL. I do ask you not —

AUDRIE. Very well. It 's hard lines that I may n't decorate my own church.

MICHAEL. I have another request to make — a favor to beg of you.

AUDRIE. It 's done, whatever it is. But make it some great thing — something very hard and desperate, that I may show you there 's nothing I would not do if you ask it.

MICHAEL. It 's something very simple. I 'm going to ask you not to be present at the dedication service to-morrow.

AUDRIE. But I came on purpose —

MICHAEL. I beg you not. I have a strong reason. You won't come?

AUDRIE. Not if you wish me to stay away. Shall I see you after to-morrow?

MICHAEL. After to-morrow I leave Cleveheddon for ever.

AUDRIE. Where are you going?

MICHAEL. I don't know.

AUDRIE. It does n't matter, I shall find you out.

MICHAEL. You 'll follow me ?

AUDRIE. Yes — all over this world, and the ten thousand others. I shall follow you. You 'll find me always with you, clawing at your heart. Au revoir. [*Takes up her basket of roses; going out with them by transept, stops.*] Do let me put some flowers on the altar — just to remind you. Your memory is so bad, you know.

> [*He raises his hand very quietly and turns his back on her. She stands very quiet and hopeless for a few seconds, then takes up the basket of flowers, goes a step or two towards transept, turns.*]

I 'm going to be very ill after this. [*He stands at altar in an attitude of prayer, his back to her.*] Do you hear, I 'm going to be very ill? There 's a little string in my heart — I 've just heard it snap. [*Pause.*] If I were dying and I sent for you, would you come ?

MICHAEL [*after a long pause, very quietly*]. Yes.   [*Pause.*]

AUDRIE. And that 's all ? And that 's all ? [*He stands unmoved at altar, his back to her. She takes a large red rose out of the basket, throws it towards him ; it falls on the white marble altar steps.*] There 's a flower for to-morrow ! Do put it on the altar for me ! You won't ? You won't ? [*No answer.*] It is hard to be turned out of my own church — It is hard —

> [*Exit AUDRIE by transept with the basket of flowers. A sob is heard, MICHAEL turns round. A door is heard to close. He puts out the altar lights, throws himself on altar steps. The curtains fall.
> The falling of the curtains signifies the passing of the night.
> A peal of joyous church bells followed by organ music and singing. The curtain rises and discovers the church in broad daylight and filled with worshipers. ANDREW and ROSE are at the corner in prominent positions. AUDRIE'S flower is lying on the altar steps. A processional hymn is being sung. A procession of surpliced priests file up the aisle and take their places in the chancel, walking over AUDRIE'S*

rose. MICHAEL *follows at the end of the procession; as he reaches the altar steps, he turns, very pale and cold, and speaks in a low, calm voice.*]

MICHAEL. Before this service begins and this church is reconsecrated I have a duty to perform to my people. [*Great attention of all.*] I have often insisted in this place on the necessity of a life of perfect openness before God and man. I have taught you that your lives should be crystal clear, that your hearts should be filled with sunlight, so that no foul thing may hide therein. I have enforced that with others, because I believe with my heart and soul that it is the foundation of all wholesome and happy human life. I stand here to affirm it to-day in the presence of God and you all. I stand here to affirm it against myself as I formerly affirmed it against another. I stand here to own to you that while I have been vainly preaching to you, my own life has been polluted with deceit and with deadly sin. I can find no repentance and no peace till I have freely acknowledged to you all that I am not worthy to continue my sacred office, not worthy to be the channel of grace to you. It was the dearest wish of my life to restore this beautiful temple, and to be Heaven's vicar here. I have raised it again, but I may not enter. I dare not enter. I have sinned — as David sinned. I have broken the sanctity of the marriage vow. It is my just sentence to go forth from you, not as your guide, your leader, your priest; but as a broken sinner, humbled in the dust before the Heaven he has offended. I bid you all farewell. I ask your pardon for having dared to continue in my office knowing I had profaned and desecrated it. It now remains for me to seek the pardon of Heaven. Let the service continue without me. Let no one leave his place. Pray for me all of you ! I have need of your prayers ! Pray for me !

> [*He comes down from the altar steps amidst the hushed and respectful surprise of the congregation, who all turn to look at him as he passes. ROSE makes a very slight gesture of sympathy as he passes her. ANDREW stands with hands over his eyes. MICHAEL passes out by transept, his head bowed, his lips moving in prayer as he goes off.*]

[*Ten months pass between Acts IV and V.*]

ACT V

SCENE — *Reception room of the Monastery of San Salvatore at Majano, in Italy. A simply furnished room in an old Italian building. At back right an open door approached by a flight of steps, at back left a large window; a mass of masonry divides the window and door. A door down stage, left. The portrait of* MICHAEL'S *mother hangs on the wall. Time, a summer evening. Discover* FATHER HILARY *reading. Enter* SIR LYOLF *up the steps and by door at back.*

FATHER HILARY. Well?

SIR LYOLF. I've been to see her again. I can't get her out of my mind.

FATHER HILARY. How is she this evening?

SIR LYOLF. In the very strangest state, laughing, crying, jesting, fainting, and chattering like a magpie. I believe she's dying.

FATHER HILARY. Dying?

SIR LYOLF. Yes. It seems she had a kind of malarial fever a month or two ago and was n't properly treated. I wish there was a good English doctor in the place. And I wish Michael was here.

FATHER HILARY. Be thankful that he is away.

SIR LYOLF. But if he finds out that she has been here, that she has sent again and again for him, and that we have hidden it from him — and that she has died?

FATHER HILARY. He must n't know it until he can bear to hear it. We must consider him first. Think what he must have suffered all these months. Now that at last he is learning to forget her, now that he is finding peace, how wrong, how cruel it would be to reopen his wounds!

SIR LYOLF. She said he promised to come to her if she sent for him. She begged so hard. She has come from England with the one hope of seeing him. I felt all the while that I was helping to crush the life out of her.

FATHER HILARY. What did you tell her?

SIR LYOLF. That he had gone away alone for a few days in the mountains. That we did n't exactly know where to find him, but that he might come back at any time, and that I would bring him to her the moment he returned.

FATHER HILARY. Well, what more can we do?

SIR LYOLF. Nothing now, I suppose. I wish we had sent after him when she came last week. We could have found him before this. Besides, she does n't believe me.

FATHER HILARY. Does n't believe you?

SIR LYOLF. She thinks that Michael is here with us, and that we are hiding it from him. I wish he'd come back.

FATHER HILARY. If she is passing away, better it should all be over before he returns.

SIR LYOLF. I don't like parting them at the last. She loves him, Ned, she loves him.

FATHER HILARY. Remember it's a guilty love.

SIR LYOLF. Yes, I know.

FATHER HILARY. Remember what it has already cost him.

SIR LYOLF. Yes, I know. But love is love, and whether it comes from heaven, or whether it comes from the other place, there's no escaping it. I believe it always comes from heaven!

[FATHER HILARY *shakes his head.*]

SIR LYOLF. I'm getting my morals mixed up in my old age, I suppose. But, by God, she loves him, Ned, she loves him — Who's that?

[FATHER HILARY *looks out of window, makes a motion of silence.*]

FATHER HILARY. Hush! He's come back.

SIR LYOLF. I must tell him.

FATHER HILARY. Let us sound him first, and see what his feelings are. Then we can judge whether it will be wise to let him know.

[*Enter up steps and by door* MICHAEL *in a traveling cloak. He enters very listlessly. He has an expression of settled pensiveness and resignation, almost despair. He comes up very affectionately to his father, shakes hands, does the same to* FATHER HILARY. *Then he sits down without speaking.*]

SIR LYOLF. Have you come far to-day, Michael?

MICHAEL. No, only from Casalta. I stayed there last night.

SIR LYOLF. You are back rather sooner than you expected?

MICHAEL. I had nothing to keep me away. One place is the same as another.

FATHER HILARY. And about the future? Have you made up your mind?

MICHAEL. Yes. I had really decided before I went away, but I wanted this week alone to be quite sure of myself, to be quite sure that I was right in taking this final step, and that I should never draw back. [*To* FATHER HILARY.] You remember at Saint Decuman's Isle, two years ago, you said you could give me a deeper peace than I could find within or around me?

FATHER HILARY. And I can. And I will.

MICHAEL. Give me that peace. I need it. When can I be received?

FATHER HILARY. When I have prepared you.

MICHAEL. Let it be soon. Let it be soon. [*To his father.*] This is a blow to you—

SIR LYOLF. You know best. I wish you could have seen your way to stay in your own Church.

MICHAEL. I was an unfaithful steward and a disobedient son to her. She is well rid of me. [*To* FATHER HILARY.] You are sure you can give me that peace—

FATHER HILARY. If you'll but give me your will entirely, and let me break it in pieces. On no other condition. Come and talk to me alone.

[*Trying to lead him off left.*]

SIR LYOLF. No—! [*Goes to* MICHAEL.] Michael, you are at peace now, are n't you?

[MICHAEL *looks at him.*]

FATHER HILARY. He will be soon. Leave him to me.

SIR LYOLF. No. I must know the truth from him.

FATHER HILARY. You're wrong to torture him.

SIR LYOLF. [*To* MICHAEL.] You are at peace now—at least, you are gaining peace, you are forgetting the past?

FATHER HILARY. He will. He shall. Say no more. [*To* MICHAEL.] Come with me,—I insist!

SIR LYOLF. No. Michael, before you take this last step answer me one question —I have a reason for asking. Tell me this truly. If by any chance some one in England — some one who was dear to you —

MICHAEL. Oh, don't speak of her — [*Turns away, hides his head for a minute, turns round with a sudden outburst.*] Yes, speak of her! Speak of her! I have n't heard her name for so long! Let me hear it again — Audrie! Audrie!

FATHER HILARY [*sternly to* SIR LYOLF]. Do you hear? Let him alone. Don't torment him by dragging up the past. He has buried it.

MICHAEL. No! No! No! Why should I deceive you? Why should I deceive myself? All this pretended peace is no peace! There is no peace for me without her, either in this world or the next!

FATHER HILARY. Hush! Hush! How dare you speak so!

MICHAEL. I must. The live agony of speech is better than the dead agony of silence, the eternal days and nights without her! Forget her? I can't forget! Look!

[*Takes out a faded red rose.*]

SIR LYOLF. What is it?

MICHAEL. A flower she threw me in church the last time I saw her. And I would n't take it! I sent her away! I sent her away! And her flower was trampled on. The next night I got up in the middle of the night and went over to the church and found it on the altar steps. I've kept it ever since. [*To his father.*] Talk to me about her. I want somebody to talk to me about her. Tell me something you remember of her — some little speech of hers. — Do talk to me about her.

SIR LYOLF. My poor fellow!

MICHAEL. I can't forget. The past is always with me! I live in it! It's my life. You think I'm here in this place with you — I've never been here. I'm living with her two years ago. I have no present, no future. I've only the past when she was with me. Give me the past! Oh! give me back only one moment of the past, one look, one word from her — and then take all that remains of me and do what you like with it. Oh!

[*Goes back to bench, sits.*]

SIR LYOLF. [*To* FATHER HILARY.] You see! I must tell him —

FATHER HILARY. No, not while he's in this mad state. Let's quiet him first.

SIR LYOLF. Then we'll take him to her!

FATHER HILARY. When he is calmer.

SIR LYOLF. Take care it is n't too late.

FATHER HILARY. [*Goes to* MICHAEL, *puts his hand on* MICHAEL'S *shoulder.*] This is weakness. Be more brave. Control yourself!

MICHAEL. Have I not controlled myself? Who trained and guided himself with more care than I? Who worked as I worked, prayed as I prayed, kept watch over himself, denied himself, sacrificed himself as I did? And to what end? Who had higher

aims and resolves than I? They were as
high as heaven, and they've tumbled all
round me! Look at my life, the inconsequence, the inconsistency, the futility, the
foolishness of it all. What a patchwork of
glory and shame! Control myself? Why?
Let me alone! Let me drift! What does it
matter where I go? I'm lost in the dark!
One way is as good as another!

[*The vesper bell heard off at some little distance.*]

FATHER HILARY. You've wandered
away from the road, and now you complain
that the maps are wrong. Get back to the
highway, and you'll find that the maps are
right.

MICHAEL. Forgive me, Uncle Ned — I'm
ashamed of this. I shall get over it. I'll
talk with you by and by. I will submit myself. I will be ruled. Father, come to me.
You nursed me yourself night after night
when I was delirious with the fever. I was a
child then. I'm a child now. Talk to me
about her. Talk to me about Audrie!

[*AUDRIE'S face, wasted and hectic,
appears just over the doorstep, coming up the steps at back; during the
following conversation she raises
herself very slowly and with great
difficulty up the steps, leaning on
the wall.*]

I've heard nothing of her. Where do you
think she is? In England? I think I
could be patient, I think I could bear my
life if I knew for certain that all was well
with her. If I could know that she is
happy — No, she isn't happy — I know
that.

SIR LYOLF. Michael, I've had some
news of her.

MICHAEL. News! Good? Bad? Quick!
Tell me.

SIR LYOLF. You can bear it?

MICHAEL. She's dead? And I never
went to her! I never went to her! She
won't forgive me!

SIR LYOLF. She's not dead.

MICHAEL. What then?

SIR LYOLF. You promised you'd go to
her if she sent for you.

MICHAEL. Yes.

SIR LYOLF. She has sent for you.

[*Sees her entering.*]

MICHAEL. She's dying?

[*She has gained the door, just enters,
leaning back against the post
MICHAEL's back is towards her.*]

AUDRIE. I'm afraid I am.

[*MICHAEL looks at her, utters a wild
cry of joy, then looks at her more
closely, realizes she is dying, goes
to her, kisses her, bursts into sobs.*]

AUDRIE [*putting her hand on his head*].
Don't cry. I'm past crying for. Help me
there. [*Points to seat.*]

[*He seats her; looks at her with great
anxiety.*]

AUDRIE [*laughing, a little weak feeble
laugh, and speaking feebly with pause between each word*]. Don't pull — that — long
— face. You'll — make me — laugh — if
you — do. And I want to be — serious now.

MICHAEL. But you're dying!

AUDRIE [*with a sigh*]. Yes. Can't help
it. Sir Lyolf, pay — coachman — [*taking
out purse feebly*] outside — No, perhaps —
better — wait — or bring another sort — of
— carriage. But no mutes — no feathers
— no mummery.

SIR LYOLF. I'll send him away. You'll
stay with us now?

AUDRIE. [*Nods.*] So sorry — to intrude.
Won't be very long about it.

[*Exit SIR LYOLF by door and steps;
MICHAEL is standing with hands
over eyes.*]

FATHER HILARY [*coming to AUDRIE*].
Can I be of any service, any comfort to you?

AUDRIE. No, thanks. I've been dreadfully wicked — does n't much — matter,
eh? Can't help it now. Have n't strength
to feel sorry. So sorry I can't feel sorry.

FATHER HILARY. There is forgiveness —

AUDRIE. Yes, I know. Not now. Want
to be with him. [*Indicating MICHAEL.*]

[*SIR LYOLF reënters by steps.*]

SIR LYOLF. Come, Ned —

AUDRIE. [*To FATHER HILARY.*] Come
back again — in — few minutes. I shall
want you. I've been dreadfully wicked.
But I've built a church — and — [*fever-
ishly*] I've loved him — with all my heart
— and a little bit over.

[*Exeunt SIR LYOLF and FATHER
HILARY, door left.*]

AUDRIE [*motioning MICHAEL*]. Why did
n't you come when I sent for you?

MICHAEL. I've only known this moment.
Why did n't you send before?

AUDRIE. I sent you hundreds — of messages — from my heart of hearts. Did n't you get them?

MICHAEL. Yes — every one.

AUDRIE. I 've crawled all over Europe after you. And you are n't worth it — Yes, you are. You would n't come —

MICHAEL. Yes — anywhere — anywhere — take me where you will.

AUDRIE. You know — he 's dead. I 'm free.

MICHAEL. Is it so? But it 's too late.

AUDRIE. Yes. Pity! Not quite a well-arranged world, is it? Hold my hand. We 're not to be parted?

MICHAEL. No.

AUDRIE. Sure?

MICHAEL. Quite sure. You 're suffering?

AUDRIE. No — that 's past — [*Shuts her eyes. He watches her.*] Very comfortable — very happy — just like going into a delicious faint — [*Sighs.*] Do you remember — beautiful sunrise — diamonds on the sea —

MICHAEL. Yes, I remember — all — every moment! And the wind that blew us together when we stood on the cliff! Oh! we were happy then — I remember all! All! All!

AUDRIE. So glad your memory 's good at last. [*A vesper hymn heard off at some distance.*] Pity to die on such a lovely evening — not quite well-arranged world? But we were happy — if the next world has anything as good it won't be much amiss.

I 'm going. Fetch — priest — [MICHAEL *is going to door left; she calls him back.*] No. No time to waste. Don't leave me. We shan't be parted?

MICHAEL. No! No! No! No!

AUDRIE. [*Gives a deep sigh of content, then looks up at his mother's picture.*] She 's there? [MICHAEL *nods.*] She 'll forgive me! [*Blows a little kiss to the picture.*] But I 'm your angel — I 'm leading you —

MICHAEL. Yes. Where?

AUDRIE. I don't know. Don't fuss about it. " Le bon Dieu nous pardonnera : c'est son métier " — [*Closes her eyes.*] Not parted? [*Looks up at him.*]

MICHAEL. No! No! No! No!

AUDRIE. You won't keep me waiting too long? [*Looks up at him, a long deep sigh of content.*] Hold my hand — Tight! tight! Oh! don't look so solemn —

> [*Begins to laugh, a ripple of bright, feeble laughter, growing louder and stronger, a little outburst, then a sudden stop, as she drops dead.* MICHAEL *kisses her lips, her face, her hands, her dress.*]

[*Enter* FATHER HILARY.]

MICHAEL. Take me! I give my life, my will, my soul, to you! Do what you please with me! I 'll believe all, do all, suffer all — only — only persuade me that I shall meet her again!

[*Throws himself on her body.*]

STRIFE

A DRAMA IN THREE ACTS

By JOHN GALSWORTHY

PERSONS OF THE PLAY

JOHN ANTHONY, *Chairman of the Trenartha Tin Plate Works*

EDGAR ANTHONY, *his son,* ⎫

FREDERIC H. WILDER, ⎪

WILLIAM SCANTLEBURY, ⎬ *Directors of the same*

OLIVER WANKLIN, ⎭

HENRY TENCH, *Secretary of the same*

FRANCIS UNDERWOOD, C.E., *Manager of the same*

SIMON HARNESS, *a Trades Union Official*

DAVID ROBERTS, ⎫

JAMES GREEN, ⎪

JOHN BULGIN, ⎬ *the workmen's committee*

HENRY THOMAS, ⎪

GEORGE ROUS, ⎭

HENRY ROUS, ⎫

LEWIS, ⎪

JAGO, ⎪

EVANS, ⎪

A BLACKSMITH, ⎬ *workmen at the Trenartha Tin Plate Works*

DAVIES, ⎪

A RED-HAIRED YOUTH, ⎪

BROWN, ⎭

FROST, *valet to John Anthony*

ENID UNDERWOOD, *wife of Francis Underwood, daughter of John Anthony*

ANNIE ROBERTS, *wife of David Roberts*

MADGE THOMAS, *daughter of Henry Thomas*

MRS. ROUS, *mother of George and Henry Rous*

MRS. BULGIN, *wife of John Bulgin*

MRS. YEO, *wife of a workman*

A PARLORMAID *to the Underwoods*

JAN, *Madge's brother, a boy of ten*

A CROWD OF MEN ON STRIKE

ACT   I. THE DINING-ROOM OF THE MANAGER'S HOUSE

ACT II. SCENE I. THE KITCHEN OF THE ROBERTS'S COTTAGE
NEAR THE WORKS

SCENE II. A SPACE OUTSIDE THE WORKS

ACT III. THE DRAWING-ROOM OF THE MANAGER'S HOUSE

The action takes place on February 7 between the hours of noon
and six in the afternoon, close to the Trenartha Tin Plate Works,
on the borders of England and Wales, where a strike has been
in progress throughout the winter.

STRIFE

ACT I

It is noon. In the Underwoods' dining-room a bright fire is burning. On one side of the fire-place are double doors leading to the drawing-room, on the other side a door leading to the hall. In the center of the room a long dining-table without a cloth is set out as a Board table. At the head of it, in the Chairman's seat, sits JOHN ANTHONY, *an old man, big, clean-shaven, and high-colored, with thick white hair, and thick dark eyebrows. His movements are rather slow and feeble, but his eyes are very much alive. There is a glass of water by his side. On his right sits his son* EDGAR, *an earnest-looking man of thirty, reading a newspaper. Next him* WANKLIN, *a man with jutting eyebrows, and silver-streaked light hair, is bending over transfer papers.* TENCH, *the Secretary, a short and rather humble, nervous man, with side whiskers, stands helping him. On* WANKLIN'S *right sits* UNDERWOOD, *the Manager, a quiet man, with a long, stiff jaw, and steady eyes. Back to the fire is* SCANTLEBURY, *a very large, pale, sleepy man, with gray hair, rather bald. Between him and the Chairman are two empty chairs.*

WILDER [*who is lean, cadaverous, and complaining, with drooping gray mustaches, stands before the fire*]. I say, this fire's the devil! Can I have a screen, Tench?

SCANTLEBURY. A screen, ah!

TENCH. Certainly, Mr. Wilder. [*He looks at* UNDERWOOD.] That is — perhaps the Manager — perhaps Mr. Underwood —

SCANTLEBURY. These fireplaces of yours, Underwood —

UNDERWOOD [*roused from studying some papers*]. A screen? Rather! I'm sorry. [*He goes to the door with a little smile.*] We 're not accustomed to complaints of too much fire down here just now.

[*He speaks as though he holds a pipe between his teeth, slowly, ironically.*]

WILDER [*in an injured voice*]. You mean the men. H'm! [UNDERWOOD *goes out.*]

SCANTLEBURY. Poor devils!

WILDER. It 's their own fault, Scantle-bury.

EDGAR [*holding out his paper*]. There 's great distress among them, according to the "Trenartha News."

WILDER. Oh, that rag! Give it to Wank-lin. Suit his Radical views. They call us monsters, I suppose. The editor of that rub-bish ought to be shot.

EDGAR [*reading*]. "If the Board of worthy gentlemen who control the Tre-nartha Tin Plate Works from their arm-chairs in London would condescend to come and see for themselves the conditions pre-vailing amongst their workpeople during this strike —"

WILDER. Well, we *have* come.

EDGAR [*continuing*]. "We cannot believe that even their leg-of-mutton hearts would remain untouched."

[WANKLIN *takes the paper from him.*]

WILDER. Ruffian! I remember that fel-low when he had n't a penny to his name; little snivel of a chap that's made his way by blackguarding everybody who takes a different view to himself.

[ANTHONY *says something that is not heard.*]

WILDER. What does your father say?

EDGAR. He says "The kettle and the pot."

WILDER. H'm!

[*He sits down next to* SCANTLEBURY.]

SCANTLEBURY [*blowing out his cheeks*]. I shall boil if I don't get that screen.

[UNDERWOOD *and* ENID *enter with a screen, which they place before the fire.* ENID *is tall; she has a small, decided face, and is twenty-eight years old.*]

ENID. Put it closer, Frank. Will that do, Mr. Wilder? It 's the highest we 've got.

WILDER. Thanks, capitally.

SCANTLEBURY [*turning with a sigh of pleasure*]. Ah! Merci, madame!

ENID. Is there anything else you want,

father? [ANTHONY *shakes his head.*] Edgar — anything?

EDGAR. You might give me a "J" nib, old girl.

ENID. There are some down there by Mr. Scantlebury.

SCANTLEBURY [*handing a little box of nibs*]. Ah! your brother uses "J's." What does the manager use? [*With expansive politeness.*] What does your husband use, Mrs. Underwood?

UNDERWOOD. A quill!

SCANTLEBURY. The homely product of the goose.   [*He holds out quills.*]

UNDERWOOD [*dryly*]. Thanks, if you can spare me one. [*He takes a quill.*] What about lunch, Enid?

ENID [*stopping at the double doors and looking back*]. We're going to have lunch here, in the drawing-room, so you need n't hurry with your meeting.

[WANKLIN and WILDER bow, and she goes out.]

SCANTLEBURY [*rousing himself, suddenly*]. Ah! Lunch! That hotel — Dreadful! Did you try the whitebait last night? Fried fat!

WILDER. Past twelve! Are n't you going to read the minutes, Tench?

TENCH [*looking for the CHAIRMAN'S assent, reads in a rapid and monotonous voice*]. "At a Board Meeting held the 31st of January at the Company's Offices, 512 Cannon Street, E.C. Present — Mr. Anthony in the chair, Messrs. F. H. Wilder, William Scantlebury, Oliver Wanklin, and Edgar Anthony. Read letters from the Manager dated January 20th, 23d, 25th, 28th, relative to the strike at the Company's Works. Read letters to the Manager of January 21st, 24th, 26th, 29th. Read letter from Mr. Simon Harness, of the Central Union, asking for an interview with the Board. Read letter from the Men's Committee, signed David Roberts, James Green, John Bulgin, Henry Thomas, George Rous, desiring conference with the Board ; and it was resolved that a special Board Meeting be called for February 7th at the house of the Manager, for the purpose of discussing the situation with Mr. Simon Harness and the Men's Committee on the spot. Passed twelve transfers, signed and sealed nine certificates and one balance certificate."

[*He pushes the book over to the CHAIRMAN.*]

ANTHONY [*with a heavy sigh*]. If it 's your pleasure, sign the same.

[*He signs, moving the pen with difficulty.*]

WANKLIN. What 's the Union's game, Tench? They have n't made up their split with the men. What does Harness want this interview for?

TENCH. Hoping we shall come to a compromise, I think, sir; he 's having a meeting with the men this afternoon.

WILDER. Harness! Ah! He 's one of those cold-blooded, cool-headed chaps. I distrust them. I don't know that we did n't make a mistake to come down. What time 'll the men be here?

UNDERWOOD. Any time now.

WILDER. Well, if we 're not ready, they 'll have to wait — won't do them any harm to cool their heels a bit.

SCANTLEBURY [*slowly*]. Poor devils! It 's snowing. *What* weather!

UNDERWOOD [*with meaning slowness*]. This house 'll be the warmest place they 've been in this winter.

WILDER. Well, I hope we 're going to settle this business in time for me to catch the 6.30. I 've got to take my wife to Spain to-morrow. [*Chattily.*] My old father had a strike at his works in '69 ; just such a February as this. They wanted to shoot him.

WANKLIN. What! In the close season?

WILDER. By George, there was no close season for employers then! He used to go down to his office with a pistol in his pocket.

SCANTLEBURY [*faintly alarmed*]. Not seriously?

WILDER [*with finality*]. Ended in his shootin' one of 'em in the legs.

SCANTLEBURY [*unavoidably feeling his thigh*]. No? Which?

ANTHONY [*lifting the agenda paper*]. To consider the policy of the Board in relation to the strike.   [*There is a silence.*]

WILDER. It 's this infernal three-cornered duel — the Union, the men, and ourselves.

WANKLIN. We need n't consider the Union.

WILDER. It 's my experience that you 've always got to consider the Union, confound them! If the Union were going to withdraw their support from the men, as they 've done, why did they ever allow them to strike at all?

EDGAR. We've had that over a dozen times.

WILDER. Well, I've never understood it! It's beyond me. They talk of the engineers' and furnacemen's demands being excessive — so they are — but that's not enough to make the Union withdraw their support. What's behind it?

UNDERWOOD. Fear of strikes at Harper's and Tinewell's.

WILDER [*with triumph*]. Afraid of other strikes — now, that's a reason! Why could n't we have been told that before?

UNDERWOOD. You were.

TENCH. You were absent from the Board that day, sir.

SCANTLEBURY. The men must have seen they had no chance when the Union gave them up. It's madness.

UNDERWOOD. It's Roberts!

WILDER. Just our luck, the men finding a fanatical firebrand like Roberts for leader.

[*A pause.*]

WANKLIN [*looking at* ANTHONY]. Well?

WILDER [*breaking in fussily*]. It's a regular mess. I don't like the position we're in; I don't like it; I've said so for a long time. [*Looking at* WANKLIN.] When Wanklin and I came down here before Christmas it looked as if the men must collapse. You thought so too, Underwood.

UNDERWOOD. Yes.

WILDER. Well, they have n't! Here we are, going from bad to worse — losing our customers — shares going down!

SCANTLEBURY [*shaking his head*]. M'm! M'm!

WANKLIN. What loss have we made by this strike, Tench?

TENCH. Over fifty thousand, sir!

SCANTLEBURY [*pained*]. You don't say!

WILDER. We shall never get it back.

TENCH. No, sir.

WILDER. Who'd have supposed the men were going to stick out like this — nobody suggested that. [*Looking angrily at* TENCH.]

SCANTLEBURY [*shaking his head*]. I've never liked a fight — never shall.

ANTHONY. No surrender!

[*All look at him.*]

WILDER. Who wants to surrender? [ANTHONY *looks at him.*] I — I want to act reasonably. When the men sent Roberts up to the Board in December — then was the time. We ought to have humored him;

instead of that the Chairman — [*dropping his eyes before* ANTHONY'S] — er — we snapped his head off. We could have got them in then by a little tact.

ANTHONY. No compromise!

WILDER. There we are! This strike's been going on now since October, and as far as I can see it may last another six months. Pretty mess we shall be in by then. The only comfort is, the men'll be in a worse!

EDGAR. [*To* UNDERWOOD.] What sort of state are they really in, Frank?

UNDERWOOD [*without expression*]. Damnable!

WILDER. Well, who on earth would have thought they'd have held on like this without support!

UNDERWOOD. Those who know them.

WILDER. I defy any one to know them! And what about tin? Price going up daily. When we do get started we shall have to work off our contracts at the top of the market.

WANKLIN. What do you say to that, Chairman?

ANTHONY. Can't be helped!

WILDER. Shan't pay a dividend till goodness knows when!

SCANTLEBURY [*with emphasis*]. We ought to think of the shareholders. [*Turning heavily.*] Chairman, I say we ought to think of the shareholders. [ANTHONY *mutters.*] What's that?

TENCH. The Chairman says he *is* thinking of you, sir.

SCANTLEBURY [*sinking back into torpor*]. Cynic!

WILDER. It's past a joke. *I* don't want to go without a dividend for years if the Chairman does. We can't go on playing ducks and drakes with the Company's prosperity.

EDGAR [*rather ashamedly*]. I think we ought to consider the men.

[*All but* ANTHONY *fidget in their seats.*]

SCANTLEBURY [*with a sigh*]. We must n't think of our private feelings, young man. That'll never do.

EDGAR [*ironically*]. I'm not thinking of our feelings. I'm thinking of the men's.

WILDER. As to that — we're men of business.

WANKLIN. That *is* the little trouble.

EDGAR. There's no necessity for pushing things so far in the face of all this suffering — it's — it's cruel.

[*No one speaks, as though* EDGAR *had uncovered something whose existence no man prizing his self-respect could afford to recognize.*]

WANKLIN [*with an ironical smile*]. I'm afraid we must n't base our policy on luxuries like sentiment.

EDGAR. I detest this state of things.

ANTHONY. We did n't seek the quarrel.

EDGAR. I know that sir, but surely we 've gone far enough.

ANTHONY. No.   [*All look at one another.*]

WANKLIN. Luxuries apart, Chairman, we must look out what we 're doing.

ANTHONY. Give way to the men once and there 'll be no end to it.

WANKLIN. I quite agree, but — [AN-THONY *shakes his head.*] You make it a question of bedrock principle ? [ANTHONY *nods.*] Luxuries again, Chairman ! The shares are below par.

WILDER. Yes, and they 'll drop to a half when we pass the next dividend.

SCANTLEBURY [*with alarm*]. Come, come! Not so bad as that.

WILDER [*grimly*]. You 'll see ! [*Craning forward to catch* ANTHONY'S *speech.*] I did n't catch —

TENCH [*hesitating*]. The Chairman says, sir, " Fais que — que — devra —

EDGAR [*sharply*]. My father says : " Do what we ought — and let things rip."

WILDER. Tcha !

SCANTLEBURY [*throwing up his hands*]. The Chairman 's a Stoic — I always said the Chairman was a Stoic.

WILDER. Much good that 'll do us.

WANKLIN [*suavely*]. Seriously, Chairman, are you going to let the ship sink under you, for the sake of — a principle ?

ANTHONY. She won't sink.

SCANTLEBURY [*with alarm*]. Not while I 'm on the Board I hope.

ANTHONY [*with a twinkle*]. Better rat, Scantlebury.

SCANTLEBURY. What a man !

ANTHONY. I 've always fought them ; I 've never been beaten yet.

WANKLIN. We 're with you in theory, Chairman. But we 're not all made of cast-iron.

ANTHONY. We 've only to hold on.

WILDER [*rising and going to the fire*]. And go to the devil as fast as we can !

ANTHONY. Better go to the devil than give in !

WILDER [*fretfully*]. That may suit you, sir, but it does n't suit me, or any one else I should think.

[ANTHONY *looks him in the face — a silence.*]

EDGAR. I don't see how we can get over it that to go on like this means starvation to the men's wives and families.

[WILDER *turns abruptly to the fire, and* SCANTLEBURY *puts out a hand to push the idea away.*]

WANKLIN. I'm afraid again that sounds a little sentimental.

EDGAR. Men of business are excused from decency, you think ?

WILDER. Nobody's more sorry for the men than I am, but if they [*lashing himself*] choose to be such a pig-headed lot, it's nothing to do with us; we 've quite enough on *our* hands to think of ourselves and the shareholders.

EDGAR [*irritably*]. It won't kill the shareholders to miss a dividend or two; I don't see that *that 's* reason enough for knuckling under.

SCANTLEBURY [*with grave discomfort*]. You talk very lightly of your dividends, young man; I don't know where we are.

WILDER. There 's only one sound way of looking at it. We can't go on ruining *ourselves* with this strike.

ANTHONY. No caving in !

SCANTLEBURY [*with a gesture of despair*]. Look at him !

[ANTHONY *is leaning back in his chair. They do look at him.*]

WILDER [*returning to his seat*]. Well, all I can say is, if that 's the Chairman's view, I don't know what we 've come down here for.

ANTHONY. To tell the men that we 've got nothing for them — [*Grimly.*] They won't believe it till they hear it spoken in plain English.

WILDER. H'm ! Should n't be a bit surprised if that brute Roberts had n't got us down here with the very same idea. I hate a man with a grievance.

EDGAR [*resentfully*]. We did n't pay him enough for his discovery. I always said that at the time.

WILDER. We paid him five hundred and a bonus of two hundred three years later. If that's not enough! What does he want, for goodness' sake?

TENCH [complainingly]. Company made a hundred thousand out of his brains, and paid him seven hundred — that's the way he goes on, sir.

WILDER. The man's a rank agitator! Look here, I hate the Unions. But now we've got Harness here let's get him to settle the whole thing.

ANTHONY. No! [Again they look at him.]

UNDERWOOD. Roberts won't let the men assent to that.

SCANTLEBURY. Fanatic! Fanatic!

WILDER [looking at ANTHONY]. And not the only one!

[FROST enters from the hall.]

FROST. [To ANTHONY.] Mr. Harness from the Union, waiting, sir. The men are here too, sir.

[ANTHONY nods. UNDERWOOD goes to the door, returning with HARNESS, a pale, clean-shaven man with hollow cheeks, quick eyes, and lantern jaw — FROST has retired.]

UNDERWOOD [pointing to TENCH's chair]. Sit there next the Chairman, Harness, won't you?

[At HARNESS's appearance, the Board have drawn together, as it were, and turned a little to him, like cattle at a dog.]

HARNESS [with a sharp look round, and a bow]. Thanks! [He sits — his accent is slightly nasal.] Well, gentlemen, we're going to do business at last, I hope.

WILDER. Depends on what you call business, Harness. Why don't you make the men come in?

HARNESS [sardonically]. The men are far more in the right than you are. The question with us is whether we shan't begin to support them again.

[He ignores them all, except ANTHONY, to whom he turns in speaking.]

ANTHONY. Support them if you like; we'll put in free labor and have done with it.

HARNESS. That won't do, Mr. Anthony. You can't get free labor, and you know it.

ANTHONY. We shall see that.

HARNESS. I'm quite frank with you. We were forced to withhold our support from your men because some of their demands are in excess of current rates. I expect to make them withdraw those demands to-day: if they do, take it straight from me, gentlemen, we shall back them again at once. Now, I want to see something fixed upon before I go back to-night. Can't we have done with this old-fashioned tug-of-war business? What good's it doing you? Why don't you recognize once for all that these people are men like yourselves, and want what's good for them just as you want what's good for you — [Bitterly.] Your motor-cars, and champagne, and eight-course dinners.

ANTHONY. If the men will come in, we'll do something for them.

HARNESS [ironically]. Is that your opinion too, sir — and yours — and yours? [The Directors do not answer.] Well, all I can say is : it's a kind of high and mighty aristocratic tone I thought we'd grown out of — seems I was mistaken.

ANTHONY. It's the tone the men use. Remains to be seen which can hold out longest — they without us, or we without them.

HARNESS. As business men, I wonder you're not ashamed of this waste of force, gentlemen. You know what it'll all end in.

ANTHONY. What?

HARNESS. Compromise — it always does.

SCANTLEBURY. Can't you persuade the men that their interests are the same as ours?

HARNESS [turning, ironically]. I could persuade them of that, sir, if they were.

WILDER. Come, Harness, you're a clever man, you don't believe all the Socialistic claptrap that's talked nowadays. There's no real difference between their interests and ours.

HARNESS. There's just one very simple question I'd like to put to you. Will you pay your men one penny more than they force you to pay them? [WILDER is silent.]

WANKLIN [chiming in]. I humbly thought that not to pay more than was necessary was the A B C of commerce.

HARNESS [with irony]. Yes, that seems to be the A B C of commerce, sir; and the A B C of commerce is between your interests and the men's.

SCANTLEBURY [whispering]. We ought to arrange something.

HARNESS [*dryly*]. Am I to understand then, gentlemen, that your Board is going to make no concessions ?

[WANKLIN *and* WILDER *bend forward as if to speak, but stop.*]

ANTHONY [*nodding*]. None.

[WANKLIN *and* WILDER *again bend forward, and* SCANTLEBURY *gives an unexpected grunt.*]

HARNESS. You were about to say something, I believe ?

[*But* SCANTLEBURY *says nothing.*]

EDGAR [*looking up suddenly*]. We're sorry for the state of the men.

HARNESS [*icily*]. The men have no use for your pity, sir. What they want is justice.

ANTHONY. Then let *them* be just.

HARNESS. For that word "just" read "humble," Mr. Anthony. Why should they be humble ? Barring the accident of money, are n't they as good as you ?

ANTHONY. Cant !

HARNESS. Well, I've been five years in America. It colors a man's notions.

SCANTLEBURY [*suddenly, as though avenging his uncompleted grunt*]. Let's have the men in and hear what they've got to say !

[ANTHONY *nods, and* UNDERWOOD *goes out by the single door.*]

HARNESS [*dryly*]. As I'm to have an interview with them this afternoon, gentlemen, I'll ask you to postpone your final decision till that's over.

[*Again* ANTHONY *nods, and taking up his glass drinks.* UNDERWOOD *comes in again, followed by* ROBERTS, GREEN, BULGIN, THOMAS, ROUS. *They file in, hat in hand, and stand silent in a row.* ROBERTS *is lean, of middle height, with a slight stoop. He has a little rat-gnawed, brown-gray beard, mustaches, high cheek-bones, hollow cheeks, small fiery eyes. He wears an old and grease-stained blue serge suit, and carries an old bowler hat. He stands nearest the Chairman.* GREEN, *next to him, has a clean, worn face, with a small gray goatee beard and drooping mustaches, iron spectacles, and mild, straightforward eyes. He wears an overcoat, green with age, and a linen collar. Next to him is* BULGIN, *a tall, strong man, with a dark mustache,*

and fighting jaw, wearing a red muffler, who keeps changing his cap from one hand to the other. Next to him is THOMAS, *an old man with a gray mustache, full beard, and weatherbeaten, bony face, whose overcoat discloses a lean, plucked-looking neck. On his right,* ROUS *the youngest of the five, looks like a soldier; he has a glitter in his eyes.*]

UNDERWOOD [*pointing*]. There are some chairs there against the wall, Roberts ; won't you draw them up and sit down ?

ROBERTS. Thank you, Mr. Underwood — we 'll stand — in the presence of the Board. [*He speaks in a biting and staccato voice, rolling his r's, pronouncing his a's like an Italian a, and his consonants short and crisp.*] How are you, Mr. Harness ? Did n't expect t' have the pleasure of seeing you till this afternoon.

HARNESS [*steadily*]. We shall meet again then, Roberts.

ROBERTS. Glad to hear that ; we shall have some news for you to take to your people.

ANTHONY. What do the men want ?

ROBERTS [*acidly*]. Beg pardon, I don't quite catch the Chairman's remark.

TENCH [*from behind the Chairman's chair*]. The Chairman wishes to know what the men have to say.

ROBERTS. It 's what the Board has to say we 've come to hear. It 's for the Board to speak first.

ANTHONY. The Board has nothing to say.

ROBERTS [*looking along the line of men*]. In that case we 're wasting the Directors' time. We 'll be taking our feet off this pretty carpet.

[*He turns, the men move slowly, as though hypnotically influenced.*]

WANKLIN [*suavely*]. Come, Roberts, you did n't give us this long cold journey for the pleasure of saying that.

THOMAS. [*A pure Welshman.*] No, sir, an' what I say iss—

ROBERTS [*bitingly*]. Go on, Henry Thomas, go on. You 're better able to speak to the — Directors than me.

[THOMAS *is silent.*]

TENCH. The Chairman means, Roberts, that it was the men who asked for the conference, the Board wish to hear what they have to say.

ROBERTS. Gad ! If I was to begin to tell ye all they have to say, I would n't be finished to-day. And there 'd be some that 'd wish they 'd never left their London palaces.

HARNESS. What 's your proposition, man ? Be reasonable.

ROBERTS. You want reason, Mr. Harness ? Take a look round this afternoon before the meeting. [*He looks at the men; no sound escapes them.*] You 'll see some very pretty scenery.

HARNESS. All right, my friend; you won't put me off.

ROBERTS. [*To the men.*] We shan't put Mr. Harness off. Have some champagne with your lunch, Mr. Harness; you 'll want it, sir.

HARNESS. Come, get to business, man !

THOMAS. What we 're asking, look you, is just simple justice.

ROBERTS [*venomously*]. Justice from London ? What are you talking about, Henry Thomas ? Have you gone silly ? [THOMAS *is silent.*] We know very well what we are — discontented dogs — never satisfied. What did the Chairman tell me up in London ? That I did n't know what I was talking about. I was a foolish, uneducated man, that knew nothing of the wants of the men I spoke for.

EDGAR. Do please keep to the point.

ANTHONY [*holding up his hand*]. There can only be one master, Roberts.

ROBERTS. Then, be Gad, it 'll be us.

[*There is a silence;* ANTHONY *and* ROBERTS *stare at one another.*]

UNDERWOOD. If you 've nothing to say to the Directors, Roberts, perhaps you 'll let Green or Thomas speak for the men.

[GREEN *and* THOMAS *look anxiously at* ROBERTS, *at each other, and the other men.*]

GREEN. [*An Englishman.*] If I 'd been listened to, gentlemen —

THOMAS. What I 'fe got to say iss what we 'fe all got to say —

ROBERTS. Speak for yourself, Henry Thomas.

SCANTLEBURY [*with a gesture of deep spiritual discomfort*]. Let the poor men call their souls their own !

ROBERTS. Aye, they shall keep their souls, for it 's not much body that you 've left them, Mr. [*with biting emphasis, as*

though the word were an offense] Scantlebury ! [*To the men.*] Well, will you speak, or shall I speak for you ?

ROUS [*suddenly*]. Speak out, Roberts, or leave it to others.

ROBERTS [*ironically*]. Thank you, George Rous. [*Addressing himself to* ANTHONY.] The Chairman and Board of Directors have honored us by leaving London and coming all this way to hear what we 've got to say; it would not be polite to keep them any longer waiting.

WILDER. Well, thank God for that !

ROBERTS. Ye will not dare to thank Him when I have done, Mr. Wilder, for all your piety. May be your God up in London has no time to listen to the working man. I 'm told He is a wealthy God; but if he listens to what I tell Him, He will know more than ever He learned in Kensington.

HARNESS. Come, Roberts, you have your own God. Respect the God of other men.

ROBERTS. That 's right, sir. We have another God down here; I doubt He is rather different to Mr. Wilder's. Ask Henry Thomas; he will tell you whether his God and Mr. Wilder's are the same.

[THOMAS *lifts his hand, and cranes his head as though to prophesy.*]

WANKLIN. For goodness' sake, let 's keep to the point, Roberts.

ROBERTS. I rather think it is the point, Mr. Wanklin. If you can get the God of Capital to walk through the streets of Labor, and pay attention to what he sees, you 're a brighter man than I take you for, for all that you 're a Radical.

ANTHONY. Attend to me, Roberts ! [*Roberts is silent.*] You are here to speak for the men, as I am here to speak for the Board. [*He looks slowly round.* WILDER, WANKLIN, *and* SCANTLEBURY *make movements of uneasiness, and* EDGAR *gazes at the floor. A faint smile comes on* HARNESS's *face.*] Now then, what is it ?

ROBERTS. Right, sir ! [*Throughout all that follows, he and* ANTHONY *look fixedly upon each other. Men and Directors show in their various ways suppressed uneasiness, as though listening to words that they themselves would not have spoken.*] The men can't afford to travel up to London; and they don't trust you to believe what they say in black and white. They know what the post is [*he darts a look at* UNDERWOOD *and* TENCH], and what Directors' meetings are: "Refer it to the manager — let the manager advise us on the men's condition. Can we squeeze them a little more?"

UNDERWOOD [*in a low voice*]. Don't hit below the belt, Roberts!

ROBERTS. Is it below the belt, Mr. Underwood? The men know. When I came up to London, I told you the position straight. An' what came of it? I was told I did n't know what I was talkin' about. I can't afford to travel up to London to be told that again.

ANTHONY. What have you to say for the men?

ROBERTS. I have this to say — and first as to their condition. Ye shall 'ave no need to go and ask your manager. Ye can't squeeze them any more. Every man of us is well-nigh starving. [*A surprised murmur rises from the men.* ROBERTS *looks round.*] Ye wonder why I tell ye that? Every man of us is going short. We can't be no worse off than we've been these weeks past. Ye need n't think that by waiting ye 'll drive us to come in. We 'll die first, the whole lot of us. The men have sent for ye to know, once and for all, whether ye are going to grant them their demands. I see the sheet of paper in the Secretary's hand. [TENCH *moves nervously.*] That 's it, I think, Mr. Tench. It 's not very large.

TENCH [*nodding*]. Yes.

ROBERTS. There 's not one sentence of writing on that paper that we can do without. [*A movement amongst the men.* ROBERTS *turns on them sharply.*] Is n't that so? [*The men assent reluctantly.* ANTHONY *takes from* TENCH *the paper and peruses it.*] Not one single sentence. All those demands are fair. We have not asked anything that we are not entitled to ask. What I said up in London, I say again now: there is not anything on that piece of paper that a just man should not ask, and a just man give. [*A pause.*]

ANTHONY. There is not one single demand on this paper that we will grant.

[*In the stir that follows on these words,* ROBERTS *watches the Directors and* ANTHONY *the men.* WILDER *gets up abruptly and goes over to the fire.*]

ROBERTS. D' ye mean that?

ANTHONY. I do.

[WILDER *at the fire makes an emphatic movement of disgust.*]

ROBERTS [*noting it, with dry intensity*]. Ye best know whether the condition of the Company is any better than the condition of the men. [*Scanning the Directors' faces.*] Ye best know whether ye can afford your tyranny — but this I tell ye: If ye think the men will give way the least part of an inch, ye 're making the worst mistake ye ever made. [*He fixes his eyes on* SCANTLEBURY.] Ye think because the Union is not supporting us — more shame to it! — that we 'll be coming on our knees to you one fine morning. Ye think because the men have got their wives an' families to think of — that it 's just the question of a week or two —

ANTHONY. It would be better if you did not speculate so much on what we think.

ROBERTS. Aye! It 's not much profit to us! I will say this for you, Mr. Anthony — ye know your own mind! [*Staring at* ANTHONY.] I can reckon on ye!

ANTHONY [*ironically*]. I am obliged to you!

ROBERTS. And I know mine. I tell ye this: The men will send their wives and families where the country will have to keep them; an' they will starve sooner than give way. I advise ye, Mr. Anthony, to prepare yourself for the worst that can happen to your Company. We are not so ignorant as you might suppose. We know the way the cat is jumping. Your position is not all that it might be — not exactly!

ANTHONY. Be good enough to allow us to judge of our position for ourselves. Go back, and reconsider your own.

ROBERTS [*stepping forward*]. Mr. Anthony, you are not a young man now; from the time I remember anything ye have been an enemy to every man that has come into your works. I don't say that ye 're a mean man, or a cruel man, but ye 've grudged them the say of any word in their own fate. Ye 've fought them down four times. I 've heard ye say ye love a fight — mark my words — ye 're fighting the last fight ye 'll ever fight —

[TENCH *touches* ROBERTS's *sleeve.*]

UNDERWOOD. Roberts! Roberts!

ROBERTS. Roberts! Roberts! I must n't speak my mind to the Chairman, but the Chairman may speak his mind to me!

WILDER. What are things coming to?

ANTHONY [*with a grim smile at* WILDER]. Go on, Roberts; say what you like!

ROBERTS [*after a pause*]. I have no
more to say.

ANTHONY. The meeting stands adjourned
to five o'clock.

WANKLIN [*in a low voice to* UNDERWOOD].
We shall never settle anything like this.

ROBERTS [*bitingly*]. We thank the Chairman and Board of Directors for their
gracious hearing.

[*He moves towards the door; the men
cluster together stupefied; then
ROUS, throwing up his head, passes
ROBERTS and goes out. The others
follow.*]

ROBERTS [*with his hand on the door —
maliciously*]. Good-day, gentlemen !

[*He goes out.*]

HARNESS [*ironically*]. I congratulate you
on the conciliatory spirit that 's been displayed. With your permission, gentlemen,
I 'll be with you again at half past five.
Good-morning !

[*He bows slightly, rests his eyes on
ANTHONY, who returns his stare
unmoved, and, followed by UNDER-
WOOD, goes out. There is a moment
of uneasy silence. UNDERWOOD
reappears in the doorway.*]

WILDER [*with emphatic disgust*]. Well !

[*The double doors are opened.*]

ENID [*standing in the doorway*]. Lunch is
ready.

[*EDGAR, getting up abruptly, walks
out past his sister.*]

WILDER. Coming to lunch, Scantlebury ?

SCANTLEBURY [*rising heavily*]. I suppose
so, I suppose so. It 's the only thing we
can do. [*They go out through the double doors.*]

WANKLIN [*in a low voice*]. Do you
really mean to fight to a finish, Chairman ?

[*ANTHONY nods.*]

WANKLIN. Take care ! The essence of
things is to know when to stop.

[*ANTHONY does not answer.*]

WANKLIN [*very gravely*]. This way disaster lies. The ancient Trojans were fools
to your father, Mrs. Underwood.

[*He goes out through the double doors.*]

ENID. I want to speak to father, Frank.

[*UNDERWOOD follows WANKLIN out.
TENCH, passing round the table, is
restoring order to the scattered pens
and papers.*]

ENID. Are n't you coming, Dad ?

[*ANTHONY shakes his head. ENID
looks meaningly at TENCH.*]

ENID. Won't you go and have some
lunch, Mr. Tench ?

TENCH [*with papers in his hand*]. Thank
you, ma'am, thank you !

[*He goes slowly, looking back.*]

ENID [*shutting the doors*]. I do hope it 's
settled, father !

ANTHONY. No !

ENID [*very disappointed*]. Oh ! Have n't
you done anything ?

[*ANTHONY shakes his head.*]

ENID. Frank says they all want to come
to a compromise, really, except that man
Roberts.

ANTHONY. *I* don't.

ENID. It 's such a horrid position for us.
If you were the wife of the manager, and
lived down here, and saw it all. You can't
realize, Dad !

ANTHONY. Indeed ?

ENID. We see *all* the distress. You remember my maid Annie, who married Roberts ? [ANTHONY *nods.*] It 's so wretched,
her heart 's weak ; since the strike began,
she has n't even been getting proper food.
I know it for a fact, father.

ANTHONY. Give her what she wants,
poor woman !

ENID. Roberts won't let her take anything from *us*.

ANTHONY [*staring before him*]. I can't
be answerable for the men's obstinacy.

ENID. They 're all suffering. Father !
Do stop it, for my sake !

ANTHONY [*with a keen look at her*]. You
don't understand, my dear.

ENID. If I were on the Board, I 'd do
something.

ANTHONY. What would you do ?

ENID. It 's because you can't bear to give
way. It 's so —

ANTHONY. Well ?

ENID. So unnecessary.

ANTHONY. What do *you* know about necessity ? Read your novels, play your music, talk your talk, but don't try and tell
me what 's at the bottom of a struggle like
this

ENID. I live down here and see it.

ANTHONY. What do you imagine stands
between you and your class and these men
that you 're so sorry for ?

ENID [*coldly*]. I don't know what you
mean, father.

ANTHONY. In a few years you and your

children would be down in the condition
they 're in, but for those who have the eyes
to see things as they are and the backbone
to stand up for themselves.

ENID. You don't know the state the men
are in.

ANTHONY. I know it well enough.

ENID. You don't, father; if you did, you
would n't —

ANTHONY. It 's you who don't know the
simple facts of the position. What sort of
mercy do you suppose you 'd get if no one
stood between you and the continual demands of labor? This sort of mercy —
[*He puts his hand up to his throat and
squeezes it.*] First would go your sentiments, my dear; then your culture, and
your comforts would be going all the
time!

ENID. I don't believe in barriers between
classes.

ANTHONY. You — don't — believe — in
— barriers — between the classes?

ENID [*coldly*]. And I don't know what
that has to do with this question.

ANTHONY. It will take a generation or
two for you to understand.

ENID. It 's only you and Roberts, father,
and you know it! [ANTHONY *thrusts out
his lower lip.*] It 'll ruin the Company.

ANTHONY. Allow me to judge of that.

ENID [*resentfully*]. I won't stand by and
let poor Annie Roberts suffer like this!
And think of the children, father! I warn
you.

ANTHONY [*with a grim smile*]. What do
you propose to do?

ENID. That 's my affair.

[ANTHONY *only looks at her.*]

ENID [*in a changed voice, stroking his
sleeve*]. Father, you *know* you ought n't to
have this strain on you — you know what
Dr. Fisher said!

ANTHONY. No old man can afford to
listen to old women.

ENID. But you *have* done enough, even if
it really is such a matter of principle with
you.

ANTHONY. You think so?

ENID. Don't, Dad! [*Her face works.*] You
— you might think of *us*!

ANTHONY. I am.

ENID. It 'll break you down.

ANTHONY [*slowly*]. My dear, I am not
going to funk; on that you may rely.

[*Reënter* TENCH *with papers; he glances at
them, then plucking up courage.*]

TENCH. Beg pardon, madam, I think
I 'd rather see these papers were disposed
of before I get my lunch.

[ENID, *after an impatient glance at
him, looks at her father, turns suddenly, and goes into the drawing-
room.*]

TENCH [*holding the papers and a pen to
ANTHONY, very nervously*]. Would you sign
these for me, please, sir?

[ANTHONY *takes the pen and signs.*]

TENCH [*standing with a sheet of blotting-
paper behind* EDGAR'S *chair, begins speaking nervously*]. I owe my position to you,
sir.

ANTHONY. Well?

TENCH. I 'm obliged to see everything
that 's going on, sir; I — I depend upon the
Company entirely. If anything were to happen to it, it 'd be disastrous for me. [AN-
THONY *nods.*] And, of course, my wife 's
just had another; and so it makes me
doubly anxious just now. And the rates are
really terrible down our way.

ANTHONY [*with grim amusement*]. Not
more terrible than they are up mine.

TENCH. No, sir? [*Very nervously.*] I
know the Company means a great deal to
you, sir.

ANTHONY. It does; I founded it.

TENCH. Yes, sir. If the strike goes on
it 'll be very serious. I think the Directors
are beginning to realize that, sir.

ANTHONY [*ironically*]. Indeed?

TENCH. I know you hold very strong
views, sir, and it 's always your habit to
look things in the face; but I don't think
the Directors — like it, sir, now they — they
see it.

ANTHONY [*grimly*]. Nor you, it seems.

TENCH [*with the ghost of a smile*]. No,
sir; of course I 've got my children, and
my wife 's delicate; in my position I *have*
to think of these things. [ANTHONY *nods.*]
It was n't *that* I was going to say, sir, if
you 'll excuse me —   [*Hesitates.*]

ANTHONY. Out with it, then!

TENCH. I know — from my own father,
sir, that when you get on in life you do feel
things dreadfully —

ANTHONY [*almost paternally*]. Come, out
with it, Tench!

TENCH. I don't like to say it, sir.

ANTHONY [*stonily*]. You must.

TENCH [*after a pause, desperately bolting
it out*]. I think the Directors are going to
throw you over, sir.

ANTHONY. [*Sits in silence.*] Ring the
bell!

[TENCH *nervously rings the bell and
stands by the fire.*]

TENCH. Excuse me for saying such a
thing. I was *only* thinking of you, sir.

[FROST *enters from the hall, he comes
to the foot of the table, and looks at*
ANTHONY; TENCH *covers his nervousness by arranging papers.*]

ANTHONY. Bring me a whiskey and soda.

FROST. Anything to eat, sir?

[ANTHONY *shakes his head.* FROST
*goes to the sideboard, and prepares
the drink.*]

TENCH [*in a low voice, almost supplicating*]. If you *could* see your way, sir, it
would be a great relief to my mind, it would
indeed. [*He looks up at* ANTHONY, *who has
not moved.*] It does make me so very anxious. I haven't slept properly for weeks,
sir, and that's a fact.

[ANTHONY *looks in his face, then
slowly shakes his head.*]

TENCH [*disheartened*]. No, sir?

[*He goes on arranging papers.*
FROST *places the whiskey and soda
on a salver and puts it down by*
ANTHONY's *right hand. He stands
away, looking gravely at* AN-
THONY.]

FROST. *Nothing* I can get you, sir? [AN-
THONY *shakes his head.*] You're aware, sir,
of what the doctor said, sir?

ANTHONY. I am.

[*A pause.* FROST *suddenly moves
closer to him, and speaks in a low
voice.*]

FROST. This strike, sir; puttin' all this
strain on you. Excuse me, sir, is it — is
it worth it, sir? [ANTHONY *mutters some
words that are inaudible.*] Very good, sir!

[*He turns and goes out into the hall.*
TENCH *makes two attempts to
speak; but meeting his Chairman's
gaze he drops his eyes, and, turning
dismally, he too goes out.* ANTHONY
*is left alone. He grips the glass,
tilts it, and drinks deeply; then
sets it down with a deep and rumbling sigh, and leans back in his
chair.*]

ACT II

SCENE I

It is half past three. In the kitchen of ROB-
ERTS's *cottage a meager little fire is burning.
The room is clean and tidy, very barely furnished, with a brick floor and white-washed
walls, much stained with smoke. There is a kettle on the fire. A door opposite the fireplace
opens inward from a snowy street. On the
wooden table are a cup and saucer, a teapot,
knife, and plate of bread and cheese. Close to
the fireplace in an old armchair, wrapped in a
rug, sits* MRS. ROBERTS, *a thin and dark-haired
woman about thirty-five, with patient eyes. Her
hair is not done up, but tied back with a piece of
ribbon. By the fire, too, is* MRS. YEO; *a red-
haired, broad-faced person. Sitting near the
table is* MRS. ROUS, *an old lady, ashen-white,
with silver hair; by the door, standing, as if
about to go, is* MRS. BULGIN, *a little, pale,
pinched-up woman. In a chair, with her elbows
resting on the table, and her face resting in her
hands, sits* MADGE THOMAS, *a good-looking
girl of twenty-two, with high cheekbones, deep-
set eyes, and dark untidy hair. She is listening
to the talk, but she neither speaks nor moves.*

MRS. YEO. So he give me a sixpence,
and that's the first bit o' money *I* seen this
week. There an't much 'eat to this fire.
Come and warm yerself, Mrs. Rous, you're
lookin' as white as the snow, you are.

MRS. ROUS [*shivering — placidly*]. Ah!
but the winter my old man was took was
the proper winter. Seventy-nine that was,
when none of you was hardly born — not
Madge Thomas, nor Sue Bulgin. [*Looking
at them in turn.*] Annie Roberts, 'ow old
were you, dear?

MRS. ROBERTS. Seven, Mrs. Rous.

MRS. ROUS. Seven — well, ther'! A tiny
little thing!

MRS. YEO [*aggressively*]. Well, I was
ten myself, I remembers it.

MRS. ROUS [*placidly*]. The Company
hadn't been started three years. Father
was workin' on the acid, that's 'ow he
got 'is pisoned leg. I kep' sayin' to 'im,
"Father, you've got a pisoned leg."
"Well," 'e said, "mother, pison or no pison,
I can't afford to go a-layin' up." An' two
days after, he was on 'is back, and never
got up again. It was Providence! There
wasn't none o' these Compensation Acts
then.

MRS. YEO. Ye had n't no strike that winter ! [*With grim humor.*] This winter 's 'ard enough for me. Mrs. Roberts, you don't want no 'arder winter, do you ? Would n't seem natural to 'ave a dinner, would it, Mrs. Bulgin ?

MRS. BULGIN. We 've had bread and tea last four days.

MRS. YEO. You got that Friday's laundry job ?

MRS. BULGIN [*dispiritedly*]. They said they 'd give it me, but when I went last Friday, they were full up. I got to go again next week.

MRS. YEO. Ah ! There 's too many after that. I send Yeo out on the ice to put on the gentry's skates an' pick up what 'e can. Stops 'im from broodin' about the 'ouse.

MRS. BULGIN [*in a desolate, matter-of-fact voice*]. Leavin' out the men — it 's bad enough with the children. I keep 'em in bed, they don't get so hungry when they 're not running about ; but they 're that restless in bed they worry your life out.

MRS. YEO. You 're lucky they 're all so small. It 's the goin' to school that makes 'em 'ungry. Don't Bulgin give you *any-thin'* ?

MRS. BULGIN. [*Shakes her head, then, as though by afterthought.*] Would if he could, I s'pose.

MRS. YEO [*sardonically*]. What ! 'Ave n't 'e got no shares in the Company ?

MRS. ROUS [*rising with tremulous cheerfulness*]. Well, good-bye, Annie Roberts, I 'm going along home.

MRS. ROBERTS. Stay an' have a cup of tea, Mrs. Rous ?

MRS. ROUS [*with the faintest smile*]. Roberts 'll want 'is tea when he comes in. I 'll just go an' get to bed ; it 's warmer there than anywhere.

[*She moves very shakily towards the door.*]

MRS. YEO [*rising and giving her an arm*]. Come on, mother, take my arm ; we 're all goin' the same way.

MRS. ROUS [*taking the arm*]. Thank you, my dearies !

[THEY *go out, followed by* MRS. BULGIN.]

MADGE [*moving for the first time*]. There, Annie, you see that ! I told George Rous, " Don't think to have my company till you 've made an end of all this trouble. You

ought to be ashamed," I said, " with your own mother looking like a ghost, and not a stick to put on the fire. So long as you 're able to fill your pipes, you 'll let us starve." " I 'll take my oath, Madge," he said, " I 've not had smoke nor drink these three weeks ! " " Well, then, why do you go on with it ? " " I can't go back on Roberts ! " . . . That 's it ! Roberts, always Roberts ! " They 'd all drop it but for him. When *he* talks it 's the devil that comes into them. [*A silence.* MRS. ROBERTS *makes a movement of pain.*] Ah ! *You* don't want him beaten ! He 's your man. With everybody like their own shadows ! [*She makes a gesture towards* MRS. ROBERTS.] If Rous wants me he must give up Roberts. If *he* gave him up — they all would. They 're only waiting for a lead. Father 's against him — they 're all against him in their hearts.

MRS. ROBERTS. You won't beat Roberts !

[*They look silently at each other.*]

MADGE. Won't I ? The cowards — when their own mothers and their own children don't know where to turn.

MRS. ROBERTS. Madge !

MADGE [*looking searchingly at* MRS. ROBERTS]. I wonder he can look *you* in the face. [*She squats before the fire, with her hands out to the flame.*] Harness is here again. They 'll have to make up their minds to-day.

MRS. ROBERTS [*in a soft, slow voice, with a slight West-country burr*]. Roberts will never give up the furnacemen and engineers. 'T would n't be right.

MADGE. You can't deceive me. It 's just his pride.

[*A tapping at the door is heard, the women turn as* ENID *enters. She wears a round fur cap, and a jacket of squirrel's fur. She closes the door behind her.*]

ENID. Can I come in, Annie ?

MRS. ROBERTS [*flinching*]. Miss Enid ! Give Mrs. Underwood a chair, Madge !

[MADGE *gives* ENID *the chair she has been sitting on.*]

ENID. Thank you ! [*To* MRS. ROBERTS.] Are you any better ?

MRS. ROBERTS. Yes, m'm ; thank you, m'm.

ENID [*looking at the sullen* MADGE *as though requesting her departure*]. Why did you send back the jelly ? I call that really wicked of you !

MRS. ROBERTS. Thank you, m'm, I'd no need for it.

ENID. Of course! It was Roberts's doing, was n't it? How can he let all this suffering go on amongst you?

MADGE [*suddenly*]. What suffering?

ENID [*surprised*]. I beg your pardon!

MADGE. Who said there was suffering?

MRS. ROBERTS. Madge!

MADGE [*throwing her shawl over her head*]. Please to let us keep ourselves to ourselves. We don't want you coming here and spying on us.

ENID [*confronting her, but without rising*]. I did n't speak to *you.*

MADGE [*in a low, fierce voice*]. Keep your kind feelings to yourself. You think you can come amongst us, but you 're mistaken. Go back and tell the Manager that.

ENID [*stonily*]. This is not your house.

MADGE [*turning to the door*]. No, it is not my house; keep clear of my house, Mrs. Underwood.

[*She goes out.* ENID *taps her fingers on the table.*]

MRS. ROBERTS. Please to forgive Madge Thomas, m'm; she 's a bit upset to-day.

[*A pause.*]

ENID [*looking at her*]. Oh, I think they 're so *stupid*, all of them.

MRS. ROBERTS [*with a faint smile*]. Yes, m'm.

ENID. Is Roberts out?

MRS. ROBERTS. Yes, m'm.

ENID. It is *his doing* that they don't come to an agreement. Now is n't it, Annie?

MRS. ROBERTS [*softly, with her eyes on* ENID, *and moving the fingers of one hand continually on her breast*]. They do say that your father, m'm —

ENID. My father 's getting an old man, and you know what old men are.

MRS. ROBERTS. I am sorry, m'm.

ENID [*more softly*]. I don't expect *you* to feel sorry, Annie. I know it 's his fault as well as Roberts's.

MRS. ROBERTS. I'm sorry for any one that gets old, m'm; it 's dreadful to get old, and Mr. Anthony was such a fine old man I always used to think.

ENID [*impulsively*]. He always liked you, don't you remember? Look here, Annie, what can I do? I do so want to know. You don't get what you ought to have. [*Going to the fire, she takes the kettle off, and looks for coals.*] And you 're so naughty sending back the soup and things!

MRS. ROBERTS [*with a faint smile*]. Yes, m'm?

ENID [*resentfully*]. Why, you have n't even got coals?

MRS. ROBERTS. If you please, m'm, to put the kettle on again; Roberts won't have long for his tea when he comes in. He 's got to meet the men at four.

ENID [*putting the kettle on*]. That means he 'll lash them into a fury again. Can't you stop his going, Annie? [MRS. ROBERTS *smiles ironically.*] Have you tried? [*A silence.*] Does he know how ill you are?

MRS. ROBERTS. It 's only my weak 'eart, m'm.

ENID. You used to be so well when you were with us.

MRS. ROBERTS [*stiffening*]. Roberts is always good to me.

ENID. But you ought to have everything you want, and you have nothing!

MRS. ROBERTS [*appealingly*]. They tell me I don't look like a dyin' woman?

ENID. Of course you don't; if you could only have proper — Will you see my doctor if I send him to you? I 'm sure he 'd do you good.

MRS. ROBERTS [*with faint questioning*]. Yes, m'm.

ENID. Madge Thomas ought n't to come here; she only excites you. As if I did n't know what suffering there is amongst the men! I do feel for them dreadfully, but you know they *have* gone too far.

MRS. ROBERTS [*continually moving her fingers*]. They say there 's no other way to get better wages, m'm.

ENID [*earnestly*]. But, Annie, that 's why the Union won't help them. My husband 's very sympathetic with the men, but he says they 're not underpaid.

MRS. ROBERTS. No, m'm?

ENID. They never think how the Company could go on if we paid the wages they want.

MRS. ROBERTS [*with an effort*]. But the dividends having been so big, m'm.

ENID [*taken aback*]. You all seem to think the shareholders are rich men, but they 're not — most of them are really no better off than working men. [MRS. ROBERTS *smiles.*] They have to keep up appearances.

MRS. ROBERTS. Yes, m'm?

ENID. You don't have to pay rates and taxes, and a hundred other things that they do. If the men did n't spend such a lot in drink and betting they 'd be quite well off !

MRS. ROBERTS. They say, workin' so hard, they must have some pleasure.

ENID. But surely not low pleasure like that.

MRS. ROBERTS [a little resentfully]. Roberts never touches a drop ; and he 's never had a bet in his life.

ENID. Oh ! but he 's not a com— I mean he 's an engineer — a superior man.

MRS. ROBERTS. Yes, m'm. Roberts says they 've no chance of other pleasures.

ENID [musing]. Of course, I know it 's hard.

MRS. ROBERTS [with a spice of malice]. And they say gentlefolk 's just as bad.

ENID [with a smile]. I go as far as most people, Annie, but you know, yourself, that 's nonsense.

MRS. ROBERTS [with painful effort]. A lot o' the men never go near the Public ; but even they don't save but very little, and that goes if there 's illness.

ENID. But they 've got their clubs, have n't they ?

MRS. ROBERTS. The clubs only give up to eighteen shillin's a week, m'm, and it 's not much amongst a family. Roberts says workin' folk have always lived from hand to mouth. Sixpence to-day is worth more than a shillin' to-morrow, that 's what they say.

ENID. But that 's the spirit of gambling.

MRS. ROBERTS [with a sort of excitement]. Roberts says a working man's life is all a gamble, from the time 'e 's born to the time 'e dies. [ENID leans forward, interested. MRS. ROBERTS goes on with a growing excitement that culminates in the personal feeling of the last words.] He says, m'm, that when a working man's baby is born, it 's a toss-up from breath to breath whether it ever draws another, and so on all 'is life ; an' when he comes to be old, it 's the workhouse or the grave. He says that without a man is very near, and pinches and stints 'imself and 'is children to save, there can't be neither surplus nor security. That 's why he would n't have no children [she sinks back], not though I wanted them.

ENID. Yes, yes, I know !

MRS. ROBERTS. No you don't, m'm. You 've got your children, and you 'll never need to trouble for them.

ENID [gently]. You ought n't to be talking so much, Annie. [Then, in spite of herself.] But Roberts was paid a lot of money, was n't he, for discovering that process ?

MRS. ROBERTS [on the defensive]. All Roberts's savin's have gone. He 's always looked forward to this strike. He says he 's no right to a farthing when the others are suffering. 'T is n't so with all o' them ! Some don't seem to care no more than that — so long as they get their own.

ENID. I don't see how they can be expected to when they 're suffering like this. [In a changed voice.] But Roberts ought to think of you ! It 's all terrible ! The kettle 's boiling. Shall I make the tea ? [She takes the teapot, and, seeing tea there, pours water into it.] Won't you have a cup ?

MRS. ROBERTS. No, thank you, m'm. [She is listening, as though for footsteps.] I 'd sooner you did n't see Roberts, m'm, he gets so wild.

ENID. Oh ! but I must, Annie ; I 'll be quite calm, I promise.

MRS. ROBERTS. It 's life an' death to him, m'm.

ENID [very gently]. I 'll get him to talk to me outside, we won't excite you.

MRS. ROBERTS [faintly]. No, m'm.

[She gives a violent start. ROBERTS has come in, unseen.]

ROBERTS [removing his hat — with subtle mockery]. Beg pardon for coming in ; you 're engaged with a lady, I see.

ENID. Can I speak to you, Mr. Roberts ?

ROBERTS. Whom have I the pleasure of addressing, ma'am ?

ENID. But surely you know me ! I 'm Mrs. Underwood.

ROBERTS [with a bow of malice]. The daughter of our Chairman.

ENID [earnestly]. I 've come on purpose to speak to you ; will you come outside a minute ?   [She looks at MRS. ROBERTS.]

ROBERTS [hanging up his hat]. I have nothing to say, ma'am.

ENID. But I must speak to you, please.

[She moves towards the door.]

ROBERTS [with sudden venom]. I have not the time to listen !

MRS. ROBERTS. David !

ENID. Mr. Roberts, *please !*

ROBERTS [*taking off his overcoat*]. I am sorry to disoblige a lady — Mr. Anthony's daughter.

ENID [*wavering, then with sudden decision*]. Mr. Roberts, I know you've another meeting of the men. [ROBERTS *bows.*] I came to appeal to you. Please, please, try to come to some compromise ; give way a little, if it's only for your own sakes !

ROBERTS [*speaking to himself*]. The daughter of Mr. Anthony begs me to give way a little, if it's only for our own sakes !

ENID. For everybody's sake ; for your wife's sake.

ROBERTS. For my wife's sake, for everybody's sake — for the sake of Mr. Anthony.

ENID. Why are you so bitter against my father? He has never done anything to you.

ROBERTS. Has he not ?

ENID. He can't help his views, any more than you can help yours.

ROBERTS. I really didn't know that I had a right to views !

ENID. He's an old man, and you —

[*Seeing his eyes fixed on her, she stops.*]

ROBERTS [*without raising his voice*]. If I saw Mr. Anthony going to die, and I could save him by lifting my hand, I would not lift the little finger of it.

ENID. You — you —

[*She stops again, biting her lips.*]

ROBERTS. I would not, and that's flat !

ENID [*coldly*]. You don't mean what you say, and you know it !

ROBERTS. I mean every word of it.

ENID. But why ?

ROBERTS [*with a flash*]. Mr. Anthony stands for tyranny ! That's why !

ENID. Nonsense !

[MRS. ROBERTS *makes a movement as if to rise, but sinks back in her chair.*]

ENID [*with an impetuous movement*]. Annie !

ROBERTS. Please not to touch my wife !

ENID [*recoiling with a sort of horror*]. I believe — you are mad.

ROBERTS. The house of a madman then is not the fit place for a lady.

ENID. I'm not afraid of you.

ROBERTS [*bowing*]. I would not expect the daughter of Mr. Anthony to be afraid. Mr. Anthony is not a coward like the rest of them.

ENID [*suddenly*]. I suppose you think it brave, then, to go on with the struggle.

ROBERTS. Does Mr. Anthony think it brave to fight against women and children ? Mr. Anthony is a rich man, I believe ; does he think it brave to fight against those who haven't a penny ? Does he think it brave to set children crying with hunger, an' women shivering with cold ?

ENID [*putting up her hand, as though warding off a blow*]. My father is acting on his principles, and you know it !

ROBERTS. And so am I !

ENID. You hate us ; and you can't bear to be beaten !

ROBERTS. Neither can Mr. Anthony, for all that he may say.

ENID. At any rate you might have pity on your wife.

[MRS. ROBERTS *who has her hand pressed to her heart, takes it away, and tries to calm her breathing.*]

ROBERTS. Madam, I have no more to say.

[*He takes up the loaf. There is a knock at the door, and* UNDERWOOD *comes in. He stands looking at them,* ENID *turns to him, then seems undecided.*]

UNDERWOOD. Enid !

ROBERTS [*ironically*]. Ye were not needing to come for your wife, Mr. Underwood. We are not rowdies.

UNDERWOOD. I know that, Roberts. I hope Mrs. Roberts is better. [ROBERTS *turns away without answering.*] Come, Enid !

ENID. I make one more appeal to you, Mr. Roberts, for the sake of your wife.

ROBERTS [*with polite malice*]. If I might advise ye, ma'am — make it for the sake of your husband and your father.

[ENID, *suppressing a retort, goes out* UNDERWOOD *opens the door for her and follows.* ROBERTS, *going to the fire, holds out his hands to the dying glow.*]

ROBERTS. How goes it, my girl ? Feeling better, are you ? [MRS. ROBERTS *smiles faintly. He brings his overcoat and wraps it round her. Looking at his watch.*] Ten minutes to four ! [*As though inspired.*] I've seen their faces, there's no fight in them, except for that one old robber.

MRS. ROBERTS. Won't you stop and eat, David ? You've 'ad nothing all day !

ROBERTS [*putting his hand to his throat*]

Can't swallow till those old sharks are out
o' the town. [*He walks up and down.*] I
shall have a bother with the men — there's
no heart in them, the cowards. Blind as
bats, they are — can't see a day before
their noses.

MRS. ROBERTS. It's the women, David.

ROBERTS. Ah! So they say! They can
remember the women when their own bellies
speak! The women never stop them from
the drink; but from a little suffering to
themselves in a sacred cause, the women
stop them fast enough.

MRS. ROBERTS. But think o' the children, David.

ROBERTS. Ah! If they will go breeding
themselves for slaves, without a thought o'
the future o' them they breed —

MRS. ROBERTS [*gasping*]. That's enough,
David; don't begin to talk of that — I won't
— I can't —

ROBERTS [*staring at her*]. Now, now, my
girl!

MRS. ROBERTS [*breathlessly*]. No, no,
David — I won't!

ROBERTS. There, there! Come, come!
That's right! [*Bitterly.*] Not one penny
will they put by for a day like this. Not
they! Hand to mouth — Gad! — I know
them! They've broke my heart. There
was no holdin' them at the start, but now
the pinch 'as come.

MRS. ROBERTS. How can you expect it,
David? They're not made of iron.

ROBERTS. Expect it? Would n't I expect what I would do meself? Would n't I
starve an' rot rather than give in? What
one man can do, another can.

MRS. ROBERTS. And the women?

ROBERTS. This is not women's work.

MRS. ROBERTS [*with a flash of malice*].
No, the women may die for all you care.
That's their work.

ROBERTS [*averting his eyes*]. Who talks
of dying? No one will die till we have
beaten these — [*He meets her eyes again, and
again turns his away. Excitedly.*] This is
what I 've been waiting for all these
months. To get the old robbers down, and
send them home again without a farthin's
worth o' change. I 've seen their faces, I tell
you, in the valley of the shadow of defeat.

[*He goes to the peg and takes down his
hat.*]

MRS. ROBERTS [*following with her eyes —*

softly]. Take your overcoat, David; it must
be bitter cold.

ROBERTS [*coming up to her — his eyes are
furtive*]. No, no! There, there, stay quiet
and warm. I won't be long, my girl.

MRS. ROBERTS [*with soft bitterness*].
You 'd better take it.

[*She lifts the coat. But* ROBERTS *puts
it back, and wraps it round her. He
tries to meet her eyes, but cannot.*
MRS. ROBERTS *stays huddled in
the coat, her eyes, that follow him
about, are half malicious, half
yearning. He looks at his watch
again, and turns to go. In the doorway he meets* JAN THOMAS, *a boy
of ten in clothes too big for him,
carrying a penny whistle.*]

ROBERTS. Hallo, boy!

[*He goes.* JAN *stops within a yard of*
MRS. ROBERTS, *and stares at her
without a word.*]

MRS. ROBERTS. Well, Jan!

JAN. Father's coming; sister Madge's
coming.

[*He sits at the table, and fidgets with
his whistle; he blows three vague
notes; then imitates a cuckoo. There
is a tap on the door. Old* THOMAS
comes in.]

THOMAS. A very coot tay to you, ma'am.
It is petter that you are.

MRS. ROBERTS. Thank you, Mr. Thomas.

THOMAS [*nervously*]. Roberts in?

MRS. ROBERTS. Just gone on to the
meeting, Mr. Thomas.

THOMAS [*with relief, becoming talkative*].
This is fery unfortunate, look you! I came
to tell him that we must make terms with
London. It is a fery great pity he is gone
to the meeting. He will be kicking against
the pricks, I am thinking.

MRS. ROBERTS [*half rising*]. He'll never
give in, Mr. Thomas.

THOMAS. You must not be fretting, that
is very pat for you. Look you, there iss
hartly any mans for supporting him now,
but the engineers and George Rous. [*Solemnly.*] This strike is no longer coing with
Chapel, look you! I have listened carefully,
an' I have talked with her. [JAN *blows.*]
Sst! I don't care what th' others say, I say
that *Chapel means us* to be stopping the
trouple, that is what I make of her; and
it is my opinion that this is the fery best
thing for all of us. If it was n't my opinion,

I ton't say — but it is my opinion, look you.

MRS. ROBERTS [*trying to suppress her excitement*]. I don't know what 'll come to Roberts, if you give in.

THOMAS. It iss no disgrace whateffer! All that a mortal man coult do he hass tone. It iss against human nature he hass gone; fery natural — any man may do that; but Chapel has spoken and he must not go against her. [JAN *imitates the cuckoo*.] Ton't make that squeaking! [*Going to the door.*] Here iss my daughter come to sit with you. A fery goot day, ma'am — no fretting — rememper!

[MADGE *comes in and stands at the open door, watching the street.*]

MADGE. You 'll be late, father; they 're beginning. [*She catches him by the sleeve.*] For the love of God, stand up to him, father — this time!

THOMAS [*detaching his sleeve with dignity*]. Leave me to do what 's proper, girl!

[*He goes out.* MADGE, *in the center of the open doorway, slowly moves in, as though before the approach of some one.*]

ROUS [*appearing in the doorway*]. Madge!

[MADGE *stands with her back to* MRS. ROBERTS, *staring at him with her head up and her hands behind her.*]

ROUS [*who has a fierce distracted look*]. Madge! I 'm going to the meeting. [MADGE, *without moving, smiles contemptuously.*] D' ye hear me?

[*They speak in quick low voices.*]

MADGE. I hear! Go, and kill your own mother, if you must.

[ROUS *seizes her by both her arms. She stands rigid, with her head bent back. He releases her, and he too stands motionless.*]

ROUS. I swore to stand by Roberts. I swore that! Ye want me to go back on what I 've sworn.

MADGE [*with slow soft mockery*]. You are a pretty lover!

ROUS. Madge!

MADGE [*smiling*]. I 've heard that lovers do what their girls ask them — [JAN *sounds the cuckoo's notes*] — but that 's not true, it seems!

ROUS. You 'd make a blackleg of me!

MADGE [*with her eyes half closed*]. Do it for me!

ROUS [*dashing his hand across his brow*]. Damn! I can't!

MADGE [*swiftly*]. Do it for me!

ROUS [*through his teeth*]. Don't play the wanton with me!

MADGE [*with a movement of her hand towards* JAN — *quick and low*]. I would be *that* for the children's sake!

ROUS [*in a fierce whisper*]. Madge! Oh, Madge!

MADGE [*with soft mockery*]. But *you* can't break your word for me!

ROUS [*with a choke*]. Then, begod, I can!

[*He turns and rushes off.* MADGE *stands, with a faint smile on her face, looking after him. She turns to* MRS. ROBERTS.]

MADGE. I have done for Roberts!

MRS. ROBERTS [*scornfully*]. Done for my man, with that — [*She sinks back.*]

MADGE [*running to her, and feeling her hands*]. You 're as cold as a stone! You want a drop of brandy. Jan, run to the "Lion"; say I sent you for Mrs. Roberts.

MRS. ROBERTS [*with a feeble movement*]. I 'll just sit quiet, Madge. Give Jan — his — tea.

MADGE [*giving* JAN *a slice of bread*]. There, ye little rascal. Hold your piping. [*Going to the fire, she kneels.*] It 's going out.

MRS. ROBERTS [*with a faint smile*]. 'T is all the same! [JAN *begins to blow his whistle.*]

MADGE. Tsht! Tsht! — you — [JAN *stops.*]

MRS. ROBERTS [*smiling*]. Let 'im play, Madge.

MADGE [*on her knees at the fire, listening*]. Waiting an' waiting. I 've no patience with it; waiting an' waiting — that 's what a woman has to do! Can you hear them at it — I can!

[JAN *begins to play his whistle;* MADGE *gets up; half tenderly she ruffles his hair; then, sitting, leans her elbows on the table, and her chin on her hands. Behind her, on* MRS. ROBERTS'S *face the smile has changed to horrified surprise. She makes a sudden movement, sitting forward, pressing her hands against her breast. Then slowly she sinks back; slowly her face loses the look of pain, the smile returns. She fixes her eyes again on* JAN, *and moves her lips and finger to the tune.*]

SCENE II

It is past four. In a gray, failing light, an open muddy space is crowded with workmen. Beyond, divided from it by a barbed wire fence, is the raised towing-path of a canal, on which is moored a barge. In the distance are marshes and snow-covered hills. The "Works" high wall runs from the canal across the open space, and in the angle of this wall is a rude platform of barrels and boards. On it, ROBERTS is standing. ROBERTS, a little apart from the crowd, leans his back against the wall. On the raised towing-path two bargemen lounge and smoke indifferently.

HARNESS [*holding out his hand*]. Well, I've spoken to you straight. If I speak till to-morrow I can't say more.

JAGO. [*A dark, sallow, Spanish-looking man with a short, thin beard.*] Mister, want to ask you! Can they get blacklegs?

BULGIN [*menacing*]. Let 'em try.

[*There are savage murmurs from the crowd.*]

BROWN. [*A round-faced man.*] Where could they get 'em then?

EVANS. [*A small, restless, harassed man, with a fighting face.*] There's always blacklegs; it's the nature of 'em. There's always men that'll save their own skins.

[*Another savage murmur. There is a movement, and old THOMAS, joining the crowd, takes his stand in front.*]

HARNESS [*holding up his hand*]. They can't get them. But that won't help you. Now men, be reasonable. Your demands would have brought on us the burden of a dozen strikes at a time when we were not prepared for them. The Unions live by Justice, not to one, but all. Any fair man will tell you — you were ill-advised! I don't say you go too far for that which you're entitled to, but you're going too far for the moment; you've dug a pit for yourselves. Are you to stay there, or are you to climb out? Come!

LEWIS. [*A clean-cut Welshman with a dark mustache.*] You've hit it, mister! Which is it to be?

[*Another movement in the crowd, and ROUS, coming quickly, takes his stand next THOMAS.*]

HARNESS. Cut your demands to the right pattern, and we'll see you through; refuse, and don't expect me to waste my

time coming down here again. I'm not the sort that speaks at random, as you ought to know by this time. If you're the sound men I take you for — no matter who advises you against it — [*he fixes his eyes on* ROBERTS] you'll make up your minds to come in, and trust to us to get your terms. Which is it to be? Hands together, and victory — or — the starvation you've got now. [*A prolonged murmur from the crowd.*]

JAGO [*sullenly*]. Talk about what you know.

HARNESS [*lifting his voice above the murmur*]. Know? [*With cold passion.*] All that you've been through, my friend, I've been through — I was through it when I was no bigger than [*pointing to a youth*] that shaver there; the Unions then were n't what they are now. What's made them strong? It's hands together that's made them strong. I've been through it all, I tell you, the brand's on my soul yet. I know what you've suffered — there's nothing you can tell me that I don't know; but the whole is greater than the part, and you are only the part. Stand by us, and we will stand by you.

[*Quartering them with his eyes, he waits. The murmuring swells; the men form little groups. GREEN, BULGIN, and LEWIS talk together.*]

LEWIS. Speaks very sensible, the Union chap.

GREEN [*quietly*]. Ah! if I 'd 'a' been listened to, you 'd 'ave 'eard sense these two months past.

[*The bargemen are seen laughing.*]

LEWIS [*pointing*]. Look at those two blanks over the fence there!

BULGIN [*with gloomy violence*]. They 'd best stop their cackle, or I 'll break their jaws.

JAGO [*suddenly*]. You say the furnace men 's paid enough?

HARNESS. I did not say they were paid enough; I said they were paid as much as the furnace men in similar works elsewhere.

EVANS. That 's a lie! [*Hubbub.*] What about Harper's?

HARNESS [*with cold irony*]. You may look at home for lies, my man. Harper's shifts are longer, the pay works out the same.

HENRY ROUS. [*A dark edition of his brother George.*] Will ye support us in double pay overtime Saturdays?

HARNESS. Yes, we will.

JAGO. What have ye done with our subscriptions?

HARNESS [*coldly*]. I have told you what we *will* do with them.

EVANS. Ah! *will*, it's always will! Ye'd have our mates desert us. [*Hubbub.*]

BULGIN [*shouting*]. Hold your row!

[EVANS *looks round angrily.*]

HARNESS [*lifting his voice*]. Those who know their right hands from their lefts know that the Unions are neither thieves nor traitors. I've said my say. Figure it out, my lads; when you want me you know where I shall be.

[*He jumps down, the crowd gives way, he passes through them, and goes away. A* BARGEMAN *looks after him jerking his pipe with a derisive gesture. The men close up in groups, and many looks are cast at* ROBERTS, *who stands alone against the wall.*]

EVANS. He wants ye to turn blacklegs, that's what he wants. He wants ye to go back on us. Sooner than turn blackleg — I'd starve, I would.

BULGIN. Who's talkin' o' blacklegs — mind what you're saying, will you?

BLACKSMITH. [*A youth with yellow hair and huge arms.*] What about the women?

EVANS. They can stand what we can stand, I suppose, can't they?

BLACKSMITH. Ye've no wife?

EVANS. An' don't want one!

THOMAS [*raising his voice*]. Aye! Give us the power to come to terms with London, lads.

DAVIES. [*A dark, slow-fly, gloomy man.*] Go up the platform, if you got anything to say, go up an' say it.

[*There are cries of "Thomas!" He is pushed towards the platform; he ascends it with difficulty, and bares his head, waiting for silence. A hush.*]

RED-HAIRED YOUTH [*suddenly*]. Coot old Thomas!

[*A hoarse laugh; the bargemen exchange remarks; a hush again, and* THOMAS *begins speaking.*]

THOMAS. We are all in the tepth together, and it iss Nature that has put us there.

HENRY ROUS. It's London put us there!

EVANS. It's the Union.

THOMAS. It iss not Lonton; nor it iss not the Union—it iss Nature. It iss no disgrace whateffer to a potty to give in to Nature. For this Nature iss a fery pig thing; it is pigger than what a man is. There iss more years to my hett than to the hett of any one here. It is fery pat, look you, this coing against Nature. It is pat to make other potties suffer, when there is nothing to pe cot py it. [*A laugh.* THOMAS *angrily goes on.*] What are ye laughing at? It is pat, I say! We are fighting for a principle; there is no potty that shall say I am not a peliever in principle. Putt when Nature says "No further," then it is no coot snapping your fingers in her face. [*A laugh from* ROBERTS, *and murmurs of approval.*] This Nature must pe humort. It is a man's pisiness to pe pure, honest, just, and merciful. That's what Chapel tells you. [*To* ROBERTS, *angrily.*] And, look you, David Roberts, Chapel tells you ye can do that without coing against Nature.

JAGO. What about the Union?

THOMAS. I ton't trust the Union; they haf treated us like tirt. "Do what we tell you," said they. I haf peen captain of the furnace men twenty years, and I say to the Union — [*excitedly*] — "Can you tell me then, as well as I can tell you, what iss the right wages for the work that these men do?" For fife and twenty years I haf paid my moneys to the Union and — [*with great excitement*] — for nothings! What iss that but roguery, for all that this Mr. Harness says! [*Murmurs.*]

EVANS. Hear, hear.

HENRY ROUS. Get on with you! Cut on with it then!

THOMAS. Look you, if a man toes not trust me, am I coing to trust him?

JAGO. That's right.

THOMAS. Let them alone for rogues, and act for ourselves. [*Murmurs.*]

BLACKSMITH. That's what we been doin', haven't we?

THOMAS [*with increased excitement*]. I wass brought up to do for meself. I wass brought up to go without a thing if I hat not moneys to puy it. There iss too much, look you, of doing things with other people's moneys. We haf fought fair, and if we haf peen beaten, it iss no fault of ours. Gif us the power to make terms with Lonton for ourself; if we ton't succeed, I say it iss petter to take our peating like men, than to tie like togs, or hang on to others' coat-tails to make them do our pisiness for us!

EVANS [*muttering*]. Who wants to?

THOMAS [*craning*]. What's that? If I stand up to a potty, and he knocks me town, I am not to go hollering to other potties to help me; I am to stand up again; and if he knocks me town properly, I am to stay there, is n't that right? [*Laughter.*]

JAGO. No Union!

HENRY ROUS. Union!

[*Others take up the shout.*]

EVANS. Blacklegs!

[BULGIN *and the* BLACKSMITH *shake their fists at* EVANS.]

THOMAS [*with a gesture*]. I am an olt man, look you.

[*A sudden silence, then murmurs again.*]

LEWIS. Olt fool, with his "No Union!"

BULGIN. Them furnace chaps! For two-pence I'd smash the faces o' the lot of them.

GREEN. If I 'd 'a' been listened to at the first —

THOMAS [*wiping his brow*]. I'm comin' now to what I was coing to say —

DAVIES [*muttering*]. An' time too!

THOMAS [*solemnly*]. Chapel says: Ton't carry on this strife! Put an end to it.

JAGO. That's a lie! Chapel says go on!

THOMAS [*scornfully*]. Inteet! I haf ears to my head.

RED-HAIRED YOUTH. Ah! long ones!

[*A laugh.*]

JAGO. Your ears have misbeled you then.

THOMAS [*excitedly*]. Ye cannot be right if I am, ye cannot haf it both ways.

RED-HAIRED YOUTH. Chapel can though!

["*The Shaver" laughs; there are mur-murs from the crowd.*]

THOMAS [*fixing his eyes on "The Shaver"*]. Ah! ye 're coing the roat to tamnation. An' so I say to all of you. If ye co against Chapel I will not pe with you, nor will any other Got-fearing man.

[*He steps down from the platform. JAGO makes his way towards it. There are cries of "Don't let 'im go up!"*]

JAGO. Don't let him go up? That's free speech, that is. [*He goes up.*] I ain't got much to say to you. Look at the matter plain; ye 've come the road this far, and now you want to chuck the journey. We 've

all been in one boat; and now you want to pull in two. We engineers have stood by you; ye 're ready now, are ye, to give us the go-by? If we 'd 'a' known that before, we 'd not 'a' started out with you so early one bright morning! That's all I 've got to say. Old man Thomas ain't got his Bible lesson right. If you give up to London, or to Harness, now, it 's givin' us the chuck — to save your skins — you won't get over that, my boys; it 's a dirty thing to do.

[*He gets down; during his little speech, which is ironically spoken, there is a restless discomfort in the crowd. ROUS, stepping forward, jumps on the platform. He has an air of fierce distraction. Sullen murmurs of disapproval from the crowd.*]

ROUS [*speaking with great excitement*]. I'm no blanky orator, mates, but wot I say is drove from me. What I say is yuman nature. Can a man set an' see 'is mother starve? Can 'e now?

ROBERTS [*starting forward*]. Rous!

ROUS [*staring at him fiercely*]. Sim 'Ar-ness said fair! I 've changed my mind!

ROBERTS. Ah! Turned your coat you mean! [*The crowd manifests a great surprise.*]

LEWIS [*apostrophizing* ROUS]. Hallo! What's turned him round?

ROUS [*speaking with intense excitement*]. 'E said fair. "Stand by us," 'e said, "and we 'll stand by you." That's where we 've been makin' our mistake this long time past; and who 's to blame for 't? [*He points at* ROBERTS.] That man there! "No," 'e said, "fight the robbers," 'e said, "squeeze the breath out o' them!" But it 's not the breath out o' them that's being squeezed; it 's the breath out of *us* and *ours*, and that's the book of truth. I 'm no orator, mates, it 's the flesh and blood in me that's speakin', it 's the heart o' me. [*With a menacing, yet half-ashamed movement towards* ROBERTS.] He'll speak to you again, mark my words, but don't ye listen. [*The crowd groans.*] It 's hell fire that 's on that man's tongue. [ROB-ERTS *is seen laughing.*] Sim 'Arness is right. What are we without the Union — handful o' parched leaves — a puff o' smoke. I 'm no orator, but I say: Chuck it up! Chuck it up! Sooner than go on starving the women and the children.

[*The murmurs of acquiescence almost drown the murmurs of dissent.*]

EVANS. What's turned *you* to blacklegging?

ROUS [*with a furious look*]. Sim 'Arness knows what he's talking about. Give us power to come to terms with London ; I'm no orator, but I say — have done wi' this black misery !

[*He gives his muffler a twist, jerks his head back, and jumps off the platform. The crowd applauds and surges forward. Amid cries of "That's enough!" "Up Union!" "Up Harness!"* ROBERTS *quietly ascends the platform. There is a moment of silence.*]

BLACKSMITH. We don't want to hear you. Shut it !

HENRY ROUS. Get down !

[*Amid such cries they surge towards the platform.*]

EVANS [*fiercely*]. Let 'im speak ! Roberts ! Roberts !

BULGIN [*muttering*]. He'd better look out that I don't crack his skull.

[ROBERTS *faces the crowd, probing them with his eyes till they gradually become silent. He begins speaking. One of the bargemen rises and stands.*]

ROBERTS. You don't want to hear me, then ? You'll listen to Rous and to that old man, but not to me. You'll listen to Sim Harness of the Union that's treated you *so fair ;* maybe you'll listen to those men from London ? Ah! You groan! What for ? You love their feet on your necks, don't you ? [*Then as* BULGIN *elbows his way towards the platform, with calm pathos.*] You'd like to break my jaw, John Bulgin. Let me speak, then do your smashing, if it gives you pleasure. [BULGIN *stands motionless and sullen.*] Am I a liar, a coward, a traitor ? If only I were, ye'd listen to me, I'm sure. [*The murmurings cease, and there is now dead silence.*] Is there a man of you here that has less to gain by striking ? Is there a man of you that had more to lose ? Is there a man of you that has given up *eight hundred* pounds since this trouble here began ? Come now, is there ? How much has Thomas given up — ten pounds or five, or what ? You listened to him, and what had he to say ? "None can pretend," he said, "that I'm not a believer in principle — [*with biting irony*] — but when Nature says : 'No fur-

ther,'t es going agenst Nature.' " *I* tell you if a man cannot say to Nature : "Budge me from this if ye can ! " — [*with a sort of exaltation*] — his principles are but his belly. "Oh, but," Thomas says, "a man can be pure and honest, just and merciful, and take off his hat to Nature ! " *I* tell you Nature's neither pure nor honest, just nor merciful. You chaps that live over the hill, an' go home dead beat in the dark on a snowy night — don't ye fight your way every inch of it ? Do ye go lyin' down an' trustin' to the tender mercies of this merciful Nature ? Try it and you'll soon know with what ye've got to deal. 'T es only by that — [*he strikes a blow with his clenched fist*] — in Nature's face that a man can be a man. "Give in," says Thomas, "go down on your knees ; throw up your foolish fight, an' perhaps," he said, "perhaps your enemy will chuck you down a crust."

JAGO. Never !

EVANS. Curse them !

THOMAS. I nefer said that.

ROBERTS [*bitingly*]. If ye did not say it, man, ye meant it. An' what did ye say about Chapel ? "Chapel's against it," ye said. "She's against it !" Well, if Chapel and Nature go hand in hand, it's the first I've ever heard of it. That young man there — [*pointing to* ROUS] — said I'ad 'ell fire on my tongue. If I had I would use it all to scorch and wither this talking of surrender. Surrendering's the work of cowards and traitors.

HENRY ROUS [*as* GEORGE ROUS *moves forward*]. Go for him, George — don't stand his lip !

ROBERTS [*flinging out his finger*]. Stop there, George Rous, it's no time this to settle personal matters. [ROUS *stops.*] But there was one other spoke to you — Mr. Simon Harness. We have not much to thank Mr. Harness and the Union for. They said to us "Desert your mates, or we'll desert you." An' they did desert us.

EVANS. They did.

ROBERTS. Mr. Simon Harness is a clever man, but he has come too late. [*With intense conviction.*] For all that Mr. Simon Harness says, for all that Thomas, Rous, for all that any man present here can say — *We've won the fight !* [*The crowd sags nearer, looking eagerly up. With withering scorn.*] You've felt the pinch o't in your bellies. You've forgotten what that fight 'as been; many times I have told you; I will tell you now this once again. The fight o' the country's body and blood against a blood-sucker. The fight of those that spend themselves with every blow they strike and every breath they draw, against a thing that fattens on them, and grows and grows by the law of *merciful* Nature. That thing is Capital! A thing that buys the sweat o' men's brows, and the tortures o' their brains, at its own price. *Don't* I know that? Was n't the work o' *my* brains bought for seven hundred pounds, and has n't one hundred thousand pounds been gained them by that seven hundred without the stirring of a finger. It is a thing that will take as much and give you as little as it can. That 's *Capital!* A thing that will say — "I 'm very sorry for you, poor fellows — you have a cruel time of it, I know," but will not give one sixpence of its dividends to help you have a better time. That 's Capital! Tell me, for all their talk, is there one of them that will consent to another penny on the Income Tax to help the poor? That 's Capital! A white-faced, stony-hearted monster! Ye have got it on its knees; are ye to give up at the last minute to save your miserable bodies pain? When I went this morning to those old men from London, I looked into their very 'earts. One of them was sitting there — Mr. Scantlebury, a mass of flesh nourished on us: sittin' there for all the world like the shareholders in this Company, that sit not moving tongue nor finger, takin' dividends — a great dumb ox that can only be roused when its food is threatened. I looked into his eyes and I saw *he was afraid* — afraid for himself and his dividends, afraid for his fees, afraid of the very shareholders he stands for; and all but one of them 's afraid — like children that get into a wood at night, and start at every rustle of the leaves. I ask you, men — [*he pauses, holding out his hand till there is utter silence*] — give me a free hand to tell them : "Go you back to London. The men have nothing for you!" [*A murmuring.*] Give me that, an' I swear to you, within a week you shall have from London all you want.

EVANS, JAGO, and OTHERS. A free hand! Give him a free hand! Bravo — bravo!

ROBERTS. 'T is not for this little moment of time we 're fighting [*the murmuring dies*],

not for ourselves, our own little bodies, and their wants, 't is for all those that come after throughout all time. [*With intense sadness.*] Oh! men — for the love o' them, don't roll up another stone upon their heads, don't help to blacken the sky, an' let the bitter sea in over them. They 're welcome to the worst that can happen to me, to the worst that can happen to us all, are n't they — are n't they? If we can shake [*passionately*] that white-faced monster with the bloody lips, that has sucked the life out of ourselves, our wives, and children, since the world began. [*Dropping the note of passion, but with the utmost weight and intensity.*] If we have not the hearts of men to stand against it breast to breast, and eye to eye, and force it backward till it cry for mercy, it will go on sucking life; and we shall stay forever what we are [*in almost a whisper*], less than the very dogs.

> [*An utter stillness, and* ROBERTS *stands rocking his body slightly, with his eyes burning the faces of the crowd.*]

EVANS and JAGO [*suddenly*]. Roberts!

> [*The shout is taken up. There is a slight movement in the crowd, and* MADGE *passing below the towing-path, stops by the platform, looking up at* ROBERTS. *A sudden doubting silence.*]

ROBERTS. "Nature," says that old man, "give in to Nature." I tell you, strike your blow in Nature's face — an' let it do its worst!

> [*He catches sight of* MADGE, *his brows contract, he looks away.*]

MADGE [*in a low voice — close to the platform*]. Your wife's dying!

> [ROBERTS *glares at her as if torn from some pinnacle of exaltation.*]

ROBERTS [*trying to stammer on*]. I say to you — answer them — answer them —

> [*He is drowned by the murmur in the crowd.*]

THOMAS [*stepping forward*]. Ton't you hear her, then?

ROBERTS. What is it? [*A dead silence.*]

THOMAS. Your wife, man!

> [ROBERTS *hesitates, then with a gesture, he leaps down, and goes away below the towing-path, the men making way for him. The standing bargeman opens and prepares to*

Is always never seen in play he is objective solemnly now like
shows feel here he is subjective we judge.

light a lantern. Daylight is fast failing.]

MADGE. He need n't have hurried! Annie Roberts is dead. [*Then in the silence, passionately.*] You pack of blinded hounds! How many more women are you going to let to die?

[*The crowd shrinks back from her, and breaks up in groups, with a confused, uneasy movement. MADGE goes quickly away below the towing-path. There is a hush as they look after her.*]

LEWIS. There 's a spitfire for ye!

BULGIN [*growling*]. I 'll smash 'er jaw.

GREEN. If I 'd 'a' been listened to, that poor woman —

THOMAS. It 's a judgment on him for co-ing against Chapel. I tolt him how 't would be!

EVANS. All the more reason for sticking by 'im. [*A cheer.*] Are you goin' to desert him now 'e 's down? Are you goin' to chuck him over, now 'e 's lost 'is wife?

[*The crowd is murmuring and cheering all at once.*]

ROUS [*stepping in front of platform*]. Lost his wife! Aye! Can't ye see? Look at home, look at your own wives! What 's to save them? You 'll have the same in all your houses before long!

LEWIS. Aye, aye!

HENRY ROUS. Right! George, right!

[*There are murmurs of assent.*]

ROUS. It 's not us that 's blind, it 's Roberts. How long will ye put up with 'im!

HENRY ROUS, BULGIN, DAVIES. Give 'im the chuck! [*The cry is taken up.*]

EVANS [*fiercely*]. Kick a man that 's down? Down?

HENRY ROUS. Stop his jaw there!

[*EVANS throws up his arm at a threat from BULGIN. The bargeman, who has lighted the lantern, holds it high above his head.*]

ROUS [*springing on to the platform*]. What brought him down then, but 'is own black obstinacy? Are ye goin' to follow a man that can't see better than that where he 's goin'?

EVANS. He 's lost 'is wife.

ROUS. An' who's fault 's that but his own. 'Ave done with 'im, I say, before he 's killed your own wives and mothers.

DAVIES. Down 'im!

HENRY ROUS. He 's finished!

BROWN. We 've had enough of 'im!

BLACKSMITH. Too much!

[*The crowd takes up these cries, excepting only EVANS, JAGO, and GREEN, who is seen to argue mildly with the BLACKSMITH.*]

ROUS [*above the hubbub*]. We 'll make terms with the Union, lads. [*Cheers.*]

EVANS [*fiercely*]. Ye blacklegs!

BULGIN [*savagely — squaring up to him*]. Who are ye callin' blacklegs, Rat?

[*EVANS throws up his fists, parries the blow, and returns it. They fight. The bargemen are seen holding up the lantern and enjoying the sight. Old THOMAS steps forward and holds out his hands.*]

THOMAS. Shame on your strife!

[*The BLACKSMITH, BROWN, LEWIS, and the RED-HAIRED YOUTH pull EVANS and BULGIN apart. The stage is almost dark.*]

ACT III

It is five o'clock. In the UNDERWOODS' *drawing-room, which is artistically furnished,* ENID *is sitting on the sofa working at a baby's frock.* EDGAR, *by a little spindle-legged table in the center of the room, is fingering a china box. His eyes are fixed on the double doors that lead into the dining-room.*

EDGAR [*putting down the china box, and glancing at his watch*]. Just on five, they 're all in there waiting, except Frank. Where 's he?

ENID. He 's had to go down to Gasgoyne's about a contract. Will you want him?

EDGAR. He can't help us. This is a director's job. [*Motioning towards a single door half hidden by a curtain.*] Father in his room?

ENID. Yes.

EDGAR. I wish he 'd stay there, Enid. [ENID *looks up at him.*] This is a beastly business, old girl!

[*He takes up the little box again and turns it over and over.*]

ENID. I went to the Roberts's this afternoon, Ted.

EDGAR. That was n't very wise.

ENID. He 's simply killing his wife.

EDGAR. We are you mean.

ENID [*suddenly*]. Roberts *ought* to give way!

EDGAR. There's a lot to be said on the men's side.

ENID. I don't feel half so sympathetic with them as I did before I went. They just set up class feeling against you. Poor Annie was looking dreadfully bad — fire going out, and nothing fit for her to eat. [EDGAR *walks to and fro.*] But she would stand up for Roberts. When you see all this wretchedness going on and feel you can do nothing, you have to shut your eyes to the whole thing.

EDGAR. If you can.

ENID. When I went I was all on their side, but as soon as I got there I began to feel quite different at once. People talk about sympathy with the working classes, they don't know what it means to try and put it into practice. It seems hopeless.

EDGAR. Ah! well.

ENID. It's dreadful going on with the men in this state. I do hope the Dad will make concessions.

EDGAR. He won't. [*Gloomily.*] It's a sort of religion with him. Curse it! I know what's coming! He'll be voted down.

ENID. They wouldn't dare!

EDGAR. They will — they're in a funk.

ENID [*indignantly*]. He'd never stand it!

EDGAR [*with a shrug*]. My dear girl, if you're beaten in a vote, you've got to stand it.

ENID. Oh! [*She gets up in alarm.*] But would he resign?

EDGAR. Of course! It goes to the roots of his beliefs.

ENID. But he's so *wrapped up in this company*, Ted! There'd be nothing left for him! It'd be dreadful! [EDGAR *shrugs his shoulders.*] Oh, Ted, he's so old now! You mustn't let them!

EDGAR [*hiding his feelings in an outburst*]. My sympathies in this strike are all on the side of the men.

ENID. He's been Chairman for more than thirty years! He made the whole thing! And think of the bad times they've had; it's always been he who pulled them through. Oh, Ted, you must —

EDGAR. What is it you want? You said just now you hoped he'd make concessions. Now you want me to back him in not making them. This isn't a game, Enid!

ENID [*hotly*]. It isn't a game to *me* that the Dad's in danger of losing all he cares

about in life. If he won't give way, and he's beaten, it'll simply break him down!

EDGAR. Didn't you say it was dreadful going on with the men in this state?

ENID. But can't you see, Ted, father'll never get over it! You must stop them somehow. The others are afraid of him. If you back him up —

EDGAR [*putting his hand to his head*]. Against my convictions — against yours! The moment it begins to pinch one personally —

ENID. It isn't personal, it's the Dad!

EDGAR. Your family or yourself, and over goes the show!

ENID [*resentfully*]. If you don't take it seriously, I do.

EDGAR. I am as fond of him as you are; that's nothing to do with it.

ENID. We can't tell about the men; it's all guess-work. But we know the Dad might have a stroke any day. D' you mean to say that he isn't more to you than —

EDGAR. Of course he is.

ENID. I don't understand you then.

EDGAR. H'm!

ENID. If it were for one's self it would be different, but for our own father! You don't seem to realize.

EDGAR. I realize perfectly.

ENID. It's your first duty to save him.

EDGAR. I wonder.

ENID [*imploring*]. Oh, Ted! It's the only interest he's got left; it'll be like a death-blow to him!

EDGAR [*restraining his emotion*]. I know.

ENID. Promise!

EDGAR. I'll do what I can.

[*He turns to the double doors. The curtained door is opened, and AN-THONY appears. EDGAR opens the double doors and passes through. SCANTLEBURY's voice is faintly heard: "Past five; we shall never get through — have to eat another dinner at that hotel!" The doors are shut. ANTHONY walks forward.*]

ANTHONY. You've been seeing Roberts, I hear.

ENID. Yes.

ANTHONY. Do you know what trying to bridge such a gulf as this is like? [ENID *puts her work on the little table, and faces him.*] Filling a sieve with sand!

ENID. Don't!

ANTHONY. You think with your gloved hands you can cure the trouble of the century. [He passes on.]

ENID. Father! [ANTHONY stops at the double doors.] I'm only thinking of you!

ANTHONY [more softly]. I can take care of myself, my dear.

ENID. Have you thought what'll happen if you're beaten — [she points] — in there?

ANTHONY. I don't mean to be.

ENID. Oh! father, don't give them a chance. You're not well; need you go to the meeting at all?

ANTHONY [with a grim smile]. Cut and run?

ENID. But they'll out-vote you!

ANTHONY [putting his hand on the doors]. We shall see!

ENID. I beg you, Dad! [ANTHONY looks at her softly.] Won't you?

[ANTHONY shakes his head. He opens the doors. A buzz of voices comes in.]

SCANTLEBURY. Can one get dinner on that 6.30 train up?

TENCH. No, sir, I believe not, sir.

WILDER. Well, I shall speak out; I've had enough of this.

EDGAR [sharply]. What?

[It ceases instantly. ANTHONY passes through, closing the doors behind him. ENID springs to them with a gesture of dismay. She puts her hand on the knob, and begins turning it; then goes to the fireplace, and taps her foot on the fender. Suddenly she rings the bell. FROST comes in by the door that leads into the hall.]

FROST. Yes, m'm?

ENID. When the men come, Frost, please show them in here; the hall's cold.

FROST. I could put them in the pantry, m'm.

ENID. No. I don't want to — to offend them; they're so touchy.

FROST. Yes, m'm. [Pause.] Excuse me, Mr. Anthony's 'ad nothing to eat all day.

ENID. I know Frost.

FROST. Nothin' but two whiskies and sodas, m'm.

ENID. Oh! you ought n't to have let him have those.

FROST [gravely]. Mr. Anthony is a little difficult, m'm. It's not as if he were a younger man, an' knew what was good for 'im; he will have his own way.

ENID. I suppose we all want that.

FROST. Yes, m'm. [Quietly.] Excuse me speakin' about the strike. I'm sure if the other gentlemen were to give up to Mr. Anthony, and quietly let the men 'ave what they want, afterwards, that'd be the best way. I find that very useful with him at times, m'm. [ENID shakes her head.] If he's crossed, it makes him violent [with an air of discovery], and I've noticed in my own case, when I'm violent I'm always sorry for it afterwards.

ENID [with a smile]. Are you ever violent, Frost?

FROST. Yes, m'm; oh! sometimes very violent.

ENID. I've never seen you.

FROST [impersonally]. No, m'm; that is so. [ENID fidgets towards the back of the door.] [With feeling.] Bein' with Mr. Anthony, as you know, m'm, ever since I was fifteen, it worries me to see him crossed like this at his age. I've taken the liberty to speak to Mr. Wanklin [dropping his voice] — seems to be the most sensible of the gentlemen — but 'e said to me: "That's all very well, Frost, but this strike's a very serious thing," 'e said. "Serious for all parties, no doubt," I said, "but yumor 'im, sir," I said, "yumor 'im. It's like this, if a man comes to a stone wall, 'e does n't drive 'is 'ead against it, 'e gets over it." "Yes," 'e said, "you'd better tell your master that." [FROST looks at his nails.] That's where it is, m'm. I said to Mr. Anthony this morning: "Is it worth it, sir?" "Damn it," he said to me, "Frost! Mind your own business, or take a month's notice!" Beg pardon, m'm, for using such a word.

ENID [moving to the double doors, and listening]. Do you know that man Roberts, Frost?

FROST. Yes, m'm; that's to say, not to speak to. But to look at 'im you can tell what he's like.

ENID [stopping]. Yes?

FROST. He's not one of these 'ere ordinary 'armless Socialists. 'E's violent; got a fire inside 'im. What I call "personal." A man may 'ave what opinions 'e likes, so long as 'e's not personal; when 'e's that 'e's not safe.

ENID. I think that's what my father feels about Roberts.

FROST. No doubt, m'm, Mr. Anthony has a feeling against him. [ENID *glances at him sharply, but finding him in perfect earnest, stands biting her lips, and looking at the double doors.*] It's a regular right down struggle between the two. I've no patience with this Roberts, from what I 'ear he's just an ordinary workin' man like the rest of 'em. If he did invent a thing he's no worse off than 'undreds of others. My brother invented a new kind o' dumb-waiter — nobody gave *him* anything for it, an' there it is, bein' used all over the place. [ENID *moves closer to the double doors.*] There's a kind o' man that never forgives the world, because 'e was n't born a gentleman. What I say is — no man that's a gentleman looks down on another because 'e 'appens to be a class or two above 'im, no more than if 'e 'appens to be a class or two below.

ENID [*with slight impatience*]. Yes, I know, Frost, of course. Will you please go in and ask if they'll have some tea; say I sent you.

FROST. Yes, m'm.

[*He opens the doors gently and goes in. There is a momentary sound of earnest, rather angry talk.*]

WILDER. I don't agree with you.

WANKLIN. We've had this over a dozen times.

EDGAR [*impatiently*]. Well, what's the proposition?

SCANTLEBURY. Yes, what does your father say? Tea? Not for me, not for me!

WANKLIN. What I understand the Chairman to say is this —

[FROST *reënters closing the door behind him.*]

ENID [*moving from the door*]. Won't they have any tea, Frost?

[*She goes to the little table, and remains motionless, looking at the baby's frock.*]

[*A Parlormaid enters from the hall.*]

PARLORMAID. A Miss Thomas, m'm.

ENID [*raising her head*]. Thomas? What Miss Thomas — d' you mean a — ?

PARLORMAID. Yes, m'm.

ENID [*blankly*]. Oh! Where is she?

PARLORMAID. In the porch.

ENID. I don't want —   [*She hesitates.*]

FROST. Shall I dispose of her, m'm?

ENID. I'll come out. No, show her in here, Ellen.

[*The* PARLORMAID *and* FROST *go out.* ENID *pursing her lips, sits at the little table, taking up the baby's frock. The* PARLORMAID *ushers in* MADGE THOMAS *and goes out;* MADGE *stands by the door.*]

ENID. Come in. What is it? What have you come for, please?

MADGE. Brought a message from Mrs. Roberts.

ENID. A message? Yes?

MADGE. She asks you to look after her mother.

ENID. I don't understand.

MADGE [*sullenly*]. That's the message.

ENID. But — what — why?

MADGE. Annie Roberts is dead.

[*There is a silence.*]

ENID [*horrified*]. But it's only a little more than an hour since I saw her.

MADGE. Of cold and hunger.

ENID [*rising*]. Oh! that's not true! the poor thing's heart — What makes you look at me like that? I tried to help her.

MADGE [*with suppressed savagery*]. I thought you'd like to know.

ENID [*passionately*]. It's so unjust! Can't you see that I want to help you all?

MADGE. I never harmed any one that had n't harmed me first.

ENID [*coldly*]. What harm have I done you? Why do you speak to me like that?

MADGE [*with the bitterest intensity*]. You come out of your comfort to spy on us! A week of hunger, that's what *you* want?

ENID [*standing her ground*]. Don't talk nonsense!

MADGE. I saw her die; her hands were blue with the cold.

ENID [*with a movement of grief*]. Oh! why would n't she let me help her? It's such senseless pride!

MADGE. Pride's better than nothing to keep your body warm.

ENID [*passionately*]. I won't talk to you! How can you tell what I feel? It's not my fault that I was born better off than you.

MADGE. We don't want your money.

ENID. You don't understand, and you don't want to; please to go away!

MADGE [*balefully*]. You've killed her, for all your soft words, you and your father —

ENID [*with rage and emotion*]. That's
wicked! My father is suffering himself
through this wretched strike.

MADGE [*with somber triumph*]. Then tell
him Mrs. Roberts is dead. That'll make
him better.

ENID. Go away!

MADGE. When a person hurts us we get
it back on them.

[*She makes a sudden and swift movement towards* ENID, *fixing her eyes
on the child's frock lying across the
little table.* ENID *snatches the frock
up, as though it were the child itself.
They stand a yard apart, crossing
glances.*]

MADGE [*pointing to the frock with a little
smile*]. Ah! You felt *that!* Lucky it's her
mother — not her children — you've to look
after, is n't it. *She* won't trouble you long!

ENID. Go away!

MADGE. I've given you the message.

[*She turns and goes out into the hall.*
ENID, *motionless till she has gone,
sinks down at the table, bending her
head over the frock, which she is
still clutching to her. The double
doors are opened, and* ANTHONY
*comes slowly in; he passes his
daughter, and lowers himself into an
armchair. He is very flushed.*]

ENID [*hiding her emotion — anxiously*].
What is it, Dad? [ANTHONY *makes a gesture, but does not speak.*] Who was it? [AN-
THONY *does not answer.* ENID *going to the
double doors meets* EDGAR *coming in. They
speak together in low tones.*] What is it, Ted?

EDGAR. That fellow Wilder! Taken to
personalities! He was downright insulting.

ENID. What did he say?

EDGAR. Said father was too old and
feeble to know what he was doing! The
Dad's worth six of him!

ENID. Of course he is.

[*They look at* ANTHONY. *The doors
open wider,* WANKLIN *appears with*
SCANTLEBURY.]

SCANTLEBURY [*sotto voce*]. I don't like
the look of this!

WANKLIN [*going forward*]. Come, Chairman! Wilder sends you his apologies. A
man can't do more.

[WILDER, *followed by* TENCH, *comes
in, and goes to* ANTHONY.]

WILDER [*glumly*]. I withdraw my words,
sir. I'm sorry. [ANTHONY *nods to him.*]

ENID. You have n't come to a decision,
Mr. Wanklin? [WANKLIN *shakes his head.*]

WANKLIN. We're all here, Chairman;
what do you say? Shall we get on with the
business, or shall we go back to the other
room?

SCANTLEBURY. Yes, yes; let's get on.
We must settle something.

[*He turns from a small chair, and
settles himself suddenly in the larg-
est chair with a sigh of comfort.*
WILDER *and* WANKLIN *also sit;
and* TENCH, *drawing up a straight-
backed chair close to his Chairman,
sits on the edge of it with the minute-
book and a stylographic pen.*]

ENID [*whispering*]. I want to speak to
you a minute, Ted.

[*They go out through the double doors.*]

WANKLIN. Really, Chairman, it's no use
soothing ourselves with a sense of false
security. If this strike's not brought to an
end before the General Meeting, the shareholders will certainly haul us over the
coals.

SCANTLEBURY [*stirring*]. What — what's
that?

WANKLIN. I know it for a fact.

ANTHONY. Let them!

WILDER. And get turned out?

WANKLIN. [*To* ANTHONY.] I don't mind
martyrdom for a policy in which I believe,
but I object to being burnt for some one
else's principles.

SCANTLEBURY. Very reasonable — you
must see that, Chairman.

ANTHONY. We owe it to other employers to stand firm.

WANKLIN. There's a limit to that.

ANTHONY. You were all full of fight at
the start.

SCANTLEBURY [*with a sort of groan*]. We
thought the men would give in, but they —
have n't!

ANTHONY. They will!

WILDER [*rising and pacing up and down*].
I can't have my reputation as a man of
business destroyed for the satisfaction of
starving the men out. [*Almost in tears.*] I
can't have it! How can we meet the shareholders with things in the state they are?

SCANTLEBURY. Hear, hear — hear, hear!

WILDER [*lashing himself*]. If any one expects me to say to them I've lost you
fifty thousand pounds and sooner than put

my pride in my pocket I'll lose you another. [*Glancing at* ANTHONY.] It's—it's unnatural ! *I don't want* to go against you, sir—

WANKLIN [*persuasively*]. Come Chairman, we're *not* free agents. We're part of a machine. Our only business is to see the Company earns as much profit as it safely can. If you blame me for want of principle : I say that we're trustees. Reason tells us we shall never get back in the saving of wages what we shall lose if we continue this struggle—really, Chairman, we *must* bring it to an end, on the best terms we can make.

ANTHONY. No.

[*There is a pause of general dismay.*]

WILDER. It's a deadlock then. [*Letting his hands drop with a sort of despair.*] Now I shall never get off to Spain !

WANKLIN [*retaining a trace of irony*]. You hear the consequences of your victory, Chairman ?

WILDER [*with a burst of feeling*]. My wife's *ill* !

SCANTLEBURY. Dear, dear ! You don't say so.

WILDER. If I don't get her out of this cold, I won't answer for the consequences.

[*Through the double doors* EDGAR *comes in looking very grave.*]

EDGAR. [*To his father.*] Have you heard this, sir ? Mrs. Roberts is dead ! [*Every one stares at him, as if trying to gauge the importance of this news.*] Enid saw her this afternoon, she had no coals, or food, or anything. It's enough !

[*There is a silence, every one avoiding the other's eyes, except* ANTHONY, *who stares hard at his son.*]

SCANTLEBURY. You don't suggest that we could have helped the poor thing ?

WILDER [*flustered*]. The woman was in bad health. Nobody can say there's any responsibility on us. At least—not on me.

EDGAR [*hotly*]. I say that we *are* responsible.

ANTHONY. War is war !

EDGAR. Not on women !

WANKLIN. It not infrequently happens that women are the greatest sufferers.

EDGAR. If we knew that, all the more responsibility rests on us.

ANTHONY. This is no matter for amateurs.

EDGAR. Call me what you like, sir. It's sickened me. We had no right to carry things to such a length.

WILDER. I don't like this business a bit —that Radical rag will twist it to their own ends ; see if they don't ! They'll get up some cock and bull story about the poor woman's dying from starvation. I wash my hands of it.

EDGAR. You can't. None of us can.

SCANTLEBURY [*striking his fist on the arm of his chair*]. But I protest against this—

EDGAR. Protest as you like, Mr. Scantlebury, it won't alter facts.

ANTHONY. That's enough.

EDGAR [*facing him angrily*]. No, sir. I tell you exactly what I think. If we pretend the men are not suffering, it's humbug ; and if they're suffering, we know enough of human nature to know the women are suffering more, and as to the children—well—it's damnable ! [SCANTLEBURY *rises from his chair.*] I don't say that we meant to be cruel, I don't say anything of the sort ; but I do say it's criminal to shut our eyes to the facts. We employ these men, and we can't get out of it. I don't care so much about the men, but I'd sooner resign my position on the Board than go on starving women in this way.

[*All except* ANTHONY *are now upon their feet,* ANTHONY *sits grasping the arms of his chair and staring at his son.*]

SCANTLEBURY. I don't—I don't like the way you're putting it, young sir.

WANKLIN. You're rather overshooting the mark.

WILDER. I should think so indeed !

EDGAR [*losing control*]. It's no use blinking things ! If *you* want to have the death of women on your hands—*I* don't !

SCANTLEBURY. Now, now, young man !

WILDER. On *our* hands ? Not on *mine*, I won't have it !

EDGAR. We are five members of this Board ; if we were four against it, why did we let it drift till it came to this ? You know perfectly well why—because we hoped we should starve the men out. Well, all we've done is to starve one woman out !

SCANTLEBURY [*almost hysterically*]. I protest, I protest ! I'm a humane man— we're all humane men !

EDGAR [*scornfully*]. There 's nothing wrong with our *humanity*. It 's our imaginations, Mr. Scantlebury.

WILDER. Nonsense! My imagination 's as good as yours.

EDGAR. If so, it is n't good enough.

WILDER. I foresaw this!

EDGAR. Then why did n't you put your foot down!

WILDER. Much good that would have done. [*He looks at* ANTHONY.]

EDGAR. If you, and I, and each one of us here who say that our imaginations are so good —

SCANTLEBURY [*flurried*]. I never said so.

EDGAR [*paying no attention*]. — Had put our feet down, the thing would have been ended long ago, and this poor woman's life would n't have been crushed out of her like this. For all we can tell there may be a dozen other starving women.

SCANTLEBURY. For God's sake, sir, don't use that word at a — at a Board meeting; it 's — it 's monstrous.

EDGAR. I *will* use it, Mr. Scantlebury.

SCANTLEBURY. Then I shall not listen to you. I shall not listen! It 's painful to me. [*He covers his ears.*]

WANKLIN. None of us are opposed to a settlement, except your father.

EDGAR. I 'm certain that if the shareholders knew —

WANKLIN. I don't think you 'll find their imaginations are any better than ours. Because a woman happens to have a weak heart —

EDGAR. A struggle like this finds out the weak spots in everybody. Any child knows that. If it had n't been for this cutthroat policy, she need n't have died like this; and there would n't be all this misery that any one who is n't a fool can see is going on. [*Throughout the foregoing* ANTHONY *has eyed his son; he now moves as though to rise, but stops as* EDGAR *speaks again.*] I don't defend the men, or myself, or anybody.

WANKLIN. You may have to! A coroner's jury of disinterested sympathizers may say some very nasty things. We must n't lose sight of our position.

SCANTLEBURY [*without uncovering his ears*]. Coroner's jury! No, no, it 's not a case for that!

EDGAR. I 've had enough of cowardice.

WANKLIN. Cowardice is an unpleasant word, Mr. Edgar Anthony. It will look very like cowardice if we suddenly concede the men's demands when a thing like this happens; we must be careful!

WILDER. Of course we must. We 've no knowledge of this matter, except a rumor. The proper course is to put the whole thing into the hands of Harness to settle for us; that 's natural, that 's what we *should* have come to any way.

SCANTLEBURY [*with dignity*]. Exactly! [*Turning to* EDGAR.] And as to you, young sir, I can't sufficiently express my — my distaste for the way you 've treated the whole matter. You ought to withdraw! Talking of starvation, talking of cowardice! Considering what our views are! Except your own father — we 're all agreed the only policy is — is one of good will — it 's most irregular, it 's most improper, and all I can say is it 's — it 's given me pain — [*He places his hand over his heart.*]

EDGAR [*stubbornly*]. I withdraw nothing. [*He is about to say more when* SCANTLEBURY *once more covers up his ears.* TENCH *suddenly makes a demonstration with the minute-book. A sense of having been engaged in the unusual comes over all of them, and one by one they resume their seats.* EDGAR *alone remains on his feet.*]

WILDER [*with an air of trying to wipe something out*]. I pay no attention to what young Mr. Anthony has said. Coroner's jury! The idea 's preposterous. I — I move this amendment to the Chairman's motion: That the dispute be placed at once in the hands of Mr. Simon Harness for settlement, on the lines indicated by him this morning. Any one second that? [*TENCH writes in his book.*]

WANKLIN. I do.

WILDER. Very well, then; I ask the Chairman to put it to the Board.

ANTHONY [*with a great sigh — slowly*]. We have been made the subject of an attack. [*Looking round at* WILDER *and* SCANTLEBURY *with ironical contempt.*] I take it on *my* shoulders. I am seventy-six years old. I have been Chairman of this Company since its inception two-and-thirty years ago. I have seen it pass through good and evil report. My connection with it began in the year that this young man was born. [EDGAR *bows his head.* ANTHONY, *gripping his chair, goes on.*] I have had to do with "men" for fifty years; I've always stood up to them; I have never been beaten yet. I have fought the men of this Company four times, and four times I have beaten them. It has been said that I am not the man I was. [*He looks at* WILDER.] However that may be, I am man enough to stand to my guns. [*His voice grows stronger. The double doors are opened.* ENID *slips in, followed by* UNDERWOOD, *who restrains her.*] The men have been treated justly, they have had fair wages, we have always been ready to listen to complaints. It has been said that times have changed; if they have, I have not changed with them. Neither will I. It has been said that masters and men are equal! Cant! There can only be one master in a house! Where two men meet the better man will rule. It has been said that Capital and Labor have the same interests. Cant! Their interests are as wide asunder as the poles. It has been said that the Board is only part of a machine. Cant! We *are* the machine; its brains and sinews; it is for us to lead and to determine what is to be done, and to do it without fear or favor. Fear of the men! Fear of the shareholders! Fear of our own shadows! Before I am like that, I hope to die. [*He pauses, and meeting his son's eyes, goes on.*] There is only one way of treating "men" — with *the iron hand.* This half and half business, the half and half manners of this generation, has brought all this upon us. Sentiment and softness, and what this young man, no doubt, would call his social policy. You can't eat cake and have it! This middle-class sentiment, or socialism, or whatever it may be, is rotten. Masters are masters, men are men! Yield one demand, and they will make it six. They are [*he smiles grimly*] like Oliver Twist, asking for more. If I were in *their* place I should be the same. But I am not in their place. Mark my words: one fine morning, when you have given way here, and given way there — you will find you have parted with the ground beneath your feet, and are deep in the bog of bankruptcy; and with you, floundering in that bog, will be the very men you have given way to. I have been accused of being a domineering tyrant, thinking only of my

pride — I am thinking of the future of this country, threatened with the black waters of confusion, threatened with mob government, threatened with what I cannot see. If by any conduct of mine I help to bring this on us, I shall be ashamed to look my fellows in the face.

> [ANTHONY *stares before him, at what he cannot see, and there is perfect stillness.* FROST *comes in from the hall, and all but* ANTHONY *look round at him uneasily.*]

FROST. [*To his master.*] The men are here, sir. [ANTHONY *makes a gesture of dismissal.*] Shall I bring them in, sir?

ANTHONY. Wait! [FROST *goes out,* ANTHONY *turns to face his son.*] I come to the attack that has been made upon me. [EDGAR, *with a gesture of deprecation, remains motionless with his head a little bowed.*] A woman has died. I am told that her blood is on my hands; I am told that on my hands is the starvation and the suffering of other women and of children.

EDGAR. I said "on *our* hands," sir.

ANTHONY. It is the same. [*His voice grows stronger and stronger, his feeling is more and more made manifest.*] I am not aware that if my adversary suffer in a fair fight not sought by me, it is *my* fault. If I fall under *his* feet — as fall I may — I shall not complain. That will be *my* lookout — and this is — his. I cannot separate, as I would, these men from their women and children. A fair fight is a fair fight! Let them learn to think before they pick a quarrel!

EDGAR [*in a low voice*]. But is it a fair fight, father? Look at them, and look at us! They've only this one weapon!

ANTHONY [*grimly*]. And you're weak-kneed enough to teach them how to use it! It seems the fashion nowadays for men to take their enemy's side. I have not learned that art. Is it my fault that they quarreled with their Union too?

EDGAR. There is such a thing as mercy.

ANTHONY. And justice comes before it.

EDGAR. What seems just to one man, sir, is injustice to another.

ANTHONY [*with suppressed passion*]. You accuse me of injustice — of what amounts to inhumanity — of cruelty —

> [EDGAR *makes a gesture of horror — a general frightened movement.*]

WANKLIN. Come, come, Chairman.

ANTHONY [*in a grim voice*]. These are the words of my own son. They are the words of a generation that I don't understand; the words of a soft breed.

[*A general murmur. With a violent effort* ANTHONY *recovers his control.*]

EDGAR [*quietly*]. I said it of *myself*, too, father.

[*A long look is exchanged between them, and* ANTHONY *puts out his hand with a gesture as if to sweep the personalities away; then places it against his brow, swaying as though from giddiness. There is a movement towards him. He moves them back.*]

ANTHONY. Before I put this amendment to the Board, I have one more word to say. [*He looks from face to face.*] If it is carried, it means that we shall fail in what we set ourselves to do. It means that we shall fail in the duty that we owe to all Capital. It means that we shall fail in the duty that we owe ourselves. It means that we shall be open to constant attack to which we as constantly shall have to yield. Be under no misapprehension — run this time, and you will never make a stand again! You will have to fly like curs before the whips of your own men. If that is the lot you wish for, you will vote for this amendment. [*He looks again, from face to face, finally resting his gaze on* EDGAR ; *all sit with their eyes on the ground.* ANTHONY *makes a gesture, and* TENCH *hands him the book. He reads.*] "Moved by Mr. Wilder, and seconded by Mr. Wanklin: 'That the men's demands be placed at once in the hands of Mr. Simon Harness for settlement on the lines indicated by him this morning.'" [*With sudden vigor.*] Those in favor: Signify the same in the usual way! [*For a minute no one moves ; then hastily just as* ANTHONY *is about to speak,* WILDER'S *hand and* WANKLIN'S *are held up, then* SCANTLEBURY'S, *and last* EDGAR'S *who does not lift his head.*] Contrary? [ANTHONY *lifts his own hand. In a clear voice.*] The amendment is carried. I resign my position on this Board. [ENID *gasps, and there is dead silence.* ANTHONY *sits motionless, his head slowly drooping ; suddenly he heaves as though the whole of his life had risen up within him.*] Fifty years! You have disgraced me, gentlemen. Bring in the men!

[*He sits motionless, staring before*

him. *The Board draws hurriedly together, and forms a group.* TENCH *in a frightened manner speaks into the hall.* UNDERWOOD *almost forces* ENID *from the room.*]

WILDER [*hurriedly*]. What's to be said to them? Why is n't Harness here? Ought we to see the men before he comes? I don't —

TENCH. Will you come in, please?

[*Enter* THOMAS, GREEN, BULGIN, *and* ROUS, *who file up in a row past the little table.* TENCH *sits down and writes. All eyes are fixed on* ANTHONY, *who makes no sign.*]

WANKLIN [*stepping up to the little table, with nervous cordiality*]. Well, Thomas, how's it to be? What's the result of your meeting?

ROUS. Sim Harness has our answer. He'll tell you what it is. We're waiting for him. He'll speak for us.

WANKLIN. Is that so, Thomas?

THOMAS [*sullenly*]. Yes. Roberts will not pe coming, his wife is dead.

SCANTLEBURY. Yes, yes! Poor woman! Yes! Yes!

FROST [*entering from the hall*]. Mr. Harness, sir!

[*As* HARNESS *enters he retires.* HARNESS *has a piece of paper in his hand, he bows to the Directors, nods towards the men, and takes his stand behind the little table in the very center of the room.*]

HARNESS. Good-evening, gentlemen.

[TENCH, *with the paper he has been writing, joins him; they speak together in low tones.*]

WILDER. We've been waiting for you, Harness. Hope we shall come to some —

FROST [*entering from the hall*]. Roberts!

[*He goes.* ROBERTS *comes hastily in, and stands staring at* ANTHONY. *His face is drawn and old.*]

ROBERTS. Mr. Anthony, I am afraid I am a little late, I would have been here in time but for something that — has happened. [*To the men.*] Has anything been said?

THOMAS. No! But, man, what made ye come?

ROBERTS. Ye told us this morning, gentlemen, to go away and reconsider our position. We have reconsidered it ; we are here to bring you the men's answer. [*To* ANTHONY.] Go ye back to London. We have nothing for you. By no jot or tittle do we abate our demands, nor will we until the whole of those demands are yielded.

[ANTHONY *looks at him but does not speak. There is a movement amongst the men as though they were bewildered.*]

HARNESS. Roberts !

ROBERTS [*glancing fiercely at him, and back to* ANTHONY]. Is that clear enough for ye ? Is it short enough and to the point ? Ye made a mistake to think that we would come to heel. Ye may break the body, but ye cannot break the spirit. Get back to London, the men have nothing for ye ?

[*Pausing uneasily he takes a step towards the unmoving* ANTHONY.]

EDGAR. We're all sorry for you, Roberts, but —

ROBERTS. Keep your sorrow, young man. Let your father speak !

HARNESS [*with the sheet of paper in his hand, speaking from behind the little table*]. Roberts !

ROBERTS. [*To* ANTHONY, *with passionate intensity.*] Why don't ye answer ?

HARNESS. Roberts !

ROBERTS [*turning sharply*]. What is it ?

HARNESS [*gravely*]. You're talking without the book ; things have traveled past you. [*He makes a sign to* TENCH, *who beckons the Directors. They quickly sign his copy of the terms.*] Look at this, man ! [*Holding up his sheet of paper.*] " Demands conceded, *with the exception of those relating to the engineers and furnace men.* Double wages for Saturday's overtime. Night-shifts as they are." These terms have been agreed. The men go back to work again to-morrow. The strike is at an end.

ROBERTS [*reading the paper, and turning on the men. They shrink back from him, all but* ROUS, *who stands his ground. With deadly stillness*]. Ye have gone back on me ? I stood by ye to the death ; ye waited for *that* to throw me over !

[*The men answer, all speaking together.*]

ROUS. It's a lie !

THOMAS. Ye were past endurance, man.

GREEN. If ye'd listen to me —

BULGIN [*under his breath*]. Hold your jaw !

ROBERTS. Ye waited for *that !*

HARNESS [*taking the Directors' copy of the terms, and handing his own to* TENCH]. That's enough, men. You had better go.

[*The men shuffle slowly, awkwardly away.*]

WILDER [*in a low, nervous voice*]. There's nothing to stay for now, I suppose. [*He follows to the door.*] I shall have a try for that train ! Coming, Scantlebury ?

SCANTLEBURY [*following with* WANKLIN]. Yes, yes ; wait for me.

[*He stops as* ROBERTS *speaks.*]

ROBERTS. [*To* ANTHONY.] But *ye* have not signed them terms ! They can't make terms without their Chairman ! Ye would never sign them terms ! [ANTHONY *looks at him without speaking.*] Don't tell me ye have ! for the love o' God ! [*With passionate appeal.*] I reckoned on ye !

HARNESS [*holding out the Directors' copy of the terms*]. The Board has signed !

[ROBERTS *looks dully at the signatures — dashes the paper from him, and covers up his eyes.*]

SCANTLEBURY [*behind his hand to* TENCH]. Look after the Chairman ! He's not well ; he's not well — he had no lunch. If there's any fund started for the women and children, put me down for — for twenty pounds.

[*He goes out into the hall, in cumbrous haste; and* WANKLIN, *who has been staring at* ROBERTS *and* ANTHONY *with twitchings of his face, follows.* EDGAR *remains seated on the sofa, looking at the ground;* TENCH, *returning to the bureau, writes in his minute-book.* HARNESS *stands by the little table, gravely watching* ROBERTS.]

ROBERTS. Then you're no longer Chairman of this Company ! [*Breaking into halfmad laughter.*] Ah ! ha — ah, ha, ha ! They've thrown ye over — thrown over their Chairman ! Ah — ha — ha ! [*With a sudden dreadful calm.*] So — they've done us both down, Mr. Anthony ?

[ENID, *hurrying through the double doors, comes quickly to her father.*]

ANTHONY. Both broken men, my friend Roberts !

HARNESS [*coming down and laying his hands on* ROBERTS'S *sleeve*]. For shame, Roberts ! Go home quietly, man ; go home !

ROBERTS [*tearing his arm away*]. Home ? [*Shrinking together — in a whisper.*] Home !

ENID [*quietly to her father*]. Come away, dear ! Come to your room !

[ANTHONY *rises with an effort. He turns to* ROBERTS *who looks at him. They stand several seconds, gazing at each other fixedly;* ANTHONY *lifts his hand, as though to salute, but lets it fall. The expression of* ROBERTS's *face changes from hostility to wonder. They bend their heads in token of respect.* ANTHONY *turns, and slowly walks towards the curtained door. Suddenly he sways as though about to fall, recovers himself, and is assisted out by* EDGAR *and* ENID; UNDERWOOD *follows, but stops at the door.* ROBERTS *remains motionless for several seconds, staring intently after* ANTHONY, *then goes out into the hall.*]

TENCH [*approaching* HARNESS]. It's a great weight off my mind, Mr. Harness ! But what a painful scene, sir ! [*He wipes his brow.* HARNESS, *pale and resolute, regards, with a grim half-smile the quavering* TENCH.] It's all been so violent ! What did he mean by : " Done us both down " ? If he has lost his wife, poor fellow, he ought n't to have spoken to the Chairman like that !

HARNESS. A woman dead ; and the two best men both broken !

TENCH [*staring at him — suddenly excited*]. D' you know, sir — these terms, they 're the *very same* we drew up together, you and I, and put to both sides before the fight began ? All this — all this — and — and what for ?

HARNESS [*in a slow grim voice*]. That's where the fun comes in !

[UNDERWOOD *without turning from the door makes a gesture of assent.*]

THE MADRAS HOUSE

A COMEDY, IN FOUR ACTS

By GRANVILLE BARKER

THE MADRAS HOUSE

ACT I

The HUXTABLES *live at Denmark Hill, for* MR. HUXTABLE *is the surviving partner in the well-known Peckham drapery establishment of Roberts & Huxtable, and the situation, besides being salubrious, is therefore convenient. It is a new house.* MR. HUXTABLE *bought it half finished, so that the interior might be to his liking; its exterior the builder said one might describe as of a Free Queen Anne Treatment; to which* MR. HUXTABLE *rejoined, after blinking at the red brick spotted with stone ornament, that after all it was inside they were going to live, you know.*

Through the stained, grained front door, rattling with colored glass, one reaches the hall, needlessly narrow, needlessly dark, but with its black-and-white tessellated pavement making for cleanliness. On the left is the stained and grained staircase, with its Brussels carpet and twisted brass stair rods, on the right the drawing-room. The drawing-room can hardly be said to express the personality of MR. HUXTABLE. *The foundations of its furnishings are in the taste of* MRS. HUXTABLE. *For fifteen years or so additions to this family museum have been disputed into their place by the six* MISS HUXTABLES: LAURA *(aged thirty-nine),* MINNIE, CLARA, JULIA, EMMA, JANE *(aged twenty-six). The rosewood cabinets, the picture from some Academy of the early Seventies, entitled* In Ye Olden Time *(this was a wedding present, most likely), the gilt clock, which is a Shakespeare, narrow-headed, but with a masterly pair of legs, propped pensively against a dial and enshrined beneath a dome of glass, another wedding present. These were the treasures of* MRS. HUXTABLE'S *first drawing-room, her solace in the dull post-honeymoon days. She was the daughter of a city merchant, wholesale as against her husband's retail; but even in the Seventies retail was lifting its head. It was considered, though, that* KATHERINE TOMBS *conferred some distinction upon young* HARRY HUXTABLE *by marrying him, and even now, as a portly lady nearing sixty, she figures by the rustle of her dress, the measure of her mellow voice, with its carefully chosen phrases, for the dignity of the household.*

The difference between one MISS HUXTABLE *and another is, to a casual eye, the difference between one lead pencil and another, as these lie upon one's table, after some weeks' use; a matter of length, of sharpening, of wear.* LAURA'S *distinction lies in her being the housekeeper; it is a solid power, that of ordering the dinner. She is very silent. While her sisters are silent with strangers, she is silent with her sisters. She does n't seem to read much, either; one hopes she dreams, if only of wild adventures with a new carpet-sweeper. When there was some family bitterness as to whether the fireplace, in summer, should hold ferns or a Chinese umbrella, it was* LAURA'S *opinion that an umbrella gathers less dust, which carried the day.* MINNIE *and* CLARA *are inclined to religion; not sentimentally; works are a good second with them to faith. They have veered, though, lately, from district visiting to an interest in Missions — missions to Poplar or China (one is almost as far as the other); good works, the results of which they cannot see. Happily, they forbear to ask why this proves the more soul-satisfying sort.*

JULIA *started life — that is to say, left school — as a genius. The head mistress had had two or three years of such dull girls that really she could not resist this excitement. Water-color sketches were the medium. So* JULIA *was dressed in brown velveteen, and sent to an art school, where they would n't let her do water-color drawing at all. And in two years she learned enough about the trade of an artist not ever to want to do those water-color drawings again.* JULIA *is now over thirty, and very unhappy. Three of her water-colors (early masterpieces) hang on the drawing-room wall. They shame her, but her mother won't have them taken down. On a holiday she'll be off now and then for a solitary day's sketching, and as she tears up the vain attempt to put on paper the things she has learned to see, she sometimes cries. It was* JULIA, EMMA, *and* JANE *who, some years ago, conspired to present their mother with that intensely conspicuous cozy corner. A cozy corner is apparently a device for making a corner just what the very nature of a corner should forbid it to be. They beggared themselves; but one wishes that* MR. HUXTABLE *were more lavish with his dress allowances, then they might at least have afforded something not quite so hideous.*

EMMA, *having* JULIA *in mind, has run rather to coats and skirts and common sense. She would have been a success in an office, and worth, perhaps, thirty shillings a week. But the* HUXTABLES *don't want another thirty shillings a week, and this gift, such as it is, has been wasted, so that* EMMA *runs also to a brusque temper.*

JANE *is meekly enough a little wild.* MRS. HUXTABLE'S *power of applying the brake of good breeding, strong enough over five daughters, waned at the sixth attempt in twelve years, and* JANE *has actually got herself proposed to twice by not quite desirable young men. Now the fact that she was old enough to be proposed to at all came as something of a shock to the family. Birthdays pass, their celebration growing less emphatic. No one likes to believe that the years are passing; even the birthday's owner, least able to escape its significance, laughs, and then changes the subject. So the* MISS HUXTABLES *never openly asked each other what the marriage of the youngest of them might imply; perhaps they never even asked themselves. Besides,* JANE *didn't marry. But if she does, unless, perhaps, she runs away to do it, there will be heart-searchings, at least.* MR. HUXTABLE *asked, though, and* MRS. HUXTABLE'S *answer — given early one morning, before the hot water came — scarcely satisfied him. "For," said* MR. HUXTABLE, *"if the girls don't marry some day, what are they to do! It's not as if they had to go into the shop." "No, thank Heaven!" said* MRS. HUXTABLE.

Since his illness MR. HUXTABLE *has taken to asking questions — of anybody and about anything; of himself oftenest of all. But for that illness he would have been a conventional enough type of successful shopkeeper, coarsely fed, whiskered, podgy. But eighteen months' nursing and dieting and removal from the world seem to have brought a gentleness to his voice, a spark of humor to his eye, a childishness to his little bursts of temper — they have added, in fact, a wistfulness which makes him rather a lovable old buffer on the whole.*

This is a Sunday morning, a bright day in October. The family are still at church, and the drawing-room is empty. The door opens, and the parlormaid — much becapped and aproned — shows in PHILIP MADRAS *and his friend,* MAJOR HIPPISLY THOMAS. THOMAS, *long-legged and deliberate, moves across the room to the big French windows, which open onto a balcony and*

look down on the garden and to many gardens beyond. THOMAS *is a good fellow.*

PHILIP MADRAS *is more complex than that. To begin with, it is obvious he is not wholly English. A certain litheness of figure, the keenness and color of his voice, and a liking for metaphysical turns of speech, show an Eastern origin, perhaps. He is kind in manner, but rather cold, capable of that least English of dispositions — intellectual passion. He is about thirty-five, a year or two younger than his friend. The parlormaid has secured* MAJOR THOMAS'S *hat, and stands clutching it. As* PHILIP *passes her into the room he asks . . .*

PHILIP. About how long?

THE MAID. In just a few minutes now, I should say, sir. Oh, I beg pardon, does it 'appen to be the third Sunday in the month?

PHILIP. I don't know. Tommy, does it?

THOMAS [*from the window*]. Don't ask me. Well, I suppose I can tell you. [*And he vaguely fishes for his diary.*]

THE MAID. No, I don't think it does, sir. Because then some of them stop for the 'Oly Communion, and that may make them late for dinner, but I don't think it is, sir.

[*She backs through the door, entangling the hat in the handle.*]

PHILIP. Is my mother still staying here?

THE MAID. Mrs. Madras, sir? Yes, sir.

[*Then having disentangled the hat, the parlormaid vanishes.* PHILIP *thereupon plunges swiftly into what must be an interrupted argument.*]

PHILIP. Well, my dear Tommy, what are the two most important things in a man's character? His attitude towards money and his attitude towards women.

THOMAS [*ponderously slowing him up*]. Yes, you're full up with moral precepts. Why behave about money as if it didn't exist? I never said don't join the County Council.

PHILIP [*deliberately, but in a breath*]. It is quite impossible for any decent man to walk with his eyes open from Waterloo to Denmark Hill on a Sunday morning without wishing me to stand for the County Council.

[THOMAS *intrenches himself on a sofa.*]

THOMAS. You've got what I call a Reformer's mind. I shouldn't cultivate it, Phil. It makes a man unhappy and discontented, not with himself, but with other people, mark you . . . so it makes him conceited, and puts him out of condition both ways. Don't you get to imagine you can make this country better by tidying it up.

PHILIP [*whimsically*]. But I'm very interested in England, Tommy.

THOMAS [*not without some answering humor*]. We all are. But we don't all need to go about saying so. Even I can be interested in England, I suppose, though I have had to chuck the Army and take to business to earn bread and treacle for a wife and four children . . . and not a bad thing for me, either. I tell you if every chap would look after himself and his family, and lead a godly, righteous and sober life — I'm sorry, but it is Sunday — England would get on a damn sight better than it will with all your interference.

[*He leans back.* PHILIP'S *eyes fix themselves on some great distance.*]

PHILIP. It's a muddled country. One's first instinct is to be rhetorical about it . . . to write poetry and relieve one's feelings. I once thought I might be self-sacrificing — give my goods to the poor, and go slumming — keeping my immortal soul superior still. There's something wrong with a world, Tommy, in which it takes a man like me all his time to find out that it's bread people want, and not either cake or crumbs.

THOMAS. There's something wrong with a man while he will think of other people as if they were ants on an ant heap.

PHILIP [*relaxing to a smile*]. Tommy, that's perfectly true. I like having a good talk with you : sooner or later you always say one sensible thing.

THOMAS. Thank you ; you're damn polite. And, as usual, we've got right off the point.

PHILIP. The art of conversation !

THOMAS [*shying at the easy epigram*]. Go on six County Councils, if you like. But why chuck up seven hundred a year and a directorship, if State wants you to keep 'em ? And you could have double or more, and manage the place, if you'd ask for it.

PHILIP [*almost venomously*]. Tommy, I loathe the Madras House. State may buy it, and do what he likes with it.

[JULIA *and* LAURA *arrive. They are the first from church. Sunday frocks, Sunday hats, best gloves, umbrellas and prayer books.*]

JULIA. Oh, what a surprise !

PHILIP. Yes, we walked down. Ah, you don't know . . . Let me introduce Major Hippisly Thomas . . . my cousin, Miss Julia Huxtable . . . and Miss Huxtable.

JULIA. How do you do ?

THOMAS. How do you do ?

LAURA. How do you do ?

JULIA. Have you come to see Aunt Amy ?

PHILIP. No, your father.

JULIA. He's walking back with her. They'll be last, I'm afraid.

LAURA. Will you stay to dinner ?

PHILIP. No, I think not.

LAURA. I'd better tell them you won't. Perhaps they'll be laying for you.

[LAURA *goes out, decorously avoiding a collision with* EMMA, *who, panoplied as the others, comes in at the same moment.*]

PHILIP. Hullo, Emma !

EMMA. Well, what a surprise !

PHILIP. You don't know . . . Major Hippisly Thomas . . . Miss Emma Huxtable.

THOMAS. How do you do ?

EMMA. How do you do ? Will you stay to dinner ?

PHILIP. No, we can't. [*That formula again completed, he varies his explanation.*] I've just brought Thomas a Sunday morning walk to help me tell Uncle Henry a bit of news. My father will be back in England to-morrow.

EMMA [*with a round mouth*]. Oh !

JULIA. It's a beautiful morning for a walk, is n't it ?

THOMAS. Wonderful for October.

[*These two look first at each other, and then out of the window.* EMMA *gazes quizzically at* PHILIP.]

EMMA. I think he knows.

PHILIP. He sort of knows.

EMMA. Why are you being odd, Philip ? [PHILIP *is more hail-fellow-well-met with* EMMA *than with the others.*]

PHILIP. Emma . . . I have enticed a comparative stranger to be present so that your father and mother cannot, in decency, begin to fight the family battle over again with me. I know it's very cunning, but we did want a walk. Besides, there's a meeting to-morrow. . . .

[JANE *peeps through the door.*]

JANE. You? Mother!

[*She has turned to the hall, and from the hall comes* MRS. HUXTABLE'S *rotund voice,* "*Yes, Jane!*"]

JANE. Cousin Philip!

[MRS. HUXTABLE *sails in, and superbly compresses every family greeting into one.*]

MRS. HUXTABLE. What a surprise! Will you stay to dinner?

EMMA [*alive to a certain redundancy*]. No, mother, they can't.

PHILIP. May I introduce my friend . . . Major Hippisly Thomas . . . my aunt, Mrs. Huxtable.

MRS. HUXTABLE [*stately and gracious*]. How do you do, Major Thomas?

PHILIP. Thomas is Mr. Eustace State's London manager.

THOMAS. How do you do?

[MRS. HUXTABLE *takes an armchair with the air of one mounting a throne, and from that vantage point begins polite conversation. Her daughters distribute themselves, so do* PHILIP *and* HIPPISLY THOMAS.]

MRS. HUXTABLE. Not in the Army, then, Major Thomas?

THOMAS. I was in the Army.

EMMA. Jessica quite well, Philip?

PHILIP. Yes, thanks.

EMMA. And Mildred?

PHILIP. I think so. She's back at school.

MRS. HUXTABLE. A wonderfully warm autumn, is it not?

THOMAS. Quite.

MRS. HUXTABLE. Do you know Denmark Hill well?

THOMAS. Not well.

MRS. HUXTABLE. We have always lived here. I consider it healthy. But London is a healthy place, I think. Oh, I beg your pardon . . . my daughter Jane.

JANE. How do you do?

[*They shake hands with ceremony.* EMMA, *in a mind to liven things up, goes to the window.*]

EMMA. We've quite a good garden, that's one thing.

THOMAS [*not wholly innocent of an attempt to escape from his hostess, makes for the window, too*]. I noticed it. I am keen on gardens.

MRS. HUXTABLE [*her attention distracted by* JULIA'S *making for the door*]. Julia, where are you going?

JULIA. To take my things off, mother.

[JULIA *departs. When they were quite little girls* MRS. HUXTABLE *always did ask her daughters where they were going when they left the room, and where they had been when they entered it, and she has never dropped the habit. They resent it only by the extreme patience of their replies.*]

EMMA [*entertainingly*]. That's the Crystal Palace.

THOMAS. Is it?

[*They both peer appreciatively at that famous landmark. In the Crystal Palace and the sunset the inhabitants of Denmark Hill have acquired almost proprietary interest. Then* MRS. HUXTABLE *speaks to her nephew with a sudden severity.*]

MRS. HUXTABLE. Philip, I don't consider your mother's health is at all the thing.

PHILIP [*amicably*]. It never is, Aunt Kate.

MRS. HUXTABLE [*admitting the justice of the retort*]. That's true.

PHILIP. Uncle Henry keeps better, I think.

MRS. HUXTABLE. He's well enough now. I have had a slight cold. Is it true that your father may appear in England again?

PHILIP. Yes, he has only been on the Continent. He arrives to-morrow.

MRS. HUXTABLE. I'm sorry.

JANE. Mother!

[MRS. HUXTABLE *has launched this with such redoubled severity that* JANE *had to protest. However, at this moment arrives* MR. HUXTABLE *himself, one glad smile.*]

MR. HUXTABLE. Ah, Phil . . . I 'ad an idea you might come over. You'll stay to dinner. Jane, tell your aunt . . . she's taking 'er bonnet off.

[JANE *obeys. He sights on the balcony* MAJOR THOMAS'S *back.*]

MR. HUXTABLE. Who's that outside?

PHILIP. Hippisly Thomas. We wanted a walk; we can't stay.

MR. HUXTABLE. Oh!

MRS. HUXTABLE. Have you come on business?

PHILIP. Well . . .

MRS. HUXTABLE. On Sunday?

PHILIP. Not exactly.

[*She shakes her head gravely deprecating.* THOMAS *comes from the balcony.*]

MR. HUXTABLE. How are you?

THOMAS. How are *you*?

MR. HUXTABLE. Fine morning, is n't it? Nice prospect, this . . . see the Crystal Palace?

[*While* THOMAS *turns, with perfect politeness, to view again this phenomenon,* PHILIP *pacifies his aunt.*]

PHILIP. You see, Aunt Katherine, tomorrow afternoon we have the first real conference with this Mr. State about buying up the two firms, and my father is passing through England again to attend it.

MRS. HUXTABLE. Of course, Philip, if it's business, I know nothing about it. But is it suggested that your uncle should attend, too?

[*Her voice has found a new gravity.* PHILIP *becomes very airy; so does* MR. HUXTABLE, *who comes back to rejoin the conversation.*]

PHILIP. My dear aunt, naturally.

MR. HUXTABLE. What's this?

MRS. HUXTABLE [*the one word expressing volumes*]. Constantine.

MR. HUXTABLE [*with elaborate innocence*]. That's definite now, is it?

MRS. HUXTABLE. You dropped a hint last night, Henry.

MR. HUXTABLE. I dessay. I dessay I did.   [*His eye shifts guiltily.*]

MRS. HUXTABLE. Quite out of the question, it seems to me.   [JANE *comes back.*]

JANE. Aunt Mary's coming.

MR. HUXTABLE [*genial again*]. Oh! My daughter Jane . . . Major Thomas, Major Hippisly Thomas.

JANE [*with discretion*]. Yes, father.

MRS. HUXTABLE [*tactfully*]. You are naturally not aware, Major Thomas, that for family reasons, into which we need not go, Mr. Huxtable has not spoken to his brother-in-law for a number of years.

[PHILIP'S *eye meets* THOMAS'S *in comic agony. But* MR. HUXTABLE, *too, plunges delightedly into the forbidden subject.*]

MR. HUXTABLE. Thirty years, very near. Wonderful, is n't it? Interested in the same business. Was n't easy to keep it up.

THOMAS. I had heard.

MR. HUXTABLE. Oh, yes, notorious.

MRS. HUXTABLE [*in reprobation*]. And well it may be, Henry.

[MRS. MADRAS *comes in. It is evident*

that PHILIP *is his father's son. He would seem so wholly but for that touch of "self-worship which is often self-mistrust"; his mother's gift, appearing nowadays less lovably in her as a sort of querulous assertion of her rights and wrongs against the troubles which have been too strong for her. She is a pale old lady, shrunk a little, the life gone out of her.*]

MRS. HUXTABLE [*some severity remaining*]. Amy, your husband is in England again.

[PHILIP *presents a filial cheek. It is kissed.*]

PHILIP. How are you, mother?

MR. HUXTABLE [*sotto voce*]. Oh, tact, Katherine, tact!

PHILIP. Perhaps you remember Reggie Thomas?

THOMAS. I was at Marlborough with Philip, Mrs. Madras.

MRS. MADRAS. Yes. Is he, Katherine?

[*Having given* THOMAS *a limp hand, and her sister this coldest of responses, she finds her way to a sofa, where she sits silent, thinking to herself.* MRS. HUXTABLE *keeps majestic hold upon her subject.*]

MRS. HUXTABLE. I am utterly unable to see, Philip, why your uncle should break through his rule now.

MR. HUXTABLE. There you are, Phil!

PHILIP. Of course it is quite for Uncle Henry to decide.

MR. HUXTABLE. Naturally . . . naturally.

[*Still he has an appealing eye on* PHILIP, *who obliges him.*]

PHILIP. But since Mr. State's offer may not be only for the Madras House, but Roberts and Huxtable into the bargain . . . if the two principal proprietors can't meet him round a table to settle the matter . . .

THOMAS [*ponderously diplomatic*]. Yes . . . a little awkward . . . if I may say so . . . as Mr. State's representative, Mrs. Huxtable.

MRS. HUXTABLE. You don't think, do you, Major Thomas, that any amount of awkwardness should induce us to pass over wicked conduct?

[*This reduces the assembly to such a shamed silence that poor* MR. HUXTABLE *can only add . . .*]

MR. HUXTABLE. Oh, talk of something else . . . talk of something else.

[*After a moment* MRS. MADRAS's *pale voice steals in, as she turns to her son.*]

MRS. MADRAS. When did you hear from your father ?

PHILIP. A letter from Marienbad two or three days ago, and a telegram yesterday morning.

[MRS. HUXTABLE, *with a hostess's authority, now restores a polite and easy tone to the conversation.*]

MRS. HUXTABLE. And have you left the Army long, Major Thomas ?

THOMAS. Four years.

MRS. HUXTABLE. Now what made you take to the Drapery Trade ?

PHILIP [*very explanatory*]. Mr. State is an American financier, Aunt Kitty, who has bought up Burrows', the big mantle place in the city, and is about to buy us up, too, perhaps.

MRS. HUXTABLE. We are not in difficulties, I hope.

PHILIP. Oh, no.

MRS. HUXTABLE. No. No doubt Henry would have told me if we had been.

[*As she thus gracefully dismisses the subject there appear up the steps and along the balcony the last arrivals from church,* MINNIE *and* CLARA. *The male part of the company unsettles itself.*]

MR. HUXTABLE. 'Ullo ! Where have you been ?

MINNIE. We went for a walk.

MRS. HUXTABLE [*in apparently deep surprise*]. A walk, Minnie ! Where to ?

MINNIE. Just the long way home. We thought we 'd have time.

CLARA. Did you notice what a short sermon ?

MR. HUXTABLE. Oh, may I . . . My daughter Clara . . . Major 'Ippisly Thomas. My daughter Minnie . . . Major Thomas.

[*The conventional chant begins.*]

MINNIE. How d' you do ?

THOMAS. How d' you do ?

CLARA. How d' you do ?

MINNIE. How d' you do, Philip ?

PHILIP. How d' you do ?

CLARA. How d' you do ?

PHILIP. How d' you do ?

[*The chant over, the company resettles;*

MR. HUXTABLE *buttonholing* PHILIP *in the process with an air of some mystery.*]

MR. HUXTABLE. By the way, Phil, remind me to ask you something before you go . . . rather important.

PHILIP. I shall be at your place in the morning. Thomas is coming to go through some figures.

MR. HUXTABLE [*with a regular snap*]. Yes . . . I shan't.

PHILIP. The State meeting is in Bond Street, three o'clock.

MR. HUXTABLE. I know, I know. [*Then, finding himself prominent, he captures the conversation.*] I 'm slacking off, Major Thomas, slacking off. Ever since I was ill I 've been slacking off.

MRS. HUXTABLE. You are perfectly well now, Henry.

MR. HUXTABLE. Not the point. I want leisure, you know, leisure. Time for reading . . . time to think a bit.

MRS. HUXTABLE. Nonsense ! [*She adds, with correctness.*] Major Thomas will excuse me.

MR. HUXTABLE [*on his hobby*]. Oh, well . . . a man must . . . some portion of his life . . .

THOMAS. Quite. I got most of my reading done early.

MRS. HUXTABLE. The natural time for it.

MR. HUXTABLE. Ah, lucky feller ! Educated, I suppose. Well, I was n't. I 've been getting the books for years — good editions. I 'd like you to see my library. But these geniuses want settling down to . . . if a man's to keep pace with the thought of the world, y' know. Macaulay, 'Erbert Spencer, Grote's 'Istory of Greece ! I 've got 'em all there.

[*He finds no further response.* MRS. HUXTABLE *fills the gap.*]

MRS. HUXTABLE. I thought the sermon dull this morning, Amy, did n't you ?

MRS. MADRAS [*unexpectedly*]. No, I did n't.

MINNIE [*to do her share of the entertaining*]. Mother, somebody ought to speak about those boys . . . it 's disgraceful. Mr. Vivian had actually to turn round from the organ at them during the last hymn.

[JULIA, *her things taken off, reappears.* MR. HUXTABLE *is on the spot.*]

MR. HUXTABLE. Ah, my daughter Julia . . . Major —

JULIA. We 've been introduced, father.

[*She says this with a hauteur which really is pure nervousness, but* MR. HUXTABLE *is sufficiently crushed.*]

MR. HUXTABLE. Oh, I beg pardon.

[*But* MRS. HUXTABLE *disapproves of any self-assertion, and descends upon the culprit, who is, for some obscure reason (or for none), more often disapproved of than the others.*]

MRS. HUXTABLE. Close the door, please, Julia.

JULIA. I 'm sorry, mother.

[PHILIP *closes the offending door.* JULIA *obliterates herself in a chair, and the conversation, hardly encouraged by this little affray, comes to an intolerable standstill. At last* CLARA *makes an effort.*]

CLARA. Is Jessica quite well, Philip?

PHILIP. Yes, thank you, Clara.

MRS. HUXTABLE. And dear little Mildred?

PHILIP. Yes, thank you, Aunt Kate.

[*Further standstill. Then* MINNIE *contrives a remark.*]

MINNIE. Do you still like that school for her?

PHILIP [*with finesse*]. It seems to provide every accomplishment that money can buy.

[MRS. HUXTABLE *discovers a sure opening.*]

MRS. HUXTABLE. Have you been away for the summer, Major Thomas?

THOMAS [*vaguely — he is getting sympathetically tongue-tied*]. Oh . . . yes . . .

PHILIP. Tommy and Jessica and I took our holidays motoring around Munich and into it for the operas.

MRS. HUXTABLE. Was that pleasant?

PHILIP. Very.

MRS. HUXTABLE. And where was dear Mildred?

PHILIP. With her aunt most of the time . . . Jessica's sister-in-law, you know.

MINNIE. Lady Ames?

PHILIP. Yes.

MRS. HUXTABLE [*innocently, genuinely snobbish*]. Very nice for her.

MR. HUXTABLE. We take a 'ouse at Weymouth, as a rule.

MRS. HUXTABLE. Do you know Weymouth, Major Thomas?

THOMAS. No, I don't.

MRS. HUXTABLE. George III used to stay there, but that is a hotel now.

MR. HUXTABLE. Keep your spare money in the country, y' know.

MRS. HUXTABLE. Oh, there is everything one wants at Weymouth.

[*But even this subject flags.*]

MRS. HUXTABLE. You think more of Bognor, Amy, I know.

MRS. MADRAS. Only to live in, Katherine.

[*They have made their last effort. The conversation is dead.* MR. HUXTABLE's *discomfort suddenly becomes physical.*]

MR. HUXTABLE. I 'm going to change my coat.

PHILIP. I think perhaps we ought to be off.

MR. HUXTABLE. No, no, no, no, no! I shan't be a minute. Don't go, Phil; there 's a good fellow.

[*And he has left them all to it. The* HUXTABLE *conversation, it will be noticed, consists mainly of asking questions. Visitors, after a time, fall into the habit, too.*]

PHILIP. Do you like this house better than the old one, Clara?

CLARA. It has more rooms, you know.

MRS. HUXTABLE. Do you live in London, Major Thomas?

THOMAS. No, I live at Woking. I come up and down every day. I think the country 's better for the children.

MRS. HUXTABLE. Not a cheerful place, is it?

THOMAS. Oh, very cheerful.

MRS. HUXTABLE. I had thought not, for some reason.

EMMA. The cemetery, mother.

MRS. HUXTABLE [*accepting the suggestion with dignity*]. Perhaps.

CLARA. And of course there 's a much larger garden. We have the garden of the next house as well.

JANE. Not all the garden of the next house.

CLARA. Well, most of it.

[*This stimulating difference of opinion takes them to the balcony.* PHILIP *follows.* JULIA *follows* PHILIP. MINNIE *departs to take her things off.*]

JULIA. Do you notice how near the Crystal Palace seems? That means rain.

PHILIP. Of course . . . you can see the Crystal Palace.

MRS. HUXTABLE. Julia, do you think you won't catch cold on the balcony without a hat?

JULIA [meek, but, before the visitor, determined]. I don't think so, mother.

[MRS. HUXTABLE turns, with added politeness, to MAJOR THOMAS.]

MRS. HUXTABLE. Yes, we used to live not so far along the hill; it certainly was a smaller house.

[PHILIP is now on the balcony, receiving more information.]

PHILIP. That's Ruskin's house, is it? Yes, I see the chimney pots.

MRS. HUXTABLE. I should not have moved, myself, but I was overruled.

EMMA. Mother, we had grown out of Hollybank.

MRS. HUXTABLE. I was overruled. Things are done on a larger scale than they used to be. Not that I approve of that.

THOMAS. Of course one's family will grow up.

MRS. HUXTABLE. People spend their money nowadays. I remember my father's practice was to live on half his income. However, he lost the greater part of his money by unwise investments in lead, I think it was. I was at school at the time, in Brighton. And he educated me above my station in life.

[At this moment CLARA breaks out of the conservatory. Something has happened.]

CLARA. Jane, the Agapanthus is out at last!

JANE. Oh!

[They crowd in to see it. PHILIP crowds in, too. MRS. HUXTABLE is unmoved.]

MRS. HUXTABLE. We are told that riches are a snare, Major Thomas.

THOMAS. It is one I have always found easy to avoid, Mrs. Huxtable.

MRS. HUXTABLE [oblivious of the joke, which, indeed, she would not have expected on such a subject]. And I have noticed that their acquisition seldom improves the character of people in my station of life. I am, of course, ignorant of my husband's affairs . . . that is to say, I keep myself as ignorant as possible . . . but it is my wish that the ordering of our household should remain as it was when we were first married.

THOMAS [forestalling a yawn]. Quite so. Quite so. [MRS. HUXTABLE takes a breath.]

MRS. HUXTABLE. A family of daughters, Major Thomas . . .

EMMA [a little agonized]. Mother!

MRS. HUXTABLE. What is it, Emma?

[But EMMA thinks better of it, and goes to join the Agapanthus party, saying . . .]

EMMA. Nothing, mother. I beg your pardon.

[MRS. HUXTABLE retakes her breath.]

MRS. HUXTABLE. What were we saying?

THOMAS [with resigned politeness]. A family of daughters.

MRS. HUXTABLE. Yes. Were you in the war?

[The inexplicable but characteristic suddenness of this rouses the MAJOR a little.]

THOMAS. I was.

MRS. HUXTABLE. I find that people look differently on family life to what they used. A man no longer seems prepared to marry and support a wife and family by his unaided exertions. I consider that a pity.

THOMAS [near another yawn]. Quite . . . quite so.

MRS. HUXTABLE. I have always determined that my daughters should be sought after for themselves alone. That should insure their happiness. Any eligible gentleman who visits here constantly is always given to understand, delicately, that nothing need be expected from Mr. Huxtable beyond his approval. You are married, I think you said, Major Thomas.

[This quite wakes him up, though MRS. HUXTABLE is really innocent of her implication.]

THOMAS. Yes. Oh, dear me, yes.

MRS. HUXTABLE. And a family?

THOMAS. Four children . . . the youngest is only three.

MRS. HUXTABLE. Pretty dear!

THOMAS. No; ugly little beggar, but has character.

MRS. HUXTABLE. I must take off my things before dinner. You'll excuse me. If one is not punctual one's self . . .

THOMAS. Quite.

MRS. HUXTABLE. We cannot induce you to join us?

THOMAS. Many thanks, but we have to meet Mrs. Phil for lunch in town at two.

MRS. HUXTABLE. I am sorry.

[THOMAS *opens the door for her with his best bow, and she graciously departs, conscious of having properly impressed him.* CLARA, *who has now her things to take off, crosses the room, saying to* PHILIP, *who follows her from the balcony . . .*]

CLARA. Yes, I'll tell father, Philip. I'm going upstairs.

[THOMAS *opens the door for her, but only with his second best bow, and then turns to* PHILIP *with a sigh.*]

THOMAS. Phil, we ought to be going.

PHILIP. Wait till you've seen my uncle again.

THOMAS. All right.

[*He heaves another sigh and sits down. All this time there has been* MRS. MADRAS *upon her sofa, silent, as forgotten as any other piece of furniture for which there is no immediate use.* PHILIP *now goes to her. When she does speak it is unresponsively.*]

PHILIP. How long do you stay in town, mother?

MRS. MADRAS. I have been here a fortnight. I generally stay three weeks.

PHILIP. Jessica has been meaning to ask you to Phillimore Gardens again.

MRS. MADRAS. Has she?

PHILIP [*a little guiltily*]. Her time's very much occupied . . . with one thing and another.

[*Suddenly* MRS. MADRAS *rouses herself.*]

MRS. MADRAS. I wish to see your father, Philip.

PHILIP [*in doubt*]. He won't be here long, mother.

MRS. MADRAS. No, I am sure he won't.

[*With three delicate strides* THOMAS *lands himself onto the balcony.*]

PHILIP. Tommy being tactful! Well, I'll say that you want to see him.

MRS. MADRAS. No, please don't. Tell him that I think he ought to come and see me.

PHILIP. He won't come, mother.

MRS. MADRAS. No, I know he won't. He came to England in May, didn't he? He

was here till July, wasn't he? Did he so much as send me a message?

PHILIP [*with unkind patience*]. No, mother.

MRS. MADRAS. What was he doing all the while, Philip?

PHILIP. I didn't see much of him. I really don't know what he came back for at all. We could have done this business without him, and anyway it hasn't materialized till now. This is why he's passing through England again. I don't think there's much to be gained by your seeing him, you know.

MRS. MADRAS. You are a little heartless, Philip.

[*This being a little true,* PHILIP *a little resents it.*]

PHILIP. My dear mother, you and he have been separated for . . . how long is it?

MRS. MADRAS [*with withered force*]. I am his wife still, I should hope. He went away from me when he was young. But I have never forgotten my duty. And now that he is an old man, and past such sin, and I am an old woman, I am still ready to be a comfort to his declining years, and it's right that I should be allowed to tell him so, and you should not let your wife put you against your own mother, Philip.

PHILIP [*bewildered*]. Really!

MRS. MADRAS. I know what Jessica thinks of me. Jessica is very clever, and has no patience with people who can only do their best to be good — I understand that. Well, it isn't her duty to love me . . . at least it may not be her duty to love her husband's mother, or it may be, I don't say. But it is your duty. I sometimes think, Philip, you don't love me any longer, though you're afraid to say so.

[*The appeal ends so pathetically that* PHILIP *is very gently equivocal.*]

PHILIP. If I didn't love you, my dear mother, I should be afraid to say so.

MRS. MADRAS. When are you to see your father?

PHILIP. We've asked him to dinner tomorrow night.

[*At this moment* EMMA *comes in with a briskness so jarring to* MRS. MADRAS's *already wrought nerves, that she turns on her.*]

MRS. MADRAS. Emma, why do you come

bouncing in like that when I 'm trying to get a private word with Philip?

EMMA. Really, Aunt Amy, the drawing-room belongs to every one.

MRS. MADRAS. I 'm sure I don't know why I come and stay here at all. I dislike your mother intensely.

EMMA. Then kindly don't tell me so. I 've no wish not to be polite to you.

PHILIP [*pacifically*]. Emma, I think Uncle Henry ought to attend this meeting to-morrow.

MRS. MADRAS [*beginning to cry*]. Of course he ought. Who is he, to go on like this about Constantine! My handkerchief 's upstairs.

EMMA [*contritely*]. Shall I fetch it for you, Aunt Amy?

MRS. MADRAS. No. I 'll be a trouble to no one.

[*She retires, injured. PHILIP continues, purposely placid.*]

PHILIP. What 's more, he really wants to attend it.

EMMA. I 'm sorry I was rude . . . but she does get on our nerves, you know.

PHILIP. Why do you invite her?

EMMA [*quite jolly with him*]. Oh, we 're all very fond of Aunt Amy, and anyhow, mother would think it our duty. I don't see how she can enjoy coming, though. She never goes out anywhere . . . never joins in the conversation . . . just sits nursing herself.

PHILIP [*quizzically*]. You 're all too good, Emma.

EMMA. Yes. I heard you making fun of Julia in the conservatory. But if one stopped doing one's duty how upside down the world would be! [*Her voice now takes that tone which is the well-bred substitute for a wink.*] I say . . . I suppose I ought n't to tell you about Julia, but it is rather a joke. You know, Julia gets hysterical sometimes, when she has her headaches.

PHILIP. Does she?

EMMA. Well, a collar marked Lewis Waller came back from the wash in mistake for one of father's. I don't think he lives near here, but it 's one of those big steam laundries. And Morgan the cook got it, and she gave it to Julia . . . and Julia kept it. And when mother found out she cried for a whole day. She said it showed a wanton mind. [*PHILIP's mocking face becomes grave.*]

PHILIP. I don't think that 's at all amusing, Emma.

EMMA [*in genuine surprise*]. Don't you?

PHILIP. How old is Julia?

EMMA. She 's thirty-four. [*Her face falls, too.*] No . . . it is rather dreadful, is n't it? [*Then wrinkling her forehead, as at a puzzle.*] It is n't exactly that one wants to get married. I dare say mother is right about that.

PHILIP. About what?

EMMA. Well, some time ago a gentleman proposed to Jane. And mother said it would have been more honorable if he had spoken to father first, and that Jane was the youngest, and too young to know her own mind. Well, you know, she 's twenty-six. And then they heard of something he 'd once done, and it was put a stop to. And Jane was very rebellious, and mother cried. . . .

PHILIP. Does she always cry?

EMMA. Yes, she does cry, if she 's upset about us. And I think she was right. One ought not to risk being unhappy for life, ought one?

PHILIP. Are you all happy now, then?

EMMA. Oh, deep down, I think we are. It would be so ungrateful not to be. When one has a good home and . . . ! But of course living together, and going away together, and being together all the time, one does get a little irritable now and then. I suppose that 's why we sit as mum as maggots when people are here; we 're afraid of squabbling.

PHILIP. Do you squabble?

EMMA. Not like we used. You know, till we moved into this house, we had only two bedrooms between us, the nursery and the old night nursery. Now Laura and Minnie have one each, and there 's one we take by turns. There was n't a bigger house to be got here, or I suppose we could have had it. They hated the idea of moving far. And it 's rather odd, you know, father seems afraid of spending money, though he must have got lots. He says if he gave *us* any more we should n't know what to do with it, . . . and of course that 's true.

PHILIP. But what occupations have you girls?

EMMA. We 're always busy. I mean there 's lots to be done about the house, and there 's calling and classes and things. Julia used to sketch quite well. You must n't think I'm grumbling, Philip. I know I talk too much. They tell me so.

[PHILIP's *comment is the question, half serious.*]

PHILIP. Why don't you go away, all six of you, or say five of you?

EMMA [*wide-eyed*]. Go away!

PHILIP [*comprehensively*]. Out of it.

EMMA [*wider-eyed*]. Where to?

PHILIP [*with a sigh — for her*]. Ah, that's just it.

EMMA. How could one! And it would upset them dreadfully. Father and mother don't know that one feels like this at times . . . they'd be very grieved.

[PHILIP *turns to her with kindly irony.*]

PHILIP. Emma, people have been worrying your father at the shop lately about the drawbacks of the living in system. Why don't you ask him to look at home for them?

[MR. HUXTABLE *returns, at ease in a jacket. He pats his daughter kindly on the shoulder.*]

MR. HUXTABLE. Now run along, Jane . . . I mean Emma . . . I want a word with your cousin.

EMMA. Yes, father.

[EMMA — *or* JANE — *obediently disappears.* PHILIP *then looks sideways at his uncle.*]

PHILIP. I've come over, as you asked me to.

MR. HUXTABLE. I didn't ask you.

PHILIP. You dropped a hint.

MR. HUXTABLE [*almost with a blush*]. Did I? I dessay I did.

PHILIP. But you must hurry up and decide about the meeting to-morrow. Thomas and I have got to go.

MR. HUXTABLE. Phil, I suppose you're set on selling.

PHILIP. Quite.

MR. HUXTABLE. You young men! The Madras 'Ouse means nothing to you.

PHILIP [*anti-sentimental*]. Nothing unsalable, uncle.

MR. HUXTABLE. Well, well, well! [*Then, in a furtive fuss.*] Well, just a minute, my boy, before your aunt comes down . . . she's been going on at me upstairs, y' know! Something you must do for me to-morrow, like a good feller, at the shop in the morning. [*He suddenly becomes portentous.*] Have you heard this yet about Miss Yates?

PHILIP. No.

MR. HUXTABLE. Disgraceful! Disgraceful!

PHILIP. She got on very well in Bond Street . . . learned a good deal. She has only been back a few weeks.

MR. HUXTABLE [*snorting derisively*]. Learned a good deal! [*Then he sights* THOMAS *on the balcony, and hails him.*] Oh, come in, Major Thomas. [*And dropping his voice again ominously.*] Shut the window, if you don't mind; we don't want the ladies to hear this.

[THOMAS *shuts the window, and* MR. HUXTABLE *spreads himself to the awful enjoyment of imparting scandal.*]

MR. HUXTABLE. I tell you, my boy, up at your place, got hold of she's been by some feller . . . some West End Club feller, I dessay . . . and he's put her in the . . . well, I tell you!! Major Thomas will excuse me. Not a chit of a girl, mind you, but first hand in our Costume room. Buyer we were going to make her, and all!

[PHILIP *frowns, both at the news and at his uncle's manner of giving it.*]

PHILIP. What do you want me to do?

MR. HUXTABLE [*more portentous than ever*]. You wait; that's not the worst of it. You know Brigstock.

PHILIP. Do I?

MR. HUXTABLE. Oh, yes; third man in the 'Osiery.

PHILIP. True.

MR. HUXTABLE. Well . . . it seems that more than a week ago Miss Chancellor had caught them kissing.

PHILIP [*his impatience of the display growing*]. Caught *who* kissing?

MR. HUXTABLE. I know it ain't clear. Let's go back to the beginning . . . Major Thomas will excuse me.

THOMAS [*showing the properest feeling*]. Not at all.

MR. HUXTABLE. Wednesday afternoon, Willoughby, that's our doctor, comes up as usual. Miss Yates goes in to see him. Miss Chancellor — that's our housekeeper, Major Thomas — over'ears, quite by accident, so she says, and afterwards taxes her with it.

PHILIP. Unwise.

MR. HUXTABLE. No! no! Her plain duty . . . she knows my principle about such things. But then she remembers about the kissing and that gets about among our young ladies. Somebody stupid there, I grant you, but you know what these things are. And then it gets about about Miss Yates . . . all over the shop. And then it turns out that Brigstock's a married man . . . been married two years . . . secret from us, you know, because he's living in and on promotion and all the rest. And yesterday morning his wife turns up in my office, and has hysterics, and says her husband's been slandered.

PHILIP. I don't see why Miss Yates should come to any particular harm at our place. A girl's only out of our sight at week ends, and then we're supposed to know where she is.

MR. HUXTABLE [*still instinctively spreading himself, but with that wistful look creeping on him now*]. Well . . . I had 'er up the day before. And I don't know what's coming over me. I scolded her well. I was in the right in all I said . . . but . . . ! Have you ever suddenly 'eard your own voice saying a thing? Well, I did . . . and it sounded more like a dog barking than me. And I went funny all over. So I told her to leave the room. [*He grows distressed and appealing.*] And you must take it on, Phil, . . . it ought to be settled to-morrow. Miss Yates must have the sack, and I'm not sure Brigstock hadn't better have the sack. We don't want to lose Miss Chancellor, but really if she can't hold 'er tongue at her age . . . well, she'd better have . . .

PHILIP [*out of patience*]. Oh, nonsense, uncle!

MR. HUXTABLE [*his old unquestioning self asserted for a moment*]. No, I will not have these scandals in the shop. We've always been free of 'em . . . almost always. I don't want to be hard on the girl. If the man's in our employ, and you can find 'im out . . . punish the guilty as well as the innocent . . . I'm for all that. [*That breath exhausted, he continues, quite pathetically, to* THOMAS.] But I do not know what's coming over me. Before I got ill I'd have tackled this business like winking. But when you're a long time in bed . . . I'd never been ill like that before . . . I dunno how it is . . . you get thinking . . . and things which used to be quite clear don't seem nearly so clear . . . and then after, when

you start to do and say the things that used to come natural . . . they don't come so natural as they did, and that puts you off something . . .

[*This is interrupted by the reappearance of* MRS. HUXTABLE, *lace-capped, and ready for dinner. She is at the pitch to which the upstairs dispute with her husband evidently brought her. It would seem he boiled in the middle of it.*]

MRS. HUXTABLE. Is it the fact, Philip, that if your uncle does not attend the meeting to-morrow that this business transaction with Mr. — I forget his name — the American gentleman . . . and which I, of course, know nothing about, will be seriously upset?

MR. HUXTABLE [*joining battle*]. Kitty, I don't see why I should n't go. If Constantine chooses to turn up . . . that is his business. I need n't speak directly to him . . . so to say.

MRS. HUXTABLE [*hurling this choice bolt from her vocabulary*]. A quibble, Henry.

MR. HUXTABLE. If he's leaving England now for good . . .

MRS. HUXTABLE. But you do as you like, of course.

MR. HUXTABLE [*wistful again*]. I should so like you to be convinced.

MRS. HUXTABLE. Don't prevaricate, Henry. And your sister is just coming into the room. We had better drop the subject.

[*And in* MRS. MADRAS *does come, but what with one thing and another* MR. HUXTABLE *is now getting what he would call thoroughly put out.*]

MR. HUXTABLE. Now if Amelia here was to propose seeing 'im —

MRS. HUXTABLE. Henry . . . a little consideration!

MR. HUXTABLE [*goaded to the truth*]. Well, I want to go, Kitty, and that's all about it. And I dropped a 'int, I did, to Phil to come over and help me through it with you. I thought he'd make it seem as if it was most pressing business . . . only he has n't . . . so as to hurt your feelings less. Because I'd been bound to have told you afterwards, or it might have slipped out somehow. Goodness gracious me, here's the Madras House, which I've sunk enough money in these last ten years to build a battleship, very nearly . . . a small battleship, y' know . . . it's to be sold because Phil won't stand by me, and his father don't care a button now. Not but what that's Constantine all over ! Marries you, Amelia, behaves like a duke and an archangel, mixed, for eighteen months, and then —

MRS. HUXTABLE [*scandalized*, "*Before visitors, too !* "]. Henry !

MR. HUXTABLE. All right, all right. And I'm not to attend this meeting, if you please !   [*The little storm subsides.*]

MRS. MADRAS. It's to be sold, is it ?

PHILIP. Yes, mother.

MRS. MADRAS [*at her brother*]. It was started with my money as well as yours.

[MR. HUXTABLE *is recovering, and takes no notice.*]

PHILIP. Yes, mother, we know.

MRS. MADRAS. And if that's all you've lost by Constantine, I don't see you've a right to be so bitter against him.

[*She is still ignored.* MR. HUXTABLE, *quite cheery again, goes on affably.*]

MR. HUXTABLE. D' you know, Major Thomas, that twenty years ago, when that shop began to be the talk of London, Duchesses have been known to go, to all intents and purposes, on their knees to him to design them a dress. Would n't do it unless he pleased — not unless he approved their figure. 'Ad Society under his thumb.

MRS. HUXTABLE [*from the height of respectability*]. No doubt he knew his business.

MR. HUXTABLE [*in an ecstasy*]. Knew his business ! Knew his business ! ! My boy, in the old days . . . asked everywhere, like one of themselves, very nearly ! First of his sort to break that barrier. D' you know, it's my belief that if Mrs. Gladstone had been thirty years younger, and a fashionable woman . . . he could have had a knighthood.

MRS. HUXTABLE [*explicitly*]. He was untrue to his wife, Henry.

[*At this* MR. HUXTABLE *is the moral man again. These sudden changes are so like him. They are genuine; he is just half conscious of their suddenness.*]

MR. HUXTABLE. Yes, I know, and Amy did what she should have done. You see, it was n't an ordinary case, Major Thomas. It was girls in the shop. And even though he

took 'em out of the shop . . . that's a slur on the whole trade. A man in his position . . . you can't overlook that.

MRS. MADRAS [*palely asserting herself*]. I could have overlooked it if I had chosen.

PHILIP [*to whom this is all so futile and foolish*]. My dear mother, you were unhappy with my father, and you left him . . . the matter is very simple.

MRS. MADRAS. I beg your pardon, Philip, . . . I was not unhappy with him.

MRS. HUXTABLE. Amy, how could you be happy with a man who was unfaithful to you ? What nonsense !

[JANE *and* JULIA, *from the balcony, finding the window locked, tap with their finger-nails upon the pane. The very sharpness of the sound begins to put out* MR. HUXTABLE *again.*]

MR. HUXTABLE. No, no ! They can't come in ! [*He mouths at them through the window.*] You can't come in.   [JANE *mouths back.*]

MR. HUXTABLE. What ? [*Then the sense of it coming to him, he looks at his watch.*] No, it is n't . . . two minutes yet.

[*And he turns away, having excluded the innocent mind from this unseemly discussion. But at the very moment* LAURA *comes in by the door. His patience flies.*]

MR. HUXTABLE. Oh, damn ! Well, I beg pardon. [*Then in desperate politeness.*] Let me introduce . . . my daughter Laura . . . Major Thomas.

LAURA [*collectedly*]. We have met, father.

MR. HUXTABLE [*giving it all up*]. Well . . . how can I tell . . . there are so many of you !

MRS. HUXTABLE [*severely*]. I think, Henry, you had better go to this meeting to-morrow.

MR. HUXTABLE [*wistful for a moment*]. You think I ought ?

MRS. HUXTABLE. You know you ought not.

MR. HUXTABLE [*disputing it manfully*]. No . . . I don't know I ought not. It is n't so easy to know what ought and ought not to be done as you always make out, Kitty. And suppose I just do something wrong for once, and see what happens.

MRS. HUXTABLE. Henry, don't say such things.

MR. HUXTABLE [*very reasonably to* MAJOR THOMAS]. Well, since I 've been ill —

[*But* EMMA *and* MINNIE *have come in now, and* JANE *and* JULIA, *finding their exile a little unreasonable, rattle hard at the window.* MR. HUXTABLE *gives it all up again.*]

MR. HUXTABLE. Oh, let 'em in, Phil, . . . there 's a good feller.

THOMAS. Allow me.   [*And he does so.*]

EMMA [*crisply*]. Oh, what 's it all been about ?

MRS. HUXTABLE. Never mind, Emma.

[*She says this to* EMMA *as she would have said it to her at the age of four. Meanwhile,* MR. HUXTABLE *has recovered.*]

MR. HUXTABLE. You know, Major Thomas, Constantine could always get the better of me in little things.

[JANE *has sighted* MINNIE, *and callously, across the breadth of the room, imparts a tragedy.*]

JANE. Minnie, your frog 's dead . . . in the conservatory.   [MINNIE *pales.*]

MINNIE. Oh, dear !

MR. HUXTABLE. . . . After the difference I began to write to him as Dear Sir ; to this day he 'll send me business letters beginning Dear 'Arry.

[MINNIE *is hurrying to the glass house of death.*]

JANE. I buried it.

MR. HUXTABLE. . . . Always at his ease, you know.

[THOMAS *escapes from him.* PHILIP *is bending over his mother a little kindlier.*]

PHILIP. I 'll try to see you again before you go back to Bognor, mother.

[*At this moment the gong rings. A tremendous gong, beloved of the English middle class, which makes any house seem small. A hollow sound; the dinner hour striking its own empty stomach.* JANE, *whose things are not taken off, gives a mitigated yelp and dashes for the door, dashes into the returning, tidy* CLARA. MRS. HUXTABLE *shakes a finger.*]

MRS. HUXTABLE. Late again, Jane.

PHILIP. We 'll be off, Aunt Katherine.

MRS. HUXTABLE [*with a common humanity she has not shown before*]. Philip . . . never think I mean to be self-righteous about your father. But he made your mother most unhappy when you were too young to know of it . . . and there is the example to others, is n't there ?

PHILIP. Yes . . . of course, Aunt Kate. I know just how you feel about it . . . I 'm not fond of him, either.

[PHILIP *must be a little mischievous with his aunt. She responds by returning at once to her own apparent self again.*]

MRS. HUXTABLE. My dear boy . . . and your own father !

[*From the balcony one hears the tag of* JULIA's *entertaining of* MAJOR THOMAS. *They have been peering at the horizon.*]

JULIA. Yes, it means rain . . . when you see it so clearly.

[*A general-post of leave-taking now begins.*]

PHILIP. Well, see you to-morrow, Uncle Henry.

MR. HUXTABLE. Yes, I suppose so. Oh, and about that other matter. . . .

PHILIP. What can I do ?

MR. HUXTABLE. I 'll telephone you in the morning.

PHILIP. Good-bye, mother.

THOMAS. Good-bye, Mrs. Huxtable.

MRS. HUXTABLE [*with a final flourish of politeness*]. You have excused this domestic discussion, I hope, Major Thomas . . . it will happen sometimes.

THOMAS. I 've been most interested.

[MINNIE *comes back sadly from the frog's grave.*]

PHILIP. Good-bye, Clara.

CLARA. Good-bye, Philip.

MR. HUXTABLE. You really won't stay to dinner ?

PHILIP. Good-bye, Laura.

THOMAS. Thanks, no. We meet to-morrow.

[*The general-post quickens, the chorus grows confused.*]

LAURA. Good-bye.

THOMAS. Good-bye.

JANE. Good-bye.

THOMAS. Good-bye.

PHILIP. Good-bye, Emma — oh, pardon.

[*There has been the confusion of crossed hands. Apologies, withdrawals, a treading on toes, more apologies.*]

EMMA. Good-bye, Major Thomas.

PHILIP. Now good-bye, Emma.

THOMAS. Good-bye, Mrs. Madras.
PHILIP. Good-bye.
THOMAS. Good-bye.

[*The chorus and the general-post continue, until at last* PHILIP *and* THOMAS *escape to a tram and a tube and their lunch, while the* HUX-TABLES *sit down in all ceremony to Sunday dinner: Roast beef, horse-radish, Yorkshire pudding, brown potatoes, Brussels sprouts, apple tart, custard and cream, Stilton cheese, dessert.*]

ACT II

The business offices of ROBERTS *and* HUX-TABLE *are tucked away upon the first floor somewhere at the back of that large drapery establishment. The waiting-room — the one in which employee sits in shivering preparation for interviews with employer — besides thus having been the silent scene of more misery than most places on earth, is one of the very ugliest rooms that ever entered into the mind of a builder and decorator. Four plain walls of brick or plaster, with seats round them, would have left it a waiting-room pure and simple. But the ugly hand of the money maker was upon it. In the person of a contractor he thrust upon the unfortunate room — as on all the others — everything that could excuse his price and disguise his profit. The walls, to start with, were distempered an unobjectionable green, but as that might seem too plain and cheap, a dado of a nice stone color was added, topped with stenciling in dirty red of a pattern that once was Greek.*

The fireplace is apparently designed to provide the maximum amount of work possible for the wretched boy who cleans it every morning, retiring from the contest well black-leaded himself. The mantelpiece above — only an expert in such abominations knows what it is made of; but it pretends, with the aid of worm-shaped dashes of paint, to be brown marble. It is too high for comfort, too low for dignity. It has to be dusted, and usually isn't.

The square lines of the two long windows, which look upon some sanitary brick airshaft, have been carefully spoilt by the ovalling of their top panes. The half-glazed door, that opens from the passage, is of the wrong shape; the green baize door, that admits to MR. PHILIP'S *room, is of the wrong color.*

And then the furnishing! Those yellow chairs upholstered in red cotton goose-flesh plush; that plush-seated, plush-backed bench, placed draughtily between the windows! There is a reasonable office table in the middle of the room. On the walls are, firstly, photographs of ROBERTS *and* HUXTABLE. ROBERTS *was a Welshman, and looks it. No prosperous drapery business in London but has its Welshman. There is also a photograph of the premises — actual; and an advertisement sketch of them — ideal. There is a ten-year-old fashion plate: twenty faultless ladies engaged in ladylike occupations or serene in the lack of any. There is an insurance almanac, the one thing of beauty in the room. On the mantelpiece lies a London Directory, the one piece of true color.*

The hand of the money maker that has wrenched awry the Greek pattern on the wall has been laid also on all the four people who sit waiting for MR. PHILIP *at noon on this Monday, and to the warping more or less of them all.*

MRS. BRIGSTOCK, *sitting stiffly on the plush bench, in brown quilled hat and coat and skirt, is, one would guess, a clerk of some sort. She lacks color; she lacks repose; she lacks — one stops to consider that she might possibly be a beautiful woman were it not for the things she lacks. But she is the product of fifteen years or so of long hours and little lunch. Certainly at this moment she is not seen at her best. She sits twisting her gloved hands, pulling at a loose thread, now and then biting it. Otherwise she bites her lips; her face is drawn, and she stares in front of her with only a twist of the eye now and then towards her husband, who is uncomfortable upon a chair a few feet away.*

If one were asked to size up MR. BRIGSTOCK *one would say: Nothing against him. The position of Third Man in the Hosiery does not require any special talents, and it doesn't get them; or if it does, they don't stay there. And* MR. BRIGSTOCK *stays there — just stays there. It sums him up — sums up millions of him —to say that in their youth they have energy enough to get into a position; afterwards, in their terror — or sometimes only because their employers have not the heart to dismiss them — they stay there. Sometimes, though, the employers have the heart, and do. And then what happens? Considered as a man rather than a wage-earner — not that it is usual for us so to consider him — he is one of those who, happily for themselves, get married by women whom apparently no other man much wants to marry. Subdued to what he works in, he is dressed as a Third Man in the Hosiery should be. He is, at the moment, as agitated as his wife, and as he has no nervous force to be agitated with, is in a state of greater wretchedness.*

On the other side of the room sits MISS CHAN-

CELLOR. *Every large living-in draper's should
have as housekeeper a lady of a certain age, who
can embody in her own person the virtues she
will expect in the young ladies under her. Decorum, sobriety of thought, tidiness, respect of
persons — these are the qualities generally necessary to a shop-assistant's salvation.* MISS CHAN-
CELLOR *radiates them. They are genuine in her,
too. She is now planted squarely on her chair,
as it might be, in easy authority, but looking
closely, one may see that it is a dignified resentment keeping her there unmovable.*

In the middle of the room, by the table, sits
MISS YATES. *While they wait this long time
the other three try hard to keep their eyes off her.
It is n't easy; partly because she is in the middle
of the room and they are not. But anyhow and
anywhere* MISS YATES *is a person that you look
at, though you may ignorantly wonder why.
She is by no means pretty, nor does she try to
attract you. But you look at her as you look at
a fire or a light in an otherwise empty room.
She is not a lady, nor is she well educated, and
ten years' shop-assisting has left its marks on her.
But there it is. To the seeing eye she glows in
that room like a live coal. She has genius — she
has life, to however low a use she — or the world
for her — may put it. And commoner people
are lustreless beside her.*

*They wait silently, and the tension increases.
At last it is slightly relieved by* PHILIP'S *arrival.
He comes in briskly, his hat on, a number of
unopened letters in his hand. They get up to
receive him with varying degrees of respect and
apprehension.*

PHILIP. Good-morning, Miss Chancellor.
Good-morning, Miss Yates. Good-morning, Mr. Brigstock.

MR. BRIGSTOCK [*introducing her*]. Mrs.
Brigstock.

[PHILIP *nods pleasantly to* MRS. BRIG-
STOCK, *who purses her lips in a half-
frightened, half-vengeful way, and
sits down again. Then he puts his
hat on the mantelpiece and settles
himself in the master position at the
table.*]

PHILIP. I 'm afraid I 've kept you waiting a little. Well, now —

[*There is a sharp knock at the door.*]

PHILIP. Come.

[*It is* BELHAVEN. BELHAVEN *is
seventeen, perhaps, on the climb
from office boy to clerk, of the usual
pattern.* PHILIP *greets him pleasantly.*]

PHILIP. Oh, good-morning, Belhaven.

BELHAVEN. I 've put Major Thomas in
your room, sir, as the papers were there,
but Mr. Huxtable's is empty, if you 'd
like . . .

PHILIP. No, this 'll do.

BELHAVEN. Major Thomas said would
you speak to him for a minute, as soon as
you came.

PHILIP. I 'll go in now.

BELHAVEN. Thank you, sir.

PHILIP. [*To the waiting four.*] Excuse
me one minute, please.

[BELHAVEN *bolts back to his outer office
by one door — his way of open-
ing and getting through it is a labor-
saving invention; and* PHILIP *goes
to find* THOMAS *through the other.
There is silence again, held by these
four at a greater tension than ever.
At last* MRS. BRIGSTOCK, *least
able to bear it, gives one desperate
wriggle-fidget.* BRIGSTOCK *looks at
her deprecatingly and says . . .*]

MR. BRIGSTOCK. Will you sit here,
Freda, if you feel the draught?

MRS. BRIGSTOCK [*just trusting herself to
answer*]. No, thank you.

[*Silence again, but soon broken by*
PHILIP, *who comes from the other
room, throwing over his shoulder the
last of his few words with* THOMAS,
"*All right, Tommy.*" TOMMY, *even
at the dullest business, always pleasantly amuses him. Then he settles
himself at the table for the second
time, conciliatory, kind.*]

PHILIP. Well, now . . .

[MRS. BRIGSTOCK, *determined to be
first heard, lets slip the torrent of her
wrath.*]

MRS. BRIGSTOCK. It 's slander, Mr. Madras, and I request that it shall be retracted
immediately . . . before everybody . . . in
the public press . . . by advertisement.

MR. BRIGSTOCK [*in an agonized whisper*]. Oh, Freda . . . not so 'eadstrong.

[PHILIP *is elaborately cool and good-
tempered.*]

PHILIP. Miss Chancellor.

[MISS CHANCELLOR *is even more
elaborately cold and dignified.*]

MISS CHANCELLOR. Yes, sir.

PHILIP. I think we might inform Mrs.
Brigstock that we 're sorry the accusation
has become so public . . . it has naturally
caused her some pain.

Mrs. Brigstock [*ascending the scale*]. I don't believe it . . . I didn't believe it . . . if I'd have believed it—

Mr. Brigstock [*interposing*]. Oh, Freda!

Miss Chancellor [*very definitely*]. I saw them kissing. I didn't know Mr. Brigstock was a married man. And even if I had known it . . . I saw them kissing.

[Miss Yates, *opening her mouth for the first time, shows an easy impatience of their anger and their attitudes, too.*]

Miss Yates. Oh . . . what sort of a kiss?

Miss Chancellor. Are there different sorts of kisses, Miss Yates?

Miss Yates. Well . . . aren't there?

Mrs. Brigstock [*growing shrill now*]. He owns he did that, and he knows he shouldn't have, and he asked my pardon . . . and whose business is it, but mine . . . ?

Mr. Brigstock [*vainly interposing this time*]. Oh, Freda!

Mrs. Brigstock [*climbing to hysterics*]. Hussy to let him . . . hussy . . . hussy!

[Philip *adds a little severity to his coolness.*]

Philip. Mrs. Brigstock.

Miss Yates [*as pleasant as possible*]. All right . . . Mr. Madras, I don't mind.

Philip. But I do. Mrs. Brigstock, I shall not attempt to clear up this business unless we can all manage to keep our tempers.

[Miss Yates *collectedly explains.*]

Miss Yates. I've been friends with Mr. Brigstock these twelve years. We both came into the firm together . . . and I knew he was married . . . p'raps I'm the only one that did. And when I told him . . . all I chose to tell him as to what had happened to me . . . I asked him to kiss me just to show he didn't think so much the worse of me. And he gave me one kiss . . . here. [*She dabs with one finger the left top corner of her forehead.*] And that is the truth of that.

Philip. You might have given this explanation to Miss Chancellor.

Miss Yates. She wouldn't have believed it.

Miss Chancellor. I don't believe it.

Mrs. Brigstock [*with gathering force*]. William! William!! William!!!

[Brigstock *desperately musters a little authority.*]

Mr. Brigstock. Freda, be quiet . . . haven't I sworn it to you on the Bible?

[Miss Chancellor *now puts her case.*]

Miss Chancellor. I may say I have known other young ladies in trouble and whether they behaved properly or improperly under the circumstances . . . and I've known them behave both . . . they did not confide in their gentlemen friends . . . without the best of reasons.

Philip. There is no reason that they shouldn't, Miss Chancellor.

Miss Chancellor. They didn't.

Miss Yates. Well . . . I did.

Miss Chancellor. I had no wish for the scandal to get about. I don't know how it happened.

Miss Yates. Ask your little favorite, Miss Jordan, how it happened.

[*This shot tells.* Miss Chancellor's *voice sharpens.*]

Miss Chancellor. Mr. Madras, if I am to be accused of favoritism—

Philip. Yes, yes . . . we'll keep to the point, I think.

Miss Chancellor. If Mr. Brigstock wasn't the man—

Mrs. Brigstock [*the spring touched*]. William!

Miss Chancellor. Why shouldn't she tell me who it was?

Miss Yates. Why should I?

Miss Chancellor. Am I here to look after the morals of these young ladies, or am I not?

Mrs. Brigstock. A set of hussies.

Mr. Brigstock [*in agony*]. Freda, you'll get me the sack.

Philip. Brigstock, if I wished to give any one the sack, I should not be taking the trouble to discuss this with you all in—I hope—a reasonable way.

[Mrs. Brigstock, *much resenting reasonableness, stands up now to give battle.*]

Mrs. Brigstock. Oh, give him the sack, if you please, Mr. Madras. It's time he had it for his own sake.

Mr. Brigstock. No, Freda!

Mrs. Brigstock. You've got your way to make in the world, haven't you? He's got to start on his own like other people, hasn't he?

Mr. Brigstock [*feeling safety and his situation slipping*]. In time, Freda.

MRS. BRIGSTOCK. Now's the time. If you're not sick of the life you lead . . . seeing me once a week for an hour or two . . . then I am. And this libel and slander makes about the last straw, I should think.

PHILIP. How long have you been married, Mrs. Brigstock?

MRS. BRIGSTOCK. Four years.

PHILIP. Four years!

MRS. BRIGSTOCK [*a little quelled by his equable courtesy*]. Four years!

PHILIP [*in amazed impatience*]. My dear Brigstock, why not have come to the firm and told them? It could have been arranged for you to live out with your wife.

MR. BRIGSTOCK. Well, I have been thinking of it lately, sir, but I never seem to happen on a really likely moment. I'm afraid I'm not a favorite in my department.

MRS. BRIGSTOCK. No fault of his!

MR. BRIGSTOCK. And it's sometimes a very little thing makes the difference between a feller's going and staying . . . when all those that aren't wanted are cleared out after sale time, I mean, for instance. And, of course, the thirty pound a year they allow you to live out on does not keep you . . . it's no use my saying it does. And when you're married . . .

MRS. BRIGSTOCK [*who has gathered her grievances again*]. I agreed to it. I have my profession, too. We've been saving quicker. It's three hundred pounds now, all but a bit . . . that's enough to start on. I've got my eye on the premises. It's near here, I don't mind telling you. Why shouldn't we do as well as others . . . and ride in our carriages when we're fifty!

MR. BRIGSTOCK [*deprecating such great optimism*]. Well, I've asked advice . . .

MRS. BRIGSTOCK. You think too much of advice. If you'd value yourself higher! Give him the sack, if you please, Mr. Madras, and I'll say thank you.

[*She finishes, and suddenly* MISS YATES *takes up this part of the tale quite otherwise.*]

MISS YATES. He has asked my advice, and I've told him to stay where he is.

MRS. BRIGSTOCK [*her breath leaving her*]. Oh, indeed!

MISS YATES. He's as steady as can be. But his appearance is against him.

MRS. BRIGSTOCK [*hardly recovering it*]. Well, I never!

MR. BRIGSTOCK. A feller does think of the future, Marion.

MISS YATES. I wouldn't if I were you. I don't know where we all get to when we're fifty, and I've never met any one who did. We're not in the shop any longer, most of us, are we? And we're not all in our carriages.

MR. BRIGSTOCK [*meekly*]. I suppose it can be done.

MISS YATES. Oh . . . premises near here and three hundred pounds. Perfect foolery, and William ought to know it is. This firm'll undersell you and eat you up and a dozen more like you . . . and the place that's trusted you for your stock will sell up every stick, and there you'll be in the gutter. I advised him to own up to *you* [*she nods at* MRS. BRIGSTOCK] and live out and do the best he could.

MRS. BRIGSTOCK [*more drenched with the cold water than she'll own*]. I'm much obliged, I'm sure . . . I've my own opinion. . . .

PHILIP [*who has been studying her rather anxiously*]. You've no children, Mrs. Brigstock? [MRS. BRIGSTOCK *goes white.*]

MRS. BRIGSTOCK. No, I've no children. How can you save when you have children? But if it was his child this hussy was going to have, and I thought God would n't strike him dead on the spot, I'd do it myself, so I would . . . and he knows I would.

MR. BRIGSTOCK. Haven't I taken my oath to you, Freda?

MRS. BRIGSTOCK. How can I tell if he's speaking the truth . . . I ask you how can I tell? I lie awake at night away from him till I could scream with thinking about it. And I do scream as loud as I dare . . . not to wake the house. And *if* somebody don't open that window, I shall go off.

PHILIP. Open the window, please, Mr. Brigstock.

[PHILIP'S *voice is serious, though he says but a simple thing.* MR. BRIGSTOCK *opens the window as a man may do in a sick room, helpless, a little dazed. Then he turns back to his wife, who is sitting, head tilted against the sharp back of the plush bench, eyes shut, mouth open. Only* MISS YATES *is ready with her bit of practical comfort.*]

MISS YATES. Look here, don't you worry.

I could have married William if I'd wanted to. That ought to be proof enough.

MR. BRIGSTOCK. There you are, Freda.

MISS YATES. Before he knew you.

MRS. BRIGSTOCK [opening her eyes]. Did you ask her?

MISS YATES. No, he never asked me . . . but you know what I mean.

[MISS YATES gives emphasis to this with what one fears must be described as a wink. MRS. BRIGSTOCK looks at the acquiescent BRIGSTOCK and acknowledges the implication.]

MRS. BRIGSTOCK. Yes, I know. Oh, I don't believe it really.

[Comforted, she discovers her handkerchief and blows her nose, after which MISS CHANCELLOR, who has been sitting all this while still, silent, and scornful, inquires in her politest voice . . .]

MISS CHANCELLOR. Do you wish me still to remain, Mr. Madras?

PHILIP. One moment.

MISS YATES. Oh, you'll excuse my back, sir. [And she turns to the table again.]

PHILIP. I don't think I need detain you any longer, Mr. and Mrs. Brigstock. Your character is now quite clear in the firm's eyes, Brigstock, and I shall see that arrangements are made for you to live out in the future. I apologize to you both for all this unpleasantness.

[They have both risen at this, and now BRIGSTOCK begins, hesitatingly.]

MR. BRIGSTOCK. Well . . . thank you . . sir . . . and . . .

MRS. BRIGSTOCK. No, William.

MR. BRIGSTOCK. All right, Freda! [He struggles into his prepared speech.] We are very much obliged to you, sir, but I do not see how I can remain with the firm unless there has been, with regard to the accusation, some definite retraction.

PHILIP [near the end of his patience]. My good man, it is retracted.

MRS. BRIGSTOCK. Publicly.

PHILIP. Nonsense, Mrs. Brigstock.

MRS. BRIGSTOCK [quite herself again]. Is it indeed . . . how would you like it? [Then becoming self-conscious.] Well, I beg pardon. I'm sure we're very sorry for Miss Yates, and I wish she were married.

MISS YATES [with some gusto]. So do I! [Suddenly MISS CHANCELLOR bursts ovt.]

MISS CHANCELLOR. Then you wicked girl, why didn't you say so before . . . when I wished to be kind to you? And we shouldn't all be talking in this outrageous, indecent way. I never did in all my life. I don't know how I manage to sit here. Didn't I try to be kind to you?

MISS YATES [unconquerable]. Yes, and you tried to cry over me. No, I don't wish I were married.

MR. BRIGSTOCK. Of course it's not for me to say, Marion, but will the way you're going on now stop the other young ladies tattling?

[The tone of the dispute now sharpens rather dangerously.]

MRS. BRIGSTOCK. How's Mr. Brigstock to remain in the firm if Miss Chancellor does?

PHILIP. That is my business, Mrs. Brigstock.

MISS CHANCELLOR. What . . . when I saw him kissing her . . . kissing her!

MRS. BRIGSTOCK. William!

PHILIP. That has been explained.

MISS CHANCELLOR. No, Mr. Madras, while I'm housekeeper here I will not countenance loose behavior. I don't believe one word of these excuses.

PHILIP. This is just obstinacy, Miss Chancellor.

MISS CHANCELLOR. And personally I wish to reiterate every single thing I said.

[And now it degenerates into a wrangle.]

MRS. BRIGSTOCK. Then the law shall deal with you.

MISS CHANCELLOR. You can dismiss me at once, if you like, Mr. Madras.

MRS. BRIGSTOCK. It's libellous . . . it's slander . . . !

MR. BRIGSTOCK. Oh, Freda, don't!

MRS. BRIGSTOCK. Yes, and she can be put in prison for it.

MISS CHANCELLOR. If Miss Yates and Mr. Brigstock stay with this firm, I go.

MRS. BRIGSTOCK. And she shall be put in prison . . . the cat!

MR. BRIGSTOCK. Don't, Freda!

MRS. BRIGSTOCK. The heartless cat! Do you swear it is n't true, William?

PHILIP. Take your wife away, Brigstock.

[PHILIP's sudden vehemence causes MRS. BRIGSTOCK to make straight for the edge of her self-control — and over it.]

MRS. BRIGSTOCK. Yes, and he takes himself away . . . leaves the firm, I should think so, and sorry enough you 'll be before we 've done. I 'll see what the law will say to her . . . and they 're not a hundred yards off . . . on the better side of the street, too, and a plate glass window as big as yours.

MR. BRIGSTOCK. Do be quiet, Freda !

MRS. BRIGSTOCK [in hysterics now]. Three hundred pounds, and how much did Maple have when he started . . . or Whiteley . . . and damages, what 's more . . . And me putting up with the life I 've led . . . !

> [They wait till the fit subsides—PHILIP with kindly impatience, BRIGSTOCK in mute apology — and MRS. BRIGSTOCK is a mass of sobs. Then BRIGSTOCK edges her towards the door.]

PHILIP. Wait . . . wait . . . wait. You can't go into the passage making that noise.

MR. BRIGSTOCK. Oh, Freda, you don't mean it.

MRS. BRIGSTOCK [relieved and contrite]. I 'm sure I hope I 've said nothing unbecoming a lady . . . I did n't mean to.

PHILIP. Not at all . . . It 's natural you should be upset.

MRS. BRIGSTOCK. And we 're very much obliged for your kind intentions to us . . .

PHILIP. Wait till you 're quite calm.

MRS. BRIGSTOCK. Thank you.

> [Then with a final touch of injury, resentment, dignity, she shakes off BRIGSTOCK's timid hold.]

MRS. BRIGSTOCK. You need n't hold me, William.

> [WILLIAM follows her out to forget and make her forget it all as best he can. PHILIP comes back to his chair, still good-humored, but not altogether pleased with his own part in the business so far.]

PHILIP. I 'm afraid you 've put yourself in the wrong, Miss Chancellor.

MISS CHANCELLOR. One often does, sir, in doing one's duty. [Then her voice rises to a sort of swan song.] Thirty years have I been with the firm . . . only thirty years. I will leave to-morrow.

PHILIP. I hope you recognize it will not be my fault if you have to.

MISS CHANCELLOR. Miss Yates can obviate it. She has only to speak the truth.

> [PHILIP now makes another effort to be frank and kindly.]

PHILIP. Miss Chancellor, are we quite appreciating the situation from Miss Yates's point of view ? Suppose she were married ?

MISS YATES. I 'm not married.

PHILIP. But if you told us you were, we should have to believe you.

MISS CHANCELLOR. Why, Mr. Madras ?

PHILIP [with a smile]. It would be good manners to believe her. We must believe so much of what we 're told in this world.

MISS YATES [who has quite caught on]. Well, I did mean to stick that up on you . . . if any one wants to know. I bought a wedding ring, and I had it on when I saw Dr. Willoughby. But when she came in with her long face and her " What can I do for you, my poor child ? " . . . well, I just could n't . . . I suppose the Devil tempted me, and I told her the truth.

PHILIP. That 's as I thought, so far. Miss Yates, have you that wedding ring with you ?

MISS YATES. Yes, I have . . . it 's not real gold.

PHILIP. Put it on.

> [MISS YATES, having fished it out of a petticoat pocket, rather wonderingly does so, and PHILIP turns, maliciously humorous, to MISS CHANCELLOR.]

PHILIP. Now, where are we, Miss Chancellor ?

MISS CHANCELLOR. I think we 're mocking at a very sacred thing, Mr. Madras.

MISS YATES. Yes . . . and I won't now.

> [With a sudden access of emotion she slams the ring upon the table. PHILIP meditates for a moment on the fact that there are some things in life still inaccessible to his light-hearted logic.]

PHILIP. True . . . true . . . I beg both your pardons. But suppose the affair had not got about, Miss Yates ?

MISS YATES. Well . . . I should have had a nice long illness. It 'd all depend on whether you wanted me enough to keep my place open.

PHILIP. You are an employee of some value to the firm.

MISS YATES. I reckoned you would. Miss McIntyre 'd be pleased to stay on a bit now she 's quarreled with her fiance. Of course if I 'd only been behind the counter . . .

MISS CHANCELLOR [*who has drawn the longest of breaths at this calculated immodesty*]. This is how she brazened it out to me, Mr. Madras. This is just what she told Mr. Huxtable ... and you 'll pardon my saying he took a very different view of the matter to what you seem to be taking.

MISS YATES. Oh, I 've got to go, now I 'm found out ... I 'm not arguing about it.

MISS CHANCELLOR [*severely*]. Mr. Madras, what sort of notions are you fostering in this wretched girl's mind ?

PHILIP [*gently enough*]. I was trying for a moment to put myself in her place.

MISS CHANCELLOR. You will excuse me saying, sir, that you are a man ...

PHILIP. Not at all !

[*A poor joke, but* MISS CHANCELLOR *remains unconscious of it.*]

MISS CHANCELLOR. Because a woman is independent, and earning her living, she 's not to think she can go on as she pleases. If she wishes to have children, Providence has provided a way in the institution of marriage. Miss Yates would have found little difficulty in getting married, I gather.

MISS YATES. Living in here for twelve years !

MISS CHANCELLOR. Have you been a prisoner, Miss Yates ? Not to mention that there are two hundred and thirty-five gentlemen employed here.

MISS YATES. Supposing I don't like any of 'em ?

MISS CHANCELLOR. My dear Miss Yates, if you are merely looking for a husband as such ... well ... we 're all God's creatures, I suppose. Personally, I don't notice much difference in men, anyway.

MISS YATES. Nor did I.

MISS CHANCELLOR. Lack of self-control ...

MISS YATES. *Is* it !

MISS CHANCELLOR. ... And self-respect. That 's what the matter is. Are we beasts of the field, I should like to know ? I simply do not understand this unladylike attitude towards the facts of life. Is there nothing for a woman to do in the world but to run after men ... or pretend to run away from them ? I am fifty-eight ... and I have passed, thank God, a busy and a happy and I hope a useful life ... and I have never thought any more or less of

men than I have of any other human beings ... or any differently. I look upon spinsterhood as an honorable state, as my Bible teaches me to. Men are different. But some women marry happily and well ... and all women can't ... and some can't marry at all. These facts have to be faced, I take it.

PHILIP. We may take it that Miss Yates has been facing them.

MISS CHANCELLOR. Yes, sir, and in what spirit ? I have always endeavored to influence the young ladies under my control towards the virtues of modesty and decorum ... so that they may regard either state with an indifferent mind. If I can no longer do that, I prefer to resign my charge. I will say before this young person that I regret the story should have got about. But when any one has committed a fault it seems to me immaterial who knows of it.

PHILIP [*reduced to irony*]. Do you really think so ?

MISS CHANCELLOR. Do you require me any more now ?

PHILIP. I am glad to have had your explanation. We 'll have a private talk to-morrow. .

MISS CHANCELLOR. Thank you, sir. I think that will be more in order. Good-morning.

PHILIP. Good-morning.

[MISS CHANCELLOR *has expressed herself to her entire satisfaction, and retires in good order.* MISS YATES, *conscientiously brazen until the enemy has quite disappeared, collapses pathetically. And* PHILIP, *at his ease at last, begins to scold her in a most brotherly manner.*]

MISS YATES. I 'm sure she 's quite right in all she says.

PHILIP. She may not be. But are you the sort of woman to have got yourself into a scrape of this kind, Miss Yates ?

MISS YATES. I 'm glad you think I 'm not, sir.

PHILIP. Then what on earth did you go and do it for ?

MISS YATES. I don't know. I did n't mean to.

PHILIP. Why are n't you married ?

MISS YATES. That 's my business. [*Then, as if making amends for the sudden snap.*] Oh, I 've thought of getting married any

time these twelve years. But look what
happens . . . look at the Brigstocks . . .

PHILIP. No, no, no . . . that's not what
I mean. Why aren't you to be married
even now ?

MISS YATES. I'd rather not say.

[MISS YATES *assumes an air of reti-
cence natural enough; but there is
something a little peculiar in the
manner of it, so* PHILIP *thinks.*]

PHILIP. Very well.

MISS YATES. I'd rather not talk about
that part of it, sir, with you, if you don't
mind. [*Then she bursts out again.*] I took
the risk. I knew what I was about. I
wanted to have my fling. And it was fun for
a bit. That sounds horrid, I know, but it
was.   [PHILIP *is watching her.*]

PHILIP. Miss Yates, I've been standing
up for you, haven't I ?

MISS YATES. Yes.

PHILIP. That's because I have uncon-
ventional opinions. But I don't do uncon-
ventional things.

MISS YATES [*naïvely*]. Why don't you ?

PHILIP. I shouldn't do them well. Now
you start on this adventure believing all the
other people say, so I'm not happy about
you. As man to man, Miss Yates . . . were
you in a position to run this risk ?

[MISS YATES *honestly thinks before
she speaks.*]

MISS YATES. Yes . . . I shall be getting
a hundred and forty a year living out. I've
planned it all. [*She grows happily confidential.*] There's a maisonette at Raynes
Park, and I can get a cheap girl to look
after it and to take care of . . . I shall call
him my nephew, like the Popes of Rome
used to . . . or why can't I be a widow ?
I can bring him up and do him well on it.
Insurance 'll be a bit stiff in case anything
happens to me. But I've got nearly two
hundred saved in the bank to see me through
till next summer.

PHILIP. Where are you going when you
leave here ? What relations have you ?

MISS YATES. I have an aunt. I hate her.

PHILIP. Where are you going for the
winter ?

MISS YATES. Evercreech.

PHILIP. Where's that ?

MISS YATES. I don't know. You get to
it from Waterloo. I found it in the A. B. C.

PHILIP [*in protest*]. But, my dear girl . . . !

MISS YATES. Well, I want a place where
nobody knows me, so I'd better go to one
which I don't know, had n't I ? I always
make friends. I'm not afraid of people.
And I've never been in the country in the
winter. I want to see what it's like.

[PHILIP *surrenders, on this point
beaten ; but takes up another more
seriously.*]

PHILIP. Well . . . granted that you don't
want a husband . . . it's your obvious duty
to make the man help you support his child.

[MISS YATES *is ready for it; serious,
too.*]

MISS YATES. I dare say. But I won't.
I've known other girls in this sort of mess
— one or two . . . with everybody being
kind to them and sneering at them. And
there they sat and cried, and were ashamed
of themselves ! What's the good of that ?
And the fellows hating them. Well, I don't
want him to hate me. He can forget all
about it if he likes . . . and of course he
will. I started by crying my eyes out.
Then I thought that if I couldn't buck up
and anyway pretend to be pleased and jolly
well proud, I might as well die. And d' you
know when I'd been pretending a bit I
found that I really was pleased and proud.
. . . And I am really proud and happy
about it now, sir, . . . I am not pretending.
I dare say I've done wrong . . . perhaps
I ought to come to grief altogether, but —

[*At this moment a telephone in the
table rings violently, and* MISS
YATES *apologizes — to it, apparently.*]

MISS YATES. Oh, I beg pardon.

PHILIP. Excuse me. [*Then answering.*]
Yes. Who ? No, no, no . . . State. Mr.
State. Put him through. [*He is evidently
put through.*] Morning ! Who ! My father
. . . not yet. Yes, from Marienbad.

[MISS YATES *gets up, apparently to
withdraw tactfully, but looking a
little startled, too.*]

MISS YATES. Shall I . . .

PHILIP. No, no ; it's all right.

[BELHAVEN *knocks, comes in, and
stands waiting by* PHILIP, *who tele-
phones on.*]

PHILIP. Yes ? Well ? . . . Who . . .
Mark who ? . . . Aurelius. No. I've not
been reading him lately . . . Certainly I
will . . . Thomas is here doing figures . .

I' you want him . . . I 'll put you through.
. . . No, wait. I 'll call him here, if it 's not
private. [*Then calling out.*] Tommy !

BELHAVEN. Major Thomas is in the
counting-house, sir.

PHILIP. Oh. [*Then through the telephone.*]
If you 'll hold the line I can get him in a
minute. Say Mr. State 's on the telephone
for him, Belhaven.

BELHAVEN. Yes, sir . . . and Mrs. Madras is below in a taxicab, sir, and would
like to speak to you. Shall she come up, or,
if you 're too busy to be interrupted, will
you come down to her ?

PHILIP. My mother ?

BELHAVEN. No, not Mrs. Madras . . .
your Mrs. Madras, sir.

PHILIP. Bring her up. And tell Major
Thomas.

BELHAVEN. Yes, sir.

> [BELHAVEN *achieves a greased de-*
> *parture, and* PHILIP *turns back to*
> MISS YATES.]

PHILIP. Where were we ?

MISS YATES [*inconsequently*]. It is hot in
here. is n't it ?

PHILIP. The window 's open.

MISS YATES. Shall I shut it ?

> [*She turns and goes up to the window;*
> *one would say to run away from*
> *him.* PHILIP *watches her steadily.*]

PHILIP. What 's the matter, Miss Yates ?

> [*She comes back more collectedly.*]

MISS YATES. Oh, I 'm sure Miss Chancellor can't expect me to marry one like
that now . . . can she ?

PHILIP. Marry who ?

MISS YATES. Not that I say anything
against Mr. Belhaven . . . a very nice young
man. And, indeed, I rather think he did try
to propose last Christmas. The fact is, y'
know, it 's only the very young men that
ever do ask you to marry them here. When
they get older they seem to lose heart . . .
or they think it 'll cost too much . . . or . . .
but anyway, I 'm sure it 's not important . . .

> [*This very out-of-place chatter dies*
> *away under* PHILIP'S *sternly in-*
> *quiring gaze.*]

PHILIP. There 's one more thing I 'm
afraid I ought to ask you. This trouble
has n't come about in any way by our sending you up to Bond Street, has it ?

MISS YATES [*diving into many words*
again]. Oh, of course it was most kind of
you to send me to Bond Street to get a polish on one's manners . . . but I tell you . . .
I could n't have stood it for long. Those
ladies that you get coming in there . . .
well, it does just break your nerve. What
with following them about, and the things
they say you 've got to hear, and the things
they 'll say . . . about you half the time . . .
that you 've got not to hear . . . and keep your
voice low and sweet, and let your arms hang
down straight. You may work more hours
in this place, and I dare say it 's commoner,
but the customers are friendly with you.

PHILIP. . . . Because, you see, Mr. Huxtable and I would feel a little more responsible if it was any one connected with us
who . . .

MISS YATES [*quite desperately*]. No, you
need n't . . . indeed you need n't . . . I will
say there 's something in that other place
that does set your mind going about men.
What he saw in me I never could think . . .
honestly, I could n't, though I think a good
deal of myself, I can assure you. But it was
my own fault, and so 's all the rest of it
going to be . . . my very own . . .

> [MAJOR THOMAS'S *arrival is to* MISS
> YATES *a very welcome interruption,*
> *as she seems, perhaps by the hypno-*
> *tism of* PHILIP'S *steady look, to be*
> *getting nearer and nearer to saying*
> *just what she means not to. He comes*
> *in at a good speed, glancing back*
> *along the passage, and saying* . . .]

THOMAS. Here 's Jessica.

PHILIP. State on the telephone.

THOMAS. Thank you.

> [*And he makes for it as* JESSICA
> *comes to the open door.* PHILIP'S
> *wife is an epitome of all that æs-*
> *thetic culture can do for a woman.*
> *More : she is the result — not of*
> *thirty-three years — but of three or*
> *four generations of cumulative re-*
> *finement. She might be a race horse !*
> *Come to think of it, it is a very won-*
> *derful thing to have raised this crop*
> *of ladyhood. Creatures, dainty in*
> *mind and body, gentle in thought*
> *and word, charming, delicate, sensi-*
> *tive, graceful, chaste, credulous of all*
> *good, shaming the world's ugliness*
> *and strife by the very ease and de-*
> *lightsomeness of their existence; fas-*
> *tidious — fastidious — fastidious;*
> *also in these latter years with their at-*

tractions more generally salted by the addition of learning and humor. Is not the perfect lady perhaps the most wonderful achievement of civilization, and worth the cost of her breeding, worth the toil and the helotage of — all the others? JESSICA MADRAS is even something more than a lady, for she is conscious of her ladyhood. She values her virtue and her charm: she is proud of her culture, and fosters it. It is her weapon; it justifies her. As she floats now into the ugly room, exquisite from her eyelashes to her shoes, it is a great relief — just the sight of her.]

JESSICA. Am I interrupting?

PHILIP. No, come in, my dear.

THOMAS [*into the telephone*]. Hullo!

PHILIP. Well, Miss Yates, I want to see, if I can, that you are not more unfairly treated than people with the courage of their opinions always are.

THOMAS. Hullo!

PHILIP. Oh, you don't know my wife. Jessica, this is Miss Yates, who is in our costume room. You're not actually working in your department now, I suppose?

MISS YATES [*as defiant of all scandal*]. I am.

THOMAS [*still to the unresponsive telephone*]. Hullo! Hullo!

PHILIP [*finding MISS YATES beyond — possibly above him*]. Very well. That'll do now.

[BUT MISS YATES, *by the presence of* JESSICA, *is now brought to her best costume department manner. She can assume at will, it seems, a new face, a new voice; can become, indeed, a black-silk being of another species.*]

MISS YATES. Thank you, sir. I'm sure I hope I've not talked too much. I always was a chatterbox, madam.

PHILIP. You had some important things to say, Miss Yates.

MISS YATES. Not at all, sir. Good-morning, madam.

JESSICA. Good-morning.

[*And there is an end of MISS YATES. Meanwhile, the telephone is reducing THOMAS to impotent fury.*]

THOMAS. They've cut him off.

[*While he turns the handle fit to break it,* JESSICA *produces an opened telegram, which she hands to PHILIP.*]

JESSICA. This . . . just after you left.

PHILIP. My dear, coming all this way with it! Why did n't you telephone?

THOMAS [*hearing something at last*]. Hullo . . . is that Mr. State's office? No! Well . . . Counting-house, are you still through to it?

[JESSICA *is watching, with an amused smile.*]

JESSICA. I hate the telephone, especially the one here. Hark at you, Tommy, poor wretch! They put you through from office to office . . . six different clerks . . . all stupid, and all with hideous voices.

[PHILIP *has now read his telegram, and is making a face.*]

PHILIP. Well, I suppose she must come if she wants to.

JESSICA. What'll your father say?

PHILIP. My dear girl . . . she has a right to see him if she insists . . . it's very foolish. Here, Tommy! [*He ousts him from the telephone and deals expertly with it.*] I want a telegram sent. Get double three double O Central, and plug through to my room . . . not here . . . my room.

THOMAS [*fervently*]. Thank yer.

JESSICA. Got over your anger at the play last night?

THOMAS. Oh, sort of play you must expect if you go to the theater on a Sunday. 'Scuse me.

[*Having admiringly sized up* JESSICA *and her costume, he bolts.* PHILIP *sits down to compose his telegram in reply.* JESSICA, *discovering that there is nothing attractive to sit on, hovers.*]

PHILIP. Can you put her up for the night?

JESSICA. Yes.

PHILIP. Shall I ask her to dinner?

JESSICA. She'll cry into the soup . . . but I suppose it does n't matter.

PHILIP. Dinner at eight?

JESSICA. I sound inhospitable.

PHILIP. Well, I've only said we shall be delighted.

JESSICA. But your mother dislikes me so. It's difficult to see much of her.

PHILIP. You have n't much patience with her, have you, Jessica?

JESSICA. Have you?

PHILIP [*whimsically*]. I've known her longer than you have.

JESSICA [*with the nicest humor*]. I only

wish she would n't write Mildred silly letters about God.

PHILIP. A grandmother's privilege.

JESSICA. The child sends me on another one this morning . . . did I tell you?

PHILIP. No.

JESSICA. Miss Gresham writes, too. She puts it quite nicely. But it 's an awful thing for a school to get religion into it.

[BELHAVEN *slides in.*]

BELHAVEN. Yessir.

PHILIP. Send this at once, please.

BELHAVEN. Yessir.

[BELHAVEN *slides out. Then* PHILIP *starts attending to the little pile of letters he brought in with him.* JESSICA, *neglected, hovers more widely.*]

JESSICA. Will you come out to lunch, Phil?

PHILIP. Lord! is it lunch time?

JESSICA. It will be soon. I 'm lunching with Margaret Inman and Walter Muirhead at the Dieudonné.

PHILIP. Then you won't be lonely.

JESSICA [*mischievous*]. Margaret may be 'f you don't come.

PHILIP. I can't, Jessica. I 'm not nearly through.

[*She comes to rest by his table, and starts to play with the things on it, finding at last a blotting roller that gives satisfaction.*]

JESSICA. Phil, you might come out with me a little more than you do.

PHILIP [*humorously final*]. My dear, not at lunch time.

JESSICA. Ugly little woman you 'd been scolding when I came in.

PHILIP. I did n't think so.

JESSICA. Are ugly women as attractive as ugly men?

PHILIP. D' you know . . . I don't find that women attract me.

JESSICA. What a husband!

PHILIP. D' you want them to?

JESSICA. Yes . . . in theory.

PHILIP. Why, Jessica?

JESSICA [*with charming finesse*]. For my own sake. Last day of Walter's pictures. He has sold all but about five . . . and there 's one I wish you 'd buy.

PHILIP. Can't afford it.

JESSICA. I suppose, Phil, you 're not altogether sorry you married me?

[*Although* PHILIP *is used enough to her*

charming and reasoned inconsequence, *he really jumps.*]

PHILIP. Good heavens, Jessica! Well, we 've got through eleven years, have n't we?

[JESSICA *puts her head on one side and is quite half serious.*]

JESSICA. Are you in the least glad you married me?

PHILIP. My dear . . . I don't think about it. Jessica, I cannot keep up this game of repartee.

[*She floats away at once, half seriously snubbed and hurt.*]

JESSICA. I 'm sorry. I know I 'm interrupting.

PHILIP [*remorseful at once, for she is so pretty*]. No, no! I did n't mean that. These are n't important.

[*But he goes on with his letters, and* JESSICA *stands looking at him, her face hardening a little.*]

JESSICA. But there are times when I get tired of waiting for you to finish your letters.

PHILIP. I know . . . I never quite finish my letters nowadays. You 've got a fit of the idle-fidgets this morning . . . that 's what brings you after me. Shall we hire a motor-car for the week-end?

[THOMAS *bundles into the tête-à-tête, saying as he comes . . .*]

THOMAS. He 'll make you an offer for the place here, Phil.

PHILIP. Good!

[JESSICA *stands there, looking her prettiest.*]

JESSICA. Tommy, come out and lunch . . . Phil won't.

THOMAS. I 'm afraid I can't.

JESSICA. I 've got to meet Maggie Inman and young Muirhead. He 'll flirt with her all the time. If there is n't a fourth I shall be fearfully in the cold.

PHILIP [*overcome by such tergiversation*]. Oh, Jessica!

[THOMAS *is nervous, apparently; at least he is neither ready nor gallant.*]

THOMAS. Yes, of course you will. But I 'm afraid I can't.

JESSICA [*in cheerful despair*]. Well, I won't drive to Peckham again of a morning. Wednesday, then, will you call for me?

THOMAS. Wednesday?

JESSICA. Symphony Concert.

THOMAS [*with sudden seriousness*]. D' you know, I 'm afraid I can't on Wednesday, either.

JESSICA. Why not?

THOMAS [*though the pretense withers before a certain sharpness in her question*]. Well . . . I 'm afraid I can't.

> [*It is evident that* JESSICA *has a temper bred to a point of control which makes it nastier, perhaps. She now becomes very cold, very civil, very swift.*]

JESSICA. We settled it only last night, What 's the time?

PHILIP. Five to one.

JESSICA. I must go. I shall be late.

THOMAS [*with great concern*]. Have you got a cab?

JESSICA. I think so.

THOMAS. We might do the next, perhaps.

JESSICA. All right, Tommy . . . don't be conscience-stricken. But when you change your mind about going out with me it 's pleasanter if you 'll find some excuse. Goodbye, you two.

> [*And she is gone;* PHILIP *calling after her* . . .]

PHILIP. I shall be in by seven, my dear.

> [THOMAS *looks a little relieved, and then considerably worried; in fact, he frowns portentously.* PHILIP *disposes of his last letter.*]

PHILIP. We 've so organized the world's work as to make companionship between men and women a very artificial thing.

THOMAS [*without interest*]. Have we?

PHILIP. I think so. What have we got to settle before this afternoon?

THOMAS. Nothing much. [*Then seeming to make up his mind to something.*] But I want three minutes' talk with you, old man.

PHILIP. Oh!

> [*And he gets up and stretches.*]

THOMAS. D' you mind if I say something caddish?

PHILIP. No.

THOMAS. Put your foot down and don't have me asked to your house quite so much.

> [PHILIP *looks at him for half a puzzled minute.*]

PHILIP. Why not?

THOMAS. I 'm seeing too much of your wife.

> [*He is so intensely solemn about it that*

> PHILIP *can hardly even pretend to be shocked.*]

PHILIP. My dear Tommy!

THOMAS. I don't mean one single word more than I say.

PHILIP [*good-naturedly*]. Tommy, you always have flirted with Jessica.

THOMAS. I don't want you to think that I 'm the least bit in love with her.

PHILIP. Naturally not . . . you 've got a wife of your own.

THOMAS [*in intense brotherly agreement*]. Right. That 's good horse sense.

PHILIP. And though, as her husband, I 'm naturally obtuse in the matter . . . I really don't think that Jessica is in love with you.

THOMAS [*most generously*]. Not for a single minute.

PHILIP. Then what 's the worry, you silly old ass?

> [THOMAS *starts to explain, a little tortuously.*]

THOMAS. Well, Phil, this is such a damned subtle world. I don't pretend to understand it, but in my old age I have got a sort of rule-of-thumb experience to go by . . . which, mark you, I 've paid for.

PHILIP. Well?

THOMAS. Phil, I don't like women, and I never did . . . but I 'm hardly exaggerating when I say I married simply to get out of the habit of finding myself once every six months in such a position with one of them that I was supposed to be making love to her.   [PHILIP *is enjoying himself.*]

PHILIP. What do they see in you, Tommy?

THOMAS. God knows, old man . . . I don't. And the time it took up! Of course I was as much in love with Mary as you like, or I could n't have asked her to marry me. And I would n't be without her and the children now for all I ever saw. But I don't believe I 'd have gone out of my way to get them if I had n't been driven to it, old man, . . . driven to it. I 'm not going to start the old game again now.

> [*And he wags his head wisely.*]

PHILIP. What 's the accusation against Jessica? Let 's have it in so many words.

> [THOMAS *gathers himself up to launch the vindicating compliment effectively.*]

THOMAS. She 's a very accomplished and a very charming and a very sweet-natured woman. I consider she 's an ornament to society.

PHILIP [*with equal fervor*]. You 're quite right, Tommy, . . . what are we to do with them ?

THOMAS [*it 's his favorite phrase*]. What d' you mean ?

PHILIP. Well . . . what 's your trouble with her ?

THOMAS [*tortuously still*]. There ain't any yet . . . but . . . well . . . I 've been dreading for the last three weeks that Jessica would begin to talk to me about you. That 's why I 'm talking to you about her. [*Then, with a certain enjoyment of his shocking looseness of behavior.*] I am a cad !

PHILIP [*still amused — but now rather subacidly*]. My standing for the County Council must be a most dangerous topic.

THOMAS. But that 's just how it begins. Then there 's hints . . . quite nice ones . . . about how you get on with each other. Last night in the cab she was talking about when she was a girl . . .

PHILIP. I walked home. Tactful husband !

THOMAS. Phil . . . don't you be French.
[PHILIP, *suddenly serious, turns to him.*]

PHILIP. But, Tommy, do you imagine that she is unhappy with me ?

THOMAS. No, I don't. But she thinks a lot . . . when she 's bored with calling on people, and her music, and her pictures. And once you begin putting your feelings into words . . . why, they grow.

PHILIP. But if she were, I 'd rather that she did confide in you.
[THOMAS *shakes his head vehemently.*]

THOMAS. No.

PHILIP. Why should n't she ? You 're friends.

THOMAS. Yes . . . there 's no reason . . . but I tell you it always begins that way.

PHILIP. You silly ass . . . can't you let a woman talk seriously to you without making love to her ?

THOMAS. Damn it, that 's what they say . . . but it never made any difference.

PHILIP. Tommy, you 're a perfect child !

THOMAS. I remember when I was twenty-four . . . there was one woman . . . years older than me . . . had a grown-up son. She took to scolding me for wasting my time flirting. Told me she 'd done it

herself once . . . then told me why she 'd done it. I kept off kissing her for six weeks, and I 'll swear she never wanted me to kiss her. But I did.

PHILIP. Did she box your ears ?

THOMAS. No . . . she said she could n't take me seriously. Well . . . if I 'd gone away that would have been priggish. And if I 'd stayed I 'd have done it again.

PHILIP [*mischievously*]. Which did you do ?

THOMAS. Oh . . . never you mind.

PHILIP [*with the utmost geniality*]. Well . . . you have my permission to kiss Jessica, if you think she wants you to.

THOMAS. Thanks, old man . . . that 's very clever and up to date, and all the rest of it . . . but I asked you to chuck me out of the house to some extent.

PHILIP. I 'm not going to.

THOMAS. Then you 're no friend of mine.

PHILIP. Let us put it quite brutally. If Jessica chooses to be unfaithful to me how am I to stop her . . . even if I 've the right to stop her ?

THOMAS. If you 're not prepared to behave like a decent married man you 've no right to be married . . . you 're a danger.

PHILIP. Also, Tommy, if you caught me making love to your wife you might talk to me . . . but you would n't talk to her about it.

THOMAS [*with a touch of sentiment*]. Mary 's different. [*Then protesting again.*] And I 'm not making love to your wife. I told you so.

PHILIP. Then if she 's making love to you, run away for yourself.

THOMAS. She is n't making love to me. But if you can't take a hint —

PHILIP. A *hint !* Well . . . I 'm dashed !

THOMAS. Well, old man, I give you fair warning of the sort of fool I am . . . and I 'll take no more responsibility in the matter.

PHILIP [*in comic desperation*]. Don't warn me . . . warn Jessica. Tell her you 're afraid of making a fool of yourself with her . . .

THOMAS [*his eyebrows up*]. But that 'd be as good as doing it. Good Lord, you can't behave towards women as if they were men !

PHILIP. Why not.

THOMAS. You try it.

PHILIP. I always do.

THOMAS. No wonder she wants to grumble about you to me.

[PHILIP *takes him seriously again*.]

PHILIP. Look here, Tommy, I know Jessica pretty well. She doesn't want to be made love to.

THOMAS [*positively and finally*]. Yes, she does. [*Then with real chivalry.*] I don't mean that unpleasantly . . . but all women do. Some of 'em want to be kissed and some want you to talk politics . . . but the principle's the same.

PHILIP [*finely contemptuous*]. What a world you live in !

THOMAS. . . . And the difficulty with me is that if I try to talk politics I find they don't know enough about it . . . or else that they know too much about it . . . and it's simpler to kiss 'em and have done.

PHILIP. Oh, much *simpler* !

THOMAS [*back to his starting-point — pathetic*]. But I'm married now, and I want a quiet life . . .

[*A knock at the door interrupts him.*]

PHILIP. Come in. [*It is* BELHAVEN.]

BELHAVEN. Will you lunch, sir ?

PHILIP. What is there ?

BELHAVEN. I'm afraid only the Usual, sir.

PHILIP. Can you manage the Usual, Tommy ? What is it, Belhaven ?

BELHAVEN. Boiled mutton and a jam pudding, I think, sir. [*Then, as confessing to a vulgarity.*] Roly-poly.

THOMAS [*with great approval*]. Right. I hope it's strawberry jam.

PHILIP. Sure to be. Put it in Mr. Huxtable's room, will you . . . that's airy.

BELHAVEN. Yessir.

[BELHAVEN *vanishes*.]

THOMAS [*as on reflection*]. Not plum, y' know . . . plum's no use.

[PHILIP *gathers up his papers*.]

PHILIP. I'll give the wicked woman your message.

[THOMAS *takes alarm. He hadn't thought of this.*]

THOMAS. No . . . do it off your own bat. She won't mind, then.

PHILIP. Tommy, I cannot assume the turban of the Turk. My sense of humor and my sense of decency towards women won't let me.

THOMAS [*frowning*]. I believe I'd better not have told you.

PHILIP [*unsympathetic*]. Why not ? Next to telling her, the most common-sense thing to do.

THOMAS. She won't think so.

PHILIP. She'll have to.

[*There is something so like cruelty in these three words that* THOMAS *stares at him. Then he says, reflectively.*]

THOMAS. Phil, d' you ever thank God you 're not a woman ?

PHILIP. No.

THOMAS. When I think what most of 'em have to choose between is soft-hearted idiots like me and hard-headed devils like you . . . I wonder they put up with us as they do.

[PHILIP *stares at him in turn with a queer smile. Then, as he turns to go . . .*]

PHILIP. You've made it again, Tommy.

THOMAS. What ?

PHILIP. Your one sensible remark. Come along.

[*And he is gone.* THOMAS *follows, protesting.*]

THOMAS. Look here . . . what d' you mean by One Sensible Remark ? It's like your infernal . . .

[*He pulls the door to after him. The room is alone with its ugliness.*]

ACT III

In 1884 the Madras House was moved to its present premises in Bond Street. In those days decoration was mostly a matter of paint and wall-paper, but MR. CONSTANTINE MADRAS, *ever daring, proceeded to beautify the home of his professional triumphs. He could neither draw nor color but he designed and saw to it all himself, and being a man of great force of character, produced something which, though extraordinarily wrong, was yet, since it was sincere, in a way effective. It added to his reputation and to the attractiveness of the Madras House.*

In twenty-six years there have been changes, but one room remains untouched from then till now. This is the rotunda, a large, lofty, sky-lighted place, done in the Moorish style. The walls are black marble to the height of a man, and from there to the ceiling the darkest red. The ceiling is of a cerulean blue, and in the middle of the skylight a golden sun, with spiked rays proceeding from its pleasant human countenance, takes credit for some of the light it intercepts. An archway with fretted top leads from the rest of the establishment. Another has behind it a platform, a few steps high, hung with black velvet. The necessary fireplace (were there hot-water pipes in 1884?) is disguised by a heavy multi-colored canopy, whose fellow hangs over a small door opposite. On the floor is a Persian carpet of some real beauty. On the walls are gas brackets (1884 again!) the Oriental touch achieved in their crescent shape. Round the wall are divans, many-cushioned; in front of them little coffee-stools. It is all about as Moorish as Baker Street Station, but the general effect is humorous, pleasant, and even not undignified.

In the old, grand days of the Madras House the rotunda was the happy preserve of very special customers, those on whom the great man himself would keep an eye. If you had been there you spoke of it casually; indeed, to be free of the ro- tunda was to be a well-dressed woman and recognized by all society as such. Ichabod! Since MR. CONSTANTINE MADRAS *retired, the Ma- dras House is on the way to becoming almost like any other shop; the special customers are nobody in particular, and the rotunda is where a de- generate management meet to consider the choice of readymade models from Paris. A large oval table had to be imported and half a dozen Moor- ish chairs. It seemed, to the surprise of the gentleman who went innocently ordering such things, that there were only that number in exist- ence. Scene of its former glories, this is now to be the scene, perhaps, of the passing of the Madras House into alien hands.*

Three o'clock on the Monday afternoon is when the deal is to be put through, if possible, and it is now five minutes to. MAJOR THOMAS *is there, sitting at the table; papers spread before him, racking his brains at a few final figures.* PHILIP *is there, in rather a schoolboyish mood. He is sitting on the table, swinging his legs.* MR. HUXTABLE *is there, too, dressed in his best, important and nervous, and he is talking to* MR. EUSTACE PERRIN STATE.

MR. STATE *is an American, and if American magazine literature is anything to go by, no American is altogether unlike him. He has a rugged, blood-and-iron sort of face, utterly belied by his soft, smiling eyes; rightly belied, too, for he has made his thirty or forty millions in the gentlest way — as far as he knows. You would not think of him as a money-maker. As a matter of fact, he has no love of money, and little use for it, for his tastes are simple. But money- making is the honorable career in his own coun- try, and he has the instinct for turning money over and the knack of doing so on a big scale. His*

shock of gray hair makes him look older than he probably is; his voice is almost childlike in its sweetness. He has the dignity and aptitude for command that power can give.

From the little canopied dome comes MR. WINDLESHAM, *present manager of the establish- ment. He is a tailor-made man; and the tailor only left off for the wax modeler and wigmaker to begin. For his clothes are too perfect to be worn by anything but a dummy, and his hair and complexion are far from human. Not that he dyes or paints them; no, they were made like that. His voice is a little inhuman, too, and as he prefers the French language, with which he has a most unripe acquaintance, to his own, and so speaks English as much like French as his French is like English, his conversation seems as unreal as the rest of him. Impossible to think of him in any of the ordinary relations of life. He is a functionary. Nature, the great inventor, will evolve, however roughly, what is necessary for her uses. Millinery has evolved the man- milliner. As he comes in — and he has the gait of a water-wagtail —* MR. HUXTABLE *is making conversation.*

MR. HUXTABLE. A perfect barometer, as you might say — when your eye gets used to it.

WINDLESHAM. [*To* PHILIP, *and with a wag of his head back to the other room.*] They 're just ready.

MR. STATE [*smiling benevolently at* MR. HUXTABLE]. Is it really? The Crystal Palace! But what a sound that has!

MR. HUXTABLE [*with modest pride*]. And a very 'ealthy locality!

PHILIP. Come along and meet State.
[*He jumps off the table, capturing* WINDLESHAM'S *arm.*]

MR. STATE [*enthusiastic*]. Denmark Hill. Compliment to Queen Alexandra!

MR. HUXTABLE [*struck by the informa- tion*]. Was it, now?

MR. STATE. Herne Hill . . . Herne the Hunter! That 's the charm of London to an American. Association. Every spot speaks.

PHILIP [*as he joins them*]. This is Mr. Windlesham . . . our manager. He 's going to show us some new models.
[MR. STATE *impressively extends a hand and repeats the name.*]

MR. STATE. Mr. Windlesham.

WINDLESHAM. Most happy. I thought you 'd like to see the very latest . . . brought them from Paris only yesterday.

MR. STATE. Most opportune! [*Then*

with a sweeping gesture.] Mr. Philip, this room inspires me. Your father's design?

PHILIP. Yes.

MR. STATE. I thought so.

PHILIP. That used to be his private office.

MR. STATE [*reverently*]. Indeed! Where the Duchess went on her knees! An historic spot. Interesting to me!

PHILIP. Something of a legend that.

[MR. STATE, *intensely solemn, seems now to ascend the pulpit of some philosophic conventicle.*]

MR. STATE. I believe in legends, sir . . . they are the spiritual side of facts. They go to form tradition. And it is not given to man to found his institutions in security of mind except upon tradition. That is why our eyes turn eastward to you from America, Mr. Huxtable.

MR. HUXTABLE [*in some awe*]. Do they, now?

MR. STATE. Has it never struck you that while the progress of man has been in the path of the sun, his thoughts continually go back to the place of its rising? I have at times found it a very illuminating idea.

PHILIP [*not indecently commonplace*]. Well, have them in now, Windlesham, while we're waiting.

WINDLESHAM. You might cast your eyes over these new girls, Mr. Philip . . . the very best I could find, I do assure you. Faces are hard enough to get, but figures . . . Well, there! [*Reaching the little door, he calls through.*] Allons, mes'moiselles! Non . . . non . . . par l'autre porte et à la gauche. [*Then back again.*] You get the best effect through a big doorway. [*He further explains this by sketching one in the air.*] One, two and four first.

[*He exhibits some costume drawings he has been carrying, distributes one or two, and then vanishes into the other room, from which his voice vibrates.*]

WINDLESHAM. En avant, s'il vous plait. Numéro un! Eh bien . . . numéro trois. Non, ma'moiselle, ce n'est pas commode . . . regardez ce corságe la . . .

MR. HUXTABLE [*making a face*]. What I'm always thinking is, why not have a manly chap in charge of the place up here.

MR. STATE [*with perfect justice*]. Mr.

Windlesham may be said to strike a note Whether it is a right note . . . ?

[*Through the big doorway WINDLESHAM ushers in a costume from Paris, the very last word in discreet and costly finery, delicate in color, fragile in texture; a creation. This is hung upon a young lady of pleasing appearance, preoccupied with its exhibition, which she achieves by slow and sinuous, never-ceasing movements. She glides into the room. She wears a smile also.*]

WINDLESHAM. One and two are both Larguillière, Mr. Philip. He can't get in the Soupçon Anglais, can he? Won't . . . I tell him. Promenez et sortez, ma'moiselle.

[*The young lady, still smiling and sinuous, begins to circle the room. She seems to be unconscious of its inhabitants, and they, in return, rather dreadfully pretend not to notice her, but only the costume.*]

WINDLESHAM. Numéro Deux.

[*Another costume, rakishly inclined, with a hat deliberately hideous. The young lady contained in them is again slow and sinuous and vacantly smiling.*]

WINDLESHAM. But this is chic, isn't it? Promenez.

MR. STATE [*in grave inquiry*]. What is the Soupçon Anglais?

PHILIP. A Frenchman will tell you that for England you must first make a design and then spoil it.

THOMAS [*whose attention has been riveted*]. Don't they speak English?

WINDLESHAM. Oh, pas un mot . . . I mean, not a word. Only came over with me yesterday . . . these three.

THOMAS. Because this frock's a bit thick, y' know.

WINDLESHAM. Numéro Trois!

[*A third costume, calculated to have an innocent effect. The accompanying young lady, with a sense of fitness, wears a pout instead of a smile.*]

PHILIP. What's this?

[*His eye is on the surmounting hat of straw.*]

WINDLESHAM [*with a little crow of delight*]. That's the new hat. La belle Hélène again.

MR. STATE [*interested ; still grave*]. La belle Hélène. A Parisian firm?

WINDLESHAM [*turning this to waggish account*]. Well . . . dear me . . . you can almost call her that, can't you? [*Suddenly he dashes at the costume and brings it to a standstill.*] Oh, mon Dieu, ma'moiselle ! La gorgette . . . vous l'avez derangé.

[*He proceeds to arrange la gorgette to satisfaction, also some other matters which seem to involve a partial evisceration of the underclothing. The young lady, passive, pouts perseveringly. He is quite unconscious of her separate existence. But* THOMAS *is considerably shocked, and whispers violently to* PHILIP.]

THOMAS. I say, he should n't pull her about like that.

WINDLESHAM [*skipping back to admire the result*]. Là . . . comme ça.

[*The costume continues its round; the others are still circling, veering, and tacking, while* WINDLESHAM *trips admiringly around and about them. It all looks like some dance of modish dervishes.*]

PHILIP [*heartlessly*]. La belle Hélène, Mr. State, is a well-known Parisian cocotte . . . who sets many of the fashions which our wives and daughters afterwards assume.

MR. HUXTABLE [*scandalized*]. Don't say that, Phil ; it 's not nice.

PHILIP. Why?

MR. HUXTABLE. I 'm sure no ladies are aware of it.

PHILIP. But what can be more natural and right than for the professional charmer to set the pace for the amateur !

WINDLESHAM [*pausing in the dance*]. Quite la haute cocotterie, of course.

MR. STATE [*solemnly*]. Do you infer, Mr. Madras, a difference in degree, but not in kind?

PHILIP [*courteously echoing his tone*]. I do.

MR. STATE. That is a very far-reaching observation, sir.

PHILIP. It is.

THOMAS. Do you know the lady personally, Mr. Windlesham?

[WINDLESHAM *turns, with some tag of a costume in his hand, thus unconsciously detaining the occupier.*]

WINDLESHAM. Oh, no . . . oh, dear me, no . . . quite the reverse, I do assure you. There 's nothing gay in Paris to me. I was blasé long ago.

MR. STATE. But touching that hat, Mr. Windlesham.

WINDLESHAM. Oh, to be sure. Attendez, ma'moiselle.

[*Tiptoeing, he dexterously tilts the straw hat from the elaborate head it is perched on.*]

WINDLESHAM. It 's not a bad story. Sortez.

[*By this two costumes have glided out. The third follows.* STATE, *who has found it hard to keep his eyes off them, gives something of a sigh.*]

MR. STATE. If they 'd only just smile or wink, I might get over the extraordinary feeling it gives me.

[WINDLESHAM, *caressing the hat, takes up an attitude for his story.*]

WINDLESHAM. Well . . . it appears that a while ago, out at the Pré Cathelan . . . there was Hélène, taking her afternoon cup of buttermilk. What should she see but Madame Erlancourt . . . one knows enough about that lady, of course . . . in a hat the very twin of hers . . . the very twin. Well . . . you can imagine ! Some one had blundered.

MR. STATE [*absorbed*]. No, I don't follow.

PHILIP. Some spy in the service of that foreign power had procured and parted with the plans of the hat.

MR. STATE. Madame What 's-her-name might have seen it on her before, and copied it.

PHILIP. Mr. State, Hélène does n't wear a hat twice.

MR. STATE. My mistake !

WINDLESHAM. So there was a terrible scene . . .

THOMAS. With madame . . . ?

WINDLESHAM [*repudiating any such vulgarity*]. Oh, no. Hélène just let fly at her chaperon, she being at hand, so to speak.

MR. STATE [*dazzled*]. Her what ! [*Then with humorous awe.*] No, I beg your pardon . . . go on . . . go on.

WINDLESHAM. She took off her own hat . . . pinned it on the head of the ugliest little gamine she could find, and sent the child walking along the grass in it. Then

she sent to the kitchens for one of those
baskets they bring the fish in . . . [*he
twirls the hat*] . . . you see. Then she ripped
a yard of lace off her underskirt and twisted
it round. Then she took off both her . . .
well . . . La Belle France, you know . . .
there is something in the atmosphere ! It
was her garters she took off . . . blue silk.

MR. STATE [*Puritan*]. In public ?

WINDLESHAM [*professional*]. Oh, . . .
it can be done. Hooked them together, and
fastened the bit of lace round the basket
this way. Très simple ! That 's what she
wore the rest of the afternoon and back to
Paris. This is what 's going to be the rage.

[*Having deftly pantomimed this creation of a fashion, he hands the hat,
with an air, to* MR. STATE, *who
examines it.* PHILIP *is smilingly
caustic.*]

PHILIP. La belle Hélène has imagination,
Mr. State. She is also, I am told, thrifty,
inclined to religion, a vegetarian, Vichy
water her only beverage ; in fact, a credit
to her profession and externally . . . to
ours.

[MR. STATE *hands back the hat, with
the solemnest humor.*]

MR. STATE. Mr. Windlesham, I am much
obliged to you for this illuminating anec-
dote.

WINDLESHAM. Not at all. . . . Will you
see the other three ?

MR. STATE. By all means.

WINDLESHAM. They won't be long in
changing . . . but there 's one I must just
pin on.

MR. STATE. No hurry.

[*He has acquired a new joy in* WIN-
DLESHAM, *whom he watches dance
away. Then a song is heard from
the next room . . .*]

WINDLESHAM. Allons . . . numéro cinq
. . . numéro sept . . . numéro dix. Ma'moiselle Ollivier . . . vous vous mettrez . . .

[*And the door closes.* PHILIP *looks at
his watch.*]

PHILIP. But it 's ten past three. We 'd
better not wait for my father.

[*They surround the table and sit down.*]

MR. STATE. Major Thomas, have you
my memoranda ?

THOMAS. Here.

[*He hands them to* STATE, *who clears
his throat, refrains from spitting,*

*and begins the customary American
oration.*]

MR. STATE. The scheme, gentlemen, for
which I desire to purchase the Madras
House and add it to the interest of the
Burrows enterprise, which I already control, is — to put it shortly — this. The Burrows provincial scheme — you are aware
of its purpose — goes well enough as far
as the shareholding by the local drapery
stores is concerned. It has been interesting
to me to discover which aspects of the Burrows scheme suit which cities . . . and why.
An absorbing problem in the psychology of
local conditions ! Now, we have eliminated
from the mass a considerable number of
cases where the local people will not join
with us. And in your Leicesters and Nor-
wiches and Plymouths and Coventrys . . .
there the unknown name, the uninspiring
name of Burrows, upon a fire-new establishment next door might anyhow be in-
effective. But beyond that I have a reason
. . . and I hope a not uninteresting reason,
to put before you gentlemen . . . why it
is in these provincial centers that we should
look to establish our Madras Houses . . .
New Edition. Is that clear so far ?

[*During this* MR. CONSTANTINE MA-
DRAS *has arrived. He turned aside
for a moment to the door that the
models came from, now he joins the
group. A man of sixty, to whom
sixty is the prime of life. Tall, quite
dramatically dignified, suave, a
little remote ; he is one of those to
whom life is an art of which they
have determined to be master. It is a
handsome face, Eastern in type, the
long beard only streaked with gray.
He does not dress like the ruck of
men, because he is not of them. The
velvet coat, brick-red tie, shepherd's-
plaid trousers, white spats and
patent boots, both suit him and express him subtly and well — the
mixture of sensuous originality and
tradition which is the man.* PHILIP
*is purposely casual in greeting him;
he has sighted him first. But* MR.
STATE *gets up, impressed. It is
part of his creed to recognize great-
ness; he insists on recognizing it.*]

PHILIP. Hullo, father !

MR. STATE. Mr. Madras ! Proud to meet
you again.

CONSTANTINE [*graciously, without emotion*]. How do you do, Mr. State.

PHILIP. You know every one, father. Oh . . . Hippisly Thomas.

CONSTANTINE [*just as graciously*]. How do you do, sir. [*Then, with a mischievous smile, he pats* HUXTABLE *on the shoulder.*] How are you, my dear Harry ?

[MR. HUXTABLE *had heard him coming, and felt himself turn purple. This was the great meeting after thirty years! He had let it come upon him unawares; purposely let it, for indeed he had not known what to say or do. He had dreaded having the inspiration to say or do anything. Now, alas, and thank goodness! it is too late. He is at a suitable disadvantage. He need only grunt out sulkily . . .*]

MR. HUXTABLE. I'm quite well, thank you.

[CONSTANTINE, *with one more pat in pardon for the rudeness, goes to his chair.*]

MR. STATE. A pleasant trip on the continent ?

CONSTANTINE. Instructive. Don't let me interrupt business. I shall pick up the thread.

MR. STATE [*serving up a little rewarmed oration*]. I was just proceeding to place on the tablecloth some preliminary details of the scheme that has been elaborating since our meeting in June last to consolidate your name and fame in some of the most important cities of England. We had not got far.

[*He consults his notes.* CONSTANTINE *produces from a case a slender cigarette holder of amber.*]

CONSTANTINE. You've some new models, Phil.

PHILIP. Yes.

CONSTANTINE. The tall girl looks well enough. May I smoke ?

MR. STATE [*whipping out his cigar case*]. Allow me.

CONSTANTINE. A cigarette, thank you, of my own.

[*He proceeds to make and light one.* MR. STATE *offers cigars generally, and then places one to his own hand.*]

MR. STATE. I occasionally derive some pleasure from a cold cigar. I was not for the moment entering upon the finance of the matter because I entertain no doubt that . . . possibly with a little adjustment of the proportion of shares and cash . . . that can be fixed.

MR. HUXTABLE [*in emulation of all this ease and grace*]. I'll 'ave a cigarette, Phil, . . . if you've got one.

[PHILIP *has one. And every one makes himself comfortable, while* MR. STATE *continues enjoyably . . .*]

MR. STATE. And I suspect that you are no more interested in money than I am, Mr. Madras. Any one can make money, if he has capital enough. The little that I have came from lumber and canned peaches. Now, there was poetry in lumber. The virgin forest . . . I'd go sit in it for weeks at a time. There was poetry in peaches . . . before they were canned. Do you wonder why I bought that mantle establishment in the city ?

PHILIP [*who is only sorry that some time he must stop*]. Why, Mr. State ?

MR. STATE. Because, Mr. Philip, I found myself a lonely man. I felt the need of getting into touch with what Goethe refers to as the woman-spirit . . . drawing us ever upward and on. That opportunity occurred, and it seemed a businesslike way of doing the trick.

CONSTANTINE [*through a little cloud of smoke*]. And satisfying ?

MR. STATE. I beg your pardon ?

CONSTANTINE. Has the readymade skirt business satisfied your craving for the eternal feminine ?

MR. STATE. Mr. Madras . . . that sarcasm is deserved. . . . No, sir, it has not. The Burrows business, I discover, lacks all inner meaning . . . it has no soul. A business can no more exist without a soul than a human being can. I'm sure I have you with me there, Mr. Huxtable.

[*Poor* MR. HUXTABLE *quite chokes at the suddenness of this summons, but shines his best.*]

MR. HUXTABLE. I should say so, quite.

[MR. STATE *begins to glow.*]

MR. STATE. There was fun, mind you . . . there still is . . . in making these provincial milliners hop . . . putting a pistol to their heads . . . saying Buy our Goods or be Froze Out. That keeps me lively and it wakes them up . . . does them good. But Burrows isn't in the Movement. The Woman's Movement. The Great Modern

Woman's Movement. It has come home to me that the man who has as much to do with Woman as manufacturing the bones of her corsets and yet is not consciously in that Movement is Outside History. Shoveling goods over a counter and adding up profits . . . that's no excuse for cumbering the earth . . . nothing personal, Mr. Huxtable.

[MR. HUXTABLE *is ready this time.*]

MR. HUXTABLE. No, no . . . I'm listening to you. I'm not too old to learn.

MR. STATE. Mind, I don't say I haven't taken pleasure in Burrows. We've had Notions . . . caused two Ideas to spring where one sprung before. There was Nottingham.

MR. HUXTABLE. I know Nottingham . . . got a shop there!

MR. STATE [*with wholesome pride*]. In two years the Burrows establishment in Nottingham has smashed competition. I've not visited the city myself. The notion was our local manager's. Simple. The Ladies' Department served by gentlemen . . . the Gentlemen's by ladies. Always, of course, within the bounds of delicacy. Do you think there is nothing in that, Mr. Huxtable?

MR. HUXTABLE [*round-eyed and open-mouthed*]. Oh . . . well . . .

MR. STATE. But are you the Mean Sensual Man?

MR. HUXTABLE [*whose knowledge of the French language hardly assists him in this startling translation*]. No . . . I hope not.

MR. STATE. Put yourself in his place. Surrounded by pretty girls . . . good girls, mind you . . . high class. Pay them well . . . let them live out . . . pay for their mothers and chaperons, if necessary. Well . . . surrounded by Gracious Womanhood, does the Sensual Man forget how much money he is spending or does he not? Does he come again? Is it a little Oasis in the desert of his business day? Is it a better attraction than Alcohol, or is it not?

PHILIP [*bitingly*]. Is it?

MR. STATE. Then, sir . . . Audi Alteram Partem. I should like you to see our Ladies' Fancy Department at its best . . . just before the football season.

PHILIP. I think I do!

MR. STATE. Athletes every one of 'em . . . not a man under six foot . . . bronzed, noble fellows! And no flirting allowed . . .

no making eyes . . . no pandering to anything Depraved. Just the Ordinary Courtesies of our Modern Civilization from Pure, Clean-minded Gentlemen towards any of the Fair Sex who step in to buy a shilling sachet or the like. And pay, sir . . . the women come in flocks!

MR. HUXTABLE [*bereft of breath*]. Is this how you mean to run your new Madras Houses?

MR. STATE. Patience, Mr. Huxtable. It's but six months ago that I started to study the Woman Question from the point of view of Burrows & Co. I attended women's meetings in London, in Manchester, and in one-horse places as well. Now, Political claims were but the narrowest, drabbest aspect of the matter as I saw it. The Woman's Movement is Woman expressing herself. Let us look at things as they are. What are a Woman's chief means . . . how often her only means of expressing herself? Anyway . . . what is the first thing that she spends her money on? Clothes, gentlemen, clothes. Therefore, I say . . . though at Cannon Street we may palp with good ideas . . . the readymade skirt is out of date . . .

[WINDLESHAM, *pins in his mouth, fashion plates under his arm, and the fish-basket hat in his hand, shoots out of the other room.*]

WINDLESHAM. Will you have the others in now? [*Then back through the door.*] Allons, mes'moiselles, s'il vous plait. Numéro cinq le premier. [*Then he turns the hat upside down on the table.*] I thought you'd like to see that they've actually left the handles on. But I don't think we can do that here, do you?

[*There comes in as before the most elaborate evening gown that ever was.*]

WINDLESHAM [*as he searches for the design*]. Numéro cinq . . . number five.

[THOMAS *is much struck.*]

THOMAS. I say . . . by Jove!

[*But the cold, searching light seems to separate from the glittering pink affair the poor, pretty, smiling creature exhibiting it, until, indeed, she seems half naked.* MR. WINDLESHAM's *æsthetic sense is outraged.*]

WINDLESHAM. Mais non, mais non . . . pas en plein jour. Mettez vous par là dans le . . . dans l'aleove . . . à côté du velour noir.

[*The costume undulates towards the*

black velvet platform. THOMAS *is lost in admiration.*]

THOMAS. That gives her a chance, don't it? Damn pretty girl!

PHILIP [*his eye twinkling*]. She'll understand that, Tommy.

THOMAS [*in good faith*]. She won't mind.

MR. STATE [*who has been studying the undulations*]. How they learn to walk like it . . . that's what beats me!

[MR. WINDLESHAM *turns on the frame of lights which bear upon the velvet platform. The vision of female loveliness is now complete.*]

WINDLESHAM. There . . . that's the coup d'œil.

[*The vision turns this way and that to show what curves of loveliness there may be. They watch, all but CONSTANTINE, who has sat silent and indifferent, rolling his second cigarette, which he now smokes serenely. At last PHILIP's voice breaks in, at its coolest, its most ironic.*]

PHILIP. And are we to assume, Mr. State, that this piece of self-decoration really expresses the nature of any woman? Rather an awful thought!

THOMAS [*in protest*]. Why?

PHILIP. Or if it expresses a man's opinion of her . . . that's rather worse.

THOMAS. It's damned smart. Ain't it, Mr. Huxtable?

MR. HUXTABLE [*who is examining closely*]. No use to us, of course. We couldn't imitate that under fifteen guineas. Look at the . . . what d' you call it?

WINDLESHAM [*loving the very word*]. Diamanté.

THOMAS [*with discretion*]. Just for England, of course, you might have the shiny stuff marking a bit more definitely where the pink silk ends and she begins.

MR. HUXTABLE [*not to be sordid*]. But it's a beautiful thing.

MR. STATE [*sweepingly*]. Fitted to adorn the presiding genius of some intellectual and artistic salon. More artistic than intellectual, perhaps . . . more likely to be the center of Emotion than Thought!

WINDLESHAM. I could almost tell you who we shall sell that to. Mrs. . . . Mrs. . . . dear me . . . you'd all know the name. Assez, ma'moiselle . . . sortez.

[*He turns off the light. The vision be-*

comes once more a ridiculously expensive dress, with a rather thin and shivering young person half inside it, who is thus unceremoniously got rid of.*]

WINDLESHAM. Numéro sept.

[*Another costume.*]

MR. STATE. Now here again. Green velvet. Is it velvet?

WINDLESHAM. Panne velvet. Promenez, s'il vous plait.

MR. STATE. And ermine.

MR. HUXTABLE. Good Lord . . . more buttons!

MR. STATE. The very thing, no doubt, in which some peeress might take the chair at a drawing-room meeting.

PHILIP [*as he eyes the buttons and the ermine*]. Either of the Humanitarian or of the Anti-Sweating League. Indeed, no peeress could dream of taking a chair without it.

MR. STATE [*in gentle reproof*]. Sarcasm, Mr. Philip.

PHILIP [*won by such sweetness*]. I really beg your pardon.

WINDLESHAM. Numéro dix.

[*A third costume.*]

PHILIP. What about this?

MR. STATE. Gray with a touch of pink . . . severely soft. An Anti-Suffrage Platform.

PHILIP [*in tune with him*]. No . . . it's cut square in the neck. Suffrage, I should say.

MR. STATE [*rubbing his hands*]. Good! There is purpose in this persiflage, Major Thomas. Woman allures us along many paths. Be it ours to attend her, doing what service we may.

CONSTANTINE. You are a poet, Mr State.

MR. STATE. I never wrote one in my life, sir.

CONSTANTINE. How many poets should cease scribbling and try to live such perfect epics as seems likely to be this purchase of yours of the Madras House!

MR. STATE [*much gratified*]. I shall be proud to be your successor. [*Then he soars.*] But it is the Middle Class Woman of England that is waiting for me. The woman who still sits at the Parlor window of her Provincial Villa, pensively gazing through the Laurel bushes. I have seen her on my Solitary Walks. She must have *her* chance to Dazzle and Conquer. That is every

woman's birthright . . . be she a Duchess
in Mayfair or a doctor's wife in the suburbs
of Leicester. And remember, gentlemen,
that the Middle Class Women of England . . . think of them in bulk . . . they
form one of the greatest Money-Spending
Machines the world has ever seen.

MR. HUXTABLE [*with a wag of the head;
he is more at his ease now*]. Yes . . . their
husbands' money.

MR. STATE [*taking a long breath and a
high tone*]. All our most advanced thinkers
are agreed that the economic independence
of women is the next step in the march of
civilization.

MR. HUXTABLE [*overwhelmed*]. Oh . . .
I beg pardon.

MR. STATE [*soaring now more than ever*].
And now that the Seed of Freedom is sown
in their Sweet Natures . . . what Mighty
Forest . . . what a Luxuriant, Tropical,
Scented growth of Womanhood may not
spring up around us. For we live in an
Ugly World. Look at my tie ! Consider
your vest, Major Thomas ! [*His eye searches
for those costumes, and finds one.*] This is
all the Living Beauty that there is. We
want more of it. I want to see that Poor
Provincial Lady burst through the Laurel
bushes and dash down the road . . . Clad
in Colors of the Rainbow.

> [WINDLESHAM *has indeed detained
> the severely soft costume and its
> young lady, and there she has stood
> for a while, still smiling, but won-
> dering, perhaps, behind the smile,
> into what peculiar company of mil-
> liners she has fallen.* THOMAS, *sud-
> denly noticing that she is standing
> there, with the utmost politeness
> jumps up to hand his chair.*]

THOMAS. I say, though . . . allow me.

WINDLESHAM. Thank you . . . but she
can't. Not in that corset.

MR. STATE. Dear me, I had not meant
to detain mademoiselle. [*Then to amend
his manners, and rather as if it were an in-
cantation warranted to achieve his purpose.*]
Bon jour.

> [*The young lady departs, a real smile
> quite shaming the unreal.*]

MR. STATE. You clean forget they 're
there. We gave some time and money to
elaborating a mechanical moving figure to
take the place of . . . a real automaton,
in fact. But sometimes it stuck and sometimes it ran away . . .

THOMAS. And the cost !

PHILIP [*finely*]. Flesh and blood is always cheaper.

MR. STATE. You approve of corsets, Mr.
Windlesham ?

WINDLESHAM. Oh, yes . . . the figure
is the woman, as we say.

MR. STATE. Have you ever gone deeply
into the Psychology of the question ? A
while ago I had a smart young Historian
write Burrows a little Monograph on Corsets . . . price one shilling. Conservative,
summing up in their favor. And we made
up a little Museum of them . . . at South-
hampton, I think . . . but that was not a
success. Major Thomas . . . we must send
Mr. Windlesham a copy of that Monograph.
You will find it very interesting.

WINDLESHAM. I 'm sure I shall. Can I
do any more for you ?

PHILIP. See me before I go, will you ?

WINDLESHAM. Then it 's au'voir.

> [*And he flutters away. There is a pause
> as if they had to recollect where they
> were. It is broken by* PHILIP *say-
> ing, meditatively* . . .]

PHILIP. I sometimes wonder if we realize
what women's clothes are like . . . or our
own, for that matter.

MR. HUXTABLE. What 's that ?

PHILIP. Have you ever tried to describe
a costume as it would appear to a strange
eye ? Can you think of this last ? A hat as
little like a hat as anything on a creature's
head may be. Lace. Flowers of a color it
never pleases God to grow them. And a
jeweled feather . . . a feather with stones
in it. The rest might be called a conspiracy
in three colors on the part of a dozen sewing women to persuade you that the creature
they have clothed can neither walk, digest
her food, nor bear children. Now . . . can
that be beautiful ?

MR. STATE [*to whom this is the real con-
versational thing*]. Mr. Philip, that notion is
a lever thrust beneath the very foundations
of Society.

MR. HUXTABLE [*showing off a little*]. Oh
. . . trying to upset people's ideas for the
sake of doing it . . . silly.

THOMAS [*with solid sense*]. I think a
crowd of well-dressed women is one of the
most beautiful things in the world.

PHILIP. Have you ever seen an Eastern woman walk into a Bond Street tea shop?

THOMAS. No.

PHILIP [*forcefully*]. I have.

CONSTANTINE. Ah!

[*With one long, meditative exhalation he sends a little column of smoke into the air.* MR. STATE *turns to him deferentially.*]

MR. STATE. We are boring you, Mr. Madras, I'm afraid. You were Facile Princeps upon all these questions so long ago.

[CONSTANTINE *speaks in the smoothest of voices.*]

CONSTANTINE. No, I am not bored, Mr. State . . . only a little horrified.

MR. STATE. Why so?

CONSTANTINE. You see . . . I am a Mohammedan . . . and this attitude towards the other sex has become loathsome to me.

[*This bombshell, so delicately exploded, affects the company very variously. It will be some time before* MR. HUXTABLE *grasps its meaning at all.* THOMAS *simply opens his mouth.* MR. STATE *has evidently found a new joy in life.* PHILIP, *to whom it seems no news, merely says in light protest . . .*]

PHILIP. My dear father!

MR. STATE [*as he beams round*]. A real Mohammedan?

CONSTANTINE. I have become a Mohammedan. If you were not, it would be inconvenient to live permanently at Hit . . . a village upon the borders of Southern Arabia . . . that is my home. Besides, I was converted.

THOMAS [*having recovered enough breath*]. I did n't know you could become a Mohammedan.

CONSTANTINE [*with some severity*]. You can become a Christian, sir.

THOMAS [*a little shocked*]. Ah . . . not quite the same sort of thing.

MR. STATE [*who feels that he really is rediscovering the Old World*]. But how very interesting! To a broadminded man . . . how extraordinarily interesting! Was it a sudden conversion?

CONSTANTINE. No . . . I had been searching for a religion . . . a common need in these times . . . and this is a very fine one, Mr. State.

MR. STATE. Is it? I must look it up.

The Koran! Yes, I 've never read the Koran . . . an oversight.

[*He makes a mental note. And slowly, slowly, the full iniquity of it has sunk into* MR. HUXTABLE. *His face has gone from red to white and back again to red. He becomes articulate and vehement. He thumps the table.*]

MR. HUXTABLE. And what about Amelia?

MR. STATE [*with conciliatory calm*]. Who is Amelia?

PHILIP. Afterwards, uncle.

MR. HUXTABLE [*thumping again*]. What about your wife? No, I won't be quiet, Phil! It 's illegal.

CONSTANTINE [*with a half-cold, half-kindly eye on him*]. Harry . . . I dislike to see you make yourself ridiculous.

[*Only this was needed.*]

MR. HUXTABLE. Who cares if I 'm ridiculous? I 've not spoken to you for thirty years . . . have I? That is . . . I 've not taken more notice of you than I could help. And I come here to-day full of forgiveness . . . and curiosity . . . to see what you 're really like now . . . and whether I 've changed my mind . . . or whether I never really felt all that about you at all . . . and damned if you don't go and put up a fresh game on me! What about Amelia? Religion this time! Mohammedan, indeed . . . at your age! Can't you ever settle down? I beg your pardon, Mr. State. All right, Phil, afterwards! I 've not done . . . but you 're quite right . . . afterwards.

[*The gust over,* MR. STATE, *who is a little be-blown by it at such close quarters, says, partly with a peacemaking intention, partly in curiosity . . .*]

MR. STATE. But do you indulge in a Harem?

[MR. HUXTABLE *is on his feet, righteously strepitant.*]

MR. HUXTABLE. If you insult my sister by answering that question . . .

[*With a look and a gesture* CONSTANTINE *can silence him. Then with the coldest dignity he replies . . .*]

CONSTANTINE. My household, sir, is that of the ordinary Eastern gentleman of my position. We do not speak of our women in public.

Mr. State. I'm sure I beg your pardon.

Constantine. Not at all. It is five years since I definitely retired from business and decided to consummate my affection for the East by settling down there. This final visit to Europe . . . partly to see you, Mr. State . . . was otherwise only to confirm my judgment on the question.

Mr. State. Has it?

Constantine. It has. I was always out of place amongst you. I was sometimes tempted to regret my scandalous conduct . . . [*A slight stir from* Mr. Huxtable.] Hush, Harry . . . hush! But I never could persuade myself to amend it. It is some slight personal satisfaction to me to discover . . . with a stranger's eye . . . that Europe in its attitude towards women is mad.

Mr. State. Mad!

Constantine. Mad.

Thomas [*who is all ears*]. I say!

Constantine. You possibly agree with me, Major Thomas.

Thomas [*much taken aback*]. No . . . I don't think so.

Constantine. Many men do, but — poor fellows — they dare not say so. For instance, Mr. State, what can be said of a community in which five men of some ability and dignity are met together to traffic in . . . what was the numéro of that aphrodisiac that so particularly attracted Major Thomas?

[Thomas *is shocked even to violence.*]

Thomas. No . . . really. I protest —

Mr. State [*utterly calm*]. Easy, Major Thomas. Let us consider the accusation philosophically. [*Then with the sweetest smile.*] Surely that is a gross construction to put on the instinct of every beautiful woman to adorn herself.

Constantine. Why gross? I delight in pretty women, prettily adorned. To come home after a day's work to the welcome of one's women folk . . . to find them unharassed by notions of business or politics . . . ready to refresh one's spirit by attuning it to the gentler, sweeter side of life . . .

Thomas [*making hearty atonement*]. Oh! Quite so . . . quite so.

Constantine. I thought you would agree with me, Major Thomas. That is the Mohammedan gentleman's domestic ideal.

Thomas [*brought up short*]. Is it?

Constantine. But you don't expect to find your wife dressed like that . . . the diamanté and the . . .

Thomas [*mental discomfort growing on him*]. No . . . that was a going-out dress.

Philip [*greatly enjoying this contest*]. Oh . . . Tommy! Tommy!

Thomas [*in tortuosity of mind — and conscience*]. But I tell you if my wife would . . . that is, if any chap's wife will . . . I mean . . . [*Then he gets it out.*] If a woman always kept herself smart and attractive at home, then a man would have no excuse for gadding about after other women.

[Mr. Huxtable *joins the fray, suddenly, snappily.*]

Mr. Huxtable. She sits looking after his children . . . what more does he want of her?

Constantine. Harry is a born husband, Major Thomas.

Mr. Huxtable. I'm not a born libertine, I hope.

Thomas. Libertine be damned.

Mr. State [*pacifically*]. Gentlemen, gentlemen . . . these are abstract propositions.

Mr. Huxtable. Gadding after another man's wife, perhaps! Though I don't think you ever did that, Constantine . . . I'll do you justice . . . I don't think you ever did.

Constantine. I never did.

Philip [*with intense mischief*]. Oh, Tommy, Tommy . . . can you say the same?

[Thomas *is really flabbergasted at the indecency.*]

Thomas. Phil, that ain't nice . . . that ain't gentlemanly. And I wasn't thinking of that, and you know I wasn't. And . . . we ain't all so unattractive to women as you are.

[Mr. State *loses himself in enjoyment of this repartee.*]

Mr. State. Ah . . . Sour Grapes, **Mr.** Philip. We mustn't be personal . . . but is it Sour Grapes?

Philip [*very coolly on his defense*]. Thank you, Tommy . . . I can attract just the sort of woman I want to attract. But as long as it's Numéro Cinq, Six, or Sept that attracts you . . . well . . . so long will Madras Houses be an excellent investment for Mr. State.

[*That is the end of that little breeze.*

and CONSTANTINE'S *voice completes
the quieting.*]

CONSTANTINE. Phil is a cold-blooded
egotist, and if women like him that is their
misfortune. I know his way with a woman
. . . coax her on to the intellectual plane,
where he thinks he can better her. You have
my sympathy, Major Thomas. I also am as
susceptible as Nature means a man to be . . .
as all women must wish him to be. And I
referred to these going-out dresses because
— candidly — I found myself obliged to
leave a country where women are let loose
with money to spend and time to waste.
Encouraged to flaunt their charms on the
very streets . . . proud if they see the 'busmen wink . . .

MR. HUXTABLE. Not 'busmen.

[*He is only gently deprecating now.*]

CONSTANTINE. Proud, my dear Harry, if
they see a cabman smile.

[MR. HUXTABLE *looks around, and
then nods solemnly and thoughtfully.*]

MR. HUXTABLE. Yes, it's true. I'd deny
it any other time, but I've been thinking a
bit lately . . . and the things you think of
once you start to think! And it's true.
[*But with great chivalry.*] Only they don't
know they do it. They don't know they do
it. [*Then a doubt occurring.*] D' you think
they know they do it, Phil?

PHILIP. Some of them suspect, uncle.

MR. HUXTABLE [*his faith unspoiled*]. No,
what I say is it's Instinct . . . and we've
just got to be as nice-minded about it as
we can. There was Julia, this summer at
Weymouth . . . that's one of my daughters. Bought herself a dress . . . not one
of the numéro sort, of course . . . but
very pretty . . . orange color, it was . . .
stripes. But you could see it a mile off on
the parade . . . and her sisters all with
their noses out of joint. I said to myself
. . . Instinct . . .

[*Suddenly MR. STATE rescues the discussion.*]

MR. STATE. Yes, sir . . . the noblest Instinct of all . . . the Instinct to Perpetuate
our Race. Let us take High Ground in this
matter, gentlemen.

CONSTANTINE [*unstirred*]. The very highest, Mr. State. If you think that to turn
Weymouth for a month a year into a cock-
pit of haphazard love-making, with all the

consequences that custom entails, is the
best way of perpetuating your race . . .
well, I disagree with you . . . but it's a
point of view. What I ask is why Major
Thomas and myself . . . already perhaps
in a creditable state of marital perpetuation
. . . should have our busy London lives ob-
sessed by . . . What is this thing?

PHILIP. La belle Hélène's new hat, father.

CONSTANTINE. Now, that may be ugly
. . . I hope I never made anything quite
so ugly myself . . . but it's attractive.

PHILIP [*with a wry face*]. No, father.

CONSTANTINE. Is n't it, Major Thomas?

THOMAS [*honestly*]. Well . . . it makes
you look at 'em when you might not otherwise.

CONSTANTINE. Yes . . . it's provoca-
tive. Its intention is that none of the world's
work shall be done while it's about. And
when it's always about I honestly confess
again that I cannot do my share. It's a
terrible thing to be constantly conscious
of women. They have their uses to the
world . . . as you so happily phrased it,
Mr. State . . . their perpetual use . . .
and the world's interest is best served by
keeping them strictly to it. Are these pro-
vocative ladies [*he fingers the hat again*] remarkable for perpetuation nowadays?

[*Once more MR. STATE bursts in —
this time almost heart-brokenly.*]

MR. STATE. I can't bear this, sir . . . I
can't bear to take such a view of life . . .
no man of feeling could. Besides, it's Re-
actionary . . . you're on the wrong tack.
You must come back to us, sir. You gave
us Joy and Pleasure . . . can we do without them? When you find yourself once
more among the Loveliness you helped us
to Worship you'll change your mind. What
was the end of that little story of the Duchess? How, on the appointed night, attired
in her Madras Creation, she swept into the
the Ballroom with a frou-frou of silk skirt,
wafting Perfume as she came . . . while
her younger rivals Pale before the Intoxication of her Beauty, and every man in the
room . . . young and old . . . struggles
for a Glimpse . . . a Word . . . a Look.
[*Once again he starts to soar.*] A Ballroom,
sir . . . is n't it one of the Sweetest Sights
in the World? When bright the lamps
shine o'er Fair Women and Brave Men

Music arises with its Voluptuous Swell.
Soft eyes look Love to eyes which speak
again. And all goes Merry as a Marriage
Bell! Byron, gentlemen, taught me at my
mother's knee. The poet of Love and Liberty . . . read in every school in America.

[*At the end of this recitation, which*
MR. HUXTABLE barely refrains
from applauding, CONSTANTINE
goes coolly on.]

CONSTANTINE. Mr. State, that is my
case. The whole of our upper class life,
which every one with a say in the government of the country tries to lead . . . is
now run as a ballroom is run. Men swaggering before women . . . the women og-
ling the men. Once a lad got some training in manliness. But now from the very
start . . . ! In your own progressive country . . . mixed education . . oh, my dear
sir . . . mixed education !

MR. STATE. A softening influence.

CONSTANTINE [*unexpectedly*]. Of course
it is. And what has it sunk to, moreover
. . . all education nowadays ? Book-learn-
ing. Because woman's a dab at that . . .
though it's of quite secondary importance
to a man.

THOMAS [*feelingly*]. That's so.

CONSTANTINE. And moral influence.
Woman's morality . . . the worst in the
world.

PHILIP. Slave morality.

CONSTANTINE. Yes. Read Nietzsche . . .
as my friend Tarleton says. [*All one gathers*
from this cryptic allusion is that MR. HUX-
TABLE, at any rate, reprobates Tarleton, and,
inferentially, Nietzsche.] At Oxford and
Cambridge it grows worse . . . married
professors . . . Newnham and Girton . . .
suffrage questions . . . purity questions.

MR. HUXTABLE. Of course, some of the
novels . . .

CONSTANTINE. From seventeen to thirty-
four . . . the years which a man should
consecrate to the acquiring of political virtue . . . wherever he turns he is distracted,
provoked, tantalized by the barefaced presence of women. How's he to keep a clear
brain for the larger issues of life ? Why
do you soldiers, Major Thomas, volunteer
with such alacrity for foreign service ?

THOMAS [*with a jump*]. Good God . . .
I never thought of that.

CONSTANTINE. What's the result ?

Every great public question . . . all politics, all religion, all economy is being
brought down to the level of women's emotion. Admirable in its way . . . charming
in its place ! But softening, sentimentalizing, enervating . . . lapping the world, if
you let it, in the nursery cotton wool of
prettiness and pettiness. Men don't realize
how far rotted by the process they are . . .
that's what's so fatal. We're used to a
whole nation's anger being vented in scold-
ings . . . or rather we're getting used to
the thought that it's naughty to be angry
at all. Justice degenerates into kindness
. . . that doesn't surprise us. Religion is a
pretty hymn tune to keep us from fear of
the dark. You four unfortunates might own
the truth just for once . . . you needn't
tell your wives.

MR. STATE. I am not married.

CONSTANTINE. I might have known it.

MR. STATE [*a little astonished*]. But no
matter.

CONSTANTINE [*with full appreciation of*
what he says]. Women haven't morals or
intellect in our sense of the words. They
have other incompatible qualities quite as
important, no doubt. But shut them away
from public life and public exhibition. It's
degrading to compete with them . . . it's
as degrading to compete for them. Perhaps
we're too late already . . . but, oh, my
dear sentimental sir [*he addresses the pained*
though admiring MR. STATE], if we could
replant the laurel bushes thick enough we
might yet rediscover the fine manly world
we are losing.

[*Except PHILIP, who sits detached and*
attentive, they are all rather de-
pressed by this judgment upon them.
THOMAS recovers sufficiently to
ask . . .]

THOMAS. Are you advocating polygamy
in England ?

CONSTANTINE. That is what it should
come to.

THOMAS. Well, I call that rather shocking. [*Then with some hopeful interest.*] And
is it practical ?

CONSTANTINE. I did not anticipate the reform in my lifetime . . . so I left for the East.

PHILIP [*finely*]. You did quite right,
father. I wish everyone of your way of
thinking would do the same.

[CONSTANTINE *is ready for him.*]

CONSTANTINE. Are you prepared for so much depopulation? Think of the women who'd be off to-morrow.

[MR. HUXTABLE *wakes from stupe-faction to say with tremendous emphasis* . . .]

MR. HUXTABLE. Never!

CONSTANTINE. Wrong, Harry.

MR. HUXTABLE. No, I'm not wrong just because you say so! You ought to listen to me a bit sometimes. I always listened to you.

CONSTANTINE. Bless your quick temper.

[*Who could resist* CONSTANTINE'S *smile* . . . *Well, not* HUXTABLE.]

MR. HUXTABLE. Oh . . . go on . . . tell me why I'm wrong . . . I dare say I am.

CONSTANTINE. Even if you have liked bringing up six daughters and not getting them married . . . how have they liked it? You should have drowned them at birth, Harry . . .

MR. HUXTABLE. You must have your joke, must n't you?

CONSTANTINE. Therefore, how much pleasanter for you . . . how much better for them . . . if you'd only to find one man ready, for a small consideration, to marry the lot.

MR. HUXTABLE [*with intense delight*]. Now if I was to tell my wife that she would n't see the 'umor of it.

CONSTANTINE. The woman emancipator's last ditch, Mr. State, is the trust that women will side with him. Don't make any mistake. This is a serious question to them . . . of health and happiness . . . and sometimes of bread and butter. Quite apart from our customers here . . . kept women, every one of them . . .

MR. STATE [*in some alarm*]. You don't say!

CONSTANTINE [*gently lifting him from the little trap*]. Economically. Kept by their husbands . . . or if they live on their dividends, kept by Society.

PHILIP. What about men who live on their dividends?

MR. STATE. No . . . now don't let us go on to politics.

CONSTANTINE. . . . And apart from the prisoners in that chaste little fortress on Denmark Hill . . . we used to employ, Harry, between us . . . what? . . . two or three hundred free and independent women . . . making clothes for the others, the ladies. They are as free as you like . . . free to go . . . free to starve. How much do they rejoice in their freedom to earn their living by ruining their health and stifling their instincts? Answer me, Harry, you monster of good-natured wickedness.

MR. HUXTABLE. What's that?

CONSTANTINE. You keep an industrial seraglio.

MR. HUXTABLE. A what!

CONSTANTINE. What else is your Roberts and Huxtable but a harem of industry. Do you know that it would sicken with horror a good Mohammedan? You buy these girls in the open market . . . you keep them under lock and key . . .

MR. HUXTABLE. I do?

CONSTANTINE. Quite right, Harry, no harm done. [*Then his voice sinks to the utmost seriousness.*] But you coin your profits out of them by putting on exhibition for ten hours a day . . . their good looks, their good manners, their womanhood. Hired out it is to any stranger to hold as cheap for a few minutes as common decency allows. And when you've worn them out you turn them out . . . forget their very names . . . would n't know their faces if you met them selling matches at your door. For such treatment of potential motherhood, my Prophet condemns a man to hell.

MR. HUXTABLE [*breathless with amazement*]. Well, I never did in all my born days! They can marry respectably, can't they? We like 'em to marry.

PHILIP. Yes, uncle . . . I went into that question with Miss Yates and the Brigstocks this morning.

CONSTANTINE [*completing his case*]. I ask you all . . . what is to happen to you as a nation? Where are your future generations coming from? What with the well-kept women you flatter and æstheticize till they won't give you children, and the free women you work at market rates till they can't give you children . . .

MR. HUXTABLE [*half-humorously sulky*]. Miss Yates has obliged us, anyhow.

PHILIP [*quickly capping him*]. And we're going to dismiss her.

[MR. HUXTABLE *flashes again into protestation.*]

MR. HUXTABLE. What else can we do? But I said you were n't to be hard on the girl. And I won't be upset like this. I want to take things as I find 'em . . . that is as I used to find 'em . . . before there was any of these ideas going around . . . and I'm sure we were happier without 'em. Stifling their instincts . . . it's a horrid way to talk. And I don't believe it. I could send for every girl in the shop, and not one of 'em would hint at it to me. [*He has triumphed with himself so far, but his new-born intellectual conscience brings him down.*] Not that that proves anything, does it? I'm a fool. It's a beastly world. But I won't make it so, do I?

PHILIP. Who does?

MR. HUXTABLE. Other people. [*Philip's eye is on him.*] Oh, I see it coming. You're going to say we're all the other people or something. I'm getting up to you.

CONSTANTINE [*very carefully*]. What is this about a Miss Yates?

PHILIP. A little bother down at Peckham. I can tell you afterwards if you like.

CONSTANTINE. No . . . there is no need.

[*Something in the tone of this last makes* PHILIP *look up quickly. But* MR. STATE, *with a sudden thought, has first dived for his watch, and then, at the sight of it, gets up from the table.*]

MR. STATE. Gentlemen, are you aware of the time? I may mention that I have a City appointment at four o'clock.

CONSTANTINE [*polite, but leisurely*]. Are we detaining you, Mr. State? Not universal or compulsory polygamy, Major Thomas. That would be nonsense. The very distribution of the sexes forbids it. But its recognition is one of the logical outcomes of the aristocratic method of government. And that's the only ultimate method . . . all others are interim plans for sifting out various aristocracies. The community of the future will specialize its functions. Women will find, I hope, some intellectual companions like my son, who will, besides, take a gentle interest in the County Council. There will be single-hearted men like Harry, content with old-fashioned domesticity. There will be poets like you, Mr. State, to dream about women and to dress them . . . their bodies in silks and their virtues in phrases. But there must also be such men as Major Thomas and myself . . .

[THOMAS *rises, yet again, to this piece of chaff.*]

THOMAS. No, no! I'm not like that . . not in the least. Because a fellow has been in the Army! Don't drag me in.

MR. STATE. As stimulating a conversation as I remember. A little hard to follow at times . . . but worth far more than the sacrifice of any mere business doings.

[CONSTANTINE *takes the hint graciously, and is apt for business at once.*]

CONSTANTINE. My fault! Shall we agree, Mr. State, to accept as much of your offer as you have no intention of altering? We are dealing for both the shops?

MR. STATE. Yes. What are we proposing to knock off their valuation, Major Thomas?

THOMAS. Eight thousand six hundred.

CONSTANTINE. Phil, what were we prepared to come down?

PHILIP. Nine thousand.

CONSTANTINE. A very creditable margin. Your offer is accepted, Mr. State.

[MR. STATE *feels he must really play up to such magnificent conducting of business.*]

MR. STATE. I should prefer to knock you down only eight thousand.

CONSTANTINE [*keeping the advantage*]. Isn't that merely romantic of you, Mr. State . . . not in the best form of business art?

THOMAS. But the conditions, you know?

CONSTANTINE. We accept your conditions. If they won't work you'll be only anxious to alter them. So the business is done.   [MR. HUXTABLE'S *eyes are wide.*]

MR. HUXTABLE. But look here.

PHILIP. Uncle Harry has something to say . . .

MR. HUXTABLE [*assertively*]. Yes.

CONSTANTINE. Something *different* to say, Harry?

MR. HUXTABLE [*after thinking it over*]. No.

[*So* CONSTANTINE *returns happily to his subject.*]

CONSTANTINE. What interests me about this Woman Question . . . now that I've settled my personal share in it . . . is to wonder how Europe, hampered by such an unsolved problem, can hope to stand up against the Oriental revival.

THOMAS. What's that?

CONSTANTINE. You'll hear of it shortly Up from the Persian gulf to where I live we could grow enough wheat to feed the British Empire. Life there is simple and spacious . . . the air is not breathed out. All we want is a happy, hardy race of men, and under a decent government we shall soon beget it. But you Europeans! Is this the symbol you are marching to the future under. [*He has found again, and lifts up, la Belle Hélène's new hat.*] A cap of slavery! You are all idolaters of women . . . and they are the slaves of your idolatry.

MR. STATE [*with undisguised admiration*]. Mr. Madras, I am proud to have met you again. If I say another word, I may be so interested in your reply that I shall miss my appointment. My coat? Thank you, Mr. Philip. I have to meet a man about a new system of country-house drainage that he wants me to finance. I can hardly hope for another Transcendental Discussion upon that.

CONSTANTINE. Why not?

MR. STATE. If you were he! Good-bye, sir. Good-day, Mr. Huxtable. Till to-morrow, Major Thomas. No, Mr. Philip, don't see me down.

[*He is off for his next deal. PHILIP civilly takes him past the door, saying . . .*]

PHILIP. Your car's at the Bond Street entrance, I expect.

[*And then he comes back. CONSTANTINE is keeping half a friendly eye on HUXTABLE, who fidgets under it. THOMAS takes breath and expounds a grievance.*]

THOMAS. That's how he settles business. But leaves us all the papers to do. I shall take mine home. The four-thirty gets me indoors by a quarter to six. Time for a cup of tea! Phil, have you got China tea?

PHILIP. Downstairs.

MR. HUXTABLE. I must be getting back, I think.

CONSTANTINE. Harry . . . you're running away from me.

MR. HUXTABLE [*in frank amused confession*]. Yes . . . I was. Habit, y' know . . . habit.

CONSTANTINE [*with the most friendly condescension*]. Suppose I go with you . . . part of the way. How do you go?

MR. HUXTABLE. On a 'bus.

CONSTANTINE. Suppose we go together . . on a 'bus.

MR. HUXTABLE [*desperately cunning*]. It's all right . . . they won't see me with you. We don't close till seven.

[CONSTANTINE'S *face sours.*]

CONSTANTINE. No, to be sure. Phil, I can't come to dinner, I'm afraid.

PHILIP. Oh, I was going to tell you. Mother will be there. Tommy, you know the tea room.

THOMAS [*all tact*]. Oh, quite!

PHILIP. Straight downstairs, first to the left and the second passage. I'll follow.

[THOMAS *departs.* CONSTANTINE *says, indifferently . . .*]

CONSTANTINE. Then I'll come in after dinner.

PHILIP. You don't mind?

CONSTANTINE. No.

[*There stands* MR. HUXTABLE, *first on one foot and then on the other, desperately nervous.* CONSTANTINE *smiling at him.* PHILIP *cannot resist it. He says . . .*]

PHILIP. It's afterwards now, uncle. Fire away.

[*And is off.* CONSTANTINE *still smiles. Poor* MR. HUXTABLE *makes a desperate effort to do the proper thing by this reprobate. He forms his face into a frown. It's no use; an answering smile will come. He surrenders.*]

MR. HUXTABLE. Look here . . . don't let's talk about Amelia.

CONSTANTINE. No . . . never rake up the past.

MR. HUXTABLE. Lord! What else has a chap got to think of?

CONSTANTINE. That's why you look so old.

MR. HUXTABLE. Do I, now?

CONSTANTINE. What age are you?

MR. HUXTABLE. Sixty.

[*The two sit down together.*]

CONSTANTINE. You should come and stay with me at Hit . . . not far from Hillel . . . Hillel is Babylon, Harry.

MR. HUXTABLE [*curious*]. What's it like there?

CONSTANTINE. The house is white, and there are palm trees about it . . . and not far off flows the Euphrates.

MR. HUXTABLE. Just like in the Bible [*His face is wistful.*] Constantine.

CONSTANTINE. Yes, Harry.

MR. HUXTABLE. You've said odder

things this afternoon than I 've ever heard you say before.

CONSTANTINE. Probably not.

MR. HUXTABLE [wondering]. And I have n't really minded 'em. But I believe it 's the first time I 've ever understood you . . . and p'r'aps that 's just as well for me.

CONSTANTINE [encouragingly]. Oh . . . why, Harry ?

MR. HUXTABLE. Because . . . d' you think it 's only not being very clever keeps us . . . well-behaved ?

CONSTANTINE. Has it kept you happy ?

MR. HUXTABLE [impatient at the petty word]. Anyone can be happy. What worries me is having got to my age and only just beginning to understand anything at all. And you can't learn it out of books, old man. Books don't tell you the truth . . . at least not any that I can find. I wonder if I'd been a bit of a dog like you . . . ? But there it is . . . you can't do things on purpose. And what 's more, don't you go to think I 'd have done them if I could . . . knowing them to be wrong. [Then comes a discovery.] But I was always jealous of you, Constantine, for you seemed to get the best of everything . . . and I know people could n't help being fond of you . . . for I was fond of you myself, whatever you did. That was odd to start with. And now here we are, both of us old chaps . . .

CONSTANTINE [as he throws back his head]. I am not old.

MR. HUXTABLE [with sudden misgiving]. You don't repent, do you ?

CONSTANTINE. What of ?

MR. HUXTABLE. Katherine said this morning that you might have . . . but I was n't afraid of that. [Now he wags his head wisely.] You know . . . you evildoers . . . you upset us all, and you hurt our feelings, and of course you ought to be ashamed of yourself. But . . . well . . . it 's like the only time I went abroad. I was sick going . . . I was 'orribly uncomfortable . . . I 'ated the cooking . . . I was sick coming back. But I would n't have missed it . . . !

CONSTANTINE [in affectionate good fellowship]. Come to Arabia, Harry.

MR. HUXTABLE [humorously pathetic about it]. Don't you make game of me. My time 's over. What have I done with it, now ? Married. Brought up a family. Been mas-

ter to a few hundred girls and fellows who never really cared a bit for me. I 've been made a convenience of . . . that 's my life. That 's where I envy you. You 've had your own way . . . and you don't look now as if you 'd be damned for it, either.

CONSTANTINE [in gentlemanly defiance]. I shan't be.

[MR. HUXTABLE shakes a fist, somewhat, though unconsciously, in the direction of the ceiling.]

MR. HUXTABLE. It 's not fair, and I don't care who hears me say so.

CONSTANTINE. Suppose we shout it from the top of the 'bus.

[As they start, MR. HUXTABLE returns to his mundane, responsible self.]

MR. HUXTABLE. But you know, old man, . . . you 'll excuse me, I 'm sure . . . and it 's all very well having theories and being able to talk . . . still, you did treat Amelia very badly . . . and those other ones, too . . . say what you like ! Let go my arm, will you !

CONSTANTINE. Why ?

MR. HUXTABLE [his scruples less strong than the soft touch of CONSTANTINE's hand]. Well, p'r'aps you need n't. [A thought strikes him.] Are you really going away for good this time ?

CONSTANTINE. To-morrow.

MR. HUXTABLE [beaming on him]. Then come home and see mother and the girls.

[MAJOR THOMAS comes back, looking about him.]

THOMAS. Excuse me . . . I left my hat.

CONSTANTINE. It will make them very uncomfortable.

MR. HUXTABLE [his smile fading]. D' you think so ? Won't it do 'em good . . . broaden their minds ?

[PHILIP comes back, too.]

MR. HUXTABLE. Phil . . . shall I take your father 'ome to call ?

PHILIP [after one gasp at the prospect, says with great cheerfulness . . .] Certainly.

CONSTANTINE. I 'll be with you by nine, Phil.

[MR. HUXTABLE's dare-devil heart fails once more.]

MR. HUXTABLE. I say . . . better not be too friendly through the shop.

[CONSTANTINE smiles still, but does not loose his arm. Off they go.]

THOMAS [*still searching*]. Where the devil did I put it?

PHILIP. Pity you can't take father's place at dinner, Tommy.

[THOMAS *stops and looks at him aggrievedly.*]

THOMAS. Are you chaffing me?

PHILIP. We might get some further light on the Woman Question. My mother's opinion and Jessica's upon such men as you and my father.

[*He picks up some papers and sits to them at the table.*]

THOMAS. Look here, Phil . . . don't you aggravate me into behaving rashly. Here it is.

[*He has found his hat on a gas-bracket — and he slams it on.*]

PHILIP. With Jessica?

THOMAS [*with ferocious gallantry*]. Yes . . . a damned attractive woman.

PHILIP. After all . . . as an abstract proposition, Tommy . . . polyandry is just as simple a way . . . and, as far as we know, as much Nature's way as the other. We ought to have put that point to the gentle Mohammedan.

THOMAS [*after vainly considering this for a moment*]. Phil, I should like to see you in love with a woman . . . It 'd serve you right.

[*Suddenly* PHILIP *drops his mocking tone and his face grows gentle and grave.*]

PHILIP. Tommy . . . what 's the purpose of it all? Apart from the sentimental wallowings of Mr. Eustace Perrin State . . . and putting that Lord of Creation, my father, on one side for a moment . . . what do we slow-breeding, civilized people get out of love . . . and the beauty of women . . . and the artistic setting that beauty demands? For which we do pay rather a big price, you know, Tommy. What do we get for it?

THOMAS [*utterly at sea*]. I don't know.

PHILIP. It 's an important question. Think it over in the train.

THOMAS. Old chap . . . I beg your pardon . . . the County Council is the best place for you. It 'll stop your addling over these silly conundrums.

PHILIP [*subtly*]. On the contrary.

THOMAS [*his favorite phrase again*]. What do you mean?

PHILIP. Get out . . . you 'll miss that four-thirty.

[THOMAS *gets out.* PHILIP *gets desperately to loathed business.*]

ACT IV

PHILIP, *his mother, and* JESSICA, *are sitting, after dinner, round the drawing-room fire in Phillimore Gardens.* JESSICA, *rather, is away upon the bench of her long, black piano, sorting bound books of music, and the firelight hardly reaches her. But it flickers over* MRS. MADRAS, *and though it marks more deeply the little bitter lines on her face, it leaves a glow there in recompense. She sits, poor, anxious old lady, gazing, not into the fire, but at the shining copper fender, her hands on her lap, as usual. Every now and then she lifts her head to listen.* PHILIP *is comfortable upon the sofa opposite; he is smoking, and is deep, besides, in some weighty volume, the Longman Edition of the Minority Report of the Poor Law Commission, perhaps.*

It is a charming room. The walls are gray, the paint is a darker gray. The curtains to the two long windows are of the gentlest pink brocade; the lights that hang on plain little brackets from the walls are a soft pink, too, and there is no other color in the room, but the maziness of some Persian rugs on the floor and the mellowed brilliancy of the Arundel prints on the walls. There is no more furniture than there need be; there is no more light than there need be; yet it is not empty or dreary. There is just nothing to jar, nothing to prevent a sensitive soul finding rest there.

The parlor maid comes in; she is dressed in gray, too, capless, some black ribbons about her. [*Really,* JESSICA'S *home inclines to be a little precious!*] *She brings letters, one for* JESSICA, *two for* PHILIP, *and departs.*

PHILIP. Last post.

JESSICA. Half past nine. I suppose your father means to come?

PHILIP. He said so.

MRS. MADRAS. Is your letter interesting, Jessica?

JESSICA. A receipt.

MRS. MADRAS. Do you run bills?

JESSICA. Lots.

MRS. MADRAS. Is that quite wise?

JESSICA. The tradesmen prefer it.

[*With that she walks to her writing table.* JESSICA'S *manner to her mother-in-law is over-courteous, an unkind weapon against which the old lady, but half conscious of it, is quite defenseless. PHILIP has opened his second letter, and whistles, at its contents, a bar of a tune that is in his head.*]

JESSICA. What's the matter, Phil?

[*To emphasize his feelings he performs the second bar with variations.*]

JESSICA. As bad as that?

[*For final comment he brings the matter to a full close on one expressive note, and puts the letter away. JESSICA flicks at him amusedly.*]

MRS. MADRAS. How absurd! You can't tell in the least what he means.

JESSICA. No.

[*With forced patience she wanders back to her piano.*]

MRS. MADRAS. You might play us something, Jessica . . . just to pass the time.

[*Unobserved, JESSICA casts her eyes up to the ceiling.*]

JESSICA. What will you have?

MRS. MADRAS. I am sure you play all the latest things.

JESSICA. I'm afraid you don't really like my playing.

MRS. MADRAS. I do think it's a little professional. I prefer something softer.

[*JESSICA leaves the piano.*]

JESSICA. I'm afraid we are giving you a dull evening.

MRS. MADRAS [*with that suddenness which seems to characterize the HUXTABLE family*]. Why do you never call me mother, Jessica?

JESSICA. Don't I?

MRS. MADRAS [*resenting prevarication*]. You know you don't.

JESSICA. I suppose I don't think of you just like that.

MRS. MADRAS. What has that to do with it?

JESSICA [*more coldly courteous than ever*]. Nothing . . . mother.

MRS. MADRAS. That's not a very nice manner of giving way, either, is it?

JESSICA [*on the edge of an outburst*]. It seemed to me sufficiently childish.

MRS. MADRAS [*parading a double injury*]. I don't know what you mean. It's easy to be too clever for me, Jessica.

[*PHILIP mercifully intervenes.*]

PHILIP. Mother, what do you think parents gain by insisting on respect and affection from grown-up children?

MRS. MADRAS. Isn't it their right?

PHILIP. But I asked what they gained.

MRS. MADRAS. Isn't it natural? When an old woman has lost her husband, or worse, if she's to lose her children, too, what has she left?

JESSICA [*recovering a little kindness*]. Her womanhood, mother.

PHILIP. Her old-womanhood. You know, it may be a very beautiful possession.

[*The parlor maid announces "MR. CONSTANTINE MADRAS." There stands CONSTANTINE in the bright light of the hall, more dramatically dignified than ever. As he comes in, though, it seems as if there was the slightest strain in his charming manners. He has not changed his clothes for the evening. He goes straight to JESSICA, and it seems that he has a curious soft way of shaking hands with women.*]

CONSTANTINE. How do you do, Jessica? I find you looking beautiful.

[*JESSICA acknowledges the compliment with a little disdainful bend of the head and leaves him, then with a glance at PHILIP leaves the room. CONSTANTINE comes towards his wife. She does not look up, but her face wrinkles pathetically. So he speaks at last.*]

CONSTANTINE. Well, Amelia?

[*For MRS. MADRAS it must be resentment or tears, or both. Resentment comes first.*]

MRS. MADRAS. Is that the way to speak to me after thirty years?

CONSTANTINE [*amicably*]. Perhaps it isn't. But there's not much variety of choice in greetings, is there?

[*PHILIP, nodding to his father, has edged to the door, and now edges out of it.*]

CONSTANTINE. They leave us alone. We might be an engaged couple.

[*She stays silent, distressfully avoiding his eye. He takes a chair and sits by her. He would say [as JESSICA would no doubt say of herself] that he speaks kindly to her.*]

CONSTANTINE. Well, Amelia? I beg your pardon. I repeat myself, and you dislike the phrase. I hope, though, that you are quite well? Don't cry, dear Amelia . . unless, of course, you want to cry. Well, then . . . cry. And, when you've finished crying ... there's no hurry ... you shall tell me why you wished to see me ... and run the risk of upsetting yourself like this.

MRS. MADRAS [*dabbing her eyes*]. I don't often cry. I don't often get a chance.

CONSTANTINE. I fear that is only one way of saying that you miss me.

[*The handkerchief is put away, and she faces him.*]

MRS. MADRAS. Are you really going back to that country to-morrow?

CONSTANTINE. To-morrow morning.

MRS. MADRAS. For good?

CONSTANTINE [*with thanksgiving*]. For-ever.

MRS. MADRAS [*desperately resolute*]. Will you take me with you?

[*It takes* CONSTANTINE *just a moment to recover.*]

CONSTANTINE. No, Amelia, I will not.

MRS. MADRAS [*reacting a little hysterically*]. I'm sure I don't want to go, and I'm sure I never meant to ask you. But you haven't changed a bit, Constantine ... in spite of your beard. [*Then the voice saddens and almost dies away.*] I have.

CONSTANTINE. Only externally, I'm sure.

MRS. MADRAS. Why did you ever marry me? You married me for my money.

CONSTANTINE [*sighting boredom*]. It is so long ago.

MRS. MADRAS. It isn't ... it seems like yesterday. Didn't you marry me for my money?

CONSTANTINE. Partly, Amelia, partly. Why did you marry me?

MRS. MADRAS. I wanted to. I was a fool.

CONSTANTINE [*evenly still*]. You were a fool, perhaps, to grumble at the consequence of getting what you wanted. It would have been kinder of me, no doubt, not to marry you. But I was more impetuous then, and, of course, less experienced. I didn't realize you never could change your idea of what a good husband must be, nor how necessary it would become that you should.

MRS. MADRAS. How dare you make excuses for the way you treated me?

CONSTANTINE. There were two excuses. I was the first. I'm afraid that you ultimately became the second.

MRS. MADRAS [*with spirit*]. I only stood up for my rights.

CONSTANTINE. You got them, too. We separated, and there was an end of it.

MRS. MADRAS. I've never been happy since.

CONSTANTINE. That is nothing to be proud of, my dear.

[MRS. MADRAS *feels the strangeness between them wearing off.*]

MRS. MADRAS. What happened to that woman and her son ... that Flora?

CONSTANTINE. The son is an engineer ... promises very well, his employers tell me. Flora lives at Hitchin ... quite comfortably, I have reason to believe.

MRS. MADRAS. She was older than me.

CONSTANTINE. About the same age, I think.

MRS. MADRAS. You've given her money?

CONSTANTINE [*his eyebrows up*]. Certainly ... they were both provided for.

MRS. MADRAS. Don't you expect me to be jealous?

CONSTANTINE [*with a sigh*]. Still, Amelia?

MRS. MADRAS. Do you ever see her now?

CONSTANTINE. I haven't seen her for years.

MRS. MADRAS. It seems to me she has been just as well treated as I have ... if not better.

CONSTANTINE. She expected less.

MRS. MADRAS. And what about the others?

CONSTANTINE [*his patience giving out*]. No, really, it's thirty years ago ... I cannot fight my battles over again. Please tell me what I can do for you beyond taking you back with me.

MRS. MADRAS [*cowering to the least harshness*]. I didn't mean that. I don't know what made me say it. But it's dreadful seeing you once more and being alone with you.

CONSTANTINE. Now, Amelia, are you going to cry again?

MRS. MADRAS [*setting her teeth*]. No.

CONSTANTINE. That's right.

[MRS. MADRAS *really does pull herself together, and becomes intensely reasonable.*]

MRS. MADRAS. What I really want you to do, if you please, Constantine, is not to go away. I don't expect us to live together

. . . after the way you have behaved I could not consent to such a thing. But somebody must look after you when you are ill, and, what's more, I don't think you ought to go and die out of your own country.

CONSTANTINE [*meeting reason with reason*]. My dear . . . I have formed other ties.

MRS. MADRAS. Will you please explain exactly what you mean by that?

CONSTANTINE. I am a Mohammedan.

MRS. MADRAS. Nonsense!

CONSTANTINE. Possibly you are not acquainted with the Mohammedan marriage laws.

MRS. MADRAS. D' you mean to say you're not married to me?

CONSTANTINE. No . . . though it was not considered necessary for me to take that into account in conforming to it . . . I did.

MRS. MADRAS. Well . . . I never thought you could behave any worse. Why weren't you satisfied in making me unhappy? If you've gone and committed blasphemy as well . . . I don't know what's to become of you, Constantine.

CONSTANTINE. Amelia, if I had been a Mohammedan from the beginning you might be living happily with me now.

MRS. MADRAS. How can you say such a horrible thing? Suppose it were true?

CONSTANTINE. I came from the East.

MRS. MADRAS. You did n't.

CONSTANTINE. Let us be quite accurate. My grandfather was a Smyrna Jew.

MRS. MADRAS. You never knew him. Your mother brought you up a Baptist.

CONSTANTINE. I was an unworthy Baptist. As a Baptist I owe you apologies for my conduct. What does that excellent creed owe me for the little hells of temptation and shame and remorse that I passed through because of it?

MRS. MADRAS [*in pathetic wonder*]. Did you, Constantine?

CONSTANTINE. I did.

MRS. MADRAS. You never told me.

CONSTANTINE [*with manly pride*]. I should think not.

MRS. MADRAS. But I was longing to have you say you were sorry, and let me forgive you. Twice and three times I'd have forgiven you . . . and you knew it, Constantine.

[CONSTANTINE *recovers his humor,*

his cool courtesy, and his inhumanity, which he had momentarily lost.]

CONSTANTINE. Yes, it was n't so easy to escape your forgiveness. If it were n't for Mahomet, the Prophet of God, Amelia, I should hardly be escaping it now.

[PHILIP *comes delicately in.*]

PHILIP. I beg pardon . . . only my book. [*Which he takes from the piano.*]

CONSTANTINE. Don't go, Phil.

[So PHILIP *joins them, and then, as silence supervenes, says, with obvious cheerfulness . . .*]

PHILIP. How are you getting on?

MRS. MADRAS [*her tongue released*]. Philip, don't be flippant. It's just as your cousin Ernest said. Your father has gone and pretended to marry a lot of wretched women out in that country you showed me on the map, and I don't know what's to be done. My head's going round.

CONSTANTINE. Not a lot, Amelia.

MRS. MADRAS. And if anybody had told me, when I was a girl at school, and learning about such things in history and geography, that I should ever find myself in such a situation as this, I would n't have believed them. [*She piles up the agony.*] Constantine, how are you going to face me Hereafter? Have you thought of that? Was n't our marriage made in Heaven? I must know what is going to happen to us . . . I simply must. I have always prayed that you might come back to me, and that I might close your eyes in death. You know I have, Philip, and I've asked you to tell him so. He has no right to go and do such wicked things. You're mine in the sight of God, Constantine, and you can't deny it.

[*Without warning,* CONSTANTINE *loses his temper, jumps up and thunders at her.*]

CONSTANTINE. Woman . . . be silent. [*Then, as in shame, he turns his back on her and says in the coldest voice . . .*] Philip, I have several things to talk over with you. Suggest to your mother that she should leave us alone.

PHILIP [*protesting against both temper and dignity*]. I shall do nothing of the sort. While my father's in England, and you're in our house, he can at least treat his wife with politeness.

MRS. MADRAS [*with meek satisfaction*]. I'd rather he did n't . . . it's only laughing at me. I'll go to bed. I'd much rather he lost his temper.

[*She gets up to go.* CONSTANTINE'S *bitter voice stops her.*]

CONSTANTINE. Phil . . . when you were a boy . . . your mother and I once quarreled in your presence.

PHILIP [*in bitterness, too*]. I remember.

CONSTANTINE. I'm ashamed of it to this day.

MRS. MADRAS [*quite pleasantly*]. Well . . . I'm sure I don't remember it. What about?

CONSTANTINE. Oh . . . this terrible country. Every hour I stay in it seems to rob me of some atom of self-respect.

[MRS. MADRAS *joins battle again at this.*]

MRS. MADRAS. Then why did you come back? And why haven't you been to see me before . . . or written to me?

CONSTANTINE [*in humorous despair*]. Amelia, don't aggravate me any more. Go to bed, if you're going.

MRS. MADRAS. I wish I'd never seen you again.

PHILIP. Good-night, mother.

[PHILIP *gets her to the door and kisses her kindly. Then* CONSTANTINE *says, with all the meaning possible* . . .]

CONSTANTINE. Good-bye, Amelia.

[*She turns, the bright hall light falling on her, looks at him hatefully, makes no other reply, goes.* PHILIP *comes back to the fire. All this is bitter to him, too. He eyes his father.*]

CONSTANTINE. I'm sorry. I'm upset. I was upset when I came here.

PHILIP. What about? The visit to Denmark Hill?

CONSTANTINE [*who has apparently forgotten that*]. No. . . I didn't go there, after all.

PHILIP. Funked it?

CONSTANTINE [*accepting the gibe*]. I dare say. Once we were off the 'bus, Harry began to mutter about hurting their feelings. I dare say I was funking it, too. I told him to tell them how unbendingly moral he had been with me. He shed three tears as we parted.

PHILIP. Yes . . . my mother was alone here. She's a disappointed woman . . . peevish with ill health. One has her at a disadvantage. But Aunt Kate . . . unveiled and confident, with six corseted daughters to back her!

CONSTANTINE. You think, of course, that I've always treated your mother badly?

PHILIP. I can't help thinking so. Was it the only way to treat her?

CONSTANTINE. Was I meant to pass the rest of a lifetime making her forget that she was as unhappy as people who have outlived their purpose always are?

PHILIP. Personally, I have this grudge against you both, my dear father. As the son of a quarrelsome marriage, I have grown up inclined to dislike men and despise women. You're so full of this purpose of getting the next generation born. Suppose you thought a little more of its upbringing.

CONSTANTINE. What was wrong with yours?

PHILIP. I had no home.

CONSTANTINE. You spent a Sunday with me every month. You went to the manliest school I could find.

PHILIP. Never mind how I learned Latin and Greek. Who taught me that every pretty, helpless woman was a man's prey . . . and how to order my wife out of the room?

CONSTANTINE [*with a shrug*]. My dear boy . . . they like it.

PHILIP. *Do* they?

CONSTANTINE. Well . . . how else are you to manage them?

PHILIP. Father, don't you realize that . . . in decadent England, at least, this manliness of yours is getting a little out of date . . . that you and your kind begin to look foolish at last?

CONSTANTINE [*voicing the discomfort that possesses him*]. I dare say. Thank God, I shall be quit of the country to-morrow! I got here late this evening because I traveled three stations too far in that Tube, sitting opposite such a pretty little devil. She was so alive . . . so crying out for conquest . . . she had that curve of the instep and the little trick of swinging her foot that I never could resist. How does a man resist it? Yes. That's ridiculous and ignominious and degrading. I escaped from England to escape from it. Old age here . . . a loose lip and a furtive eye. I'd have asked you to shoot me first.

PHILIP. Was it that upset you ?

CONSTANTINE. No.

[*He frowns; his thoughts are much elsewhere. There is a moment's silence.* PHILIP *breaks it.*]

PHILIP. Father, what do you know about his Miss Yates affair ?

[CONSTANTINE *gives him a sharp look; then carefully casual* . . .]

CONSTANTINE. What you 've told me.

PHILIP. No more ?

CONSTANTINE. Is there more to know ?

[PHILIP *fishes out and hands across the letter over which he whistled.*]

PHILIP. This has just come from Miss Chancellor.

CONSTANTINE. Who 's she ?

PHILIP. The housekeeper at Peckham, who rashly accused Brigstock of being the other responsible party.

CONSTANTINE. Is he ?

PHILIP. I think not. But she incloses a letter she has just had from Brigstock's solicitors, to the effect that both an apology and compensation is due to him unless the slander is to come into court. Hers faithfully, Meyrick & Hodges.

CONSTANTINE. I don't know them.

PHILIP. We were all still making personal remarks at half past twelve to-day . . . so by their expedition I should say they both are and are not a first-class firm. But suppose the whole thing is made public . . . then the question of the parentage must be cleared up. Miss Yates says it 's nobody's business but hers. That 's an odd idea, in which, if she chooses to have it, the law seems to support her.

[*The steady eye and the steady voice have seemed to make the tension unbearable, and* PHILIP *has meant them to. But he hardly expected this outburst.* CONSTANTINE, *in his own dramatically dignified way, has a fit of hysterics.*]

CONSTANTINE. Phil, I saw the little baggage when the shop closed. I insisted on her meeting me. You know how I 've always behaved over these matters. No one could have been kinder. But she refused money.

PHILIP [*calling on the gods to witness this occasion*]. Well . . . I might have guessed. Oh . . . you incorrigible old man !

CONSTANTINE. She insulted me . . . said she 'd done with me . . . denied me the right to my own child. I 'd even have taken her away. But you 're helpless. I never felt so degraded in my life.

PHILIP. Serve you right !

CONSTANTINE. . . . But the girl 's mad ! Think of my feelings. What does it make of *me* ? Did she know what she was saying ?

PHILIP [*framing his thoughts at last*]. Possibly not . . . but I 'm thankful some woman 's been found at last to put you in your place.

[*These parental-filial passages have brought the two of them face to face, strung to shouting pitch. They become aware of it when* JESSICA *walks in very gently.*]

JESSICA. Your mother gone ?

PHILIP. To bed.

JESSICA [*conscious of thunder*]. Am I intruding ? I sent Phil in for his book a while ago. He did n't return, so I judged that he was. Perhaps I 'm not ?

[CONSTANTINE *is master of himself again, though the hand holding the letter which* PHILIP *gave him does tremble a little still.*]

CONSTANTINE. Well . . . what does Miss Chancellor want ?

PHILIP. She asks my advice.

CONSTANTINE. Dismiss Baxter.

PHILIP. D' you mean Brigstock ?

CONSTANTINE. Brigstock, then. Dismiss him.

PHILIP. What 's he done to deserve it ?

CONSTANTINE. He seems a nonentity of a fellow, and without grit enough to own up to his wife and risk his place. D' you want to protect a man from the consequences of what he *is* ?

PHILIP. Society conspires to.

CONSTANTINE. Then pay him fifty pounds for the damage to his silly little reputation. That 'll be a just consequence to you of sentimentalizing over him.

PHILIP. And stick to Miss Chancellor ?

CONSTANTINE. Certainly. Thank her from the firm for nosing out such a scandal.

PHILIP. And what about Miss Yates ?

JESSICA. The girl in your office this morning ?

PHILIP. Yes.

JESSICA. In the usual trouble ?

PHILIP. How d'you know that?

JESSICA. By the tone of your voice.

CONSTANTINE [*more slowly, more carefully, a little resentfully*]. Dismiss Miss Yates. Keep your eye on her . . . and in a year's time find her a better place . . . if you can . . . in one of these new Madras Houses of State's. He seems to pay very well. [*Then with a breath of relief he becomes his old charming self again.*] Let us change the subject. How is Mildred, Jessica?

JESSICA. Growing.

CONSTANTINE. I've an appointment with my solicitor to-night . . . ten o'clock. There will be two or three thousand pounds to come to that young lady by my will. I mean to leave it as a dowry for her marriage . . . its interest to be paid to her if she's a spinster at thirty . . . which Heaven forbid.

PHILIP. What are you doing with the rest, father?

CONSTANTINE. There are one or two . . . legacies of honor, shall I call them? What remains will come to you.

PHILIP. Yes . . . I don't want it, thank you.

CONSTANTINE. It is n't much.

PHILIP. Take it to Hit, that charming village on the borders of Southern Arabia. Stick it in the ground . . . let it breed more corn and oil for you. We've too much of it already . . . it breeds idleness here.

CONSTANTINE. Dear me!

[*They settle into a chat.*]

JESSICA. We're discussing a *reduction* of our income by a few hundreds a year.

PHILIP. I'm refusing State's directorship.

JESSICA. Though I'm waiting for Phil to tell me where the saving's to come in.

PHILIP. We ought to change that school of Mildred's, for one thing.

JESSICA. Nonsense, Phil!

PHILIP. My dear father, I spent a day there with the child, and upon my word, the only thing she's being taught which will not be a mere idle accomplishment is gardening. And even in their gardens . . . No vegetables allowed!

JESSICA. Phil, I don't mean to have any nonsense with Mildred about earning her living. Accomplished women have a very good time in this world . . . serious women don't. I want my daughter to be happy.

PHILIP. If we've only enough life left to be happy with we must keep ourselves decently poor.   [CONSTANTINE *gets up.*]

CONSTANTINE. Could you get me a taxi, I wonder? It had started raining when I came.

PHILIP. There'll be one on the stand opposite.

CONSTANTINE. I must n't be too late for Voysey. He makes a favor of coming after hours.

JESSICA. I frankly cultivate expensive tastes. I like to have things beautiful around me. I don't know what else civilization means.

CONSTANTINE. I am sure that Philip can refuse you nothing.

PHILIP. If I do dismiss Miss Yates, I wonder if I could do it brutally enough to induce her to accept some compensation.

JESSICA. What for?

PHILIP. She won't take money from this gentleman . . . whoever he is . . . that is, she won't be bribed into admitting her shame.

JESSICA. When a woman has gone wrong may n't it be her duty to other women to own up to it?

CONSTANTINE [*who has stood still the while, stroking his beard*]. If your auditors won't pass any decent sum, I should be happy to send you a check, Phil.

PHILIP [*with a wry smile*]. That would be very generous of you, father.

CONSTANTINE. Good-bye, Jessica.

JESSICA. Good-bye.

CONSTANTINE. Philip is fortunate in his marriage.

JESSICA. So good of you to remind him of that.

CONSTANTINE. You have a charming home. I wonder how much of your womanly civilization it would have needed to conquer *me*. Well . . . I leave you to your conversation. A pleasant life to you.

[*He bends over her hand as if to kiss it. She takes it, as if fastidiously, out of his soft grasp. So he bows again and leaves her.*]

CONSTANTINE. Victoria at eleven o'clock to-morrow, Philip.

PHILIP. Yes . . . I'll see you off.

CONSTANTINE. I have to do a little shopping quite early.

PHILIP. Shopping! What can the West send the East?

CONSTANTINE. I must take back a trinket or two.

PHILIP. To be sure. We do the same on our travels.

[PHILIP *sees him through the hall to the front door, hails a stray cab, and is quit of him.* JESSICA *moves about as if to free the air of this visitation, and when* PHILIP *comes back . . .*]

JESSICA. Does your father usually scatter checks so generously and carelessly?

PHILIP. Jessica, while I have every respect for that young lady's independence . . . still, two hundred pounds would be all to the good of the child's upbringing . . . and why should n't Miss Yates keep her secret?

JESSICA. Yes. I don't like your father. And I 'm sometimes afraid that you 're only an intellectual edition of him. It 's very vital, of course, to go about seducing everybody to your own way of thinking. But really it 's not quite civilized. You ought to learn to talk about the weather.

PHILIP. I cannot talk about what can't be helped.

[*He had settled to a chair and a cigarette, but on the impulse he abandons both and starts a lively argument instead.* PHILIP'S *excited arguments are carried on in short dashes about the room and with queer un-English gestures.*]

PHILIP. And I wonder more and more what the devil you all mean by civilization. This room is civilization. Whose civilization? Not ours.

JESSICA [*in mock despair*]. Oh, dear!

PHILIP. Cheer up. Did n't you marry me because I thought more of Bach than Offenbach? Why should n't you share a fresh set of convictions? This sort of marriage is worth while, you know. Even one's quarrels have a certain dignity.

JESSICA. Go ahead . . . bless your heart.

PHILIP [*shaking his fist at the world in general*]. Whitechapel High Street 's our civilization.

JESSICA. I don't know it.

PHILIP. Therefore you don't much matter, my dear . . . any more than my father did with his view of life as a sort of love-chase. [*He surveys the charming room that is his home.*] Persian carpet on the floor. Last

Supper, by Ghirlandajo, over the mantel-piece. The sofa you 're sitting on was made in a forgotten France. This is a museum. And down at that precious school what are they cultivating Mildred's mind into but another museum . . . of good manners and good taste and . . . [*He catches* JESSICA'S *half scornful, half kindly-quizzical look.*] Are we going to have a row about this?

JESSICA. If you Idealists want Mildred to live in the Whitechapel Road . . . make it a fit place for her.

PHILIP [*taking the thrust and enjoyably returning it*]. When she lives in it it will become so. Why do I give up designing dresses and running a fashion shop to go on the County Council . . . if I can get on? And not to cut a fine figure there, either. But to be on a committee or committees. Not to talk finely even then . . . Lord keep me from the temptation . . . but to do dull, hard work over drains and disinfectants and . . .

JESSICA. Well . . . why, Phil? I may as well know.

PHILIP. To save my soul alive.

JESSICA. I 'm sure I hope you may. But what is it we 're to cultivate in poor Mildred's soul?

[PHILIP *stops in his walk, and then . . .*]

PHILIP. Why not a sense of ugliness? Have you ever really looked at a London street . . . walked slowly up and down it three times . . . carefully testing it with every cultured sense?

JESSICA. Yes . . . it 's loathsome.

PHILIP. Then what have you done?

JESSICA. What can one do?

PHILIP. Come home to play a sonata of Beethoven! Does that drown the sights and the sounds and the smell of it?

JESSICA. Yes . . . it does.

PHILIP [*in fierce revolt*]. Not to me . . . my God . . . not to me!

JESSICA [*gently bitter*]. For so many women, Phil, art has to make life possible.

PHILIP. Suppose we teach Mildred to look out of the window at the life outside. We want to make that *impossible*. Neither Art nor Religion nor good manners have made the world a place I 'll go on living in if I can help it. [*He throws himself into a chair.*] D' you remember in my young days when I used to spend part of a holiday lecturing on Shelley ?

JESSICA. Yes.

PHILIP. I remember once traveling in the train with a poor wretch who lived . . . so he told me . . . on what margins of profit he could pick up by standing rather incompetently between the cornfield and the baker . . . or the coal mine and the fire . . . or the landowner and the tenant . . . I forget which. And he was weary and irritable and unhealthy. And he hated Jones . . . because Jones had done him out of a half per cent on two hundred and fifty pounds . . . and if the sum had been bigger he'd have sued him, so he would. And the end of Prometheus was running in my head . . .

This, like thy glory, Titan, is to be
Good, great and joyous, beautiful and free . . .

and I thought him a mean fellow. And then he told me how he dreaded bankruptcy, and how his uncle, who had been a clerk, had come to the workhouse . . . and what a disgrace that was. And I'm afraid he was a little drunk. And I wondered whether it would be possible to interest *him* in the question of Shelley's position as a prosodist . . . or whether even the beauties of Prometheus would comfort him at all. But when he asked me what I was going to Manchester for . . . do you know, I was ashamed to tell him ?

[*There falls a little silence. Their voices hardly break it.*]

JESSICA. Yes . . . a terrible world . . . an ugly, stupid, wasteful world. A hateful world !

PHILIP. And yet we have to teach Mildred what love of the world means, Jessica. Even if it's an uncomfortable business. Even if it means not adding her to that aristocracy of good feeling and good taste . . . the very latest of class distinctions. I tell you I haven't come by these doubts so easily. Beautiful sounds and sights and thoughts are all of the world's heritage I care about. Giving them up is like giving my carefully created soul out of my keeping before I die.

JESSICA [*with a sudden fling of her hands*]. And into whose ?

PHILIP [*shaking his head at the fire*]. I'm afraid into the keeping of everybody we are at present tempted to dislike and despise. For that's Public Life. That's Democracy. But that's the Future. [*He looks across at his wife half curiously.*] I know it's even harder for you women. You put off your armor for a man you love. But otherwise you've your Honor and Dignity and Purity . . .

JESSICA. Do you want a world without that, either ?

PHILIP. I rather want to know just what the world gets by it. Those six thin girls at my uncle's . . . what do we get from them or they from the world ? Little Miss Yates, now . . . her transgressions may be the most profitable thing about her . . .

JESSICA. Two wrongs don't make a right.

PHILIP [*quaintly*]. They often do . . . properly mixed. Of course you women could serve yourselves up to such lords of creation as my father quite profitably, in one sense, if you would.

JESSICA [*her lip curling*]. Thank you . . . we're not cattle.

PHILIP. No. Then there's a price to be paid for free womanhood, I think . . . and how many of you ladies are willing to pay it ? Come out and be common women among us common men ? [*He leans towards her, and his voice deepens.*] Jessica, do you feel that it was you shot that poor devil six months ago ? . . . that it's you who are to be hanged to-morrow ?

JESSICA. I don't think I do.

PHILIP. That it's your body is being sold on some street this evening ?

[*She gives a little most genuine shudder.*]

JESSICA. I hate to think about such things.

PHILIP [*summing up*]. Then there's precious little hope for the Kingdom of Heaven upon earth. I know it sounds mere nonsense, but I'm sure it's true. If we can't love the bad as well as the beautiful . . . if we won't share it all out now . . . fresh air and art . . . and dirt and sin . . . then we good and clever people are costing the world too much. Our brains cost too much if we don't give them freely. Your beauty costs too much if I only admire it because of the uglier women I see . . . even your virtue may cost too much, my dear. Rags pay for finery and ugliness for beauty, and sin pays for virtue. Why can nothing keep for long more beauty in a good man's eyes than the ugliest thing on earth ? Why need no man be wiser than the biggest fool on earth ? Why does it profit neither man nor woman to be more righteous than the greatest sinner on earth ? [*He clenches his hands.*] These are the riddles this Sphinx of a world is asking me. Your artists and scholars and preachers don't answer them . . . so I must turn my back for a bit on artist and scholar and preacher . . . all three.

[JESSICA *looks at him as he completes his apologia, sympathetic, if not understanding. Then she rallies him cheerfully.*]

JESSICA. Meanwhile, my dear Phil, I shall not stop subscribing to the London Symphony Concerts . . . and I shall expect you to take me occasionally.

PHILIP [*jumping back from his philosophic world*]. Oh . . . that reminds me . . . I 've a message for you from Tommy.

JESSICA. Have you ? He was really irritating this morning.

PHILIP. We must take Tommy with a sense of humor. It was n't so much a message as one of those little bursts of childlike confidence . . . he endears himself to one with them from time to time.

JESSICA. About me ?

PHILIP. Yes. What it comes to is this. Will you please not flirt with him any more, because he has n't the time, and he 's too fond both of me and his wife to want to find himself seriously in love with you.

[*Now* PHILIP *has not said this unguardedly, and* JESSICA *knows it. She'll walk into no little trap set for her vanity or the like. Still, it is with hardly a steady voice that she says simply* . . .]

JESSICA. Thank you for the message.

[PHILIP *goes cheerfully on; he is turning the pages of his book.*]

PHILIP. He does n't at all suppose you are in love with him . . . seriously or otherwise.

JESSICA [*steadily*]. Do you ?

PHILIP. No.

JESSICA [*her tone sharpening still*]. And is this the first time you 've discussed me with Tommy or any one ? Please let it be the last.

PHILIP. Are you angry, Jessica ?

JESSICA. I 'm more than angry.

PHILIP. I 'm sorry.

[*Having kept her temper successfully, if not the sense of humor which* PHILIP *warned her he was appealing to,* JESSICA *now allows herself a deliberate outburst of indignation.*]

JESSICA. I despise men. I despised them when I was fifteen . . . the first year I was conscious of them. I 've been through many opinions since . . . and I come back to despising them.

PHILIP. He was afraid you would n't be pleased with him. But he has my sympathies, Jessica.

JESSICA [*throwing back her head*]. Has he !

PHILIP. Tommy is what the entertaining State called this afternoon the Mean Sensual Man.

JESSICA [*with utter contempt*]. Yes. When we 're alone, having a jolly talk about things in general, he 's all the time thinking I want him to kiss me.

PHILIP. While what you really want is to have him wanting to kiss you but never to kiss you.

JESSICA [*in protest*]. No.

PHILIP [*fixing her with a finger*]. Oh, yes, Jessica.

[JESSICA'S *sense of humor returns for a moment.*]

JESSICA. Well . . . I can't help it if he does.

PHILIP. You can, of course. And the Mean Sensual Man calls it being made a fool of.

[*She puts a serious face on it again; not that she can keep one with* PHILIP'S *twinkling at her.*]

JESSICA. I give you my word I 've never tried to flirt with Tommy . . . except once or twice when he has been boring me. And perhaps once or twice when I was in the dumps . . . and there he was . . . and I was boring him. I know him too well to flirt with him . . . you can't flirt with a man you know well. But he 's been boring me lately, and I suppose I 've been a bit bored. But suppose I have been flirting with him . . . I thought he was safe enough. [*That attempt failing, there is a tack left, and on this she really manages to work herself back to indignation.*] And a caddish thing to go speaking to you about it.

PHILIP. So he said . . . so he said.

JESSICA. Worse than caddish . . . outrageous! I never heard of such a thing . . . you should n't have let him.

PHILIP. Should I have knocked him down when he mentioned your name?

JESSICA. Yes . . . I wish you had.

PHILIP. Little savage!

JESSICA. I can't laugh about this. I'm hurt.

PHILIP. My dear, if you have any sense at all, you 'll ask him to dinner and chaff him about it . . . before me.

JESSICA. Have you any understanding of what a woman feels when men treat her like this? Degraded and cheapened.

[*But the high moral tone* PHILIP *will not stand. He drops chaff and tackles her.*]

PHILIP. I can tell you what the man feels. He'll be either my father or me. That's your choice. Tommy's my father when you 've put on your best gown to attract him, or he 's me when he honestly says that he 'd rather you would n't. Do you want him to be me or my father? That's the first question for you.

JESSICA. I want a man to treat a woman with courtesy and respect.

PHILIP. And what does that come to? My dear, don't you know that the Mean Sensual Man . . . no, not Tommy for the moment, but say Dick or Harry . . . looks on you all as choice morsels . . . with your prettinesses, your dressings-up, your music and art, as so much sauce to his appetite? Which only a mysterious thing called your virtue prevents him from indulging . . . almost by force, if it were n't for the police, Jessica? Do you like that?

JESSICA. I don't believe it.

PHILIP. Do you really believe that most men's good manners towards most pretty women are anything else but good manners?

JESSICA. I prefer good manners to yours. [*Then, both fine taste and sense of humor to the rescue again.*] No . . . that's rude.

PHILIP [*with much more affection than the words convey*]. I treat you as a man would treat another man . . . neither better nor worse. Is the compliment quite wasted?

JESSICA [*as amazed at this unreasonable world*]. I want to be friends with men. I 'd sooner be friends with them. It's they who flirt with me. Why?

PHILIP [*incurably mischievous*]. Of course I've forgotten what you look like, and I never notice what you have on . . . but I suspect it 's because you 're rather pretty and attractive.

JESSICA. Do you want women not to be?

PHILIP. No.

JESSICA. It's perfectly sickening. Of course, if I had dozens of children, and grew an old woman with the last one, I should be quite out of danger. But we can't all be like that . . . you don't want us to be.

PHILIP [*purely negative*]. No.

[*He leaves her free to justify herself.*]

JESSICA. I do my share of things. I make a home for you. I entertain your friends. It may cost your precious world too much . . . my civilization . . . but you want all this done. [*Then with a certainly womanly reserve.*] And Phil . . . suppose I 'm not much nicer by nature than some of you men? When I was a baby, if I 'd not been fastidious I should have been a sad glutton. My culture . . . my civilization . . . may n't be quite up to keeping the brilliant Tommy a decent friend to me, but it has its uses.

[*But* PHILIP *means to laugh this out of court, too.*]

PHILIP. Look here, if it 's only your culture keeps you from kissing Tommy . . . kiss him.

[*To be so driven from pillar to post really does exasperate her.*]

JESSICA. Phil . . . I sometimes think I 'd sooner have been married to your father.

PHILIP. Why?

JESSICA. If you went on as he did instead of as you do . . . I should be sorry . . . I should despise you . . . but it would string me up and add to my self-respect enormously! [*Then a little appealingly.*] But it 's when you 're inhuman, Phil . . . that I 'm ever so little tempted.

PHILIP [*contrite at once*]. I know I am. [*Then he gets up to stand looking into the fire, and what he says is heartfelt.*] But I do so hate that farmyard world of sex . . . men and women always treating each other in this unfriendly way . . . that I 'm afraid it hardens me a bit.

JESSICA [*from her side, gently, with just a look at him*]. I hate it, too . . . but I happen to love you, Phil.

[*They smile at each other.*]

PHILIP. Yes, my dear. If you'd kindly come over here . . . I should like to kiss you.

JESSICA. I won't. You can come over to me.

PHILIP. Will you meet me halfway?

[*They meet halfway, and kiss as husband and wife can. They stand together, looking into the fire.*]

PHILIP. Do you know the sort of world I want to live in?

JESSICA. Should I like it?

PHILIP. Hasn't Humanity come of age at last?

JESSICA. Has it?

PHILIP. Mayn't we hope so? Finery sits so well on children. And they strut and make love absurdly . . . even their quarreling is in all good faith and innocence. But I don't see why we men and women should not find all happiness . . . and beauty, too, . . . in soberer purposes. And with each other . . . why not always some touch of the tranquil understanding which is yours and mine, dear, at the best of moments?

JESSICA [*happily*]. Do you mean when we sometimes suddenly want to shake hands?

PHILIP [*happily, too*]. That's it. And I want an art and a culture that shan't be just a veneer on savagery . . . but it must spring in good time from the happiness of a whole people.

[JESSICA *gives herself one little shake of womanly common sense.*]

JESSICA. Well, what's to be done?

PHILIP [*nobody more practical than he*]. I've been making suggestions. We must learn to live on a thousand a year . . . put Mildred to a sensible school . . . and I must go on the County Council. That's how these great spiritual revolutions work out in practice, to begin with.

JESSICA [*as one who demands a right*]. Where's my share of the job?

PHILIP [*conscious of some helplessness*]. How is a man to tell you? There's enough to choose from.

JESSICA [*the burden of her sex's present fate upon her*]. Ah, you're normal. Nobody sizes you up as a good man or a bad man . . . pretty or plain. There's a trade for bad women and several professions for plain ones. But I've been taught how to be charming and to like dainty clothes. And I dare say I'm excitable and emotional . . . but I can't help it. I'm well off, married to you, I know. You do make me forget I'm a female occasionally.

PHILIP. Male and female created He them . . . and left us to do the rest. Men and women are a long time in the making . . . aren't they?

JESSICA [*enviously*]. Oh . . . you're all right.

PHILIP [*with some humble knowledge of himself*]. Are we?

JESSICA. But I tell you, Phil, it isn't so easy for us. You don't always let us have the fairest of chances, do you?

PHILIP. No, I grant it's not easy. But it's got to be done.

JESSICA. Yes . . .

[*She doesn't finish, for really there is no end to the subject. But for a moment or two longer, happy together, they stand looking into the fire.*]

THE HOUR-GLASS

A MORALITY

By W. B. YEATS

DRAMATIS PERSONÆ

A WISE MAN
A FOOL
SOME PUPILS
AN ANGEL
THE WISE MAN'S WIFE AND TWO CHILDREN

THE HOUR–GLASS

SCENE: *A large room with a door at the back and another at the side opening to an inner room. A desk and a chair in the middle. An hour-glass on a bracket near the door. A creepy stool near it. Some benches. The* WISE MAN *sitting at his desk.*

WISE MAN [*turning over the pages of a book*]. Where is that passage I am to explain to my pupils to-day? Here it is, and the book says that it was written by a beggar on the walls of Babylon : "There are two living countries, the one visible and the one invisible ; and when it is winter with us it is summer in that country; and when the November winds are up among us it is lambing-time there." I wish that my pupils had asked me to explain any other passage, for this is a hard passage. [*The* FOOL *comes in and stands at the door, holding out his hat. He has a pair of shears in the other hand.*] It sounds to me like foolishness ; and yet that cannot be, for the writer of this book, where I have found so much knowledge, would not have set it by itself on this page, and surrounded it with so many images and so many deep colors and so much fine gilding, if it had been foolishness.

FOOL. Give me a penny.

WISE MAN. [*Turns to another page.*] Here he has written : "The learned in old times forgot the visible country." That I understand, but I have taught my learners better.

FOOL. Won't you give me a penny ?

WISE MAN. What do you want ? The words of the wise Saracen will not teach you much.

FOOL. Such a great wise teacher as you are will not refuse a penny to a Fool.

WISE MAN. What do you know about wisdom ?

FOOL. Oh, I know ! I know what I have seen.

WISE MAN. What is it you have seen ?

FOOL. When I went by Kilcluan where the bells used to be ringing at the break of every day, I could hear nothing but the people snoring in their houses. When I went by Tubbervanach where the young men used to be climbing the hill to the blessed well, they were sitting at the cross-roads playing cards. When I went by Carrigoras where the friars used to be fasting and serving the poor, I saw them drinking wine and obeying their wives. And when I asked what misfortune had brought all these changes, they said it was no misfortune, but it was the wisdom they had learned from your teaching.

WISE MAN. Run round to the kitchen, and my wife will give you something to eat.

FOOL. That is foolish advice for a wise man to give.

WISE MAN. Why, Fool ?

FOOL. What is eaten is gone. I want pennies for my bag. I must buy bacon in the shops, and nuts in the market, and strong drink for the time when the sun is weak. And I want snares to catch the rabbits and the squirrels and the hares, and a pot to cook them in.

WISE MAN. Go away. I have other things to think of now than giving you pennies.

FOOL. Give me a penny and I will bring you luck. Bresal the Fisherman lets me sleep among the nets in his loft in the winter-time because he says I bring him luck ; and in the summer-time the wild creatures let me sleep near their nests and their holes. It is lucky even to look at me or to touch me, but it is much more lucky to give me a penny. [*Holds out his hand.*] If I was n't lucky, I 'd starve.

WISE MAN. What have you got the shears for ?

FOOL. I won't tell you. If I told you, you would drive them away.

WISE MAN. Whom would I drive away ?

FOOL. I won't tell you.

WISE MAN. Not if I give you a penny ?

FOOL. No.

WISE MAN. Not if I give you two pennies.

FOOL. You will be very lucky if you give me two pennies, but I won't tell you.

WISE MAN. Three pennies?

FOOL. Four, and I will tell you!

WISE MAN. Very well, four. But I will not call you Teigue the Fool any longer.

FOOL. Let me come close to you where nobody will hear me. But first you must promise you will not drive them away. [WISE MAN *nods*.] Every day men go out dressed in black and spread great black nets over the hills, great black nets.

WISE MAN. Why do they do that?

FOOL. That they may catch the feet of the angels. But every morning, just before the dawn, I go out and cut the nets with my shears, and the angels fly away.

WISE MAN. Ah, now I know that you are Teigue the Fool. You have told me that I am wise, and I have never seen an angel.

FOOL. I have seen plenty of angels.

WISE MAN. Do you bring luck to the angels too.

FOOL. Oh, no, no! No one could do that. But they are always there if one looks about one; they are like the blades of grass.

WISE MAN. When do you see them?

FOOL. When one gets quiet; then something wakes up inside one, something happy and quiet like the stars — not like the seven that move, but like the fixed stars.

[*He points upward.*]

WISE MAN. And what happens then?

FOOL. Then all in a minute one smells summer flowers, and tall people go by, happy and laughing, and their clothes are the color of burning sods.

WISE MAN. Is it long since you have seen them, Teigue the Fool?

FOOL. Not long, glory be to God! I saw one coming behind me just now. It was not laughing, but it had clothes the color of burning sods, and there was something shining about its head.

WISE MAN. Well, there are your four pennies. You, a fool, say "Glory be to God," but before I came the wise men said it. Run away now. I must ring the bell for my scholars.

FOOL. Four pennies! That means a great deal of luck. Great teacher, I have brought you plenty of luck!

[*He goes out shaking the bag.*]

WISE MAN. Though they call him Teigue the Fool, he is not more foolish than everybody used to be, with their dreams and their preachings and their three worlds; but I have overthrown their three worlds with the seven sciences. [*He touches the books with his hands.*] With Philosophy that was made for the lonely star, I have taught them to forget Theology; with Architecture, I have hidden the ramparts of their cloudy heaven; with Music, the fierce planets' daughter whose hair is always on fire, and with Grammar that is the moon's daughter, I have shut their ears to the imaginary harpings and speech of the angels; and I have made formations of battle with Arithmetic that have put the hosts of heaven to the rout. But, Rhetoric and Dialectic, that have been born out of the light star and out of the amorous star, you have been my spearman and my catapult! Oh! my swift horseman! Oh! my keen darting arguments, it is because of you that I have overthrown the hosts of foolishness! [*An* ANGEL, *in a dress the color of embers, and carrying a blossoming apple bough in his hand and with a gilded halo about his head, stands upon the threshold.*] Before I came, men's minds were stuffed with folly about a heaven where birds sang the hours, and about angels that came and stood upon men's thresholds. But I have locked the visions into heaven and turned the key upon them. Well, I must consider this passage about the two countries. My mother used to say something of the kind. She would say that when our bodies sleep our souls awake, and that whatever withers here ripens yonder, and that harvests are snatched from us that they may feed invisible people. But the meaning of the book must be different, for only fools and women have thoughts like that; their thoughts were never written upon the walls of Babylon. [*He sees the* ANGEL.] What are you? Who are you? I think I saw some that were like you in my dreams when I was a child — that bright thing, that dress that is the color of embers! But I have done with dreams, I have done with dreams.

ANGEL. I am the Angel of the Most High God.

WISE MAN. Why have you come to me?

ANGEL. I have brought you a message.

WISE MAN. What message have you got for me?

ANGEL. You will die within the hour. You will die when the last grains have fallen in this glass. [*He turns the hour-glass.*]

WISE MAN. My time to die has not come. I have my pupils. I have a young wife and children that I cannot leave. Why must I die?

ANGEL. You must die because no souls have passed over the threshold of heaven since you came into this country. The threshold is grassy, and the gates are rusty, and the angels that keep watch there are lonely.

WISE MAN. Where will death bring me to?

ANGEL. The doors of heaven will not open to you, for you have denied the existence of heaven; and the doors of purgatory will not open to you, for you have denied the existence of purgatory.

WISE MAN. But I have also denied the existence of hell!

ANGEL. Hell is the place of those who deny.

WISE MAN [*kneeling*]. I have indeed denied everything and have taught others to deny. I have believed in nothing but what my senses told me. But, oh! beautiful Angel, forgive me, forgive me!

ANGEL. You should have asked forgiveness long ago.

WISE MAN. Had I seen your face as I see it now, oh! beautiful Angel, I would have believed, I would have asked forgiveness. Maybe you do not know how easy it is to doubt. Storm, death, the grass rotting, many sicknesses, those are the messengers that came to me. Oh! why are you silent? You carry the pardon of the Most High; give it to me! I would kiss your hands if I were not afraid — no, no, the hem of your dress!

ANGEL. You let go undying hands too long ago to take hold of them now.

WISE MAN. You cannot understand. You live in that country people only see in their dreams. You live in a country that we can only dream about. Maybe it is as hard for you to understand why we disbelieve as it is for us to believe. Oh! what have I said! You know everything! Give me time to undo what I have done. Give me a year — a month — a day — an hour! Give me to this hour's end, that I may undo what I have done!

ANGEL. You cannot undo what you have done. Yet I have this power with my message. If you can find one that believes before the hour's end, you shall come to heaven after the years of purgatory. For, from one fiery seed, watched over by those that sent me, the harvest can come again to heap the golden threshing-floor. But now farewell, for I am weary of the weight of time.

WISE MAN. Blessed be the Father, blessed be the Son, blessed be the Spirit, blessed be the Messenger They have sent!

ANGEL [*at the door and pointing at the hour-glass*]. In a little while the uppermost glass will be empty. [*Goes out.*]

WISE MAN. Everything will be well with me. I will call my pupils; they only say they doubt. [*Pulls the bell.*] They will be here in a moment. I hear their feet outside on the path. They want to please me; they pretend that they disbelieve. Belief is too old to be overcome all in a minute. Besides, I can prove what I once disproved. [*Another pull at the bell.*] They are coming now. I will go to my desk. I will speak quietly, as if nothing had happened.

[*He stands at the desk with a fixed look in his eyes.*]

[*Enter* PUPILS *and the* FOOL.]

FOOL. Leave me alone. Leave me alone. Who is that pulling at my bag? King's son, do not pull at my bag.

A YOUNG MAN. Did your friends the angels give you that bag? Why don't they fill your bag for you?

FOOL. Give me pennies! Give me some pennies!

A YOUNG MAN. Let go his cloak, it is coming to pieces. What do you want pennies for, with that great bag at your waist?

FOOL. I want to buy bacon in the shops, and nuts in the market, and strong drink for the time when the sun is weak, and snares to catch rabbits and the squirrels that steal the nuts, and hares, and a great pot to cook them in.

A YOUNG MAN. Why don't your friends tell you where buried treasures are?

ANOTHER. Why don't they make you dream about treasures? If one dreams three times, there is always treasure.

FOOL [*holding out his hat*]. Give me pennies! Give me pennies!

[*They throw pennies into his hat. He is standing close to the door, that he may hold out his hat to each new-comer.*]

A YOUNG MAN. Master, will you have Teigue the Fool for a scholar ?

ANOTHER YOUNG MAN. Teigue, will you give us pennies if we teach you lessons ? No, he goes to school for nothing on the mountains. Tell us what you learn on the mountains, Teigue ?

WISE MAN. Be silent all. [*He has been standing silent, looking away.*] Stand still in your places, for there is something I would have you tell me.

[*A moment's pause. They all stand round in their places.* TEIGUE *still stands at the door.*]

WISE MAN. Is there any one amongst you who believes in God ? In heaven ? Or in purgatory ? Or in hell ?

ALL THE YOUNG MEN. No one, Master ! No one !

WISE MAN. I knew you would all say that ; but do not be afraid. I will not be angry. Tell me the truth. Do you not believe?

A YOUNG MAN. We once did, but you have taught us to know better.

WISE MAN. Oh ! teaching, teaching does not go very deep ! The heart remains unchanged under it all. You believe just as you always did, and you are afraid to tell me.

A YOUNG MAN. No, no, master.

WISE MAN. If you tell me that you believe I shall be glad and not angry.

A YOUNG MAN. [*To his neighbor.*] He wants somebody to dispute with.

HIS NEIGHBOR. I knew that from the beginning.

A YOUNG MAN. That is not the subject for to-day ; you were going to talk about the words the beggar wrote upon the walls of Babylon.

WISE MAN. If there is one amongst you that believes, he will be my best friend. Surely there is one amongst you. [*They are all silent.*] Surely what you learned at your mother's knees has not been so soon forgotten.

A YOUNG MAN. Master, till you came, no teacher in this land was able to get rid of foolishness and ignorance. But every one has listened to you, every one has learned the truth. You have had your last disputation.

ANOTHER. What a fool you made of that monk in the market-place ! He had not a word to say.

WISE MAN. [*Comes from his desk and stands among them in the middle of the room.*] Pupils, dear friends, I have deceived you all this time. It was I myself who was ignorant. There is a God. There is a heaven. There is fire that passes, and there is fire that lasts for ever.

[TEIGUE, *through all this, is sitting on a stool by the door, reckoning on his fingers what he will buy with his money.*]

A YOUNG MAN [*to another*]. He will not be satisfied till we dispute with him. [*To the* WISE MAN.] Prove it, master. Have you seen them ?

WISE MAN [*in a low, solemn voice*]. Just now, before you came in, some one came to the door, and when I looked up I saw an angel standing there.

A YOUNG MAN. You were in a dream. Anybody can see an angel in his dreams.

WISE MAN. Oh, my God ! It was not a dream. I was awake, waking as I am now. I tell you I was awake as I am now.

A YOUNG MAN. Some dream when they are awake, but they are the crazy, and who would believe what they say ? Forgive me, master, but that is what you taught me to say. That is what you said to the monk when he spoke of the visions of the saints and the martyrs.

ANOTHER YOUNG MAN. You see how well we remember your teaching.

WISE MAN. Out, out from my sight ! I want some one with belief. I must find that grain the Angel spoke of before I die. I tell you I must find it, and you answer me with arguments. Out with you, or I will beat you with my stick ! [*The young men laugh.*]

A YOUNG MAN. How well he plays at faith ! He is like the monk when he had nothing more to say.

WISE MAN. Out, out, or I will lay this stick about your shoulders ! Out with you, though you are a king's son !

[*They begin to hurry out.*]

A YOUNG MAN. Come, come ; he wants us to find some one who will dispute with him.   [*All go out.*]

WISE MAN [*alone. He goes to the door at the side*]. I will call my wife. She will believe; women always believe. [*He opens the door and calls.*] Bridget! Bridget! [BRIDGET *comes in wearing her apron, her sleeves turned up from her floury arms.*] Bridget, tell me the truth ; do not say what you think will please me. Do you sometimes say your prayers ?

BRIDGET. Prayers ! No, you taught me to leave them off long ago. At first I was sorry, but I am glad now, for I am sleepy in the evenings.

WISE MAN. But do you not believe in God ?

BRIDGET. Oh, a good wife only believes what her husband tells her !

WISE MAN. But sometimes when you are alone, when I am in the school and the children asleep, do you not think about the saints, about the things you used to believe in ? What do you think of when you are alone ?

BRIDGET [considering]. I think about nothing. Sometimes I wonder if the pig is fattening well, or I go out to see if the crows are picking up the chickens' food.

WISE MAN. Oh, what can I do ! Is there nobody who believes ? I must go and find somebody ! [He goes toward the door but stops with his eyes fixed on the hour-glass.] I cannot go out ; I cannot leave that !

BRIDGET. You want somebody to get up an argument with.

WISE MAN. Oh, look out of the door and tell me if there is anybody there in the street. I cannot leave this glass ; somebody might shake it ! Then the sand would fall more quickly !

BRIDGET. I don't understand what you are saying. [Looks out.] There is a great crowd of people talking to your pupils.

WISE MAN. Oh, run out, Bridget, and see if they have found somebody that believes !

BRIDGET [wiping her arms in her apron and pulling down her sleeves]. It's a hard thing to be married to a man of learning that must be always having arguments. [Goes out and shouts through the kitchen door.] Don't be meddling with the bread, children, while I'm out.

WISE MAN. [Kneels down.] " Salvum me fac, Deus — salvum — salvum. . . ." I have forgotten it all. It is thirty years since I have said a prayer. I must pray in the common tongue, like a clown begging in the market, like Teigue the Fool ! [He prays.] Help me, Father, Son, and Spirit !
[BRIDGET enters, followed by the FOOL, who is holding out his hat to her.]

FOOL. Give me something ; give me a

penny to buy bacon in the shops, and nuts in the market, and strong drink for the time when the sun grows weak.

BRIDGET. I have no pennies. [To the WISE MAN.] Your pupils cannot find anybody to argue with you. There is nobody in the whole country who had enough belief to fill a pipe with since you put down the monk. Can't you be quiet now and not always be wanting to have arguments ? It must be terrible to have a mind like that.

WISE MAN. I am lost ! I am lost !

BRIDGET. Leave me alone now ; I have to make the bread for you and the children.

WISE MAN. Out of this, woman, out of this, I say ! [BRIDGET goes through the kitchen door.] Will nobody find a way to help me ! But she spoke of my children. I had forgotten them. They will believe. It is only those who have reason that doubt ; the young are full of faith. Bridget, Bridget, send my children to me !

BRIDGET [inside]. Your father wants you ; run to him now.

> [The two children come in. They stand together a little way from the threshold of the kitchen door, looking timidly at their father.]

WISE MAN. Children, what do you believe ? Is there a heaven ? Is there a hell ? Is there a purgatory ?

FIRST CHILD. We haven't forgotten, father.

THE OTHER CHILD. Oh, no, father. [They both speak together as if in school.] There is no heaven ; there is no hell ; there is nothing we cannot see.

FIRST CHILD. Foolish people used to think that there were, but you are very learned and you have taught us better.

WISE MAN. You are just as bad as the others, just as bad as the others ! Out of the room with you, out of the room ! [The children begin to cry and run away.] Go away, go away ! I will teach you better — no, I will never teach you again. Go to your mother — no, she will not be able to teach them. . . . Help them, O God ! [Alone.] The grains are going very quickly. There is very little sand in the uppermost glass. Somebody will come for me in a moment ; perhaps he is at the door now ! All creatures that have reason doubt. O that the grass and the planets could speak ! Somebody has said that they would wither if they doubted. O speak to me, O grass blades ! O fingers of God's certainty, speak to me. You are millions and you will not speak. I dare not know the moment the messenger will come for me. I will cover the glass. [*He covers it and brings it to the desk, and the* FOOL *is sitting by the door fiddling with some flowers which he has stuck in his hat. He has begun to blow a dandelion head.*] What are you doing ?

FOOL. Wait a moment. [*He blows.*] Four, five, six.

WISE MAN. What are you doing that for ?

FOOL. I am blowing at the dandelion to find out what time it is.

WISE MAN. You have heard everything ! That is why you want to find out what hour it is ! You are waiting to see them coming through the door to carry me away. [FOOL *goes on blowing.*] Out through the door with you ! I will have no one here when they come. [*He seizes the* FOOL *by the shoulders, and begins to force him out through the door, then suddenly changes his mind.*] No, I have something to ask you. [*He drags him back into the room.*] Is there a heaven ? Is there a hell ? Is there a purgatory ?

FOOL. So you ask me now. I thought when you were asking your pupils, I said to myself, if he would ask Teigue the Fool, Teigue could tell him all about it, for Teigue has learned all about it when he has been cutting the nets.

WISE MAN. Tell me ; tell me !

FOOL. I said, Teigue knows everything. Not even the owls and the hares that milk the cows have Teigue's wisdom. But Teigue will not speak; he says nothing.

WISE MAN. Tell me, tell me ! For under the cover the grains are falling, and when they are all fallen I shall die; and my soul will be lost if I have not found somebody that believes ! Speak, speak !

FOOL [*looking wise*]. No, no, I won't tell you what is in my mind, and I won't tell you what is in my bag. You might steal away my thoughts. I met a bodach on the road yesterday, and he said, "Teigue, tell me how many pennies are in your bag. I will wager three pennies that there are not twenty pennies in your bag ; let me put in my hand and count them." But I pulled the strings tighter, like this ; and when I go to sleep every night I hide the bag where no one knows.

WISE MAN. [*Goes toward the hour-glass as if to uncover it.*] No, no, I have not the courage ! [*He kneels.*] Have pity upon me, Fool, and tell me !

FOOL. Ah ! Now, that is different. I am not afraid of you now. But I must come near you ; somebody in there might hear what the Angel said.

WISE MAN. Oh, what did the Angel tell you ?

FOOL. Once I was alone on the hills, and an Angel came by and he said, "Teigue the Fool, do not forget the Three Fires : the Fire that punishes, the Fire that purifies, and the Fire wherein the soul rejoices for ever ! "

WISE MAN. He believes ! I am saved ! Help me. The sand has run out. I am dying. . . . [FOOL *helps him to his chair.*] I am going from the country of the seven wandering stars, and I am going to the country of the fixed stars ! Ring the bell. [FOOL *rings the bell.*] Are they coming ? Ah ! now I hear their feet. . . . I will speak to them. I understand it all now. One sinks in on God; we do not see the truth ; God sees the truth in us. I cannot speak, I am too weak. Tell them, Fool, that when the life and the mind are broken, the truth comes through them like peas through a broken peascod. But no, I will pray — yet I cannot pray. Pray, Fool, that they may be given a sign and save their souls alive. Your prayers are better than mine.

[FOOL *bows his head.* WISE MAN'S *head sinks on his arm on the books.* PUPILS *enter.*]

A YOUNG MAN. Look at the Fool turned bell-ringer !

ANOTHER. What have you called us in for, Teigue ? What are you going to tell us ?

ANOTHER. No wonder he has had dreams ! See, he is fast asleep now. [*Goes over and touches the* WISE MAN.] Oh, he is dead !

FOOL. Do not stir ! He asked for a sign that you might be saved. [*All are silent for a moment.*] Look what has come from his mouth . . . a little winged thing . . . a little shining thing. It has gone to the door. [*The* ANGEL *appears in the doorway, stretches out her hands and closes them again.*] The Angel has taken it in her hands . . . she will open her hands in the Garden of Paradise.

[*They all kneel.*]

RIDERS TO THE SEA

A PLAY IN ONE ACT

By JOHN MILLINGTON SYNGE

PERSONS

Maurya, *an old woman*
Bartley, *her son*
Cathleen, *her daughter*
Nora, *a younger daughter*
Men and Women

RIDERS TO THE SEA

SCENE. — *An Island off the west of Ireland. Cottage kitchen, with nets, oil-skins, spinning-wheel, some new boards standing by the wall, etc.* CATHLEEN, *a girl of about twenty, finishes kneading cake, and puts it down in the pot-oven by the fire; then wipes her hands, and begins to spin at the wheel.* NORA, *a young girl, puts her head in at the door.*

NORA [*in a low voice*]. Where is she?

CATHLEEN. She's lying down, God help her, and may be sleeping, if she's able.

[NORA *comes in softly, and takes a bundle from under her shawl.*]

CATHLEEN [*spinning the wheel rapidly*]. What is it you have?

NORA. The young priest is after bringing them. It's a shirt and a plain stocking were got off a drowned man in Donegal.

[CATHLEEN *stops her wheel with a sudden movement, and leans out to listen.*]

NORA. We're to find out if it's Michael's they are, some time herself will be down looking by the sea.

CATHLEEN. How would they be Michael's, Nora? How would he go the length of that way to the far north?

NORA. The young priest says he's known the like of it. "If it's Michael's they are," says he, "you can tell herself he's got a clean burial by the grace of God, and if they're not his, let no one say a word about them, for she'll be getting her death," says he, "with crying and lamenting."

[*The door which* NORA *half closed is blown open by a gust of wind.*]

CATHLEEN [*looking out anxiously*]. Did you ask him would he stop Bartley going this day with the horses to the Galway fair?

NORA. "I won't stop him," says he, "but let you not be afraid. Herself does be saying prayers half through the night, and the Almighty God won't leave her destitute," says he, "with no son living."

CATHLEEN. Is the sea bad by the white rocks, Nora?

NORA. Middling bad, God help us. There's a great roaring in the west, and it's worse it'll be getting when the tide's turned to the wind. [*She goes over to the table with the bundle.*] Shall I open it now?

CATHLEEN. Maybe she'd wake up on us, and come in before we'd done. [*Coming to the table.*] It's a long time we'll be, and the two of us crying.

NORA. [*Goes to the inner door and listens.*] She's moving about on the bed. She'll be coming in a minute.

CATHLEEN. Give me the ladder, and I'll put them up in the turf-loft, the way she won't know of them at all, and maybe when the tide turns she'll be going down to see would he be floating from the east.

[*They put the ladder against the gable of the chimney;* CATHLEEN *goes up a few steps and hides the bundle in the turf-loft.* MAURYA *comes from the inner room.*]

MAURYA [*looking up at* CATHLEEN *and speaking querulously*]. Isn't it turf enough you have for this day and evening?

CATHLEEN. There's a cake baking at the fire for a short space [*throwing down the turf*] and Bartley will want it when the tide turns if he goes to Connemara.

[NORA *picks up the turf and puts it round the pot-oven.*]

MAURYA [*sitting down on a stool at the fire*]. He won't go this day with the wind rising from the south and west. He won't go this day, for the young priest will stop him surely.

NORA. He'll not stop him, mother, and I heard Eamon Simon and Stephen Pheety and Colum Shawn saying he would go.

MAURYA. Where is he itself?

NORA. He went down to see would there be another boat sailing in the week, and I'm thinking it won't be long till he's here now, for the tide's turning at the green head, and the hooker's tacking from the east.

CATHLEEN. I hear some one passing the big stones.

NORA [*looking out*]. He's coming now, and he in a hurry.

BARTLEY. [*Comes in and looks round the room; speaking sadly and quietly.*] Where is the bit of new rope, Cathleen, was bought in Connemara?

CATHLEEN [*coming down*]. Give it to him, Nora; it's on a nail by the white boards. I hung it up this morning, for the pig with the black feet was eating it.

NORA [*giving him a rope*]. Is that it, Bartley?

MAURYA. You'd do right to leave that rope, Bartley, hanging by the boards. [*Bartley takes the rope.*] It will be wanting in this place, I'm telling you, if Michael is washed up to-morrow morning, or the next morning, or any morning in the week, for it's a deep grave we'll make him by the grace of God.

BARTLEY [*beginning to work with the rope*]. I've no halter the way I can ride down on the mare, and I must go now quickly. This is the one boat going for two weeks or beyond it, and the fair will be a good fair for horses I heard them saying below.

MAURYA. It's a hard thing they'll be saying below if the body is washed up and there's no man in it to make the coffin, and I after giving a big price for the finest white boards you'd find in Connemara.

[*She looks round at the boards.*]

BARTLEY. How would it be washed up, and we after looking each day for nine days, and a strong wind blowing a while back from the west and south?

MAURYA. If it wasn't found itself, that wind is raising the sea, and there was a star up against the moon, and it rising in the night. If it was a hundred horses, or a thousand horses you had itself, what is the price of a thousand horses against a son where there is one son only?

BARTLEY [*working at the halter, to* CATHLEEN]. Let you go down each day, and see the sheep aren't jumping in on the rye, and if the jobber comes you can sell the pig with the black feet if there is a good price going.

MAURYA. How would the like of her get a good price for a pig?

BARTLEY. [*To* CATHLEEN.] If the west wind holds with the last bit of the moon let you and Nora get up weed enough for another cock for the kelp. It's hard set we'll

be from this day with no one in it but one man to work.

MAURYA. It's hard set we'll be surely the day you're drownd'd with the rest. What way will I live and the girls with me, and I an old woman looking for the grave?

[*Bartley lays down the halter, takes off his old coat, and puts on a newer one of the same flannel.*]

BARTLEY. [*To* NORA.] Is she coming to the pier?

NORA [*looking out*]. She's passing the green head and letting fall her sails.

BARTLEY [*getting his purse and tobacco*]. I'll have half an hour to go down, and you'll see me coming again in two days, or in three days, or maybe in four days if the wind is bad.

MAURYA [*turning round to the fire, and putting her shawl over her head*]. Isn't it a hard and cruel man won't hear a word from an old woman, and she holding him from the sea?

CATHLEEN. It's the life of a young man to be going on the sea, and who would listen to an old woman with one thing and she saying it over?

BARTLEY [*taking the halter*]. I must go now quickly. I'll ride down on the red mare, and the gray pony'll run behind me. . . . The blessing of God on you.

[*He goes out.*]

MAURYA [*crying out as he is in the door*]. He's gone now, God spare us, and we'll not see him again. He's gone now, and when the black night is falling I'll have no son left me in the world.

CATHLEEN. Why wouldn't you give him your blessing and he looking round in the door? Isn't it sorrow enough is on every one in this house without your sending him out with an unlucky word behind him, and a hard word in his ear?

[MAURYA *takes up the tongs and begins raking the fire aimlessly without looking round.*]

NORA [*turning toward her*]. You're taking away the turf from the cake.

CATHLEEN [*crying out*]. The Son of God forgive us, Nora, we're after forgetting his bit of bread. [*She comes over to the fire.*]

NORA. And it's destroyed he'll be going till dark night, and he after eating nothing since the sun went up.

CATHLEEN [*turning the cake out of the*

oven]. It's destroyed he'll be, surely. There's no sense left on any person in a house where an old woman will be talking forever. [MAURYA *sways herself on her stool*.]

CATHLEEN [*cutting off some of the bread and rolling it in a cloth ; to* MAURYA]. Let you go down now to the spring well and give him this and he passing. You'll see him then and the dark word will be broken, and you can say "God speed you," the way he'll be easy in his mind.

MAURYA [*taking the bread*]. Will I be in it as soon as himself?

CATHLEEN. If you go now quickly.

MAURYA [*standing up unsteadily*]. It's hard set I am to walk.

CATHLEEN [*looking at her anxiously*]. Give her the stick, Nora, or maybe she'll slip on the big stones.

NORA. What stick?

CATHLEEN. The stick Michael brought from Connemara.

MAURYA [*taking a stick* NORA *gives her*]. In the big world the old people do be leaving things after them for their sons and children, but in this place it is the young men do be leaving things behind for them that do be old.

[*She goes out slowly.* NORA *goes over to the ladder.*]

CATHLEEN. Wait, Nora, maybe she'd turn back quickly. She's that sorry, God help her, you would n't know the thing she'd do.

NORA. Is she gone round by the bush?

CATHLEEN [*looking out*]. She's gone now. Throw it down quickly, for the Lord knows when she'll be out of it again.

NORA [*getting the bundle from the loft*]. The young priest said he'd be passing tomorrow, and we might go down and speak to him below if it's Michael's they are surely.

CATHLEEN [*taking the bundle*]. Did he say what way they were found?

NORA [*coming down*]. "There were two men," says he, "and they rowing round with poteen before the cocks crowed, and the oar of one of them caught the body, and they passing the black cliffs of the north."

CATHLEEN [*trying to open the bundle*]. Give me a knife, Nora, the string's perished with the salt water, and there's a black knot on it you would n't loosen in a week.

NORA [*giving her a knife*]. I've heard tell it was a long way to Donegal.

CATHLEEN [*cutting the string*]. It is surely. There was a man in here a while ago — the man sold us that knife — and he said if you set off walking from the rocks beyond, it would be seven days you'd be in Donegal.

NORA. And what time would a man take, and he floating?

[CATHLEEN *opens the bundle and takes out a bit of a stocking. They look at them eagerly.*]

CATHLEEN [*in a low voice*]. The Lord spare us, Nora! is n't it a queer hard thing to say if it's his they are surely?

NORA. I'll get his shirt off the hook the way we can put the one flannel on the other. [*She looks through some clothes hanging in the corner.*] It's not with them, Cathleen, and where will it be?

CATHLEEN. I'm thinking Bartley put it on him in the morning, for his own shirt was heavy with the salt in it [*pointing to the corner*]. There's a bit of a sleeve was of the same stuff. Give me that and it will do.

[NORA *brings it to her and they compare the flannel.*]

CATHLEEN. It's the same stuff, Nora; but if it is itself are n't there great rolls of it in the shops of Galway, and is n't it many another man may have a shirt of it as well as Michael himself?

NORA [*who has taken up the stocking and counted the stitches, crying out*]. It's Michael, Cathleen, it's Michael; God spare his soul, and what will herself say when she hears this story, and Bartley on the sea?

CATHLEEN [*taking the stocking*]. It's a plain stocking.

NORA. It's the second one of the third pair I knitted, and I put up threescore stitches, and I dropped four of them.

CATHLEEN [*Counts the stitches.*] It's that number is in it [*crying out*]. Ah, Nora, is n't it a bitter thing to think of him floating that way to the far north, and no one to keen him but the black hags that do be flying on the sea?

NORA [*swinging herself round, and throwing out her arms on the clothes*]. And is n't it a pitiful thing when there is nothing left of a man who was a great rower and fisher. but a bit of an old shirt and a plain stocking?

CATHLEEN [*after an instant*]. Tell me is herself coming, Nora? I hear a little sound on the path.

NORA [*looking out*]. She is, Cathleen. She's coming up to the door.

CATHLEEN. Put these things away before she'll come in. Maybe it's easier she'll be after giving her blessing to Bartley, and we won't let on we've heard anything the time he's on the sea.

NORA [*helping CATHLEEN to close the bundle*]. We'll put them here in the corner.

[*They put them into a hole in the chimney corner. CATHLEEN goes back to the spinning-wheel.*]

NORA. Will she see it was crying I was?

CATHLEEN. Keep your back to the door the way the light'll not be on you.

[*NORA sits down at the chimney corner, with her back to the door. MAURYA comes in very slowly, without looking at the girls, and goes over to her stool at the other side of the fire. The cloth with the bread is still in her hand. The girls look at each other, and NORA points to the bundle of bread.*]

CATHLEEN [*after spinning for a moment*]. You didn't give him his bit of bread?

[*MAURYA begins to keen softly, without turning round.*]

CATHLEEN. Did you see him riding down? [*MAURYA goes on keening.*]

CATHLEEN [*a little impatiently*]. God forgive you; isn't it a better thing to raise your voice and tell what you seen, than to be making lamentation for a thing that's done? Did you see Bartley, I'm saying to you.

MAURYA [*with a weak voice*]. My heart's broken from this day.

CATHLEEN [*as before*]. Did you see Bartley?

MAURYA. I seen the fearfulest thing.

CATHLEEN. [*Leaves her wheel and looks out.*] God forgive you; he's riding the mare now over the green head, and the gray pony behind him.

MAURYA. [*Starts, so that her shawl falls back from her head and shows her white tossed hair. With a frightened voice.*] The gray pony behind him.

CATHLEEN [*coming to the fire*]. What is it ails you, at all?

MAURYA [*speaking very slowly*]. I've seen the fearfulest thing any person has

seen, since the day Bride Dara seen the dead man with a child in his arms.

CATHLEEN AND NORA. Uah.

[*They crouch down in front of the old woman at the fire.*]

NORA. Tell us what it is you seen.

MAURYA. I went down to the spring well, and I stood there saying a prayer to myself. Then Bartley came along, and he riding on the red mare with the gray pony behind him. [*She puts up her hands, as if to hide something from her eyes.*] The Son of God spare us, Nora!

CATHLEEN. What is it you seen.

MAURYA. I seen Michael himself.

CATHLEEN [*speaking softly*]. You did not, mother; It wasn't Michael you seen, for his body is after being found in the Far North, and he's got a clean burial by the grace of God.

MAURYA [*a little defiantly*]. I'm after seeing him this day, and he riding and galloping. Bartley came first on the red mare; and I tried to say, "God speed you," but something choked the words in my throat. He went by quickly; and "the blessing of God on you," says he, and I could say nothing. I looked up then, and I crying, at the gray pony, and there was Michael upon it — with fine clothes on him, and new shoes on his feet.

CATHLEEN. [*Begins to keen.*] It's destroyed we are from this day. It's destroyed, surely.

NORA. Didn't the young priest say the Almighty God wouldn't leave her destitute with no son living?

MAURYA [*in a low voice, but clearly*]. It's little the like of him knows of the sea. . . . Bartley will be lost now, and let you call in Eamon and make me a good coffin out of the white boards, for I won't live after them. I've had a husband, and a husband's father, and six sons in this house — six fine men, though it was a hard birth I had with every one of them and they coming to the world — and some of them were found and some of them were not found, but they're gone now the lot of them. . . . There were Stephen, and Shawn, were lost in the great wind, and found after in the Bay of Gregory of the Golden Mouth, and carried up the two of them on the one plank, and in by that door.

[*She pauses for a moment, the girls*

start as if they heard something through the door that is half open behind them.]

NORA [in a whisper]. Did you hear that, Cathleen? Did you hear a noise in the northeast?

CATHLEEN [in a whisper]. There's some one after crying out by the seashore.

MAURYA. [Continues without hearing anything.] There was Sheamus and his father, and his own father again, were lost in a dark night, and not a stick or sign was seen of them when the sun went up. There was Patch after was drowned out of a curagh that turned over. I was sitting here with Bartley, and he a baby, lying on my two knees, and I seen two women, and three women, and four women coming in, and they crossing themselves, and not saying a word. I looked out then, and there were men coming after them, and they holding a thing in the half of a red sail, and water dripping out of it — it was a dry day, Nora — and leaving a track to the door.

[She pauses again with her hand stretched out toward the door. It opens softly and old women begin to come in, crossing themselves on the threshold, and kneeling down in front of the stage with red petticoats over their heads.]

MAURYA [half in a dream, to CATHLEEN]. Is it Patch, or Michael, or what is it at all?

CATHLEEN. Michael is after being found in the Far North, and when he is found there how could he be here in this place?

MAURYA. There does be a power of young men floating round in the sea, and what way would they know if it was Michael they had, or another man like him, for when a man is nine days in the sea, and the wind blowing, it's hard set his own mother would be to say what man was it.

CATHLEEN. It's Michael, God spare him, for they're after sending us a bit of his clothes from the Far North.

[She reaches out and hands MAURYA the clothes that belonged to MICHAEL. MAURYA stands up slowly, and takes them in her hands. NORA looks out.]

NORA. They're carrying a thing among them and there's water dripping out of it and leaving a track by the big stones.

CATHLEEN [in a whisper to the women who have come in]. Is it Bartley it is?

ONE OF THE WOMEN. It is surely, God rest his soul.

[Two younger women come in and pull out the table. Then men carry in the body of BARTLEY, laid on a plank, with a bit of a sail over it, and lay it on the table.]

CATHLEEN [to the women, as they are doing so]. What way was he drowned?

ONE OF THE WOMEN. The gray pony knocked him into the sea, and he was washed out where there is a great surf on the white rocks.

[MAURYA has gone over and knelt down at the head of the table. The women are keening softly and swaying themselves with a slow movement. CATHLEEN and NORA kneel at the other end of the table. The men kneel near the door.]

MAURYA [raising her head and speaking as if she did not see the people around her]. They're all gone now, and there is n't anything more the sea can do to me. . . . I'll have no call now to be up crying and praying when the wind breaks from the south, and you can hear the surf is in the east, and the surf is in the west, making a great stir with the two noises, and they hitting one on the other. I'll have no call now to be going down and getting Holy Water in the dark nights after Samhain, and I won't care what way the sea is when the other women will be keening. [To NORA.] Give me the Holy Water, Nora, there's a small sup still on the dresser.

[NORA gives it to her.]

MAURYA. [Drops MICHAEL's clothes across BARTLEY's feet, and sprinkles the Holy Water over him.] It is n't that I have n't prayed for you, Bartley, to the Almighty God. It is n't that I have n't said prayers in the dark night till you would n't know what I'd be saying; but it's a great rest I'll have now, and it's time surely. It's a great rest I'll have now, and great sleeping in the long nights after Samhain, if it's only a bit of wet flour we do have to eat, and maybe a fish that would be stinking.

[She kneels down again, crossing herself, and saying prayers under her breath.]

CATHLEEN. [To an old man.] Maybe yourself and Eamon would make a coffin when the sun rises. We have fine white boards herself bought, God help her, thinking Michael would be found, and I have a new cake you can eat while you 'll be working.

THE OLD MAN [*looking at the boards*]. Are there nails with them ?

CATHLEEN. There are not, Colum ; we did n't think of the nails.

ANOTHER MAN. It 's a great wonder she would n't think of the nails, and all the coffins she 's seen made already.

CATHLEEN. It 's getting old she is, and broken.

> [MAURYA *stands up again very slowly and spreads out the pieces of* MICHAEL's *clothes beside the body, sprinkling them with the last of the Holy Water.*]

NORA [*in a whisper to* CATHLEEN]. She 's quiet now and easy ; but the day Michael was drowned you could hear her crying out from this to the spring well. It 's fonder she was of Michael, and would any one have thought that ?

CATHLEEN [*slowly and clearly*]. An old woman will be soon tired with anything she will do, and is n't it nine days herself is after crying and keening, and making great sorrow in the house ?

MAURYA. [*Puts the empty cup mouth downwards on the table, and lays her hands together on* BARTLEY's *feet.*] They 're all together this time, and the end is come. May the Almighty God have mercy on Bartley's soul, and on Michael's soul, and on the souls of Sheamus and Patch, and Stephen and Shawn [*bending her head*] ; and may He have mercy on my soul, Nora, and on the soul of every one is left living in the world.

> [*She pauses, and the keen rises a little more loudly from the women, then sinks away.*]

MAURYA [*continuing*]. Michael has a clean burial in the Far North, by the grace of the Almighty God. Bartley will have a fine coffin out of the white boards, and a deep grave surely. What more can we want than that ? No man at all can be living forever, and we must be satisfied.

> [*She kneels down again and the curtain falls slowly.*]

THE RISING OF THE MOON

By LADY GREGORY

PERSONS

SERGEANT
POLICEMAN X
POLICEMAN B
A RAGGED MAN

THE RISING OF THE MOON

SCENE: *Side of a quay in a seaport town. Some posts and chains. A large barrel. Enter three policemen. Moonlight.*

SERGEANT, *who is older than the others, crosses the stage to right and looks down steps. The others put down a pastepot and unroll a bundle of placards.*

POLICEMAN B. I think this would be a good place to put up a notice.

[*He points to barrel.*]

POLICEMAN X. Better ask him. [*Calls to* SERGEANT.] Will this be a good place for a placard? [*No answer.*]

POLICEMAN B. Will we put up a notice here on the barrel? [*No answer.*]

SERGEANT. There's a flight of steps here that leads to the water. This is a place that should be minded well. If he got down here, his friends might have a boat to meet him; they might send it in here from outside.

POLICEMAN B. Would the barrel be a good place to put a notice up?

SERGEANT. It might; you can put it there. [*They paste the notice up.*]

SERGEANT [*reading it*]. Dark hair — dark eyes, smooth face, height five feet five — there's not much to take hold of in that — It's a pity I had no chance of seeing him before he broke out of jail. They say he's a wonder, that it's he makes all the plans for the whole organization. There isn't another man in Ireland would have broken jail the way he did. He must have some friends among the jailers.

POLICEMAN B. A hundred pounds is little enough for the Government to offer for him. You may be sure any man in the force that takes him will get promotion.

SERGEANT. I'll mind this place myself. I wouldn't wonder at all if he came this way. He might come slipping along there [*points to side of quay*], and his friends might be waiting for him there [*points down steps*], and once he got away it's little chance we'd have of finding him; it's maybe under a load of kelp he'd be in a fishing boat, and not one to help a married man that wants it to the reward.

POLICEMAN X. And if we get him itself, nothing but abuse on our heads for it from the people, and maybe from our own relations.

SERGEANT. Well, we have to do our duty in the force. Haven't we the whole country depending on us to keep law and order? It's those that are down would be up and those that are up would be down, if it wasn't for us. Well, hurry on, you have plenty of other places to placard yet, and come back here then to me. You can take the lantern. Don't be too long now. It's very lonesome here with nothing but the moon.

POLICEMAN B. It's a pity we can't stop with you. The Government should have brought more police into the town, with *him* in jail, and at assize time too. Well, good luck to your watch. [*They go out.*]

SERGEANT. [*Walks up and down once or twice and looks at placard.*] A hundred pounds and promotion sure. There must be a great deal of spending in a hundred pounds. It's a pity some honest man not to be the better of that.

[*A ragged man appears at left and tries to slip past.* SERGEANT *suddenly turns.*]

SERGEANT. Where are you going?

MAN. I'm a poor ballad-singer, your honor. I thought to sell some of these [*holds out bundle of ballads*] to the sailors. [*He goes on.*]

SERGEANT. Stop! Didn't I tell you to stop? You can't go on there.

MAN. Oh, very well. It's a hard thing to be poor. All the world's against the poor.

SERGEANT. Who are you?

MAN. You'd be as wise as myself if I told you, but I don't mind. I'm one Jimmy Walsh, a ballad-singer.

SERGEANT. Jimmy Walsh? I don't know that name.

MAN. Ah, sure, they know it well enough in Ennis. Were you ever in Ennis, sergeant?

SERGEANT. What brought you here?

MAN. Sure, it's to the assizes I came, thinking I might make a few shillings here or there. It's in the one train with the judges I came.

SERGEANT. Well, if you came so far, you may as well go farther, for you'll walk out of this.

MAN. I will, I will; I'll just go on where I was going. [Goes toward steps.]

SERGEANT. Come back from those steps; no one has leave to pass down them to-night.

MAN. I'll just sit on the top of the steps till I see will some sailor buy a ballad off me that would give me my supper. They do be late going back to the ship. It's often I saw them in Cork carried down the quay in a hand-cart.

SERGEANT. Move on, I tell you. I won't have any one lingering about the quay to-night.

MAN. Well, I'll go. It's the poor have the hard life! Maybe yourself might like one, sergeant. Here's a good sheet now. [Turns one over.] "Content and a pipe" — that's not much. "The Peeler and the goat" — you wouldn't like that — "Johnny Hart" — that's a lovely song.

SERGEANT. Move on.

MAN. Ah, wait till you hear it. [Sings.]

There was a rich farmer's daughter lived near the town of Ross;
She courted a Highland soldier, his name was Johnny Hart;
Says the mother to her daughter, "I'll go distracted mad
If you marry that Highland soldier dressed up in Highland plaid."

SERGEANT. Stop that noise.
[MAN wraps up his ballads and shuffles toward the steps.]

SERGEANT. Where are you going?

MAN. Sure you told me to be going, and I am going.

SERGEANT. Don't be a fool. I didn't tell you to go that way; I told you to go back to the town.

MAN. Back to the town, is it?

SERGEANT [taking him by the shoulder and shoving him before him]. Here, I'll show you the way. Be off with you. What are you stopping for?

MAN [who has been keeping his eye on the notice, points to it]. I think I know what you're waiting for, sergeant.

SERGEANT. What's that to you?

MAN. And I know well the man you're waiting for — I know him well — I'll be going. [He shuffles on.]

SERGEANT. You know him? Come back here. What sort is he?

MAN. Come back is it, sergeant? Do you want to have me killed?

SERGEANT. Why do you say that?

MAN. Never mind. I'm going. I would n't be in your shoes if the reward was ten times as much. [Goes on off stage to left.] Not if it was ten times as much.

SERGEANT [rushing after him]. Come back here, come back. [Drags him back.] What sort is he? Where did you see him?

MAN. I saw him in my own place, in the County Clare. I tell you you would n't like to be looking at him. You'd be afraid to be in the one place with him. There is n't a weapon he does n't know the use of, and as to strength, his muscles are as hard as that board [slapping barrel].

SERGEANT. Is he as bad as that?

MAN. He is then.

SERGEANT. Do you tell me so?

MAN. There was a poor man in our place, a sergeant from Ballyvaughan. — It was with a lump of stone he did it.

SERGEANT. I never heard of that.

MAN. And you would n't, sergeant. It's not everything that happens gets into the papers. And there was a policeman in plain clothes, too. . . . It is in Limerick he was. . . . It was after the time of the attack on the police barrack at Kilmallock. . . . Moonlight . . . just like this . . . waterside. . . . Nothing was known for certain.

SERGEANT. Do you say so? It's a terrible county to belong to.

MAN. That's so, indeed! You might be standing there, looking out that way, thinking you saw him coming up this side of the quay [points], and he might be coming up this other side [points], and he'd be on you before you knew where you were.

SERGEANT. It's a whole troop of police they ought to put here to stop a man like that.

MAN. But if you'd like me to stop with you, I could be looking down this side. I could be sitting up here on this barrel.

SERGEANT. And you know him well, too?

MAN. I'd know him a mile off, sergeant.

SERGEANT. But you would n't want to share the reward?

MAN. Is it a poor man like me, that has to be going the roads and singing in fairs, to have the name on him that he took a reward? But you don't want me. I'll be safer in the town.

SERGEANT. Well, you can stop.

MAN [getting up on barrel]. All right, sergeant. I wonder, now, you 're not tired out, sergeant, walking up and down the way you are.

SERGEANT. If I 'm tired I 'm used to it.

MAN. You might have hard work before you to-night yet. Take it easy while you can. There 's plenty of room up here on the barrel, and you see farther when you 're higher up.

SERGEANT. Maybe so. [Gets up beside him on barrel, facing right. They sit back to back, looking different ways.] You made me feel a bit queer with the way you talked.

MAN. Give me a match, sergeant [he gives it, and MAN lights pipe]; take a draw yourself? It 'll quiet you. Wait now till I give you a light, but you need n't turn round. Don't take your eye off the quay for the life of you.

SERGEANT. Never fear, I won't. [Lights pipe. They both smoke.] Indeed, it 's a hard thing to be in the force, out at night and no thanks for it, for all the danger we 're in. And it 's little we get but abuse from the people, and no choice but to obey our orders, and never asked when a man is sent into danger, if you are a married man with a family.

MAN. [Sings.]

As through the hills I walked to view the hills
  and shamrock plain,
I stood awhile where nature smiles to view the
  rocks and streams,
On a matron fair I fixed my eyes beneath a
  fertile vale,
As she sang her song it was on the wrong of
  poor old Granuaile.

SERGEANT. Stop that; that 's no song to be singing in these times.

MAN. Ah, sergeant, I was only singing to keep my heart up. It sinks when I think of him. To think of us two sitting here, and he creeping up the quay, maybe, to get to us.

SERGEANT. Are you keeping a good lookout?

MAN. I am; and for no reward too. Am n't I the foolish man? But when I saw a man in trouble, I never could help trying to get him out of it. What 's that? Did something hit me? [Rubs his heart.]

SERGEANT [patting him on the shoulder]. You will get your reward in heaven.

MAN. I know that, I know that, sergeant, but life is precious.

SERGEANT. Well, you can sing if it gives you more courage.

MAN. [Sings.]

Her head was bare, her hands and feet with
  iron bands were bound,
Her pensive strain and plaintive wail mingles
  with the evening gale,
And the song she sang with mournful air, I am
  old Granuaile.
Her lips so sweet that monarchs kissed . . .

SERGEANT. That 's not it. . . . "Her gown she wore was stained with gore." . . . That 's it — you missed that.

MAN. You 're right, sergeant, so it is; I missed it. [Repeats line.] But to think of a man like you knowing a song like that.

SERGEANT. There 's many a thing a man might know and might not have any wish for.

MAN. Now, I dare say, sergeant, in your youth, you used to be sitting up on a wall, the way you are sitting up on this barrel now, and the other lads beside you, and you singing "Granuaile"? . . .

SERGEANT. I did then.

MAN. And the "Shan Bhean Bhocht"? . . .

SERGEANT. I did then.

MAN. And the "Green on the Cape"?

SERGEANT. That was one of them.

MAN. And maybe the man you are watching for to-night used to be sitting on the wall, when he was young, and singing those same songs. . . . It 's a queer world. . . .

SERGEANT. Whisht! . . . I think I see something coming. . . . It 's only a dog.

MAN. And is n't it a queer world? . . . Maybe it 's one of the boys you used to be singing with that time you will be arresting to-day or to-morrow, and sending into the dock. . . .

SERGEANT. That 's true, indeed.

MAN. And maybe one night, after you had been singing, if the other boys had told you some plan they had, some plan to free the country, you might have joined with them . . . and maybe it is you might be in trouble now.

SERGEANT. Well, who knows but I might? I had a great spirit in those days.

MAN. It's a queer world, sergeant, and it's little any mother knows when she sees her child creeping on the floor what might happen to it before it has gone through its life, or who will be who in the end.

SERGEANT. That's a queer thought now, and a true thought. Wait now till I think it out . . . If it wasn't for the sense I have, and for my wife and family, and for me joining the force the time I did, it might be myself now would be after breaking jail and hiding in the dark, and it might be him that's hiding in the dark and that got out of jail would be sitting up where I am on this barrel. . . . And it might be myself would be creeping up trying to make my escape from himself, and it might be himself would be keeping the law, and myself would be breaking it, and myself would be trying maybe to put a bullet in his head, or to take up a lump of a stone the way you said he did . . . no, that myself did . . . Oh! [Gasps. After a pause.] What's that? [Grasps MAN's arm.]

MAN. [Jumps off barrel and listens, looking out over water.] It's nothing, sergeant.

SERGEANT. I thought it might be a boat. I had a notion there might be friends of his coming about the quays with a boat.

MAN. Sergeant, I am thinking it was with the people you were, and not with the law you were when you were a young man.

SERGEANT. Well, if I was foolish then, that time's gone.

MAN. Maybe, sergeant, it comes into your head sometimes, in spite of your belt and your tunic, that it might have been as well for you to have followed Granuaile.

SERGEANT. It's no business of yours what I think.

MAN. Maybe, sergeant, you'll be on the side of the country yet.

SERGEANT. [Gets off barrel.] Don't talk to me like that. I have my duties and I know them. [Looks round.] That was a boat; I hear the oars.

[Goes to the steps and looks down.]

MAN. [Sings.]

Oh, then, tell me, Shawn O'Farrell,
  Where the gathering is to be.
In the old spot by the river
  Right well known to you and me!

SERGEANT. Stop that! Stop that, I tell you!

MAN. [Sings louder.]

One word more, for signal token,
  Whistle up the marching tune,
With your pike upon your shoulder,
  At the Rising of the Moon.

SERGEANT. If you don't stop that, I'll arrest you.

[A whistle from below answers, repeating the air.]

SERGEANT. That's a signal. [Stands between him and steps.] You must not pass this way. . . . Step farther back. . . . Who are you? You are no ballad-singer.

MAN. You needn't ask who I am; that placard will tell you. [Points to placard.]

SERGEANT. You are the man I am looking for.

MAN. [Takes off hat and wig. SERGEANT seizes them.] I am. There's a hundred pounds on my head. There is a friend of mine below in a boat. He knows a safe place to bring me to.

SERGEANT [looking still at hat and wig]. It's a pity! it's a pity! You deceived me. You deceived me well.

MAN. I am a friend of Granuaile. There is a hundred pounds on my head.

SERGEANT. It's a pity, it's a pity!

MAN. Will you let me pass, or must I make you let me?

SERGEANT. I am in the force. I will not let you pass.

MAN. I thought to do it with my tongue. [Puts hand in breast.] What is that?

Voice of POLICEMAN X outside. Here, this is where we left him.

SERGEANT. It's my comrades coming.

MAN. You won't betray me . . . the friend of Granuaile. [Slips behind barrel.]

Voice of POLICEMAN B. That was the last of the placards.

POLICEMAN X [as they come in]. If he makes his escape it won't be unknown he'll make it.

[SERGEANT puts hat and wig behind his back.]

POLICEMAN B. Did any one come this way?

SERGEANT [*after a pause*]. No one.

POLICEMAN B. No one at all?

SERGEANT. No one at all.

POLICEMAN B. We had no orders to go back to the station; we can stop along with you.

SERGEANT. I don't want you. There is nothing for you to do here.

POLICEMAN B. You bade us to come back here and keep watch with you.

SERGEANT. I'd sooner be alone. Would any man come this way and you making all that talk? It is better the place to be quiet.

POLICEMAN B. Well, we'll leave you the lantern anyhow.   [*Hands it to him.*]

SERGEANT. I don't want it. Bring it with you.

POLICEMAN B. You might want it. There are clouds coming up and you have the darkness of the night before you yet. I'll leave it over here on the barrel.

[*Goes to barrel.*]

SERGEANT. Bring it with you I tell you. No more talk.

POLICEMAN B. Well, I thought it might be a comfort to you. I often think when I have it in my hand and can be flashing it about into every dark corner [*doing so*] that it's the same as being beside the fire at home, and the bits of bogwood blazing up now and again.

[*Flashes it about, now on the barrel, now on* SERGEANT.]

SERGEANT [*furious*]. Be off the two of you, yourselves and your lantern!

[*They go out.* MAN *comes from behind barrel. He and* SERGEANT *stand looking at one another.*]

SERGEANT. What are you waiting for?

MAN. For my hat, of course, and my wig. You wouldn't wish me to get my death of cold?   [SERGEANT *gives them.*]

MAN [*going toward steps*]. Well, good-night, comrade, and thank you. You did me a good turn to-night, and I'm obliged to you. Maybe I'll be able to do as much for you when the small rise up and the big fall down . . . when we all change places at the Rising [*waves his hand and disappears*] of the Moon.

SERGEANT [*turning his back to audience and reading placard*]. A hundred pounds reward! A hundred pounds! [*Turns toward audience.*] I wonder now, am I as great a fool as I think I am?

THE TRUTH
A PLAY IN FOUR ACTS
By CLYDE FITCH

THE PERSONS IN THE PLAY

WARDER

ROLAND

LINDON

SERVANT AT THE WARDERS'

BECKY WARDER

EVE LINDON

LAURA FRASER

MRS. GENEVIEVE CRESPIGNY

MESSENGER BOY

ACT I. AT THE WARDERS', NEW YORK
(*Thursday Afternoon*)

ACT II. AT THE WARDERS'
(*Saturday Afternoon, just after lunch*)

ACT III. AT STEPHEN ROLAND'S, BALTIMORE
(*Saturday Night*)

ACT IV. AT STEPHEN ROLAND'S
(*Monday Morning*)

THE TRUTH

ACT I

At Mrs. Warder's. *An extremely attractive room, in the best of taste, gray walls with dull soft green moldings, old French chintz curtains, furniture painted to match the walls and covered with the same chintz. Some old colored engravings are on the mantel-shelf and a couple of eighteenth-century French portraits on the wall. On the left is a mantel, and near it a large writing table against the back of a low sofa which faces the audience; on the table a telephone; an arm-chair and a small table on the left; a baby grand piano in the upper left corner of the room. Some consols and tables in the room; four windows at the back, through which one sees the park. Doors, right and left; books, photographs, flowers, etc., on the tables and consols.*

A smart, good-looking man-servant, Jenks, *shows in* Mrs. Lindon *and* Laura Fraser. *The former is a handsome, nervous, overstrung woman of about thirty-four, very fashionably dressed;* Miss Fraser, *on the contrary, a matter-of-fact, rather commonplace type of good humor — wholesomeness united to a kind sense of humor —* Mrs. Lindon *is the sort of woman warranted to put any one on edge in the course of a few hours' consecutive association, while friction with* Miss Fraser *is equally certain to smooth down the raw edges.*

Mrs. Lindon [*coming in to a chair near the center with quick determination*]. You have no idea when Mrs. Warder will be in?

Servant. No, madam.

Mrs. Lindon. She was lunching out?

Servant. Yes, madam.

Laura [*with a movement to go*]. Come! She may be playing bridge and not come home for hours.

Mrs. Lindon [*firm, though irritable*]. I will wait till half past five. [*To* Servant.] If Mrs. Warder comes in before that, we will be here.

[*Nervously picks up check-book from the writing-table, looks at it but not in it, and puts it down.*]

Servant. Very good, madam.

[*Goes out left.*]

Laura. [*Goes to* Eve.] My dear, you must control yourself. That man, if he has half a servant's curiosity, could easily see you are excited.

Mrs. Lindon. Yes, but think! She's been meeting Fred probably every day for the last two months, although she knew I had left his house, and always pretended to me she never saw him!

[*Sitting beside the writing-table.*]

Laura [*sitting left*]. You should n't have come here at once. You should have waited till you had time to think over your information and calm yourself a little.

Mrs. Lindon. I could n't wait! Becky! One of my oldest friends! One of my bridesmaids!

Laura. What!

Mrs. Lindon. No, she was n't, but she might have been ; she was my next choice if any one had backed out.

Laura. Probably Fred 's appealing to her sympathy, — you know your own husband!

Mrs. Lindon [*with a disagreeable half-laugh*]. Yes, I know him better than she does! What I don't like is her secrecy about it after I 'd made her the confidante of my trouble!

Laura. I thought *I* was that?

Mrs. Lindon. You are — another! But you must n't forget that I have gone to Becky in hysterics and begged her to make it up for me with Fred.

Laura. Were you perfectly frank with her?

Mrs. Lindon. Perfectly! I told her the truth, and more too! I told her I loved Fred in spite of his faults — Good Heavens! if a woman had to find a *faultless* man to love ! — I 've asked her advice.

[*Rising nervously and going to the sofa.*]

Laura. You have n't taken it!

Mrs. Lindon. That does n't make any

difference ! Who ever does ? [*Sitting on the sofa.*] She *owed* me her loyalty instead of flirting with Fred behind my back.

[*She opens the cigar box on the writing-table behind her and then bangs it shut.*]

LAURA. Perhaps she's really trying to make peace between you in her own way !

MRS. LINDON. Does it look like it ? Actually telling me yesterday she would n't trust herself in his presence for fear she'd lose her control and tell him what she thought of him ! — and all the time she had an appointment to meet him this afternoon — in the *Eden Musée*, if you please !

LAURA [*with comic disgust*]. Oh ! Horrors !

MRS. LINDON. Yes, in the chamber of them ! If that is n't compromising !

LAURA. Eve !

MRS. LINDON. And Tom Warder so nice ! *Everybody* likes him !

[*Picks up stamp box amd bangs it down.*]

LAURA. Including Becky. That's the point. Becky *loves* her own husband. What does she want of yours ?

MRS. LINDON. She loved Tom Warder when she married him, but that was in 1903 ! Besides, Becky always liked having men fond of her whether she cared for them or not.

LAURA. Nonsense !

MRS. LINDON. She's what the French call an "*allumeuse*" — leads them on till they lose their heads, then she gets frightened and feels insulted!

LAURA. But you claim she *does* care for Fred !

MRS. LINDON. My dear, a magnetic man like Fred has a way of winding himself around a woman and keeping himself wound as long as he wishes ! even when *she does n't* wish, — look at me ! I'd give anything to throw him off for good, but I can't stop being in love with him !

LAURA [*who has moved over to the chair beside the sofa, pats* EVE'S *hand*]. Poor old Eve ! Well, when she comes, what are you going to do ?

MRS. LINDON. Give her one more chance to tell me the truth ! I'll ask her outright when she saw Fred last.

LAURA. But if she keeps on with her "bluff" of not seeing him, you can't tell

her she lies without making a horrid scene, and what good would that do ?

MRS. LINDON. Exactly! She'd never acknowledge she was lying but just go on ! I may appeal to Tom Warder himself !

[*Rises and goes to mantel, looking at the fly-leaves of two books on a table which she passes.*]

LAURA. No !

MRS. LINDON. Why not ? We've been friends since babies.

LAURA. You *would n't !*

MRS. LINDON. I don't accuse Becky of anything dreadful ! Besides, it will be for his good too, as well as mine, — he knows Fred, and I'll wager anything he'll be as eager as I to stop any excess of friendship with him. [*Goes up to the window.*] Sh ! here she is ! and a man with her !

LAURA. [*Rises, excited, and joins her.*] Who ?

MRS. LINDON [*going to the other window*]. I can't see.

LAURA [*joining her at the second window*]. Suppose it should be —

MRS. LINDON. Exactly! If she hears I'm here, she'll never let him in. [*She starts with a new idea and goes to the door right.*] The window in that hall juts out ; perhaps we can see the front door from there. Come quickly ! [*Tries to pull* LAURA *out right.*]

LAURA. I don't approve of what you're doing at all.

MRS. LINDON. Oh, come !

[*They go out and close the door behind them.*]

[*The* SERVANT *shows in* BECKY *and* LINDON, *left.* BECKY *is a pretty, charming, volatile young woman, sprightly, vivacious, lovable. She is dressed ultra-smartly, and in the best of taste.* LINDON *is dapper, rather good-looking, though not particularly strong in character, and full of a certain personal charm. He also wears very fashionable clothes. He is a man whose chief aim in life is to amuse himself.*]

SERVANT. Mrs. Lindon and Miss Fraser were waiting to see you, madam ; they must have gone.

BECKY [*with a humorous raising of the eyebrows and a look to* LINDON]. Oh ! — I'm so sorry ! [*The* SERVANT *goes out.*]

LINDON. Gee ! what a narrow escape.

LAURA [*off stage right, pleading loudly*].
Eve ! Eve ! ! Come ! ! !

MRS. LINDON [*off stage right, loudly*]. I
will not. I will run my own affairs my own
way.

BECKY [*who has heard this, with an amused,
mischievous expression*]. They are there ! Do
you suppose they saw you ?
          [*They lower their voices slightly.*]

LINDON. Well, — Eve can see through
most things, but not through the walls !
Good-bye.
          [*He starts to hurry out, but* BECKY
          stops him.]

BECKY. You must come back ! That 's
what I brought you home with me to-day
for — to talk about Eve. This estrangement has gone on long enough. I 've come
to the conclusion you 're as much to blame
as she is — or more.

LINDON. I like *that* from *you !*

BECKY. I mean it, and if she wants you
back, you 've got to go.

LINDON. Well, let me get a cocktail
first.

BECKY. I 'm serious.

LINDON. So 'll I be if Eve comes in and
catches me.   [*Going.*]

BECKY [*going with him*]. I 'll let you out
— but I expect you again in half an
hour. Do you understand ? [*They go out
left. Off stage.*] You 're to come back at
six.

LINDON [*off stage, at a distance*]. All
right.

          [EVE *comes in excitedly from the right.*]

MRS. LINDON. I think it is Fred ! Watch
from the window ! I 'll stay here in case
Becky comes in. [*She comes to the writing-
table.*] I 'd like to scratch her eyes out !

          [LAURA *comes in and goes to right of the sofa.*]

LAURA. It *was* Fred.

MRS. LINDON. [*Gives a tigerish, half-con-
trolled, hushed cry of rage.*] The *wretched
little beast !*

          [BECKY *comes in with a start of surprise. She
          beams.*]

BECKY. My dears ! What a pleasant surprise ! Why did n't Jenks tell me ? Where
in the world did you drop from ? Laura,
darling !
          [*She kisses* LAURA, *who is very unre-
          sponsive, having pressed* MRS. LIN-
          DON'S *hand as she passed her.*]

MRS. LINDON. We heard you come in, —
we thought *with* some one, — and as I 'm
rather upset, we went in there till you
should be alone. If you are busy, don't let
us interrupt.
          [BECKY *shows that she is relieved when
          she hears they don't know* FRED *was
          there.*]

BECKY. Oh, dear, no, I 'm not busy. I
came home alone, — you must have heard
me talking with the servant. I 've been
playing bridge since luncheon.
          [BECKY *and* LAURA *sit on the sofa.*]

MRS. LINDON. Where ?

BECKY. Clara Ford's, our usual four.
          [LAURA *and* EVE *exchange glances.*]

MRS. LINDON. Why ! I saw her lunching
at Sherry's.

BECKY [*quickly, after only a second's hesitation*]. Yes, she could n't play to-day, but
it was her turn at her house, so we went all
the same — and — er — er — Belle Prescott
took her place.
          [*Another surreptitious look passes
          between* LAURA *and* MRS. LINDON.]

LAURA. Did you win ?

BECKY. Yes, a hundred and fifty !

LAURA. A hundred and fifty ? Good !

MRS. LINDON [*who has seated herself in
the chair beside the sofa*]. Becky, Laura
knows all my troubles ; she 's the bosom I
weep them out on.

BECKY. Oh, come, I 've gathered a few
dewy diamonds off my laces ! Well, how is
Fred behaving ? Has he shown any sign
yet ?

MRS. LINDON. Not one. I thought perhaps you 'd have some news.

BECKY [*looking away*]. I? How should I
have ?
          [*Leans over and smooths her skirt.*
          MRS. LINDON *exchanges a look
          with* LAURA.]

MRS. LINDON. You said two days ago
for me to keep silent and wait, and Fred
would make an advance.

BECKY. And so he will, I 'm sure ! unless
you do what you threatened. [*To* LAURA.]
I tell Eve if she starts a suit for separation
or does anything of that sort publicly, Fred
may be furious and accept the situation, no
matter how much of a bluff it might be on
Eve's part.

LAURA. Very likely.

MRS. LINDON. I thought perhaps you

meant to see Fred and have a talk with him?

BECKY. No! [MRS. LINDON *and* LAURA *exchange glances, as* BECKY, *rising, rings bell right.*] What good would that do? To have the reconciliation mean anything it must be of his own volition. He must come for you, Eve, because he misses you, because he wants you back. [MRS. LINDON *joins* LAURA *on the sofa and talks in a loud and excited whisper to her as to* BECKY's *very evident prevarication.* SERVANT *enters right;* BECKY *speaks to him aside, amusedly watching them, and then comes above table. As she comes back.*] Well?

MRS. LINDON. I believe there's another woman in it!

BECKY [*laughing*]. I knew she was jealous! [*To* MRS. LINDON.] That's just the sort of thing that has made quarrels all along between you and Fred.

[*She comes to her.*]

MRS. LINDON. Well, if you knew all I've had to forgive Fred, and all I have forgiven, you'd realize I had good reason always for my share of the quarrels.

BECKY. Listen to me, Eve. You're a luckier woman than you know!

MRS. LINDON [*startled*]. How do you mean?

[LAURA *puts her hand on* EVE's *shoulder to calm her.*]

BECKY. Because, instead of having the forgiveness always on his side, you have the blessed privilege of doing the forgiveness yourself. [MRS. LINDON *gives a falsetto snort.*] You may smile if you like —

MRS. LINDON [*interrupting*]. Oh, no, thank you. I don't feel at all like smiling!

BECKY. Well, honestly, I envy you. [*Takes* EVE's *hands in hers.* MRS. LINDON *looks once at* LAURA *questioningly, and back again quickly to* BECKY.] You know I love Tom with my whole heart — and it's a big heart for a little woman — and yet I keep him forgiving me — forgiving me something or other all the time. I'd be afraid his forgiveness would wear out, only it's in his soul instead of his body, and if our bodies wear out, our souls don't — do they? Already at the very beginning of our life together I owe him more dear forgiveness than I can ever repay, and believe me, Eve, such a debt would be unbearable for a woman unless she *adored* her husband.

MRS. LINDON. You've too much sentiment — I'm practical.

BECKY [*sitting down in the chair at center*]. Does being practical give you one half the happiness my "sentiment" gives me?

MRS. LINDON. Nonsense! My sympathies are with the one who has the forgiving to do.

BECKY. You mean, like all selfish people, you sympathize with yourself, so you'll never be happy, even if you get Fred back.

MRS. LINDON [*startled, angry*]. If? What do you mean by that?

[*Looks at* BECKY, *then at* LAURA, *sharply, then back at* BECKY.]

BECKY [*smiling*]. Say *when* instead! — *when* you get Fred back. Trust me, teach yourself to be grateful that it is *you* who have to forgive, and not the other way round.

MRS. LINDON. [*Rises, facing her, almost triumphantly, fully persuaded that* BECKY *is in the wrong.*] I knew when I came here you'd make excuses for him.

BECKY [*smiling*]. You've misunderstood me. I'm *trying* to make them for you.

MRS. LINDON. Thank you. *You* need excuses more than I do.

LAURA. [*Rises, alarmed.*] Eve!

MRS. LINDON. I am perfectly well aware that I made a very serious mistake in coming to *you* of all women!

BECKY. [*Rises.*] In that case I think it best to consider the matter closed between us.

MRS. LINDON. You can think what you please, but I have no such intention!

LAURA. Eve! [*She sits again on the sofa.*] Really Becky has shown herself reasonable and kind, and you've said enough to-day. We'd better go.

BECKY. I should have to ask you to excuse me in any case, as I have an engagement in a few minutes.

[MRS. LINDON *looks meaningly at* LAURA.]

MRS. LINDON. [*To* BECKY.] I intend to have the whole thing out now!

[WARDER *enters left.* WARDER *is a strong and sensible, unsuspicious man, — no nerves and no "temperament," nothing subtle about him; he is straightforward and lovable.*]

WARDER. Oh, excuse me!

BECKY. No, come in, Tom; it's Laura and Mrs. Lindon.

[LAURA *and* MRS. LINDON *say "Ho*

do you do," as WARDER *comes into the room. He greets them in turn.* BECKY *writes in pencil on a sheet of paper on the desk.*]

TOM. I wanted to ask Becky if she wished to go to a theater to-night.

BECKY. Yes, I should like to. [*She indicates to* TOM *that she wants* EVE *and* LAURA *to go, and having finished writing, comes to him.*] I'm sorry, but you really must excuse me. [*Slipping into* WARDER'S *hand the note she had secretly written.*] Mrs. Lindon and Laura *are going.* What are *you* going to do now?

[MRS. LINDON *looks again meaningly at* LAURA.]

WARDER. I thought I'd go round to the club till dinner.

BECKY [*relieved*]. That's right. I shall be engaged till half past six, — er — Mrs. Clayton is coming to see me about the Golf Club at Roslyn — and — lots of things. You need n't hurry back.

[*She gives him an affectionate little squeeze of the arm and goes out right. He looks down at the paper slyly and reads it.*]

MRS. LINDON. [*Rises and goes to* TOM.] Tom, if you've nothing in particular on at the club, would you give me half an hour?

LAURA. [*Rises and goes to* EVE.] Eve, you have n't the time yourself; you must come with me.

WARDER [*suppressing a smile as he finishes reading the note; he is a little embarrassed*]. Well — really — Eve — I don't know, — I'll tell you how it is —

MRS. LINDON. Oh, I don't mean here! I know Becky wrote you a note telling you not to let me stay, did n't she?

WARDER [*laughing*]. She did — you see, she has an engagement. [*Reading from the paper, good-naturedly.*] "Get rid of Eve, I want the room."

MRS. LINDON. At six o'clock.

[*Glances meaningly at* LAURA.]

WARDER [*casually*]. Is it?

MRS. LINDON. To see *Fred* in!

LAURA. Eve! be sensible!

WARDER. No, it's for Mrs. Clayton about Roslyn.

MRS. LINDON. Then, why must she be rid of me? Georgia Clayton and I are the best of friends, and I have as much to do with Roslyn as Becky.

WARDER [*still pleasantly*]. I suppose Becky has a good reason, if she cared to tell us.

MRS. LINDON. I *know* Becky has an appointment *here,* at *six,* with Fred.

LAURA. You don't *know* it, Eve!

MRS. LINDON. I *do.*

WARDER [*still pleasantly*]. In any case that is Becky's and Fred's business, is n't it?

MRS. LINDON. You *know* Fred?

WARDER. Yes!

MRS. LINDON. Well?

WARDER. You don't want my opinion of Fred, at this late day! I also know Becky!

MRS. LINDON. Becky and Fred meet every single day.

LAURA. [*Interpolates.*] She *thinks* so.

WARDER. What are you talking about?

MRS. LINDON. What I *know!* And if you'll wait here with me a few minutes now, in spite of what Becky said, you'll see *Fred* and not Mrs. Clayton arrive.

WARDER. If your husband is really coming, it was probably to spare you that Becky spoke of Mrs. Clayton, and I should n't think of embarrassing her by waiting.

MRS. LINDON [*disagreeably, irritatingly*]. Oh, you don't mind, then?

WARDER. Almost any man, my dear Eve, would mind your husband meeting his wife every day! I only think you've been misinformed, or only half informed, that's all.

MRS. LINDON. You are aware that Fred and I have been separated for two months?

WARDER. Yes, Becky told me.

LAURA [*looking at her watch*]. It's almost six now. Come, Eve.

WARDER [*going toward the door, left*]. Yes, I'm afraid I must ask you —

[*Rings electric bell on wall beside the door.*]

MRS. LINDON [*going to him*]. Tom, for the sake of our boy and girl friendship, walk home with me, and let me speak plainly.

LAURA [*on the other side of* WARDER]. Mr. Warder, please don't go.

MRS. LINDON. [*To* LAURA, *angrily.*] What do you mean? [*To* WARDER, *pleadingly.*] I've no other man in the world to go to; I need advice. Won't you give me yours?

WARDER. [*Looks at her a moment, hesi-*

tates, then says.] My advice? Of course, if you wish that. [*The* SERVANT *appears in the doorway in answer to the bell. To* SERVANT.] My hat and coat — and say to Mrs. Warder I'm walking home with Mrs. Lindon. [*He goes out left.*]

SERVANT. Yes, sir. [*Follows him out.*]

[LAURA *looks significantly at* MRS. LINDON.]

LAURA. If you keep on, there soon won't be a soul left in New York whose advice you haven't asked and not taken!

MRS. LINDON. Well, it's my *own trouble;* I can do what I like with it. What are *you* going to do now?

[*She sits in the armchair at the left.*]

LAURA [*going to her*]. Don't tell him all you think you know about Becky.

MRS. LINDON. *Think!*

LAURA. It will be a very great mistake.

MRS. LINDON. Laura, I'll tell you the truth; I've had Fred watched by private detectives for over a month, and I have a list of dates and places of their meetings to more than prove what I say.

LAURA. How dreadful of you!

MRS. LINDON. Oh, wait till you get a husband, and then you'll sympathize more with a woman who is trying to keep one!

LAURA. But these places where they meet?

MRS. LINDON. Are respectable so far as I know. But *daily* meetings my dear, *daily!*

LAURA. And you'll tell Mr. Warder?

MRS. LINDON. I don't know yet how much I shall tell. What are you going to do now?

LAURA. Wait till to-morrow! Give yourself time to recover, to consider.

MRS. LINDON. [*Simply repeats.*] What are you going to do now?

LAURA. [*Deliberately crosses to the chair at center and sits.*] Stay and see Becky.

MRS. LINDON. [*Rises, delighted.*] Oh, do! Stay till Fred comes, and catch her!

LAURA. No, no! I've finished with this now. I don't sympathize with what you're going to do.

WARDER [*with hat and coat, in the doorway left*]. Ready?

MRS. LINDON. Yes.

WARDER. Good-bye, Laura.

LAURA. Good-bye. [MRS. LINDON *goes out left with* WARDER. *After the outside door is heard to close* BECKY *comes into the room* hurriedly. *She stops suddenly on seeing* LAURA, *turns and tries to steal out. Just as she gets to the door,* LAURA *catches her.*] Becky!

[BECKY *turns and their eyes meet.* BECKY *laughs, realizing she is caught.*]

BECKY. Oh, you didn't go with them?

LAURA. No!

BECKY. Had enough of Eve to-day?

LAURA. Not enough of you.

BECKY. [*Sings instead of speaks.*] "Thank you!"

[*She puts her arm around* LAURA, *and they sit on the sofa.*]

LAURA. Becky, why won't you be frank with Eve?

BECKY. I was.

LAURA. No, you didn't tell the truth about seeing Fred.

BECKY. Oh, that!

LAURA. Yes, that!

BECKY. I may have seen him once or twice, that's all.

LAURA. Exactly what Eve says — you don't tell the truth!

BECKY. It's false! I never told a malicious lie in my life. I never told a fib that hurt any one but myself!

LAURA. Tell Eve the truth. Make her have confidence in you. She says if you cross the ferry to Jersey City, you say you've been abroad.

BECKY [*laughing*]. Well, so I *have!* Laura! I'm doing my best to make Eve happy. I can't do any more than my best, and if I do it at all, I must do it my own way!

LAURA. You've seen Fred to-day.

BECKY. No, I haven't.

LAURA. Becky! He came home with you just now!

BECKY. What makes you think so?

LAURA. I saw his back on the steps with you.

BECKY. Oh, I see — spying on me? Well, you made a mistake in the back.

LAURA. I know it was Fred Lindon.

BECKY. And I know it wasn't.

LAURA. You're not seeing him every day?

BECKY. Certainly not! But what affair is it of yours, if I do?

LAURA. We're all friends, and you're making Eve wildly jealous.

BECKY. That is entirely her own fault, not mine.

[*The* SERVANT *enters left with a bill on a small silver tray.*]

SERVANT. Pardon me, madam, a man with a box and a bill to collect.

BECKY [*taking bill*]. A bandbox?
[*She opens bill.*]

SERVANT. Yes, madam.

BECKY. [*To* LAURA.] Oh, my dear, such a duck of a hat! And only sixty-five dollars. I saw it on my way here and could n't resist buying. Are hats a passion with you?

LAURA [*uninterested*]. Yes, rather.

BECKY. I told them to send it C.O.D., but I did n't suppose it would come till to-morrow and I have n't a cent!

LAURA. I thought you said you won a hundred and fifty at bridge?

BECKY. No, no, my dear, you misunderstood me; I lost. [*To* SERVANT.] Tell the man if he can't leave the box, to take it back and call later; say Mrs. Warder is out.

SERVANT. Yes, madam.
[*Goes out with the bill, left.*]

LAURA. You said you *won* at bridge!

BECKY. Oh, you tedious person! You hang on to anything like a terrier, don't you! I said I won because I did n't want Eve to think I 'd lost; I never can bear to own up I 've lost anything before Eve. [*Laughs, pulls* LAURA *by the arm.*] Good-bye!

LAURA. I won't go yet.

BECKY [*urging her*]. You must. I have an engagement.

LAURA. *With Fred Lindon!*

BECKY. It is not. [SERVANT *enters and announces* "MR. LINDON." LINDON *follows in. He is surprised to see* LAURA, *but instantly covers his surprise. Going to* LINDON, *quickly.*] Oh, what a surprise!

LINDON. Surprise? Am I early?

BECKY [*indicating* LAURA]. Sh! Yes, surprise. [LINDON *sees* LAURA *and makes an amused grimace.*] But I can only give you a very few minutes. I have an engagement, have n't I, Laura?
[*As they shake hands.*]

LINDON. Oh, hello, Laura!

LAURA [*very dryly*]. How d' you do, Fred?

LINDON. How 's Eve?

LAURA [*embarrassed*]. Very well — at least not very — yes, she is of course very well! She 's just left here.
[*She adds this pointedly.*]

LINDON. Oh! sorry I missed her! Give her my regards when you see her, and say I 'm glad she 's well.
[*He goes to the piano, sits on the bench, and plays.*]

LAURA. [*Rises indignant.*] I shall do nothing of the kind.
[*She starts to leave the room.* LINDON *runs what he is playing into* "*Good-bye, little girl, Good-bye.*"]

BECKY [*offering her hand*]. Good-bye.

LAURA. [*Pretends not to see* BECKY'S *hand.*] Good-bye. [*She goes out left.*]

BECKY [*going to the piano*]. They both saw you come back with me!

LINDON [*still playing, improvising. Laughing*]. No! Did they?

BECKY [*laughing*]. Yes, but it 's no laughing matter! Eve is jealous.

LINDON. [*Stops playing.*] What right has she? Did she expect me to sit alone in the drawing-room for two months straining my ears to hear her ring the front door bell?
[*He continues playing.*]

BECKY. They know we 've been meeting every day — at least they think so. Have we?

LINDON [*still playing*]. No!

BECKY. Yes we *have! Have*n't we?

LINDON. [*Stops playing.*] Well, yes, if you want the truth.

BECKY. [*Goes to sofa and sits.*] There 's no use telling a story about it. I 've nothing to be ashamed of — I did it with the best of motives.

LINDON. [*Goes to* BECKY.] Oh, don't spoil it all, Becky, with motives!
[*He leans over the arm of the sofa to talk to her.*]

BECKY. [*Laughs.*] You know Eve mustn't be jealous of me!

LINDON [*earnestly*]. Now you 're not going to let her break up our little —

BECKY [*interrupting*]. Fred, how much do you like me?

LINDON [*smiling*]. I dare n't tell you!

BECKY. No, I mean *really!*

LINDON. So do I!

BECKY. I believe you are fond of me.

LINDON. I am!

BECKY. And I like you to be.

LINDON [placing his hand on hers on the sofa's arm]. Because?

BECKY [slowly drawing her hand from his]. I like men to like me, even though it really means nothing.

LINDON. Nothing? [Rather chagrined.]

BECKY [amused]. I like it for myself, and besides I think it's a compliment to Tom!

LINDON [mockingly]. Oh! Oh! I say! Becky!

[He moves to the chair right beside BECKY and drawing it nearer sits facing her.]

BECKY. But with you there was a special reason.

LINDON. [Is encouraged. Draws a little nearer to her.] Yes?

BECKY. Of course you have perfectly understood why I've seen so much of you.

LINDON. You've been my friend.

BECKY. I've sympathized with you.

LINDON. You've been the only real glimpse of happiness I've had for months in my life.

BECKY. Don't be rhetorical! no man sounds sincere, when he talks pictures. I'll tell you why I wanted you to come back this afternoon.

LINDON [taking her two hands]. To make me happy!

BECKY [pulling her hands away, and patting his half seriously]. Yes [he leans over toward her], by making you realize it's time you went to Eve and asked her to come back.

LINDON [sinking back in his chair]. Nonsense; Eve's made a row and frightened you.

BECKY. How frightened me? I always meant when I'd got you where I wanted you, to influence you to make it up with Eve. She adores you!

LINDON. She has an odd way of showing it.

[He rises and leans against the mantel beside the sofa.]

BECKY. You don't want every woman to show her love in the same way.

LINDON. I don't want any other woman to show me she loves me in Eve's way.

BECKY. Come now, you're unfair to Eve! I'm going to sympathize with her a little. Granted that she is jealous, granted that she doesn't always control her temper! — what woman worth while does!

LINDON [laughing]. But she ought to trust me — as you do.

BECKY [laughing]. Oh, I'm not your wife. I wouldn't trust you for a minute if I were married to you!

LINDON. How about Tom?

BECKY. Of course I trust Tom.

LINDON. And I trust Eve. [Laughing.]

BECKY. Oh! but it's not the same thing. You trust Eve because you don't care enough. I trust Tom because — well, in one little word, he is perfect and I adore him!

LINDON. Sounds boring!

BECKY. Eve's proved she loves you with a big love! She's proved it by forgiveness. That's the proof of a love it's not easy to get and even harder to deserve! You've got it — [he moves toward her]. We won't go into the deserving part! But if only half that she says and one quarter of what every one else says of you is true, you ought to go on your knees to her in gratitude if she is willing to take you back.

LINDON. [Sits on the arm of sofa, half laughing.] She will! She's left before.

BECKY. You love her, Fred?

LINDON [casually]. No, I love you!

BECKY. Nonsense! I mean really! Promise me you'll go to Eve to-morrow and ask her to come back.

LINDON. [Slides down on to sofa.] Not yet — give me another month!

BECKY. You'll lose her!

LINDON. No, there are certain things you can't lose — try as hard as you like!

BECKY. That isn't funny.

LINDON. She's been urging you to do this.

BECKY. Nothing of the sort! She's too proud. And she mustn't dream I've had anything to do with your going to her. No woman really wants to accept her happiness like a pauper at the Lady Bountiful hands of another woman. She might think she was grateful to me, but she wouldn't be! With a disposition like Eve's you'd have another quarrel inside a fortnight. No! Eve must think you've come to her spontaneously because you can't live without her. [He whistles. She rises.] You can whistle, but you'll never get another woman half so good to you as Eve! Make her think you want her back. Make yourself think you want her back, and you don't know how happy you 'll be — first in making her happy, and second in finding you are yourself.

[He takes hold of her hand; she draws it away quickly and sits in the armchair on the opposite side of the room.]

LINDON. What are you doing away over there?

BECKY. Oh, I thought it was getting a little crowded on the sofa.

LINDON. And must I give up my visits with you?

BECKY. Of course.

LINDON. Oh, well, if that 's the price, I don't want happiness, it costs too much!

BECKY. You won't need sympathy any more. You can write me a little note and say: "Becky, I thought I loved you, but it was only a heart being caught on the rebound. Thank you for being sensible and pitching the heart back! Thank you for seeing my real happiness was in making Eve happy."

LINDON. You know that does n't sound like me!

BECKY. Not like your foolish *old you*, but like your sensible *new you*, who has found out you can have a woman friend without getting sued for damages, — which has been your usual experience, I believe!

LINDON. Becky! Don't rob the graves!

BECKY. Well, will you go to Eve and beg her to come back?

LINDON. *[Rises.]* No!

BECKY. Fred! The price of my friendship is your peace with Eve!

LINDON *[going to BECKY]*. But if I consent, I may come to see you?

BECKY. Yes.

LINDON. Eve, my darling wife, forgive me! Come to my arms and stay there — for five minutes — consider it done! Where, to-morrow?

BECKY. The Metropolitan?

LINDON. No, let me come here to-morrow, and what time?

BECKY. *[Rises.]* Four — but to say *Goodbye! [She means it.]* The *last* visit!

LINDON. Oh! well, we won't cross that bridge till we come to it! and I 'll make you a bet if you ever do send me away for good, do you know what will happen?

BECKY *[amused]*. No, what?

LINDON. In a day or two you 'd send for me to come again after all!

BECKY *[laughing]*. Why?

LINDON. Because you like me better than you think you do?

BECKY *[going to the writing-table]*. Oh, really!!

LINDON *[following her]*. Yes, really! and you know — though you may not acknowledge it to yourself, still you know just how strong my feeling is for you.

BECKY *[turning toward him]*. But I do acknowledge it, and I am grateful and pleased to have you care for me.

[She pulls the chair beside the table in front of her.]

LINDON *[pushing chair away]*. "Care for you!"

BECKY *[pulling chair back]*. Yes! and I want to show my appreciation by making you happy.

LINDON. Eve's jealousy has frightened you, but you 'll forget it to-morrow!

BECKY *[really not understanding]*. How do you mean?

[She looks at him questioningly, innocently. He looks back knowingly with a half smile, not believing her. A pause. WARDER comes in left. He looks from one to the other, then speaks pleasantly.]

WARDER. Oh! How are you, Lindon?

LINDON. Good-evening, Warder.

[Both men stand; an awkward pause.]

BECKY *[sitting in the armchair right]*. Sit down, Tom.

[He does so on the chair by the table. LINDON sits on the sofa. A moment's pause.]

LINDON. Do you come uptown generally as late as this?

WARDER. Oh, no, I 've been up some time.   *[Second awkward pause.]*

BECKY. Did you get the theater tickets?

WARDER. No, I forgot; I did n't go to the club. I 'll telephone from here. *[Very casually.]* Has Mrs. Clayton gone?

BECKY. Who?

WARDER. Mrs. Clayton. You said —

[BECKY interrupting.]

BECKY. Mrs. Cl—? Oh! Yes! She 's gone.   *[Awkward pause.]*

LINDON. Have you been to the club?

WARDER *[very casually]*. No, I walked back with your wife to her mother's.

[Awkward pause. BECKY and LINDON exchange glances.]

LINDON [*half-humorously*]. I hear Eve is looking very well. [*Pause.*]

WARDER. By the way, will you have a whiskey and soda, a cocktail or something?

BECKY. Or *tea?*

LINDON. Tea? — poison to me! No, thanks, I must be getting on.

[*All rise; then, after a moment of embarrassment,* WARDER *speaks.*]

WARDER. Yes?

LINDON. I 've an early, melancholy, bachelor's dinner at seven.

BECKY. It 's your own fault! Think how well Eve looks in a dinner dress, and what a delightful hostess she always is.

LINDON. Yes, Eve 's all right in a crowd! [*Shaking hands. To* WARDER.] Forgive my domestic affairs intruding. Mrs. Warder has been kind enough to advise me a little! Good-bye! [*Going.*]

WARDER. I'm sure her advice is good. You 'd better take it!

LINDON. Perhaps! — but in homœopathic doses! [*To* BECKY.] Good-bye! [*To* WARDER.] Bye, Warder.

[*Laughing, he goes out.* WARDER *and* BECKY, *alone, look at each other* — BECKY *questioningly,* WARDER *half puzzled.*]

BECKY. Well! Has Eve been weeping on *your* bosom, too?

WARDER. No, I think she *scratched* it, if she did anything!

BECKY [*half amused, half worried*]. How do you mean? [*The* SERVANT *enters with a letter which he gives to* BECKY.] When did this come?

SERVANT. A little while ago, but madam gave orders not to be interrupted.

[*He goes out.* WARDER *gives* BECKY *a quick, sharp look, which, however, she does n't notice.*]

BECKY. From father! He can't want more money already!

WARDER. *You* sent him how much two days ago?

BECKY. [*Goes above the writing-table as she opens the letter.*] *You* sent him, you generous darling, three hundred dollars. I had given him his allowance the beginning of the month.

WARDER. And gone already! Of course, he 's been at the races this week! No more. Becky — is it true you 've been seeing Lindon every day lately?

BECKY [*while she reads her letter*]. No! — yes! [*Looks up at him.*] I mean no, certainly not!

WARDER [*smiling*]. Which is it? — or do I take my choice?

BECKY [*with a little laugh*]. I 've seen something of him. I 'm sorry for him. — Father 's in more trouble.

WARDER. That 's an old story, and this is something new. Eve is jealous of you.

BECKY. [*Looks up at him.*] Are you, of Fred Lindon?

WARDER. No!

BECKY. [*Goes quickly to him and kisses him and pushes him down on to the sofa.*] Bless you! You 're right, and that 's my answer to Eve! — Father does want more money!

WARDER. We send no more till next month, not one penny. Come here! [*He makes her sit on the arm of the sofa beside him. She puts her arm about his neck and hugs him.* WARDER *continues.*] You have n't seen Lindon almost daily for the past month, have you?

BECKY. No.

WARDER. You have n't met him by appointment at the Metropolitan, Eden Musée, or any such places?

BECKY. Eve's jealousy gives her the most ridiculous ideas! When I have been with Mr. Lindon, it has been principally to talk about Eve, and entirely with the desire to try and reconcile them.

WARDER. Grant that! But it 's not true about all these appointments?

BECKY. No!

WARDER [*with his arm about her waist*]. I believe you love me better than all the world?

BECKY. Than all the world, and every world, and all the planets put together, Mars, Saturn, and Venus. Yes. I love you *even* more than Venus!

[*Laughing and giving him another caress.*]

WARDER. I have every confidence in you and your motives. But I have none in Lindon's — so I want to-day's visit to be his last, my dear.

BECKY [*rising, a little uncomfortable*]. All right.

WARDER. Own up, now, has n't he tried to make love to you?

BECKY [*leaning on the back of the chair, facing him*]. No!

WARDER. Not a bit?

BECKY [*smiling*]. Well — maybe — just a tiny bit — but not in earnest.

WARDER [*rising, angrily*]. I was sure of it! the damn puppy! Becky, I've heard him swear there's no such thing as a decent woman if a man goes about it in the right way!

BECKY. Oh, you men are always hard on another man whom women like.

WARDER. I know what I'm talking about *this* time, and you don't.

BECKY [*with dignity*]. I judge by his behavior to me. He may have led me to believe he likes me very much, — he ought to like me, I've been very nice to him, — and I suppose it flattered me — [*smiling*] it always does flatter me when men like me, — and I think one feeling I have is pride that you have a wife whom other men admire! If Mr. Lindon has made — er — respectful love to me, that's a compliment to *you*. [WARDER *laughs, sincerely amused.*] But he has *not* insulted me.

WARDER [*smiling*]. That's your fault. You are the kind of woman he does n't believe exists, and he can't make up his mind just what tactics to adopt.

BECKY. He knows perfectly, unless he's deaf and blind, that my seeing him — a few times only — has been solely to reconcile him with Eve.

WARDER. That sort of man *is* deaf and blind except to his own rotten mental suggestions. He is incapable of believing in your philanthropic motive, so let it go, dear.

BECKY. [*Places the letter on the writing-table and sits behind it.*] Eve has frightened you!

WARDER. [*Walks away.*] Not a bit; I laughed at her fears that you were fascinated by her precious worm! But I do consider that unwittingly you have been playing a dangerous and — forgive me, darling — [*going to her*] a very foolish game. Already some one believes you've been seeing Lindon every day. You have n't! But that does n't make any difference! Every one will believe you have seen him twice a day in another month if you continue seeing him at all. No woman can have the "friendship" of a man like Lin-

don for long without — justly or unjustly — paying the highest price for it. [*He places his hand tenderly on her shoulder.*] You would n't know what the price was till the bill came in — and then no matter how well you knew and those who love you knew you had not danced, all the same the world would make you pay the piper!

BECKY. I do your sex greater justice than you! I don't believe there's any man, no matter what he has been, whom some sincere woman can't waken to some good that is in him!

WARDER [*smiling*]. That's all right, but you please let Eve wake up Lindon! [*He moves away.*] Had you made any arrangements to ring a little friendly alarm on him to-morrow?

BECKY. No! And that, of course, was Eve's suggestion!

WARDER. Well, never mind so long as it's understood his visits here are at an end. You don't expect him to-morrow, and should he come, you won't see him, eh?

BECKY. Exactly! [*Smiling.*] When I told him to-day his visits were over, what do you think he said?

WARDER. I could n't guess.

BECKY. He said I'd change my mind and send for him!

WARDER. And if you did, do you know what he would do?

BECKY. No — what?

WARDER. Consider it a signal of capitulation — and ten to one take you in his arms and kiss you!

BECKY. [*Rises.*] He would n't dare!

WARDER. I'm not sure, but at any rate I am serious about one thing in this discussion.

BECKY. [*Goes to him and places her hands lovingly on his arms.*] Our first "domestic row."

WARDER. [*Turns her about and holds her in his arms — she leans against him.*] And last!

BECKY. Amen!

WARDER [*very seriously*]. And I echo the sentiment, I know, of every sane husband in New York — Lindon's attentions to a man's wife are an insult, and as your husband I won't have them.

BECKY [*leaving his arms, pushes him playfully into a chair and sits near him in the corner of the sofa*]. Well, give me my woman's last word. I still think you are unfair to him — but I love you all the same ! !

WARDER. You'd better !

BECKY. I'm so afraid you 'll get — not tired, but — well — too used to me !

WARDER. Not till I find you twice the same ! Now — what about your father ?

BECKY. He only wants fifty dollars, and says he must have it ; let's send it.

WARDER. No, that's the way it's been always. Our "no" has always ended "yes," so of course he has n't believed in it. This time it must stay "no."

BECKY [*plaintively*]. You won't send it ?

WARDER. No, and you must n't.

BECKY. Oh, I have n't got a cent. But he says he's in real trouble and he must have it.

WARDER. It's always the same thing ! And we must put a stop to his inveterate, indiscriminate gambling. If we don't teach him the lesson he needs soon, before we know it he will be in real trouble that ten thousand times fifty dollars might n't get him out of.

BECKY. But he promises not to —

WARDER [*interrupting*]. My dear ! He has given his word over and over again, and broken it twice as many times ! If it is n't a race course, it's a bucket shop — or some cheap back door roulette table, and it's got to stop ! Stop now !

BECKY. But, Tom —

WARDER [*interrupting*]. Now, Becky ! You know how hard it is for me to refuse you.

BECKY. It's only —

WARDER [*interrupting*]. You must trust my judgment, and your father must learn, and a small matter of fifty dollars is a good chance to begin ; it can't be so very serious ! so that's ended.

BECKY [*half-humorously, half-discouragedly*]. Yes, I guess it's ended !

WARDER. Now, will you try to realize that I only want to do what's best and right ?

BECKY. [*Kisses him.*] Yes, but I can't help feeling sorry for father.   [*Smiling.*] [*The* SERVANT *enters left with a bill and a bandbox.*]

SERVANT. Beg pardon, madam, but the man has come back.

BECKY. [*Takes the bill.*] Oh, my hat ! Very well, I 'll ring when I'm ready. Leave the box on the chair.

SERVANT. [*Puts bandbox on the chair at left.*] Very good, madam.   [*He goes out.*]

BECKY [*smiling, embarrassed*]. I'm nearly as bad as father !

WARDER. Lose at bridge to-day ?

BECKY. No, I did n't play to-day, but I could n't resist a hat, my dear, the most adorable hat ! [WARDER *laughs* " Oh, Becky."] No, honestly ! Much more beautiful than the one I bought day before yesterday ! I'm ashamed, but I did order it to come home, and I have n't a penny.

WARDER [*teasing her*]. Send it back !

BECKY. Oh, you would n't be so heartless ! — and what would they think at the shop ?

WARDER [*getting out his pocketbook*]. How much is it ?

BECKY. [*Hesitates a moment.*] Fifty dollars !

WARDER [*with a slight quizzing look*]. Just what your father wants.

BECKY. Yes ! Give the money to father and I 'll send back the bonnet.

WARDER. No, my darling. You know it is n't the money with your father, it's the principle of the thing. I've not got the money, I must write a check.

[*He looks for the check-book. She quickly gets a check-book from table and hides it behind her back.*]

BECKY. Your check-book's upstairs.

[*She rings the bell on the desk.*]

WARDER. I thought perhaps yours was here ?

BECKY. No, mine's used up, as usual !

WARDER. All right.

[*He goes out right, as the* SERVANT *enters.*]

BECKY [*opening the bandbox*]. Send the man here, Jenks.

SERVANT. Yes, madam.

[*He goes out, left.*]

BECKY. [*Takes out the hat and looks at it admiringly.*] What a duck ! [*Heaves a great sigh and puts it back and starts to re-tie the strings, as the* MAN *enters.*] I want you to take this back to Mme. Flora, and say Mrs. Warder is extremely sorry, but Mr. Warder has taken a violent dislike to the hat, so she cannot have it. She will be in later to choose another.

MAN. Yes, ma'am.

[*He goes out with the bandbox, left.* BECKY *sits down and starts to write a letter hurriedly.* WARDER *comes in with check.* BECKY *hides the letter she is writing.*]

WARDER [*coming to the table*]. Here's the check, all but the name of the payee. Where's the bill?

BECKY. Make it out to me, and I'll indorse it.

WARDER. Why?

BECKY. [*Half worried, half smiling.*] Oh, dear! I told you a sort of fib! The hat was only thirty-five dollars, but I wanted the extra fifteen for something else. Please don't be angry —

WARDER [*laughing*]. I'm not angry, though you know I dislike even little fibs. Why did n't you tell me if you 're hard up? I'll give you this and make out another for the bonnet shop.

BECKY. No, you need n't do that; the man's gone now for the change — I told him.

WARDER. [*Finishes the check and gives it to her.*] Becky! you 're not going to send this to your father? I forbid that.

BECKY. No, no, darling! [*Takes the check.*] And now you get dressed. I'll be up in a minute. You know it always takes you twice as long as it does me when you wear a white tie! It's a long play and begins early.

WARDER. I'll bet you I'll be dressed before you start! [*He hurries out, right.*]

BECKY. [*Rings the telephone on the desk.*] Hello! Hello, 6304–72d. [*Writes on her interrupted letter with one hand and listens with the receiver in the other. After a moment.*] Hello! 6304–72d? Is Mr. Lindon — yes, ask him to come to the 'phone and speak to 2759–38th. [*Listens as she writes.*] Hello! Is that you? Yes — yes — Oh [*laughs*], don't be silly! I called you to say I am very sorry, but our engagement for to-morrow is off! *O double f!* No, for good! For *Good!* [*She adds very quickly.*] Good-bye! [*Hangs up the receiver and writes. In a moment the telephone bell rings furiously; at first she ignores it; then she makes a grimace at it; then she takes up the receiver.*] Hello! No, Central, I was n't cut off. No, I don't want the number back; thank you, I hung up the receiver. I can't

help that! You need n't re-connect us — say the line is busy! [*Hangs up the receiver.*] Mercy! when you don't want them!! [*Rings the electric bell on the desk, indorses the check, puts it in the letter, and seals the envelope. The* SERVANT *enters as she addresses letter.*] I want you to take this at once and put a special delivery stamp on it. I want it to reach my father in Baltimore to-night.

SERVANT. Yes, madam.

BECKY. Have you any idea whether it would be delivered there to-night or to-morrow morning?

SERVANT. One or the other, madam.

BECKY [*smiling*]. That I know! Make haste.

[*The* SERVANT *goes out left, as* WARDER *all dressed, save that his tie hangs loose, rushes in, right. She rises quickly.*]

WARDER. Who's ready first?

BECKY [*laughing*]. Oh, you 've raced! But while you 're tying your tie I'll —

WARDER. [*Interrupts.*] No, I came down purposely to get you to tie it for me!

[*He stands ready.*]

BECKY. [*Ties it during the following speeches.*] You forgive me for telling you that little fib?

WARDER. Yes, if it 's to be your last one.

BECKY. My *very* last.

WARDER. No more of those wicked little white lies, even, that you know you do amuse yourself with, and distress me?

BECKY. No, no! Really! I've opened the cage door and let all the little white mice fibs out for good!

WARDER. And you do love me?

BECKY. Do you want to know how much I love you?

WARDER. Yes, how much?

BECKY. How deep is the ocean in its deepest spot?

WARDER. As deep as your love for me.

BECKY. Oh, that is n't fair! You 're stealing my thunder! There! [*The tie is finished, and she pushes him playfully into the chair by the writing-table.*] One good turn deserves another. [*With her arms about his neck she slides on to his knee, like a child.*] I've let Perkins go out, and you *must* hook me up the back.

[*And both laugh gayly as he embraces her and the curtain falls.*]

ACT II

At the Warders' early Saturday afternoon, just after lunch.

The same scene as Act I. BECKY and WAR-DER are sitting on the sofa, both drinking coffee after lunch. WARDER puts his coffee-cup on the table as the curtain rises.

BECKY. Are n't you going to smoke, darling?

[*Putting her coffee on the table behind her.*]

WARDER. Yes. [*Getting out cigar.*]

BECKY. Give it to me. [*She takes it, and cuts the tip with a gold jeweled cutter which she wears on a chain about her neck.*] For six years you 've not smoked a cigar in my presence that I have n't clipped, have you?

WARDER. No. And how about anybody else's cigars? That has n't cut off any tips for — Lindon, I hope!

BECKY. No, indeed! He only smokes cigarettes.

WARDER [*amused*]. Is that the only reason?

BECKY. Oh, you darling! I believe you are a little jealous of Lindon and I adore you for it. [*Hugging and kissing him.*]

WARDER. Well, you go on adoring, but I 'm not a bit jealous of Lindon.

[*Rises, and lights his cigar with a match from the table behind them.*]

BECKY. You 're not going back to the office? It 's Saturday.

WARDER. No — I think I 'll have a game of racquets with Billy Weld.

BECKY. Do! You love it so. I 've regretted their invitation to dine with them next week, Friday. I said we 're going out of town.

WARDER. But we 're not. We 've people dining here, have n't we?

BECKY. Yes, but I think going out of town sounds so much more interesting. Besides, then they can't possibly be offended that they are n't asked here. Grace 'll be consumed with curiosity, too, as to where we 're going! [*Amused.*]

WARDER. But if they see us Friday?

BECKY. They 'll think we have n't gone yet.

WARDER. But if Billy meets me downtown Saturday morning?

BECKY. He 'll think you took an early train back.

WARDER. The truth 's so simple, so much easier — why not tell it?

BECKY. Don't worry, it 'll be all right. I 'm sorry I told you if you 're going to worry! [*He goes to kiss her; she stops him.*]

WARDER [*sitting beside her*]. What 's up?

BECKY. I 've decided I kiss you too often. I 'm a shopkeeper with only one line of goods — no variety, and I 'm cheapening my wares. [WARDER *laughs.*] I don't want you to feel you 're getting a left-over stock of stale, shopworn kisses! I want you to feel the supply does n't equal the demand.

[*She kisses him. The* SERVANT *enters and they move apart.*]

SERVANT. Mrs. Lindon to see Mr. Warder.

BECKY. [*To* WARDER.] Eve! [*To* SERVANT.] Ask her to come in here and have a cup of coffee and a cigarette.

SERVANT. Yes, madam. [*Goes out.*]

BECKY [*beaming*]. Come to tell us of the reconciliation!

WARDER. Why she did n't let him go and be thankful! I don't see what she can love in a little outsider like Lindon!

BECKY. Thank Heaven, all women don't love the same kind of a man! [*Steals a caress.*] Think what an awful fight there 'd be!

SERVANT [*coming back*]. Mrs. Lindon sends this message — she wishes to see Mr. Warder.

[BECKY *and* WARDER *look at each other, surprised and amused.* BECKY *makes a grimace.*]

WARDER. Very well, show Mrs. Lindon in.

SERVANT. Yes, sir. [*Goes out.*]

WARDER. More trouble!

BECKY. They 've quarreled again already! It must have been *his* fault.

[SERVANT *shows in* MRS. LINDON *and goes out.*]

MRS. LINDON. [*To* WARDER, *not noticing* BECKY.] How do you do?

WARDER. How do you do, Eve?

BECKY. How do you do, Eve! Sit down.

MRS. LINDON. I wish to see Tom for a moment, Becky.

BECKY. What for?

MRS. LINDON. I wish to see him alone.

BECKY. Why?

MRS. LINDON. That, Becky, is my affair — and *his*, perhaps!

BECKY. Oh, really! I suppose I ought to become very jealous now, and do dreadful things. [*Smiles.*] But don't have me for a moment on your mind, Tom.

[*Kisses her finger, puts it to* TOM'S *lips, he kisses it, and she goes out right.*]

WARDER. What is it, Eve? You know I have no earthly secrets from Becky.

MRS. LINDON. It's about her secrets from you!

WARDER. Nonsense! [*Half laughs.*]

MRS. LINDON [*sitting in the chair by the table near center*]. I only hinted at things the other day — and only hinted at one half the truth.

WARDER [*sitting on the sofa*]. Excuse me, Eve, but you've got hold of the wrong half. I asked Becky outright — that is our way always. She denied practically all you said.

MRS. LINDON. You can't make me believe you've lived as long as you have with Becky Roland and not found out — she lies.

WARDER. [*Rises quickly in anger.*] It's because you're a woman you dare say that to me, but you know I don't have to listen to you, so don't push our old friendship's claim too far.

MRS. LINDON. I said Becky and Fred met often on the sly.

WARDER [*sitting again*]. Which is n't true!

MRS. LINDON. No! They meet *every day!*

WARDER. Eve, I think your trouble has gone to your brain.

MRS. LINDON [*still quietly, but with the quiet of the crater when the volcano is alive beneath*]. I can prove to you that Becky has seen Fred every day and more than that! When we had our talk two days ago, they had agreed together that he was to go through a form of reconciliation with me for appearance' sake, and their meetings were to continue. She had an appointment with him for yesterday.

WARDER. That I know is n't true, for she swore to me the opposite.

MRS. LINDON. Yes, you frightened her off and she broke the engagement by telephone, which made Fred perfectly furious!

WARDER [*rising, goes to mantel and knocks his cigar ashes into the grate; absolutely unconvinced, he continues with a cynical smile*].

And how did you obtain this decidedly intimate information?

MRS. LINDON [*in an outburst, the volcano becoming a little active*]. From him! I knew they had n't met for two days —

WARDER [*interrupting*]. How?

[*He looks up curiously.*]

MRS. LINDON. [*Rises and turns away, a little ashamed.*] I've had Fred watched for weeks!

WARDER [*astonished, rises*]. You mean you've — [*He hesitates.*]

MRS. LINDON. Yes! [*Coming to the desk, and speaking across it to him.*] I took their not meeting for a sign that after all Becky had given him up, and I had the impulse to go to him — to go back home. He turned on me like a wolf — said I'd meddled with his affairs once too often — that I'd frightened Becky into breaking off with him — that he had been on the point of making up with me for the reason I've told you, but now it was done for! I'd raised your suspicions, I'd given the whole thing away to everybody, and I could congratulate myself on having broken off his and my relations for good — forever! Oh, how could he insult me so when it was only his love I was asking for?

[*She sinks down in the chair above the table, and buries her face in her hands and sobs.*]

WARDER. [*Forgets himself and exclaims.*] But can you — how can you still care for him after everything you've gone through? It's beyond my understanding!

[*He throws his cigar angrily into the fireplace.*]

MRS. LINDON. The history of the world is full of women who love like me, but no men — I don't know why; but I suppose that's why you can't understand it. Why could n't he realize it is for happiness not appearances I've been fighting? And now it's over, for I know when he means what he says — and he told me, like a low brute, I could go to — where you can imagine — for all he cares, or for all he'll ever live with me again. [*Her voice fills up again.*]

WARDER. I should think if you went to the address he proposed, it would insure at least an eventual meeting!

MRS. LINDON [*who has not heard and does not understand*]. What?

WARDER. I beg your pardon! I made

a foolish joke ! Well ? [*With a hearty long breath of relief.*] Now do you feel better ?

MRS. LINDON [*feebly, not understanding*]. Better ?

WARDER. Yes, now you've got it all "off your chest" ? To-morrow you'll be all right and ready to forgive again. Shall I call Becky ?

[*Going toward the bell beside the mantel.*]

MRS. LINDON. [*Rises.*] You're going to accuse her before me ?

WARDER. [*Stops and turns.*] Accuse her ? [*Laughs.*] No — I don't believe a word you've told me. I'd take Becky's unspoken denial against Fred's sworn statement any day.

MRS. LINDON [*going to him*]. Then here's yesterday's report from the agency ! — and Thursday's, and Thursday's includes the report of the telephone central who connected Becky with our house when she broke off the appointment with Fred — that telephone girl has told us many interesting things !

WARDER. Stop ! Stop this ! I won't listen to you — at any rate, not behind Becky's back. I'm not a jealous, suspicious woman with good reason to believe the worst. I'm a straightforward, decent man, I hope, and I know I've every reason to believe absolutely in my wife, God bless her ! [*He moves away and then turns upon her.*] Why have you come and told me this, anyway ?

MRS. LINDON [*staggered*]. Why — why ?

WARDER [*angry*]. Yes, why ? — to me of all people ! I was the last person you should have told, as a matter of breeding, as a matter of tact, as a matter of the friendship you talk about.

MRS. LINDON. But that was just it !

WARDER. Do you dream what it would mean to me to shake even by a miserable tremor my confidence in my wife ? But you have n't !

MRS. LINDON. I thought, and I still think, it's to your advantage to know.

WARDER [*with a complete change of voice, from anger to the tone one adopts with a silly child*]. My dear Eve, while I don't for a minute excuse him, still I do now understand, perhaps, how even Fred Lindon must have found your ideas of devotion at times over the endurance line.

MRS. LINDON. You don't understand —

I thought if you knew everything, together we could separate them — could arrange something. .

WARDER. Eve ! Believe me, there's nobody to separate in this case ; there's nothing, so far as I and mine are concerned, to arrange.

[*He goes again to the bell by the mantel.*]

MRS. LINDON. Who are you going to ring for ?

WARDER. You know.

MRS. LINDON [*stopping him quickly*]. Not before me ! I don't want to see her humiliated. I don't want a public revenge or triumph ; that's not the feeling I have.

WARDER. What in the world do you mean ? [*He rings.*] Becky will deny the —

MRS. LINDON [*interrupting*]. Very likely! But these proofs are uncombatable, and if that's her attitude, I shall go straight from your door to the divorce court.

[*She places the envelope of reports on the table with a blow.*]

WARDER. [*Goes to her.*] You're mad ! If your proofs are all right, then Becky'll not deny, she'll explain them. You forget you can only see everything red now, but I'm sane and quiet and sure [*smiling*], and I see things in their true color. You must be guided by me in this. [*He takes her hand almost cruelly and speaks strongly, with the manner and voice of the man who is and means to remain master.*] Do you understand that ? [*She draws her hand away as if in pain.*] I beg your pardon. I am afraid you are one of those dangerous "well-meaning" persons who do more harm than the people who are purposely malicious. You are to take no step without my sanction.

[BECKY *comes in with a certain air of bravado.*]

BECKY. Excuse me, I heard the bell and I was waiting — am I right !

WARDER. [*Goes to her.*] Come right in, dear.

BECKY. Well ! Has Eve thrown a bomb, or a trump card ? Am I to be taken into the secret or conspiracy or what ?

WARDER [*after a second's pause, in which he thinks how to begin*]. Eve has convinced herself, and would convince me, of some very — [*he thinks for the word*] — wrong — worse than wrong things, but I prefer to be convinced of the contrary by you. And

I prefer to come to you with my confidence, my conviction complete. And together we'll try to keep Eve from harming others as well as herself and Lindon — the latter seems unavoidable. [EVE *pushes her papers on the desk pointedly nearer to him. He ignores them.*] Eve says you've not been seeing Lindon often, but every day.

BECKY. Do you want me to deny it?

WARDER [*indulgently*]. I want you to tell the truth.

BECKY. Of course, the accusation and the idea behind it are absurd. [WARDER *turns and looks at* MRS. LINDON, *who meets his glance and then looks down at the evidence on the table, pushing the papers a little farther toward him. He does not follow her glance.* BECKY *half laughs.*] It's like a trial, is n't it! By what right does Eve —

MRS. LINDON [*interrupting*]. The supreme right of any married woman who cares for her husband. Shall I be more explicit?

BECKY. No, you need n't trouble! What next, Tom?

WARDER. Eve claims you had an engagement with Fred —

[*Hesitates, trying to remember the day.*]

MRS. LINDON [*quickly*]. Day before yesterday.

WARDER. Which you broke off over the telephone.

BECKY. How does she know that? Does she tap our wire? Merciful Heavens, Eve, you've become so morbid over your trouble your mind's diseased on the subject of Fred — and everybody else apparently.

MRS. LINDON. Ha!

WARDER. But is this true, Becky?

BECKY [*to gain time*]. Is what true?

WARDER. About this appointment with Fred which you broke over the —

BECKY [*interrupting*]. Of course not!

WARDER [*who begins to doubt her*]. If it were, you could easily explain it, I'm sure.

[*Hoping to suggest this course to her.*]

BECKY [*her head lost*]. Of course — but there's nothing to explain! The whole thing's false! What do you take me for, Eve? If you think I'm a home destroyer, you've made a mistake in the bird! And what do you mean by coming into my precious home and trying to make trouble for me?

[*Sitting on the sofa, frightened, and almost in tears.*]

WARDER. Wait a minute, Becky, it's partly my fault.

BECKY. It is not! I know whose fault it is, and I must say that, at last, I don't blame Fred Lindon!

MRS. LINDON. Oh!

BECKY. There! I'm sorry I said that. When I'm excited like this I speak the truth straight out, no matter what happens!

WARDER. Well, really it was I who insisted on your joining us, against Eve's will. [*To* MRS. LINDON.] Your way was best. It was my man's point of view — [*To* BECKY.] And you are right, under the circumstances, no doubt, to answer as you do.

BECKY. My dear Tom, there's no **other** way to answer.

WARDER. [*Looks at her, then takes up the envelope containing the detective reports and holds them tightly in his hand. He comes down to* MRS. LINDON.] If you will leave us alone, I will go over the whole matter with Becky — by ourselves will be much better.

MRS. LINDON. I need hardly tell you those papers are most valuable to me.

BECKY [*looking up, her curiosity aroused*]. What papers?

[*Nobody answers her. She tries to see.*]

MRS. LINDON. Will you promise me not to let them out of your hands till you put them back into mine?

WARDER. I will.

MRS. LINDON [*as she moves to go, stops*]. You will find the entries which are of particular interest to you marked on the margin with a red cross!

WARDER [*satirically*]. Thank you!

[BECKY *rises and rings for the* SERVANT. MRS. LINDON *goes out.*]

BECKY [*coming to meet* WARDER]. I think I'm a pretty good-natured woman to let Eve —

WARDER. [*Stands before* BECKY *with his hands on her shoulders, making her look straight into his eyes.*] Now be careful, dearest. You've married a man who does n't understand a suspicious nature — who has every confidence in you and the deepest — a confidence that could n't be easily disturbed; but once it was shaken, every unborn suspicion of all the past years would spring to life full-grown and strong at their birth, and God knows if my confidence could ever come back. It never has in any of the smaller trials of it I've made in my life

So you'll be careful, won't you, dearest? I mean even in little things. My faith in you is what gives all the best light to my life, but it's a live wire — neither you nor I can afford to play with it.

[*Goes to the writing-table and takes the papers out of* Eve's *envelope.*]

Becky. Tom, you frighten me! Eve has made you jealous again. [*Goes to him and puts both arms about his neck.*] Now, my darling, I give you my word of honor I love only you and never have loved Fred Lindon and never could! Say you believe me!

Warder. Have n't I always believed you?

Becky. Ye—s.

Warder. But if I find your word of honor is broken in one thing, how can I ever trust it in another?

Becky. Of course you can't — but you need n't worry, because it won't be broken.

Warder. Then, now we're alone, tell me the truth, which you did n't tell me when you said you 'd not seen Lindon often.

Becky. [*Turns away.*] It was the truth. I have n't — so very often.

Warder. Not every day?

Becky. [*Sits in the chair by the writing-table.*] How could I?

Warder. Nor telephoned him Thursday, breaking off an engagement *after you told me absolutely you 'd parted with him for good — and had no appointment?*

Becky. Of course not? The idea! [*But she shows she is a little worried.*] Eve Lindon never could tell the truth!

Warder. The telephone girl must have lied, too, or else the statement was made out of whole cloth.

[*Throwing the envelope on the desk.*]

Becky. What statement?

Warder [*sitting on sofa*]. From these detectives.

[*He begins to look through the papers.*]

Becky. Detectives! [*Stunned.*] What detectives?

[*Picks up envelope and looks at it, puts it back on desk.*]

Warder. Eve's, who have shadowed her husband for the past two months.

Becky [*thoroughly alarmed*]. You don't mean —

Warder. [*Interrupts, not hearing what*

Becky *says; his thoughts on the papers which he is reading, he speaks very quietly.*] These certainly do make out a case of daily meetings for you two.

Becky. It 's not true!

Warder. Though not so very many here.   [*Turning over a fresh paper.*]

Becky. [*Rises, gets above desk.*] All! All the meetings there have been — practically. This is simply awful! Eve is capable of making the most terrific scandal for nothing. Don't let her, Tom, will you? Tear those things up!

Warder [*smiling indulgently, not taking her seriously*]. Becky!

Becky [*leaning over the table, stretches out her hand toward him*]. Well, let me! Let me take them from you without your noticing till it 's too late!

Warder [*seriously*]. You 're not serious?

Becky. I am!

Warder. You heard me give Eve my word?

Becky. To a mad woman like that it does n't count.

Warder. I wonder just how much your word does count with you, Becky!

Becky [*with great and injured dignity*]. It counts everything!

Warder. They seem to have hit on some very out-of-the-way places for your rendezvous. [*He smiles.*] Where is Huber's Museum?

Becky. Why, it 's down on Fourteenth — [*She interrupts herself quickly.*] I don't know where it is!

[*She moves away to collect herself.*]

Warder [*still smiling*]. And why the Washington Heights Inn in February? Or the Eden Musée ever?

Becky. Of course, some one else has been mistaken for me.

Warder. [*Looks up.*] Ah! yes, that 's a very possible idea.

Becky. [*Goes to the sofa and sits beside him.*] Tom, don't read any more of the horrid things! Listen to me, don't let Eve go on. She 'll ruin everything if she does. He 'll never forgive her, never take her back.

Warder [*reading and smiling*]. I did n't know you skated!

Becky. I always loved skating. I only gave it up because it bored you. But I did n't skate then!

WARDER. When?

BECKY. I — I don't — oh, whenever that beast says!

WARDER. St. Nicholas Rink, Friday, February eighteenth. [*He has noticed the slip she made, but hides the fact; he speaks as he goes on reading.*] Eve and her husband have had a big row, and he swears he'll never see her again, not even in the other place, that she's come between you and him and that he'll never forgive.

[*He finishes seriously, his bantering manner gone.*]

BECKY. Oh, how untrue! I don't believe he said any such thing. Eve's jealous mind has distorted something else. The reason for our friendship — [*he rises with a half-angry movement, goes above the table looking for the envelope*] — such as it is — was to bring Eve and him together.

WARDER. From *your* point of view.

BECKY. No, believe me, he is n't as bad as you think.

WARDER [*showing the papers*]. And what about these? They agree with me.

BECKY. If you believe those papers about him, then you must believe them about me.

WARDER [*coming to her*]. Heaven forbid, Becky! They would prove you a liar and a terrible one — which you're *not*, are you?

BECKY. How can you ask?

WARDER. If these were true — if I thought you had deceived me to such an extent — I could never trust you again so long as I lived, Becky.

BECKY. Shall you speak to Mr. Lindon about them?

WARDER. No, I would n't insult you by discussing you with Lindon, unless I was convinced every word and more here was true. I will see Eve to-morrow and perhaps get hold of these detectives myself.

BECKY [*almost trembling with dread*]. And now go and have your game. You need it! You're getting morbid. You'll be believing these beastly things if you don't get some exercise.

WARDER. What time is it?

BECKY. [*She looks at clock on the mantel, and speaks with her face still away from him.*] Three. When will you be back?

[*She conceals her anxiety to hear his answer.*]

WARDER. Oh, six, I suppose.

BECKY [*facing him with a certain relief*]. Not till six — you're sure?

WARDER. Yes, you know your father's coming and there's no necessity of my seeing him.

BECKY. Oh! I forgot all about father's telegram! If it's money, I'm to be firm?

WARDER. Absolutely.

BECKY [*taking hold of the envelope which he has in his left hand away from her*]. What are you going to do with those?

WARDER. You heard me tell Eve they should n't go out of my hands except into hers.

[*He gently but firmly removes her hand from the envelope.*]

BECKY. And you meant it?

WARDER. Don't you mean a promise you give like that?

BECKY. Yes, of course . . .

WARDER [*taking out his keys*]. I'm going to put them away in my room. I want to have a thorough, careful look through them later. Of course I can't let it rest here. The detectives must learn their mistake at once.

BECKY. Yes, of course. But you are going to the Welds' now for your game?

WARDER. Yes, good-bye.

[*Presses her hand. Gives her a tender but questioning look, but does not kiss her, and then goes out.*]

BECKY. He's begun to distrust me already. Dear God in Heaven, if I ever get out of this, I'll never tell another lie so long as I live! [*She turns to the window. Smiles to* WARDER *outside and throws him a kiss, but afterward her face at once assumes its frightened look. Coming from the window, she sinks upon the piano stool.*] He's got to save me! Now he can prove that he is worthy a decent woman's friendship. [*She goes to the telephone and calls.*] Hello! Hello! [*She suddenly realizes.*] But I can't use the telephone! Central has told things already! [*She hangs up the receiver. The telephone bell rings.*] I must write him. [*The bell rings again. She takes up the receiver and speaks angrily.*] Hello? . . . No, I did n't ring. You've made a mistake. [*Hangs up the receiver.*] You telltale toad you! [*She writes.*] "If this note reaches you in time, please come over" — I ought to be able to get rid of father in half an hour [*she looks up at the clock*] — "at half past three." [*Seals note* and addresses it.] "Important." [*Which she underlines.*]

SERVANT [*entering left, announces*]. Mr. Roland.

> [ROLAND *is an elderly, dried-up little man with an air of the dandy jockey still clinging to him underneath his gray hairs and dyed mustache. A vivid carnation is in his buttonhole and a somewhat rusty springiness in his gait.*]

ROLAND [*coming in jauntily*]. Hello, Beck !

BECKY [*with fictitious spirit*]. Father !

> [*He starts to kiss her, forgetting the ever-present cigarette in his mouth; then he stops to remove it, and does kiss her.*]

ROLAND. How are you ?

BECKY. I'm awfully glad to see you, but you can't stay long. Excuse me just a moment. Jenks, I want you to ring for a messenger and give him — [*stops*] — no, when he comes, send him to me.

> [*She has started to give* JENKS *the note, but changes her mind.* JENKS *bows and turns to leave.*]

ROLAND. I say, Becky, might I have a glass of brandy ? I took coffee after lunch on the train and it's poisoned me. Must have been canned coffee !

BECKY. Very well, Jenks.

> [*The* SERVANT *goes out left.*]

ROLAND [*lolling on the sofa*]. What the devil did you mean by sending me fifty dollars instead of five hundred ?

BECKY [*surprised*]. I read it fifty ! I never dreamed you'd ask for five hundred more ! [*Going toward him.*]

ROLAND. I wrote five hundred and I must have it !

BECKY. My dear father, it's impossible. I tried as it was to get a little more from Tom, but he said "no," to send you the fifty dollars, with his love, but not one penny more, and to make you understand — and, father, he means it — that for the future you must keep within your allowance.

> [*The* SERVANT *enters with the brandy on a salver, and pours out a liqueur glass full.*]

ROLAND. But *you'll* help me ?

BECKY [*sitting on the opposite end of the sofa*]. No, he forbids it, and in the future I'm going to do what Tom wishes, and never deceive him even in a little thing

again. [*To the* SERVANT *who hands the glass of brandy to* ROLAND.] The messenger boy has n't come yet ?

SERVANT. No, madam.

BECKY. If he does n't come in five minutes, ring again.

SERVANT. Yes, madam.

> [*Starting to go,* ROLAND *stops him.*]

ROLAND. Not so fast !

> [*He points to the glass which he has emptied and the* SERVANT *pours out another glass.* ROLAND *takes it and puts it on the table behind him. The* SERVANT *busies himself with gathering up the after-dinner coffee-cups and trying to overhear all that he can.*]

BECKY. How is Mrs. Crespigny ?

ROLAND. That woman will be the death or the marriage of me !

BECKY. Don't be absurd, father ! She's given you the most comfortable home you've had for years. In that letter she wrote me she said she'd been a real mother to you.

ROLAND. The *mother* is a blind, a false lead to hide her hand ! her trumps are marriage.

BECKY. Nonsense ! Mrs. Crespigny must realize the difference in your positions.

ROLAND. You have n't lived with her social souvenirs as I have for four years ! [*The* SERVANT *starts to take up the glass which* ROLAND *has put aside, but the latter stops him. The* SERVANT *has delayed over his work as long as he dares in his desire to listen, and now goes out left.*] Becky, are you and Tom hungering for a mother-in-law ?

BECKY. I don't know what you mean ?

ROLAND. It's a question of five hundred dollars for me or a new Mrs. Roland !

BECKY [*astounded*]. You don't mean you owe Mrs. Crespigny that money ?

ROLAND. Well, I've not paid my board bill as regularly as I might have wished.

BECKY. [*Rises, indignant.*] I'm ashamed of you !

ROLAND. I'm ashamed of myself, but shame won't pay bills ; if it would, there'd have been many an unpaid debt washed off the slate in this world.

> [*The* SERVANT *returns with a messenger boy.*]

SERVANT. The messenger, madam.

> [BECKY *goes to the boy. During*

BECKY'S *talk with the messenger,* ROLAND *fills his pocket with cigars from the box on the table.*]

BECKY. I want you to take this note to its address, but only leave it in case the gentleman is in. Do you understand?

MESSENGER. Yes, ma'am.

BECKY. And come back and tell me.

MESSENGER. Yes, ma'am.

[*He goes out with the* SERVANT, *who has waited for him.*]

ROLAND. I confess, my child, I have flirted a little with the dame in question.

BECKY. Father!

ROLAND. I have, in a way, led her on!

BECKY. And you always told me my mother's memory was the one precious thing left, that you meant to keep always untouched by your life!

ROLAND. I don't deny, Becky, I'd be ashamed of it. I don't pretend Mrs. Crespigny would be a solace or a substitute; she would, at the best, perhaps, be a resource, — but what she threatens to become unless I pay is a legal necessity!

BECKY. *Could* she do that?

ROLAND. I have been obliged at times by desperate need of ready money to suggest to her certain things as probabilities which were barely remote possibilities! And unfortunately — *unfortunately* — once or twice in writing.

BECKY. She has compromising letters of yours?

ROLAND. She has a large collection of illustrated postal cards from every place I've been since I lodged with her — they are her chief artistic dissipation — and a double set of Baltimore Duplicates, which I am afraid are the most foolish; as I am in the habit of making up with her in that way after little tiffs when she takes the stand of not being on speaking terms with me.

BECKY. Father! You've been a terrible idiot.

ROLAND. I have, my dear!

BECKY. Can't you get those cards back?

ROLAND. The rent due is "Mother's" price for them. [*Rising.*] You will make Tom give it to me, won't you? and I'll promise not to make such a fool of myself again.

[*Sitting on the arm of the sofa, drawing* BECKY *toward him and putting both his arms about her.*]

BECKY. Tom's idea now is that you deserve all you get. He'll say you deserve Mrs. Crespigny.

[*Leaving him, she goes above the table.*]

ROLAND. Oh, come, she's not so bad as that!

BECKY. How old is she?

ROLAND. She has told me several ages. The general average would make her about forty-seven and a quarter.

BECKY. Pretty?

ROLAND. A fine figure of a woman and plays an A-one game of piquet.

BECKY. I see! When did her husband die?

ROLAND. He did n't die. He stole from the bank in which he was employed and went to jail, and she says for social reasons she was naturally obliged to take advantage of the divorce law. I have a suspicion myself he may have preferred jail!

BECKY. [*Comes quickly to him.*] Father, I would never forgive you if you did such a thing! It's degrading to me and to my mother's memory for you to accept any sort of indulgence at that woman's hands! When we get her paid, you must leave her house.

ROLAND. That I can't and won't do, because I'm far too comfortable!

SERVANT [*entering left, announces*]. Mrs. Crespigny!

ROLAND. [*Jumps up.*] Mrs. who?

[MRS. CRESPIGNY *comes in flamboyantly. She is a woman past the age of uncertainty, dressed gaudily, with an hour-glass figure; she has innumerable bracelets and bangles, and an imitation jeweled chain flaunts a heavy pair of lorgnettes, like a gargoyle hanging over a much-curved bust. Enormous wax pearls in her ears are in direct contrast to the dark beginnings of her otherwise russet-gold hair. Neither her shoes nor her stays fit, and both are too tight. She is brightly rouged, and yet the very failure of the façade reveals, somehow, the honest interior of a human if forlornly foolish female.*]

MRS. CRESPIGNY. Excuse me for intruding myself which I know is not social good form. Mis' Warder, I take it?

[BECKY *bows.*]

ROLAND [*angrily*]. What do you mean by following me here?

MRS. CRESPIGNY [*after a severe look at him, turns back to* BECKY]. I want you to know the facts as between your father and me, and just how the matter is, and get your support that I done right! [*To* ROLAND.] I know your daughter is a lady if you ain't, and being a lady myself I have a certain pride. [*To* BECKY.] I've had a good deal of trouble persuading your father that though a lady sometimes takes in a paying guest she still holds her own in the social scale. I have friends of my own in the New York Smart Set! My niece married a Mr. Gubenhamers and lives in a perfectly elegant house of her own on Lennox Avenue. Do you know her? One thousand two hundred and fifty-three?

BECKY. No.

MRS. CRESPIGNY. Oh, don't you? Well, of course I know New York is big. Still, perhaps you know her husband's cousin, who is also in a way a relation? You will know her by name — Mrs. Otto Gurtz, President of the West Side Ladies' Saturday Afternoon Social Gathering?

BECKY. No, I'm afraid I don't know her.

MRS. CRESPIGNY. Well! I guess you don't read the Harlem society notes in the papers; if you did, you'd know what she stands for socially.

BECKY. Suppose we keep to the reason of your visit — I understand my father owes you money — [MRS. CRESPIGNY *turns sharply to* ROLAND] — and that you insist on being paid, which is natural —

MRS. CRESPIGNY. A trumped-up story! [*Going to* ROLAND.] I guess I done just about the right thing to chase on here after you! I'm sorry to say it, Mis' Warder, 'specially as it ain't exactly ladylike, but your father, with all his superfine qualities, is a liar! Yes, ma'am, between us two as ladies, he's an ornery liar!

[*Sinks into a chair in tears.* ROLAND *lights a cigarette angrily and goes up to the window.*]

BECKY. Mrs. Crespigny, wouldn't it be better to behave more like a lady and talk less about one? Why break into the house of a woman you don't know and make a scene over a matter of rent due you —

MRS. CRESPIGNY. It ain't the rent! It's all a question of horses. When he left my house this morning, he said he was leaving for good unless I let him have —

ROLAND [*interrupting her*]. Mrs. Crespigny! You're hysterical! You're saying things you'll regret —

SERVANT [*entering, left*]. The messenger has come back, madam.

BECKY. Oh, I want to see that boy! Excuse me a minute.

[*She hurries out and the* SERVANT *follows her.*]

ROLAND. I knew you were in the train; that's why I stayed in the smoker. And it decided me to keep my word never to go back to your house!

[*He sits determinedly in the armchair at left.*]

MRS. CRESPIGNY. And you told her I was dunning you for the rent!

ROLAND. She has no more sympathy with my betting than you have! I wouldn't tell her the money was to put on Wet Blanket, Monday!

MRS. CRESPIGNY. [*Rises and goes to him.*] No, you'd rather let her think I was a grasping harpy, when you know, if the truth's told, you owe me at least five times five hundred dollars with your borrowings and your losses at cards!

ROLAND [*smilingly*]. You haven't won lately.

MRS. CRESPIGNY. Do you know why?

ROLAND. Oh, of course! You got out of the wrong side of the bed or you dreamed of a black horse!

MRS. CRESPIGNY [*pathetically and a little ashamed*]. No. I've let you win a-purpose — because I was ashamed for you to owe me any more money. I'm trying to keep a little pride in you somehow, even if I have to cheat to do it.

[*She almost breaks down again, and turning away, takes a powder puff from a little gilt box and powders her nose to cover up the traces of tears.*]

ROLAND. Well, do you think it's pleasant for me to owe you money? A kind friend like you! [*Going to the mantel and flicking his cigarette ash in the fireplace.*] One reason I want to take advantage of this tip for Monday is to pay you if I win.

MRS. CRESPIGNY. Yes, and then go board somewhere else? Is that your idea? Or to stay here?

ROLAND. Well, my daughter and her husband want me. [*Leaning on the mantel.*] They say their home is my home.

MRS. CRESPIGNY [*going toward him, alarmed*]. But you won't stay, will you? I left word with Josephine to have your favorite meenoo cooked for a late supper in case you'd come back. We'll have a game to-night. I'll play you a rubber for the five hundred — it's against my conscience to give it to you outright for horse-racing.

ROLAND. *Loan* it to me!

MRS. CRESPIGNY. Yes, of course! I always mean loan. Oh, the flat'd be just too dreadful lonesome without you! Say you'll come back! Quick, before Mis' Warder comes in! Won't you?

ROLAND [*coming toward her*]. Well, if you make it a personal favor to you in this way, I can't exactly refuse! And that ends the most serious quarrel we've had yet.

MRS. CRESPIGNY [*embarrassedly*]. If we was man and wife, there would n't be any need of such quarrels. The money'd be yours then to do as you liked with.

ROLAND. Don't tempt me! You know you're a great deal too kind to me as it is and I'm no good to take as much advantage of you as I do.

MRS. CRESPIGNY. Oh, pshaw! Say! I wish you'd help me to get on the right side of your daughter. You're too delicate to say anything, but I always suspect it's her that stands between us.

BECKY [*coming back*]. I'm very sorry, but you must go at once. I have an important engagement here in a few minutes and must change my dress. I will promise you, Mrs. Crespigny —

ROLAND. [*Interrupts.*] I have made an arrangement with Mrs. Crespigny that is agreeable to her, without Tom's and your assistance —

BECKY [*alarmed*]. Father, not —

ROLAND. [*Shakes his head.*] It seems I exaggerated my indebtedness a little and Mrs. Crespigny exaggerated her desire to be paid this month and —

MRS. CRESPIGNY. Yes, I was just mad clean through and would have said anything!

BECKY. Well, I'm glad it's settled, but it seems a pity you could n't have accomplished it without the railway journey, especially as I must ask you to excuse me at once.

[*She guides* MRS. CRESPIGNY *toward the door left, but* MRS. CRESPIGNY,

instead of going out, makes a circle around an armchair and settles herself in it. BECKY *goes despairingly to* ROLAND.]

MRS. CRESPIGNY. Oh, I don't regret the trip over, because I've been dying to meet you, Mis' Warder, ever since I had the pleasure of knowing your father in a taty-taty sort of way. And we can catch the four-fifteen.

BECKY. Good! [*Crossing to her, and holding out her hand.*] I'm sorry I can't ask you to stay.

MRS. CRESPIGNY. Oh, I can come over nearly any day! I've got such a perfectly lovely servant girl now. I give her every night out and she works like a dog all day — and you can trust her with everything! Can't you, Mr. Roland?

ROLAND. You can trust her with me all right. [MRS. CRESPIGNY *laughs loudly.*]

BECKY. Father!

MRS. CRESPIGNY. Ain't he killing! Do you inherit his sense of humor? He can get anything he wants out of me with just one of them witticisms. [ROLAND *winks aside to* BECKY.] Of course, I won't say that he ain't an expensive boarder — [BECKY *sinks in the chair near center, discouraged*] but I consider he cuts both ways and at the finish the ends meets.

BECKY. I think I gather what you mean I'm afraid you'll lose your train!

MRS. CRESPIGNY. I mean it's hard for a lady what's got it in her blood, to take boarders, because usually the boarders is beneath what the lady's been accustomed to and she don't feel at home with 'em. Now with your father it's different, because he's a Roland and I'm a Crespigny.

BECKY. Oh, is that your own name? I thought —

ROLAND [*interrupting*]. No, Mrs. Crespigny's maiden name was Ruggles.

MRS. CRESPIGNY. Yes, mamma made what we'd call a messyliance, — married beneath her, you know. But she never descended, nor allowed us to neither, to papa's social level. Mamma was a O'Roorke. You know, one of them early high-toned families that came over from Amsterdam in the Mayflower.

BECKY. I see!

MRS. CRESPIGNY. Mamma often said to me, says she, "Jennie — "

BECKY [*with her patience exhausted, jumps up, interrupting her*]. I must say good-bye now — I've no time to dress.

[*She hurries out right.*]

MRS. CRESPIGNY [*rising*]. Well, do you think I made any sort of a hit with her?

ROLAND. My dear friend, I've told you before, you're not quite my daughter's style.

MRS. CRESPIGNY. But why not? She seems real refined.

[ROLAND *groans.* WARDER *comes in left. He does not see* MRS. CRESPIGNY *on his entrance.*]

WARDER. Hello, father! I did n't think I was going to have this pleasure. I had an engagement to play racquets with Billy Weld, but he broke down in his motor somewhere between Tuxedo and here and I could n't wait.

[MRS. CRESPIGNY *comes a few steps and beckons to* ROLAND *to introduce* WARDER.]

ROLAND. Mrs. Crespigny, Mr. Warder.

MRS. CRESPIGNY. [*Bows.*] Pleased to make your acquaintance.

[*She turns away with a rather grand manner.* WARDER *looks from her to* ROLAND *and shakes his head, then goes to the writing-table with some letters he has brought in from the hall.*]

ROLAND. Excuse me one moment. [*Beckons to* MRS. CRESPIGNY *and whispers to her aside.*] Wait for me!

MRS. CRESPIGNY. In the hall?

ROLAND. Lord, no! At the station!

MRS. CRESPIGNY. Oh! [*Going, she turns at door to bid* WARDER *good-bye.*] If you should ever be coming over to Baltimore, Mr. Warder, why, just drop in!

[*She goes out left.*]

WARDER. Where's Becky?

ROLAND [*going to him*]. She's upstairs. I just wanted to thank you for the money you sent me day before yesterday.

WARDER. What money?

ROLAND. The check for fifty dollars Becky mailed me.

WARDER. [*Starts, but controls it immediately.*] Oh, a check for fifty dollars —

ROLAND. The joke on me is that what I wanted was five hundred!

[*Digs* TOM *in ribs.*]

WARDER [*looking off where* BECKY *went, absorbed in his thoughts*]. Oh, five hundred!

ROLAND. Yes, just five hundred. [*He looks at* WARDER, *and waits; hums a song and dances a few steps.*] Nothing doing, I suppose?

WARDER. No. Father, the fact is —

ROLAND. Yes, I know, Becky told me. Excuse me, I've got to catch a train. Good-bye, my boy.

WARDER [*with his thoughts elsewhere*]. Good-bye!

[ROLAND *goes out whistling "Waiting at the Church."* WARDER *stands a moment thinking, then takes out his key-chain.*]

SERVANT [*entering, shows in* LINDON]. Mr. Lindon to see Mrs. Warder, sir.

[WARDER *looks up with a start, which he immediately controls, and disguises completely his thoughts and emotions.*]

LINDON. How are you, Warder?

WARDER. [*Speaks very casually and pleasantly, with complete self-control.*] Good afternoon, Lindon. [*Sees* SERVANT *about to go to* BECKY, *stops him.*] Jenks! [JENKS *goes to him.* WARDER *gives him a key from his chain.*] Go to my room and get me a large blue envelope from the upper right-hand drawer of the desk.

JENKS. Yes, sir. [*He goes out left.*]

WARDER. Excuse me, Mrs. Warder is out. She'll be sorry.

LINDON [*surprised*]. Out?

WARDER. Yes.

LINDON. But surely there must be some mistake?

WARDER. No, I'm sorry. I assure you she's out.

LINDON. Oh! Then do you mind if I wait?

WARDER. Is that scarcely worth while? I must be off at once, and I imagine Mrs. Warder is out for her usual bridge afternoon.

LINDON. I think, on the contrary, she must be surely coming back, and if you don't mind, I'll wait.

WARDER [*with an apparently good-natured laugh*]. I don't like to insist against your apparently superior knowledge —

LINDON [*also smiling*]. No, no, it's only a note I received a few moments ago at the club. Here it is. [*Takes it from his pocket.*] That she must see me this afternoon. You know your wife is kindly acting as intermediary between Eve and myself. It is in regard to that. [*He hands the note to* WARDER, *who glances at it and returns it without reading.*] As it only came half an hour ago, I feel sure Mrs. Warder must expect to return soon.

SERVANT [*entering with an envelope, which he gives to* WARDER]. That is all I can find, sir.

WARDER [*humorously*]. That's all I want, so it's all right. Jenks, am I wrong in understanding that Mrs. Warder is out?

SERVANT. Yes, sir. Mrs. Warder is in, sir.

WARDER. Oh! I beg your pardon, Lindon.

LINDON. That's all right.

WARDER. [*To* JENKS.] Jenks, say to Mrs. Warder, Mr. Lindon is here. You need n't say anything about me. I'm off.

SERVANT. Yes, sir.   [*Goes out right.*]

LINDON. I'm not driving you away, I hope.

WARDER. Oh, no, I have some important papers to go over. Make yourself comfortable. Good-bye.

LINDON. Thanks, old man. Good-bye.

[*He sits on the sofa, as* WARDER *goes out left.*]

LINDON. Well! She did send for you, Freddy, old son! Now's your chance!

SERVANT [*reëntering*]. Mrs. Warder will be down at once.

LINDON. Thank you. [*The* SERVANT *goes out left.* LINDON *goes to the piano and sings a verse of a song, "Everything comes to him who waits," etc. An idea comes to him. He weighs it, accepts it, smiles, and stops playing.*] I will! By George, I will!

[*He rises.*]

[BECKY *hurries in from the right and goes quickly toward him, crying, "Fred!" in a tone of distress and excitement. She leaves the door open behind her.* LINDON, *before she realizes what he is doing, has met her, taken her in his arms, and kissed her. She forces herself away from him, standing for a moment speechless with rage and astonishment.*]

LINDON. I told you, did n't I, Becky.

[*Tries to embrace her again.*]

BECKY [*slowly and deliberately*]. That's just exactly what Tom said you'd do!

LINDON. *What!*

BECKY. Ten to one, he said, if I sent for you again, you'd kiss me.

LINDON [*in alarm and astonishment*]. Yes, but what —

BECKY. But I would n't believe him! I said, and I believed, he did you an injustice.

LINDON. So you talked me all over with him, did you! Then why did you send for me to-day?

BECKY. Because I was a fool, if you want the true reason!

LINDON. My dear Becky —

BECKY. Oh, you'll hear more and worse than that if you stay to listen! I advise you to go! You can't help me. I don't trust you. You might even make matters worse. It may have been all done purposely as it is.

LINDON. Oh!

BECKY. You see I'm ready to believe all I've heard of you, now that you've shown your true silly self to me in that one sickening moment, and I'd rather not be saved at all than be saved by you!

[*She leans for a second against the corner of the writing-table.*]

LINDON. How saved? From what?

BECKY. Never mind! I only want to say one more thing to you and then go, please. But I want this to ring in your ears so long as you remember me! There is only one man in this world I love, and that's Tom, and there's only one man I despise, and that's you! Lindon, Fred Lindon! You know who I mean! I know now what our friendship meant to you and I wish I could cut out of my life every second of every hour I've spent with you! I've been a fool woman, and you've been a cad, — but, thank God, there are men in the world — real men — and one is my husband. Now, go, please! Eve's a fool not to jump at the chance of getting rid of you and I shall tell her so.

[*She turns away from him with a movement of dismissal.*]

LINDON [*going toward her*]. Do! For that, at least, I shall thank you, as well as for our delightful friendship, which I am sorry to have end so contrary to my expectations.

BECKY [*with her eyes down, speaks in a low, shamed voice*] This room is too small for you and me at this moment, — which leaves ?

[*He smiles, hesitates a moment, then sits in the armchair at left.* BECKY *gives a half-smothered exclamation of rage and starts to leave the room.* LINDON *rises quickly.*]

LINDON. No, no, I was only joking! I 'm sorry you take the whole affair so seriously. Allow me.

[*He bows and goes out left.*]

BECKY. [*Stands quietly thinking a moment, then makes up her mind.*] Eve herself is the one to help me! But I can't go to her till I 'm sure she 'll listen and understand — Laura ! [*She sits by the table and takes up the receiver of the telephone.*] Seven eight Plaza. Yes! It 's a lady this time, so I hope you won't have to listen ! Hello! Is Miss — Oh, is that you, Laura ? Can you come over at once ? I am in dreadful trouble ! Oh, well, after dinner, then ! No, I was going out, but I won't — it 's too important. You were right — and Eve 's right, too. Never mind, I can't tell you over the 'phone. I 'll explain everything to-night, only don't fail me. You can prevent a real catastrophe that has no need to happen. — Oh, that 's all right, don't stop another minute, then. Thank you with all my heart. [*She hangs up the receiver, gives a long sigh, and sits worriedly thinking.* WARDER *comes in, serious but calm. Looking at him, half frightened, she makes a great effort to be natural, and to be in a good humor.*] Hello, Tom ! Your game finished already ?

WARDER. We did n't play. Weld did n't get back to town. Any callers ?

BECKY. No.

WARDER. I thought I saw some one leaving — from the top of the street.

BECKY. Did you ? Oh ! it was probably father ; he came.

WARDER. No, I spoke with your father some fifteen minutes ago. He told me about the money you gave him.

[*A second's pause ;* BECKY *looks down and then up at him.*]

BECKY. Are you angry?

WARDER. You gave me your word you would n't.

BECKY. But I was so sorry for him — that 's why he came to-day; he said he must have it ; I could n't refuse him and you were n't here !

WARDER. He said you mailed him my check day before yesterday.

[BECKY *is silent, trapped, frightened. A pause, then she speaks in a low voice.*]

BECKY. I 'm so sorry —

[*A second's pause.*]

WARDER. It looked to me like Fred Lindon.

[BECKY, *more frightened, realizing what is hanging over her, like a drowning person who cannot swim, flounders helplessly about in the next few speeches, trying to save herself by any and every means that she thinks may help her for the moment.*]

BECKY. Well, I 'll be honest, it *was* Fred Lindon !

WARDER [*anger getting the best of him*]. After everything — your word of honor, Eve's accusations, my absolute desire — you sent for him to come and see you !

BECKY. No, no, you must n't think that, Tom ! He came of his own accord, of course, — I suppose to see if I would see him ! I did n't know it !

WARDER [*wary, suspicious, to lead her on*]. Then, why did you see him ? You could easily excuse yourself.

BECKY. No, you don't understand. [*She flounders hopelessly.*] I did n't know it was he ! Don't you see ?

WARDER. No, I don't see !

[*Watches her with a face growing harder and harder with each lie she tells.*]

BECKY. But I 'm telling you — it was just like this ; I was upstairs and Jenks came — and said a gentleman wanted to see me in the drawing-room. Just that, don't you see — a gentleman. [*She sees the doubting look in his face and, mistaking it, tries to make her story more plausible.*] I was surprised, too, and said, " Who ? " and Jenks said the gentleman gave no name — [*He turns sharply away from her, unable to face her as she tells the lies.*] Yes, I know it was funny — I thought so then. I suppose Jenks considered it a joke, — and I suppose he did n't give his name for that very reason, for fear I would n't see him — [WARDER, *looking up as if to stop her, sees the door right open and quickly closes it.*] Of course the moment I came into the room and saw who it was, I excused myself, and he left.

WARDER [*in a voice not loud but full of anger and emotion*]. Lies! all of it! Every word a lie, and another and another and another!

BECKY [*breathless with fright, gasping*]. Tom!

WARDER [*going to her*]. You sent for him! [*She is too frightened to speak, but she shakes her head in a last desperate effort at denial.*] Don't shake your head! I know what I'm talking about and for the first time with you, I believe! [*She puts up her hands helplessly and backs away from him.*] I saw your note to him! [*She starts with a sense of anger added to her other emotions.*] I read it here, in this room; he gave it to me before you came down.

BECKY. The beast!

WARDER [*with biting satire*]. You're going to misjudge him too!

BECKY. No, Tom, I'll tell you the truth and all of it!

WARDER. Naturally, now you've *got to!*

BECKY. No — wait! I did send for him — it was to tell him about those papers of Eve's.

WARDER. Yes, you must plan your escape together!

BECKY. No! because I still believed he was decent. I thought it was his duty, that he would claim it as his right, to prevent such a scandal as Eve threatened to make, which he knew I didn't deserve.

WARDER. Hah!

BECKY. You may sneer, but I don't! Yes, I broke my promise to you — what else could I do? You wouldn't let me send for him! And he came! And he did what you said he would. He took me in his arms before I could stop him, and kissed me.

[*She bends over the back of the chair at center on which she is leaning, and sobs.*]

WARDER. [*Goes to her, speaking with bitter irony.*] Charming! And you turned on him, of course! Played the shocked and surprised wife and ordered him out of the house!

BECKY. Yes. But I did! Why do you speak as if I didn't?

WARDER. Do you expect me to believe this, too?

BECKY [*facing him*]. I don't expect, — you've got to!

WARDER. Do you think you can go on

telling lies forever and I'll go on blindly believing them as I have for three years?

BECKY. Even you couldn't have turned on him with more anger and disgust than I did!

WARDER. I couldn't believe you if I wanted to! You've destroyed every breath of confidence in me!

BECKY. It's the truth I'm telling you now!

WARDER. In everything — everything that has come up since my eyes were first forced half open — you have told me a lie!

BECKY. It's the truth! It's the truth!

WARDER. [*Continues, hardly hearing her.*] The money to your father, the first lie, and to-day made a double one! All this rotten evidence of Eve's — another dozen! Your promise that Lindon's visit Thursday should be his last, the next!

BECKY. I meant it then — I meant it truthfully.

WARDER [*ignoring her interruption*]. His visit after all to-day — that led of course to a mass of lies! And then the truth! He kissed you! And then another lie and another dozen to try and save yourself!

BECKY [*quietly, in a hushed, frightened voice*]. By everything in this world and in the next that I hold dear and reverence, I've told you the truth at last.

WARDER. You don't know what's true when you hear it or when you speak it! I could never believe in you again! Never have confidence! How could I? Ask any man in the world, and his answer would be the same!

[*He turns and goes away from her, to control his anger, which threatens to get the best of him.*]

BECKY [*sobbing*]. No, no, Tom! Don't! don't say that! You must believe in me! You must believe in me!

WARDER [*after a pause, collects himself and comes to the writing-table*]. Becky, you and I must say good-bye to each other. We must finish separately. [*A silence. She looks at him in dumb horror and surprise.*] Do you understand?

BECKY [*in a low voice*]. No!

WARDER. We must separate. Quietly — no fuss, no divorce unless you wish it. [*A pause; she does not answer. He goes toward her and repeats.*] No divorce unless you wish it.

BECKY [*with simple but deep pathos*]. I love you.

WARDER. You must stay on in the house for the present, till you can make your plans. That will help keep the thing quiet, too.

BECKY. Tom! Do you really mean all you 're saying? Do you realize what it must mean for me — for both of us?

WARDER. Yes.

BECKY. To-morrow, perhaps — ?

WARDER. No. I shall go to Boston to-night for a few days; when I come back, you may have settled on something. If you have n't, I can manage all right. I don't want to press you about that, only —

BECKY. I will not stay in your house one single day without you.

WARDER. You 'll have to! My price for hushing up Lindon and Eve, and every one else, is that you on your side act with dignity, and as I think wisest.

BECKY [*going to the armchair at left*]. No! A woman like me whose heart is breaking, whether she 's right or wrong, can't act like that. *She can't do it!*

[*She sinks into the chair, bursting into tears.*]

WARDER [*beside her*]. Try. For your sake as well as mine. Good-bye, Becky.

BECKY [*with the tears choking her voice*]. I told you the truth the last time. Oh, can't you believe me?

WARDER. No — good-bye. [*Going.*]

BECKY. I love you and only you and you always —

WARDER. [*Turns in the doorway.*] The club address will reach me!

[*He goes out, closing the door behind him. BECKY sits still a moment thinking; then she goes to the writing-table, rings the bell, and takes up a time-table. Her hands drop upon the table in utter dejection and her head lowers as the tears come again fast and thick.*]

SERVANT [*entering left*]. Yes, madam?

BECKY [*controlling her emotion and hiding as best she can the traces of it*]. Tell Perkins to pack my small trunk and hand-bag. I am going to Baltimore to spend a day or so with my father.

SERVANT. Yes, madam.

BECKY. And then come back, please.

SERVANT. Very good, madam. [*Goes out.*]

BECKY [*taking up the telephone*]. Hello! 78 Plaza. [*As she listens for the answer she looks about the room, the control goes from her face, and the tears come once more; she brushes them away and tries to speak in a conventional tone without displaying her emotion, which is, however, plainly evident.*] Hello; I want Miss Fraser please. . . . Oh, ask her to call me the minute she 's free, please. Mrs. Warder. [*She hangs up the receiver and writes.*] "I am leaving now. You will at least believe that I cannot turn you out of your house, nor can I live in it one single day without you. It is ready waiting for you as I shall be all the rest of my life if you can ever again believe — "

[*She stops as the SERVANT enters and comes to her.*]

SERVANT. Madam?

[*BECKY finishes writing silently.*]

BECKY [*sealing the note*]. Has Mr. Warder gone yet?

SERVANT. Only just this second went out, madam. He told me to pack his bag and meet him at the station with it.

BECKY [*rising*]. Give this to Mr. Warder with his things. [*Gives the note.*]

SERVANT. Yes, madam.

[*He goes out left. The telephone bell rings.*]

BECKY. [*Goes to the table, sits, and takes up the receiver. Again she does her best to keep the emotion out of her voice, but only partly succeeds.*] Hello! Laura? I 'm so sorry, after all, I can't see you to-night. Tom has been called to — Chicago suddenly on business — yes, is n't it too bad? And I 've had a telegram that father is n't very well, so I am taking the five-twenty train for Baltimore. Yes, I 'll write. No, I don't think he 's seriously ill. Good-bye!

[*She hangs up the receiver, dropping her head on the table and sobbing heart-brokenly as the curtain falls.*]

ACT III

The same night.

MR. ROLAND's *rooms in* MRS. CRESPIGNY's *flat in Baltimore. This is the parlor of a cheap flat, with the bedroom, through an arch, originally intended for the dining-room and lit by a narrow window on a wall. There is red paper on the walls and red globes for the electric lights. An ugly set of furniture, with many tidies, a strange conglomeration of cheap feminine "knick-knacks," relieved by a sporting print or two, a frame of prize ribbons, and a few other masculine belongings which have been added to the original condition of the room, like a thin coat of paint. At back is a bow-window beside a sofa. On the left is the opening into the bedroom, and beside this a door leads to the hall. There is a center-table with chairs on either side and a Morris chair down on the right. A side-board in the upper left corner.*

ROLAND *and* MRS. CRESPIGNY *are playing piquet at the center-table. A "Teddy-Bear" with a pink ribbon bow about its neck is sitting on the table near* MRS. CRESPIGNY. *They play on through part of the scene.* ROLAND *stops to light a cigarette, and* MRS. CRESPIGNY *takes advantage of the pause to powder her face and preen herself in a pocket mirror.*

MRS. CRESPIGNY. You don't think you smoke too many of them?

ROLAND. If my smoking is disagreeable to you, I might spend my evenings at the club.

MRS. CRESPIGNY. You know different! You can't make that an excuse for skinning out of spending your evenings at home. I only wish 't I smoked 'em myself. I 've read in the papers that real ladies do now — but I guess it 's the fast set, and I always was conservative.

ROLAND [*playing*]. Don't talk; study your cards. If you don't take care, you 'll win!

MRS. CRESPIGNY. Will I? Excuse me, I was n't thinking. [*She plays a card, and as* ROLAND *takes the trick she takes up her mirror and examines wrinkles.*] I believe I 'll have massage. I heard of a fine massoor yesterday.

ROLAND. Masseuse, you mean, I hope.

MRS. CRESPIGNY. Massoor! Massoose is plural. The singular is massoor. You forget I was educated in New Orleans.

[*She rises and goes to the sideboard and pours out a brandy and soda.*]

ROLAND. Where 's my brandy and soda?

MRS. CRESPIGNY. I 'm getting it.

[*Bringing the glass down to the table.*]

ROLAND. That 's a good girl. Thank you, Mrs. Crespigny.

MRS. CRESPIGNY. Ain't it funny, good friends as we 've been for so long now, we 've kep' on calling each other " Mr." and " Mrs." ? S'pose it would n't be etiquay to call each other by our first names.

ROLAND. Etiquette.

MRS. CRESPIGNY. *Etiquay!* You can correct my English when you want to, but my French I 've kep' pure since school, and I remember perfeckly — all words ending in *e-t* you pernounce *A*.

ROLAND. What is your first name?

MRS. CRESPIGNY. Genevieve, but I was always called Jenny by my first h— ! I mean — I was always called Jenny by my schoolgirl friends.

ROLAND [*playing*]. Very interesting.

MRS. CRESPIGNY [*playing*]. I think your first name 's real pretty!

ROLAND [*taking the trick*]. Tut, tut! You 're getting too skittish, Mrs. Crespigny. [*She laughs a little embarrassedly.*]

MRS. CRESPIGNY. It 's your fault!

ROLAND [*playing card, and laughing*]. Then I apologize!

MRS. CRESPIGNY [*playing card, and giggling*]. Oh, you need n't!

ROLAND [*laughing more at her than with her, but realizing that she will not know the difference*]. I insist. [*He takes the trick.*]

MRS. CRESPIGNY. Anybody 'd think we was engaged to be married or something of that sort, would n't they?

ROLAND. I hope not!

MRS. CRESPIGNY. Oh, I don't know! I remember some postal cards what I 've read that might be construed to lean that way. [ROLAND *rises and gets a cigarette from the box on the table in the bow-window.*] There was one from Atlantic City that was just too sweet for anything! You sent it after we had that ridickerlous quarrel on the Board Walk.

ROLAND. What about?

MRS. CRESPIGNY. I lost my self-respect and asked you to kiss me, 'cause you said you was grateful for the fifty dollars I gave you for your poker losses the night before. And you handed me back my money and said if that was the price of the loan — oh, how you hurt my feelings!

[*With a touch of futile emotion.*]

ROLAND [*coming back to his chair*]. That was only a bluff! Come along, I 'll play you a game for the whole bunch of postal cards. [*Takes up the second deck and shuffles.*]

MRS. CRESPIGNY [*rising, speaks rather grandly*]. Nobody won't never get them postal cards from me except over my dead body. [*Cuts the cards, and* ROLAND *deals.*]

And I intend to refer to 'em every chance I get in hopes that some day — just in a desperate fit, maybe — you 'll up and marry me to stop me. [*Sits again.*]

ROLAND. Go on, play.

MRS. CRESPIGNY. You 've owned up you 're comfortable in my cute little flat — and I don't nag.

[*Both take up their hands, both play, and she takes trick.*]

ROLAND. You have n't the right, but as my wife — nay, nay, Pauline.

MRS. CRESPIGNY. You 've got the best rooms here, and if you ever do pay any board, don't I lend it right back to you the next day ?

ROLAND. Is n't it a little indelicate to remind me of that, Mrs. Crespigny ?

[*Playing.*]

MRS. CRESPIGNY [*getting a little angry*]. Well, I guess the indelicacy 's even ! [*She plays and starts to take the trick. He stops her and takes it himself.*] Oh, excuse me, I 'm at your beck and nod, and I 've even so far forgot my family pride as to hint that you was n't unacceptable to me in a nearer relation.

ROLAND. There you go again ! Keep off the thin ice !

MRS. CRESPIGNY. [*Throws down her cards and loses her temper outright.*] Well, why won't you marry me ? I may have forgot my pride, but I never forget myself. You know you would n't dare step over the invisible line between the dumb-waiter and the bathroom, what separates your apartment from mine in the flat.

ROLAND. One moment, please. Have I ever even hinted at taking the slightest advantage of your unprotected position in this house ? [*He rises in mock dignity.*] Who 's kept further from that invisible line, you or I ?

MRS. CRESPIGNY. Well, I must say you 've always behaved toward me like a perfect gentleman. [*He sits again and takes another cigarette.*] But jes' let 's speak the truth — if you can about anything ! [*He fumbles in his vest pockets.*] Matches ? [*She rises, goes to the sideboard, and finding a box of matches, brings it back to the table. During the first part of the following speech she makes nervous and ineffectual efforts to strike matches, in each case breaking off the heads without any result.*] You know you ain't wanted at your clubs ; that 's why you first took to playin' evenings with me — that, and 'cause I was easy ! You know that here in Baltimore you 're called a tout, a broken-down gambler, and a has-been, but I 've always hoped you was a will-be for me. [*Irritated by her repeated failures, he takes the match-box from her and lights his cigarette with the first match he strikes.*] You know your old friends 'd rather go 'round the block than stop and talk to you in the street. Yes, you know it as well as I do ! And you 've lived off me, borrowed money of me, led me to caring for you, let me take care of you as if you was — my own child, and I 've saved you from bein' a drunken sot ! [*Her voice fills with tears, but her anger gets the best of her, and she finishes strongly, striking the table with her beringed hand as she leans across toward him.*] Now, why ain't I good enough for you ?

ROLAND [*rising, really angry, and his dignity offended*]. Mrs. Crespigny —

MRS. CRESPIGNY. Oh, you need n't get on your high horse or I 'll win this rubber for the five hundred ! I know you 're worthless, and I know you don't always tell the truth, but through it all you 've been a real gentleman to me, and I realized yesterday, when I thought you was gone for good, what it meant to me. I 'm a decent woman, Mr. Roland, if I am a fool, and I swear I 'm good enough for you !

ROLAND. So far as that goes, you 're too good for me, but I 've got others to consider. My daughter —

MRS. CRESPIGNY [*interrupting him*]. Yes, I know she 's against me. [*She sits again, and with determination.*] Well, I 'm against her, and perhaps some day I 'll have a chance to pay her back !

ROLAND. That 's talking foolishly ! In the first place, my allowance would stop the day I married.

MRS. CRESPIGNY. Well, have n't I got enough for two ? It 's looked mighty like it the last couple a years.

[*She nervously takes the "Teddy Bear" from the table to hide her embarrassment at her boldness, and laying it flat on her knee, face downward, reties the pink bow on its neck.*]

ROLAND [*sitting, he gathers the cards together and shuffles them*]. Come, come, here we are again on one of those useless discussions. Come along, give me another brandy and soda.

MRS. CRESPIGNY [*resignedly*]. All right. [*Rises, and takes his glass, replacing the "Teddy Bear" on the table.*] This will be your second before twelve o'clock and it's got to be a little weakish. [*She goes to the sideboard. The front doorbell is heard ring.*] My goodness! who can that be?

[*The bell rings again.*]

ROLAND. Don't know, old girl, but go on, I'll deal for you. [*He deals.*]

MRS. CRESPIGNY [*going to the table, cuts the cards*]. I just love to have you call me "old girl" — it seems so nice and familiar.

[*The bell rings again, and* MRS. CRESPIGNY, *taking the "Teddy Bear" with her, places it on the side table at left and goes out.* ROLAND *deals. After a moment's pause* BECKY *comes in, carrying a handbag. She enters with an air of bravado, which fades instantly when she observes* ROLAND *does not see her. But her pathetic, timid look vanishes immediately when he looks up.*]

ROLAND [*going on dealing, without looking up*]. Who was it?

BECKY [*with forced gayety*]. Hello, father!

ROLAND. Good Heavens!

BECKY [*putting her bag on the table at left*]. Are n't you surprised?

ROLAND [*dryly*]. Very.

BECKY. And pleased?

ROLAND. Where in the world did you come from?

BECKY. New York; the next train after you. Give me a kiss. How are you?

[*Kisses him.*]

ROLAND. What have you come for? Where are you stopping?

BECKY. Here!

ROLAND. At what hotel?

BECKY. No hotel — here with you!

ROLAND. Nonsense! There's no place for you in the flat.

BECKY. Why not? I gave my check to the expressman and my trunk will be around in the morning.

ROLAND. These two rooms are all I have. [*Showing the opening to the left.*] Take a look at the bedroom — a beastly, dark little hole with one window that does n't look out — it

looks in! The bedroom of the flat we use for a dining-room. Mrs. Crespigny sleeps in the servant's room — so she tells me.

BECKY. Father!

ROLAND. Now you can see what nice sort of surroundings your poor old father's had to put up with these last years.

BECKY. [*Takes off her hat and cloak and puts them on sofa at right.*] You have only yourself to blame! You could live splendidly on the allowance Tom makes you in the one club you 've got left.

ROLAND. You need n't take off your things; you can't stay here.

BECKY. Oh, can't I? I 've come to pay you a little visit, and here I stay to-night and several nights.

[*Comes to the center-table and starts to collect cards.*]

ROLAND. Be careful! That's Genevieve's hand and we must finish this some time — I 'm well ahead. [*Carefully places the cards, properly divided, on the table at left.*] And really, Becky, you can't stay here. You can go to a hotel if you want to, or back to New York. You 're in the way here! I 'm an old man; this sort of thing upsets me! There 's no room and there 's no bed for you. [*Crosses to the Morris chair and sits.*] What the devil do you mean, turning up here well toward midnight, and threatening to stay, when for years I 've been trying to get you to come to Baltimore, and you know you were ashamed to come?

BECKY [*sitting in the chair left of the center-table*]. That is n't true, father; I always said I 'd come if you 'd give up certain things.

ROLAND. Well, I have n't given them up, so why have you come? What's the joke? And where's Tom?

BECKY [*after a second's pause*]. That's just it. Tom has been called to — San Francisco — suddenly — just after you left, on business — and the idea came to me, at last I 'll make that visit to father! It 'll be a good chance for me to settle Mrs. Crespigny, too!

ROLAND. You could n't have come at a more inopportune time! I was very busy this evening.

BECKY. Yes, I know — piquet with Mrs. C.! I 'll finish it with you.

[*Rises and goes to get the cards.*]

ROLAND. No, you won't! You'll go to a

hotel for the night and I'll come and have a decent lunch with you to-morrow.

BECKY. I can't go to a hotel. I've come away without a penny. I had to borrow half the money for my ticket from Perkins.

ROLAND. Where is Perkins?

BECKY. In New York. I knew, of course, there'd be no place for her here.

ROLAND. Any of the hotel people here will trust you.

BECKY. I won't ask them. I forgot to get Tom's address, so I can't send to him for any money. I've got to stay with you, father.

[*She sits on the arm of the Morris chair and puts her arm about her father.*]

ROLAND. You're a very boring person!

BECKY. That's a kind welcome for a dear and only daughter!

ROLAND. And I'm not going to have myself made uncomfortable by you!

BECKY. Please let me stay for a day or two, maybe a little longer or maybe not so long. I'll promise not to be any trouble; I'll sleep on the sofa!

ROLAND. Humph! You don't know that sofa! That was made in the antebellum and the antespringum days! Even a cat couldn't sleep on it without chloroform.

BECKY. Well, I don't expect to sleep, father, and if I don't, you won't know it. I've got to stay.

[*Rises and goes away and stands by the table with her back toward him.*]

ROLAND. [*Looks at her, suddenly suspicious.*] Becky, you're not telling me the truth. Something's the matter.

BECKY [*turning toward him, taking a high moral stand*]. Really, father!

ROLAND. There's something wrong. What is it?

BECKY. Nothing.

ROLAND. Oh, come, I'm your father, and I know the look in your eyes when you're not telling the truth; you get that look from me! You're telling me a lie — tell me the truth. What does it mean?

BECKY [*after a second's pause, bursts out with all her pent-up feelings, which she has been trying to hide*]. I've left Tom.

ROLAND. How do you mean — "Left Tom"?

BECKY. Left him for good. I'll never live with him again.

ROLAND. Nonsense!

BECKY. Never! You don't understand.

[*She sits again beside the table, leaning her elbows upon it and resting her face between her two hands.*]

ROLAND. No, I don't! and I don't want to!

BECKY. I've left his house in New York for good.

ROLAND. What's your reason? What's he done?

BECKY. He's deceived me.

ROLAND [*rising*]. Tom! Never!

BECKY. Father, I can't go back to him; I can't! Don't ask me any more questions, only keep me with you — please, keep me with you. . . .

ROLAND [*going to her*]. You're upset about matters. You've had a quarrel, that's all, and you're going back to-night.

BECKY. No. I've told him I'll never come back and I've come to stay — with you.

ROLAND. But I won't have it! In the first place, Mrs. Crespigny wouldn't have it either. She'd be jealous of your being here — and after all it's her flat. And I don't believe what you tell me about Tom.

BECKY. We can go somewhere else. Who is Mrs. Crespigny? [*Rises, and going to him takes hold of his sleeve.*] And I'm your daughter. Besides, Tom's allowance will stop. From now on you and I must get on together with the little money I have from mother.

ROLAND. Nothing of the sort. Even if you did leave Tom, you can make him take care of you.

BECKY. I won't take any money from Tom! No more money! Do you hear me, father?

ROLAND [*becoming more angry*]. No, I don't hear you! And I have something to say about my end of all this, which is that you've got to go back to your husband before it's too late for him to take you back, and give him a chance to explain! You'll go back to Tom to-night!

[*He goes determinedly to the sofa and gets her hat and cloak for her.*]

BECKY. [*Takes her hat from him and puts it on the center-table with equal determination.*] I shall sleep here, in this room, to-night!

ROLAND. You'll sleep in a Pullman car and wake up to-morrow, happy and in your right senses, in Jersey City.

BECKY. [*Moves back from him a little.*] You can't turn me out!

[*A pause.* ROLAND *reads the real trouble in her face and becomes serious and sympathetic.*]

ROLAND. Becky, you don't really believe what you say about Tom? [*She lowers her head in assent.*] You *know*? [*She lowers her head again.*] There must be a mistake somewhere! [*Puts the cloak on the Morris chair.*] If I ever knew a man who loved his wife! Go back, Becky!

BECKY. It's impossible!

ROLAND [*going to her*]. I speak to you with years of bitter experience behind me, and it's only what good there is left in me that is urging me to say this to you. I know in the end that you'll be nearer happiness than you ever can be any other way. Go back to Tom.

BECKY. No, no, I tell you, father, I've left Tom for good! Keep me with you — [*A knock on the door.*]

ROLAND. Come in!

[MRS. CRESPIGNY *comes in left and* BECKY *sinks down into the Morris chair.*]

MRS. CRESPIGNY [*worried*]. It's getting pretty late! I did n't know as Mis' Warder knew the street car don't run past here after twelve-thirty.

ROLAND. That's all right. Mrs. Warder is taking the one o'clock train to New York. We'll catch the last car.

MRS. CRESPIGNY [*relieved, smiles*]. Oh, well, then, you've got plenty of time. I'd better let you have my latchkey, though. I'll leave it on the hall table. [*To* BECKY.] Would you like anything? A glass of raspberry vinegar and a piece of jell cake?

BECKY. No, thanks.

MRS. CRESPIGNY [*offended*]. Good-evening.

BECKY. Good-evening. [MRS. CRESPIGNY *goes out.*] Why did you say I was going? I'm not!

ROLAND. You are. If you love Tom, you'll go. [*He goes to her and puts his arm around her shoulder.*] Do you love Tom still?

BECKY. Yes, father.

ROLAND. Then go back, Becky!

BECKY. No.

ROLAND. Your religion teaches you that the greatest love always carries with it the power of forgiveness.

BECKY [*eagerly*]. Oh, it's what I want to believe. If it's only true — if it's only true of *us!*

ROLAND. You've got to *make* it true by going back! [*He moves away.*] Good God! you shan't repeat your mother's and my mistake and make a miserable failure of both your lives! [BECKY *looks up surprised.*]

BECKY. What mistake?

ROLAND [*quietly, ashamed*]. Your mother left me, just as you want to leave Tom.

BECKY. Mother — [*rises*] — left you?

ROLAND. And for the same reason, do you understand me — that you want to leave Tom.

BECKY. But you never told me!

ROLAND. No.

BECKY. How long before she died?

ROLAND. A year.

BECKY. And how long were you and mother happy together?

ROLAND. A few months — not many.

BECKY. Tom and I have been blissfully happy for six years!

ROLAND. That's an argument for me! Go back!

BECKY. What a lot of lies you've always told me about yourself and mother — all my life! You always said you were an ideal couple and that it was sorrow over her death that made you what you are!

ROLAND. I was ashamed when you found me out — I wanted some excuse to try and keep your sympathy and affection. Besides, what good would it have done to have told you the truth?

[*He crosses to the table left, and taking up a photograph of his wife, stands looking at it.*]

BECKY. If you had always told me the truth about everything, I think it would have saved me this night. I've about decided that the truth in everything is the best for everything in the end — if one could only learn to tell it.

ROLAND. You must begin young and you did n't.

BECKY. By whose fault? [ROLAND *turns away from her, feeling the sting.*] Tell me now about you and mother.

[*She sits again in the Morris chair.*]

ROLAND [*by the center-table*]. Well, your mother accused me as you do Tom. But it was n't true of me, Becky! it was n't true — then.

BECKY. I 'm afraid I don't believe you, father.

ROLAND. You don't believe me when, even now, after all these years, I tell you it was n't true ?

BECKY. No. I want to believe you, father, but I can't ! You 've just admitted you 've lied to me all my life about you and mother ! Why should I believe you would suddenly turn around and tell me the truth now ?

ROLAND. At last, one trait in you like your mother ! Do all that I could, swear by everything she or I held holy, I could n't persuade her I was telling the truth !

BECKY. Perhaps you had already destroyed her confidence in you ! You can do that, even with some one who loves you, in a day, in an hour, in even less !

ROLAND. It did look ugly against me, and your mother was already disappointed in me. I could n't live up to her standard. [*He smiles.*] I was sort of good-looking, when she married me, — too foppish, perhaps, — and I rode my own horses, generally to win, too, — and what part of my income I did n't make on the race-track I made with the ace and right bower ! I promised your mother to give up the gambling side of it — but I could n't ; it was in my blood ; I tried, Becky, but I failed. I lied to her about it and she found me out and began to distrust me. She was a crank on the subject of lying, anyway. One of those straightforward, narrow-minded, New England women who think everything that is n't the truth is a lie ! I always hated the plain truth. I liked to trim it up a little.

BECKY [*with a nervous, pathetic little laugh*]. Like me !

ROLAND. Yes. I remember how we used to laugh at you as a child ! Almost the first words you spoke were fibs, and gad, the fairy stories you used to tell about yourself ! [*Goes up to table.*]

BECKY. Yes. Do you remember the time, father, after I 'd been reading Grimm's fairy tales about the wicked step-parents, how I told all over Baltimore you were my stepfather and beat me ? It made me a real heroine, to the other children, and I loved it ! And you found it out, and gave me my choice of being punished or promising never to tell another story ! Do you remember ?

ROLAND. [*Sits on the arm of the chair*

and puts his arm about her.] I could never bear to punish you !

BECKY. I always made up stories about everything. I did n't see any harm — then —

ROLAND. Well, your mother said I 'd proved I could n't tell the truth ! She did n't often use plain and ugly words, but she called me a liar, and I 've never heard the word since without hearing her voice and seeing her face as she said it !

BECKY. You loved her ! Oh, I know how it must have hurt !

ROLAND. She would n't believe me, she would n't forgive, and she left me ! I don't blame her ; it was my own fault at bottom. But it 's true as land and water, Becky, as true as you 're my daughter, God help you, and that I 've loved you in my useless, selfish old way, I *was true to your mother*. I loved her, and no other woman existed for me then. I was willing to own up I had broken my word and was a gambler ! I was willing to own up I was a liar, even, and perhaps I deserved all I got, but I loved your mother, and when she went back on me and believed the one thing about me that was n't true, I gritted my teeth like a damn fool and said, " To hell with women and to the dogs for me ! "

BECKY. And it was n't true ! Father ! I believe you, it was n't true !

ROLAND. No; but it was true enough soon after ! I kept my word to myself and gave her plenty of reasons not to love me afterwards — and that was the beginning of the end of me.

BECKY. But if you 'd only waited, if you 'd only given her a chance, would n't she have realized ?

ROLAND [*going to her, puts his hand on her shoulder*]. Yes, and that 's why you must go back to Tom to-night. Do you want to repeat your mother's and my story ? Go back, Becky !

BECKY. I can't.

ROLAND. Well, I can tell you what Tom 'll do if you put off going back to him till it 's too late. He 'll let you go, and help you to divorce him, so he can marry some other woman, your opposite, and be happy the rest of his life.

BECKY. Father !

[BECKY *shows a new element, jealousy, added to her trouble.*]

ROLAND. Or else he 'll grow hard and

bitter about all women, and the gold years of a man's life will be brass in his mouth — thanks to you!

BECKY. Yes, and I'll live here with you and grow dowdy and slattern, till I'm slovenly all through — body and soul! I won't care how I look or what company I keep in place of the friends who will surely drop me. I'll take up your life here, and my face'll grow flabby and my heart dry and my spirit fogged, and I'll have nobody to thank for the dead end but myself!

ROLAND. But I won't have it! You've got to go back to Tom to-night! You were happy enough with him this afternoon! He's been a wonderful husband to you and I know the run of them! I don't blame him for not wanting me around — a father-in-law who was a disgrace to his wife. He did right to keep me here where I'm an old story and nobody cares. I'll own up to this now that you want to turn your back on him. But you shan't do it! You shan't break up his home with a beastly scandal and spoil your whole life and perhaps his, all in one hysterical hour! Listen! [*He goes to her and places his two hands on her shoulders.*] It's true that no one was to blame for what I've sunk to but myself. Still, it's also true that in the beginning, perhaps, a great deal of patience, and more forgiveness, might have made both your mother's life and mine a little more worth living!

[*He turns aside, surprised by a welling up of an almost forgotten emotion.*]

BECKY. You don't dream how every word you say cuts and saws into me! But I can't go back!

ROLAND. You will. For if it comes down to this point, I won't keep you here!

BECKY. But I can't go to a hotel. I have n't any money.

ROLAND. I have enough for your ticket, and I'll take you to the station and send a telegram to Tom to expect you in the morning.

BECKY. No, I can't — I can't.

ROLAND [*sternly*]. You've *got to!* You can't stay here and I won't give you a cent to stay anywhere else!

BECKY. You would n't turn me out into the streets!

ROLAND. Yes, I will, if I must to force you to go back to your husband.

[*He gets her cloak.*]

BECKY. [*Rises, desperate.*] Father!

ROLAND [*struck by her tone, pauses*]. Well?

BECKY. [*Drops her head and with a great effort speaks, her voice sinking almost to a whisper.*] I have n't left Tom — it's Tom's left me —

[*A pause. ROLAND stands looking at her and her cloak drops from his hand, as he slowly takes in what she means.*]

ROLAND. What do you say?

BECKY. Tom has left me — now you know why I can't go back.

ROLAND. What for?

BECKY. He called me what mother called you. He's lost confidence in me. He believes — there's some one else.

[*The last in agony of shame and grief.*]

ROLAND. No wonder you made me worm out the truth! I would n't have believed it of you, Becky! I would n't have believed it of you!

BECKY [*frightened*]. But it is n't true, father!

ROLAND. Why did n't you tell me the right story in the beginning?

BECKY [*aghast*]. Father! Don't you believe me?

ROLAND. You denied it to him, I suppose?

BECKY. Of course.

ROLAND. And he turned you out all the same?

BECKY. He did n't turn me out; he only refused to stay in the house with me. I came away!

ROLAND. Well, if your husband does n't believe in you, how can you expect me to, who've known all your life you could n't tell the truth?

BECKY. Father, I've told you the truth now! For God's sake, believe me, for if *you* won't believe me either, what will become of me?

ROLAND. I can help you better if you'll be honest with me. A man like Tom Warder is n't putting the wife he's been a slave to out of his life without good reason.

[*He turns away from her.*]

BECKY. You said you knew the look in my face when I lied, because it was your look. [*Goes to him and stands close, facing him.*] Look in my face now and tell me what you see there. [*She speaks very simply and clearly.*] I love Tom and only Tom and never have loved any other man and have never been anything but faithful and true in my love for him. [ROLAND *stands silently looking into her face, still unconvinced.*] I stand with Tom exactly, father, where you stood the day mother left you —

[*His face begins to change. A knock on the door left.*]

MRS. CRESPIGNY [*outside*]. If Mis' Warder wants to catch that train, I hear the car coming!

BECKY [*breathlessly seizing hold of him with her two hands*]. Father!

ROLAND. Mrs. Warder's changed her mind. She's stopping here to-night.

[*Putting his arms about her.*]

BECKY. Father!

[*Her tension gives way, and she lies limp in his arms, her slender body shaking with the emotion which now masters her as the curtain falls.*]

ACT IV

MR. ROLAND'S *rooms in* MRS. CRESPIGNY'S *flat, the following Monday. The sun pours in through the bow-window; folded bedclothes and a pillow are placed neatly on one end of the sofa.* BECKY *and* ROLAND *are having coffee together at the center-table. The cloth is soiled, other things in the room are in disorder, and everything is decidedly unappetizing.* ROLAND *is wearing a slovenly bathrobe; a newspaper is propped against the coffee-pot before him.*

BECKY. How horrid and messy everything is!

ROLAND [*who is smoking a cigarette as he eats*]. Oh, you'll get used to it. Before you know it you'll like things best this way.

BECKY. Not if I can help it. I shall fight against it.

ROLAND. You think so now; you've only had one day at it.

BECKY. To begin with, my dear father, you mustn't come to breakfast with me in that disgusting bathrobe.

ROLAND. If you imagine for a minute I'm going to let you come here and upset everything to rob me of my comfort, you'll have your hands full.

[MRS. CRESPIGNY *is heard playing a piano in a farther room through most of the scene. Her repertoire is varied, and consists of an old waltz, a coon song, the "Melody in F," and "Waiting at the Church."*]

BECKY [*with an effort at a smile*]. It will be another fight then, father, such as we used to have. Only this time I'm stronger by six years' life with a splendid character, which will help me bring you and myself up to Tom's level, rather than go down with you to this.

ROLAND [*to change the subject*]. Have you written Tom?

BECKY [*sighing*]. A hundred letters, I should think.

ROLAND. And no answer?

BECKY. No, there isn't time.

ROLAND. Yes, he could telegraph.

BECKY. But I didn't send any of the letters.

ROLAND [*looking up from his newspaper*]. You aren't eating anything.

BECKY [*rising in disgust, goes and sits in Morris chair*]. Father, we can't live here, can we? You must tell Mrs. Crespigny, and I'll find a little flat, just for us two —

ROLAND [*irritably*]. I knew it would come to that! Not satisfied with upsetting Warder's existence and your own, you've got to come here and upset mine! No, sir! I'll marry Mrs. C. before I'll leave here.

BECKY. That's a threat I know you won't carry out. I've had two long, long nights to think things over. I wish I could die, but I know one can't die when one wants to. I know sorrow, however heartbreaking, doesn't kill, — and I'm so horribly healthy I'll probably live forever. I may even have to stand aside and see Tom happy with some one else. Well, all the same I mean to live exactly as I would if I were still with Tom. I'm going to live as if every day, every hour, I was expecting him back. I'm going to live so that if he ever should come back to me — I will be ready to go home with him.

[*The music stops for a moment.*]

ROLAND. That's all very well for you, but I don't see why I should have to live a life to please Tom — just so you can leave me in the lurch when he comes back after you. The odds are pretty strong against his wanting me to go home with him too! I've never ridden yet according to his rules, and I don't intend to begin now.

[*Goes to far table in the bow-window and takes a fresh cigarette and changes his paper for another.*]

BECKY [*rising, takes the bedclothes from the sofa*]. Don't forget, father, what little money we have is mine, so you'll have to live as I wish. And in the end I believe you'll thank me. [*She goes into the bedroom.*]

ROLAND. But in the beginning I'll damn you, and in the end, too! I'm too old a leopard to change my spots.

[*He makes himself comfortable in the Morris chair.*]

BECKY [*coming out of the bedroom*]. I'm going to try just as hard as I can not to tell even little lies, no matter how small, just to see if I can't get into the habit of always telling the truth. Because he might come back, father, don't you think so? Don't you think maybe he'll come back?

ROLAND. I'm doing my best to make him.

BECKY [*surprised and eager*]. How?

ROLAND. Never mind how. I'll tell you if it works.

BECKY [*piling the breakfast dishes on the tray*]. I hoped he'd answer the note I sent by Jenks, but he didn't. No; when Tom says a thing, he means it. I'm going out for a little while.

[*She places the tray on the table left.*]

ROLAND. Where?

BECKY. There's a small empty flat two doors below here; I'm going to look it over. I think it may do for us.

[*She goes into the bedroom.*]

ROLAND. Don't be gone long, because I might need you.

BECKY [*in the bedroom*]. For what?

ROLAND. To help receive Tom!

BECKY [*coming out quickly*]. Father!

ROLAND. Don't get your expectations too high, but I telegraphed him yesterday to come here.

[*The piano is heard again, but stops during BECKY's long speech.*]

BECKY. If he would n't come for me, he would n't come because you asked him.

ROLAND. I feel if only you could get face to face with him, Becky, especially now when he's had time to think things over, to realize calmly, away from the heat of anger, that whatever your faults might be —

BECKY. [*Interrupts eagerly, going toward him.*] Yes, yes —

ROLAND. Lack of love for him and faithlessness could n't be among them.

BECKY. Yes, if I could see him! [*She kneels on the floor beside him, her arms on the arm of the chair.*] I feel that if there's left in the bottom of his heart — no matter how deep down — just a little love for me, if it's only the memory of what he once had, would n't my own love be some sort of a magnet to bring him back? If I could sit and talk to him, hold his hand, go back over our life a little, make him see that I loved him — and only him, that what I'd done had been foolish — wrong not to do as he wished — but only *that* wrong — and that I've learned something by this terrible lesson? And if I promised to try with all my might and main not to lie any more, if I promised I would n't be discouraged with failure if he would n't be, but would keep on trying, would n't he on his side try to have a little confidence again? Would n't he let me come back into his life just for that trial anyway? . . .

ROLAND. I think so. A man like Warder can't get over loving a woman all in a moment, especially if he finds out before it's too late he's misjudged her. Wrong as you may have been, we know you're not so wrong as he thinks.

BECKY. But he won't come. You see you have n't heard from him — he won't come.

[*She goes up to the bow-window and looks out.*]

ROLAND. I'm a little worried myself. I told him to telegraph and said it was urgent.

BECKY. How — urgent?

ROLAND. Well, my dear, as you say, if I had simply said, "Come and see Becky," of course he would n't have paid any attention. I had to make the telegram so he would come.

BECKY. Yes, but how did you?

ROLAND. It was a stroke of genius! I said, "Becky is dying. Come at once!"

BECKY [*going to the sofa and sitting on it*]. But I'm not dying. He'll find out as soon as he gets here.

ROLAND. No, he must n't. My idea was that he would think you had tried to kill yourself — don't you see? It would rouse his sympathies — perhaps some remorse — and he would hurry on.

[*Dropping the paper carelessly on the floor, he rises.*]

BECKY. But he has n't!

ROLAND. He could n't get here till this morning; still, I ought to have had an answer to the telegram.

[*He goes into the bedroom.*]

BECKY. [*Rises and goes toward the opening.*] And if he should come?

ROLAND [*coming out of the bedroom in his shirt-sleeves, without the bathrobe*]. Well, you must be careful not to give me away till you are solid with him again. You must be weak and ill — just getting over it — the doctor's saved you! Anyway, I thought that might bring him.

BECKY. I don't like it.

ROLAND [*going back into the bedroom offended*]. I did my best!

BECKY. But it seems to me as if I would be telling Tom a lie again.

ROLAND. Not at all. I'm telling it. And besides, does n't the end justify the means?

BECKY. I think Tom 'd call it a lie. I don't want to do it!

ROLAND. Well, if he comes in answer to my telegram, you've *got* to do it!

BECKY. No, father, I won't!

ROLAND. Nonsense! You can't get out of it. And, good Heavens, why should you, if it 's going to give you back what you want and prevent a terrible upheaval?

[*The piano is heard again.*]

BECKY. Well, anyway, he has n't answered, so perhaps he won't come. I 'm going out.   [*Gets her hat from table left.*]

ROLAND. Don't be long in any case. He might have forgot to send word, or not have time, or even have suspected something and not answered purposely, and be coming all the same on this morning's train!

BECKY [*putting on her hat*]. I 'll see the flat and come straight back. [*She starts to go, stops and turns in the doorway.*] Thank you, father, for trying to help me. If he only *will* come!   [*She goes out left.*]

ROLAND [*lighting another cigarette*]. Move into another flat! To live with everything so filthy clean you can't be easy and let things go! Ta, ta to the bucket-shop, and never a cent to put on anything again! Nothing but cleanth and economy! No, no, Stephen Roland, not at your age. [*He stands gazing at a portrait of* MRS. CRESPIGNY *on the right wall, with a half-humorous expression of resignation, then crosses to the electric bell on the left wall.*] Listen, don't you hear wedding bells? [*He rings the bell.*] Do you hear them, Stephen! [*He rings again. The piano off stage stops.*] Wedding bells! [*He turns and walks toward the portrait again, nodding his head definitely. A knock on the door left.*] Come in — *Jennie!*

[MRS. CRESPIGNY *comes in.*]

MRS. CRESPIGNY. Did you ring?

ROLAND. I believe I did.

MRS. CRESPIGNY. What 's the matter? My piano-playing disturb Mis' Warder?

ROLAND. Oh — is the pianola mended?

MRS. CRESPIGNY. Yes. The man said I worked the pedals too emotionally.

ROLAND. I wanted to see you.

MRS. CRESPIGNY [*pulling her belt down and her marcel wave out*]. Well, I 'm visible!

ROLAND. Mrs. Crespigny, I 'm in trouble.

MRS. CRESPIGNY [*going to him*]. Now look here, Mr. Roland, true as Gospel I can't let you have another cent, not before the first of the month. Your daughter's here now; you 've got to go to her.

ROLAND. Not so fast, please! It is n't money. At least that is n't this moment's trouble. My daughter and her husband have quarreled.

MRS. CRESPIGNY. I suspected something was wrong. [*She starts, aghast and angry at a new idea which comes to her.*] She don't mean to come here and live?

ROLAND. No, she wants to take me away to live with her.

MRS. CRESPIGNY. Did n't I always tell you she'd separate us if she could! Now show your character! I guess you 're your own boss, ain't you? You won't go, Mr. Roland?

ROLAND. But you see if they don't make up their quarrel, my allowance stops and I won't have a cent. I 'll have to live where my daughter wants me.

MRS. CRESPIGNY [*taking from the bosom of her shirt-waist a second-hand natural rose with a wired stem and destitute of green leaves, she twists the wired part nervously about*]. Why ain't one woman's money just as good as another's for you to live on?

ROLAND. Mrs. Crespigny, you 've come straight to the point, and you 've come pretty bluntly, but that 's just as well in view of the poor figure I cut in the matter.

[*He turns up toward the center-table and places on it his newspaper, which he has picked up from the floor.*]

MRS. CRESPIGNY. Why, I think, con-sidering your age, your figger's great!

ROLAND [*looking at her despairingly*]. I spoke figuratively! Now I'm doing my best to bring about a reconciliation. Of course, if I succeed, I can keep on living here just as usual — I'll have my allowance.

MRS. CRESPIGNY. But if you don't bring about the reconciliation? . . .

ROLAND. Well, in that case, frankly, I should have to leave you or marry you!

MRS. CRESPIGNY [*going to the table*]. Look here, Mr. Roland, I want this in black and white! Are you proposing to me?

ROLAND. Well, Mrs. Crespigny, in a way —

MRS. CRESPIGNY. But there's a string to it?

ROLAND. You know you have once or twice delicately suggested that a marriage would n't be altogether disagreeable to you, but it's a poor bargain for you, and in case the proposal should ever be definitely made, I want to be sure you know what you're getting!

MRS. CRESPIGNY. I guess I know well enough. I ain't lived in the same flat with you for four solid years without finding out whether or not you was worth it *to me*. I know your faults, Mr. Roland, but they 're swell faults.

ROLAND. [*He goes to the table in the window to get a cigarette.*] Mrs. Crespigny, suppose you keep to the point, which is, if I marry — if you marry me, you do it with your eyes open. I'm to have all the liberty I've ever had. None of my habits are to be interfered with, none of my ways of spending money.

MRS. CRESPIGNY. All right. I know I won't be marrying a hero, but I'll be getting a high-toned name and the company I want for keeps, for if once we 're married, your daughter nor nobody else won't sneak you away from me, and you can't get nothing in this world for nothing.

[*She sits right of the table with a lugubrious expression on her poor powdered face.*]

ROLAND. Very well, then [*coming down to her*], if there 's no reconciliation to-day, we 'll consider it settled without another word.

MRS. CRESPIGNY. And if she does make it up with her husband?

ROLAND. We 'll let that stand for the present. I would still have my allowance and I would n't have to leave the flat.

MRS. CRESPIGNY. Then, so far as I'm concerned, — and I don't make no bones about saying it, — I'd rather they kep' separate.

ROLAND. Don't be selfish! I think you 'll win without that. [*He lifts her head tenderly, smiling sweetly; then, as he turns away from her, the sweetness fades, and he looks at least twenty years older.* MRS. CRESPIGNY, *happy but embarrassed, tears the faded rose to pieces petal by petal.*] I don't understand it. I ought to have had a telegram long ago!

MRS. CRESPIGNY. [*Starts and rises.*] A telegram! My stars! This telegram came before you was up and I forgot all about it.
[*Giving him a telegram.*]

ROLAND. That won't do! You 'll have to be more thoughtful than that! [*Reading the telegram.*] He's coming! He 's due here any minute! And Beck out! Quick! help me make this look like a sick-room.

MRS. CRESPIGNY. A sick-room?

ROLAND. I 'll put this chair here for Becky to sit in!
[*Moving the Morris chair near to the table.*]

MRS. CRESPIGNY. And I 'll put a towel on the table. [*Getting one from the bedroom.*] But why a sick-room, Mr. Roland. Who 's sick?

ROLAND. That 's how I got him here. Telegraphed Becky was dying — and it 's worked — he 's coming!

MRS. CRESPIGNY. You ought to have some bottles for medicine!

ROLAND. Bottles? Here 's a couple!
[*Getting a whiskey bottle and a brandy bottle from the sideboard.*]

MRS. CRESPIGNY [*taking the bottles from him*]. You don't want him to think she 's been on a spree, do you? [*She puts them on the table left.*] Put a glass of water on the table. [*He gets a glass from the sideboard.*] And I 'll put this saucer and spoon on top — that 'll look like homœopathic stuff. [*She places a saucer on the table and breathes on the spoon and polishes it on a corner of table-cloth.* ROLAND *gets a pillow and a blanket from the bedroom and arranges them in the Morris chair.*] Do you know what we ought to have on that table? An orange on a plate! I don't know why it is, but it always looks like sick folks, having an orange on a plate by 'em ! Wait a minute. I've got a marble orange just like real. I'll get it. I'll take the tray. [MRS. CRESPIGNY *with the tray at the door left.*] Josephine ! Josephine ! Oh, never mind if your hands are in the suds ! [ROLAND *gets a hassock, which he places in front of the Morris chair. He pulls down the window shades, takes the siphon, and fills the glass on the table, putting the saucer and spoon on top of it. MRS. CRESPIGNY enters with an imitation orange on a plate.*] Here it is ! And I brought a knife with it — don't it look natural ?

[*The front bell rings.*]

ROLAND. Becky !

MRS. CRESPIGNY. No — I let her take the key !

ROLAND. Maybe it's he ! And Becky not back ! Don't let Josephine open the door yet !

MRS. CRESPIGNY. [*Opens the left door and calls.*] Josephine ! Josy ! I'll tend door ; you go on with your washing !

[*She shuts the door.*]

ROLAND. Show him here —

MRS. CRESPIGNY. Huh, huh ?

ROLAND. And I'll tell him the doctor's with Becky —

MRS. CRESPIGNY. Huh, huh ?

ROLAND. Then you watch for her, and when she comes, knock on the door and tell me the doctor's gone —

MRS. CRESPIGNY [*doubtfully*]. Huh, huh —

ROLAND. Then I'll go "to find out if she feels able to see him," and bring her in as if from her bedroom.

[*He goes to the Morris chair and arranges the pillow and blanket.*]

MRS. CRESPIGNY. It's lucky I don't have to tell him all that ! You know, I have n't got your — *imagination !*

ROLAND. That's all right — you'll see, — they'll be reconciled !

[*Gets a fan from behind the book-rack on the back wall and puts it on the table.*]

MRS. CRESPIGNY. Reconciled !

ROLAND. Yes, yes, they'll be reconciled !

MRS. CRESPIGNY. *Our* marriage is as good as off, then !

ROLAND. Yes, yes — I mean we'll see ! [*The front bell rings again.*] Don't keep him waiting — he might get suspicious !

MRS. CRESPIGNY [*turning the matter over in her mind, speaks very abstractedly*]. Our marriage is as good as off, then !

[*She goes out slowly, weighing this sudden complication in her affairs.*]

ROLAND. Well, you never know your luck ! No, no, don't close the door ! I'll be here, expecting him.

MRS. CRESPIGNY [*off stage*]. How do you do ? Won't you come right in ?

[WARDER *enters.*]

ROLAND. So you 've come, Tom ?

WARDER [*very serious*]. How is she, father ?

ROLAND. The doctor is with her now. Mrs. Crespigny will let me know when he's gone. I have n't let her know I telegraphed you.

WARDER. But will she get well ? Is she no worse ?

ROLAND. We have every hope of her getting well.

WARDER. [*He turns aside to control a sudden flood of emotion.*] Thank God !

ROLAND. I think a good deal now depends upon you. [WARDER *faces* ROLAND. ROLAND *goes to him.*] Are you ready to take my daughter back ?

WARDER [*very quietly, soberly*]. Yes.

ROLAND. For good ?

WARDER. If I can only feel sure Becky will try — only *try* — to be straightforward and honest with me, that's all I ask. God knows what I've suffered these two days, and when your message came — it would, to have that on my shoulders too — it would have been more than a man could bear !

ROLAND. Whatever Becky's faults may have been, you did her one terrible injustice !

WARDER. Yes, I know that now ! Becky — never ! Father, hour after hour since the one in which I left her, I've paced up and down my room, or sat and gritted my teeth in the train, and thought — and thought — and *thought* — till the anger died out of me and I began to see things white and clear both ahead and behind me. And all the time Becky's final words kept ringing in my ears, and they rang *true:* "I love you, and only you, and you always." . . . And the further away from the excitement and anger I got, the saner I grew. And as I passed over our life together, second by second of happiness, I found only proof after proof of her love for me! Yes, I did Becky one great injustice, and I want to ask her to forgive me.

ROLAND [*his better self moved. Takes* TOM's *hand*]. Tom —

WARDER. After all, life is made up of compromises and concessions, and if Becky will only try, and let me help her —

ROLAND. I believe you love her still?

WARDER. I can only answer you by saying that I want more than anything else in the world to believe in her again — to have at least the beginning of confidence.

[*With a knock on the door,* MRS. CRESPIGNY *comes in, frightened at what she is going to do.* ROLAND *hesitates one moment, but his old habit soon reasserts itself.*]

ROLAND. The doctor gone? [MRS. CRESPIGNY *nods her head.*] Excuse me.

[*He hurries out left.* MRS. CRESPIGNY *stands looking after* ROLAND, *evidently trying to nerve herself up to the task of telling* WARDER *the truth. She makes several ineffectual gasping efforts to speak, and finally gets started, rushing her words and not daring to speak slowly for fear she'd stop.*]

MRS. CRESPIGNY. I'm going to do something awful, and I only hope I won't be punished for it all the rest of my life. Lord knows, seems as if I'd been punished enough in advance. Can I trust you?

WARDER. In what way?

MRS. CRESPIGNY. As a gentleman. If I tell you something — something that you ought to know — will you promise to see it through and not let on I told you?

WARDER. I don't know if I can promise that. Is it anything you have a right to tell me?

MRS. CRESPIGNY [*going toward him*]. It won't do you no harm to pertect me, and I give you my sacred word of honor it's the truth instead of the lie you've been told! And all I ask is that you'll pertect me as regards Mr. Roland.

WARDER [*astounded, bewildered, but his suspicions rearoused*]. What lie? Go on. I give you the promise!

MRS. CRESPIGNY. [*Whispers.*] She ain't sick!

WARDER. Who?

MRS. CRESPIGNY. Mis' Warder! She ain't been sick — that was all a story to get you here!

WARDER [*catching her two hands by the wrists and holding them tight, so she can't get away from him*]. No! Don't say that!

MRS. CRESPIGNY. Ssh! I will say it! It's true! The doctor was n't here when you came! Mis' Warder was out and only came in when I knocked on the door just now!

WARDER. Do you realize what you're saying?

MRS. CRESPIGNY. Perfeckly!

WARDER. And you're telling me the truth?

MRS. CRESPIGNY. Keep your eyes open and judge for yourself, that's all! Maybe you think *that's* the truth!

[*Snatching up the imitation orange from the table, she smashes it on the floor.* WARDER *moves to go; she stands in front of the door to stop him.*]

WARDER. Let me go! I won't stay for this brutal farce!

MRS. CRESPIGNY. You promised to pertect me, and if you go now Mr. Roland 'll catch on, and I want him to marry me! Now you know —

WARDER. Was this his idea or hers?

MRS. CRESPIGNY. His, and she —

[*Listens.*]

WARDER [*eagerly*]. She what —

MRS. CRESPIGNY [*moving away from the door*]. Ssh! they're here!

[WARDER *controls himself and goes to the other side of the room.* ROLAND *comes, bringing* BECKY, *who leans on him. Her eyes are down.* WARDER *stands immovable and watches.*]

ROLAND [*pointedly*]. Thank you, Mrs. Crespigny.

[*She goes out unwillingly.* BECKY *looks up and sees* WARDER. *He stands motionless, watching her.*]

BECKY [*as she meets* WARDER's *eyes, breaks away from* ROLAND]. No, father! I can't do it! I won't do it!

ROLAND [*frightened*]. Becky!

BECKY. No! I tell you it's only another lie and a revolting one!

ROLAND. You're ill! You don't know what you're saying!

BECKY. No, I'm not ill, and you know it, and I have n't been! And if I can't win his love back by the truth, I'll never be able to keep it, so what's the use of getting it back at all?

[*The tears fill her eyes and her throat.*]

WARDER. Becky!

[*He wants to go to her, but still holds himself back. His face shows his joy, but neither* BECKY *nor* ROLAND *see this.*]

BECKY [*continuing after a moment, pathetically*]. I thought I might creep back, through pity, first into your life, and then into your heart again. But, after all, I can't do it. [*She sits in the Morris chair, hopelessly.*] Something's happened to me in these two days — even if I tell lies, I've learned to loathe them and be afraid of them, and all the rest of my life I'll try —

WARDER [*in a choked voice*]. Thank God!

[*He goes to her, almost in tears himself.* ROLAND *looks at* WARDER, *and realizes what it means; a smile comes over his own face, and at the same time his eyes fill with his almost-forgotten tears.*]

BECKY. You can't forgive me!

WARDER. We don't love people because they are perfect.

[*He takes her two trembling hands in his, and she rises.*]

BECKY. Tom!

WARDER. We love them because they are themselves.

[*And he takes her in his arms close to him, as the final curtain falls.*]

THE GREAT DIVIDE

A PLAY IN THREE ACTS

By WILLIAM VAUGHN MOODY

TO

HENRY MILLER

IN GRATITUDE AND FRIENDSHIP

PERSONS OF THE PLAY

PHILIP JORDAN

POLLY JORDAN, *Philip's wife*

MRS. JORDAN, *his mother*

RUTH JORDAN, *his sister*

WINTHROP NEWBURY

DR. NEWBURY, *Winthrop's father*

STEPHEN GHENT

LON ANDERSON

BURT WILLIAMS

DUTCH

A MEXICAN

A CONTRACTOR

AN ARCHITECT

A BOY

THE GREAT DIVIDE

ACT I

Interior of PHILIP JORDAN'S *cabin in southern Arizona, on a late afternoon in spring. A large room rudely built, adorned with blankets, pottery, weapons, and sacred images of the local Indian tribes, and hung with trophies of the chase, together with hunting-knives, saddles, bridles, nosebags for horses, lariats, and other paraphernalia of frontier life. Through a long, low window at the back the desert is seen, intensely colored, and covered with the uncouth shapes of giant cacti, dotted with bunches of gorgeous bloom. The entrance door is on the left (from the spectator's standpoint), in a projecting elbow of the room; farther to the left is a door leading to the sleeping-quarters. On the right is a cook-stove, a cupboard for dishes and household utensils, and a chimney-piece, over which hangs a bleached cow's skull supporting a rifle.*

At a rude table in the center sits PHILIP JORDAN, *a man of thirty-four, mending a bridle.* POLLY, *his wife, kneels before an open trunk, assisted in her packing by* WINTHROP NEWBURY, *a recent graduate of an Eastern medical college.* RUTH JORDAN, PHILIP'S *sister, a girl of nineteen, stands at the window looking out.*

WINTHROP [*as he hands the last articles to* POLLY]. What on earth possessed you to bring such a load of duds to Arizona?

POLLY. They promised me a good time, meaning one small shindig — one — in the three months I've spent in this unholy place.

[PHILIP *makes an impatient movement with the bridle; speaks gruffly.*]

PHILIP. You'd better hurry. It's getting late.

RUTH [*from the window*]. It's getting cooler, which is more to the point. We can make the railroad easily by sunrise, with this delicious breeze blowing.

POLLY. [*Gives the finishing touches to the trunk and locks the lid.*] There, at last! Heaven help the contents.

PHILIP [*gruffly, as he rises*]. Give me a lift with the trunk, Win.

[*They carry the trunk outside.* POLLY, *with the aid of a cracked mirror, puts on her traveling-hat and cloak.*]

RUTH. My, Pollikins! You'll be the talk of all the jackrabbits and sage hens between here and the railroad.

POLLY. Phil is furious at me for going, and it *is* rather mean to sneak off for a visit in a grand house in San Francisco, when you poor dears have to slave on here. But really, I can't endure this life a day longer.

RUTH. It isn't in nature that you should. Fancy *that* [*she indicates* POLLY *with a grandiose gesture*] nourishing itself on salt pork, chickory beans, and air-tight!

POLLY. Do you really mean to say that apart from your pride in helping your brother, making the project go, and saving the family fortunes, you really *enjoy* yourself here?

RUTH. Since Phil and I came out, one day has been more radiantly exciting than the other. I don't know what's the matter with me. I think I shall be punished for being so happy.

POLLY. Punished for being happy! There's your simonpure New Englander.

RUTH. True! I was discovered at the age of seven in the garret perusing *The Twelve Pillars and Four Cornerstones of a Godly Life.*

POLLY [*pointing at* RUTH'S *heart, speaks with mock solemnity*]. If Massachusetts and Arizona ever get in a mixup in there, woe be! — Are you ever going to have that coffee done?

RUTH. I hope soon, before you get me analyzed out of existence.

POLLY [*as* RUTH *busies herself at the stove*]. The main point is this, my dear, and you'd better listen to what the old lady is a-tellin' of ye. Happiness is its own justification, and it's the sacreder the more unreasonable it is. It comes or it does n't, that's all you can say about it. And when it comes, one has the sense to grasp it or one hasn't. There you have the Law and the Prophets.

[WINTHROP *and* PHILIP *enter from*

outside. RUTH, *who has set out the coffee and sandwiches on the table, bows elaborately, with napkin over arm.*]

RUTH. *Messieurs et Mesdames!*

WINTHROP. Coffee! Well, rather, with an all-night ride in the desert ahead of us. [*They drink their coffee,* PHILIP *standing sullenly apart.*] Where do we get our next feed?

RUTH. With luck, at Cottonwood Wash.

WINTHROP. And how far may Cottonwood Wash be?

RUTH. Thirty miles.

WINTHROP [*sarcastically*]. Local measurement?

POLLY [*poking* PHILIP]. Phil, for Heaven's sake, say something. You diffuse the gloom of the Pit.

PHILIP. I've had my say out, and it makes absolutely no impression on you.

POLLY. It's the impression on the public I'm anxious about.

PHILIP. The public will have to excuse me.

POLLY. I *am* horribly sorry for you two poor dears, left alone in this dreadful place. When Dr. Newbury goes, I don't see how you'll support life. I should like to know how long this sojourn in the wilderness is going to last, anyhow. [*During the following,* RUTH *takes a candle from the shelf, lights it, and brings it to the table. The sunset glow has begun to fade.*]

RUTH. Till Cactus Fiber makes our eternal fortune.

WINTHROP. And how long will that be?

RUTH [*Counts on her fingers.*] Two years to pay back the money we raised on mother's estate, two years of invested profits, two years of hard luck and marking time, two years of booming prosperity. Say eight years!

POLLY. Shades of the tomb! How long do you expect to live?

RUTH. Forever! [*The sound of a galloping horse is heard, muffled by the sand.*]

WINTHROP. Listen. What's that? [*A boy of fifteen, panting from his rapid ride, appears at the open door.*]

PHILIP [*rising and going toward the door*]. What's the matter?

BOY. I've come for the doctor.

PHILIP. Who wants the doctor?

BOY. Your man Sawyer, over to Lone Tree. — He's broke his leg.

RUTH. Broken his leg! Sawyer? Our foreman?

PHILIP. There's a nice piece of luck! — How did it happen?

BOY. They was doin' some Navajo stunts on horseback, pullin' chickens out of the sand at a gallop and takin' a hurdle on the upswing. Sawyer's horse renigged, and lunged off ag'in' a 'dobe wall. Smashed his leg all to thunder. [WINTHROP *looks vaguely about for his kit and traveling necessaries, while* POLLY *gives the boy food, which he accepts shyly as he goes outside with* PHILIP. RUTH *has snatched saddle and bridle from their peg.*]

RUTH. I'll have Buckskin saddled for you in a jiffy. How long will it take you to set the leg?

WINTHROP. Perhaps an hour, perhaps three.

RUTH. It's a big détour, but you can catch us at Cottonwood Wash by sunrise, allowing three hours for Sawyer. Buckskin has done it before. [*She goes out.*]

POLLY [*pouting*]. This will spoil all our fun! Why can't the creature wait till you get back?

WINTHROP Did you ever have a broken leg?

POLLY. Well, no, not exactly a leg. But I've had a broken heart! In fact, I've got one now, if you're not going with us.

WINTHROP. To tell you the truth, mine is broken too. [*Pause.*] Did you ever dream of climbing a long hill, and having to turn back before you saw what was on the other side? [POLLY *nods enthusiastically.*] I feel as if I'd had my chance to-night to see what was over there, and lost it.

POLLY. You'll excuse me if it sounds personal, Dr. Newbury, but did you expect to discern a — sort of central figure in the outrolled landscape?

WINTHROP [*embarrassed, repenting of his sentimental outburst*]. No. That is —

POLLY [*with a sweep of her arm*]. Oh, I see. Just scenery! [*She laughs and goes into the inner room, left.* RUTH *reënters. The sky has partly faded and a great full moon begins to rise.*]

RUTH. Buckskin is ready, and so is the moon. The boy knows the trails like an Indian. He will bring you through to Cottonwood by daylight.

WINTHROP [*taking heart*]. We shall have the ride back together, at any rate.

RUTH. Yes. — I would go with you, and try to do something to make poor Sawyer comfortable, but we have n't another horse that can do the distance. [*She holds out her hand.*] Good-bye.

WINTHROP [*detaining her hand*]. Won't you make it up to me?

[*He draws her toward him.*]

RUTH [*gently but firmly*]. No Win. Please not.

WINTHROP. Never?

RUTH. Life is so good just as it is! Let us not change it.

[*He drops her hand, and goes out, without looking back. POLLY reënters. The women wave WINTHROP good-bye.*]

POLLY. [*Takes RUTH by the shoulders and looks at her severely.*] Conscience clear?

RUTH [*humoring her*]. Crystal!

POLLY. [*Counts on her fingers.*] Promising young physician, charming girl, lonely ranch, horseback excursions, spring of the year!

RUTH. Not guilty.

POLLY. Gracious! Then it's not play, it's earnest.

RUTH. Neither the one nor the other. It's just your little blonde romantic noddle.

[*She takes POLLY's head between her hands and shakes it as if to show its emptiness.*]

Do you think if I wanted to flirt, I would select a youth I've played hookey with, and seen his mother spank? [*Suddenly sobered.*] Poor dear Win! He's so good, so gentle and chivalrous. But — [*with a movement of lifted arms, as if for air*] — ah, me, he's — finished! I want one that is n't finished!

POLLY. Are you out of your head, you poor thing?

RUTH. You know what I mean well enough. Winthrop is all rounded off, a completed product. But the man I sometimes see in my dreams is — [*pausing for a simile*] — well, like this country out here, don't you know — ?

[*She breaks off, searching for words,*

and makes a vague outline in the air, to indicate bigness and incompletion.]

POLLY [*dryly*]. Yes, thank you. I do know. Heaven send you joy of him!

RUTH. Heaven won't, because, alas, he does n't exist! I am talking of a sublime abstraction — of the glorious unfulfilled — of the West — the Desert.

POLLY. [*Lifts RUTH's chin, severely.*] We have n't by chance, some spring morning, riding over to the trading-station or elsewhere — just by the merest chance beheld a sublime abstraction — say in blue overalls and jumper? [*Ruth shakes her head.*] Honest?

[*More emphatic head-shaking. POLLY drops RUTH's chin with a shrug of the shoulders. PHILIP enters.*]

RUTH [*putting on her riding-hat*]. Is Pinto saddled?

PHILIP. Pinto is gone.

RUTH [*astonished*]. Gone where?

PHILIP. To that Mexican blow-out over at Lone Tree. Every man-jack on the ranch has disappeared, without leave asked or notice given, except this paper which I just found nailed to the factory door.

[*RUTH takes the note and reads it anxiously. Then she slowly removes her hat and lays it away.*]

What are you up to now? We've no time to lose!

RUTH [*with quiet determination*]. I am not going.

POLLY [*as PHILIP turns in surprise*]. Not going?

RUTH. I must stay and look after the ranch.

PHILIP. Oh, come, that's out of the question!

RUTH. We have put all mother's money into this venture. We can't take any risks.

PHILIP. The men will be back to-morrow. It's not to be thought of — your staying here all alone.

POLLY. [*Seats herself with decision.*] One thing is certain : either Ruth goes or I stay.

PHILIP. [*Takes off his hat and sets down the provision basket.*] That suits me perfectly!

POLLY [*hysterical*]. But I can't stay! I won't stay! I shall go mad if I spend another night in this place.

RUTH. No, you must n't stay. You would

never get us worked up to the point of letting you go, another time.

[*She lifts* POLLY, *and with arm around her waist leads her to the door.*]

PHILIP. I refuse to leave you here alone, just to satisfy a whim of Polly's. That's flat!

RUTH. But, Phil, you forget the stores you're to fetch back. They will be dumped out there on the naked sand, and by to-morrow night —

[*She blows across her palm, as if scattering thistledown.*]

PHILIP. Well, what of it? A few hundred dollars' worth of stuff!

RUTH. A few hundred dollars means sink or swim with us just now. — Besides, there's poor Sawyer. He'll be brought back here to-morrow, and nobody to nurse him. Then inflammation, fever, and good-bye Sawyer.

[PHILIP, *with a gesture of accepting the inevitable, picks up the grain-sacks and basket.*]

POLLY [*at the door, embracing* RUTH]. Good-bye, dear. Are n't you really afraid to stay?

RUTH. I'm awfully sorry to miss the fun, but as for danger, the great Arizona Desert is safer than Beacon Hill.

POLLY. You're sure?

RUTH. If marauders prowl, I'll just fire the blunderbuss out the window, and they won't stop running this side of the Great Divide.

POLLY [*kissing her*]. Good-bye, dear.

RUTH. Good-bye. [POLLY *goes out.*]

PHILIP [*pausing beside* RUTH, *at the door*]. Mind you put out the light early. It can be seen from the Goodwater Trail. There's no telling what riff-raff will be straggling back that way after the dance.

RUTH. Riff-raff! They're my sworn knights and brothers.

PHILIP. In that case, what makes you uneasy about the property?

RUTH. Oh, property! That's different.

PHILIP. Well, you mind what I say and put out the light.

RUTH. Yours for prudence!

[*She puts her arm around his waist and draws him to her, kissing him tenderly.*]

Good-bye, Phil.

[*He kisses her and starts to go. She still detains him. When she speaks*

again, her voice is softened and awed.]

What a lovely night! Who would ever think to call this a desert, this moonlit ocean of flowers? What millions of cactus blooms have opened since yesterday!

PHILIP [*looking at her dubiously*]. What's the matter with you to-night?

RUTH. Nothing. Everything. Life! — I don't know what's got into me of late. I'm just drunk with happiness the whole time.

PHILIP. Well, you're a queer one. — Good-bye. I shall get back as soon as horse-flesh will do it. [*He goes out.*]

RUTH [*as the rumble of the wagon is heard*]. Good-bye! Good-bye, Pollikins! Good-bye!

[*She takes the candle from the table and stands in the door for a time, then raises the light in one hand and waves her handkerchief with the other. She sets the candle again on the table, goes to the mantel-shelf, and takes down a photograph.*]

Dear Win! I forgot how disappointed *you* were going to be.

[*Pause, during which she still gazes at the picture.*]

Clear, kind heart!

[*After a moment she replaces it brusquely on the mantel-shelf, and raises her arms above her head with a deep breath. She stands thus, with arms crossed behind her head, looking at the photograph. Her gaze becomes amused and mischievous; she points her finger at the picture and whispers mockingly.*]

Finished! Finished!

[*She begins to prepare for bed, taking down her hair, and re-coiling it loosely during the following. She hums a tune vaguely and in snatches, then with a stronger rhythm; at last she sings.*]

Heart, wild heart,
Brooding apart,
Why dost thou doubt, and why art thou sullen?
Flower and bird
Wait but thy word —

[*She breaks off, picks up a photograph from the table, and looks at it for a moment in silence.*]

Poor little mother! You look out at me with such patient, anxious eyes. There are better days coming for you, and it's troublesome me that's bringing them. Only you trust me!

[*A man's face appears at the edge of the window, gazing stealthily in. As* RUTH *turns, he disappears. She lays down the picture and sings again.*]

This is the hour,
And thine is the power.
Heart, high heart, be brave to begin it.
Dare you refuse?
Think what we lose!
Think what we gain —

[*The words grow indistinct as she takes up the candle and passes into the other room, from which her voice sounds from time to time in interrupted song. The man again appears, shading his face with a peaked Mexican hat so as to see into the darkened room. He turns and waves his hand as if signaling distant persons to approach, then enters through the open door. He looks cautiously about the room, tiptoes to the inner door and listens, then steals softly out, and is seen again at the window, beckoning.* RUTH *reënters, carrying the candle. She is shod in moccasins, and clad in a loose, dark sleeping-dress, belted at the waist, with wide, hanging sleeves and open throat. As she crosses to the table she sings.*]

Heart which the cold
Long did enfold —
Hark, from the dark eaves the night thaw drummeth!
Now as a god,
Speak to the sod,
Cry to the sky that the miracle cometh!

[*She passes her hand over a great bunch of wild flowers on the table.*]

Be still, you beauties! You'll drive me to distraction with your color and your odor. I'll take a hostage for your good behavior.

[*She selects a red flower, puts it in the dark mass of her hair, and looks out at the open door.*]

What a scandal the moon is making, out there in that great crazy world! Who but me could think of sleeping on such a night?

[*She sits down, folds the flowers in her arms, and buries her face in them. After a moment she starts up, listens, goes hurriedly to the door, and peers out. She then shuts and bolts*

the door, draws the curtains before the window, comes swiftly to the table, and blows out the light. The room is left in total darkness. There are muttering voices outside, the latch is tried, then a heavy lunge breaks the bolt. A man pushes in, but is hurled back by a taller man, with a snarling oath. A third figure advances to the table, and strikes a match. As soon as the match is lighted* RUTH *levels the gun, which she has taken from its rack above the mantel. There is heard the click of the hammer, as the gun misses fire. It is instantly struck from her hand by the first man (*DUTCH*), who attempts to seize her. She evades him, and tries to wrest a pistol from a holster on the wall. She is met by the second man (*SHORTY*), who frustrates the attempt, pocketing the weapon. While this has been going on the third man (*GHENT*) has been fumbling with the lamp, which he has at last succeeded in lighting. All three are dressed in rude frontier fashion; the one called* SHORTY *is a Mexican half-breed, the others are Americans.* GHENT *is younger than* DUTCH, *and taller, but less powerfully built. All are intoxicated, but not sufficiently so to incapacitate them from rapid action. The* MEXICAN *has seized* RUTH *and attempts to drag her toward the inner room. She breaks loose, and flies back again to the chimney-place, where she stands at bay.* GHENT *remains motionless and silent by the table, gazing at her.*]

DUTCH [*uncorking a whiskey flask*]. Plucky little catamount. I drink its health.
[*Drinks.*]

RUTH. What do you want here?

DUTCH. [*Laughs, with sinister relish.*] Did you hear that, Steve?

[*He drinks again, and reaches out the flask to* RUTH.]

Take one, and pull in its purty little claws, eh? Jolly time. No more fuss and fury.

[RUTH *reaches for a knife, hidden behind the elbow of the chimney.* DUTCH *wrests the knife from her and seizes her in his arms.*]

Peppery little devil!

[*With desperate strength she breaks*

from his clutch and reels from him in sickness of horror. GHENT remains gazing at her in a fascinated semi-stupor. Meanwhile, after closing the door, the MEXICAN has taken dice from his pocket, and, throwing them into a small vase on the table, shakes them and holds out the vase to DUTCH. He takes it and turns to GHENT; the latter has moved a step or two toward RUTH, who in her retreat has reached the chimney-piece and stands at bay.]

DUTCH. Come, get into the game, curse you, Steve! This is going to be a free-for-all, by God!

[As he rattles the dice, RUTH makes a supplicating gesture to GHENT.]

RUTH. Save me! save me!

[Her gesture is frozen by his advancing toward her. She looks wildly about, shrinking from him, then with sudden desperate resolution speaks.]

Save me, and I will make it up to you!

[GHENT again advances; she goes on pantingly, as she stands at bay.]

Don't touch me! Listen! Save me from these others, and from yourself, and I will pay you — with my life.

GHENT *[with dull wonder]*. With — your life?

RUTH. With all that I am or can be.

GHENT. What do you mean? — *[Pause.]* You mean you'll go along with me out of this? Stick to me — on the square?

RUTH *[in a tragic whisper]*. Yes.

GHENT. On the dead square?

RUTH. Yes.

GHENT. You won't peach, and spoil it?

RUTH. No.

[Pause, during which he looks at her fixedly.]

GHENT. Give me your hand on it!

[She gives him her hand. The other men, at the table, have drawn their weapons, and hold them carelessly, but alert to the slightest suspicious movement on the part of GHENT.]

DUTCH *[as GHENT turns to them]*. Shorty and me 's sittin' in this game, and interested, eh, Shorty?

[The MEXICAN nods. GHENT comes slowly to the table, eyeing the two. DUTCH holds out the vase containing the dice.]

Shake for her!

GHENT. Shake how?

DUTCH. Any damn way! Sole and exclusive rights. License to love and cherish on the premises!

[GHENT takes the vase, shakes the dice meditatively, is about to throw, then sets the vase down. He searches through his pockets and produces a few bills and a handful of silver, which he lays on the table.]

GHENT. There's all I've got in my clothes. Take it, and give me a free field, will you?

DUTCH *[leaning over the table to GHENT in plaintive remonstrance]*. You don't mean me, Steve!

GHENT. *[To the MEXICAN.]* Well, you, then!

[The MEXICAN spreads the money carelessly with his left hand to ascertain its amount, then thrusts it away with a disgusted grunt of refusal.]

DUTCH. Don't blame you, Shorty! A ornery buck of a dirt-eatin' Mojave 'd pay more 'n that for his squaw.

[RUTH covers her face shudderingly. GHENT stands pondering, watching the two men under his brows, and slowly gathering up the money. As if on a sudden thought, he opens his shirt, and unwinds from his neck a string of gold nuggets in the rough, strung on a leather thread.]

GHENT. Well, it ain't much, that's sure. But there's a string of gold nuggets I guess is worth some money. *[He throws it on the table, speaking to both men.]* Take that, and clear out.

DUTCH. *[Draws up angrily.]* I've give you fair warning!

GHENT. We'll keep everything friendly between me and you. A square stand-up shoot, and the best man takes her.

DUTCH *[mollified]*. Now you're comin' to!

GHENT. *[To the MEXICAN.]* Then it's up to you, and you'd better answer quick!

THE MEXICAN *[eyeing GHENT and RUTH, points to the gun lying on the floor]*. I take him, too.

GHENT. No, you don't. You leave everything here the way you found it.

THE MEXICAN. Alla right.

[He pockets the chain and starts for the door.]

GHENT. Hold on a minute. You've got to promise to tie the man who falls, on

his horse, and take him to Mesa Grande.
Bargain?   [*The* MEXICAN *nods.*]
And mouth shut, mind you, or —
    [*He makes a sign across his throat.*]
THE MEXICAN. [*Nods.*] Alla right.
                          [*He goes out.*]
GHENT [*motioning toward the door*]. Out-
side.
DUTCH [*surprised*]. What for?
GHENT [*sternly*]. Outside!
    [*They move toward the door.* DUTCH
    stops and waves his hand to RUTH.]
DUTCH. Don't worry, my girl. Back soon.
GHENT [*threateningly*]. Cut that out!
DUTCH. What's eatin' you? She ain't
yours yet, and I guess she won't be, not till
hell freezes over.
    [*He taps his pistol and goes out.* GHENT
    *picks up the rifle which has pre-
    viously missed fire; he unloads it,
    throws it on the window-seat, and
    follows* DUTCH. RUTH *stands be-
    side the table, listening. Four shots
    are heard. After a short time* GHENT
    *appears and watches from the door
    the vanishing horses. He comes to
    the table opposite* RUTH.]
RUTH [*in a low voice*]. Is he dead?
GHENT. No; but he'll stay in the coop
for a while.
    [*She sinks down in a chair.* GHENT
    *seats himself at the other side of the
    table, draws a whiskey flask from
    his pocket, and uncorks it awk-
    wardly, using only his right hand.*]
RUTH [*as he is about to drink*]. Don't!
GHENT [*lowers the bottle and looks at her
in a dazed way*]. Is this on the square?
RUTH. I gave you my promise.
    [*Gazing at her, he lets the bottle sink
    slowly by his side; the liquor runs
    out, while he sits as if in a stupor.*
    RUTH *glances toward the door, and
    half starts from her seat, sinking
    back as he looks up.*]
GHENT. Give me a drink of water.
    [*She brings the water from a bucket in
    the corner. He sets the empty bottle
    on the table, drinks deeply of the
    water, takes a handkerchief from his
    neck, wets it, and mops his face.*]
GHENT. Where are your folks?
RUTH. My brother has gone out to the
railroad.
GHENT. Him and you ranching it here
by yourselves?

RUTH. Yes.
GHENT. Write him a note. [*He shoves
paper, pen, and ink before her.*] Fix it up
any way you like.
RUTH. Tell me first what you mean to
do with me.
GHENT. [*Ponders awhile in silence.*] Have
you got a horse to ride?
RUTH. Yes.
GHENT. We can reach San Jacinto before
sun-up. Then we're off for the Cordilleras.
I've got a claim tucked away in them hills
that'll buy you the city of Frisco some day,
if you have a mind to it!
                    [*She shrinks and shudders.*]
What you shivering at?
    [RUTH *does not answer, but begins to
    write.* GHENT, *still using only one
    hand, takes a pistol from his pocket,
    examines it, and lays it carelessly
    on the table, within* RUTH'S *reach.
    He rises and goes to the fireplace,
    takes a cigarette from his pocket and
    lights it, and examines the objects
    on the mantel-shelf.* RUTH *stops
    writing, takes up the pistol, then lays
    it down, as he speaks without turn-
    ing round.*]
Read what you've written.
    [RUTH, *about to read, snatches up
    the pistol again, rises, and stands
    trembling and irresolute.*]
Why don't you shoot? [*He turns round de-
liberately.*] You promised on the square, but
there's nothing square about this deal. You
ought to shoot me like a rattlesnake!
RUTH. I know that.
GHENT. Then why don't you?
RUTH [*slowly*]. I don't know.
GHENT. I guess you've got nerve enough,
for that or anything.— Answer me; why
not?
RUTH. I don't — know. — You laid it
there for me. — And — you have no right
to die.
GHENT. How's that?
RUTH. You must live — to pay for hav-
ing spoiled your life.
GHENT. Do you think it is spoiled?
RUTH. Yes.
GHENT. And how about your life?
RUTH. I tried to do it.
GHENT. To do what?
RUTH. To take my life. I ought to die.
I have a right to die. But I cannot, I can-

not! I love my life, I must live. In torment, in darkness — it does n't matter. I want my life. I will have it!

[*She drops the weapon on the table, pushes it toward him, and covers her eyes.*]

Take it away! Don't let me see it. If you want me on these terms, take me, and may God forgive you for it; but if there is a soul in you to be judged, don't let me do myself violence.

[*She sinks down by the table, hiding her face in her hands.*]

O God have pity on me!

[Ghent *puts the pistol back into his belt, goes slowly to the outer door, opens it, and stands for some moments gazing out. He then closes the door, and takes a step or two toward the table. As he speaks,* Ruth's *sobs cease, she raises her head and looks strangely at him.*]

Ghent. I've lived hard and careless, and lately I've been going downhill pretty fast. But I have n't got so low yet but what I can tell one woman from another. If that was all of it, I'd be miles away from here by now, riding like hell for liquor to wash the taste of shame out of my mouth. But that ain't all. I 've seen what I 've been looking the world over for, and never knew it. — Say your promise holds, and I'll go away now.

Ruth. Oh, yes, go, go! You will be merciful. You will not hold me to my cruel oath.

Ghent. And when I come back?

[Ruth *does not answer. He takes a step nearer.*]

And when I come back?

Ruth. You never — could — come back.

Ghent. No, I guess I never could.

Ruth [*eager, pleading*]. You *will* go?

Ghent. For good?

Ruth. Yes.

Ghent. Do you mean that?

Ruth [*wildly*]. Yes, yes, ten thousand times!

Ghent. Is that your last word?

Ruth. Yes.

[*Pause. She watches him with strained anxiety.*]

Oh, why did you come here to-night?

Ghent. I come because I was blind-drunk and sun-crazy, and looking for damnation the nearest way. That 's why I come.

But that 's not why I 'm staying. I 'm talking to you in my right mind now. I want you to try and see this thing the way it is.

Ruth. Oh, that is what I want you to do! You did yourself and me a hideous wrong by coming here. Don't do us both a more hideous wrong still! I was in panic fear. I snatched at the first thing I could. Think what our life would be, beginning as we have begun! Oh, for God's pity go away now, and never come back! Don't you see there can never be anything between us but hatred, and misery, and horror?

Ghent [*hardening*]. We 'll see about that! — Are you ready to start?

[Ruth, *conscious for the first time of her undress condition, shrinks, and folds her gown closer about her neck.*]

Go, and be quick about it.

[*She starts toward her room; he detains her.*]

Where 's your saddle?

[*She points at it and goes out.* Ghent *picks up the note she has written, reads it, and stands for a moment in reflection before laying it down. He gets more water from the bucket, drinks deeply, mops his face, and rolls up the sleeve of his left arm, which is soaked with blood. He tries awkwardly to stanch a wound in his forearm, gives it up in disgust, and rolls down his sleeve again. He reads the note once more, then takes* Ruth's *saddle and bridle from the wall and goes out.* Ruth *comes in; her face is white and haggard, but her manner determined and collected. She comes to the table, and sees the bloody handkerchief and basin of water. As* Ghent *enters, she turns to him anxiously.*]

Ruth. You are hurt.

Ghent. It 's no matter.

Ruth. Where?

[*He indicates his left arm. She throws off her hooded riding-cloak, and impulsively gathers together water, towels, liniment, and bandages; she approaches him, quite lost in her task, flushed and eager.*]

Sit down. — Roll up your sleeve.

[*He obeys mechanically. She rapidly and deftly washes and binds the wound, speaking half to herself, between long pauses.*]

Can you lift your arm? — The bone is not

touched. — It will be all right in a few
days. — This balsam is a wonderful thing
to heal.

GHENT [*watching her dreamily, as she
works*]. What's your name?

RUTH. Ruth — Ruth — Jordan. [*Long
pause.*] There, gently. — It must be very
painful.

[*He shakes his head slowly, with half-
humorous protest.*]

GHENT. It's not fair!

RUTH. What isn't fair?

GHENT. To treat me like this. It's not
in the rules of the game.

RUTH [*as the sense of the situation again
sweeps over her*]. Binding your wound? I
would do the same service for a dog.

GHENT. Yes, I dare say. But the point
is, I ain't a dog; I'm a human — the worst
way!

[*She rises and puts away the liniment
and bandages. He starts up with
an impulsive gesture.*]

Make this bad business over into something
good for both of us! You'll never regret
it! I'm a strong man!

[*He holds out his right arm, rigid.*]

I used to feel sometimes, before I went to
the bad, that I could take the world like
that and tilt her over. And I can do it, too,
if you say the word! I'll put you where
you can look down on the proudest. I'll
give you the kingdoms of the world and all
the glory of 'em.

[*She covers her face with her hands. He
comes nearer.*]

Give me a chance, and I'll make good. By
God, girl, I'll make good! — I'll make a
queen of you. I'll put the world under your
feet!

[RUTH *makes a passionate gesture, as
if to stop her ears.*]

What makes you put your hands over your
ears like that? Don't you like what I'm
saying to you?

RUTH [*taking the words with difficulty*].
Do you remember what that man said just
now?

GHENT. What about?

RUTH. About the Indian — and — his
squaw.

GHENT. Yes. There was something in it,
too. I was a fool to offer him that mean
little wad.

RUTH. For — me!

GHENT. Well, yes, for you, if you want to
put it that way.

RUTH. But — a chain of nuggets — that
comes nearer being a fair price?

GHENT. Oh, to buy off a greaser!

RUTH. But to buy the soul of a woman
— one must go higher. A mining-claim!
The kingdoms of the world and all the glory
of them! [*Breaking down in sudden sobs.*]
Oh, be careful how you treat me! Be careful! I say it as much for your sake as mine.
Be careful!

GHENT. [*Turns from her, his bewilderment
and discomfiture translating itself into gruff-
ness.*] Well, I guess we'll blunder through.
— Come along! We've no time to lose. —
Where are your things?

[*At her gesture, he picks up the saddle-
pack which she has brought out of
the bedroom with her, and starts
toward the door.*]

RUTH [*taking a hammer from the window-
ledge and handing it to* GHENT]. Fix the
bolt. My brother must not know.

[*He drives in the staple of the bolt,
while she throws the blood-stained
water and handkerchief into the
fire. He aids her in replacing the
weapons on the walls, then takes the
saddle-pack and stands at the door,
waiting. She picks up her mother's
picture, and thrusts it in her bosom.
After standing a moment in hesitation, she takes the picture out, kisses
it, lays it on the mantel, face down.
She extinguishes the lamp, and goes
out hastily. He follows, closing the
door.*]

ACT II

STEPHEN GHENT'S *home, in the Cordilleras.
At the right, crowning a rude terrace, is an
adobe cabin, stained a pale buff, mellowed to
ivory by sun and dust. Over it clamber vines
loaded with purple bloom. The front of the cabin
is turned at an angle toward the spectator, the
farther side running parallel with the brink of
a cañon, of which the distant wall and upper
reaches are crimsoned by the afternoon light.
In the level space before the rocky terrace is a
stone table and seats, made of natural rocks
roughly worked with the chisel. The rude materials have manifestly been touched by a refined
and artistic hand, bent on making the most of the
glorious background. Against the rocks on the
left stands a large hand-loom of the Navajo type,*

*with weaving-stool, and a blanket half woven.
On the table lies a half-finished Indian basket,
and heaps of colored weaving-materials lie in a
heap on the ground. Cactus plants in blossom
fill the niches of the rocks and lift their fantastic
forms above the stones which wall the cañon brink.
At one point this wall is broken, where a path
descends into the cañon.*

LON ANDERSON, *a venerable-looking miner,
with gray hair and beard, sits smoking before the
cabin.* BURT WILLIAMS, *a younger man, peeps
up over the edge of the cañon, from the path.*

BURT. Hello, Lon. Is the missus inside?
[LON *smokes on, without looking at
the questioner.*]
Look here, I put a nickel in you, you blame
rusty old slot-machine. Push out something!

LON. [*Removes his pipe deliberately.*] What
you wantin' off 'n her now? A music lesson or a headache powder?

BURT. Boss's waitin' down at the mine,
with a couple o' human wonders he's
brought back with him from wherever he's
been this time. Something doin' on the
quiet.

LON. You can tell him his wife ain't no-
wheres about.
[BURT *produces an enormous bandana
from his pocket, mounts the wall, and
waves it. He sits on the wall and
smokes for a moment in silence, looking down into the cañon, as if watching the approaching party. He points
with his pipe at the cabin.*]

BURT. Funny hitch-up — this here one
— I think.

LON [*after a pause*]. How much you
gittin' a day now?

BURT. Same little smilin' helpless three
and six-bits.

LON. Anything extry for thinkin'?

BURT. Nope! Throwed in.
[*They smoke again.* BURT *glances
down to reassure himself, then
points at the loom and basket.*]
Queer business — this rug-weavin' and
basket-makin', ain't it? — What d' ye
s'pose she wants to sit, day in and day out,
like a half-starved Navajo, slavin' over
them fool things fur? — Boss ain't near, is
he? Don't keep her short of ice-cream
sodas and trolley-rides, does 'e?
[LON *rises and approaches* BURT,
regarding him grimly.]

Saw 'er totin' a lot o' that stuff burro-back
over to the hotel week 'fore last. — An'
Dod Ranger — you know what a disgustin'
liar Dod is — he tells how he was makin'
tests over in the cross-cañon, an' all of a
sudden plump he comes on her talkin' to a
sawed-off Mexican hobo, and when she sees
Dod, she turns white 's a sheet.

LON [*with suppressed ferocity*]. You tell
Dod Ranger to keep his mouth shet, and
you keep yourn shet too — or by Jee-
hosophat, I'll make the two of ye eat yer
Adam's-apples and swaller the core!

BURT. Oh, git down off 'n yer hind legs,
Lon! Nobody's intendin' any disrespect.

LON. You boys keep yer blatherin'
tongues off 'n her! Or you'll get mixed
up with Alonzo P. Anderson — [*he taps his
breast*] — so 's it'll take a coroner to un-
tangle ye!

BURT [*deprecatingly*]. I guess I'd stick
up fur 'er 's quick as you would, come to
that.

LON. Well, we don't need no stickin' up
fur 'er. What we need is less tongue.
[*He leans down and speaks lower.*]
Especially when the boss is round. You
tell the boys so.
[BURT *looks at him in surprise and is
about to speak;* LON *makes a warning signal, indicating the approach
of the party below.* BURT *descends,
saluting* GHENT *respectfully.*]

GHENT [*peeping up over the edge of the
cañon*]. Coast clear, eh, Lon?

LON. Yes, sir.

GHENT. Where is she?

LON. [*Points along the brink of the cañon.*]
Kind o' think she went out to Look-off
Ledge. — Guess she did n't expect you back
to-day.

GHENT [*speaking below*]. Come up, gentlemen.
[GHENT *emerges from the cañon, followed by an architect, a dapper
young Easterner, and a contractor,
a bluff Western type.* GHENT *is
neatly dressed in khaki, with riding-
boots and broad felt hat. He has a
prosperous and busy air, and is
manifestly absorbed in the national
game of making money.*]
Take a seat.

CONTRACTOR. [*Seats himself by the table.*]
Don't care if I do. That new stage of yours

just jumped stiff-legged from the go-off.
And the trail up here from the mine is a good
deal of a proposition for the seedentary.

ARCHITECT [*as he takes in the stupendous
view*]. What a wonderful place! Even
better than you described it.

GHENT. Yes. My wife picked it out. —
Let's see your plans.

[*He removes basket from the table,
where the* ARCHITECT *unrolls several
sheets of blue paper.*]

ARCHITECT. I have followed your instructions to the letter. I understand that
nothing is to be touched except the house.

GHENT. Not a stone, sir; not a head of
cactus. Even the vines you've got to keep,
exactly as they are.

ARCHITECT [*smiling*]. That will be a little difficult.

GHENT. You can put 'em on a temporary
trellis. — A little pains will do it.

CONTRACTOR. Maybe, with a man to
shoo the masons off with a shot-gun.

GHENT [*over the plans*]. Provide a dozen
men, if necessary, with machine guns.

CONTRACTOR. As you please, Mr. Ghent.
The owner of the Verde Mine has a right
to his whims, I reckon.

ARCHITECT. I have designed the whole
house in the Spanish style, very broad and
simple. This open space where we stand —
[*points to the plans*] — I have treated as a
semi-inclosed *patio*, with arcaded porches.

GHENT [*dubiously*]. Good.

ARCHITECT. This large room fronting
the main arcade is the living-room.

GHENT. I guess we'll have 'em all liv-
ing-rooms. This place is to be lived in,
from the word go.

ARCHITECT [*humoring him*]. To be sure,
everything cheerful and open. — Here on
the left of the inner court is the library and
music-room.

GHENT. I'm afraid we won't have much
use for that. My wife don't go in much for
frills. I used to play the concertina once,
but it was a long while ago.

ARCHITECT. It can be used for other
purposes. For instance, as a nursery, though
I had put that on the other side.

GHENT [*embarrassed and delighted*]. Um,
yes, nursery. — Stamping-ground for the —?

[*The* ARCHITECT *nods; the* CONTRAC-
TOR *follows suit, with emphasis.*
LON *nods solemnly over his pipe.*]

Good.

[*The* ARCHITECT *bends over to make a
note with his pencil.* GHENT *restrains him and says somewhat
sheepishly in his ear.*]

You can leave it music-room on the map.

ARCHITECT [*continuing his explanation*].
This wing —

[GHENT, *interrupting him, holds the
plan at arm's length, with head on
one side and eyes squinted, as he
looks from the drawings to the cabin
and surroundings.*]

GHENT. Looks a little — *sprawly* on
paper. I had sort of imagined something
more — more up in the air, like them swell
tepees on the Hill in Frisco.

[*He makes a grandiose outline of high
roofs and turrets in the air.*]

ARCHITECT. I think this is more harmonious with the surroundings.

CONTRACTOR [*in answer to* GHENT'S *in-
quiring look*]. Won't look so showy from
the new hotel across yonder.

[*He points to the left, down the curve of
the cañon wall.*]

GHENT. What's your estimate on this
plan, now you've seen the location?

CONTRACTOR. It's a long way to haul
the stuff. — Say somewheres between twenty
and twenty-five thousand. Twenty-five will
be safe.

GHENT [*slightly staggered*]. That's a big
lot of money, my friend!

CONTRACTOR [*with cold scorn*]. I thought
we was talkin' about a *house!* I can build
you a good sheep-corral for a right smart
less.

GHENT. Well, I guess we don't want any
sheep-corrals.

CONTRACTOR. I should think not, with
the Verde pumping money at you the way
they tell she does.

GHENT. [*Holds up the plans again and
looks at them in perplexed silence.*] I'll tell
you, gentlemen, I'll have to consult my
wife about this before I decide. The fact is,
I've been working the thing out on the sly,
up to now.

CONTRACTOR. Expect to build it of an
afternoon, while the lady was takin' her
see-ester?

GHENT. I thought I'd smuggle her off
somewhere for a while.

[*He is silent a moment, pondering.*]

No! It's her house, and she must O.K. the plans before ground is broke.

[*He looks along the cañon rim.*]

Would you mind waiting a few minutes till I see if I can find her?

[*He starts irresolutely, then turns back.*]

Or, better still, leave the plans, and I'll see you at the hotel to-morrow morning. I have n't been over there since it was opened. I'd like to know what they 're making of it.

CONTRACTOR [*astonished*]. Hain't been over to the Buny Visty yet?

GHENT. Too busy.

CONTRACTOR. Well, you 'll find it an up-to-date joint, and chock full of tourist swells and lungers.

GHENT. Good - afternoon, gentlemen. You 'll excuse me. You can find your way back all right? Take the left-hand path. It 's better going.

[*The* ARCHITECT *bows ceremoniously, the* CONTRACTOR *nods.* GHENT *disappears along the cañon brink behind the cabin.*]

ARCHITECT. [*Has been examining the work on the loom, and has then picked up the unfinished basket, admiringly.*] What a beautiful pattern! I say, this is like those we saw at the hotel. [*To* LON.] May I ask who is making this?

[LON *smokes in silence; the architect raises his voice, slightly sharp.*]

May I ask who is making this?

LON [*benignly*]. You kin, my friend, you kin!

ARCHITECT. Well, then, the question is put.

LON. And very clear-put, too. You 'd ought to be in the law business, young man. [*He gets up deliberately.*] Or some other business that 'd take up all yer time.

ARCHITECT [*between wrath and amusement*]. Well, I 'll be hanged!

[*He follows his companion down the cañon path, stopping a moment at the brink to look round with a professional air at the house and surroundings, then at* LON.]

Tart old party!

[*He descends.* LON *crosses to the table, looks over the plans, makes outlines in the air in imitation of* GHENT, *then shakes his head dubiously, as he rolls up the plans.*

RUTH *appears, emerging from the* cañon path. *She wears the same dress as at the close of Act I, with a dark scarf-like handkerchief thrown over her head. She is pale and exhausted. She sinks on the rocks at the edge of the cañon.*]

LON [*approaching her, anxiously*]. It 's too much fer you, ma'am. You 'd oughter let me go.

[*He brings her a glass of water from an Indian water-jar before the cabin.*]

RUTH [*tasting the water*]. Oh, I thought I should never get back!

[*She leans against a rock, with closed eyes then rouses herself again.*]

Lon, take the glass, and see if you can make out any one down yonder, on the nearer trail. I — I thought some one was following me.

LON. [*Speaks low.*] Excuse me askin', Mis' Ghent, but is that dod-blamed Mexican a-botherin' you again?

RUTH. No. He has gone away, for good. It 's some one I saw at the hotel — some one I used to know. — Look if you can make out a man's figure, coming up.

LON. [*Takes the glass from the niche in the rocks, and scans the cañon path.*] Can't see nothin' but a stray burro, an' he ain't got no figger to speak of. — Might be t' other side o' Table Rock, down in the pinyon scrub.

[RUTH *gets up with an effort, takes the glass and looks through it, then lays it on the ledge.*]

Excuse me, ma'am, but — Mister Ghent come home this afternoon.

RUTH [*startled*]. Where is he?

LON. Huntin' for you down Look-off Ledge way. I 'lowed you was there, not knowin' what else to say.

RUTH. Thank you, Lon. — You can go now.

[*He goes down the cañon path.* RUTH *looks once more through the glass, then crosses to the table, where she sits down and begins to finger the roll of plans.* GHENT *reënters. He approaches with soft tread and bends over* RUTH. *She starts up with a little cry, avoiding his embrace.*]

You frightened me. — When did you come back?

GHENT. An hour ago.

RUTH. Was your journey successful?

GHENT. Yes. But my home-coming —

that looks rather like a failure. [*Pause.*] I expected to find you out on the bluff.

RUTH. Lou was mistaken. I had gone the other way.

[*As she stands at the table, she begins to unroll the plans.*]

What are these papers?

GHENT. Have n't you one word of welcome for me, after five days?

[RUTH *remains silent, with averted head, absently unrolling the packet.*]

Not a look even?

[*He waits a moment, then sighs and seats himself moodily by the table.*]

I never can remember! After I 've been away from you for twelve hours, I forget completely.

RUTH. Forget what?

GHENT. How it stands between us. It 's childish, but for the life of me I can't help it. — After I 've been away a few hours, this place gets all lit up with bright colors in my mind, like — [*searching for a simile*] — well, like a Christmas tree! I dare say a Christmas tree don't amount to much in real life, but I saw one once, in a play, — I was a little mining-camp roustabout, so high, — and ever since it has sort of stood to me for the gates o' glory.

RUTH [*with a hysterical laugh*]. A Christmas tree!

[*She bows her head in her hands, and repeats the words, as if to herself, in a tone in which bitterness has given place to tragic melancholy.*]

A Christmas tree!

[GHENT, *watching her moodily, crumples up the plans and throws them upon the ground. He goes toward the cabin, hesitates, turns, and comes back to the table, where* RUTH *still sits with buried head. He draws from his pocket a jewel-case, which he opens and lays before her.*]

GHENT. There is a little present I brought home for you. And here are some more trinkets.

[*He takes out several pieces of jewelry and tumbles them together on the table.*]

I know you don't care much for these things, but I had to buy something, the way I was feeling. And these papers — [*picks them up and spreads them out on the table*] — these mean that you 're not to live much longer

in a mud shanty, with pine boxes for furniture. These are the drawings for a new house that I want to talk over with you.

[*He points at the map and speaks glibly, trying to master his discomfiture at her lack of interest.*]

Spanish style, everything broad and simple! Large living-room opening on inner court. Library and music-room, bless your heart. Bedrooms; kitchen and thereunto pertaining. Wing where the proprietor retires to express his inmost feelings. General effect sprawly, but harmonious with the surroundings. Twenty thousand estimated, twenty-five limit. Is she ours?

RUTH [*in a dead, flat tone*]. How much did you say the house is to cost?

GHENT. Twenty-five thousand dollars at the outside.

RUTH. And these — trinkets?

GHENT. Oh, I don't know. — A few hundred.

RUTH. [*Draws the plans toward her and pours the jewels in a heap upon them from her lifted hands.*] Twenty-five thousand dollars and the odd hundreds!

[*She laughs suddenly and jarringly.*]

My price has risen! My price has risen!

[*She laughs again, as she rises from the table and looks down the cañon path.*]

Keep those displayed to show to our visitors! My honor is at stake.

[*She points down the path.*]

There is one coming now!

GHENT. Visitors? What visitors?

RUTH. Only an old school friend of mine: a Mr. Winthrop Newbury.

GHENT. What are you talking about? Are you crazy?

[*He joins her, where she stands looking down into the cañon.*]

This fellow, is he really what you say?

[RUTH *nods, with unnaturally bright eyes and mocking smile.*]

What does this mean?

RUTH. It means that he caught sight of me, an hour ago, in the hotel.

GHENT. In the hotel? What were you doing there?

RUTH [*with biting calm*]. Nothing wicked — as yet. They don't pay twenty-five thousand dollars over there — at least not yet!

[GHENT *turns sharply, as if stung by a physical blow. She raises her hands to him, in a swift revulsion of feeling.*]

Oh, don't judge me ! Don't listen to me ! I am not in my right mind.

GHENT. [*Sweeps the jewels together, and throws them over the cliff.*] Do you want me to be here, while you see him ? [*She does not answer.*] Won't you answer me ?

RUTH [*again cold*]. Act as you think best.

GHENT. It's a question of what will be easiest for you.

RUTH. Oh, it's all easy for me !

[GHENT *stands irresolute, then raises his hand in a gesture of perplexity and despair, and goes into the house, closing the door.* WINTHROP NEW-BURY *appears at the top of the cañon path, looks curiously about, catches sight of* RUTH'S *averted figure, and rushes toward her.*]

WINTHROP. Ruth ! Is it really you !

[RUTH *starts involuntarily toward him, stretching out her arms. As he advances, she masters herself, and speaks in a natural voice, with an attempt at gayety, as she takes his hand.*]

RUTH. Well, of all things ! Winthrop Newbury ! How did you find your way to this eagle's nest ?

WINTHROP. I — we saw you — we caught a glimpse of you at the hotel, but we were n't sure. We followed you, but lost you in the cañon.

RUTH. We ? Who is we ?

WINTHROP. Your brother and his wife.

RUTH [*turning the shock, which she has been unable to conceal, into conventional surprise*]. Philip and Polly here !

WINTHROP. They took the other turn, down there where the path forks. We did n't know which way you had gone.

RUTH. Yes, but why on earth are they here at all ?

WINTHROP. They are on their way East. They stopped over to see me.

RUTH. To see you ? Are you — living here ?

WINTHROP. I have been here only a week.

[*He starts impulsively, trying to break through the conventional wall which she has raised between them.*]

Ruth — for God's sake — !

RUTH [*interrupting him, with exaggerated animation*]. But tell me ! I am all curiosity. How do you happen to be here — of all places ?

WINTHROP. What does it matter ? I am here. We have found you, after all these miserable months of anxiety and searching. O Ruth, — why —

RUTH. I have acted badly, I know. But I wish not to talk of that. Not now. I will explain everything later. Tell me about yourself — about Philip and Polly — and mother. I am thirsty for news. What have you been doing all these months, since — our queer parting ?

WINTHROP [*solemnly*]. Looking for you. [*Pause.*] O Ruth — how could you do it ? How could you do it ?

RUTH. [*Touches him on the arm and looks at him with dumb entreaty, speaking low.*] Winthrop !

WINTHROP [*in answer to her unspoken words*]. As you will.

RUTH. [*Resumes her hard, bright tone.*] You have n't told me about mother. How is she ?

WINTHROP. Well. Or she will be, now. Ruth, you ought at least to have written to her. She has suffered cruelly.

RUTH [*quickly, with a nervous uplift of her arms*]. Yes, yes, I know that ! — And you are — settled here ? You mean to remain ?

WINTHROP. I am the physician at the End-of-the-Rainbow Mines, three miles below. At least I — I am making a trial of it.
[*Pause.*]
How pale and worn you are. — Don't turn away. Look at me.

[*She flinches, then summons her courage and looks him steadily in the face.*]

You are — you are ill — I fear you are desperately ill !

RUTH [*moving away nervously*]. Nonsense. I was never better in my life. [*She goes toward the cañon brink.*] You have n't praised our view. We are very proud of it.

WINTHROP [*following her*]. Yes, very fine. Magnificent.

RUTH. But you're not looking at it at all ! Do you see that bit of smoke far down yonder ? That is the stamp mill of the Rio Verde Mine.

WINTHROP [*compelling himself to follow her lead*]. Yes — the Rio Verde. One of the big strikes of the region. Dispute about the ownership, I believe.

RUTH. None that I ever heard of, and I ought to know. For — [*she makes a sweeping bow*] — *we* are the Rio Verde, at your service.

WINTHROP. You — your — husband is the owner of the Verde Mine?

RUTH. No less!

WINTHROP [*embarrassed*]. We found the record of your marriage at San Jacinto. The name was Ghent — Stephen Ghent.

RUTH. Yes. He will be so glad to see some of my people.

[WINTHROP's *eyes have fallen on the basket at the foot of the table. He picks it up, examines it curiously, and looks meaningly at* RUTH, *who snatches it from his hand and throws it over the cliff.*]

A toy I play with! You know I always have to keep my hands busy pottering at some rubbishy craft or other.

WINTHROP [*is about to speak, but checks himself. He points at the loom*]. And the blanket, too?

RUTH. Yes, another fad of mine. It is really fascinating work. The Indian women who taught me think I am a wonder of cleverness.

WINTHROP. So do — the women — over there. [*He points across the cañon.*]

RUTH [*flushing*]. Ah, yes, you saw some of my stuff at the hotel. You know how vain I am. I had to show it.

WINTHROP. Perhaps. But why should the wife of the man who owns the Verde Mine *sell* her handiwork, and under such — such vulgar conditions?

RUTH [*brilliantly explanatory*]. To see if it *will* sell, of course! That is the test of its merit.

[*He looks at her in mute protest, then with a shake of the head, rises and puts on his hat.*]

WINTHROP. Do you want to see the others?

RUTH. Why, yes, to be sure I do. How should I not?

WINTHROP. You haven't seemed very anxious — these last eight months.

RUTH. True. I have been at fault. I so dread explanations. And Phil's tempests of rage! Poor boy, he must feel sadly ill-used.

WINTHROP. He does. [*Hesitates.*] If

there is any reason why you would rather he didn't see you, just now —

RUTH. There is no reason. At least, none valid.

WINTHROP. Then I will bring them up.

RUTH. By all means. [*She holds out her hand, smiling.*] *Auf wiedersehen!*

[WINTHROP *releases her hand and goes toward the cañon path. He waves, and turns to* RUTH.]

WINTHROP. They are just below.

[*As* RUTH *advances he takes her hand and looks searchingly into her eyes.*]

For old friendship's sake, won't you give me one human word before they come? At least answer me honestly one human question?

RUTH [*keeping up her hard, bright gayety*]. In the great lottery of a woman's answers there is always one such prize!

WINTHROP [*dejectedly, as he drops her hand*]. It's no use, if that is your mood.

RUTH. My mood! Your old bugbear! I am as sober-serious as my stars ever let me be.

WINTHROP. Did you, that night you bade me good-bye, know that — this was going to happen?

RUTH [*cordially explanatory*]. No. It was half accident, half wild impulse. Phil left me at the ranch alone. My lover came, impatient, importunate, and I — went with him.

WINTHROP. And your — this man — to whom you are married — pardon me, you don't need to answer unless you wish — for how long had you known him?

RUTH [*solemnly, as she looks him straight in the eyes*]. All my life! And for æons before.

[*He looks at her for a moment, then goes toward the cañon path.* POLLY's *voice is heard calling.*]

POLLY [*not yet visible*]. Win! Win!

WINTHROP. [*Calls down the cañon.*] Come up! Come up!

[RUTH *goes past him down the cañon path. In a moment she reappears, with* POLLY. *They are laughing and talking as they come.*]

POLLY. Ruth!

RUTH. Dear old Polly!

POLLY. You *naughty* girl!

RUTH. If our sins must find us out, you are the kind of Nemesis I choose.

POLLY. My! But you 're a shady character. And sly!

[PHILIP *appears.* RUTH *hurries to embrace him, while* POLLY, *fanning herself with her handkerchief, examines the house and surroundings with curiosity.*]

RUTH. O Phil! — Dear old man!

[*She covers his face lightly with her hands.*]

No scolding, no frowns. This is the finding of the prodigal, and she expects a robe and a ring.

POLLY [*seating herself on a rock*]. Heavens, what a climb! — I 'm a rag.

RUTH. [*Motions to the men to be seated.*] The cabin would n't hold us all, but there 's one good thing about this place; there 's plenty of outdoors.

WINTHROP [*looking about*]. I should say there was!

POLLY. To think of our practical Ruth doing the one really theatrical thing known in the annals of Milford Corners, Mass.! — And what a setting! My dear, your stage arrangements are perfect.

RUTH. In this case Providence deserves the credit. We may have come here to have our pictures taken, but we stayed to make a living.

[PHILIP *has drawn apart, gloomy and threatening.* POLLY *keeps up her heroic efforts to give the situation a casual and humorous air.*]

POLLY [*with jaunty challenge*]. Well, where is he?

RUTH. Who?

POLLY. He!

[RUTH *points at the cabin, smiling.*]

Well, produce him!

RUTH [*following, with gratitude in her eyes, the key of lightness and raillery which* POLLY *has struck*]. You insist?

POLLY. Absolutely.

RUTH. Oh, very well!

[*She goes up the rocky incline, and enters the cabin, calling: "Steve! Steve!"* POLLY *goes to* PHILIP, *and shakes him.*]

POLLY. Now, you behave! [*Indicates* WINTHROP.] He 's behaving.

[RUTH *reappears in the doorway, followed by* GHENT.]

RUTH [*with elaborate gayety, as they descend the rocks*]. Well, Stephen, since they 've run us to earth, I suppose we must put a good face on it, and acknowledge them. — This is Polly, of whom I 've talked so much. Polly the irresistible. Beware of her! [POLLY *shakes his hand cordially.*] And this is — my brother Philip.

[GHENT *extends his hand, which* PHILIP *pointedly ignores.* RUTH *goes on hastily, to cover the insult.*]

And this is my old school friend, Winthrop Newbury. [*They shake hands.*]

WINTHROP. [*To* PHILIP, *formally explanatory.*] Mr. Ghent is the owner of the famous Verde Mine.

GHENT. Part owner, sir. I had n't the capital to develop with, so I had to dispose of a half-interest.

WINTHROP. Is n't there some litigation under way?

RUTH [*looking at* GHENT, *surprised*]. Litigation?

GHENT. Yes — a whole rigmarole.

POLLY [*catching at a straw to make talk*]. Heaven help you if you have got entangled in the law! I can conceive of nothing more horrible or ghostly than a court of law; unless [*she glances at* PHILIP] it is that other court of high justice, which people hold in private to judge their fellows, from hearsay and half-knowledge!

RUTH [*keeping up the play desperately, as she blesses* POLLY *with a look*]. But there must be law, just the same, and penalties and rewards and all that. Else what 's the use of being good?

POLLY. Like you — for instance!

RUTH. Well, yes, like me!

POLLY. You are not good, you are merely magnificent. I want to be magnificent! I want to live on the roof of the world and own a gold mine! [*To* GHENT.] Show me where the sweet thing is.

GHENT. We can get a better view of the plant from the ledge below. Will you go down?

[GHENT, POLLY, *and* WINTHROP *go down the cañon path.* RUTH *takes* PHILIP *by the arm, to lead him after.*]

PHILIP. No. We must have a word together, before the gabble begins again. Winthrop has given me your explanation, which explains nothing.

RUTH [*trying to keep up the light tone*] Has n't that usually been the verdict on explanations of my conduct?

PHILIP. Don't try to put me off! Tell me in two words how you came to run away with this fellow.

RUTH [*hardening*]. Remember to whom you are speaking, and about whom.

PHILIP. I got your note, with its curt announcement of your resolve. Later, by mere accident, we found the record of your marriage at San Jacinto — if you call it a marriage, made hugger-mugger at midnight by a tipsy justice of the peace. I don't want to question its validity. I only pray that no one will. But I want to know how it came to be made, in such hurry and secrecy — how it came to be made at all, for that matter. How did you ever come to disgrace yourself and your family by clandestine meetings and a hedge-row marriage with a person of this class? And why, after the crazy leap was taken, did you see fit to hide yourself away without a word to me or your distracted mother? Though that, perhaps, is easier to understand!

RUTH. The manner of your questions absolves me from the obligation to answer them.

PHILIP. I refuse to be put off with any such patent subterfuge.

RUTH. Subterfuge or not, it will have to suffice, until you remember that my right to choose my course in life is unimpeachable, and that the man whose destiny I elect to share cannot be insulted in my presence.

PHILIP. Very well, I can wait. The truth will come out some day. Meanwhile, you can take comfort from the fact that your desertion at the critical moment of our enterprise has spelled ruin for me.

RUTH [*overwhelmed*]. Philip, you don't mean — !

PHILIP. Absolute and irretrievable ruin.

RUTH. Then you are going back East — for good!

PHILIP. Yes.

RUTH. But — mother's money! What will she do? [PHILIP *shrugs his shoulders.*] Is everything gone — everything?

PHILIP. I shall get something from the sale. Perhaps enough to make a fresh start, somewhere, in some small way.

RUTH. [*Comes to him, and lays her arms on his shoulders.*] Phil, I am sorry, sorry!

[*He caresses her; she bursts into suppressed convulsive weeping and clings to him, hiding her face in his breast.*]

PHILIP. Ruth, you are not happy! You have made a hideous mistake. Come home with me. [RUTH *shakes her head.*] At least for a time. You are not well. You look really ill. Come home with us, if only for a month.

RUTH. No, no, dear Phil, dear brother!

[*She draws down his face and kisses him; then lifts her head, with an attempt at lightness.*]

There! I have had my cry, and feel better. The excitement of seeing you all again is a little too much for me.

PHILIP. If there is anything that you want to tell me about all this, tell me now.

RUTH. Oh, there will be plenty of time for explanations and all that! Let us just be happy now in our reunion.

PHILIP. There will not be plenty of time. We leave to-morrow morning.

RUTH. Then you will take me on trust — like a dear good brother. Perhaps I shall never explain! I like my air of mystery.

PHILIP. Remember that if you ever have anything to complain of — in your life — it is my right to know it. The offender shall answer to me, and dearly, too.

RUTH. [*Takes his head between her hands, and shakes it, as with recovered gayety.*] Of course they will, you old fire-eater!

PHILIP [*pointing to the blanket on the loom*]. Ruth, at least tell me why —

[RUTH *does not see his gesture, as she is looking at the others, who come up from below. The men linger in the background,* GHENT *pointing out objects in the landscape.*]

RUTH. [*To* POLLY, *who advances.*] Well, what do you think of us, in a bird's-eye view?

POLLY. In a bird's-eye view you are superb!

[*She draws* RUTH *to her, and speaks in a lower tone.*]

And looked at near, you are an enthralling puzzle.

RUTH [*half to herself*]. If you only knew how much!

POLLY [*taking* RUTH *by the chin as in Act I*]. So you had — just by chance — riding over to the trading-station or so — met the glorious unfulfilled — in blue overalls and a jumper! I thought so!

[RUTH *bows her head in a spasm of pain.* POLLY, *who does not see her face, goes on teasingly.*]

I see now what you meant about wanting one that was n't finished. This one certainly is n't finished. But when he is, he 'll be grand !

[RUTH *moves away with averted head.* POLLY *follows her, peeping round to view her face.*]

Don't sulk ! I meant nothing disrespectful. On the contrary, I 'm crazy about him.

[*In a louder tone.*]

And now that I 've seen the outside of you, I *must* peep into that fascinating little house !

RUTH. [*To* GHENT, *who has drawn nearer.*] Polly wants to go inside the cabin. I can't let her until we have shown her what it 's going to be.

[*With* GHENT'S *aid she spreads out the plans, which* POLLY *examines with curiosity.*]

These are the plans for our new house. You call us magnificent. We will show you that we are not. We are overwhelming !

WINTHROP [*looking at his watch*]. I am afraid we must be getting back. It grows dark very suddenly in the cañon.

RUTH. [*To* POLLY]. Well, then you may come in, if you will promise to view the simple present in the light of the ornate future.

[POLLY *goes in.* RUTH, *lingering at the door for an instant, looks back anxiously at the men.*]

PHILIP [*curtly, to* GHENT]. If you will permit me, I should like a word with you.

GHENT. Certainly.

[WINTHROP *effaces himself, making and lighting a cigarette, as he looks out over the cañon.*]

PHILIP. In deference to my sister's wishes, I refrain from asking you for the explanation which is due me. [GHENT *bows in silence.*] But there is one thing which I think I am at liberty to question.

GHENT. Do so.

PHILIP. I hear of your interest in a valuable mine. I hear of plans for an elaborate house. Why, then, is my sister compelled to peddle her own handiwork in a public caravansary ?

GHENT. What do you mean ? I don't understand you.

PHILIP. [*Points at the loom.*] Her rugs and baskets are on sale in the corridor of the hotel, fingered and discussed by the tourist mob.

GHENT [*astonished*]. This can't be true ! PHILIP. It is, however.

GHENT. I know nothing of it. I 've had to be away a great deal. I knew she worked too hard over these things, but I took it for a mere pastime. Perhaps — No, I can't understand it at all !

PHILIP. I advise you to make inquiries. She has taken pains to conceal her identity, but it is known, nevertheless, and the subject of public curiosity.

[POLLY *and* RUTH *come out from the cabin.*]

POLLY. [*To* PHILIP.] Take me away quickly, or I shall never enjoy upholstery again ! [*To* RUTH.] Please change your mind, dear, and come with us for the night.

RUTH. No. I will see you in the morning.

WINTHROP. We leave by the early stage.

RUTH [*looking at him quickly*]. You, too?

WINTHROP. Yes, I have decided so.

RUTH. I will be there in good time, trust me. [*She kisses* POLLY *and* PHILIP.] Good-bye, till morning. [*Gives her hand to* WINTHROP.] Good-bye.

[PHILIP *ignores* GHENT *pointedly in the leave-takings.* POLLY *bids him farewell with corresponding cordiality.*]

POLLY. Good-bye, Mr. Ghent.

[*As they descend the cañon path, she is heard chatting enthusiastically.*]

Oh, Phil, you ought to have seen the inside of that delightful little house !

[*Her voice is heard for some time, indistinctly.* RUTH, *at the top of the path, waves to them as they descend.*]

GHENT. [*Looks long at her, with deep gratitude.*] God bless you !

[*She sits down on the rocks of the cabin terrace. He walks up and down in anxious thought. Once or twice he makes as if to speak. At length he stops before her.*]

You must go in and lie down. You are worn out.

RUTH [*rousing herself*]. No, there is something I must tell you first.

GHENT. [*Points at the rug.*] It 's about this — work you have been doing ?

RUTH [*slightly startled*]. You know of that ?

GHENT. Your brother told me. I should

have found it out to-morrow anyhow. [*Pause.*] Have you wanted money?

RUTH. Yes.

GHENT. I thought I — I thought you had enough. I have often begged you to take more.

RUTH. I haven't spent what you gave me. It is in there. [*She points toward the house.*]

GHENT [*astonished*]. You haven't spent — any of it?

RUTH. A little. Nothing for myself.

GHENT. But there has been no need to save, not after the first month or two. You surely knew that!

RUTH. Yes, I knew it. It was not economy.

GHENT [*slowly*]. You haven't been willing to take money from me?

RUTH. No. I know it was small of me, but I couldn't help it. I have paid for everything. — I have kept account of it — oh, to the last dreadful penny! These clothes are the ones I wore from my brother's house that night. This shelter — you know I helped to raise that with my own hands. And — and some things I paid for secretly, from the little hoard I brought away with me. You were careless; you did not notice.

GHENT. [*Sits down, dizzy from the shock of her words.*] I must try to grasp this!

[*There is a silence, during which he sits perfectly motionless. At last he turns to her.*]

Why — why did you stand up so plucky, so splendid, just now? Put a good face on everything about our life? Call me by my first name and all that — before your own people?

RUTH. We are man and wife. Beside that, my own people are as strangers.

GHENT [*eagerly*]. You say that? You can still say that?

RUTH. [*Looks up, startled.*] Can't you? [*She awaits his answer tensely.*]

GHENT [*desperately*]. Oh, I don't know. I can't say or think anything, after what you have just told me!

RUTH. [*Wails.*] You can't say it! And it isn't true! It is we who are strangers. — Worse, a thousand times worse!

GHENT. [*Rises and stands over her.*] Don't let us dash ourselves to hell in one crazy minute!

[*He pauses and hesitates. When he speaks again it is with wistful tenderness.*]

Ruth, do you remember our journey here? [*She lifts her head, looking at him with white, thirsty face.*]

I thought — it seemed to me you had — begun to care for me.

RUTH. That night, when we rode away from the justice's office at San Jacinto, and the sky began to brighten over the desert — the ice that had gathered here — [*she touches her heart*] — began to melt in spite of me. And when the next night and the next day passed, and the next, and still you spared me and treated me with beautiful rough chivalry, I said to myself, "He has heard my prayer to him. He knows what a girl's heart is." As you rode before me down the arroyos, and up over the mesas, through the dazzling sunlight and the majestic silence, it seemed as if you were leading me out of a world of little codes and customs into a great new world. — So it was for those first days. — And then — and then — I woke, and saw you standing in my tent-door in the starlight! I knew before you spoke that we were lost. You hadn't had the strength to save us!

GHENT [*huskily*]. Surely it hasn't all been — hateful to you? There have been times, since that. — The afternoon we climbed up here. The day we made the table; the day we planted the vines.

RUTH [*in a half whisper*]. Yes! — Beautiful days!

[*She puts her hands suddenly before her face and sobs.*]

Oh, it was not my fault! I have struggled against it. You don't know how I have struggled!

GHENT. Against what? Struggled against what?

RUTH. Against the hateful image you had raised up beside your own image.

GHENT. What do you mean?

RUTH. I mean that sometimes — often — when you stand there before my eyes, you fade away, and in your place I see — the Other One!

GHENT. Speak plainly, for God's sake! I don't understand this talk.

RUTH [*looking steadfastly, as at an invisible shape, speaks in a horrified whisper*]. There he stands behind you now! — The human beast, that goes to its horrible

pleasure as not even a wild animal will go
— *in pack, in pack!*

> [GHENT, *stung beyond endurance, rises
> and paces up and down. RUTH con-
> tinues in a broken tone, spent by
> the violence of her own words.*]

I have tried — Oh, you don't know how
I have tried to save myself from these
thoughts. — While we were poor and struggling I thought I could do it. — Then —
[*she points toward the cañon*] — then that
hole down there began belching its stream
of gold. You began to load me with gifts
— to force easy ways upon me —

GHENT. Well, what else did I care to
make money for?

> [RUTH *does not answer for a moment,
> then speaks slowly, taking the words
> with loathing upon her tongue.*]

RUTH. Every time you give me anything, or talk about the mine and what it
is going to do there rings in my ears that
dreadful sneer: "A dirt-eating Mojave
would pay more than that for his squaw!"
[*She rises, lifting her arms.*] I held myself
so dear! And you bought me for a handful
of gold, like a woman of the street! You
drove me before you like an animal from
the market!

> [GHENT *has seated himself again,
> elbows on knees and face in his
> hands. RUTH takes slowly from her
> bosom the nugget chain and holds
> it crumpled up in her palm. Her
> tone is quiet, almost matter-of-fact.*]

I have got back the chain again.

GHENT. [*Looks up.*] Chain? — What
chain?

RUTH [*in the same tone, as she holds it up,
letting it unwind*]. The one you bought me
with.

GHENT [*dumbfounded*]. Where the devil
— ? Has that fellow been around here?

RUTH. It would have had no meaning
for me except from his hand.

GHENT. So that's what you've been doing with this rug-weaving and basket-mak-
ing tomfoolery?

> [RUTH *does not answer, but continues
> looking at the chain, running it
> through her fingers and weighing it
> in her hand.*]

How long has this been going on?

RUTH. How long? — How long can one
live without breathing? Two minutes? A
few lifetimes? How long!

GHENT. It was about a month after we
came here that you began to potter with
this work.

RUTH. [*Draws her hand about her neck
as if loosening something there; convulsively.*]
Since then this has been round my neck,
round my limbs, a chain of eating fire. Link
by link I have unwound it. You will never
know what it has cost me, but I have paid
it all. Take it and let me go free. [*She
tries to force it upon him, with wailing entreaty.*] Take it, take it, I beseech you!

GHENT [*holding himself under stern control*]. You are killing yourself. You must n't
go on this way. Go and rest. We will talk
of this to-morrow.

RUTH. Rest! To-morrow! Oh, how little you have understood of all I have said!
I know it is only a symbol — a make-believe.
I know I am childish to ask it. Still, take
it and tell me I am free.

> [GHENT *takes the chain reluctantly,
> stands for a moment looking at it,
> then speaks with iron firmness.*]

GHENT. As you say, your price has risen.
This is not enough.

> [*He throws the chain about her neck
> and draws her to him by it.*]

You are mine, mine, do you hear? Now
and forever!

> [*He starts toward the house. She holds
> out her hand blindly to detain him.*]

RUTH [*in a stifled voice*]. Wait! There
is — something else.

> [*He returns to her, anxiously, and
> stands waiting. She goes on, touch-
> ing the chain.*]

It is n't only for my sake I ask you to take
this off me, nor only for your sake. There
is — another life — to think of.

GHENT [*leaning to look into her averted
face*]. Ruth! — Is it true? — Thank God!

RUTH. Now, will you take this off me?

GHENT. [*Starts to do so, then draws back.*]
No. Now less than ever. For now, more
than ever, you are mine.

RUTH. But — *how* yours? Oh, remember, have pity! *How* yours?

> [PHILIP *appears at the head of the
> cañon path. Hearing their voices,
> he waits, half concealed.*]

GHENT. No matter how! Bought if you
like, but mine! Mine by blind chance and
the hell in a man's veins, if you like! Mine by
almighty Nature, whether you like it or not!

RUTH. Nature! Almighty Nature!

[*She takes the chain slowly from her neck.*]

Not yours! By everything my people have held sacred! [*She drops the chain.*] Not yours! Not yours!

[*She turns slowly.* PHILIP *has come forward, and supports her as she sinks half fainting upon his neck.*]

PHILIP. [*To* GHENT.] I came back to get my sister for the night. — I don't know by what ugly spell you have held her, but I know, from her own lips, that it is broken. [*To* RUTH.] Come! I have horses below.

GHENT. No!

PHILIP [*measuring him*]. Yes. [*Pause.*]

GHENT. Let her say!

RUTH. [*Looks long at* GHENT, *then at the house and surroundings. At last she turns to her brother.*] Take me — with you. Take me — home!

[PHILIP, *supporting her, leads her down the cañon path.* GHENT *stands gazing after them as they disappear below the rim. He picks up the chain and goes back, looking down after the descending figures. The sunset light has faded, and darkness has begun to settle over the mountain world.*]

ACT III

Sitting-room of MRS. JORDAN'S *house at Milford Corners, Massachusetts. An old-fashioned New England interior, faded but showing signs of former distinction. The walls are hung with family portraits, several in clerical attire of the eighteenth century, one in the uniform of the Revolutionary War. Doors open right and left. At the back is a fireplace, flanked by windows, the curtains of which are drawn. On the left is a small table, with a lamp, books, and magazines; on the right, near the fireplace, a sewing-table, with lamp and sewing-basket. A bookcase and a writing-desk occupy opposite corners of the room, forward.*

WINTHROP *and* PHILIP *stand near the desk, chatting.* POLLY *is reading a newspaper at the table, left.* RUTH *sits before the grate, sewing; her face is turned away toward the fire.*

PHILIP. [*Offers* WINTHROP *his cigarcase.*] Have another cigar.

WINTHROP. Well, as a celebration.

[*Takes one and lights it.*]

PHILIP. Rather small business for the Jordan family, to be celebrating a bare escape from the poorhouse.

WINTHROP. Where did you scare up the benevolent uncle? I never heard of him before.

PHILIP. Nor I, scarcely. He's always lived abroad.

[WINTHROP, *strolling about, peeps over* POLLY'S *shoulder.*]

WINTHROP. [*To* PHILIP, *with a scandalized gesture*]. Stock reports!

PHILIP. Her latest craze!

WINTHROP. Last week it was Japanese Samurai.

POLLY [*crushingly*]. And next week it will be — Smart Alecks.

[*The door on the left opens, and* MRS. JORDAN *enters, with* DR. NEWBURY. *During the preceding conversation* RUTH *has sat sewing, paying no heed to the chatter.* MRS. JORDAN *and the doctor look at her as they come in, but she does not look up.*]

MRS. JORDAN. Sit down, doctor, at least for a moment.

DR. NEWBURY. [*Seats himself,* MRS. JORDAN *near him.*] I can never resist such an invitation, in this house.

MRS. JORDAN. Dear doctor, you've been a wonderful friend to me and mine all these years, since poor Josiah was taken.

DR. NEWBURY. But just when you needed help most —

MRS. JORDAN. I know how gladly you would have offered it, if you could.

DR. NEWBURY. Your brother-in-law in England was able to redeem the property?

MRS. JORDAN [*hastily*]. Yes, yes. — But what we are to do for the future, with my little capital gone — [*She speaks lower.*] Oh, that dreadful West! If my children had only stayed where they were born and bred.

[*She glances at* RUTH, *who has let her sewing fall in her lap and sits staring into the fire.*]

DR. NEWBURY [*sotto voce*]. Poor child.

[POLLY *looks up from the newspaper excitedly, holding her finger at a place on the sheet.*]

POLLY. I say, Phil! Win! Look here.

[PHILIP *and* WINTHROP, *who have been chatting and smoking apart, come to the table.*]

PHILIP. What is it now?

POLLY [*tapping on the paper*]. Something about your Arizona scheme.

PHILIP [*bending over her, reads*]. "Alleghany pig-iron, 93¾, National Brick —"

POLLY [*pointing*]. No, there!

PHILIP. "Arizona Cactus Fiber, 84."

[*He picks up the paper, astounded.*]

Cactus Fiber listed! Selling at 84!

[*He tosses the paper to* WINTHROP.]

This is the last straw!

MRS. JORDAN [*who has been listening anxiously*]. What does it mean, Phil?

PHILIP. Only that the people who bought our plant and patents for a song, have made a fortune out of them.

[RUTH *has resumed her needlework.* WINTHROP *offers her the paper, with his finger at the line. She takes it, looks at it vaguely, and lays it on the table.*]

POLLY [*leaning across*]. Does n't that interest you?

RUTH [*tonelessly*]. Oh, yes.

[*She rises, lays her work aside, and goes toward the door, left.*]

DR. NEWBURY [*as she passes him*]. Won't you bid me good-night, my child?

RUTH [*giving him her hand*]. Good-night, doctor.

DR. NEWBURY [*shaking his finger*]. Remember, no more moping! And from to-morrow, outdoors with you.

[RUTH *looks at him vacantly, attempting to smile. She moves toward the door, which* WINTHROP *opens for her.*]

WINTHROP [*holding out his hand*]. You must bid me good-night, too, and good-bye.

RUTH [*with a faint kindling of interest*]. Are you going away?

WINTHROP. Only back to Boston. Some time, when you are stronger, you will come down and see our new sailors' hospital.

RUTH. Yes. — Good-bye.

[*She goes out,* WINTHROP *closing the door.*]

WINTHROP. [*To* DR. NEWBURY.] I must be going along, father. Good-night, everybody! [*Patting* PHILIP'S *shoulder.*] Hard luck, old man!

[*He goes out by the hall door on the right,* PHILIP *accompanying him.*]

DR. NEWBURY [*looking after his son*]. Brave boy! Brave boy! He keeps up a good show.

MRS. JORDAN. You think he still grieves over her?

DR. NEWBURY. Ah, poor chap! He's made of the right stuff, if he is mine.

MRS. JORDAN. Let us not talk of it. It is too sad, too dreadful.

[PHILIP *reënters.*]

DR. NEWBURY. About part of it we must talk.

[*He speaks so as to include* PHILIP *and* POLLY *in the conversation.*]

Mrs. Jordan, I don't want to alarm you, but your daughter — I may as well put it bluntly — is in a dangerous state.

MRS. JORDAN [*frightened*]. Doctor, I thought she seemed so much stronger.

DR. NEWBURY. She is, so far as her body is concerned.

[MRS. JORDAN *sits in an attitude of nervous attention, gazing at the doctor as if trying to formulate one of many questions pressing. upon her.* PHILIP *comes forward and sits by the table, near them.*]

PHILIP. Don't you think that the routine of life which she has taken up will soon restore her to a normal state of mind?

DR. NEWBURY. Perhaps. — I hope so. — I would have good hope of it, if it were not for her attitude toward her child.

MRS. JORDAN [*overwhelmed*]. You noticed that, too! I have n't spoken to you of it, because — I have n't been willing to see it myself.

PHILIP. I can't see that there is anything particularly strange in her attitude. She takes care of the brat scrupulously enough.

POLLY. Brat!

MRS. JORDAN. Brat!

[*To* DR. NEWBURY, *after a reproachful gaze at* PHILIP.]

With the most watchful, the minutest care, but — [*she speaks in a constrained voice, with a nervous glance at the door*] — exactly as if it were a piece of machinery! — Phil, do please lay down that paper-knife before you break it! Your father brought that to me from India.

[*He obeys, but picks it up again absent-mindedly, after a few seconds.*]

Pardon me, Doctor. She goes about her daily business, and answers when she is spoken to, but as for her really being here — [*She breaks out.*] Doctor, what *shall* we do?

DR. NEWBURY. She must be roused from this state, but how to do it, I don't know.

POLLY [*rising, with heightened color and nervous emphasis*]. Well, I do!

MRS. JORDAN [*looking at her with frightened interrogation*]. Polly — ?

POLLY. What she needs is her husband, and I have sent for him!

PHILIP [*inarticulate with surprise and anger*]. You — !

POLLY. Yes, I. He 's been here a week. And he 's an angel, is n't he, mother ?

[PHILIP *snaps the paper-knife in two, flings the pieces to the floor, and rises, pale with rage.*]

MRS. JORDAN [*gathering up the pieces with a wail*]. Oh, Phil! How could you! One of my most precious relics !

PHILIP. [*To* MRS. JORDAN.] Is this true, or is it another of her tedious jokes ?

POLLY [*protesting*]. Oh, my dear, tedious !

MRS. JORDAN. [*Wipes her eyes, after ruefully fitting the broken pieces of the knife together and laying them tenderly on the table.*] You don't deserve to have me answer you, but it is true.

PHILIP. Was this action taken with your knowledge ?

MRS. JORDAN. I do not expect to be spoken to in that tone. Polly telegraphed merely the facts. He came at his own instance.

PHILIP. But you have consented to enter into relations with him ?

MRS. JORDAN. I have seen him several times.

POLLY [*triumphantly*]. And yesterday we showed him the baby! Such fun, was n't it, mother ?

MRS. JORDAN [*wiping her eyes, sheepishly*]. Yes, it was rather — enjoyable.

PHILIP. He can't be in this town. I should have heard of it.

POLLY. We 've hid him safe.

PHILIP. Where ?

POLLY. Never mind. He 's on tap, and the sooner we turn on the spigot the better, is what I think. Doctor, what do you think ?

DR. NEWBURY. Let me ask you again to state your view of Ruth's case. I don't think I quite grasp your view.

POLLY [*pluming herself, doctrinaire*]. Well! Here on the one hand is the primitive, the barbaric woman, falling in love with a romantic stranger, who, like some old Viking on a harry, cuts her with his two-handed sword from the circle of her kinsmen, and bears her away on his dragon ship toward the midnight sun. Here on the other hand is the derived, the civilized woman, with a civilized nervous system, observing that the creature eats bacon with his bowie knife, knows not the manicure, has the conversation of a preoccupied walrus, the instincts of a jealous caribou, and the endearments of a dancing crab in the mating season.

MRS. JORDAN. Polly! What ideas! What language !

DR. NEWBURY. Don't be alarmed, Mrs. Jordan. The vocabulary has changed since our day, and — the point of view has shifted a little. [*To* POLLY.] Well ?

POLLY. Well, Ruth is one of those people who can't live in a state of divided feeling. She sits staring at this cleavage in her life, like — like that man in Dante, don't you know, who is pierced by the serpent, and who stands there in hell staring at his wound, yawning like a sleepy man.

MRS. JORDAN. Oh, Polly, do please try not to get our heads muddled up with literature !

POLLY. All I mean is that when she married her man she married him for keeps. And he did the same by her.

[PHILIP *rises, with uncontrollable impatience, and goes back to the mantelpiece, against which he leans, nervously tearing a bit of paper to pieces.*]

DR. NEWBURY. Don't you think that a mere difference of cultivation, polish — or — or something of that sort — is rather small to have led to a rupture, and so painful a one, too ?

POLLY [*a little nonplussed*]. Well, yes, perhaps it *does look* small. But we don't know the particulars; and men *are* such *colossal* brutes, you know, dear doctor !

DR. NEWBURY [*judicially*]. Yes, so they are, so they are !

POLLY. And then her pride! You know when it comes to pride, Ruth would make Lucifer look like a charity-boy asking for more soup.

DR. NEWBURY. I think perhaps the plan should be tried. [*After a pause.*] Yes, I think so decidedly.

PHILIP. I call this a plot against her dignity and peace of mind !

DR. NEWBURY [*rising*]. Well, this conspirator must be going.

[*He shakes hands with* POLLY *and* MRS. JORDAN, *takes his hat and stick.* PHILIP *remains plunged in angry reflection.* DR. NEWBURY *taps* PHILIP *jestingly on the shoulder with the tip of his cane.*]

When you have lived as long as I have, my boy, you 'll — you 'll be just as old as I am !

[*He goes out,* POLLY *accompanying him to the door.* PHILIP, *disregarding his mother's conciliatory look and gesture as he passes her, goes out left.* POLLY *stretches her arms and draws a deep breath as the door closes after him.*]

MRS. JORDAN [*looking at her severely*]. Pray what does that mean ?

POLLY. Oh, Phil is such a walking thunder-cloud, these days. It 's a relief to get rid of him.

MRS. JORDAN. Have you done what you could to make his life brighter ?

POLLY. I never had a chance. He has always been too much wrapped up in Ruth to think of me.

MRS. JORDAN. How can you say such a thing ? What do you suppose he married you for ?

POLLY. Heaven knows ! What do they ever do it for ? It is a most curious and savage propensity. But immensely interesting to watch.

MRS. JORDAN [*with a despairing gesture*]. If you hold such heathenish views, why are you so bent on bringing those two together ?

POLLY [*soberly*]. Because they represent — what Philip and I have missed.

MRS. JORDAN. And pray what have " Philip and I " missed ?

POLLY. Oh, we 're all right. But we 're not like those two.

MRS. JORDAN. I should hope not !

POLLY. Even I believe that now and then a marriage is made in heaven. This one was. They are predestined lovers !

MRS. JORDAN [*mournfully, hypnotized by the evangelical note*]. I pray it may be so. [*She looks suspiciously at* POLLY.] You wretched girl ! Predestined lovers and marriages made in heaven, after all you 've just been saying about how impossible he is.

POLLY. He is quite impossible, but he 's the kind we can't resist, any of us. He 'd only have to crook his little finger at me.

MRS. JORDAN [*lifting her hands in despair*]. What are you young women coming to ! [*Pause.*] He seems to be a good man.

POLLY [*delighted*]. Oh, he 's *good !* So is a volcano between eruptions. And commonplace, too, until you happen to get a glimpse down one of the old volcanic rifts in his surface, and see — far below — underneath the cold lava-beds — fire, fire, the molten heart of a continent !

MRS. JORDAN. I only hope you have some vague general notion of what you are talking about.

POLLY. Amen. — And now let 's consider when, where, and how we are to hale this dubious pair together.

MRS. JORDAN. One thing is sure, it must n't be here.

POLLY. Why not ?

MRS. JORDAN. On Philip's account.

POLLY. Oh, bother Philip ! — Was n't that the doorbell ?

MRS. JORDAN. Yes. You had better go.

[POLLY *goes out. After a moment she reënters, excitedly.*]

POLLY. It 's Mr. Ghent !

MRS. JORDAN [*amazed*]. Mr. Ghent ?

[POLLY *nods enthusiastically.* GHENT *enters. He is conventionally dressed, a black string tie and the broad-brimmed hat which he carries being the only suggestions of Western costume remaining.* MRS. JORDAN *receives him in a flutter of excitement and alarm.*]

Mr. Ghent — ! Surely at this hour — !

GHENT. I beg your pardon. There was no other way. I am going West to-night. — Can I see you alone ?

MRS. JORDAN. [*Looks at* POLLY, *who goes out, pouting.*] Going West to-night ?

GHENT. Yes. Trouble at the mine.

MRS. JORDAN. Is n't your business partner competent to attend to it ?

GHENT. He 's competent to steal the whole outfit. In fact, is doing it, or has done it already.

MRS. JORDAN [*vaguely alarmed*]. And — my property here ? Is that involved in the danger ?

GHENT. Certainly not.

MRS. JORDAN [*relieved*]. I have gone

through such months of misery at the thought of losing the dear old place ! — If Ruth only knew that we owe the very roof over our heads to you —

GHENT. Well, she is n't to know, that 's understood, is n't it ? Besides, it 's nothing to speak of. Glad if you think it a service. She would n't.

MRS. JORDAN. You mean — ?

GHENT. I mean that if she knew about it, she would n't stay here overnight.

MRS. JORDAN. Sit down.

[*She motions him to a seat at the table; she sits near him, speaking with nervous impulsiveness.*]

Tell me what is the trouble between you ! It has all been a dreadful mystery from the beginning !

GHENT. Is it a mystery that a woman like your daughter — ?

[*He stops and sinks into gloomy thought.*]

MRS. JORDAN. Should have chosen you ? — Pardon me, I don't mean anything unkind —

[*He makes a gesture of brusque exoneration.*]

But having chosen — and broken faith with her brother to do it —

GHENT [*nervously*]. Let 's drop that ! [*Pause.*] Mrs. Jordan, you come of the old stock. Do you believe in the devil ?

MRS. JORDAN. Perhaps not in the sense you mean.

GHENT [*tapping his breast*]. I mean the devil inside of a man — the devil in the heart !

MRS. JORDAN. Oh, yes. We are all forced by our lives to believe in that.

GHENT. Our lives !

[*He looks slowly round the room.*]

How long have you lived here ?

MRS. JORDAN. For thirty years, in this house. Before I was married I lived in the old house down the road yonder, opposite the church.

GHENT. [*To himself.*] Think of it !

MRS. JORDAN. What did you say ?

GHENT. [*Gathers himself together.*] Mrs. Jordan, I want you to promise that what I put in your hands from time to time comes to your daughter as if from another source.

MRS. JORDAN. You are going away for good ?

GHENT. Yes.

MRS. JORDAN. You give her up ?

GHENT. A man can't give up what is n't his.

MRS. JORDAN. What is n't his ? She is your wife.

GHENT. No. Never has been.

MRS. JORDAN [*terrified*]. Oh, pitiful heavens !

GHENT I beg your pardon. — I was only trying to say — I used to think that when a couple was married, there they were, man and wife, and that was the end of it. I used to think that when they had a child, well, sure enough it was their child, and all said. — And there 's something in that, too.

[*He stares before him, smiting the table and speaking with low intensity.*]

Damn me if there ain't something eternal in it !

[*He sits for a moment more in gloomy thought.*]

Do you think she 'll make up to the young one, after a bit.

MRS. JORDAN. Oh, surely ! To think otherwise would be too dreadful !

GHENT. I 'd give a good deal to know. — It 's kind of lonesome for the little rooster, sitting out there all by himself on the world's doorstep ! — I must see her for a minute before I go. — Do your best for me.

MRS. JORDAN. I will do what I can.

GHENT. You can put it as a matter of business. There is a matter of business I want to talk over with her, if I can get up the gumption.

MRS. JORDAN. Had n't you better tell me what it is ?

GHENT. Well, it 's about your son Philip. That little scheme he started out in my country — the Cactus Fiber industry.

MRS. JORDAN. Yes ?

GHENT. I believe he thinks his sister's going away when she did queered his game.

MRS. JORDAN. It was a severe blow to him in every way. She was the life and soul of his enterprise.

GHENT. I want her to give him back the Cactus Fiber outfit, worth something more than when he dropped it.

MRS. JORDAN. Give it back to him ? She ?

GHENT. [*Takes papers from his pocket.*]

Yes. I happened to hear it was knocking around for nothing in the market, and I bought it — for the house, really. Hated to see that go to the dogs. Then I looked over the plant, and got a hustler to boom it. I thought as a matter of transfer, to cancel her debt, or what she thinks her debt —

[*Pause.*]

MRS. JORDAN [*fingering the paper with hesitation*]. Mr. Ghent, we really can't accept such a thing. Your offer is quixotic.

GHENT. Quix— what?

MRS. JORDAN. Quixotic, it really is.

GHENT [*doubtfully*]. I guess you're right. It depends on the way you look at it. One way it looks like a pure business proposition — so much lost, so much made good. The other way it looks, as you say, quix— um —. Anyway, there are the papers! Do what you think best with them.

[*He lays the papers on the table, and picks up his hat.*]

MRS. JORDAN. Wait in the parlor.

[*He opens the hall door.*]

The second door on the left.

[*With an awkward bow to* MRS. JORDAN, *he partly closes the door after him, when the inner door opens and* RUTH *appears. She goes to the sewing-table and picks up her sewing. Her mother, with a frightened glance, at the half-open hall door, draws her back and kisses her.* GHENT, *unseen by* RUTH, *remains standing, with his hand on the doorknob.*]

MRS. JORDAN. Ruth, you are a brave girl, and I will treat you like one. — Your husband is here.

RUTH. Here? — Where?

[GHENT *pushes the door open, and closes it behind him.* RUTH, *sinking back against the opposite wall, stares at him blankly.*]

MRS. JORDAN. He is leaving for the West again to-night. He has asked to see you before he goes.

[RUTH *covers her face with her hands, then fumbles blindly for the latch of the door. Her mother restrains her.*]

It is your duty to hear what he has to say. You owe that to the love you once bore him.

RUTH. He killed my love before it was born!

MRS. JORDAN. It is your duty to hear

him, and part with him in a Christian spirit, for our sakes, if not for your own.

RUTH. For whose sake?

MRS. JORDAN. For mine and your brother's. — We owe it to him, as a family.

GHENT [*raising his hand restrainingly*]. Mrs. Jordan — !

RUTH. Owe!

MRS. JORDAN. We owe it to him, for what he has done and wishes to do.

RUTH. What he has done? — Wishes to do?

MRS. JORDAN. Yes, don't echo me like a parrot! He has done a great deal for us, and is anxious to do more, if you will only let him.

RUTH. What is this? Explain it to me quickly.

MRS. JORDAN [*with growing impatience*]. Don't think to judge your mother!

RUTH. I demand to hear what all this is! Tell me.

MRS. JORDAN [*losing control of herself*]. He has kept us from being turned into the street!

[GHENT, *who has tried dumbly to restrain her, turns away in stoic resignation to his fate.*]

He has given us the very roof over our heads!

RUTH. You said that uncle —

MRS. JORDAN. Well, it was not your uncle! I said so to shield you in your stubborn and cold-hearted pride.

RUTH. Is there more of this?

MRS. JORDAN. Yes, there is more. You wronged your brother to follow your own path of willful love, and now you wrong him again by following your own path of willful aversion. Here comes your husband, offering to make restitution —

RUTH. What restitution?

MRS. JORDAN. He has bought Philip's property out there, and wants you to give it back to him.

[RUTH *stands motionless for a moment, then looks vacantly about, speaking in a dull voice, as at first.*]

RUTH. I must go away from this house.

MRS. JORDAN. You don't understand. He claims nothing. He is going away himself immediately. Whatever this dreadful trouble is between you, you are his wife, and he has a right to help you and yours.

RUTH. I am not his wife.

MRS. JORDAN. Ruth, don't frighten me. He said those same words —

RUTH. He said — what?

MRS. JORDAN. That you were not his wife.

RUTH. He said — that?

MRS. JORDAN. Yes, but afterward he explained —

RUTH [*flaming into white wrath*]. Explained! Did he explain that when I was left alone that night at the ranch he came — with two others — and when gun and knife had failed me, and nothing stood between me and their drunken fury, I sold myself to the strongest of them, hiding my head behind the name of marriage? Did he explain that between him and the others money clinked — [*she raps on the table*] — my price in hard money on the table? And now that I have run away to the only refuge I have on earth, he comes to buy the very house where I have hidden, and every miserable being within it!

[*Long pause. She looks about blankly and sinks down by the table.*]

MRS. JORDAN [*cold and rigid*]. And you — married him — after that?

[*She turns away in horror-stricken judgment.*]

You ought to have — died — first!

[*Philip opens the door and enters, staring at* GHENT *with dislike and menace.*]

Oh, Philip, she has told me! — You can't imagine what horrors!

[*RUTH rises, with fright in her face, and approaches her brother to restrain him.*]

PHILIP. Horrors? What horrors?

MRS. JORDAN. It was your fault! You ought never to have left her alone in that dreadful place! She — she married him — to save herself — from — Oh, horrible!

[*PHILIP waits an instant, the truth penetrating his mind slowly. Then, with mortal rage in his face, he starts toward* GHENT.]

PHILIP. You — dog!

[*RUTH throws herself in* PHILIP'S *path.*]

RUTH. No, no, no!

PHILIP. Get out of my way. This is my business now.

RUTH. No, it is mine. I tell you it is mine.

PHILIP. We'll see whose it is. I said

that if the truth ever came out, this man should answer to me, and now, by God, he shall answer?

[*With another access of rage he tries to thrust* RUTH *from his path.* MRS. JORDAN, *terrified at the storm she has raised, clings desperately to her son's arm.*]

RUTH. I told him long ago it should be between us. Now it shall be between us.

MRS. JORDAN. Philip! For my sake, for your father's sake! Don't, don't! You will only make it worse. In pity's name, leave them alone together. Leave them alone — together!

[*They force* PHILIP *back to the door, where he stands glaring at* GHENT.]

PHILIP. [*To* GHENT.] My time will come. Meanwhile, hide behind the skirts of the woman whose life you have ruined and whose heart you have broken. Hide behind her. It is the coward's privilege. Take it.

[*PHILIP, with* MRS. JORDAN *still clinging to his arm, goes out,* RUTH *closing the door after them. She and* GHENT *confront each other in silence for a moment, across the width of the room.*]

RUTH. God forgive me! You never can.

GHENT. It was a pity — but — you were in a corner. I drove you to it, by coming here.

RUTH. It was base of me — base!

GHENT. The way your mother took it showed me one thing. — I've never understood you, because — I don't understand your people.

RUTH. You mean — her saying I ought to have died rather than accept life as I did?

GHENT. Yes.

RUTH. She spoke the truth. I have always seen it.

GHENT. Ruth, it's a queer thing for me to be saying, but — it seems to me, you've never seen the truth between us.

RUTH. What is the truth — between us?

GHENT. The truth is —

[*He pauses, then continues with a disconsolate gesture.*]

Well, there's no use going into that.

[*He fumbles in his pocket, and takes from it the nugget chain, which he looks at in silence for a time, then speaks in quiet resignation.*]

I 've got here the chain, that 's come, one way and another, to have a meaning for us. For you it 's a bitter meaning, but, all the same, I want you to keep it. Show it some day to the boy, and tell him — about me.

[*He lays it on the desk and goes toward the door.*]

RUTH. What is the truth — between us ?

GHENT. I guess it was only of myself I was thinking.

RUTH. What is it — about yourself ?

GHENT [*after a pause*]. I drifted into one of your meeting-houses last Sunday, not knowing where else to go, and I heard a young fellow preaching about what he called "The Second Birth." A year and a half ago I should have thought it was all hocus-pocus, but you can believe me or not, the way he went on he might have been behind the door that night in that little justice den at San Jacinto, saying to the Recording Angel : " Do you see that rascal ? Take notice ! There ain't an ounce of bone or a drop of blood in him but what 's new man ! "

RUTH. You think it has been all my fault — the failure we 've made of our life ?

GHENT. It 's been no failure. However it is, it 's been our life, and in my heart I think it 's been — all — right !

RUTH. All right ! Oh, how can you say that ?

[*She repeats the words with a touch of awe and wonder.*]

All right !

GHENT. Some of it has been wrong, but as a whole it has been right — right ! I know that does n't happen often, but it has happened to us, because — [*he stops, unable to find words for his idea*] — because — because the first time our eyes met, they burned away all that was bad in our meeting, and left only the fact that we *had* met — pure good — pure joy — a fortune of it — for both of us. Yes, for both of us ! You 'll see it yourself some day.

RUTH. If you had only heard my cry to you, to wait, to cleanse yourself and me — by suffering and sacrifice — before we dared begin to live ! But you would n't see the need ! — Oh, if you could have felt for yourself what I felt for you ! If you could have said, " The wages of sin is death ! " and suffered the anguish of death, and risen again purified ! But instead of that, what you had done fell off from you like any daily trifle.

GHENT. [*Steps impulsively nearer her, sweeping his hand to indicate the portraits on the walls.*] Ruth, it 's these fellows are fooling you ! It 's they who keep your head set on the wages of sin, and all that rubbish. What have we got to do with suffering and sacrifice ? That may be the law for some, and I 've tried hard to see it as our law, and thought I had succeeded. But I have n't ! Our law is joy, and selfishness ; the curve of your shoulder and the light on your hair as you sit there says that as plain as preaching. — Does it gall you the way we came together ? You asked me that night what brought me, and I told you whiskey, and sun, and the devil. Well, I tell you now I 'm thankful on my knees for all three ! Does it rankle in your mind that I took you when I could get you, by main strength and fraud ? I guess most good women are taken that way, if they only knew it. Don't you want to be paid for ? I guess every wife is paid for in some good coin or other. And as for you, I 've paid for you not only with a trumpery chain, but with the heart in my breast, do you hear? That 's one thing you can't throw back at me — the man you 've made of me, the life and the meaning of life you 've showed me the way to !

[RUTH'S *face is hidden in her hands, her elbows on the table. He stands over her, flushed and waiting. Gradually the light fades from his face. When he speaks again, the ring of exultation which has been in his voice is replaced by a sober intensity.*]

If you can't see it my way, give me another chance to live it out in yours.

[*He waits, but she does not speak or look up. He takes a package of letters and papers from his pocket, and runs them over, in deep reflection.*]

During the six months I 've been East —

RUTH [*looking up*]. Six months ? Mother said a week !

GHENT. Your sister-in-law's telegram was forwarded to me here. I let her think it brought me, but as a matter of fact, I came East in the next train after yours. It was rather a low-lived thing to do, I suppose, hanging about and bribing your servant for news —

[RUTH *lets her head sink in her hands. He pauses and continues ruefully.*]

I might have known how that would strike you! Well, it would have come out sooner or later. — That's not what I started to talk about. — You ask me to suffer for my wrong. Since you left me I *have* suffered — God knows! You ask me to make some sacrifice. Well — how would the mine do? Since I've been away they've as good as stolen it from me. I could get it back easy enough by fighting; but supposing I don't fight. Then we'll start all over again, just as we stand in our shoes, and make another fortune — for our boy.

[RUTH *utters a faint moan as her head sinks in her arms on the table. With trembling hands,* GHENT *caresses her hair lightly, and speaks between a laugh and a sob.*]

Little mother! Little mother! What does the past matter, when we've got the future — and him?

[RUTH *does not move. He remains bending over her for some moments, then straightens up, with a gesture of stoic despair.*]

I know what you're saying there to yourself, and I guess you're right. Wrong is wrong, from the moment it happens till the crack of doom, and all the angels in heaven, working overtime, can't make it less or different by a hair. That seems to be the law. I've learned it hard, but I guess I've learned it. I've seen it written in mountain letters across the continent of this life. — Done is done, and lost is lost, and smashed to hell is smashed to hell. We fuss and potter and patch up. You might as well try to batter down the Rocky Mountains with a rabbit's heartbeat!

[*He goes to the door, where he turns.*]

You've fought hard for me, God bless you for it. — But it's been a losing game with you from the first! — You belong here, and I belong out yonder — beyond the Rockies, beyond the Great Divide!

[*He opens the door and is about to pass out.* RUTH *looks up with streaming eyes.*]

RUTH. Wait!

[*He closes the door and stands waiting for her to speak.* RUTH *masters herself and goes on, her eyes shining, her face exalted.*]

Tell me you know that if I could have followed you, and been your wife, without struggle and without bitterness, I would have done it.

GHENT [*solemnly*]. I believe you would.

RUTH. Tell me you know that when I tore down with bleeding fingers the life you were trying to build for us, I did it only — because — I loved you!

GHENT. [*Comes slowly to the table, looking at her with bewilderment.*] How was that?

RUTH. Oh, I don't wonder you ask! Another woman would have gone straight to her goal. You might have found such a one. But instead you found me, a woman in whose ears rang night and day the cry of an angry Heaven to us both — "Cleanse yourselves!" And I went about doing it in the only way I knew — [*she points at the portraits on the wall*] — the only way my fathers knew — by wretchedness, by self-torture, by trying blindly to pierce your careless heart with pain. And all the while you — Oh, as I lay there and listened to you, I realized it for the first time — you had risen, in one hour, to a wholly new existence, which flooded the present and the future with brightness, yes, and reached back into our past, and made of it — made of all of it — something to cherish!

[*She takes the chain, and comes closer.*]

You have taken the good of our life and grown strong. I have taken the evil and grown weak, weak unto death. Teach me to live as you do!

[*She puts the chain about her neck.*]

GHENT [*puzzled, not yet realizing the full force of her words*]. Teach you — to live — as I do?

RUTH. And teach — *him!*

GHENT [*unable to realize his fortune*]. You'll let me help make a kind of a happy life for — the little rooster?

RUTH. [*Holds out her arms, her face flooded with happiness.*] And for us! For us!

THE WITCHING HOUR

A PLAY

By AUGUSTUS THOMAS

CAST OF CHARACTERS

JACK BROOKFIELD, *professional gambler*

JUSTICE PRENTICE

FRANK HARDMUTH

CLAY WHIPPLE

HARVEY, *a servant*

TOM DENNING

COLONEL BAYLEY

LEW ELLINGER

MR. EMMETT, *Reporter*

JUSTICE HENDERSON

JO, *a servant*

MRS. HELEN WHIPPLE, *Clay's mother*

MRS. ALICE CAMPBELL, *Jack's sister*

VIOLA CAMPBELL, *her daughter*

THE WITCHING HOUR

ACT I

SCENE — *The library and card-room at "*JACK
BROOKFIELD'S,*" Louisville.*

*There is a large doorway, center, at the back,
which lets into a hallway, in which the banister
of a stairway which descends to the street level
is seen. A second and smaller doorway is near
the front in the wall to the left of the stage. This
doorway leads to the dining-room. The second
plan of the left wall is occupied by a fireplace
and mantel, surmounted by a marine painting.
The fireplace is surrounded by a garde au feu
club seat.*

*The rest of the left wall, as well as the rear
wall on both sides of the center door and all of the
right wall, is fitted with bookcases about five
feet high, in which are books handsomely bound.*

*The walls above these bookcases are hung with
heavy brocaded Genoese velvet of a deep maroon
in color and loosely draped. The ceiling is of
carved wood, gilded. On the wall velvet, at proper
intervals, are paintings by celebrated modern
artists. Some of these paintings are fitted with
hooded electric lights. Such a fitting is above a
noticeable Corot, which hangs to the right of the
center door.*

*A dark-red rug of luxuriant thickness is on
the floor. The furniture is simple, massive, and
Colonial in type. It consists of a heavy sofa
above the fireplace and running at right angles
to the wall. A heavy table fitted with books is in
the center; a smaller table for cards is at the
stage, right. Chairs are at both tables.*

*Above the center door is a marble bust of
Minerva, surmounted by a bronze raven, lac-
quered black, evidently illustrating Poe's poem.
The Antommarchi death-mask of Napoleon in
bronze hangs on the dark wood fireplace. A
bronze mask of Beethoven is on one of the bookcases and on another is a bust of Dante. A
bronze Sphinx is on another bookcase.*

*The room is lighted by a standing lamp at
the back and by the glow from the fireplace. Over
the table, center, is suspended an electric lamp
in a large bronze shade. This lamp, while not
lighted, is capable of being turned on by a push
button, which depends from it.*

*On the table, center, is a large paper-cutter
made of an ivory tusk.*

*Empty stage. After pause, sound of laughter
and dishes, left.*

[*Enter* JO, *sleek negro of Pullman car variety,
by stairway and center door. He goes to
door, left, and pauses — laughter ceases.*]

JO. Massar Brookfield.
JACK [*outside, left*]. Well, Jo?
JO. Mr. Denning, sah.
JACK. Ask Mr. Denning to come up.
JO. Yes, sah.

  [*Exit center. More talk and laughter,
  left.*]

[JACK *enters left. He walks to center on way
toward main door. Pauses. Returns, left.*]

JACK [*at door, left*]. Lew! I say — Lew
— you ladies excuse Mr. Ellinger a moment?

HELEN, ALICE, VIOLA [*outside*]. Oh —
yes. Certainly.

[*Enter* LEW ELLINGER, *from dining-room,
left.*]

LEW. See me?
JACK. Tom Denning's here — he expects
a game. My sister and Mrs. Whipple ob-
ject to the pasteboards — so don't mention
it before them.
LEW. Not a word — but, Tom — ?
JACK. I'll attend to Tom.
LEW. Good. [*Starts back to dining-room.*]

[*Enter* TOM DENNING, *right center; he is fat,
indolent type.*]

TOM. Hello, Lew.

  [LEW *stops and turns.* JACK *motions
  him out and* LEW *goes.*]

What you got to-night? Young Rocke-
feller?
JACK. Some ladies —
TOM [*grinning*]. What —
JACK [*sternly*]. My sister and her daugh-
ter — and a lady friend of theirs.
TOM [*disappointed*]. — No game?
JACK. Not until they go.

TOM [*getting a peek off into dining-room*]. Oh — chafing-dish.

JACK. They 've been to the opera. — I had Harvey brew them some terrapin.

TOM [*complaining*]. My luck!

[*His hands hang limp.*]

JACK. No, I think there 's some left. [*Pause.*] I 'm going to take a long chance and introduce you, Tom, only don't say anything about poker before the ladies.

TOM. Thought you said your *sister* —

JACK. I did.

TOM. Well, she 's on, is n't she?

JACK. But she does n't like it — and my niece — my niece does n't like it.

[*Enter HARVEY, old negro servant, from dining-room, left.*]

HARVEY. I 've made some coffee, Mars Jack. You have it in the dining-room or heah, sah?

JACK [*going*]. I 'll ask the ladies.

TOM. How are you, Harvey?

HARVEY [*bowing*]. Mars Denning —

JACK [*who has paused at door, left*]. Got some terrapin for Mr. Denning, Harvey?

HARVEY. Yas, sah. [*To TOM.*] Yas, sah.

[*Exit JACK, left.*]

TOM. They left some of the rum, too, I hope.

HARVEY. Could n't empty my ice-box in one evening, Mars Denning.

[*Starts off. Pause.*]

De ladies getting up.

[*Stands up stage in front of fire. TOM goes right. A pause.*]

[*Enter JACK.*]

JACK. The ladies will have their coffee in here, Harvey.

HARVEY. Yes, sir.

[*Enter ALICE. She is smartly gowned and is energetic.*]

JACK. Alice — this is my friend, Mr. Denning — my sister — Mrs. Campbell.

ALICE. Mr. Denning.

[*Enter HELEN and VIOLA. HELEN is thoroughly feminine in type, and is young-looking for the mother of a boy of twenty — VIOLA is an athletic Kentucky girl.*]

HELEN. I never take coffee even after dinner and at this hour — never!

[*Exit HARVEY.*]

JACK. Mrs. Whipple, may I present Mr. Denning?

HELEN. Mr. Denning.

TOM. Good-evening!

JACK. My niece, Miss Viola Campbell.

TOM. How are you? [*VIOLA bows.*]

JACK. Mr. Denning 's just left the *foundry* and he 's very hungry.

TOM. And thirsty —

JACK [*pushing him toward dining-room*]. Yes, and thirsty. Uncle Harvey 's going to save his life.

TOM. Ha, ha! Excuse me! [*Exit.*]

ALICE. The foundry?

[*Sits right of table.*]

JACK. Never did a day's work in his life. That 's Tom Denning.

VIOLA [*on sofa at fireplace*]. Tom Denning 's the name of the big race-horse.

JACK. Yes — he 's *named after* the race-horse.

HELEN [*on sofa, beside VIOLA*]. *What* does he do?

JACK. His father — father 's in the packing business — Kansas City; this fellow has four men *shoveling* money away from him so he can breathe.

[*Starts toward dining-room.*]

ALICE [*in amused protest*]. Oh, Jack!

JACK. Yes — I 'm one of them — you 'll find cigarettes in that box.

ALICE. Jack! [*Rises.*]

JACK [*apologizing*]. Not *you*, Alice, but —

VIOLA [*protesting*]. Well, certainly not for *me*, Uncle Jack?

JACK. Of course, not you . . .

HELEN. Thank you, Mr. Brookfield!

ALICE [*joining JACK*]. My dear brother, you confuse the Kentucky ladies with some of your Eastern friends.

JACK. Careful, Alice. *Helen* lived in the East twenty years, remember.

HELEN. But even my *husband* did n't smoke.

JACK. No?

HELEN. *Never* — in his life —

JACK. In his *life?* Why make such a pessimistic distinction?

[*HELEN turns away right.*]

ALICE. Jack! [*After a look to HELEN.*] How can you say a thing like that?

JACK. She 's the man's widow — I 've got to say it if any one does.

[*Enter HARVEY, with coffee.*]

Mr. Denning 's got his tortoise, Uncle Harvey?

HARVEY [*offering tray to* HELEN]. He's got the same as we all had, Mars Jack. Yas, sah. [*Laughs.*]

HELEN. None, thank you.

[HARVEY *moves on.*]

JACK. I'll take it, Uncle Harvey. I think three or four of them'll help this head of mine.

ALICE [*taking coffee*]. Why don't you let Viola cure your headache?

VIOLA [*taking coffee*]. Yes, Uncle Jack.

JACK. No, the coffee'll fix it, I'm sure.

[*Exit* HARVEY.]

VIOLA. Sit here while you drink it.

JACK. No — no, Viola. It isn't enough for that. I'll conserve your mesmeric endowment for a real occasion.

[*Swallows coffee in one mouthful.*]

VIOLA. Goodness! Just to please me?

JACK [*shaking head*]. Don't want to spoil your awful stories. [*Exit to dining-room.*]

HELEN. Is Viola a magnetic healer, too?

[*Sits right of table.*]

VIOLA. [*She takes a book, and returns to sofa, carrying also a large ivory tusk paper-cutter.*] Oh, no.

ALICE [*sitting left of table.*] Yes — a remarkable one.

VIOLA. Only headaches, Mrs. Whipple. Those I *crush* out of my victims.

HELEN. I remember Jack used to have a wonderful ability that way as a young man.

VIOLA. He says only with the girls.

ALICE. We know better, don't we?

HELEN. Yes.

VIOLA. Well, for myself, I'd rather have Uncle Jack sit by me than any regular physician I ever saw.

HELEN. You mean if you were ill?

VIOLA. Of course.

ALICE. You must be very clear with Mrs. Whipple on that point, Viola, because she used to prefer your Uncle Jack to sit by her, even when she was n't ill.

HELEN. [*To* VIOLA.] But especially when ill, my dear. [*To* ALICE.] And has he quit it?

ALICE. Yes — you know Jack went into politics for a while.

HELEN. Did he?

ALICE. *Local* politics — yes — something about the police did n't please him and then he quit all of his curative work.

HELEN. Why?

ALICE. Well, in politics, I believe there's something unpleasant about the word "heeler."

HELEN. Oh!

VIOLA. Entirely different spelling, however.

HELEN. Our English language is so elastic in that way.

ALICE. Yes, the papers joked about his magnetic touch. The word "touch" is used offensively also. So Jack dropped the whole business.

HELEN. And Viola inherits the ability?

ALICE. Well, if one can inherit ability from an uncle.

HELEN. From a family.

ALICE. That's even more generous, but Viola is like Jack in every way in which a girl may resemble a man. Horses and boats and every kind of personal risk — and —

VIOLA. [*Rises.*] I'm *proud* of it.

ALICE. And Jack spoils her.

VIOLA. Am I spoiled?

[*Goes to back of table.*]

ALICE. He could n't love her more if he were her father —

[*Enter* CLAY, *a boy of twenty.*]

CLAY [*pausing at door*]. May I come in?

VIOLA. Certainly.

CLAY. Is n't this a jolly room, mother?

HELEN. Beautiful.

CLAY [*waving hand above*]. And the sleeping apartments are what I take pride in. Private bath to every bedroom, reading-lamps just over the pillows —

VIOLA. Have n't you seen the house, Mrs. Whipple?

HELEN. Not above this floor.

ALICE. Would it interest you?

[*Rises and goes left.*]

HELEN. Very much.

ALICE [*at door of dining-room*]. Jack —

JACK [*outside*]. Yes —

ALICE. [*To* HELEN.] Will I do as your guide?

HELEN. [*Rises.*] Oh, yes.

[*Enter* JACK.]

ALICE. I want to show Helen over the house.

JACK. Do.

ALICE. The rooms are empty?

JACK. Empty, of course.

ALICE. Don't be too indignant, they're not always empty. [*To* HELEN.] In *Jack's* house one is liable to find a belated pilgrim in any room.

HELEN [*laughing*]. And a lady walking in unannounced would be something of a surprise, would n't she?

JACK. Well — two ladies would, certainly.

ALICE. Jack!

JACK. My dear sister — they *would*. Hard lines when the reputation of a man's house is n't respected by his own sister — ha!   [*Exit left, with mock indignation.*]

HELEN [*smiling*]. The same Jack.

ALICE. Intensified and confirmed! [*Pausing at door.*] Will you come, too, Viola?

VIOLA. No, thank you, mother.

[HELEN *looks at* ALICE. *She and* ALICE *go.*]

CLAY. What was Frank Hardmuth saying to you?

VIOLA. When?

CLAY. At supper — and in the box at the theater, too?

VIOLA. Oh — Frank Hardmuth — nobody pays any attention to him.

CLAY. I thought *you* paid a great deal of attention to what he was saying.

VIOLA. In the same theater party a girl's got to listen — or leave the box.

CLAY. Some persons listen to the opera.

VIOLA. I told him that was what I wanted to do.

CLAY. Was he making love to you, Viola?

VIOLA. I should n't call it that.

CLAY. Would anybody else have called it that if they'd overheard it?

VIOLA. I don't think so.

CLAY. Won't you tell me what it was about?

VIOLA. I don't see why you ask.

CLAY. I asked because he seemed so much in earnest — and because *you* seemed so much in earnest.

VIOLA. Well?

CLAY. And Frank Hardmuth's a fellow that 'll stand watching.   [*Looks off left.*]

VIOLA [*smiling*]. He stood a good deal to-night.

CLAY. I mean that he 's a clever lawyer and would succeed in making a girl commit herself in some way to *him* before she knew it.

VIOLA. I think that depends more on the way the *girl* feels.

CLAY. Well — I don't want you to listen to Frank Hardmuth under the idea that he 's the only chance in Kentucky.

VIOLA. Why, Clay Whipple —

CLAY. You know very well *I've* been courting you myself, Viola, don't you?

VIOLA. You have n't. You've been coming round like a big boy.

CLAY. [*Follows right.*] Have I gone with any other girl — anywhere?

VIOLA. I don't know.   [*Sits right.*]

CLAY. And I've spoken to your Uncle Jack about it.

VIOLA. To Uncle Jack?

CLAY. Yes.

VIOLA. [*Rises.*] Nobody told you to speak to Uncle Jack.

CLAY. Mother did.

VIOLA. *Your* mother?

CLAY. Yes. Mother 's got regular old-fashioned ideas about boys and young ladies and she said, "if you think Viola *likes* you, the *honorable* thing to do is to speak to her guardian first."

VIOLA. Oh! — you *thought* that, did you?

CLAY. I certainly did.

VIOLA. I can't imagine why.

CLAY. I thought that because you 're Jack Brookfield's niece, and nobody of his blood would play a game that is n't fair.

VIOLA. I wish you would n't always throw that up to me. [*Goes to sofa.*] 'T is n't our fault if Uncle Jack 's a sporting man.   [*Sits.*]

CLAY [*following*]. Why, Viola, I was praising him. I think your Uncle Jack the gamest man in Kentucky.

VIOLA. Nor that either. I don't criticize my Uncle Jack, but he 's a lot better man than just a fighter or a card-player. I love him for his big heart.

CLAY. So do I. If I'd thought you cared I 'd have said you were too much like him at heart to let a fellow come a-courtin' if you meant to refuse him — and that was all that was in my mind when I asked about Frank Hardmuth — and I don't care what Hardmuth said either, if it was n't personal that way.

VIOLA. Frank Hardmuth's nothing to me.

CLAY. And he won't be? [*Pause.*] Will

he — ? [*Pause.*] Say that. Because I'm awfully in love with you.

VIOLA. Are you?

CLAY. You bet I am. Just Tom-fool heels over head in love with you.

VIOLA. You never said so.

CLAY. Mother said a boy in an architect's office had better wait till he was a partner — but I can't wait, Viola, if other fellows are pushing me too hard.

VIOLA. [*Rises.*] Uncle Jack says you *are* a regular architect if there ever was one.

CLAY. It's what *you* think that makes the difference to me.

VIOLA. Well, I think — [*Pause.*] — Uncle Jack certainly *knows*.

CLAY. And an architect's just as good as a lawyer.

VIOLA. Every bit.

CLAY. Viola.   [*Takes her in his arms.*]

VIOLA. Now — I don't *mind* tellin' you — he was speakin' for himself — Frank Hardmuth.

CLAY. By Jove — on this very night.

VIOLA. Yes.

CLAY. Seems like the Hand of Providence that I was here. Let's sit down. [*They sit.*] You've got confidence in me, have n't you?

VIOLA. Yes — I've always said to mother — Clay Whipple 'll make his mark some day — I should say I *had* confidence in you.

CLAY. Huh. [*Laughs.*] Of course the *big* jobs *pay*. Things like insurance buildings — but my heart's in domestic architecture — and if you don't laugh at me, I'll *tell* you something.

VIOLA. Laugh at you — about your work and your ambition! Why, Clay!

CLAY. I do most of the domestic interiors for the firm already — and whenever I plan a second floor or a staircase I can see *you* plain as day walkin' through the rooms — or saying good-night over the banisters.

VIOLA. Really? [CLAY *nods.*] You mean in your mind?

CLAY. No, with my eyes. Domestic architecture's the most poetic work a man can get into outside of *downright* poetry itself.

VIOLA. It must be if you can *see* it all that way.

CLAY. Every room — I can see your short sleeves as you put your hands on the

banisters — and sometimes you push up your front hair with the back of your hand that way —   [*Brushes his forehead.*]

VIOLA. Oh, this — [*repeats the gesture*] — all girls do that.

CLAY. But not just the same way as you do it. Yes, sir! I can see every little motion *you* make.

VIOLA. Whenever you care to think about me.

CLAY. Bless you, no — that's the trouble of it.

VIOLA. What trouble?

CLAY. The pictures of you — don't come just when I *want* them to come — and they don't go when I want them to go — especially in the dark.

VIOLA. Why, how funny.

CLAY. Sometimes I've had to light the gas in order to go to sleep.

VIOLA. Why, I never heard of anything like that.

CLAY. Well, it happens with me often. I designed this room for your Uncle Jack — but before I put a brush in my color-box I saw this very Genoese velvet and the picture frames in their places — and that Corot right there — I've got kind of a superstition about that picture.

VIOLA. [*Rises.*] A superstition!
        [*Regards the Corot.*]

CLAY. I said to Jack, have anything else you want on the other walls, but right there I want you to put a Corot that I've seen at a dealer's in New York — and he did it.

VIOLA. Uncle Jack generally has his own way about pictures.

CLAY. I only mean that he approved my taste in the matter — but my idea of this house really started *with* — and grew around that canvas of Corot's.

VIOLA. Then it is n't always *me* that you see?

CLAY. Always you when I think about a real house, you bet — a house for *me* — and you'll be there, won't you?
        [*Takes her in his arms.*]

VIOLA. Will I?

CLAY. Yes — say, "I will."

VIOLA. I will.

[*Reënter* ALICE *and* HELEN.]

ALICE [*astonished*]. Viola!
        [VIOLA *goes left.*]

CLAY. I 've asked her — mother.

ALICE. Helen, you knew ?

HELEN. Yes.

CLAY. [*To* ALICE.] And I asked Jack, too.

ALICE. You mean —

CLAY. We 're engaged — if you say it 's all right.

ALICE. And you — Viola ?

VIOLA [*nodding*]. Yes —

ALICE [*going to chair left of table*]. Well, if Jack 's been consulted and you *all* know of it — I should make a very hopeless minority.

CLAY. Why any minority ?

ALICE. Only the necessary considerations. [*To* HELEN.] Clay's prospects — his youth.

VIOLA. Why, he designs most of the work for his firm now.

CLAY. That is, dwellings.

HELEN. I should advise waiting — myself — until Clay is in the firm — [*To* CLAY.] And I did advise delay in speaking to Viola herself.

CLAY. I 'd 'a' waited, mother, only Frank Hardmuth proposed to Viola *to-night!*

ALICE. To-night ?

VIOLA. At the opera.

ALICE. One is n't safe anywhere.

CLAY. You would n't want *him!* So you do consent, don't you ?

ALICE. I think your mother and I should talk it over.

CLAY. Well, it 's a thing a fellow does n't usually ask his mother to arrange, but —
[*Pause.*]

VIOLA. You mean privately ?

ALICE. Yes.

CLAY. We can go to the billiard room, I suppose ?

VIOLA. Come on.

CLAY [*at the center door with* VIOLA]. You know, mother — how I feel about it.
[*Exit with* VIOLA.]

HELEN. I supposed you had guessed it.
[*Sits right of table.*]

ALICE. I had — but when the moment arrives after all, it 's such a surprise that a mother can't act naturally.

HELEN. Clay is really very trustworthy for his years.

ALICE. There 's only one thing to discuss. I have n't mentioned it because — well, because I 've seen so little of you since it began and because the fault is in my own family.

HELEN. Fault ?

ALICE. Yes — Jack's fault — [*Pause.*] Clay is playing.

HELEN. You mean —

ALICE. Here with Jack's friends.

HELEN. Clay gambling !

ALICE [*wincing*]. I don't quite get used to the word, though we 've had a lifetime of it — [*sits left of table*] — gambling.

HELEN. I should n't have thought Jack would do that — with *my* boy.

ALICE. Jack has n't our feminine viewpoint, Helen — and, besides, Jack is calloused to it.

HELEN. You should have talked to Jack yourself.

ALICE. Talked to him ? I did much more — that is, as much more as a sister dependent on a brother for support could do. You know Jack really *built* this place for me and Viola.

HELEN. I 'd thought so — yes.

ALICE. Viola is the very core of Jack's heart — well, we both left the house and went into our little apartment and are there now. A woman can't do much more than that and still take her living from a man, can she ?

HELEN. No —

ALICE. And it hurt him — hurt him past any idea.

HELEN. You did that because my Clay was — was playing here ?

ALICE. Not entirely Clay — everybody ! [*Pause — a distant burst of laughter comes from the men in the dining-room.*] There is n't a better-hearted man nor an abler one in the State than Jack Brookfield, but I had my daughter to consider. There were two nights under our last city government when nothing but the influence of Frank Hardmuth kept the police from coming to this house and arresting everybody — think of it.

HELEN. Dreadful —

ALICE. Now, that 's something, Helen, that I would n't tell a soul but you. *Viola* does n't know it — but Jack's card-playing came between you and him years ago and you — *may* know it. [*Rises and looks toward dining-room.*] You may even have some influence with Jack.

HELEN. I — ah, no.

ALICE. Yes — this supper to-night was Jack's idea for you. The box at the opera for you.

HELEN. Why, Jack didn't even sit with us.

ALICE. Also — for you — Jack Brookfield is a more notable character in Louisville to-day than he was twenty-two years ago. His company would have made you the subject of unpleasant comment. That's why he left us alone in the box.

HELEN. Isn't it a pity — a terrible pity! [Laughter off left. HELEN rises.]

[Enter HARDMUTH, JACK, DENNING, and LEW. HARDMUTH is the aggressive prosecutor.]

HARDMUTH. I tell the gentlemen we've left the ladies to themselves long enough, Mrs. Campbell.

ALICE. Quite long enough, Mr. Hardmuth.

DENNING. Where's the young lady? Jack's niece?

HELEN. In the billiard room, I believe.

DENNING. [To HELEN, disappointed.] Oh — Jack's been telling us what a great girl she is.

HARDMUTH. Some of us knew that without being told.

DENNING. And she's wonderfully like you — wonderfully.

HELEN. You compliment me —

JACK. Are you under the impression you're speaking to Viola's mother?

DENNING. Ain't I?

JACK. This lady is Mrs. Whipple.

DENNING. Oh, Clay's mother? [HELEN bows.] Well, your boy, Mrs. Whipple, plays in the hardest luck of all the people I ever sat next to.

HELEN. You mean —

JACK [interrupting and putting his arm about DENNING]. You depreciate yourself, Tom. There's no hard luck in merely sitting next to you.

DENNING. Ha, ha.

HELEN. [To ALICE.] I think Clay and I should be going.

JACK [consulting his watch]. Oh, no — only a little after twelve and no one ever goes to sleep here before two. [To DENNING.] I told you to keep still about card games.

DENNING. I meant unlucky at billiards. They're all right, ain't they?

JACK. Oh — [Walks away impatiently.]

DENNING. Let's go and see the young lady play billiards with Clay. [To ALICE.] I can see now your daughter resembles you. [Moves up with ALICE toward door. LEW follows.]

JACK. Shall we join them?

HELEN. I'd like it. [JACK and HELEN start up.]

HARDMUTH. Jack! Just a minute.

JACK. [To HELEN.] Excuse me —

DENNING. [To ALICE as they go.] No, Kansas City's my home, but I don't live there. [Exit with ALICE.]

JACK. Be right in, Lew. [Exit HELEN with LEW.]

Well, Frank —

HARDMUTH. I took advantage of your hospitality, old man, to-night.

JACK. Advantage?

HARDMUTH. Yes — I've been talking to your niece.

JACK. Oh!

HARDMUTH. Proposed to her.

JACK. Yes?

HARDMUTH. Yes —

[Enter Jo from downstairs.]

Jo. A gentleman called you on the telephone, sah.

JACK [regarding watch]. Who?

Jo. Judge Brennus — name sounds like. Holdin' the wire, sah.

JACK. I don't know any Judge Brennus.

Jo. Says you don't know him, sah, but he's got to leave town in the mornin' and he'd be very much obliged if you'd see him to-night.

JACK. Did you tell him we were dark to-night?

Jo. He didn't want no game. It's about a picture — a picture you've got.

JACK. A picture?

Jo. He wants to look at it. [JACK looks at HARDMUTH.]

HARDMUTH. It's a blind.

JACK [consulting watch]. Well, this is a good night to work a blind on me. [To Jo.] Tell the gentleman I'll be up for half an hour.

Jo. Yes, sah. [Exit.]

JACK. So you proposed to Viola?

HARDMUTH. Yes. How do you feel about that?

JACK. You know the story of the barkeeper asking the owner, "Is Grady good for a drink ? " — " Has he had it ? " — " He has." — " He is."

HARDMUTH. Just that way, eh ? [JACK *nods*.] Well — she has n't answered me.

JACK [*musing*]. Ha —

HARDMUTH. And under those conditions, how 's Grady's credit with you ?

JACK. Well, Frank, on any *ordinary* proposition you 're aces with me. You know that.

HARDMUTH [*seated right of table*]. But for the girl ?

JACK. It 's different.

HARDMUTH. Why ?

JACK. She 's only nineteen — you know.

HARDMUTH. My sister married at *eighteen*.

JACK. I mean *you 're* thirty-five.

HARDMUTH. That 's not an unusual difference.

JACK. Not an impossible difference, but I think unusual — and rather unadvisable.

HARDMUTH. That 's what *you* think.

JACK. That 's what I think.

HARDMUTH. But suppose the lady is willing to give that handicap ? [*Pause —* JACK *shrugs his shoulders*.] What then ?

JACK. Let 's cross the bridge when we come to it.

HARDMUTH. You mean *you 'd* still drag a little ?

JACK. [*Pause*.] Do you think Viola likes you well enough to say yes?

HARDMUTH. Let 's cross *that* bridge when we come to it.

JACK. We have come to that one, Frank. There 's another man in the running and I think she likes him.

HARDMUTH. You mean young Whipple ? [*Rises, goes to fireplace*.] Well, he took second money in the box party to-night — at the supper table, too. I 'll agree to take care of him if you 're with *me*.

JACK [*at table, center*]. I think *he 's* your biggest opposition.

HARDMUTH. But you. Can I count on *you* in the show-down ?

JACK. [*Pause. Sits right of table*.] If Viola did n't care enough for you, Frank, to accept you in spite of everything, I should n't try to influence her in your favor.

[*Enter* LEW, *center, from left*.]

LEW. I think a bum game of billiards is about as thin an entertainment for the outsiders as " Who 's got the button."

HARDMUTH [*meeting* LEW *up left center*]. I 've got a little business, Lew, with Jack for a minute.

LEW. Well, I can sit in by the bottle, can't I ? [*Moves toward dining-room*.]

JACK. Help yourself, Lew.

LEW. Such awful stage waits while they chalk their cues. [*Exit left*.]

HARDMUTH. But you would n't try to influence her against me.

JACK. [*Pause*.] She 's about the closest thing to me there *is* — that niece of mine.

HARDMUTH. [*Pause*.] Well ?

JACK. I 'd protect her happiness to the limit of my ability.

HARDMUTH. If she likes me — or should come to like me — enough — her — happiness would be with *me*, would n't it ? [*Sits again*.]

JACK. She might think so.

HARDMUTH. Well ?

JACK. But she 'd be mistaken. It would be a mistake, old chap.

HARDMUTH. I know twenty men — twelve to fifteen years older than their wives — all happy — wives happy, too.

JACK. 'T is n't just that.

HARDMUTH. What is it ?

JACK. She 's a fine girl — that niece of mine — not a blemish.

HARDMUTH. Well —

JACK. I want to see her get the best — the very best — in family position — character —

HARDMUTH. Anything against the Hardmuths ? [JACK *shakes head*.] I 'm assistant district attorney — and next trip I 'll be *the* district attorney.

JACK. I said character.

HARDMUTH. Character ?

JACK. Yes.

HARDMUTH. You mean there 's anything against my reputation ?

JACK. No — I mean character pure and simple — I mean the moral side of you !

HARDMUTH. Well, by God !

JACK. You see, I 'm keeping the *girl* in mind all the time.

HARDMUTH. *My morals !*

JACK. Let 's say your moral fiber.

HARDMUTH. [*Rises*.] Well, for richness this beats anything I 've struck. Jack Brookfield talking to me about my moral fiber ! [*Goes toward fire*.]

JACK. You asked for it.

HARDMUTH. [*Returns aggressively.*] Yes — I did, and now I'm going to ask for the show-down. What do you mean by it?

JACK [*with fateful repression*]. I mean — as long as you've called attention to the "richness" of Jack Brookfield talking to you on the subject — that Jack Brookfield is a professional gambler — people get from Jack Brookfield just what he promises — a square game. Do you admit that?

HARDMUTH. I admit that. Go on.

JACK. [*Rises, front of table.*] You're the assistant prosecuting attorney for the city of Louisville; the people *don't* get from you just what *you* promised — not by a jugful —

HARDMUTH. I'm the *assistant* prosecuting attorney, remember — I promised to assist in prosecution, not to institute it.

JACK. I expect technical defense, old man, but this was to be a show-down.

HARDMUTH. Let's have it — I ask for particulars.

JACK. Here's one. You *play* here in my house and you know it's against the law that you've sworn to support.

HARDMUTH. I'll support the law whenever it's invoked. Indict me and I'll plead guilty.

JACK. This evasion is what I mean by lack of moral fiber.

HARDMUTH. Perhaps we're a little shy somewhere on mental fiber.

JACK. You make me say it, do you, Frank? Your duty, at least, is to keep secret the information of your office; contrary to that duty you've betrayed the secrets of your office to warn me and other men of this city when their game was in danger from the police.

HARDMUTH. You *throw* that up to me?

JACK. [*Sits on left end of table.*] Throw nothing — you asked for it.

HARDMUTH. I stand by my friends.

JACK. Exactly — and you've taken an oath to stand by the people.

HARDMUTH. Do you know any sure politician that does n't stand by his friends?

JACK. Not one.

HARDMUTH. Well, there!

JACK. But I don't know any sure politician that I'd tell my niece to marry.

HARDMUTH. That's a little too fine-haired for me! [*Turns to fire.*]

JACK. I think it is.

HARDMUTH. [*Returns.*] I'll bet you a thousand dollars I'm the next prosecuting attorney of this city.

JACK. I'll take half of that if you can place it. I'll bet even money you're anything in politics that you go after for the next ten years.

HARDMUTH. Then I don't understand your kick.

JACK. But I'll give odds that the time 'll come when you're way up there — full of honor and reputation and pride — that somebody 'll drop to you, Frank, and flosh! *You* for the down and outs.

HARDMUTH. Rot!

JACK. It's the same in every game in the world — the crook either gets too gay or gets too slow, or both, and the "come on" sees him make the pass. I've been pallbearer for three of the slickest men that ever shuffled a deck in Kentucky — just a little *too* slick, that's all — and they've always got it when it was hardest for the family.

HARDMUTH. So that 'll be my finish, will it?

JACK. Sure.

HARDMUTH [*going back of table*]. You like the moral fiber of this Whipple kid?

JACK. I don't know. [*Crosses to fireplace.*]

HARDMUTH. Weak as dishwater.

JACK. I don't think so.

HARDMUTH. I'll do him at any game you name.

JACK. He's only a boy — you should.

HARDMUTH. I'll do him at this game.

JACK. What game?

HARDMUTH. The girl! I thought I could count on you because — well, for the very tips you hold against me; but you're only her uncle, old man, after all.

[*Swaggers down right.*]

JACK. That's all.

HARDMUTH. And if she says "yes" —

JACK. [*Comes to front of table. Pause. The men confront each other.*] Frank! Some day the truth 'll come out — as to who murdered the governor-elect of this State.

HARDMUTH. Is there any doubt about that?

JACK. Is n't there?

HARDMUTH. The man who fired that shot's in jail.

JACK. I don't want my niece mixed up in it.

HARDMUTH [*angrily*]. What do you mean by that?

[*Enter* HELEN, *center. An awkward pause.*] The young people still playing?

HELEN. Yes.

HARDMUTH. I'll look 'em over. [*Exit.*]

HELEN. Won't you come, too?

JACK. I'd rather stay here with you.

HELEN. That gentleman that called after supper —

JACK. Mr. Denning —

HELEN. Yes. He seems to take pleasure in annoying Clay —

JACK [*seriously*]. Yes — I know that side of Denning! [*Goes to door of dining-room.*] Lew!

LEW. Yes.

JACK. I wish you'd go into the billiard room and look after Tom Denning.

LEW [*entering left*]. What's he doing?
[*Jack turns to* HELEN.]

HELEN. [*To* JACK.] Commenting humorously — hiding the chalk and so on.

LEW [*as he goes up*]. Lit up a little I suppose.

JACK [*nodding*]. Just ride hard on him.
[*Exit* LEW.]

HELEN [*going left to sofa*]. He does n't seem much of a gentleman, this Mr. Denning.

JACK. He was n't expected to-night.

HELEN. Is he one of your "clients"?

JACK [*smiling*]. One of my "*clients*"?

HELEN. Clay meets him here?

JACK. Yes — *has* met him here.

HELEN. I did n't think you'd do that — Jack — with *my* boy.

JACK. Do what?

HELEN. Gamble.

JACK [*smiling*]. It's no gamble with your boy, Helen — sure thing. He has n't won a dollar!

HELEN. I'm glad you're able to smile over it.

JACK. Perhaps it would be more humorous to you if he'd won.

HELEN. If he plays — I'd rather see him win, of course.

JACK. [*Beside sofa.*] That's what puts me in the *business* — winning. The thing that makes every gambler stick to it is winning occasionally. I've never let your boy get up from the table a dollar to the good and because he *was* your boy.

HELEN. Why let him play at all?

JACK. He'll play somewhere till he gets sick of it — or marries.

HELEN. Will marriage cure it?

JACK. It would have cured me — but you don't see it that way.

HELEN. You made your choice.

JACK. I asked you to trust me — you wanted some ironclad pledge — well, my dear Helen — that was n't the best way to handle a fellow of spirit.
[*Goes front of table.*]

HELEN. So *you* chose the better way?

JACK. No choice — I stood pat — that's all.

HELEN. And wasted your life.

JACK [*sitting on edge of table*]. That depends on how you look at it. You married a doctor who wore himself out in the Philadelphia hospitals. I've had three meals a day — and this place — and — a pretty fat farm and a stable with some good blood in it — and —

HELEN [*coming to him*]. And every one of them, Jack, is a monument to the worst side of you.

JACK. [*Stands and takes her hands; he smiles.*] Prejudice, my dear Helen. You might say that if I'd earned these things in some respectable business combination that starved out all its little competitors — but I've simply furnished a fairly expensive entertainment — to eminent citizens — looking for rest.

HELEN. I know all the arguments of your — profession — Jack, and I don't pretend to answer them any more than I answer the arguments of reckless women who claim that they are more commendable than their sisters who make loveless marriages.

JACK. [*Goes to chair, right.*] I'm not flattered by the implied comparison — still —

HELEN. I only feel sure that anything which the majority of good people condemn is wrong. [*Sits left of table.*]

JACK. [*Sits right of table.*] I'm sorry —

HELEN. I'd be glad if you meant that — but you're not sorry.

JACK. I *am* sorry — I'm sorry not to have public respect — as long as you think it's valuable.

HELEN. I amuse you — don't I?

JACK [*elbows on knees*]. Not a little bit — but you make me blue as the devil, if that's any satisfaction.

HELEN. I'd be glad to make you blue as the devil, Jack, if it meant discontent with what you're doing — if it could make you do better.

JACK. I'm a pretty old leopard to get nervous about my spots.

HELEN. Why are you blue?

JACK. You.

HELEN. In what way?

JACK. I had hoped that twenty years of charitable deeds had made you also charitable in your judgment.

HELEN. I hope it has.

JACK. Don't seem to ease up on my specialty.

HELEN. You called your conduct "wild oats" twenty years ago.

JACK. It was — but I found such an excellent market for my wild oats that I had to stay in that branch of the grain business. Besides, it has been partly your fault, you know.

[HELEN *plays with the ivory paper-knife, balancing it on the front edge of table.*]

HELEN. Mine?

JACK. Your throwing me over for my wild oats — put it up to me to prove that they were a better thing than you thought.

HELEN. Well — having demonstrated that —

JACK. Here we are —

HELEN. Yes — here we are.

JACK. Back in the old town. Don't you think it would be rather a pretty finish, Helen, if despite all my — my leopard's spots — and despite that — [*pause*] — that Philadelphia episode of yours —

HELEN. You call twenty years of marriage episodic.

JACK. I call any departure from the main story episodic.

HELEN. And the main story is —

JACK. You and I —

HELEN. Oh —

[*Paper-knife falls to floor — JACK rises and picks it up, stands in front of table left hand on HELEN's — his right gesticulating with paper-knife.*]

JACK. Wouldn't it be a pretty finish if you took my hand and I could walk right up to the camera and say, "I told you so" — ? You know I always felt that you were coming back.

HELEN. Oh, did you?

JACK [*playfully, and going right center*]. Had a candle burning in the window every night.

HELEN. You're sure it wasn't a red light?

JACK [*remonstrating*]. Dear Helen! have some poetry in your composition. Literally "red light" of course — but the real flame was here — [*hand on breast*] — a flickering hope that somewhere — somehow — somewhen I should be at rest — with the proud Helen that loved and — rode away.

HELEN [*almost accusingly*]. I — believe — you.

JACK. Of course you believe me.

HELEN. You had a way, Jack — when you were a boy at college, of making me write to you.

JACK. Had I? [*Goes back of table.*]

HELEN. You know you had — at nights — about this hour — I'd find it impossible to sleep until I'd got up and written to you — and two days later I'd get from you a letter that had crossed mine on the road. I don't believe the word "telepathy" had been coined then — but I guessed something of the force — and all these years, I've felt it — nagging! Nagging!

JACK. Nagging?

HELEN. Yes — I could not keep you out of my waking hours — out of my thought — but when I surrendered myself to sleep the call would come — and I think it was rather cowardly of you, really.

JACK [*back of table*]. I plead guilty to having thought of you, Helen — lots — and it was generally when I was alone — late — my — clients gone. This room —

"Whose lights are fled,
Whose garlands dead,
And all but he departed."

HELEN. And as you say — here we are.

JACK. Well, what of my offer? Shall we say to the world — "We told you so?" What of my picturesque finish?

HELEN. You know my ideas — you've known them twenty-two years.

JACK. No modification?

HELEN. None!

JACK. I'll be willing to sell the tables. [*Points above to second floor.*] And — well — I don't think I could get interested in this bridge game that the real good people play — would you object to a gentleman's game of "draw" now and then?

HELEN. You called it a gentleman's game in those days.

JACK. No leeway at all?

HELEN. No compromise, Jack — no —

. JACK. M— [*Pause.*] I trust you won't consider my seeming hesitation uncomplimentary?

HELEN. Not unprecedented, at least.

JACK. You see it opens up a new line of thought — and —

[*Passes his hand over forehead.*]

HELEN [*rising in sympathy*]. And you have a headache, too, — it is n't kind I 'm sure.

[*Enter* Jo.]

JACK. Oh, nothing — nothing. [*To* Jo.] Well?

Jo. That gentleman, sah, about the picture.

JACK. I 'll see him. [*Exit* Jo.]

HELEN. A caller?

JACK. Won't be a minute — don't go away, because I think we can settle this question to-night, you and I.

HELEN. Please don't put me in the light of waiting for an answer.

JACK. Dear Helen — we 're both past that — are n't we? If I can only be sure that I could be worthy of you. I 'm the one that 's waiting for an answer — from my own weak character and rotten irresolution.

[JACK *goes with* HELEN *to door, center, kisses her hand. She goes;* JACK *retains her hand as long as possible and when he lets it go, it falls limply to* HELEN'S *side as she disappears.*]

They say cards make a fellow superstitious. [*Pause.*] Well — I — guess they do —

[*Enter* Jo *and* JUSTICE PRENTICE. PRENTICE *wears overcoat, carries cane and silk hat.*]

JACK. Judge de Brennus?

PRENTICE [*after amused look at* Jo]. Justice Prentice. [*Exit* Jo.]

JACK. Oh, Justice Prentice! Good-evening!

PRENTICE. You are Mr. Brookfield?

JACK. Yes.

PRENTICE. I should n't have attempted so late a call but that a friend pointed you out to-night at the opera, Mr. Brookfield, and said that your habit was — well —

JACK. Not to retire immediately?

PRENTICE. Yes.

JACK. Will you be seated?

PRENTICE. I 'm only passing through the city. I called to see a Corot that I understand you bought from Knoedler.

JACK. That 's it.

PRENTICE. Oh — thank you. [*Starts.*] You don't object to my looking at it?

JACK. Not at all.

[*Touches button, light shows on picture.*]

PRENTICE [*after regard*]. That 's fine. [*Pause.*] I thought at one time that I would buy this picture.

JACK. You know it, then?

PRENTICE. Yes. [*Pause.*] Are you particularly attached to it, Mr. Brookfield?

JACK [*sitting*]. I think not irrevocably.

[*Takes pad of paper and figures mechanically.*]

PRENTICE. Oh.

[*Pause, during which the* JUSTICE *looks at the picture.*]

Do I understand that is what you paid for it, or what you intend to ask me for it?

[*Jack starts.*]

JACK. What?

PRENTICE. Sixty-five hundred.

JACK [*astonished*]. I did n't speak the price, did I?

PRENTICE. Did n't you — oh. [*Pause.*] I could n't pay that amount.

JACK [*puzzled*]. That 's its price — however.

PRENTICE. I regret I did n't buy it from the dealer when I had my chance.

[*Looks about at other pictures on back wall.*]

I could n't have given it so beautiful a setting, Mr. Brookfield, nor such kindred — but it would not have been friendless —

[*At fireplace.*]

That 's a handsome marine.

JACK. Yes.

PRENTICE. Pretty idea I read recently in an essay of Dr. van Dyke's. His pictures were for him his windows by which he looked out from his study onto the world. [*Pause.*] Yes?

JACK. Quite so.

PRENTICE [*regarding a picture over dining-room door*]. M— Washington!

JACK [*again astonished*]. What?

PRENTICE. My home is Washington — I thought you asked me?

JACK. No, I did n't.

PRENTICE. I beg your pardon —

JACK [*front of table ; aside*]. But I 'm damned if I was n't going to ask him.

PRENTICE [*viewing other pictures*]. And the phases of your world, Mr. Brookfield, have been very prettily multiplied.

JACK. Thank you — may I offer you a cigar? [*Opens box on table.*]

PRENTICE. Thank you, I won't smoke.

JACK. Or a glass of wine?

PRENTICE. Nothing. I 'll return to the hotel — first asking you again to excuse my untimely call.

JACK. I wish you 'd sit down awhile.

PRENTICE. But I did n't know until I 'd missed it from Knoedler's how large a part of my world — my dream world — I had been looking at through this frame.

[*Regards the Corot again.*]

JACK. Well, if it 's a sentimental matter, Mr. Justice, we might talk it over.

PRENTICE. I must n't submit the sentimental side of it, Mr. Brookfield, and where I have so — so intruded.

JACK. That 's the big side of anything for me — the sentimental.

PRENTICE. I 'm sure of it — and I must n't take advantage of that knowledge.

JACK. You 're sure of it?

PRENTICE. Yes.

JACK. Is that my reputation?

PRENTICE. I don't know your reputation.

JACK. Then, how are you sure of it?

PRENTICE [*impressively*]. Oh — I see you — and — well, we have *met*.

JACK. Ah —

PRENTICE. Good-night. [*Going up.*]

JACK. One moment. [*Pause.*] You said your address was Washington?

PRENTICE. Yes.

JACK. You thought at the time I was about to ask you that question?

PRENTICE. I thought you had asked it.

JACK. And you thought a moment before I had said sixty-five hundred for the picture?

PRENTICE. Yes.

JACK. Do you often — pick answers that way?

PRENTICE. Well, I think we all do — at times.

JACK. We all do?

PRENTICE. Yes — but we speak the answers only as we get older and less atten-

tive and mistake a person's thought for his spoken word.

JACK. A person's thought?

PRENTICE. Yes.

JACK. Do you mean you know what I think?

PRENTICE [*returning to table*]. I had n't meant to claim any monopoly of that power. It 's my opinion that every one reads the thoughts of others — that is, some of the thoughts.

JACK. Every one?

PRENTICE. Oh, yes.

JACK. That *I* do?

PRENTICE [*regarding him*]. I should say *you* more generally than the majority of men.

JACK. There was a woman said something like that to me not ten minutes ago.

PRENTICE. A woman would be apt to be conscious of it.

JACK. You really believe that — that stuff? [*Sits left of table.*]

PRENTICE. Oh, yes — and I 'm not a pioneer in the belief. The men who declare the stuff most stoutly are scientists who have given it most attention.

JACK. How do they prove it?

PRENTICE. They *don't* prove it — that is, not universally. Each man must do that for himself, Mr. Brookfield.

JACK. How —

PRENTICE. [*Pause. Smiles.*] Well, I 'll tell you all I know of it. [*Becoming serious.*] Every thought is active — that is, born of a desire — and travels from us — or it is born of the desire of some one else and comes to us. We send them out — or we take them in — that is all.

JACK. How do we know which we are doing?

PRENTICE. If we are idle and empty-headed, our brains are the playrooms for the thought of others — frequently rather bad. If we are active, whether benevolently or malevolently, our brains are workshops — *power-houses*. I was passively regarding the pictures ; your active idea of the price — registered, that 's all — so did your wish to know where I was from.

JACK. You say "*our* brains" — do you still include mine?

PRENTICE. Yes.

JACK. You said mine more than the majority of men's.

PRENTICE. I think so.

JACK. Why has n't this whatever it is — effect — happened to me, then?

PRENTICE. It has.

JACK. [Pause.] Why did n't I know it?

PRENTICE. Vanity? Perhaps.

JACK. Vanity?

PRENTICE. Yes — often some — friend has broached some independent subject and you have said, " I was just about to speak of that myself."

JACK. Very often, but —

PRENTICE. Believing the idea was your own — your vanity shut out the probably proper solution — that it was his.

JACK. Well, how, then, does a man tell which of his thoughts are his own?

PRENTICE. It 's difficult. Most of his idle ones are not. When we drift we are with the current. To go against it or to make even an eddy of our own we must swim — Most everything less than that is hopeless.

JACK [smiling]. Well — I have n't been exactly helpless.

PRENTICE. No one would call you so, Mr. Brookfield. [Going.] You have a strong psychic — a strong hypnotic ability.

JACK [smiling]. You think so?

PRENTICE. I know it.

JACK. This business?

[Makes slight pass after manner of the professional hypnotist.]

PRENTICE [smiling]. That business for the beginner, yes —

JACK. You mean that I could hypnotize anybody?

PRENTICE. Many persons — yes — but I would n't do it if I were you —

JACK. Why not?

PRENTICE. Grave responsibility.

JACK. In what way?

PRENTICE. [Pause. Smiles.] I 'll send you a book about it — if I may.

JACK. Instructions?

PRENTICE. And cautions — yes —

[Goes up to picture again.]

If you tire of your Corot, I 'd be glad to hear from you.

JACK. Why could n't I save postage by just thinking another price?

PRENTICE. The laws on contracts have n't yet recognized that form of tender.

Enter TOM, center. He laughs and shows signs of drink.]

TOM. I say, Jack — here 's the greatest joke you ever saw — [Sees the JUSTICE.] Oh, excuse me.

[Enter LEW, following.]

LEW. That won't do, Tom. — [To JACK.] Excuse me, Jack, but I had to get him out of there.

JACK. I 'll go downstairs with him, Mr. Justice. [Exit with the JUSTICE.]

TOM. Who 's that old bird?

LEW. You 'll offend Jack if you 're not careful, Tom. You 've got half a jag now.

TOM. J' ever see anything 's as funny as that? He don't like my scarf-pin — ha, ha — well I don't like it — but my valet put it on me and what 's difference —

[Enter HARDMUTH.]

HARDMUTH. What was that?

TOM. My scarf-pin!

HARDMUTH. Scarf-pin?

TOM. Yes — he pushed me away from him and I said what 's matter. He said I don't like your scarf-pin — ha, ha — I said don't? I don't like your face.

LEW. Very impolite with the ladies there.

HARDMUTH. Why should he criticize Tom's scarf-pin?

TOM. 'Zactly. I said I can change my scarf-pin — but I don't like your face.

[Enter CLAY from dining-room excitedly.]

CLAY. Where 's Jack?

LEW. Saying good-night to some old gentleman below.

TOM [interposing as CLAY starts up left center]. And I don't like your face.

CLAY. That 's all right, Mr. Denning. [Tries to pass.] Excuse me.

TOM [with scarf-pin in hand]. Excuse me. What 's the matter with that scarf-pin?

CLAY. It 's a cat's-eye and I don't like them, that 's all — I don't like to look at them.

LEW. Let him alone, Tom.

TOM. Damn 'f 'ee ain't scared of it, ha, ha!

[Pushing pin in front of CLAY's face.]

CLAY [greatly excited]. Don't do that.

HARDMUTH [sneering]. 'T won't bite you, will it?

CLAY. [Averts his face.] Go away, I tell you.

TOM. [Holds CLAY with left hand. Has pin in right.] 'T will bite him — bow — wow — wow —

CLAY. Don't, I tell you — don't.

TOM [*still holding him*]. Bow — wow — wow —

LEW. Tom !

HARDMUTH [*laughing*]. Let them alone.

CLAY. Go away.

TOM. Bow — wow —

[*Enter* JACK.]

JACK. What 's the matter here ?

TOM [*pursuing* CLAY]. Wow —

[CLAY *in frenzy swings the large ivory paper-knife from table, blindly strikes* TOM, *who falls.*]

JACK. Clay !

CLAY [*horrified*]. He pushed that horrible cat's-eye right against my face.

JACK. What cat's-eye ?

HARDMUTH. [*Picks up the pin which* DENNING *has dropped.*] Only playing with him — a scarf-pin.

LEW [*kneeling by* DENNING]. He 's out, Jack.

[*Enter* Jo.]

CLAY. I did n't mean to hurt him ; really I did n't mean that.

HARDMUTH [*taking the paper-cutter from* CLAY]. The hell you did n't. You could kill a bull with that ivory tusk.

JACK. Put him on the window seat — give him some air.

[*Enter* ALICE, *left center.*]

ALICE. Jack, we 're going now — all of us.

[*Enter* HARVEY.]

JACK [*turning to* ALICE]. Wait a minute. [*To* Jo.] Help Mr. Ellinger there.

[Jo, LEW, *and* HARVEY *carry off* TOM *into the dining-room.*]

ALICE. What is it ?

JACK. An accident — keep Helen and Viola out of these rooms.

ALICE. Had n't we better go ? Clay is with us.

CLAY. I can't go just now, Mrs. Campbell — [*Looks off.*] I hope it is n't serious — I did n't mean to hurt him, really. [*Exit left.*]

ALICE. A quarrel ?

[LEW *enters and waves hand, meaning "All over."*]

HARDMUTH [*with paper-knife*]. A murder !

[*Enter* HELEN *and* VIOLA.]

VIOLA. What 's the matter ?

[*Enter* CLAY.]

CLAY [*in panic and up right center. To* HELEN]. Oh, mother, I 've killed him.

HELEN [*taking* CLAY *in her arms*]. Killed him — whom ?

HARDMUTH. Tom Denning.

CLAY. But I never meant it — Jack ; I just struck — struck wild.

HARDMUTH. With this.

HELEN. With that ! Oh, my boy !

JACK. That will do ! Everybody — Lew, telephone Dr. Monroe it 's an emergency case and to come in dressing-gown and slippers. [*Exit* LEW, *right center.*] Alice, I know you 're not afraid of a sick man — or — that sort of thing. Help me and Jo.

[*Leads* ALICE, *left. She braces herself.*]

Viola, you take Mrs. Whipple upstairs and wait there.

HARDMUTH [*starting up right*]. I 'll notify the police.

HELEN. Oh !

JACK [*interposing*]. *Stop !* You 'll stay just where you are !

HARDMUTH. You tryin' to hide this thing ?

JACK. The doctor 'll tell us exactly what this thing is. And then the boy 'll have the credit himself *of notifying the police.*

ACT II

SCENE — *The library-living room of* JUSTICE PRENTICE, *Washington, D.C.*

The walls of this room are bookcases glassed quite to the ceiling, and filled with books mostly in sheepskin binding. This array is broken by a large bay window at the back, center, which is equipped with a window seat, and by two doors near the front of the stage, one on the right and one on the left.

At the left is also a fireplace with a log fire. In the upper left-hand corner of the room there is a buffet, fitted with glasses and decanters. A dark rug is on the floor.

The furniture of the room is dark oak in Gothic. It consists of a table and three chairs at the center, sofa and smaller table up right. The smaller table holds a lamp.

Over the buffet there is a small canvas by Rousseau showing a sunset.

JUSTICE PRENTICE *and* JUDGE HENDERSON *are playing chess.*

HENDERSON. Checkmate in three moves.

PRENTICE. I don't see that.

HENDERSON. Well, Knight to —

PRENTICE. Yes, yes, I see. Checkmate in three moves. That's one game each. Shall we play another?

HENDERSON. Let us look at the enemy. [*Draws watch.*] By Jove! Quarter of twelve. I guess Mrs. Henderson will be expecting me soon. [*Pause.*] I'll play a rubber with you, and its result shall decide your position on the Whipple case.

PRENTICE. Why, Mr. Justice, I'm surprised at you. A United States Supreme Court decision — shaped by a game of chess. We'll be down to the level of the intelligent jurymen soon — flipping pennies for the verdict.

HENDERSON. And a very good method in just such cases as this. Well, if you won't play — [*rises*] — I'll have to go.

PRENTICE. [*Rises.*] Not without another toddy.

HENDERSON. Yes.

PRENTICE [*at sideboard up left*]. Oh, no. Come, now, don't you like this liquor?

HENDERSON. Immensely. Where did you say you got it?

PRENTICE. Kentucky. One lump?

HENDERSON. Only one!

PRENTICE. My old home, sir, — and a bit of lemon?

HENDERSON. A piece of the peel — yes.

PRENTICE. They make it there.

HENDERSON. I'll pour the water.

PRENTICE. There, there, don't drown me.

HENDERSON. My folks were Baptists, you see. What do you say it costs you?

PRENTICE. Fifty cents a gallon.

HENDERSON. What!! I think I'll take water. [*Puts down glass.*]

PRENTICE. That's what it cost me. Its value I don't know. An old friend sends it to me. Fifty cents for express.

HENDERSON. Oh!

PRENTICE. That's different, is n't it?

HENDERSON. [*Recovers glass.*] Very!

PRENTICE. He makes it down there. Why, it's in the same county in which this Whipple murder occurred.

HENDERSON. How about that point? We might as well admit it and remand the case.

PRENTICE. No. There's no constitutional point involved.

HENDERSON. A man's entitled to an open trial.

PRENTICE. Well, Whipple had it.

HENDERSON. No, he did n't. They would n't admit the public.

PRENTICE. Oh, come, now; the courtroom was crowded and the Judge refused admission to others — only when there was danger of the floor breaking.

HENDERSON. But, my dear Mr. Justice, that would have been all right to limit the attendance —

PRENTICE. Well, that's all he did.

HENDERSON. Only he did it by having the sheriff issue tickets of admission. That placed the attendance entirely in the control of the prosecution and the defense is right in asking a rehearing.

PRENTICE. Oh, nonsense! Justice is a little too slow in my old State and I'm impatient with technical delays. It is two years since they openly assassinated the governor-elect and the guilty man is still at large.

HENDERSON. Why should the killing of Scovill bear on this case!

PRENTICE. It bears on me. I'm concerned for the fair fame of Kentucky.

HENDERSON. Well, if you won't, you won't and there's an end of it.

[*Rings call bell.*]

PRENTICE. Have another?

HENDERSON. Not another drop.

[*Enter* SERVANT.]

Get my coat!

PRENTICE. A nightcap.

SERVANT. I beg pardon, sir.

PRENTICE. Speaking to the Justice.

[*Exit* SERVANT.]

HENDERSON. No, I must n't. Mrs. Henderson filed her protest against my coming home loaded and I've got to be moderate.

PRENTICE. Well, if you won't, you won't.

HENDERSON [*front of table, picks up book*]. Hello! Reading the Scriptures in your old age?

PRENTICE. It does look like a Bible, does n't it? That's a flexible binding I had put on a copy of Bret Harte. I admire him very much.

HENDERSON. I like some of his stuff.

PRENTICE. When I get home from the Capitol and you prosy lawyers, I'm too tired to read Browning and those heavy

guns, so I take Bret Harte — very clever,
I think ; I was reading before you came —
[*takes book*] — "A Newport Romance." Do
you know it ?

HENDERSON. I don't think I do.

PRENTICE. It's about an old house at
Newport — that's haunted — a young girl
in the colonial days dies of a broken heart
in this house, it seems. Her sweetheart
sailed away and left her — and here's the
way Bret Harte tells of her coming back.
[HENDERSON *sits.*] Oh, I'm not going to
read all of it to you — only one verse.
[*Looks at book. — Pause.*] Oh, I forgot to
tell you that when this chap left the girl he
gave her a little bouquet — understand ?
That's a piece of material evidence necessary to this summing up.

[HENDERSON *nods.* PRENTICE *reads.*]

"And ever since then when the clock strikes
  two,
She walks unbidden from room to room,
And the air is filled, that she passes through,
With a subtle, sad perfume.

The delicate odor of mignonette,
The ghost of a dead-and-gone bouquet,
Is all that tells of her story; yet
Could she think of a sweeter way ? "

Is n't that charming, eh ?

HENDERSON. A very pretty idea.

PRENTICE. Beautiful to have a perfume
suggest her. I suppose it appeals to me
especially because I used to know a girl
who was foolishly fond of mignonette.

HENDERSON. Well, you don't believe in
that stuff, do you?

PRENTICE. What stuff ?

HENDERSON. That Bret Harte stuff —
the dead coming back — ghosts and so
forth ?

PRENTICE. Yes, in one way I do. I find
as I get older, Judge, that the things of
memory become more real every day —
every day. Why, there are companions of
my boyhood that I have n't thought of for
years — that seem to come about me —
more tangibly, or as much so as they were
in life.

HENDERSON. Well, how do you account
for that ? Spiritualism ?

PRENTICE. Oh, no. It's Time's perspective.

HENDERSON. Time's perspective ?

PRENTICE. Yes. [*Pause.*] I'll have to
illustrate my meaning. [*Indicates a paint-*

ing.] Here's a sunset by Rousseau. I
bought it in Paris last summer. Do you
see what an immense stretch of land there
is in it ?

HENDERSON. Yes.

PRENTICE. A bird's-eye view of that
would require a chart reaching to the ceiling. But see Rousseau's perspective. The
horizon line is n't two inches from the
base.

HENDERSON. Well ?

PRENTICE. [*Returns to table.*] Well, my
dear Judge, that is the magic in the perspective of Time. My boyhood's horizon is
very near to my old eyes now. The dimmer
they grow, the nearer it comes, until I
think sometimes that when we are through
with it all — we go out almost as we entered — little children.

HENDERSON. [*Pause.*] That's a very
beautiful painting, Judge — a Russell, you
say ?

PRENTICE. A Rousseau.

HENDERSON. Oh —

PRENTICE. Yes — cost me three thousand
only, and a funny thing about it : the canvas just fitted into the top of my steamer
trunk, and it came through the custom-
house without a cent of duty. I completely
forgot it.

HENDERSON. Your memory is n't so re-
tentive, then, as it seems ?

PRENTICE. Not on those commercial matters.

[*Enter* SERVANT *with coat. In crossing front
of table to* HENDERSON, *the coat knocks a
miniature from the table to the floor.*]

PRENTICE. You dropped your tobacco-
box, I guess, Mr. Justice.

HENDERSON. [*Examines pocket.*] No.

SERVANT. [*Picks up miniature.*] It was
this picture, sir.

PRENTICE. My gracious — my gracious !
It might have been broken.

SERVANT. Oh, it often falls when I'm
dusting, sir.

PRENTICE. Oh, does it ? Well, I'll put
it away. [*Exit* SERVANT.] An ivory miniature by Wimar. I prize it highly — old-
fashioned portrait, see ! Gold back.

HENDERSON. A beautiful face.

PRENTICE [*eagerly*]. Is n't it ? Is n't it ?
[*Looks over* HENDERSON's *shoulder.*]

HENDERSON. Very. What a peculiar

way of combing the hair — long, and over the ears.

PRENTICE. The only becoming way women ever wore their hair. I think the scrambly style they have now is disgraceful.

HENDERSON. Your mother?

PRENTICE. Dear, no, a young girl I used to know. Oh, don't smile, she's been dead a *good* thirty years — married and had a large family.

HENDERSON. Very sweet — very sweet, indeed.

PRENTICE. Isn't it?

[*Enter* SERVANT.]

Well?

SERVANT. Card, sir.

PRENTICE. Gentleman here?

[*Takes card.*]

SERVANT. Yes, sir.

PRENTICE. I'll see him. [*Exit* SERVANT.]

HENDERSON. Call?

PRENTICE. Yes. The man owns a picture that I've been trying to buy — a Corot.

HENDERSON. Oh — another of these perspective fellows?

PRENTICE. Yes — his call doesn't surprise me, for he's been in my mind all day.

HENDERSON. Seems to be in a hurry for the money — coming at midnight.

PRENTICE. I set him the example — besides, midnight is just the shank of the evening for Mr. Brookfield. He's supposed to be a sporting man — ahem.

[*Enter* SERVANT *and* JACK. JACK *is paler and less physical than in first act.*]

PRENTICE. Good-evening.

JACK. You remember me, Mr. Justice?

PRENTICE. Perfectly, Mr. Brookfield — this is Justice Henderson.

HENDERSON. Mr. Brookfield.

JACK. Pleased to meet you, Mr. Justice. [*To* PRENTICE.] I hope I'm not intruding.

HENDERSON. I'm just going, Mr. Brookfield. [*To* PRENTICE.] To-morrow?

PRENTICE. To-morrow!

HENDERSON [*at door, inquiringly*]. No constitutional point about it? Eh?

PRENTICE. None.

HENDERSON. Good-night.

PRENTICE. Good-night. [*To* JACK.] Have a chair.

JACK. Thank you.

[*Stands by chair left of table.*]

PRENTICE [*toward buffet*]. I've some medicine here that comes directly from your city.

JACK. I don't think I will — if you'll excuse me.

PRENTICE. Ah — [*Pause. Smiles.*] Well, have you brought the picture?

JACK. The picture is still in Louisville — I — I'm in Washington with my niece.

PRENTICE. Yes?

JACK. And — a lady friend of hers. They're very anxious to meet you, Mr. Justice.

PRENTICE. Ah. [*Pause.*] Well — I go to the Capitol at noon to-morrow and —

JACK. To-night! — They're leaving the city to-morrow — as you were when I had the pleasure of receiving you.

PRENTICE. I remember.

JACK [*with watch*]. They were to come after me in five minutes if I didn't return, and those five minutes, Mr. Justice, I hoped you would give to me.

PRENTICE. With pleasure.

[*Sits right of table.*]

JACK [*plunging at once into his subject*]. Those two books you sent me —

PRENTICE. Yes?

JACK. I want to thank you for them again — and to ask you how far you go — with the men that wrote them — especially the second one. Do you believe that book?

PRENTICE. Yes.

JACK. You do?

PRENTICE. I do. I know the man who wrote it — and I believe him.

JACK. Did he ever do any of his stunts for you — that he writes about?

PRENTICE. He didn't call them "stunts," but he has given me many demonstrations of his ability — and mine.

JACK. For example?

PRENTICE. For example? He asked me to think of him steadily at some unexpected time and to think of some definite things. A few days later — this room — two o'clock in the morning — I concentrated my thoughts — I mentally pictured him going to his telephone and calling me.

JACK. And did he do it?

PRENTICE. No — [*pause*] — but he came here at my breakfast hour and told me that at two o'clock he had waked and risen from his bed — and walked to his 'phone in the hallway with an *impulse* to call me — and then had stopped — because he had no message to deliver and because he thought his imagination might be tricking him.

JACK. You had n't given him any tip, such as asking how he 'd slept?

PRENTICE. None. Five nights after that I repeated the experiment.

JACK. Well?

PRENTICE. That time he called me.

JACK. What did he say?

PRENTICE. He said, "Old man, you ought to be in bed asleep and not disturbing honest citizens," which was quite true.

JACK. By Jove, it 's a devilish creepy business, is n't it?

PRENTICE. Yes.

JACK. And if it 's so —

PRENTICE. And it is so.

JACK. Pay a man to be careful what he thinks — eh?

PRENTICE. It will very well pay your type of men to do so.

JACK. I don't want to be possessed by any of these bughouse theories, but I 'll be blamed if a few things have n't happened to me, Mr. Justice, since you started me on this subject.

PRENTICE. Along this line?

JACK. Yes. [Pause.] And I 've tried the other side of it, too.

PRENTICE. What other side?

JACK. The mesmeric business. [Pause. Makes passes.] I can do it.

PRENTICE. Then I should say, Mr. Brookfield, that for you the obligation for clean and unselfish thinking was doubly imperative.

JACK. Within this last year I 've put people — well — practically asleep in a chair and I 've made them tell me what a boy was doing — a mile away — in a jail.

PRENTICE. I see no reason to call clairvoyance a "bughouse" theory.

JACK. I only know that I do it.

PRENTICE. Yes — you have the youth for it — the glorious strength. Does it make any demand on your vitality?

JACK. [Passes hand over his eyes.] I 've fancied that a headache to which I 'm subject is more frequent — that 's all.

PRENTICE. But you find the ability — the power — increases — don't you?

JACK. Yes — in the last month I 've put a man into a hypnotic sleep with half a dozen waves of the hand. [Makes pass.]

PRENTICE. Why motion?

JACK. Fixed his attention, I suppose.

PRENTICE [shaking head]. Fixes your attention. When in your own mind your belief is sufficiently trained, you won't need this. [Another slight pass.]

JACK. I won't?

PRENTICE. No.

JACK. What 'll I do?

PRENTICE. Simply think. [Pause.] You have a headache, for example.

JACK. I have a headache for a fact.

[JACK again passes hand over eyes and forehead.]

PRENTICE. Well — some persons could cure it by rubbing your forehead.

JACK. I know that.

PRENTICE. Others could cure it by the passes of the hypnotist. Others by simply willing that it should — [pause] — be cured.

JACK. Well, that 's where I can't follow you — and your friend the author.

PRENTICE. You simply think your headache.

JACK. I know it aches.

PRENTICE. I think it does n't.

JACK [astonished]. What?

PRENTICE. I — think — it does n't.

JACK. [Pause.] Well, just this moment, it does n't, but — [Pause.] — is n't that — simply mental excitement — won't it come back?

PRENTICE. It won't come back to-day.

JACK. That 's some comfort. The blamed things have made it busy for me since I 've been studying this business.

PRENTICE. It is a two-edged sword —

JACK. You mean it 's bad for a man who tries it?

PRENTICE. I mean that it constantly opens to the investigator new mental heights, higher planes — and every man, Mr. Brookfield, is ill in some manner who lives habitually on a lower level — than the light he sees.

[Enter SERVANT.]

SERVANT. Two ladies, sir.

PRENTICE. Your friends?

JACK. I think so.

[PRENTICE and JACK look at SERVANT.]

SERVANT. Yes, sir.

PRENTICE. Ask them up.

[Exit SERVANT.]

JACK. Thank you.

PRENTICE. [*Rises.*] I'll put away Judge Henderson's glass.

JACK. They're Kentucky ladies, Mr. Justice.

PRENTICE [*indicating* JACK]. But I don't want any credit for a hospitality I haven't earned.

JACK. I see.

[*Enter* SERVANT *with* HELEN *and* VIOLA.]

JACK. My niece, Miss Campbell.

PRENTICE. Miss Campbell.

JACK. And —

HELEN. One moment, Jack. I prefer to introduce myself.

PRENTICE. Won't you be seated, ladies?

[*Exit* SERVANT. HELEN *sits right of table.* VIOLA *goes to the window-seat.* JACK *stands center.*]

HELEN. You are not a married man, Justice Prentice?

PRENTICE. I am not.

HELEN. But you have the reputation of being a very charitable one.

PRENTICE. [*Sits left of table.*] That's pleasant to hear — what charity do you represent?

HELEN. None. I hardly know how to tell you my object.

PRENTICE. It's a personal matter, is it?

JACK [*back of table*]. Yes, a very personal matter.

PRENTICE. Ah!

HELEN. I have here an autograph book —

PRENTICE. [*To* JACK.] I usually sign my autograph for those who wish it — at the —

HELEN. I did not come for an autograph, Justice Prentice, I have brought one.

PRENTICE. Well, I don't go in for that kind of thing very much. I have no collection — my taste runs more toward —

HELEN. The autograph I have brought is one of yours, written many years ago. It is signed to a letter. Will you look at it?

[*Opens autograph book and gives small folded and old lace handkerchief from book to* VIOLA, *who joins her.*]

PRENTICE. With pleasure. [*Takes book.*] Is this the letter? Ah — [*Reads.*] "June 15, 1860." Dear me, that's a long time ago. [*Reads.*] "My dear Margaret: The matter passed satisfactorily — a mere scratch. Boland apologized. — Jim." What is this?

HELEN. A letter from you.

PRENTICE. And my dear Margaret — 1860. Why, this letter — was it written to Margaret?

HELEN. To Margaret Price —

PRENTICE. Is it possible — well — well. [*Pause.*] I wonder if what we call coincidences are ever mere coincidences. Margaret Price. Her name was on my lips a moment ago.

JACK. Really, Mr. Justice?

PRENTICE. [*To* JACK.] Yes. Did you know Margaret Price?

JACK. Yes.

[*Looks at* HELEN — PRENTICE'S *gaze follows.*]

HELEN. She was my mother —

PRENTICE. Margaret Price was —

HELEN. Was my mother.

PRENTICE. Why, I was just speaking of her to Justice Henderson whom you saw go out. Her picture dropped from the table here. [*Gets it.*] This miniature! Margaret Price gave it to me herself. And you are her daughter?

HELEN. Yes, Justice Prentice.

PRENTICE. Yes, I can see the likeness. At twenty you must have looked very like this miniature. [*Passes miniature to* HELEN.]

HELEN [*as* JACK *and* VIOLA *look at miniature*]. I have photographs of myself that are very like this. [*To* PRENTICE.] And you were speaking of her just now?

PRENTICE. Not five minutes ago. — But be seated, please.

[VIOLA *sits again at window.*] I'm very delighted to have you call.

HELEN. Even at such an hour?

PRENTICE. At any hour. Margaret Price was a very dear friend of mine; and to think, you're her daughter. And this letter 1860 — what's this?

HELEN. Oh, don't touch that. It will break. It's only a dry spray of mignonette, pinned to the note when you sent it.

PRENTICE [*musingly*]. A spray of mignonette.

HELEN. My mother's favorite flower and perfume.

PRENTICE. I remember. Well, well, this is equally astonishing.

JACK. Do you remember the letter, Mr Justice?

PRENTICE. Perfectly.

JACK. And the circumstances it alludes to?

PRENTICE. Yes. It was the work of a romantic boy. I — I was very fond of your mother, Mrs. — by the way, you have n't told me your name.

HELEN. Never mind that now. Let me be Margaret Price's daughter for the present.

PRENTICE. Very well. Oh, this was a little scratch of a duel — they 've gone out of fashion now, I 'm thankful to say.

HELEN. Do you remember the cause of this one?

PRENTICE. Yes; Henry Boland had worried Margaret some way. She was frightened, I think, and fainted.

HELEN. And you struck him?

PRENTICE. Yes, and he challenged me.

HELEN. I 've heard mother tell it. Do you remember what frightened her?

PRENTICE. I don't believe I do. Does the letter say?

HELEN. No. Try to think.

PRENTICE. Was it a snake or a toad?

HELEN. No — a jewel.

PRENTICE. A jewel? I remember now — a — a — cat's-eye. A cat's-eye jewel, was n't it?

HELEN [with excitement]. Yes, yes, yes. [Weeping.]

PRENTICE. My dear madam, it seems to be a very emotional subject with you.

HELEN. It is. I 've hoped so you would remember it. On the cars I was praying all the way you would remember it. And you do — you do.

PRENTICE. I do.

VIOLA. [Comes to HELEN.] Compose yourself, dear. Remember what depends on it.

PRENTICE. It is evidently something in which I can aid you.

HELEN. It is — and you will?

PRENTICE. There is nothing I would not do for a daughter of Margaret Price. You are in mourning, dear lady; is it for your mother?

HELEN. For my son.

PRENTICE. [To JACK.] How long has he been dead?

HELEN. He is not dead. Justice Prentice, my boy — the grandson of Margaret Price — is under a sentence of death.

PRENTICE. Sentence of death?

HELEN. Yes. I am the mother of Clay Whipple.

PRENTICE. [Rises.] But, madam —

HELEN. He is to die. I come —

PRENTICE. [Retreats toward second door.] Stop! You forget yourself. The case of Whipple is before the Supreme Court of the United States. I am a member of that body — I cannot listen to you.

HELEN. You must.

PRENTICE. You are prejudicing his chances. [To JACK.] You are making it necessary for me to rule against him. [To HELEN.] My dear madam, for the sake of your boy, do not do this. It is unlawful — without dignity or precedent. [To JACK.] If the lady were not the mother of the boy I should call your conduct base —

VIOLA. But she is his mother.

HELEN [following]. And Justice Prentice, I am the daughter of the woman you loved.

PRENTICE. I beg you to be silent.

JACK. Won't you hear us a moment?

PRENTICE. I cannot. I dare not — I must leave you. [Going.]

VIOLA. Why?

PRENTICE. I have explained — the matter is before the court. For me to hear you would be corrupt.

HELEN. I won't talk of the question before your court. That our attorneys tell us, is a constitutional point.

PRENTICE. That is its attitude.

HELEN. I will not talk of that. I wish to speak of this letter.

JACK. You can listen to that, can't you, Mr. Justice?

PRENTICE. Do you hope for its influence indirectly?

HELEN. No; sit down, Justice Prentice, and compose yourself. I will talk calmly to you.

PRENTICE. My dear madam, my heart bleeds for you. [To JACK.] Her agony must be her judicial measurement.

JACK. Only God knows, sir!

[HELEN sits at table; VIOLA stands by her side; PRENTICE sits by the fire; JACK remains standing.]

HELEN. [Pause.] Justice Prentice.

PRENTICE. Mrs. Whipple.

HELEN. You remember this letter — you have recalled the duel. You remember — thank God — its cause?

PRENTICE. I do.

HELEN. You know that my mother's

aversion to that jewel amounted almost to an insanity?

PRENTICE. I remember that.

HELEN. I inherited that aversion. When a child, the sight of one of them would throw me almost into convulsions.

PRENTICE. Is it possible?

HELEN. It is true. The physicians said I would outgrow the susceptibility, and in a measure I did so. But I discovered that Clay had inherited the fatal dislike from me.

JACK. You can understand that, Mr. Justice?

PRENTICE. Medical jurisprudence is full of such cases. Why should we deny them? Is nature faithful only in physical matters? You are like this portrait. Your voice is like that of Margaret Price. Nature's behest should have also embraced some of the less apparent possessions, I think.

JACK. We urged all that at the trial, but they called it invention.

PRENTICE. Nothing seems more probable to me.

HELEN. Clay, my boy, had that dreadful and unreasonable fear of the jewel. I protected him as far as possible, but one night over a year ago, some men — companions — finding that the sight of this stone annoyed him, pressed it upon his attention. He did not know, Justice Prentice, he was not responsible. It was insanity, but he struck his tormentor and the blow resulted in the young man's death.

PRENTICE. Terrible — terrible!

HELEN. My poor boy is crushed with the awful deed. He is not a murderer. He was never that, but they have sentenced him, Justice Prentice — he — is to die.

[Rises impulsively.]

JACK [catching her]. Now — now — my dear Helen, compose yourself.

VIOLA [embracing her]. You promised.

HELEN. Yes, yes, I will.

[Viola leads Helen aside.]

PRENTICE. All this was ably presented to the trial court, you say?

JACK. By the best attorneys.

PRENTICE. And the verdict?

JACK. Still was guilty. But, Mr. Justice, the sentiment of the community has changed very much since then. We feel that a new trial would result differently.

HELEN. When our lawyers decided to go to the Supreme Court, I remembered some letters of yours in this old book. Can you imagine my joy when I found the letter was on the very point of this inherited trait on which we rested our defense?

JACK. We have ridden twenty-four hours to reach you. The train came in only at ten o'clock.

HELEN. You — you are not powerless to help me. What is an official duty to a mother's love? To the life of her boy?

PRENTICE. My dear, dear madam, that is not necessary — believe me. This letter comes very properly under the head of new evidence. [To Jack.] The defendant is entitled to a rehearing on that.

HELEN. Justice Prentice! Justice Prentice!   [Turns again to Viola.]

VIOLA. There — there —
[Comforts Helen.]

PRENTICE. Of course that is n't before us, but when we remand the case on this constitutional point —

HELEN. Then you will — you will remand it?

PRENTICE [prevaricating]. Justice Henderson had convinced me on the point as you called. So I think there is no doubt of the decision.

HELEN. You can never know the light you let into my heart.

[Viola returns lace handkerchief to book which Helen opens for the purpose, closing it again on handkerchief.]

PRENTICE. What is that perfume? Have you one about you?

HELEN. Yes, on this handkerchief.

PRENTICE. What is it?

HELEN. Mignonette.

PRENTICE. Mignonette.

HELEN. A favorite perfume of mother's. This handkerchief of hers was in the book with the letter.

PRENTICE. Indeed.

HELEN. Oh, Justice Prentice, do you think I can save my boy?

PRENTICE. [To Jack.] On the rehearing I will take pleasure in testifying as to this hereditary aversion — and what I know of its existence in Margaret Price.

JACK. May I tell the lawyers so?

PRENTICE. No. They will learn it in the court to-morrow. They can stand the suspense. I am speaking comfort to the mother's heart.

HELEN. Comfort. It is life !

PRENTICE. [*To* JACK.] Say nothing of this call, if you please. Nothing to any one.

JACK. We shall respect your instructions, Mr. Justice. My niece, who has been with Mrs. Whipple during this trouble, is the fiancée of the boy who is in jail.

PRENTICE. You have my sympathy, too, my dear.

VIOLA. Thank you.

[*Goes to* PRENTICE *and gives him her hand.*]

PRENTICE. And now good-night.

VIOLA. Good-night.

[*Goes to door where* JACK *joins her.*]

HELEN. Good-night, Justice Prentice. You must know my gratitude — words cannot tell it. [*Exit* VIOLA.]

PRENTICE. Would you do me a favor ?

HELEN. Can you ask it ?

[JACK *waits at the door.*]

PRENTICE. If that was the handkerchief of Margaret Price, I 'd like to have it.

[*With a moment's effort at self-control,* HELEN *gives* PRENTICE *the handkerchief. She does not dare to speak, but turns to* JACK *who leads her out.* PRENTICE *goes to the table and takes up the miniature. A clock strikes two.*]

PRENTICE. Margaret Price. People will say that she has been in her grave thirty years, but I 'll swear her spirit was in this room to-night and directed a decision of the Supreme Court of the United States.

[*Noticing the handkerchief which he holds he puts it to his lips.*]

" The delicate odor of mignonette,
The ghost of a dead-and-gone bouquet,
Is all that tells of her story ; yet
Could she think of a sweeter way ? "

ACT III

SCENE — *Same as Act I.*

JACK *in chair with elbows on knees apparently in deep thought.*

[*Enter* HARVEY, *left.*]

HARVEY. Mars Jack.

JACK. Well, Uncle Harvey ?

HARVEY. 'Scuse me, sah, when you wants to be alone, but I 'se awful anxious myself. Is dey any word from the court-house ?

JACK. None, Uncle Harvey.

HARVEY. 'Cause Jo said Missus Campbell done come in, an' I thought she 'd been to the trial, you know.

JACK. She has. You 're not keeping anything from me, Uncle Harvey ?

HARVEY. 'Deed, no, sah. Ah jes' like to ask you, Mars Jack, if I 'd better have de cook fix sumpun' to eat — maybe de other ladies comin' too ?

JACK. Yes, Uncle Harvey, but whether they 'll want to eat or not 'll depend on what word comes back with the jury.

HARVEY. Yes, sah. [*Exit left.*]

[*Enter* ALICE, *right center.*]

ALICE [*in astonishment and reproach*]. Jack —

JACK. Well —

ALICE. Why are you here ?

JACK. Well — I live here.

ALICE. But I thought you 'd gone to Helen and Viola.

JACK. No.

ALICE. You should do so, Jack. Think of them alone when that jury returns — as it may at any moment — with its verdict.

JACK. The lawyers are there and Lew Ellinger is with them.

ALICE. But Helen — Helen needs you.

JACK. I may be useful here.

ALICE. How ?

JACK. There 's one man on that jury that I think is a friend.

ALICE. One man ?

JACK. Yes.

ALICE. Out of a jury of twelve.

JACK. One man can stop the other eleven from bringing in an adverse verdict — and this one is with us.

ALICE. Would your going to Helen and Viola in the court-house stop his being with us ?

JACK. Perhaps not, but it would stop my being with him.

ALICE. What ? [*Looks about.*] I don't understand you.

JACK. Justice Prentice told me that he could sit alone in his room and make another man get up and walk to the telephone and call him by simply thinking steadily of that other man.

ALICE. Superstitious people imagine anything.

JACK. Imagine much — yes — but this is n't imagination.

ALICE. It's worse — Jack. I call it spiritualism.

JACK. Call it anything you like — spiritualism — or socialism — or rheumatism — it's there. I know nothing about it scientifically, but I've tried it on and it works, my dear Alice, it works.

ALICE. You've tried it on?

JACK. Yes.

ALICE. With whom?

JACK. With you.

ALICE. I don't know it if you have.

JACK. That is one phase of its terrible subtlety.

ALICE. When did you try it on?

JACK [inquiringly]. That night, a month ago, when you rapped at my door at two o'clock in the morning and asked if I was ill in any way?

ALICE. I was simply nervous about you.

JACK. Call it "nervousness" if you wish to — but that was an experiment of mine — a simple experiment.

ALICE. Oh!

JACK. Two Sundays ago you went right up to the church door — hesitated, and turned home again.

ALICE. Lots of people do that.

JACK. I don't ask you to take stock in it, but that was another experiment of mine. The thing appeals to me. I can't help Helen by being at the court-house, but, as I'm alive and my name's Jack Brookfield, I do believe that my thought reaches that particular juryman.

ALICE. That's lunacy, Jack, dear.

JACK. [Rises and walks.] Well, call it "lunacy." I don't insist on "rheumatism."

ALICE. Oh, Jack, the boy's life is in the balance. Bitter vindictive lawyers are prosecuting him, and I don't like my big strong brother, who used to meet men and all danger face to face, treating the situation with silly mind-cure methods — hidden alone in his rooms. I don't like it.

JACK. You can't acquit a boy of murder by having a strong brother thrash somebody in the court-rooms. If there was anything under the sun I could do with my physical strength, I'd do it; but there is n't. Now, why not try this? Why not, if I believe I can influence a juryman by my thought, — why not try?

[ALICE turns away.]

[Enter Jo, right center.]

JACK. Well?

Jo. Mistah Hardmuth.

ALICE [astonished]. Frank Hardmuth?

Jo. Yes.

JACK. Here's one of the "bitter vindictive" men you want me to meet face to face. You stay here while I go and do it.

[Starts up.]

[Enter HARDMUTH.]

HARDMUTH. Excuse me, but I can't wait in an anteroom.

JACK. That 'll do, Jo.   [Exit Jo.]

HARDMUTH. I want to see you alone.

JACK. [To ALICE.] Yes —

ALICE [going]. What do you think it is?

JACK. Nothing to worry over.

[Conducts her to door. Exit ALICE.]

HARDMUTH [threateningly]. Jack Brookfield.

JACK. Well?   [Confronts HARDMUTH.]

HARDMUTH. I've just seen Harvey Fisher — of the Courier.

JACK. Yes.

HARDMUTH. He says you've hinted at something associating me with the shooting of Scovill.

JACK. Right.

HARDMUTH. What do you mean?

JACK. I mean, Frank Hardmuth, that you shan't hound this boy to the gallows without reckoning with me and the things I know of you.

HARDMUTH. I'm doing my duty as a prosecuting attorney.

JACK. You are, and a great deal more — you're venting a personal hatred.

HARDMUTH. That has n't anything to do with this insinuation you've handed to a newspaper man, an insinuation for which anybody ought to kill you.

JACK. I don't deal in "insinuations." It was a charge.

HARDMUTH. A statement?

JACK. A charge! You understand English — a specific and categorical charge.

HARDMUTH. That I knew Scovill was to be shot.

JACK. That you knew it? No. That you planned it and arranged and procured his assassination.

HARDMUTH [in low tone]. If the newspapers print that, I'll kill you — damn you, I'll kill you.

JACK. I don't doubt your willingness.
And they 'll print it — if they have n't done
so already — and if they don't print it, by
God, I 'll print it myself and paste it on
the fences.

HARDMUTH [*weakening*]. What have I
ever done to you, Jack Brookfield, except
to be your friend ?

JACK. You 've been much too friendly.
With this murder on your conscience, you
proposed to take to yourself, as wife, my
niece, dear to me as my life. As revenge
for her refusal and mine, you 've persecuted
through two trials the boy she loved, and
the son of the woman whose thought regu-
lates the pulse of my heart, an innocent,
unfortunate boy. In your ambition you 've
reached out to be the governor of this State,
and an honored political party is seriously
considering you for that office to-day.

HARDMUTH. That Scovill story 's a lie —
a political lie. I think you mean to be honest, Jack Brookfield, but somebody 's strung
you.

JACK. Wait ! The man that 's now hiding
in Indiana — a fugitive from your feeble
efforts at extradition — sat upstairs drunk
and desperate — his last dollar on a case
card. I pitied him. If a priest had been
there he could n't have purged his soul
cleaner than poor Raynor gave it to me.
If he put me on, am I strung ?

HARDMUTH [*frightened*]. Yes, you are.
I can't tell you why, because this jury is
out and may come in any moment and I 've
got to be there, but I can square it. So
help me God, I can square it.

JACK. You 'll have to square it.

[*Enter* ALICE, *left, followed by* PRENTICE.]

ALICE. Jack.

[*Indicates* PRENTICE.]

PRENTICE. Excuse me, I —

HARDMUTH. Oh — Justice Prentice.

JACK. Mr. Hardmuth — the State's attorney.

PRENTICE. I recognize Mr. Hardmuth.
I did n't salute him because I resent his
disrespectful treatment of myself during
his cross-examination.

HARDMUTH. Entirely within my rights
as a lawyer and —

PRENTICE. Entirely — and never within
the opportunities of a gentleman.

HARDMUTH. Your side foresaw the

powerful effect on a local jury of any testimony by a member of the Supreme Court,
and my wish to break that —

PRENTICE. Was quite apparent, sir, —
quite apparent,— but the testimony of every
man is entitled to just such weight and
consideration as that man's character commands. But it is not that disrespect which
I resent. I am an old man — That I am unmarried — childless — without a son to inherit the vigor that time has reclaimed, is
due to — a sentiment that you endeavored
to ridicule, Mr. Hardmuth, a sentiment
which would have been sacred in the hands
of any true Kentuckian, which I am glad
to hear you are not.

JACK. That 's all.

HARDMUTH. Perhaps not.   [*Exit.*]

PRENTICE. My dear Mr. Brookfield, that
man certainly has n't seen this newspaper ?

JACK. No — but he knows it 's coming.

PRENTICE. When I urged you as a citizen to tell anything you knew of the man,
I had n't expected a capital charge.

ALICE. What is it, Jack, — what have
you said ?

JACK. [*To* ALICE.] All in the headlines — read it. [*To* PRENTICE.] That
enough for your purpose, Justice Prentice ?

PRENTICE. I never dreamed of an attack
of that — that magnitude — Enough !

ALICE. Why — why did you do this,
Jack ?

JACK. Because I 'm your big strong
brother — and I had the information.

PRENTICE. It was necessary, Mrs. Campbell, — necessary.

ALICE. Why necessary ?

JACK. My poor sister, you don't think.
If that jury brings in a verdict of guilty —
what then ?

ALICE. What then ? I don't know.

JACK. An appeal to the governor — for
clemency.

ALICE. Well ?

JACK. Then we delay things until a new
governor comes in. But suppose that new
governor is Hardmuth himself.

ALICE. How can the new governor be
Hardmuth ?

PRENTICE. Nothing can stop it if he gets
the nomination, and the convention is in
session at Frankfort to-day with Mr. Hardmuth's name in the lead.

JACK [*indicating paper*]. I 've served

that notice on them and they won't dare nominate him. That is, I think they won't.

ALICE. But to charge him with murder?

PRENTICE. The only thing to consider there is, — have you your facts?

JACK. I have.

PRENTICE. Then it was a duty and you chose the psychological moment for its performance. "With what measure you mete — it shall be measured to you again." I have pity for the man whom that paper crushes, but I have greater pity for the boy he is trying to have hanged. [*Goes to* ALICE.] You know, Mrs. Campbell, that young Whipple is the grandson of an old friend of mine.

ALICE. Yes, Justice Prentice, I know that.

[*Enter* JO, *followed by* HELEN *and* VIOLA.]

JO. Mars Jack!

JACK [*turning*]. Yes?

HELEN. Oh, Jack! —

　　　[*Comes down to* JACK. VIOLA *goes to* ALICE.]

JACK. What is it?

　　　[*Catches and supports* HELEN.]

VIOLA. The jury returned and asked for instructions.

JACK. Well?

HELEN. There's a recess of an hour.

VIOLA. The court wishes them locked up for the night, but the foreman said the jurymen were all anxious to get to their homes and he felt an agreement could be reached in an hour.

PRENTICE. Did he use exactly those words — "to their homes"?

VIOLA. "To their homes" — yes.

PRENTICE [*smiling at* JACK]. There you are.

HELEN. What, Jack?

JACK. What?

PRENTICE. Men with vengeance or severity in their hearts would hardly say they're "anxious to get to their homes." They say, "the jury is anxious to get away," or "to finish its work."

HELEN. Oh, Justice Prentice, you pin hope upon such slight things.

PRENTICE. That is what hope is for, my dear Mrs. Whipple; the frail chances of this life.

VIOLA. And now, Uncle Jack, Mrs. Whipple ought to have a cup of tea and something to eat.

HELEN. Oh, I could n't — we must g: back at once.

VIOLA. Well, I could — I — I must.

ALICE. Yes — you must — both of you.

　　　[*Exit to dining-room.*]

VIOLA [*returning to* HELEN]. You don' think it's heartless, do you?

HELEN. You dear child. [*Kisses her.*]

VIOLA. You come, too.

HELEN [*refusing*]. Please.

　　　[*Exit* VIOLA. HELEN *sinks to sofa.*]

JACK. And now, courage, my dear Helen it's almost over.

HELEN. At the other trial the jury delayed — just this way.

PRENTICE. Upon what point did the jury ask instruction?

HELEN. Degree.

PRENTICE. And the court?

HELEN. Oh, Jack, the Judge answered — guilty in the first degree, or not guilty.

PRENTICE. That all helps us.

HELEN. It does?

JACK. Who spoke for the jury?

HELEN. The foreman — and one other juryman asked a question.

JACK. Was it the man in the fourth chair — first row?

HELEN [*inquiringly*]. Yes — ?

JACK. Ah.

HELEN. Why?

JACK. I think he's a friend, that's all.

HELEN. I should die, Jack, if it was n't for your courage. You won't get tired of it — will you — and forsake my poor boy — and me?

JACK [*encouragingly*]. What do you think?

HELEN. All our lawyers are kindness itself, but — but — you — Jack — you somehow —

　　　[*Enter* VIOLA.]

VIOLA. Oh, Uncle Jack — here's a note our lawyer asked me to give to you — I forgot it until this minute.

JACK. Thank you. [*Takes note.*]

VIOLA. Please try a cup of tea.

HELEN. No — no — Viola. [*Exit* VIOLA.] What is it, Jack? Are they afraid?

JACK. It's not about the trial at all.

　　　[*Hands note to* PRENTICE.]

HELEN. Really?

JACK. Yes.

HELEN. But why don't you show it to us, then?

JACK. [PRENTICE *returns note.*] I will —
if my keeping it gives you so much alarm
as that. [*Turns on the large drop light and
stands under it.*] Colonel Bayley says —
"Dear Jack, I've seen the paper; Hardmuth will shoot on sight."

HELEN [*quickly to* JACK's *side*]. Oh, Jack,
if anything should happen to you —

JACK. "Anything" is quite as likely to
happen to Mr. Hardmuth.

HELEN. But not even that — my boy has
killed a man — and — you — Jack — you —
well, you just must n't let it happen, that's
all.

JACK. I must n't let it happen because —?

HELEN. Because — I — could n't bear
it.

[JACK *lifts her hand to his face and
kisses it.*]

[*Enter* ALICE.]

ALICE. What was the letter, Jack?

JACK. [*Hands letter to* ALICE *as he passes,
leading* HELEN *to door.*] And, now I'll agree
to do the best I can for Mr. Hardmuth if
you'll take a cup of tea and a biscuit.

HELEN. There is n't time.

JACK. There's plenty of time if the ad-
journment was for an hour.

ALICE [*in alarm*]. Jack!

JACK. Eh — [*Turns to* ALICE.] Wait one
minute. [*Goes on to door with* HELEN.] Go.
[*Exit* HELEN.]

ALICE [*as* JACK *returns*]. He threatens
your life.

JACK. Not exactly. Simply Colonel Bayley's opinion that he will shoot on sight.

ALICE [*impatiently*]. Oh —

JACK. There is a difference, you know.

[*Enter* Jo.]

Jo. Mr. Ellinger, sah.

[*Enter* LEW.]

LEW [*briskly*]. Hello, Jack.   [*Exit* Jo.]

JACK. Well, Lew?

LEW [*with newspaper*]. Why, that's the
damnedest thing — [*To* ALICE.] I beg your
pardon.

ALICE. Don't, please, — some manly emphasis is a real comfort, Mr. Ellinger.

LEW. That charge of yours against Hardmuth is raisin' more h-h-high feeling than
anything that ever happened.

JACK. I saw the paper.

LEW. You did n't see this — it's an extra.

[*Reads.*] "The charge read to the convention in night session at Frankfort — Bill
Glover hits Jim Macey on the nose — De
Voe of Carter County takes Jim's gun
away from him. The delegation from Butler get down to their stomachs and crawl
under the benches — some statesmen go
through the windows. Convention takes
recess till morning. Local sheriff swearin'
in deputies to keep peace in the barrooms."
— That's all you've done.

JACK. [*To* ALICE.] Good! [*To* PREN-
TICE.] Well, they can't nominate Mr.
Hardmuth now.

LEW. [*To* ALICE.] I been hedgin' — I
told the fellows I'd bet Jack had n't said
it.

JACK. Yes — I did say it.

LEW. In just those words — ? [*Reads.*]
"The poor fellow that crouched back of a
window sill and shot Kentucky's governor
deserves hanging less than the man whom
he is shielding — the man who laid the plot
of assassination. The present prosecuting
attorney by appointment — Frank Allison
Hardmuth." Did you say that?

JACK. Lew, that there might be no mistake — I wrote it.

[LEW *whistles;* JACK *takes the paper
and scans it.*]

LEW. Is it straight?

JACK. Yes.

[*Pushes hanging button and turns off
the large drop.*]

LEW. He *was* in the plot to kill the governor?

JACK. He organized it.

LEW. Well, what do you think of that?
And now he's runnin' for governor himself
— a murderer!

JACK. Yes.

LEW. [*To* PRENTICE.] And for six months
he's been houndin' every fellow in Louisville that sat down to a game of cards.
[JACK *nods.*] The damned rascal's nearly
put me in the poorhouse.

JACK. Poor old Lew!

LEW. [*To* PRENTICE.] Why, before I
could get to that court-house to-day I had
to take a pair of scissors that I used to cut
coupons with and trim the whiskers off o'
my shirt cuffs. [*To* JACK.] How long have
you known this?

JACK. Ever since the fact.

PRENTICE. Mm —

LEW. Why do you spring it only now?

JACK. Because until now I lacked the character and the moral courage. I spring it now by the advice of Justice Prentice to reach that convention at Frankfort.

LEW. Well, you reached them.

PRENTICE. The convention was only a secondary consideration with me — my real object was this jury with whom Mr. Hardmuth seemed too powerful.

LEW. Reach the jury?

JACK [enthusiastically]. The jury? Why, of course, — the entire jury, — and I was hoping for one man —

LEW. Why, they don't see the papers — the jury won't get a line of this.

JACK. I think they will.

LEW. You got 'em fixed?

JACK. Fixed? No.

LEW. Then how will they see it.

PRENTICE [firmly and slowly to LEW, who is half dazed]. How many people in Louisville have already read that charge as you have read it?

LEW. Thirty thousand, maybe, but —

PRENTICE. And five hundred thousand in the little cities and the towns. Do you think, Mr. Ellinger, that all those minds can be at white heat over knowledge and none of it reach the thought of those twelve men? Ah, no —

JACK. To half a million good Kentuckians to-night Frank Hardmuth is a repulsive thing — and that jury's faith in him — is dead.

LEW. [Pause.] Why, Jack, old man, you 're dippy.

[ALICE turns away wearily, agreeing with LEW.]

PRENTICE. Then, Mr. Ellinger, I am dippy, too.   [ALICE turns back.]

LEW. You mean you think the jury gets the public opinion — without anybody tellin' them or their reading it.

PRENTICE. Yes.

[Pause. LEW looks stunned.] In every widely discussed trial the defendant is tried not alone by his twelve peers, but by the entire community.

LEW. Why, blast it! The community goes by what the newspaper says!

PRENTICE. That is often the regrettable part of it — but the fact remains.

JACK. And that 's why you asked me to expose Frank Hardmuth?

PRENTICE. Yes.

LEW. Well, the public will think you did it because he closed your game.

JACK. Hardmuth did n't close my game.

LEW. Who did?

JACK [pointing to PRENTICE]. This man.

PRENTICE. [To JACK.] Thank you.

LEW. How the he— er — heaven's name did he close it?

JACK. He gave my self-respect a slap on the back and I stood up.   [Exit.]

LEW [thoroughly confused. Pause.] Stung.   [Turns to PRENTICE.]

So you are responsible for these — these new ideas of Jack's?

PRENTICE. In a measure. Have the ideas apparently hurt Mr. Brookfield?

LEW. They 've put him out of business — that 's all.

PRENTICE. Which business?

LEW. Why, this house of his.

PRENTICE. I see. But his new ideas? Don't you like them, Mr. Ellinger?

LEW. I love Jack Brookfield — love him like a brother — but I don't want even a brother askin' me if I 'm sure I 've "thought it over" when I 'm startin' to take the halter off for a pleasant evenin'. Get my idea?

PRENTICE. I begin to.

LEW. In other words — I don't want to take my remorse first. It dampens fun. The other day a lady at the races said, "We 've missed you, Mr. Ellinger." And I said, "Have you? — Well I 'll be up this evening," and I 'm pressing her hand and hanging on to it till I 'm afraid I 'll get the carriage grease on my coat — feelin' only about thirty-two, you know, then I turn round and Jack has those sleepy lamps on me — and "bla" —   [Turns and sinks onto sofa.]

PRENTICE. And you don't go?

LEW [bracing up]. I do go — as a matter of self-respect — but I don't make a hit. I 'm thinking so much more about those morality ideas of Jack's than I am about the lady that it cramps my style and we never get past the weather, and "when did you last hear from So-and-so?" [Rises.] I want to reform all right. I believe in reform. But first I want to have the fun of fallin' and fallin' hard.

Jo [distant and outside]. 'Fore God, Mars Clay!

CLAY. Jo, is my mother here?

ALICE [*entering left*]. Why, that's Clay.
[*Voices off continue together and approach.*]
LEW. [*To* PRENTICE.] It's the boy.
ALICE. His mother!
[*Starts to call* HELEN, *then falters in indecision.*]
Oh! [*The outside voices grow louder.*]
PRENTICE. Acquittal!

[*Enter* CLAY, *followed by* COLONEL BAYLEY, *his attorney.*]

ALICE. Clay, Clay!
CLAY. Oh, Mrs. Campbell.
[ALICE *embraces him.*]

[*Enter* JACK, HELEN, *and* VIOLA.]

JACK [*seeing* CLAY *and speaking back to* HELEN]. Yes.
HELEN [*as she enters*]. My boy!
CLAY. Mother!
[*They embrace.* CLAY *slips to his knee with his face hidden in* HELEN'S *lap, repeating her name.* HELEN *standing sways and is caught by* JACK. CLAY *noting this weakness rises and helps support her.*]
JACK [*rousing her*]. He's free, Helen, he's free.
CLAY. Yes, mother, I'm free.
[VIOLA, *who has crossed back of* CLAY *and* HELEN, *weeps on shoulder of* ALICE, *who comforts her.*]
HELEN. My boy, my boy!
[VIOLA *looks at them.* HELEN *sees* VIOLA *and turns* CLAY *toward her.* CLAY *takes* VIOLA *in his arms.*]
CLAY. Viola, my brave sweetheart!
VIOLA. It's really over?
CLAY. Yes.
JACK. It's a great victory, Colonel.
BAYLEY. Thank you.
JACK. If ever a lawyer made a good fight for a man's life, you did. Helen, Viola, you must want to shake this man's hand.
VIOLA. I could have thrown my arms around you when you made that speech.
BAYLEY [*laughing*]. Too many young fellows crowding into the profession as it is.
HELEN [*taking his hand*]. Life must be sweet to a man who can do so much good as you do.
BAYLEY. I couldn't stand it, you know, if it wasn't that my ability works both ways.

[*Enter* HARVEY, *left.*]
HARVEY. Mars Clay.
CLAY. Harvey! Why, dear old Harvey.
[*Half embraces* HARVEY *and pats him affectionately.*]
HARVEY. Yes, sah. Could — could you eat anything, Mars Clay?
CLAY. Eat anything! Why, I'm starvin', Harvey.
HARVEY. Ha, ha. Yes, sah. [*Exit quickly.*]
CLAY. But you with me, mother — and Viola.
HELEN. My boy! Colonel!
[*Turns to* BAYLEY. *Exit* CLAY, VIOLA, HELEN, BAYLEY, *and* ALICE *to dining-room.*]
JACK. [*Alone with* PRENTICE. *Picks up* BAYLEY'S *letter; takes hold of push button over head.*] I shall never doubt you again.
PRENTICE. Mr. Brookfield, never doubt yourself.
[*Enter* HARDMUTH. *He rushes down toward dining-room and turns back to* JACK *who is under the lamp with his hand on its button.*]
HARDMUTH. You think you'll send me to the gallows, but, damn you, you go first yourself.
[*Thrusts a derringer against* JACK'S *body.*]
JACK. Stop!
[*The big light flashes on above* HARDMUTH'S *eyes. At* JACK'S *"Stop,"* PRENTICE *inclines forward with eyes on* HARDMUTH *so that there is a double battery of hypnotism on him. A pause.*]
You can't shoot — that — gun. You can't pull the trigger. [*Pause.*] You can't even hold the gun.
[*Pause. The derringer drops from* HARDMUTH'S *hand.*]
Now, Frank, you can go.
HARDMUTH [*recoiling slowly*]. I'd like to know — how in hell you did that — to me.

ACT IV

SCENE — *Same as Act III. All lights on including big electric.*

CLAY *and* VIOLA *seated on sofa near the fireplace.*

VIOLA. I must really say good-night and let you get some sleep.
CLAY. Not before Jack gets home. Our

mothers have considerately left us alone together. They'll just as considerately tell
us when it's time to part.

VIOLA. *My* mother said it was time half
an hour ago.

CLAY. Wait till Jack comes in.

[*Enter* JO.]

JO. Mars Clay?

CLAY. Well, Jo?

JO. Dey's another reporter to see you,
sah?

VIOLA. Send him away — Mr. Whipple
won't see any more reporters.

CLAY. [*Rises.*] Wait a minute — who is
he? [JO *hands card.*] I've got to see this
one, Viola.

VIOLA [*complaining*]. Why "got to"?

CLAY. He's a friend — I'll see him, Jo.

JO. Yas, sah —   [*Exit.*]

VIOLA. [*Rises.*] You've said that all day
— they're all friends.

CLAY. Well, they are — but this boy especially. It was fine to see you and mother
and Jack when I was in that jail — great —
but you were there daytimes. This boy
spent hours on the other side of the bars
helping me pass the awful nights. I tell
you — death-cells would be pretty nearly
hell if it wasn't for the police reporters —
ministers ain't in it with 'em.

[*Enter* EMMETT, *a reporter.*]

EMMETT. Good-evening.

CLAY. How are you, Ned? You know
Miss Campbell?

EMMETT [*bowing*]. Yes.

VIOLA. Good-evening.

CLAY. Have a chair.

EMMETT. Thank you.

[*Defers to* VIOLA *who sits first on
sofa. Pause.*]

This is different.   [*Looks around the room.*]

CLAY. Some.

EMMETT. Satisfied? The way we handled the story?

CLAY. Perfectly. You were just bully,
old man.

EMMETT. [*To* VIOLA.] That artist of
ours is only a kid — and they work him to
death on the "Sunday" — so — [*Pause.*]
[*To* CLAY.] You understand.

CLAY. Oh — I got used to the — pictures a year ago.

EMMETT. Certainly. [*Pause.*] Anything
you want to say?

VIOLA. For the paper?

EMMETT. Yes.

CLAY. I think not.

[*Enter* HELEN *and* ALICE. EMMETT *rises.*]

HELEN. Clay, dear — [*Pause.*] Oh —

CLAY. You met my mother?

EMMETT. No —

CLAY. Mother — this is Mr. Emmett of
whom I've told you so often.

HELEN. Oh — the good reporter.

EMMETT. [*To* CLAY.] Gee! That'd be
a wonder if the gang heard it. [*Taking*
HELEN'S *hand as she offers it.*] We got pretty
well acquainted — yes, 'm.

CLAY [*introducing* ALICE]. Mrs. Campbell.

ALICE. Won't you sit down, Mr. Emmett?

EMMETT. Thank you. I guess we've covered everything, but the chief wanted me
to see your son — [*turns to* CLAY] and see
if you'd do the paper a favor?

CLAY. If possible — gladly —

EMMETT. I don't like the assignment because — well for the very reason that it was
handed to me — and that is because we're
more or less friendly.

[*Enter* JACK *in fur coat with cap and goggles in
hand.*]

JACK. Well, it's a wonderful night outside.

ALICE. You're back early.

JACK. Purposely. [*To* EMMETT.] How
are you?

EMMETT [*rising*]. Mr. Brookfield.

JACK. I thought you girls might like a
little run in the moonlight before I put in
the machine.

HELEN. Mr. Emmett has some message
from his editor.

JACK. What is it?

EMMETT. There's a **warrant** out **for**
Hardmuth — you saw that?

VIOLA. Yes, we saw that. [*Goes to* JACK.]

JACK. To-night's paper —

EMMETT. If they get him and he comes
to trial and all that, it'll be the biggest trial
Kentucky ever saw.

CLAY. Well?

EMMETT. Well — the paper wants you to
agree to report it for them — the trial —
there'll be other papers after you, of course.

VIOLA. Oh, no —

EMMETT. Understand, Clay, I'm **not**

asking it. [*To* VIOLA.] I'm here under orders just as I'd be at a fire or a bread riot.

CLAY [*demurring*]. And — of course — you understand, don't you?

EMMETT. Perfectly — and I told the chief myself you would n't see it.

CLAY. Paper's been too friendly for me to assume any — any —

JACK. Unnecessary dignity —

CLAY. Exactly — but — I just could n't, you see —

EMMETT [*going*]. Oh, leave it to me — I 'll let 'em down easy.

CLAY. Thank you.

EMMETT. You expect to be in Europe or—

CLAY. But I don't.

[JACK *removes fur coat, puts it on chair up right center.*]

VIOLA. We 're going to stay right here in Louisville —

CLAY. And work out my — my own future among the people who know me.

EMMETT. Of course — Europe 's just to stall off the chief — get him on to some other dope —

HELEN [*rising*]. But —

JACK [*interrupting*]. It 's all right.

HELEN. [*To* JACK.] I hate to begin with a falsehood.

EMMETT. Not your son — me — Saw some copy on our telegraph desk, Mr. Brookfield, that 'd interest you.

JACK. Yes.

EMMETT. Or maybe you know of it? Frankfort —

JACK. No.

EMMETT. Some friend named you in the caucus.

JACK. What connection?

EMMETT. Governor.

VIOLA. [*To* EMMETT.] Uncle Jack?

EMMETT. Yes, 'm — that is, for the nomination.

JACK. It 's a joke.

EMMETT. Grows out of these Hardmuth charges, of course.

JACK. That 's all.

EMMETT. Good-night — [*Bows.*] Mrs. Whipple — ladies — [*Exit.*]

CLAY [*going to door with* EMMETT]. You 'll make that quite clear, won't you?

EMMETT [*outside*]. I 'll fix it.

CLAY [*returning*]. If it was n't for the notoriety of it, I 'd like to do that.

[*Sits right of table.*]

HELEN [*reproachfully*]. My son!

JACK. Why would you like to do it?

CLAY. To get even. I 'd like to see Hardmuth suffer as he made me suffer. I 'd like to watch him suffer and write of it.

JACK. That 's a bad spirit to face the world with, my boy.

CLAY. I hate him. [*Goes to* VIOLA.]

JACK. Hatred is heavier freight for the shipper than it is for the consignee.

CLAY. I can't help it.

JACK. Yes, you can help it. Mr. Hardmuth should be of the utmost indifference to you. To hate him is weak.

VIOLA. Weak?

JACK. Yes, weak-minded. Hardmuth was in love with you at one time — he hated Clay. He said Clay was as weak as dishwater — [*to* CLAY] — and you were at that time. You 've had your lesson — profit by it. Its meaning was self-control. Begin now if you 're going to be the custodian of this girl's happiness.

HELEN. I 'm sure he means to, Jack.

JACK. You can carry your hatred of Hardmuth and let it embitter your whole life — or you can drop it — so — [*Drops a book on table.*] The power that any man or anything has to annoy us we give him or it by our interest. Some idiot told your great-grandmother that a jewel with different colored strata in it was " bad luck " — or a " hoodoo " — she believed it, and she nursed her faith that passed the lunacy on to your grandmother.

HELEN. Jack, don't talk of that, please.

JACK. I 'll skip one generation — but I 'd like to talk of it.

ALICE [*rising, comes to* HELEN]. Why talk of it?

JACK. It was only a notion, and an effort of will can banish it.

CLAY. It was more than a notion.

JACK. Tom Denning's scarf-pin which he dropped there [*indicates floor*] was an exhibit in your trial — Judge Bayley returned it to me to-day.

[*Puts hand in pocket.*]

VIOLA. I wish you would n't, Uncle Jack.

[*Turns away.*]

JACK. [*To* CLAY.] You don't mind, do you?

CLAY. I 'd rather not look at it — to-night.

JACK. You need n't look at it. I 'll hold

it in my hand and you put your hands over mine.

ALICE. I really don't see the use in this experiment, Jack.

JACK [*with* CLAY's *hand over his*]. That does n't annoy you, does it?

CLAY. I'm controlling myself, sir — but I feel the influence of the thing all through and through me.

HELEN. Jack!

[VIOLA *turns away in protest.*]

JACK. Down your back, is n't it, and in the roots of your hair — tingling — ?

CLAY. Yes.

HELEN. Why torture him?

JACK. Is it torture?

CLAY [*with brave self-control*]. I shall be glad when it's over.

JACK [*severely*]. What rot! That's only my night-key — look at it. I have n't the scarf-pin about me.

CLAY. Why make me think it was the scarf-pin?

JACK. To prove to you that it's only thinking — that's all. Now, be a man — the cat's-eye itself is in that table drawer. Get it and show Viola that you're not a neuropathic idiot. You're a child of *the everlasting God* and nothing on the earth or under it can harm you in the slightest degree. [CLAY *opens drawer and takes pin.*] That's the spirit — look at it — I've made many a young horse do that to an umbrella. Now, give it to me. [*To* VIOLA.] You're not afraid of it.

VIOLA. Why, of course I'm not.

JACK [*putting pin on her breast*]. Now, if you want my niece, go up to that hoodoo like a man. [CLAY *embraces* VIOLA.]

HELEN. Oh, Jack, do you think that will last?

JACK. Which — indifference to the hoodoo or partiality to my niece?

CLAY. They'll both last.

JACK. Now, my boy, drop your hatred of Hardmuth as you drop your fear of the scarf-pin. Don't look back — your life's ahead of you. Don't mount for the race over-weight.

[*Enter* Jo.]

Jo. Mr. Ellinger.

[*Enter* LEW.]

LEW. I don't intrude, do I?

JACK. Come in.

LEW. [*To* LADIES.] Good-evening. Ah, Clay. [*Shakes hands with* CLAY.] Glad to see you looking so well. Glad to see you in such good company. [*To* JACK, *briskly.*] I've got him.

JACK. Got whom?

LEW. Hardmuth. [*To* LADIES.] Detectives been hunting him all day, you know.

HELEN. He's caught, you say?

LEW. No — but I've treed him — [*to* JACK] — and I thought I'd just have a word with you before passing the tip. [*To* LADIES.] He's nearly put me in the poorhouse with his raids and closing laws, and I see a chance to get even.

JACK. In what way?

LEW. They've been after him nearly twenty-four hours — morning paper's going to offer a reward for him, and I understand the State will also. If I had a little help I'd hide him for a day or two and then surrender him for those rewards.

JACK. Where is Hardmuth?

[*Sits at table.*]

LEW. Hiding.

JACK [*writing a note*]. Naturally.

LEW. You remember Big George?

JACK. The darkey?

LEW. Yes — used to be on the door at Phil Kelly's?

JACK. Yes.

LEW. He's there. In Big George's cottage — long story — Big George's wife — that is, she — well, his wife used to be pantry maid for Hardmuth's mother. When they raided Kelly's game, Big George pretended to turn State's evidence, but he really hates Hardmuth like a rattler — so it all comes back to me. You see, if I'd win a couple of hundred at Kelly's I used to slip George a ten going out. Your luck always stays by you if you divide a little with a nigger or a humpback — and in Louisville it's easier to find a nigger — so —

JACK. He's there now?

LEW. Yes. He wants to get away. He's got two guns and he'll shoot before he gives up — so I'd have to con him some way. George's wife is to open the door to Kelly's old signal, you remember — [*raps*] — one knock, then two, and then one.

JACK. Where is the cottage?

LEW. Number 7 Jackson Street — little dooryard-border of arbor-vitæ on the path.

JACK. One knock — then two — and then one — [*Rises with note written.*]

LEW. What you gonta do?

JACK. Send for him.

LEW. Who you gonta send?

JACK. That boy there.

CLAY. Me?

JACK. Yes.

HELEN. Oh, no — no.

JACK. And my niece.

VIOLA. What! To arrest a man?

JACK. [*To* CLAY.] My machine is at the door. Give Hardmuth this note. He'll come with you quietly. Bring him here. We'll decide what to do with him after that.

ALICE. I can't allow Viola on such an errand.

JACK. When the man she's promised to marry is going into danger —

VIOLA. If Mr. Hardmuth will come for that note — why can't I deliver it?

JACK. You may — if Clay'll let you.

CLAY [*quietly taking note as* JACK *offers it to* VIOLA]. I'll hand it to him.

JACK. I hope so. [*Gives goggles and coat.*] Take these — remember — one rap, then two, then one.

CLAY. I understand — number seven —?

LEW. Jackson Street.

ALICE. I protest.

HELEN. So do I.

JACK. [*To* CLAY *and* VIOLA.] You're both of age. I ask you to do it. If you give Hardmuth the goggles, nobody'll recognize him and with a lady beside him you'll get him safely here.

CLAY. Come. [*Exit with* VIOLA.]

LEW [*following to door*]. I ought to be in the party.

JACK. No — you stay here.

ALICE. That's scandalous.

JACK. But none of us will start the scandal, will we?

HELEN. Clay knows nothing of that kind of work — a man with two guns — think of it.

JACK. After he's walked barehanded up to a couple of guns a few times, he'll quit fearing men that are armed only with a scarf-pin.

HELEN [*hysterically*]. It's cruel to keep constantly referring to that — that — mistake of Clay's — I want to forget it.

JACK [*going to* HELEN. *Tenderly*]. The way to forget it, my dear Helen, is not to guard it as a sensitive spot in your memory, but to grasp it as the wise ones grasp a nettle — crush all its power to harm you in one courageous contact. We think things are calamities and trials and sorrows — only names. They are spiritual gymnastics and have an eternal value when once you front them and make them crouch at your feet. Say once for all to your soul and thereby to the world — "Yes, my boy killed a man — because I'd brought him up a half-effeminate, hysterical weakling, but he's been through the fire and I've been through the fire, and we're both the better for it."

HELEN. I can say that truthfully, but I don't want to make a policeman of him, just the same. [*Exit to dining-room.*]

ALICE [*following*]. Your treatment's a little too heroic, Jack. [*Exit.*]

LEW. Think they'll fetch him?

JACK. [*Sits left of table.*] Yes.

LEW. He'll come, of course, if he does, under the idea that you'll help him when he gets here.

JACK. Yes.

LEW. Pretty hard double-cross, but he deserves it. I've got a note of fifteen thousand to meet to-morrow, or, damn it, I don't think I'd fancy this man-hunting. I put up some Louisville-Nashville bonds for security, and the holder of the note'll be only too anxious to pinch 'em.

JACK. You can't get your rewards in time for that.

LEW. I know — and that's one reason I come to you, Jack. If you see I'm in a fair way to get a reward —

JACK. I'll lend you money, Lew.

LEW. Thank you.

[JACK *takes check-book and writes.*] I thought you would. If I lose those bonds they'll have me selling programs for a livin' at a grand stand. You see, I thought hatin' Hardmuth as you do, and your reputation bein' up through that stuff to the papers —

JACK. There. [*Gives check.*]

LEW. Thank you, old man. I'll hand this back to you in a week.

JACK. [*Rises.*] You need n't.

LEW. What?

JACK. You need n't hand it back. It's only fifteen thousand and you've lost a hundred of them at poker in these rooms.

LEW. Never belly-ached, did I?

JACK. Never — but you don't owe me that fifteen.

LEW. Rot! I'm no baby — square game, was n't it?

JACK. Perfectly.

LEW. And I'll sit in a square game any time I get a chance.

JACK. I know, Lew, all about that.

LEW. I'll play you for this fifteen right away.   [*Displays check.*]

JACK. No.   [*Walks aside.*]

LEW. Ain't had a game in three weeks — and, besides, I think my luck's changin'? When Big George told me about Hardmuth I took George's hand before I thought what I was doin' — and you know what shakin' hands with a nigger does just before any play.

JACK [*resisting* LEW's *plea*]. No, thank you, Lew.

LEW. My money's good as anybody else's, ain't it?

JACK. Just as good, but —

LEW. It ain't a phoney check, is it?
          [*Examines check.*]

JACK. The check's all right.

LEW [*taunting*]. Losing your nerves?

JACK. No [*pause*] — suppose you shuffle those and deal a hand.
          [*Indicates small table, right.*]

LEW. That's like old times; what is it — stud-horse or draw?   [*Sits at table.*]

JACK. [*Goes to fireplace.*] Draw if you say so.

LEW. I cut 'em?

JACK. You cut them.

LEW [*dealing two poker hands*]. Table stakes — check goes for a thousand.

JACK. That suits me.

LEW [*taking his own cards*]. Sit down.

JACK [*at other side of room looking into fire*]. I don't need to sit down just yet.

LEW. As easy as that, am I?

JACK. Lew!

LEW. Yes?

JACK. [*Pause.*] Do you happen to have three queens?

          [LEW *looks at* JACK, *then carefully at back of his own cards, then at the deck.*]

LEW. Well, I can't see it.

JACK. No use looking — they're not marked.

LEW. Well, I shuffled 'm all right.

JACK. Yes.

LEW. And cut 'm?   [JACK *nods.*]
Could n't 'a' been a cold deck?

JACK. No.

LEW. Then, how did you know I had three queens?

JACK. I did n't know it. I just thought you had.

LEW. Can you do it again?

JACK. I don't know. Draw one card.

LEW [*drawing one card from deck*]. All right.

JACK. [*Pause.*] Is it the ace of hearts?

LEW. It is.

JACK. Mm — turns me into a rotter, does n't it? [*Comes gloomily to the big table.*]

LEW. Can you do that every time?

JACK. I never tried it until to-night — that is, consciously. I've always had luck and I thought it was because I took chances on a game — same as any player — but that don't look like it, does it?

LEW. Beats me.

JACK. And what a monster it makes of me — these years I've been in the business.

LEW. You say you did n't know before?

JACK. I did n't know it — no — but — some things have happened lately that have made me think it might be so; that jury yesterday — some facts I've had from Justice Prentice. Telepathy of a very common kind — and I guess it's used in a good many games, old man, we are n't on to.

LEW. Well — have you told anybody?

JACK. No.

LEW [*excitedly*]. Good! [*Rises and comes to* JACK.] Now, see here, Jack, if you can do that right along I know a game in Cincinnati where it'd be like takin' candy from children.

JACK. Good God! you're suggesting that I keep it up?

LEW. Don't over-do it — no — [*Pause.*] Or you show me the trick and I'll collect all right.

JACK [*slowly*]. Lew — [*Pause.*] Some of the fellows I've won from in this house have gone over to the park and blown their heads off.

LEW. Some of the fellows anybody wins from in any house go somewhere and blow their heads off.

JACK. True —   [*Pause.*]

LEW. Three queens — before the draw —

well, you could 'a' had me all right — and
you won't tell me how you do it?

JACK. I don't know how I do it; the
thought just comes to my mind stronger
than any other thought.

LEW [*reprovingly*]. God A'mighty gives
you a mind like that and you won't go with
me to Cincinnati.

[*Goes to card table; studies cards.*]

[*Enter* JO.]

JO. Justice Prentice, sah.

JACK. Ask him to step up here.

JO. Yes, sah.   [*Exit.*]

JACK. [*Goes to door, left.*] Alice — Helen
— Justice Prentice has called; I'd like you
to join us.

LEW. Can the old man call a hand like
that, too?

JACK. I'm sure he could.

LEW. And — are there others?

JACK. I believe there are a good many
others who unconsciously have the same
ability.

LEW. Well, it's a God's blessin' there's
a sucker born every minute. I'm a widow
and an orphan 'longside o' that.

[*Throws cards in disgust onto table.*]

[*Enter* ALICE *and* HELEN.]

ALICE. Been losing, Mr. Ellinger?

LEW. Losing? I just saved fifteen thousand I was gonta throw 'way like sand in a
rathole. I'm a babe eatin' spoon victuals
and only gettin' half at that.

[*Enter* PRENTICE.]

JACK. Good-evening.

PRENTICE. Good-evening.

[*Shakes hands with* ALICE *and*
HELEN.]

JACK. I stopped at your hotel, Mr. Justice, but you were out.

[*Enter* VIOLA.]

ALICE [*anxiously*]. Viola.

HELEN. Where's Clay?

VIOLA. Downstairs. Good-evening.

PRENTICE. Good-evening.

JACK. [*To others.*] Pardon. [*To* VIOLA.]
Did the — gentleman come with you?

VIOLA. Yes.

[*Lew flutters and shows excitement.*]

JACK. Won't you ask Clay, my dear, to
take him through the lower hall and into
the dining-room until I'm at liberty?

VIOLA. Certainly.   [*Exit.*]

PRENTICE. I am keeping you from other
appointments?

JACK. Nothing that can't wait.

PRENTICE. I am leaving for Washington
in the morning.

JACK. We'll all be at the train to see
you off.

PRENTICE. That's good, because I should
like to say good-bye to — to the young people — I can see them there — I shan't see
you then, Mr. Ellinger —

[*Goes to* LEW, *who stands at card
table.*]

LEW. Good-bye, Judge — you — you've
given me more of a "turn over" than you
know.

PRENTICE. Really?

LEW. I'd 'a' saved two hundred thousand dollars if I'd 'a' met you thirty years
ago.

PRENTICE. Well, that's only about six
thousand a year, is n't it?

LEW. That's so — and, damn it, I have
lived.

[*Smiles — looks dreamily into the
past.*]

PRENTICE. Good-night. [*Exit* PRENTICE.]

JACK. Good-night — good-night.

ALICE. Is that Hardmuth in there?

[*Points to dining-room.*]

JACK. Yes.

ALICE. I don't want to see him.

JACK. Very well, dear, I'll excuse you.

ALICE [*going*]. Come, Helen.

JACK [*at door, left*]. Come in. [*To*
HELEN, *who is going with* ALICE.] Helen!
I'd like *you* to stay.

HELEN. Me?

JACK. Yes.   [*Exit* ALICE.]

[*Enter* CLAY, HARDMUTH, *and* VIOLA. VIOLA
lays automobile coat on sofa. HARDMUTH
bows to HELEN. HELEN *bows.*]

JACK. Your mother has just left us,
Viola. You'd better join her.

VIOLA. Very well.

JACK [*taking her hand as she passes him*].
And I want you to know — I appreciate
very much, my dear, your going on this
errand for me — you're the right stuff.

[*Kisses her. Exit* VIOLA.]

[*To* HARDMUTH.] You're trying to get
away?

HARDMUTH. This your note?

JACK. Yes.

HARDMUTH. You say you'll help me out of the State?

JACK. I will.

HARDMUTH. When?

JACK. Whenever you're ready.

HARDMUTH. I'm ready now.

JACK. Then I'll help you now.

LEW. Now?

JACK. Yes.

HELEN. Doesn't that render you liable in some way, Jack, to the law?

JACK. Yes — but I've been liable to the law in some way for the last twenty years. [To CLAY.] You go down and tell the chauffeur to leave the machine and walk home. I'm going to run it myself and I'll turn it in.

CLAY. Yes, sir.   [Exit.]

HARDMUTH. You're going to run it yourself?

JACK. Yes.

HARDMUTH. Where to?

JACK. Across the river, if that's agreeable to you — or any place you name.

HARDMUTH. Is anybody — waiting for you — across the river?

JACK. No.

HARDMUTH [again with note]. This is all on the level?

JACK. Completely.

LEW. Why, I think you mean that.

JACK. I do.

LEW [aggressively]. But I've got something to say, haven't I?

JACK. I hope not.

LEW [quitting]. If you're in earnest, of course. But I don't see your game.

JACK. I'm not fully convinced of Mr. Hardmuth's guilt.

LEW. Why, he's running away?

[Enter CLAY.]

HARDMUTH. I know what a case they'd make against me, but I'm not guilty in any degree.

JACK. I want to do this thing for you, Frank — don't make it too difficult by any lying. When I said I wasn't fully convinced of your guilt, my reservation was one you wouldn't understand. [To CLAY.] He gone?

CLAY. Yes.

JACK. My coat and goggles?

CLAY. Below in the reception-room.

JACK. Thank you. I wish now you'd go to Viola and her mother and keep them wherever they are.

CLAY. All right.   [Exit.]

JACK. [To HARDMUTH.] Hungry?
                        [Touches push button.]

HARDMUTH. No, thank you.

JACK. Got money?

HARDMUTH. Yes.

[Enter JO.]

JACK. Jo, take Mr. Hardmuth below and lend him one of the fur coats. [To HARDMUTH.] I'll join you immediately.
                   [Exit HARDMUTH with JO.]

HELEN. What does it all mean, Jack?

JACK. Lew, I called that ace of hearts, didn't I?

LEW. And the three queens.

JACK. Because the three queens and the ace were in your mind.

LEW. I don't see any other explanation.

JACK. Suppose, instead of the cards there'd been in your mind a well-developed plan of assassination — the picture of a murder —

LEW. Did you drop to him that way?

JACK. No. Raymor told me all I know of Hardmuth — but here's the very hell of it. Long before Scovill was killed I thought he deserved killing and I thought it could be done just — as — it — was done.

HELEN. Jack!

JACK. I never breathed a word of it to a living soul, but Hardmuth planned it exactly as I dreamed it — and by God, a guilty thought is almost as criminal as a guilty deed. I've always had a considerable influence over that poor devil that's running away to-night, and I'm not sure that before the Judge of both of us the guilt isn't mostly mine.

HELEN. That's morbid, Jack, dear, perfectly morbid.

JACK. I hope it is — we'll none of us ever know — in this life — but we can all of us —   [Pause.]

LEW. What?

JACK. Live as if it were true.
            [Change of manner to brisk command.]

I'm going to help him over the line — the roads are watched, but the police won't suspect me and they won't suspect Lew — and all the less if there's a lady with us — [*To* LEW.] Will you go?

LEW. The limit.

JACK. Get a heavy coat from Jo.

LEW. Yes.   [*Exit.*]

JACK [*alone with* HELEN]. You know you said I used to be able to make you write to me when I was a boy at college?

HELEN. Yes.

JACK. And you were a thousand miles away — while this fellow — Hardmuth — was just at my elbow half the time.

HELEN. It can't help you to brood over it.

JACK. It can help me to know it, and make what amend I can. Will you go with me while I put this poor devil over the line?

HELEN [*taking* VIOLA'S *fur coat*]. Yes, I'll go with you.

JACK. Helen, you stood by your boy in a fight for his life.

HELEN. Did n't you?

JACK. Will you stand by *me* while I make my fight?

HELEN [*giving her hand*]. You've made your fight, Jack, and you've won.

[JACK *kisses her hand, which he reverently holds in both of his.*]

THE SCARECROW

A TRAGEDY OF THE LUDICROUS

By
PERCY MACKAYE

AUTHOR'S NOTE

THE version of "The Scarecrow" here printed is the first publication of the text which embodies the practical revisions made by me during rehearsals which I conducted in New York and on the road, when the play was first produced under the management of Mr. Henry B. Harris.

It is the version made for the professional use [during two theatrical seasons] of Mr. Frank Reicher in the United States, and of Miss Muriel Pratt in England, at the Theatre Royal, Bristol [in repertory].

It is also the version translated into German by Dr. Walther Fischer, of the University of Pennsylvania, for the professional use of Herr Rudolf Schildkraut in Germany, at the Deutscher Theater, Berlin, under direction of Prof. Max Reinhardt.

PERCY MACKAYE

CORNISH, N.H.,
September 25, 1914.

TO

MY MOTHER

IN MEMORY OF AUSPICIOUS
"COUNTINGS OF THE CROWS"
BY OLD NEW ENGLAND CORNFIELDS

DRAMATIS PERSONÆ

JUSTICE GILEAD MERTON

GOODY RICKBY ("*Blacksmith Bess*")

LORD RAVENSBANE ("*Marquis of Oxford, Baron of Wittenberg, Elector of Worms, and Count of Cordova*"), *their hypothetical son*

DICKON, *a Yankee improvisation of the Prince of Darkness*

RACHEL MERTON, *niece of the Justice*

MISTRESS CYNTHIA MERTON, *sister of the Justice*

RICHARD TALBOT, *Esquire, betrothed to Rachel*

SIR CHARLES REDDINGTON, *Lieutenant-Governor*

MISTRESS REDDINGTON } *his daughters.*
AMELIA REDDINGTON

CAPTAIN BUGBY, *the Governor's Secretary*

MINISTER DODGE

MISTRESS DODGE, *his wife*

REV. MASTER RAND, *of Harvard College*

REV. MASTER TODD, *of Harvard College*

MICAH, *a servant of the Justice*

Time — Late Seventeenth Century
Place — A Town in Massachusetts

THE SCARECROW

ACT I

The interior of a blacksmith shop. Right center, a forge. Left, a loft, from which are hanging dried cornstalks, hay, and the yellow ears of cattle-corn. Back center, a wide double door, closed when the curtain rises. Through this door — when later it is opened — is visible a New England landscape in the late springtime: a distant wood; stone walls, high elms, a well-sweep; and, in the near foreground, a ploughed field, from which the green shoots of early corn are just appearing. The blackened walls of the shop are covered with a miscellaneous collection of old iron, horseshoes, cart-wheels, etc., the usual appurtenances of a smithy. In the right-hand corner, however, is an array of things quite out of keeping with the shop proper: musical instruments, puppets, tall clocks, and fantastical junk. Conspicuous amongst these articles is a large standing mirror, framed grotesquely in old gold and curtained by a dull stuff, embroidered with peaked caps and crescent moons.

Just before the scene opens, a hammer is heard ringing briskly upon steel. As the curtain rises there is discovered, standing at the anvil in the flickering light of a bright flame from the forge, a woman — powerful, ruddy, proud with a certain masterful beauty, white-haired (as though prematurely), bare-armed to the elbows, clad in a dark skirt (above her ankles), a loose blouse, open at the throat; a leathern apron and a workman's cap. The woman is GOODY RICKBY. *On the anvil she is shaping a piece of iron. Beside her stands a framework of iron formed like the ribs and backbone of a man. For a few moments she continues to ply her hammer, amid a shower of sparks, till suddenly the flame on the forge dies down.*

GOODY RICKBY. Dickon ! More flame.

A VOICE [*above her*]. Yea, Goody.

[*The flame in the forge spurts up high and suddenly.*]

GOODY RICKBY. Nay, not so fierce.

THE VOICE [*at her side*]. *Votre pardon,* madame. [*The flame subsides.*]
Is that better ?

GOODY RICKBY. That will do.

[*With her tongs, she thrusts the iron into the flame; it turns white-hot.*]

Quick work; nothing like brimstone for the smithy trade.

[*At the anvil, she begins to weld the iron rib onto the framework.*]

There, my beauty ! We 'll make a stout set of ribs for you. I 'll see to it this year that I have a scarecrow can outstand all the nor'easters that blow. I 've no notion to lose my corn-crop this summer.

[*Outside, the faint cawings of crows are heard. Putting down her tongs and hammer,* GOODY RICKBY *strides to the double door, and flinging it wide open, lets in the gray light of dawn. She looks out over the fields and shakes her fist.*]

So ye 're up before me and the sun, are ye?

[*Squinting against the light.*]

There 's one ! Nay, two. Aha !

> One for sorrow,
> Two for mirth —

Good ! This time we 'll have the laugh on our side.

[*She returns to the forge, where again the fire has died out.*]

Dickon ! Fire ! Come, come, where be thy wits ?

THE VOICE [*sleepily from the forge*]. 'T is early, dame.

GOODY RICKBY. The more need —

[*Takes up her tongs.*]

THE VOICE. [*Screams.*] Ow !

GOODY RICKBY. Ha ! Have I got thee ?

[*From the blackness of the forge she pulls out with her tongs, by the right ear, the figure of a devil, horned and tailed. In general aspect, though he resembles a mediæval familiar demon, yet the suggestions of a goatish beard, a shrewdly humorous smile, and (when he speaks) the slightest of nasal drawls, remotely simulate a species of Yankee rustic.* GOODY RICKBY *substitutes her fingers for the tongs.*]

Now, Dickon !

DICKON. *Deus !* I have n't been nabbed

like that since St. Dunstan tweaked my nose. Well, sweet Goody?

GOODY RICKBY. The bellows!

DICKON [*going slowly to the forge*]. Why, 't is hardly dawn yet. Honest folks are still abed. It makes a long day.

GOODY RICKBY [*working, while* DICKON *plies the bellows*]. Aye, for your black pets, the crows, to work in. That 's why we must be at it early. You heard 'em. We must have this scarecrow of ours out in the field at his post before sunrise. Here, I 've made the frame strong, so as to stand the weather; *you* must make the body lifelike so as to fool the crows. This year, we must make 'em think it 's a real human crittur.

DICKON. To fool the philosophers is my specialty, but the crows — hm!

GOODY RICKBY. Pooh! That staggers thee!

DICKON. Madame Rickby, prod not the quick of my genius. I am Phidias, I am Raphael, I am the Lord God! — You shall see — [*Demands with a gesture.*] Yonder broom-stick.

GOODY RICKBY [*fetching him a broom from the corner*]. Good boy!

DICKON [*straddling the handle*]. Ha, ha! gee up! my Salem mare.

[*Then, pseudo-philosophically.*]
A broomstick — that 's for imagination!

[*He begins to construct the scarecrow, while* GOODY RICKBY, *assisting, brings the constructive parts from various nooks and corners.*]

We are all pretty artists, to be sure, Bessie. Phidias, he sculptures the gods; Raphael, he paints the angels; the Lord God, he creates Adam; and Dickon — fetch me the poker — aha! Dickon! What doth Dickon? He nullifies 'em all; he endows the Scarecrow! A poker: here 's his conscience. There 's two fine legs to walk on, — imagination and conscience. Yonder flails now! The ideal — the *beau idéal*, dame — that 's what we artists seek. The apotheosis of scarecrows! And pray, what 's a scarecrow? Why, the antithesis of Adam. — "Let there be candles!" quoth the Lord God, sitting in the dark. "Let there be candle-extinguishers," saith Dickon. "I am made in the image of my maker," quoth Adam. "Look at yourself in the glass," saith Goodman Scarecrow.

[*Taking two implements from* GOODY RICKBY.*]

Fine! fine! here are flails — one for wit, t' other for satire. *Sapristi!* with two such arms, my lad, how thou wilt work thy way in the world!

GOODY RICKBY. You talk as if you were making a real mortal, Dickon.

DICKON. To fool a crow, Goody, I must fashion a crittur that will first deceive a man.

GOODY RICKBY. He 'll scarce do that without a head. [*Pointing to the loft.*] What think ye of yonder Jack-o'-lantern? 'T was made last Hallowe'en.

DICKON. Rare, my Psyche! We shall collaborate. Here!

[*Running up the ladder, he tosses down a yellow hollowed pumpkin to* GOODY RICKBY, *who catches it. Then rummaging forth an armful of cornstalks, ears, tassels, dried squashes, gourds, beets, etc., he descends and throws them in a heap on the floor.*]

Whist! [*As he drops them.*] Gourd, carrot, turnip, beet : — the anatomy.

GOODY RICKBY [*placing the pumpkin on the shoulders*]. Look!

DICKON. *O Johannes Baptista!* What wouldst thou have given for such a head! I helped Salome to cut his off, dame, and it looked not half so appetizing on her charger. Tut! Copernicus wore once such a pumpkin, but it is rotten. Look at his golden smile! Hail, Phœbus Apollo!

GOODY RICKBY. 'T is the finest scarecrow in town.

DICKON. Nay, poor soul, 't is but a skeleton yet. He must have a man's heart in him.

[*Picking a big red beet from among the cornstalks, he places it under the left side of the ribs.*]

Hush! Dost thou hear it *beat*?

GOODY RICKBY. Thou merry rogue!

DICKON. Now for the lungs of him.

[*Snatching a small pair of bellows from a peg on the wall.*]

That 's for eloquence! He 'll preach the black knaves a sermon on theft. And now —

[*Here, with* GOODY RICKBY'S *help, he stuffs the framework with the gourds, corn, etc., from the loft, weaving the husks about the legs and arms.*]

Here goes for digestion and inherited instincts! More corn, Goody. Now he 'll fight for his own flesh and blood!

GOODY RICKBY [*laughing*]. Dickon, I am proud of thee.

DICKON. Wait till you see his peruke.

[*Seizing a feather duster made of crow's feathers.*]

Voici! Scalps of the enemy!

[*Pulling them apart, he arranges the feathers on the pumpkin, like a gentleman's wig.*]

A rare conqueror!

GOODY RICKBY. Oh, you beauty!

DICKON. And now a bit of comfort for dark days and stormy nights.

[*Taking a piece of corn-cob with the kernels on it, DICKON makes a pipe, which he puts into the scarecrow's mouth.*]

So! There, Goody! I tell thee, with yonder brand-new coat and breeches of mine — those there in my cupboard! — we 'll make him a lad to be proud of.

[*Taking the clothes, which GOODY RICKBY brings — a pair of fine scarlet breeches and a gold-embroidered coat with ruffles of lace — he puts them upon the scarecrow. Then, eying it like a connoisseur, makes a few finishing touches.*]

Why, dame, he 'll be a son to thee.

GOODY RICKBY. A son? Aye, if I had but a son!

DICKON. Why, here you have him. [*To the scarecrow.*] Thou wilt scare the crows off thy mother's cornfield — won't my pretty? And send 'em all over t'other side the wall to her dear neighbor's, the Justice Gilead Merton's.

GOODY RICKBY. Justice Merton! Nay, if they 'd only peck his eyes out, instead of his corn.

DICKON [*grinning*]. Yet the Justice was a dear friend of "Blacksmith Bess."

GOODY RICKBY. Aye, "Blacksmith Bess"! If I had n't had a good stout arm when he cast me off with the babe, I might have starved for all his worship cared.

DICKON. True, Bessie; 't was a scurvy trick he played on thee — and on me, that took such pains to bring you together — to steal a young maid's heart —

GOODY RICKBY. And then toss it away like a bad penny to the gutter! And the child — to die! [*Lifting her hammer in rage.*] Ha! If I could get the worshipful Justice Gilead into my power again —

[*Drops the hammer sullenly on the anvil.*]

But no! I shall beat my life away on this anvil, whilst my justice clinks his gold, and drinks his port to a fat old age. Justice! Ha — justice of God!

DICKON. Whist, dame! Talk of angels and hear the rustle of their relatives.

GOODY RICKBY [*turning, watches outside a girl's figure approaching*]. His niece — Rachel Merton! What can she want so early? Nay, I mind me; 't is the mirror. She 's a maid after our own hearts, boy, — no Sabbath-go-to-meeting airs about *her*! She hath read the books of the *magi* from cover to cover, and paid me good guineas for 'em, though her uncle knows naught on 't. Besides, she 's in love, Dickon.

DICKON [*indicating the scarecrow*]. Ah? With *him*? Is it a rendezvous?

GOODY RICKBY [*with a laugh*]. Pff! Begone!

DICKON. [*Shakes his finger at the scarecrow.*] Thou naughty rogue!

[*Then, still smiling slyly, with his head placed confidentially next to the scarecrow's ear, as if whispering, and with his hand pointing to the maiden outside, DICKON fades away into air. RACHEL enters, nervous and hesitant. GOODY RICKBY makes her a curtsy, which she acknowledges by a nod, half absent-minded.*]

GOODY RICKBY. Mistress Rachel Merton — so early! I hope your uncle, our worshipful Justice, is not ill?

RACHEL. No, my uncle is quite well. The early morning suits me best for a walk. You are — quite alone?

GOODY RICKBY. Quite alone, mistress. [*Bitterly.*] Oh, folks don't call on Goody Rickby — except on business.

RACHEL [*absently, looking round in the dim shop*]. Yes — you must be busy. Is it — is it here?

GOODY RICKBY. You mean the —

RACHEL [*starting back, with a cry*]. Ah! who 's that?

GOODY RICKBY [*chuckling*]. Fear not, mistress; 't is nothing but a scarecrow. I 'm going to put him in my cornfield yonder. The crows are so pesky this year.

RACHEL. [*Draws her skirts away with a shiver.*] How loathsome!

GOODY RICKBY [*vastly pleased*]. He 'll do.

RACHEL. Ah, here! — This is *the* mirror?

GOODY RICKBY. Yea, mistress, and a wonderful glass it is, as I told you. I would n't sell it to most comers, but seeing how you and Master Talbot —

RACHEL. Yes ; that will do.

GOODY RICKBY. You see, if the town folks guessed what it was, well — You 've heard tell of the gibbets on Salem Hill ? There 's not many in New England like you, Mistress Rachel. You know enough to approve some miracles — outside the Scriptures.

RACHEL. You are quite sure the glass will do all you say ? It — never fails ?

GOODY RICKBY. Ah, now, mistress, how could it ? 'T is the glass of truth — [*insinuatingly*] — the glass of true lovers. It shows folks just as they are ; no shams, no varnish. If a wolf should dress himself in a white sheep's wool, this glass would reflect the black beast inside it.

RACHEL [*with awe*]. The black beast ! But what of the sins of the soul, Goody ? Vanity, hypocrisy, and — and inconstancy ? Will it surely reveal them ?

GOODY RICKBY. I have told you, my young lady. If it doth not as I say, bring it back and get your money again. Oh, trust me, sweeting, an old dame hath eyes in her heart yet. If your lover be false, this glass shall pluck his fine feathers !

RACHEL [*with aloofness*]. 'T is no question of that. I wish the glass to — to amuse me.

GOODY RICKBY [*laughing*]. Why, then, try it on some of your neighbors.

RACHEL. You ask a large price for it.

GOODY RICKBY. [*Shrugs.*] I run risks. Besides, where will you get another ?

RACHEL. That is true. Here, I will buy it. That is the sum you mentioned, I believe ?

[*She hands a purse to* GOODY RICKBY, *who opens it and counts over some coins.*]

GOODY RICKBY. Let see ; let see.

RACHEL. Well ?

GOODY RICKBY. Good : 't is good. Folks call me a witch, mistress. Well — harkee — a witch's word is as good as a justice's gold. The glass is yours — with my blessing.

RACHEL. Spare yourself that, dame. But the glass : how am I to get it ? How will you send it to me — quietly ?

GOODY RICKBY. Trust me for that. I 've a willing lad that helps me with such errands ; a neighbor o' mine. [*Calls.*] Ebenezer !

RACHEL [*startled*]. What ! is he here ?

GOODY RICKBY. In the hayloft. The boy 's an orphan ; he sleeps there o' times. Ebenezer !

[*A raw, disheveled country boy appears in the loft, slides down the ladder, and shuffles up sleepily.*]

THE BOY. Evenin'.

RACHEL [*drawing* GOODY RICKBY *aside*]. You understand ; I desire no comment about this purchase.

GOODY RICKBY. Nor I, mistress, be sure.

RACHEL. Is he — ?

GOODY RICKBY [*tapping her forehead significantly*]. Trust his wits who hath no wit ; he 's mum.

RACHEL. Oh !

THE BOY [*gaping*]. Job ?

GOODY RICKBY. Yea, rumple-head ! His job this morning is to bear yonder glass to the house of Justice Merton — the big one on the hill ; to the side door. Mind, no gabbing. Doth he catch ?

THE BOY [*nodding and grinning*]. 'E swallows.

RACHEL. But is the boy strong enough ?

GOODY RICKBY. Him ? [*Pointing to the anvil.*] Ebenezer !

[*The boy spits on his palms, takes hold of the anvil, lifts it, drops it again, sits on it, and grins at the door, just as* RICHARD TALBOT *appears there, from outside.*]

RACHEL. Gracious !

GOODY RICKBY. Trust him. He 'll carry the glass for you.

RACHEL. I will return home at once, then. Let him go quietly to the side door, and wait for me. Good-morning.

[*Turning, she confronts* RICHARD.]

RICHARD. Good-morning.

RACHEL. Richard ! — Squire Talbot, you — you are abroad early.

RICHARD. As early as Mistress Rachel. Is it pardonable ? I caught sight of you walking in this direction, so I thought it wise to follow, lest —

[*Looks hard at* GOODY RICKBY.]

RACHEL. Very kind. Thanks. We can return together. [*To* GOODY RICKBY.] You

will make sure that I receive the — the
article.

GOODY RICKBY. Trust me, mistress.

[*She curtsies to* RICHARD.]

RICHARD [*bluntly, looking from one to the
other*]. What article?

[RACHEL *ignores the question and
starts to pass out.* RICHARD
frowns at GOODY RICKBY, *who
stammers.*]

GOODY RICKBY. Begging your pardon,
sir?

RICHARD. What article? I said. [*After
a short, embarrassed pause, more sternly.*]
Well?

GOODY RICKBY. Oh, the article! Yonder
old glass, to be sure, sir. A quaint piece,
your honor.

RICHARD. Rachel, you have n't come
here at sunrise to buy — that thing?

RACHEL. Verily, "that thing," and at
sunrise. A pretty time for a pretty purchase. Are you coming?

RICHARD [*in a low voice*]. More witchcraft nonsense? Do you realize this is serious?

RACHEL. Oh, of course. You know I am
desperately mystical, so pray let us not discuss it. Good-bye.

RICHARD. Rachel, just a moment. If
you want a mirror, you shall have the prettiest one in New England. Or I will import
you one from London. Only — I beg of
you — don't buy stolen goods.

GOODY RICKBY. Stolen goods?

RACHEL [*aside to* RICHARD]. Don't! don't!

RICHARD. [*To* GOODY RICKBY.] Can you
account for this mirror — how you came by
it?

GOODY RICKBY. I 'll show ye! I 'll show
ye! Stolen — ha!

RICHARD. Come, old swindler, keep your
mirror, and give this lady back her money.

GOODY RICKBY. I 'll damn ye both, I
will! — Stolen!

RACHEL [*imploringly*]. Will you come?

RICHARD. Look you, old Rickby; this
is not the first time. Charm all the broom-
sticks in town, if you like; bewitch all the
tables and saucepans and mirrors you
please; but gull no more money out of
young girls. Mind you! We 're not so en-
terprising in this town as at Salem; but —
it may come to it! So look sharp! I 'm not
blind to what 's going on here.

GOODY RICKBY. Not blind, Master Puritan? Oho! You can see through all my
counterfeits, can ye? So! you would scrape
all the wonder out'n the world, as I 've
scraped all the meat out'n my punkin-head
yonder! Aha! wait and see! Afore sun-
down, I 'll send ye a nut to crack, shall
make your orthodox jaws ache. Your servant, Master Deuteronomy!

RICHARD. [*To* RACHEL, *who has seized his
arm.*] We 'll go.

[*Exeunt* RICHARD *and* RACHEL.]

GOODY RICKBY. [*Calls shrilly after them.*]
Trot away, pretty team; toss your heads.
I 'll unhitch ye and take off your blinders.

THE SLOUCHING BOY [*capering and
grimacing in front of the mirror, shrieks with
laughter*]. Ohoho!

GOODY RICKBY [*returning, she mutters
savagely*]. "Stolen goods!" [*Screams.*]
Dickon! Stop laughing.

THE BOY. O Lord! O Lord!

GOODY RICKBY. What tickles thy mirth
now?

THE BOY. For to think that the soul of
an orphan innocent, what lives in a hayloft, should wear horns.

[*On looking into the mirror, the spectator perceives therein that the reflection of the slouching boy is the
horned demon figure of* DICKON,
*who performs the same antics in
pantomime within the glass as the
boy does without.*]

GOODY RICKBY. Yea; 't is a wise devil
that knows his own face in the glass. But
hark now! thou must find me a rival for
this cock-squire, — dost hear? A rival, that
shall steal away the heart of his Mistress
Rachel.

DICKON. And take her to church?

GOODY RICKBY. To church or to hell.
All 's one.

DICKON. A rival! [*Pointing at the glass.*]
How would *he* serve — in there? Dear
Ebenezer! Fancy the deacons in the vestry,
Goody, and her uncle, the Justice, when they
saw him escorting the bride to the altar, with
his tail round her waist!

GOODY RICKBY. Tut, tut! Think it over
in earnest, and meantime take her the glass.
Wait, we 'd best fold it up small, so as not
to attract notice on the road. [DICKON, *who
has already drawn the curtains over the glass,
grasps one side of the large frame,* GOODY

RICKBY *the other.*] Now! [*Pushing their shoulders against the two sides, the frame disappears and* DICKON *holds in his hand a mirror about a foot square, of the same design.*] So! Be off! And mind, a rival for Richard !
DICKON.

> For Richard a rival,
> Dear Goody Rickby
> Wants Dickon's connival:
> Lord! What can the trick be ?

[*To the scarecrow.*] By-by, Sonny; take care of thy mother.

> [DICKON *slouches out with the glass, whistling.*]

GOODY RICKBY. Mother! Yea, if only I had a son — the Justice Merton's and mine ! If the brat had but lived now to remind him of those merry days, which he has forgotten. Zooks, would n't I put a spoke in his wheel ! But no such luck for me ! No such luck !

> [*As she goes to the forge, the stout figure of a man appears in the doorway behind her. Under one arm he carries a large book, in the other hand a gold-headed cane. He hesitates, embarrassed.*]

THE MAN. Permit me, madam.
GOODY RICKBY [*turning*]. Ah, him ! — Justice Merton !
JUSTICE MERTON [*removing his hat, steps over the sill, and lays his great book on the table; then with a supercilious look, he puts his hat firmly on again*]. Permit me, dame.
GOODY RICKBY. You !

> [*With confused, affected hauteur, the* JUSTICE *shifts from foot to foot, flourishing his cane. As he speaks,* GOODY RICKBY, *with a shrewd, painful expression, draws slowly backward toward the door, left, which opens into an inner room. Reaching it, she opens it part way, stands facing him, and listens.*]

JUSTICE MERTON. I have had the honor — permit me — to entertain suspicions; to rise early, to follow my niece, to meet just now Squire Talbot; to hear his remarks concerning — hem ! — you, dame ! to call here — permit me — to express myself and inquire —
GOODY RICKBY. Concerning your waistcoat?

> [*Turning quickly, she snatches an article of apparel which hangs on the inner side of the door, and holds it up.*]

JUSTICE MERTON [*starting, crimson*]. Woman !
GOODY RICKBY. You left it behind — the last time.
JUSTICE MERTON. I have not the honor to remember —
GOODY RICKBY. The one I embroidered ?
JUSTICE MERTON. 'T is a matter of —
GOODY RICKBY. Of some two-and-twenty years. [*Stretching out the narrow width of the waistcoat.*] Will you try it on now, dearie ?
JUSTICE MERTON. Unconscionable ! Un-un-unconscionable witch !
GOODY RICKBY. Witchling — thou used to say.
JUSTICE MERTON. Pah ! pah ! I forget myself. Pride, permit me, goeth before a fall. As a magistrate, Rickby, I have already borne with you long ! The last straw, however, breaks the camel's back.
GOODY RICKBY. Poor camel !
JUSTICE MERTON. You have soiled, you have smirched, the virgin reputation of my niece. You have inveigled her into notions of witchcraft; already the neighbors are beginning to talk. 'T is a long lane which hath no turning, saith the Lord. Permit me — as a witch, thou art judged. Thou shalt hang.
A VOICE [*behind him*]. And me, too ?
JUSTICE MERTON. [*Turns about and stares.*] I beg pardon.
THE VOICE [*in front of him*]. Not at all.
JUSTICE MERTON. Did — did somebody speak ?
THE VOICE. Don't you recognize my voice ? *Still and small*, you know. If you will kindly let me out, we can chat.
JUSTICE MERTON [*turning fiercely on* GOODY RICKBY]. These are thy sorceries. But I fear them not. The righteous man walketh with God. [*Going to the book which lies on the table.*] Satan, I ban thee ! I will read from the Holy Scriptures !

> [*Unclasping the Bible, he flings open the ponderous covers. —* DICKON *steps forth in smoke.*]

DICKON. Thanks; it was stuffy in there.
JUSTICE MERTON [*clasping his hands*]. Dickon !
DICKON [*moving a step nearer on the table*]. Hullo, Gilly ! Hullo, Bess !
JUSTICE MERTON. Dickon ! No ! No !

DICKON. Do ye mind Auld Lang Syne — the chorus that night, Gilly ? [*Sings.*]

> Gil-ead, Gil-ead, Gil-ead Merton,
> He was a silly head, silly head, Certain,
> When he forgot to steal a bed-Curtain.

Encore, now !

JUSTICE MERTON. No, no, be merciful ! I will not harm her; she shall not hang ; I swear it, I swear it ! [DICKON *disappears.*] I swear — ah ! Is he gone ? Witchcraft ! Witchcraft ! I have witnessed it. 'T is proved on thee, slut. I swear it : thou shalt hang. [*Exit wildly.*]

GOODY RICKBY. Ay, Gilead ! I shall hang *on !* Ahaha ! Dickon, thou angel ! Ah, Satan ! Satan ! For a son now !

DICKON [*reappearing*]. *Videlicet,* in law — a bastard. *N' est ce pas ?*

GOODY RICKBY. Yea, in law and in justice, I should 'a' had one now. Worse luck that he died.

DICKON. One-and-twenty years ago ? [GOODY RICKBY *nods.*] Good; he should be of age now. One-and-twenty — a pretty age, too, for a rival. Haha ! — For arrival ? — Marry, he shall arrive, then ; arrive and marry and inherit his patrimony — all on his birthday ! Come, to work !

GOODY RICKBY. What rant is this ?

DICKON. Yet, Dickon, it pains me to perform such an anachronism. All this mediævalism in Massachusetts ! — These old-fashioned flames and alchemic accompaniments, when I 've tried so hard to be a native American product; it jars. But *che vuole !* I 'm naturally middle-aged. I have n't been really myself, let me think, — since 1492 !

GOODY RICKBY. What art thou mooning about ?

DICKON [*still impenetrable*]. There was my old friend in Germany, Dr. Johann Faustus; he was nigh such a bag of old rubbish when I made him over. Ain't it trite ! No, you can't teach an old dog like me new tricks. Still, a scarecrow ! that 's decidedly local color. Come, then; a Yankee masterpiece !

> [*Seizing* GOODY RICKBY *by the arm, and placing her before the scarecrow, he makes a bow and wave of introduction.*]

Behold, madam, your son — illegitimate; the future affianced of Mistress Rachel Merton, the heir-elect, through matrimony, of Merton House, — Gilead Merton second :

Lord Ravensbane ! Your lordship — your mother.

GOODY RICKBY. Dickon ! Can you do it ?

DICKON. I can — try.

GOODY RICKBY. You will create him for me ? — [*wickedly*] — and for Gilead !

DICKON. I will — for a kiss.

GOODY RICKBY [*about to embrace him*]. Dickon !

DICKON [*dodging her*]. Later. Now, the waistcoat.

GOODY RICKBY [*handing it*]. Rare ! rare ! He shall go wooing in 't — like his father.

DICKON [*shifting the scarecrow's gold-trimmed coat, slips on the embroidered waistcoat and replaces the coat*]. Stand still, Jack! So, my macaroni. *Perfecto !* Stay — a walking-stick !

GOODY RICKBY [*wrenching a spoke out of an old rickety wheel*]. Here : the spoke for Gilead. He used to take me to drive in the chaise it came out of.

DICKON [*placing the spoke as a cane, in the scarecrow's sleeve, views him with satisfaction*]. *Sic !* There, Jacky ! *Filius fit non nascitur.* — Sam Hill ! My Latin is stale. "In the beginning, was the — gourd !" Of these thy modest ingredients may thy spirit smack !

> [*Making various mystic passes with his hands,* DICKON *intones, now deep and solemn, now with fanciful shrill rapidity, this incantation.*]

> Flail, flip ;
> Broom, sweep ;
>   *Sic itur !*
> Cornstalk
> And turnip, talk !
>   Turn crittur !

> Pulse, beet ;
> Gourd, eat ;
>   *Ave* Hellas !
> Poker and punkin,
> Stir the old junk in;
>   Breathe, bellows !

> Corn-cob,
> And crow's feather,
> End the job ;
> Jumble the rest o' the rubbish together ;
>   Dovetail and tune 'em.
>   *E pluribus unum !*

> [*The scarecrow remains stock still.*]

The devil ! Have I lost the hang of it ? Ah *!*

Hullo ! He 's dropped his pipe. What 's a dandy without his 'baccy !

> [*Picking up the pipe, he shows it to* GOODY RICKBY, *pointing into the pipe-bowl.*]

'T is my own brand, Goody : brimstone. Without it he 'd be naught but a scare-crow.

> [*Restoring the corn-cob pipe to the scarecrow's mouth.*]

'T is the life and breath of him. So ; hand me yon hazel switch, Goody.   [*Waving it.*] Presto !

> Brighten, coal,
> I' the dusk between us !
> Whiten, soul !
> *Propinquat Venus !*

> [*A whiff of smoke puffs from the scarecrow's pipe.*]

Sic ! Sic ! Jacobus ! [*Another whiff.*] Bravo !

> [*The whiffs grow more rapid and the thing trembles.*]

GOODY RICKBY. Puff ! puff, manny, for thy life !

DICKON. *Fiat, fœtus !* — Huzza ! *Noch einmal !* Go it !

> [*Clouds of smoke issue from the pipe, half fill the shop, and envelop the creature, who staggers.*[1]]

GOODY RICKBY. See ! See his eyes !

DICKON [*beckoning with one finger*]. *Veni, fili ! Veni !* Take 'ee first step, *bambino !* — Toddle !

> [*The* SCARECROW *makes a stiff lurch forward and falls sidewise against the anvil, propped half-reclining against which he leans rigid, emitting fainter puffs of smoke in gasps.*]

GOODY RICKBY. [*Screams.*] Have a care ! He 's fallen.

DICKON. Well done, Punkin Jack ! Thou shalt be knighted for that !

> [*Striking him on the shoulder with the hazel rod.*]

Rise, Lord Ravensbane !

> [*The* SCARECROW *totters to his feet, and makes a forlorn rectilinear salutation.*]

GOODY RICKBY. Look ! He bows. — He

---

[1] At Dickon's words, "Come, to work !" on p. 369, the living actor, concealed by the smoke, and disguised, has substituted hifuself for the elegantly clad effigy. His make-up, of course, approximates to the latter, but the grotesque contours of his expression gradually, throughout the remainder of the act, become refined and sublimated till, at the *finale*, they are of a lordly and distinguished caste.

flaps his flails at thee. He smiles like a tik-doo-loo-roo !

DICKON [*with a profound reverence, backing away*]. Will his lordship deign to follow his tutor ?

> [*With hitches and jerks, the* SCARE-CROW *follows* DICKON.]

GOODY RICKBY. O Lord ! Lord ! the style o' the broomstick !

DICKON [*holding ready a high-backed chair*]. Will his lordship be seated and rest himself ?

> [*Awkwardly the* SCARECROW *half falls into the chair; his head sinks side-ways, and his pipe falls out.* DICKON *snatches it up instantly and restores it to his mouth.*]

Puff ! Puff, *puer ;* 't is thy life.

> [*The* SCARECROW *puffs again.*]

Is his lordship's tobacco refreshing ?

GOODY RICKBY. Look, now ! The red color in his cheeks. The beet-juice is pumping, oho !

DICKON [*offering his arm*]. Your lordship will deign to receive an audience ? [*The* SCARECROW *takes his arm and rises.*] The Marchioness of Rickby, your lady mother, entreats leave to present herself.

GOODY RICKBY [*curtsying low*]. My son !

DICKON [*holding the pipe, and waving the hazel rod*]. *Dicite !* Speak !

> [*The* SCARECROW, *blowing out his last mouthful of smoke, opens his mouth, gasps, gurgles, and is silent.*]

In principio erat verbum ! Accost thy mother !

> [*The* SCARECROW, *clutching at his side in a struggle for coherence, fixes a pathetic look of pain on* GOODY RICKBY.]

THE SCARECROW. Mother !

GOODY RICKBY [*with a scream of hyster-ical laughter, seizes both* DICKON'S *hands and dances him about the forge*]. O Beelzebub ! I shall die !

DICKON. Thou hast thy son.

> [DICKON *whispers in the* SCARE-CROW'S *ear, shakes his finger, and exit.*]

GOODY RICKBY. He called me "mother." Again, boy, again.

THE SCARECROW. From the bottom of my heart — mother.

GOODY RICKBY. "The bottom of his heart " ! — Nay, thou killest me.

THE SCARECROW. Permit me, madam !

Goody Rickby. Gilead ! Gilead himself !
Waistcoat, "permit me," and all : thy father
over again, I tell thee.

The Scarecrow [*with a slight stammer*].
It gives me — I assure you — lady — the
deepest happiness.

Goody Rickby. Just so the old hypocrite spoke when I said I 'd have him. But
thou hast a sweeter deference, my son.

[*Reënter* Dickon; *he is dressed all in
black, save for a white stock — a
suit of plain elegance.*]

Dickon. Now, my lord, your tutor is
ready.

The Scarecrow. [*To* Goody Rickby.]
I have the honor — permit me — to wish
you — good-morning.

[*Bows and takes a step after* Dickon,
*who, taking a three-cornered cocked
hat from a peg, goes toward the
door.*]

Goody Rickby. Whoa ! Whoa, Jack !
Whither away ?

Dickon [*presenting the hat*]. Deign to
reply, sir.

The Scarecrow. I go — with my tutor
— Master Dickonson — to pay my respects
— to his worship — the Justice — Merton
— to solicit — the hand — of his daughter
— the fair Mistress — Rachel. [*With another bow.*] Permit me.

Goody Rickby. Permit ye ? God speed
ye ! Thou must teach him his tricks, Dickon.

Dickon. Trust me, Goody. Between
here and Justice Merton's, I will play the
mother-hen, and I promise thee, our bant-
ling shall be as stuffed with compliments
as a callow chick with caterpillars.

[*As he throws open the big doors, the
cawing of crows is heard again.*]

Hark ! your lordship's retainers acclaim
you on your birthday. They bid you welcome to your majority. Listen ! "Long
live Lord Ravensbane ! Caw !"

Goody Rickby. Look ! Count 'em,
Dickon.

One for sorrow,
Two for mirth,
Three for a wedding,
Four for a birth —

Four on 'em ! So ! Good luck on thy birthday ! And see ! There 's three on 'em flying
into the Justice's field.

— Flight o' the crows
Tells how the wind blows ! —

A wedding ! Get ye gone. Wed the girl,
and sting the Justice. Bless ye, my son !

The Scarecrow [*with a profound reverence*]. Mother — believe me — to be — your
ladyship's — most devoted — and obedient
— son.

Dickon [*prompting him aloud*]. Ravensbane.

The Scarecrow [*donning his hat, lifts
his head in hauteur, shakes his lace ruffle over
his hand, turns his shoulder, nods slightly, and
speaks for the first time with complete mastery
of his voice*]. Hm ! Ravensbane !

[*With one hand in the arm of* Dickon,
*the other twirling his cane (the con-
verted chaise-spoke), wreathed in
halos of smoke from his pipe, the
fantastical figure hitches elegantly
forth into the daylight, amid louder
acclamations of the crows.*]

ACT II

The same morning. Justice Merton's
*parlor, furnished and designed in the style of the
early colonial period. On the right wall hangs a
portrait of the* Justice *as a young man; on the
left wall, an old-fashioned looking-glass. At
the right of the room stands the glass of truth,
draped — as in the blacksmith shop — with the
strange, embroidered curtain.*

In front of it are discovered Rachel *and*
Richard; Rachel *is about to draw the curtain.*

Rachel. Now ! Are you willing ?

Richard. So you suspect me of dark,
villainous practices ?

Rachel. No, no, foolish Dick.

Richard. Still, I am to be tested ; is
that it ?

Rachel. That 's it.

Richard. As your true lover.

Rachel. Well, yes.

Richard. Why, of course, then, I consent. A true lover always consents to the
follies of his lady-love.

Rachel. Thank you, Dick ; I trust the
glass will sustain your character. Now ;
when I draw the curtain —

Richard [*staying her hand*]. What if I
be false ?

Rachel. Then, sir, the glass will reflect
you as the subtle fox that you are.

Richard. And you — as the goose ?

Rachel. Very likely. Ah ! but, Richard
dear, we must n't laugh. It may prove very

serious. You do not guess — you do not dream all the mysteries —

RICHARD [*shaking his head, with a grave smile*]. You pluck at too many mysteries. Remember our first mother Eve !

RACHEL. But this is the glass of truth ; and Goody Rickby told me —

RICHARD. Rickby, forsooth !

RACHEL. Nay, come ; let 's have it over.

[*She draws the curtain, covers her eyes, steps back by RICHARD'S side, looks at the glass, and gives a joyous cry.*]

Ah ! there you are, dear ! There we are, both of us — just as we have always seemed to each other, true. 'T is proved. Is n't it wonderful ?

RICHARD. Miraculous ! That a mirror bought in a blacksmith shop, before sunrise, for twenty pounds, should prove to be actually — a mirror !

RACHEL. Richard, I 'm so happy.

[*Enter JUSTICE MERTON and MISTRESS MERTON.*]

RICHARD [*embracing her*]. Happy, art thou, sweet goose ? Why, then, God bless Goody Rickby.

JUSTICE MERTON. Strange words from you, Squire Talbot.

[*RACHEL and RICHARD part quickly; RACHEL draws the curtain over the mirror; RICHARD stands stiffly.*]

RICHARD. Justice Merton ! Why, sir, the old witch is more innocent, perhaps, than I represented her.

JUSTICE MERTON. A witch, believe me, is never innocent.

[*Taking their hands, he brings them together and kisses RACHEL on the forehead.*]

Permit me, young lovers. I was once young myself, young and amorous.

MISTRESS MERTON [*in a low voice*]. Verily !

JUSTICE MERTON. My fair niece, my worthy young man, beware of witchcraft.

MISTRESS MERTON. And Goody Rickby, too, brother ?

JUSTICE MERTON. That woman shall answer for her deeds. She is proscribed.

RACHEL. Proscribed ? What is that ?

MISTRESS MERTON [*examining the mirror*]. What is this ?

JUSTICE MERTON. She shall hang.

RACHEL. Uncle, no ! Not merely because of my purchase this morning.

JUSTICE MERTON. Your purchase ?

MISTRESS MERTON [*pointing to the mirror*]. That, I suppose.

JUSTICE MERTON. What ! you purchased that mirror of her ? You brought it here ?

RACHEL. No, the boy brought it ; I found it here when I returned.

JUSTICE MERTON. What ! From her shop ? From her infamous den, into my parlor ! [*To MISTRESS MERTON.*] Call the servant. [*Himself calling.*] Micah ! Away with it ! Micah !

RACHEL. Uncle Gilead, I bought —

JUSTICE MERTON. Micah, I say ! Where is the man ?

RACHEL. Listen, uncle. I bought it with my own money.

JUSTICE MERTON. Thine own money ! Wilt have the neighbors gossip ? Wilt have me, thyself, my house, suspected of complicity with witches ?

[*Enter MICAH.*]

Micah, take this away.

MICAH. Yes, sir ; but, sir —

JUSTICE MERTON. Out of my house !

MICAH. There be visitors.

JUSTICE MERTON. Away with —

MISTRESS MERTON [*touching his arm*]. Gilead !

MICAH. Visitors, sir ; gentry.

JUSTICE MERTON. Ah !

MICAH. Shall I show them in, sir ?

JUSTICE MERTON. Visitors ! In the morning ? Who are they ?

MICAH. Strangers, sir. I should judge they be very high gentry; lords, sir.

ALL. Lords !

MICAH. At least, one on 'em, sir. The other — the dark gentleman — told me they left their horses at the inn, sir.

MISTRESS MERTON. Hark !

[*The faces of all wear suddenly a startled expression.*]

Where is that unearthly sound ?

JUSTICE MERTON [*listening*]. Is it in the cellar ?

MICAH. 'T is just the dog howling, madam. When he spied the gentry he turned tail and run below.

MISTRESS MERTON. Oh, the dog !

JUSTICE MERTON. Show the gentlemen here, Micah. Don't keep them waiting.

[*Exit MICAH.*]

A lord ! [*To* RACHEL.] We shall talk of this matter later. — A lord !

[*Turning to the small glass on the wall, he arranges his peruke and attire.*]

RACHEL. [*To* RICHARD.] What a fortunate interruption ! But, dear Dick ! I wish we need n't meet these strangers now.

RICHARD. Would you really rather we were alone together ?

[*They chat aside, absorbed in each other.*]

JUSTICE MERTON. Think of it, Cynthia, a lord !

MISTRESS MERTON [*dusting the furniture hastily with her handkerchief*]. And such dust !

RACHEL. [*To* RICHARD.] You know, dear, we need only be introduced, and then we can steal away together.

[*Reënter* MICAH.]

MICAH [*announcing*]. Lord Ravensbane : Marquis of Oxford, Baron of Wittenberg, Elector of Worms, and Count of Cordova ; Master Dickonson.

[*Enter* RAVENSBANE *and* DICKON.]

JUSTICE MERTON. Gentlemen, permit me, you are excessively welcome. I am deeply gratified to meet —

DICKON. Lord Ravensbane, of the Rookeries, Somersetshire.

JUSTICE MERTON. Lord Ravensbane — his lordship's most truly honored.

RAVENSBANE. Truly honored.

JUSTICE MERTON [*turning to* DICKON]. His lordship's —?

DICKON. Tutor.

JUSTICE MERTON [*checking his effusiveness*]. Ah, so !

DICKON. Justice Merton, I believe.

JUSTICE MERTON. Of Merton House. — May I present — permit me, your lordship — my sister, Mistress Merton.

RAVENSBANE. Mistress Merton.

JUSTICE MERTON. And my — and my — [*under his breath*] — Rachel ! [RACHEL *remains with a bored expression behind* RICHARD.] — My young neighbor, Squire Talbot, Squire Richard Talbot of — of —

RICHARD. Of nowhere, sir.

RAVENSBANE. [*Nods.*] Nowhere.

JUSTICE MERTON. And permit me, Lord Ravensbane, my niece — Mistress Rachel Merton.

RAVENSBANE. [*Bows low.*] Mistress Rachel Merton.

RACHEL. [*Curtsies.*] Lord Ravensbane.

[*As they raise their heads, their eyes meet and are fascinated.* DICKON *just then takes* RAVENSBANE'S *pipe and fills it.*]

RAVENSBANE. Mistress Rachel !

RACHEL. Your lordship !

[DICKON *returns the pipe.*]

MISTRESS MERTON. A pipe ! Gilead ! — in the parlor !

[JUSTICE MERTON *frowns silence.*]

JUSTICE MERTON. Your lordship — ahem ! — has just arrived in town ?

DICKON. From London, via New Amsterdam.

RICHARD [*aside*]. Is he staring at *you?* Are you ill, Rachel ?

RACHEL [*indifferently*]. What ?

JUSTICE MERTON. Lord Ravensbane honors my humble roof.

DICKON. [*Touches* RAVENSBANE'S *arm.*] Your lordship — " roof."

RAVENSBANE [*starting, turns to* MERTON]. Nay, sir, the roof of my father's oldest friend bestows generous hospitality upon his only son.

JUSTICE MERTON. Only son — ah, yes ! Your father —

RAVENSBANE. My father, I trust, sir, has never forgotten the intimate companionship, the touching devotion, the unceasing solicitude for his happiness which you, sir, manifested to him in the days of his youth.

JUSTICE MERTON. Really, your lordship, the — the slight favors which — hem ! some years ago, I was privileged to show your illustrious father —

RAVENSBANE. Permit me ! — Because, however, of his present infirmities — for I regret to say that my father is suffering a temporary aberration of mind —

JUSTICE MERTON. You distress me !

RAVENSBANE. My lady mother has charged me with a double mission here in New England. On my quitting my home, sir, to explore the wideness and the mystery of this world, my mother bade me be sure to call upon his worship, the Justice Merton ; and deliver to him, first, my father's remembrances ; and secondly, my mother's epistle.

DICKON [*handing to* JUSTICE MERTON *a sealed document*]. Her ladyship's letter, sir.

JUSTICE MERTON [*examining the seal with awe, speaks aside to* MISTRESS MERTON]. Cynthia ! — a crested seal !

DICKON. His lordship's crest, sir : rooks rampant.

JUSTICE MERTON [*embarrassed, breaks the seal*]. Permit me.

RACHEL [*looking at* RAVENSBANE]. Have you noticed his bearing, Richard : what personal distinction ! what inbred nobility ! Every inch a true lord !

RICHARD. He may be a lord, my dear, but he walks like a broomstick.

RACHEL. How dare you !

[*Turns abruptly away; as she does so, a fold of her gown catches in a chair.*]

RAVENSBANE. Mistress Rachel — permit me.

[*Stooping, he extricates the fold of her gown.*]

RACHEL. Oh, thank you.

[*They go aside together.*]

JUSTICE MERTON. [*To* DICKON, *glancing up from the letter.*] I am astonished — overpowered !

RICHARD. [*To* MISTRESS MERTON.] So Lord Ravensbane and his family are old friends of yours ?

MISTRESS MERTON [*monosyllabically*]. I never heard the name before, Richard.

RAVENSBANE. [*To* RACHEL, *taking her hand after a whisper from* DICKON.] Believe me, sweet lady, it will give me the deepest pleasure.

RACHEL. Can you really tell fortunes ?

RAVENSBANE. More than that ; I can bestow them.

[RAVENSBANE *leads* RACHEL *off, left, into an adjoining room, the door of which remains open.* RICHARD *follows them.* MISTRESS MERTON *follows him, murmuring,* "RICHARD !" DICKON *stands where he can watch them in the room off scene, while he speaks to the* JUSTICE.]

JUSTICE MERTON. [*To* DICKON, *glancing up from the letter.*] I am astonished — overpowered ! But is her ladyship really serious ? An offer of marriage !

DICKON. Pray read it again, sir.

JUSTICE MERTON. [*Reads.*] "To the Worshipful, the Justice Gilead Merton, Merton House.

"My Honorable Friend and Benefactor:

"With these brief lines I commend to you our son " — *our* son !

DICKON. She speaks likewise for his young lordship's father, sir.

JUSTICE MERTON. Ah ! of course. [*Reads.*] " In a strange land, I entrust him to you as to a father." Honored, believe me ! " I have only to add my earnest hope that the natural gifts, graces, and inherited fortune " — ah — !

DICKON. Twenty thousand pounds — on his father's demise.

JUSTICE MERTON. Ah ! — "fortune of this young scion of nobility will so propitiate the heart of your niece, Mistress Rachel Merton, as to cause her to accept his proffered hand in matrimony " ; — but — but — but Squire Talbot is betrothed to — well, well, we shall see ; — "in matrimony, and thus cement the early bonds of interest and affection between your honored self and his lordship's father ; not to mention, dear sir, your worship's ever grateful and obedient admirer,

" ELIZABETH,
" Marchioness of ·R."

Of R. ! of R. ! Will you believe me, my dear sir, so long is it since my travels in England — I visited at so many — hem ! noble estates — permit me, it is so awkward, but —

DICKON [*with his peculiar intonation of Act I*]. Not at all.

RAVENSBANE. [*Calls from the adjoining room.*] Dickon, my pipe !

[DICKON *glides away.*]

JUSTICE MERTON [*starting in perturbation. To* DICKON]. Permit me, one moment ; I did not catch your name.

DICKON. My name ? Dickonson.

JUSTICE MERTON [*with a gasp of relief*]. Ah, Dickonson ! Thank you. I mistook the word.

DICKON. A compound, your worship. [*With a malignant smile.*] Dickon-[*then, jerking his thumb toward the next room*] son ! [*Bowing.*] Both at your service.

JUSTICE MERTON. Is he — he there ?

DICKON. Bessie's brat ; yes ; it did n't die, after all, poor suckling ! Dickon weaned it. Saved it for balm of Gilead. Raised it for joyful home-coming. Prodigal's return ! Twenty-first birthday ! Happy son ! Happy father !

JUSTICE MERTON. My — son ! .

DICKON. Felicitations !

JUSTICE MERTON [*faintly*]. What — what do you want?

DICKON. Only the happiness of your dear ones — the union of these young hearts and hands.

JUSTICE MERTON. What! he will dare — an illegitimate —

DICKON. Fie, fie, Gilly! Why, the brat is a lord now.

JUSTICE MERTON. Oh, the disgrace! Spare me that, Dickon. And she is innocent; she is already betrothed.

DICKON. Twiddle-twaddle! 'T is a brilliant match; besides, her ladyship's heart is set upon it.

JUSTICE MERTON. Her ladyship — ?

DICKON. The Marchioness of Rickby.

JUSTICE MERTON [*glowering*]. Rickby! — I had forgotten.

DICKON. Her ladyship has never forgotten. So, you see, your worship's alternatives are most simple. Alternative one: advance his lordship's suit with your niece as speedily as possible, and save all scandal. Alternative two: impede his lordship's suit, and —

JUSTICE MERTON. Don't, Dickon! don't reveal the truth; not disgrace now!

DICKON. Good; we are agreed, then?

JUSTICE MERTON. I have no choice.

DICKON [*cheerfully*]. Why, true; we ignored that, did n't we?

MISTRESS MERTON [*reëntering*]. This young lord — Why, Gilead, are you ill?

JUSTICE MERTON [*with a great effort, commands himself*]. Not in the least.

MISTRESS MERTON. Rachel's deportment, my dear brother — I tell you, they are fortune-telling!

JUSTICE MERTON. Tush! Tush!

MISTRESS MERTON. Tush? "Tush" to me? Tush! [*She goes out, right.*]

[RAVENSBANE *and* RACHEL *reënter from the adjoining room followed shortly by* RICHARD.*]

RACHEL. I am really at a loss. Your lordship's hand is so very peculiar.

RAVENSBANE. Ah! Peculiar.

RACHEL. This, now, is the line of life.

RAVENSBANE. Of life, yes?

RACHEL. But it begins so abruptly, and see! it breaks off and ends nowhere. And just so here with this line — the line of — of love.

RAVENSBANE. Of love. So; it breaks?

RACHEL. Yes.

RAVENSBANE. Ah, then, that must be the *heart* line.

RACHEL. Why, Lord Ravensbane, your pulse. Really, if I am cruel, you are quite heartless. I declare I can't feel your heart beat at all.

RAVENSBANE. Ah, mistress, that is because I have just lost it.

RACHEL [*archly*]. Where?

RAVENSBANE [*faintly*]. Dickon, my pipe!

RACHEL. Alas! my lord, are you ill?

DICKON [*restoring the lighted pipe to* RAVENSBANE, *speaks aside*]. Pardon me, sweet young lady, I must confide to you that his lordship's heart is peculiarly responsive to his emotions. When he feels very ardently, it quite stops. Hence the use of his pipe.

RACHEL. Oh! Is smoking, then, necessary for his heart?

DICKON. Absolutely — to equilibrate the valvular palpitations. Without his pipe — should his lordship experience, for instance, the emotion of love — he might die.

RACHEL. You alarm me!

DICKON. But this is for you only, Mistress Rachel. We may confide in you?

RACHEL. Oh, utterly, sir.

DICKON. His lordship, you know, is so sensitive.

RAVENSBANE. [*To* RACHEL.] You have given it back to me. Why did not you keep it?

RACHEL. What, my lord?

RAVENSBANE. My heart.

RICHARD. Intolerable! Do you approve of *this*, sir? Are Lord Ravensbane's credentials satisfactory?

JUSTICE MERTON. Eminently, eminently.

RICHARD. Ah! So her ladyship's letter is —

JUSTICE MERTON. Charming; charming. [*To* RAVENSBANE.] Your lordship will, I trust, make my house your home.

RAVENSBANE. My home, sir.

RACHEL. [*To* DICKON, *who has spoken to her.*] Really? [*To* JUSTICE MERTON.] Why, uncle, what is this Master Dickonson tells us?

JUSTICE MERTON. What! What! he has revealed —

RACHEL. Yes, indeed.

JUSTICE MERTON. Rachel! Rachel!

RACHEL [*laughingly to* RAVENSBANE]. My uncle is doubtless astonished to find you so grown.

RAVENSBANE [*laughingly to* JUSTICE MERTON]. I am doubtless astonished, sir, to be so grown.

JUSTICE MERTON. [*To* DICKON.] You have —

DICKON. Merely remarked, sir, that your worship had often dandled his lordship — as an infant.

JUSTICE MERTON [*smiling lugubriously*]. Quite so — as an infant merely.

RACHEL. How interesting! Then you must have seen his lordship's home in England.

JUSTICE MERTON. As you say.

RACHEL. [*To* RAVENSBANE.] Do describe it to us. We are so isolated here from the grand world. Do you know, I always imagine England to be an enchanted isle, like one of the old Hesperides, teeming with fruits of solid gold.

RAVENSBANE. Ah, yes! my mother raises them.

RACHEL. Fruits of gold?

RAVENSBANE. Round like the rising sun. She calls them — ah! punkins.

MISTRESS MERTON. "Punkins"!

JUSTICE MERTON [*aside, grinding his teeth*]. Scoundrel! Scoundrel!

RACHEL [*laughing*]. Your lordship pokes fun at us.

DICKON. His lordship is an artist in words, mistress. I have noticed that in whatever country he is traveling, he tinges his vocabulary with the local idiom. His lordship means, of course, not pumpkins, but pomegranates.

RACHEL. We forgive him. But, your lordship, please be serious and describe to us your hall.

RAVENSBANE. Quite serious: the hall. Yes, yes; in the middle burns a great fire — on a black — ah! black altar.

DICKON. A Druidical heirloom. His lordship's mother collects antiques.

RACHEL. How fascinating!

RAVENSBANE. Fascinating! On the walls hang pieces of iron.

DICKON. Trophies of Saxon warfare.

RAVENSBANE. And rusty horseshoes.

GENERAL MURMURS. Horseshoes!

DICKON. Presents from the German Em-

peror. They were worn by the steeds of Charlemagne.

RAVENSBANE. Quite so; and broken cart-wheels.

DICKON. Relics of British chariots.

RACHEL. How mediæval it must be! [*To* JUSTICE MERTON.] And to think you never described it to us!

MISTRESS MERTON. True, brother; you have been singularly reticent.

JUSTICE MERTON. Permit me; it is impossible to report all one sees on one's travels.

MISTRESS MERTON. Evidently.

RACHEL. But surely your lordship's mother has other diversions besides collecting antiques. I have heard that in England ladies followed the hounds; and sometimes — [*looking at her aunt and lowering her voice*] — they even dance.

RAVENSBANE. Dance — ah, yes; my lady mother dances about the — the altar; she swings high a hammer.

DICKON. Your lordship, your lordship! Pray, sir, check this vein of poetry. Lord Ravensbane symbolizes as a hammer and altar a golf-stick and tee — a Scottish game, which her ladyship plays on her Highland estates.

RICHARD. [*To* MISTRESS MERTON.] What do you think of this?

MISTRESS MERTON [*with a scandalized look toward her brother*]. He said to me "tush."

RICHARD. [*To* JUSTICE MERTON, *indicating* DICKON.] Who is this magpie?

JUSTICE MERTON. [*Hisses in fury.*] Satan!

RICHARD. I beg pardon!

JUSTICE MERTON. Satan, sir, — makes you jealous.

RICHARD. [*Bows stiffly.*] Good-morning. [*Walking up to* RAVENSBANE.] Lord Ravensbane, I have a rustic colonial question to ask. Is it the latest fashion to smoke incessantly in ladies' parlors, or is it — mediæval?

DICKON. His lordship's health, sir, necessitates —

RICHARD. I addressed his lordship.

RAVENSBANE. In the matter of fashions, sir — [*Hands his pipe to be refilled.*] My pipe, Dickon!

[*While* DICKON *holds his pipe — somewhat longer than usual* —RA-

VENSBANE, *with his mouth open as if about to speak, relapses into a vacant stare.*]

RICHARD. Well ?

DICKON [*as he lights the pipe for* RAVENSBANE, *speaks suavely and low as if not to be overheard by him*]. Pardon me. The fact is, my young pupil is sensitive ; the wound from his latest duel is not quite healed ; you observe a slight lameness, an occasional — absence of mind.

RACHEL. A wound — in a real duel ?

DICKON [*aside*]. You, mistress, know the *true* reason — his lordship's heart.

RICHARD. [*To* RAVENSBANE, *who is still staring vacantly into space.*] Well, well, your lordship. [RAVENSBANE *pays no attention.*] You were saying — ? [DICKON *returns the pipe*] — in the matter of fashions, sir — ?

RAVENSBANE [*regaining slowly a look of intelligence, draws himself up with affronted hauteur*]. Permit me ! [*Puffs several wreaths of smoke into the air.*] I am the fashions.

RICHARD [*going*]. Insufferable !
[*He pauses at the door.*]

MISTRESS MERTON. [*To* JUSTICE MERTON.] Well — what do you think of that ?

JUSTICE MERTON. Spoken like King Charles himself.

MISTRESS MERTON. Brother ! brother ! is there nothing wrong here ?
[*Going out, she passes* DICKON, *starts at a look which he gives her, and goes out, right, flustered. Following her,* JUSTICE MERTON *is stopped by* DICKON, *and led off left by him.*]

RACHEL. [*To* RAVENSBANE.] I — object to the smoke ? Why, I think it is charming.

RICHARD [*who has returned from the door, speaks in a low, constrained voice*]. Rachel !

RACHEL. Oh ! — you ?

RICHARD. You take quickly to European fashions.

RACHEL. Yes ? To what one in particular ?

RICHARD. Two ; smoking and flirtation.

RACHEL. Jealous ?

RICHARD. Of an idiot ? I hope not. Manners differ, however. Your confidences to his lordship have evidently not included — your relation to me.

RACHEL. Oh, our relations !

RICHARD. Of course, since you wish him to continue in ignorance —

RACHEL. Not at all. He shall know at once. Lord Ravensbane !

RAVENSBANE. Fair mistress !

RICHARD. Rachel, stop ! I did not mean —

RACHEL. [*To* RAVENSBANE.] My uncle did not introduce to you with sufficient elaboration this gentleman. Will you allow me to do so now ?

RAVENSBANE. I adore Mistress Rachel's elaborations.

RACHEL. Lord Ravensbane, I beg to present Squire Talbot, *my betrothed.*

RAVENSBANE. Betrothed ! Is it — [*noticing* RICHARD'S *frown*] — is it pleasant ?

RACHEL. [*To* RICHARD.] Are you satisfied ?

RICHARD [*trembling with feeling*]. *More* than satisfied. [*Exit.*]

RAVENSBANE [*looking after him*]. Ah ! Betrothed is *not* pleasant.

RACHEL. Not always.

RAVENSBANE [*anxiously*]. Mistress Rachel is not pleased ?

RACHEL [*biting her lip, looks after* RICHARD]. With him.

RAVENSBANE. Mistress Rachel will smile again ?

RACHEL. Soon.

RAVENSBANE [*ardent*]. Ah ! What can Lord Ravensbane do to make her smile ? See ! will you puff my pipe ? It is very pleasant. [*Offering the pipe.*]

RACHEL [*smiling*]. Shall I try ?
[*Takes hold of it mischievously.*]

[*Enter* JUSTICE MERTON *and* DICKON, *left.*]

JUSTICE MERTON [*in a great voice*]. Rachel !

RACHEL. Why, uncle !

JUSTICE MERTON. [*Speaks suavely to* RAVENSBANE.] Permit me, your lordship — Rachel, you will kindly withdraw for a few moments ; I desire to confer with Lord Ravensbane concerning his mother's — her ladyship's letter — [*obsequiously to* DICKON] —that is, if you think, sir, that your noble pupil is not too fatigued.

DICKON. Not at all ; I think his lordship will listen to you with much pleasure.

RAVENSBANE [*bowing to* JUSTICE MERTON, *but looking at* RACHEL]. With much pleasure.

DICKON. And in the mean time, if Mistress Rachel will allow me, I will assist her in writing those invitations which your worship desires to send in her name.

JUSTICE MERTON. Invitations — from my niece?

DICKON. To his Excellency, the Lieutenant-Governor; to your friends, the Reverend Masters at Harvard College, etc., etc.; in brief, to all your worship's select social acquaintance in the vicinity — to meet his lordship. It was so thoughtful in you to suggest it, sir, and believe me, his lordship appreciates your courtesy in arranging the reception in his honor for this afternoon.

RACHEL. [To JUSTICE MERTON.] This afternoon! Are we really to give his lordship a reception? And will it be here, uncle?

DICKON [looking at him narrowly]. Your worship said here, I believe?

JUSTICE MERTON. Quite so, sir; quite so, quite so.

DICKON. Permit me to act as your scribe, Mistress Rachel.

RACHEL. With pleasure. [With a curtsy to RAVENSBANE.] Till we meet again!
[Exit, right.]

DICKON [aside to JUSTICE MERTON]. I advise nothing rash, Gilly; the brat has a weak heart. [Aside, as he passes RAVENSBANE.] Remember, Jack! Puff! Puff!

RAVENSBANE [staring at the door]. She is gone.

JUSTICE MERTON. Impostor! You, at least, shall not play the lord and master to my face.

RAVENSBANE. Quite — gone!

JUSTICE MERTON. I know with whom I have to deal. If I be any judge of my own flesh and blood — permit me — you shall quail before me.

RAVENSBANE [dejectedly]. She did not smile — [Joyously.] She smiled!

JUSTICE MERTON. Affected rogue! I know thee. I know thy feigned pauses, thy assumed vagaries. Speak; how much do you want?

RAVENSBANE [ecstatically]. Ah! Mistress Rachel!

JUSTICE MERTON. Her! Scoundrel, if thou dost name her again, my innocent — my sweet maid! If thou dost — thou godless spawn of temptation — mark you, I will put an end —
[Reaching for a pistol that rests in a rack on the wall, — the intervening form of DICKON suddenly appears, pockets the pistol, and exit.]

DICKON. I beg pardon; I forgot something.

JUSTICE MERTON [sinking into a chair]. God, Thou art just!
[He holds his head in his hands and weeps.]

RAVENSBANE [for the first time, since RACHEL's departure, observing MERTON]. Permit me, sir, are you ill?

JUSTICE MERTON [recoiling]. What art thou!

RAVENSBANE [monotonously]. I am Lord Ravensbane: Marquis of Oxford, Baron of Wittenberg, Elector of Worms, and — [As JUSTICE MERTON covers his face again.] Shall I call Dickon? [Walking quickly toward the door, calls.] Dickon!

JUSTICE MERTON [starting up]. No, do not call him. Tell me: I hate thee not; thou wast innocent. Tell me! — I thought thou hadst died as a babe. — Where has Dickon, our tyrant, kept thee these twenty years?

RAVENSBANE [with gentle courtesy]. Master Dickonson is my tutor.

JUSTICE MERTON. And why has thy mother — Ah, I know well; I deserve all. But yet, it must not be published now! I am a justice now, an honored citizen — and my young niece — Thy mother will not demand so much.

RAVENSBANE. My mother is the Marchioness of Rickby.

JUSTICE MERTON. Yes, yes; 't was well planned, a clever trick. 'T was skillful of her. But surely thy mother gave thee commands to —

RAVENSBANE. My mother gave me her blessing.

JUSTICE MERTON. Ah, 't is well, then. Young man, my son, I too will give thee my blessing, if thou wilt but go — go instantly — go with half my fortune — but leave me my honor — and my Rachel?

RAVENSBANE. Rachel? Rachel is yours? No, no, Mistress Rachel is mine. We are ours.

JUSTICE MERTON [pleadingly]. Consider the disgrace — you, an illegitimate — and she — oh, think what thou art!

RAVENSBANE [monotonously, puffing smoke at the end]. I am Lord Ravensbane: Marquis of Oxford, Baron of Wittenberg, Elector of Worms, and Count —

JUSTICE MERTON [*wrenching the pipe from* RAVENSBANE'S *hand and lips*]. Devil's child! Boor! Buffoon! [*Flinging the pipe away.*] I will stand thy insults no longer. If thou hast no heart —

RAVENSBANE [*putting his hand to his side, staggers*]. Ah! my heart!

JUSTICE MERTON. Hypocrite! Thou canst not fool me. I am thy father.

RAVENSBANE [*faintly, stretches out his hand to him for support*]. Father!

JUSTICE MERTON. Stand away. Thou mayst break thy heart and mine and the devil's, but thou shalt not break Rachel's.

RAVENSBANE [*faintly*]. Mistress Rachel is mine —

[*He staggers again, and falls, half reclining, upon a chair. More faintly he speaks, beginning to change expression.*]

Her eyes are mine; her smiles are mine.

[*His eyes close.*]

JUSTICE MERTON. Good God! Can it be — his heart? [*With agitated swiftness, he feels and listens at* RAVENSBANE'S *side.*] Not a motion; not a sound! Yea, God, Thou art good! 'T is his heart. He is — ah! he is my son. Judge Almighty, if he should die now; may I not be still a moment more and make sure. No, no, my son — he is changing. [*Calls.*] Help! Help! Rachel! Master Dickonson! Help! Richard! Cynthia! Come hither!

[*Enter* DICKON *and* RACHEL.]

RACHEL. Uncle!

JUSTICE MERTON. Bring wine. Lord Ravensbane has fainted.

RACHEL. Oh! [*Turning swiftly to go.*] Micah, wine.

DICKON [*detaining her*]. Stay! His pipe! Where is his lordship's pipe?

RACHEL. Oh, terrible!

[*Enter, at different doors,* MISTRESS MERTON *and* RICHARD.]

MISTRESS MERTON. What's the matter?

JUSTICE MERTON. [*To* RACHEL.] He threw it away. He is worse. Bring the wine.

MISTRESS MERTON. Look! How strange he appears!

RACHEL [*searching distractedly*]. The pipe! His lordship's pipe! It is lost, Master Dickonson.

DICKON [*stooping, as if searching, with his back turned, having picked up the pipe, is filling and lighting it*]. It must be found. This is a heart attack, my friends; his lordship's life depends on the nicotine.

[*Deftly he places the pipe in* RACHEL'S *way.*]

RACHEL. Thank God! Here it is.

[*Carrying it to the prostrate form of* RAVENSBANE, *she lifts his head and is about to put the pipe in his mouth.*]

Shall I — shall I put it in?

RICHARD. No! not you.

RACHEL. Sir!

RICHARD. Let his tutor perform that office.

RACHEL [*lifting* LORD RAVENSBANE'S *head again*]. My lord!

RICHARD AND JUSTICE MERTON [*together*]. Rachel!

DICKON. Pardon me, Mistress Rachel; give the pipe at once. Only a token of true affection can revive his lordship now.

RICHARD [*as* RACHEL *puts the pipe to* RAVENSBANE'S *lips*]. I forbid it, Rachel.

RACHEL [*watching only* RAVENSBANE]. My lord — my lord!

MISTRESS MERTON. Give him air; unbutton his coat.

[RACHEL *unbuttons* RAVENSBANE'S *coat, revealing the embroidered waistcoat.*]

Ah, Heavens! What do I see?

JUSTICE MERTON [*looks, blanches, and signs silence to* MISTRESS MERTON]. Cynthia!

MISTRESS MERTON [*aside to* JUSTICE MERTON, *with deep tensity*]. That waistcoat! that waistcoat! Brother, hast thou never seen it before?

JUSTICE MERTON. Never, my sister.

DICKON. See! He puffs — he revives. He is coming to himself.

RACHEL [*as* RAVENSBANE *rises to his feet*]. At last!

DICKON. Look! he is restored.

RACHEL. God be thanked!

DICKON. My lord, Mistress Rachel has saved your life.

RAVENSBANE [*taking* RACHEL'S *hand*]. Mistress Rachel is mine; we are ours.

RICHARD. Dare to repeat that.

RAVENSBANE [*looking at* RACHEL]. Her eyes are mine.

RICHARD [*flinging his glove in his face*]. And that, sir, is yours.

RACHEL. Richard!

RICHARD. I believe such is the proper fashion in England. If your lordship's last dueling wound is sufficiently healed, perhaps you will deign a reply.

RACHEL. Richard! Your lordship!

RAVENSBANE [*stoops, picks up the glove, pockets it, bows to* RACHEL, *and steps close to* RICHARD]. Permit me!

[*He blows a puff of smoke full in* RICHARD's *face*.]

ACT III

The same day. Late afternoon. The same scene as Act II.

RAVENSBANE *and* DICKON *discovered at table, on which are lying two flails.* RAVENSBANE *is dressed in a costume which, composed of silk and jewels, subtly approximates in design to that of his original grosser composition. So artfully, however, is this contrived that, to one ignorant of his origin, his dress would appear to be merely an odd personal whimsy; whereas, to one initiated, it would stamp him grotesquely as the apotheosis of scarecrows.*

DICKON *is sitting in a pedagogical attitude;* RAVENSBANE *stands near him, making a profound bow in the opposite direction.*

RAVENSBANE. Believe me, ladies, with the true sincerity of the heart.

DICKON. Inflection a little more lachrymose, please: "The *true* sincerity of the *heart*."

RAVENSBANE. Believe me, ladies, with the *true* sincerity of the *heart*.

DICKON. Prettily, prettily! Next!

RAVENSBANE [*changing his mien, as if addressing another person*]. Verily, sir, as that prince of poets, the immortal Virgil, has remarked: —

" Adeo in teneris consuescere multum est."

DICKON. *Basta!* The next.

RAVENSBANE [*with another change to courtly manner*]. Trust me, your Excellency, I will inform his Majesty of your courtesy.

DICKON. "His Majesty" more emphatic. Remember! You must impress all of the guests this afternoon. But continue, Cobby, dear; the retort now to the challenge!

RAVENSBANE [*with a superb air*]. The second, I believe.

DICKON. Quite so, my lord.

RAVENSBANE. Sir! the local person whom you represent has done himself the honor of submitting to me a challenge to mortal combat. Sir! Since the remotest times of my feudal ancestors, in such affairs of honor, choice of weapons has ever been the —

DICKON. Prerogative!

RAVENSBANE. Prerogative of the challenged. Sir! This right of etiquette must be observed. Nevertheless, believe me, I have no selfish desire that my superior —

DICKON. Attainments!

RAVENSBANE. Attainments in this art should assume advantage over my challenger's ignorance. I have, therefore, chosen those combative utensils most appropriate both to his own humble origin and to local tradition. Permit me, sir, to reveal my choice. [*Pointing grandly to the table.*] There are my weapons!

DICKON. Delicious! O thou exquisite flower of love! How thy natal composites have burst in bloom! — The pumpkin in thee to a golden collarette; thy mop of crow's wings to these raven locks; thy broomstick to a lordly limp; thy corn-silk to these pale-tinted tassels. Verily in the gallery of scarecrows, thou art the Apollo Belvedere!

RAVENSBANE. Mistress Rachel — I may see her now?

DICKON. Romeo! Romeo! Was ever such an amorous puppet show!

RAVENSBANE. Mistress Rachel!

DICKON. Wait; let me think! Thou art wound up now, my pretty apparatus, for at least six-and-thirty hours. The wooden angel Gabriel that trumpets the hours on the big clock in Venice is not a more punctual manikin than thou with my speeches. Thou shouldst run, therefore, —

RAVENSBANE [*frowning darkly at* DICKON]. Stop talking; permit me! A tutor should know his place.

DICKON [*rubbing his hands*]. Nay, your lordship is beyond comparison.

RAVENSBANE [*in a terrible voice*]. She will come? I shall see her?

[*Enter* MICAH.]

MICAH. Pardon, my lord.

RAVENSBANE [*turning joyfully to* MICAH]. Is it she?

MICAH. Captain Bugby, my lord, the Governor's secretary.

DICKON. Good. Squire Talbot's second. Show him in.

RAVENSBANE [*flinging despairingly into a chair*]. Ah! ah!

MICAH [*lifting the flails from the table*]. Beg pardon, sir; shall I remove —

DICKON. Drop them; go.

MICAH. But, sir —

DICKON. Go, thou slave! [*Exit* MICAH.]
[DICKON *hands* RAVENSBANE *a book*.]
Here, my lord; read. You must be found reading.

RAVENSBANE [*in childlike despair*]. She will not come! I shall not see her! [*Throwing the book into the fireplace*.] She does not come!

DICKON. Fie, fie, Jack; thou must not be breaking thy Dickon's apron-strings with a will of thine own. Come!

RAVENSBANE. Mistress Rachel.

DICKON. Be good, boy, and thou shalt see her soon.

[*Enter* CAPTAIN BUGBY.]

Your lordship was saying — Oh! Captain Bugby?

CAPTAIN BUGBY [*nervous and awed*]. Captain Bugby, sir, ah! at Lord Ravensbane's service — ah!

DICKON. I am Master Dickonson, his lordship's tutor.

CAPTAIN BUGBY. Happy, sir.

DICKON. [*To* RAVENSBANE.] My lord, this gentleman waits upon you from Squire Talbot. [*To* CAPTAIN BUGBY.] In regard to the challenge of this morning, I presume?

CAPTAIN BUGBY. The affair, ah! the affair of this morning, sir.

RAVENSBANE [*with his former superb air — to* CAPTAIN BUGBY]. The second, I believe?

CAPTAIN BUGBY. Quite so, my lord.

RAVENSBANE. Sir! the local person whom you represent has done himself the honor of submitting to me a challenge to mortal combat. Sir! Since the remotest times of my feudal ancestors, in such affairs of honor, choice of weapons has ever been the pre-pre- [DICKON *looks at him intensely*] prerogative of the challenged. Sir! this right of etiquette must be observed.

CAPTAIN BUGBY. Indeed, yes, my lord.

DICKON. Pray do not interrupt. [*To* RAVENSBANE.] Your lordship : "observed."

RAVENSBANE. — observed. Nevertheless, believe me, I have no selfish desire that my superior a-a-at-attainments in this art should assume advantage over my challenger's ignorance. I have, therefore, chosen those combative utensils most appropriate both to his own humble origin and to local tradition. Permit me, sir, to reveal my choice. [*Pointing to the table*.] There are my weapons!

CAPTAIN BUGBY [*looking, bewildered*]. These, my lord?

RAVENSBANE. Those.

CAPTAIN BUGBY. But these are — are flails.

RAVENSBANE. Flails.

CAPTAIN BUGBY. Flails, my lord? — Do I understand that your lordship and Squire Talbot —

RAVENSBANE. Exactly.

CAPTAIN BUGBY. But your lordship — flails!

[DICKON'S *intense glance focusses on* RAVENSBANE'S *face with the faintest of smiles*.]

RAVENSBANE. My adversary should be deft in their use. He has doubtless wielded them frequently on his barn floor.

CAPTAIN BUGBY. Ahaha! I understand now. Your lordship — ah! is a wit. Haha! Flails!

DICKON. His lordship's satire is poignant.

CAPTAIN BUGBY. Indeed, sir, so keen that I must apologize for laughing at my principal's expense. But — [*soberly to* RAVENSBANE] — my lord, if you will deign to speak one moment seriously —

RAVENSBANE. Seriously?

CAPTAIN BUGBY. I will take pleasure in informing Squire Talbot — ah! as to your *real* preference for —

RAVENSBANE. For flails, sir. I have, permit me, nothing further to say. Flails are final. [*Turns away haughtily*.]

CAPTAIN BUGBY. Eh! What! Must I really report — ?

DICKON. Lord Ravensbane's will is inflexible.

CAPTAIN BUGBY. And his wit, sir, incomparable. I am sorry for the Squire, but 't will be the greatest joke in years. Ah! will

you tell me — is it — [*indicating* RAVENS-
BANE'S *smoking*] — is it the latest fashion?

DICKON. Lord Ravensbane is always the
latest.

CAPTAIN BUGBY. Obliged servant, sir.
Aha ! Such a joke as — O Lord ! flails !

[*Exit.*]

DICKON [*gayly to* RAVENSBANE]. Bravo,
my pumpky dear! That squelches the
jealous betrothed. Now nothing remains
but for you to continue to dazzle the enamored Rachel, and so present yourself to
the Justice as a pseudo-son-nephew-in-law.

RAVENSBANE. I may go to Mistress
Rachel ?

DICKON. She will come to you. She is
reading now a poem from you, which I left
on her dressing-table.

RAVENSBANE. She is reading a poem
from me ?

DICKON. With your pardon, my lord, I
penned it for you. I am something of a poet-
aster. Indeed, I flatter myself that I have
dictated some of the finest lines in literature.

RAVENSBANE. Dickon ! She will come ?

DICKON. She comes !

[*Enter* RACHEL, *reading from a piece of paper.*]

[DICKON *draws* RAVENSBANE *back.*]

RACHEL. [*Reads.*] " To Mistress R——,
enchantress : —

" If faith in witchcraft be a sin,
    Alas ! what peril he is in
Who plights his faith and love in thee,
    Sweetest maid of sorcery.

" If witchcraft be a whirling brain,
    A roving eye, a heart of pain,
Whose wound no thread of fate can stitch,
    How hast thou conjured, cruel witch, —

With the brain, eye, heart, and total mortal
residue of thine enamored.

" JACK LANTHORNE,
    " [LORD R——.]"

[DICKON *goes out.*]

RACHEL. " To Mistress R——, enchantress : " R ! It *must* be. R—— must mean —

RAVENSBANE [*with passionate deference*].
Rachel !

RACHEL. Ah ! How you surprised me,
my lord.

RAVENSBANE. You are come again ; you
are come again.

RACHEL. Has anything happened ? Oh,
my lord, I have been in such terror. Promise
me that there shall be — no — duel !

RAVENSBANE. No duel.

RACHEL. Oh, I am so gratefully happy !

RAVENSBANE. I know I am only a thing
to make Mistress Rachel happy. Ah ! look at
me once more. When you look at me, I live.

RACHEL. It is strange, indeed, my lord,
how the familiar world, the daylight, the
heavens themselves have changed since
your arrival.

RAVENSBANE. This is the world ; this is
the light ; this is the heavens themselves.
Mistress Rachel is looking at me.

RACHEL. For me, it is less strange, perhaps. I never saw a real lord before. But
you, my lord, must have seen so many,
many girls in the great world.

RAVENSBANE. No, no; never.

RACHEL. No other girls before to-day,
my lord !

RAVENSBANE. Before to-day ? I do not
know ; I do not care. I was not — here.
To-day I was born — in your eyes. Ah !
my brain whirls !

RACHEL [*smiling*].

" If witchcraft be a whirling brain,
    A roving eye, a heart of pain, — "

[*In a whisper.*] My lord, do you really believe in witchcraft ?

RAVENSBANE. With all my heart.

RACHEL. And approve of it ?

RAVENSBANE. With all my soul.

RACHEL. So do I — that is, innocent
witchcraft ; not to harm anybody, you
know, but just to feel all the dark mystery
and the trembling excitement — the way
you feel when you blow out your candle all
alone in your bedroom and watch the little
smoke fade away in the moonshine.

RAVENSBANE. Fade away in the moonshine !

RACHEL. Oh, but we must n't speak of
it. In a town like this, all such mysticism
is considered damnable. But your lordship
understands and approves ? I am so glad !
Have you read the *Philosophical Considerations* of Glanville, the *Saducismus Trium-
phatus*, and the *Presignifications of Dreams* ?
What kind of witchcraft, my lord, do you
believe in ?

RAVENSBANE. In all yours.

RACHEL. Nay, your lordship must not
take me for a real witch. I can only tell
fortunes, you know — like this morning.

RAVENSBANE. I know ; you told how
my heart would break.

RACHEL. Oh, that's palmistry, and that is n't always certain. But the surest way to prophesy — do you know what it is?

RAVENSBANE. Tell me.

RACHEL. To count the crows. Do you know how?

One for sorrow —

RAVENSBANE. Ha, yes! —

Two for mirth!

RACHEL.

Three for a wedding —

RAVENSBANE.

Four for a birth —

RACHEL.

And five for the happiest thing on earth!

RAVENSBANE. Mistress Rachel, come! Let us go and count five crows.

RACHEL [delightedly]. Why, my lord, how did you ever learn it? I got it from an old goody here in town — a real witchwife. If you will promise not to tell a secret, I will show you. — But you must promise!

RAVENSBANE. I promise.

RACHEL. Come, then. I will show you a real piece of witchcraft that I bought from her this morning — the glass of truth. There! Behind that curtain. If you look in, you will see — But come; I will show you. [They put their hands on the cords of the curtain.] Just pull that string, and — ah!

DICKON [stepping out through the curtain]. My lord, your pipe.

RACHEL. Master Dickonson, how you frightened me!

DICKON. So excessively sorry!

RACHEL. But how did you — ?

DICKON. I believe you were showing his lordship —

RACHEL [turning hurriedly away]. Oh, nothing; nothing at all.

RAVENSBANE [sternly to DICKON]. Why do you come?

DICKON [handing back RAVENSBANE'S pipe filled]. Allow me. [Aside.] 'T is high time you came to the point, Jack; 't is near your lordship's reception. Woo and win, boy; woo and win.

RAVENSBANE [haughtily]. Leave me.

DICKON. Your lordship's humble, very humble. [Exit.]

RACHEL [shivering]. My dear lord, why do you keep this man?

RAVENSBANE. I — keep this man?

RACHEL. Pardon my rudeness — I cannot endure him.

RAVENSBANE. You do not like him? Ah, then, I do not like him also. We will send him away — you and I.

RACHEL. You, my lord, of course; but I —

RAVENSBANE. You will be Dickon! You will be with me always and light my pipe. And I will live for you, and fight for you, and kill your betrothed!

RACHEL [drawing away]. No, no!

RAVENSBANE. Ah! but your eyes say "yes." Mistress Rachel leaves me; but Rachel in her eyes remains. Is it not so?

RACHEL. What can I say, my lord! It is true that since my eyes met yours, a new passion has entered into my soul. I have felt — but 't is so impertinent, my lord, so absurd in me, a mere girl, and you a nobleman of power — yet I have felt it irresistibly, my dear lord, — a longing to help you, I am so sorry for you — so sorry for you! I pity you deeply. — Forgive me; forgive me, my lord!

RAVENSBANE. It is enough.

RACHEL. Indeed, indeed, 't is so rude of me, — 't is so unreasonable.

RAVENSBANE. It is enough. I grow — I grow — I grow! I am a plant; you give it rain and sun. I am a flower; you give it light and dew; I am a soul, you give it love and speech. I grow. Toward you — toward you I grow!

RACHEL. My lord, I do not understand it, how so poor and mere a girl as I can have helped you. Yet I do believe it is so; for I feel it so. What can I do for you?

RAVENSBANE. Be mine. Let me be yours.

RACHEL. But, my lord — do I love you?

RAVENSBANE. What is "I love you"? Is it a kiss, a sigh, an embrace? Ah! then, you do not love me. — "I love you": is it to nourish, to nestle, to lift up, to smile upon, to make greater — a worm? Ah! then, you love me.

[Enter RICHARD at left back, unobserved.]

RACHEL. Do not speak so of yourself, my lord; nor exalt me so falsely.

RAVENSBANE. Be mine.

RACHEL. A great glory has descended upon this day.

RAVENSBANE. Be mine.

RACHEL. Could I but be sure that this glory is love — Oh, *then!*

[*Turns toward* RAVENSBANE.]

RICHARD [*stepping between them*]. It is *not* love ; it is witchcraft.

RACHEL. Who are you ? — Richard ?

RICHARD. You have, indeed, forgotten me ? Would to God, Rachel, I could forget you.

RAVENSBANE. Ah, permit me, sir —

RICHARD. Silence ! [*To* RACHEL.] Against my will, I am a convert to your own mysticism ; for nothing less than damnable illusion could so instantly wean your heart from me to — this. I do not pretend to understand it ; but that it is witchcraft I am convinced ; and I will save you from it.

RACHEL. Go ; please go.

RAVENSBANE. Permit me, sir ; you have not replied yet to flails !

RICHARD. Permit *me*, sir. [*Taking something from his coat.*] My answer is — bare cob ! [*Holding out a shelled corn-cob.*] Thresh this, sir, for your antagonist. 'T is the only one worthy your lordship.

[*Tosses it contemptuously toward him.*]

RAVENSBANE. Upon my honor, as a man —

RICHARD. As a *man*, forsooth ! Were you, indeed, a man, Lord Ravensbane, I would have accepted your weapons, and flailed you out of New England. But it is not my custom to chastise runagates from asylums, or to banter further words with a natural and a ninny.

RACHEL. Squire Talbot ! Will you leave my uncle's house ?

RAVENSBANE. One moment, mistress : — I did not wholly catch the import of this gentleman's speech, but I fancy I have insulted him by my reply to his challenge. One insult may perhaps be remedied by another. Sir, permit me to call *you* a ninny, and to offer you — [*drawing his sword and offering it*] — swords.

RICHARD. Thanks ; I reject the offer.

RAVENSBANE [*turning away despondently*]. He rejects it. Well !

RACHEL. [*To* RICHARD.] And *now* will you leave ?

RICHARD. At once. But one word more. Rachel — Rachel, have you forgotten this morning and the Glass of Truth ?

RACHEL [*coldly*]. No.

RICHARD. Call it a fancy now if you will. I scoffed at it ; yes. Yet *you* believed it. I loved you truly, you said. Well, have I changed ?

RACHEL. Yes.

RICHARD. Will you test me again — in the glass ?

RACHEL. No. Go ; leave us.

RICHARD. I will go. I have still a word with your aunt.

RAVENSBANE. [*To* RICHARD.] I beg your pardon, sir. You said just now that had I been a man —

RICHARD. I say, Lord Ravensbane, that the straight fiber of a true man never warps the love of a woman. As for yourself, you have my contempt and pity. Pray to God, sir, pray to God to make you a man.

[*Exit, right.*]

RACHEL. Oh ! it is intolerable ! [*To* RAVENSBANE.] My dear lord, I do believe in my heart that I love you, and if so, I will with gratitude be your wife. But, my lord, strange glamors, strange darknesses reel, and bewilder my mind. I must be alone ; I must think and decide. Will you give me this tassel ?

RAVENSBANE [*unfastening a silk tassel from his coat and giving it to her*]. Oh, take it.

RACHEL. If I decide that I love you, that I will be your wife — I will wear it this afternoon at the reception. Good-bye.

[*Exit, right.*]

RAVENSBANE. Mistress Rachel ! —

[*He is left alone. As he looks about gropingly, and raises his arms in vague prayer,* DICKON *appears from the right and watches him, with a smile.*]

God, are you here ? Dear God, I pray to you — make me to be a man !

[*Exit, left.*]

DICKON. Poor Jacky ! Thou shouldst 'a' prayed to t' other one.

[*Enter, right,* JUSTICE MERTON.]

JUSTICE MERTON. [*To* DICKON.] Will you not listen ? Will you not listen !

DICKON. Such a delightful room !

JUSTICE MERTON. Are you merciless ?

DICKON. And such a living portrait of your Worship ! The waistcoat is so beautifully executed.

JUSTICE MERTON. If I pay him ten thousand pounds —

[*Enter, right,* MISTRESS MERTON, *who goes toward the table. Enter, left,* MICAH.]

MISTRESS MERTON. Flails! Flails in the parlor!

MICAH. The minister and his wife have turned into the gate, madam.

MISTRESS MERTON. The guests! Is it so late?

MICAH. Four o'clock, madam.

MISTRESS MERTON. Remove these things at once.

MICAH. Yes, madam.

[*He lifts them, and starts for the door where he pauses to look back and speak.*]

Madam, in all my past years of service at Merton House, I never waited upon a lord till to-day. Madam, in all my future years of service at Merton House, I trust I may never wait upon a lord again.

MISTRESS MERTON. Micah, mind the knocker.

MICAH. Yes, madam.

[*Exit at left back. Sounds of a brass knocker outside.*]

MISTRESS MERTON. Rachel! Rachel!

[*Exit, left.*]

JUSTICE MERTON. [*To* DICKON.] So you are contented with nothing less than the sacrifice of my niece!

[*Enter* MICAH.]

MICAH. Minister Dodge, your Worship; and Mistress Dodge. [*Exit.*]

[*Enter the* MINISTER *and his* WIFE.]

JUSTICE MERTON [*stepping forward to receive them*]. Believe me, this is a great privilege. — Madam! [*Bowing.*]

MINISTER DODGE [*taking his hand*]. The privilege is ours, Justice; to enter a righteous man's house is to stand, as it were, on God's threshold.

JUSTICE MERTON [*nervously*]. Amen, amen. Permit me—ah! Lord Ravensbane, my young guest of honor, will be here directly — permit me to present his lordship's tutor, Master Dickonson; the Reverend Master Dodge, Mistress Dodge.

MINISTER DODGE [*offering his hand*]. Master Dickonson, sir —

DICKON [*barely touching the minister's fingers, bows charmingly to his wife*]. Madam, of all professions in the world, your husband's most allures me.

MISTRESS DODGE. 'T is a worthy one, sir.

DICKON. Ah! Mistress Dodge, and so arduous — especially for a minister's wife.

[*He leads her to a chair.*]

MISTRESS DODGE [*accepting the chair*]. Thank you.

MINISTER DODGE. Lord Ravensbane comes from abroad?

JUSTICE MERTON. From London.

MINISTER DODGE. An old friend of yours, I understand.

JUSTICE MERTON. From London, yes. Did I say from London? Quite so; from London.

[*Enter* MICAH.]

MICAH. Captain Bugby, the Governor's secretary. [*Exit.*]

[*Enter* CAPTAIN BUGBY. *He walks with a slight lameness, and holds daintily in his hand a pipe, from which he puffs with dandy deliberation.*]

CAPTAIN BUGBY. Justice Merton, your very humble servant.

JUSTICE MERTON. Believe me, Captain Bugby.

CAPTAIN BUGBY [*profusely*]. Ah, Master Dickonson! my dear friend Master Dickonson — this is, indeed — ah! How is his lordship since — aha! but discretion! Mistress Dodge — her servant! Ah! yes — [*indicating his pipe with a smile of satisfaction*] — the latest, I assure you; the very latest from London. Ask Master Dickonson.

MINISTER DODGE [*looking at* CAPTAIN BUGBY]. These will hatch out in the spring-time.

CAPTAIN BUGBY [*confidentially to* DICKON]. But really, my good friend, may not I venture to inquire how his lordship — ah! has been in health since the — ah! since —

DICKON [*impressively*]. Oh! quite, quite!

[*Enter* MISTRESS MERTON; *she joins* JUSTICE MERTON *and* MINISTER DODGE.]

CAPTAIN BUGBY. You know, I informed Squire Talbot of his lordship's epigrammatic retort — his retort of — shh! ha haha! Oh, that reply was a stiletto; 't was sharper than a sword-thrust, I assure you. To have conceived it — 't was inspiration; but to have expressed it — oh! 't was genius. Hush! "Flails"! Oh! It sticks me now in the ribs. I shall die with concealing it.

MINISTER DODGE. [*To* MISTRESS MER-
TON.] 'T is true, mistress; but if there
were more like your brother in the parish,
the conscience of the community would be
clearer.

[*Enter* MICAH.]

MICAH. The Reverend Master Rand of
Harvard College; the Reverend Master
Todd of Harvard College. [*Exit.*]

[*Enter two elderly, straight-backed divines.*]

JUSTICE MERTON [*greeting them*]. Permit
me, gentlemen; this is fortunate — before
our return to Cambridge.

> [*He conducts them to* MISTRESS MER-
> TON *and* MINISTER DODGE, *center.
> Seated left,* DICKON *is ingratiating
> himself with* MISTRESS DODGE;
> CAPTAIN BUGBY, *laughed at by
> both parties, is received by neither.*]

CAPTAIN BUGBY [*puffing smoke toward the
ceiling*]. Really, I cannot understand what
keeps his Excellency, the Lieutenant-Governor, so long. He has two such charming
daughters, Master Dickonson —

DICKON. [*To* MISTRESS DODGE.] Yes,
yes; such suspicious women with their
charms are an insult to the virtuous ladies
of the parish.

CAPTAIN BUGBY. How, sir!

MISTRESS DODGE. And to think that she
should actually shoe horses herself!

CAPTAIN BUGBY [*piqued, walks another
way*]. Well!

REV. MASTER RAND. [*To* JUSTICE MER-
TON.] It would not be countenanced in the
college yard, sir.

REV. MASTER TODD. A pipe! Nay,
mores inhibitæ!

JUSTICE MERTON. 'T is most unfortunate,
gentlemen; but I understand 't is the new
vogue in London.

[*Enter* MICAH.]

MICAH. His Excellency, Sir Charles
Reddington, Lieutenant - Governor; the
Mistress Reddingtons.

CAPTAIN BUGBY. At last!

MISTRESS MERTON [*aside*]. Micah.

[MICAH *goes to her.*]

[*Enter* SIR CHARLES, MISTRESS REDDINGTON,
and AMELIA REDDINGTON.]

JUSTICE MERTON. Your Excellency, this
is, indeed, a distinguished honor.

SIR CHARLES [*shaking hands*]. Fine
weather, Merton. Where's your young
lord?

THE TWO GIRLS [*curtsying*]. Justice
Merton, Mistress Merton. [MICAH *goes out.*]

CAPTAIN BUGBY. Oh, my dear Mistress
Reddington! Charming Mistress Amelia!
You are so very late, but you shall hear —
hush!

MISTRESS REDDINGTON [*noticing his
pipe*]. Why, what is this, Captain?

CAPTAIN BUGBY. Oh, the latest, I assure
you, the very latest. Wait till you see his
lordship.

AMELIA. What! is n't he here? [*Laughing.*] La, Captain! Do look at the man!

CAPTAIN BUGBY. Oh, he's coming directly. Quite the mode — what?

> [*He talks to them aside, where they
> titter.*]

SIR CHARLES. [*To* DICKON.] What say?
Traveling for his health?

DICKON. Partially, your Excellency; but
my young pupil and master is a singularly
affectionate nature.

THE TWO GIRLS. [*To* CAPTAIN BUGBY.]
What! flails — really!

> [*They burst into laughter among
> themselves.*]

DICKON. He has journeyed here to Massachusetts peculiarly to pay this visit to
Justice Merton — his father's dearest
friend.

SIR CHARLES. Ah! knew him abroad,
eh?

DICKON. In Rome, your Excellency.

MISTRESS DODGE. [*To* JUSTICE MER-
TON.] Why, I thought it was in London.

JUSTICE MERTON. London, true, quite
so; we made a trip together to Lisbon —
ah! Rome.

DICKON. Paris, was it not, sir?

JUSTICE MERTON [*in great distress*].
Paris, Paris, very true; I am — I am —
sometimes I am —

[*Enter* MICAH, *right.*]

MICAH. [*Announces.*] Lord Ravensbane.

[*Enter right,* RAVENSBANE *with* RACHEL.]

JUSTICE MERTON [*with a gasp of relief*].
Ah! his lordship is arrived.

> [*Murmurs of "his lordship" and a
> flutter among the girls and* CAPTAIN
> BUGBY.]

CAPTAIN BUGBY. Look! — Now!

JUSTICE MERTON. Welcome, my lord ! [*To* SIR CHARLES.] Your Excellency, let me introduce — permit me —

RAVENSBANE. Permit *me ;* [*addressing her*] Mistress Rachel ! — Mistress Rachel will introduce —

RACHEL [*curtsying*]. Sir Charles, allow me to present my friend, Lord Ravensbane.

MISTRESS REDDINGTON [*aside to* AMELIA]. Her *friend* — did you hear ?

SIR CHARLES. Mistress Rachel, I see you are as pretty as ever. Lord Ravensbane, your hand, sir.

RAVENSBANE. Trust me, your Excellency, I will inform his Majesty of your courtesy.

CAPTAIN BUGBY [*watching* RAVENSBANE *with chagrin*]. On my life ! he 's lost his limp.

RAVENSBANE [*apart to* RACHEL]. You said : " A great glory has descended upon this day."

RACHEL [*shyly*]. My lord !

RAVENSBANE. Be sure — O mistress, be sure — that this glory is love.

SIR CHARLES. My daughters, Fanny and Amelia — Lord Ravensbane.

THE TWO GIRLS [*curtsying*]. Your lordship !

SIR CHARLES. Good girls, but silly.

THE TWO GIRLS. Papa !

RAVENSBANE. Believe me, ladies, with the *true* sincerity of the *heart*.

MISTRESS REDDINGTON. Is n't he perfection !

CAPTAIN BUGBY. What said I ?

AMELIA [*giggling*]. I can't help thinking of flails.

SIR CHARLES [*in a loud whisper aside to* JUSTICE MERTON]. Is it congratulations for your niece ?

JUSTICE MERTON. Not — not precisely.

DICKON. [*To* JUSTICE MERTON.] Your worship — a word. [*Leads him aside.*]

RAVENSBANE [*whom* RACHEL *continues to introduce to the guests, to* MASTER RAND]. Verily, sir, as that prince of poets, the immortal Virgil, has remarked :

" Adeo in teneris consuescere multum est."

REV. MASTER TODD. His lordship is evidently a university man.

REV. MASTER RAND. Evidently most accomplished.

JUSTICE MERTON [*aside to* DICKON]. A song ! Why, it is beyond all bounds of custom and decorum.

DICKON. Believe me, there is no such flatterer to win the maiden heart as music.

JUSTICE MERTON. And here ; in this presence ! Never !

DICKON. Nevertheless, it will amuse me vastly, and you will announce it.

JUSTICE MERTON [*with hesitant embarrassment, which he seeks to conceal*]. Your Excellency and friends, I have great pleasure in announcing his lordship's condescension in consenting to regale our present company — with a song.

SEVERAL VOICES [*in various degrees of amazement and curiosity*]. A song !

MISTRESS MERTON. Gilead ! What is this ?

JUSTICE MERTON. The selection is a German ballad — a particular favorite at the court of Prussia, where his lordship last rendered it. His tutor has made a translation which is entitled —

DICKON. " The Prognostication of the Crows."

ALL. Crows !

JUSTICE MERTON. And I am requested to remind you that in the ancient heathen mythology of Germany, the crow or raven, was the fateful bird of the god Woden.

CAPTAIN BUGBY. How prodigiously novel !

MINISTER DODGE [*frowning*]. Unparalleled !

SIR CHARLES. A ballad ! Come now, that sounds like old England again. Let 's have it. Will his lordship sing without music ?

JUSTICE MERTON. Master Dickonson, hem ! has been — persuaded — to accompany his lordship on the spinet.

AMELIA. How delightful !

REV. MASTER RAND [*aside to* TODD]. Shall we remain ?

REV. MASTER TODD. We must.

RAVENSBANE. [*To* RACHEL.] My tassel, dear mistress ; you do not wear it ?

RACHEL. My heart still wavers, my lord. But whilst you sing, I will decide.

RAVENSBANE. Whilst I sing ? My fate, then, is waiting at the end of a song ?

RACHEL. At the end of a song.

DICKON [*calling to* RAVENSBANE]. Your lordship !

RAVENSBANE [*starting, turns to the company*]. Permit me.

[DICKON *sits, facing left, at the spinet. At first, his fingers in playing give sound only to the soft tinkling notes of that ancient instrument; but gradually, strange notes and harmonies of an aërial orchestra mingle with, and at length drown, the spinet. The final chorus is produced solely by fantastic symphonic cawings, as of countless crows, in harsh but musical accord. During the song* RICHARD *enters.* DICKON'S *music, however, does not cease but fills the intervals between the verses. To his accompaniment, amid the whispered and gradually increasing wonder, resentment, and dismay of the assembled guests,* RAVENSBANE, *with his eyes fixed upon* RACHEL, *sings.*]

Baron von Rabentod arose;
 (The golden sun was rising)
Before him flew a flock of crows:
 Sing heigh! Sing heigh! Sing heigh! Sing —

" Ill speed, ill speed thee, baron-wight;
 Ill speed thy palfrey pawing!
Blithe is the morn but black the night
 That hears a raven's cawing."

[*Chorus.*]
Caw! Caw! Caw!

MISTRESS DODGE. [*Whispers to her husband.*] Did you hear them?

MINISTER DODGE. Hush!

AMELIA [*sotto voce*]. What *can* it be?

CAPTAIN BUGBY. Oh, the latest, be sure.

DICKON. You note, my friends, the accompanying harmonics; they are an intrinsic part of the ballad, and may not be omitted.

RAVENSBANE. [*Sings.*]

The baron reckèd not a pin;
 (For the golden sun was rising)
He rode to woo, he rode to win;
 Sing heigh! Sing heigh! Sing heigh! Sing —

He rode into his prince's hall
 Through knights and damsels flow'ry:
" Thy daughter, prince, I bid thee call;
 I claim her hand and dowry."

[*Enter* RICHARD. MISTRESS MERTON *seizes his arm nervously.*]

SIR CHARLES. [*To* CAPTAIN BUGBY.] This gentleman's playing is rather ventriloquistical.

CAPTAIN BUGBY. Quite, as it were.

REV. MASTER TODD. This smells unholy.

REV. MASTER RAND. [*To* TODD.] Shall we leave?

RAVENSBANE. [*Sings.*]

" What cock is this, with crest so high,
 That crows with such a pother? "
" Baron von Rabentod am I;
 Methinks we know each other."

" Now welcome, welcome, dear guest of mine,
 So long why didst thou tarry?
Now, for the sake of auld lang syne,
 My daughter thou shalt marry."

AMELIA. [*To* BUGBY.] And he kept right on smoking!

MINISTER DODGE [*who, with* RAND *and* TODD, *has risen uneasily*]. This smacks of witchcraft.

RAVENSBANE. [*Sings.*]

The bride is brought, the priest as well;
 (The golden sun was passing)
They stood beside the altar rail;
 Sing ah! Sing ah! Sing ah! Sing —

. " Woman, with this ring I thee wed."
 What makes his voice so awing?
The baron by the bride is dead:
 Outside the crows were cawing.

[*Chorus, which grows tumultuous, seeming to fill the room with the invisible birds.*]
Caw! Caw! Caw!

[*The guests rise in confusion.* DICKON *still plays delightedly, and the strange music continues.*]

MINISTER DODGE. This is no longer godly. — Justice Merton! Justice Merton, sir! —

RAVENSBANE. [*To* RACHEL, *who holds his tassel in her hand.*] Ah! and you have my tassel!

RACHEL. See! I will wear it now. You yourself shall fasten it.

RAVENSBANE. Rachel! Mistress!

RACHEL. My dear lord!

[*As* RAVENSBANE *is placing the silken tassel on* RACHEL'S *breast to fasten it there,* RICHARD, *by the mirror, takes hold of the curtain strings.*]

RICHARD. I told you — witchcraft, like murder will out! Lovers! Behold yourselves! [*He pulls the curtain back.*]

RACHEL [*looking into the glass, screams and turns her gaze fearfully upon* RAVENSBANE]. Ah! Do not look!

DICKON [*who, having turned round from*

the spinet, has leaped forward, now turns back again, biting his finger]. Too late !

[*In the glass are reflected the figures of* RACHEL *and* RAVENSBANE — RACHEL *just as she herself appears, but* RAVENSBANE *in his essential form of a scarecrow, in every movement reflecting* RAVENSBANE'S *motions. The thing in the glass is about to pin a wisp of corn-silk on the mirrored breast of the maiden.*]

RAVENSBANE. What is there ?

RACHEL [*looking again, starts away from* RAVENSBANE]. Leave me ! Leave me ! — Richard !   [*She faints in* RICHARD'S *arms.*]

RAVENSBANE. Fear not, mistress, I will kill the thing.

[*Drawing his sword, he rushes at the glass. Within, the scarecrow, with a drawn wheel-spoke, approaches him at equal speed. They come face to face and recoil.*]

Ah ! ah ! Fear'st thou me ? What art thou ? Why, 't is a glass. Thou mockest me ? Look, look, mistress, it mocks me ! O God, no ! no ! Take it away. Dear God, do not look ! — It is I !

ALL [*rushing to the doors*]. Witchcraft ! Witchcraft !

[*As* RAVENSBANE *stands frantically confronting his abject reflection, struck in a like posture of despair, the curtain falls.*]

ACT IV

The same. Night. The moon, shining in broadly at the window, discovers RAVENSBANE *alone, prostrate before the mirror. Raised on one arm to a half-sitting posture, he gazes fixedly at the vaguely seen image of the scarecrow prostrate in the glass.*

RAVENSBANE. All have left me — but not thou. Rachel has left me ; her eyes have turned away from me ; she is gone. All that I loved, all that loved me, have left me. A thousand ages — a thousand ages ago, they went away ; and thou and I have gazed upon each other's desertedness. Speak ! and be pitiful ! If thou art I, inscrutable image, if thou dost feel these pangs thine own, show then self-mercy ; speak ! What art thou ? What am I ? Why are we here ? How comes it that we feel and guess and suffer ? Nay, though thou answer not these doubts, yet mock them, mock them aloud, even as there, monstrous, thou counterfeitest mine

actions. Speak, abject enigma ! — Speak, poor shadow, thou —

[*Recoiling wildly.*]

Stand back, inanity ! Thrust not thy mawkish face in pity toward me. Ape and idiot ! Scarecrow ! — to console me ! Haha ! — A flail and broomstick ! a cob, a gourd and pumpkin, to fuse and sublimate themselves into a mage-philosopher, who discourseth metaphysics to itself — itself, God ! Dost Thou hear ? Itself ! For even such am I — I whom Thou madest to love Rachel. Why, God — haha ! dost Thou dwell in this thing ? Is it Thou that peerest forth *at* me — *from* me ? Why, hark then ; Thou shalt listen, and answer — if Thou canst. Between the rise and setting of a sun, I have walked in this world of Thine. I have been thrilled with wonder ; I have been calmed with knowledge ; I have trembled with joy and passion. Power, beauty, love have ravished me. Infinity itself, like a dream, has blazed before me with the certitude of prophecy ; and I have cried, "This world, the heavens, time itself, are mine to conquer," and I have thrust forth mine arm to wear Thy shield forever — and lo ! for my shield Thou reachest me — a mirror, and whisperest : "Know thyself ! Thou art — a scarecrow : a tinkling clod, a rigmarole of dust, a lump of ordure, contemptible, superfluous, inane !" Haha ! Hahaha ! And with such scarecrows Thou dost people a planet ! O ludicrous ! Monstrous ! Ludicrous ! At least, I thank Thee, God ! at least this breathing bathos can laugh at itself. Thou hast vouchsafed to me, Spirit, — hahaha ! — to know myself. Mine, mine is the consummation of man — even self-contempt ! [*Pointing in the glass with an agony of derision.*] Scarecrow ! Scarecrow ! Scarecrow !

THE IMAGE IN THE GLASS [*more and more faintly*]. Scarecrow! Scarecrow! Scarecrow!

[RAVENSBANE *throws himself prone upon the floor, beneath the window, sobbing. There is a pause of silence, and the moon shines brighter. — Slowly then* RAVENSBANE, *getting to his knees, looks out into the night.*]

RAVENSBANE. What face are you, high up through the twinkling leaves ? Do you not, like all the rest, turn, aghast, your eyes away from me — me, abject enormity, groveling at your feet ? Gracious being, do you not fear — despise me ? O white peace of

the world, beneath your gaze the clouds
glow silver, and the herded cattle, slumbering far afield, crouch — beautiful. The
slough shines lustrous as a bridal veil.
Beautiful face, you are Rachel's, and you
have changed the world. Nothing is mean,
but you have made it miraculous ; nothing
is loathsome, nothing ludicrous, but you
have converted it to loveliness, that even
this shadow of a mockery myself, cast by
your light, gives me the dear assurance I
am a man. Rachel, mistress, mother, out
of my suffering you have brought forth my
soul. I am saved !

THE IMAGE IN THE GLASS. A very pretty
sophistry.

> [*The moonlight grows dimmer, as at
> the passing of a cloud.*]

RAVENSBANE. Ah ! what voice has
snatched you from me ?

THE IMAGE. A most poetified pumpkin !

RAVENSBANE. Thing ! dost thou speak
at last ? My soul abhors thee.

THE IMAGE. I *am* thy soul.

RAVENSBANE. Thou liest.

THE IMAGE. Our daddy Dickon and our
mother Rickby begot and conceived us at
sunrise, in a Jack-o'-lantern.

RAVENSBANE. Thou liest, torturing illusion. Thou art but a phantom in a glass.

THE IMAGE. Why, very true. So art
thou. *We* are a pretty phantom in a glass.

RAVENSBANE. It is a lie. I am no longer
thou. I feel it ; I am a man.

THE IMAGE.
And prithee, what 's a man? Man 's but a mirror,
Wherein the imps and angels play charades,
Make faces, mope, and pull each other's hair—
Till crack ! the sly urchin Death shivers the
    glass,
And the bare coffin boards show underneath.

RAVENSBANE. Yea ! if it be so, thou
coggery ! if both of us be indeed but illusions, why, now let us end together. But
if it be not so, then let *me* for evermore
be free of thee. Now is the test—the glass!

> [*Springing to the fireplace, he seizes an
> iron crosspiece from the andirons.*]

I 'll play your urchin Death and shatter it.
Let see what shall survive !

> [*He rushes to strike the glass with the
> iron.* DICKON *steps out of the mir-
> ror, closing the curtain.*]

DICKON. I would n't, really !

RAVENSBANE. Dickon ! dear Dickon ! is
it you ?

DICKON. Yes, Jacky ! it 's dear Dickon,
and I really would n't.

RAVENSBANE. Would n't what, Dickon ?

DICKON. Sweep the cobwebs off the sky
with thine aspiring broomstick. When a
man questions fate, 't is bad digestion. When
a scarecrow does it, 't is bad taste.

RAVENSBANE. At last, *you* will tell me the
truth, Dickon ! Am I, then — that thing ?

DICKON. You must n't be so skeptical.
Of course you 're that thing.

RAVENSBANE. Ah me despicable ! Rachel,
why didst thou ever look upon me ?

DICKON. I fear, cobby, thou hast never
studied woman's heart and hero-worship.
Take thyself now. I remarked to Goody
Bess, thy mother, this morning, as I was
chucking her thy pate from the hayloft, that
thou wouldst make a Mark Antony or an
Alexander before night.

RAVENSBANE. Cease ! cease ! in pity's
name. You do not know the agony of being
ridiculous.

DICKON. Nay, Jacky, all mortals are
ridiculous. Like you, they were rummaged
out of the muck ; and like you, they shall
return to the dunghill. I advise 'em, like
you, to enjoy the interim, and smoke.

RAVENSBANE. This pipe, this ludicrous
pipe that I forever set to my lips and puff !
Why must I, Dickon ? Why ?

DICKON. To avoid extinction — merely.
You see, 't is just as your fellow in there
[*pointing to the glass*] explained. You yourself are the subtlest of mirrors, polished
out of pumpkin and pipe-smoke. Into this
mirror the fair Mistress Rachel has pro-
jected her lovely image, and thus provided
you with what men call a soul.

RAVENSBANE. Ah ! then, I have a soul
— the truth of me ? Mistress Rachel has
indeed made me a man ?

DICKON. Don't flatter thyself, cobby.
Break thy pipe, and whiff — soul, Mistress
Rachel, man, truth, and this pretty world
itself, go up in the last smoke.

RAVENSBANE. No, no ! not Mistress
Rachel.

DICKON. Mistress Rachel exists for your
lordship merely in your lordship's pipe-
bowl.

RAVENSBANE. Wretched, niggling caricature that I am ! All is lost to me — lost !

DICKON. "Paradise Lost" again ! Always blaming it on me. There 's that gaunt

fellow in England has lately wrote a parody on me when I was in the apple business.

RAVENSBANE [*falling on his knees and bowing his head*]. O God! I am so contemptible!

[*Enter, at door back,* GOODY RICKBY; *her blacksmith garb is hidden under a dingy black mantle with peaked hood.*]

DICKON. Good verse, too, for a parody!

[*Ruminating, raises one arm rhetorically above* RAVENSBANE.]

— "Farewell, happy fields
Where joy forever dwells! Hail, horrors; hail,
Infernal world! and thou, profoundest hell,
Receive thy new possessor."

GOODY RICKBY [*seizing his arm*]. Dickon!

DICKON. Hullo! You, Bess!

GOODY RICKBY. There's not a minute to lose. Justice Merton and the neighbors have ended their conference at Minister Dodge's, and are returning here.

DICKON. Well, let 'em come. We're ready.

GOODY RICKBY. But thou toldst me they had discovered —

DICKON. A scarecrow in a mirror. Well? The glass is bewitched; that's all.

GOODY RICKBY. All? Witchcraft is hanging — that's all! And the mirror was bought of me — of me, the witch. Wilt thou be my hangman, Dickon?

DICKON. Wilt thou give me a kiss, Goody? When did ever thy Dickon desert thee?

GOODY RICKBY. But how, boy, wilt thou —

DICKON. Trust me, and thy son. When the Justice's niece is thy daughter-in-law, all will be safe. For the Justice will cherish his niece's family.

GOODY RICKBY. But when he knows —

DICKON. But he shall *not* know. How can he? When the glass is denounced as a fraud, how will he, or any person, ever know that we made this fellow out of rubbish? Who, forsooth, but a poet — or a devil — *would* believe it? You must n't credit men with our imaginations, my dear.

GOODY RICKBY. Then thou wilt pull me through this safe?

DICKON. As I adore thee — and my own reputation.

GOODY RICKBY [*at the window*]. I see their lanterns down the road.

DICKON. Stay, marchioness — his lordship! My lord — your lady mother.

GOODY RICKBY [*curtsying, laughs shrilly*]. Your servant — my son! [*About to depart.*]

RAVENSBANE. Ye lie! both of you! — I was born of Rachel.

DICKON. Tut, tut, Jacky; you must n't mix up mothers and prospective wives at your age. It's fatal.

GOODY RICKBY [*excitedly*]. They're coming! [*Exit.*]

DICKON [*calling after her*]. Fear not; I'll overtake thee.

RAVENSBANE. She is coming; Rachel i coming, and I may not look upon her!

DICKON. Eh? Why not?

RAVENSBANE. I am a monster.

DICKON. Fie! fie! Thou shalt have her.

RAVENSBANE. Have her, Dickon?

DICKON. For lover and wife.

RAVENSBANE. For wife?

DICKON. For wife and all. Thou hast but to obey.

RAVENSBANE. Ah! who will do this for me?

DICKON. I!

RAVENSBANE. Dickon! Wilt make me a man — a man and worthy of her?

DICKON. Fiddlededee! I make over no masterpieces. Thy mistress shall be Cinderella, and drive to her palace with her gilded pumpkin.

RAVENSBANE. It is the end.

DICKON. What! You'll not?

RAVENSBANE. Never.

DICKON. Harkee, manikin. Hast thou learned to suffer?

RAVENSBANE [*wringing his hands*]. O God!

DICKON. *I* taught thee. Shall I teach thee further?

RAVENSBANE. Thou canst not.

DICKON. Cannot — ha! What if I should teach Rachel, too?

RAVENSBANE. Rachel! — Ah! now I know thee.

DICKON [*bowing*]. Flattered.

RAVENSBANE. Devil! Thou wouldst not torment Rachel?

DICKON. Not if my lord —

RAVENSBANE. Speak! What must I do?

DICKON. *Not* speak. Be silent, my lord, and acquiesce in all I say.

RAVENSBANE. I will be silent.

DICKON. And acquiesce?

RAVENSBANE. I will be silent.

[*Enter* MINISTER DODGE, *accompanied by* SIR CHARLES REDDINGTON, CAPTAIN BUGBY, *the* REVEREND MASTERS RAND *and* TODD, *and followed by* JUSTICE MERTON, RICHARD, MISTRESS MERTON, *and* RACHEL. RICHARD *and* RACHEL *stand somewhat apart*, RACHEL *drawing close to* RICHARD *and hiding her face. All wear their outer wraps, and two or three hold lanterns, which, save the moon, throw the only light upon the scene. All enter solemn and silent.*]

MINISTER DODGE. Lord, be Thou present with us, in this unholy spot.

SEVERAL MEN'S VOICES. Amen.

DICKON. Friends! Have you seized her?

MINISTER DODGE. Stand from us.

DICKON. Sir, the witch! Surely you did not let her escape?

ALL. The witch!

DICKON. A dame in a peaked hood. She has but now fled the house. She called herself — Goody Rickby.

ALL. Goody Rickby!

MISTRESS MERTON. She here!

DICKON. Yea, mistress, and hath confessed all the damnable art, by which all of us have lately been so terrorized.

JUSTICE MERTON. What confessed she?

MINISTER DODGE. What said she?

DICKON. This: It appeareth that, for some time past, she hath cherished revengeful thoughts against our honored host, Justice Merton.

MINISTER DODGE. Yea, he hath often righteously condemned her!

DICKON. Precisely! So, in revenge, she bewitched yonder mirror, and this very morning unlawfully inveigled this sweet young lady into purchasing it.

SIR CHARLES. Mistress Rachel!

MINISTER DODGE. [*To* RACHEL.] Didst thou purchase that glass?

RACHEL [*in a low voice*]. Yes.

MINISTER DODGE. From Goody Rickby?

RACHEL. Yes. [*Clinging to* RICHARD.] O Richard!

MINISTER DODGE. But the image; what was the damnable image in the glass?

DICKON. A familiar devil of hers — a sly imp, who wears to mortal eyes the shape of a scarecrow. It seems she commanded this devil to reveal himself in the glass as my lord's own image, that thus she

might wreck Justice Merton's family felicity.

MINISTER DODGE. Infamous!

DICKON. Indeed, sir, it was this very devil whom but now she stole here to consult withal, when she encountered me, attendant here upon my poor prostrate lord, and — held by the wrath in my eye — confessed it all.

SIR CHARLES. Thunder and brimstone! Where is this accursed hag?

DICKON. Alas — gone, gone! If you had but stopped her.

MINISTER DODGE. I know her den — the blacksmith shop. Let us seize her there!

SIR CHARLES [*starting*]. Which way?

MINISTER DODGE. To the left.

SIR CHARLES. Go on, there.

MINISTER DODGE. My honored friends, come with us. Heaven shield, with her guilt, the innocent!

[*Exeunt all but* RICHARD, RACHEL, DICKON, *and* RAVENSBANE.]

DICKON. So, then, dear friends, this strange incident is happily elucidated. Bygones, therefore, be bygones. The future brightens — with orange-blossoms. Hymen and Felicity stand with us here ready to unite two amorous and bashful lovers. His lordship is reticent; yet to you alone, of all beautiful ladies, Mistress Rachel —

RAVENSBANE [*in a mighty voice*]. Silence!

DICKON. My lord would —

RAVENSBANE. Silence! Dare not to speak to her!

DICKON [*biting his lip*]. My babe is weaned.

[*He steps back, and disappears, left, in the dimness.*]

RACHEL [*still at* RICHARD's *side*]. Oh, my lord, if I have made you suffer —

RICHARD [*appealingly*]. Rachel!

RAVENSBANE [*approaching her, raises one arm to screen his face*]. Gracious lady! let fall your eyes; look not upon me. If I dare now speak once more to you, 't is because I would have you know — Oh, forgive me! — that I love you.

RICHARD. Sir! This lady has renewed her promise to be my wife.

RAVENSBANE. Your wife, or not, I love her.

RICHARD. Zounds!

RAVENSBANE. Forbear, and hear me! For one wonderful day I have gazed upon this, your world. A million forms — of trees, of stones, of stars, of men, of common things — have swum like motes before my eyes; but one alone was wholly beautiful. That form was Rachel: to her alone I was not ludicrous; to her I also was beautiful. Therefore, I love her.

RICHARD. Sir!

RAVENSBANE. You talk to me of mothers, mistresses, lovers, and wives and sisters, and you say men love these. What is love? The night and day of the world — the *all* of life, the all which must include both you and me and God, of whom you dream. Well, then, I love you, Rachel. What shall prevent me? Mistress, mother, wife — thou art all to me!

RICHARD. My lord, I can only reply for Mistress Rachel, that you speak like one who does not understand this world.

RAVENSBANE. O God! Sir, and do you? If so, tell me — tell me before it be too late — why, in this world, such a thing as *I* can love and talk of love. Why, in this world, a true man and woman, like you and your betrothed, can look upon this counterfeit and be deceived.

RACHEL AND RICHARD. Counterfeit?

RAVENSBANE. Me — on me — the ignominy of the earth, the laughing-stock of the angels!

RACHEL. Are you not Lord Ravensbane?

RAVENSBANE. No, I am *not* Lord Ravensbane. I am a nobleman of husks, bewitched from a pumpkin. I am Lord Scarecrow!

RACHEL. Ah me, the image in the glass was true?

RAVENSBANE. Yes, true. It is the glass of truth — Thank God for you, dear.

DICKON [*his face only reappearing in the mirror, speaks low*]. Remember! if you dare — Rachel shall suffer for it.

RAVENSBANE. You lie. She is above your power.

DICKON. Still, thou darest not —

RAVENSBANE. Fool, I dare. [RAVENSBANE *turns to* RACHEL. *While he speaks,* DICKON'S *face slowly fades and disappears.*] Mistress, this pipe is I. This intermittent smoke holds, in its nebula, Venus, Mars, the world. If I should break it — Chaos and the dark! And this of me that now stands up will sink jumbled upon the floor — a scarecrow. See! I break it. [*He breaks the pipe in his hands, and flings the pieces to the ground; then turns, agonized, to* RACHEL.] Oh, Rachel, could I have been a man — ! [*He sways, staggering.*]

RACHEL. Richard! Richard! support him.

[*She draws the curtain of the mirror, just opposite which* RAVENSBANE *has sunk upon the floor. At her cry, he starts up faintly and gazes at his reflection, which is seen to be a normal image of himself.*]

Look, look: the glass!

RAVENSBANE. Who is it?

RACHEL. Yourself, my lord — 't is the glass of truth.

RAVENSBANE [*his face lighting with an exalted joy, starts to his feet, erect, before the glass*]. A man! [*He falls back into the arms of the two lovers.*] Rachel! [*He dies.*]

RICHARD [*bending over him*]. Dead!

RACHEL [*with an exalted look*]. But a man!

THE WEAVERS

A DRAMA OF THE FORTIES

By GERHART HAUPTMANN

Translated from the German by MARY MORISON

I DEDICATE THIS DRAMA

TO MY FATHER

ROBERT HAUPTMANN

*You, dear Father, know what feelings lead me to dedicate this
work to you, and I am not called upon to analyse them here.
Your stories of my grandfather, who in his young days sat at
the loom, a poor weaver like those here depicted, contained the
germ of my drama. Whether it possesses the vigor of life or
is rotten at the core, it is the best, "so poor a man as Hamlet
is" can offer.*

Yours,

GERHART.

COMPLETE LIST OF CHARACTERS

DREISSIGER, *fustian manufacturer*

MRS. DREISSIGER

PFEIFER, *manager*
NEUMANN, *cashier*
AN APPRENTICE } *in* DREISSIGER'S *employment*
JOHN, *coachman*
A MAID

WEINHOLD, *tutor to* DREISSIGER'S *sons*

PASTOR KITTELHAUS

MRS. KITTELHAUS

HEIDE, *Police Superintendent*

KUTSCHE, *policeman*

WELZEL, *publican*

MRS. WELZEL

ANNA WELZEL

WIEGAND, *joiner*

A COMMERCIAL TRAVELER

A PEASANT

A FORESTER

SCHMIDT, *surgeon*

HORNIG, *rag dealer*

WITTIG, *smith*

WEAVERS

BERKER

MORITZ JAEGER

OLD BAUMERT

MOTHER BAUMERT

BERTHA } BAUMERT
EMMA

FRITZ, EMMA's *son* (*four years old*)

AUGUST BAUMERT

OLD ANSORGE

MRS. HEINRICH

OLD HILSE

MOTHER HILSE

GOTTLIEB HILSE

LUISE, GOTTLIEB's *wife*

MIELCHEN, *their daughter* (*six years old*)

REIMANN, *weaver*

HEIBER, *weaver*

A WEAVER'S WIFE

A number of weavers, young and old, of both sexes.

The action passes in the Forties, at Kaschbach, Peterswaldau
and Langenbielau, in the Eulengebirge.

THE WEAVERS

THE FIRST ACT

A large whitewashed room on the ground floor of DREISSIGER'S *house at Peterswaldau, where the weavers deliver their finished webs and the fustian is stored. To the left are uncurtained windows, in the back wall there is a glass door, and to the right another glass door, through which weavers, male and female, and children, are passing in and out. All three walls are lined with shelves for the storing of the fustian. Against the right wall stands a long bench, on which a number of weavers have already spread out their cloth. In the order of arrival each presents his piece to be examined by* PFEIFER, DREISSIGER'S *manager, who stands, with compass and magnifying-glass, behind a large table, on which the web to be inspected is laid. When* PFEIFER *has satisfied himself, the weaver lays the fustian on the scale, and an office apprentice tests its weight. The same boy stores the accepted pieces on the shelves.* PFEIFER *calls out the payment due in each case to* NEUMANN, *the cashier, who is seated at a small table.*

It is a sultry day toward the end of May. The clock is on the stroke of twelve. Most of the waiting work-people have the air of standing before the bar of justice, in torturing expectation of a decision that means life or death to them. They are marked, too, by the anxious timidity characteristic of the receiver of charity, who has suffered many humiliations, and, conscious that he is barely tolerated, has acquired the habit of self-effacement. Add to this an expression on every face that tells of constant, fruitless brooding. There is a general resemblance among the men. They have something about them of the dwarf, something of the schoolmaster. The majority are flat-breasted, short-winded, sallow, and poor looking — creatures of the loom, their knees bent with much sitting. At a first glance the women show fewer typical traits. They look over-driven, worried, reckless, whereas the men still make some show of a pitiful self-respect; and their clothes are ragged, while the men's are patched and mended. Some of the young girls are not without a certain charm, consisting in a wax-like pallor, a slender figure, and large, projecting, melancholy eyes.

NEUMANN [*counting out money*]. **Comes** to one and sevenpence halfpenny.

WEAVER'S WIFE. [*About thirty, emaciated, takes up the money with trembling fingers.*] Thank you, sir.

NEUMANN [*seeing that she does not move on*]. Well, something wrong this time, too?

WEAVER'S WIFE [*agitated, imploringly*]. Do you think I might have a few pence in advance, sir? I need it that bad.

NEUMANN. And I need a few pounds. If it was only a question of needing it — ! [*Already occupied in counting out another weaver's money, shortly.*] It's Mr. Dreissiger who settles about pay in advance.

WEAVER'S WIFE. Could n't I speak to Mr. Dreissiger himself, then, sir?

PFEIFER. [*Now manager, formerly weaver. The type is unmistakable, only he is well fed, well dressed, clean-shaven; also takes snuff copiously. He calls out roughly.*] Mr. Dreissiger would have enough to do if he had to attend to every trifle himself. That's what we are here for. [*He measures, and then examines through the magnifying-glass.*] Mercy on us! what a draught! [*Puts a thick muffler round his neck.*] Shut the door, whoever comes in.

APPRENTICE [*loudly to* PFEIFER]. You might as well talk to stocks and stones.

PFEIFER. That's done! — Weigh! [*The weaver places his web on the scales.*] If you only understood your business a little better! Full of lumps again. . . . I hardly need to look at the cloth to see them. Call yourself a weaver, and "draw as long a bow" as you've done there!

[BECKER *has entered. A young, exceptionally powerfully-built weaver; offhand, almost bold in manner.* PFEIFER, NEUMANN, *and the* APPRENTICE *exchange looks of mutual understanding as he comes in.*]

BECKER. Devil take it! This is a sweating job, and no mistake.

FIRST WEAVER [*in a low voice*]. This blazing heat means rain.

[OLD BAUMERT *forces his way in at the glass door on the right, through which the crowd of weavers can be seen, standing shoulder to shoulder, waiting their turn. The old man stumbles forward and lays his bundle on the bench, beside BECKER'S. He sits down by it, and wipes the sweat from his face.*]

OLD BAUMERT. A man has a right to a rest after that.

BECKER. Rest's better than money.

OLD BAUMERT. Yes, but we *needs* the money, too. Good-mornin' to you, Becker!

BECKER. Morning, Father Baumert! Goodness knows how long we'll have to stand here again.

FIRST WEAVER. And what does that matter? What's to hinder a weaver waitin' for an hour, or for a day if need be? What else is he there for?

PFEIFER. Silence there! We can't hear our own voices.

BECKER [*in a low voice*]. This is one of his bad days.

PFEIFER. [*To the weaver standing before him.*] How often have I told you that you must bring cleaner cloth? What sort of mess is this? Knots, and straw, and all kinds of dirt.

REIMANN. It's for want of a new picker, sir.

APPRENTICE. [*Has weighed the piece.*] Short weight, too.

PFEIFER. I never saw such weavers. I hate to give out the yarn to them. It was another story in my day! I'd have caught it finely from my master for work like that. The business was carried on in different style then. A man had to know his trade — that's the last thing that's thought of nowadays. Reimann, one shilling.

REIMANN. But there's always a pound allowed for waste.

PFEIFER. I've no time. Next man! — What have you to show?

HEIBER. [*Lays his web on the table. While* PFEIFER *is examining it, he goes close up to him; eagerly in a low tone.*] Beg pardon, Mr. Pfeifer, but I wanted to ask you, sir, if you would perhaps be so very kind as do me the favor an' not take my advance money off this week's pay.

PFEIFER [*measuring and examining the texture; jeeringly*]. Well! What next, I wonder? This looks very much as if half the weft had stuck to the bobbins again.

HEIBER. [*Continues.*] I'll be sure to make it all right next week, sir. But this last week I've had to put in two days' work on the estate. And my missus is ill in bed. . . .

PFEIFER [*giving the web to be weighed*]. Another piece of real slop-work. [*Already examining a new web.*] What a selvage! Here it's broad, there it's narrow; here it's drawn in by the wefts goodness knows how tight, and there it's torn out again by the temples. And hardly seventy threads weft to the inch. What's come of the rest? Do you call this honest work? I never saw anything like it.

[HEIBER, *repressing tears, stands humiliated and helpless.*]

BECKER [*in a low voice to* BAUMERT]. To please that brute you would have to pay for extra yarn out of your own pocket.

[*The* WEAVER'S WIFE, *who has remained standing near the cashier's table, from time to time looking round appealingly, takes courage and once more comes forward.*]

WEAVER'S WIFE. [*To cashier imploringly.*] I don't know what's to come of me, sir, if you won't give me a little advance this time — O Lord, O Lord!

PFEIFER. [*Calls across.*] It's no good whining, or dragging the Lord's name into the matter. You're not so anxious about Him at other times. You look after your husband and see that he's not to be found so often lounging in the public-house. We can give no pay in advance. We have to account for every penny. It's not our money. People that are industrious, and understand their work, and do it in the fear of God, never need their pay in advance. So now you know.

NEUMANN. If a Bielau weaver got four times as much pay, he would squander it four times over and be in debt into the bargain.

WEAVER'S WIFE [*in a loud voice, as if appealing to the general sense of justice*]. No one can't call me idle, but I'm not fit now for what I once was. I've twice had a miscarriage. And as to John, he's but a poor creature. He's been to the shepherd at

Zerlau, but he could n't do him no good, and . . . you can't do more than you've strength for. . . . We works as hard as ever we can. This many a week I've been at it till far on into the night. An' we'll keep our heads above water right enough if I can just get a bit of strength into me. But you must have pity on us, Mr. Pfeifer, sir. [*Eagerly, coaxingly.*] You'll please be so very kind as to let me have a few pence on the next job, sir?

PFEIFER [*paying no attention*]. Fiedler, one and twopence.

WEAVER'S WIFE. Only a few pence, to buy bread with. We can't get no more credit. We've a lot of little ones.

NEUMANN [*half aside to the* APPRENTICE, *in a serio-comic tone*]. "Every year brings a child to the linen-weaver's wife, heigh-ho, heigh-ho, heigh."

APPRENTICE. [*Takes up the rhyme, half singing.*] "And the little brat it's blind the first weeks of its life, heigh-ho, heigh-ho, heigh."

REIMANN [*not touching the money which the cashier has counted out to him*]. We've always got one and fourpence for the web.

PFEIFER. [*Calls across.*] If our terms don't suit you, Reimann, you have only to say so. There's no scarcity of weavers — especially of your sort. For full weight we give full pay.

REIMANN. How anything can be wrong with the weight is past . . .

PFEIFER. You bring a piece of fustian with no faults in it, and there will be no fault in the pay.

REIMANN. It's not possible that there's too many knots in this web.

PFEIFER [*examining*]. If you want to live well, then be sure you weave well.

HEIBER. [*Has remained standing near* PFEIFER, *so as to seize on any favorable opportunity. He laughs at* PFEIFER'S *little witticism, then steps forward and again addresses him.*] I wanted to ask you, sir, if you would perhaps have the great kindness not to take my advance of sixpence off to-day's pay? My missus has been bedridden since February. She can't do a hand's turn for me, and I've to pay a bobbin girl. And so . . .

PFEIFER. [*Takes a pinch of snuff.*] Heiber, do you think I have no one to attend to but you? The others must have their turn.

REIMANN. As the warp was given me I took it home and fastened it to the beam. I can't bring back better yarn than I get.

PFEIFER. If you are not satisfied, you need come for no more. There are plenty ready to tramp the soles off their shoes to get it.

NEUMANN. [*To* REIMANN.] Do you not want your money?

REIMANN. I can't bring myself to take such pay.

NEUMANN [*paying no further attention to* REIMANN]. Heiber, one shilling. Deduct sixpence for pay in advance. Leave sixpence.

HEIBER. [*Goes up to the table, looks at the money, stands shaking his head as if unable to believe his eyes, then slowly takes it up.*] Well, I never! — [*Sighing.*] Oh, dear, oh, dear!

OLD BAUMERT [*looking into* HEIBER'S *face*]. Yes, Franz, that's so! There's matter enough for sighing.

HEIBER [*speaking with difficulty*]. I've a girl lying sick at home, too, an' she needs a bottle of medicine.

OLD BAUMERT. What's wrong with her?

HEIBER. Well, you see, she's always been a sickly bit of a thing. I don't know. . . . I need n't mind tellin' you — she brought her trouble with her. It's in her blood, and it breaks out here, there, and everywhere.

OLD BAUMERT. It's always the way. Let folks be poor, and one trouble comes to them on the top of another There's no help for it and there's no end to it.

HEIBER. What are you carryin' in that cloth, Father Baumert?

OLD BAUMERT. We have n't so much as a bite in the house, and so I've had the little dog killed. There's not much on him, for the poor beast was half starved. A nice little dog he was! I could n't kill him myself. I had n't the heart to do it.

PFEIFER. [*Has inspected* BECKER'S *web — calls.*] Becker, one and threepence.

BECKER. That's what you might give to a beggar: it's not pay.

PFEIFER. Every one who has been attended to must clear out. We have n't room to turn round in.

BECKER. [*To those standing near, without lowering his voice.*] It's a beggarly pittance, nothing else. A man works his treadle from early morning till late at night, an' when he has bent over his loom for days an' days, tired to death every evening, sick with the dust and the heat, he finds he 's made a beggarly one and threepence !

PFEIFER. No impudence allowed here.

BECKER. If you think I 'll hold my tongue for your telling, you 're much mistaken.

PFEIFER. [*Exclaims.*] We 'll see about that ! [*Rushes to the glass door and calls into the office.*] Mr. Dreissiger, Mr. Dreissiger, will you be good enough to come here ?

[*Enter* DREISSIGER. *About forty, full-bodied, asthmatic. Looks severe.*]

DREISSIGER. What is it, Pfeifer ?

PFEIFER [*spitefully*]. Becker says he won't be told to hold his tongue.

DREISSIGER. [*Draws himself up, throws back his head, stares at* BECKER ; *his nostrils tremble.*] Oh, indeed ! — Becker. [*To* PFEIFER.] Is he the man ? . . .

[*The clerks nod.*]

BECKER [*insolently*]. Yes, Mr. Dreissiger, yes ! [*Pointing to himself.*] This is the man. [*Pointing to* DREISSIGER.] And that 's a man, too !

DREISSIGER [*angrily*]. Fellow, how dare you ?

PFEIFER. He 's too well off. He 'll go dancing on the ice once too often, though.

BECKER [*recklessly*]. You shut up, you Jack-in-the-box. Your mother must have gone dancing once too often with Satan to have got such a devil for a son.

DREISSIGER. [*Now in a violent passion, roars.*] Hold your tongue this moment, sir, or . . .

[*He trembles and takes a few steps forward.*]

BECKER [*holding his ground steadily*]. I 'm not deaf. My hearing 's quite good yet.

DREISSIGER. [*Controls himself, asks in an apparently cool business tone.*] Was this fellow not one of the pack . . . ?

PFEIFER. He 's a Bielau weaver. When there 's any mischief going, they are sure to be in it.

DREISSIGER [*trembling*]. Well, I give you all warning : if the same thing happens again as last night — a troop of half-drunken cubs marching past my windows singing that low song . . .

BECKER. Is it "Bloody Justice" you mean ?

DREISSIGER. You know well enough what I mean. I tell you that if I hear it again I 'll get hold of one of you, and — mind, I 'm not joking — before the justice he shall go. And if I can find out who it was that made up that vile doggerel . . .

BECKER. It 's a beautiful song, that 's what it is !

DREISSIGER. Another word and I send for the police on the spot, without more ado. I 'll make short work with you young fellows. I 've got the better of very different men before now.

BECKER. I believe you there. A real thoroughbred manufacturer will get the better of two or three hundred weavers in the time it takes you to turn round — swallow them up, and not leave as much as a bone. He 's got four stomachs like a cow, and teeth like a wolf. That 's nothing to him at all !

DREISSIGER. [*To his clerks.*] That man gets no more work from us.

BECKER. It 's all the same to me whether I starve at my loom or by the roadside.

DREISSIGER. Out you go, then, this moment ! . . .

BECKER [*determinedly*]. Not without my pay.

DREISSIGER. How much is owing to the fellow, Neumann ?

NEUMANN. One and threepence.

DREISSIGER. [*Takes the money hurriedly out of the cashier's hand, and flings it on the table, so that some of the coins roll off on to the floor.*] There you are, then ; and now, out of my sight with you !

BECKER. Not without my pay.

DREISSIGER. Do you not see it lying there ? If you don't take it and go . . . It 's exactly twelve now . . . The dyers are coming out for their dinner . . .

BECKER. I get my pay into my hand — here.

[*Points with the fingers of his right hand at the palm of his left.*]

DREISSIGER. [*To the* APPRENTICE.] Pick up the money, Tilgner.

[*The* APPRENTICE *lifts the money and puts it into* BECKER'S *hand.*]

BECKER. Everything in proper order.

[*Deliberately takes an old purse out*

of his pocket and puts the money into it.]

DREISSIGER [*as* BECKER *still does not move away*]. Well? Do you want me to come and help you?

[*Signs of agitation are observable among the crowd of weavers. A long, loud sigh is heard, and then a fall. General interest is at once diverted to this new event.*]

DREISSIGER. What's the matter there?

CHORUS OF WEAVERS AND WOMEN. "Some one's fainted." — "It's a little sickly boy." — "Is it a fit, or what?"

DREISSIGER. What do you say? Fainted? [*He goes nearer.*]

OLD WEAVER. There he lies, any way.

[*They make room. A boy of about eight is seen lying on the floor as if dead.*]

DREISSIGER. Does any one know the boy?

OLD WEAVER. He's not from our village.

OLD BAUMERT. He's like one of Weaver Heinrich's boys. [*Looks at him more closely.*] Yes, that's Heinrich's little Philip.

DREISSIGER. Where do they live?

OLD BAUMERT. Up near us in Kaschbach, sir. He goes round playin' music in the evenings, and all day he's at the loom. They've nine children an' a tenth a-coming.

CHORUS OF WEAVERS AND WOMEN. "They're terrible put to it." — "The rain comes through their roof." — "The woman has n't two shirts among the nine."

OLD BAUMERT [*taking the boy by the arm*]. Now then, lad, what's wrong with you? Wake up, lad.

DREISSIGER. Some of you help me, and we'll get him up. It's disgraceful to send a sickly child this distance. Bring some water, Pfeifer.

WOMAN [*helping to lift the boy*]. Surely you're not going to die, lad!

DREISSIGER. Brandy, Pfeifer, brandy will be better.

BECKER [*forgotten by all, has stood looking on. With his hand on the door-latch, he now calls loudly and tauntingly*]. Give him something to eat, an' he'll soon be all right. [*Goes out.*]

DREISSIGER. That fellow will come to a bad end. — Take him under the arm, Neu-

mann. Easy now, easy; we'll get him into my room. What?

NEUMANN. He said something, Mr. Dreissiger. His lips are moving.

DREISSIGER. What — what is it, boy?

BOY. [*Whispers.*] I'm h — hungry.

WOMAN. I think he says . . .

DREISSIGER. We'll find out. Don't stop. Let us get him into my room. He can lie on the sofa there. We'll hear what the doctor says.

[DREISSIGER, NEUMANN, *and the woman lead the boy into the office. The weavers begin to behave like school-children when their master has left the classroom. They stretch themselves, whisper, move from one foot to the other, and in the course of a few moments are conversing loudly.*]

OLD BAUMERT. I believe as how Becker was right.

CHORUS OF WEAVERS AND WOMEN. "He did say something like that." — "It's nothing new here to fall down from hunger." — "God knows what's to come of them in winter if this cutting down of wages goes on." — "An' this winter the potatoes are n't no good at all." — "Things'll get worse and worse till we're all done for together."

OLD BAUMERT. The best thing a man could do would be to put a rope round his neck and hang hisself on his own loom, like Weaver Nentwich. [*To another old weaver.*] Here, take a pinch. I was at Neurode yesterday. My brother-in-law, he works in the snuff factory there, and he give me a grain or two. Have you anything good in your handkercher?

OLD WEAVER. Only a little pearl barley. I was coming along behind Ulbrich the miller's cart, and there was a slit in one of the sacks. I can tell you we'll be glad of it.

OLD BAUMERT. There's twenty-two mills in Peterswaldau, but of all they grind, there's never nothing comes our way.

OLD WEAVER. We must keep up heart. There's always something comes to help us on again.

HEIBER. Yes, when we're hungry, we can pray to all the saints to help us, and if that don't fill our bellies we can put a pebble in our mouths and suck it. Eh, Baumert?

[*Reënter* DREISSIGER, PFEIFER, AND NEUMANN.]

DREISSIGER. It was nothing serious. The boy is all right again. [*Walks about excitedly, panting.*] But all the same it's a disgrace. The child's so weak that a puff of wind would blow him over. How people, how any parents can be so thoughtless is what passes my comprehension. Loading him with two heavy pieces of fustian to carry good six miles! No one would believe it that had n't seen it. It simply means that I shall have to make a rule that no goods brought by children will be taken over. [*He walks up and down silently for a few moments.*] I sincerely trust such a thing will not occur again. — Who gets all the blame for it? Why, of course the manufacturer. It's entirely our fault. If some poor little fellow sticks in the snow in winter and goes to sleep, a special correspondent arrives posthaste, and in two days we have a blood-curdling story served up in all the papers. Is any blame laid on the father, the parents, that send such a child? — Not a bit of it. How should they be to blame? It's all the manufacturer's fault — he's made the scapegoat. They flatter the weaver, and give the manufacturer nothing but abuse — he's a cruel man, with a heart like a stone, a wicked fellow, at whose calves every cur of a journalist may take a bite. He lives on the fat of the land, and pays the poor weavers starvation wages. In the flow of his eloquence the writer forgets to mention that such a man has his cares too and his sleepless nights; that he runs risks of which the workman never dreams; that he is often driven distracted by all the calculations he has to make, and all the different things he has to take into account; that he has to struggle for his very life against competition; and that no day passes without some annoyance or some loss. And think of the manufacturer's responsibilities, think of the numbers that depend on him, that look to him for their daily bread. No, No! none of you need wish yourselves in my shoes — you would soon have enough of it. [*After a moment's reflection.*] You all saw how that fellow, that scoundrel Becker, behaved. Now he'll go and spread about all sorts of tales of my hard-heartedness, of how my weavers are turned off for a mere trifle, without a moment's notice. Is that true? Am I so very unmerciful?

CHORUS OF VOICES. No, sir.

DREISSIGER. It does n't seem to me that I am. And yet these ne'er-do-wells come round singing low songs about us manufacturers — prating about hunger, with enough in their pockets to pay for quarts of bad brandy. If they would like to know what want is, let them go and ask the linen-weavers: they can tell something about it. But you here, you fustian-weavers, have every reason to thank God that things are no worse than they are. And I put it to all the old, industrious weavers present: Is a good workman able to gain a living in my employment, or is he not?

MANY VOICES. Yes, sir; he is, sir.

DREISSIGER. There now! You see! Of course such a fellow as that Becker can't. I advise you to keep these young lads in check. If there's much more of this sort of thing, I'll shut up shop — give up the business altogether, and then you can shift for yourselves, get work where you like — perhaps Mr. Becker will provide it.

FIRST WEAVER'S WIFE. [*Has come close to* DREISSIGER, *obsequiously removes a little dust from his coat.*] You've been an' rubbed ag'in' something, sir.

DREISSIGER. Business is as bad as it can be just now, you know that yourselves. Instead of making money, I am losing it every day. If, in spite of this, I take care that my weavers are kept in work, I look for some little gratitude from them. I have thousands of pieces of cloth in stock, and don't know if I'll ever be able to sell them. Well, now, I've heard how many weavers hereabouts are out of work, and — I'll leave Pfeifer to give the particulars — but this much I'll tell you, just to show you my good will. . . . I can't deal out charity all round; I'm not rich enough for that; but I can give the people who are out of work the chance of earning at any rate a little. It's a great business risk I run by doing it, but that's my affair. I say to myself: Better that a man should work for a bite of bread than that he should starve altogether. Am I not right?

CHORUS OF VOICES. Yes, yes, sir.

DREISSIGER. And therefore I am ready to give employment to two hundred more

weavers. Pfeifer will tell you on what conditions.   [*He turns to go.*]

FIRST WEAVER'S WIFE. [*Comes between
him and the door, speaks hurriedly, eagerly,
imploringly.*] Oh, if you please, sir, will you
let me ask you if you'll be so good . . .
I've been twice laid up for . . .

DREISSIGER [*hastily*]. Speak to Pfeifer,
good woman. I'm too late as it is.
              [*Passes on, leaving her standing.*]

REIMANN. [*Stops him again. In an injured, complaining tone.*] I have a complaint
to make, if you please, sir. Mr. Feifer refuses to . . . I've always got one and two-
pence for a web . . .

DREISSIGER. [*Interrupts him.*] Mr. Pfeifer's my manager. There he is. Apply to
him.

HEIBER [*detaining* DREISSIGER ; *hurriedly
and confusedly*]. O sir, I wanted to ask if
you would p'r'aps, if I might p'r'aps . . .
if Mr. Feifer might . . . might . . .

DREISSIGER. What is it you want ?

HEIBER. That advance pay I had last
time, sir ; I thought p'r'aps you would
kindly . . .

DREISSIGER. I have no idea what you are
talking about.

HEIBER. I'm awful hard up, sir, because . . .

DREISSIGER. These are things Pfeifer
must look into — I really have not the
time. Arrange the matter with Pfeifer.
          [*He escapes into the office. The sup-
          plicants look helplessly at one an-
          other, sigh, and take their places
          again among the others.*]

PFEIFER [*resuming his task of inspection*].
Well, Annie, let us see what yours is like.

OLD BAUMERT. How much are we to get
for the web, then, Mr. Pfeifer ?

HEIBER. One shilling a web.

OLD BAUMERT. Has it come to that !
          [*Excited whispering and murmuring
          among the weavers.*]

THE SECOND ACT

A small room in the house of WILHELM
ANSORGE, *weaver and house-owner in the village of Kaschbach, in the Eulengebirge.*

*In this room, which does not measure six feet
from the dilapidated wooden floor to the smoke-
blackened rafters, sit four people. Two young
girls,* EMMA *and* BERTHA BAUMERT, *are working at their looms;* MOTHER BAUMERT, *a de-
crepit old woman, sits on a stool beside the bed,
with a winding-wheel in front of her; her idiot
son* AUGUST *sits on a footstool, also winding.
He is twenty, has a small body and head, and
long, spider-like legs and arms.*

*Faint, rosy evening light makes its way
through two small windows in the right wall,
which have their broken panes pasted over with
paper or stuffed with straw. It lights up the
flaxen hair of the girls, which falls loose on their
slender white necks and thin bare shoulders, and
their coarse chemises. These, with a short petticoat of the roughest linen, form their whole attire.
The warm glow falls on the old woman's face,
neck, and breast — a face worn away to a skeleton, with shriveled skin and sunken eyes, red
and watery with smoke, dust, and working by
lamplight; a long goître neck, wrinkled and
sinewy; a hollow breast covered with faded,
ragged shawls.*

*Part of the right wall is also lighted up, with
stove, stove-bench, bedstead, and one or two
gaudily colored sacred prints. On the stove rail
rags are hanging to dry, and behind the stove is
a collection of worthless lumber. On the bench
stand some old pots and cooking-utensils, and
potato-parings are laid out on it, on paper, to
dry. Hanks of yarn and reels hang from the
rafters; baskets of bobbins stand beside the
looms. In the back wall there is a low door without fastening. Beside it a bundle of willow
wands is set up against the wall, and beyond
them lie some damaged quarter-bushel baskets.
The room is full of sound — the rhythmic
thud of the looms, shaking floor and walls, the
click and rattle of the shuttles passing back and
forward, and the steady whirr of the winding-
wheels, like the hum of gigantic bees.*

MOTHER BAUMERT [*in a querulous, feeble
voice, as the girls stop weaving and bend over
their webs*]. Got to make knots again already, have you ?

EMMA. [*The elder of the two girls, about
twenty-two, tying a broken thread.*] It's the
plaguyest web, this !

BERTHA. [*Fifteen.*] Yes, it's real bad yarn
they've given us this time.

EMMA. What can have happened to
father ? He's been away since nine.

MOTHER BAUMERT. You may well ask.
Where in the wide world can he be ?

BERTHA. Don't you worry yourself,
mother.

MOTHER BAUMERT. I can't help it,
Bertha lass.   [EMMA *begins to weave again.*]

BERTHA. Stop a minute, Emma !

EMMA. What is it!

BERTHA. I thought I heard some one.

EMMA. It 'll be Ansorge coming home.

[*Enter* FRITZ, *a little, barefooted, ragged boy of four.*]

FRITZ [*whimpering*]. I 'm hungry, mother.

EMMA. Wait, Fritzel, wait a bit! Gran'-father will be here very soon, an' he 's bringin' bread along with him, an' coffee, too.

FRITZ. But I 'm awful hungry, mother.

EMMA. Be a good boy now, Fritz. Listen to what I 'm tellin' you. He 'll be here this minute. He 's bringin' nice bread an' nice corn-coffee; an' when we stop working mother 'll take the tater peelin's and carry them to the farmer, and the farmer 'll give her a drop o' good skim milk for her little boy.

FRITZ. Where 's grandfather gone?

EMMA. To the manufacturer, Fritz, with a web.

FRITZ. To the manufacturer?

EMMA. Yes, yes, Fritz; down to Dreissiger's at Peterswaldau.

FRITZ. Is it there he gets the bread?

EMMA. Yes; Dreissiger gives him money, and then he buys the bread.

FRITZ. Does he give him a heap of money?

EMMA [*impatiently*]. Oh, stop that chatter, boy.

[*She and* BERTHA *go on weaving for a time, and then both stop again.*]

BERTHA. August, go and ask Ansorge if he 'll give us a light.

[AUGUST *goes out accompanied by* FRITZ.]

MOTHER BAUMERT [*overcome by her childish apprehension, whimpers*]. Emma! Bertha! where can father be?

BERTHA. He 'll have looked in to see Hauffen.

MOTHER BAUMERT [*crying*]. What if he 's sittin' drinkin' in the public house?

EMMA. Don't cry, mother! You know well enough father 's not the man to do that.

MOTHER BAUMERT [*half distracted by a multitude of gloomy forebodings*]. What . . . what . . . what 's to become of us if he does n't come home? — if he drinks the money, and brings us nothin' at all? There 's not so much as a handful of salt in the house

— not a bite o' bread, nor a bit o' wood for the fire.

BERTHA. Wait a bit, mother! It 's moonlight just now. We 'll take August with us and go into the wood and get some sticks.

MOTHER BAUMERT. Yes, an' be caught by the forester.

[ANSORGE, *an old weaver of gigantic stature, who has to bend down to get into the room, puts his head and shoulders in at the door. Long, unkempt hair and beard.*]

ANSORGE. What 's wanted?

BERTHA. Light, if you please.

ANSORGE [*in a muffled voice, as if speaking in a sick-room*]. There 's good daylight yet.

MOTHER BAUMERT. Are we to sit in the dark next?

ANSORGE. I 've to do the same myself.

[*Goes out.*]

BERTHA. It 's easy to see that he 's a miser.

EMMA. Well, there 's nothin' for it but to sit an' wait his pleasure.

[*Enter* MRS. HEINRICH, *a woman of thirty, enceinte; an expression of torturing anxiety and apprehension on her worn face.*]

MRS. HEINRICH. Good-evenin' t' you all.

MOTHER BAUMERT. Well, Jenny, and what 's your news?

MRS. HEINRICH [*who limps*]. I 've got a piece o' glass into my foot.

BERTHA. Come an' sit down, then, an' I 'll see if I can get it out.

[MRS. HEINRICH *seats herself.* BERTHA *kneels down in front of her, and examines her foot.*]

MOTHER BAUMERT. How are you all at home, Jenny?

MRS. HEINRICH. [*Breaks out despairingly.*] Things is in a terrible way with us! [*She struggles in vain against a rush of tears; then weeps silently.*]

MOTHER BAUMERT. The best thing as could happen to the likes of us, Jenny, would be if God had pity on us an' took us away out o' this weary world.

MRS. HEINRICH. [*No longer able to control herself, screams, still crying*]. My children 's starvin'. [*Sobs and moans.*] I 'm at my wits' ends. Let me work till I fall down — I 'm more dead than alive — it 's all no use. Am I able to fill nine hungry mouths? We got a bit o' bread last night, but it wasn't enough even for the two smallest ones. Who was I to give it to, eh? They all cried: Me, me, mother! give it to me! . . . An' if it's like this while I'm still on my feet, what'll it be when I've to take to bed? Our few taters was washed away. We haven't a thing to put in our mouths.

BERTHA [*Has removed the bit of glass and washed the wound.*] We'll put a rag round it. Emma, see if you can find one.

MOTHER BAUMERT. We're no better off than you, Jenny.

MRS. HEINRICH. You have your girls, anyway. You've a husband as can work. Mine was taken with one of his fits last week again — so bad that I didn't know what to do with him, and was half out o' my mind with fright. And when he's had a turn like that, he can't stir out of bed under a week.

MOTHER BAUMERT. Mine's no better. His breathin''s bad now as well as his back. An' there's not a farthin' nor a farthin's worth in the house. If he don't bring a few pence with him to-day, I don't know what we're to do.

EMMA. It's the truth she's tellin' you, Jenny. We had to let father take the little dog with him to-day, to have him killed, that we might get a bite into our stomachs again!

MRS. HEINRICH. Have you not got as much as a handful of flour to spare?

MOTHER BAUMERT. And that we have not, Jenny. There's not as much as a grain of salt in the house.

MRS. HEINRICH. Oh, whatever am I to do? [*Rises; stands still, brooding.*] I don't know what'll be the end of this! It's more nor I can bear. [*Screams in rage and despair.*] I would be contented if it was nothin' but pigs' food! — But I can't go home again empty-handed — that I can't. God forgive me, I see no other way out of it.

[*She limps quickly out.*]

MOTHER BAUMERT. [*Calls after her in a warning voice.*] Jenny, Jenny! don't you be doin' anything foolish, now!

BERTHA. She'll do herself no harm, mother. You need n't be afraid.

EMMA. That's the way she always goes on.

[*Seats herself at the loom and weaves for a few seconds.*]

[AUGUST *enters, carrying a tallow candle, and lighting his father,* OLD BAUMERT, *who follows close behind him, staggering under a heavy bundle of yarn.*]

MOTHER BAUMERT. Oh, father, where have you been all this long time? Where have you been?

OLD BAUMERT. Come now, mother, don't fall on a man like that. Give me time to get my breath first. An' look who I've brought with me.

[MORITZ JAEGER *comes stooping in at the low door. Reserve soldier, newly discharged. Middle height, rosy-cheeked, military carriage. His cap on the side of his head, hussar fashion, whole clothes and shoes, a clean shirt without collar. Draws himself up and salutes.*]

JAEGER [*in a hearty voice*]. Good-evening, Auntie Baumert!

MOTHER BAUMERT. Well, well, now! And to think you've got back! An' you've not forgotten us? Take a chair, then, lad.

EMMA [*wiping a wooden chair with her apron, and pushing it toward* MORITZ]. An' so you've come to see what poor folks are like again, Moritz?

JAEGER. I say, Emma, is it true that you've got a boy nearly old enough to be a soldier? Where did you get hold of him, eh?

[BERTHA, *having taken the small supply of provisions which her father has brought, puts meat into a saucepan, and shoves it into the oven, while* AUGUST *lights the fire.*]

BERTHA. You knew Weaver Finger, did n't you?

MOTHER BAUMERT. We had him here in the house with us. He was ready enough to marry her; but he was too far gone in consumption; he was as good as a dead man. It did n't happen for want of warning from me. But do you think she would listen? Not she. Now he's dead an' forgotten long ago, an' she's left with the boy to provide for as best she can. But now tell us how you've been gettin' on, Moritz.

OLD BAUMERT. You've only to look at him, mother, to know that. He's had luck. It'll be about as much as he can do to speak to the likes of us. He's got clothes like a prince, an' a silver watch, an' thirty shillings in his pocket into the bargain.

JAEGER [*stretching himself consequentially, a knowing smile on his face*]. I can't complain. I did n't get on at all badly in the regiment.

OLD BAUMERT. He was the major's own servant. Just listen to him — he speaks like a gentleman.

JAEGER. I 've got so accustomed to it that I can't help it.

MOTHER BAUMERT. Well, now, to think that such a good-for-nothing as you were should have come to be a rich man. For there was n't nothing to be made of you. You would never sit still to wind more than a hank of yarn at a time, that you would n't. Off you went to your tom-tit boxes an' your robin redbreast snares — they was all you cared about. Is it not the truth I 'm telling?

JAEGER. Yes, yes, auntie, it 's true enough. It was n't only redbreasts. I went after swallows, too.

EMMA. Though we were always tellin' you that swallows were poison.

JAEGER. What did I care ? — But how have you all been getting on, Auntie Baumert ?

MOTHER BAUMERT. Oh, badly, lad, badly these last four years. I 've had the rheumatics — just look at them hands. And it 's more than likely as I 've had a stroke o' some kind, too, I 'm that helpless. I can hardly move a limb, an' nobody knows the pains I suffers.

OLD BAUMERT. She 's in a bad way, she is. She 'll not hold out long.

BERTHA. We 've to dress her in the mornin' an' undress her at night, an' to feed her like a baby.

MOTHER BAUMERT [*speaking in a complaining, tearful voice*]. Not a thing can I do for myself. It 's far worse than bein' ill. For it 's not only a burden to myself I am, but to every one else. Often and often do I pray to God to take me. For oh ! mine 's a weary life. I don't know . . . p'r'aps they think . . . but I 'm one that 's been a hard worker all my days. An' I 've always been able to do my turn too ; but now, all at once, [*she vainly attempts to rise*] I can't do nothing. — I 've a good husband an' good children, but to have to sit here and see them . . . ! Look at the girls ! There 's hardly any blood left in them — faces the color of a sheet. But on they must work at these weary looms whether they earn enough to keep theirselves or not. What sort o' life is it they lead ? Their feet never off the treadle from year's end to year's end. An' with it all they can't scrape together as much as 'll buy them clothes that they can let theirselves be seen in ; never a step can they go to church, to hear a word of comfort. They 're liker scarecrows than young girls of fifteen and twenty.

BERTHA [*at the stove*]. It 's beginnin' to smoke again !

OLD BAUMERT. There now ; look at that smoke. And we can't do nothin' for it. The whole stove 's goin' to pieces. We must let it fall, and swallow the soot. We 're coughin' already, one worse than the other. We may cough till we choke, or till we cough our lungs up — nobody cares.

JAEGER. But this here is Ansorge's business ; he must see to the stove.

BERTHA. He 'll see us out of the house first ; he has plenty against us without that.

MOTHER BAUMERT. We 've only been in his way this long time past.

OLD BAUMERT. One word of complaint an' out we go. He 's had no rent from us this last half-year.

MOTHER BAUMERT. A well-off man like him need n't be so hard.

OLD BAUMERT. He 's no better off than we are, mother. He 's hard put to it, too, for all he holds his tongue about it.

MOTHER BAUMERT. He 's got his house.

OLD BAUMERT. What are you talkin' about, mother ? Not one stone in the wall is the man's own.

JAEGER. [*Has seated himself, and taken a short pipe with gay tassels out of one coat-pocket, and a quart bottle of brandy out of another.*] Things can't go on like this. I 'm dumbfoundered when I see the life the people live here. The very dogs in the towns live better.

OLD BAUMERT [*eagerly*]. That 's what I say ! Eh ? eh ? You know it, too ! But if you say that here, they 'll tell you that it 's only bad times.

[*Enter ANSORGE, an earthenware pan with soup in one hand, in the other a half-finished quarter-bushel basket.*]

ANSORGE. Glad to see you again, Moritz !

JAEGER. Thank you, Father Ansorge — same to you !

ANSORGE [*shoving his pan into the oven*]. Why, lad, you look like a duke !

OLD BAUMERT. Show him your watch, Moritz ! An' he 's got a new suit of clothes besides them he 's on, an' thirty shillings in his purse.

ANSORGE [*shaking his head*]. Is that so ? Well, well !

EMMA. [*Puts the potato-parings into a bag.*] I must be off ; I 'll maybe get a drop o' skim milk for these. [*Goes out.*]

JAEGER [*the others hanging on his words*]. You know how you all used to be down on me. It was always : Wait, Moritz, till your soldiering time comes — you 'll catch it then. But you see how well I 've got on. At the end of the first half-year I had got my good conduct stripes. You 've got to be willing — that 's where the secret lies. I brushed the sergeant's boots ; I groomed his horse ; I fetched his beer. I was as sharp as a needle. Always ready, accoutrements clean and shining — first at stables, first at roll-call, first in the saddle. And when the bugle sounded to the assault — why, then, blood and thunder, and ride to the devil with you! ! I was as keen as a pointer. Says I to myself : There 's no help for it now, my boy, it 's got to be done; and I set my mind to it and did it. Till at last the major said before the whole squadron : There 's a hussar now that shows you what a hussar should be ! [*Silence. He lights his pipe.*]

ANSORGE [*shaking his head*]. Well, well, well ! You had luck with you, Moritz.

[*Sits down on the floor, with his willow twigs beside him, and continues mending the basket, which he holds between his legs.*]

OLD BAUMERT. Let 's hope you 've brought some of it to us. — Are we to have a drop to drink your health in ?

JAEGER. Of course you are, Father Baumert. And when this bottle 's done, we 'll send for more. [*He flings a coin on the table.*]

ANSORGE [*open-mouthed with amazement*]. Oh, my ! Oh, my ! What goings on to be sure ! Roast meat frizzlin' in the oven ! A bottle o' brandy on the table ! [*He drinks out of the bottle.*] Here 's to you, Moritz ! — Well, well, well !

[*The bottle circulates freely after this.*]

OLD BAUMERT. If we could anyway have a bit o' meat on Sundays and holidays, instead of never seein' the sight of it from year's end to year's end ! Now we 'll have to wait till another poor little dog finds its way into the house like this one did four weeks gone by — an' that 's not likely to happen soon again.

ANSORGE. Have you killed the little dog ?

OLD BAUMERT. We had to do that or starve.

ANSORGE. Well, well !

MOTHER BAUMERT. A nice, kind little beast he was, too !

JAEGER. Are you as keen as ever on roast dog hereabouts ?

OLD BAUMERT. My word, if we could only get enough of it !

MOTHER BAUMERT. A nice little bit o' meat like that does you a lot o' good.

OLD BAUMERT. Have you lost the taste for it, Moritz ? Stay with us a bit, and it 'll soon come back to you.

ANSORGE [*sniffing*]. Yes, yes! That will be a tasty bite — what a good smell it has !

OLD BAUMERT [*sniffing*]. Splendid !

ANSORGE. Come, then, Moritz, tell us your opinion, you that 's been out and seen the world. Are things at all like improving for us weavers, eh ?

JAEGER. They would need to.

ANSORGE. We 're in an awful state here. It 's not livin' an' it 's not dyin'. A man fights to the bitter end, but he 's bound to be beat at last — to be left without a roof over his head, you may say without ground under his feet. As long as he can work at the loom he can earn some sort o' poor, miserable livin'. But it 's many a day since I 've been able to get that sort o' job. Now I tries to put a bite into my mouth with this here basket-makin'. I sits at it late into the night, and by the time I tumbles into bed I 've earned three-halfpence. I put it to you if a man can live on that, when everything 's so dear ? Nine shillin' goes in one lump for house tax, three shillin' for land tax, nine shillin' for mortgage interest — that makes one pound one. I may reckon my year's earnin' at just double that money, and that leaves me twenty-one shillin' for a whole year's food, an' fire, an' clothes, an' shoes ; and I 've got to keep up some sort of a place to live in. Is it any wonder if I 'm behind-hand with my interest payments ?

OLD BAUMERT. Some one would need to go to Berlin an' tell the King how hard put to it we are.

JAEGER. Little good that would do, Father Baumert. There's been plenty written about it in the newspapers. But the rich people, they can turn and twist things round . . . as cunning as the devil himself.

OLD BAUMERT [*shaking his head*]. To think they've no more sense than that in Berlin!

ANSORGE. And is it really true, Moritz? Is there no law to help us? If a man has n't been able to scrape together enough to pay his mortgage interest, though he's worked the very skin off his hands, must his house be taken from him? The peasant that's lent the money on it, he wants his rights — what else can you look for from him? But what's to be the end of it all, I don't know. — If I'm put out o' the house . . . [*In a voice choked by tears.*] I was born here, and here my father sat at his loom for more than forty year. Many was the time he said to mother: Mother, when I'm gone, the house'll still be here. I've worked hard for it. Every nail means a night's weaving, every plank a year's dry bread. A man would think that . . .

JAEGER. They're quite fit to take the last bite out of your mouth — that's what they are.

ANSORGE. Well, well, well! I would rather be carried out than have to walk out now in my old days. Who minds dyin'? My father, he was glad to die. At the very end he got frightened, but I crept into bed beside him, an' he quieted down again. I was a lad of thirteen then. I was tired and fell asleep beside him — I knew no better — and when I woke he was quite cold.

MOTHER BAUMERT [*after a pause*]. Give Ansorge his soup out o' the oven, Bertha.

BERTHA. Here, Father Ansorge, it'll do you good.

ANSORGE [*eating and shedding tears*]. Well, well, well!

[*OLD BAUMERT has begun to eat the meat out of the saucepan.*]

MOTHER BAUMERT. Father, father, can't you have patience an' let Bertha serve it up properly?

OLD BAUMERT [*chewing*]. It's two years now since I took the sacrament. I went straight after that an' sold my Sunday coat, an' we bought a good bit o' pork, an' since then never a mouthful of meat has passed my lips till to-night.

JAEGER. How should *we* need meat? The manufacturers eat it for us. It's the fat of the land *they* live on. Whoever does n't believe that has only to go down to Bielau and Peterswaldau. He'll see fine things there — palace upon palace, with towers and iron railings and plate-glass windows. Who do they all belong to? Why, of course, the manufacturers! No signs of bad times there! Baked and boiled and fried — horses and carriages and governesses — they've money to pay for all that and goodness knows how much more. They're swelled out to bursting with pride and good living.

ANSORGE. Things was different in my young days. Then the manufacturers let the weaver have his share. Now they keep everything to theirselves. An' would you like to know what's at the bottom of it all? It's that the fine folks nowadays believes neither in God nor devil. What do they care about commandments or punishments? And so they steal our last scrap o' bread, an' leave us no chance of earnin' the barest living. For it's their fault. If our manufacturers was good men, there would be no bad times for us.

JAEGER. Listen, then, and I'll read you something that will please you. [*He takes one or two loose papers from his pocket.*] I say, August, run and fetch another quart from the public-house. Eh, boy, do you laugh all day long?

MOTHER BAUMERT. No one knows why, but our August's always happy — grins an' laughs, come what may. Off with you, then, quick! [*Exit* AUGUST *with the empty brandy-bottle.*] You've got something good now, eh, father?

OLD BAUMERT [*still chewing; spirits rising from the effect of food and drink*]. Moritz, you're the very man we want. You can read an' write. You understand the weavin' trade, and you've a heart to feel for the poor weavers' sufferin's. You should stand up for us here.

JAEGER. I'd do that quick enough! There's nothing I'd like better than to give the manufacturers round here a bit of a fright — dogs that they are! I'm an easy-going fellow, but let me once get worked up into a real rage, and I'll take Dreissiger in the one hand and Dittrich in the other, and knock their heads together till the sparks fly out of their eyes. — If we could only arrange all to join together, we 'd soon give the manufacturers a proper lesson . . . without help from King or Government . . . all we 'd have to do would be to say, We want this and that, and we don't want the other thing. There would be a change of days then. As soon as they see that there 's some pluck in us, they 'll cave in. I know the rascals; they 're a pack of cowardly hounds.

MOTHER BAUMERT. There 's some truth in what you say. I 'm not an ill-natured woman. I 've always been the one to say as how there must be rich folks as well as poor. But when things come to such a pass as this . . .

JAEGER. The devil may take them all, for what I care. It would be no more than they deserve.

[OLD BAUMERT *has quietly gone out.*]

BERTHA. Where 's father?

MOTHER BAUMERT. I don't know where he can have gone.

BERTHA. Do you think he 's not been able to stomach the meat, with not gettin' none for so long?

MOTHER BAUMERT [*in distress, crying*]. There, now, there! He 's not even able to keep it down when he 's got it. Up it comes again, the only bite o' good food as he 's tasted this many a day.

[*Reënter* OLD BAUMERT, *crying with rage.*]

OLD BAUMERT. It 's no good! I 'm too far gone! Now that I 've at last got hold of somethin' with a taste in it, my stomach won't keep it.

[*He sits down on the bench by the stove crying.*]

JAEGER [*with a sudden violent ebullition of rage*]. And yet there are people not far from here, justices they call themselves too, over-fed brutes, that have nothing to do all the year round but invent new ways of wasting their time. And these people say that the weavers would be quite well off if only they were n't so lazy.

ANSORGE. The men as say that are no men at all, they 're monsters.

JAEGER. Never mind, Father Ansorge; we 're making the place hot for 'em. Becker and I have been and given Dreissiger a piece of our mind, and before we came away we sang him "Bloody Justice."

ANSORGE. Good Lord! Is that the song?

JAEGER. Yes; I have it here.

ANSORGE. They call it Dreissiger's song, don't they?

JAEGER. I 'll read it to you.

MOTHER BAUMERT. Who wrote it?

JAEGER. That 's what nobody knows. Now listen.

[*He reads, hesitating like a schoolboy, with incorrect accentuation, but unmistakably strong feeling. Despair, suffering, rage, hatred, thirst for revenge, all find utterance.*]

The justice to us weavers dealt
Is bloody, cruel, and hateful;
Our life 's one torture, long drawn out:
For Lynch law we 'd be grateful.

Stretched on the rack day after day,
Hearts sick and bodies aching,
Our heavy sighs their witness bear
To spirits slowly breaking.

[*The words of the song make a strong impression on* OLD BAUMERT. *Deeply agitated, he struggles against the temptation to interrupt* JAEGER. *At last he can keep quiet no longer.*]

OLD BAUMERT. [*To his wife, half laughing, half crying, stammering.*] Stretched on the rack day after day. Whoever wrote that, mother, wrote the truth. You can bear witness . . . eh, how does it go? "Our heavy sighs their witness bear" . . . what 's the rest?

JAEGER. "To spirits slowly breaking."

OLD BAUMERT. You know the way we sigh, mother, day and night, sleepin' and wakin'.

[ANSORGE *has stopped working, and cowers on the floor, strongly agitated.* MOTHER BAUMERT *and* BERTHA *wipe their eyes frequently during the course of the reading.*]

JAEGER. [*Continues to read.*]

The Dreissigers true hangmen are,
Servants no whit behind them;
Masters and men with one accord
Set on the poor to grind them.

You villains all, you brood of hell . . .

OLD BAUMERT [*trembling with rage, stamping on the floor*]. Yes, brood of hell!!!

JAEGER. [*Reads.*]

You fiends in fashion human,
A curse will fall on all like you,
Who prey on man and woman.

ANSORGE. Yes, yes, a curse upon them !
OLD BAUMERT [*clenching his fist threateningly*]. You prey on man and woman.
JAEGER. [*Reads.*]

> The suppliant knows he asks in vain,
> Vain every word that 's spoken.
> " If not content, then go and starve —
> Our rules cannot be broken."

OLD BAUMERT. What is it ? "The suppliant knows he asks in vain"? Every word of it 's true . . . every word . . . as true as the Bible. He knows he asks in vain.

ANSORGE. Yes, yes ! It 's all no good.

JAEGER. [*Reads.*]

> Then think of all our woe and want,
> O ye who hear this ditty !
> Our struggle vain for daily bread
> Hard hearts would move to pity.
>
> But pity 's what *you* 've never known, —
> You 'd take both skin and clothing,
> You cannibals, whose cruel deeds
> Fill all good men with loathing.

OLD BAUMERT. [*Jumps up, beside himself with excitement.*] Both skin and clothing. It 's true, it 's all true ! Here I stand, Robert Baumert, master-weaver of Kaschbach. Who can bring up anything against me ? I 've been an honest, hard-working man all my life long, an' look at me now ! What have I to show for it ? Look at me ! See what they 've made of me ! Stretched on the rack day after day. [*He holds out his arms.*] Feel that ! Skin and bone ! "You villains all, you brood of hell ! !"

[*He sinks down on a chair, weeping with rage and despair.*]

ANSORGE. [*Flings his basket from him into a corner, rises, his whole body trembling with rage, gasps.*] And the time 's come now for a change, I say. We 'll stand it no longer ! We 'll stand it no longer ! Come what may !

THE THIRD ACT

The common room of the principal public-house in Peterswaldau. A large room with a raftered roof supported by a central wooden pillar, round which a table runs. In the back wall, a little to the right of the pillar, is the entrance door, through the opening of which the spacious lobby or outer room is seen, with barrels and brewing utensils. To the right of this door, in the corner, is the bar — a high wooden counter with receptacles for beer-mugs, glasses, etc.; a cupboard with rows of brandy and liqueur bottles on the wall behind, and between counter and cupboard a narrow space for the barkeeper. In front of the bar stands a table with a gay-colored cover, a pretty lamp hanging above it, and several cane chairs placed around it. Not far off, in the right wall, is a door with the inscription: Bar Parlor. Nearer the front on the same side an old eight-day clock stands ticking. At the back, to the left of the entrance door, is a table with bottles and glasses, and beyond this, in the corner, is the great stove. In the left wall there are three small windows. Below them runs a long bench; and in front of each stands a large oblong wooden table, with the end towards the wall. There are benches with backs along the sides of these tables, and at the end of each facing the window stands a wooden chair. The walls are washed blue and decorated with advertisements, colored prints and oleographs, among the latter a portrait of Frederick William III.

WELZEL, *the publican, a good-natured giant, upwards of fifty, stands behind the counter, letting beer run from a barrel into a glass.*

MRS. WELZEL *is ironing by the stove. She is a handsome, tidily dressed woman in her thirty-fifth year.*

ANNA WELZEL, *a good-looking girl of seventeen, with a quantity of beautiful, fair, reddish hair, sits, nicely dressed, with her embroidery, at the table with the colored cover. She looks up from her work for a moment and listens, as the sound of a funeral hymn sung by school-children is heard in the distance.*

WIEGAND, *the joiner, in his working clothes, is sitting at the same table, with a glass of Bavarian beer before him. His face shows that he understands what the world requires of a man if he is to attain his ends — namely, craftiness, sharpness, and relentless determination.*

A COMMERCIAL TRAVELER *is seated at the pillar-table, vigorously masticating a beefsteak. He is of middle height, stout and thriving-looking, inclined to jocosity, lively, and impudent. He is dressed in the fashion of the day, and his portmanteau, pattern-case, umbrella, overcoat, and traveling-rug lie on chairs beside him.*

WELZEL [*carrying a glass of beer to the* TRAVELER, *but addressing* WIEGAND]. The devil 's loose in Peterswaldau to-day.

WIEGAND [*in a sharp, shrill voice*]. That 's because it 's delivery day at Dreissiger's.

MRS. WELZEL. But they don't generally make such an awful row.

WIEGAND. It 's maybe because of the

two hundred new weavers that he's going to take on.

MRS. WELZEL [*at her ironing*]. Yes, yes, that'll be it. If he wants two hundred, six hundred's sure to come. There's no lack of *them*.

WIEGAND. You may well say that. There's no fear of their dying out, let them be ever so badly off. They bring more children into the world than we know what to do with. [*The strains of the funeral hymn are suddenly heard more distinctly.*] There's a funeral to-day, too. Weaver Nentwich is dead, as no doubt you know.

WELZEL. He's been long enough about it. He's been goin' about like a livin' ghost this many a long day.

WIEGAND. You never saw such a little coffin, Welzel; it was the tiniest, miserablest little thing I ever glued together. And what a corpse! It didn't weigh ninety pounds.

TRAVELER. [*His mouth full.*] What I don't understand's this. . . . Take up whatever paper you like and you'll find the most heartrending accounts of the destitution among the weavers. You get the impression that three quarters of the people in this neighborhood are starving. Then you come and see a funeral like what's going on just now. I met it as I came into the village. Brass band, schoolmaster, schoolchildren, pastor, and such a procession behind them that you would think it was the Emperor of China that was getting buried. If the people have money to spend on this sort of thing, well . . . ! [*He takes a drink of beer; puts down the glass; suddenly and jocosely.*] What do you say to it, Miss? Don't you agree with me?

[ANNA *gives an embarrassed laugh, and goes on working busily.*]

TRAVELER. Now, I'll take a bet that these are slippers for papa.

WELZEL. You're wrong, then; I wouldn't put such things on my feet.

TRAVELER. You don't say so! Now, I would give half of what I'm worth if these slippers were for me.

MRS. WELZEL. Oh, you don't know nothing about such things.

WIEGAND. [*Has coughed once or twice, moved his chair, and prepared himself to speak.*] You were saying, sir, that you wondered to see such a funeral as this. I

tell you, and Mrs. Welzel here will bear me out, that it's quite a small funeral.

TRAVELER. But, my good man . . . what a monstrous lot of money it must cost! Where does that all come from?

WIEGAND. If you'll excuse me for saying so, sir, there's a deal of foolishness among the poorer working-people hereabouts. They have a kind of inordinate idea, if I may say so, of the respect an' duty an' honor they're bound to show to such as are taken from their midst. And when it comes to be a case of parents, then there's no bounds whatever to their superstitiousness. The children and the nearest family scrapes together every farthing they can call their own, an' what's still wanting, that they borrow from some rich man. They run themselves into debt over head and ears; they're owing money to the pastor, to the sexton, and to all concerned. Then there's the victuals an' the drink, an' such like. No, sir, I'm far from speaking against dutifulness to parents; but it's too much when it goes the length of the mourners having to bear the weight of it for the rest of their lives.

TRAVELER. But surely the pastor might reason them out of such foolishness.

WIEGAND. Begging your pardon, sir, but I must mention that every little place hereabouts has its church an' its respected pastor to support. These honorable gentlemen has their advantages from big funerals. The larger the attendance is, the larger the offertory is bound to be. Whoever knows the circumstances connected with the working classes here, sir, will assure you that the pastors are strong against quiet funerals.

[*Enter* HORNIG, *the rag-dealer, a little bandy-legged old man, with a strap round his chest.*]

HORNIG. Good-mornin', ladies and gentlemen! A glass of schnapps, if you please, Mr. Welzel. Has the young mistress anything for me to-day? I've got beautiful ribbons in my cart, Miss Anna, an' tapes, an' garters, an' the very best of pins an' hairpins an' hooks an' eyes. An' all in exchange for a few rags. [*He changes his voice.*] An' out of them rags fine white paper's to be made, for your sweetheart to write you a letter on.

ANNA. Thank you, but I've nothing to do with sweethearts.

MRS. WELZEL [*putting a bolt into her*

tron]. No, she 's not that kind. She 'll not hear of marrying.

TRAVELER. [*Jumps up, affecting delighted surprise, goes forward to* ANNA'S *table, and holds out his hand to her across it.*] That 's right, miss. You and I think alike in this matter. Give me your hand on it. We 'll both remain single.

ANNA [*blushing scarlet, gives him her hand*]. But you are married already!

TRAVELER. Not a bit of it. I only pretend to be. You think so because I wear a ring. I only have it on my finger to protect my charms against shameless attacks. I 'm not afraid of you, though. [*He puts the ring into his pocket.*] But tell me, truly, miss, are you quite determined never, never, never, to marry?

ANNA. [*Shakes her head.*] Oh, get along with you!

MRS. WELZEL. You may trust her to remain single unless something very extra good turns up.

TRAVELER. And why should it not? I know of a rich Silesian proprietor who married his mother's lady's maid. And there 's Dreissiger, the rich manufacturer, his wife is an innkeeper's daughter too, and not half so pretty as you, miss, though she rides in her carriage now, with servants in livery. And why not? [*He marches about, stretching himself, and stamping his feet.*] Let me have a cup of coffee, please.

[*Enter* ANSORGE *and* OLD BAUMERT, *each with a bundle. They seat themselves meekly and silently beside* HORNIG, *at the front table to the left.*]

WELZEL. How are you, Father Ansorge? Glad to see you once again.

HORNIG. Yes, it 's not often as you crawl down from that smoky old nest.

ANSORGE [*visibly embarrassed, mumbles*]. I 've been fetchin' myself a web again.

BAUMERT. He 's goin' to work at a shilling the web.

ANSORGE. I would n't have done it, but there 's no more to be made now by basket-weavin'.

WIEGAND. It 's always better than nothing. He does it only to give you employment. I know Dreissiger very well. When I was up there taking out his double windows last week we were talking about it, him and me. It 's out of pity that he does it.

ANSORGE. Well, well, well! That may be so.

WELZEL [*setting a glass of schnapps on the table before each of the weavers*]. Here you are, then. I say, Ansorge, how long is it since you had a shave? The gentleman over there would like to know.

TRAVELER. [*Calls across.*] Now, Mr. Welzel, you know I did n't say that. I was only struck by the venerable appearance of the master-weaver. It is n't often one sees such a gigantic figure.

ANSORGE [*scratching his head, embarrassed*]. Well, well!

TRAVELER. Such specimens of primitive strength are rare nowadays. We 're all rubbed smooth by civilization . . . but I can still take pleasure in nature untampered with. . . . These bushy eyebrows! That tangled length of beard!

HORNIG. Let me tell you, sir, that these people have n't the money to pay a barber, and as to a razor for themselves, that 's altogether beyond them. What grows, grows. They have n't nothing to throw away on their outsides.

TRAVELER. My good friend, you surely don't imagine that I would . . . [*Aside to* WELZEL.] Do you think I might offer the hairy one a glass of beer?

WELZEL. No, no; you must n't do that. He would n't take it. He 's got some queer ideas in that head of his.

TRAVELER. All right, then, I won't. With your permission, miss. [*He seats himself at* ANNA'S *table.*] I declare, miss, that I 've not been able to take my eyes off your hair since I came in — such glossy softness, such a splendid quantity! [*Ecstatically kisses his finger-tips.*] And what a color! . . . like ripe wheat. Come to Berlin with that hair and you 'll create no end of a sensation. On my honor, with hair like that you may go to Court. . . . [*Leans back, looking at it.*] Glorious, simply glorious!

WIEGAND. They 've given her a name because of it.

TRAVELER. And what may that be?

HORNIG. The chestnut filly, is n't it?

WELZEL. Come, now, we 've had enough o' this. I 'm not goin' to have the girl's head turned altogether. She 's had a-plenty of silly notions put into it already. She 'll hear of nothing under a count to-day, and to-morrow it 'll be a prince.

MRS. WELZEL. You let her alone, father. There's no harm in wantin' to rise in the world. It's as well that people don't all think as you do, or nobody would get on at all. If Dreissiger's grandfather had been of your way of thinkin', they would be poor weavers still. And now they're rollin' in wealth. An' look at old Tromtra. He was nothing but a weaver, too, and now he owns twelve estates, an' he's been made a nobleman into the bargain.

WIEGAND. Yes, Welzel, you must look at the thing fairly. Your wife's in the right this time. I can answer for that. I'd never be where I am, with seven workmen under me, if I had thought like you.

HORNIG. Yes, you understand the way to get on; that your worst enemy must allow. Before the weaver has taken to bed, you're gettin' his coffin ready.

WIEGAND. A man must attend to his business if he's to make anything of it.

HORNIG. No fear of you for that. You know before the doctor when death's on the way to knock at a weaver's door.

WIEGAND [attempting to laugh, suddenly furious]. And you know better than the police where the thieves are among the weavers, that keep back two or three bobbins full every week. It's rags you ask for, but you don't say No, if there's a little yarn among them.

HORNIG. An' your corn grows in the churchyard. The more that are bedded on the sawdust, the better for you. When you see the rows of little children's graves, you pats yourself on the belly, and says you: This has been a good year; the little brats have fallen like cockchafers off the trees. I can allow myself a quart extra in the week again.

WIEGAND. And supposing this is all true, it still doesn't make me a receiver of stolen goods.

HORNIG. No; perhaps the worst you do is to send in an account twice to the rich fustian manufacturers, or to help yourself to a plank or two at Dreissiger's when there's building goin' on and the moon happens not to be shinin'.

WIEGAND [turning his back]. Talk to any one you like, but not to me. [Then suddenly.] Hornig the liar!

HORNIG. Wiegand the coffin-jobber!

WIEGAND. [To the rest of the company.] He knows charms for bewitching cattle.

HORNIG. If you don't look out, I'll try one of 'em on you. [WIEGAND turns pale.]

MRS. WELZEL. [Had gone out; now returns with the TRAVELER's coffee; in the act of putting it on the table.] Perhaps you would rather have it in the parlor, sir?

TRAVELER. Most certainly not! [With a languishing look at ANNA.] I could sit here till I die.

[Enter a YOUNG FORESTER and a PEASANT, the latter carrying a whip. They wish the others "Good-Morning," and remain standing at the counter.]

PEASANT. Two brandies, if you please.

WELZEL. Good-morning to you, gentlemen.

[He pours out their beverage; the two touch glasses, take a mouthful, and then set the glasses down on the counter.]

TRAVELER. [To FORESTER.] Come far this morning, sir?

FORESTER. From Steinseiffersdorf — that's a good step.

[Two old WEAVERS enter, and seat themselves beside ANSORGE, BAUMERT, and HORNIG.]

TRAVELER. Excuse me asking, but are you in Count Hochheim's service?

FORESTER. No. I'm in Count Keil's.

TRAVELER. Yes, yes, of course — that was what I meant. One gets confused here among all the counts and barons and other gentlemen. It would take a giant's memory to remember them all. Why do you carry an axe, if I may ask?

FORESTER. I've just taken this one from a man who was stealing wood.

OLD BAUMERT. Yes, their lordships are mighty strict with us about a few sticks for the fire.

TRAVELER. You must allow that if every one were to help himself to what he wanted . . .

OLD BAUMERT. By your leave, sir, but there's a difference made here as elsewhere between the big an' the little thieves. There's some here as deals in stolen wood wholesale, and grows rich on it. But if a poor weaver . . .

FIRST OLD WEAVER. [Interrupts BAUMERT.] We're forbid to take a single branch; but their lordships, they take the very skin off of us — we've assurance money to pay, an' spinning-money, an' charges in kind — we must go here an' go there, an' do so an' so much field work, all willy-nilly.

ANSORGE. That's just how it is — what the manufacturer leaves us, their lordships takes from us.

SECOND OLD WEAVER. [*Has taken a seat at the next table.*] I've said it to his lordship himself. By your leave, my lord, says I, it's not possible for me to work on the estate so many days this year. For why — my own bit of ground, my lord, it's been next to carried away by the rains. I've to work both night and day if I'm to live at all. For oh, what a flood that was! . . . There I stood an' wrung my hands, an' watched the good soil come pourin' down the hill, into the very house! And all that dear, fine seed! . . . I could do nothing but roar an' cry until I couldn't see out o' my eyes for a week. And then I had to start an' wheel eighty heavy barrow-loads of earth up that hill, till my back was all but broken.

PEASANT [*roughly*]. You weavers here make such an awful outcry. As if we hadn't all to put up with what Heaven sends us. An' if you *are* badly off just now, whose fault is it but your own? What did you do when trade was good? Drank an' squandered all you made. If you had saved a bit then, you'd have it to fall back on now when times is bad, and not need to be goin' stealin' yarn and wood.

FIRST YOUNG WEAVER [*standing with several comrades in the lobby or outer room, calls in at the door*]. What's a peasant but a peasant, though he lies in bed till nine?

FIRST OLD WEAVER. The peasant an' the count, it's the same story with 'em both. Says the peasant when a weaver wants a house: I'll give you a little bit of a hole to live in, an' you'll pay me so much rent in money, an' the rest of it you'll make up by helpin' me to get in my hay an' my corn — an' if that doesn't please you, why, then you may go elsewhere. He tries another, and the second he says the same as the first.

BAUMERT [*angrily*]. The weaver's like a bone that every dog takes a gnaw at.

PEASANT [*furious*]. You starving curs, you're no good for anything. Can you yoke a plough? Can you draw a straight furrow or throw a bundle of sheaves on to a cart. You're fit for nothing but to idle about an' go after the women. A pack of scoundrelly ne'er-do-wells!

[*He has paid and now goes out. The* FORESTER *follows, laughing.* WELZEL, *the joiner, and* MRS. WELZEL *laugh aloud; the* TRAVELER *laughs to himself. Then there is a moment's silence.*]

HORNIG. A peasant like that's as stupid as his own ox. As if I didn't know all about the distress in the villages round here. Sad sights I've seen! Four and five lyin' naked on one sack of straw.

TRAVELER [*in a mildly remonstrative tone*]. Allow me to remark, my good man, that there's a great difference of opinion as to the amount of distress here in the Eulengebirge. If you can read . . .

HORNIG. I can read straight off, as well as you. An' I know what I've seen with my own eyes. It would be queer if a man that's traveled the country with a pack on his back these forty years an' more did n't know something about it. There was Fullern, now. You saw the children scraping about among the dung-heaps with the peasants' geese. The people up there died naked, on the bare stone floors. In their sore need they ate the stinking weavers' glue. Hunger carried them off by the hundred.

TRAVELER. You must be aware, since you are able to read, that strict investigation has been made by the Government, and that . . .

HORNIG. Yes, yes, we all know what that means. They send a gentleman that knows all about it already better nor if he had seen it, an' he goes about a bit in the village, at the lower end, where the best houses are. He doesn't want to dirty his shining boots. Thinks he to himself: All the rest 'll be the same as this. An' so he steps into his carriage, an' drives away home again, an' then writes to Berlin that there's no distress in the place at all. If he had but taken the trouble to go higher up into a village like that, to where the stream comes in, or across the stream on to the narrow side — or, better still, if he'd gone up to the little out-o'-the-way hovels on the hill above, some of 'em that black an' tumble-down as it would be the waste of a good match to set fire to 'em — it's another kind of report he'd have sent to

Berlin. They should have come to me, these government gentlemen that would n't believe there was no distress here. I would have shown them something. I 'd have opened their eyes for 'em in some of these starvation holes.

[*The strains of the Weavers' Song are heard, sung outside.*]

WELZEL. There they are, roaring at that devil's song again.

WIEGAND. They 're turning the whole place upside down.

MRS. WELZEL. You 'd think there was something in the air.

[JAEGER *and* BECKER *arm in arm, at the head of a troop of young weavers, march noisily through the outer room and enter the bar.*]

JAEGER. Halt! To your places!

[*The new arrivals sit down at the various tables, and begin to talk to other weavers already seated there.*]

HORNIG. [*Calls out to* BECKER.] What 's up now, Becker, that you 've got together a crowd like this?

BECKER [*significantly*]. Who knows but something may be going to happen? Eh, Moritz?

HORNIG. Come, come, lads. Don't you be a-gettin' of yourselves into mischief.

BECKER. Blood's flowed already. Would you like to see it?

[*He pulls up his sleeve and shows bleeding tattoo-marks on the upper part of his arm. Many of the other young weavers do the same.*]

BECKER. We 've been at Father Schmidt's gettin' ourselves vaccinated.

HORNIG. Now the thing's explained. Little wonder there's such an uproar in the place, with a band of young rapscallions like you paradin' round.

JAEGER [*consequentially, in a loud voice*]. You may bring two quarts at once, Welzel! I pay. Perhaps you think I have n't got the needful. You 're wrong, then. If we wanted we could sit an' drink your best brandy an' swill coffee till to-morrow morning with any bagman in the land.

[*Laughter among the young weavers.*]

TRAVELER [*affecting comic surprise*]. Is the young gentleman kind enough to take notice of me?

[*Host, hostess, and their daughter,* WIEGAND, *and the* TRAVELER *all laugh.*]

JAEGER. If the cap fits wear it.

TRAVELER. Your affairs seem to be in a thriving condition, young man, if I may be allowed to say so.

JAEGER. I can't complain. I 'm a traveler in made-up goods. I go shares with the manufacturers. The nearer starvation the weaver is, the better I fare. His want butters my bread.

BECKER. Well done, Moritz! You gave it to him that time. Here 's to you!

[WELZEL *has brought the cornbrandy. On his way back to the counter he stops, turns round slowly, and stands, an embodiment of phlegmatic strength, facing the weavers.*]

WELZEL [*calmly but emphatically*]. You let the gentleman alone. He 's done you no harm.

YOUNG WEAVERS. And we 're doing him no harm.

[MRS. WELZEL *has exchanged a few words with the* TRAVELER. *She takes the cup with the remains of his coffee and carries it into the parlor. The* TRAVELER *follows her amidst the laughter of the weavers.*]

YOUNG WEAVERS [*singing*].

"The Dreissigers the hangmen are,
  Servants no whit behind them."

WELZEL. Hush-sh! Sing that song anywhere else you like, but not in my house.

FIRST OLD WEAVER. He 's quite right. Stop that singin', lads.

BECKER. [*Roars.*] But we must march past Dreissiger's, boys, and let them hear it once more.

WIEGAND. You 'd better take care — you may march once too often.

[*Laughter and cries of Ho, ho!*]

[WITTIG *has entered; a gray-haired old smith, bareheaded, with leather apron and wooden shoes, sooty from the smithy. He is standing at the counter waiting for his schnapps.*]

YOUNG WEAVER. Wittig, Wittig!

WITTIG. Here he is. What do you want with him?

YOUNG WEAVERS. "It 's Wittig!" — "Wittig, Wittig!" — "Come here, Wittig." — "Sit beside us, Wittig."

WITTIG. Do you think I would sit beside a set of rascals like you?

JAEGER. Come and take a glass with us.

WITTIG. Keep your brandy to yourselves. I pay for my own drink. [*Takes his glass and sits down beside* BAUMERT *and* ANSORGE. *Clapping the latter on the stomach.*] What's the weavers' food so nice? Sauerkraut and roasted lice!

OLD BAUMERT [*excitedly*]. But what would you say now if they'd made up their minds as how they would put up with it no longer.

WITTIG [*with pretended astonishment, staring open-mouthed at the old weaver*]. Heinerle! you don't mean to tell me that that's you? [*Laughs immoderately.*] O Lord, O Lord! I could laugh myself to death. Old Baumert risin' in rebellion! We'll have the tailors at it next, and then there'll be a rebellion among the baa-lambs, and the rats and the mice. Damn it all, but we'll see some sport. [*He nearly splits with laughter.*]

OLD BAUMERT. You need n't go on like that, Wittig. I'm the same man I've always been. I still say 't would be better if things could be put right peaceably.

WITTIG. Peaceably! How could it be done peaceably? Did they do it peaceably in France? Did Robespeer tickle the rich men's palms? No! It was: Away with them, every one! To the gilyoteen with them! Allongs onfong! You've got your work before you. The geese 'll not fly ready roasted into your mouths.

OLD BAUMERT. If I could make even half a livin' —

FIRST OLD WEAVER. The water's up to our chins now, Wittig.

SECOND OLD WEAVER. We're afraid to go home. It's all the same whether we works or whether we lies abed; it's starvation both ways.

FIRST OLD WEAVER. A man's like to go mad at home.

OLD ANSORGE. It's that length with me now that I don't care how things go.

OLD WEAVERS [*with increasing excitement*]. "We've no peace anywhere." — "We've no spirit left to work." — "Up with us in Steenkunzendorf you can see a weaver sittin' by the stream washin' hisself the whole day long, naked as God made him. It's driven him clean out of his mind."

THIRD OLD WEAVER [*moved by the spirit, stands up and begins to "speak with tongues," stretching out his hand threateningly*]. Judg-

ment is at hand! Have no dealings with the rich and the great! Judgment is at hand! The Lord God of Sabaoth . . .

[*Some of the weavers laugh. He is pulled down on to his seat.*]

WELZEL. That's a chap that can't stand a single glass — he gets wild at once.

THIRD OLD WEAVER. [*Jumps up again.*] But they — they believe not in God, not in hell, not in heaven. They mock at religion . . .

FIRST OLD WEAVER. Come, come now, that's enough!

BECKER. You let him do his little bit o' preaching. There's many a one would be the better for taking it to heart.

VOICES [*in excited confusion*]. "Let him alone!" — "Let him speak!"

THIRD OLD WEAVER [*raising his voice*]. But hell is opened, saith the Lord; its jaws are gaping wide, to swallow up all those that oppress the afflicted and pervert judgment in the cause of the poor. [*Wild excitement.*]

THIRD OLD WEAVER [*suddenly declaiming schoolboy fashion*].

When one has thought upon it well,
It's still more difficult to tell
Why they the linen-weaver's work despise.

BECKER. But we're fustian-weavers, man. [*Laughter.*]

HORNIG. The linen-weavers is ever so much worse off than you. They're wandering about among the hills like ghosts. You people here have still got the pluck left in you to kick up a row.

WITTIG. Do you suppose the worst's over here? It won't be long till the manufacturers drain away that little bit of strength they still have left in their bodies.

BECKER. You know what he said: It will come to the weavers working for a bite of bread. [*Uproar.*]

SEVERAL OLD AND YOUNG WEAVERS. Who said that?

BECKER. Dreissiger said it.

A YOUNG WEAVER. The damned rascal should be hung up by the heels.

JAEGER. Look here, Wittig. You've always jawed such a lot about the French Revolution, and a good deal too about your own doings. A time may be coming, and that before long, when every one will have a chance to show whether he's a braggart or a true man.

WITTIG [*flaring up angrily*]. Say another word if you dare ! Have you heard the whistle of bullets ? Have you done outpost duty in an enemy's country ?

JAEGER. You need n't get angry about it. We 're comrades. I meant no harm.

WITTIG. None of your comradeship for me, you impudent young fool.

[*Enter* KUTSCHE, *the policeman.*]

SEVERAL VOICES. Hush — sh ! Police ! [*This calling goes on for some time, till at last there is complete silence, amidst which* KUTSCHE *takes his place at the central pillar-table.*]

KUTSCHE. A small brandy, please.

[*Again complete silence.*]

WITTIG. I suppose you 've come to see if we 're all behaving ourselves, Kutsche ?

KUTSCHE [*paying no attention to* WITTIG]. Good-morning, Mr. Wiegand.

WIEGAND [*still in the corner in front of the counter*]. Good-morning t' you, sir.

KUTSCHE. How 's trade ?

WIEGAND. Thank you, much as usual.

BECKER. The chief constable 's sent him to see if we 're spoiling our stomach on these big wages we 're getting. [*Laughter.*]

JAEGER. I say, Welzel, you will tell him how we 've been feasting on roast pork an' sauce an' dumplings and sauerkraut, and now we 're sitting at our champagne wine. [*Laughter.*]

WELZEL. The world 's upside down with them to-day.

KUTSCHE. An' even if you had the champagne wine and the roast meat, you would n't be satisfied. I 've to get on without champagne wine as well as you.

BECKER [*referring to* KUTSCHE'S *nose*]. He waters his beet-root with brandy and gin. An' it thrives upon it, too. [*Laughter.*]

WITTIG. A p'liceman like that has a hard life. Now it 's a starving beggar boy he has to lock up, then it 's a pretty weaver girl he has to lead astray ; then he has to get roarin' drunk an' beat his wife till she goes screamin' to the neighbors for help ; and there 's the ridin' about on horseback and the lyin' in bed till nine — nay, faith, but it 's no easy job !

KUTSCHE. Jaw away ; you 'll jaw a rope round your neck in time. It 's long been known what sort of a fellow you are. The magistrates know all about that dangerous tongue of yours. I know who 'll drink wife and child into the poorhouse an' himself into jail before long, who it is that 'll go on agitatin' and agitatin' till he brings down judgment on himself and all concerned.

WITTIG. [*Laughs bitterly.*] It 's true enough — no one knows what 'll be the end of it. You may be right yet. [*Bursts out in fury.*] But if it does come to that, I know who I 've got to thank for it, who it is that 's blabbed to the manufacturers an' all the gentlemen round, an' blackened my character to that extent that they never give me a hand's turn of work to do — an' set the peasants an' the millers against me, so that I 'm often a whole week without a horse to shoe or a wheel to put a tire on. I know who 's done it. I once pulled the damned brute off his horse, because he was givin' a little stupid boy the most awful flogging for stealin' a few unripe pears. But I tell you this, Kutsche, and you know me — if you get me put into prison, you may make your own will. If I hear as much as a whisper of it, I 'll take the first thing as comes handy, whether it 's a horseshoe or a hammer, a wheel-spoke or a pail ; I 'll get hold of you if I 've to drag you out of bed from beside your wife, and I 'll beat in your brains, as sure as my name 's Wittig.

[*He has jumped up and is going to rush at* KUTSCHE.]

OLD AND YOUNG WEAVERS [*holding him back*]. Wittig, Wittig ! Don't lose your head !

KUTSCHE. [*Has risen involuntarily, his face pale. He backs toward the door while speaking. The nearer the door the higher his courage rises. He speaks the last words on the threshold, and then instantly disappears.*] What are you goin' on at me about ? I did n't meddle with you. I came to say something to the weavers. My business is with them an' not with you, and I 've done nothing to you. But I 've this to say to you weavers : The Superintendent of Police herewith forbids the singing of that song — Dreissiger's song, or whatever it is you call it. And if the yelling of it on the streets is n't stopped at once, he 'll provide you with plenty of time and leisure for going on with it in jail. You may sing there, on bread and water, to your hearts' content. [*Goes out.*]

WITTIG. [*Roars after him.*] He's no right to forbid it — not if we were to roar till the windows shook an' they could hear us at Reichenbach — not if we sang till the manufacturers' houses tumbled about their ears an' all the Superintendents' helmets danced on the top of their heads. It's nobody's business but our own.

[BECKER *has in the mean time got up, made a signal for singing, and now leads off, the others joining in.*]

The justice to us weavers dealt
  Is bloody, cruel, and hateful ;
Our life 's one torture, long drawn out ;
  For Lynch law we 'd be grateful.

[WELZEL *attempts to quiet them but they pay no attention to him.* WIEGAND *puts his hands to his ears and rushes off. During the singing of the next verse the weavers rise and form into procession behind* BECKER *and* WITTIG, *who have given pantomimic signs for a general break-up.*]

Stretched on the rack, day after day,
  Hearts sick and bodies aching,
Our heavy sighs their witness bear
  To spirit slowly breaking.

[*Most of the weavers sing the following verse out on the street, only a few young fellows, who are paying, being still in the bar. At the conclusion of the verse no one is left in the room except* WELZEL *and his wife and daughter,* HORNIG, *and* OLD BAUMERT.]

You villains all, you brood of hell,
  You fiends in fashion human,
A curse will fall on all like you
  Who prey on man and woman.

WELZEL [*phlegmatically collecting the glasses*]. Their backs are up to-day, and no mistake.

HORNIG. [*To* OLD BAUMERT, *who is preparing to go.*] What in the name of Heaven are they up to, Baumert ?

BAUMERT. They 're goin' to Dreissiger's to make him add something on to the pay.

WELZEL. And are you joining in these foolish ongoings ?

OLD BAUMERT. I 've no choice, Welzel. The young men may an' the old men must.
  [*Goes out rather shamefacedly.*]

HORNIG. It 'll not surprise me if this ends badly.

WELZEL. To think that even old fellows like him are goin' right off their heads !

HORNIG. We all set our hearts on something !

THE FOURTH ACT

Peterswaldau. Private room of DREISSIGER, *the fustian manufacturer — luxuriously furnished in the chilly taste of the first half of this century. Ceiling, doors, and stove are white, and the wall paper, with its small, straight-lined floral pattern, is dull and cold in tone. The furniture is mahogany, richly-carved, and upholstered in red. On the right, between two windows with crimson damask curtains, stands the writing-table, a high bureau with falling flap. Directly opposite to this is the sofa, with the strong-box beside it; in front of the sofa a table, with chairs and easy-chairs arranged about it. Against the back wall is a gun-cupboard. All three walls are decorated with bad pictures in gilt frames. Above the sofa is a mirror with a heavily gilt rococo frame. On the left an ordinary door leads into the hall. An open folding-door at the back shows the drawing-room, over-furnished in the same style of comfortless splendor. Two ladies,* MRS. DREISSIGER *and* MRS. KITTELHAUS, *the Pastor's wife, are seen in the drawing-room, looking at pictures.* PASTOR KITTELHAUS *is there too, engaged in conversation with* WEINHOLD, *the tutor, a theological graduate.*

KITTELHAUS [*a kindly little elderly man, enters the front room, smoking and talking to the tutor, who is also smoking ; he looks round and shakes his head in surprise at finding the room empty*]. You are young, Mr. Weinhold, which explains everything. At your age we old fellows held — well, I won't say the same opinions — but certainly opinions of the same tendency. And there 's something fine about youth — youth with its grand ideals. But unfortunately, Mr. Weinhold, they don't last; they are as fleeting as April sunshine. Wait till you are my age. When a man has said his say from the pulpit for thirty years — fifty-two times every year, not including saints' days — he has inevitably calmed down. Think of me, Mr. Weinhold, when you come that length.

WEINHOLD [*nineteen, pale, thin, tall, with lanky fair hair ; restless and nervous in his movements*]. With all due respect, Mr. Kittelhaus — I can't think — people have such different natures.

KITTELHAUS. My dear Mr. Weinhold, however restless-minded and unsettled a man may be — [*in a tone of reproof*] — and you are a case in point — however violently and wantonly he may attack the existing order of things, he calms down in the end. I grant you, certainly, that among our professional brethren individuals are to be found, who, at a fairly advanced age, still play youthful pranks. One preaches against the drink evil and founds temperance societies, another publishes appeals which undoubtedly read most effectively. But what good do they do? The distress among the weavers, where it does exist, is in no way lessened — but the peace of society is undermined. No, no; one feels inclined in such cases to say: Cobbler, stick to your last; don't take to caring for the belly, you who have the care of souls. Preach the pure Word of God, and leave all else to Him who provides shelter and food for the birds, and clothes the lilies of the field. But I should like to know where our good host, Mr. Dreissiger, has suddenly disappeared to.

[MRS. DREISSIGER, *followed by* MRS. KITTELHAUS, *now comes forward. She is a pretty woman of thirty, of a healthy, florid type. A certain discordance is noticeable between her deportment and way of expressing herself and her rich, elegant toilette.*]

MRS. DREISSIGER. That's what I want to know, too, Mr. Kittelhaus. But it's what William always does. No sooner does a thing come into his head than off he goes and leaves me in the lurch. I've said enough about it, but it does no good.

KITTELHAUS. It's always the way with business men, my dear Mrs. Dreissiger.

WEINHOLD. I'm almost certain that something has happened downstairs.

[DREISSIGER *enters, hot and excited.*]

DREISSIGER. Well, Rosa, is coffee served?

MRS. DREISSIGER [*sulkily*]. Fancy your needing to run away again!

DREISSIGER [*carelessly*]. Ah! these are things you don't understand.

KITTELHAUS. Excuse me — has anything happened to annoy you, Mr. Dreissiger?

DREISSIGER. Never a day passes without that, my dear sir. I am accustomed to it. What about that coffee, Rosa?

[MRS. DREISSIGER *goes ill-humor-*

edly and gives one or two violent tugs at the broad embroidered bell-pull.]

DREISSIGER. I wish you had been down stairs just now, Mr. Weinhold. You'd have gained a little experience. Besides ... But now let us have our game of whist.

KITTELHAUS. By all means, sir. Shake off the dust and burden of the day, Mr. Dreissiger; forget it in our company.

DREISSIGER. [*Has gone to the window, pushed aside a curtain, and is looking out.*] Vile rabble!! Come here, Rosa! [*She goes to the window.*] Look ... that tall red-haired fellow there! ...

KITTELHAUS. That's the man they call Red Becker.

DREISSIGER. Is he the man that insulted you the day before yesterday? You remember what you told me — when John was helping you into the carriage?

MRS. DREISSIGER [*pouting, carelessly*]. I'm sure I don't know.

DREISSIGER. Come now, what's the use of being cross? I must know. If he's the man, I mean to have him arrested. [*The strains of the Weavers' Song are heard.*] Listen to that! Just listen!

KITTELHAUS [*highly incensed*]. Is there to be no end to this nuisance? I must acknowledge now that it is time for the police to interfere. Permit me. [*He goes forward to the window.*] See, see, Mr. Weinhold! These are not only young people. There are numbers of steady-going old weavers among them, men whom I have known for years and looked upon as most deserving and God-fearing. There they are, taking part in this intolerable uproar, trampling God's law under foot. Do you mean to tell me that you still defend these people?

WEINHOLD. Certainly not, Mr. Kittelhaus. That is, sir ... *cum grano salis*. For after all, they are hungry and they are ignorant. They are giving expression to their dissatisfaction in the only way they understand. I don't expect that such people ...

MRS. KITTELHAUS. [*Short, thin, faded, more like an old maid than a married woman.*] Mr. Weinhold, Mr. Weinhold, how can you?

DREISSIGER. Mr. Weinhold, I am sorry to be obliged to ... I did n't bring you into my house to give me lectures on philanthropy, and I must request that you will confine yourself to the education of my boys, and leave my other affairs entirely to me — entirely ! Do you understand ?

WEINHOLD. [*Stands for a moment rigid and deathly pale, then bows, with a strained smile. In a low voice.*] Certainly, of course I understand. I have seen this coming. It is my wish too. [*Goes out.*]

DREISSIGER [*rudely*]. As soon as possible then, please. We require the room.

MRS. DREISSIGER. William, William !

DREISSIGER. Have you lost your senses, Rosa, that you 're taking the part of a man who defends a low, blackguardly libel like that song ?

MRS. DREISSIGER. But, William, he did n't defend it.

DREISSIGER. Mr. Kittelhaus, did he defend it or did he not ?

KITTELHAUS. His youth must be his excuse, Mr. Dreissiger.

MRS. KITTELHAUS. I can't understand it. The young man comes of such a good, respectable family. His father held a public appointment for forty years, without a breath on his reputation. His mother was overjoyed at his getting this good situation here. And now . . . he himself shows so little appreciation of it.

PFEIFER [*suddenly opens the door leading from the hall and shouts in*]. Mr. Dreissiger, Mr. Dreissiger ! they 've got him ! Will you come, please ? They 've caught one of them.

DREISSIGER [*hastily*]. Has some one gone for the police ?

PFEIFER. The Superintendent 's on his way upstairs.

DREISSIGER [*at the door*]. Glad to see you, sir. We want you here.

[KITTELHAUS *makes signs to the ladies that it will be better for them to retire. He, his wife, and* MRS. DREISSIGER *disappear into the drawing-room.*]

DREISSIGER [*exasperated, to the* POLICE SUPERINTENDENT, *who has now entered*]. I have at last had one of the ringleaders seized by my dyers. I could stand it no longer — their insolence was beyond all bounds — quite unbearable I have visitors in my house, and these blackguards dare to . . . They insult my wife whenever she shows herself; my boys' lives are not safe. My visitors run the risk of being jostled and cuffed. Is it possible that in a well-ordered community incessant public insult

offered to unoffending people like myself and my family should pass unpunished ? If so . . . then . . . then I must confess that I have other ideas of law and order.

SUPERINTENDENT. [*A man of fifty, middle height, corpulent, full-blooded. He wears cavalry uniform with a long sword and spurs.*] No, no, Mr. Dreissiger . . . certainly not ! I am entirely at your disposal. Make your mind easy on the subject. Dispose of me as you will. What you have done is quite right. I am delighted that you have had one of the ringleaders arrested. I am very glad indeed that a settling day has come. There are a few disturbers of the peace here whom I have long had my eye on.

DREISSIGER. Yes, one or two raw lads, lazy vagabonds, that shirk every kind of work, and lead a life of low dissipation, hanging about the public-houses until they 've sent their last halfpenny down their throats. But I 'm determined to put a stop to the trade of these professional blackguards once and for all. It 's in the public interest to do so, not only my private interest.

SUPERINTENDENT. Of course it is ! Most undoubtedly, Mr. Dreissiger ! No one can possibly blame you. And everything that lies in my power . . .

DREISSIGER. The cat-o'-nine tails is what should be taken to the beggarly pack.

SUPERINTENDENT. You 're right, quite right. We must make an example.

[KUTSCHE, *the policeman, enters and salutes. The door is open, and the sound of heavy steps stumbling up the stair is heard.*]

KUTSCHE. I have to inform you, sir, that we have arrested a man.

DREISSIGER. [*To* SUPERINTENDENT.] Do you wish to see the fellow ?

SUPERINTENDENT. Certainly, most certainly. We must begin by having a look at him at close quarters. Oblige me, Mr. Dreissiger, by not speaking to him at present. I 'll see to it that you get complete satisfaction, or my name 's not Heide.

DREISSIGER. That 's not enough for me, though. He goes before the magistrates. My mind 's made up.

[JAEGER *is led in by five dyers, who have come straight from their work — faces, hands, and clothes stained with dye. The prisoner, his cap set jauntily on the side of his head.*

presents an appearance of impudent gayety; he is excited by the brandy he has just drunk.]

JAEGER. Hounds that you are ! — Call yourselves workingmen ! — Pretend to be comrades ! Before I would do such a thing as lay my hands on a mate, I'd see my hand rot off my arm !

[*At a sign from the* SUPERINTENDENT, KUTSCHE *orders the dyers to let go their victim.* JAEGER *straightens himself up, quite free and easy. Both doors are guarded.*]

SUPERINTENDENT. [*Shouts to* JAEGER.] Off with your cap, sir. [JAEGER *takes it off, but very slowly, still with an impudent grin on his face.*] What's your name !

JAEGER. What's yours? I'm not your swineherd.

[*Great excitement is produced among the audience by this reply.*]

DREISSIGER. This is too much of a good thing.

SUPERINTENDENT. [*Changes color, is on the point of breaking out furiously, but controls his rage.*] We'll see about this afterwards. — Once more, what's your name ? [*Receiving no answer, furiously.*] If you don't answer at once, fellow, I'll have you flogged on the spot.

JAEGER. [*Perfectly cheerful, not showing ny so much as the twitch of an eyelid that he has heard the* SUPERINTENDENT'S *angry words, calls over the heads of those around him to a pretty servant girl, who has brought in the coffee and is standing open-mouthed with astonishment at the unexpected sight.*] Hullo, Emmy, do you belong to this company now ? The sooner you find your way out of it, then, the better. A wind may begin to blow here, an' blow everything away overnight.

[*The girl stares at* JAEGER, *and as soon as she comprehends that it is to her he is speaking, blushes with shame, covers her eyes with her hands, and rushes out, leaving the coffee things in confusion on the table. Renewed excitement among those present.*]

SUPERINTENDENT. [*Half beside himself, to* DREISSIGER.] Never in all my long service . . . such a case of shameless effrontery . . . [JAEGER *spits on the floor.*]

DREISSIGER. I'll thank you to remember that this is not a stable.

SUPERINTENDENT. My patience is at an end now. For the last time: What's your name ?

[KITTELHAUS, *who has been peering out at the partly opened drawing-room door, listening to what has been going on, can no longer refrain from coming forward to interfere. He is trembling with excitement.*]

KITTELHAUS. His name is Jaeger, sir. Moritz . . . is it not ? Moritz Jaeger. [*To* JAEGER.] And, Jaeger, you know me.

JAEGER [*seriously*]. You are Pastor Kittelhaus.

KITTELHAUS. Yes, I am your pastor, Jaeger ! It was I who received you, a babe in swaddling clothes, into the Church of Christ. From my hands you took for the first time the body of the Lord. Do you remember that, and how I toiled and strove to bring God's Word home to your heart ? Is this your gratitude ?

JAEGER [*like a scolded schoolboy, in a surly voice*]. I paid my half-crown like the rest.

KITTELHAUS. Money, money . . . Do you imagine that the miserable little bit of money . . . Such utter nonsense ! I'd much rather you kept your money. Be a good man, be a Christian ! Think of what you promised. Keep God's law. Money, money ! . . .

JAEGER. I'm a Quaker now, sir. I don't believe in anything.

KITTELHAUS. Quaker ! What are you talking about ? Try to behave yourself, and don't use words you don't understand. Quaker, indeed ! They are good Christian people, and not heathens like you.

SUPERINTENDENT. Mr. Kittelhaus, I must ask you . . . [*He comes between the Pastor and* JAEGER.] Kutsche ! tie his hands !

[*Wild yelling outside: "Jaeger, Jaeger! come out !"*]

DREISSIGER. [*Like the others, slightly startled, goes instinctively to the window.*] What's the meaning of this next ?

SUPERINTENDENT. Oh, I understand well enough. It means that they want to have the blackguard out among them again. But we're not going to oblige them. Kutsche, you have your orders.. He goes to the lock-up.

KUTSCHE [*with the rope in his hand, hesitating*]. By your leave, sir, but it'll not be an easy job. There's a confounded big crowd out there — a pack of raging devils. They 've got Becker with them, and the smith . . .

KITTELHAUS. Allow me one more word ! — So as not to rouse still worse feeling, would it not be better if we tried to arrange things peaceably ? Perhaps Jaeger will give his word to go with us quietly, or . . .

SUPERINTENDENT. Quite impossible ! Think of my responsibility. I could n't allow such a thing. Come, Kutsche ! lose no more time.

JAEGER [*putting his hands together, and holding them out*]. Tight, tight, as tight as ever you can ! It 's not for long.

[KUTSCHE, *assisted by the workmen, ties his hands.*]

SUPERINTENDENT. Now, off with you, march ! [*To* DREISSIGER.] If you feel anxious, let six of the weavers go with them. They can walk on each side of him, I 'll ride in front, and Kutsche will bring up the rear. Whoever blocks the way will be cut down.

[*Cries from below: "Cock-a-doodle-doo-oo-oo! Bow, wow, wow!"*]

SUPERINTENDENT [*with a threatening gesture in the direction of the window*]. You rascals, I 'll cock-a-doodle-doo and bow-wow you ! Forward ! March !

[*He marches out first, with drawn sword; the others, with* JAEGER, *follow.*]

JAEGER. [*Shouts as he goes.*] An' Mrs. Dreissiger there may play the lady as proud as she likes, but for all that she 's no better than us. Many a hundred times she 's served my father with a half penny-worth of schnapps. Left wheel — march !

[*Exit laughing.*]

DREISSIGER [*after a pause, with apparent calmness*]. Well, Mr. Kittelhaus, shall we have our game now ? I think there will be no further interruption. [*He lights a cigar, giving short laughs as he does so; when it is lighted, bursts into a regular fit of laughing.*] I 'm beginning now to think the whole thing very funny. That fellow ! [*Still laughing nervously.*] It really is too comical : first came the dispute at dinner with Weinhold — five minutes after that he takes leave — off to the other end of the world ; then this affair crops up — and now we 'll proceed with our whist.

KITTELHAUS. Yes, but . . . [*Roaring is*

heard outside.] Yes, but . . . that 's a terrible uproar they 're making outside.

DREISSIGER. All we have to do is to go into the other room ; it won't disturb us in the least there.

KITTELHAUS [*shaking his head*]. I wish I knew what has come over these people. In so far I must agree with Mr. Weinhold, or at least till quite lately I was of his opinion, that the weavers were a patient, humble, easily-led class. Was it not your idea of them, too, Mr. Dreissiger ?

DREISSIGER. Most certainly that is what they used to be — patient, easily managed, peaceable people. They were that as long as these so-called humanitarians let them alone. But for ever so long now they 've had the awful misery of their condition held up to them. Think of all the societies and associations for the alleviation of the distress among the weavers. At last the weaver believes in it himself, and his head 's turned. Some of them had better come and turn it back again, for now he 's fairly set a-going there 's no end to his complaining. This does n't please him, and that does n't please him. He must have everything of the best.

[*A loud roar of "Hurrah !" is heard from the crowd.*]

KITTELHAUS. So that with all their humanitarianism they have only succeeded in almost literally turning lambs into wolves.

DREISSIGER. I won't say that, sir. When you take time to think of the matter coolly, it 's possible that some good may come of it yet. Such occurrences as this will not pass unnoticed by those in authority, and may lead them to see that things can't be allowed to go on as they are doing — that means must be taken to prevent the utter ruin of our home industries.

KITTELHAUS. Possibly. But what is the cause, then, of this terrible falling off of trade ?

DREISSIGER. Our best markets have been closed to us by the heavy import duties foreign countries have laid on our goods. At home the competition is terrible, for we have no protection, none whatever.

PFEIFER. [*Staggers in, pale and breathless.*] Mr. Dreissiger, Mr. Dreissiger !

DREISSIGER [*in the act of walking into the drawing-room, turns round, annoyed*]. Well, Pfeifer, what now ?

PFEIFER. Oh, sir! Oh, sir! . . . It's worse than ever!

DREISSIGER. What are they up to next?

KITTELHAUS. You're really alarming us — what is it?

PFEIFER [still confused]. I never saw the like. Good Lord! — The Superintendent himself . . . they'll catch it for this yet.

DREISSIGER. What's the matter with you, in the devil's name? Is any one's neck broken?

PFEIFER. [Almost crying with fear, screams.] They've set Moritz Jaeger free — they've thrashed the Superintendent and driven him away — they've thrashed the policeman and sent him off to — without his helmet . . . his sword broken . . . Oh dear, oh dear!

DREISSIGER. I think you've gone crazy, Pfeifer.

KITTELHAUS. This is actual riot.

PFEIFER [sitting on a chair, his whole body trembling]. It's turning serious, Mr. Dreissiger! Mr. Dreissiger, it's serious now!

DREISSIGER. Well, if that's all the police . . .

PFEIFER. Mr. Dreissiger, it's serious now!

DREISSIGER. Damn it all, Pfeifer, will you hold your tongue?

MRS. DREISSIGER [coming out of the drawing-room with MRS. KITTELHAUS]. This is really too bad, William. Our whole evening's being spoiled. Here's Mrs. Kittelhaus saying that she'd better go home.

KITTELHAUS. You mustn't take it amiss, dear Mrs. Dreissiger, but perhaps, under the circumstances, it would be better . . .

MRS. DREISSIGER. But, William, why in the world don't you go out and put a stop to it?

DREISSIGER. Go you and try if you can do it. Try! Go and speak to them! [Standing helplessly in front of the pastor.] Am I such a tyrant? Am I a cruel master?

[Enter JOHN the coachman.]

JOHN. If you please, m'm, I've put to the horses. Mr. Weinhold's put Georgie and Charlie into the carriage. If it comes to the worst, we're ready to be off.

MRS. DREISSIGER. If what comes to the worst?

JOHN. I'm sure I don't know, m'm. But the crowd's gettin' bigger and bigger, an' they've sent the Superintendent an' the p'liceman to the right-about.

PFEIFER. It's serious now, Mr. Dreissiger! It's serious!

MRS. DREISSIGER [with increasing alarm]. What's going to happen? — What do the people want? — They're never going to attack us, John?

JOHN. There's some rascally hounds among 'em, ma'am.

PFEIFER. It's serious now! serious!

DREISSIGER. Hold your tongue, fool! — Are the doors barred?

KITTELHAUS. I ask you as a favor, Mr. Dreissiger . . . as a favor . . . I am determined to . . . I ask you as a favor . . . [To JOHN.] What demands are the people making?

JOHN [awkwardly]. It's higher wages they're after, the blackguards.

KITTELHAUS. Good, good! — I shall go out and do my duty. I shall speak seriously to these people.

JOHN. Oh, sir, please, sir, don't do any such thing. Words is quite useless.

KITTELHAUS. One little favor, Mr. Dreissiger. May I ask you to post men behind the door, and to have it closed at once after me?

MRS. KITTELHAUS. O Joseph, Joseph! you're not really going out?

KITTELHAUS. I am. Indeed I am. I know what I'm doing. Don't be afraid. God will protect me.

[MRS. KITTELHAUS presses his hand, draws back, and wipes tears from her eyes.]

KITTELHAUS [while the murmur of a great, excited crowd is heard uninterruptedly outside]. I'll go . . . I'll go out as if I were simply on my way home. I shall see if my sacred office . . . if the people have not sufficient respect for me left to . . . I shall try . . . [He takes his hat and stick.] Forward, then, in God's name!

[Goes out accompanied by DREISSIGER, PFEIFER, and JOHN.]

MRS. KITTELHAUS. Oh, dear Mrs. Dreissiger! [She bursts into tears and embraces her.] I do trust nothing will happen to him.

MRS. DREISSIGER [absently]. I don't know how it is, Mrs. Kittelhaus, but I . . . I can't tell you how I feel. I didn't think such a thing was possible. It's . . . it's as if it was a sin to be rich. If I had been told about all this beforehand, Mrs. Kittelhaus,

I don't know but what I would rather have been left in my own humble position.

MRS. KITTELHAUS. There are troubles and disappointments in every condition of life, Mrs. Dreissiger.

MRS. DREISSIGER. True, true, I can well believe that. And suppose we have more than other people . . . goodness me! we did n't steal it. It 's been honestly got, every penny of it. It 's not possible that the people can be going to attack us! If trade 's bad, that 's not William's fault, is it?

[Loud, confused yelling is heard outside. While the two women stand gazing at each other, pale and startled, DREISSIGER rushes in.]

DREISSIGER. Quick, Rosa, — put on something, and get into the carriage. I 'll be after you this moment.

[He rushes to the strong-box, and takes out papers and various articles of value.]

[Enter JOHN.]

JOHN. We 're ready to star   But come quickly, before they get round to the back door.

MRS. DREISSIGER [in a transport of fear, throwing her arms around JOHN'S neck]. John, John, dear, good John! Save us, John. Save my boys! Oh, what is to become of us?

DREISSIGER. Rosa, try to keep your head. Let John go.

JOHN. Yes, yes, ma'am! Don't you be frightened. Our good horses 'll soon leave them all behind; an' whoever does n't get out of the way 'll be driven over.

MRS. KITTELHAUS [in helpless anxiety]. But my husband . . . my husband? But, Mr. Dreissiger, my husband?

DREISSIGER. He 's in safety now, Mrs. Kittelhaus. Don't alarm yourself; he 's all right.

MRS. KITTELHAUS. Something dreadful has happened to him. I know it. You need n't try to keep it from me.

DREISSIGER. You must n't take it to heart — they 'll be sorry for it yet. I know exactly whose fault it was. Such a detestable, shameful outrage will not go unpunished. A community laying hands on its own pastor and maltreating him — abominable! Mad dogs they are — raging brutes — and they 'll be treated as such. [To his wife who still stands petrified.] Go, for my sake, Rosa, go quickly! [The clatter of window panes being smashed on the ground floor is heard.] They 've gone quite mad. There 's nothing for it but to get away as fast as we can.

[Cries of "Feifer, come out!" — "We want Feifer!" — "Feifer, come out!" are heard.]

MRS. DREISSIGER. Feifer, Feifer, they want Feifer!

PFEIFER. [Dashes in.] Mr. Dreissiger, there are people at the back gate already, and the house door won't hold much longer. The smith 's battering it in with a stable pail.

[The cry sounds louder and clearer: "Feifer! Feifer! Feifer! come out!" MRS. DREISSIGER rushes off as if pursued. MRS. KITTELHAUS follows. PFEIFER listens, and changes color as he hears what the cry is. A perfect panic of fear seizes him; he weeps, entreats, whimpers, writhes, all at the same moment. He overwhelms DREISSIGER with childish caresses, strokes his cheeks and arms, kisses his hands, and at last, like a drowning man, throws his arms round him and prevents him moving.]

PFEIFER. Dear, good, kind Mr. Dreissiger, don't leave me behind. I 've always served you faithfully. I 've always treated the people well. I could n't give them more wages than the fixed rate. Don't leave me here — they 'll do for me! If they find me, they 'll kill me. O God! O God! My wife, my children!

DREISSIGER [making his way out, vainly endeavoring to free himself from PFEIFER'S clutch]. Can't you let me go, fellow? It 'll be all right; it 'll be all right.

[For a few seconds the room is empty. Windows are broken in the drawing-room. A loud crash resounds through the house, followed by shouts of "Hurrah!" For an instant there is silence. Then gentle, cautious steps are heard on the stair, then timid, hushed ejaculations: "To the left!" — "Up with you!" — "Hush!" — "Slow, slow!" — "Don't shove like that!" — "It 's a wedding we 're goin' to!" — "Stop that crowding!" — "You go first!" — "No, you go!"]

[Young weavers and weaver girls appear at the door leading from the hall, not daring to enter, but each trying to shove the other in. In the course of a few moments their timidity is overcome, and the poor, thin, ragged or patched figures, many of them sickly-looking, disperse themselves through DREISSIGER'S *room and the drawing-room, first gazing timidly and curiously at everything, then beginning to touch things. Girls sit down on the sofas, whole groups admire themselves in the mirrors, men stand up on chairs, examine the pictures and take them down. There is a steady influx of miserable-looking creatures from the hall.]*

FIRST OLD WEAVER *[entering]*. No, no, this is carryin' it too far. They 've started smashing things downstairs. There 's no sense nor reason in that. There 'll be a bad end to it. No man in his wits would do that. I 'll keep clear of such ongoings.

*[*JAEGER, BECKER, WITTIG *carrying a wooden pail,* BAUMERT, *and a number of other old and young weavers, rush in as if in pursuit of something, shouting hoarsely.]*

JAEGER. Where has he gone?

BECKER. Where 's the cruel brute?

BAUMERT. If we can eat grass, he may eat sawdust.

WITTIG. We 'll hang him whenever we catch him.

FIRST YOUNG WEAVER. We 'll take him by the legs and fling him out at the window, onto the stones. He 'll never get up again.

SECOND YOUNG WEAVER. *[Enters.]* He 's off!

ALL. Who?

SECOND YOUNG WEAVER. Dreissiger.

BECKER. Feifer too?

VOICES. Let 's get hold of Feifer. Look for Feifer!

BAUMERT. Yes, yes! Feifer! Tell him there 's a weaver here for him to starve.

[Laughter.]

JAEGER. If we can't lay hands on that brute Dreissiger himself . . . we 'll at any rate make a poor man of him.

BAUMERT. As poor as a church mouse . . . we 'll see to that!

[All, bent on the work of destruction, rush towards the drawing-room door.]

BECKER *[who is leading, turns round and stops the others]*. Halt! Listen to me! This is nothing but a beginning. When we 're done here, we 'll go straight to Bielau, to Dittrich's, where the steam power-looms are. The whole mischief 's done by these factories.

OLD ANSORGE. *[Enters from hall. Takes a few steps, then stops and looks round, bewildered; shakes his head, taps his forehead.]* Who am I? Weaver Anton Ansorge. Has he gone mad, Old Ansorge? My head 's goin' round like a humming-top, sure enough. What 's he doing here? He 'll do whatever he 's a mind to. Where is Ansorge? *[He taps his forehead repeatedly.]* Something 's wrong! I 'm not answerable! I 'm off my head! Off with you, off with you, rioters that you are! Heads off, legs off, hands off! If you take my house, I take your house. Forward, forward!

[Goes yelling into the drawing-room, followed by a yelling, laughing mob.]

THE FIFTH ACT

Langen-Bielau. OLD WEAVER HILSE'S *workroom. On the left a small window, in front of which stands the loom. On the right a bed, with a table pushed close to it. Stove, with stove-bench, in the right-hand corner. Family worship is going on.* HILSE, *his old, blind, and almost deaf wife, his son* GOTTLIEB, *and* LUISE, GOTTLIEB'S *wife, are sitting at the table, on the bed and wooden stools. A winding-wheel and bobbins on the floor between table and loom. Old spinning, weaving, and winding implements are disposed of on the smoky rafters; hanks of yarn are hanging down. There is much useless lumber in the low narrow room. The door, which is in the back wall, and leads into the big outer passage, or entry-room of the house, stands open. Through another open door on the opposite side of the passage, a second, in most respects similar weaver's room is seen. The large passage, or entry-room of the house, is paved with stone, has damaged plaster, and a tumble-down wooden staircase leading to the attics; a washing-tub on a stool is partly visible; dirty linen of the most miserable description and poor household utensils lie about untidily. The light falls from the left into all three apartments.*

OLD HILSE *is a bearded man of strong build, but bent and wasted with age, toil, sickness, and hardship. He is an old soldier, and has lost an arm. His nose is sharp, his complexion ashen-gray, and he shakes; he is nothing but skin and bone, and has the deep-set, sore weaver's eyes.*

OLD HILSE. [*Stands up, as do his son and daughter-in-law ; prays.*] O Lord, we know not how to be thankful enough to Thee, for that Thou hast spared us this night again in thy goodness . . . an' hast had pity on us . . . an' hast suffered us to take no harm. Thou art the All-Merciful, an' we are poor, sinful children of men — that bad that we are not worthy to be trampled under thy feet. Yet Thou art our loving Father, an' Thou will look upon us an' accept us for the sake of thy dear Son, our Lord and Savior Jesus Christ. "Jesus' blood and righteousness, Our covering is and glorious dress." An' if we're sometimes too sore cast down under thy chastening — when the fire of thy purification burns too raging hot — oh, lay it not to our charge; forgive us our sin. Give us patience, heavenly Father, that after all these sufferin's we may be made partakers of thy eternal blessedness. Amen.

MOTHER HILSE [*who has been bending forward, trying hard to hear*]. What a beautiful prayer you do say, father !

[LUISE *goes off to the wash-tub,* GOTTLIEB *to the room on the other side of the passage.*]

OLD HILSE. Where's the little lass ?

LUISE. She's gone to Peterswaldau, to Dreissiger's. She finished all she had to wind last night.

OLD HILSE [*speaking very loud*] You'd like the wheel now, mother, eh ?

MOTHER HILSE. Yes, father, I'm quite ready.

OLD HILSE [*setting it down before her*]. I wish I could do the work for you.

MOTHER HILSE. An' what would be the good of that, father ? There would I be, sittin' not knowin' what to do.

OLD HILSE. I'll give your fingers a wipe, then, so that they'll not grease the yarn.

[*He wipes her hands with a rag.*]

LUISE [*at her tub*]. If there's grease on her hands, it's not from what she's eaten.

OLD HILSE. If we've no butter, we can eat dry bread — when we've no bread, we can eat potatoes — when there's no potatoes left, we can eat bran.

LUISE [*saucily*]. An' when that's all eaten, we'll do as the Wenglers did —

we'll find out where the skinner's buried some stinking old horse, an' we'll dig it up an' live for a week or two on rotten carrion — how nice that'll be !

GOTTLIEB [*from the other room*]. There you are, letting that tongue of yours run away with you again.

OLD HILSE. You should think twice, lass, before you talk that godless way. [*He goes to his loom, calls.*] Can you give me a hand, Gottlieb ? — there's a few threads to pull through.

LUISE [*from her tub*]. Gottlieb, you're wanted to help father.

[GOTTLIEB *comes in, and he and his father set themselves to the troublesome task of "drawing and slaying," that is, pulling the strands of the warp through the "heddles" and "reed" of the loom. They have hardly begun to do this when* HORNIG *appears in the outer room.*]

HORNIG [*at the door*]. Good luck to your work !

HILSE AND HIS SON. Thank you, Hornig.

GOTTLIEB. I say, Hornig, when do you take your sleep ? You're on your rounds all day, an' on watch all night.

HORNIG. Sleep's gone from me nowadays.

LUISE. Glad to see you, Hornig !

OLD HILSE. And what's the news?

HORNIG. It's queer news this mornin'. The weavers at Peterswaldau have taken the law into their own hands, an' chased Dreissiger an' his whole family out of the place.

LUISE [*perceptibly agitated*]. Hornig's at his lies again.

HORNIG. No, missus, not this time, not to-day. — I've some beautiful pinafores in my cart. — No, it's God's truth I'm telling you. They've sent him to the right-about. He came down to Reichenbach last night, but, Lord love you ! they dare n't take him in there, for fear of the weavers — off he had to go again, all the way to Schweinitz.

OLD HILSE. [*Has been carefully lifting threads of the web and approaching them to the holes, through which, from the other side,* GOTTLIEB *pushes a wire hook, with which he catches them and draws them through.*] It's about time you were stopping now, Hornig !

HORNIG. It 's as sure as I 'm a livin' man. Every child in the place 'll soon tell you the same story.

OLD HILSE. Either your wits are a-wool-gatherin' or mine are.

HORNIG. Not mine. What I 'm telling you 's as true as the Bible. I would n't believe it myself if I had n't stood there an' seen it with my own eyes — as I see you now, Gottlieb. They 've wrecked his house from the cellar to the roof. The good china came flyin' out at the garret windows, rattlin' down the roof. God only knows how many pieces of fustian are lying soakin' in the river! The water can't get away for them — it 's running over the banks, the color of washin'-blue with all the indigo they 've poured out at the windows — it was flyin' like clouds of sky-blue dust. Oh, it 's a terrible destruction they 've worked! And it 's not only the house — it 's the dye-works, too, — an' the stores! They 've broken the stair rails, they 've torn up the fine flooring — smashed the lookin'-glasses — cut an' hacked an' torn an' smashed the sofas an' the chairs. — It 's awful — it 's worse than war.

OLD HILSE. An' you would have me believe that my fellow weavers did all that?

[He shakes his head incredulously. Other tenants of the house have collected at the door and are listening eagerly.]

HORNIG. Who else, I 'd like to know? I could put names to every one of 'em. It was me took the sheriff through the house, an' I spoke to a whole lot of 'em, an' they answered me back quite friendly like. They did their business with little noise, but my word! they did it well. The sheriff spoke to them, and they answered him mannerly, as they always do. But there was n't no stoppin' of them. They hacked on at the beautiful furniture as if they were workin' for wages.

OLD HILSE. You took the sheriff through the house?

HORNIG. An' what would I be frightened of? Every one knows me. I 'm always turning up, like a bad penny. But no one has anything agin' me. They 're all glad to see me. Yes, I went the rounds with him, as sure as my name 's Hornig. An' you may believe me or not as you like, but my heart 's sore yet from the sight — an' I could see by the sheriff's face that he felt queer enough, too. Not a living word did we hear — they were doin' their work and holdin' their tongues. It was a solemn an' a woeful sight to see the poor starving creatures for once in a way takin' their revenge.

LUISE [with irrepressible excitement, trembling, wiping her eyes with her apron]. An' right they are! It 's only what should be!

VOICES AMONG THE CROWD AT THE DOOR. "There 's some of the same sort here." — "There 's one no farther away than across the river." — "He 's got four horses in his stable an' six carriages, an' he starves his weavers to keep them."

OLD HILSE [still incredulous]. What was it set them off?

HORNIG. Who knows? Who knows? One says this, another says that.

OLD HILSE. What do they say?

HORNIG. The story as most of them tells is that it began with Dreissiger sayin' that if the weavers were hungry they might eat grass.

[Excitement at the door, as one person repeats this to the other, with signs of indignation.]

OLD HILSE. Well, now, Hornig — if you was to say to me: Father Hilse, says you, you 'll die to-morrow, I would answer back: That may be — an' why not? You might even go to the length of saying: You 'll have a visit to-morrow from the King of Prussia. But to tell me that weavers, men like me an' my son, have done such things as that — never! I 'll never in this world believe it.

MIELCHEN. [A pretty girl of seven, with long, loose flaxen hair, carrying a basket on her arm, comes running in, holding out a silver spoon to her mother.] Mammy, mammy! look what I 've got! An' you 're to buy me a new frock with it.

LUISE. What d' you come tearing in like that for, girl? [With increased excitement and curiosity.] An' what 's that you 've got hold of now? You 've been runnin' yourself out o' breath, an' there — if the bobbins are n't in her basket yet? What 's all this about?

OLD HILSE. Mielchen, where did that spoon come from?

LUISE. She found it, maybe.

HORNIG. It's worth its seven or eight shillin's at least.

OLD HILSE [*in distressed excitement*]. Off with you, lass — out of the house this moment — unless you want a lickin'! Take that spoon back where you got it from. Out you go! Do you want to make thieves of us all, eh? I'll soon drive that out of you.

[*He looks round for something to beat her with.*]

MIELCHEN [*clinging to her mother's skirts, crying*]. No, grandfather, no! don't lick me! We — we did find them. All the other bob — bobbin . . . girls has . . . has them too.

LUISE [*half frightened, half excited*]. I was right, you see. She found it. Where did you find it, Mielchen?

MIELCHEN [*sobbing*]. At — at Peterswal — dau. We — we found them in front of — in front of Drei — Dreissiger's house.

OLD HILSE. This is worse an' worse! Get off with you this moment, unless you would like me to help you.

MOTHER HILSE. What's all the to-do about?

HORNIG. I'll tell you what, Father Hilse. The best way'll be for Gottlieb to put on his coat an' take the spoon to the police office.

OLD HILSE. Gottlieb, put on your coat.

GOTTLIEB [*pulling it on, eagerly*]. Yes, an' I'll go right in to the office an' say they're not to blame us for it, for what can a child like that understand about it? an' I brought the spoon back at once. Stop your crying now, Mielchen!

[*The crying child is taken into the opposite room by her mother, who shuts her in and comes back.*]

HORNIG. I believe it's worth as much as nine shillin's.

GOTTLIEB. Give us a cloth to wrap it in, Luise, so that it'll take no harm. To think of the thing bein' worth all that money!

[*Tears come into his eyes while he is wrapping up the spoon.*]

LUISE. If it was only ours, we could live on it for many a day.

OLD HILSE. Hurry up, now! Look sharp! As quick as ever you can. A fine state o' matters, this! Get that devil's spoon out o' the house.

[GOTTLIEB *goes off with the spoon.*]

HORNIG. I must be off now, too.

[*He goes, is seen talking to the people in the entry-room before he leaves the house.*]

SURGEON SCHMIDT. [*A jerky little ball of a man, with a red, knowing face, comes into the entry-room.*] Good-morning, all! These are fine goings on! Take care! Take care! [*Threatening with his finger.*] You're a sly lot — that's what you are. [*At* HILSE's *door without coming in.*] Morning, Father Hilse. [*To a woman in the outer room.*] And how are the pains, mother? Better, eh? Well, well. And how's all with you, Father Hilse? [*Enters.*] Why the deuce! what's the matter with mother?

LUISE. It's the eye veins, sir — they've dried up, so as she can't see at all now.

SURGEON SCHMIDT. That's from the dust and weaving by candle-light. Will you tell me what it means that all Peterswaldau's on the way here? I set off on my rounds this morning as usual, thinking no harm; but it wasn't long till I had my eyes opened. Strange doings these! What in the devil's name has taken possession of them, Hilse? They're like a pack of raging wolves. Riot — why, it's revolution! they're plundering and laying waste right and left . . . Mielchen! where's Mielchen? [MIELCHEN, *her face red with crying, is pushed in by her mother.*] Here, Mielchen, put your hand into my coat pocket. [MIELCHEN *does so.*] The ginger-bread nuts are for you. Not all at once, though, you baggage! And a song first! The fox jumped up on a . . . come, now . . . The fox jumped up . . . on a moonlight . . . Mind, I've heard what you did. You called the sparrows on the churchyard hedge a nasty name, and they're gone and told the pastor. Did any one ever hear the like? Fifteen hundred of them agog — men, women, and children. [*Distant bells are heard.*] That's at Reichenbach — alarm-bells! Fifteen hundred people! Uncomfortably like the world coming to an end!

OLD HILSE. An' is it true that they're on their way to Bielau?

SURGEON SCHMIDT. That's just what I'm telling you. I've driven through the middle of the whole crowd. What I'd have liked to do would have been to get down and give each of them a pill there and then. They were following on each other's heels like grim death, and their singing was more than enough to turn a man's stomach. I was nearly sick, and Frederick was shaking on the box like an old woman. We had to take a stiff glass at the first opportunity. I would n't be a manufacturer, not though I could drive my carriage and pair. [*Distant singing.*] Listen to that! It 's for all the world as if they were beating at some broken old boiler. We 'll have them here in five minutes, friends. Good-bye! Don't you be foolish. The troops will be upon them in no time. Keep your wits about you. The Peterswaldau people have lost theirs. [*Bells ring close at hand.*] Good gracious! There are our bells ringing too! Every one 's going mad. [*He goes upstairs.*]

GOTTLIEB. [*Comes back. In the entry-room, out of breath.*] I 've seen them, I 've seen them! [*To a woman.*] They 're here, auntie, they 're here! [*At the door.*] They 're here, father, they 're here! They 've got bean-poles, an' ox-goads, an' axes. They 're standin' outside the upper Dittrich's kickin' up an awful row. I think he 's payin' them money. O Lord! whatever 's goin' to happen? What a crowd! Oh, you never saw such a crowd! Dash it all — if once they make a rush, our manufacturers 'll be hard put to it.

OLD HILSE. What have you been runnin' like that for? You 'll go racin' till you bring on your old trouble, and then we 'll have you on your back again, strugglin' for breath.

GOTTLIEB [*almost joyously excited*]. I had to run, or they would have caught me an' kept me. They were all roarin' to me to join them. Father Baumert was there too, and says he to me: You come an' get your sixpence with the rest — you 're a poor starving weaver too. An' I was to tell you, father, from him, that you were to come an' help to pay out the manufacturers for their grindin' of us down. Other times is coming, he says. There 's going to be a change of days for us weavers. An' we 're all to come an' help to bring it about. We 're to have our half-pound of meat on Sundays, and now and again on a holiday sausage with our cabbage. Yes, things is to be quite different, by what he tells me.

OLD HILSE [*with repressed indignation*]. An' that man calls himself your godfather! and he bids you take part in such works of

wickedness? Have nothing to do with them, Gottlieb. They 've let themselves be tempted by Satan, an' it 's his works they 're doin'.

LUISE [*no longer able to restrain her passionate excitement, vehemently*]. Yes, Gottlieb, get into the chimney corner, an' take a spoon in your hand, an' a dish of skim milk on your knee, an' put on a petticoat an' say your prayers, an' then father 'll be pleased with you. And *he* sets up to be a man!

[*Laughter from the people in the entry-room.*]

OLD HILSE [*quivering with suppressed rage*]. An' you set up to be a good wife, eh? You call yourself a mother, an' let your evil tongue run away with you like that? You think yourself fit to teach your girl, you that would egg on your husband to crime an' wickedness?

LUISE [*Has lost all control of herself.*] You an' your piety an' religion — did they serve to keep the life in my poor children? In rags an' dirt they lay, all the four — it did n't as much as keep them dry. Yes! I set up to be a mother, that 's what I do — an' if you 'd like to know it, that 's why I would send all the manufacturers to hell — because I 'm a mother! — Not one of the four could I keep in life! It was cryin' more than breathin' with me from the time each poor little thing came into the world till death took pity on it. The devil a bit you cared! You sat there prayin' and singin', and let me run about till my feet bled, tryin' to get one little drop o' skim milk. How many hundred nights have I lain an' racked my head to think what I could do to cheat the churchyard of my little one? What harm has a baby like that done that it must come to such a miserable end — eh? An' over there at Dittrich's they 're bathed in wine an' washed in milk. No! you may talk as you like, but if they begin here, ten horses won't hold me back. An' what 's more — if there 's a rush on Dittrich's, you 'll see me in the forefront of it — an' pity the man as tries to prevent me — I 've stood it long enough, so now you know it.

OLD HILSE. You 're a lost soul — there 's no help for you.

LUISE [*frenzied*]. It 's you that there 's no help for! Tatter-breeched scarecrows — that 's what you are — an' not men at all

Whey-faced gutter-scrapers that take to your heels at the sound of a child's rattle. Fellows that say "thank you" to the man as gives you a hidin'. They 've not left that much blood in you as that you can turn red in the face. You should have the whip taken to you, an' a little pluck flogged into your rotten bones.   [*She goes out quickly.*]

[*Embarrassed pause.*]

MOTHER HILSE. What 's the matter with Liesl, father?

OLD HILSE. Nothin', mother! What should be the matter with her?

MOTHER HILSE. Father, is it only me that 's thinkin' it, or are the bells ringin'?

OLD HILSE. It 'll be a funeral, mother.

MOTHER HILSE. An' I 've got to sit waitin' here yet. Why must I be so long a-dyin', father?   [*Pause.*]

OLD HILSE. [*Leaves his work, holds himself up straight; solemnly.*] Gottlieb! — you heard all your wife said to us. Look here, Gottlieb! [*He bares his breast.*] Here they cut out a bullet as big as a thimble. The King knows where I lost my arm. It was n't the mice as ate it. [*He walks up and down.*] Before that wife of yours was ever thought of, I had spilled my blood by the quart for King an' country. So let her call what names she likes — an' welcome! It does me no harm. — Frightened? Me frightened? What would I be frightened of, will you tell me that? Of the few soldiers, maybe, that 'll be comin' after the rioters? Good gracious me! That would be a lot to be frightened at! No, no, lad; I may be a bit stiff in the back, but there 's some strength left in the old bones; I 've got the stuff in me yet to make a stand against a few rubbishin' bay'nets. — An' if it came to the worst! Willin', willin' would I be to say good-bye to this weary world. Death would be welcome — welcomer to me to-day than to-morrow. For what is it we leave behind? That old bundle of aches an' pains we call our body, the care an' the oppression we call by the name of life. We may be glad to get away from it. — But there 's something to come after, Gottlieb! — an' if we 've done ourselves out of that too — why, then it 's all over with us!

GOTTLIEB. Who knows what 's to come after? Nobody 's seen it.

OLD HILSE. Gottlieb! don't you be throwin' doubts on the one comfort us poor people have. Why have I sat here an' worked my treadle like a slave this forty year an' more? — sat still an' looked on at him over yonder livin' in pride an' wastefulness — why? Because I have a better hope, something as supports me in all my troubles. [*Points out at the window.*] You have your good things in this world — I 'll have mine in the next. That 's been my thought. An' I 'm that certain of it — I 'd let myself be torn in pieces. Have we not His promise? There 's a Day of Judgment coming; but it 's not us as are the judges — no: vengeance is mine, saith the Lord.

[*A cry of "Weavers, come out!" is heard outside the window.*]

OLD HILSE. Do what you will for me. [*He seats himself at his loom.*] I stay here.

GOTTLIEB [*after a short struggle*]. I 'm going to work, too, — come what may.

[*Goes out.*]

[*The Weavers' Song is heard, sung by hundreds of voices quite close at hand; it sounds like a dull monotonous wail.*]

INMATES OF THE HOUSE [*in the entry-room*]. "Oh, mercy on us! there they come swarmin' like ants!" — "Where can all these weavers be from?" — "Don't shove like that, I want to see too." — "Look at that great maypole of a woman leadin' on in front!" — "Gracious! they 're comin' thicker an' thicker."

HORNIG. [*Comes into the entry-room from outside.*] There 's a theayter play for you now! That 's what you don't see every day. But you should go up to the other Dittrich's an' look what they 've done there. It 's been no half work. He 's got no house now, nor no factory, nor no wine-cellar, nor nothing. They 're drinkin' out of the bottles — not so much as takin' the time to get out the corks. One, two, three, an' off with the neck, an' no matter whether they cut their mouths or not. There 's some of them runnin' about bleedin' like stuck pigs. — Now they 're goin' to do for this Dittrich.

[*The singing has stopped.*]

INMATES OF THE HOUSE. There 's nothin' so very wicked-like about them.

HORNIG. You wait a bit! you 'll soon see! All they 're doin' just now is makin' up their minds where they 'll begin. Look, they 're inspectin' the palace from every side. Do you see that little stout man there, him with the stable pail? That's the smith from Peterswaldau — an' a dangerous little chap he is. He batters in the thickest doors as if they were made o' pie-crust. If a manufacturer was to fall into his hands it would be all over with him!

INMATES OF THE HOUSE. "That was a crack!" — "There went a stone through the window!" — "There's old Dittrich, shakin' with fright." — "He's hangin' out a board." — "Hangin' out a board?" — "What's written on it?" — "Can you not read?" — "It would be a bad job for me if I could n't read!" — "Well, read it, then!" — "You — shall have — full — satisfaction! You — shall have full satisfaction.'"

HORNIG. He might ha' spared himself the trouble — *that* won't help him. It's something else they've set their minds on here. It's the factories. They're goin' to smash up the power-looms. For it's them that are ruinin' the hand-loom weaver. Even a blind man might see that. No! the good folks know what they're after, an' no sheriff an' no p'lice superintendent'll bring them to reason — much less a bit of a board. Him as has seen them at work already knows what's comin'.

INMATES OF THE HOUSE. "Did any one ever see such a crowd?" — "What can these ones be wantin'?" — [*Hastily.*] "They're crossin' the bridge!" — [*Anxiously.*] "They're never comin' over on this side, are they?" — [*In excitement and terror.*] "It's to us they're comin'!" — "They're comin' to us!" — "They're comin' to fetch the weavers out of their houses!"

[*General flight. The entry-room is empty. A crowd of dirty, dusty rioters rush in, their faces scarlet with brandy and excitement; tattered, untidy-looking, as if they had been up all night. With the shout: "Weavers, come out!" they disperse themselves through the house. BECKER and several other young weavers, armed with cudgels and poles, come into OLD HILSE'S room. When they see the old man at his loom they start, and cool down a little.*]

BECKER. Come, Father Hilse, stop that. Leave your work to them as wants to work. There's no need now for you to be doin' yourself harm. You'll be well taken care of.

FIRST YOUNG WEAVER. You'll never need to go hungry to bed again.

SECOND YOUNG WEAVER. The weaver's goin' to have a roof over his head and a shirt on his back once more.

OLD HILSE. An' what's the devil sendin' you to do now, with your poles an' axes?

BECKER. These are what we're goin' to break on Dittrich's back.

SECOND YOUNG WEAVER. We'll heat them red hot an' stick them down the manufacturers' throats, so as they'll feel for once what burnin' hunger tastes like.

THIRD YOUNG WEAVER. Come along, Father Hilse! We'll give no quarter.

SECOND YOUNG WEAVER. No one had mercy on us — neither God nor man. Now we're standin' up for our rights ourselves.

[OLD BAUMERT *enters, somewhat shaky on the legs, a newly killed cock under his arm.*]

OLD BAUMERT [*stretching out his arms*]. My brothers — we're all brothers! Come to my arms, brothers! [*Laughter.*]

OLD HILSE. And that's the state you're in, Willem?

OLD BAUMERT. Gustav, is it you? My poor starvin' friend! Come to my arms, Gustav!

OLD HILSE. [*Mutters.*] Let me alone.

OLD BAUMERT. I'll tell you what, Gustav. It's nothin' but luck that's wanted. You look at me. What do I look like? Luck's what's wanted. Do I not look like a lord? [*Pats his stomach.*] Guess what's in there! There's food fit for a prince in that belly. When luck's with him a man gets roast hare to eat an' champagne wine to drink. — I'll tell you all something: We've made a big mistake — we must help ourselves.

ALL [*speaking at once*]. We must help ourselves, hurrah!

OLD BAUMERT. As soon as we get the first good bite inside us we're different men. Damn it all! but you feel the power comin' into you till you're like an ox, an' that wild with strength that you hit out right an' left without as much as takin' time to look. Dash it, but it's grand!

JAEGER [*at the door, armed with an old cavalry sword*]. We've made one or two first-rate attacks.

BECKER. We know how to set about it now. One, two, three, an' we're inside the house. Then, at it like lightning — bang, crack, shiver ! till the sparks are flyin' as if it was a smithy.

FIRST YOUNG WEAVER. It would n't be half bad to light a bit o' fire.

SECOND YOUNG WEAVER. Let 's march to Reichenbach an' burn the rich folks' houses over their heads !

JAEGER. That would be nothing but butterin' their bread. Think of all the insurance money they 'd get. [Laughter.]

BECKER. No, from here we 'll go to Freiburg, to Tromtra's.

JAEGER. What would you say to givin' all them as holds Government appointments a lesson ? I 've read somewhere as how all our troubles come from them birocrats, as they call them.

SECOND YOUNG WEAVER. Before long we 'll go to Breslau, for more an' more 'll be joining us.

OLD BAUMERT. [To HILSE.] Won't you take a drop, Gustav ?

OLD HILSE. I never touches it.

OLD BAUMERT. That was in the old world; we 're in a new world to-day, Gustav.

FIRST YOUNG WEAVER. Christmas comes but once a year. [Laughter.]

OLD HILSE [impatiently]. What is it you want in my house, you limbs of Satan ?

OLD BAUMERT [a little intimidated, coaxingly]. I was bringin' you a chicken, Gustav. I thought it would make a drop o' soup for mother.

OLD HILSE [embarrassed, almost friendly]. Well, you can tell mother yourself.

MOTHER HILSE [who has been making efforts to hear, her hand at her ear, motions them off]. Let me alone. I don't want no chicken soup.

OLD HILSE. That 's right, mother. An' I want none, an' least of all that sort. An' let me say this much to you, Baumert : The devil stands on his head for joy when he hears the old ones jabberin' and talkin' as if they was infants. An' to you all I say — to every one of you : Me and you, we 've got nothing to do with each other. It 's not with my will that you 're here. In law an' justice you 've no right to be in my house.

A VOICE. Him that 's not with us is against us.

JAEGER [roughly and threateningly]. You 're a cross-grained old chap, and I 'd have you remember that we 're not thieves.

A VOICE. We 're hungry men, that 's all.

FIRST YOUNG WEAVER. We want to live — that 's all. An' so we 've cut the rope we were hung up with.

JAEGER. And we were in our right ! [Holding his fist in front of the old man's face.] Say another word, and I 'll give you one between the eyes.

BECKER. Come now, Jaeger, be quiet. Let the old man alone. — What we say to ourselves, Father Hilse, is this: Better dead than begin the old life again.

OLD HILSE. Have I not lived that life for sixty years an' more ?

BECKER. That does n't help us — there 's got to be a change.

OLD HILSE. On the Judgment Day.

BECKER. What they 'll not give us willingly we 're going to take by force.

OLD HILSE. By force. [Laughs.] You may as well go an' dig your graves at once. They 'll not be long showin' you where the force lies. Wait a bit, lad !

JAEGER. Is it the soldiers you 're meaning ? We 've been soldiers, too. We 'll soon do for a company or two of them.

OLD HILSE. With your tongues, maybe. But supposin' you did — for two that you 'd beat off, ten 'll come back.

VOICES. [Call through the window.] The soldiers are comin'! Look out !

[General, sudden silence. For a moment a faint sound of fifes and drums is heard; in the ensuing silence a short, involuntary exclamation, " The devil ! I'm off !" followed by general laughter.]

BECKER. Who was that ? Who speaks of running away ?

JAEGER. Which of you is it that 's afraid of a few paltry helmets ? You have me to command you, and I 've been in the trade. I know their tricks.

OLD HILSE. An' what are you goin' to shoot with ? Your sticks, eh ?

FIRST YOUNG WEAVER. Never mind that old chap ; he 's wrong in the upper story.

SECOND YOUNG WEAVER. Yes, he 's a bit off his head.

GOTTLIEB. [Has made his way unnoticed among the rioters ; catches hold of the speaker.] Would you give your impudence to an old man like him ?

SECOND YOUNG WEAVER. Let me alone. 'T was n't anything bad I said.

OLD HILSE [*interfering*]. Let him jaw, Gottlieb. What would you be meddlin' with him for? He'll soon see who it is that's been off his head to-day, him or me.

BECKER. Are you comin', Gottlieb?

OLD HILSE. No, he's goin' to do no such thing.

LUISE. [*Comes into the entry-room, calls.*] What are you puttin' off your time with prayin' hypocrites like them for? Come quick to where you're wanted! Quick! Father Baumert, run all you can! The Major's speakin' to the crowd from horseback. They're to go home. If you don't hurry up, it'll be all over.

JAEGER [*as he goes out*]. That's a brave husband of yours.

LUISE. Where is he? I've got no husband!

[*Some of the people in the entry-room sing.*]

Once on a time a man so small,
 Heigh-ho, heigh!
Set his heart on a wife so tall,
 Heigh diddle-di-dum-di!

WITTIG, THE SMITH. [*Comes downstairs, still carrying the stable pail; stops on his way through the entry-room.*] Come on! all of you that are not cowardly scoundrels! — hurrah!

[*He dashes out, followed by* LUISE, JAEGER, *and others, all shouting "Hurrah!"*]

BECKER. Good-bye, then, Father Hilse; we'll see each other again. [*Is going.*]

OLD HILSE. I doubt that. I've not five years to live, and that'll be the soonest you'll get out.

BECKER. [*Stops, not understanding.*] Out o' what, Father Hilse?

OLD HILSE. Out of prison — where else?

BECKER. [*Laughs wildly.*] Do you think I would mind that? There's bread to be had there anyhow! [*Goes out.*]

OLD BAUMERT. [*Has been cowering on a low stool, painfully beating his brains; he now gets up.*] It's true, Gustav, as I've had a drop too much. But for all that I know what I'm about. You think one way in this here matter; I think another. I say Becker's right: even if it ends in chains an' ropes — we'll be better off in prison than at home. You're cared for there, an' you don't need to starve. I would n't have joined them, Gustav, if I could have let it be; but once in a

lifetime a man's got to show what he feels. [*Goes slowly toward the door.*] Good-bye, Gustav. If anything happens, mind you put in a word for me in your prayers.

[*Goes out.*]

[*The rioters are now all gone. The entry-room gradually fills again with curious onlookers from the different rooms of the house.* OLD HILSE *knots at his web.* GOTTLIEB *has taken an axe from behind the stove and is unconsciously feeling its edge. He and the old man are silently agitated. The hum and roar of a great crowd penetrate into the room.*]

MOTHER HILSE. The very boards is shakin', father — what's goin' on? What's goin' to happen to us?

[*Pause.*]

OLD HILSE. Gottlieb!

GOTTLIEB. What is it?

OLD HILSE. Let that axe alone.

GOTTLIEB. Who's to split the wood, then?

[*He leans the axe against the stove.*]

[*Pause.*]

MOTHER HILSE. Gottlieb, you listen to what father says to you.

[*Some one sings outside the window.*]

Our little man does all that he can,
 Heigh-ho, heigh!
At home he cleans the pots an' the pan,
 Heigh-diddle-di-dum-di!

[*Passes on.*]

GOTTLIEB. [*Jumps up, shakes his clenched fist at the window.*] Brute that you are, would you drive me crazy?

[*A volley of musketry is heard.*]

MOTHER HILSE. [*Starts and trembles.*] Good Lord! is that thunder again?

OLD HILSE [*instinctively folding his hands*]. Oh, our Father in heaven! defend the poor weavers, protect my poor brothers!

[*A short pause ensues.*]

OLD HILSE. [*To himself, painfully agitated.*] There's blood flowing now.

GOTTLIEB. [*Had started up and grasped the axe when the shooting was heard; deathly pale, almost beside himself with excitement.*] And am I to lie to heel like a dog still?

A GIRL. [*Calls from the entry-room.*] Father Hilse, Father Hilse! get away from the window. A bullet's just flown in at ours upstairs. [*Disappears.*]

MIELCHEN. [*Puts her head in at the window, laughing.*] Gran'father, gran'father, they've shot with their guns. Two or three's been knocked down, an' one of them's turnin' round and round like a top, an' one's twistin' himself like a sparrow when its head's bein' pulled of. An' oh, if you saw all the blood that came pourin' — ! [*Disappears.*]

A WEAVER'S WIFE. Yes, there's two or three'll never get up again.

AN OLD WEAVER [*in the entry-room*]. Look out! They're goin' to make a rush on the soldiers.

A SECOND WEAVER [*wildly*]. Look, look, look at the women! — skirts up', an' spittin' in the soldiers' faces already!

A WEAVER'S WIFE. [*Calls in.*] Gottlieb, look at your wife. She's more pluck in her than you. She's jumpin' about in front o' the bay'nets as if she was dancin' to music.

[*Four men carry a wounded rioter through the entry-room. Silence, which is broken by some one saying in a distinct voice, "It's Weaver Ulbrich." Once more silence for a few seconds, when the same voice is heard again: "It's all over with him; he's got a bullet in his ear." The men are heard climbing the wooden stair. Sudden shouting outside: "Hurrah, hurrah !"*]

VOICES IN THE ENTRY-ROOM. "Where did they get the stones from?" — "Yes, it's time you were off !" — "From the new road." — "Ta-ta, soldiers !" — "It's raining paving-stones."

[*Shrieks of terror and loud roaring outside, taken up by those in the entry-room. There is a cry of fear, and the house door is shut with a bang.*]

VOICES IN THE ENTRY-ROOM. "They're loading again." — "They'll fire another vol-

ley this minute." — "Father Hilse, get away from that window."

GOTTLIEB. [*Clutches the axe.*] What! are we mad dogs? Are we to eat powder an' shot now instead of bread? [*Hesitating instant: to the old man.*] Would you have me sit here an' see my wife shot? Never! [*As he rushes out.*] Look out! I'm coming!

OLD HILSE. Gottlieb, Gottlieb!

MOTHER HILSE. Where's Gottlieb gone?

OLD HILSE. He's gone to the devil.

VOICES FROM THE ENTRY-ROOM. Go away from the window, Father Hilse.

OLD HILSE. Not I! Not if you all go crazy together! [*To MOTHER HILSE, with rapt excitement.*] My heavenly Father has placed me here. Is n't that so, mother? Here we'll sit, an' do our bounden duty — ay, though the snow was to go on fire.

[*He begins to weave.*]

[*Rattle of another volley. OLD HILSE mortally wounded, starts to his feet and then falls forward over the loom. At the same moment loud shouting of "Hurrah !" is heard. The people who till now have been standing in the entry-room dash out, joining in the cry. The old woman repeatedly asks: "Father, father, what's wrong with you?" The continued shouting dies away gradually in the distance. MIELCHEN comes rushing in.*]

MIELCHEN. Gran'father, gran'father, they're drivin' the soldiers out of the village; they've got into Dittrich's house, an' they're doin' what they did at Dreissiger's. Gran'father !

[*The child grows frightened, notices that something has happened, puts her finger in her mouth, and goes up cautiously to the dead man.*]

Gran'father !

MOTHER HILSE. Come now, father, can't you say something? You're frightenin' me.

THE VALE OF CONTENT

DAS GLÜCK IM WINKEL

A DRAMA IN THREE ACTS

By HERMANN SUDERMANN

Translated by WILLIAM ELLERY LEONARD

DRAMATIS PERSONÆ

WIEDEMANN, *Principal of an intermediate school of a township*

ELIZABETH, *his second wife*

HELENE,
FRITZ, } *his children by his first wife*
EMIL,

FREIHERR VON ROECKNITZ, *of Witzlingen*

BETTINA, *his wife*

DOCTOR ORB, *School Inspector of the district*

FRAU ORB

DANGEL, *second teacher*

FRÄULEIN GOEHRE, *woman teacher*

ROSA, *maid at the Wiedemanns'*

Place — *A small district seat in North Germany*
Time — *The present*

THE VALE OF CONTENT

ACT I

The School Principal's farmyard.
To the left the dwelling-house with a veranda, and with a wing that extends at right angles into the scene. A large linden, in the shadow of which stands a white-covered table with chairs. To the right the gable-end of the schoolhouse; before it gymnastic apparatus, toward the yard and the footlights, inclosed by a low picket-fence. In the house a door. In the background a stable, with farm apparatus, wagons, etc., in front. A picket-gate leads out to the street beyond.

To the left, at the table, are seated ELIZABETH *and* HELENE, *busied with woman's work,* ELIZABETH *with embroidery,* HELENE *with knitting. From the schoolhouse is heard an anthem, sung by the children in two voices, accompanied by a violin, and now and then by a powerful male voice.*

HELENE. How fine papa sings to-day.

ELIZABETH. I've noticed it, too, my child.

HELENE. Often now he has a something — something glad in his voice. Again and again it seems as if he wanted to thank the dear God for something — and with such a full heart. [*Tenderly.*] And I know, too, what for. . . . Mamma, don't scold me; I've lost my ball of yarn.

ELIZABETH. I'll pick it up, darling.
[*Lays down her work.*]

HELENE. If I should feel along the ground, I could find it well enough, but then I'm always sure to unravel it. . . . Thank you, thank you, mamma. But why are n't they singing any more?

ELIZABETH. Why, you know to-day he's going to explain the notes to the little tots.

HELENE. Oh, yes, so he is. . . . Herr Dangel wanted to explain them to me, too, the other day, but I did n't comprehend them a bit. . . . As a child I was really stupid at them. I used to think the notes were round little angels, sitting on a long fence and beating their wings. The sixteenth notes very fast, and the half very slow. . . . And I'm still the same. . . . Anyway, Herr Dangel is taking an awful lot of trouble with me. That's probably because he intends to become a teacher of the blind, and so he's practicing on me. . . . Yesterday he had on a coat that felt as soft as clouds. . . . But listen, mamma.

ELIZABETH. What is it, darling?

HELENE. Papa's laughing . . . papa's so happy. . . . Do you know, too, why? Now guess.

ELIZABETH [*smiling*]. M—m, because — his rape has been growing so well.

HELENE. No.

ELIZABETH. Or because he got first prize at the bee-show.

HELENE. Oh, no.

ELIZABETH [*smiling*]. Then, I don't know, I'm sure.

HELENE. Because he has you . . . because he has you! . . . And I'm so happy, too, because I have you! During the three years that you've been here, it's all the time like harps in the house. . . . There's music in every corner. . . . Oh, when I think of the times before you were here, oh, how dreadful it all was! . . . the youngsters so naughty — and papa so sullen — and I everywhere in the way. . . . Here a cuff . . . and soon another cuff. . . . And now how good the youngsters are to me. . . . And my first mamma, she was always so sad. And she was always weeping to strangers about me. . . . And that made me so sorry.

ELIZABETH. Let that rest, my child; that's a long time ago.

HELENE. Dear, dear, what if you had n't come . . . what if you had n't . . .
[*Noise to the right.*]

ELIZABETH. Listen, listen! Is n't that Herr Dangel's class?

HELENE [*nodding*]. Hm! . . . Mamma, do you suppose he'll come to take leave?

ELIZABETH [*smiling*]. Why, he usually does, my child; and he'll surely —

HELENE. Do you hear? There he is! Oh, he has such a melodious step.

[DANGEL *comes out of the schoolhouse.*]

DANGEL. [*With blond and very youthful full beard,—somewhat narrow-chested—gray coat, too tight.*] Good afternoon, Frau Wiedemann. I only wanted to —

ELIZABETH. Well, did things go hard to-day, Herr Dangel?

DANGEL. I find things never really hard enough, Frau Wiedemann. When I reflect how little we do and —

HELENE [*interrupting*]. How much our Lord Jesus does — you mean?

ELIZABETH. Well, every one has his own field of influence, Herr Dangel.

DANGEL. And to have to say to one's self: Perhaps thou failest even there.

ELIZABETH. Well, you 'll soon be having a harder one.

HELENE [*eagerly*]. When are you going away, Herr Dangel?

DANGEL. I don't know, Fräulein Helene. I 've applied to School Inspector Orb and told him that I 'm at the service of the Institutes for the Blind and ready to take any and every examination.

ELIZABETH. Will that succeed?

DANGEL. Whatever I will succeeds, Frau Wiedemann.

ELIZABETH [*with warning finger*]. Tut, tut, not too chesty.

DANGEL. Oh, Frau Wiedemann, you 're such a highly respected, motherly friend to me —

HELENE. Pooh! Herr Dangel! Such a big son! I think mamma would rather be excused.

ELIZABETH. Call me so, if you will, Herr Dangel.

DANGEL. But you must n't be always humbling me.

ELIZABETH [*calm, almost serene*]. If nobody else does, life itself humbles us, my good friend.

DANGEL. You say that so bitterly.

ELIZABETH. Why bitterly? I say it, because it 's so.

HELENE [*listening at something*]. Mamma!
[*Points to the rear.*]

ELIZABETH. Who 's coming there?

HELENE. School Inspector Orb.

ELIZABETH. Do you recognize him, too?

HELENE. Why, I recognize every one.

DANGEL. Good-bye, then, Frau Wiedemann. [*Attempts to hasten off.*]

[DOCTOR ORB *enters from the street.*]

ORB [*benignantly*]. Now, now, my young friend, am I then so dreaded that at my mere appearance you take to your heels?

DANGEL. Oh, not in the least dreaded, Herr Inspector.

ORB. But also not beloved — eh?
[DANGEL *is silent with embarrassment.*]

ELIZABETH [*coming to his rescue*]. Shyness before such a mighty man, Herr School-Inspector-of-the-District, you must reckon to the credit of us poor souls. And by the way, how do you do? [*Extends her hand.*]

ORB. How do you do, Frau Principal — How do you do, Fräulein Hel—bah! I declare, there 's another running away from me. [HELENE *disappears into the house.*]

ELIZABETH [*smiling*]. Well, she 's running for a fact because she 's afraid.

ORB. The poor child! And, my friend, we 'll talk over later your philanthropic plans for the blind. I 'm expecting any day the decision of the provincial school board.
[*Extends his hand.*]

DANGEL. I would be, indeed, so happy, if —

ORB [*formally*]. As I said, we 'll talk later. [*Exit DANGEL, bowing.*]

ORB. This increasing ardor of the young man gives me an idea; has something been brewing?

ELIZABETH [*dryly*]. Perhaps.

ORB. Hm! [*They sit.*] And you permit that?

ELIZABETH. Yes.

ORB. Mm . . . cool!

ELIZABETH. Oh, no. But let 's leave that. The affair will be subject to the judgment of the board of control only after some years. In the mean time the chief parties themselves don't know anything about it as yet.

ORB. Do you know, Frau Principal, that I admire you?

ELIZABETH. Now, that 's very nice of you.

ORB. So calm — so full of plans — so sure of your own affairs. . . . The only thing I don't understand is that you 've been able to adapt yourself to these petty conditions — for which — frankly — you 're too good.

ELIZABETH. Did n't you want to speak with my husband?

ORB. I wanted to, for a fact, but I hear with regret that he's still holding recitations. [*Looks at his watch.*] Half past four. Is he keeping them in for punishment?

ELIZABETH. Oh, no, thank goodness, my husband has n't much to punish.

ORB. Yes, he accomplishes much with kindness. I've observed that. An extraordinary man. Too bad, too bad! . . . Why should this man, who, just as much as any of us was called to a higher career, suffer shipwreck on his way. . . . Now, there are so many people, and no more gifted than he, who pass the higher examinations easily. And yet he must make shift with this position, at best so inferior. Too bad, as I said, altogether too bad!

ELIZABETH. Herr Inspector, do you suppose it amuses me to hear such talk about my husband?

ORB. Come, now, come, I'm assuming that we two, as his best friends and well-wishers, we've surely a right to converse about his luck.

ELIZABETH. About his luck, yes — about his lack, no.

ORB. Well, as to his luck, my dear madame, we would have to talk about — you.

ELIZABETH. You are really too kind, Herr Doctor.

ORB. Ah, men of our walk follow a world of human life through the most diverse phases of development. . . . To be sure, I've not been here long, but — let's see — did you know him in the days when he was a family tutor at Witzlingen?

ELIZABETH. Oh, no.

ORB. But it was at Witzlingen manor house that you made his acquaintance?

ELIZABETH. Very true. . . . Only fifteen years later. His pupils certainly had to have time to grow up and marry, for I came, you know, first to Witzlingen as the friend of Frau von Roecknitz.

ORB. Ah, so it was. . . . Besides, it was very creditable to the Herr Baron; I'd heard him variously well spoken of, as an influential and brilliant personality, but really I'd never suspected so much gratitude and loyalty.

ELIZABETH. How so?

ORB. Why, in maintaining so genuinely his associations with his former tutor . . . that's not usually the way with grand gentlemen. But, Frau Principal, when you came here, out of the splendor of the house of Roecknitz, out of the circles of gentlefolk and culture —

ELIZABETH [*rising*]. I hope, Herr Inspector, that in this house you will have to lack neither for gentility nor for culture.

[*To the left a noise of school-children going home.*]

ORB. Oh, as to that I've never doubted — I only meant —

ELIZABETH. Pardon; see, there is my husband.

[WIEDEMANN *comes from the school with a bundle of exercise-books under his arm.*]

WIEDEMANN. Ah, Herr Inspector Orb . . . at such an unexpected moment. . . . If I'd had any inkling, I'd have had the children at least sing a closing anthem.

ELIZABETH [*turning around as she leaves*]. Pardon, but would you drink a cup of coffee with us, Herr Doctor?

ORB. Very kind of you . . . you know my notions in these matters are pretty strict ; — but, as I'm here this time unprofessionally, I may, in lieu of the lacking anthem . . . [*Makes a bow.*]

WIEDEMANN. I beg you, Herr School Inspector, — I have them sing it regularly; only because to-day it was already so —

ELIZABETH [*stroking her husband's arm*]. Well, is it going to cost him his head, Herr Doctor?

ORB [*with deprecating smile*]. Ah!

ELIZABETH. Shall I take the exercise-books along?

WIEDEMANN. Please be so good, dear.

ELIZABETH. So, auf wiedersehen.

[*Goes in through the veranda.*]

ORB [*sitting down, after she has disappeared*]. On the contrary, my dear Principal, if I may use this opportunity to allow myself a small friendly observation, I am much more inclined to warn you against a certain — over-zealousness.

WIEDEMANN. How? Have I — ?

ORB. You have not . . . indeed not at all. . . . Understand me rightly. But there can be too much of a good thing. . . . Four o'clock is the prescribed hour for closing. The children are needed at home. The distance is in some cases long. The Superintendent was saying to me only the other day, Wiedemann's pupils have a sort of haggard look.

WIEDEMANN. Is that the judgment of the Herr Superintendent about me?

ORB. Oh, no, he merely let it fall in passing.

WIEDEMANN. I am a father to my pupils, Herr School Inspector. [EMIL *and* FRITZ *bob up by the schoolhouse, and are about to shy back.*] Everybody knows that. . . . Look, there come my two youngsters — tut, come here, youngsters. . . . The Herr School Inspector won't hurt you. . . . [*Softer.*] Look you, every one loves his own flesh and blood best; that's a matter of course, and it's sheer cant for any one to argue to the contrary — but you'll find that the last boy on the last seat goes home feeling he's just as dear to me as these here.

ORB. Oh, I'm convinced of that, — quite convinced. . . . And I did n't intend, either, to — How'do, youngsters, studying hard?

FRITZ. Yes, sir, I'm studying Greek, too, now.

ORB. Ah!

FRITZ. By next Michaelmas I'll be to the *mi*-verbs —

ORB. Ei, ei, ei. And you? What can you do?

EMIL. I can do any day what Fritz can.

ORB. So? And when will you be going to the Gymnasium?

EMIL. Father says he does n't know yet.

WIEDEMANN. I intend to carry them as far as Unter-Secunda myself, Herr School Inspector. They've been too long without a mother for me to withdraw them from a mother's influence yet. . . . So, now make your bows to the Herr Inspector.

FRITZ. Father, can we go down to the market-place a little while?

WIEDEMANN. Why, what's there?

EMIL. 'S a man come to the horse-fair with a cemul.

ORB. We say "a camel," my son.

EMIL. Yes, sir, a ca-ame-el.

WIEDEMANN. First ask mother.

[*Exeunt* FRITZ *and* EMIL.]

ORB. After all, you are really in enviable circumstances, my dear Principal. About to send two sons to the higher schools. Not many teachers can afford that.

WIEDEMANN. To be perfectly frank, Herr School Inspector, our fortune is the school land which we farm ourselves. For-

merly, you know, I leased it out. But my wife, who grew up in a country home, longed for agricultural work, and under her blessed hands the little enterprise is thriving so famously.

ORB. Now that's all very well and fine, and I congratulate you heartily; but you yourself, my very dear Principal, don't you feel to a degree — uh — distracted?

WIEDEMANN. Di — dis — ?

ORB. I mean by that, a man, you see, must give his undivided attention to his profession — really, he must — uh —

WIEDEMANN. Well, now I'm *quite* at sea —

ELIZABETH. [*Comes with the coffee-tray through the door, with an air of superior gayety.*] Well, Herr School Inspector, are you nagging again a bit?

WIEDEMANN. Why, Elizabeth!

ORB. Mm! Mm!

ELIZABETH. I'd like to ask you one favor, dear Doctor; leave my husband in peace — he's doing his duty.

WIEDEMANN. I do my duty, to be sure. But, Elizabeth, dear, you must n't say so.

ELIZABETH. Cup of coffee, Doctor?

ORB. Oh, thank you — very kind.

[*Helps himself. Exit* ELIZABETH.]

WIEDEMANN. I beseech you most earnestly, Herr School Inspector, not to count that against my wife. She is still in entire ignorance how the —

ORB. You don't smoke?

WIEDEMANN. No, I don't smoke — but permit me — [*Starts to rise.*]

ORB. I beg you, — I have my own. [*Draws out his cigar-case.*] Look you, my good friend, that's also a matter we'll have to talk over some time. Your partner comes from the manor house of Roecknitz, which by hearsay we all know and prize so, even though we've not all had the advantage of frequenting it — by the way, if the opportunity offers, you might make me acquainted with the Baron. I understand you're still on friendly terms?

WIEDEMANN. Friendly terms — that is —

ORB. Oh, well, well, — but he calls on you, does n't he?

WIEDEMANN. The Baron and his lady have n't been here for a good while.

ORB. But won't he be coming to to-morrow's horse-fair? One would suppose —

WIEDEMANN. It's not impossible — perhaps even probable. In short, I'm sure I don't know.

ORB. Now, what was it I was going to say? Oh, your wife has been accustomed at the Witzlingen manor house to a nonchalant, rather patronizing tone which truly does n't altogether fit her present situation. You heard yourself just now . . . that will never do . . . that is, I don't mean to blame her, for, thank Heaven, there was n't any one else of the teaching staff [*looks about him*] around. But now, tell me, my very dear friend ; in a word, how did you happen upon the idea of — a young woman of such pretensions, who played a part in society — why, that is really a puzzle. . . . How did it happen? Did somebody give you encouragement? . . . Have you something or other — somehow or other —

WIEDEMANN. Herr Inspector Orb, if this question is not perhaps of a professional character —

ORB. But, my dear friend, how can you ascribe a dictated interest to my purely human good will — how —

ELIZABETH [*who has been standing some minutes in the open door*]. Well, then, Herr Inspector, permit me, instead of my husband, to be responsible for the answer you seem so exceedingly to desire. . . . Look you . . . I was an orphan . . . and poor, and from my twelfth year bandied about among my fashionable relations. Fetched from the railway station, shipped back to the station — nothing but unclaimed goods. Oh, it 's then one begins to long for a protector. I was so weary and broken that in the end I wanted, oh, merely some still little nook where I could serve and labor in peace. And if I 'd had to filch my happiness and rend it even from high heaven, I would have done so — and would have bundled it off in secret into my nook and set it down before me — like a magpie with his shining trinket. And if I 'd stolen it a thousand times over — my little happiness — and if a thousand times over I don't belong here, yet here I 'll stand on guard before it, and spread my arms out over it, and he who would touch it will have to step across my body. . . . So, Herr School Inspector, — and if you still desire to know more, ask me, just ask me — I 'm at your service.

ORB. But, my most honored friend, I don't know why you are so excited.

ELIZABETH. Oh, I 'm not excited.

ORB. I came as a friend, as a sympathetic friend, as a well-wishing friend — and there was nothing I more desired than to be a humble witness of your happiness.

[*Takes hat and cane.*]

ELIZABETH. Are you going so soon?

ORB. Unfortunately, my time, — my dear Principal, I leave you with the greatest admiration [*with an attempt to jest*], and if I were n't a good, Christian father of a family, I verily believe I 'd be envious.

[*Toward the rear with a bow, accompanied by the Principal.* ELIZABETH *walks thoughtfully back and forth.* WIEDEMANN *comes back and sinks, as if exhausted, into a chair.*]

ELIZABETH. What is it, Georg? Why, you 're all . . . Shall I bring you your medicine, dear? [*He shakes his head ; she remains by him standing and stroking his hair.*] They 've got to leave us in peace. . . . What do they want of us? We 're not hurting a soul. . . . We only ask that they leave us in peace.

WIEDEMANN. Yes, yes. What must be, comes.

ELIZABETH. What comes? What must? [WIEDEMANN *shakes his head.*]

ELIZABETH. Now, dear, don't make me coax ; speak one little word.

WIEDEMANN. They begrudge it us.

ELIZABETH. Begrudge what?

WIEDEMANN. Our happiness.

ELIZABETH [*reflectively*]. Our happiness!

WIEDEMANN. No, no, — forgive me ! I mean, mine, *mine* . . . altogether selfishly, only *my* happiness. . . . For you — oh, thanks for all. . . . You 've been speaking out for us warmly, splendidly. . . . And you mean it, too, — indeed, you do. . . . Rather — you try to force yourself to mean it. . . . Yet, for all that, you must find life here one continual penance. Such a visitor as this fellow who 's just gone ! What secret contempt you must feel.

ELIZABETH. Dear, you know I never feel contempt.

WIEDEMANN. They all ask me : How could you dare — how could you dare to do it, fellow ? And do you see, Elizabeth, I could n't have dared, indeed not . . . for, after all, what was I ? The reduced scholar without his degree, the poor schoolmaster, the widower no longer young, with three children and one of them a cripple. I had merely looked up at you, shyly as at one in a higher sphere, and at your sorrowful eyes . . . for I was only tolerated among the guests at Witzlingen. . . . Had that night not come in the manor garden, where I met you weeping behind the Neptune grotto and where your dear heart told me of its loneliness —

ELIZABETH. How nobly you gave me courage there. Dear man that you are.

WIEDEMANN. See, from then on, I conceived I might . . . for, after all, the happiness that's fused from a twofold unhappiness holds the firmest. . . . But my hopes never mounted as high as this. . . . I thought only: It lasts as long as it lasts . . . she needs help . . . she'll get strong again in a quiet retreat. . . . And then in Heaven's name I will have her shake the dust of my house from her feet. And if I have her only a year to myself — that will be more than enough for a whole lifetime. . . . And now it's already going on three years. . . . And that seems to me more and more a crime against you.

ELIZABETH. See, Georg, dear, you all make the same mistake, you and all of you here — even the sniff-nose who just went: you all take me for something quite uncommon. But I'm nothing uncommon. . . . I'm no princess bewitched. . . . I'm quite an ordinary mortal: and where I used to live they knew it well enough.

WIEDEMANN. You're wrong there. . . . They were all raving about you — the women and the men.

ELIZABETH [with bitter smile]. Oh, yes, especially the men. [As he flinches slightly.] What's the matter, Georg?

WIEDEMANN. With me? — Nothing.

ELIZABETH. Now and then you seem to be hiding something from me.

WIEDEMANN. Tell me, are you hiding nothing from me?

ELIZABETH. Dearest friend, you remember: trust for trust. You said to me: "If you will be mine, dearest, — or perhaps you had n't begun to say 'dearest' then, — you need explain me nothing, dear lady, and let the past be buried. I'm begging the same for myself." . . . Did n't you say just that?

WIEDEMANN. Oh, don't remind me.

ELIZABETH. Why not?

WIEDEMANN. Good Heavens, what was I to do? To belch up all that I'd swallowed for such a long time? — all the humbling and humiliation and self-degradation — there would have been surely no sense in that. I would have won the fight for daily bread, that's certain enough — for you may be sure of one thing: I was never without earnestness.

ELIZABETH [smiling]. There's nothing I'm quite so sure of.

WIEDEMANN. But harder and harder grew the fight with my own dull and weary brain. . . . When the whole world cries out at you, every comrade that outstrips you, every fop that tries his wit on you, every bright and successful fellow whose questions balk you, when everybody cries: "It's brains that count, brains that count" . . . and you feel that you've come to the end of your rope, your mind has lost its spring in the long struggle. . . . And then when all private-tutordom has patched up with much good sweat a passable examination for a job in the intermediate schools . . . merely to have at last a roof on his head . . . for such a poor devil is sure to have a girl waiting for him, besides.

ELIZABETH. Let the girl rest, Georg. . . . We'll put a wreath on her grave — and so, enough.

WIEDEMANN. All right — I'll let her rest. . . . But should I have repeated to you all the wretched business? No, Elizabeth, that would have been suicide. The little respect you cherished toward me, — I had to guard that at least. But now that I have you, dear, and happiness has really come to this little nook, with you here, now that I've learned again a little cheerfulness, I can't get rid of the dread of losing it all again.

ELIZABETH. But, Georg, who is to take it from you?

WIEDEMANN. I don't know. . . . But what must happen, happens. For, you see, it does n't belong to me at all. . . . Why, I've stolen it. . . . Everybody has the same feeling and — [hesitating, uneasy] — I have it, too.

ELIZABETH. Stolen it from whom? Georg, stop and think, from whom?

WIEDEMANN. That's not so easy to say

I 'd have to be clearer about much in you and in me. . . . But just now, as you mentioned the magpie carrying its shining trinket into the nook, every limb of my body began to burn, on fire with —

[HELENE *appears on the veranda.*]

ELIZABETH. Sh-sh ! . . . What is it, my darling !

HELENE. Mamma, Rosa wants to know where to set the table for supper.

ELIZABETH. Come here, Lenchen.

HELENE. What do you want, mamma ?

ELIZABETH [*taking her hand*]. Give papa a kiss and tell him that he 's plaguing himself foolishly, and how we all love him so.

HELENE [*stroking his cheek*]. Papa, yes — lots and lots, papa.

WIEDEMANN. And you tell mamma, Lenchen child, how it used to be here and how we will thank her to the last —

EMIL AND FRITZ [*storming into the yard, pell-mell*]. Mamma, papa, oh, to think ! — Uncle Roecknitz and Aunt Bettina are here !

WIEDEMANN. Ah, but that 's good news ! Is n't it, Elizabeth ?

ELIZABETH [*quietly*]. Certainly. I 'm always glad when Bettina comes.

EMIL. Oh, to think ! — Uncle Roecknitz has brought along nine horses — three sorrels — and a black with a white spot and white feet — and two grays — and —

FRITZ. No, only one gray; the other was a dappled gray.

EMIL. Mamma, he thinks I don't know a dappled gray.

WIEDEMANN. And where did you meet them ?

FRITZ. Before the Black Eagle Inn. They were just coming out — over to us — Uncle Roecknitz was just as awfully funny as ever. " Run on home ahead and make a racket," that 's what he said.

EMIL. " The point is to make a racket," that 's what he said.

WIEDEMANN. That 's just like him. The wild boy — that 's the way he was, Elizabeth.

ELIZABETH [*agreeing.*] Mm !

HELENE. Mamma, what ails you ?

ELIZABETH. Nothing, my darling.

[*Enter the* FREIHERR VON ROECKNITZ *and* BETTINA.]

EMIL AND FRITZ [*going toward them*]. Hurrah, Uncle Roecknitz !

ROECKNITZ. Come, forward ! forward ! Scream, you rascals ! Well, what 's up ?

FRITZ AND EMIL [*louder*]. Hurrah ! !

ROECKNITZ. That 's it ! [*Extending his hand to* WIEDEMANN, *while* ELIZABETH *and* BETTINA *are embracing.*] Well, then, how are you, my lord and master ?

WIEDEMANN. Very well, thank you, my old friend Roecknitz. And you ?

ROECKNITZ. Oh, you know, you know, one swindles his way along — so-so — Keep still, youngsters, keep still there ! — first comes mamma. . . . What the devil, Frau Elizabeth ! — ta-ta — you need n't be afraid, — my demonstrations of regard I 'll keep to myself . . . [*Kisses her hand.*] It would be too easy to singe my mouth.

EMIL. Why would he singe his mouth, papa ?

WIEDEMANN. Uncle Roecknitz is joking.

ELIZABETH. What lodgings have you, Bettina ?

BETTINA. [*Smiles as she shrugs her shoulders.*] Ach, my dearest Elizabeth, God bless any one who 'll put at our disposal even a cast-off dog kennel.

WIEDEMANN. Won't you make an exception, then, and for this once accept our —

ELIZABETH [*hurriedly breaking in*]. Why, but you know, Georg, much as we 'd. . . . Oh, it could be arranged for Bettina, easily enough — but —

WIEDEMANN. I don't comprehend you, Elizabeth. As for me, at a pinch I can go over to the schoolhouse.

ROECKNITZ. My pretty housewife, cross your heart ! Does n't there lurk just a grain of unwillingness in this ?

BETTINA. Elizabeth fosters no unwillingness toward us, Alfred. . . . Do you, my love ?

ELIZABETH. It 's likely you know that best, Bettina.

ROECKNITZ. Good ; then matters would be straightened out, after all. Why should n't he go to the schoolhouse. Even if we are n't invited, we 'll accept with thanks. . . . And you youngsters, run now, quick, over to the Black Eagle and tell my stable-boy, August, where we are. He 'll manage the rest himself. For you know August, with his red Turk's fez, don't you ?

FRITZ. Why, August is a friend of mine.

EMIL. He showed me his watch, too. He did n't show it to Fritz.

ROECKNITZ. So. Well, then, perhaps he confided to you besides where he stole it! The fellow's a sad dog, for a fact, but quite indispensable with the horses. [*To the youngsters.*] Come, use your legs! [*Exeunt* FRITZ *and* EMIL.] Yes, sir, I and my August — we're the only two people left who understand anything about horses. And by the way, Elizabeth, you yourself used to be rather knowing. Something might have been made of you, sooner or later.

ELIZABETH [*smiling*]. But yet I would never have got so far as stable-boy.

ROECKNITZ. Too bad, too bad. There are people who botch their destiny right in the bud. . . . Don't they, my old Doctor that was to be? Oh, you, you indeed befool and mock us all.

WIEDEMANN. I rather think I have n't much talent for mockery, dear Roecknitz.

ROECKNITZ. A man with such a wife, he has talent for anything. . . . Hello — what's hiding there behind that tree? There's something hiding there, still as a mouse, behind that tree.

BETTINA [*hastening toward* HELENE]. Lenchen, since when have you grown so shy?

HELENE [*flying into her arms*]. Dear, dear Aunt Bettina.

ROECKNITZ. Well, and don't I get a kiss, too?

[HELENE *goes slowly up to him and begins to offer him her brow, then turns suddenly around and feels her way hastily into the house, stumbling on the steps.*]

ELIZABETH. Lenchen!

WIEDEMANN. What ails the child?

ROECKNITZ. Little girls grow into young ladies — that's all.

ELIZABETH. Excuse me, Bettina, dear, only I'll have to see what —

BETTINA. Take me along, sweetheart; I'm tired.

ROECKNITZ [*tapping her cheek idly*]. Yes, take her along. I've talked her to death.

ELIZABETH. We'll revive her for you. Auf wiedersehen.

ROECKNITZ. Auf wiedersehen, pretty housewife! [*Both women go into the house.*] [*Staring after the ladies.*] Do you know, Wiedemann, she's grown even more beautiful, since she's your wife. The grace with which she went up the steps . . . and my wife beside her! . . . Tell me, man; have you the least idea what you've got there?

WIEDEMANN. I believe so, Roecknitz.

ROECKNITZ [*doubtfully*]. Well, well! . . . yes . . . yes, yes . . . Well, and, for the rest, how goes the noble schoolmaster business? Still as gayly? A god-forsaken job. . . . In Siberia — round the corner over yonder to the left — there's an arsenic-pit. . . . People have often been seen going in, but no one ever yet came out . . . That's about my notion of school-teaching. [WIEDEMANN *clucks smilingly with his tongue.*] Nix! these brats! . . . Lay a train of powder under 'em and blow 'em up, — that would be my pedagogy. . . . And I was the wildest of all — eh?

WIEDEMANN. Well, and that's why you've become such a top-notcher, too.

ROECKNITZ. Oh, yes, — so they say. At least things have to buzz with me. When I can't drudge, I'm up to fool's pranks . . . for I tell you, the women, how they get a fellow into hot water! Thus I've gone in for drudgery. Since you were last at Witzlingen, I've drained sixty acres of meadow — I've doubled the productive area of the lowlands — I've introduced goat-breeding — I've delivered thirty-two head of cavalry horses — I've bought a portable railway for carting off sugar-beets. I'm renting them out one after the other to the neighbors and making a pile of money at it. For I'm a divil of a chap and everything comes my way.

WIEDEMANN [*beaming*]. Yes, yes, Roecknitz — a man like you — such a masterly nature — it's good merely to stand by and see it spread its wings.

ROECKNITZ. You mean by that, to see it thrashing around, eh! — Tut, never mind . . . By the way, old chap, your school land, — my compliments! . . . Just now as I was driving by, I said to my wife: "Dear, we could n't do it better ourselves" . . . the grass-fodder and the vegetables . . .

WIEDEMANN. Ah, but you just ought to see my rape.

ROECKNITZ. And the like of that is only a schoolmaster! the like of that plies the ruler!

WIEDEMANN [*smiling*]. Or sometimes even the violin bow.

ROECKNITZ. And the way everything

looks around the yard here . . . the wagons and the dung-heap . . . just like a guest chamber. . . . Man, why did n't you let your gifts be known sooner ? . . . Why, my father would never have let you out of the house. . . . We 'd have wrapped you in cotton-batting, — tell you that !

WIEDEMANN. But I 've explained already, dear Roecknitz, that most of all this is the work of my wife.

ROECKNITZ. Yes, and now, your wife ! now, your wife ! Look here, don't I know women ! And I know your wife, too ! — of my wife's friends I know her perhaps the best of all. . . . And I can assure you of one thing, old man : She 's not at all happy here.

WIEDEMANN. Roecknitz, you believe that ? — you believe that, too — ?

ROECKNITZ. Why, now, I fancy that 's clear enough.

WIEDEMANN [looking about him, softly]. It 's true she 's never complained ; she goes her ways calmly and apparently joyously. . . . She looks like happiness itself. . . . And I 'd do anything for her. . . . I 'd lay my very hands under her footsteps. . . . But how am I to change things here ?

ROECKNITZ. Just wait — just let me. . . . Be perfectly calm . . . you 're a substantial fellow — always were — a little heavy, but reliable to the last ditch. . . . So — now they want to elect me for the Reichstag. . . . Lord, why not, then ? With so many little sticks there, there 's always room for a bigger. If I only had the palest shimmer who could manage things on the place. . . . My wife 's a good creature, surely, but enough, one must n't cast reflections on the ladies. . . . So, as I was saying, I need a man on whom I can rely blindly — a man of genius — a man of character — and the thought struck me that perhaps I could hack your wretched schoolmaster legs out of the ice.

WIEDEMANN. So I 'm this man of genius ?

ROECKNITZ. We 'll arrange matters thus : that you may feel independent, you take one of my farms on lease or on commission — or any way you will, and meanwhile you keep an eye on all the rest. . . . Rather a clever scheme, eh !

WIEDEMANN. My dear friend, now that 's only another of your wild ideas.

ROECKNITZ. How so, then ?

WIEDEMANN. I 'm no agriculturalist — I 'm a schoolmaster. . . . I studied languages and by dint of digging I 've got as far as the principalship of the three grades of an intermediate school in a township. That 's not a brilliant position, but I 'm an unpretending man and I 'm happy in it.

ROECKNITZ. And your wife ?

WIEDEMANN [startled, without spirit]. Yes, my wife.

ROECKNITZ. This very minute you avow to me that you 'd do anything under heaven to alter this existence here ; and now, when I give you the chance, you shrink back afraid. Have you no fear that she 'll inevitably pine away in this shopkeeper atmosphere, when she won't even pass muster with madame, the District Judge's wife, and with madame, the Doctor's ? . . . If you don't know it, old man, your wife has in her nature the most remarkable mixture possible to a human temperament : she is at once kind-hearted and proud. . . . But take care what will become of her kind-heartedness if day in and day out her pride is trodden under foot.

WIEDEMANN. Oh, if you knew how near right you are.

ROECKNITZ. Consider in time : such a chance will never be offered you again. . . . She must be got out of this scurvy hole. She must go back among friends — back to the world. . . . And you yourself, my old friend, how you would pick up —

WIEDEMANN. Oh, leave me out of the game. It 's not a question of me. But I 'll speak to her this very day. I 'll —

ROECKNITZ. No, no. Let me do the speaking.

WIEDEMANN. Why you ?

ROECKNITZ. I know your wife, I take it ! If she gets the least notion that anything on earth is done her as a favor —

WIEDEMANN. Yes, I confess then she 'd say no, even if she went to wrack and ruin.

ROECKNITZ. Well, good. . . . The preliminaries you can undertake, but the master-stroke I 'll manage myself. Agreed ?

WIEDEMANN. And one thing still, Roecknitz, on your honor now ! Is not the whole affair in the end perhaps nothing more or less than a service of friendship ?

ROECKNITZ. Not much, little man ! Be quite easy there. I 'm a rank egoist. . .

If you were n't necessary to me, I 'd leave you without ado sitting in your nook.

WIEDEMANN [*looking about him*]. My nook, my beloved nook! It has become so dear to me through her. It 's as if consecrated through her.

ROECKNITZ [*shrugging his shoulders*]. Well, very good, stay there.

WIEDEMANN [*hastily*]. No, no, no! It must be done! You are right. [*Seizing his hands.*] I thank you. I thank you! I will —

ROECKNITZ. Be still! Is n't that she?

[*The glass door to the veranda opens.*]

WIEDEMANN. I 'm going — I 'm too much agitated. She 'd mark at once how —

[*Turns to the rear.*]

ROECKNITZ. Wiedemann, that 's not wise.

[WIEDEMANN *goes.*]

[ELIZABETH *comes leading* HELENE *by the hand.*]

ELIZABETH. Where did my husband go to?

ROECKNITZ. He had to look after something about the farm. He 'll be back in a minute.

ELIZABETH. Bettina 's asleep. She was very tired from the long drive.

ROECKNITZ. Well, praise the Lord! — when Bettina is n't sleeping, she 's out of sorts.

ELIZABETH. So, Lenchen, now go and say: "Beg pardon, Uncle Roecknitz, that I ran off."

HELENE [*without expression*]. Beg pardon, Uncle Roecknitz, that I ran off.

ROECKNITZ. No matter, little chicken, no matter! [HELENE *whirls about and runs off.*] Queer child, she 's become.

ELIZABETH. [*Calls after her.*] Lenchen!

ROECKNITZ. Elizabeth! [*She turns around.*] No greetings?

[ELIZABETH *looks him full in the face with a glance of gentle reproach and then turns to go.*]

[*Passionately.*] Elizabeth!

ACT II

The Principal's living-room and study.

In the background at the left a door to the dining-room; at the right a glass door to the veranda; between them a china-closet. On the left side a door to the kitchen, pantry, etc.; further to the front a sofa with table and easy- chairs. *On the right side a window; near it bookcases surmounted by plaster busts of Schiller and Goethe. On the walls a picture of Bismarck, collections of bugs and butterflies, a violin and bow, models of beehives, a pendulum clock, etc. A desk, and, at right angles to it, a card-table piled with volumes and exercise-books. Before it an armchair. Bourgeois furnishings, which with slender means attempt to give the impression of elegance and culture.*

ELIZABETH *and* HELENE *are busy shelling peas, in linen aprons, with small platters before them.* BETTINA *watching.*

BETTINA. Have n't you an apron and a plate for me, too, Lisbeth? I don't like to be just looking on when you 're at work.

ELIZABETH. Let it be, Bettina, love, you 're not used to it.

BETTINA. Once you were n't used to it either.

ELIZABETH. Ach, I!

BETTINA. To be sure, you have to.

HELENE. No, Aunt Bettina, she did n't have to — did you, mamma? For, you see, Rosa and I, we could just as soon have done everything. . . . I 'm not quite so helpless as people may suppose. I can stitch the coarser things myself, I can iron, too, — and feed the geese and ducks, too, —

BETTINA. Indeed you can, Lenchen.

HELENE. I believe I could even drive a coach out into the country.

ELIZABETH. Now, it would be just as well not to try that, Lenchen.

HELENE. Besides, we have n't any coach.

BETTINA. But you 'd like one?

HELENE. Not for myself, Aunt Bettina; only for mamma.

BETTINA. That 's so, Elizabeth; — you with the reins in your hand, that was —

[ELIZABETH *lays a finger on her lips.*]

BETTINA. Yes, what I wanted to say was, when I go would n't you like to have me take Lenchen along as I pay my calls?

HELENE. Me?

BETTINA. The District President's wife remarked only recently she wished I 'd bring the child over sometime.

ELIZABETH. Why, the District President's wife knows me. . . . How is it she never breathed her wish to me?

BETTINA [*embarrassed*]. You and your husband have never called, you see.

ELIZABETH. At the District President's?

Surely, that would have been an impertinence.

BETTINA. Anyhow, just let me take her along. Who knows but what good may come of it.

ELIZABETH. Yes, you are right. Go, dress yourself, Lenchen.

HELENE. Must I, mamma, dear?

ELIZABETH. Yes, my child. Papa will thank you for it.

HELENE. Yes — then, I will.   [*Exit.*]

BETTINA. Poor Lisbeth!

ELIZABETH. Why *poor* Lisbeth? . . . Everybody pities me! Everybody acts as if he had to beg my pardon for some — I know not what — injustice or other. Why, I 've chosen my fate myself. . . . And I 'm requesting nothing better. . . . Why, I 'm altogether happy as it is.

BETTINA. One may say so, of course.

ELIZABETH. Good Heavens, one has to sacrifice many things. Why, our youthful dreams, for that matter, don't exactly exist for the purpose of coming true. Who dares say of himself, "I have a right to happiness"? . . . When one has come to some terms merely with the demands of every day, then there 's — already — much —
    [*Listens.*]

BETTINA. What 's the matter, love?

ELIZABETH. Nothing. I seemed to hear your husband.

BETTINA. Oh, we won't have much sight of him to-day. . . . With him it 's always a horse before even a woman — especially before his own.

ELIZABETH. See now — how resigned that sounds — from you too — who now have this man, the much-sought-for! — and I 'll wager if one were to ask you on your conscience —

BETTINA. Ach, I! Why, I 'm entirely out of the question. . . . Good Heavens, why, I only sleep.

ELIZABETH [*startled*]. What does that mean, child?

BETTINA. You heard it, did n't you? — "When she is n't sleeping, she 's out of sorts; — when she is n't sleeping, she is n't happy" — So it goes a hundred times — day after day.

ELIZABETH. But he does n't mean it that way, Bettina! Why, he must always have something to tease — we know that, surely

BETTINA. True enough, he must be teasing somebody. . . . But yet this is something different. Toward me, there 's always malice behind it — Ach, one gets used to it — and then it hardly hurts any more. . . . If I only did n't have the feeling: You were n't the right one for him. . . . No, I don't measure up to him — not in energy — and not in intelligence. . . . Do you know, dear, who 'd have been the right one for him?

ELIZABETH. Well? —

BETTINA. You!

ELIZABETH [*startled*]. What sort of joking is this, Bettina?

BETTINA [*laughing*]. Now I *can* say it. In those days, when you were with us at the house, and you two discussed hour after hour everything under the sun till your heads were hot, often I thought to myself: How long perhaps will it be before I get word: "Bettina, clear out!"

ELIZABETH. What? You endured me in your house and yet carried about with you the secret thought that I wanted to crowd you out?

BETTINA. Not wanted to — no, no — but it would have come about of itself. . . . I don't believe I could have been even angry at you. . . . For at that time my child had n't come yet. . . . And my fortune was guaranteed . . . and there was n't anybody in the world I begrudged him less than you, dear.

ELIZABETH. Do you know, Bettina, that you 're tormenting me?

BETTINA. Don't be angry, Lieselchen. I 'm just pouring my heart out to you, that 's all. . . . See now, why, for all of them he has. . . . Whether he plays with them, or they with him, it 's all the same to me! . . . I 'm already used to it. . . . Then whenever they 're staring so wistfully into a corner — as you 're doing now —

ELIZABETH [*startled*]. What am I doing?

BETTINA [*laughing*]. And especially, then, whenever they start up so, as you even now —

ELIZABETH. Do you mean by that —?

BETTINA. But, Lieselchen — shame! See, otherwise I trust no one out of my sight. . . . Only of you was I always absolutely sure. Ah, the sun could sooner have fallen out of heaven — I know you could have stepped up to me and said: "I love him, and I am

stronger than you — give me your place."
. . . Yes, you could have done that.

ELIZABETH. Do you think so?

BETTINA. But behind my back — in my
own house — ugh! — no, you? — never!

ELIZABETH [embracing her]. You are right
in that, Bettina. God knows you are right
in that.

BETTINA. And so, you see, now I'm
merely living alongside him. Oh, believe
me, I loved him as only a girl can. I could
have offered up my last breath for him —
but he's said too often to me : "Go — sleep
— sleep." . . . And so one feeling after
another has really gone to sleep. . . . Many
a time I almost wonder even if I still love
my child.

ELIZABETH. Bettina, this is infinitely sad,
all this you're saying.

BETTINA. Why sad? — It does n't grieve
me any more. . . . One changes so, in time.
. . . But I'm sorry for him. He could have
had so many joys in his house, if he had
taken a little trouble to be contented with
me. . . . Now he must be running after all
these strange women, who still either are n't
worthy of him, or if — then they are made
unhappy by him — And to be such a dumb
spectator of it all —

ELIZABETH. Stop!

BETTINA. What's the matter?

ELIZABETH. That *was* he. [Pause.] —
[Knocking.] Come in!

[Enter ROECKNITZ.]

ROECKNITZ. Good-morning, noble ladies!
— Well, been gossiping a bit about me? —
for you seem so embarrassed — Morning,
Frau Elizabeth!

ELIZABETH [extending her hand]. We let
you go off early this morning without something warm, my dear Roecknitz. Many
apologies.

ROECKNITZ. But, dear hostess, it was
only half past four. I slunk down the stairs
in my stocking-feet, like a successful lover.
. . . And anyway, I always carry for such
emergencies a pocket-pistol of cognac.

ELIZABETH. But perhaps now you'd —?

ROECKNITZ. Thanks, my sweet one,
thanks, thanks! . . . I've breakfasted with
four jockeys to-day. . . . It was swell, I can
assure you — well, it gave me a chance to do
the duffers — damn if it did n't! . . . You
there, I got two hundred thalers for that

lop-sided sorrel — that's the talented sort
you have for a wedded lord! Yes, yes, Frau
Elizabeth — horse-trading, there's where a
man is still of some account — quite the
opposite from love — there he's o' no 'count
't all.

BETTINA. That's a fact.

ROECKNITZ [laughing]. Hm-ha-ha! On
such an occasion even you wake up again,
too . . . Donnerwetter, but what did I
come for? . . . Oh, of course — the certificate. You there, have n't you seen the
pocket-book with the pedigrees? — It surely
lay before the mirror —

BETTINA. If you wish, I'll look for it.
[Starts to rise.]

ROECKNITZ [with a glance at ELIZABETH].
Ach, yes, be so good.

ELIZABETH [jumping up]. Oh, let me.
Bettina.

ROECKNITZ. But I beg of you.

ELIZABETH. Oh, no, no, no!
[Exit hurriedly.]

ROECKNITZ. It seems, indeed, almost a.
if she — [Goes about awhile whistling.] Well,
is she pretty?

BETTINA [smiling]. You ask if she's
pretty!

ROECKNITZ. There's something or other
restrained in her conduct now. . . . Often
she seems a madonna, and often there lurks
inside her something or other like a bacchante. Does n't there — eh?

BETTINA. A bacchante? — how so?

ROECKNITZ. Oh, well, then, there don't.
. . . Has she told you anything of a forth-
coming change in her affairs?

BETTINA. A change?

ROECKNITZ. Well, then don't ask her
either, understand? — say!

BETTINA. What, Alfred?

ROECKNITZ. Nothing, nothing, nothing.
. . . Yes, are you going out after a while?

BETTINA. Yes, I'm going to pay calls.

ROECKNITZ. Oh, of course! Do that.
That's right. — Shall I send over the
coach?

BETTINA Oh, no. It's only a little ways.

ROECKNITZ. But you snap it out so —
jealous?

BETTINA. I? Of whom?

ROECKNITZ [winking, with admonishing
finger]. Tut!

BETTINA. Ought to be ashamed of your
self, Alfred.

ROECKNITZ. Good, I am ashamed of myself — apropos, I 've met our late friend Johann.

BETTINA [gladly]. Old Johann? How is he? Dear me!

ROECKNITZ. Fine — excellent — absolutely splendid! — A brandy nose and a beggar.

BETTINA. A beggar — and you say *that* so?

ROECKNITZ. Heavens, child, why, everything 's already arranged. Day after tomorrow he 's to move over to Witzlingen — there I 'll first break him of his guzzling, and then you can stuff him to death.

BETTINA [wiping her eyes]. Forgive me, Alfred; ach, you 're so good.

[ELIZABETH reënters, a pocket-book in her hand.]

ELIZABETH. That 's it, is n't it?

ROECKNITZ. My dearest friend, my soul struggles for appropriate expressions of gratitude — but don't find 'em.

ELIZABETH. Crying, Bettina? [Chiding.] Roecknitz!

BETTINA [quickly]. You 're mistaken, Lieselchen.

ROECKNITZ. She 's only a little moved, because I 'm so generous-hearted — that is, you know, my specialty. Recommend me in all subsequent cases as doer-of-good, friend-of-man, rescuer-of-the-wretched, anything you like — only it must n't cost anything.

BETTINA. Don't believe him! Don't believe him!

ROECKNITZ [counts the certificates]. One, two, three, four — number four — that 's a rascally beast. Now as to him if I could once — ach, he 's got, you see, the concealed limp. Do you know what that is? — We have it, too! — When our spirits begin to drag — when there is n't one feeling that any longer really dares to speak out — when the — [with emphasis] — do you know what the concealed limp is?

ELIZABETH. My dear Roecknitz, truly your philosophy of life is altogether too much borrowed from the horse-market for us to be able to follow it.

ROECKNITZ. Do you want to provoke me?

[ELIZABETH shakes her head with a serious smile.]

ROECKNITZ. My dear madame, I gather

from this you know exactly what sort of a friend you have in me — I thank you. . . . Bettina, when are you going to pay your calls?

BETTINA. By eleven I think — I could —

ROECKNITZ. Good! — Auf wiedersehen, my very dear lady!

ELIZABETH. We eat at half past twelve, my dear Roecknitz.

ROECKNITZ [stiffly polite]. You 'll find me even earlier on the spot! [With a bow, toward the door. Falling back into his previous tone.] Good-morning, noble ladies!
[Exit.]

BETTINA. Really, that was n't right of you, Elizabeth.

ELIZABETH. Yes, forgive me; you are my guests; forgive me, dear.

BETTINA. It 's not on that account — truly it is n't! — But if you knew, how often — he thinks of you and how he —

ELIZABETH. Don't, I beseech you, don't!

BETTINA. Good, — as you will. Oh, about what I wanted to ask you. What, then, has been happening, as a matter of fact? — I won't repeat it — Have you and your husband — another position in prospect — or will your husband even —

ELIZABETH. My husband — what?

BETTINA. I thought you knew it. I 'm supposed, you see, not to mention it. Please, please, don't ask either.

ELIZABETH. Well, what *is* this going on here? Behind my back things are happening which I —

BETTINA. Perhaps they want to surprise you.

ELIZABETH. I 'm no child. I need no surprises.

BETTINA. Has n't your husband, then —

ELIZABETH. He has n't — not a — yes, this morning he let fall a hint or so that — if something better offered, something — that must have been by way of preparation. Forgive me, Bettina; after all, of what interest can this be to you? . . . I 'm entirely — [pressing her hands to her face] — oh, I want my peace! It 's my peace I want!

[HELENE appears and behind her in the doorway ROSA with a coffee-tray.]

HELENE. The bell will ring in a minute, mamma. Can Rosa bring in the breakfast?

ELIZABETH. Rosa can bring in the breakfast.

HELENE [*hastening to her*]. Mamma, dear, mamma, dear!

ELIZABETH. What, child?

HELENE. Had n't I better stay with you?

ELIZABETH [*rising*]. For Heaven's sake, go, darling!

> [*The school-bell rings. One hears forthwith a buzzing of children's voices that continues during the following scenes until the bell rings a second time.*]

ELIZABETH [*stepping up to the table on which* ROSA *has laid the tray with bread, butter, ham, and a jug of fresh milk*]. Would n't you have just a bite, Bettina?

BETTINA. No, thanks — only a glass of real cold milk, if you will, please.

HELENE [*listening at the window, with her face turned toward the audience*]. Just hear, Aunt Bettina, how the youngsters are cutting up again. Now, the girls are always so much better behaved. There's a boy called Jerschke who fights everybody — but Michaelmas he's going to the Gymnasium; then things will be quiet again. [*Crying out with delight.*] Oh, there's Herr Dangel, too, — Aunt Bettina, do you hear Herr Dangel?

BETTINA. No, my child.

HELENE. Mamma, but you hear Herr Dangel, don't you?

ELIZABETH. Lenchen, our ears are not so sharp.

HELENE. Is n't that funny!

[EMIL *and* FRITZ *come storming in.*]

EMIL [*bowing and scraping*]. Good-morning.

FRITZ [*likewise*]. Good-morning.

> [BETTINA *nods to them.*]

EMIL. Breakfast, please.

FRITZ. Oh, yes, breakfast please, real quick!

ELIZABETH. But go first, kiss Aunt Bettina's hand, and ask her how she slept at our house.

EMIL [*kissing* BETTINA'S *hand*]. Aunt Bettina, how did you sleep at our house?

BETTINA [*stroking his head*]. Many thanks, my little boy.

EMIL [*with a sharp turn*]. Breakfast, please!

FRITZ. Aunt Bettina, how —

BETTINA [*laughing*]. Thanks, thanks, thanks! I slept well.

FRITZ. Mamma, please, do hurry up! We've got to beat up that Jerschke boy yet. He's too fresh.

HELENE. But you can't fix *him*.

FRITZ. Pooh — ha!

EMIL [*at the same time*]. We'll fix him all right.

HELENE. He does n't mind anybody but Herr Dangel.

EMIL. Oh, you, forever with your beloved Herr Dangel.

ELIZABETH [*with warning finger*]. Ei, youngsters!

> [FRITZ *and* EMIL, *with their buttered bread, slip noiselessly past* WIEDEMANN *as he enters.*]

WIEDEMANN. Very good-morning! [*Extending* BETTINA *his hand.*] Now, what do you say, dear Frau von Roecknitz, to all this noise?

BETTINA. It takes me back most pleasantly to my own school-days, my good Herr Principal.

WIEDEMANN. It's a jolly uproar, is n't it? — It's something I would n't for all the world — [*with a glance at* ELIZABETH, *correcting himself hastily*] — that is, if one has n't, indeed, a sense for something higher — [*As the noise outside becomes suddenly louder.*] Ah, but yet that's going too far. What can they be up to to-day?

HELENE. They're beating up the Jerschke boy, papa.

WIEDEMANN. What's become of Dangel, then?

HELENE [*very warmly*]. But Herr Dangel must have at least a second's relief sometimes, too, papa. You absolutely can't expect of him that he —

WIEDEMANN [*calling into the yard*]. Quiet outside there!

> [*The noise suddenly subsides into a low buzzing till the ringing of the school-bell, then slightly increases, and stops in a moment altogether.*]

BETTINA [*softly*]. Do you want to talk with him now? [ELIZABETH *nods.*]

BETTINA. Come, Lenchen, let's get ready.

HELENE. Only think, papa, Aunt Bettina's going to take me along to the District President's.

WIEDEMANN [*startled, dubious*]. Ah, ah, dear Frau von Roecknitz, is n't that, after all —

BETTINA. Let me assume the entire responsibility. Auf wiedersehen, my dear Principal.

WIEDEMANN. Auf wiedersehen, Frau von Roecknitz.

[*Exeunt* BETTINA *and* HELENE.]

WIEDEMANN. Mm, well — Have you sent a note to the School Inspector's, Elizabeth, with regard to this evening?

ELIZABETH. Oh, yes — they 're coming.

WIEDEMANN. What will you have?

ELIZABETH. There 's a leg of veal and young peas. Besides, I did n't send the peaches to market to-day.

WIEDEMANN. That 's right, that 's all right. What about the dessert and punch? — well, we 'll think that over. There 's some Mosel on hand, too. — Has Roecknitz turned up yet?

ELIZABETH. He was here — but off again right away.

WIEDEMANN. So! Mm! — How goes it, then, at the fair?

ELIZABETH. First-rate, I think.

WIEDEMANN. Oh, farming 's the thing! [*Starts to go.*] Well —

ELIZABETH. Have you still a moment's time for me?

WIEDEMANN. Only that it will ring right away, Elizabeth.

ELIZABETH. No matter, — Georg, — straight out with it, what are you withholding from me?

WIEDEMANN [*confused*]. Allow me, Elizabeth, how —

ELIZABETH. Georg, see, I don't deserve this. We joined hands to share all. . . . You 've found me in joy and sorrow — found me always at your side! . . . Georg!

WIEDEMANN. Forgive me, Elizabeth — I did n't want to hurt you. Everything is so — I will explain these events — I will. See, dear, — that I 've been discontented with my lot here, that 's something you 've surely noticed in me for some time now.

ELIZABETH. Till early this morning — no.

WIEDEMANN. But just stop and think! How often I 've said, My life is botched — my — my —

ELIZABETH. Oh, that you did n't pass the examinations for Gymnasium teacher — why, there 's nothing more to do about that.

WIEDEMANN. See, and there you are blaming me for it.

ELIZABETH. So many people have blamed you for it, it would be cruel if I did, too.

WIEDEMANN. And even if you hide it from me — out of tact, out of compassion — I don't know what! — still, in yourself you 'll have contempt enough — why, it simply can't be otherwise. . . . For such an existence! Dependent on every tomfool about! I 've always been for liberty — But this!

ELIZABETH. But reflect, Georg, — in any other position you 'd be, why, just as dependent — even in a Gymnasium. And there, in fact, still more. . . . That lies in the very nature of your profession.

WIEDEMANN. And a fine profession — digging arsenic — that would be better — upon my soul!

ELIZABETH. Georg, dear, have n't you often told me how happy you are in this nook of ours?

WIEDEMANN [*to whom her words come home*]. In — this nook — of ours. . . . Yes, yes — oh, yes — one can say so. . . . But that 's not enough — a man must out — his tasks grow. [*Outside the school-bell rings — he starts to go out.*] However — we 'll talk it over later.

ELIZABETH. Georg, are you going to leave me so alone?

WIEDEMANN. But, sweetheart, dearest, darling, have n't I said the bell will ring right off, — and besides, I can't lop a single minute from the Latin class. That would be a regular crime.

ELIZABETH. Now, that does n't look exactly — does it? — as if you were sick of your profession.

WIEDEMANN [*silent, abashed*]. Good, let them wait — Believe me, that may deceive one, Elizabeth! A fellow in the treadmill has to tread, and no help for it. . . . And it 's all to be only for our own best interest — just think, with our talents for agriculture — just think, I with first prize as beekeeper — and you — ach — what a landed proprietress you 'd make — oh, that 's something I must see before I die. And now, just suppose there was offered us a sphere of activity — as manager or as trustee, or — where, unhampered by snoopers and sniffnoses, — I 'm only using your expression, Elizabeth, — industrious and happy — even happier than here — we —

ELIZABETH. Even happier than here, you say — don't forget that.

WIEDEMANN. Oh, well — much happier — incomparably happier — where we 'd be respected and honored, where we could plough, sow, and reap, at our own pleasure.

ELIZABETH. Dear, don't you plough, sow, and reap here, too ?

WIEDEMANN. Ach, this trifle. The few miserable acres.

ELIZABETH. I mean in human hearts, Georg, and I use only your own expression, too.

WIEDEMANN. [*Sinks into a chair, as her words come home. After a pause.*] Oh, really there's no discussing with you. You're too obstinate, Elizabeth ! There'll have to come somebody who's stronger than I am. Just wait ; Roecknitz, he'll make the matter clear enough to you.

ELIZABETH [*with a start — half to herself*]. So — it *is* Roecknitz.

WIEDEMANN. Yes, indeed, Roecknitz ! — See, that's a man ! He knows how to appraise us better than we do ourselves — and now excuse me, dear, if I —

[*About to go.*]

ELIZABETH [*following him, anxious*]. One word more. Is the sphere of activity you mention offered us perchance by any recommendation of his ?

WIEDEMANN. No, my dear child ! He's not the man to let matters rest there. He's the one I educated into a whole man, something I, poor chump, had n't the stuff to become. If he gets it into his head that we'd be a valuable acquisition, he's not the one to wait till somebody else snaps us up.

ELIZABETH [*in a panic*]. Ah !

WIEDEMANN. Well, but you're rather good at concealing your joy. And I thought precisely — Just say a word, Elizabeth ; are n't you, then, at all glad ?

ELIZABETH [*who has sunk into a chair*]. Go now, please, Georg, — later ! — go now !

WIEDEMANN. Oh, it is n't on your account, Elizabeth — for Heaven's sake, no ! [*Begging.*] But say : are n't you at all glad ?

[*She does n't answer; he goes off shaking his head.*]

ELIZABETH. [*Walks about in great agitation, then forces herself to be calm and calls through the door.*] Rosa !

ROSA. What do you wish, Frau Principal ?

ELIZABETH. If the Herr Baron comes sooner than — no, no, say nothing — I'm not well — I'll —

ROSA. I think, Frau Principal, that's the Herr Baron coming already.

ELIZABETH [*after a short struggle, raising herself erect*]. Good ! [*Exit* ROSA.]

ROECKNITZ [*sticking his head through the door*]. May I come in, my dear lady ?

ELIZABETH. By all means.

ROECKNITZ [*looking about*]. Are you alone ?

ELIZABETH. I am all alone.

ROECKNITZ. Ah — you were expecting me, then ?

ELIZABETH. Oh, yes, — I was expecting you.

ROECKNITZ. Just look at that, will you ! — I was n't in the least prepared for such good treatment. For the way you've handled me ever since yesterday — Donnerwetter !

ELIZABETH. If as a housewife I was n't polite enough to you a little while ago, I ask your pardon.

ROECKNITZ. But, Elizabeth, I beg of you, — between us two !

ELIZABETH. Why between us two ? Between us two, my dear Roecknitz, — or better, between you and me, — exists nothing in common. I beg you to take that most kindly into account.

ROECKNITZ. More's the pity ! — I know that the best.

ELIZABETH. And nothing ever did exist in common.

ROECKNITZ. So ? Cross your heart ?

ELIZABETH. I was Bettina's girl friend. I was for two years the guest of your house and as such made myself useful, as far as I could. . . . That justifies, I take it, a certain easy familiarity with one's associates —

ROECKNITZ. But not a serious understanding ?

ELIZABETH. No.

ROECKNITZ. Very kind of you. Really extraordinarily kind of you. . . . Now, tell me, are you merely putting on, or is your memory really so short that, under the three years' matrimonial yoke, all the pretty unspoken things that hovered between us in the air have been shattered to fragments ?

ELIZABETH. My dear Roecknitz, I could say to you : That concerns us no longer — but I'd rather not slink behind a subterfuge. . . . And now that you've made bold to touch on matters that were better left unmentioned for all time, I'll ask you straight in the eye: What did you want of me? — I was a lone waif: I had no protection in the world but you — you could so beautifully have spread your hands out over me. Why did you want to make me your strumpet?

ROECKNITZ. Elizabeth!

ELIZABETH. Surely, there were women enough. Why my poor self? — You know, I take life not lightly — there is in my nature something of moral earnestness that, if toyed with, brings nothing but misery. Why did n't you leave me my little peace?

ROECKNITZ. Have you left me mine?

ELIZABETH. What harm did I do you, then? Can you dare to accuse me of ever having played the coquette with you?

ROECKNITZ. No — everything that's fair and good — that was far from your thoughts — Elizabeth, look at me; I'm not a base fellow! — But down in me somewhere I've a strain of blood, with the very devil in it, that's not to be controlled. . . . God, what battles I've fought from my twelfth — what am I saying! — it seems from my very cradle, — beyond all counting! . . . I demand women — I need women — I can't live without women.

ELIZABETH. And Bettina?

ROECKNITZ. Oh, now, let me alone with Bettina.

ELIZABETH. Why, you don't know Bettina.

ROECKNITZ. Very well, then — we'll let her sleep! — But you can believe me in this: if ever in the same breath with all the rest I had named that name — I mean yours — that would have been — have been — without fine phrases — that would have been the profanation of a shrine.

ELIZABETH. You've had to say that to every one, have n't you?

ROECKNITZ. Elizabeth, I'm not lying — I don't need to lie — [with wild energy] — for what I will, I put through! — Don't you know that? — Have you never yet been in dread of my will?

[ELIZABETH is silent, turning away.]

ROECKNITZ. See, when I let you enter upon this marriage, — pardon, I do not intend any criticism, — it was not perchance because I felt myself beaten, but simply: I would not! — For two years, as long as you were under my roof, every morning I

waked up trembling with thoughts of you; every evening I threw myself upon my bed trembling with thoughts of you; day by day I yearned to snatch you to me. . . . But I understood you, I knew it would have been your death. . . . A beast of prey that has pity — uh! . . . And now accuse me, if you can — eh! eh! [A pause.] Yes, lovely they were, those times in spite of all! — God, those were lovely times! — For once a helpmeet at one's side — a woman with your eyes in her head! — who reads one's plans from out his soul, ere ever he knows them himself. . . . Elizabeth, those summer nights when we were sitting up there on the terrace, stretched out in the steamer-chairs with heads toward the stars — and Bettina beside us — she was fast asleep, of course, in her plaid — eh! eh! — were those lovely times, Elizabeth?

ELIZABETH [dreamily]. Oh, yes; those were lovely times.

ROECKNITZ. Well, there you are.

ELIZABETH. Why could n't you have kept silent?

ROECKNITZ. Silent? Oh, yes! — I've choked it down well-nigh all these two years. Till it got too much for me! — And all the stages one has to go through before he can make up his mind to show his good wife the door. That's no small matter.

ELIZABETH [shocked]. This? — have you — ?

ROECKNITZ. How, then? Were you, I wonder, in earnest just now, with that horrible word there? — Be at rest, Elizabeth; you're not made of the clay they fashion courtesans of.

ELIZABETH. The poor girl, the poor girl! If she ever guessed it, what she must have suffered!

ROECKNITZ. Well, everything's to the good now. Everything's once more admirably adjusted in this best of all worlds. My old girl has a bouncing boy — and you are the Frau Principal! . . . That you in the first passion had to rush headlong into just this — if this at least had n't happened!

ELIZABETH. I must remind you, Roecknitz; you're in the house of my husband.

ROECKNITZ. I beseech you, Elizabeth; no sensitiveness. Much really depends upon this hour — for you and — for me too — I presume your husband has told you what it's about? [ELIZABETH nods.]

ROECKNITZ. And you surely assent?

ELIZABETH. Oh, no.

ROECKNITZ [*painfully mastering himself*]. Mm! — May one at least know your grounds?

ELIZABETH. It would be perhaps rather my place to ask you for your grounds. For surely it's not for amusement that one uproots from its plot of earth a family honestly supporting itself, and exposes it to a hazardous future.

ROECKNITZ. Ah, you desire guarantees.

ELIZABETH. I desire no guarantees. I desire to be left in peace.

ROECKNITZ. Elizabeth, now just sit down here — so. See now — that time you told us, out of a clear sky, that you had accepted my former tutor, it was not for an instant unclear to me that here was a case of desperation.

ELIZABETH. But you see now well enough that you were deceived.

ROECKNITZ. So? — well! And it was forthwith just as clear that I — no other than I — had driven you to it. . . . Had it been in my power to — but you were balking again, you see. My letters you sent back unopened, and you denied me an interview. Come to think of it, to-day is absolutely the first time that we've had another talk alone.

ELIZABETH. It's likely to be the last, too.

ROECKNITZ. Who knows? . . . See here, a delicate conscience is not exactly my failing, but damn if I've ever once ceased to feel myself responsible for the whole transaction. Day after day I've said to myself : She went to pieces through you. . . . Please, let me say my say. . . . Your middle-class surroundings, everything in the way of humiliation and deadening of spirit in the way of — ach, what shall I say? This playing the stepmother, all this miserable subserviency that's inevitable in the situation of your husband and that with good grace or bad you have to share with him — for all this I've blamed myself continually. . . . And I had no rest till I came to the decision : "Make it good!" — I will make it good. . . . See, that is it.

ELIZABETH. And it's with this design that you came yesterday to our house?

ROECKNITZ. Design? — no! I suppose I came wishing to set things here a little to rights, but I didn't yet know how. . . . My idea came to me first as I saw how splendidly you two are farming it here. . . . What you're doing on a small scale, you can do on a large — and so you profit, and so I profit. . . . Thus if you had the intention of upbraiding me for an eventual abasement of your husband, let the dagger rest in its sheath, my dearest friend. It's not a question of a sinecure, and I value my dear old tutor quite as much as you do.

ELIZABETH [*extending her hand*]. I thank you, Roecknitz, for taking the trouble to give matters this concluding turn.

ROECKNITZ. And?

ELIZABETH. We won't speak of it further.

ROECKNITZ [*holding her hand tight*]. Elizabeth — see — I — I — if not — on your account, then do it — for — me.

ELIZABETH. For you!

ROECKNITZ. Elizabeth, since you've gone out of my life — I don't know what is becoming of me; I've been going to ruin since you've been away.

ELIZABETH. You, Roecknitz? The most esteemed man in the district, the most brilliant in society [*smiling bitterly*], the most gallant in affairs of the heart? — Ah, it's not right of you to frighten me so.

ROECKNITZ. What I'm telling you, Elizabeth, is like a cry for help. . . . It's merely my life that I'm trying to save, for this is no longer life — it's a mere existing, an aimless, hollow, feverish reeling about — hither and thither. And how coarse I've become! — and how small I've become — everything big has gone out of my life, since you are away . . . the fresh air seems cut off from me, and I have so much room for breathing there. I work from four in the morning on into the night, but that does no good. For a man wants to know what he's working for. Don't come at me with the child — that's a plaything, nothing more. For a man must have a human being with whom he — ah, if one might feel you again near at hand — think, evenings I'd come riding over to Angerershof or Brickyard — no matter which — your husband can choose for himself — or you two would come to us and we'd sit again on the terrace as of old, and discuss what we'd been doing and what we intended to do. When one pictures all that! — To become a living man again through you — to grow in peace and power — day by day! And never will I talk to you again of love. That I'll swear to you with the most solemn of oaths. . . . Besides, would be no use — would seem in fact merely an insult to you. . . . Don't worry; I'll know how to hold myself in. You'll see. [*Silence.*] Elizabeth — not a word?

ELIZABETH [*after continued silence, deeply moved, though outwardly calm*]. Dear friend, what you're recounting me here is indeed all very fine and tempting, but it's out of the question, no less.

ROECKNITZ [*hoarsely*]. Why out of the question?

ELIZABETH. I see I must tell you the reason which will convince you; otherwise we'll be tormenting each other still, who knows how long. I still love you, Roecknitz — I've never ceased to feel love for you — now you see, surely, that it's out of the question — don't you?

ROECKNITZ [*pressing up to her with outstretched arms*]. Elizabeth!

ELIZABETH [*fleeing into a corner, warding him off in horror*]. Have mercy! Spare me!

ROECKNITZ. At last! at last!
[*About to snatch her to him.*]

ELIZABETH. At last!
[*She flings herself with a cry of joy upon his breast, and remains, after he has kissed her long, with shut eyes, as if lifeless, hanging in his arms.*]

ROECKNITZ. Elizabeth! [*She doesn't reply; he leads her to a chair. She sinks with head against the arm; he kneels down before her.*] Elizabeth! come to yourself! Or I'll have to fetch help!

ELIZABETH [*opening her eyes wildly, raises herself slowly up and lays her hands on his shoulders, as she looks into his eyes*]. And this is his face! — And so I have him! This once! this once!

ROECKNITZ. Woman — adored!

ELIZABETH [*laying a hand on his mouth*]. Still! not a word! not a word!

ROECKNITZ [*springing up*]. Ah, won't that be a life now! Won't that be a life now! All one great festival! — What say, Elizabeth — ha — oho!

ELIZABETH [*anxiously*]. What do you mean by that?

ROECKNITZ. What do I mean by it? Well, is that so hard, then? — Is that so hard, then?

ELIZABETH. You and I, are we not, after all, seeing each other for the last time in this world? After all, we dare not meet again — Roecknitz, that stands to reason, if we wish for the courage still to live.

ROECKNITZ. No, no, no! Everything that — but Elizabeth, why, we're both no longer children — we've not exactly dropped out of the moon. God, woman, — you — woman — she can kiss, the woman can! No more refusals! I will have no more resistance, else I'll go mad. I'll sooner raze your house and my house to the ground than ever let you out of my hands again. I'll give you time till this evening, and then if you don't say yes, then —

ELIZABETH. What — then?

ROECKNITZ. You'll see soon enough. Then I'll have to act on my own hook. There's no way out of that! — Good-bye — sweet, my —
[*About to embrace her. ELIZABETH draws back with a shudder.*]

ROECKNITZ. Well, what's up, then? [*Shaking his head.*] Women, women, who can fathom you! — Well, I'd better be going, then. [*Exit.*]
[ELIZABETH *collapses in tearless sobbing.*]

ROSA [*entering from the left*]. Ach, Frau Principal, it's almost twelve. Because to-day the Baron and his lady are here, won't you see to dinner a little again?

ELIZABETH [*dazed*]. Yes. I'm coming right away to see to dinner.
[ROSA *goes off.* ELIZABETH *lifts herself wearily; the bell rings; she shudders and goes staggering to the door. Amid the muffled noise of the children pouring out of the school, the curtain falls.*]

ACT III

Setting of the previous act.
Lamps with tissue-paper shades are burning on both tables. Through the shut glass door one looks out upon the veranda, where another lamp burns on the table round which the company sits. Pale moonlight falls through the window.
Outside on the veranda are WIEDEMANN, ELIZABETH, VON ROECKNITZ, BETTINA, DOCTOR ORB, FRÄULEIN GOEHRE. *The lamp is flickering in the wind. Merry laughter.*
HELENE *sits to the right at the window, dreaming away to herself, half listening.*

DANGEL *steps in through the glass door, looking cautiously about.*

HELENE [*starting up joyously*]. Herr Dangel — you!

DANGEL. Pardon me, Fräulein Helene, but I was sent to get the fire screen out of the dining-room — the lamp is flickering so.

HELENE [*standing up*]. Are you having a nice time out there?

DANGEL. Oh, charming! And everything makes such an impression of distinction. One feels absolutely elevated in one's social standing. Now, if you, too, were with us. . . . Fräulein Helene, are n't you coming, then, out there to the company even a minute?

HELENE. Why, you know, Herr Dangel, that 's nothing for me. . . . And besides, I always make the others so sad . . . for every one thinks: Ach, the poor little girl! And in a jiffy it 's all up with the fun.

DANGEL. You must n't talk so, Lenchen. That pierces one's heart.

HELENE. Does the peach-punch taste good, Herr Dangel?

DANGEL. I would never have thought, Fräulein Helene, that there existed anything so delicious in the world.

HELENE. See, I prepared the peaches myself. They have to be peeled carefully, and soaked eight hours in the Mosel.

DANGEL. Oh, I suspected that at once.

[*Laughter outside.*]

HELENE. Only hear how they 're laughing!

DANGEL. The Herr Baron tells such comical stories. Oh, often they 're perfectly killing. . . . The School Inspector has already twice given me a very rebuking glance. But I don't pay any attention to it. Well, — he 's got the wrong fellow there.

HELENE [*anxiously*]. And how is mamma? Is she gay?

DANGEL. Why do you ask it so?

HELENE [*softly*]. She was so strange — all this afternoon. . . . She did n't once hear what one said to her, and her hands were all hot.

DANGEL. Now that you remind me, I must say, too, she is n't quite herself. . . . Oh, no, she is in fact very absent-minded.

HELENE. Does she laugh?

DANGEL. Often a great deal. But then

again not a bit. . . . The most comical things she seems not to have heard at all.

HELENE. You see, you see. Ach, Herr Dangel, I can't be with her, I know; besides I 'm too stupid. But you will look out, you will protect her. You 'll promise me that, won't you, Herr Dangel?

DANGEL. Certainly, Lenchen — if I only —

ELIZABETH [*coming in*]. Herr Dangel!

DANGEL [*with a start*]. Ach!

ELIZABETH. But you were going to be so kind as to fetch the screen.

DANGEL. Ach, pardon — I —

[*Exit to the left and rear.*]

ELIZABETH. My Lenchen! [HELENE *encircles dumbly her waist.*] Not coming out, child? [HELENE *shakes her head.*]

ELIZABETH. [*To* DANGEL, *coming back with the fire screen.*] Herr Dangel, come in here for a moment a little later, please.

DANGEL. Very well, Frau Principal!

[*Exit.*]

ELIZABETH. It 's half past ten, my darling. . . . Instead of sitting here, it would be better to go to bed — would n't it?

HELENE. If you wish me to, mamma, dear, of course I will.

ELIZABETH. Good-night, then, my child.

HELENE. Good-night!

[*Kisses* ELIZABETH's *hand.* ELIZABETH *lays a hand on the child's brow, looks her in the face with devotion, then kisses her softly on the brow.* HELENE *goes to the door.*]

ELIZABETH. [*Gazes after her with great emotion, then half-choking.*] Len—

HELENE. Did you call me, mamma dear?

ELIZABETH. No, no, no, my darling. Sleep well!

HELENE. You, too, mamma dear!

[*Exit.*]

[ELIZABETH *goes to the glass door.* ROECKNITZ *steps in; she starts back.*]

ROECKNITZ. Well? Yes or no? [ELIZABETH *turns away.*] Girl, just look here! [*Shows her his shut right hand.*] Now I have you so. By this you may know. . . . And I don't let you go any more. . . . Be sure of that.

ELIZABETH. What harm can you do me if I am not willing?

ROECKNITZ. You 'll see soon enough. This very evening. . . . I 'll have no toy-

ing with me. . . . Whether the whole ca-
boodle here goes a-flying through the air
or not is utterly all one to me.

ELIZABETH. How extraordinary ! Why,
I thought I knew you, Roecknitz. That you
can be so —

ROECKNITZ. Brutal ! . . . Say it briskly now : brutal. . . . Be perfectly at ease
about it — This is the dear old song that
— one so often has heard.

ELIZABETH. The shame ! — the shame !

ROECKNITZ. Yes or no, Elizabeth ?

ELIZABETH [as DANGEL appears at the
glass door]. But you need n't go, Herr Dangel. . . . Does the lamp burn steadier
now, Herr Dangel ?

DANGEL. It seems to, Frau Principal, that
is, unless a regular gust comes — then —

ROECKNITZ [with meaning]. I bet it will
soon be coming, Frau Principal.

ELIZABETH [pointing to DANGEL]. Ach,
dear Roecknitz, will you leave me a moment with —

ROECKNITZ [shrugging his shoulders]. As
you command, dear lady.   [Exit.]

          [ELIZABETH sinks into a chair at the
          left.]

DANGEL. Frau Principal, are you not
well ?

ELIZABETH. Quite well, my good friend,
thank you kindly. . . . Sit down here a
little beside me — so.

DANGEL. Pardon, Frau Principal, but
won't they be missing you ?

ELIZABETH. Perhaps so. But I'd like to
impart some news which will certainly give
you pleasure. Your application is as good
as granted.

DANGEL. Oh ? Did the Herr School Inspector give you the —

ELIZABETH. Yes. But for the time being
don't seem to know. My husband must first
make his official statement concerning you.

DANGEL. Ach, I am absolutely —

ELIZABETH. And so you'll be leaving us
before long, Herr Dangel. I'm sorry — for
all of us — for you've become a reliable
friend. . . . I'm sorry for Lenchen, too,
who is so fond of you.

DANGEL. Yes, is that true ?

ELIZABETH. The child is so in need of
protection. And you've always been so attentive and friendly.

DANGEL. Ach, Frau Principal, if it were
permitted me to say —

ELIZABETH. Rather, say nothing — words
bind one — and I won't have that. . . . But
circumstances can arise — pretty soon —
when she'll be yet more in need of your
protection, of your sympathy.

DANGEL [disconcerted]. What do you
mean by that, Frau Principal ?

ELIZABETH. Good Heavens, we're all in
God's hands, are n't we ? . . . It's easily
possible that hereafter I can't be with her
as much as I gladly would. . . . In such
event, I may count on you — may I not ?
— to be to her — let us say — a dear
brother ? —

DANGEL. Frau Principal, my whole
power, my whole life —

ELIZABETH. No, no, no ! — not too much.
And now give me your hand ! God bless
you my dear boy ! [Whilst he inclines his
head to her hand, she adds softly, half turning aside with eyes to the ground.] God bless
you both !

DANGEL. Why, that's like a parting for
life, Frau Principal. . . . What, then, can —

ELIZABETH. Nothing — nothing of importance — only — But just look and see
what's the matter out there ?

[It has become dark on the veranda. Laughter.]

DANGEL [from the doorway]. Now the
lamp's gone out, after all.

[FRAU ORB, FRÄULEIN GOEHRE, VON ROECK-
NITZ, DOCTOR ORB, WIEDEMANN, and BET-
TINA come into the room.]

FRAU ORB [with a wineglass in her hand].
Well, I never, such a lamp. Such a lamp.

ELIZABETH [who has come some steps
nearer the ladies]. I hope you were not
frightened, Frau School Inspector.

FRAU ORB. Oh, I beg of you — not the
least. [Sits down. With benignant superiority.] It's wisest, of course, in such cases to
use a wind lamp. . . . However, one can't
possess everything, and you're still such a
young wife !

BETTINA [who has likewise sat down]. For
all that, I've already learned very much
from my dear friend Elizabeth.

FRAU ORB [piqued, yet zealous]. Well,
of course, if you say that, Lady von Roecknitz, you with your splendid ménage, then
of course —

          [ELIZABETH goes out on the veranda
          to fetch the punch-bowl and glasses;
          DANGEL assists her.]

ORB [*with two glasses in his hand*]. I have taken the liberty to bring your glass, esteemed Lady von Roecknitz.

BETTINA [*friendly*]. Many thanks.

ORB. I was just permitting myself to lay before your consort, Lady von Roecknitz, some of the cases where the discipline of the Church has presumably a vigorous word to add, without, however, essentially restricting the personal competency of the nobility . . . in cases of drunkenness, unchastity, and idleness — entirely apart from the specific paragraphs of the legal —

ROECKNITZ [*who has thrown himself into the easy-chair*]. Now that we 're just talking of drunkenness, my dear Elizabeth, give me another glass of punch.

[*Stands up and walks to the card-table, where she has set the bowl.*]

ELIZABETH. Permit me.

ROECKNITZ. Thanks most humbly. [*Softly.*] Yes or no ?

ELIZABETH [*hastily*]. Who else of our guests will have a glass ? Don't you drink anything at all, Fräulein Goehre ?

FRÄULEIN GOEHRE [*with constrained laugh*]. Really, I don't know whether I —

BETTINA [*kindly*]. Just come now, dear Fräulein. Both of us are always good for one more. The constituted authorities will keep an eye shut — what say, my dear Principal ?

WIEDEMANN. Seeing that we are all poor sinners — that is, excuse me, I speak only for myself.

ORB. Now, now, I am myself no inhuman creature either. . . . The Horatian *desipere in loco* was written for me too — in a way.

FRAU ORB [*gazing about*]. No, how nice everything is here, is n't it, Lady von Roecknitz ? So tasteful and genuine. . . . You must feel, after all, really quite happy here, Frau Principal ?

WIEDEMANN [*as she does n't hear*]. Elizabeth !

ELIZABETH [*starting*]. What were you saying, please ?

BETTINA. Now — happiness makes one silent. That 's the case with her.

ROECKNITZ [*with emphasis*]. For a fact it 's an awful shame that everything here 's coming so soon to an end.

[*ELIZABETH shrinks with a start.*]

WIEDEMANN [*confused*]. But. Roecknitz!

ORB. What for, then ? I think there 's no one more secure in his position than our dear Principal.

ROECKNITZ. That you don't intend to oust him, I take for granted, my honored sir.

ORB. But ?

WIEDEMANN. Why, you see, Herr School Inspector, he 's having his joke.

ROECKNITZ. So ? . . . Mm yes. . . . Oh, please, my dearest housewife, fill my glass again.

[*Draws near to* ELIZABETH. *She wants to talk to him, but dares not.*]

ORB. [*Takes* WIEDEMANN *in the mean time aside.*] Now, tell me, — for you gave such a start, — what did he mean by that ?

WIEDEMANN. I know — absolutely nothing.

ORB. Won't you be so friendly as to explain yourself more clearly, Herr Baron ? . . . It 's a matter that interests us, too, in a way.

ROECKNITZ. Oh, what is there here to explain, then ? Why, there 's nothing at all to explain. One can hold what notions about it he will. What say, dearest housewife, surely every one can hold what notions he will ?

ELIZABETH [*desperately*]. Oh, certainly.

BETTINA. What can be the matter with my husband ?

ROECKNITZ. Now, tell me, my dear Herr School Inspector — for it 's all right to tell me — have you ever stolen silver spoons ?

[*All laugh.*]

ORB [*joining in the laughter*]. But, permit me —

ROECKNITZ. Neither have I . . . I swear it : neither have I — I 'm in every way a model youth. . . . When I want to take anything from one, I do it eye to eye, shoulder against shoulder. . . . You see, this fine trait of character I 've inherited from my ancestors . . . there was one especially — a sturdy knight — who carried on a thriving business in silk-stuffs, rosewood, Genoese brocade, precious stones, whiting and pomade — what one calls a dealer in sundries. . . . Nix, he was n't particular . . . he took everything that the grace of God brought along by his castle. [*Wildly.*] Eye to eye, shoulder against shoulder. That 's the traffic for me . . . we 'll try it too ! . . . What, my old tutor ? This very day ! . . . We'll try — what ? . . . this very day — mm ?

WIEDEMANN [*perplexed at his wild talk*]. But, my dear Roecknitz, now I really don't know what I — [*Turns to* ORB.]

ROECKNITZ. Ha ha, ha ha, ha ha — yes, yes, yes !

ELIZABETH [*behind him — softly*]. Have pity — be still !

ROECKNITZ [*relieved, to himself*]. Mm, mm !

ORB. That is all so incoherent — one would suppose — yes, will you not, in the interest of our guests, permit me again the question, Herr Baron : now, how do you explain, then, the mysterious words that everything here will soon be at an end ?

ROECKNITZ. Now — since — uh — since it's time to go to bed. That's very simple, surely. [*The other guests rise laughing.*]

ORB. Oh, yes. . . . You've been amusing yourself, to be sure, somewhat at our expense, Herr Baron — but I may, I trust, express the hope [*putting forth his hand for leave-taking*] of meeting you shortly again in a vein so jocose.

ROECKNITZ. Don't mention it. . . . We've missed you and your wife for some time at our house.

ORB. Ah — this pleasure comes — so unexpectedly, Herr Baron.

ROECKNITZ. And so — auf wiedersehen !
[*Turns to the rear. General leave-taking.*]

WIEDEMANN. I'll unlock the garden gate for the company, Elizabeth. [*To* ROECKNITZ.] Excuse me a moment.

ELIZABETH. [*Nods. To* DANGEL, *who lingers by the door.*] Good-night, my dear Herr Dangel !

DANGEL [*choked*]. Frau Principal —

ELIZABETH. Yes — can I do anything for you ?

DANGEL [*constrained*]. Good-night.
[*Exit, with a bow.*]

BETTINA. Nice people, these Orbs.

ROECKNITZ. Ugh ! — Earwigs !

BETTINA. If they're so distasteful to you, why, then, did you invite them, dear ?

ROECKNITZ. I say, Bettina — go to bed.

BETTINA. But I'm not the least bit —

ROECKNITZ. Quick, quick, quick, say good-night. It's time. I'll be with you right away.

BETTINA [*sighing*]. And so good-night, Lieschen !

[ELIZABETH *looks earnestly into her eyes and then kisses her lovingly.*]

ROECKNITZ. Children, keep your tenderness for to-morrow. Quick, quick !
[*Exit* BETTINA.]

ROECKNITZ. You said I should keep silent. So I have kept silent. Elizabeth — for the last time —

ELIZABETH [*pressing her hands against her brow and eyes*]. Why have you been baiting me so to my terror. I'm hardly a wild beast that one —

ROECKNITZ. Before he comes in again — at once ! — yes or no ?

ELIZABETH. It is, then, your fixed determination to ruin my life, in case I did not as you —

[ROECKNITZ *utters a short, impatient laugh.*]

ELIZABETH. Roecknitz, even if I tell you that I —

ROECKNITZ. It is my fixed determination to possess you. I've nothing further to say.

ELIZABETH. And you would tell my husband what to-day — between us — ?

ROECKNITZ. Here — right off — on the spot ! In two minutes, you can see for yourself, my girl.

ELIZABETH [*after some silence*]. It is well, Roecknitz. And so — I — yield —

ROECKNITZ [*lifting himself in triumph*]. Ah ! . . . And just wait till we have you in the new conditions. O woman — it's you, and of course I'll —

ELIZABETH. And with you that means : eye to eye, shoulder against shoulder ?

ROECKNITZ. Every time that it's necessary. . . . But why, then, — now any longer ? And when he comes back, we'll set in order the matter of the lease at once. There must be order. Obviously.

ELIZABETH. I beg you urgently : wait till to-morrow.

ROECKNITZ. What's the good of that ? Why to-morrow ?

ELIZABETH. I beg you !

ROECKNITZ. Good, good, good ! Gallant to a fault ! [*With awakening suspicion.*] That is, Elizabeth — in case, my girl, you may be playing me some trick before to-morrow — it won't do any good — mark me — I'll find you for all that.

ELIZABETH. Go now ! please !

Roecknitz. Yet I must say good-night to him. What may he — ?

Elizabeth. I'll attend to that for you! For to-morrow will —

Roecknitz [suspiciously]. Everything to-morrow! — Oh, well, good — and so to-morrow. [Tenderly, from the doorway.] Good-night!

Elizabeth. Good-night!

[Elizabeth goes to the door at the right, toward Wiedemann.]

Wiedemann. Have the Roecknitzes gone to bed?

Elizabeth. They were all tired out and begged to be excused.

Wiedemann. It was doubtless a little careless of me to make them wait so long, but Orb simply would hold on to me . . . yes, — say, what got into Roecknitz all of a sudden that he seemed about to trumpet the affair from the house-tops? My heart stood still with fright. . . . It was almost as if he intended to devise a fait accompli right over our heads. Now, one can't permit one's self to be treated after that fashion. . . . It would really be better — one — well, I'll say nothing — nothing at all . . . you're to do the deciding.

Elizabeth [mildly]. Wait till to-morrow, Georg.

Wiedemann. Anything you will, child! . . Anything you —

[Laughs aloud to himself, as he recalls something.]

Elizabeth. And you laugh?

Wiedemann. Oho, for everything in the world has its humorous side, too. . . . Orb quite correctly smelt a rat . . . for he's a sly one. . . . But, instead of being offended, he's put a higher price on me. . . . You know well enough how he usually bulldozes me. Just now on leaving he literally showered me with sugar-plums. . . . He even hinted the prospect of a raise in salary. . . . Yes, yes, one must make one's self a rarity and play the part of the much-sought-after. . . . That's what I've neglected all my life.

Elizabeth. So you'd be — glad enough — to stay — right here?

Wiedemann. [Takes a book from the shelf — sighing.] Ach, Heavens — I — after all —

Elizabeth [with energy]. And you shall stay, Georg!

Wiedemann. No — no — no — not for all the world. [He seats himself at the desk.]

Elizabeth. Are you still going to work, Georg?

Wiedemann. Heavens, I'm only going to — Why, one can't come to class without at least a glimmer — [With covert bitterness.] Even for a prospective overseer that's hardly the square thing — I'll do the rest in bed.

Elizabeth. Do you sleep well over in the schoolhouse?

Wiedemann. Thank you, very well.

Elizabeth. [Extinguishes the lamp on the table to the left.] Are you going over pretty soon?

Wiedemann. Of course — I've only got to —

Elizabeth. Then shove the key in here again — so we can unlock to-morrow morning.

Wiedemann. Certainly. We'll do that.

Elizabeth. Good-night, then, Georg.

[Offers him her hand.]

Wiedemann. How the affair does upset you! . . . You're perfectly pale. . . . I've noticed it — the whole evening! . . . Oh, Heaven . . . and all was so good and so fine and so rich. . . . One can scarce trust himself to believe that he has all this in his his own house. . . . Thank you so, dear. [About to kiss her. Elizabeth starts back.] Don't want to give me a kiss?

Elizabeth. Surely!

[Leans toward his hand, which she touches hastily with her lips.]

Wiedemann [startled, withdrawing his hand]. But, Elizabeth!

[Exit Elizabeth hastily. Wiedemann peers after her in deep emotion, then takes a bundle of books under his arm, and is about to extinguish the lamp. One hears in the yard muffled steps, which stop before the house. He listens and calls through the glass door.]

Wiedemann. Any one there?

Dangel's Voice. Herr Principal — it's me.

Wiedemann. Dangel! you? What do you want now? [Dangel enters.] How did you get into the yard, anyway?

Dangel. I climbed over the fence, Herr Principal.

Wiedemann. Man, why that's hardly the thing for you to be doing. . . . If anybody had — Why did n't you ring?

DANGEL. Before I left I wanted to — but I thought I — That is to say, I want to speak with you in private, Herr Principal.

WIEDEMANN. So? . . . Dangel, before you begin telling me any yarns, — our Rosa there in the kitchen is a pretty girl. You're both young — I will seem not to have remarked anything — but hereafter spare my house anything of this sort — if you please.

DANGEL [*indignantly*]. Herr Principal, do not insult me. . . . There is some one in this house I love, but that is your Lenchen.

WIEDEMANN. Dangel! . . . Dangel, I don't know whether I ought to rejoice. . . . That can easily ruin your life, Dangel. And my poor child shall ruin no man's life.

DANGEL. Herr Principal, my life is already mapped out.

WIEDEMANN. And so it was for this — your plans — about becoming a teacher of the blind! Does she know anything?

[DANGEL *shakes his head.*]

WIEDEMANN. That is good, Dangel. . . . That is honorable of you.

DANGEL. Herr Principal, I did n't come on that account. . . . I 've come — because — Herr Principal — I suspect, something dreadful 's going to happen in your house.

WIEDEMANN. Dangel! . . . Sh! . . . [*Opens the door to the corridor, listens, and says, coming back.*] Now, tell me.

DANGEL. Well, then, Herr Principal, to-day Lenchen drew me aside and fervently besought me to keep an eye on Frau Wiedemann, — for she seemed so different.

WIEDEMANN. My wife? . . . Yes, yes — there are reasons for that.

DANGEL. Herr Principal, but your wife then bade me good-bye.

WIEDEMANN. Good - bye ? — to you ? Why, then, precisely to you?

DANGEL. Because she knows — or rather sees through — this matter with Lenchen. And then she urged me to watch over the child — if she — should n't be here — any more.

WIEDEMANN. [*Lifts himself to his full height, speechless. His features become stone-calm.*] Did she say anything more?

DANGEL. No. But I observed her then.

WIEDEMANN. And?

DANGEL. Well, if, in my inexperience, I 've a right to an opinion, she intends — she intends —

WIEDEMANN. To leave this house ?

DANGEL. Yes.

WIEDEMANN. [*Sinks into his chair again, brooding with head in his hands.*] That — may — well — be.

DANGEL. Herr Principal — my dear Herr Principal!

WIEDEMANN. And this very night — is n't it?

DANGEL. Well, one can't tell as to that, Herr Principal.

WIEDEMANN. And so I 'll stay here all night, for any chance. It 's here that she 'll have to pass through. If she — can one see the light shine very far ? [DANGEL *makes a motion of not understanding.*] I mean, the light from the house.

DANGEL. I rather think so, Herr Principal.

WIEDEMANN. Then, I 'll close up. . . . I thank you, Dangel ! — Here 's the key to the garden gate . . . you can leave that open.

DANGEL. Shan't I rather —

WIEDEMANN. If she intends to go, the way must be left free. Good-night, Dangel.

DANGEL. Good-night, Herr Principal.

[*Exit.*]

[WIEDEMANN *closes the shutters of the window and of the glass door, listens at the corridor door and hangs his handkerchief over the keyhole, then sits down at his desk and tries to read, but his agitation overmasters him. A soft sound becomes audible from the adjacent room. He starts up and listens with averted face. The door opens; there's a cry — then shuts quickly.*]

WIEDEMANN. Is any one there still up?

[*Goes a few steps toward the door.*]

ELIZABETH [*coming in fearsomely with a dark crocheted kerchief over her head*]. It 's only me, Georg.

WIEDEMANN. Are you going out into the air again?

ELIZABETH [*panting*]. Yes, I just wanted to go down to the river. . . . I wanted to see if there are any fish in the box — the Roecknitzes are likely to stay over till dinner, you know — [*Totters.*]

WIEDEMANN. You must sit down, Elizabeth. Why, you can hardly keep your feet.

ELIZABETH [*trying to steady herself*]. Oh, no — I —

WIEDEMANN. Just come, now. This day's been too much for you. Then I'll go down with you.

[*He leads her to the easy-chair, into which she sinks heavily.*]

ELIZABETH. But — you were — going — to bed — right away?

WIEDEMANN. True, but I found a little more work to tend to.

ELIZABETH. What, then?

WIEDEMANN. Ach, nothing of . . . Elizabeth!

ELIZABETH. What, Georg?

WIEDEMANN. Elizabeth, if it's now at an end between us — I've seen it coming, you know that — but to slink out of the house in night and darkness, see, now, — you don't have to do that.

ELIZABETH. Where — did you know — what — I — ?

WIEDEMANN. In reality I know nothing . . . nothing, except what you said to Dangel. . . . But now that we stand here face to face for the last time, we're surely not going to play each other a comedy. And I won't hold you back . . . the gate is already open, Elizabeth.

ELIZABETH [*a moment undecided; then with sudden resolution*]. Then, farewell!

[*About to rush forth.*]

WIEDEMANN. Elizabeth!

ELIZABETH. What still do you wish of me?

WIEDEMANN. You've, indeed, nothing more to say to me, I see that. . . . And what could it possibly be? You go your own way . . . whither? I won't even ask you. . . . You've been to me all love and kindness — and I've broken your life . . .

ELIZABETH. How, then, Georg? . . . You came to me in my hour of grief and I said yes. . . . In a joyful hour I would have said no. I admit it. . . . But ultimately — it was my own free will . . . or what one calls free will when one's drowning and snatches at an outstretched hand. . . . I fled then from the same man from whom I'm fleeing to-night.

WIEDEMANN [*stammering*]. I — don't — understand — you —

ELIZABETH [*simply, without gesture*]. Who's sleeping there upstairs?

WIEDEMANN [*precipitously*]. Elizabeth! . . . [*Controlling himself forthwith, without expression.*] Were you his mistress, Elizabeth?

ELIZABETH. In that case I would n't be here. . . . One is n't likely to deliver one's self up quite so entirely. . . .

WIEDEMANN. True — then I fancy this house ought to be the best protection you have on earth.

ELIZABETH. It was, Georg. It was until to-day. . . . But your house has guarded me ill. Or rather, indeed, you've the right to say: I've guarded your house ill. . . . Georg, I've thrown myself upon his neck, in your own house.

[WIEDEMANN *presses toward her, reels back and then sinks dumbly into a chair.*]

ELIZABETH [*after a pause*]. I've not sought this interview, Georg. I did n't *want* to hurt you. . . . On the contrary. . . . More dearly one could n't purchase one's silence. . . . You'd both have found me to-morrow — and there an end.

WIEDEMANN. Elizabeth — have pity — child, what did you — Thank God, I stayed up. Thank God, thank God.

ELIZABETH. Do not thank God. . . . We two have no occasion for that. True, if we'd been different from what we are — hard, or self-righteous, or something else — ah, then we'd have an easy parting . . . then we'd throw in each other's faces all sorts of accusations, and in the end I'd shut the door blandly behind me. . . . Indeed, that's the way married people usually separate. . . . But we two! . . . Oh, dear Georg, . . . never has there been one harsh word between us . . . from you have I had nothing but kindness and forethought. . . . We were destined to be happy, and if we were not, woe to us now.

WIEDEMANN. Did the fault lie in me, my child?

ELIZABETH. Ah, it's easy for you to talk. . . . You were done with your youth, but I was not. In me all was still on fire — every nerve still. . . . I was full to the brim of longing. [*Softly, half to herself.*] Ah, what a world of experience I have craved for! And then there come the winter evenings when one stares at the lamp, and the summer nights when the linden blooms before the door — ach, Georg! and one says to one's self: Off beyond somewhere lies the great world and life and happiness — but you sit here and knit stockings.

WIEDEMANN. Oh, yes, child, perhaps

that 's what every one must go through, who has chosen his lot . . . perhaps in every one there was once a whole hell of such hopes and desires.

ELIZABETH. But all that I hoped and desired was riveted to that man there upstairs. . . . It was madness, I knew that perfectly. Ah, it was madness! But for that very reason I clung so tight to it — Indeed, I don't know myself how it all hangs together! But, Georg, I have not deceived you — I 've come to care for you and the children with my whole soul ; I 've grown used to it here as to my daily bread. . . . And yet — if I have lived here among you till this day, I 've been able to do so only through this one longing. . . . So drive me out, if you will.

WIEDEMANN [after a pause, hurt but calm]. You are mistress here. Go or stay, as it pleases you.

ELIZABETH. Then say at least one hard word to me. . . . So much kindness — that 's too much to bear.

WIEDEMANN. Where are you going to? Have you any plan as yet ?

[ELIZABETH shakes her head.]

WIEDEMANN. What does he desire of you?

ELIZABETH. Have n't you yourself contrived that with him ? [WIEDEMANN starts.]

ELIZABETH. Ah, now I understand him! Now I know on what sort of a man I 've thrown away my best of life ! . . . Be at rest, Georg, I would not have sold myself and you — [with the laughter of pain] — God knows, no !

WIEDEMANN. Is it for this, Elizabeth, that this night you have —

ELIZABETH. Whether this night — or some other time ! . . . I 'm too weary to begin anew. . . . Anyway, it would be likely to come to the same in the end.

WIEDEMANN [after some silence]. Elizabeth !

ELIZABETH. What, Georg ?

WIEDEMANN. Will you stay with us ?

ELIZABETH. Georg !

WIEDEMANN. Will you stay with us ?

ELIZABETH. Georg, how am I to live here among you with this stain on my soul ? . . . How am I to look you in the eye ? . . . Where am I to get a little self-respect when depressed by some reproach ? It won't do — why, you see it won't. . . . And you will get over it. . . .

WIEDEMANN. Ah, what of it whether I get over it or not ! . . . But the children ! . . . I 'm so grieved for Lenchen.

ELIZABETH. Don't think of Lenchen ! Don't make it too hard for one.

WIEDEMANN. Now that you speak of a stain, Elizabeth, and suppose you 'd have to be in dread of me, I 'll confess something to you — a suspicion — a — something that I 've always been carrying about within me! . . . As I found you that night so forlorn in the manor garden I believed you 'd been forsaken by some one or other in your world — I mean — I mean — become a sacrifice — Now you know why I said I 'd stolen you . . . yet in spite of the suffering it cost me, did I ever once let you feel it ? . . . Do you still suppose you dare n't look me in the eye any more ?

ELIZABETH. Georg ! Georg !

[She buries her face in his arm.]

WIEDEMANN [stroking her hair]. My youth, indeed, — that I cannot bring back to you. . . . But little by little yours too will pass away. . . . The desires will become more still . . . the longing will go to sleep . . . every one must resign one's self — even the happiest. . . . And who knows but then there 'll be once more some happiness in this old nook of ours.

[ELIZABETH nods again and again amid her tears.]

WIEDEMANN. Now go to bed, child. . . . Just go to bed. . . . To-morrow morning our house shall be cleansed ; let me take care of that. . . . Why are you looking at me this way ?

ELIZABETH. It seems as if I saw you to-night for the first time.

THE RED ROBE

LA ROBE ROUGE

A PLAY IN FOUR ACTS

Crowned by the French Academy

By BRIEUX
OF THE FRENCH ACADEMY

Translated by F. O. REED.

PERSONS OF THE PLAY

MOUZON

VAGRET

ETCHEPARE

MONDOUBLEAU

LA BOUZULE

BUNERAT

ATTORNEY-GENERAL

PRESIDENT OF THE ASSIZES

DELORME

ARDEUIL

BRIDET

POLICE SERGEANT

CLERK

PLACAT

JANITOR OF THE COURT

YANETTA

ETCHEPARE'S MOTHER

MADAME VAGRET

MADAME BUNERAT

BERTHA

CATIALÉNA

Time — the present, at Mauléon

THE RED ROBE

ACT I

A modest drawing-room in an old house at Mauléon.

As the curtain rises MADAME VAGRET, *in evening dress, is arranging the position of the chairs in her drawing-room.*

[*Enter* BERTHA, *also in evening dress, holding a newspaper.*]

BERTHA. Here's the paper. I have had the *Record* taken to father. He is just back from court and is dressing.

MADAME VAGRET. Is the hearing over?

BERTHA. Not yet.

MADAME VAGRET [*taking the paper*]. The paper is still full of it?

BERTHA. As usual.

MADAME VAGRET. It does n't take long to find it. . . . Here it is in the headlines, in large letters : " THE IRISSARRY CRIME." They are after your father now ! [*Reading.*] " M. Vagret, our prosecuting attorney . . ." [*Continuing to herself.*] And subheadings : " Murderer still at large." As if it were our fault ! . . . "Justice asleep." Asleep, indeed ! The idea of writing things like that when your father has n't had a wink of sleep for two weeks ! Has n't he done his duty ? Is n't Delorme, the examining magistrate, doing his ? He has made himself sick over it, poor man ! . . . Just day before yesterday he arrested another vagabond with scarcely a shred of evidence against him ! Well, then ! No, I tell you, these reporters are mad !

BERTHA. It seems there's going to be an article in the Basque paper too . . .

MADAME VAGRET. The *Eskual Herria* !

BERTHA. So the apothecary told me just now.

MADAME VAGRET. What do I care for a paper like that ? The A.G. does n't read it.

BERTHA. On the contrary, father was saying the other day that the Attorney-General has a translation sent him of all articles bearing on the magistracy.

MADAME VAGRET. Is that so ? Then it's a pretty state of affairs ! Well, we 'll not talk of it any more. . . . How many of us will there be this evening ? Have you the list ?

BERTHA. Yes. . . . [*Getting it from the mantel and reading.*] The Judge of the Assizes . . . the Judge of the Court . . .

MADAME VAGRET. All right, all right ! . . . Nine in all, are n't there ?

BERTHA. Yes, nine.

MADAME VAGRET. Nine ! To have nine people to dinner and not to know at what time they will come — that's the worst of these session-end dinners which we are obliged to give in honor of the Judge of the Assizes. . . . We dine after the hearing ! . . . After the hearing ! Well ! Let us await the good pleasure of these gentlemen. . . . [*Sighing.*] Well, my child ?

BERTHA. Mamma ?

MADAME VAGRET. Do you still want to marry a magistrate ?

BERTHA [*decidedly*]. Oh, no !

MADAME VAGRET. To think that you had that idea two years ago !

BERTHA. I'm over it now !

MADAME VAGRET. Just look at us ! Consider your father. . . . Public Prosecutor — in a court of the third class, just because he is not a schemer, and has never known how to take advantage of politics. . . . Well — there's no use talking ! he's an able man. Since he has been in office he has obtained three life-imprisonments ! And in a district like this, where cases are hopelessly rare ! Is n't that doing pretty well ? Of course, he has just had two acquittals in this last session. Granted ! But that was only bad luck. . . . And for defending Society as he does, what does he get ? Do you even know ?

BERTHA. Oh, yes, I know. You have told me often enough, mother.

MADAME VAGRET. And I'll tell you again. Counting what is kept back for his pension, he gets in all, three hundred ninety-five francs and eighty-three centimes per month. . . . And we find ourselves obliged to give a dinner for nine to receive the counselor, Judge of the Assizes. . . . I hope everything is ready, at least. Let us see. . . . Is my *Revue des Deux Mondes* there ? . . . Yes. . . . Is my chair placed right ? [*Sitting down in it.*] Yes. . . . [*Bowing by way of rehearsal.*] " Judge, be seated, I beg you . . ." I hope it will go off like that. . . . And to think that Dufour, who was a simple judge when we were at Castelnaudary, is to-day Judge of the second class at Douai after serving only at Brest ! . . .

BERTHA. Really ?

MADAME VAGRET [*getting a book from the mantel*]. Look it up in the *Year Book.*

BERTHA. I'll take your word for it.

MADAME VAGRET. You well may ! *The Year Book of the Magistracy*, I know that by heart !

BERTHA. But as father is going to receive his appointment as counselor almost any day . . .

MADAME VAGRET. It's been a long time coming — that counselor's appointment of his.

BERTHA. But it's all settled now. He is slated for the first vacancy — since the death of Lefèvre.

MADAME VAGRET. I hope to goodness you're right ! If we miss it again this time, it's all up. We'll have to stay at Mauléon until we're pensioned. What a shame they can't lay hands on that accursed murderer ! Such a beautiful crime ! . . . This time we might hope for the death sentence — the very first !

BERTHA. Never mind, little mother, there is still a chance.

MADAME VAGRET. You take it lightly, I must say ! You see that the papers are beginning to growl. They are attacking us for indolence. My child, I suppose you do *not* know that there is talk of sending to Paris for a member of the police ! That would be disgrace itself ! Everything promised so well. . . . You have no idea how excited your father was when they woke him up to tell him that an old man, eighty-seven years old, had just been murdered in his district ! He had on his clothes in less than five minutes and he said to me, mastering his feelings, but vigorously pressing my hand : " I think I've got it this time, my appointment ! " [*She sighs.*] And now here's everything going to smash through the fault of this good-for-nothing who refuses to be caught ! [*She sighs again.*] What time is it ?

BERTHA. It has just struck six.

MADAME VAGRET. Go make the menus . . . Don't forget that only the titles are put on : " Judge of the Assizes . . . Judge of the Court of Mauléon . . ." and so on.

BERTHA. That's a good deal to write.

MADAME VAGRET. There's no way to get out of it ! Here's your father. Go take a look into the kitchen as if by accident. . . .

[BERTHA *goes out.*]

[*Enter* VAGRET, *in evening dress.*]

MADAME VAGRET. Isn't the hearing over ?

VAGRET. No. When I left, my Substitute was rising to demand the application of the penalty.

MADAME VAGRET. Anything new ?

VAGRET. About the crime ? Nothing. . . .

MADAME VAGRET. And is Delorme, your examining magistrate, making thorough investigations ?

VAGRET. He is doing all he can.

MADAME VAGRET. Oh ! If *I* were in his place, it seems to me. . . . There ! The examining magistrates ought to be women ! [*Absent-mindedly.*] Nothing in the *Record ?*

VAGRET [*annoyed*]. Yes.

MADAME VAGRET. And you did n't tell me. . . . Something for us ?

VAGRET. No. . . . Nanteuil has been appointed Advocate-General.

MADAME VAGRET. Nanteuil ?

VAGRET. Yes.

MADAME VAGRET. That's the last straw ! He was Assistant Judge at Lunéville when you were Substitute there !

VAGRET. Yes, but he has a cousin who is a Deputy — you can't beat that combination !

[*Silence.* MADAME VAGRET *sits down and begins to cry.*]

MADAME VAGRET. We never have any luck!

VAGRET. Come, come! my dear, don't cry.

MADAME VAGRET [still weeping]. My poor dear, I know well enough it's not your fault . . . you do the best you can . . . the only trouble with you is that you are too honest, and I would be the last one to reproach you for it . . . only, what's the use of talking! Everybody gets ahead of us . . . before long you will be the oldest Prosecutor . . .

VAGRET. What! I? Where is the Year Book?

MADAME VAGRET [still in tears]. Look under Length of Service — farther over.

VAGRET [throwing aside the Year Book]. Don't cry like that! You know I have been picked out as Lefèvre's successor.

MADAME VAGRET. Yes, I know.

VAGRET. I am slated for advancement.

MADAME VAGRET. So is everybody else.

VAGRET. But I have the definite promise of the Attorney-General and of the Chief Justice.

MADAME VAGRET. It's the Deputy's you need.

VAGRET. Oh!

MADAME VAGRET. Certainly. Until now you have waited for advancement; you must meet it halfway, my dear. If you don't do as others do, you are only a simpleton.

VAGRET. A man of principle, you mean!

MADAME VAGRET. And for the very reason that you are a man of principle you ought to strive to attain to higher duties. If the independent and capable magistrates let the others outstrip them, what will be the future of the magistracy?

VAGRET. There is some truth in that . . .

MADAME VAGRET. Since you can better our situation through the influence of a Deputy, and still scrupulously retain your integrity, you would be wrong not to do so. . . . What do they want you to do in return, anyway? — to defend the Ministry . . .

VAGRET. As it happens, I am on that side anyway.

MADAME VAGRET. Hurry, then: a Ministry doesn't last long. . . . To defend the Ministry is to defend the Government, that is, the State, that is, Society. It is to do one's duty.

VAGRET. You are ambitious.

MADAME VAGRET. Ambitious! No, my dear . . . but really one must think of the future. . . . If you knew how hard it is for me to make both ends meet. . . . We ought to be getting Bertha married; our sons are going to cost us more every year; on account of our position we are constrained to certain useless expenditures which we could well dispense with, but we must keep up appearances, we must maintain our position. We want George to enter the Polytechnic, and that's going to take money! And then, there is Henry who is going to study law. . . . The better position you hold the better you will be able to help him.

VAGRET [after a pause]. I haven't told you all.

MADAME VAGRET. What is it now?

VAGRET [timidly]. Cortan has been appointed Counselor at Amiens.

MADAME VAGRET [angrily]. What! That idiot Cortan?

VAGRET. Yes.

MADAME VAGRET. Worse than ever!

VAGRET. What did you expect? The new Keeper of the Seals is from his Department; you can't beat that combination!

MADAME VAGRET. There is always something. . . . Cortan! What a splurge she will make! — Madame Cortan! A woman who writes "judiciary" with an s. . . . I suppose she'll trot out that yellow hat! Don't you remember that yellow hat?

VAGRET. No.

MADAME VAGRET. It's the husband who should wear that color.

VAGRET. Rosa, you are unjust.

MADAME VAGRET [nervously]. I know it, but it relieves me . . .

[Enter CATIALÉNA.]

CATIALÉNA. Madame, where shall I put that bundle that we took out of the linen-closet this morning?

MADAME VAGRET. What bundle?

CATIALÉNA. That bundle, you know, — when we took the linen-closet for the cloak-room . . .

MADAME VAGRET [suddenly]. Yes, yes . . . take it to my room.

CATIALÉNA. This way?

MADAME VAGRET. No; just leave it here. I will put it away myself.

CATIALÉNA. Very well, madame. [*Goes out.*]

MADAME VAGRET. [*To herself, smelling of the bundle.*] For all my moth-balls, it will be all worm-eaten before you ever get a chance to wear it.

VAGRET. What is it ?

MADAME VAGRET [*putting the bundle on the table and opening the wrapper*]. Look.

VAGRET. Ah, yes, my red robe . . . the one you bought me ahead of time two years ago.

MADAME VAGRET. Yes. That time it was Gamard who was chosen in your place.

VAGRET. How else could it be ! Gamard was brother-in-law of a Deputy. You can't beat that combination ! Of course, the Ministry has to assure itself of a majority.

MADAME VAGRET. And to think that in spite of all my hunting I have not been able to discover even among my cousins as much as an alderman !

VAGRET. Here, put it away. I don't like to look at it. . . . [*Giving back the robe which he has unfolded.*] Perhaps it would n't fit me now . . .

MADAME VAGRET. Oh, those things fit every one !

VAGRET. Let 's see. [*Takes off his coat.*]

MADAME VAGRET. And they bring you a thousand francs more a year !

VAGRET. It has n't faded.

[*Enter* BERTHA; *he hides his red robe.*] What is it ?

BERTHA. It is I.

VAGRET. You frightened me.

BERTHA [*seeing the robe*]. You are appointed ! You are appointed !

VAGRET. Be quiet ! Go lock the door !

BERTHA. Papa is appointed ?

MADAME VAGRET. Do as you 're told ! No, he is not appointed.

VAGRET. It 's just as good as new, is n't it ? [*Putting on the robe.*]

MADAME VAGRET. Well, it ought to be ! I got the best there was.

VAGRET. Ah, if I only had that on to demand the head of the Irissarry murderer ! There 's no use talking, the man who planned that costume was no fool. What an effect it does have on the jury ! And just as much on the prisoner ! I remember one fellow who did not take his eyes from the robe of the Prosecutor during a whole hearing.

You feel stronger with it on, you have more dignity, a freer gesture. . . . "Gentlemen of the court, gentlemen of the jury !" Would n't my demand have an effect, though ! "Gentlemen of the court, gentlemen of the jury; 't is in the name of Society, which voices its vengeance through me, 't is in the name of the sacred interests of humanity, in the name of the eternal principles, 't is in the strength of my right and of my duty, that I rise — [*recommencing his gesture*] — that I rise to demand of you the head of the wretch who is before you . . ."

MADAME VAGRET. How well you speak !

[VAGRET, *after shrugging his shoulders, sighs, takes off his robe slowly in silence and gives it to his wife.*]

VAGRET. Here, put it away.

MADAME VAGRET. There 's the bell.

BERTHA. Yes.

MADAME VAGRET. [*To her daughter.*] Here, take it !

BERTHA. Yes, mother.

[*Does up the bundle and starts to go out.*]

MADAME VAGRET. Bertha.

BERTHA. Mother ?

MADAME VAGRET [*weeping*] Put some more mothballs in it, my poor child !

[BERTHA *goes out.*]

[*Enter* CATIALÉNA.]

CATIALÉNA. [*Hands a note to* VAGRET.] Some one just brought this for you.

[*Goes out.*]

VAGRET. What is it ? The Basque paper, the *Eskual Herria* . . . an article marked with blue pencil. [*Reading.*] "Eskual herri guzia, hamabartz égun huntan . . ." Just try to make something out of that language of savages, will you !

MADAME VAGRET [*who has been reading over his shoulder*]. It is something about you.

VAGRET. No !

MADAME VAGRET. Yes, there . . . "Vagret procuradoreak galdegin . . ." Wait a minute. [*Calling at the door in the background.*] Catialéna ! Catialéna !

VAGRET. What are you doing ?

MADAME VAGRET. Catialéna will translate it for us. . . . [*To* CATIALÉNA *who has just entered.*] Here, Catialéna, read us this, will you ?

CATIALÉNA. Yes, madame. [*Reading.*] " Eta gaitzegilea ozda oraino gakopian Irissarryko."

VAGRET. What does that mean?

CATIALÉNA. That means that the Iris-sarry murderer has not been arrested yet . . .

VAGRET. We know that. What else?

CATIALÉNA. "Baginakien yadanik dona Mauléano tribunala yuye bourru arin edo tzarrendka ko béréchiazela" . . . that means that at Mauléon there are only judges who have been driven away from everywhere else and who don't know how to do anything . . . who have n't much sense.

VAGRET. Very well, that 's enough . . .

MADAME VAGRET. No, no; go on, Catialéna.

CATIALÉNA. "Yaun hoyen Biribi . . ."

MADAME VAGRET. Biribi?

CATIALÉNA. Yes, madame.

MADAME VAGRET. What does that mean in Basque, — "Biribi?"

CATIALÉNA. I don't know.

MADAME VAGRET. You don't know? — You mean you don't want to say it? Is it a coarse word?

CATIALÉNA. Oh, madame, in that case I would understand it . . .

VAGRET. Biribi . . .

BERTHA. Perhaps it is a nickname they have given you . . .

MADAME VAGRET. Perhaps . . . [*A silence. To* CATIALÉNA.] Go on.

CATIALÉNA. It 's about Monsieur Vagret.

MADAME VAGRET. [*To her husband.*] I told you so . . . [*To* CATIALÉNA.] Anything bad?

VAGRET. Enough of this, I tell you! [*Snatches the paper from* CATIALÉNA *and puts it in his pocket.*] Go to your kitchen, you! And be mighty quick about it!

CATIALÉNA. Sir, I swear I will not tell you the other words there . . .

VAGRET. Nobody wants you to. Go!

CATIALÉNA, I knew you would get angry . . . [*Starts to go out.*]

MADAME VAGRET. Catialéna!

CATIALÉNA. Madame?

MADAME VAGRET. So you really don't know what Biribi means?

CATIALÉNA. No, madame, . . . on my word . . .

MADAME VAGRET. All right. There 's the bell. Go see what it is. [CATIALÉNA *goes out.*] That girl 's going to get her week's notice — and no later than to-morrow.

VAGRET. Well, now . . .

CATIALÉNA [*returning*]. It is Monsieur Delorme, sir.

MADAME VAGRET. Your examining magistrate?

VAGRET. Yes, he has come to give me his reply. [*To* CATIALÉNA.] Show him in.

MADAME VAGRET. What reply?

VAGRET. He has come to give up the case.

MADAME VAGRET. Give up the case . . .

VAGRET. Yes, I asked him to think it over until this evening.

MADAME VAGRET. Perhaps he has only come to dinner.

VAGRET. No, you know, of course, his health . . . Here he is. Leave us.

[*Enter* MONSIEUR DELORME.]

MADAME VAGRET [*amiably, going out*]. Good-evening, Monsieur Delorme.

DELORME. Madame . . .

VAGRET. Well, my friend . . .

DELORME. It 's no; that 's final.

VAGRET. Why?

DELORME. I 've already told you. [*A silence.*]

VAGRET. And the *alibi* of your prisoner?

DELORME. I have verified it.

VAGRET. It holds?

DELORME. Beyond the shadow of a doubt.

VAGRET [*sadly*]. Then you let the fellow go?

DELORME [*regretfully*]. There was nothing else to do.

VAGRET [*still sad*]. Of course. [*Pause.*] It 's too bad, though.

DELORME. Yes.

VAGRET. And what, then?

DELORME. I wish you would give the case to some one else.

VAGRET. There 's no appeal?

DELORME. I 'm afraid not; you see, my dear Vagret, I am too old to adapt myself to the customs of the present day. . . . I am a magistrate of the old school, like yourself. I inherited from my father certain scruples which are no longer the fashion. These daily attacks in the papers are driving me wild.

VAGRET. They would stop soon enough at the news of an arrest.

DELORME. Precisely! The result would be that I would do something foolish — in fact, I have already: I would not have arrested that fellow if I had n't been hounded as I was.

VAGRET. He was only a vagabond ; you gave him shelter for a few days — there 's no harm done.

DELORME. All the same . . .

VAGRET. You are too easily discouraged; this very evening or to-morrow some chance may put you on a new track. .

DELORME. Even so . . . By the way, they say Placat, the Bordeaux attorney, will come to defend the accused.

VAGRET. I don't see what interest he can have in the matter.

DELORME. He expects to run at the next elections in our district and counts on his plea, in which he will not fail to lodge certain attacks, to work up a little popularity here.

VAGRET. What difference will that make?

DELORME. Don't you see? He will be able to be present at all the examinations of the prisoner — the law allows it — and, as he is thirsting for notoriety, he will communicate to the papers whatever he may wish and they will insult me every morning if my proceedings do not suit him.

VAGRET. You take it too seriously.

DELORME. Not a bit. Nowadays examinations are n't conducted by the magistrate, but by the public and by the newspapers.

VAGRET. That is true for the big criminals — in reality the new law is an advantage to no one else. You know as well as I that for the common run of offenders . . .

DELORME. Really, I must beg you to let me off.

VAGRET. Come, now, you do not imagine that Placat, who has a hundred cases to look after, will come to all your examinations. You know well enough what these fellows generally do. . . . He will send some subordinate — if, indeed, he sends any one at all.

DELORME. Please don't insist, my mind is made up.

VAGRET. In that case . . .

DELORME. Allow me to withdraw. I don't want to meet my colleagues who are dining here.

VAGRET. Until to-morrow, then . . . I am very sorry . . .

DELORME. To-morrow.   [Goes out.]

[Enter immediately MADAME VAGRET by another door.]

MADAME VAGRET. Well, I was listening ; he gives up the case.

VAGRET. Yes . . . his health . . . the papers . . .

MADAME VAGRET. Well ?

VAGRET. Don't tell any one. No one suspects yet.

MADAME VAGRET. Never fear. [Listens.] This time it 's our guests.

BERTHA [entering]. Here they are.

MADAME VAGRET. Your work, Bertha ! My Revue des Deux Mondes . . .
        [They settle down in their chairs. Silence.]

BERTHA. They are taking their time . . .

MADAME VAGRET. It 's that Madame Bunerat with her ceremony . . .

BUTLER. Judge of the Court and Madame Bunerat . . .

MADAME VAGRET. Good-evening, Madame . . .   [Effusive greetings.]

BUTLER. Judge La Bouzule . . . Judge Mouzon.
        [Deep bows. They all take seats.]

MADAME VAGRET. [To MADAME BUNERAT.] Well, madame, there 's one more session over.

MADAME BUNERAT. Yes, at last !

MADAME VAGRET. Your husband probably is n't sorry . . .

MADAME BUNERAT. Nor yours either, I am sure . . .

MADAME VAGRET. Is n't the judge of the Assizes coming ?

BUNERAT. He will be a little late. He expects to leave early to-morrow morning and he has a lot of things to sign. You must remember the hearing is only just over. . . . When we saw that there was no end to it, we sent for our evening clothes while the jury was out, put them on, and then put our robes over them to pronounce the sentence . . .

MADAME VAGRET. What was it ?

BUNERAT. Acquittal.

MADAME VAGRET. Another ! Jurors are such idiots !

VAGRET. Are n't you a little immoderate in your speech, my dear ?

MADAME BUNERAT. Come, madame, don't take it so hard . . .
        [The two go together toward the rear of the stage.]

BUNERAT. [*To* VAGRET.] Yes, my dear attorney, an acquittal . . . that makes three for the session.

MOUZON. [*Forty years of age, side whiskers, handsome but of coarse type.*] Three prisoners released, all because we had no excuse for holding them any longer.

BUNERAT. A veritable run of black . . .

LA BOUZULE. [*Seventy years of age.*] No doubt, you would have preferred one of red, my dear colleagues . . .

BUNERAT. La Bouzule, you're a cynic. I don't see how you have the heart to joke on such a subject.

LA BOUZULE. I wouldn't be joking if your prisoners had been convicted.

MOUZON. Never you mind the prisoners. It's ourselves we have to think of. If you think we shall receive congratulations from the Chancery, you are very much mistaken.

BUNERAT. A lot he cares whether the Mauléon court is in bad odor at Paris or not!

LA BOUZULE. You are right, Bunerat, I don't care a fig. I have nothing more to hope for. I am seventy years old next week and shall be retired on pension. Nothing more to hope for: I have the right to judge according to my conscience. I'm free! Oho! Oho! [*Executes a step.*] Don't get angry, I won't say anything more. I see the *Year Book* over there; I will look up the approaching vacancies for you.

[*Sits down at the left.*]

BUNERAT. Go ahead! [*To* VAGRET.] The Judge of the Assizes is furious.

MOUZON. This won't help him any, either.

VAGRET. And my substitute?

BUNERAT. That's true . . .

MOUZON. It's all his fault. . . . He asked for extenuating circumstances.

BUNERAT. Where does the idiot come from?

VAGRET. He is far from an idiot, I assure you. He has been Secretary of the Conference at Paris, he is Doctor of Laws, and a very capable man.

BUNERAT. Capable?

VAGRET. Yes, capable — he has real oratorical gifts.

BUNERAT. Ah, we noticed it.

VAGRET. He is a very distinguished young man.

BUNERAT [*vehemently*]. Yes, I suppose so! But when one has as much talent as that, he goes into practice, he does not enter the magistracy!

MADAME VAGRET. [*To* LA BOUZULE, *who has come up to her.*] So, really, Judge La Bouzule, it was the fault of the new substitute, it seems . . .

MADAME BUNERAT. Tell us all about it.

LA BOUZULE. It was like this . . .

[*Goes toward the ladies and continues in a low voice.* BERTHA *has come in and has joined the group of which* VAGRET *also is a member.*]

MOUZON. [*To* BUNERAT.] All this is not going to hasten the appointment of poor Vagret . . .

BUNERAT [*with a smile*]. The fact is, poor Vagret is playing in bad luck just now.

MOUZON. Is it true that he was seriously thought of when there is at the Mauléon court a man so much better qualified . . .

BUNERAT [*with an air of false modesty*]. I don't see. . . . Whom have you in mind?

MOUZON. Yourself, Judge.

BUNERAT. In fact, I *have* been considered by the Ministry.

MOUZON. When you preside at the Assizes, the debates will be different from these lately . . .

BUNERAT. Why do you say that, Mouzon?

MOUZON. Because I have seen you preside at the police court. [*Laughs.*]

BUNERAT. What are you laughing at?

MOUZON. Something you said comes to my mind — what you said the other day.

BUNERAT [*radiant*]. I've forgotten . . .

MOUZON. So funny . . . [*Laughs.*]

BUNERAT. What was it? I said something funny? I don't remember . . .

MOUZON. I should say you did! A hundred times! You were in such spirits, that day. And what a face he made, the prisoner, you know, the ragged fellow; his name was Fawcett . . .

BUNERAT. Oh, yes! When I said to him: "Fawcett, turn on the confession!"

MOUZON. That's it! That's it! And the witness for the prisoner, that idiot! Did n't you disconcert him, though! He couldn't finish, they laughed so hard, when you said to him: "If you wish to direct the hearing, say so! Do you want my place?"

BUNERAT. Oh, yes. . . . Ladies, Mouzon has just recalled to me a rather amusing incident. The other day at the police court . . .

BUTLER [announcing]. Monsieur Gabriel Ardeuil, Substitute.

ARDEUIL. [To MADAME VAGRET.] Pray, pardon me, madame, for my tardiness. I was detained until just this minute.

MADAME VAGRET. Certainly, and the more readily in view of your success of to-day. They say it was enough to make all the lawyers of the district jealous.

[Leaves ARDEUIL by himself.]

LA BOUZULE [touching ARDEUIL on the shoulder]. Young man, sit down by me, please do ! . . . You know, of course, that it would not take many hearings like that of to-day to get yourself recalled . . .

ARDEUIL. Do you mean to say they would recall me . . .

LA BOUZULE. Believe me, it does n't do one any good to be considered odd !

ARDEUIL. Odd ! But you — in spite of the secrecy of the deliberations, I know that you stand for independence and leni-ency.

LA BOUZULE. Yes, for some little time I have been indulging in that luxury.

ARDEUIL. For some little time ?

LA BOUZULE. Yes, my young friend ; for I have been recently cured of the malady which makes bad judges out of so many decent people. This malady is the madness for advancement. Look at those over there. If they had not been infected by this microbe, they would be kind and just men, instead of cruel and servile magistrates.

ARDEUIL. You are exaggerating, sir. The French magistracy is not . . .

LA BOUZULE. Is not venal, very true : among the four thousand magistrates, perhaps you would not find one — not one ! Do you understand ? — even among the poorest and most humble . . . especially among the poorest and most humble . . . who would accept money to modify his decision. That is the glory and the peculiar possession of the magistracy of our country. Let us pay it that respect ! But a large number of them are ready to make concessions and to compromise if it is a matter of being agreeable either to the influential elector, or to the Deputy, or to the Ministry which dispenses places and favors. Universal suffrage is the God and the tyrant of magistrates. You are, therefore, right, and I am not wrong.

ARDEUIL. No one can rob us of our independence.

LA BOUZULE. True enough, but, as De Tocqueville said somewhere, we surrender it ourselves.

ARDEUIL. You are pessimistic. There are magistrates on whom no promise . . .

LA BOUZULE. Yes, there are some : — those without needs, or without ambition, — certain obscure fellows who give up their whole lives without ever soliciting anything. But you may believe me, these are exceptions ; and the Mauléon court which you have before your eyes represents a good average integrity of our magistrates. I exaggerate ? Granted ! Let 's say that in France there are only fifty courts like this, only twenty ; one would be too many ! Ah, young man, what kind of an idea have you of the magistracy, anyway ?

ARDEUIL. I am afraid of it.

LA BOUZULE. Are you serious ?

ARDEUIL. Certainly.

LA BOUZULE. Then why are you Substitute ?

ARDEUIL. Did I have any choice ? My parents put me into this career.

LA BOUZULE. Yes, the magistracy is considered a career. . . . The main thing is to succeed !   [Pause.]

ARDEUIL. It would be so wonderful to dispense justice, tempered with mercy !

LA BOUZULE. Yes, it would be wonderful. [Pause.] Do you want the advice of a man who has been for forty years a judge of the third class ?

ARDEUIL. By all means.

LA BOUZULE. Hand in your resignation ; you have chosen the wrong robe. Only in that of a priest could you attempt to put into practice the ideas which you are voic-ing.

ARDEUIL. [As if to himself.] Yes, but it would take a simple heart, capable of faith.

BUNERAT. [In the group.] If only we were lucky enough to have for Keeper of the Seals a Deputy from the Department — just for one week !

LA BOUZULE. [To ARDEUIL.] Those are the things you ought to be thinking about, my boy.

BUTLER [entering]. From the Judge of the Assizes.

[Gives a letter to MADAME VAGRET.]

VAGRET. He's not coming?

MADAME VAGRET [after reading it]. No, he's not coming!

BUNERAT. I was almost expecting it . . .

MADAME VAGRET. He says he has a headache . . . He took the six-forty-nine train.

MOUZON. That means something.

MADAME BUNERAT. He could n't have shown his displeasure more clearly.

BUNERAT. Three acquittals, too!

MADAME BUNERAT. If only they had had to deal with celebrated attorneys there might have been some excuse — but these local pettifoggers!

BUNERAT. Mere nobodies!

MADAME VAGRET. [To her daughter.] Oh, my poor child, what kind of report will he make!

BERTHA. What report?

MADAME VAGRET. Did n't you know that the Judge makes a report to the Minister at the end of each session? . . . Oh, my poor Madame Bunerat!

[The three women go and sit down at the rear.]

MOUZON. Three acquittals . . . the Irissarry crime . . . a horrible showing. . . . We are in a pretty muddle!

BUNERAT. You know, my dear Vagret, I am an outspoken man; I am not accustomed to beating about the bush. When I hunt the boar I drive him hard. I am speaking to you frankly, with my heart on my sleeve — I am a peasant's son, and not ashamed of it, either! Well! In my opinion, your administration — of course you direct it with your characteristic integrity and honesty — but it seems to me — how shall I say it? — that it is losing its hold. Mouzon, you remember, we were just speaking of it, as we were looking over the statistics . . .

MOUZON. Yes, not much prospect for a good showing this year.

BUNERAT. You know, of course, that there was a question of making us an exception to the general rule and raising us one class. . . . Well, if the number of cases diminishes like this, Mauléon will certainly not be promoted from the third class to the second.

MOUZON. We must show that there is a great deal to do here.

BUNERAT. And many cases which you dismiss could very well furnish grounds for prosecution.

MOUZON. Just think! We imposed this year one hundred and eighteen years of imprisonment less than last year!

BUNERAT. And it's not the fault of the court, either. We defend the interests of Society with the utmost vigilance.

MOUZON. But, before we can convict, you must furnish us the accused.

VAGRET. It is only recently that I gave the strictest orders for the suppression of the smuggling that is so common in this region.

BUNERAT. A good idea, too. You understand, of course, our point of view . . . it is a question of public safety.

MOUZON. We are behind the other courts of the same class. Look here — I have worked it out. [Draws a paper from his portfolio and accidentally drops other papers which LA BOUZULE picks up.] See here!

LA BOUZULE. You are losing your papers, Mouzon. . . . Is this envelope yours? [Reads:] "Mr. Benoît, Officer of the Navy, Hôtel Terminal, Bordeaux . . ." perfumed.

MOUZON [taking the envelope, embarrassed]. Yes, this letter belongs to one of my friends . . .

LA BOUZULE. And this? The Irissarry Crime . . .

MOUZON. Ah, yes, I will tell you about that. . . . It is . . . it is about the Irissarry crime, — it is the translation which Bunerat gave me of the article which appeared in to-day's Eskual Herria. . . . It is very unkind. It says that Mauléon is the place of discipline for judges, something like the Coventry of the magistracy.

VAGRET. But I really can't invent this murderer, can I? — if he persists in not allowing himself to be caught. Delorme has sent to every center the description which was given us . . .

MOUZON. Delorme! Do you want me to tell you what I think! Well! Our colleague Delorme is wrong to persist in the idea that a vagabond is the criminal . . .

VAGRET. But there is a witness . . .

MOUZON. The witness is lying or is mistaken.

BUNERAT. A witness who saw some gypsies come out of the victim's house in the morning.

MOUZON. The witness is lying or is mistaken, I tell you.

VAGRET. How do you make that out?

MOUZON. I am sure of it.

VAGRET. How so?

MOUZON. Because I am convinced the murderer was not a gypsy.

VAGRET. I don't understand you.

MOUZON. Please don't insist, Vagret; I know too well my duties toward my colleague Delorme; I have said too much already.

VAGRET. No, you haven't! Go on!

BUNERAT. Yes, go on!

MOUZON. With the utmost delicacy I warned our colleague, who was kind enough to consult me frequently and show me the results of his investigations day by day — I warned him that he was on the wrong track. He wouldn't listen and persists in looking for his vagabond . . . let him look! There are fifty thousand vagabonds in France. After all, I am probably mistaken. . . . It would surprise me, though, if I were, for in the large cities where I have served as magistrate and where I came, not accidentally, but, so to speak, every day, face to face with difficulties of this sort, I succeeded in acquiring some little familiarity with criminal cases and some little insight into them.

VAGRET. Of course. Delorme, you know, has never had a chance to handle such a fine crime . . .

MOUZON. At Bordeaux, in the case of the fair Toulousaine, which made a good deal of talk, it was I who forced the prisoner to a confession which brought him to the guillotine.

BUNERAT [admiringly]. Indeed?

VAGRET. My dear Mouzon, I am speaking most seriously, and if I insist, it is because I have grave reasons for so doing. Just between ourselves, I beg of you, tell us what are the grounds for your opinion.

MOUZON. Since you're so insistent, I will.

BUNERAT. We're all attention.

MOUZON. Let us recall the facts. In a house, isolated as are the majority of the Basque houses, there is found in his bed, one morning, an old man of eighty-seven, beaten to death. Servants sleeping in a neighboring building had heard nothing. The dogs hadn't barked; there was theft, it was true, but not simply of money, but also of family papers. Keep this point in mind. I will call your attention to another detail. It had rained the evening before. In the garden are found footprints, which are immediately attributed to the murderer, a man who was so badly shod that the big toe of his right foot protruded from his shoe. Delorme starts out on this clue; he receives evidence which encourages him and he declares that a vagabond was the murderer. All false, I tell you! The murderer was not a vagabond! The house of the crime is, indeed, an isolated one. It is known that within a radius of six to seven miles no tramp came to ask for food prior to the crime. Therefore, this tramp, if it was one, would have eaten and drunk at the scene of the murder, either before or after the deed. No evidence has been found to warrant the belief that this was the case. We have, therefore, a man who arrives worn out with fatigue. He asks for alms; he is refused; then he hides and, after nightfall, he kills and steals. There is wine there, bread, eatables of various kinds: he leaves without touching them. Is that likely? No! Don't tell me he was interrupted and fled. That won't do, since your witness himself declares that he saw him in the morning some few yards from the house — now the crime was committed before midnight. If Delorme, in addition to his other rare qualities, had also had experience in things of this sort, he would have known that empty bottles, glasses, remnants of eatables left on a table, constitute, so to speak, the signature which vagabond murderers leave on the scene of their crime.

BUNERAT. In fact, I knew that point.

LA BOUZULE [in a low voice to ARDEUIL]. Mouzon would have a man convicted simply for looking intelligent.

VAGRET. Go on, go on . . .

MOUZON. Delorme might have known this also: there is, in the life of the vagabond, one pressing need, second in importance only to hunger, the need of shoes. This is so true that sometimes they use the subterfuge of appealing their case. Now the trip to the court of appeal is generally made on foot, and the State furnishes them with shoes for the journey. These they hardly wear during their detention and find them accordingly in good condition on their release. Now the foot of the alleged vagabond is about the same size as that of his victim. His shoes, as you say yourself, are in very bad condition. Well, gentlemen! This ill-shod vagabond did not take any of the stout, serviceable shoes which were there! I will add only one word more. If the crime was committed by a chance passer, by a professional beggar, will some one tell me what this strange murderer was doing on the road which passes before the house of the crime, — a road devoid of attraction for beggars, — on which the houses are several miles apart, — when there is quite near at hand another road passing through villages and connecting numerous farmhouses where it is a tradition never to refuse hospitality to a fellow man? One word more — why, then, does this vagabond steal family papers which will identify him as the criminal at his first encounter with the police? No, gentlemen; the criminal is not a vagabond. If you wish to discover him, you must not look for him wandering on the highways; you must look for him right in the neighborhood of his victim; you must look for him among those who would profit by his death — relatives, friends, or debtors.

VAGRET. That is very true . . .

BUNERAT. There's logic and clearness for you!

MOUZON. You may take my word for it, the case is simple. If I were entrusted with the investigation, I guarantee that the culprit would be under lock and key within three days.

VAGRET. Well, my dear colleague, I have some news to impart to you. Delorme, whose health is very frail, gave up the case this afternoon and it devolves on you. It is you henceforth who are entrusted with the investigation of the Irissarry crime.

MOUZON. I don't need to say that I accept, my dear attorney. My duty is to obey. I retract nothing of what I have said; within three days the murderer will be arrested.

BUNERAT. Good for you!

VAGRET. In the name of all of us I thank you for this promise. . . . I must acknowledge that you have relieved me of a great burden. [To his wife.] Listen, my dear, M. Mouzon takes charge of the case and promises us the solution within three days . . .

MADAME VAGRET. We are very grateful to M. Mouzon . . .

MADAME BUNERAT. Very . . .

VAGRET. Bertha! Give the order to serve, — and have some old Bordeaux wine brought up! I wish to drink to your success, Mouzon.

BUTLER. Madame is served.

[The couples assemble, and all pass to the dining-room.]

ACT II

Office of MOUZON, *examining magistrate. Door in the background; also at the right. At the left, two desks. Files, armchairs, a chair. As the curtain rises the* CLERK, *sitting in the* JUDGE's *armchair, is drinking his coffee.*

[*Enter the* JANITOR.]

CLERK. Well, Sir Janitor of the Court, what's the news?

JANITOR. Here's the old man.

CLERK. So soon?

JANITOR. He came back from Bordeaux yesterday evening. He seemed tired.

CLERK [*loftily*]. A magistrate of Mauléon is always tired when he comes back from Bordeaux!

JANITOR. Why?

CLERK [*after a pause*]. I don't know.

JANITOR. It is the Irissarry case which brings him so early.

CLERK. Probably. [*While speaking, he has put away his things — cup, saucer, coffeepot, sugar-bowl — in a cabinet. Takes his own place at the desk in the rear. Enter* MOUZON. *The* JANITOR *puts on an air of dignity and goes out. The* CLERK *rises with effusive politeness.*] Good-morning, Judge.

MOUZON. Good-morning. You have n't summoned any one, have you, except on the Irissarry case?

CLERK. I have summoned the police officer, the accused, and his wife.

MOUZON. I am tired out, Benoît . . . I have such a headache. No telegram for me?

CLERK. No, Judge.

MOUZON. Has the Prosecutor asked for me?

CLERK. No, sir . . . but I have something for you, though . . .

[*Gives him an envelope.*]

MOUZON [*opening the envelope*]. Stamps

for my collection! Ah, that's fine, that is, Benoît. Let us see what it is, let us see. [*Takes a stamp-album from the drawer of his desk which was locked.*] Uruguay . . . I have that, it will do to exchange . . . that one, too. Oh, Benoît, a George Albert, first issue! . . . Where *did* you get that, Benoît?

CLERK. A lawyer's clerk found it among some papers.

MOUZON. Beautiful! . . . I must stick it in at once. . . . Hand me the mucilage, will you. [*Trims the stamp delicately with the scissors and sticks it in with the greatest care, speaking all the while.*] It is rare, very rare! According to the *Stamp Collector* it will exchange for three Blue Amadeuses or for a canceled Khedive of '70. There! [*Running through his album.*] Now! That commences to look like something, eh! It's beginning to fill up, eh, friend? And do you know, I think I'm going to get that Haiti one? [*Gleefully.*] Look here! Here's a page full! All filled up! And such beautiful specimens. [*Closes the album and utters a sigh.*] Oh, Lord!

CLERK. Don't you feel well?

MOUZON. No, I had some annoyances at Bordeaux . . .

CLERK. In connection with stamps?

MOUZON. No. [*Sighs; then to himself.*] Accursed women, I really needed something like that! [*Takes up his album again.*] When I get that Haiti one I shall need only three to fill up this page . . . yes . . . [*Closes the album.*] What's in the mail? Ah, ha! here are the reports from Paris on the Etchepare woman and the court record of her husband.

[*Enter the JANITOR with a visiting card.*]

Who's coming to disturb me now? [*Mollified after having read it.*] Ah! [*To the CLERK.*] You may leave us, Benoît.

CLERK. Yes, sir. [*Goes out.*]

MOUZON. [*To the JANITOR.*] Show him in.

[*Hides his album, seizes a file of papers which he pretends to be reading with the greatest attention.*]

[*Enter MONDOUBLEAU.*]

MONDOUBLEAU. [*Gascon accent.*] I was passing by the court-house and I thought I would come in and shake hands with you. I hope I'm not intruding . . .

MOUZON [*smiling and closing his file of papers*]. An examining magistrate, my dear Deputy, is always busy . . . but it is restful and agreeable to receive from time to time pleasant calls. Be seated, I beg you, please do . . .

MONDOUBLEAU. I will keep you but a moment.

MOUZON. I'm sorry.

MONDOUBLEAU. What's the news on the Irissarry crime?

MOUZON. Nothing, so far. I have heard the accused. He has a bad look and makes a poor defense. He denied everything, got angry, and I had to remand him to confinement without getting anything out of him.

MONDOUBLEAU. Are you really sure you have the right man?

MOUZON. Sure? No — but I would be surprised if I were mistaken.

MONDOUBLEAU. I saw Delorme yesterday; he is a little better.

MOUZON. I know. He still holds that the murderer is a vagabond. And in that connection, Deputy, I must call your attention to a peculiarity of us examining magistrates — it takes the devil himself to make us abandon the first idea which has come to our mind. I guard against this professional failing as much as I can. I am going to question Etchepare; I am awaiting the result of an investigation conducted by the police . . . if all that does not give me any results, I shall set him at liberty and shall look elsewhere . . . but I repeat, sir, I think I am on the right track.

MONDOUBLEAU. Delorme is an old magistrate, very clear-sighted, and, I confess, the reasons which he gave me . . .

MOUZON. I know my colleague is an able man. Notice, I do not claim that he is wrong. . . . We shall see. I have up to the present time only a moral certainty. I shall have a material certainty when I find out the antecedents of the accused and when I have established beyond question the motive for the deed. Just as you came in I was about to open my mail. Here is a letter from the court at Pau; it is the court record of the fellow.

[*Takes a paper-cutter to open the envelope.*]

MONDOUBLEAU. You have a strange paper-cutter.

Mouzon. That? It is the knife-blade used in the murder of the fair Toulousaine at Bordeaux. Quite a weapon, eh? I had it made into a paper-cutter . . . [*Opens the envelope.*] There! Just it! Four convictions for assault and battery. See . . .

Mondoubleau. You don't say so! Four convictions!

Mouzon. This is significant. Moreover, I have neglected nothing. I have learned that his wife, Yanetta Etchepare . . .

Mondoubleau. Is that the young woman I saw in the corridor a moment ago?

Mouzon. Yes. I have summoned her as a witness. I am going to examine her in a moment.

Mondoubleau. She looks to me like a good sort.

Mouzon. Very likely. I learned, as I was saying, that she had lived in Paris before her marriage. I sent for information and here it is. [*Opens the envelope. Smiles.*] Well! This young woman who "looks like a good sort" was once sentenced to a month's imprisonment for complicity in theft. . . . We will now listen to the police sergeant who is coming to report officially the results of the examination which I entrusted to him and which he will draw up formally this evening . . . I'll see . . .

Mondoubleau. You think he brings something new?

Mouzon. If you are interested I will receive him in your presence. [*Goes to the door and beckons. Returns and sits down.*] Bear in mind that I am asserting nothing. It is very possible that my colleague has been nearer right than I. . . .

[*Enter the* Police Officer.]

Officer. Good-morning, your honor.

Mouzon. Good-morning, Sergeant. You may speak before this gentleman.

Officer [*bowing*]. Mr. Deputy . . .

Mouzon. Well?

Officer. You were right! It is he . . .

Mouzon [*after a look at* Mondoubleau]. Not so fast. On what do you base your statement?

Officer. You will see. In the first place, he has been convicted four times.

Mouzon. Yes, I know.

Officer. In the next place, fifteen years ago he bought of old man Goyetche, the victim, a vineyard payable by annuity.

Mouzon. Good.

Officer. He claimed to have made a very bad bargain and used to call old man Goyetche a robber.

Mouzon. Exactly.

Officer. Five years ago he sold this vineyard.

Mouzon. So that for five years he had been paying an annuity to the victim, although the vineyard no longer belonged to him.

Officer. Yes, your honor.

Mouzon. Go on.

Officer. After his arrest gossip started; the neighbors began to talk.

Mouzon. That's the way it always is.

Officer. To a certain girl, Gracieuse Mendione, whom I have examined as witness, Etchepare said: "What a nuisance to have to give money to that old rapscallion."

Mouzon. Wait a minute. You say Gracieuse . . . ?

Officer. Mendione.

Mouzon [*writing*]. "Mendione . . . what a nuisance . . . money . . . to that old rapscallion." Now I call that good! What next?

Officer. I have another witness, Piarrech Artola . . .

Mouzon [*writing*]. "Piarrech Artola . . ."

Officer. About two months ago Etchepare said to him, speaking of old man Goyetche: "Did you ever hear anything like it! the Good Lord must have forgotten him."

Mouzon [*still writing*]. "The Good Lord must have forgotten him." Excellent. Is that all you have.

Officer. About all, your honor.

Mouzon. When was the next annuity to old man Goyetche due?

Officer. A week after Ascension.

Mouzon. That is, about a week after the crime?

Officer. Yes, your honor!

Mouzon. [*To* Mondoubleau.] Remarkable coincidence. . . . [*To the* Officer.] Was this Etchepare well off?

Officer. On the contrary, he was hard up. Three months ago he borrowed eight hundred francs from a Mauléon merchant.

Mouzon. And what do the neighbors say?

Officer. They say that Etchepare was

tricky and miserly, and they are not surprised that he is the guilty party. On the other hand, they are all kindly disposed to the wife, Yanetta, and used to cite her as a model wife and mother.

MOUZON. How many children?

OFFICER. Two : George, and . . . I have forgotten the name of the other.

MOUZON. The morals of the woman?

OFFICER. Irreproachable.

MOUZON. Very well.

OFFICER. I almost forgot something. . . . One of my men, one of those sent to arrest Etchepare, told me that Etchepare, seeing him coming, said to his wife : " They 've got me ! "

MOUZON. " They 've got me." . . . Well, that 's rather important !

OFFICER. And he said to his wife in Basque : " Don't let on, for anything, that I was out last night."

MOUZON. He said that before the policeman?

OFFICER. No, your honor. . . . the policeman was outside . . . by an open window. Etchepare did n't see him.

MOUZON. Have that man summoned.

OFFICER. Yes, your honor. . . . There is also that witness for the prisoner, Bridet.

MOUZON. Oh, yes. . . . I have read the deposition which he made before you — it does n't amount to anything. However, if he is there, I will hear him. Thank you. So, then, draw up a very detailed report and procure summons for the witnesses.

OFFICER. Yes, your honor.

[Bows; goes out.]

MONDOUBLEAU. Delorme is a fool.

MOUZON [laughing]. I did n't say so, Deputy.

MONDOUBLEAU. A wonderful faculty of intuition you have !

MOUZON. Wonderful, no . . . I assure you . . .

MONDOUBLEAU. How did you come to suspect this Etchepare, anyhow?

MOUZON. There are, you know, Deputy, professional accomplishments. The search for a criminal is an art in itself. I mean that a good examining magistrate is less guided by the facts themselves than by a sort of inspiration.

MONDOUBLEAU. Wonderful ! I repeat it, wonderful ! And this witness for the prisoner ?

MOUZON. He must be a false witness.

MONDOUBLEAU. What makes you think so ?

MOUZON. He accuses gypsies of the crime ! Besides that, he was in business relations with Etchepare. The Basques, you know, consider us still somewhat as enemies, as conquerors, and think nothing of perjuring themselves to us.

MONDOUBLEAU. So you have never been willing to accept the hypothesis of your predecessor . . .

MOUZON. Vagabonds . . . The unfortunate ! . . . I know your love for the humble, Deputy, and I had the same feelings as you, in not directing my suspicions exclusively upon the outcast, homeless, and hungry.

MONDOUBLEAU. Good for you ! I am delighted to see that you are not merely a capable judge, but that you hold political views which are not at variance with mine . . .

MOUZON. I am only too glad . . .

MONDOUBLEAU. I hope that henceforth the Basque paper will cease its attacks on you . . .

MOUZON. I hardly think . . .

MONDOUBLEAU. Come now . . .

MOUZON. How can it, Deputy? This paper is your enemy, and as I am not backward in supporting openly your candidacy, they make me pay as magistrate for my opinions as a citizen . . .

MONDOUBLEAU. I am overwhelmed . . . and I thank you, my dear friend, with all my heart. Continue, but be prudent, won't you? The Keeper of the Seals was saying just day before yesterday : " I am counting upon you to avoid for me all trouble in your district. No scandals ; especially no scandals." I must tell you that Eugène is much attacked at this moment . . .

MOUZON. Are you on terms of such intimacy with the Keeper of the Seals ?

MONDOUBLEAU [with a wave of his hand, simply]. We fought together in the Commune.

MOUZON. I understand . . .

MONDOUBLEAU. By the way, tell me. What sort of a man is your Public Prosecutor ?

MOUZON. Vagret ?

MONDOUBLEAU. Yes.

MOUZON. Oh, he is a very conscientious magistrate, punctilious, even.

MONDOUBLEAU. No, I mean from the political point of view.

MOUZON. You ought not to bear him any ill-will, Deputy, for being in the camp diametrically opposed to ours. Don't get the idea that he 's a bad fellow, though.

MONDOUBLEAU. He 's narrow-minded. [*For some little time he has been looking over the desk of* MOUZON.] I just happen to see on your desk the Labastide case . . . there 's not enough in the case to whip a cat for. I know Labastide well; he is one of my best lieutenants, and I assure you he is incapable of committing the things of which he is accused. I have already told Vagret, but I see that he has gone ahead with the case just the same.

MOUZON. I can assure you of only one thing, Deputy. I will look into the Labastide case with particular care.

MONDOUBLEAU. I esteem you too highly, sir, to ask more. Well! I won't take any more of your time. Good luck!

MOUZON. Good-day. [DEPUTY *goes out.*] I think the Deputy won't have too bad an idea of me. [*Smiling.*] The fact is, I *was* pretty clever in suspecting Etchepare. Now, the point is to make him confess as soon as possible.

[*Enter* JANITOR *with a telegram.*]

MOUZON. A telegram for me?

JANITOR. Yes, your honor.

MOUZON. Give it to me. All right. [JANITOR *goes out. He reads:*] " Diana still in jail. Report of yesterday's affair sent Attorney-General. — Lucian." [*Aloud.*] That puts me in a pretty fix! [*Silence.*] Well! There 's work to do. [*Goes to the door in the rear, calls his clerk.*] Benoît!

[*The* CLERK *enters.*]

MOUZON. [*Seated, gives a file of papers to the* CLERK.] Draw up for me a discharge for this Labastide and a warrant for his immediate release. You can do that during the examination. Come, let 's get started! It is already two o'clock and we have done nothing yet. Hurry up, won't you? What are you waiting for? Give me a list of the witnesses, don't you understand? What is the matter with you to-day? All right. . . . Well! Send in this famous witness for the prisoner so we can get rid of him. Is Etchepare here?

CLERK. Yes, Judge.

MOUZON. His wife, too?

CLERK. Yes, Judge.

MOUZON. Come, now! What are you looking at me like that for? Send him in . . .

CLERK. Who, Etchepare?

MOUZON. Of course not! The witness for the prisoner — the wit—ness for the pris—on—er! Do you understand?

CLERK. [*Outside, angrily.*] Bridet! Come, Bridet, are you deaf? Come in. [*Roughly.*] Hurry up!

[*Enter* BRIDET.]

BRIDET. Your honor, I came to tell you . . .

MOUZON. Keep still. You can speak when you are spoken to. Name, given names, age, occupation, address . . .

BRIDET. Bridet, Jean-Pierre, thirty-eight, sandal manufacturer at Baïgorry.

MOUZON [*without stopping to take breath*]. You swear to tell the truth, the whole truth, and nothing but the truth — say: I do. You are neither kith nor kin of the prisoner, you are not in his service nor he in yours. [*To the* CLERK.] Is he sworn?

CLERK. Yes, your honor.

MOUZON. [*To* BRIDET.] Speak. [*Silence.*] Speak, can't you!

BRIDET. I am waiting to be questioned.

MOUZON. A minute ago there was no keeping you still; now that I want you to speak, you don't find anything to say. What 's your object in taking the defense of Etchepare?

BRIDET. My object?

MOUZON. Yes, your object. Don't you understand your own language?

BRIDET. Yes, sir. . . . Why, no object, sir.

MOUZON. No object? That 's the truth, is it? Eh? No object? Well, I am willing to believe you. [*Very sternly.*] However, it is my duty to remind you that according to the Penal Code, Article 361, perjury is punishable by solitary confinement. Now that you understand the consequences of not telling the truth, I am willing to listen.

BRIDET [*confused*]. I was going to tell you that old man Goyetche was murdered by some gypsies who crossed the frontier and who came down from the mountain.

MOUZON. Are you sure of that?

BRIDET. That's what I think.

MOUZON. You are not here to tell me what you think. Tell me what you have seen or heard. That is all that is required of you.

BRIDET. Why, you meet them all the time, these gypsies. Just the other day again they robbed a tobacco shop — there were three of them. Two went in — for I must tell you that they had examined the neighborhood in the day time.

MOUZON. Did you come here to make a jest of the law?

BRIDET. I? Why . . . sir . . .

MOUZON. I asked you if you came here to make a jest of the law.

BRIDET. No, sir.

MOUZON. You are wise, for that wouldn't be a safe thing to do. Do you understand?

BRIDET. Yes, sir.

MOUZON. Have you anything more to say?

BRIDET. Yes, sir.

MOUZON. Well, then! Say it! Lord Almighty! And don't make me waste my time like this. Do you think I have nothing else to do but listen to your gossip? If you have anything to say, say it!

BRIDET. It was like this; the day after Ascension, on a Monday — no, on a Friday . . .

MOUZON. Well, which was it?

BRIDET. On a Friday . . . I thought at first it was Monday, being the day after a holiday — anyway, the day after old man Goyetche was found murdered I saw a band of gypsies coming away from there.

MOUZON. Then you were close to the house?

BRIDET. No, I was going along the road . . .

MOUZON. Did they shut the door after them?

BRIDET. I don't know, sir.

MOUZON. Then, why do you say you saw them coming away?

BRIDET. I saw them coming from the field in front of the house.

MOUZON. Well?

BRIDET. That's all.

MOUZON [lying back in his chair]. And is that all you came to disturb me for? Say! Is that all?

BRIDET. But, sir . . . I beg your pardon . . . I thought . . . I beg your pardon . . .

MOUZON. Wait a minute. . . . How many gypsies were there? Think hard, don't make any mistake . . .

BRIDET. Five.

MOUZON. Are you sure of it?

BRIDET. Yes, sir.

MOUZON. You are? Well, to the police officers you said there were five or six. So you are more sure of something a month after it happened than the day you saw it! On the other hand, you have forgotten whether the thing took place Monday or Friday, and whether the gypsies were coming out of the house or whether they were simply crossing the fields. [Sternly.] Tell me, you know the prisoner, Etchepare, don't you?

BRIDET. Yes, sir . . .

MOUZON. You have business dealings with him; you used to sell him sheep?

BRIDET. Yes, sir . . .

MOUZON. That's all I want of you. Go!

BRIDET. Yes, sir.

MOUZON. And you may call yourself lucky that I let you off so easy.

BRIDET. Yes, sir.

MOUZON. In future, before asking to appear as witness for the defense, I advise you to think twice.

BRIDET. You needn't worry, sir; you won't catch me again, I can tell you.

MOUZON. Sign your examination and go. If there were not so many simpletons and blunder-heads like you, there would not be so often occasion to complain of the delays and hesitations which justice is blamed for, but cannot help.

BRIDET. Yes, sir.

MOUZON. [To the CLERK.] Send Etchepare in.

CLERK [returning immediately]. Sir . . .

MOUZON. Well?

CLERK. The counsel for the defense, M. Placat.

MOUZON. Is he there?

CLERK. Yes, your honor. He would like to see you before the examination.

MOUZON. Well, show him in, will you? What are you waiting for? Leave us; come back when I send for the prisoner.

[Clerk goes out.]

[Enter PLACAT.]

MOUZON. Good-afternoon, Placat. How goes it?

PLACAT. Quite well, thank you. How are you? I caught a glimpse of you at the Grand yesterday evening; you were with a very pretty woman.

MOUZON. Yes, in fact, I . . .

PLACAT. I did n't mean to be indiscreet. . . . By the way . . . I wanted to have a word with you about the Etchepare case.

MOUZON. If you are free now, we will proceed at once to the examination.

PLACAT. The fact is . . . I have n't a minute.

MOUZON. Would you like to have it put off until to-morrow?

PLACAT. No. I have just had a conversation with the prisoner. The case is without interest. He denies and denies, and that is all there is to it. He is willing to be examined without me. [*Laughing.*] I may as well tell you, of course, that I advised him to keep on denying. Well, good-day. If he asks for counsel later, let me know and I 'll send one of my clerks.

MOUZON. All right. I 'll see you soon . . .

[PLACAT *goes out.* MOUZON *comes back to his desk.*]

[*Enter the* CLERK; *then* ETCHEPARE *between two officers.*]

CLERK. Come forward.

MOUZON. [*To the* CLERK.] Take this down. [*Very hastily, mumbling.*] In the year eighteen hundred ninety-nine, etc. . . . before me, examining magistrate, aided by . . . etc. . . . was brought Etchepare, Jean-Pierre, whose first appearance is recorded in the report of the . . . etc. . . . be it hereby attested that the prisoner, having consented to be examined without the presence of his counsel . . . [*To* ETCHEPARE.] You consent, don't you?

ETCHEPARE. I am innocent. I have no need of counsel.

MOUZON. All right. [*Continuing his mumbling.*] We proceeded. In consequence, we passed without delay as follows to the examination of the aforesaid Etchepare, Jean-Pierre. [*Speaking to* ETCHEPARE.] Etchepare, at the time of your first appearance, you refused to answer — a thing which was not very wise on your part, but within your rights. You became angry and I even had to recall to your mind the respect due the law. Will you speak to-day?

ETCHEPARE [*confused*]. Yes, your honor.

MOUZON. So, my fine fellow! You are off your high horse now!

ETCHEPARE. Yes. I have thought it over and want to get out of this as soon as possible.

MOUZON. Well, for my part, I ask nothing better than to release you. So far we understand each other; let us hope it will last. Be seated. First of all, I advise you to abandon the line of defense which consists in laying the crime to a band of gypsies. A certain Bridet who is in business relations with you has tried, doubtless at your instigation, to have us accept this story. . . . I must tell you that he has not been successful.

ETCHEPARE. I have no idea what Bridet may have told you . . .

MOUZON. Ah! You do not acknowledge him? Very well, you are more clever than I thought. Is it you who murdered old man Goyetche?

ETCHEPARE. No, sir.

MOUZON. You had an interest in his death?

ETCHEPARE. No, sir.

MOUZON. Oh, really? I thought that you had to pay him an annuity.

ETCHEPARE [*after hesitating*]. Yes, sir.

MOUZON. Then you did have an interest in his death? [*Silence.*] Well, you 're not going to answer? Let 's go on. You said to one witness . . . a certain . . . Mendione, Gracieuse Mendione: " What a nuisance to have to give money to that old rapscallion."

ETCHEPARE [*feebly*]. That 's not true.

MOUZON. Not true . . . the witness lies, eh?

ETCHEPARE. I don't know.

MOUZON. You don't know! . . . [*Silence.*] You thought it was time for old man Goyetche to die?

ETCHEPARE. No, sir . . .

MOUZON. No, sir. . . : Then why did you say to another witness, Piarrech Artola by name . . . why did you say to him, speaking of your creditor : " Did you ever hear anything like it? The Good Lord must have forgotten him "?

ETCHEPARE. I did n't say it . . .

MOUZON. You did n't. . . . That witness lies too. . . . Answer me, does he lie? [*Silence.*] You 're not going to answer? It is just as well. . . . Come, Etchepare, what 's the use? Is n't it clear? You are miserly, self-seeking, greedy for gain . . .

ETCHEPARE. It is so hard to earn one's living.

MOUZON. You are quick-tempered. You get drunk once in a while, and then you become dangerous. You have been convicted four times for assault and battery. You are quick with the knife. Is n't it all clear enough? You were tired of paying — without return — an annuity of considerable amount to the old man. This year's payment was approaching. You were short of funds. You thought it was time for old man Goyetche to die and you murdered him . . . You can't help seeing it, can you? Is n't it true?

ETCHEPARE [gradually recovering his self-possession]. I did n't murder him.

MOUZON. Let 's not trifle over words. . . . Did you pay some one else to kill him?

ETCHEPARE. I had nothing to do with his death. You say yourself that I was hard up. How could I have paid any one to kill him?

MOUZON. Then you did it yourself . . .

ETCHEPARE. I did not.

MOUZON. Listen, Etchepare. . . . You will confess some day or other — your defense is already weakening . . .

ETCHEPARE. If I screamed it at you, you would say I was putting on . . .

MOUZON. Sooner or later, I tell you, you will make up your mind to confess. You already acknowledge facts which in themselves are serious charges against you.

ETCHEPARE. I say what is the truth without being concerned about the consequences.

MOUZON. Well! You ought to be concerned about the consequences because they may be particularly serious for you . . .

ETCHEPARE. I have no fear of death.

MOUZON. For others . . .

ETCHEPARE. Nor for myself.

MOUZON. So much the better. But you are Basque, you are Catholic. After death, there is hell . . .

ETCHEPARE. I have no fear of hell because I have n't done anything wrong.

MOUZON. There is the dishonor which will fall upon your children. You love them, your children, don't you? They ask for you . . . they love you because they don't know yet.

ETCHEPARE. [Suddenly bursting into tears.] My poor little ones, my poor little ones!

MOUZON. Come, now! Not all good instincts are extinguished in you. Believe me, Etchepare, the jury will give you credit for your confession, your repentance. You will escape the severest penalty. You are still young . . . you have long years before you to expiate your crime. Good behavior may reduce your sentence, and perhaps you will again see your children, who will have forgiven you. Believe me, believe me, in your own interest, confess. . . . [MOUZON has approached him during the preceding. Puts his hand on his shoulder. Continues with great kindness.] Well, is it true? If you cannot speak, just nod your head, eh? It is true I know it, anyway. . . . What? I don't hear what you say. It was you, was n't it? It was you?

ETCHEPARE [still weeping]. It was n't I, sir! I swear to you I did n't do it. I swear it.

MOUZON. [Back in his place; speaking sternly.] Oh, you don't need to swear; all you need to do is to tell me the truth.

ETCHEPARE. I am telling the truth, I am . . . but I can't say that I did it when I did n't!

MOUZON. Well! We 'll get nothing out of him to-day. [To the CLERK.] Read him his examination and have him taken back to his cell. . . . Wait a minute, Etchepare.

ETCHEPARE. Yes, sir.

MOUZON. There is one way to prove your innocence, since you claim to be innocent. Prove in some way or other that you were somewhere else than at Irissarry the night of the crime and I will release you. Where were you?

ETCHEPARE. Where was I?

MOUZON. Yes; I want to know where you were the night of Ascension. Were you at home?

ETCHEPARE. Yes.

MOUZON. Is that really the truth?

ETCHEPARE. Yes.

MOUZON. [Rising, somewhat theatrically with his finger pointed at ETCHEPARE.] Well! Etchepare. That convicts you. I happen to know that you were out. When you were arrested, you said to your wife: "Don't let on, for anything, that I was out last night." I may as well tell you all.

Some one saw you, a maid. She has testified to the police that just as she was leaving a young man with whom she had been to a dance — at ten o'clock — she met you a few hundred yards from your house. Well?

ETCHEPARE. It is true. I went out.

MOUZON [*triumphantly*]. Ah; — well, my good fellow, it is hard enough to make you say anything. But it shows on your face when you lie. It shows! I read it on your face as if it were written in letters as big as that! To prove it, no witness claims to have seen you go out, neither your own maid, nor any other, and still I would have sworn it with my head under the knife! Come, now, we have made some progress in the last few minutes. [*To the* CLERK.] You have his first confession down? . . . good! [*To* ETCHEPARE.] Collect yourself a moment . . . we are going on with our little talk. . . .

[*Goes to the fireplace rubbing his hands, pours himself a glass of brandy, utters a sigh of satisfaction, returns and sits down at his place.*]

FIRST POLICEMAN. [*To his companion.*] That Judge is a wonder!

SECOND POLICEMAN. I should say so.

MOUZON. Let's go on; while you're at it, confess everything — why not? Look at those good policemen who are dying to go to supper. [POLICEMEN, CLERK, *and* MOUZON *laugh.*] You confess? No? Well, then, tell me, why did you persist in claiming that you were not out?

ETCHEPARE. Because I had said so to the police and did n't want to go back on what I had said.

MOUZON. But why did you say it to the police in the first place?

ETCHEPARE. Because I thought they had come to arrest me for smuggling.

MOUZON. Very well. Then you did not go to Irissarry that night?

ETCHEPARE. No.

MOUZON. Then, where did you go?

ETCHEPARE. To the mountain, to look for a horse that had run off the night before from a troop which we were bringing in from Spain.

MOUZON. Very well, fine! Not a bad thought. It is capable of defense. You went to look for a horse lost in the mountain, a horse which had escaped from a troop which you were smuggling in the night before — precisely. If it's the truth, it lies in your own power to be released at once. You will simply tell me to whom you sold this horse; we will send for the purchaser, and, if he confirms your statement, I shall at once sign your release. To whom did you sell it?

ETCHEPARE. I did n't sell it.

MOUZON. You gave it away. . . . You did *something* with it?

ETCHEPARE. No, I did n't find it.

MOUZON. Oh, you did n't find it! The devil, you did n't — that changes the situation. Anyway, we 'll try another tack. You did n't go all alone to the mountain?

ETCHEPARE. Yes, all alone.

MOUZON. That 's unfortunate. Next time, you see, you should take along a companion. Did you stay out long?

ETCHEPARE. All night. I came back at five o'clock in the morning.

MOUZON. That was a long time.

ETCHEPARE. We are not rich and for us a horse is a fortune.

MOUZON. Very well. But you did n't stay all night in the mountain without meeting a single soul — a shepherd, customs officers?

ETCHEPARE. It was raining torrents.

MOUZON. Then you met no one?

ETCHEPARE. No one.

MOUZON. I suspected it. [*In a tone of pouting reproach, with a show of pity.*] Tell me, Etchepare, do you take the jury for idiots? [*Silence.*] So this is all you have been able to think up, my poor man? . . . I was saying just a little while ago that you were clever — I take it back. What you 're telling me is enough to put one to sleep standing up. Why, a child of eight would have done better. It 's ridiculous, I tell you, ridiculous! The jury will shrug their shoulders when they hear it. Out all night in a driving rain-storm, looking for a horse which you don't find. . . . And without meeting a living soul, neither shepherds, nor customs officers — coming back at five o'clock in the morning . . . it is light this time of year and has been for some time — But no! No one saw you and you saw no one. . . . Everybody had become blind, eh? There was a miracle and everybody was blind that night. . . . You don't claim that? No? Why? It is just as plausible as the rest of your story. . . . Was n't everybody blind? [*The* CLERK *bursts out laughing; the* POLICEMEN *follow his example.*] You see what it's worth, your defense! It makes even the officers and my clerk laugh. Don't you agree that your new line of defense is ridiculous?

ETCHEPARE [*stupefied, half to himself*]. I don't know.

MOUZON. If *you* don't, *we* do. Anyway, I have no advice to give you. Just repeat that at the hearing, — you will see what an effect it will produce. But why not confess? Why not confess? I really don't understand your stubbornness. . . . I don't understand it, I tell you.

ETCHEPARE. Well, if I didn't do it, have I got to say, just the same, that I did?

MOUZON. Then you still persist in your phantom horse story, do you?

ETCHEPARE. How do I know? How do I know what to say? It would be better for me not to say anything. Everything I say turns against me!

MOUZON. It's because you invent stories which are altogether too ridiculous. It is because you think I am more stupid than I am that you believe I am going to take stock in such ridiculous inventions. I liked your first way better. You at least had two witnesses on your side — two witnesses without great weight, to be sure, but still two witnesses. You adopt a new plan . . . that is your right. . . . Let's go after the lost horse. . . .

ETCHEPARE. Well? [*A long silence.*]

MOUZON. Come, now! Out with it!

ETCHEPARE [*weakly, hesitatingly, looking at the clerk as if to read in his eyes whether he is answering as he ought to*]. Well! I will tell you, sir, you are right. . . . It is not the truth. . . . I did not go to the mountain. . . . I told the truth in the first place. I did n't leave the house. Just a moment ago, I was confused. In the first place I denied everything, even what was true, I was so afraid of you; then when you said to me . . . I have forgotten what — because my head is getting weak — I have forgotten, I have forgotten . . . I am sure that I'm innocent, though . . . well, a moment ago, I almost wanted to acknowledge myself guilty so you would leave me in peace. What was I saying? I have forgotten . . . Oh, yes, when

you said to me . . . those things which I can't remember . . . it seemed to me that it was better to say that I had gone out . . . I lied . . . [*With earnestness.*] But what I swear to, though, is that I am not the criminal. . . . That I swear to, I swear to you . . .

MOUZON. I repeat that I ask nothing better than to believe it. This time, we agree, you were at home?

ETCHEPARE. Yes, sir.

MOUZON. We will hear your wife. You have no other witnesses to bring forward?

ETCHEPARE. No, sir.

MOUZON. Very well. Take away the prisoner . . . but stay in the court-house. I shall probably need him in a few moments to face his wife. His examination is not over yet.

[*The* POLICEMEN *take* ETCHEPARE *out.*]

MOUZON. [*To the* CLERK.] What a rascal, eh? You could have caught him in the act with knife in hand and he would still have denied it. And he's a sly one, too! He puts up an excellent defense!

CLERK. I thought for a moment that your honor had him.

MOUZON. When I spoke to him of his children?

CLERK. Yes, it brought tears to one's eyes. It made one want to confess without having done anything.

MOUZON. Did n't it, though? Ah, if I only did n't have this headache! [*Silence.*] I have just put my foot in it.

CLERK. Oh, your honor!

MOUZON. I did, just the same! I was wrong to show him the weakness of his new story. . . . It is so absurd that it would have ruined him. Whereas, if he continues to assert that he did n't leave the house, if his maid persists, if his wife says the same thing, it will be enough to cast a doubt in the mind of the jury . . . he was well aware of it, the brute! He perceived well enough that of his two methods, the first was the better. It is I who was outwitted, Benoît. . . . [*To himself.*] The question, now, is how to repair the damage! Let us reflect. . . . Etchepare committed the crime . . . of that there is no doubt. I am as sure of it as if I had seen him. Therefore he was not at home the night of the crime and his wife knows it. . . . After his hesitation of a moment ago, if I succeed in making his wife confess that he was out until morning, we get back the ridiculous story of the lost horse — I'll catch him twice in a lie and I have him ! ... Yes ! The thing to do now is to put the woman through the third degree and it will be a wonder if I don't succeed. [*To the* CLERK.] What did I do with the police report from Paris about the Etchepare woman ?

CLERK. You put it with the other papers.

MOUZON. Yes, here it is . . . the extract from her police record. Bulletin number two, one month's imprisonment . . . complicity . . . I suspected it ! Send her in.

[*The* CLERK *goes to the door and calls.* YANETTA *comes in.*]

MOUZON. Come forward, madame. I do not administer the oath to you, since you are the wife of the prisoner. But I must urge you most earnestly to tell the truth. I warn you that a lie on your part might necessitate my accusing you of complicity with your husband in the crime of which he is accused and make me proceed to your immediate arrest.

YANETTA. I am not afraid. I cannot be an accomplice of my husband since he is not guilty.

MOUZON. I am not of your opinion, and, I may add, it is my conviction that you know more about this matter than you are willing to testify.

YANETTA. I ? It's an outrage, sir !

MOUZON. Come, come ! Don't get excited ! I don't say you took part directly in the murder. I mean, it is very probable that you knew of it, perhaps advised it, and that you profited by it. That is enough to bring you to the bar of the Assizes beside your husband. On the frankness of your replies will depend my conduct toward you ; and according as you tell the truth or not, I shall have you released or arrested. You can't say you have not been warned, can you ? Now, be kind enough to inform me if you persist in your first declaration, namely, that Etchepare passed the night of Ascension Day at home.

YANETTA. I do.

MOUZON. Well, it is false !

YANETTA [*excitedly*]. The night old man Goyetche was murdered my husband did not go out of the house.

MOUZON. It is false, I tell you.

YANETTA [*still excited*]. The night old man Goyetche was murdered my husband did not leave the house.

MOUZON. You are so stubborn, you'll do nothing but repeat the same thing.

YANETTA. Yes, I shall do nothing but repeat the same thing.

MOUZON. Then we shall examine the worth of your testimony. Since your marriage . . . for ten years . . . your conduct has been above reproach. You are thrifty, faithful, industrious, honest . . .

YANETTA. What of it ?

MOUZON. Don't interrupt. Wait. You have two children whom you adore. You are an excellent mother. People even talk of almost heroic deeds of devotion at the time your oldest boy — George, I think — was sick . . .

YANETTA. Yes, George . . . but what's that got to do with the charge against my husband ?

MOUZON. Be patient ; you'll see.

YANETTA. I'm waiting.

MOUZON. You are especially meritorious in being what you are in that your husband does not furnish an example of the same virtues. He drinks to excess occasionally.

YANETTA. He does not.

MOUZON. Come, now ! Everybody knows it. He is quarrelsome.

YANETTA. He is not quarrelsome.

MOUZON. So much so that he has been convicted four times for assault and battery.

YANETTA. It is possible : evenings of holidays there are disputes. And, besides, that was a long time ago. Lately he has been gentler and I am very happy with him.

MOUZON. I am surprised . . .

YANETTA. Anyway, how does that prove that he killed old man Goyetche ?

MOUZON. Your husband is very miserly.

YANETTA. The poor must be miserly, sir, or drop in their tracks of hunger.

MOUZON. You defend him well.

YANETTA. Did you think I was going to accuse him ?

MOUZON. Have n't you ever been convicted in court ?

YANETTA [*embarrassed*]. I ?

MOUZON. Yes, you.

YANETTA [*weakly*]. No, I have never been convicted.

MOUZON. That is strange. There was, however, a girl with the same name who once served a month's imprisonment at Paris for complicity in theft.

YANETTA [*weakly*]. For complicity . . .

MOUZON. You are not so confident. You seem embarrassed . . .

YANETTA [*still weakly.*] No, no . . .

MOUZON. You are pale, you are trembling — are you faint? Give her a chair, Benoît. [*The* CLERK *obeys.*] Pull yourself together.

YANETTA. My God! How did you find that out?

MOUZON. The record which has been sent me reads as follows: "The herein mentioned Yanetta X. was brought to Paris at the age of sixteen as companion, or waiting-maid by the M—— family who took her into their employ at Saint-Jean-de-Luz." Is that correct?

YANETTA. Yes.

MOUZON. To continue: "It was not long before a love affair developed between the girl Yanetta and the son of the house, aged twenty-three. Two years later the lovers took flight, carrying with them eight thousand francs which young M—— had stolen from his father. On the complaint of this latter, Yanetta was arrested and sentenced to one month's imprisonment for complicity in the theft. After serving this sentence she disappeared. It is believed that she went back to her native district." I suppose you are the one?

YANETTA. Yes. My God! I thought that was so far off and so forgotten! It is all true, sir, but for ten years I have devoted every minute of my life to expiation, to an attempt to redeem myself. . . . Just now, sir, I answered you rudely. . . . I implore your pardon. You hold in your hands now not only my life, but my husband's life, and the honor of my children . . .

MOUZON. Your husband does n't know?

YANETTA. No, sir. Oh! You won't tell him, will you! I beg you on my knees. It would be criminal, yes, criminal! Listen, listen to me! I came back home, I hid . . . I would have preferred to die . . . I did n't want to stay in Paris, you understand why. And then, after a little while, I lost mamma. Etchepare was in love with me and kept urging me to marry him. I refused . . . I had the courage to refuse for three years. . . . Then I was so lonely, so sad and he so unhappy, that I finally yielded. I ought to have told him everything. I wanted to,

but I could n't. He would have suffered too much. For he is good, sir, I swear it. . . . [*At a gesture of* MOUZON.] Yes, yes . . . sometimes, it is true, when he has been drinking, he is brutal . . . I was going to tell you. I won't lie to you any more, sir . . . but he does it less and less. [*Weeping.*] Oh! Don't let him know, sir, don't let him know! He would go away, he would leave me . . . he would take away my children. [*A shriek.*] Oh! He would take my children from me! I don't know what to say to you, but it can't be that you would tell him — now that you know all the harm it would do . . . Please don't! Of course I was to blame, but how was I to understand? Did I know? — I was n't sixteen years old, sir, when I went to Paris. My employers had a son; he took me almost by force . . . and then I came to love him . . . and then he wanted to take me with him because his parents wanted to send him away. I did what he wanted me to. . . . That money — I did n't know he had stolen it . . . I swear, sir, that I did n't know it.

MOUZON. All right, calm yourself.

YANETTA. Yes, sir.

MOUZON. Let us drop that for a moment.

YANETTA. Yes, sir.

MOUZON. And return to your husband.

YANETTA. Yes, sir.

MOUZON [*bluntly*]. Try to be brave, my poor woman. Your husband is guilty.

YANETTA. It can't be, it can't be! . . .

MOUZON [*with engaging frankness*]. He has n't confessed yet, himself, but very near it. I know, as a matter of fact, that he passed that night away from home. . . . I have witnesses to that effect . . .

YANETTA. No, sir! My God, my God! Witnesses, what witnesses? It is n't so!

MOUZON. Now, for your own sake, don't be so obstinate! Do you want me to tell you where you will come out? You will ruin your husband! If you persist, in the face of evidence, in your assertion that he spent the night at home, you will ruin him, I tell you. . . . On the other hand, if you tell me the truth, if he is not the murderer, he will tell us what he did do; he will tell us who his companions were.

YANETTA. He did n't have any.

MOUZON. Then he went out alone?

YANETTA. Yes.

MOUZON. At ten o'clock?

YANETTA. Yes.

MOUZON. And came back alone at five o'clock in the morning?

YANETTA. Yes, all alone.

MOUZON. But you may be mistaken in the evening. Are you sure that it was the evening of Ascension that he went out alone? . . .

YANETTA. Yes.

MOUZON. Have you got that down, Benoît?

CLERK. Yes, your honor . . .

MOUZON. Madame, I understand what your sorrow must be, but I beg of you to listen to me with the greatest attention. Your husband was short of funds, wasn't he?

YANETTA. No.

MOUZON. Yes, he was.

YANETTA. I tell you he wasn't.

MOUZON. Here's the proof of it. Three months ago he borrowed eight hundred francs from a Mauléon merchant.

YANETTA. He never told me anything about it . . .

MOUZON. Besides that, he was in debt for a considerable amount to old man Goyetche.

YANETTA. I never heard of it . . .

MOUZON. Here is a promise to pay written by your husband; I suppose it is his signature?

YANETTA. Yes, but I didn't know . . .

MOUZON. You didn't know of the existence of this debt . . . that supports still more what I know. Your husband went to Irissarry.

YANETTA. No, sir.

MOUZON. He told you that he was going to the mountain, but he went to Irissarry.

YANETTA. No, sir; he tells me everything he does.

MOUZON. You can see plainly that he does not, since you did not know of the existence of this debt. He went to Irissarry. . . . Don't you believe it?

YANETTA. Yes, sir, I believe it, but he never murdered a man for money; that is false, false, I tell you!

MOUZON. False? How do you expect me to see that? Your husband begins by denying everything, blindly; then he offers me in succession two methods of defense.

You begin by false testimony yourself. All this, I repeat, is ruining him.

YANETTA. I don't know anything about that, but what I do know and what I shall keep on repeating as long as I live is that he never killed a man for money.

MOUZON. Well, after all. . . . Perhaps he is not as guilty as I thought a moment ago. Perhaps he acted without premeditation. It may have happened like this: Etchepare, somewhat under the influence of liquor, goes to Goyetche's to ask him to wait a little for the payment of the debt. A dispute ensues between the two men; old man Goyetche was still very vigorous; there may have been, on his part, provocation, and a struggle may have followed with the tragic end which you know. In this case the situation of your husband changes absolutely. He is no longer the criminal planning his crime in advance; and the penalty pronounced against him may be one of the very lightest. So you see, madame, how important it is for you to obtain from him a complete confession. If he persists in his denials I fear for him, at the hands of the jury, the greatest severity. That he killed old man Goyetche there is not the slightest doubt. Under what circumstances did he kill him? That is the whole question. If he persists in his attempt to make himself pass for entirely innocent, he runs the risk of being held more guilty than he is. Do you get my meaning?

YANETTA. Yes, sir.

MOUZON. Are you willing to speak to him from this point of view? Shall I send for him?

YANETTA. Yes, sir.

MOUZON. [To the CLERK.] Bring in the prisoner. Tell the officers I won't need them.

[Enter ETCHEPARE.]

YANETTA. Pierre! You! Is this the way I find you, my Pierre, in prison, like a thief! . . . My poor husband, my poor husband! Come, prove to him that you haven't done anything! Tell the Judge! Tell him the truth. . . . That will be the best way. I beg you, tell him the truth.

ETCHEPARE. What's the use now? I see well enough that I am lost. Nothing I could do, nothing I could say, would do any good.

Every one of my words turns against me. The Judge will have it I am guilty. For him, I must be guilty. So then! . . . How else can it be, my poor wife? . . . I am not strong enough to struggle against him. Let them do what they want with me, — I shan't say anything more.

YANETTA. Oh, yes, do speak! You must speak, you must defend yourself. I beg you, Pierre, I implore you, defend yourself.

ETCHEPARE. What's the use?

YANETTA. I implore you in the name of your children . . . they know nothing yet, but they cry when they see me cry . . . because, you see, in spite of my hiding, in spite of my trying to control myself before them, I can't be gay, can I? Then, as they love me, they see it! And there are questions and more questions. . . . If you only knew! They ask for you . . . André was saying to me just this morning: "Where is papa? You'll go and get him, won't you? Say you will!" I said I would and ran off. . . . You see you must defend yourself, so you can come back to them as soon as possible. . . . If you have anything, the least little thing, to reproach yourself for, say so . . . you are rough sometimes; then, I don't know . . . if you went to Irissarry, say so. . . . Perhaps you got into a quarrel with the wretched man. . . . If that is it, say so, say so . . . perhaps you had a fight with him and . . . I say that . . . I don't know . . . you understand . . . you see, the Judge promised me a moment ago that, in that case, you wouldn't be punished, or not so much. . . . My God, what ought I to say to you? What ought I to do?

ETCHEPARE. So you believe me guilty, too, do you? You believe it too; do you?

YANETTA. I don't know what to think, I don't know . . .

ETCHEPARE. [To MOUZON.] Ah! So you have thought out another way, have you? You have thought that out, too! To have me tortured by my wife, and it is you who have prompted her to speak to me of my children. . . . I don't know what you may have told her, but you have almost convinced her that I am a scoundrel, and you hoped that she would succeed in having me sent to the guillotine in the name of my children by speaking to me of them, because you know that I adore them and because they are everything to me. You are

right, perhaps there isn't a father in the world who loves his little ones as much as I love mine. [To YANETTA.] You know it, too, Yanetta! You know it! And you also know that, in spite of my faults, I am a good Christian, that I believe in God, in Almighty God. . . . Well! Listen; my two sons, — my little George, my little André, — I pray God to kill them both, if I am guilty!

YANETTA [at the highest pitch of feeling]. He is innocent! He is innocent, I tell you! [Pause.] Ah! Now you may bring on your proofs and ten witnesses, — a hundred if you want to, and you could tell me that you saw him do it and I would tell you, "It is not true. It's a lie!" Even if you should prove to me that he had confessed, I would still tell you, he is innocent. Oh, Judge, you must have felt it . . . you have a heart . . . you know how it is when one loves one's children. . . . So you must be sure now that he is innocent. . . . You are going to give him back to me, aren't you? It is all settled now, and you are going to give him back to me?

MOUZON. If he is innocent, why did he lie to me just a moment ago?

ETCHEPARE. It was you who lied! Yes, you! You told me that you had witnesses who saw me leave the house that evening . . . and you didn't have any!

MOUZON. If I didn't have any then, I do now. Yes, there is a witness who has testified that on the night of the crime you were not at home, and that witness — is your wife!

ETCHEPARE. [To YANETTA.] You?

MOUZON. [To the CLERK.] Give me her examination.

[While MOUZON is looking among his papers, YANETTA looks a long time at her husband and then at MOUZON. She reflects deeply. Finally she seems to have made up her mind.]

MOUZON. There! Your wife has just testified that you went out at ten o'clock and didn't return until five in the morning.

YANETTA [very short]. It's a lie, I didn't say any such thing.

MOUZON. You went on to testify that he returned alone at five o'clock in the morning.

YANETTA. I did not!

MOUZON. I will read you your examination. [Reads.] "Question: Then he went

out alone? *Answer:* Yes. *Question:* At ten
o'clock? *Answer:* Yes."

YANETTA. I never said it.

MOUZON. Come, now! I even took the
trouble to be more exact and said to you:
"But you may be mistaken in the evening.
Are you sure that it was the evening of
Ascension that he went out alone?" You
answered: "Yes."

YANETTA. It's a lie!

MOUZON. But I have it down here in
black and white.

YANETTA. You can put down anything
you want to.

MOUZON. So, then, I am a liar! The
clerk is a liar, too!

YANETTA. The night old man Goyetche
was murdered my husband did not leave the
house.

MOUZON. Sign this paper and be quick
about it . . . it is your examination.

YANETTA. Everything in it is false! It is
false, I tell you. [*With a shriek.*] The night
old man Goyetche was murdered my husband did not leave the house . . . my husband did not leave the house!

MOUZON [*pale with wrath*]. You'll pay
for that! [*To the* CLERK.] Draw up for me
at once an order for her detention; call the
officers. [*To* YANETTA.] Yanetta Etchepare, I hereby put you under arrest on the
charge of complicity in murder. . . . [*To the
officers.*] The man you may take back to
his cell; then come back and get the woman.

[*The officers take* ETCHEPARE *out.*]

YANETTA. Ah! You are furious, aren't
you, eh, not to have gained your point!
Oh! You have done everything you could,
though—except to have us burned with slow
fire! You have pretended to be kind—you
spoke gently! You wanted to have me send
my husband to the scaffold! [MOUZON *has
taken his file of papers and pretends to be running through them with indifference.*] It is
your trade to furnish heads to be cut off . . .
you must have victims! You must have
them at any price. When a man has fallen
into your claws he is lost. One enters here
innocent, he must go out a criminal. It is
your trade, it is your glory to succeed in it.
You put questions which don't seem to be
anything and which may send a man into
the other world, and when you have forced
the wretch to convict himself, you feel a
cannibal's joy!

MOUZON. [*To the officers.*] Take her away;
hurry up, can't you!

YANETTA. Yes! A cannibal's joy! That,
justice? Is that what you call justice? . . .
[*To the officers.*] You won't get me out so
easy! No, you won't! [*Grasps a heavy piece
of furniture.*] You are a torturer! You are
as bloodthirsty as those of the olden days,
who used to crush your bones to make you
confess! [*The officers have torn her loose;
she throws herself to the floor and roars out
the following while the officers drag her to the
door at the rear:*] Yes! Cruel! You don't
even realize it and probably think yourself
a decent man, but you are only a torturer . . .

MOUZON. Come, take her out, won't you!
What! Can't the two of you rid me of that
mad woman?

[*The officers put forth renewed efforts.*]

YANETTA. Hangman! Coward! Judas!
Heartless! Yes, heartless! And still more
false and still more cruel when you have to
deal with poor people like us! [*At the door
where she holds on:*] Oh! The brutes, they
are breaking my fingers! Yes, the poorer
people are, the worse you are to them! [*She
is taken away. Her shrieks are still heard outside as the curtain falls.*] The poorer people
are, the worse you are to them . . .

THIRD ACT

*The office of the Public Prosecutor. A door, on
a cant, opening upon a corridor at the left. It
opens inward allowing the sign to be read: "Public Prosecutor." Desk, chairs, files.*

As the curtain goes up, the CLERK *is collecting
into a cardboard folder various papers which he
is taking from the desk.*

[*Enter* LA BOUZULE.]

LA BOUZULE. Good afternoon, Benoît.

CLERK [*hesitating to take the hand which*
LA BOUZULE *extends to him*]. Sir, you do
me too much honor . . .

LA BOUZULE. Come, come, Benoît, give
me your hand. I ceased to be a magistrate
this morning: my dignity no longer requires
me to be impolite to my inferiors. . . .
How far are they in the Etchepare case?

CLERK. The hearing so far has been entirely devoted to the demand for punishment
and to the pleas . . .

LA BOUZULE. Will they get through to
day?

CLERK. Without a doubt. . . . Even if Monsieur Vagret should reply — seeing that the Judge of the Assizes is going hunting to-morrow morning.

LA BOUZULE. Are you looking for an acquittal, Benoît ?

CLERK. I am inclined to, your honor.
[*About to go out.*]

LA BOUZULE. Who is that old woman waiting in the corridor ?

CLERK. Etchepare's mother, sir.

LA BOUZULE. Poor woman ! She must be very anxious.

CLERK. Not at all. She is confident of the verdict. She has n't the least concern. She spent all yesterday afternoon there and came back this morning as tranquil as you please . . . except that to-day she wanted at all odds to see the Prosecuting Attorney or a Substitute . . . Monsieur Ardeuil is away, and Monsieur Vagret . . .

LA BOUZULE. Is at the hearing . . .

CLERK. She seemed greatly disappointed not to be able to find any one.

LA BOUZULE. Well, send her in ; perhaps I can give her some good advice. Placat will speak for some little time yet, won't he ?

CLERK. I think so.

LA BOUZULE. Then tell her to come and speak to me — this good woman. It won't disturb anybody, and perhaps will be of some help to her in her trouble.

CLERK. Very well, your honor.
[*Goes to the door at the right, beckons to ETCHEPARE's mother and goes out of the door at the rear.*]

LA BOUZULE. [*Alone.*] It's remarkable how kindly disposed I've been feeling since this morning.

[*Enter ETCHEPARE's mother in the costume of the old Basque women.*]

LA BOUZULE. They tell me, madame, that you wish to see some member of the administration.

MOTHER. Yes, sir.

LA BOUZULE. You would like to attend the hearing ?

MOTHER. No, sir. . . . I am so sure that my son cannot be convicted that I am not a bit interested in all they are saying inside there. I'm just waiting for him. I only came because we have been driven from our home.

LA BOUZULE. Driven from your home ?

MOTHER. Some officers came.

LA BOUZULE. Your son had debts, then ?

MOTHER. After he was arrested our men left us. We could n't get the crops in, nor pay our debts. But I know they will make all that up to us as soon as my son is acquitted.

LA BOUZULE. [*To himself.*] Poor woman !

MOTHER. I am so glad to see the end of our troubles coming. . . . He will come back, he will go and get his house and lands again. He will have our cattle given back. That is why I wanted to see one of the magistrates.

LA BOUZULE. I don't understand.

MOTHER. Two weeks after the officers came to arrest my son, Monsieur Claudet had the water from his factory turned into the stream which flows through our land and where our cattle drink. That was also one of the causes of our ruin. If Etchepare sees that when he comes back, God knows what he will do ! Justice must stop the wrong that is being done us.

LA BOUZULE. Justice ! Ah, madame, how much better it would be for you if you could avoid recourse to it.

MOTHER. Why ? Is n't it for everybody ?

LA BOUZULE Of course.

MOTHER. Does Monsieur Claudet have a right . . .

LA BOUZULE. Certainly not.

MOTHER. Then I come to ask the judges to make him stop.

LA BOUZULE. That is not so simple as you think, madame. You must first go to a bailiff.

MOTHER. All right, I will.

LA BOUZULE. He will authenticate your statement.

MOTHER. What does that mean ?

LA BOUZULE. He will examine whether your water-course has been contaminated.

MOTHER. There is no use of bothering a bailiff, a child could see it.

LA BOUZULE. That is the law.

MOTHER. What next ?

LA BOUZULE. Then you will have to go to a solicitor and get an opinion.

MOTHER. All right, if there is no other way . . .

LA BOUZULE. That is not all. If Claudet contests the facts the Judge will appoint an expert who will visit the spot and make a report. You would have to petition the judge to assign an early date in view of the urgency of the matter. . . . Your case once on the docket, it would be heard in its turn after the recess . . .

MOTHER. After the recess!

LA BOUZULE. And that is not all. Monsieur Claudet's attorney might make default, in which case you would have to take judgment by default. Then Monsieur Claudet might take issue or any sort of exceptions, require a decision on these exceptions, appeal from the decision before coming to a final issue . . . all that would cost a great deal.

MOTHER. Who would pay it?

LA BOUZULE. You, of course — and Claudet.

MOTHER. That would be nothing for him, he is rich; but for us, who have nothing now! . . .

LA BOUZULE. Then you will have to sue *in forma pauperis*.

MOTHER. Will that take still more time?

LA BOUZULE. A great deal . . .

MOTHER. But I always heard that justice was free in France.

LA BOUZULE. So it is, but the means to obtain it are sometimes expensive, that is all.

MOTHER. And how long would that take?

LA BOUZULE. If Monsieur Claudet appeals, it might take two years.

MOTHER. It can't be! Haven't I the right on my side, sir?

LA BOUZULE. My poor woman, it is not enough to have the right on your side . . . you need the law, too.

MOTHER. I understand. What is called justice — we poor know of it only when it swoops down on us — by the wrong it does us. Then we will have to go away, no matter where. Anyway, I shall not miss the place . . . they insult us everywhere. . . . Etchepare could never stand that.

LA BOUZULE. On that point the law protects you. Lodge a complaint and those who insult you will be punished.

MOTHER. I don't believe it. . . . I have already lodged one complaint, as you say . . . but they didn't do anything to the man who was hurting us . . . so he keeps on.

LA BOUZULE. Is it a man of your place?

MOTHER. Yes, a neighbor, Labastide, a friend of Monsieur Mondoubleau, the Deputy.

LA BOUZULE. Very well, I shall do all I can, I promise you. . . .

MOTHER. I thank you sir. . . . [*A pause.*] Well, then, I will wait for them to give me back my son.

LA BOUZULE. That's right.

[*She goes out slowly.*]

CLERK [*entering by the door in the rear*]. The court has adjourned for a recess, your honor.

LA BOUZULE. Has Placat finished?

CLERK. In the midst of applause. Two jurors were seen to wipe their eyes. No one doubts an acquittal.

LA BOUZULE. I am glad of it.

CLERK. Does your honor know the great news?

LA BOUZULE. What news?

CLERK. The arrival of the Attorney-General. .

LA BOUZULE. No, I had n't heard.

CLERK. The Attorney-General has just arrived. . . . They say he is bringing the appointment of some one here as Counsellor at the Court of Appeal.

LA BOUZULE. Ah, ha! Benoît, in your opinion, who is going to capture the plum? Vagret?

CLERK. That was my opinion. . . . I hesitated a long time between the Prosecutor and the Judge, and had about decided for the Prosecutor, but I think I was wrong.

LA BOUZULE. Is it Bunerat?

CLERK. No, your honor, I am proud to say that I think it is my employer who has the honor . . .

LA BOUZULE. Mouzon!

CLERK. Yes, your honor.

LA BOUZULE. What makes you think that?

CLERK. The Attorney-General instructed me to ask Monsieur Mouzon to come and speak with him before the end of the hearing.

LA BOUZULE. My congratulations, Benoît

[*Enter* MADAME BUNERAT.]

MADAME BUNERAT [*in tears*]. Oh, my dear Monsieur La Bouzule . . .

LA BOUZULE. What has happened, Madame Bunerat?

MADAME BUNERAT. It was that lawyer! What talent! What feeling! What talent! I am overcome with emotion.

LA BOUZULE. An acquittal?

MADAME BUNERAT. It is hoped so. . . .

MADAME VAGRET [*entering*]. Well, my dear sir . . . did you hear that famous lawyer? What a clown!

LA BOUZULE. They say he had quite an effect on the jury, — the prisoner will be acquitted.

MADAME VAGRET. I am afraid so.

[*Enter* BUNERAT, *in a black robe.*]

BUNERAT. Do you know what they tell me? The Attorney-General is here.

MADAME BUNERAT. Is that so?

MADAME VAGRET. Are you sure?

LA BOUZULE. Absolutely . . . he is bringing to Monsieur Mouzon his appointment at the Court of Pau . . .

BUNERAT. Mouzon!

MADAME BUNERAT AND MADAME VAGRET. And my husband! We had a definite promise.

[*Enter the* JUDGE OF THE ASSIZES *in a red robe.*]

JUDGE OF THE ASSIZES. Good-afternoon, gentlemen. . . . You have n't seen the Attorney-General, have you?

LA BOUZULE. No, Judge . . . but if you wish to wait for him . . .

JUDGE OF THE ASSIZES. No . . . By the way, La Bouzule, you old veteran, were you at the hearing?

LA BOUZULE. I stayed until the lawyers began to talk.

JUDGE OF THE ASSIZES. You did not see me overlook any ground for appeal, did you?

LA BOUZULE. I can't say that I did . . .

JUDGE OF THE ASSIZES. That is my bogy . . . that 's all I can think of during the whole hearing. . . . I always keep the Judges' Handbook wide open before me, but I am always afraid of forgetting some formality. . . . Think of the effect at the Chancery. My mind is not easy until the time of limitation has elapsed. . . . [*Pause.*] They tell me there were reporters from Toulouse and Bordeaux present.

LA BOUZULE. And one from Paris.

JUDGE OF THE ASSIZES. One from Paris? Are you sure?

LA BOUZULE. He was standing up near the prisoners' bench.

JUDGE OF THE ASSIZES. Standing up! A reporter from Paris, and he had to stand? [*Noticing the* CLERK.] You knew it, and did n't tell me? Is that the way you do your duty? Go at once and present him my regrets and find him a good place, you understand?

CLERK. Yes, Judge. [*Starts to go out.*]

JUDGE OF THE ASSIZES [*running after him*]. Look here! [*In a low voice.*] Try to find out if he is displeased.

CLERK. Yes, Judge.

JUDGE OF THE ASSIZES. And then . . . [*Meeting* MADAME BUNERAT *at the door.*] I beg your pardon, madame.

[*Goes out running, holding up his robe.*]

LA BOUZULE. When I was at Montpelier, I knew an old tenor who had the same anxiety at the beginning of his third season.

[*Enter* MOUZON; *cool bows.*]

MADAME BUNERAT [*after a silence*]. Is it true, Monsieur Mouzon? . . .

MADAME VAGRET. . . . That the Attorney-General . . .

BUNERAT. . . . Has arrived at Mauléon?

MOUZON [*loftily*]. Precisely . . .

BUNERAT. They say that he is bringing a Counsellor's appointment . . .

MOUZON. So they say!

MADAME BUNERAT. And you don't know?

MADAME VAGRET. You don't know?

MOUZON. Have n't the slightest idea.

CLERK [*entering*]. Here comes the Attorney-General . . .

MADAME BUNERAT. Goodness! . . .
[*Arranges her hair.*]

[*Enter the* ATTORNEY-GENERAL; *handsome, dignified, impressive bearing.*]

ALL [*bowing low, in a murmur*]. Attorney-General . . .

ATTORNEY-GENERAL. I think you may go on with the hearing, gentlemen. I am only passing through Mauléon. I am planning to return before long and receive you all . . .

ALL. Oh, Attorney-General . . .
[*They prepare to go out.*]

ATTORNEY-GENERAL. Mouzon, will you stay a moment? [MOUZON *bows.*]

MADAME VAGRET [*going out*]. My respects, I am very honored, Attorney . . .

ATTORNEY-GENERAL [*bowing*]. Judge, madame, madame . . .

BUNERAT. [*To his wife.*] You were right!
[*They go out.*]

MOUZON. [*To the* CLERK *who starts to go*

nut.] Well, Benoît, I think that my appointment is assured.

CLERK. I am very glad, Counsellor.

[*Goes out.*]

MOUZON [*obsequiously*]. Attorney-General . . .

ATTORNEY-GENERAL. Be seated. [MOUZON *takes a chair.*] There has come to my office at Bordeaux a certain report which concerns you, Judge. [*Looking in his portfolio.*] Here it is. [*Reading.*] Case of Mouzon and the Pecquet Girl. Do you know anything about it?

MOUZON [*not taking the matter seriously and trying to smile. After a long silence*]. Yes, Attorney-General.

ATTORNEY-GENERAL. I await your explanations.

MOUZON [*as before*]. You were young once yourself, Attorney . . .

ATTORNEY-GENERAL. Not in that way, Judge.

MOUZON. I did go a little beyond bounds, I confess.

ATTORNEY-GENERAL [*reading*]. " Under the influence of liquor accompanied by the Pecquet girl and two other women of immoral life in the same condition Monsieur Mouzon insulted and abused the officers, whom he threatened with discharge." (*Speaking.*) Is that what you call going a little beyond bounds?

MOUZON. To tell the truth, the expression is a little weak . . .

ATTORNEY-GENERAL. And you allow the name of a magistrate to figure in a police record in conjunction with that of the Pecquet girl?

MOUZON. She said her name was Diana de Montmorency.

ATTORNEY - GENERAL [*continuing*]. " Questioned by me, Police Commissioner, the next morning, about his disguise as officer in the navy which he had adopted . . . "

[*Looks at* MOUZON *again; continued silence.*]

MOUZON [*still smiling*]. Yes, on account of my sidewhiskers . . .

ATTORNEY-GENERAL. Indeed?

MOUZON. When I . . . that is . . . when I go to Bordeaux, I always go in the character of officer in the navy in order to safeguard the dignity of the magistracy.

ATTORNEY-GENERAL. Your solicitude is a little tardy.

MOUZON. I will beg you to observe, Attorney, that my solicitude dated from the very beginning, since I took care to leave the district, and even the jurisdiction . . .

ATTORNEY-GENERAL. To continue . . . " Monsieur Mouzon revealed to me his real identity as examining magistrate. He made use of this title to request us to drop further proceedings . . . "

MOUZON. The idiot! Did he put that in his report? The idea! Didn't he know any better than that? That's not it; I tell you, it is a question of politics; the Police Commissioner is one of our opponents. I asked him . . . Well, anyway, I wanted to avoid a scandal — any one would have done the same in my place . . .

ATTORNEY-GENERAL. Have you anything more to say? . . .

MOUZON. Anything more to say? Certainly, sir, if you wish to insist in this conversation on the relations of superior and subordinate, I have nothing more to say. If, on the other hand, you would deign to allow me to forget for a moment your lofty position, if you would consent to speak with me as man to man, I would add that it was a youthful escapade, an unfortunate incident, of course, but explicable by the profound *ennui* which rises from the streets of Mauléon. I admit, I had dined too well . . . there are a lot of decent people who find themselves in the same situation every evening. . . . It is a trifling matter which does not compromise the character of any one.

ATTORNEY-GENERAL. Sir, when one has the honor to be a magistrate, when one has accepted the responsibility of judging one's fellow-men, he is in duty bound to observe more decorum, more dignity than any one else. A thing which does not compromise the character of the one judged, does compromise the character of the judge. Let that be said once for all.

MOUZON. In view of the fact, Attorney, that you do not deign to treat with me on any other than an official footing, I can do nothing but request you to inform me of your decision.

ATTORNEY-GENERAL. Have you no idea?

MOUZON. I am examining magistrate. You will degrade me to the rank of simple judge, — a decrease of five hundred francs per year. I accept.

ATTORNEY-GENERAL. Unfortunately,

this simple solution will not suffice. To speak more clearly, I have to inform you that Coire, director of the paper which is most open in its hostility toward us, is cognizant of all the facts of which you are accused, and consents to withhold them only on condition that you leave Mauléon before the end of the month. I find myself, therefore, under the painful necessity of requesting your resignation.

MOUZON. I shall not give it.

ATTORNEY-GENERAL. You won't give it!

MOUZON. It grieves me greatly to be unable to comply with one of your desires, Attorney, but my mind is made up; I shall not resign.

ATTORNEY-GENERAL. Well, . . . but . . . are you not aware . . .

MOUZON. I am aware of everything.

ATTORNEY - GENERAL. Well, sir, we should let the law take its course. [Rises.]

MOUZON. Pray do!

ATTORNEY-GENERAL. Have you considered the scandal which will devolve upon you from your appearance before the court, from your probable conviction?

MOUZON. My conviction is not so probable as you seem to think. I am quite able to defend myself and to choose my counsel. As for the scandal, it is not upon me that it will devolve ; — I am a bachelor without a family. I know no one, so to speak, at Mauléon — which has been to me hardly more than an exile. My friends are all at Bordeaux ; they belong to the gay set, and I would not be disgraced in their eyes by the proceedings in question. Even if I have to leave the magistracy, I have, fortunately, enough to live on, over and above the three thousand francs which the State allows me each year.

ATTORNEY-GENERAL. That is sufficient. You may go.

MOUZON. I wish you a very good day, sir.   [Goes out.]

JANITOR. [Comes in.] Mr. Attorney-General, the Deputy . . . he says you are expecting him.

ATTORNEY-GENERAL. Yes, I am. Ask him to come in.

[Enter MONDOUBLEAU. The ATTORNEY-GENERAL rises to greet him and grasps his hand.]

MONDOUBLEAU. How do you do, Attorney?

ATTORNEY-GENERAL. Quite well, Deputy, thank you ; how are you?

MONDOUBLEAU. Delighted to see you. I am just in from Paris. I took dinner yesterday with my friend, the Keeper of the Seals . . . the Cabinet is a little worried just for the moment . . .

ATTORNEY-GENERAL. How's that?

MONDOUBLEAU. They fear an interpellation, — at any moment, so to speak. I'll tell you about it some time. . . . By the way, they say you have a young Substitute here who is making a little too much stir . . .

ATTORNEY-GENERAL. Ardeuil?

MONDOUBLEAU. Ardeuil, that's it. Eugène is so well posted . . .

ATTORNEY-GENERAL. Eugène?

MONDOUBLEAU. Yes, my friend, Eugène, the Keeper of the Seals. He said to me : "I am relying on the Attorney-General to do his duty."

ATTORNEY-GENERAL. I ask nothing better, provided some one will tell me in what it consists . . .

MONDOUBLEAU. That is just what they want to avoid . . . By the way, you certainly do know how to keep your own counsel, don't you?

ATTORNEY-GENERAL. I ? What do you mean?

MONDOUBLEAU. You are asking to be transferred . . .

ATTORNEY-GENERAL. Who told you that?

MONDOUBLEAU. The only one who knows it, of course . . . who did you think?

ATTORNEY-GENERAL. Eu . . . [Quickly.] The Keeper of the Seals?

MONDOUBLEAU. You desire to be appointed at Orléans . . . Am I correctly informed?

ATTORNEY-GENERAL. To tell the truth, we do have family there.

MONDOUBLEAU. I believe you are already on the slate.

ATTORNEY-GENERAL. Are changes already in consideration?

MONDOUBLEAU. Yes. Speaking of Monsieur Ardeuil — the Minister confined himself to saying that he had confidence in your firmness and zeal.

ATTORNEY-GENERAL. The Keeper of the Seals may rely upon me. I have to do a little pruning here in several directions and shall lack neither firmness nor zeal, I assure you.

MONDOUBLEAU. All right, but, above all, have tact! Eugène repeated it ten times: "Especially no scandals! No scandals! Just now less than ever. . . . We are being watched. . . . So, perfect quiet!"

ATTORNEY-GENERAL. Be assured. . . . It is a question of Mouzon.

MONDOUBLEAU. Mouzon . . . Mouzon . . . the examining magistrate?

ATTORNEY-GENERAL. Yes.

MONDOUBLEAU. Of Mauléon?

ATTORNEY-GENERAL. Exactly.

MONDOUBLEAU. You can't mean it. . . . He's one of my best friends. . . . Exceedingly favorable to us. . . . A thoroughly good fellow! An excellent magistrate, energetic and discerning. . . . Why, I have even spoken of him to Eugène for the Counsellor's vacancy.

ATTORNEY-GENERAL [handing him the papers concerning MOUZON]. You certainly chose a good time! Here are some papers which concern him. Anyway, the place is promised to Vagret.

MONDOUBLEAU. What's the trouble?

ATTORNEY-GENERAL. Just this: I shall have to report him to the Superior Council of the Magistracy or bring suit against him before the Court of Appeal.

MONDOUBLEAU. What has he done? —

ATTORNEY-GENERAL. Read it.

MONDOUBLEAU [after having glanced at the papers which have been handed him]. Yes, I see, . . . a matter of no consequence. At all events, if you keep quiet nobody will know anything about it. No scandal! The enemies of the magistracy are too active now, anyway, without our furnishing them ammunition.

ATTORNEY - GENERAL. Unfortunately Coire is aware of the facts and threatens to publish them unless Mouzon is removed from Mauléon . . .

MONDOUBLEAU. The devil . . .
[Commences to laugh.]

ATTORNEY-GENERAL. What are you laughing at?

MONDOUBLEAU. Nothing, — a fantastic idea . . . just a joke . . . [Laughs.] Listen, — now don't get angry, will you . . . it's just a joke . . .

ATTORNEY-GENERAL. What is it?

MONDOUBLEAU. I was just thinking . . .

just a strange idea, of course . . . after all, if you should propose Mouzon for Counsellor at Pau, everybody would be satisfied . . .

ATTORNEY-GENERAL. But, Deputy. . . .

MONDOUBLEAU. I told you I was only joking . . . it's only a jest . . . and the funny thing about it all is that you would be satisfying Coire, myself, Mouzon, and Eugène, who does n't want any scandal, all of us at the same time. . . .

ATTORNEY-GENERAL. But that would be a scandal . . .

MONDOUBLEAU. You are wrong there. In politics there is no scandal until the scandal is out.

ATTORNEY-GENERAL. But still . . .

MONDOUBLEAU. I quite agree with you. I know perfectly well all that may be said . . . I told you I was only joking . . . and do you know that the curious part of it, really, when you think it over, is that this extravagant solution is the only one which does not have evident and serious objections. . . . Certainly, if you leave Mouzon here, Coire will tell everything. If you bring suit against him, you will give to a certain press an occasion to undermine one of the bases of Society which it will be only glad to have. Exactly! — they will confound the whole magistracy with Mouzon . . . it will not be Mouzon, who will be the ribald, it will be the tribunal, the Court of Pau . . . there will be mud on every gown.

ATTORNEY-GENERAL. But you cannot be asking seriously . . .

MONDOUBLEAU. I tell you what let's do . . . let's go and talk it over with Rollet, the Senator; he lives only a step away.

ATTORNEY-GENERAL. I assure you . . .

MONDOUBLEAU. Oh, come on! You will drop a word about Orléans at the same time . . . what do you risk? I tell you my solution is the best. . . . You will come to it, believe me! I will take you over. . . .
[Takes him by the arm.]

ATTORNEY-GENERAL. Well, I did have a word to say to him.

[Enter CLERK.]

ATTORNEY-GENERAL. How far have they got? To the verdict?

CLERK. Not yet . . . Monsieur Vagret has just replied . . .

ATTORNEY-GENERAL. Are the jury out?

CLERK. No, Attorney-General . . . they were just going when Monsieur Vagret asked for an intermission.

MONDOUBLEAU. That's a great idea . . . anyway, let's be going, friend, you will come around . . .

ATTORNEY-GENERAL [*weakly*]. Never, never!

CLERK [*deeply moved*]. Wonderful!

JANITOR [*half opening the door at the rear*]. Benoît, what's the news?

CLERK. Wonderful! Our prosecutor has just been magnificent . . . and that Etchepare is the lowest of the low . . .

[*Enter* MADAME VAGRET, *deeply moved.* CLERK *goes to her;* JANITOR *disappears.*]

MADAME VAGRET. Oh, dear me!

CLERK. Madame Vagret, I am only a clerk, but allow me to say that it was wonderful!

MADAME VAGRET. Wonderful.

CLERK. How Monsieur Vagret did give it to that Bordeaux lawyer.

MADAME VAGRET. Did n't he, though?

CLERK. It's settled now, the death penalty. . . .

MADAME VAGRET. Without any doubt.

CLERK. Madame, the jurors kept looking at that Etchepare, the scoundrel, in a way that made me afraid — as Monsieur Vagret went on speaking you could feel that they would have liked to settle his case, themselves, the wretch!

MADAME VAGRET. Yes, I saw it!

CLERK. I beg your pardon, madame, I am forgetting myself, but there are times when one is so happy, so happy that differences in station don't count.

MADAME VAGRET. You are right, my good Benoît.

[*Enter* JUDGE OF THE ASSIZES *and* BUNERAT.]

JUDGE OF THE ASSIZES. Oh, madame, let me congratulate you. We have it this time — the death penalty . . .

MADAME VAGRET. Yes, Judge, we have it at last, have n't we?

JUDGE OF THE ASSIZES. Beyond a doubt . . . but where is the victor? He was simply sublime . . . was n't he, Bunerat?

BUNERAT. Yes, Judge, but you had prepared the way so well, by the way you presided . . .

JUDGE OF THE ASSIZES. Oh, of course,

I don't mean I had nothing to do with the result, but Vagret must be given credit. [*To* MADAME VAGRET.] You ought to be happy, very happy and very proud, my dear madame . . .

MADAME VAGRET. Oh, yes, Judge . . .

JUDGE OF THE ASSIZES. But what kind of an idea was it, anyhow, to ask for a recess? . . . Is he sick?

MADAME VAGRET. Oh!

JUDGE OF THE ASSIZES. No, here he is.

[*Enter* VAGRET. *He looks worried.*]

MADAME VAGRET. Oh, my dear!
[*Takes his hand in hers. She can say nothing more, overcome by her feelings.*]

JUDGE OF THE ASSIZES. It was wonderful!

BUNERAT. I really must congratulate you, too!

VAGRET. Really, you overwhelm me . . . you deserve all the credit, Judge.

JUDGE OF THE ASSIZES. Not at all . . . do you know what carried everything before it? . . .   [*Lights a cigarette.*]

VAGRET. No.

JUDGE OF THE ASSIZES. It was when you exclaimed: "Gentlemen of the jury, you have homes, farms, property; you have wives whom you love, you have daughters whom you have tenderly nurtured . . . beware . . ." At that point you were grand! [*Going on.*] "Beware, if you allow yourselves to be misled by the eloquent sentimentality of the defense; beware, I say, if you prove unfaithful to your lofty rôle of dispensers of justice, lest One on high pick up the glaive fallen from your feeble hands and shower upon you and yours the blood which you shall have left unavenged!" That was sublime, and it produced a tremendous effect!

BUNERAT. But it was you, my dear Judge, who moved them most when, recalling quite opportunely that the accused loved the sight of blood . . .

JUDGE OF THE ASSIZES. Oh, yes, that did have some effect . . .

ALL. What? What was it?

BUNERAT. The Judge puts this question: "The morning of the crime did you not kill two sheep?" "Yes," the prisoner replies . . . and then the Judge looking him straight in the face . . .

JUDGE OF THE ASSIZES. Yes, I said to him: "You were practicing, were n't you?" . . . [*To* VAGRET.] Anyhow, if I did have something to do with the result, it is to you that the greater part of the honor of the day will fall.

VAGRET. You are too kind.

JUDGE OF THE ASSIZES. By no means . . . and your conclusion! [*With an artist's curiosity.*] You were really under the influence of a powerful emotion, of a very powerful emotion, were n't you?

VAGRET [*soberly*]. Yes, under the influence of a very powerful emotion.

JUDGE OF THE ASSIZES. You became very pale as you looked at the jury and you added with your voice sunk almost to a whisper . . . "Gentlemen, I demand of you the head of this man!"

VAGRET [*with staring eyes*]. Yes.

JUDGE OF THE ASSIZES. Then you made a sign to the counsel for the defense.

VAGRET. Yes, I thought he might have something to add . . .

JUDGE OF THE ASSIZES. But why delay the verdict? You had won the victory.

VAGRET. That was just the trouble.

JUDGE OF THE ASSIZES. What do you mean?

VAGRET. During my demand for punishment something took place which troubled me . . .

JUDGE OF THE ASSIZES. Troubled you?

BUNERAT. What was it?

VAGRET. It was n't exactly anything . . . but . .*. in short . . . [*Pause.*] Excuse me, I am very tired . . .

JUDGE OF THE ASSIZES. I understand your emotion very well, Vagret. One always has it at the time one wins his first death penalty . . . but . . . you'll see . . . you'll get used to it. [*Going out; to* BUNERAT.] It is true, he does seem tired . . .

BUNERAT. I think he is too sentimental for his place . . .

VAGRET. As I left the court-room, I met the Attorney-General and asked him urgently to give me a moment's conversation —I would like to speak alone with him . . . and with you, Judge.

BUNERAT. As you like.

MADAME VAGRET. I am afraid you are not well, my dear. . . . I will stay outside here and will come back as soon as the gentlemen have gone.

VAGRET. All right.

MADAME BUNERAT [*going out, to her husband*]. I know somebody who is going to make a blunder.

BUNERAT. What do we care?
[*They go out.*]

JUDGE OF THE ASSIZES. Can it be that you noticed anything out of order on my part in the judicial procedure?

VAGRET. No, if there was anything wrong, I am to blame.
[*Enter* ATTORNEY-GENERAL.]

ATTORNEY-GENERAL. What is there so serious, my dear Attorney?

VAGRET. It is this . . . I am worried beyond all power of expression . . . I need the consciences of both of you to reassure me . . .

ATTORNEY-GENERAL. Explain yourself . . .

VAGRET. A whole array of facts, the attitude of the prisoner, certain details which had escaped me, have aroused in my mind a doubt as to the guilt of this man.

ATTORNEY-GENERAL. Was there any indication of these facts, of these details in the papers on the case?

VAGRET. Certainly.

ATTORNEY-GENERAL. Did the attorney for the defense have access to these papers?

VAGRET. Of course.

ATTORNEY-GENERAL. Well, then, why this concern of yours?

VAGRET. But, supposing this man were not guilty?

ATTORNEY-GENERAL. The jury will decide. We have nothing to do, any of us, but bow to their decision.

VAGRET. Allow me to tell you, Attorney-General, how my conviction was shaken.

ATTORNEY-GENERAL. I don't care to know. All that is only a matter between you and your conscience. You have the right to set forth your scruples to the jury. You know the proverb — the pen is servile, speech is free.

VAGRET. I shall follow your advice.

ATTORNEY-GENERAL. I am not giving any advice.

VAGRET. I shall set forth my doubts to the jury.

ATTORNEY-GENERAL. That means acquittal.

VAGRET. I can't help it.

ATTORNEY-GENERAL [*angrily*]. Do any

thing you like; but I must tell you one thing, my dear sir. Any one planning such revolutionary proceedings generally has the courage to carry them out alone, and to accept the undivided responsibility of the follies which he may commit. . . . You are shrewder and have succeeded in finding the means of forcing others to share the consequences of your doubts . . .

VAGRET. I, shrewd? How?

ATTORNEY-GENERAL. Come, come, now, we're no children; I see plainly enough the trap into which you have led me. You have laid your responsibilities on another. If you are criticized at the Chancery for your attitude, you will reply that you consulted your superior and it is I who will be the victim . . . and there I am in difficulties with the Chancery. What do you care for my interests or for a situation which doesn't affect you? You get some notion or other into your head and you make me responsible for it in spite of myself. Once more, it is very shrewd of you, I compliment you, but I am not grateful . . .

VAGRET. You misunderstand me, Attorney-General; I have not the slightest intention of unloading upon you any responsibilities which I may incur. . . . It is certainly not at the moment that I expect to receive a Counsellor's appointment that I would be guilty of such an error. . . . I am telling you my trouble and asking you for advice, that is all.

JUDGE OF THE ASSIZES. Have you any proof?

VAGRET. If I had proof I would n't be asking for advice, would I? [Silence.] If we only had a ground for appeal — a good one . . .

JUDGE OF THE ASSIZES [wrathfully]. What's that! Ground for appeal! Based on an oversight or an error on my part, I suppose! Well, you are ingenious, my dear Attorney. . . . You arrive at some doubt or other, and in order to obtain peace with your morbidly sensitive conscience, you invite me to be kind enough to commit an error! Really, that would be convenient — to unload errors which you may have committed on others who have done their duty . . .

ATTORNEY-GENERAL [again self-possessed]. I quite agree.

JUDGE OF THE ASSIZES. And at the Chancery, speaking of me, they will say: "What kind of a Counsellor is this, anyhow, who is not even capable of presiding over an Assize session at Mauléon!" A man we have had such trouble to convict, too! And to sacrifice me to such a scoundrel! Oh, no! Find some other way, my dear sir; this is not the one for you, take my word for it!

VAGRET. Then I shall find some other way, but I shall not leave the situation as it is.

ATTORNEY-GENERAL. I don't care what you do! Only don't forget that I have given you no advice one way or another.

VAGRET. I recognize that.

JUDGE OF THE ASSIZES. When you make up your mind to go on with the hearing, please let us know.

VAGRET. I will.

ATTORNEY-GENERAL. [To the JUDGE OF THE ASSIZES.] Shall we be going? . . .
[They go out.]

MADAME VAGRET. [Enters.] What's the trouble?

VAGRET. Nothing.

MADAME VAGRET. Nothing! Why are you so depressed in spite of a success which will mean so much in your career?

VAGRET. It's this very success that frightens me.

MADAME VAGRET. Frightens you?

VAGRET. Yes, I am afraid.

MADAME VAGRET. Of what?

VAGRET. Of having gone too far.

MADAME VAGRET. Too far! Does n't he deserve death a hundred times, the murderer?

VAGRET [after a silence]. Are you sure that he is a murderer?

MADAME VAGRET. Yes.

VAGRET [in a low tone]. Well, I . . .

MADAME VAGRET. What?

VAGRET. For myself, I don't know what to think . . .

MADAME VAGRET. Good Heavens!

VAGRET. Yes, there occurred within me during the course of my demand for the penalty a terrible thing. . . . While I, representative of the State, while I, Official Prosecutor, was performing my duty, another judgment within me was examining the case with coolness; an inner voice was reproaching me for my violence and was insinuating into my mind a doubt which increased — there took place in my soul a grievous combat, a bitter combat, and a cruel one . . . that emotion as I closed of which the judge spoke, that low voice with which I demanded the penalty, was because I had reached the end of my strength; it was because, in this combat, my conscience was on the point of winning the day — and I hastened to finish because I was afraid that its voice would burst out in spite of me. When I saw the counsel for the defense remain seated without rising to say the things that I would have liked to have him say to the jury . . . then I was truly afraid of myself, afraid of my acts, of my words, of their horrible consequences, and I wanted to gain time . . .

MADAME VAGRET. But, my dear, you have done your duty; the counsel for the defense has not done his — that is no concern of yours.

VAGRET. That same reply! If I were an honest man, in a few moments, at the reopening of the hearing, I would tell the jury of the doubt which has taken possession of me. I would explain how it arose in me. . . . I would call their attention to a point which I deliberately kept back because I thought that the prisoner's counsel would point it out to them.

MADAME VAGRET. You know, dear, how I respect your scruples, but I must call your attention to this fact : Etchepare will not be pronounced innocent or guilty by you, but by the jury. If any one ought to be worried, it is Placat, not you . . .

VAGRET. I ought to represent justice!

MADAME VAGRET. Here you have a prisoner who comes before you with a record of previous convictions, with a whole mass of overwhelming circumstances which confirm his guilt. He is defended ; by whom? By a leader in the profession, famous for his integrity as well as for his skill and oratorical talent. You expound the facts to the jury. If the jury decides in your favor, I don't see how your responsibility as a magistrate is compromised.

VAGRET. As a magistrate, perhaps not; as a man, certainly. No! I have no right to be silent . . . no right! I tell you, there is in this case a series of circumstances of which no one has spoken and of such a kind as to make me believe in the innocence of the accused . . .

MADAME VAGRET. But how is it you overlooked these circumstances until now?

VAGRET [with lowered head]. Do you think that I did overlook them? In the name of Heaven, do I dare tell you all? I am not a wicked man ; I wouldn't have any one suffer through my fault, would I? Well . . . oh, how ashamed am I to confess it, to say it openly after having confessed it to myself! Well, as I studied the case, I had my mind so firmly made up in advance that Etchepare was guilty that when an argument in his favor presented itself to me, I rejected it with a shrug of the shoulders. As to the facts of which I am speaking, and from which my doubt arose . . . I at first simply tried to prove to myself that they were false, choosing in the depositions of the witnesses only what served to disprove them, repudiating all the rest with a horrible unquestioning simplicity in my bad faith . . . and at last, in order to dissipate my final scruples, I said to myself, as you are doing now, — "It is the concern of the defense, not mine!" Listen! Just see to what extent the exercise of the profession of magistrate deforms us, makes us unjust and cruel: At first I had a feeling of joy when I saw the Judge in his examination leave all these little facts in the background! That's the trade! Do you understand, the trade! Oh, poor creatures that we are, poor creatures!

MADAME VAGRET. Perhaps the jury will not convict.

VAGRET. They will, though.

MADAME VAGRET. They may take into account extenuating circumstances.

VAGRET. No. I insisted too urgently on the contrary. How I insisted! How violent I was!

MADAME VAGRET. True. . . . Why did you speak with such passion?

VAGRET. Ah, why! why! For a long time before the hearing it was so well understood by everybody that the prisoner was guilty! And how they had turned my head, how they had intoxicated me! I was the voice of humanity, I was to make the public highways safe, make the family secure, and I don't know what. Then I felt that I must rise to what was expected of me. My first demand for the penalty had been comparatively moderate . . . but when

I saw the celebrated lawyer make the jurors weep, I thought I was lost; I felt that I was losing my grip on the accusation, and, contrary to my custom, I replied. When I rose the second time I was like a fighter who has caught a glimpse of defeat and who struggles with despair. From that moment Etchepare no longer existed for me, so to speak. I no longer was concerned with the defense of Society nor with the support of the accusation, I was struggling with the attorney; it was a contest of orators, a competition between comedians — I must come out victorious at any price. I must convince the jury, win it back again, wrest from them the two "Ayes" of the verdict. It was no longer a question of Etchepare, I tell you, it was a question of myself, of my vanity, of my reputation, of my honor, of my future. . . . It is shameful, I repeat, it is shameful! At all hazards, I wished to prevent the acquittal which I felt was certain. And I was so afraid of not succeeding that I employed every argument, both good and bad, even to picturing to the terrified jury their houses in flames, their dear ones murdered . . . I spoke of the vengeance of God upon indulgent judges. And all that with a clear conscience — or rather absolutely unconsciously, in the heat of passion and in the heat of anger against the lawyer whom I hated then with all my power. My success went beyond my wishes; the jury is ready to obey me, and, my dear, I have allowed myself to be congratulated, I have taken the hands which were held out to me. . . . That's what a magistrate is!

MADAME VAGRET. Don't take it so seriously — there are n't, perhaps, ten men in France who would have done otherwise.

VAGRET. You are right. But, when you think of it, that is precisely what is so terrible.

CLERK [entering]. Attorney, the Judge wants to know when the hearing may be resumed.

VAGRET. At once.

MADAME VAGRET. What are you going to do?

VAGRET. What a man of honor ought to do. [Prepares to go out.]

ACT IV

Setting as in Act II.

[BUNERAT, JUDGE OF THE ASSIZES, *then* VAGRET.]

BUNERAT. Well, there's another session over.

JUDGE OF THE ASSIZES [*wearing a red gown*]. I was scared to death for fear those animals would make me miss my train . . . you see I am going hunting to-morrow on the Cambo lakes, and after this evening's train it's all off! [*Looking at his watch.*] Oh, I have still an hour and a half . . .

BUNERAT. What do you think of it, Judge?

JUDGE OF THE ASSIZES. Of what? The verdict? What do you suppose I care? In fact, I prefer it that way: I am sure that the defense will not dig up some unexpected error in procedure. . . . Where is my hat-box?

[*Climbs on a chair to reach the hat-box which is on top of a wardrobe.* BUNERAT *anticipates him.*]

BUNERAT. Allow me, Judge! You are our guest. [*From the chair.*] I'm afraid I'll have the pleasure of receiving you here again at the next session.

[*Sighs, handing down the hat-box.*]

JUDGE OF THE ASSIZES. The pleasure will be mine. . . .

[*Takes from the hat-box a small round hat.*]

BUNERAT. Do you want a brush? . . . There is Mouzon's . . . [*Sigh.*] Oh, Lord, when shall I ever leave Mauléon? I would so much like to live at Pau!

JUDGE OF THE ASSIZES. Pshaw! It is a much over-rated town, believe me. . . .

BUNERAT. So, then, new duties don't take me there yet?

JUDGE OF THE ASSIZES. That's nothing! It is a good enough place in the winter . . . but the summers — goodness, what summers!

BUNERAT. So I did not get the appointment?

JUDGE OF THE ASSIZES. Ah, you know it already?

BUNERAT. Yes, — I . . . that is, I did not know that it was official.

JUDGE OF THE ASSIZES [*brushing his hat and noticing a dent*]. It is already dented.

Nowadays, the hats they sell you for felt are nothing but pasteboard.

BUNERAT. That's so. No, I did n't know that it was official. . . . Mouzon is very fortunate. . . .

[*Enter* VAGRET *in citizen's dress.*]

JUDGE OF THE ASSIZES. Well, well, here is Vagret. Already dressed ! Yes, you are at home, while I must pack all this up. . . . Where in the devil is my robe-box ? [BUNERAT *starts to get it for him, but stops.*] That's strange, what has become of it . . . in this wardrobe. . . . You have n't seen it, have you, Bunerat ?

BUNERAT. No.

JUDGE OF THE ASSIZES. Ah, here it is . . . and my coat in it . . . [*Opens the box and takes out his cutaway which he puts beside the table.*] Well, you made them acquit him, my dear sir ; are you satisfied ?

VAGRET. Yes. I am very glad.

JUDGE OF THE ASSIZES. But suppose they were guilty ?

VAGRET. I shall console myself with that saying from Berryer : "It is better to let ten guilty men go free than to punish one who is innocent."

JUDGE OF THE ASSIZES. You are sentimental.

VAGRET. Must one have a heart of stone to be a magistrate ?

JUDGE OF THE ASSIZES [*tying up the box where he has put his judge's cap*]. One must rise above the petty misfortunes of mankind.

VAGRET. That is, above the misfortunes of others . . .

JUDGE OF THE ASSIZES. Oh, well. . . .

VAGRET. That's what I call selfishness.

JUDGE OF THE ASSIZES. Do you mean that for me ?

VAGRET. For all three of us.

BUNERAT. Good-day, gentlemen . . . Good-day !

[*Shakes hands with both and goes out.*]

JUDGE OF THE ASSIZES [*taking off his robe*]. My dear Attorney, I must ask you to be a little more careful in your choice of words.

VAGRET. I assure you, Judge, I am careful. . . . If I should speak out what is in my heart, you would hear some very disagreeable things.

JUDGE OF THE ASSIZES [*in his shirtsleeves*]. Do not forget to whom you are speaking. I am Counsellor at the Court, Mr. Attorney.

VAGRET. I am not speaking simply with reference to you, sir. The disagreeable things which I might say would condemn me also. I am thinking of those poor people . . .

JUDGE OF THE ASSIZES [*brushing his robe*]. What poor people ? The prisoners of this afternoon ? Well, they are acquitted ; what more do you want — give them pensions ?

VAGRET. They were acquitted, it is true, but they have been sentenced for all that. They have been sentenced to misery for their natural lives . . .

JUDGE OF THE ASSIZES. What are you talking about ?

VAGRET. And it was your fault, too, Judge.

JUDGE OF THE ASSIZES [*stopping in the midst of folding up his robe*]. My fault ?

VAGRET. And the worst of it is that you did n't even see the harm you did !

JUDGE OF THE ASSIZES. What harm have I done, pray ?

VAGRET. Well, when you disclosed to Etchepare that his wife had once been convicted of complicity in theft and that she had been seduced before he married her . . . that was really too bad of you !

JUDGE OF THE ASSIZES. Don't be so quixotic ! Do you think he did n't know it ?

VAGRET. If you had seen his emotion when his wife replied "yes," when you asked if it were so, you would be as convinced as I that he did n't know anything about it.

JUDGE OF THE ASSIZES [*closing the box where he has put his robe*]. Well, even so ; you are ascribing to people like that feelings which they don't possess.

VAGRET. "People like that" have hearts as well as we, Judge.

JUDGE OF THE ASSIZES. Let's grant it. . . . Did n't my duty compel me to do what I did ?

VAGRET. That's not for me to say.

JUDGE OF THE ASSIZES [*still in his shirtsleeves*]. Is the law at fault, then ? Well, sir ! If I did my duty, as I did, you are certainly not doing yours in attacking the law, whose faithful servant you are and which I am proud to represent.

VAGRET. You need n't be !

JUDGE OF THE ASSIZES. Sir !

VAGRET. It's an atrocity, I tell you, that it is permitted to throw up to a prisoner, innocent or guilty, a fault which he committed ten years before and which he has expiated. Yes, sir, it is revolting that after having punished, the law does not pardon.

JUDGE OF THE ASSIZES [*who has put on his coat and hat*]. If you find that the law is bad, have it changed . . . run for Deputy at the next elections.

VAGRET. Alas! . . . If I were Deputy, I should probably do as the others do, and instead of thinking of that, I would be thinking of nothing but the probable duration of the Cabinet.

JUDGE OF THE ASSIZES [*with his box under his arm*]. In that case, of course — is the janitor . . .

VAGRET [*ringing the bell*]. He will be right here. — So Mouzon is appointed in my place?

JUDGE OF THE ASSIZES. Yes; Mouzon.

VAGRET. Because he is the henchman of a Deputy, of a Mondoubleau —

JUDGE OF THE ASSIZES. I shall not allow you to speak ill of Monsieur Mondoubleau before me . . .

VAGRET. You imagine you may need him . . .

JUDGE OF THE ASSIZES. Precisely. [JANITOR *appears.*] Will you carry that for me to my hotel, my good man? — the hotel near the station. . . . You will recognize it easily; my orderly is at the door . . . [*Gives him his boxes.*] Good-day, Vagret, — I don't bear you any grudge.

[*Goes out,* VAGRET *puts on his hat and also prepares to go out.*]

[*The* CLERK *comes in.*]

CLERK. You are going, sir?

VAGRET. Yes.

CLERK. Do you have any objections to my letting Etchepare come in here? He is waiting, in the hall, for the formalities of release and complains of being exposed to public curiosity.

VAGRET. Let him come in, by all means.

CLERK. Shall I tell them to bring his wife here, too, when she comes from the office.

VAGRET. Certainly.

CLERK. I shall tell the officers, but the wife cannot be released immediately . . .

VAGRET. Why not?

CLERK. She is held on another complaint. She is accused of insulting a magistrate in the exercise of his functions.

VAGRET. Mouzon?

CLERK. Yes, your honor.

VAGRET. I will try to arrange that.

CLERK. Good-day, your honor.

VAGRET. Good-day. [*Goes out.*]

CLERK [*at the door*]. Come in, Etchepare. You will like it better here while you are waiting for your definite release . . . it won't be long.

ETCHEPARE. Thank you, sir.

CLERK. Well, at last you are acquitted, my poor man! It is over at last.

ETCHEPARE. It is over as far as the trial is concerned, sir, but it is not over for me. I am acquitted, it is true, but for me it's all up now!

CLERK. You did n't know?

ETCHEPARE. No, sir.

CLERK. It was so long ago . . . you will forgive her . . .

ETCHEPARE. A Basque never forgives those things . . . it was like a thunderbolt falling on my heart . . . and all our trouble has come to us because of her. . . . God has avenged himself . . . all is lost.

CLERK [*after a pause*]. I feel for you from the bottom of my heart.

ETCHEPARE. Thank you, sir . . . [*A pause.*] Since you are so kind, sir, will you let my mother, who is waiting outside in the hall, come in and speak to me?

CLERK. I will send her in to you. Good-bye.

ETCHEPARE. Good-bye.

[CLERK *goes out.*]

[*The* MOTHER *comes in.*]

ETCHEPARE [*pressing his mother's head to his breast*]. My poor old mother, how the grief of these three months has changed you! . . .

MOTHER. My poor child, how you must have suffered!

ETCHEPARE. That woman!

MOTHER. Yes, they have just told me.

ETCHEPARE. For ten years I have lived with that thief . . . with that wench! How well she could lie! Ah! When I heard that Judge say to her: "You were sentenced for theft in complicity with your lover," and when before all the public she con-

fessed . . . do you know, mother, I thought
Heaven was falling on my head . . . and
when she acknowledged that she had been
the mistress of that man . . . I don't know
what did happen after that! Nor whom I
would have liked to kill — the Judge who
was saying those things with such indifference ; or her, who was acknowledging them
with her head turned away from me . . .
I almost felt like confessing myself guilty
in spite of my innocence, in order not to
know any more about it, in order to be freed
. . . but I thought of you and the children !
. . . [*A long silence.*] Come ! We must decide what to do . . . did you leave them at
home ?

MOTHER. No, I had to send them away
to our cousin at Bayonne; we have no home
now, nor anything else, we are ruined . . .
Anyway, it got so I couldn't stand it here
. . . the women turned aside and crossed
themselves when I met them; at church
they left me all alone in the middle of an
empty space. . . . Already I had been obliged
to take the children out of school . . .

ETCHEPARE. Good God !

MOTHER. No one spoke to them any more.
One day George provoked the biggest boy
in the school; they had a fight, and as George
was the stronger, the other to get even
called him a murderer's son.

ETCHEPARE. And George . . .

MOTHER. He came home crying and refused to go out of the house again. It is
then that I sent them to Bayonne.

ETCHEPARE. I 'll tell you what we will
do. Go there and get them. To-morrow or
this evening I will meet you. There are
emigration offices for America there. They
will take the four of us and trust us for the
tickets on account of the children.

MOTHER. And if they ask for their
mother ?

ETCHEPARE [*after a pause*]. You will tell
them, she is dead.

[*Enter* YANETTA *whom some one brings to the
door.*]

YANETTA [*as the door is being closed*].
Yes, sir.

MOTHER [*without looking at* YANETTA].
Well, I am going.

ETCHEPARE [*also without looking at* YA-
NETTA]. Well, I shall meet you either here
this evening or there to-morrow.

MOTHER. All right.

ETCHEPARE. As soon as you get there,
you will inquire about the day and hour . . .

MOTHER. Very well.

ETCHEPARE. Until to-morrow.

MOTHER. All right.

[*Goes out without a glance at* YANETTA.]

YANETTA. [*Takes a few steps toward her
husband, falls on her knees and clasps her
hands. In a low voice.*] Forgive me !

ETCHEPARE. Never !

YANETTA. No, don't say that !

ETCHEPARE. Did the Judge lie ?

YANETTA. No, the Judge did not lie.

ETCHEPARE. You are a bad woman !

YANETTA. Yes, I am a bad woman, forgive me !

ETCHEPARE. Forgive you ! I would like
to kill you !

YANETTA. Yes, yes, but forgive me !

ETCHEPARE. You are nothing but a
wench, a Paris wench without shame or
morals !

YANETTA. Yes, insult me, strike me !

ETCHEPARE. You have lived a lie to me
for ten years !

YANETTA. Oh ! How I wanted to tell
you all ! Oh ! How many times I com-
menced that terrible confession ! I never
had the courage, Pierre ; I was always
afraid of your anger and of the pain I
would cause you. . . . You were so happy !

ETCHEPARE. You came back fresh from
vice, just out of prison, and took me for
your victim . . .

YANETTA. And to think that he believes
that, my God !

ETCHEPARE. You came to me — the leav-
ings of a thief . . . and you stole in my
house the place of a good woman. . . . Your
lie has brought the curse of God on my
family and you are the cause of it all. The
misfortune which has just stricken us was
caused by you, I tell you ! You leper ! Accursed ! Damned ! Don't talk to me any
more ! Don't talk to me any more !

YANETTA. Won't you have pity, Pierre ?
Do you think that I don't suffer !

ETCHEPARE. If you do you deserve it !
What had I done to you that you should
choose me for your victim ? What have I
done to suffer as I do ? You have made a
coward of me ! You have degraded me almost to your own level ; I ought already to
have succeeded in putting you out of my

head and my heart! And I cannot! And I
suffer terribly . . . for I suffer in the love
which I bore you . . . You! You have been
all in my life for ten years . . . you have
been all, all! . . . And I have nothing but
one hope left,— to forget you!

YANETTA. Forgive me!

ETCHEPARE. Never, never!

YANETTA. Don't say that . . . it is only
God who has the right to say that. I will
come back to your house; I shall only be
the first of the servants . . . the most humble, if you wish! I shall not take my place
at the fireside until you tell me to . . .

ETCHEPARE. We have n't any fireside,
we have n't any home . . . we have nothing now! And I repeat it, it is all your
fault . . . and it is because you used to sit
there in the place of the mother, of my
mother, you! false and faithless! that misfortune has fallen upon us!

YANETTA. I swear to you that I will
make you forget all that by my humility,
my devotion, and my repentance . . . and
wherever you go I shall follow you; Pierre,
reflect, your children still need me . . .

ETCHEPARE. My children! You shall
never see them again! Nor speak to them!
I won't have you kiss them, nor even touch
them!

YANETTA [changing her tone]. Not that!
Not that! The children? You are mistaken
there! Ah, no! Deprive me of all, condemn
me to every shame, force me to beg my
bread — I am quite willing! Don't even
look at me, don't speak to me except to insult me . . . anything you like . . . but my
children! My children! They belong to
me: they came from my womb; they are
still a part of me . . . and always, always
will be my flesh and blood. . . . You can
cut off one of my arms — it would be a dead
thing and not a part of me . . . but you
can't keep my children from being my children . . .

ETCHEPARE. You have made yourself
unworthy of keeping them . . .

YANETTA. Unworthy! Don't talk that
to me! Have I ever failed in my duties toward them? Have I been a bad mother?
Answer! I have n't, have I? Well, if I have
n't been a bad mother, my rights upon my
children remain entire and absolute! Unworthy! I could be a thousand times more
guilty! More unworthy, as you say, and

still neither you, nor the law, nor priests,
nor God would have the right to take them
from me. . . . As a woman I may have been
guilty — it is possible . . . as mother, nobody
can accuse me of anything. . . . Well, then!
Well, then! They cannot be stolen from
me . . . and you who have this project . . .
you are a scoundrel! Yes! Yes! To avenge
yourself you wish to take them from me!
You coward! You are only a man! Father!
You don't know what the word means! You
have no thought for your children. . . . Yes!
Yes! You lie, I tell you! When you say
that I am unworthy of bringing them up,
you lie! Those are only words, words! You
know it is not true; you know well enough
that I have nourished them, cared for them,
loved them, counseled them, and that I used
to have them say their prayers every evening and that I would continue. . . . You
know well that no woman could fill my
place with them . . . but what do you care
for all that! You forget them . . . you
want to punish me and so you are going to
take them from me. . . . I have the right
to tell you that it is cowardly and mean and
is only a horrible vengeance! Ah! Ah! The
children! Now he wants to lug them in!!
No! Take them from me? Ah, just think,
Pierre, it is impossible, what you are saying!

ETCHEPARE. You have spoken truly — I
am avenging myself! What you say is impossible is already done. My mother has
taken the children and has gone off with
them.

YANETTA. I will find them again.

ETCHEPARE. America is large.

YANETTA. I shall find them again!

ETCHEPARE. Then, I shall tell them why
I took them from you.

YANETTA. Never! That, never! I will
obey you, but swear to me . . .

[Enter the CLERK.]

CLERK. Come and sign your release,
Etchepare. You will be released at once.

YANETTA. Wait, sir, wait! [To ETCHE-
PARE.] I accept the separation since I must
. . . I will disappear. . . . You will never
hear of me again. But, in return for this
atrocious sacrifice, swear to me a solemn
oath that you will never tell them . . .

ETCHEPARE. I swear it . . .

YANETTA. You swear never to tell them

a word which might diminish their affection for me?

ETCHEPARE. I swear it . . .

YANETTA. Promise me also — I implore you, Pierre, in the name of our happiness, and of my suffering — promise me to keep alive in them the memory of their mother . . . you will have them pray for me, won't you?

ETCHEPARE. I swear it to you . . .

YANETTA. Then go, my life is over. . . .

ETCHEPARE. Good-bye.

[*Goes out with the* CLERK. *On the threshold of the door the latter meets* MOUZON.]

CLERK. [*To* ETCHEPARE.] They will show you the way out . . .

CLERK. The Etchepare woman is here . . .

MOUZON. So she is here! Vagret has just spoken to me of her. Well, I withdraw my complaint; I ask nothing better than to release her. Now that I am Counsellor, I have no desire to come back from Pau every week for the examination. Proceed with the necessary formalities. [*To* YANETTA.] Well, in consideration of the disciplinary confinement which you have undergone, I am willing to release you provisionally . . . perhaps I shall even withdraw my complaint if you apologize for having insulted me . . .

YANETTA. I do not regret having insulted you.

MOUZON. Do you want to go back to prison?

YANETTA. Ah, my poor man, if you only knew how little I care for your prison!

MOUZON. How so?

YANETTA. Because I have nothing left, neither house nor home, nor husband nor children. [*Looks at him.*] And it occurs to me, the more I think of it . . .

MOUZON. What?

YANETTA. That it is you who are the cause of all the trouble.

MOUZON. You have both of you been acquitted, have n't you? What more do you want?

YANETTA. Yes, we have been acquitted, it is true. But now, for my husband, for my children, for everybody, I am a bad woman just the same.

MOUZON. If any one throws up to you your former conviction, if any one makes allusion to your disciplinary detention, you have the right to prosecute the slanderer before the law. He will be punished.

YANETTA. Well! It is because some one has thrown up to me my conviction that my husband has taken away my children . . . this some one is a judge — can I have him sentenced?

MOUZON. No.

YANETTA. Why? Because he is a magistrate?

MOUZON. No. Because it is the law.

YANETTA. The law! [*Violently.*] Well! Your law is contemptible.

MOUZON. Come, now, no shrieks, nor insults, please. [*To the* CLERK.] Are you through? Then go to the office and get an order for her release.

YANETTA. For me I am not learned: I have not studied the law as you have out of books, and perhaps for that very reason I know what is just and what is not. And I have come to ask you simply this: How does the law propose to give me back my children and undo the wrong it has done me?

MOUZON. The law is not beholden to you.

YANETTA. Not beholden to me? Then what are you going to do about it? You, the judge?

MOUZON. A magistrate is not responsible.

YANETTA. Ah, you are not responsible! Then you could, just for a whim, arrest people, on a shadow of suspicion, even without suspicion; you might bring shame and dishonor on whole families, torture the unhappy, dig down deep into their existence, parade their misfortunes, bring to light forgotten and expiated faults, faults which go back ten years; you might, by your cunning, your tricks, your lies, and your cruelty, send a man to the foot of the scaffold, and what is worse, rob a mother of her little ones! And after that, like Pontius Pilate, you would say and would believe that you were not responsible! Not responsible! Before your law, you may not be responsible, as you say, but before justice itself, before the justice of decent people, before God's own justice, I swear to you that you are responsible and that is why I have come to bring you to account!

[*Sees upon the desk of* MOUZON, *whose back is turned, the dagger used as a paper-cutter. Seizes it and lays it down again.*]

MOUZON. I order you to go.

YANETTA. Listen to me . . . for the last time, I ask you what you are going to do to relieve me, to return to me all that I have lost through your fault ; what are you going to do to lessen my anguish, and how do you propose to get my children back for me ?

MOUZON. I have nothing to say to you ; I owe you nothing.

YANETTA. You owe me nothing ! You owe me more than life, more than everything . . . My children . . . I shall never see them . . . what you have taken from me is the happiness of every minute, it is their kisses every evening, it is the pride which I had in watching them grow. Never, never again, shall I hear them say mamma ! It is as if they were dead ! It is just the same as if you had killed them. [*Seizes the knife.*] Yes ! Now look at your work, all you wicked judges : Of an innocent man you almost made a criminal, and of an honest woman, of a mother, you have made a murderess !

[*Strikes him; he falls.*]

KNOW THYSELF

CONNAIS–TOI

A PLAY IN THREE ACTS

By PAUL HERVIEU
OF THE FRENCH ACADEMY

Translated by BARRY CERF

CAST OF CHARACTERS

GENERAL DE SIBÉRAN

DONCIÈRES

JEAN DE SIBÉRAN

PAVAIL

A FOOTMAN

CLARISSE DE SIBÉRAN

ANNA DONCIÈRES

The action takes place in the country, at the present day.

KNOW THYSELF

ACT I

The drawing-room of a country-house. In the background through two windows and a glass door, which open on a piazza, a park is seen. On the left, folding-doors opening on a corridor. On the right, folding-doors affording access to a small drawing-room. On the left, a large office-desk. On the right, a small table with an ink-stand on it. Consoles with vases of flowers, bronze statuettes. Chairs here and there. The fireplace is set at an angle, right, center.

As the curtain rises, CLARISSE is seated at the little table on the right, busied with her correspondence. PAVAIL, in undress uniform of a lieutenant of dragoons, appears at the rear entrance; he hesitates on the threshold. CLARISSE sees him.

CLARISSE. What! you, Pavail? My husband has just gone to his headquarters and he'll be in a rage when he does n't find his lieutenant there.

PAVAIL. The general did not instruct me to hold myself at his disposal.

CLARISSE. And you remained peacefully slumbering in your bed!

PAVAIL. No. I have not come directly from home. I left early. I strolled about, wandering from place to place. In fact I expected to pass by here on my return.

CLARISSE. Why do you come at this hour?

PAVAIL [*still slightly embarrassed*]. I brought the book I spoke to you about recently.   [*He gives it to her.*]

CLARISSE. What a strange idea, when you were going for a walk, to burden yourself with this!

PAVAIL. It is n't very heavy.

CLARISSE. I was to send for it one of these days. Pavail, this is nothing but a pretext. You have another reason for coming.

PAVAIL. Madame, your manner of examining me is enough to put one out of countenance.

CLARISSE. Exactly, you are embarrassed. And . . . I can guess why you are here.

PAVAIL. Indeed?

CLARISSE. Your conscience is not at rest.

PAVAIL. I beg you to be good enough to explain yourself.

CLARISSE. With pleasure. Listen! Yesterday evening, while the General was at that card table and you were with Anna and me, he darted a caustic remark at you over his shoulder. The subject was of little importance; the tone had no more than the usual brusqueness. You replied by a look only, but a look that was very sharp, very hostile, and which you saw me intercept. I infer that your purpose this morning must be to efface in all haste the unfavorable impression which I may have retained.

PAVAIL. Let us suppose that that is it. It would be a great joy to me, I confess, to secure your indulgence for occasions in which I am at fault.

CLARISSE [*kindly*]. I ask only this, that whenever you cause shadows to darken my thoughts, you make haste to dissipate them. I am still no farther than mere conjectures as to the sort of person you really are.

PAVAIL [*timidly*]. I will enter into those details at another time.

CLARISSE. Come, now, Pavail, why do you take this attitude toward my husband? Are n't you under great obligations to him? Was it not he who cared for your education?

PAVAIL. I see that you know something about my story.

CLARISSE. The General told me that at the time when he was a captain, he happened to be in command of a detachment sent to repress some agitation in the region where you were born. Your father, it seems, was a professor, a humanitarian, who wished to interpose between the mob and the armed force . . .

PAVAIL. Yes. He had been imprisoned many a time as a revolutionist. His intervention in the circumstances which you mention earned him his death on a barricade. It was never known from which side the bullet came. I was only three years old at the time. My mother had died in giving me birth. The wife of the young captain had a little boy, Jean de Sibéran, who is to-day your stepson. She adored him so much that she was deeply moved to learn that another child, only slightly older than her son, was bereft of shelter and sustenance as a result of events in which her own husband had played a rôle. She saw in me the seed of insurgency, a future brigand, whom there was perhaps yet time to reform according to her desires. She watched over my education. And Monsieur de Sibéran was generous enough to permit her to do so. I learned only after a considerable lapse of time whence I came and what lawless blood flowed in my veins. I may add even that I learned all that too late, when I found myself in a social position to which I had apparently not been destined. Madame de Sibéran had had me enter upon that career which most naturally presented itself to her mind: I was a second lieutenant, like her son, when that saintly woman died. I can say that no one mourned her more than I. I felt, at her grave, the distress of a broken-hearted dog.

CLARISSE. I readily infer that you did not feel for my husband a devotion as complete as this.

PAVAIL. I should be unjust if I did not acknowledge that though he has not been kind to me, he has never really done me any wrong.

CLARISSE. I am surprised that you are able to discriminate with such precision the part of each of your benefactors in the assistance you have received.

PAVAIL. For a long time I had felt in this matter only the promptings of instinct. The General himself confirmed this intuitive judgment one day when I had provoked his anger.

CLARISSE. On what occasion?

PAVAIL [hesitating]. I should feel peculiarly embarrassed to answer.

CLARISSE. Excuse my indiscretion.

PAVAIL. After all, with a person like you absolute frankness ought to be a sign of still greater respect than certain scruples of politeness. The thing happened five years ago, when the General remarried.

CLARISSE. It was apropos of my marriage?

PAVAIL. At that time, with importunate constancy, I held the opinion that the first Madame de Sibéran was one of those women who ought not to be replaced. As was quite proper, I had not openly formulated my opinion. But I abstained from appearing at the ceremony. The General called for an explanation, in the course of which it pleased him to demonstrate disdainfully that I was after all exempt from every obligation of gratitude toward him, and that he personally had never interested himself in me. His exposition was clearness itself.

CLARISSE. How is it, then, that a definitive rupture between you two did not result?

PAVAIL. The son of his dead wife, Jean de Sibéran, constrained me to seek his pardon. He made every effort to see that I obtained it, and he rendered it impossible for me to avoid the consequences. I feel for your stepson the warm affection of an older brother. It seems to me that his mother in placing me at the side of that spoiled child bequeathed to me the mission of satisfying blindly his every wish. Furthermore, Jean was the only one, intermediary as he was between the memory of his mother and the action of his father, qualified to dictate to me the proper attitude.

CLARISSE. So that after all you did not renounce the functions which attach you to the person of the General.

PAVAIL. He ordered me to this post as he has always proceeded in regard to me: by an imperious command. Nothing can alter the fact that at the beginning I was in his eyes a captive, a little living thing conquered from the enemy. Even now I cannot feel myself other than a freedman. That word evokes ideas of perfidy and ingratitude, does it not? As far as I am concerned, it makes me think, when I probe myself, of independence far off in the distance, of racial hostility surviving stubbornly.

CLARISSE. Do you know, Pavail, you are not a very reassuring person.

PAVAIL. Oh, madame, do not misunderstand me. Not one of those who serve the General would fulfill the strict duties of my office more scrupulously than I. In the field I would lay down my life to insure his safety. I claim only before you the right to restore mastery to the instincts of my heart, to my intimate thoughts, to the freedom of my manhood.

CLARISSE. I shall not arrogate any title to judge you. I disapprove, of course, your attitude toward the General. But I regard you as a wounded soul, in pain.

PAVAIL. True.

CLARISSE. Up to the present time your countenance seemed to me very different from others, impenetrable. It caused in me a sort of uneasiness, almost irritation.

PAVAIL. And now?

CLARISSE. My opinion of you has, in some particulars, just now taken somewhat more definite shape.

PAVAIL. Ah!

CLARISSE. Your reverence for her who was your second mother bears witness to a sensibility which I was not sure I perceived in you. I begin to see that your affection is bestowed only grudgingly, but that it is capable, perhaps, of a rare devotion.

PAVAIL. Oh! you would only have to put it to the test!

CLARISSE. I do not flatter myself that you are my friend. On the contrary, you have shown me how entirely I was, in your eyes, the detested intruder who was to take the place of your benefactress.

PAVAIL. My ill-will did not survive the first occasions on which we met. I quickly understood how Monsieur de Sibéran had sacrificed her memory as soon as he found himself in your presence.

CLARISSE. Ah! indeed! You were as prompt as that to make amends, were you? I am grateful to you. But you would have refrained, doubtless, from bearing me even an initial ill-will if you had informed yourself about me.

PAVAIL. Is it possible? I never even knew when or how your marriage was decided.

CLARISSE. No intrigue of mine played a part in the circumstances which made me the wife of the General. He had expressed to an aged relative the intention of not remaining a widower. He demanded neither wealth nor beauty. A poor girl would suit him, provided that she were of good birth, well brought-up, and also of sufficient poise not to humiliate him. He preferred that his future wife be beyond the bloom of youth. And above all, he asked that she be not romantic, announcing his desire to provide for himself a tranquil old age at the side of one whose nature should be all repose. Such was the ideal whose requirements I was believed to fulfill. You see that the shade of my predecessor had no reason to take umbrage at my installation in the home which had been hers; it was not unbridled passion nor mad love that was to take up its abode there with me.

PAVAIL. It has seemed to me, however, that the General was moved by a strong affection for you, I might even say violent.

CLARISSE. There was probably more fire left in him than he had supposed. It is quite likely that that made him resign himself to my being less commonplace, more high-spirited, than the type of woman he had expected to choose.

PAVAIL [as if in spite of himself]. Will you permit me to ask you a question?

CLARISSE. What?

PAVAIL [with trepidation at his own daring]. Your hopes, the desires you had formed when you were a young girl, have you found their realization in this marriage?

CLARISSE. If there were a disappointment in my life, I am bound to avoid confiding it to any one.

PAVAIL. Why?

CLARISSE. From a sense of duty, from pride, from lack of sufficient intimacy with anybody.

PAVAIL. Yet . . .

CLARISSE. [To a FOOTMAN who has come in from the left.] What is it?

FOOTMAN. Monsieur Doncières has returned. He sent me to see if Madame Doncières were not here.

[At these words PAVAIL shows haste to be leaving.]

CLARISSE. [To the FOOTMAN.] No, she will not return until lunch-time. [Exit FOOTMAN.] My husband's cousin is becoming impatient, while his wife is lingering over a sketch at the edge of the pond.

PAVAIL [in a hurry to go]. On my way home I'll pass by there and look for her.

CLARISSE. As you like. Will you tell her, please, that she is wanted?

PAVAIL [already going]. Certainly.

CLARISSE. Excuse me for having detained you so long.

PAVAIL [*his eagerness to depart suddenly checked by his natural courtesy*]. Oh, on the contrary, it is I who trespassed . . .

CLARISSE. It has given me great pleasure to have this chat with you.

PAVAIL. I shall always feel deep gratitude to you for this conversation.

CLARISSE. Good-bye.

[PAVAIL *kisses her hand and goes.*]

[CLARISSE *pensively gazes after his disappearing form.* SIBÉRAN *enters from the left in the undress uniform of a Brigadier-General.*]

CLARISSE. Have n't you anything to say to Lieutenant Pavail?

SIBÉRAN. Why do you ask me that?

CLARISSE. He might be called back; he has just left here.

SIBÉRAN. Pavail! [*He leaps toward the door as if to pursue him.*] How long was he here?

CLARISSE. Half an hour.

SIBÉRAN. Yes! He had time enough! He came with brazen effrontery to dupe us, to create an alibi!

CLARISSE. What do you mean?

SIBÉRAN. My dear Clarisse, Pavail is our cousin's lover.

CLARISSE. Pavail! Oh! . . . How can you make such an assertion?

SIBÉRAN. You know that at sunrise Anna left the house saying that she was going to make a sketch. You remember that about an hour and a half ago I left you to attend to a matter touching the service. Doncières accompanied me for the sake of the walk. We went by way of the park. We were still in the woods, approaching the lodge that Pavail rented as a dwelling. All at once we saw a woman come out. The silhouette we caught sight of from afar, the color of the dress, indicated that it was Anna. Furthermore, the person, startled by our unexpected appearance in the distance, sprang immediately from the road and slipped away through the underbrush. Doncières and I had not exchanged a word, but his impression coincided with mine, for he dashed off suddenly in pursuit. All this happened so quickly that I did not have time to think of taking a part in the affair. I listened without detecting any sound of loud voices. I waited, but no one returned. The fugitive had a good start and a nimble foot. Under cover of the

early-morning fog which clung to the branches and lingered in the bushes, she probably succeeded in making her escape.

CLARISSE. At all events, Doncières returned alone. He is upstairs, trying to find out where his wife is. She will soon be here; and she will answer that you have a mote in the eye.

SIBÉRAN. There is one thing that will render disproof rather difficult for her: before Doncières disappeared among the trees, I saw him stop to pick up a glove which had just been dropped in front of him. As he at once resumed his pursuit with redoubled vigor, I concluded that he had recognized his find as the property of his wife. As far as my part in the matter is concerned, all that was left for me to do was to go up to the Lieutenant's door and knock. I wished to lose no time in calling him to account. But my peremptory summons was of no avail; the door remained closed. Subsequent to that, being called to town to give various orders, I was able to ascertain that Pavail had, indeed, been at home and had pretended not to hear me, for he had been seen neither in the quarters, nor in the offices, nor anywhere else.

CLARISSE. I cannot believe, nevertheless, that he would have hurried straight here to play such a villainous comedy before me.

SIBÉRAN. Did he give you a valid reason for his call?

CLARISSE. Not precisely . . .

SIBÉRAN. You must have found him harassed, uneasy?

CLARISSE. At first, yes.

SIBÉRAN. Naturally! Everything is against him! By this impudent expedient he sought to discover, even under our very roof, what was the fate of his mistress.

CLARISSE. The fact is he withdrew hastily, on learning that Anna had not yet returned.

SIBÉRAN. You see: he rushed off in the hope of happening upon her, and of arranging a course of action with her.

CLARISSE. No, I tell you, no! I'm determined to refuse to believe all false appearances. I'm determined to, at least, out of consideration for Anna. How is it possible that she could have ceased to be virtuous?

SIBÉRAN. In that little brain of hers she

has doubtless decided that she cannot stand her husband.

CLARISSE [*to herself*]. That's no reason.

SIBÉRAN. Nothing interests her. She has n't any children.

CLARISSE [*sadly*]. I know what it is not to have any. And I should not see in that any palliation of the dishonor she has brought upon herself.

SIBÉRAN. [*Seeing* ANNA *in the distance.*] Here she is!

CLARISSE. Oh!

SIBÉRAN. Let her enlighten you herself. I shall be at hand; call me.

[*He goes out by the right.* ANNA *enters from the rear.*]

CLARISSE [*agitated*]. It's you, Anna, at last! Quick, tell me where you were!

ANNA [*in distress*]. I can tell by your manner that you know everything.

CLARISSE. What! Is it possible that it is you who are implicated in what the General has just disclosed to me? It was really you they saw?

ANNA [*twisting and wringing her remaining glove*]. Yes, I am the woman who is incriminated by the evidence they have.

CLARISSE. Can you explain satisfactorily why you crossed the threshold of that house?

ANNA. If I had been able to do that I should not have run away.

CLARISSE. But you have n't come back without having invented some explanation?

ANNA [*discouraged, despairingly*]. I could only invent some cock-and-bull story. I have n't the impudence, I have n't the energy to build up lie on lie. I should break down at the very start.

CLARISSE. Your husband is upstairs. You are not going to present yourself for his cross-examination without any defense? You can concede that you have been imprudent, harebrained. You can allege that in going to that place you took up a dare, accepted a challenge. But they cannot have proof that you are irreparably guilty!

ANNA. It will be useless for me to declare that I am innocent; I shall not be able to prove that either. My life from now on will be a perpetual struggle against horrible doubts and frantic suspicions. There are moments when I wonder if it would n't be better to confess right away and make a clean breast of the matter.

CLARISSE. And then?

ANNA. Why, then, my husband would either keep me or turn me out. I should know where I stand. It would put an end to this life of snares and subterfuges, these questionings, these maddening insinuations.

CLARISSE [*severely*]. I hope, at least, I may credit you with regretting your mistake, that you feel remorse?

ANNA [*in tears*]. I have never had any ill-will toward my husband. I would give anything in the world not to have caused him pain. Ah, if I could have foreseen such consequences, you may be sure that I should never have gone wrong!

CLARISSE. You yielded, then, to a lover without having the excuse of an irresistible passion?

ANNA. Ah, I should like to see what goes on in the souls of the victims of an irresistible passion at the moment when they are caught! There are many like me who must say to themselves the same things — when it is too late.

CLARISSE. Let us confine ourselves to you.

ANNA [*pleading*]. Then, you do not admit the possibility of a sudden frenzy sweeping away a woman's reason, of a passing madness of all her being?

CLARISSE [*nervously*]. Oh, do not invoke irresponsibility, suggestion, somnambulism. Consider the matter in good faith: you met a person who contrasted advantageously with the accustomed husband, younger and more handsome than he, rather different from other men, and very captivating. You gave yourself up to him, to the intoxication of his presence. That implies no supernatural causes: it is quite natural, too natural!

ANNA [*regaining her self-possession*]. I see that I have exhausted your fund of compassion.

CLARISSE. Don't take it that way.

ANNA. You no longer speak to me like a friend who wishes to help.

CLARISSE [*less severely*]. I allowed myself to be betrayed into an untimely remonstrance. I am sorry I did so, and I am ready to do anything I can for you.

ANNA. The moment has come when I must appear before my husband — you can do nothing to forestall that!

CLARISSE. Why go to him yourself? If

the meeting took place here, I might be useful to you.

ANNA. No, I must face him alone, and once for all settle this matter.

CLARISSE. Do you not wish me to follow you, at least, so as to be near enough to interpose?

ANNA [*bravely*]. Thanks. I no longer feel the abject fear that hounded me as I fled through the woods. Let me rise by my unaided efforts from this added humiliation.

CLARISSE. Really, you insist?

ANNA. Yes, I insist on going alone.

CLARISSE. May God help you! [ANNA *goes out by the left.* CLARISSE *goes to the door on the right and calls her husband.*] Will you come? She is no longer here.

SIBÉRAN. [*Comes in.*] Well?

CLARISSE. The husband and wife will soon find themselves face to face. She is going up to him.

SIBÉRAN. Did she exonerate herself?

CLARISSE. She did not try to with me.

SIBÉRAN. I should think not!

CLARISSE [*ill at ease*]. It remains to be seen how she will act upstairs, and what the result may be.

SIBÉRAN [*reassured*]. Doncières has had time to reflect. He'll not create a scandal in the house.

CLARISSE. I should have liked to assist the poor girl.

SIBÉRAN [*sharply*]. Be kind enough to reserve your good offices for more respectable misfortunes.

CLARISSE. I cannot repress a feeling of compassion when I see, so near me, a fellow-being helplessly slipping into the abyss.

SIBÉRAN [*peremptorily*]. In the first place, Anna is no longer one of your fellows. After what has been laid at her door, you ought to consider her as no longer belonging even to the same species with yourself.

CLARISSE. She quite took my breath away, I must confess. I had, indeed, noticed in her a tendency to coquetry, a little sentimentality. These are traits of the imagination which sometimes cannot be mastered. A woman may even feel an attraction toward a man; she may say to herself that he is the man she would have wished to love. But how could Anna allow herself to be carried farther than that? One does not give one's self without having definitely

made up one's mind to do it. Modesty gives forewarnings of physical surprises. There is a revulsion of one's whole being which would protect against the slightest contact.

SIBÉRAN. Let us not try to understand certain creatures, but let us be careful to avoid them. Had it not been for my kinship with Doncières, I should have been more cautious about suffering that little minx to become an intimate friend of yours.

CLARISSE. Her conduct has never been open to blame. No one could suspect . . .

SIBÉRAN. The fact is we have been very blind, all these days when intrigue had chosen to take up its abode with us. And my cousin, first and foremost, is without any doubt the traditional ninny! Deuce take it! the very essence of marital vigilance is to know one's wife well enough to guess what sort of man would be most particularly calculated to imperil her honor. But not at all! Doncières comes here to pass his summer with us, knowing that a handsome youth lives near by, a brooding hero of romance! And he had not discovered that Anna is one of those women who cannot resist the magic of a doleful mien! But, unseconded though I was, I saw more than one thing to rouse my suspicions, I assure you. For some time I have noticed in Pavail a certain inattention to his duties, a preoccupied, inexplicable air.

CLARISSE [*with deep meaning*]. Ah, Pavail! I owe him a grudge! While he was bringing me to look upon him as a soul in pain, a starving heart, he was, in fact, a successful lover. I was on the point of pitying him, of hoping that he would find a little happiness! Yes, I owe him a grudge for his hypocrisy.

SIBÉRAN [*pompously*]. You see, my dear, you are the most honest creature on earth. I have an unbounded esteem and affection for you. But, this aside, you irritate me constantly by the readiness with which you extend your confidence, by the extraordinary trust you place in those who deserve it least. I am continually having to set you right. For instance, only the other day, in the case of those poachers. No, don't protest! It is undoubtedly involuntary in you, but I may say that as soon as a contemptible rascal appears anywhere, you make it a point to go and be duped by his folderol.

CLARISSE [*gently*]. At any rate, as far as Pavail is concerned, you yourself would have taught me to forget my distrust since you have attached him to your person.

SIBÉRAN [*with authority*]. Do not discuss that. I trained Pavail to obey me. I had to break him in as you break in a pair of new shoes. But he had become useful; he suited my needs. I thought him tractable. And that is why I clung to him.

CLARISSE [*more gently still*]. You ought perhaps to have gone about it in such a manner that it would have been he who clung to you.

SIBÉRAN. Ah, be careful, please! Do not try to teach me how to conduct myself. Let people think of me what they like. My only concern is to remain at peace with my conscience; and for that it's enough for me to feel that during my life everybody will have received from me his due, without my ever having been beholden to anybody under the sun.

CLARISSE [*with melancholy bitterness*]. I have not missed anything of what you intended for me in those remarks.

SIBÉRAN. Well, your pertinacity made me lose patience.

CLARISSE. I interposed only timid objection.

SIBÉRAN. I ask you on every occasion to accept my judgment. It is the correct one.

CLARISSE [*ready to burst into tears*]. I know, yes, I know.

SIBÉRAN. Now what is it? What's the matter. Why! if your eyes aren't filling with tears! Are you going to say now that it's I who make you weep?

CLARISSE [*controlling herself*]. No! no! I don't say anything. I'm not weeping.

SIBÉRAN [*calmed*]. I'm glad to hear it! Don't get nervous like that. It's ridiculous! Come now. I won't scold you any more. Kiss me.

CLARISSE [*avoiding him and pointing to the door at the left which opens*]. Your cousin.

[DONCIÈRES *enters.*]

SIBÉRAN. Are you looking for me?

DONCIÈRES. I have something I want to talk over with you.

CLARISSE. [*To* DONCIÈRES.] You wish me to go?

DONCIÈRES. [*To* CLARISSE.] It is very difficult for me to say what I have to say;

it would be still more difficult if I were not alone with your husband.

CLARISSE. I'm going.

DONCIÈRES. [*To* CLARISSE.] But you'll coöperate with me, won't you?

CLARISSE. [*To* DONCIÈRES.] In what way?

DONCIÈRES. [*To* CLARISSE.] In leaving my wife to herself.

SIBÉRAN. [*To* DONCIÈRES.] Of course! [*To* CLARISSE.] Do not go to her.

CLARISSE. I have no desire to do so.

[*She goes out by the right.*]

DONCIÈRES. It is no longer possible for me to doubt, to hope : Anna is guilty.

SIBÉRAN. She admitted that she was unfaithful to you?

DONCIÈRES. She did not prove to me the contrary. After some silly lies of which I spare you the repetition, she suddenly declared : "Believe what you like, and do as you please."

SIBÉRAN. And you have come to tell me what you are going to do?

DONCIÈRES. You are, in a certain sense, the head of our family. I have the highest esteem for your character. Staggering under the blow that I have received, I feel the need of leaning upon you, of being guided by your advice.

SIBÉRAN. I must first have some inkling of your own intentions.

DONCIÈRES. Above all, I want to avoid a scandal.

SIBÉRAN. That is?

DONCIÈRES. You do not, I presume, advise me to send a challenge to your officer?

SIBÉRAN. That is not the sort of thing about which advice can be given.

DONCIÈRES. But, in my place, you would fight?

SIBÉRAN. I should be wrong, perhaps.

DONCIÈRES. But you would do it?

SIBÉRAN. No two men have the same temperament. As for me, I'd see red.

DONCIÈRES. Yes, a man can see red, — and think of other things, too.

SIBÉRAN. I am speaking, you understand, as a man who is furiously in love with his wife.

DONCIÈRES. I, too, loved mine. The idea of being betrayed by her would have seemed as unnatural to me, as overwhelming, as the idea of having an arm cut off.

SIBÉRAN. And now?

DONCIÈRES. Now, the question of amputation is before me; and I tremble as I ask myself if it is inevitable. The decision rests with me as to whether or not I shall put my wife outside of my existence. With her last words she subscribed to what I shall decide: if I dictate divorce, she will submit.

SIBÉRAN. In that case, things are easy.

DONCIÈRES. Easy, yes, in what concerns my treatment of her; in what concerns my treatment of myself, no. I am sorely embittered, there's no doubt of that. I despise my wife; I hate her. And yet, she is so light-headed that I fear for her. To what lamentable depth she may sink when she is once alone in the world!

SIBÉRAN [with energy]. Her lover is there to make reparation. He owes her marriage.

DONCIÈRES [timorously]. The fact is that, on my account, too, — I'm afraid of having in me a weakness, a pusillanimity, that might make me feel later that I am still bound to my wife.

SIBÉRAN [losing interest]. In that case, my dear fellow, go ahead and question yourself, meditate. You are sole master of your actions.

DONCIÈRES. I do not yet know what I shall decide upon. But if, as is very unlikely, I saw the possibility of resigning myself, perhaps of pardoning in the end . . . What would you think of me?

SIBÉRAN. I should think that you had resolved upon the course of action that pleased you most, and that it is nobody's business but yours.

DONCIÈRES. The bonds of kinship unite us too closely to permit of your avoiding the obligation of a personal opinion.

SIBÉRAN. Members of a family are not responsible for each other's actions. You are perfectly free to arrange your life in accordance with your preferences.

DONCIÈRES. Your replies are so manifestly evasive that I cannot but desire absolute clearness. This is the crucial point: if I made an effort to forget the errors of my wife, would they be forgotten on your side, too?

SIBÉRAN. What do you mean by that?

DONCIÈRES. My question is whether or not the relations existing between your family and mine could continue without modification.

SIBÉRAN. Since you put the question in that way, I cannot play false with you. I prefer to wound you by my frankness.

DONCIÈRES. Go ahead.

SIBÉRAN. Well, I see a chasm henceforth between our wives.

DONCIÈRES. Ah! Very well.

SIBÉRAN. I do not say that Anna is a monster. There are many others, unhappily, in whom there is just as much to blame. It is n't that; but my wife is a very exceptional woman. I cannot imagine her in contact with anything that does not seem to me purity itself. Believe me, I am extremely sorry to be obliged to take this stand. In the crisis which you are passing through I should like to extend both my hands to you without reserve. But, from now on, I should not like my wife to remain the friend of yours. Do you see?

DONCIÈRES. Perfectly.

SIBÉRAN. It goes without saying, that, on our side, we shall not publish the breach with you. We shall adopt an attitude which will not be embarrassing for anybody. All that would be eliminated would be the occasions on which our families live under the same roof, our intimacy, our visits.

DONCIÈRES. Ah, then we might exchange greetings!

SIBÉRAN. Now you're angry with me. I can't help it. Why did you force me to express myself? Knowing me as you do, you ought to have been able to foresee my inflexibility in such a matter as this.

DONCIÈRES. Another reason why you see me vacillate in this manner is that the semi-avowals of Anna, her confused restrictions, her contradictory protestations, all these things make my head swim. She went clandestinely to this Pavail's house: that fact has been demonstrated. But does that prove absolutely that she is his mistress? How far did she abandon herself? Is it adultery, or only grave imprudence? That is the uncertainty under which I labor, for it may be that her vexation at having been caught, her fury at having been tracked, her false pride have prevented her from defending herself.

SIBÉRAN [exasperated]. Let me tell you, my dear fellow, that fidelity is all or nothing. Even if a woman is not in the most literal sense the mistress of her seducer, if, nevertheless, she has gone to him, she has at least affianced herself to him. She has by that act rent the marriage compact, abjured her faith. Even though she should be only morally adulterous, she has committed adultery. That woman is no longer the wife of her husband. She has in her heart another image, a new hope, a different longing. What! be reduced to asking yourself just how far your wife may have been unfaithful to you! Whether it 's from top to toe, or only halfway! Can't you think? Can't you see? Can't you feel?

DONCIÈRES [*partially convinced*]. I see, I feel what kind of man I should become in your eyes if I did not take action.

SIBÉRAN. Well, I won't deny it! My opinion, understand, is that to condone such an escapade of one's companion one must be suffering from an atrophy of that pride which is instinctive in every man. There is no longer any dignity in marriage, existence in common is no longer possible, when one must acknowledge to himself, must bear constantly in mind that his wife has been held in the embrace of another. If you could not be brought to share my ideas on this subject, I do not see how I could maintain my esteem and friendship for you.

DONCIÈRES [*coming to a decision*]. Enough! You will not have to look upon me as the shame of the family. I shall conquer my repugnance and act without delay.

SIBÉRAN. What am I to understand by that?

DONCIÈRES. I know that I can find at the present time in Paris one of my friends who is a lawyer. The next train will bring me to him before three o'clock this afternoon. In the mean time my wife, under pretext of a headache, will not leave her room. Her lunch will be brought to her. Under these conditions, she could not be an embarrassment to you here. I shall be back about eight o'clock this evening; and I shall instruct her then as to the steps to be taken so that all may be over between her and me.

SIBÉRAN. You are resolved to repudiate her?

DONCIÈRES. Yes. I was abject, I confess. You made me see the right road. I thank you.

SIBÉRAN. I may have treated you pretty roughly, I may have hurt you, but I spoke

according to the dictates of my conscience. There is no reason, therefore, why I should ask your pardon.

DONCIÈRES. I agree with you. You did what was right. I 'll take just time to notify my wife that she is to await my return upstairs ; and I 'll hasten to do whatever is necessary.

SIBÉRAN. You have my full approbation. Go ahead!

DONCIÈRES. Good-bye ; till to-night.

SIBÉRAN. Till to-night. [DONCIÈRES *goes out by the left. To the* FOOTMAN *who has come in from the right in response to his ring.*] Go tell Lieutenant Pavail to be here, after lunch, in an hour. I shall have something to say to him.

ACT II

Same setting. As the curtain rises, PAVAIL, *waiting for* SIBÉRAN, *is walking to and fro. He has saber and gloves.* SIBÉRAN *enters by the door on the right, which he leaves open. He is still in the same costume.*

PAVAIL. You sent for me, General.

SIBÉRAN. You have some idea what it 's about, I suppose ?

PAVAIL. Not the slightest.

SIBÉRAN. This morning my cousin and I discovered his wife coming out of your house.

PAVAIL [*without weakening*]. I refer you to whatever explanations Madame Doncières has given.

SIBÉRAN. She had no explanations. She is your mistress.

PAVAIL. No, sir, that is not true, I swear to you.

SIBÉRAN. Useless to deny it. Passing through this room, before my wife, the sinner admitted her sin.

PAVAIL. Madame Doncières said whatever she wished. In my ignorance of what that may have been I shall remain silent.

SIBÉRAN. That 's the best thing you can do. In all this, so far as you are concerned, I see only aggravating circumstances. The knavery of the adulterer is all the more repugnant in those who, like you, engaging upon the career of arms, have, above all others, made profession of uprightness and loyalty.

PAVAIL [*mastering himself with difficulty*] General !

SIBÉRAN. To make sport of a husband, to wear a mask before all who surround you, to scheme, to work in the dark, to fear the law and the police, is a rôle unworthy of your uniform. I do not pardon it in an officer, but your case above all others, *your* case, is worse still.

PAVAIL. General, do not go any farther in your reproaches. Restrain yourself, just as I force myself to refrain from replying.

SIBÉRAN. Know that the most elementary scruples forbade you to bring shame upon relatives of mine. I do not appeal to the sentiments of simple deference which at least I ought to have inspired in you. But I tell you that it is only your duties in attendance upon me that have brought you near a woman of my family. And to have thus abused my confidence resembles theft under exceptionally damnatory conditions : by a person in one's service.

PAVAIL [*losing control of himself*]. Enough !

SIBÉRAN [*drawing himself up to his full height*]. I beg your pardon ?

PAVAIL [*his voice choked with anger*]. I tell you I 'll stand no more. You have n't the right to insult me.

SIBÉRAN. But I have the right to punish. Your profession has been too easy thus far, my boy. You will be sent to some gloomy spot in Tonquin, to meditate. If you do not wish this rigorous measure to be taken at my instigation, you have only to cut the knot yourself by a request to the Minister.

PAVAIL. I welcome as a deliverance the definitive breach you open between us. I am ready to sign whatever is necessary.

SIBÉRAN [*pointing to his desk*]. Sit down there. Compose your letter. You will leave the envelope unsealed so that I may add a postscript. I shall see that it arrives at its destination. Do you understand.

PAVAIL [*having taken off his saber, and sat down to write*]. Yes.

SIBÉRAN. I am going to attend to some affairs. A pleasant voyage.

PAVAIL [*saluting*]. Good-bye.

[SIBÉRAN *goes out by the rear door. While he is finishing his letter,* CLARISSE *enters by the door on the right, which* SIBÉRAN *had left open, and closes it.*]

PAVAIL [*rising on seeing her*]. Madame !

CLARISSE [*ironically*]. Yes, it 's I. I happened to be near enough to hear. I was rather curious to know what your attitude would be.

PAVAIL. Oh, spare me that tone of raillery !

CLARISSE. You did not seek to deceive the General ; quite right ! But I congratulate you less on having completely beguiled my simplicity this morning.

PAVAIL. Madame !

CLARISSE. You lost by it. I had formed a loftier, more or less exceptional, idea of your character.

PAVAIL. The fault I have committed is not the one attributed to me. All that I could with justice be censured for is a disastrous laxity, a deplorable complaisance.

CLARISSE. I do not catch your meaning.

PAVAIL. I told you and I repeat that during all of this morning I was out for a walk. I had yielded to the solicitations of one to whom my friendship could refuse nothing, just as his has no secrets for me. It is thus that my lodge was at the disposal of your stepson.

CLARISSE. Jean ? He left to be gone twenty-four hours. It 's only a moment now before some one is to go to the station to meet him.

PAVAIL. But since half past nine he has been my guest.

CLARISSE. He probably returned by the first train.

PAVAIL. Exactly.

CLARISSE. Then he knows the results of his escapade ?

PAVAIL. If he knew them he would be here to face them. He would not continue to hide.

CLARISSE. I know, however, that his father issued his summons in no uncertain terms, and knocked loudly at your door, just after Anna had come out.

PAVAIL. Doubtless there was no longer any one there. Jean must have slipped away first. He was obliged to calculate his time. He wished, I imagine, to reach some station on the line so as to appear to be really getting off the train at the hour agreed upon. In any case I did not find him in the lodge when I returned. You remember that I left you hastily.

CLARISSE. I noticed it.

PAVAIL. The reason was that the words of a servant had revealed to me a peril which threatened the couple. I thought it urgent to warn my guests that they were forgetting themselves.

CLARISSE. Everything is becoming clear, in all truth ! [*In a very much softened tone.*] I should prefer for you that you had not facilitated the evil. But I begin to see plainly that youth and comradeship lend themselves to such arrangements as this without many scruples. Besides, you have already endured more stinging reproaches than you deserved while it pleased you to keep my husband laboring under a delusion.

PAVAIL. The General declared to me at the very outset that Madame Doncières had confessed all to you. Since I was incriminated I felt sure that she had not divulged the other name. Under those circumstances the thought could not enter my mind to denounce the friend who had trusted in me.

CLARISSE. And yet, it is inevitable that the truth be brought to light.

PAVAIL. Why ?

CLARISSE. Why, as a matter of simple justice, so that you be not made to expiate the faults of others.

PAVAIL. The turn that things have taken is for the best. A remnant of obscurity protects the love of two persons who have some chance still of being happy together. I shall not give them up to the mercy of whatever measures Monsieur de Sibéran may take to separate them. After all, in me, who am nothing, there will be banished only one who is alone in the world, a Bohemian, an outcast, about whom no one will worry or grieve.

CLARISSE. Since you propose to allow this to remain a mystery for my husband, what reason led you to admit me to your confidence.

PAVAIL. I was very anxious that you should not retain a false opinion of me.

CLARISSE. I thank you for your delicacy.

PAVAIL [*impelled by an inner force*]. I should not like to have let you think that, where you were, I had looked upon any other woman than you.

CLARISSE [*in consternation*]. What's that you say ?

PAVAIL. I say that I had come to hope for some event momentous enough to tear me away from here. I say that for months, for years, with profound humility, with alternate exasperation and fervor, I have been eating my heart out with love for you.

CLARISSE. Oh, how dare you ? There has been nothing in my conduct to warrant such words. It is wrong of you to have allowed yourself this freedom.

PAVAIL. I make this revelation to you only at the moment when I am going to disappear forever from your sight. Do not be alarmed.

CLARISSE [*struggling with her emotion*]. It is not anger that I feel. I am stupefied, crushed.

PAVAIL. My words are without hope. They are words of farewell. Grant me a moment of indulgence, as the price of the eternal resignation to which I am condemned.

CLARISSE. You were on the point of leaving in voluntary sacrifice, to take upon yourself the burden of another's responsibilities. I should like to have remained under that last impression. Do not detract from it further. It is good, be assured, it is deep.

PAVAIL. Let me, however, add some words of explanation to the information which you desired of me this morning. You saw me approach, awkward, timid. I had come, as it were, in spite of myself, with no audacious purpose, no thought of declaring myself to you. But, without my knowing it, the time was at hand. An instinct had impelled me. Destiny was carrying me onward.

CLARISSE. Very well. I understand. Don't dwell upon considerations which lay so heavy an embarrassment upon us.

PAVAIL. Upon one point still I desire to enlighten you : my attitude toward the General doubtless seemed quite odious as long as I refrained from being more explicit regarding you. Now I have no longer any occasion to conceal from you the fact that my hostility to him was increased above all things by the suffering his tyranny made you endure.

CLARISSE. Do not attack Monsieur de Sibéran on my account. You and I accepted with their advantages the situations which he created for us.

PAVAIL. But you understand now the motive that has for such a long time kept me here in bondage at his side, at your side : my love was inflamed in our common oppression beneath that relentless will.

CLARISSE. I understand, yes. I thought myself alone with my tears. It would have been a boon to me, I confess it freely, to know that, somewhere near, a brotherly sympathy was attentive to my sorrows. It would have comforted me, it would have brought into my life a sweetness which it always lacked.

PAVAIL. Oh, why did I delay ? I ought to have told you, it is clear to me now, that I shared with all my soul the sufferings from Monsieur de Sibéran's brutality which showed in deep lines upon your face.

CLARISSE. You exaggerate; and yet, I protest only half-heartedly. Alas ! all the illusions in regard to myself that I should have liked to keep, of the modest merits of my brain, of my person, — and then, too, my vanities, sympathies, fancies, childish whims even ; may I call all those little stars which he has dimmed in me, little flowers which he has mowed down ?

PAVAIL. Worse, it's worse than that !

CLARISSE. And thus I have arrived at a dismal state, in which I have only the sentiment of duty, dimmed and without charm, the state of wifely resignation, bitter constancy, in which one waits with impatience for old age and the end.

PAVAIL. I saw all this, saw it clearly. How many times have I started when a galling contradiction froze on your lips the utterance of the very thoughts that were in my mind at that moment !

CLARISSE. The truth is I have often felt that there existed a certain affinity between your nature and mine.

PAVAIL [his face lightening]. Is it possible ! You had noticed things that brought us near to each other ?

CLARISSE. Perhaps so ; it was vague, unreasoned.

PAVAIL. Oh, try to read within yourself !

CLARISSE. What would be the good ?

PAVAIL. Out of pity, out of kindness, find the words which would prove to me that I was not an object of indifference to you !

CLARISSE. How is it that I was led to question you so much just now ? Was it not the contrary of indifference that stirred in me a desire to know you better ? And a moment ago, why did I accost you with bitter words ? Did I then feel a peculiar irritation because you were said to possess Anna's love ? You perceive with what frankness I examine myself.

PAVAIL. Speak ! Go on !

CLARISSE. I realize, too, that I should have lent myself less readily to the turn our conversation had taken, if my thoughts never before then had strayed toward you. From gazing and gazing in the time that has gone by, into the emptiness of my heart, I saw pass there, no doubt, in the dizzy whirl, a dream of an affection all innocent between us. But I let myself run on regardless ! What tales are you making me tell ? I have told too much, far too much !

PAVAIL. Oh, do not stop, I beg you ! Tell me again that your thoughts were of a tenderness which might unite us one to the other !

CLARISSE. It was the stuff that dreams are made of ! The distance that is going to separate us will make you dream again.

PAVAIL [rebelling]. Ah, why must it be ?

CLARISSE. You will be henceforth absent, eternally absent. It is by virtue of the right of the eternally absent that you may have the right to be still dear to me.

PAVAIL. But now that I have seen in your soul a ray of hope for me, I have no other thought than to appeal from the decree which expels me from here.

CLARISSE. You . . . ? What . . . ? What do you hope ?

PAVAIL. Yes ! I am considering now only how I may remain.

CLARISSE. Oh, that, you must not ! You cannot ! It would mean that you had surprised my confessions, that you had abused my confidence ! The only excuses for the things that we have said is that they will never be said again.

PAVAIL. Suffer me to remain near you, and I shall appear before you only with your permission.

CLARISSE. Impossible !

PAVAIL. I shall be submissive, distant, timid, silent ! You will know that a man is there, burning for you in the most fervid passion. But no complaint will remind you that to suspend my torture you would only have to let the breath of your lips pass lightly over my brow.

CLARISSE [*quivering*]. I will never endure the thought that, near me, some one is suffering through me. From the moment you spoke to me of your love, from the moment when our eyes unguardedly met in a manner before unknown to us both, I have felt instinctively that I might find it needful to distrust my strength.

PAVAIL. On the day when I seem too importunate you would still have time to send me away. But do not inflict upon me the pain of separation before it seems necessary.

CLARISSE. It is necessary now. Say no more. You were bidding me farewell. Let us make an end of it. I insist!

PAVAIL. Oh, reflect!

CLARISSE. No, no! Go!

PAVAIL. A last word!

CLARISSE [*imperiously*]. No!

PAVAIL. Ah, I cannot mistake that tone! This time it is all over! It is all over!

CLARISSE. Yes.

PAVAIL. Have no fear: you will never see me again! Forget me!

CLARISSE. I shall not forget that in you I have had madness at my side, grief also, and devotion, perhaps danger!

PAVAIL. Madame!

CLARISSE. Good-bye!

PAVAIL. Good-bye!

[*He has picked up his saber; he goes out, in despair.*]

CLARISSE [*alone, her strength gone*]. Oh! . . . Oh! . . .

[*She goes to the desk, takes the letter* PAVAIL *has written, runs through it, and puts it back, suppressing a sob.*]

[ANNA *enters from the left.*]

ANNA. Excuse me for coming to you.

CLARISSE. You are in traveling costume.

ANNA. Yes. Ask my husband to address his legal proceedings against me to my sister's house. I am going to beg refuge there.

CLARISSE. You do not, then, wish, first of all, to deliberate with your stepson?

ANNA. What! You know that it is he!

CLARISSE. Yes.

ANNA. Through whom?

CLARISSE. Through the man who was accused unjustly.

ANNA. Monsieur Pavail told?

CLARISSE. Me only, not the General.

ANNA. I had accused no one. It's all

right since it's done. And, yes, I do propose to see Jean. I delayed my departure until the time when I should not fail to meet him on the road.

CLARISSE. What makes you leave this house in such haste?

ANNA. There is no place for me here any longer. You yourself were not able to hide from me this morning the repulsion that I inspired in you.

CLARISSE. Do not bear me ill-will for the brusqueness of a first reaction. Since then I have been taking into consideration the circumstances in which you may have had to struggle.

ANNA. Ah! indeed! You would admit that a woman who has suffered temptation is not on that account necessarily an unpardonable wretch?

CLARISSE [*grave and indulgent*]. Do not impute to me any more cruel judgments. Do not be distrustful of me; confide in me, rather.

ANNA. Ah, that would do me good!

CLARISSE. Yes, tell me; I shall listen with the most sincere interest.

ANNA. Really?

CLARISSE. Really.

ANNA. There was so much imprudence on my part, so little perversity! Events followed each other so rapidly.

CLARISSE. It seems to me that one cannot fail to be aware of the moment when a person ceases to be an object of indifference to one.

ANNA. In his relations with me Jean had always been sarcastic, teasing, capricious. I was persuaded that he disliked me; and I never suspected myself of feeling kindly toward him. One evening when my husband was absent, Jean came to see me. It was not long before he became so satirical, so exasperating, that he irritated me as he had never done before. The discussion unnerved me so that stupidly I began to weep. That made him change his tone immediately. In a voice choked with emotion he declared that all his persecution of me had never been other than suffering, jealousy, desire. He swore to me that he loved me tenderly, passionately. You will answer that one must be already very depraved to listen to things of that sort.

CLARISSE [*with spirit*]. I don't say that It is possible to lose one's composure.

have a sensation that unnerves and overpowers you; a sensation of the most painful sort and which, however, one may not wish to bring to an end immediately. I am not expressing a judgment; I am stating an opinion; I imagine . . .

ANNA. A violent agitation seized me. Am I to suppose that these protestations of love enlightened me all of a sudden as to a condition of my heart of which I had not been conscious?

CLARISSE. Is it really true, then, that one's ignorance of one's self can reach such a point as that?

ANNA. Otherwise, why that burst of tears which served as prelude to the scene that was to follow? Or, can this be a phenomenon comparable to that of the iron and the loadstone? Is there for animate beings a magnetic attraction? What is that force with masculine will? What is that mysterious sway? that magnetism?

CLARISSE. Who knows?

ANNA. I was attracted because I was loved. Because I was loved, I went on — to the belief that I loved; I went on — to a love that destroyed me.

CLARISSE [pensively]. I begin to see, indeed, that the safeguard of many women may be the respect which makes men refrain from attacking them, the presumption that there would be nothing gained. But, when these conditions have been overstepped, when a man has had the audacity to declare himself . . . then, to be harried by him without respite! To see constantly hovering over you a will never diverted from its prey! The fascination of being coveted! There is in that, yes, a test whose terrors I can easily understand.

ANNA. I forbade Jean to return to my house. He made several ineffectual efforts to be received. But how was I to elude the invitation to your country-house? Ever since I have been living here your stepson has pursued me, persecuted me. He was always at my heels. He kept writing to me, frightening me. I lost my head when he declared to me that he would kill himself! Ought I not to have laughed at this threat which all men make?

CLARISSE. Some carry it out. There are some whom one would not dare defy!

ANNA. In short, he induced me to consent to to-day's meeting.

CLARISSE. This was the first time?

ANNA [hiding her face]. Yes.

CLARISSE. My poor child! [Perceiving her stepson.] Ah, here is Jean!

ANNA. At last!

[JEAN enters from the rear.]

JEAN. Pavail came to meet me. I know everything!

ANNA. What!

CLARISSE. You know, then, that he assumed all the responsibility.

JEAN. And that is a situation which I do not accept.

ANNA. You are going to tell your father the truth?

JEAN. Necessarily.

CLARISSE. Have you and your friend agreed upon this?

JEAN. On the point in question I have only myself to consult.

CLARISSE. I have learned from Pavail that he has reasons for exiling himself.

JEAN. He told me nothing about them.

CLARISSE. He gave me to understand as much. He is under an obligation to do it.

JEAN. He will remain free to choose whatever course suits him best.

CLARISSE. Do not insist upon marring what has been mended.

ANNA. You mean?

CLARISSE. It is in the interest of all that Pavail determined upon his rôle.

ANNA. Yes, yes, indeed!

CLARISSE. The General will be most irreparably embittered toward our cousin if he imputes to her the fault of having rendered culpable, not a stranger, but you, the son of the house, you, his own son.

ANNA. Clarisse is right. Do not add fuel to the flame!

JEAN. Since you are compromised I shall let no one believe that it is with any other than me. Such a thought would be odious to me.

CLARISSE. Yet, consider . . .

JEAN. No! On this point, no insistence will make me waver.

CLARISSE. Alas! You are no less headstrong than your father! Do as you will!
[She starts to go.]

ANNA. Do not go!

CLARISSE. How should I not feel that in the presence of you two I am in the way?

JEAN. Your kindness can serve us better

than by leaving us to ourselves. Pavail was not able to inform me of the intentions of Anna's husband. Help us with your advice.

ANNA. Yes, do not abandon us! The General may come! [*Perceiving him.*] Ah, here he is!

[SIBÉRAN *enters from the rear, in civilian's attire.*]

SIBÉRAN. [*To* JEAN, *pretending not to notice* ANNA'S *presence.*] So you're back, my boy!

JEAN. I was going to look for you, father. I have something to say to you.

SIBÉRAN. We'll choose another moment. [*Goes to the desk, and looks at the letter left by* PAVAIL, *while* CLARISSE *talks in a low voice with* ANNA.]

CLARISSE. Your presence could do nothing but harm. Go back to your room.

ANNA. You will bring me news?

CLARISSE. Yes; I am staying to try to deaden the shock.

ANNA. Oh, yes, try!

[*She goes out.*]

SIBÉRAN. [*To* JEAN.] What did you wish to communicate to me?

[*During the following speeches he busies himself adding a postscript to* PAVAIL'S *letter and affixing his seal.*]

JEAN. It's about what has just passed between Pavail and you.

SIBÉRAN. Is it possible that you mean to intercede for him?

JEAN. Grant that the action with which you reproach him is not one of those crimes which cannot be redeemed.

SIBÉRAN. I have nothing to retrench from the judgment I have pronounced.

JEAN. And yet, father, love, the allurement of pleasure, the enticement of the senses; you know that that may be irresistible. You were young like Pavail — and me.

SIBÉRAN. For your guidance, bear in mind that I sympathize only with permissible love. At Pavail's age, and yours, I had been already once married. If you young fellows have a good time with the girls of the streets — I close my eyes to that! But to turn from her path a woman who is the property of another, that for me is criminality. It is confounded in my mind with those crimes to which the law attaches an infamous penalty, outrage to modesty, or incitement to debauch. Pavail is for me henceforth the lowest of knaves.

JEAN. By expressing yourself in these terms, you render it impossible for me to delay any longer rehabilitating him in your eyes. Pavail is not the criminal; I am.

SIBÉRAN [*turning toward his son*]. What nonsense is this?

JEAN. While you still thought me far away, I had arrived secretly at Pavail's house. The man who had a rendezvous there this morning, I repeat, that man was I.

SIBÉRAN. Why should Pavail not have undeceived me?

JEAN. From a spirit of self-sacrifice, of chivalry.

SIBÉRAN. Nonsense! [*To* CLARISSE.] Do you believe this tale?

CLARISSE. I heard it a moment ago.

SIBÉRAN [*indicating* JEAN]. From him?

CLARISSE. No. From — from Anna.

SIBÉRAN. You are all trying to mystify me. [*To* JEAN.] This is a scheme you have devised on the spur of the moment for getting your friend out of difficulty.

JEAN. Regard for the truth and that only impels me to expose myself to your severity.

SIBÉRAN. Fiddlesticks! You flatter yourself that in your case I shall end by showing leniency.

JEAN. On the contrary, I understand perfectly that I cannot escape any of the accusations which, according to what he told me in a few words, you hurled into Pavail's face. All that you have charged him with in his capacity of officer, you will make me expiate likewise, since I wear the same epaulette.

SIBÉRAN. I surrender to your reasoning: all right! And so it's really you, then, that I am to treat as a blackguard!

CLARISSE. Oh, please!

SIBÉRAN [*more grieved than irritated*]. To have betrayed me in this way, betrayed my hospitality! I am mortified beyond all expression! I ought! I don't know what restrains me! [*To* JEAN.] This is a very painful blow — and from you!

JEAN. Father!

SIBÉRAN. Have you considered the consequences of your action?

JEAN. Not yet, no.

SIBÉRAN. Well; our cousin has realized

what his honor, at least, requires. You will not only have brought dishonor upon his household ; you have destroyed it !

JEAN. They are going to be divorced ?

SIBÉRAN. Yes, she is to be expelled from the family, as she deserves.

JEAN. If that is the case, Anna can be sure that she will have me at her side.

SIBÉRAN [*sharply*]. What is the significance of that remark ?

JEAN. If my cousin should be cast off on my account, I should have no other course than to marry her immediately.

SIBÉRAN [*his brow contracted*]. Marry her ! You ! You 're joking !

CLARISSE. Be calm ! In Heaven's name, be calm !

SIBÉRAN. [*To* CLARISSE.] Leave me alone. [*To* JEAN.] Continue your explanation. Unfold your scheme ! The lady is four or five years your senior. But that does n't make any difference, does it ? Marriage; that 's how you decide the matter ! And it is very possible that you promised it to each other !

JEAN. That idea did not occur to me. I did not foresee, I confess, that all my destiny could be involved. I do not know whether or not that prospect would have stopped me. But, in the position in which I am now, I see before me an obligation to make reparation which I could not fail to fulfill, without being a dishonorable man.

SIBÉRAN. You 've lost your wits ! You 're mad ! [*To* CLARISSE.] He 's becoming a raving lunatic !

CLARISSE. Be patient ! Contain yourself !

SIBÉRAN. See here, my dear boy, you would not like to take as legitimate companion a light woman, convicted of frailty ?

JEAN [*indignantly*]. Oh !

CLARISSE [*also protesting vigorously*]. Anna is not a woman of that sort !

SIBÉRAN. Oh, pshaw !

JEAN. You make use of terms which I cannot permit with reference to her.

SIBÉRAN. What guarantee have you that a woman who has proved to you her immodesty would be faithful to you in the future ? What guarantee have you that in her misconduct you were the first ?

JEAN. This is outrageous !

CLARISSE. It is too much, yes ! You have not the right !

SIBÉRAN [*in a voice which admits of no reply*]. When I ascribe to a woman habits in harmony with one of her verified actions, I am not making a very bold supposition.

CLARISSE. [*To* JEAN.] Do not reply ! Do not argue !

JEAN. [*To* CLARISSE.] See then that my father does not continue in that tone.

CLARISSE. My dear General . . .

SIBÉRAN. You, silence, I beg you !

CLARISSE [*overwhelmed*]. Has it come to this ?

SIBÉRAN. [*To* JEAN.] You, make haste to tell me that you will never again speak to me of such a marriage.

JEAN. I declare to you that Anna will cease to be Madame Doncières only to find a husband in me.

SIBÉRAN. And I, I assure you that you will not make me accept that creature as my daughter.

JEAN. All you will have to do is to drive us away, both of us.

SIBÉRAN. I shall not let you transmit the name you have received from me to an adulteress, excluded from her home !

JEAN. I have passed the age when you could forbid me to do it.

CLARISSE. Jean !

SIBÉRAN. What ! You invoke the aid of the law against me ? You would pass over my prohibition ? You would dispense with my consent ?

JEAN. If necessary, yes.

SIBÉRAN. You defy me. You have offended me. Do not appear before me again until you come with apologies. Go reflect ! Go ! Go !

JEAN. Reflect, you, too !

[*He goes out by the right.*]

SIBÉRAN. The scoundrel ! The scoundrel ! He has put me in a fury ! And you, see here, you encouraged him to hold out against me.

CLARISSE. Jean refused to abandon a woman whom he had led astray. I could not find it in my heart to blame him.

SIBÉRAN. 'Pon my word ! This adventure has unsettled your mind. What infection have you breathed ? A few hours ago, we agreed, it seems to me, that Anna had forfeited all her rights.

CLARISSE. I had not reckoned with the decrees of fate.

SIBÉRAN. What 's that word fate ? You have, then, let the woman circumvent you, and put ideas into your head, have you ?

CLARISSE. All that I can answer is that I pity her. I should like to be of some service to her, to deliver her from affliction.

SIBÉRAN. Direct your attention, rather, to breaking off all relations with her. I am surprised that I have to lay this injunction upon you.

CLARISSE. Oh, I beg of you, do not treat me again like a child!

SIBÉRAN. I am justified in doing it when your moral sense gives evidence suddenly of a laxity which I did not suspect in you.

CLARISSE. Do you think that you yourself are made all of one piece?

SIBÉRAN. What do you insinuate?

CLARISSE. In the dispute that you have just had, you no longer spoke of banishing the seducer to the end of the world, when it was your son who would have suffered this chastisement. So, do not maintain any more that there are only principles. There are also questions of persons, there are sentiments, sensations, instinct, the unforeseen . . .

SIBÉRAN. I confess that I had two standards of measurement without realizing it. Do not conclude from that, however, that Jean can count on a further weakness on my part. Unless he makes prompt submission, it is he whom I shall send away.

CLARISSE. Where will you get that power? You possessed it only in relation to another, who did not resist you. If your son retorts that he does not wish to go away . . .

SIBÉRAN. Eh?

CLARISSE. Yes. What can you do? What will you do?

SIBÉRAN. I . . . I . . . Then, you admit the reasonableness of his mad threat? You approve of his carrying out his nasty scheme?

CLARISSE. You are not looking for the way out of the difficulty where it might be.

SIBÉRAN. Where is that?

CLARISSE. After all, Jean has not said that he ever dreamed of this attachment as continuing eternally. Furthermore, I saw clearly that Anna would be quite ready to return to her duty. Make it your business to bring about a reconciliation between her and her husband.

SIBÉRAN. What's this you are proposing to me?

CLARISSE. You reported to me that it was you who had strengthened Doncières in his resolution to secure a divorce. Your influence over him could probably undo what it has done.

SIBÉRAN. Recant in that fashion! Disavow in the matter of conjugal honor all intolerance I profess! all that I believe unreservedly! Shame! Faugh!

CLARISSE. If you prevent Anna's becoming free to marry again, you have in that the real means of rendering it impossible for Jean to marry her.

SIBÉRAN. But picture to yourself what I should be guilty of if I did that! Can you imagine me, me, striving to bring back that worthy man into the arms of the woman of the town?

CLARISSE. Nevertheless, you must make a choice. I repeat, either Anna is to remain Doncières's wife, or she is to be your son's. Would you rather have her for a cousin or for a daughter-in-law? All the problem is in that. Which do you prefer?

SIBÉRAN [striving to recover possession of himself]. I am displeased with you for pressing me in this way to a categorical answer. I am displeased with you because I am humiliated to perceive that a feeling of hesitation is creeping in upon me. Be still! Be still!

CLARISSE. Yet . . .

SIBÉRAN [himself again]. Enough! I must find myself face to face with myself again. I must have a little air. Besides, I have to make my apologies to Lieutenant Pavail.

CLARISSE [terror-stricken]. Oh, not yet! In our present situation with relation to your cousin, who accuses no one but him . . .

SIBÉRAN. Pavail is innocent. It is not for me to weigh what would be the more convenient for us, to his detriment.

CLARISSE. You are not going to tell him that he can keep his place in your service?

SIBÉRAN. I am going to order him to.

CLARISSE. Oh!

SIBÉRAN. It is thus that I shall have the feeling of having retracted to the full extent of my debt to him.

CLARISSE. Wait! Listen!

SIBÉRAN. I shall listen to nothing more. [He goes out by the rear.]

CLARISSE [alone, overwhelmed]. He is going to stay!

ACT III

Same setting. The window-shutters are closed. The lamps are lighted. Through the piazza-door, the sky is seen to grow dimmer gradually and night falls on the park.

As the curtain rises, ANNA *is alone on the stage.* JEAN *enters by the door on the right.*

JEAN. I was told you were waiting for me.

ANNA. Yes. The General had to go out. Clarisse undertook to let you know that for the moment we should be uninterrupted here.

JEAN. She related to you the scene that my father and I had here a little while ago?

ANNA [*sighing*]. It is not the sort of thing to relieve my mind.

JEAN. You approve of my having asserted that in spite of everybody I should make you my wife?

ANNA. I am very much affected to learn that you conducted yourself with such loyalty to me.

JEAN. You did not doubt me, did you?

ANNA. Certainly not!

JEAN. My poor dear Anna!

ANNA [*warding off a movement of affection*]. Restrain yourself!

JEAN. Oh! You are filled with bitterness toward me on account of what has happened!

ANNA. It is not for me to take you to task any more than myself. But we are here together at this moment to examine a question which takes precedence of all else.

JEAN. I am at your orders.

ANNA. I must not be the cause of a frightful estrangement between your father and you.

JEAN. You don't have to consider that.

ANNA. You are so young! I should add a crime to my fault if I accepted the sacrifice of your brilliant prospects —

JEAN. But it will be no sacrifice! I shall be very happy.

ANNA. First of all, permit me to make known to you the substance of my recent conversation with Clarisse.

JEAN. Tell me.

ANNA. According to her, I need not entirely despair of a reconciliation with my husband.

JEAN. Ah!

ANNA. I may receive aid toward obtaining his pardon. This pardon, you understand, I should solicit in complete good faith, without mental reserve, with the firm resolution to belong to you no more.

JEAN. I understand.

ANNA. As my husband does not suspect that it is you who . . .

JEAN [*relieving her of the burden of continuing*]. Yes. Well?

ANNA. Well, then, the effort might be made to see that his grievance is never laid at your door. The ordinary associations of kinship would thus remain possible among us all.

JEAN. Go on.

ANNA. In short, if the arrangement were made, you would from that moment on, be no longer in conflict with your father. You would not have to show yourself in your true colors to your cousin. As for me, my conduct would not be exposed, my reputation would remain intact, my life would not be thrown into confusion. So, I 'm wondering now if that way of ending the whole thing would not be the most satisfactory.

JEAN [*in earnest meditation*]. Hum! It would be hard to deny it! It 's possible! It 's obvious.

ANNA [*eagerly*]. That is what I wanted to make you realize!

JEAN. What?

ANNA. That is the opinion it was important for me to let you formulate yourself!

JEAN. What! Was it a trap?

ANNA. Not at all. I placed at your disposal the resource which had just afforded me too the means of reading my conscience. Henceforth, it is settled for both of us just how much each one of us cared for the other.

JEAN. It is utterly unjust of you to speak so! Supposing that your husband should prove inexorable, does the fact not remain that I am here, ready to unite myself once and for all with you?

ANNA. Oh, pshaw! Each in turn confessed that we looked on marriage only as a last resort. Could I now think it an enviable fate if we married out of mutual concession, from resignation? Could I consent to being married simply because neither you nor I would see anything better to do? Ah, no! not that! And, look here! do you want me to tell you what you might have answered when I announced to you the plan of effecting a reconciliation between me and my husband?

JEAN [*nettled*]. I am certainly curious to hear the lesson you are preparing for me. I am impatient to learn why your manner is becoming so hostile.

ANNA [*excited by her own words*]. Well, the most ordinary courtesy commanded you, a minute ago, to reply to me that the misfortune which had befallen us was in reality not a misfortune. That opportunity of getting a divorce which would have brought me to you entirely and forever, — you might have maintained that we ought not to have let it slip, that we ought to profit by it, rejoice in it! Such are the words you would have spoken if you had been the same as you were before receiving from me what you desired! And then, listening to you, I should have questioned myself, distracted. I should have asked myself whether, after having given myself, I had thus the right to take myself back. I should have experienced a moment of painful, but sweet uncertainty.

JEAN. I did not think of all these complications, it's true. I answered you candidly, like an honest fellow.

ANNA. You ought to have been thrilled with emotion! You ought to have flown into a passion at the idea of possessing me no more! You ought to have wished to seize me and run away with me! I would have answered you with the most categorical refusal.

JEAN. Well, then?

ANNA. But I should have found in all that a caress, a consolation for the debasement I incurred for love of you, sir. You did not say what you ought to have said, because you're a heartless wretch!

[*Her voice has begun to tremble.*]

JEAN. Be calm, Anna, I beg you! do not carry on so!

ANNA. Go away! Go away!

JEAN. My stars, I almost want to! I don't know which way to turn. I don't pretend to know much about women. But it isn't a mistake, I guarantee that, to declare them incomprehensible.

ANNA [*still in tears*]. You're a little fool!

JEAN. Instead of censuring me, think how you confused me from the very beginning of our talk by your changeableness.

ANNA. Oh!

JEAN. Yes, I tell you! You explained to me right away that your dearest wish was to reëstablish your life in common with a man whom you detest.

ANNA. I, detest my husband! Where did you get that idea?

JEAN. I'm only translating your own expressions; this morning, in our cottage, you protested that your existence seemed to you to be only just beginning.

ANNA. Under such circumstances, one says a lot of things! — oh, incredible things!

JEAN. You told me that the being with whom you had lived up to that time would be thenceforth an object of horror to you.

ANNA. I didn't say that!

JEAN. Anna! come now! You added . . .

ANNA. It's a lie!

JEAN. Why, Anna!

ANNA. It was you who made every effort to make me talk. But, of my own accord, I never had any inclination to criticize my husband. And, above all, I am not the sort of woman to take advantage of a moment when he was not there to defend himself.

JEAN. All right! I must have misunderstood you. I'll not worry you any longer.

ANNA. Yes, let's drop the subject. Anything further we might say would only be more disagreeable still. Forget my sharp words.

JEAN [*with emotion*]. That will be the easiest for me to forget, Anna!

ANNA [*sadly*]. And, besides, forgetting will surely cost you less effort than it will one other!

[*She accompanies this last word with a gesture which indicates, on the left, the apartment she occupies with her husband.*]

JEAN. You desire me to leave you?

ANNA. Yes, I desire it.

JEAN. Then, there remains only for me to wish you good luck.

ANNA. Thanks. I thank you.

[*JEAN goes out by the right.*]

CLARISSE [*entering from the rear*]. You have seen Jean?

ANNA. He has just left.

CLARISSE. Was it wisdom that prevailed?

ANNA. Yes. It's done. It's settled.

CLARISSE. You must think of nothing now except winning back your husband.

ANNA. I presume that the success of the enterprise will depend on the aid that may be lent me by you and your husband. Will you succeed in bringing the General to intercede in my favor?

CLARISSE. Probably he stopped at his club and is there now. I cannot predict in what state of mind he will return. I used all my influence to bend him before he left. It's true that his desire to put obstacles in the way of Jean's marrying you made his principles waver for a moment. But it hasn't uprooted them. So, count largely upon yourself.

ANNA. Alas!

CLARISSE. Doncières will be here at any moment. Do not receive him with that helpless air, that dejected countenance, which would recall to his mind too bluntly the scenes of this day. Try to relax. Bathe your eyes. Try to resume your usual expression so as to remind him of past happiness.

ANNA. I have put myself in your hands. I have only to obey you blindly. But before I go, one thing would make me very glad.

CLARISSE. What?

ANNA. I should like to have the impression that you feel for me now something better than pity.

CLARISSE. I am as profoundly moved as I should be if my own fate were at stake.

ANNA. I need so much to believe that, in spite of everything, I have retained in your eyes something of my womanly dignity.

CLARISSE. Kiss me.

ANNA. Ah, that is what I wanted! [*They embrace.*] Ah, how good you are! I felt that you were almost sisterly.

CLARISSE. Yes.

ANNA. I can go now, with comfort in my heart. [*She goes out by the left.*]

[PAVAIL *enters from the rear, in civilian's attire.*]

CLARISSE [*greatly perturbed*]. You! already!

PAVAIL. Monsieur de Sibéran just left my house. His action has effaced what passed between us. He commanded me to stay.

CLARISSE. And you come to ask me to subscribe to that?

PAVAIL. I come to beg you to understand that I accepted immediately, without hesitation, without examination.

CLARISSE. I merit what has befallen me. It is my fault, I know, for having talked so imprudently with you.

PAVAIL. Do not regret having confided to me that there may be a certain alleviation in a lot like yours in feeling near at hand a mind ever suffering with yours, darkened by every shade of sadness detected in your face.

CLARISSE. You led me much further astray even than that. I proved to myself, I made unmistakably apparent to you, the extraordinary interest you inspired in me. I went so far as to admit that I was almost jealous already. I have thus thrown aside the mask under which I should have had my last chance, as things are now, to force you to maintain a decorous attitude toward me.

PAVAIL. After having shown me that thoughts full of promise for me have begun to come to your mind, you will never again prevent my believing, I assure you, that happiness may sometime spread its full bloom above us. I no longer despair of being loved; I hope with an ardent hope.

CLARISSE. Oh, do not hope! Do not hope for anything! What do you hope for? If I came to the point of truly sharing your love, the result would be only horrible suffering for both of us!

PAVAIL. Why would we suffer? Why would we not be happy? Why?

CLARISSE. Evidently you do not allow yourself to be embarrassed by any obstacle. Your own dwelling is a witness to the fact that there was a way of coming to an understanding with the other woman of this house. And the arrangements immediately suggest themselves to your mind which would lead me, after her, to the same trysting-place.

PAVAIL. My reverence for you ought to protect me from that cruel tone. What animosity rouses in you the desire to take back the happiness you gave me so short a time ago, when your words were, more than once, so soft and gentle? Remember how deeply you were moved, how divinely tender you were! Remember how your voice trembled!

CLARISSE. I remember only too well! I thought my whole life was to be made up of renunciations; but you brought into being that dead self which I had been forced to hide away in my heart. Under your influence, in fact, I saw for a moment the hope of another fate. It was a flash, a flame, which, thanks to you, passed over my bleak existence. Yes, I said to myself then distractedly : " Who knows whether the being for whom I was brought into the world, who knows, who knows whether that being was not you, you and no other ? "

PAVAIL. Oh, that vision came to you ?

CLARISSE. And during the instant of your farewell, I said to myself that, at the hour of destiny which was ringing then, the great event, love, can come but once. When you disappeared, something expired in me : I lost at the very moment that it had come into being my only hope of a second life upon this earth.

PAVAIL. How could you defend yourself against premonitions as strong as these ? What chain can bind you henceforth in a duty which is odious to you, in this ill-sorted union, where you clash with a nature so different from yours, with an age that has nothing in common with yours ? There is not one of your glances, there is not one of your words but is filled with yearning. All that weeps in the bottom of the soul, all that, in the heart, calls and sings, all this repeats to you that my passion offers you what you were awaiting. You know full well that never woman has been more discreetly cherished, desired. You divine full well the passionate gratitude, the joys, that will bless you, if you love me, if you love me !

CLARISSE [intoxicated]. When I listen to you, a fever unknown mounts to my brain. The gate of the future opens again, perspectives unroll before my eyes. Ah ! to escape from loneliness of the heart, and, even if one is alone, to feel that one is always two, the other and one's self, mingled in one's self ! To speak, laugh, be silent, dream, act, leave him and find him again, with the ever-present impression of being enveloped in love as in the perfume of a perpetual summer. To have one's tenderest feelings tortured no longer ; no longer to hide them timidly away under the continual menace of a reproof, of a sarcasm, nor yet under the anguish of unwelcome ardors. For the worst, do you see ? is not that the master to whom one belongs, should be tyrannical

in conversation, a disagreeable companion. That would perhaps be tolerable, if only he did not at certain moments transform himself into an amorous creditor, claiming a debt of love from one who has nothing to give.

PAVAIL [vehemently]. You shall belong to him no longer !

CLARISSE. Be still !

PAVAIL. You shall be mine, only mine !

CLARISSE [drawing away from him]. Do not mistake ! If I am to love you, if I should come to love you to the point of giving myself to you, at that very instant I should say to my husband that I am going to leave his house, to be entirely my own mistress, to receive from him no longer any benefit. I should go away from him, taking with me only the dress upon my back, for I had at least some clothes when I became his wife. It is under these conditions that you would risk seeing me come to you ?

PAVAIL. Ah, dear one ! since you do not fear privations, hardships, the struggle for life, since you do not fear these, unite your lot with mine, do not hesitate ! Let us go away together ! Let us go !

[He makes a motion to take her in his arms.]

CLARISSE [freeing herself]. I beg you !

PAVAIL. Do not repel me !

CLARISSE. Yes ! Leave me ! I told you that the day when I could no longer have any doubt as to my intention of being yours, I should go to you and throw myself into your arms. But, first of all, I must examine myself profoundly, must regain mastery of myself, unaffected by your presence. I demand time, weeks, without seeing you again.

PAVAIL. Ah, how can you !

CLARISSE. If we persisted in meeting each other, you would become from day to day more insistent, and I weaker. I do not wish to weigh myself down with the baseness of successive compromises. I do not wish to give myself piecemeal. You will have me all at once, you will have me without reserve, if you have me at all. I could not say now that you will ever have me : as to all this I am in utter darkness, in a mad frenzy. But, what I see with absolute certainty, is that I should never forgive your remaining day after day, to do violence to my decision by your ascendancy over my nerves, by the physical power of your presence.

PAVAIL. Hold myself aloof? Withdraw now? Do you think I do not see that that would mean to give you up? Do you think me rash enough to hazard my destiny thus?

CLARISSE. I ask this delay of you with the utmost determination. I shall not relent. Submit! Go!

PAVAIL. Then, put in my veins an imperishable sensation. Give me the intoxication I must have!

CLARISSE. What is it you wish?

PAVAIL. Your lips!

CLARISSE. Oh!

PAVAIL. I shall live from having had them. Your lips!

CLARISSE. Oh, Pavail!

PAVAIL. Your lips, so I may go!

CLARISSE [giving him a hasty kiss]. Go!
[He holds her in his embrace.]

[SIBÉRAN enters from the right and stands in a stupefaction that is terrible to see.]

SIBÉRAN. The wretches!
[CLARISSE has broken from PAVAIL's embrace with cries of terror.]

PAVAIL [having thrown himself between CLARISSE and her husband]. Avenge yourself only on me!

SIBÉRAN [arming himself with a bronze]. You! yes, I'll kill you!

CLARISSE [in a desperate protest]. Not that horror! Not that, not that!

SIBÉRAN [after a moment of awful hesitation, throwing the bronze to the floor]. That is not so easy as it seems!

PAVAIL. I alone am to blame. I did violence.

SIBÉRAN. You! out of here!

CLARISSE. [To PAVAIL.] Go!

PAVAIL. [To CLARISSE.] But you?

CLARISSE [with the gesture of one sinking into the unknown]. Ah!

SIBÉRAN. [To PAVAIL.] Will you go?

CLARISSE. [To PAVAIL with irresistible authority.] Go!

PAVAIL. [To CLARISSE.] I obey you!

SIBÉRAN. [To PAVAIL.] Be gone! Be gone!

[PAVAIL walking backward goes out by the rear.]

SIBÉRAN [beside himself]. It is you, it is you who have done this? While I accorded you my absolute confidence, you were deriding me, you were making fun of me! You were deceiving me basely!

CLARISSE. I am still in your presence only to fix the limits of your judgment of me. I will not let you believe that I could have lived at your side by means of ruse and hypocrisy: the sole act of my existence which is an affront to you is the one you have just witnessed.

SIBÉRAN. Old as the hills, that refrain is! You women always resort to it when you are caught, so as to have something left to deny. Come, now, don't lie any more: how long have you had this lover?

CLARISSE. If an intrigue had existed between him and me, would we have allowed your error of this morning to make you separate us from each other? I made no attempt to turn you from the decision which would have taken him away from me. I even strove, at the last, to prevent your keeping him. And he, when it was very easy to do it, did not deign to clear himself. Would they have proceeded thus who were lover and mistress?

SIBÉRAN. It looks somewhat as if you were telling the truth. But, if I surprised you in your first instant of treachery, you were already abandoned to that man, you were falling into his possession!

CLARISSE. The idea of being his, the idea of being unfaithful to you, had never occurred to me. During the last few hours I have been assailed with passionate declarations. I had not expected them. I protested against them as long as I could. In the end I suffered an irresistible, indefinable weakness.

SIBÉRAN. Ah, yes! You listened to a seducer without thinking of evil, did n't you? You exposed yourself to his advances in entire good faith, of course! It was not love that made you falter, nor the enticement of sin, nor the temptation of vice. It was n't these ordinary incentives; it was something superhuman, inconceivable!

CLARISSE. A short time ago I spoke as mockingly as you do, and already I am crying my mea culpa for having indulged in irony of that sort. At any rate, I have placed before you all the facts that the whole truth calls for.

SIBÉRAN. Do you think I'll let you off so easily?

CLARISSE. You could beat my head against the walls without being able to force me to make any further explanations. I told you all it is possible for me to say.

SIBÉRAN. The idea does n't occur to you to burst into a flood of excuses, and beg for mercy?

CLARISSE. You have taught me that an action like mine is unpardonable to a mind like yours. All that is left for me is to anticipate the command which will drive me from your house.

SIBÉRAN. That's what would just suit you, would n't it? You would be straightway free to go to the man who thrilled you a moment ago. So, confess that your sole aim now is to be entirely his.

CLARISSE. I have furnished you with the facts I owe you. I end there all accounts to be rendered you.

SIBÉRAN. You have no voice in the decision of this matter. I shall place barriers between your accomplice and you. Until matters take a new turn, you are not to stir from my house.

CLARISSE. I will not remain here at your discretion. I will not remain here for you to torture me with the jealousy I rouse in you, just as you have so long throttled me with your tyranny.

SIBÉRAN. What you reveal to me is abominable! What! I had in you an enemy of long standing that you kept concealed from me? Your reserve, your coldness, which I was fool enough to attribute to chastity, were only fierce antipathy? You hated me from the bottom of your soul? You have always hated me?

CLARISSE. Not always! I vowed to you at our marriage a perfect affection. You justified it by your probity and personal merit. But the harshness of your character has too many times brought pain to me. The impulses of my heart, my ways of thinking and acting, you did not accept them simply and frankly, as I brought them to you. To train and discipline is your favorite sport. You wished to train my manners, my reasonings, my convictions, my nature. One can be trained to do everything, perhaps, except to love, for fear enters in, which is a kind of hate. Listen! Let me tell you what made me see most clearly the state to which you had reduced me: from time to time, when we left the table, you took me to see you distribute a part of what was left of the meal to your saddle-horses. While one or the other of them was eating from your hand, I could not detach my attention from his black eye, which a semi-circle of white suddenly stamped with the terror that was always lurking there. His quick recoil, his slow and suspicious approach, that uneasy manner of looking upon his master of every day as eternally unknown, as one who flatters with the voice as he would attack with the spurs . . . well . . . yes! that picture, each time, made me think that, at the moments when you were kind to me, I had my image in that half-shuddering beast.

SIBÉRAN. But, you might weigh in the balance the advantages you have received from me. You forget too completely the disinterestedness which I flattered myself I was showing in choosing you.

CLARISSE. As to that last remark, let me say that I do not wish to hear from you any further allusion to the fact that you took me without fortune. And to go from your house poorer than I came, at least if my value as an innocent girl is taken into account, is a charge that gives me pleasure, a relief which I enjoy.

SIBÉRAN. Turn everything into a weapon against me! Concede me nothing; very well! But it was before your fall that it became you to protest; when you still had the right to raise your voice. Why did you not come and accuse me to my face? Why did you not summon me to be on my guard against my own weaknesses? Why did you not do it deliberately, like an honest woman, — such as you were?

CLARISSE. There is an energy that one finds only in tempest and shipwreck. To be able to revolt there must be in the soul something besides virtue! I do not know what name to give to the forces which animate me at this moment. It cannot be real love for another, yet. And it has already ceased to be revolt against you. It is a whole new personality in me that is coming to the light. It is the instinct to live my share of life. It is the thirst to breathe at last with the freedom that is my birthright. It is a breath of resurrection!

SIBÉRAN. If I have made a martyr of you, I protest that I have played the executioner without knowing it. I am harsh, I grant it. I have doubtless been cruel, but there was something sacred in my respect for you. I was fidelity itself and you have been my single passion.

CLARISSE. I have nothing to say in reply. To-day, that according to every law I have become guilty in relation to you, I acknowledge that you have never given me any tangible reason for hostility to you, nor cause for any positive complaints. I must henceforth recall only your constant austerity, and your presumable superiority to myself. Yes, shame at the spectacle that I have inflicted upon you here, the sincerest esteem for you: those are the sentiments which, now all is over, I am carrying away with me.

SIBÉRAN. One moment! I want to tell you that over against your faults you have led me to array mine.

CLARISSE. Let's not talk about that!

SIBÉRAN. Yes, I was a boor a minute ago when I declared that you ought to have placed your complaints before me earlier. It was my duty to discover the sorrows you were concealing from me. It was my duty to discover by myself what a timid dignity, a graceful delicacy made you suppress.

CLARISSE. I beg you . . . Abstain from kind words, which might render my step less firm as I leave you.

SIBÉRAN. Leave me! In any case it is you, not I, who see only that issue!

CLARISSE. In ridding you of a woman who has outraged you, I am procuring for you what a man of your type must consider most desirable under the circumstances.

SIBÉRAN [with subsiding rage]. I did not suppose, it is true, that in a broken happiness any comfort could be found in picking up the pieces. That is where I am now. I am taking refuge in this resource; I am struggling for this paltry consolation. I am thinking only of trying, notwithstanding everything, to reconstruct my life with you!

CLARISSE. No, no! You have heard how it is only apart from you, in freedom from you, that happiness appears to me. I repeat that I crave happiness! I wish later in my life to feel that I was happy once! I must have happiness!

SIBÉRAN. Yes, I have that cry ringing in my ears! And yet, in spite of the wounds that make my pride bleed, I feel that I love you still. I love you madly. I shall love you always!

CLARISSE. Oh!

SIBÉRAN. After you have been literally half of my being for so many years, I cannot detach you from me! I cannot!

CLARISSE. But, remember for a moment what was irreparable in the words I spoke. What can you wish to reëstablish between us? All illusion for you is reduced to nothing. What oaths can we find which would restore to you a shadow of confidence in me?

SIBÉRAN. As long as you consented to remain here, we should know, both of us, to what that binds you. I shall repose my entire trust in you for the keeping of this new compact.

CLARISSE. No, I beg you! No! Do not ask that I consent to be entombed a second time in an existence of which I have raised the stone.

SIBÉRAN. Whatever you may have had to endure from me, you have taken a terrible revenge. I shall remain warned for all time to come, amply corrected. How far must I humiliate myself to bend you? Nothing will seem too much, neither supplications, nor lamentations.

CLARISSE. Ah, do not take from me the freedom to will!

SIBÉRAN [his voice broken by sobs]. I do not ask for love any longer. But, when you see me suffer and tremble in every fiber of my body, justice and charity will move you.

CLARISSE. I don't know! I don't know!

SIBÉRAN. Because I was dictatorial, can it be right that I should suffer abandonment, gloom, ridicule, at my age, public dishonor: things which I could not survive!

CLARISSE [frightened at the suggestion of suicide]. Ah, yes, there is that!

SIBÉRAN. If I have merited all that sorrow and shame, say it now. Declare it to me once more. And all will be said and done!

CLARISSE. You are right! I no longer have any will! Keep me!

SIBÉRAN. Ah, it's decided, then?

CLARISSE [with a gesture of assent]. I will expiate. [She bursts into tears.]

SIBÉRAN. Clarisse!

CLARISSE [choking]. Do not make me talk any more!

SIBÉRAN. I should like to say . . .

CLARISSE. Say no more!

SIBÉRAN. Ah! Here's Doncières!

[DONCIÈRES *enters from the rear.*]

DONCIÈRES. I have lost no time. [*To* SIBÉRAN.] Everything will proceed according to your ideas.

SIBÉRAN. What does that mean?

DONCIÈRES. I succeeded in finding the lawyer I went to consult.

CLARISSE. Oh, my dear Doncières, you are not going to wreak vengeance on Anna! She's a frolicsome, bewitching, little creature, not at all fitted to face great vicissitudes. If you threw her from your path, what do you think would become of her?

DONCIÈRES. She chose a lover: let her keep him! Let her have him marry her!

SIBÉRAN. What a pace you're setting!

DONCIÈRES. The idea is yours.

SIBÉRAN. Granted; but you must be divorced first.

DONCIÈRES. I bring back the assurance that I can be divorced in a few weeks, since I have the acquiescence of my wife.

SIBÉRAN. She no longer consents.

DONCIÈRES [*casting questioning glances at them, alternately*]. Who dissuaded her?

CLARISSE. I had a long talk with her. Her fault of to-day is her first and will be her last. You wouldn't like her to have ruined herself for all time in one day, would you?

DONCIÈRES. But it's as a ruined woman that you two propose to treat her.

CLARISSE. What makes you think that?

DONCIÈRES. Your husband warned me that, even if I kept her, you would not continue your relations with her. [*To* SIBÉRAN.] Did n't you say that?

SIBÉRAN. I say it no longer.

DONCIÈRES. Ah, it's your wife's influence that made you change your mind?

SIBÉRAN. Yes.

DONCIÈRES. That could, of course, not be without effect upon my way of looking at the matter. Yet, I cannot put aside all that you said to me in this very room. You laid out for me with rigorous exactness the line of conduct to be followed. You impressed upon me that if any one had taken your wife, you would thirst for blood.

SIBÉRAN. It's tradition for a man to imagine that, and atavism to repeat it. But when you consider the emergency at close range, how much of that which has been stolen from us would a murder or a duel restore?

DONCIÈRES. However, you would have approved, just the same, of my going to fight with this Pavail.

SIBÉRAN. Don't utter his name again! Hours have already passed since I thought myself obliged for your sake to take action against him. I have here a letter in which, obeying my injunction, he begs to be sent four thousand leagues away. [*To* CLARISSE.] Is this not true?

CLARISSE. Yes.

SIBÉRAN [*having rung a bell*]. Until a decision has been reached as to his destination, he is banished from my house. No one of us will see him again. [*To the* FOOTMAN *who has entered.*] Mail this. [*The* FOOTMAN *goes out.*] That's settled.

DONCIÈRES. But that does n't settle everything between my wife and me. You ought to be the first to understand: it's you who, only a short time ago, urged me on in a path which you have deserted.

SIBÉRAN. I spoke too hastily.

DONCIÈRES. And I was accustomed to see you so stubborn in your opinions. All of a sudden you contradict yourself with a readiness that bewilders me.

CLARISSE. It's what you hear now that you must heed: be sure of that!

DONCIÈRES. I admit that Sibéran's theories ruled me. Respect for the opinion of others made me immediately suppress a secret desire not to break up my home.

CLARISSE. Then obey your first spontaneous impulse!

DONCIÈRES. Yes, but here's the trouble: reflection has shown me that to forgive might become as painful as to separate. To find one's self day after day face to face with one's wife, with that thought, that apparition intervening . . .

SIBÉRAN [*nervously to* CLARISSE]. Answer. Answer!

CLARISSE. [*To* DONCIÈRES.] You will have recovered your wife at the cost of your suffering, at the price of the laceration of your heart. She will feel that you have rights which she is even more strictly bound to recognize than on the day when you felt only the joy of marriage in making her your companion. Do not resist the spirit of generosity. Aid in effacing the memory of a day's folly. Lend a helping hand; and you will not regret it. Believe me, believe me!

SIBÉRAN [*with deep feeling*]. Yes, believe her !

DONCIÈRES. Well, deuce take it ! when I sound my heart, when I recall the years that my wife brought so much happiness to me !

CLARISSE. You can imagine with what impatience she is awaiting your decision.

DONCIÈRES. If she can swear to me that she is repentant, for my part, I shall try to believe it. Then we 'll travel, travel. I shall doubtless find calm in our travels, the eradication of the recollection. Some day, perhaps, you will see in me the type of the husband who has persuaded himself that his wife has never loved any man but himself, even while she was in the arms of another.

CLARISSE [*uncomfortable*]. I beg you . . .

DONCIÈRES. [*To* SIBÉRAN.] And you will smile at me ?

SIBÉRAN. No.

CLARISSE. [*To* DONCIÈRES.] I beg you, delay no longer : go to her.

DONCIÈRES. The die is cast. I 'm going, I 'm going.

[*He goes out at the left.*]

SIBÉRAN [*following* DONCIÈRES *with a gesture*]. Yesterday I should have thought him grotesque and abject.

CLARISSE. Were you a better man yesterday ?

SIBÉRAN. I did n't know myself as well.

CLARISSE [*with humility*]. Who knows himself ?

PÉLLÉAS AND MÉLISANDE

By MAURICE MAETERLINCK

Translated by RICHARD HOVEY

TO
OCTAVE MIRBEAU
IN WITNESS OF DEEP FRIENDSHIP
ADMIRATION AND GRATITUDE
M. M.

PERSONS

ARKËL, *King of Allemonde*

GENEVIÈVE, *mother of Pélléas and Golaud*

PÉLLÉAS,
GOLAUD, } *grandsons of Arkël*

MÉLISANDE

LITTLE YNIOLD, *son of Golaud (by a former marriage)*

A PHYSICIAN

THE PORTER

Servants, Beggars, etc.

PÉLLÉAS AND MÉLISANDE

ACT I

SCENE I— *The gate of the castle.*

MAIDSERVANTS [*within*]. Open the gate ! Open the gate !

PORTER [*within*]. Who is there ? Why do you come and wake me up? Go out by the little gates; there are enough of them ! . . .

A MAIDSERVANT [*within*]. We have come to wash the threshold, the gate, and the steps ; open, then ! open !

ANOTHER MAIDSERVANT [*within*]. There are going to be great happenings !

THIRD MAIDSERVANT [*within*]. There are going to be great fêtes ! Open quickly !

THE MAIDSERVANTS. Open ! open !

PORTER. Wait ! wait ! I do not know whether I shall be able to open it; . . . it is never opened. . . . Wait till it is light. . . .

FIRST MAIDSERVANT. It is light enough without; I see the sunlight through the chinks. . . .

PORTER. Here are the great keys. . . . Oh ! oh ! how the bolts and the locks grate ! . . . Help me ! help me ! . . .

MAIDSERVANTS. We are pulling ; we are pulling. . . .

SECOND MAIDSERVANT. It will not open. . . .

FIRST MAIDSERVANT. Ah ! ah ! It is opening ! it is opening slowly !

PORTER. How it shrieks ! how it shrieks ! It will wake up everybody. . . .

SECOND MAIDSERVANT [*appearing on the threshold*]. Oh, how light it is already out-of-doors !

FIRST MAIDSERVANT. The sun is rising on the sea !

PORTER. It is open. . . . It is wide open !
[*All the maidservants appear on the threshold and pass over it.*]

FIRST MAIDSERVANT. I am going to wash the sill first. . . .

SECOND MAIDSERVANT. We shall never be able to clean all this.

OTHER MAIDSERVANTS. Fetch the water ! fetch the water !

PORTER. Yes, yes ; pour on water ; pour on water ; pour on all the water of the Flood ! You will never come to the end of it. . . .

SCENE II— *A forest.* MÉLISANDE *discovered at the brink of a spring.*

[*Enter* GOLAUD.]

GOLAUD. I shall never be able to get out of this forest again. — God knows where that beast has led me. And yet I thought.I had wounded him to death; and here are traces of blood. But now I have lost sight of him; I believe I am lost myself — my dogs can no longer find me — I shall retrace my steps. . . . I hear weeping . . . Oh ! oh ! what is there yonder by the water's edge ? . . . A little girl weeping by the water's edge ? [*He coughs.*] She does not hear me. I cannot see her face. [*He approaches and touches* MÉLISANDE *on the shoulder.*] Why weepest thou ? [MÉLISANDE *trembles, starts up, and would flee.*] Do not be afraid. You have nothing to fear. Why are you weeping here all alone ?

MÉLISANDE. Do not touch me ! do not touch me !

GOLAUD. Do not be afraid. . . . I will not do you any . . . Oh, you are beautiful !

MÉLISANDE. Do not touch me ! do not touch me ! or I throw myself in the water ! . . .

GOLAUD. I will not touch you. . . . See, I will stay here, against the tree. Do not be afraid. Has any one hurt you ?

MÉLISANDE. Oh ! yes ! yes ! yes ! . . .
[*She sobs profoundly.*]

GOLAUD. Who has hurt you ?

MÉLISANDE. Every one ! every one !

GOLAUD. What hurt have they done you ?

MÉLISANDE. I will not tell ! I cannot tell ! . . .

GOLAUD. Come; do not weep so. Whence come you ?

MÉLISANDE. I have fled ! . . . fled . . . fled. . . .

GOLAUD. Yes; but whence have you fled ?

MÉLISANDE. I am lost ! . . . lost ! . . . Oh ! oh ! lost here. . . . I am not of this place. . . . I was not born there. . . .

GOLAUD. Whence are you ? Where were you born ?

MÉLISANDE. Oh ! oh ! far away from here ! . . . far away . . . far away. . . .

GOLAUD. What is it shining so at the bottom of the water ?

MÉLISANDE. Where ? — Ah ! it is the crown he gave me. It fell as I was weeping. . . .

GOLAUD. A crown ? — Who was it gave you a crown ? — I will try to get it. . . .

MÉLISANDE. No, no ; I will have no more of it ! I will have no more of it ! . . . I had rather die . . . die at once. . . .

GOLAUD. I could easily pull it out. The water is not very deep.

MÉLISANDE. I will have no more of it ! If you take it out, I throw myself in its place ! . . .

GOLAUD. No, no ; I will leave it there. It could be reached without difficulty, nevertheless. It seems very beautiful. — Is it long since you fled ?

MÉLISANDE. Yes, yes ! . . . Who are you ?

GOLAUD. I am Prince Golaud, — grandson of Arkël, the old King of Allemonde.

MÉLISANDE. Oh, you have gray hairs already. . . .

GOLAUD. Yes ; some, here, by the temples . . .

MÉLISANDE. And in your beard, too. . . . Why do you look at me so ?

GOLAUD. I am looking at your eyes. — Do you never shut your eyes ?

MÉLISANDE. Oh, yes ; I shut them at night. . . .

GOLAUD. Why do you look so astonished?

MÉLISANDE. You are a giant.

GOLAUD. I am a man like the rest. . . .

MÉLISANDE. Why have you come here ?

GOLAUD. I do not know, myself. I was hunting in the forest. I was chasing a wild boar. I mistook the road. — You look very young. How old are you ?

MÉLISANDE. I am beginning to be cold.

GOLAUD. Will you come with me ! ●

MÉLISANDE. No, no ; I will stay here.

GOLAUD. You cannot stay here all alone. You cannot stay here all night long. . . . What is your name ?

MÉLISANDE. Mélisande.

GOLAUD. You cannot stay here, Mélisande. Come with me. . . .

MÉLISANDE. I will stay here. . . .

GOLAUD. You will be afraid, all alone. We do not know what there may be here . . . all night long . . . all alone . . . it is impossible. Mélisande, come, give me your hand. . . .

MÉLISANDE. Oh, do not touch me ! . . .

GOLAUD. Do not scream. . . . I will not touch you again. But come with me. The night will be very dark and very cold. Come with me. . . .

MÉLISANDE. Where are you going ? . . .

GOLAUD. I do not know. . . . I am lost too. . . .   [Exeunt.]

SCENE III — *A hall in the castle.* ARKËL *and* GENEVIÈVE *discovered.*

GENEVIÈVE. Here is what he writes to his brother Pélléas : " I found her all in tears one evening, beside a spring in the forest where I had lost myself. I do not know her age, nor who she is, nor whence she comes, and I dare not question her, for she must have had a sore fright ; and when you ask her what has happened to her, she falls at once a-weeping like a child, and sobs so heavily you are afraid. Just as I found her by the springs, a crown of gold had slipped from her hair and fallen to the bottom of the water. She was clad, besides, like a princess, though her garments had been torn by the briers. It is now six months since I married her and I know no more about it than on the day of our meeting. Meanwhile, dear Pélléas, thou whom I love more than a brother, although we were not born of the same father ; meanwhile make ready for my return. . . . I know my mother will willingly forgive me. But I am afraid of the King, our venerable grandsire, I am afraid of Arkël, in spite of all his kindness, for I have undone by this strange marriage all his plans of state, and I fear the beauty of Mélisande will not excuse my folly to eyes so wise as his. If he consents nevertheless to receive her as he would receive his own daughter, the third night following this letter, light a lamp at the top of the tower that overlooks the sea.

I shall perceive it from the bridge of our ship; otherwise I shall go far away again and come back no more. . . ." What say you of it ?

ARKËL. Nothing. He has done what he probably must have done. I am very old, and nevertheless I have not yet seen clearly for one moment into myself ; how would you that I judge what others have done ? I am not far from the tomb and do not succeed in judging myself. . . . One always mistakes when one does not close his eyes. That may seem strange to us; but that is all. He is past the age to marry and he weds, like a child, a little girl he finds by a spring. . . . That may seem strange to us, because we never see but the reverse of destinies . . . the reverse even of our own. . . . He has always followed my counsels hitherto ; I had thought to make him happy in sending him to ask the hand of Princess Ursula. . . . He could not remain alone ; since the death of his wife he has been sad to be alone ; and that marriage would have put an end to long wars and old hatreds. . . . He would not have it so. Let it be as he would have it ; I have never put myself athwart a destiny ; and he knows better than I his future. There happen perhaps no useless events. . . .

GENEVIÈVE. He has always been so prudent, so grave and so firm. . . . If it were Pélléas, I should understand. . . . But he . . . at his age. . . . Who is it he is going to introduce here ? — An unknown found along the roads. . . . Since his wife's death, he has no longer lived for aught but his son, the little Yniold, and if he were about to marry again, it was because you had wished it. . . . And now . . . a little girl in the forest. . . . He has forgotten everything. . . . — What shall we do ? . . .

[*Enter* PÉLLÉAS.]

ARKËL. Who is coming in there ?

GENEVIÈVE. It is Pélléas. He has been weeping.

ARKËL. Is it thou, Pélléas ? — Come a little nearer, that I may see thee in the light. . . .

PÉLLÉAS. Grandfather, I received another letter at the same time as my brother's ; a letter from my friend Marcellus. . . . He is about to die and calls for me. He would see me before dying. . . .

ARKËL. Thou wouldst leave before thy brother's return ? — Perhaps thy friend is less ill than he thinks. . . .

PÉLLÉAS. His letter is so sad you can see death between the lines. . . . He says he knows the very day when death must come. . . . He tells me I can arrive before it if I will, but that there is no more time to lose. The journey is very long, and if I await Golaud's return, it will be perhaps too late. . . .

ARKËL. Thou must wait a little while, nevertheless. . . . We do not know what this return has in store for us. And, besides, is not thy father here, above us, more sick perhaps than thy friend. . . . Couldst thou choose between the father and the friend ? . . .   [*Exit.*]

GENEVIÈVE. Have a care to keep the lamp lit from this evening, Pélléas. . . .
                              [*Exeunt severally.*]

SCENE IV — *Before the castle.*
[*Enter* GENEVIÈVE *and* MÉLISANDE.]

MÉLISANDE. It is gloomy in the gardens. And what forests, what forests all about the palaces. . . .

GENEVIÈVE. Yes ; that astonished me too when I came hither ; it astonishes everybody. There are places where you never see the sun. But one gets used to it so quickly. . . . It is long ago, it is long ago. . . . It is nearly forty years that I have lived here. . . . Look toward the other side, you will have the light of the sea. . . .

MÉLISANDE. I hear a noise below us. . . .

GENEVIÈVE. Yes ; it is some one coming up toward us. . . . Ah ! it is Pélléas. . . . He seems still tired from having waited so long for you. . . .

MÉLISANDE. He has not seen us.

GENEVIÈVE. I think he has seen us but does not know what he should do. . . . Pélléas, Pélléas, is it thou ? . . .

[*Enter* PÉLLÉAS.]

PÉLLÉAS. Yes ! . . . I was coming toward the sea. . . .

GENEVIÈVE. So were we ; we were seeking the light. It is a little lighter here than elsewhere ; and yet the sea is gloomy.

PÉLLÉAS. We shall have a storm tonight. There has been one every night for some time, and yet it is so calm now. . . .

One might embark unwittingly and come back no more.

MÉLISANDE. Something is leaving the port. . . .

PÉLLÉAS. It must be a big ship. . . . The lights are very high, we shall see it in a moment, when it enters the band of light. . . .

GENEVIÈVE. I do not know whether we shall be able to see it . . . there is still a fog on the sea. . . .

PÉLLÉAS. The fog seems to be rising slowly. . . .

MÉLISANDE. Yes; I see a little light down there, which I had not seen. . . .

PÉLLÉAS. It is a lighthouse; there are others we cannot see yet.

MÉLISANDE. The ship is in the light. . . . It is already very far away. . . .

PÉLLÉAS. It is a foreign ship. It looks larger than ours. . . .

MÉLISANDE. It is the ship that brought me here! . . .

PÉLLÉAS. It flies away under full sail. . . .

MÉLISANDE. It is the ship that brought me here. It has great sails. . . . I recognized it by its sails.

PÉLLÉAS. There will be a rough sea to-night.

MÉLISANDE. Why does it go away to-night? . . . You can hardly see it any longer. . . . Perhaps it will be wrecked. . . .

PÉLLÉAS. The night falls very quickly. . . . [A silence.]

GENEVIÈVE. No one speaks any more? . . . You have nothing more to say to each other? . . . It is time to go in. Pélléas, show Mélisande the way. I must go see little Yniold a moment. [Exit.]

PÉLLÉAS. Nothing can be seen any longer on the sea. . . .

MÉLISANDE. I see more lights.

PÉLLÉAS. It is the other lighthouses. . . . Do you hear the sea? . . . It is the wind rising. . . . Let us go down this way. Will you give me your hand?

MÉLISANDE. See, see, my hands are full. . . .

PÉLLÉAS. I will hold you by the arm, the road is steep and it is very gloomy there. . . . I am going away perhaps to-morrow. . . .

MÉLISANDE. Oh! . . . why do you go away? [Exeunt.]

ACT II

SCENE I — *A fountain in the park.*

[*Enter* PÉLLÉAS *and* MÉLISANDE.]

PÉLLÉAS. You do not know where I have brought you? — I often come to sit here, toward noon, when it is too hot in the gardens. It is stifling to-day, even in the shade of the trees.

MÉLISANDE. Oh, how clear the water is! . . .

PÉLLÉAS. It is as cool as winter. It is an old abandoned spring. It seems to have been a miraculous spring, — it opened the eyes of the blind, — they still call it "Blind Man's Spring."

MÉLISANDE. It no longer opens the eyes of the blind?

PÉLLÉAS. Since the King has been nearly blind himself, no one comes any more. . . .

MÉLISANDE. How alone one is here! . . . There is no sound.

PÉLLÉAS. There is always a wonderful silence here. . . . One could hear the water sleep. . . . Will you sit down on the edge of the marble basin? There is one linden where the sun never comes. . . .

MÉLISANDE. I am going to lie down on the marble. — I should like to see the bottom of the water. . . .

PÉLLÉAS. No one has ever seen it. It is as deep, perhaps, as the sea. It is not known whence it comes. Perhaps it comes from the bottom of the earth. . . .

MÉLISANDE. If there were anything shining at the bottom, perhaps one could see it. . . .

PÉLLÉAS. Do not lean over so. . . .

MÉLISANDE. I would like to touch the water. . . .

PÉLLÉAS. Have a care of slipping. . . . I will hold your hand. . . .

MÉLISANDE. No, no, I would plunge both hands in it. . . . You would say my hands were sick to-day. . . .

PÉLLÉAS. Oh! oh! take care! take care! Mélisande! . . . Mélisande! . . . Oh! your hair! . . .

MÉLISANDE [*starting upright*]. I cannot . . . I cannot reach it. . . .

PÉLLÉAS. Your hair dipped in the water. . . .

MÉLISANDE. Yes, it is longer than my arms. . . . It is longer than I. . . .

[*A silence.*]

PÉLLÉAS. It was at the brink of a spring, too, that he found you?

MÉLISANDE. Yes. . . .

PÉLLÉAS. What did he say to you?

MÉLISANDE. Nothing; — I no longer remember. . . .

PÉLLÉAS. Was he quite near you?

MÉLISANDE. Yes; he would have kissed me.

PÉLLÉAS. And you would not?

MÉLISANDE. No.

PÉLLÉAS. Why would you not?

MÉLISANDE. Oh! oh! I saw something pass at the bottom of the water. . . .

PÉLLÉAS. Take care! take care! — You will fall! What are you playing with?

MÉLISANDE. With the ring he gave me.

PÉLLÉAS. Take care; you will lose it. . . .

MÉLISANDE. No, no; I am sure of my hands. . . .

PÉLLÉAS. Do not play so, over so deep a water. . . .

MÉLISANDE. My hands do not tremble.

PÉLLÉAS. How it shines in the sunlight! — Do not throw it so high in the air. . . .

MÉLISANDE. Oh! . . .

PÉLLÉAS. It has fallen?

MÉLISANDE. It has fallen into the water!

PÉLLÉAS. Where is it? where is it? . . .

MÉLISANDE. I do not see it sink? . . .

PÉLLÉAS. I think I see it shine. . . .

MÉLISANDE. My ring?

PÉLLÉAS. Yes, yes; down yonder. . . .

MÉLISANDE. Oh! oh! It is so far away from us! . . . no, no, that is not it . . . that is not it . . . It is lost . . . lost. . . . There is nothing any more but a great circle on the water. . . . What shall we do? What shall we do now? . . .

PÉLLÉAS. You need not be so troubled for a ring. It is nothing. . . . We shall find it again, perhaps. Or else we shall find another. . . .

MÉLISANDE. No, no; we shall never find it again; we shall never find any others either. . . . And yet I thought I had it in my hands. . . . I had already shut my hands, and it is fallen in spite of all. . . . I threw it too high, toward the sun. . . .

PÉLLÉAS. Come, come, we will come back another day; . . . come, it is time. They will come to meet us. It was striking noon at the moment the ring fell.

MÉLISANDE. What shall we say to Golaud if he asks where it is?

PÉLLÉAS. The truth, the truth, the truth. . . .   [*Exeunt.*]

SCENE II— *An apartment in the castle.* GOLAUD *discovered, stretched upon his bed;* MÉLISANDE, *by his bedside.*

GOLAUD. Ah! ah! all goes well; it will amount to nothing. But I cannot understand how it came to pass. I was hunting quietly in the forest. All at once my horse ran away, without cause. Did he see anything unusual? . . . I had just heard the twelve strokes of noon. At the twelfth stroke he suddenly took fright and ran like a blind madman against a tree. I heard no more. I do not yet know what happened. I fell, and he must have fallen on me. I thought I had the whole forest on my breast; I thought my heart was crushed. But my heart is sound. It is nothing, apparently. . . .

MÉLISANDE. Would you like a little water?

GOLAUD. Thanks, thanks; I am not thirsty.

MÉLISANDE. Would you like another pillow? . . . There is a little spot of blood on this.

GOLAUD. No, no; it is not worth while. I bled at the mouth just now. I shall bleed again, perhaps. . . .

MÉLISANDE. Are you quite sure? . . . You are not suffering too much?

GOLAUD. No, no; I have seen a good many more like this. I was made of iron and blood. . . . These are not the little bones of a child; do not alarm yourself. . . .

MÉLISANDE. Close your eyes and try to sleep. I shall stay here all night. . . .

GOLAUD. No, no; I do not wish you to tire yourself so. I do not need anything; I shall sleep like a child. . . . What is the matter, Mélisande? Why do you weep all at once? . . .

MÉLISANDE [*bursting into tears*]. I am . . . I am ill too. . . .

GOLAUD. Thou art ill? . . . What ails thee, then; what ails thee, Mélisande? . . .

MÉLISANDE. I do not know. . . . I am ill here. . . . I had rather tell you to-day; my lord, my lord, I am not happy here. . . .

GOLAUD. Why, what has happened, Mélisande? What is it? . . . And I suspecting nothing. . . . What has happened? . . . Some one has done thee harm? . . . Some one has given thee offense ?

MÉLISANDE. No, no ; no one has done me the least harm. . . . It is not that. . . . It is not that. . . . But I can live here no longer. I do not know why. . . . I would go away, go away!. . . I shall die if I am left here. . . .

GOLAUD. But something has happened ? You must be hiding something from me ? . . . Tell me the whole truth, Mélisande. . . . Is it the King ? . . . Is it my mother ? . . . Is it Pélléas ? . . .

MÉLISANDE. No, no ; it is not Pélléas. It is not anybody. . . . You could not understand me. . . .

GOLAUD. Why should I not understand ? . . . If you tell me nothing, what will you have me do ? . . . Tell me everything and I shall understand everything.

MÉLISANDE. I do not know myself what it is. . . . I do not know just what it is. . . . If I could tell you, I would tell you. . . . It is something stronger than I. . . .

GOLAUD. Come ; be reasonable, Mélisande. — What would you have me do ? — You are no longer a child. — Is it I whom you would leave ?

MÉLISANDE. Oh ! no, no ; it is not that. . . . I would go away with you. . . . It is here that I can live no longer. . . . I feel that I shall not live a long while. . . .

GOLAUD. But there must be a reason, nevertheless. You will be thought mad. It will be thought child's dreams. — Come, is it Pélléas, perhaps ? — I think he does not often speak to you.

MÉLISANDE. Yes, yes ; he speaks to me sometimes. I think he does not like me ; I have seen it in his eyes. . . . But he speaks to me when he meets me. . . .

GOLAUD. You must not take it ill of him. He has always been so. He is a little strange. And just now he is sad ; he thinks of his friend Marcellus, who is at the point of death, and whom he cannot go to see. . . . He will change, he will change, you will see ; he is young. . . .

MÉLISANDE. But it is not that . . . it is not that. . . .

GOLAUD. What is it, then ? — Can you not get used to the life one leads here ? Is it too gloomy here ? — It is true the castle is very old and very somber. . . . It is very cold, and very deep. And all those who dwell in it, are already old. And the country may seem gloomy too, with all its forests, all its old forests without light. But that may all be enlivened if we will. And then, joy, joy, one does not have it every day ; we must take things as they come. But tell me something ; no matter what ; I will do everything you could wish. . . .

MÉLISANDE. Yes, yes ; it is true. . . . You never see the sky here. I saw it for the first time this morning. . . .

GOLAUD. It is that, then, that makes you weep, my poor Mélisande ? — It is only that, then ? — You weep, not to see the sky ? — Come, come, you are no longer at the age when one may weep for such things. . . . And then, is not the summer yonder ? You will see the sky every day. — And then, next year. . . . Come, give me your hand ; give me both your little hands. [*He takes her hands.*] Oh ! oh ! these little hands that I could crush like flowers. . . . — Hold ! where is the ring I gave you ?

MÉLISANDE The ring ?

GOLAUD. Yes ; our wedding-ring, where is it ?

MÉLISANDE. I think . . . I think it has fallen. . . .

GOLAUD. Fallen ? — Where has it fallen? — You have not lost it ?

MÉLISANDE. No, no ; it fell . . . it must have fallen . . . but I know where it is. . . .

GOLAUD. Where is it ?

MÉLISANDE. You know . . . you know well . . . the grotto by the seashore ? . . .

GOLAUD. Yes.

MÉLISANDE. Well then, it is there. . . . It must be it is there. . . . Yes, yes ; I remember. . . . I went there this morning to pick up shells for little Yniold. . . . There were some very fine ones. . . . It slipped from my finger . . . then the sea came in ; and I had to go out before I had found it.

GOLAUD. Are you sure it is there ?

MÉLISANDE. Yes, yes ; quite sure. . . . I felt it slip . . . then, all at once, the noise of the waves. . . .

GOLAUD. You must go look for it at once.

MÉLISANDE. I must go look for it at once ?

GOLAUD. Yes.

MÉLISANDE. Now ? — at once ? — in the dark ?

GOLAUD. Now, at once, in the dark. You must go look for it at once. I had rather have lost all I have than have lost that ring. You do not know what it is. You do not know whence it came. The sea will be very high to-night. The sea will come to take it before you. . . . Make haste. You must go look for it at once. . . .

MÉLISANDE. I dare not. . . . I dare not go alone. . . .

GOLAUD. Go, go with no matter whom. But you must go at once, do you understand ? — Make haste ; ask Pélléas to go with you.

MÉLISANDE. Pélléas ? — With Pélléas ? — But Pélléas would not. . . .

GOLAUD. Pélléas will do all you ask of him. I know Pélléas better than you do. Go, go ; hurry ! I shall not sleep until I have the ring.

MÉLISANDE. Oh ! oh ! I am not happy ! . . . I am not happy ! . . .   [Exit, weeping.]

SCENE III — Before a grotto.

[Enter PÉLLÉAS and MÉLISANDE.]

PÉLLÉAS [speaking with great agitation]. Yes ; it is here ; we are there. It is so dark you cannot tell the entrance of the grotto from the rest of the night. . . . There are no stars on this side. Let us wait till the moon has torn through that great cloud ; it will light up the whole grotto, and then we can enter without danger. There are dangerous places, and the path is very narrow between two lakes whose bottom has not yet been found. I did not think to bring a torch or a lantern, but I think the light of the sky will be enough for us. — You have never gone into this grotto ?

MÉLISANDE. No. . . .

PÉLLÉAS. Let us go in ; let us go in. . . . You must be able to describe the place where you lost the ring, if he questions you. . . . It is very big and very beautiful. There are stalactites that look like plants and men. It is full of blue darks. It has not been explored to the end. There are great treasures hidden there, it seems. You will see the remains of ancient shipwrecks there. But you must not go far in it without a guide. There have been some who never have come back. I myself dare not go forward too far. We will stop the moment we no longer see the light of the sea or the sky. When you strike a little light there, you would say the vault was covered with stars like the sky. It is bits of crystal or salt, they say, that shine so in the rock. — Look, look, I think the sky is going to clear. . . . Give me your hand ; do not tremble, do not tremble so. There is no danger ; we will stop the moment we no longer see the light of the sea. . . . Is it the noise of the grotto that frightens you ? It is the noise of night or the noise of silence. . . . Do you hear the sea behind us ? — It does not seem happy to-night. . . . Ah ! look, the light ! . . .

[The moon lights up abundantly the entrance and part of the darkness of the grotto; and at a certain depth are seen three old beggars with white hair, seated side by side, leaning upon each other and asleep against a boulder.]

MÉLISANDE. Ah !

PÉLLÉAS. What is it ?

MÉLISANDE. There are . . . there are. . . .   [She points out the three beggars.]

PÉLLÉAS. Yes, yes ; I have seen them too. . . .

MÉLISANDE. Let us go ! . . . Let us go ! . . .

PÉLLÉAS. Yes . . . it is three old poor men fallen asleep. . . . There is a famine in the country. . . . Why have they come to sleep here ? . . .

MÉLISANDE. Let us go ! . . . Come, come. . . . Let us go ! . . .

PÉLLÉAS. Take care ; do not speak so loud. . . . Let us not wake them. . . . They are still sleeping heavily. . . . Come.

MÉLISANDE. Leave me, leave me ; I prefer to walk alone. . . .

PÉLLÉAS. We will come back another day. . . .   [Exeunt.]

SCENE IV — An apartment in the castle. ARKËL and PÉLLÉAS discovered.

ARKËL. You see that everything retains you here just now and forbids you this useless journey. We have concealed your father's condition from you until now; but it is perhaps hopeless; and that alone should suffice to stop you on the threshold. But there are so many other reasons. . . . And it is not in the day when our enemies awake, and when the people are dying of hunger and murmur about us, that you have the right to desert us. And why this journey? Marcellus is dead ; and life has graver duties than the visit to a tomb. You are weary, you say, of your inactive life ; but activity and duty are not found on the highways. They must be waited for upon the threshold, and let in as they go by; and they go by every day. You have never seen them ? I hardly see them any more myself ; but I will teach you to see them, and I will point them out to you the day when you would make them a sign. Nevertheless, listen to me; if you believe it is from the depths of your life this journey is exacted, I do not forbid your undertaking it, for you must know better than I the events you must offer to your being or your fate. I shall ask you only to wait until we know what must take place ere long. . . .

PÉLLÉAS. How long must I wait ?

ARKËL. A few weeks ; perhaps a few days. . . .

PÉLLÉAS. I will wait. . . .

ACT III

SCENE I— *An apartment in the castle.* PÉLLÉAS *and* MÉLISANDE *discovered.* MÉLISANDE *plies her distaff at the back of the room.*

PÉLLÉAS. Yniold does not come back; where has he gone?

MÉLISANDE. He had heard something in the corridor; he has gone to see what it is.

PÉLLÉAS. Mélisande . . .

MÉLISANDE. What is it ?

PÉLLÉAS. . . . Can you see still to work there ? . . .

MÉLISANDE. I work as well in the dark. . . .

PÉLLÉAS. I think everybody is already asleep in the castle. Golaud does not come back from the chase. It is late, nevertheless. . . . He no longer suffers from his fall ? . . .

MÉLISANDE. He said he no longer suffered from it.

PÉLLÉAS. He must be more prudent; his body is no longer as supple as at twenty years. . . . I see the stars through the window and the light of the moon on the trees. It is late ; he will not come back now. [*Knocking at the door.*] Who is there ? . . . Come in ! . . .

[*Little* YNIOLD *opens the door and enters the room.*]

It was you knocking so ? . . . That is not the way to knock at doors. It is as if a misfortune had arrived; look, you have frightened little mother. ·

YNIOLD. I only knocked a tiny little bit.

PÉLLÉAS. It is late; little father will not come back to-night; it is time for you to go to bed.

YNIOLD. I shall not go to bed before you do.

PÉLLÉAS. What ? . . . What is that you are saying ?

YNIOLD. I say . . . not before you . . . not before you . . .

[*Bursts into sobs and takes refuge by* MÉLISANDE.]

MÉLISANDE. What is it, Yniold ? . . . What is it ? why do you weep all at once ?

YNIOLD [*sobbing*]. Because . . . oh ! oh ! because . . .

MÉLISANDE. Because what ? . . . Because what ? . . . Tell me . . .

YNIOLD. Little mother . . . little mother . . . you are going away. . . .

MÉLISANDE. But what has taken hold of you, Yniold ? . . . I have never dreamed of going away. . . .

YNIOLD. Yes, you have ; yes, you have; little father has gone away. . . . Little father does not come back, and you are going to go away too. . . . I have seen it . . . I have seen it. . . .

MÉLISANDE. But there has never been any idea of that, Yniold. . . . Why, what makes you think that I would go away ? . . .

YNIOLD. I have seen it . . . I have seen it. . . . You have said things to uncle that I could not hear . . .

PÉLLÉAS. He is sleepy. . . . He has been dreaming. . . . Come here, Yniold; asleep already ? . . . Come and look out at the window; the swans are fighting with the dogs. . . .

YNIOLD [*at the window*]. Oh ! oh ! they are chasing the dogs ! . . . They are chasing them ! . . . Oh ! oh ! the water ! . . . the wings ! . . . the wings ! . . . they are afraid. . . .

PÉLLÉAS [*coming back by* MÉLISANDE]. He is sleepy; he is struggling against sleep; his eyes were closing. . . .

MÉLISANDE [*singing softly as she spins*].

Saint Daniel and Saint Michaël. . . .
Saint Michaël and Saint Raphaël. . . .

YNIOLD [*at the window*]. Oh! oh! little mother! . . .

MÉLISANDE [*rising abruptly*]. What is it, Yniold? . . . What is it? . . .

YNIOLD. I saw something at the window? [PÉLLÉAS *and* MÉLISANDE *run to the window.*]

PÉLLÉAS. What is there at the window? . . . What have you seen? . . .

YNIOLD. Oh! oh! I saw something! . . .

PÉLLÉAS. But there is nothing. I see nothing. . . .

MÉLISANDE. Nor I. . . .

PÉLLÉAS. Where did you see something? Which way? . . .

YNIOLD. Down there, down there! . . . It is no longer there. . . .

PÉLLÉAS. He does not know what he is saying. He must have seen the light of the moon on the forest. There are often strange reflections . . . or else something must have passed on the highway . . . or in his sleep. For see, see, I believe he is quite asleep. . . .

YNIOLD [*at the window*]. Little father is there! little father is there!

PÉLLÉAS [*going to the window*]. He is right; Golaud is coming into the courtyard.

YNIOLD. Little father! . . . little father! . . . I am going to meet him! . . .
[*Exit, running. — A silence.*]

PÉLLÉAS. They are coming up the stair.

[*Enter* GOLAUD *and little* YNIOLD *with a lamp.*]

GOLAUD. You are still waiting in the dark?

YNIOLD. I have brought a light, little mother, a big light! . . . [*He lifts the lamp and looks at* MÉLISANDE.] You have been weeping, little mother? . . . You have been weeping? . . . [*He lifts the lamp toward* PÉLLÉAS *and looks in turn at him.*] You too, you too, you have been weeping? . . . Little father, look, little father; they have both been weeping. . . .

GOLAUD. Do not hold the light under their eyes so. . . .

SCENE II — *One of the towers of the castle. A watchman's round passes under a window in the tower.*

MÉLISANDE [*at the window, combing her unbound hair*].

My long locks fall foaming
    To the threshold of the tower, —

My locks await your coming
    All along the tower,
And all the long, long hour,
    And all the long, long hour.

Saint Daniel and Saint Michaël,
Saint Michaël and Saint Raphaël.

I was born on a Sunday,
    A Sunday at high noon. . . .

[*Enter* PÉLLÉAS *by the watchman's round.*]

PÉLLÉAS. Holà! Holà! ho! . . .

MÉLISANDE. Who is there?

PÉLLÉAS. I, I, and I! . . . What art thou doing there at the window, singing like a bird that is not native here?

MÉLISANDE. I am doing my hair for the night. . . .

PÉLLÉAS. Is it that I see upon the wall? . . . I thought you had some light. . . .

MÉLISANDE. I have opened the window; it is too hot in the tower. . . . It is beautiful to-night. . . .

PÉLLÉAS. There are innumerable stars; I have never seen so many as to-night; . . . but the moon is still upon the sea. . . . Do not stay in the shadow, Mélisande; lean forward a little till I see your unbound hair. . . .

MÉLISANDE. I am frightful so. . . .
[*She leans out at the window.*]

PÉLLÉAS. Oh! oh! Mélisande! . . . oh, thou art beautiful! . . . thou art beautiful so! . . . Lean out! lean out! . . . Let me come nearer thee . . .

MÉLISANDE. I cannot come nearer thee. . . . I am leaning out as far as I can. . . .

PÉLLÉAS. I cannot come up higher; . . . give me at least thy hand to-night . . . before I go away. . . . I leave to-morrow. . . .

MÉLISANDE. No, no, no! . . .

PÉLLÉAS. Yes, yes, yes; I leave, I shall leave to-morrow. . . . Give me thy hand, thy hand, thy little hand upon my lips. . . .

MÉLISANDE. I give thee not my hand if thou wilt leave. . . .

PÉLLÉAS. Give, give, give! . . .

MÉLISANDE. Thou wilt not leave?

PÉLLÉAS. I will wait; I will wait. . . .

MÉLISANDE. I see a rose in the shadows. . . .

PÉLLÉAS. Where? . . . I see only the boughs of the willow hanging over the wall. . . .

MÉLISANDE. Farther down, farther down,

in the garden ; farther down, in the somber green. . . .

Pélléas. It is not a rose. . . . I will go see by and by, but give me thy hand first ; first thy hand. . . .

Mélisande. There, there ; . . . I cannot lean out farther. . . .

Pélléas. I cannot reach thy hand with my lips. . . .

Mélisande. I cannot lean out farther. . . . I am on the point of falling. . . . — Oh ! oh ! my hair is falling down the tower !
[*Her tresses fall suddenly over her head, as she is leaning out so, and stream over* Pélléas.]

Pélléas. Oh ! oh ! what is it ? . . . Thy hair, thy hair is falling down to me ! . . . All thy locks, Mélisande, all thy locks have fallen down the tower ! . . . I hold them in my hands ; I hold them in my mouth. . . . I hold them in my arms ; I put them about my neck. . . . I will not open my hands again to-night. . . .

Mélisande. Let me go ! let me go ! . . . Thou wilt make me fall ! . . .

Pélléas. No, no, no ; . . . I have never seen such hair as thine, Mélisande ! . . . See, see, see ; it comes from so high and yet it floods me to the heart ! . . . And yet it floods me to the knees ! . . . And it is sweet, sweet as if it fell from heaven ! . . . I see the sky no longer through thy locks. Thou seest, thou seest ? . . . I can no longer hold them with both hands ; there are some on the boughs of the willow. . . . They are alive like birds in my hands, . . . and they love me, they love me more than thou ! . . .

Mélisande. Let me go ; let me go ! . . . Some one might come. . . .

Pélléas. No, no, no ; I shall not set thee free to-night. . . . Thou art my prisoner to-night ; all night, all night ! . . .

Mélisande. Pélléas ! Pélléas ! . . .

Pélléas. I tie them, I tie them to the willow boughs. . . . Thou shalt not go away now ; . . . thou shalt not go away now. . . . Look, look, I am kissing thy hair. . . . I suffer no more in the midst of thy hair. . . . Hearest thou my kisses along thy hair ? . . . They mount along thy hair. . . . Each hair must bring thee some. . . . Thou seest, thou seest, I can open my hands. . . . My hands are free, and thou canst not leave me now. . . .

Mélisande. Oh ! oh ! thou hurtest me.

. . . [*Doves come out of the tower and fly about them in the night.*] — What is that, Pélléas ? — What is it flying about me ?

Pélléas. It is the doves coming out of the tower. . . . I have frightened them ; they are flying away. . . .

Mélisande. It is my doves, Pélléas. — Let us go away, let me go ; they will not come back again. . . .

Pélléas. Why will they not come back again ?

Mélisande. They will be lost in the dark. . . . Let me go ; let me lift my head. . . . I hear a noise of footsteps. . . . Let me go ! — It is Golaud ! . . . I believe it is Golaud ! . . . He has heard us. . . .

Pélléas. Wait ! Wait ! . . . Thy hair is about the boughs. . . . It is caught there in the darkness. . . . Wait, wait ! . . . It is dark. . . .

[*Enter* Golaud, *by the watchman's round.*]

Golaud. What do you here ?

Pélléas. What do I here ? . . . I . . .

Golaud. You are children. . . . Mélisande, do not lean out so at the window ; you will fall. . . . Do you not know it is late ? It is nearly midnight. — Do not play so in the darkness. — You are children. . . . [*Laughing nervously.*] What children ! . . . What children ! . . .

[*Exit, with* Pélléas.]

Scene III — *The vaults of the castle.*

[*Enter* Golaud *and* Pélléas.]

Golaud. Take care ; this way, this way. — You have never penetrated into these vaults ?

Pélléas. Yes ; once, of old ; but it was long ago. . . .

Golaud. They are prodigious great ; it is a succession of enormous crypts that end, God knows where. The whole castle is builded on these crypts. Do you smell the deathly odor that reigns here ? — That is what I wished to show you. In my opinion, it comes from the little underground lake I am going to have you see. Take care ; walk before me, in the light of my lantern. I will warn you when we are there. [*They continue to walk in silence.*] Hey ! hey ! Pélléas ! stop ! stop ! [*He seizes him by the arm.*] For God's sake ! . . . Do you not see ? — One step more, and you had been in the gulf ! . . .

PÉLLÉAS. But I did not see it! ... The lantern no longer lighted me. ...

GOLAUD. I made a misstep ... but if I had not held you by the arm ... Well, this is the stagnant water that I spoke of to you. ... Do you perceive the smell of death that rises? — Let us go to the end of this overhanging rock, and do you lean over a little. It will strike you in the face.

PÉLLÉAS. I smell it already; ... you would say a smell of the tomb.

GOLAUD. Farther, farther. ... It is this that on certain days has poisoned the castle. The King will not believe it comes from here. — The crypt should be walled up in which this standing water is found. It is time, besides, to examine these vaults a little. Have you noticed those lizards on the walls and pillars of the vaults? — There is a labor hidden here you would not suspect; and the whole castle will be swallowed up one of these nights, if it is not looked out for. But what will you have? Nobody likes to come down this far. ... There are strange lizards in many of the walls. ... Oh! here ... do you perceive the smell of death that rises?

PÉLLÉAS. Yes; there is a smell of death rising about us. ...

GOLAUD. Lean over; have no fear. ... I will hold you ... give me ... no, no, not your hand ... it might slip ... your arm, your arm! ... Do you see the gulf? [*Moved.*] — Pélléas? Pélléas? ...

PÉLLÉAS. Yes; I think I see the bottom of the gulf. ... Is it the light that trembles so? ... You ...

[*He straightens up, turns, and looks at* GOLAUD.]

GOLAUD [*with a trembling voice*]. Yes; it is the lantern. ... See, I shook it to lighten the walls. ...

PÉLLÉAS. I stifle here; ... let us go out. ...

GOLAUD. Yes; let us go out. ...

[*Exeunt in silence.*]

SCENE IV — *A terrace at the exit of the vaults.*

[*Enter* GOLAUD *and* PÉLLÉAS.]

PÉLLÉAS. Ah! I breathe at last! ... I thought, one moment, I was going to be ill in those enormous crypts; I was on the point of falling. ... There is a damp air there, heavy as a leaden dew, and darkness thick as a poisoned paste. ... And now, all the air of all the sea! ... There is a fresh wind, see; fresh as a leaf that has just opened, over the little green waves. ... Hold! the flowers have just been watered at the foot of the terrace, and the smell of the verdure and the wet roses comes up to us. ... It must be nearly noon; they are already in the shadow of the tower. ... It is noon; I hear the bells ringing, and the children are going down to the beach to bathe. ... I did not know that we had stayed so long in the caverns. ...

GOLAUD. We went down toward eleven o'clock. ...

PÉLLÉAS. Earlier; it must have been earlier; I heard it strike half past ten.

GOLAUD. Half past ten or a quarter to eleven. ...

PÉLLÉAS. They have opened all the windows of the castle. It will be unusually hot this afternoon. ... Look, there is mother with Mélisande at a window of the tower. ...

GOLAUD. Yes; they have taken refuge on the shady side. — Speaking of Mélisande, I heard what passed and what was said last night. I am quite aware all that is but child's play; but it need not be repeated. Mélisande is very young and very impressionable; and she must be treated the more circumspectly that she is perhaps with child at this moment. ... She is very delicate, hardly woman; and the least emotion might bring on a mishap. It is not the first time I have noticed there might be something between you. ... You are older than she; it will suffice to have told you. ... Avoid her as much as possible; without affectation, moreover; without affectation. ... — What is it I see yonder on the highway toward the forest? ...

PÉLLÉAS. Some herds they are leading to the city. ...

GOLAUD. They cry like lost children; you would say they smelt the butcher already. — It will be time for dinner. — What a fine day! What a capital day for the harvest! ... [*Exeunt.*]

SCENE V — *Before the castle.*

[*Enter* GOLAUD *and little* YNIOLD.]

GOLAUD. Come, we are going to sit down here, Yniold; sit on my knee; we shall see from here what passes in the forest. I do

not see you any more at all now. You
abandon me too; you are always at little
mother's. . . . Why, we are sitting just
under little mother's windows. — Perhaps
she is saying her evening prayer at this
moment. . . . But tell me, Yniold, she is
often with your uncle Pélléas, is n't she?

YNIOLD. Yes, yes ; always, little father ;
when you are not there, little father. . . .

GOLAUD. Ah! — Look ; some one is going by with a lantern in the garden. — But
I have been told they did not like each
other. . . . It seems they often quarrel ;
. . . no? Is it true?

YNIOLD. Yes, yes ; it is true.

GOLAUD. Yes? — Ah! ah! — But what
do they quarrel about?

YNIOLD. About the door.

GOLAUD. What? — about the door? —
What are you talking about? — No, come,
explain yourself ; why do they quarrel about
the door?

YNIOLD. Because it won't stay open.

GOLAUD. Who wants it to stay open? —
Come, why do they quarrel?

YNIOLD. I don't know, little father ;
about the light.

GOLAUD. I am not talking to you about
the light ; we will talk of that by and by.
I am talking to you about the door. Answer
what I ask you ; you must learn to talk ; it
is time. . . . Do not put your hand in your
mouth so ; . . . come. . . .

YNIOLD. Little father! little father! . . .
I won't do it any more. . . .   [He cries.]

GOLAUD. Come ; what are you crying for
now? What has happened?

YNIOLD. Oh! oh! little father, you hurt
me. . . .

GOLAUD. I hurt you? — Where did I
hurt you? I did not mean to. . . .

YNIOLD. Here, here; on my little arm. . . .

GOLAUD. I did not mean to ; come, don't
cry any more, and I will give you something to-morrow.

YNIOLD. What, little father?

GOLAUD. A quiver and some arrows ; but
tell me what you know about the door.

YNIOLD. Big arrows?

GOLAUD. Yes, yes ; very big arrows. —
But why don't they want the door to be
open? — Come, answer me sometime! —
No, no ; do not open your mouth to cry. I
am not angry. We are going to have a quiet
talk, like Pélléas and little mother when
they are together. What do they talk about
when they are together?

YNIOLD. Pélléas and little mother?

GOLAUD. Yes ; what do they talk about?

YNIOLD. About me ; always about me.

GOLAUD. And what do they say about you?

YNIOLD. They say I am going to be very
big.

GOLAUD. Oh, plague of my life! . . . I
am here like a blind man searching for his
treasure at the bottom of the ocean! . . . I
am here like a new-born child lost in the
forest, and you . . . Come, come, Yniold,
I was wandering ; we are going to talk seriously. Do Pélléas and little mother never
speak of me when I am not there? . . .

YNIOLD. Yes, yes, little father ; they are
always speaking of you.

GOLAUD. Ah! . . . And what do they say
of me?

YNIOLD. They say I shall grow as big as
you are.

GOLAUD. You are always by them?

YNIOLD. Yes, yes, always, always, little
father.

GOLAUD. They never tell you to go play
somewhere else?

YNIOLD. No, little father; they are afraid
when I am not there.

GOLAUD. They are afraid? . . . What
makes you think they are afraid?

YNIOLD. Little mother always says,
"Don't go away ; don't go away!" . . .
They are unhappy, but they laugh. . . .

GOLAUD. But that does not prove they
are afraid.

YNIOLD. Yes, yes, little father ; she is
afraid. . . .

GOLAUD. Why do you say she is afraid?

YNIOLD. They always weep in the dark.

GOLAUD. Ah! ah! . . .

YNIOLD. That makes one weep too.

GOLAUD. Yes, yes! . . .

YNIOLD. She is pale, little father.

GOLAUD. Ah! ah! . . . patience, my God,
patience! . . .

YNIOLD. What, little father?

GOLAUD. Nothing, nothing, my child. —
I saw a wolf go by in the forest. — Then they
get on well together? — I am glad to learn
they are on good terms. — They kiss each
other sometimes? — No? . . .

YNIOLD. Kiss each other, little father?
— No, no, — ah! yes, little father, yes, yes ;
once . . . once when it rained. . . .

GOLAUD. They kissed ? — But how, how did they kiss ?

YNIOLD. So, little father, so ! . . . [*He gives him a kiss on the mouth, laughing.*] Ah ! ah ! your beard, little father ! . . . It pricks ! it pricks ! it pricks ! It is getting all gray, little father, and your hair, too ; all gray, all gray, all gray. . . . [*The window under which they are sitting is lighted up at this moment, and the light falls upon them.*] Ah ! ah ! little mother has lit her lamp. It is light, little father ; it is light. . . .

GOLAUD. Yes ; it is beginning to be light. . . .

YNIOLD. Let us go there, too, little father ; let us go there, too. . . .

GOLAUD. Where do you want to go ?

YNIOLD. Where it is light, little father.

GOLAUD. No, no, my child ; let us stay in the dark a little longer. . . . One cannot tell, one cannot tell yet. . . . Do you see those poor people down there trying to kindle a little fire in the forest ? — It has rained. And over there, do you see the old gardener trying to lift that tree the wind has blown down across the road ? — He cannot ; the tree is too big ; the tree is too heavy, and it will lie where it fell. All that cannot be helped. . . . I think Pélléas is mad. . . .

YNIOLD. No, little father, he is not mad ; he is very good.

GOLAUD. Do you want to see little mother?

YNIOLD. Yes, yes ; I want to see her !

GOLAUD. Don't make any noise ; I am going to hoist you up to the window. It is too high for me, for all I am so big. . . . [*He lifts the child.*] Do not make the least noise ; little mother would be terribly afraid. . . . Do you see her ? — Is she in the room?

YNIOLD. Yes. . . . Oh, how light it is !

GOLAUD. She is alone ?

YNIOLD. Yes ; . . . no, no ; Uncle Pélléas is there, too.

GOLAUD. He — . . . !

YNIOLD. Ah ! ah ! little father ! you have hurt me ! . . .

GOLAUD. It is. nothing ; be still ; I will not do it any more ; look, look, Yniold ! . . . I stumbled ; speak lower. What are they doing ? —

YNIOLD. They are not doing anything, little father ; they are waiting for something.

GOLAUD. Are they near each other ?

YNIOLD. No, little father.

GOLAUD. And . . . and the bed ? Are they near the bed ?

YNIOLD. The bed, little father ? — I can't see the bed.

GOLAUD. Lower, lower ; they will hear you. Are they speaking ?

YNIOLD. No, little father ; they do not speak.

GOLAUD. But what are they doing ? — They must be doing something. . . .

YNIOLD. They are looking at the light.

GOLAUD. Both ?

YNIOLD. Yes, little father.

GOLAUD. They do not say anything ?

YNIOLD. No, little father ; they do not close their eyes.

GOLAUD. They do not come near each other ?

YNIOLD. No, little father ; they do not stir.

GOLAUD. They are sitting down ?

YNIOLD. No, little father ; they are standing upright against the wall.

GOLAUD. They make no gestures ? — They do not look at each other ? — They make no signs ? . . .

YNIOLD. No, little father. — Oh ! oh ! little father ; they never close their eyes. . . . I am terribly afraid. . . .

GOLAUD. Be still. They do not stir yet?

YNIOLD. No, little father. — I am afraid, little father ; let me come down ! . . .

GOLAUD. Why, what are you afraid of ? — Look ! look ! . . .

YNIOLD. I dare not look any more, little father ! . . . Let me come down ! . . .

GOLAUD. Look ! look ! . . .

YNIOLD. Oh ! oh ! I am going to cry, little father ! — Let me come down ! let me come down ! . . .

GOLAUD. Come ; we will go see what has happened. [*Exeunt.*]

ACT IV

SCENE I — *A corridor in the castle.*

[*Enter* PÉLLÉAS *and* MÉLISANDE, *meeting.*]

PÉLLÉAS. Where goest thou ? I must speak to thee to-night. Shall I see thee ?

MÉLISANDE. Yes.

PÉLLÉAS. I have just left my father's room. He is getting better. The physician has told us he is saved. . . . And yet this morning I had a presentiment this day

would end ill. I have had a rumor of misfortune in my ears for some time. . . .
Then, all at once there was a great change;
to-day it is no longer anything but a question of time. All the windows in his room
have been thrown open. He speaks; he
seems happy. He does not speak yet like
an ordinary man, but already his ideas no
longer all come from the other world. . . .
He recognized me. He took my hand and
said with that strange air he has had since
he fell sick: "Is it thou, Pélléas? Why, why,
I had not noticed it before, but thou hast the
grave and friendly look of those who will
not live long. . . . You must travel; you
must travel. . . ." It is strange; I shall
obey him. . . . My mother listened to him
and wept for joy. — Hast thou not been
aware of it? — The whole house seems already to revive, you hear breathing, you
hear speaking, you hear walking. . . .
Listen; I hear some one speaking behind
that door. Quick, quick! answer quickly!
where shall I see thee?

MÉLISANDE. Where wouldst thou?

PÉLLÉAS. In the park; near "Blind
Man's Spring." — Wilt thou? — Wilt thou
come?

MÉLISANDE. Yes.

PÉLLÉAS. It will be the last night; — I
am going to travel, as my father said.
Thou wilt not see me more. . . .

MÉLISANDE. Do not say that, Pélléas.
. . . I shall see thee always; I shall look
upon thee always. . . .

PÉLLÉAS. Thou wilt look in vain. . . .
I shall be so far away thou couldst no
longer see me. . . . I shall try to go very
far away. . . . I am full of joy, and you
would say I had all the weight of heaven
and earth on my body to-day. . . .

MÉLISANDE. What has happened, Pélléas? — I no longer understand what you
say. . . .

PÉLLÉAS. Go, go; let us separate. I
hear some one speaking behind that door.
. . . It is the strangers who came to the
castle this morning. . . . They are going
out. . . . Let us go; it is the strangers. . . .
[Exeunt severally.]

SCENE II — An apartment in the castle. ARKËL
and MÉLISANDE discovered.

ARKËL. Now that Pélléas's father is
saved, and sickness, the old handmaid of

Death, has left the castle, a little joy and
a little sunlight will at last come into the
house again. . . . It was time! — For, since
thy coming, we have only lived here whispering about a closed room. . . . And truly
I have pitied thee, Mélisande. . . . Thou
camest here all joyous, like a child seeking
a gala-day, and at the moment thou enter-
edst in the vestibule I saw thy face change,
and probably thy soul, as the face changes
in spite of us when we enter at noon into a
grotto too gloomy and too cold. . . . And
since, — since, on account of all that, I
have often no longer understood thee. . . .
I observed thee, thou wert there, listless,
perhaps, but with the strange, astray look
of one awaiting ever a great trouble, in the
sunlight, in a beautiful garden. . . . I cannot explain. . . . But I was sad to see thee
so; for thou art too young and too beautiful to live already day and night under the
breath of death. . . . But now all that will
change. At my age, — and there, perhaps,
is the surest fruit of my life, — at my age
I have gained I know not what faith in the
fidelity of events, and I have always seen
that every young and beautiful being creates about itself young, beautiful, and
happy events. . . . And it is thou who wilt
now open the door for the new era I have
glimpses of. . . . Come here; why dost
thou stay there without answering and
without lifting thine eyes? — I have kissed
thee but once only hitherto — the day of
thy coming; and yet old men need sometimes to touch with their lips a woman's
forehead or a child's cheek, to believe still
in the freshness of life and avert awhile
the menaces. . . . Art thou afraid of my
old lips? How I have pitied thee these
months! . . .

MÉLISANDE. Grandfather, I have not
been unhappy. . . .

ARKËL. Perhaps you were of those who
are unhappy without knowing it, . . . and
they are the most unhappy. . . . Let me
look at thee, so, quite near, a moment:
. . . we have such need of beauty beside
Death. . . .

[Enter GOLAUD.]

GOLAUD. Pélléas leaves to-night.

ARKËL. Thou hast blood on thy forehead. — What hast thou done?

GOLAUD. Nothing, nothing. . . . I have
passed through a hedge of thorns.

MÉLISANDE. Bend down your head a little, my lord. . . . I will wipe your forehead. . . .

GOLAUD [*repulsing her*]. I will not that you touch me, do you understand? Go, go! — I am not speaking to you. — Where is my sword? — I came to seek my sword. . . .

MÉLISANDE. Here; on the praying-stool.

GOLAUD. Bring it. [*To* ARKËL.] They have just found another peasant dead of hunger, along by the sea. You would say they all meant to die under our eyes. [*To* MÉLISANDE.] Well, my sword? — Why do you tremble so? — I am not going to kill you. I would simply examine the blade. I do not employ the sword for these uses. Why do you examine me like a beggar? — I do not come to ask alms of you. You hope to see something in my eyes without my seeing anything in yours? — Do you think I may know something? [*To* ARKËL.] — Do you see those great eyes? — It is as if they were proud of their richness. . . .

ARKËL. I see there only a great innocence. . . .

GOLAUD. A great innocence! . . . They are greater than innocence. . . . They are purer than the eyes of a lamb. . . . They would give God lessons in innocence! A great innocence! Listen: I am so near them I feel the freshness of their lashes when they wink; and yet I am less far away from the great secrets of the other world than from the smallest secret of those eyes! . . . A great innocence! . . . More than innocence! You would say the angels of heaven celebrated there an eternal baptism! . . . I know those eyes! I have seen them at their work! Close them! close them! or I shall close them for a long while! . . . Do not put your right hand to your throat so; I am saying a very simple thing. . . . I have no under-thought. . . . If I had an under-thought, why should I not say it? Ah! ah! — Do not attempt to flee! — Here! — Give me that hand! — Ah! your hands are too hot. . . . Go away! Your flesh disgusts me! . . . Here! — There is no more question of fleeing now! [*He seizes her by the hair.*] You shall follow me on your knees! — On your knees! — On your knees before me! — Ah! ah! your long hair serves some purpose at last! . . .

Right, . . . left! — Left, . . . right! — Absalom! Absalom. — Forward! back! To the ground! to the ground! . . . You see, you see; I laugh already like an old man. . . .

ARKËL [*running up*]. Golaud! . . .

GOLAUD [*affecting a sudden calm*]. You will do as you may please, look you. — I attach no importance to that. — I am too old; and, besides, I am not a spy. I shall await chance; and then . . . Oh! then! . . . simply because it is the custom; simply because it is the custom. . . .

[*Exit.*]

ARKËL. What ails him? — He is drunk?

MÉLISANDE [*in tears*]. No, no; he does not love me any more. . . . I am not happy! . . . I am not happy! . . .

ARKËL. If I were God, I would have pity on men's hearts. . . .

SCENE III — *A terrace of the castle. Little* YNIOLD *discovered, trying to lift a boulder.*

YNIOLD. Oh, this stone is heavy! . . . It is heavier than I am. . . . It is heavier than everybody. . . . It is heavier than everything that ever happened. . . . I can see my golden ball between the rock and this naughty stone, and I cannot reach it. . . . My little arm is not long enough, . . . and this stone won't be lifted. . . . I can't lift it, . . . and nobody could lift it. . . . It is heavier than the whole house; . . . you would think it had roots in the earth. . . . [*The bleatings of a flock heard far away.*] — Oh! oh! I hear the sheep crying. . . . [*He goes to look, at the edge of the terrace.*] Why! there is no more sun. . . . They are coming . . . the little sheep . . . they are coming. . . . There is a lot of them! . . . There is a lot of them! . . . They are afraid of the dark. . . . They crowd together! They crowd together! . . . They can hardly walk any more. . . . They are crying! They are crying! And they go quick! . . . They go quick! . . . They are already at the great crossroads. Ah! ah! They don't know where they ought to go any more. . . . They don't cry any more. . . . They wait. . . . Some of them want to go to the right. . . . They all want to go to the right. . . . They cannot! . . . The shepherd is throwing earth at them. . . . Ah! ah! They are going to pass by here. . . . They obey! They obey! They are going to pass under the terrace. . . . They are going to pass under the rocks. I am going to see them near by. . . . Oh! oh! what a lot of them! . . . What a lot of them! The whole road is full of them! . . . They all keep still now. . . . Shepherd! shepherd! why don't they speak any more?

THE SHEPHERD [*who is out of sight*]. Because it is no longer the road to the stable . . .

YNIOLD. Where are they going? — Shepherd! shepherd! — Where are they going? — He does n't hear me any more. They are too far away already. . . . They go quick. . . . They are not making a noise any more. . . . It is no longer the road to the stable. . . . Where are they going to sleep tonight? — Oh! oh! — It is too dark. . . . I am going to tell something to somebody. . . . [*Exit.*]

SCENE IV — *A fountain in the park.*

[*Enter* PÉLLÉAS.]

PÉLLÉAS. It is the last evening . . . the last evening. It must all end. I have played like a child about a thing I did not guess. . . . I have played a-dream about the snares of fate. . . . Who has awakened me all at once? I shall flee, crying out for joy and woe like a blind man fleeing from his burning house. . . . I am going to tell her I shall flee. . . . My father is out of danger; and I have no more reason to lie to myself. . . . It is late; she does not come. . . . I should do better to go away without seeing her again. . . . I must look well at her this time. . . . There are some things that I no longer recall. . . . It seems at times as if I had not seen her for a hundred years. . . . And I have not yet looked upon her look. . . . There remains nought to me if I go away thus. And all those memories . . . it is as if I were to take away a little water in a muslin bag. . . . I must see her one last time, to the bottom of her heart. . . . I must tell her all that I have never told her.

[*Enter* MÉLISANDE.]

MÉLISANDE. Pélléas!

PÉLLÉAS. Mélisande! — Is it thou, Mélisande?

MÉLISANDE. Yes.

PÉLLÉAS. Come hither; do not stay at the edge of the moonlight. — Come hither.

We have so many things to tell each other. . . . Come hither in the shadow of the linden.

MÉLISANDE. Let me stay in the light. . . .

PÉLLÉAS. We might be seen from the windows of the tower. Come hither; here, we have nothing to fear. — Take care; we might be seen . . .

MÉLISANDE. I wish to be seen. . . .

PÉLLÉAS. Why, what doth ail thee? — Thou wert able to come out without being seen?

MÉLISANDE. Yes; your brother slept. . . .

PÉLLÉAS. It is late. — In an hour they will close the gates. We must be careful. Why art thou come so late?

MÉLISANDE. Your brother had a bad dream. And then my gown was caught on the nails of the gate. See, it is torn. I lost all this time, and ran. . . .

PÉLLÉAS. My poor Mélisande! . . . I should almost be afraid to touch thee. . . . Thou art still out of breath, like a hunted bird. . . . It is for me, for me, thou doest all that? . . . I hear thy heart beat as if it were mine. . . . Come hither . . . nearer, nearer me. . . .

MÉLISANDE. Why do you laugh?

PÉLLÉAS. I do not laugh; — or else I laugh for joy, unwittingly. . . . It were a weeping matter, rather. . . .

MÉLISANDE. We have come here before. . . . I recollect. . . .

PÉLLÉAS. Yes . . . yes . . . Long months ago. — I knew not then. . . . Knowest thou why I asked thee to come here to-night?

MÉLISANDE. No.

PÉLLÉAS. It is perhaps the last time I shall see thee. . . . I must go away forever. . . .

MÉLISANDE. Why sayest thou always thou wilt go away? . . .

PÉLLÉAS. I must tell thee what thou knowest already? — Thou knowest not what I am going to tell thee?

MÉLISANDE. Why, no; why, no; I know nothing — . . .

PÉLLÉAS. Thou knowest not why I must go afar. . . . Thou knowest not it is because . . . [*He kisses her abruptly.*] I love thee. . . .

MÉLISANDE [*in a low voice*]. I love thee, too. . . .

PÉLLÉAS. Oh! oh! What saidst thou, Mélisande? . . . I hardly heard it! . . . Thou sayest that in a voice coming from the end of

the world ! . . . I hardly heard thee. . . .
Thou lovest me ? — Thou lovest me, too ?
. . . Since when lovest thou me ? . . .

MÉLISANDE. Since always. . . . Since I
saw thee. . . .

PÉLLÉAS. Oh, how thou sayest that ! . . .
Thy voice seems to have blown across the
sea in spring ! . . . I have never heard
it until now; . . . one would say it had
rained on my heart ! . . . Thou sayest that
so frankly ! . . . Like an angel questioned !
. . . I cannot believe it, Mélisande ! . . .
Why shouldst thou love me ? — Nay, why
dost thou love me ? — Is what thou sayest true ? — Thou dost not mock me ? —
Thou dost not lie a little, to make me
smile ? . . .

MÉLISANDE. No ; I never lie ; I lie but
to thy brother. . . .

PÉLLÉAS. Oh, how thou sayest that ! . . .
Thy voice ! thy voice ! . . . It is cooler
and more frank than the water is ! . . .
It is like pure water on my lips ! . . . It is
like pure water on my hands. . . . Give
me, give me thy hands ! . . . Oh, how small
thy hands are ! . . . I did not know thou
wert so beautiful ! . . . I have never seen
anything so beautiful before thee. . . .
I was full of unrest ; I sought throughout
the house. . . . I sought throughout the
country. . . . And I found not beauty. . . .
And now I have found thee ! . . . I have
found thee ! . . . I do not think there could be
on the earth a fairer woman ! . . . Where art
thou ? — I no longer hear thee breathe. . . .

MÉLISANDE. Because I look on thee. . . .

PÉLLÉAS. Why dost thou look so gravely
on me ? — We are already in the shadow.
— It is too dark under this tree. — Come
into the light. We cannot see how happy
we are. Come, come ; so little time remains
to us. . . .

MÉLISANDE. No, no; let us stay here.
. . . I am nearer thee in the dark. . . .

PÉLLÉAS. Where are thine eyes ? —
Thou art not going to fly me ? — Thou dost
not think of me just now.

MÉLISANDE. Oh, yes ; oh, yes ; I only
think of thee. . . .

PÉLLÉAS. Thou wert looking elsewhere. . . .

MÉLISANDE. I saw thee elsewhere. . . .

PÉLLÉAS. Thy soul is far away. . . .
What ails thee, then ? — Meseems thou art
not happy. . . .

MÉLISANDE. Yes, yes ; I am happy. but
I am sad. . . .

PÉLLÉAS. One is sad often when one
loves. . . .

MÉLISANDE. I weep always when I think
of thee. . . .

PÉLLÉAS. I, too. . . . I, too, Mélisande. . . .
I am quite near thee ; I weep for joy, and
yet . . . [He kisses her again.] — Thou art
strange when I kiss thee so. . . . Thou art
so beautiful that one would think thou wert
about to die. . . .

MÉLISANDE. Thou, too. . . .

PÉLLÉAS. There, there. . . . We do not
what we will. . . . I did not love thee the
first time I saw thee. . . .

MÉLISANDE. Nor I . . . nor I. . . . I was
afraid. . . .

PÉLLÉAS. I could not admit thine eyes.
. . . I would have gone away at once . . . and
then . . .

MÉLISANDE. And I — I would not have
come. . . . I do not yet know why — I was
afraid to come. . . .

PÉLLÉAS. There are so many things one
never knows. We are ever waiting ; and
then. . . . What is that noise ? — They are
closing the gates ! . . .

MÉLISANDE. Yes, they have closed the
gates. . . .

PÉLLÉAS. We cannot go back now ? —
Hearest thou the bolts ? — Listen ! Listen !
. . . The great chains ! . . . The great chains !
. . . It is too late; it is too late ! . . .

MÉLISANDE. All the better ! all the better ! all the better ! . . .

PÉLLÉAS. Thou — . . . ? Behold, behold !
. . . It is no longer we who will it so ! . . .
All 's lost, all 's saved ! All is saved to-
night ! — Come, come. . . . My heart beats
like a madman, — up to my very throat. . . .
[They embrace.] Listen ! Listen ! My heart
is almost strangling me. . . . Come! come! . . .
Ah, how beautiful it is in the shadows ! . . .

MÉLISANDE. There is some one behind us!

PÉLLÉAS. I see no one. . . .

MÉLISANDE. I heard a noise. . . .

PÉLLÉAS. I hear only thy heart in the
dark. . . .

MÉLISANDE. I heard the crackling of
dead leaves. . . .

PÉLLÉAS. Because the wind is silent all
at once. . . . It fell as we were kissing. . . .

MÉLISANDE. How long our shadows are
to-night ! . . .

PÉLLÉAS. They embrace to the very end of the garden. Oh, how they kiss far away from us! . . . Look! look! . . .

MÉLISANDE [*in a stifled voice*]. A-a-h! — He is behind a tree!

PÉLLÉAS. Who?

MÉLISANDE. Golaud!

PÉLLÉAS. Golaud! — Where? — I see nothing. . . .

MÉLISANDE. There . . . at the end of our shadows. . . .

PÉLLÉAS. Yes, yes; I saw him. . . . Let us not turn abruptly. . . .

MÉLISANDE. He has his sword. . . .

PÉLLÉAS. I have not mine. . . .

MÉLISANDE. He saw us kiss. . . .

PÉLLÉAS. He does not know we have seen him. . . . Do not stir; do not turn your head. . . . He would rush headlong on us. . . . He will remain there while he thinks we do not know. He watches us. . . . He is still motionless. . . . Go, go at once this way. . . . I will wait for him. . . . I will stop him. . . .

MÉLISANDE. No, no, no! . . .

PÉLLÉAS. Go! Go! He has seen all! . . . He will kill us! . . .

MÉLISANDE. All the better! all the better! all the better! . . .

PÉLLÉAS. He comes! He comes! . . . Thy mouth! . . . Thy mouth! . . .

MÉLISANDE. Yes! . . . yes! yes! . . .

[*They kiss desperately.*]

PÉLLÉAS. Oh! oh! All the stars are falling! . . .

MÉLISANDE. Upon me, too! upon me, too!

PÉLLÉAS. Again! Again! . . . Give! Give!

MÉLISANDE. All! all! all! . . .

[GOLAUD *rushes upon them, sword in hand, and strikes* PÉLLÉAS, *who falls at the brink of the fountain.* MÉLISANDE *flees terrified.*]

MÉLISANDE [*fleeing*]. Oh! Oh! I have no courage! . . . I have no courage! . . .

[GOLAUD *pursues her through the wood in silence.*]

ACT V

SCENE I — *A lower hall in the castle. The women servants discovered, gathered together, while without children are playing before one of the ventilators of the hall.*

AN OLD SERVANT. You will see, you will see, my daughters; it will be to-night. — Some one will come to tell us by and by. . . .

ANOTHER SERVANT. They will not come to tell us. . . . They don't know what they are doing any longer. . . .

THIRD SERVANT. Let us wait here. . . .

FOURTH SERVANT. We shall know well enough when we must go up. . . .

FIFTH SERVANT. When the time is come, we shall go up of ourselves. . . .

SIXTH SERVANT. There is no longer a sound heard in the house. . . .

SEVENTH SERVANT. We ought to make the children keep still, who are playing before the ventilator.

EIGHTH SERVANT. They will be still of themselves by and by.

NINTH SERVANT. The time has not yet come. . . .

[*Enter an old Servant.*]

THE OLD SERVANT. No one can go in the room any longer. I have listened more than an hour. . . . You could hear the flies walk on the doors. . . . I heard nothing. . . .

FIRST SERVANT. Has she been left alone in the room?

THE OLD SERVANT. No, no; I think the room is full of people.

FIRST SERVANT. They will come, they will come, by and by. . . .

THE OLD SERVANT. Lord! Lord! It is not happiness that has come into the house. . . . One may not speak, but if I could say what I know. . . .

SECOND SERVANT. It was you who found them before the gate?

THE OLD SERVANT. Why, yes! why, yes! It was I who found them. The porter says it was he who saw them first; but it was I who waked them. He was sleeping on his face and would not get up. — And now he comes saying, "It was I who saw them first." Is that just? — See, I burned myself lighting a lamp to go down cellar. — Now what was I going to do down cellar? — I can't remember any more what I was going to do down cellar. — At any rate, I got up very early; it was not yet very light; I said to myself, I will go across the courtyard, and then I will open the gate. Good; I go down the stairs on tiptoe, and I open the gate as if it were an ordinary gate. . . . My God! My God! What do I see? Divine a little what I see! . . .

FIRST SERVANT. They were before the gate?

THE OLD SERVANT. They were both stretched out before the gate ! . . . Exactly like poor folk that are too hungry. . . . They were huddled together like little children who are afraid. . . . The little princess was nearly dead, and the great Golaud had still his sword in his side. . . . There was blood on the sill. . . .

SECOND SERVANT. We ought to make the children keep still. . . . They are screaming with all their might before the ventilator. . . .

THIRD SERVANT. You can't hear yourself speak. . . .

FOURTH SERVANT. There is nothing to be done : I have tried already; they won't keep still. . . .

FIRST SERVANT. It seems he is nearly cured ?

THE OLD SERVANT. Who ?

FIRST SERVANT. The great Golaud.

THIRD SERVANT. Yes, yes ; they have taken him to his wife's room. I met them just now, in the corridor. They were holding him up as if he were drunk. He cannot yet walk alone.

THE OLD SERVANT. He could not kill himself ; he is too big. But she is hardly wounded, and it is she who is going to die. . . . Can you understand that ?

FIRST SERVANT. You have seen the wound ?

THE OLD SERVANT. As I see you, my daughter. — I saw everything, you understand. . . . I saw it before all the others. . . . A tiny little wound under her little left breast, — a little wound that would n't kill a pigeon. Is it natural ?

FIRST SERVANT. Yes, yes; there is something underneath. . . .

SECOND SERVANT. Yes; but she was delivered of her babe three days ago. . . .

THE OLD SERVANT. Exactly! . . . She was delivered on her death-bed; is that a little sign? — And what a child ! Have you seen it ? — A wee little girl a beggar would not bring into the world. . . . A little wax figure that came much too soon ; . . . a little wax figure that must live in lambs' wool. . . . Yes, yes ; it is not happiness that has come into the house. . . .

FIRST SERVANT. Yes, yes; it is the hand of God that has been stirring. . . .

SECOND SERVANT. Yes, yes; all that did not happen without reason. . . .

THIRD SERVANT. It is as good Lord Pélléas . . . where is he? — No one knows. . . .

THE OLD SERVANT. Yes, yes; everybody knows. . . . But nobody dare speak of it. . . . One does not speak of this ; . . . one does not speak of that ; . . . one speaks no more of anything; . . . one no longer speaks truth . . . But I know he was found at the bottom of Blind Man's Spring; . . . but no one, no one could see him. . . . Well, well, we shall only know all that at the last day. . . .

FIRST SERVANT. I dare not sleep here any longer. . . .

THE OLD SERVANT. Yes, yes; once ill-fortune is in the house, one keeps silence in vain. . . .

THIRD SERVANT. Yes ; it finds you all the same. . . .

THE OLD SERVANT. Yes, yes; but we do not go where we would. . . .

FOURTH SERVANT. Yes, yes; we do not do what we would. . . .

FIRST SERVANT. They are afraid of us now. . . .

SECOND SERVANT. They all keep silence. . . .

THIRD SERVANT. They cast down their eyes in the corridors.

FOURTH SERVANT. They do not speak any more except in a low voice.

FIFTH SERVANT. You would think they had all done it together.

SIXTH SERVANT. One does n't know what they have done. . . .

SEVENTH SERVANT. What is to be done when the masters are afraid ? . . .

[A silence.]

FIRST SERVANT. I no longer hear the children screaming.

SECOND SERVANT. They are sitting down before the ventilator.

THIRD SERVANT. They are huddled against each other.

THE OLD SERVANT. I no longer hear anything in the house. . . .

FIRST SERVANT. You no longer even hear the children breathe. . . .

THE OLD SERVANT. Come, come; it is time to go up. . . . [Exeunt, in silence.]

SCENE II — An apartment in the castle. ARKËL, GOLAUD, and the PHYSICIAN discovered in one corner of the room. MÉLISANDE is stretched upon her bed.

THE PHYSICIAN. It cannot be of that little wound she is dying; a bird would not have died of it. . . . It is not you, then, who have killed her, good my lord; do not be so disconsolate. . . . She could not have lived. . . . She was born without reason . . . to die; and she dies without reason. . . . And then, it is not sure we shall not save her. . . .

ARKËL. No, no; it seems to me we keep too silent, in spite of ourselves, in her room. . . . It is not a good sign. . . . Look how she sleeps . . . slowly, slowly; . . . it is as if her soul was cold forever. . . .

GOLAUD. I have killed her without cause! I have killed her without cause! . . . Is it not enough to make the stones weep? . . . They had kissed like little children. . . . They had simply kissed. . . . They were brother and sister. . . . And I, and I at once! . . . I did it in spite of myself, look you. . . . I did it in spite of myself. . . .

THE PHYSICIAN. Stop; I think she is waking. . . .

MÉLISANDE. Open the window; . . . open the window. . . .

ARKËL. Shall I open this one, Mélisande?

MÉLISANDE. No, no; the great window . . . the great window. . . . It is to see . . .

ARKËL. Is not the sea air too cold to-night?

THE PHYSICIAN. Do it; do it. . . .

MÉLISANDE. Thanks. . . . Is it sunset?

ARKËL. Yes; it is sunset on the sea; it 's late. — How are you, Mélisande?

MÉLISANDE. Well, well. — Why do you ask that? I have never been better. — And yet it seems to me I know something. . . .

ARKËL. What sayest thou? — I do not understand thee. . . .

MÉLISANDE. Neither do I understand all I say, you see. . . . I do not know what I am saying. . . . I do not know what I know. . . . I no longer say what I would. . . .

ARKËL. Why, yes! why, yes! . . . I am quite happy to hear thee speak so; thou hast raved a little these last days, and one no longer understood thee. . . . But now all that is far away. . . .

MÉLISANDE. I do not know. . . . — Are you all alone in the room, grandfather?

ARKËL. No; there is the physician, besides, who cured thee. . . .

MÉLISANDE. Ah! . . .

ARKËL. And then there is still some one else. . . .

MÉLISANDE. Who is it?

ARKËL. It is . . . thou must not be frightened. . . . He does not wish thee the least harm, be sure. . . . If thou 'rt afraid, he will go away. . . . He is very unhappy. . . .

MÉLISANDE. Who is it?

ARKËL. It is thy . . . thy husband. . . . It is Golaud. . . .

MÉLISANDE. Golaud is here? Why does he not come by me?

GOLAUD [dragging himself toward the bed]. Mélisande . . . Mélisande. . . .

MÉLISANDE. Is it you, Golaud? I should hardly recognize you any more. . . . It is the evening sunlight in my eyes. . . . Why look you on the walls? You have grown thin and old. . . . Is it a long while since we saw each other?

GOLAUD. [To ARKËL and the PHYSICIAN.] Will you withdraw a moment, if you please, if you please? . . . I will leave the door wide open. . . . One moment only. . . . I would say something to her; else I could not die. . . . Will you? — Go clear to the end of the corridor; you can come back at once, at once. . . . Do not refuse me this. . . . I am a wretch. . . . [Exit ARKËL and the PHYSICIAN.] — Mélisande, hast thou pity on me, as I have pity on thee? . . . Mélisande? . . . Dost thou forgive me, Mélisande? . . .

MÉLISANDE. Yes, yes, I do forgive thee. . . . What must I forgive? . . .

GOLAUD. I have wrought thee so much ill, Mélisande. . . . I cannot tell thee the ill I have wrought thee. . . . But I see it, I see it so clearly to-day . . . since the first day. . . . And all I did not know till now leaps in my eyes to-night. . . . And it is all my fault, all that has happened, all that will happen. . . . If I could tell it, thou wouldst see as I do! . . . I see all! I see all! . . . But I loved thee so! . . . I loved thee so! . . . But now there is some one dying. . . . It is I who am dying. . . . And I would know . . . I would ask thee. . . . Thou 'lt bear me no ill-will . . . I would . . . The truth must be told to a dying man. . . . He must know the truth, or else he could not sleep. . . . Swearest thou to tell me the truth?

MÉLISANDE. Yes.

GOLAUD. Didst thou love Pélléas?

MÉLISANDE. Why, yes; I loved him. — Where is he?

GOLAUD. Thou dost not understand me?

—Thou wilt not understand me ? — It seems to me . . . it seems to me . . . Well, then, here : I ask thee if thou lovedst him with a forbidden love ? . . . Wert thou . . . were you guilty ? Say, say, yes, yes, yes ! . . .

MÉLISANDE. No, no ; we were not guilty. — Why do you ask that ?

GOLAUD. Mélisande ! . . . tell me the truth, for the love of God !

MÉLISANDE. Why have I not told the truth ?

GOLAUD. Do not lie so any more, at the moment of death !

MÉLISANDE. Who is dying ? — Is it I ?

GOLAUD. Thou, thou ! And I, I too, after thee ! . . . And we must have the truth. . . . We must have the truth at last, dost thou understand ? . . . Tell me all ! Tell me all ! I forgive thee all ! . . .

MÉLISANDE. Why am I going to die ? — I did not know it. . . .

GOLAUD. Thou knowest it now ! . . . It is time ! It is time ! . . . Quick ! quick ! . . . The truth ! the truth ! . . .

MÉLISANDE. The truth . . . the truth . . .

GOLAUD. Where art thou ? — Mélisande ! — Where art thou ? — It is not natural ! Mélisande ! Where art thou ! — Where goest thou ? [*Perceiving* ARKËL *and the* PHYSICIAN *at the door of the room.*] — Yes, yes ; you may come in. . . . I know nothing ; it is useless. . . . It is too late ; she is already too far away from us. . . . I shall never know ! . . . I shall die here like a blind man ! . . .

ARKËL. What have you done ? You will kill her. . . .

GOLAUD. I have already killed her. . . .

ARKËL. Mélisande. . . .

MÉLISANDE. Is it you, grandfather ?

ARKËL. Yes, my daughter. . . . What would you have me do ?

MÉLISANDE. Is it true that the winter is beginning ? . . .

ARKËL. Why dost thou ask ?

MÉLISANDE. Because it is cold, and there are no more leaves. . . .

ARKËL. Thou art cold ? — Wilt thou have the windows closed ?

MÉLISANDE. No, no, . . . not till the sun be at the bottom of the sea. — It sinks slowly ; then it is the winter beginning ?

ARKËL. Yes. — Thou dost not like the winter ?

MÉLISANDE. Oh ! no. I am afraid of the cold. — I am so afraid of the great cold. . . .

ARKËL. Dost thou feel better ?

MÉLISANDE. Yes, yes ; I have no longer all those qualms. . . .

ARKËL. Wouldst thou see thy child ?

MÉLISANDE. What child ?

ARKËL. Thy child. — Thou art a mother. . . . Thou hast brought a little daughter into the world. . . .

MÉLISANDE. Where is she ?

ARKËL. Here. . . .

MÉLISANDE. It is strange. I cannot lift my arms to take her. . . .

ARKËL. Because you are still very weak. . . . I will hold her myself ; look. . . .

MÉLISANDE. She does not laugh. . . . She is little. . . . She is going to weep too. . . . I pity her. . . .

[*The room has been invaded, little by little, by the women servants of the castle, who range themselves in silence along the walls and wait.*]

GOLAUD [*rising abruptly*]. What is the matter ? — What are all these women coming here for ? . . .

THE PHYSICIAN. It is the servants. . . .

ARKËL. Who was it called them ?

THE PHYSICIAN. It was not I. . . .

GOLAUD. Why do you come here ? — No one has asked for you. . . . What come you here to do ? — But what is it, then ? — Answer me ! . . .

[*The servants make no answer.*]

ARKËL. Do not speak too loud. . . . She is going to sleep ; she has closed her eyes. . . .

GOLAUD. It is not . . . ?

THE PHYSICIAN. No, no ; see, she breathes. . . .

ARKËL. Her eyes are full of tears. — It is her soul weeping now. . . . Why does she stretch her arms out so ? — What would she ?

THE PHYSICIAN. It is toward the child, without doubt. . . . It is the struggle of motherhood against . . .

GOLAUD. At this moment ? — At this moment ? — You must say. Say ! Say ! . . .

THE PHYSICIAN. Perhaps.

GOLAUD. At once ? . . . Oh ! oh ! I must tell her. . . . — Mélisande ! . . . Mélisande ! . . . Leave me alone ! leave me alone with her ! . . .

ARKËL. No, no ; do not come near. . . . Trouble her not. . . . Speak no more to her. . . . You know not what the soul is. . . .

GOLAUD. It is not my fault! . . . It is not my fault!

ARKËL. Hush! . . . Hush! . . . We must speak softly now. — She must not be disturbed. . . . The human soul is very silent. . . . The human soul likes to depart alone. . . . It suffers so timorously. . . . But the sadness, Goland . . . the sadness of all we see! . . . Oh! oh! oh! . . .

> [At this moment, all the servants fall suddenly on their knees at the back of the chamber.]

ARKËL [turning]. What is the matter!

THE PHYSICIAN [approaching the bed and feeling the body]. They are right. . . .

> [A long silence.]

ARKËL. I saw nothing. — Are you sure?

THE PHYSICIAN. Yes, yes.

ARKËL. I heard nothing. . . . So quick, so quick! . . . All at once! . . . She goes without a word. . . .

GOLAUD [sobbing]. Oh! oh! oh!

ARKËL. Do not stay here, Goland. . . . She must have silence now. . . . Come, come. . . . It is terrible, but it is not your fault. . . . 'T was a little being, so quiet, so fearful, and so silent. . . . 'T was a poor little mysterious being, like everybody. . . . She lies there as if she were the big sister of her child. . . . Come, come. . . . My God! My God! . . . I shall never understand it at all. . . . Let us not stay here. — Come; the child must not stay here in this room. . . . She must live now in her place. . . . It is the poor little one's turn. . . .

> [They go out in silence.]

BEYOND HUMAN POWER

OVER ÆVNE, I

By BJÖRNSTJERNE BJÖRNSON

Translated by LEE M. HOLLANDER

Björnson does not supply a List of Persons for his later plays. For convenience such a list for Beyond Human Power may be found in the notes on the play in the appendix.

BEYOND HUMAN POWER

ACT I

A plain room with log walls. In the right-hand wall, two partitioned windows; to the left, a door.

In the foreground, on the right, stands a bed which is placed in such manner that its head is in a line with the door.

By the bed is a little table with bottles and cups. There are also a dresser, chairs, etc.

On the bed, which is covered with a white bed-spread, lies CLARA SANG, *dressed in white. At one of the windows stands her sister,* MRS. HANNAH ROBERTS.

MRS. HANNAH ROBERTS. How the sun shines on the birch leaves out there! And how delicate the leaves are here in the North!

CLARA SANG. But now there is a smell of wild cherry, Hannah!

HANNAH. I am looking for it; why, but there is no wild cherry here?

CLARA. You can't see it from there; but there are wild cherry trees here. The morning breeze brings the fragrance right toward us.

HANNAH. But I don't notice it.

CLARA. Ah, after such a rain I can detect the least current of fragrance from outside.

HANNAH. And you can smell wild cherry?

CLARA. Quite distinctly! — At any rate, close the lower window.

HANNAH. If you wish!

[*Closes the window.*]

CLARA. Who was it that said we had reason to fear a mountain-slide?

HANNAH. The old man, — the foreman on the boat that brought us here, you know. It rained and rained, and so he said: "This is dangerous, this is. After a long rain like this the soil becomes loose on the mountains up here."

CLARA. I have been thinking of that all night. There have been mountain-slides here, time and again, you know. Once — but that was before our time — the church was swept away.

HANNAH. The church?

CLARA. Not as it stands here now. It stood some distance away then.

HANNAH. Is that the reason why it was moved so near to the garden wall?

CLARA. Yes. Now, when the church windows are opened in the summer, I can hear Adolf sing before the altar as I lie here. That is, when the door to my room is open, and the door into the living-room — and of course, also, the window in the living-room. He sings so beautifully. When both doors are open I can see the church from here. Come and look! That is why my bed was placed here.

HANNAH [*going to her*]. My dear Clara, to think I should see you again in this condition!

CLARA. Hannah!

HANNAH. Why did n't you write?

CLARA. Oh, America is so far away; and then — Oh well, some other time.

HANNAH. I did n't understand your answer yesterday, when I asked about the doctor.

CLARA. Adolf was in the room, so I evaded your question. We have no doctor.

HANNAH. You have no doctor?

CLARA. He used to come here quite often — he lives very far away — and he did n't help me. So when I had lain a whole month without sleeping —

HANNAH. A whole month without sleeping? Why, but that is impossible —?

CLARA. It is almost one and a half now, dear! — Well, then we thought it did n't make any difference whether we had a doctor or not. Don't you see? My husband asked him about my sickness, and he gave it some ugly name. Adolf has n't told me what it was, so I don't know. After that we did not send for him any longer.

HANNAH. Are n't you talking too much?

CLARA. I don't talk at all for whole days. At other times I talk incessantly. I can't help it. Now Adolf will soon be back from his morning walk. He will bring me some flowers.

HANNAH. May I not gather you some, since you long so for them?

CLARA. No. There are some kinds I can't endure. He knows which. Hannah, you have n't told me about your meeting my children on the steamer. I am so very anxious to hear about it, dear!

HANNAH. There was such bustling in the house, yesterday.

CLARA. Yes, and you were all so tired. Just think, the children are sleeping still? From seven till seven! That's youth, that!

HANNAH. They needed it, too. While I can sleep only a few hours at a time. And I am not very tired either, now.

CLARA. No, it is the same with all who come under the spell of the midnight sun. One becomes so altogether wakeful. — But the children? Are n't they dear?

HANNAH. And so innocent! But they don't resemble you in the face, and not Sang, either, really, except the eyes; and that I saw only later on.

CLARA. Go on, go on!

HANNAH. If they had resembled you, I should have known them, of course. — I have n't seen any of you, since you yourselves were young. Keep that in mind! But I saw them go aboard, and I saw them later on also, although they went into the steerage . . .

CLARA. The poor dears, they could n't afford better!

HANNAH. . . . and I did n't recognize them. Then one morning, I was standing on the bridge, and they walked to and fro rapidly below me; trying to keep warm. Every time they turned their backs to me to walk forward again I could not forget their eyes. For I knew those eyes. All at once, some sea-birds darted down so close to Rachel that she threw up her arms; she was frightened, because they screeched right into her ears. But that movement of her arms — well, it was exactly yours. And then, too, I recognized the eyes. They were Sang's.

CLARA. You went down to them at once?

HANNAH. How can you ask! "Is your name Sang?" I asked. They did not need to answer. Now I saw it so clearly. "I am

your Aunt Hannah from America," I said. — And then we were all so moved.

[Both sisters weep.]

CLARA. Rachel had written to you and prayed you to come to see me? Is n't that so?

HANNAH. Yes. And I shall always thank her for it. How sweet she was! I got them right up into the cabin, and her I bundled up in a big shawl, because she was cold. And he got a plaid to wrap himself in.

CLARA. Dear Hannah!

HANNAH. But, dear, — yes, this belongs to it! — just then a black squall blew into the fjord behind us. We were right under a high mountain, bare and gray. A lot of sea-gulls came out to us; some of them shrieked over our heads. And how cold it was! Some miserable huts stood by the shore, farther in — and they were the only ones we could see and we had traveled many miles without seeing any others. Only mountains and skerries! That is Northland, I thought. Here these frozen children were reared. No, I shall never forget it! Terrible!

CLARA. But that is not so terrible.

HANNAH. Clara! — To think of you lying there! Do you remember what a fine, graceful girl you used to be?

CLARA. Yes, yes! — I don't know myself where I should begin to explain it all to you. Oh, God!

HANNAH. Why did n't you shriek over to me? — I who am so well off — and could have saved you in so many ways from becoming overworked?

Why did n't you write the truth? You have concealed it the whole time. — Only Rachel wrote me the truth.

CLARA. Yes! — That is so — and had to be so.

HANNAH. Why?

CLARA. Supposing I had written how matters stood, and you had all come hurrying here. . . ?

I don't want to be helped. For I cannot be helped.

HANNAH. But — why, then, you lied?

CLARA. Yes, of course. I lied all the time, and to every one. How could I do anything else?

HANNAH. These things are incomprehensible to me! — From beginning to end!

CLARA. Hannah? You said "overworked." You said you could have saved me in so many ways from becoming overworked. Did you ever know any one who was overworked, who was able to ask for help, or who knew how to make resistance?

HANNAH. But *before* you had become overworked?

CLARA. You don't understand what you are talking about!

HANNAH. Then explain it to me! I mean, if you can!

CLARA. No, I can't do it all at once. — But little by little, perhaps.

HANNAH. At the beginning you did n't share his faith, did you? Strange! Was *that* the reason?

CLARA. No. — Oh, it's a long story! — But it is n't *that*. Our temperaments are so different; — although that is n't it, either. If Sang had been like other men, noisy and domineering — oh, then matters would not have gone so — perhaps! But long before he knew me all his strength — and strength he has, you may be sure — was taken up with work; it had become a matter of love, of sacrifice. It was beautiful, *only* beautiful! Do you know that not one harsh word has ever been spoken in our house? — that there has never been a "scene"? And we have been married these twenty-five years, almost. He is always beaming with the gladness of Sunday. Because it is Sunday with him all the year around.

HANNAH. Oh, how you love him!

CLARA. It is too little to say that I love him. I *am* not without him. And yet you speak about making resistance? — I had to, of course, sometimes, when things went too much beyond our strength.

HANNAH. What do you mean by that?

CLARA. I will explain it to you, later on. But who can resist sheer goodness? — sheer sacrifice for others? — sheer rapture? And who can resist, when his childlike faith and his supernatural power carry everybody away?

HANNAH. Supernatural power, you say?

CLARA. Have n't you heard of that? Have n't the children told you — ?

HANNAH. — What? —

CLARA. — That Sang, when he prays fervently, obtains what he prays for?

HANNAH. That he works miracles, you mean?

CLARA. Yes!

HANNAH. Sang!

CLARA. Have n't the children told you about it?

HANNAH. No!

CLARA. Is n't that strange!

HANNAH. We never talked about such matters.

CLARA. Why, but then they have n't — Oh, they thought you knew about it! Because Sang — yes, he is the "miracle priest," the country over! They thought you knew about it! They are so modest, the children.

HANNAH. But does he work miracles? *Miracles?*

CLARA. Did you not have the impression of something supernatural about him, the moment you saw him?

HANNAH. It would never have occurred to me to use that word; — but, since you have said it — he does make a most — well, what shall I call it? — decided impression of spirituality? — a very strange impression, he certainly does. As if he did not belong to this world!

CLARA. Ah, precisely!

HANNAH. Yes, indeed!

CLARA. Do you know, I sometimes lie all contracted, with my legs gathered up to my chest, and my arms . . . no, I don't care to show you; for else I might bring it on again. . . . I sometimes lie that way *all day* when he is gone, without being able to right my limbs. I tell you, it is terrible! Once — he had gone over the mountains; oh, those journeys over the mountains! — that time I lay that way for eight whole days. And no sooner did he stand there in the doorway, and I saw him, and he me, than my arms and legs began to grow limber again, and he came and stroked them, and then I lay as straight as I do now! That is the way — over and over again! It suffices that he is in the room and all is over.

HANNAH. Strange!

CLARA. What do you say to this — that invalids, that is to say, those having real faith, who were invalids — and it has happened not once, but a hundred times! — when he came and prayed with them, they became well again!

HANNAH. Really well?

CLARA. Altogether well! And what do you think about this — that sick people whom he could not come to — for the distances are so great here ! — he wrote to them that at a certain hour he would pray for them, and that they must pray with him ; — and from that same hour their sickness took a turn ! That is true ! I know a number of such cases !

HANNAH. Strange ! But you never wrote me about this !

CLARA. Oh, I knew you two ! Do you believe I wanted to expose him to your doubts ? — There is a pastor's widow here — oh, her you must see ! She lives close by. She is the most venerable person I can imagine ! She had been paralyzed for fifteen years, when Sang came here ; that is now twenty-five years ago. *Now she walks to church every Sunday !* And she is nearly a hundred years old.

HANNAH. He restored her to health ?

CLARA. Merely by praying and getting her to pray ! For you may be sure, he can pray ! And then this case of Agatha Florvaagen. That is the strangest of all. For to our eyes she was dead. He takes one of her hands in his, and lays her other hand upon her heart and warms it, and then she begins to breathe again. Now she lives with the old clergyman's widow — right close by ! — I could lie here till to-morrow, and tell and tell about him. There is a glory about him, here and all around among thousands of believers in the whole land, — there has never been the like of it. And now it is beginning to *grow* to such a degree that there is n't a day but people come to us.

HANNAH. So I may also see it, — what you speak of, — while I am here ?

CLARA. As certainly as I am lying here and cannot more than raise myself on my elbows.

HANNAH. Then why can't the miracle help *you*, Clara ? Why has n't he healed you long ago ?

CLARA. — There is a — particular reason for that. —

HANNAH. But you will certainly tell me ?

CLARA. No. — That is, I shall. But later on.

You will have to raise a window again ! It has become so close here ! More air, dear !

HANNAH. Very well.

[*She opens the topmost window pane.*]

CLARA. He ought to be here pretty soon

now. He really is staying a long time to-day. If I only could smell the flowers. After the rain there must be an abundance of them. It is almost seven o'clock ; in fact, almost exactly seven.

HANNAH [*looking at her watch*]. Yes, it is.

CLARA. Since I have been lying here I always know what time it is. — Won't that fresh air ever reach me ? — The wind must have died down ? — You don't answer me ?

HANNAH. No, I was n't listening to what you said. I can't get over my astonishment.

CLARA. Yes, it is indeed the most remarkable thing in our land — perhaps in our time.

HANNAH. What do the people say ? What do the country people think of him ?

CLARA. I believe it would have caused twenty, oh, a hundred times, greater sensation at any other place than just here. Here it seems quite natural.

HANNAH. But, Clara ! A miracle is a miracle !

CLARA. Yes, for us. But there is something in nature here *which demands the unusual of us, also.* Nature herself is beyond all reasonable limits. We have a night which lasts almost the whole winter. And our day lasts almost all summer — and *then* the sun is above the horizon both night and day. You have seen the sun at night ? Do you know that behind the sea-mists it seems three, and sometimes four times as big as otherwise ? And the colors it spreads over sky, sea, and mountain ! From the ruddiest glow to the most delicate, exquisite golden-white. — And then the colors in the wintry sky during the Northern lights ! Although they are more subdued, they make up for it in their fantastic lines and their incessant, infinite changes ! And then the other marveis of nature ! Swarms of birds in millions ; "shoals of fish as long as from Paris to Strassburg," as somebody has written. Do you see these mountains that rise sheer out of the sea ? They don't resemble any other mountains. And the whole Atlantic breaks upon them.

And the people's conceptions are naturally in harmony. They are boundless. Their legends and their tales are like piling up one land upon another and then rolling icy mountains from the North Pole upon them. Yes, just you laugh ! But listen to the legends here, dear ! And talk with the people, and then you will soon know that Pastor Adolf Sang is the man according to their heart! His faith suits the place! He came here with a large fortune and gave away almost all of it. So it should be! That is Christianity, they think! And then, when he journeys for miles to visit some poor sick person and prays, they are opened up, as it were, and the light penetrates in to them, directly—! Sometimes they catch sight of him, out at sea in impossible weather; alone, in a little, tiny boat; maybe with one or both of the children with him; because he took them along ever since they were six years old! Performs a miracle there, perhaps, and then away again to some other fishing-village—and performs another there! They almost expect it of him. And more than that! If I had not made resistance, why, we should n't now have enough to live on and he himself would n't be alive—nor, perhaps, the children either—I won't even mention myself. For it is all over with me.

HANNAH. Then you have not made resistance, after all!—

CLARA. It may look that way. But I have. Not by remonstrating with him; that would do no good! No, I have had to think of some stratagem—always a new one, every time; else he will see through it. Oh, I am in despair about it!

HANNAH. Think of some stratagem, you say?

CLARA. He is lacking in one whole sense, the sense of reality. He never sees anything but what he wants to see. Therefore, for example, nothing bad in any one. That is to say, he sees it well enough; but he pays no attention to it. "I look at the bright side in people," he says. And when he speaks with them, all are good, altogether good, absolutely all of them! When he looks at them with those childlike eyes—who could be otherwise? But then things are bound to go wrong. Because he ruins us on such people.

But in this way he is beyond all control, you see, in great matters as well as in small. If he were permitted, he would take the last thing we owned—what we had to eat for to-morrow! "God will assuredly repay us; for he commanded us to do so."

When there is such a storm that the most experienced sailors do not dare to go out in a ship, not to speak of the pastor's long-boat—then he sets out in a little four-oar, he does—and perhaps with his little child in the stern!

He has started out over the mountains in a fog and wandered about there for three days and three nights without a morsel passing over his lips. People went out to search for him and led him back to human habitations. And then, a week later, he wants to make the same journey in foggy weather! There was a sick person who expected him, he said!

HANNAH. But can he stand it?

CLARA. He stands anything. He falls asleep like a tired child, and sleeps, and sleeps, and sleeps. Then he awakes, eats, and begins all over. He is entirely *unconcerned;* for he is perfectly innocent.

HANNAH. How you do love him!

CLARA. Yes, that is the only thing that is left of me. The worry I had about the children has completely worn me out.

HANNAH. About the children?

CLARA. It was n't good for them to be here, you see. Nothing was regular and fixed; they were becoming confused. Never any objection to anything that was thought right. Never any deliberation—only inspiration! They were grown up and hardly knew more than how to read and write.

And how I fought to get them away from here! And then, for five years, to be able to support them when they were away, and provide instruction for them! Yes, that took away my last strength. Now it is all over.

HANNAH. Dear, dear sister!

CLARA. You don't mean . . . ? I certainly hope you are not sorry for me! For *me,* who have made life's journey with the best man in all the world?—with the purest spirit of all mankind?

One lives a shorter life that way—to be sure. One cannot have everything.

But change?—How could I?

HANNAH. Has he then broken down *all* of you?

CLARA. He has! Exactly! That is, he has not broken down *everybody;* for that he was n't allowed to do. He would have ruined himself also, if I had permitted it. Because he works beyond his own powers.

HANNAH. Beyond his powers? When he really works miracles?—and each time is saved?

CLARA. Don't you think that the miracles come from the fact that he works with powers beyond his own?

HANNAH. You frighten me! What do you mean?

CLARA. I mean that this was perhaps the case with the prophets, too, — both the Jews and the Gentiles. They could do more than we in a certain direction, because they lacked so much in all other directions. At any rate, that is what I have thought.

HANNAH. But have you no *faith*, then?

CLARA. Faith? Now, what do you mean by that? We are descended from an old nervous family of doubters, we two, — I dare say, an intelligent family. I admired Sang. He was unlike all other men, better than all others. I admired him, until I loved him. It was n't his faith; that was something *altogether peculiar* to himself. How far I now believe as he does — why, that I don't know.

HANNAH. You don't know?

CLARA. I have always been in such a state of excitement, dear, that I have never had time to make up my mind. These things need time. And I had my hands full enough to take care of things, from one time to another. My constitution was undermined too soon by it. My mind was no longer fit to debate such great questions.

I hardly know the difference between right and wrong. In a rough manner, of course; — but the finer distinctions. I must confine myself to doing what I can. And it's the same way with my faith. I can't do any more.

HANNAH. Does he know this?

CLARA. He knows all about it. Do you believe I would conceal anything?

HANNAH. But does n't he want to make you believe what he himself believes?

CLARA. Not in the least! This question of belief, he says, is for God to decide, *if one is not to stand judged*. It is our business to be sincere. Then faith will come of itself — here or hereafter. Oh, he is true, he is!

HANNAH. Yet he labors to spread the faith?

CLARA. In his own way. Never, no, never by bringing pressure to bear. He is absolutely considerate with all alike. Do you hear — with all! Oh, there is no one like him!

HANNAH. You look up to him as you did during the first enchanting days! And that, although your eyes have grown old.

CLARA. Although my eyes have grown old.

HANNAH. But now, concerning your belief in his miracles, . . . in reality, you don't actually believe in them?

CLARA. What is that you say? There is nothing that exists I believe in more implicitly!

HANNAH. If you do not dare to let him start out in a hurricane, and if you do not believe that you will get again what he gives away, even though it be your last, . . . then you do not believe in them.

CLARA. Before I would consent to one of those things . . . ! Yes, it is right here that my strength lies, let me tell you.

HANNAH. Well and good. But it is n't the strength of faith.

CLARA. No, no. You are right. But if there is a contradiction here — what difference does it make? Every one of us has his contradictions — he alone excepted.

For that matter, I will tell you that to cast one's self or one's child into the stormy sea — that is more than faith; that is tempting God.

HANNAH. It seems to me that a miracle ought to occur just as well when our own life is concerned as when others' lives are.

CLARA. But to *put* one's self into danger of one's life!

HANNAH. When it is done to save others? That can certainly not be called tempting God.

CLARA. Listen — no more now! I can bear it no longer. I only know that when he wants to take the children's substance, and give it to bad, worthless men, or when he wants to start out by himself over the mountains in a fog, or to go to sea in a storm, — then, why, then I put myself right in his way! I then do all, absolutely all, I can hit upon to prevent it!

Supposing he wanted to do it now . . . ! I have n't been able to stand on my legs these many months; . . . but then I could! Then I could! I am certain of it! Then I also could work a miracle. For I love him and his children.

[*There is silence for a long time.*]

HANNAH. Is there anything I can do for you?

CLARA. Let me have some *eau-de-Cologne!* Here, over my temples. And let me smell it! I mean the kind you gave me yesterday. Quick! Can't you get the cork out? — The cork-screw is there! There, there! And open the lower window. The lowest one also!

HANNAH. Yes, yes!

CLARA. Thanks! — If the ground were not so damp after that terrible rain, I would like to go outside. Can't you get the cork out?

HANNAH. Oh, yes, in a moment.

CLARA. Screw it further in. Not too far. That's it! That's it! Come! — Ah! — jasmine!

HANNAH. Jasmine? *Nothing of the kind.*

CLARA. Jasmine, jasmine! — There he is! I hear him! There he is! Thank God! I become calm at once. — Calm. Ah, it is indeed a blessing! There . . . he . . . is.

[SANG *comes in.*]

SANG. Good-morning, again! — Good-morning, dear Hannah! How good it is to have you here! How good!

Such a morning, so full of song and fragrance you surely do not have in America! And nowhere else in the world!

CLARA. But my flowers?

SANG. Do you know what has happened to me to-day, Clara?

CLARA. You have given them away?

SANG. No. Ha-ha! No, not this time, said Tordenskjold![1] Oh, that was naughty of you! Now, have n't we just been complaining and scolding about this continuous, fearful rain, and been fearing mountain-slides and avalanches — and all kinds of calamities. . . . *And yet the rain has done nothing but produce a wonder of blessed beauty!* When at last I saw the sun, to-day, and went out . . . *Oh, the wonderful vegetation I found! There never was a year like this!* I went out into a wealth of fragrance and color, Clara dear, . . . and I felt so deeply moved, all at once, that, really, I thought it a shame to tread upon the grass that grew there and filled one with such joy. So I turned to one side and found a path, and there I walked and looked down into the wet eyes of the flowers. There was such crowding among them! Such life in their crowding! Such aspiration! The very

[1] A famous Dano-Norwegian naval hero.

smallest among them tried to stretch their necks toward the sun, even they. So open-mouthed, so greedy! Why, I really believe some started out to blossom so early that the rogues will be sending pollen out a-wooing before the day is over! I have already seen some bumble-bees! They did not know where to turn first, in all these seas of fragrance! For the one thousand only smelt sweeter and called more hotly than the next, and there were a thousand times a thousand! Now things are going on. Is n't there individuality in this million-headed multiplicity also? Ah, yes, there is! And so I could n't pluck one of them.

But I have something else for you to-day!

CLARA [*who has been making signs to her sister while he has been speaking*]. Have you?

SANG. I too shall try to open my cup to-day!

CLARA. What is it, dear?

SANG. Perhaps you don't think I am wicked enough to conceal anything, do you? But I can!

CLARA. I have noticed for a long time that there was something — ?

SANG. Now, really, have you? For, indeed, I have not said a word about it, this time.

But if I have not been as alarmed about your sickness as all the others, there has been a good reason for it.

CLARA. What is it?

HANNAH. Yes, what is it? She is getting excited.

SANG. I shall be quick about it! — I have helped so many and cannot help her, because I can't really pray with her as I should wish to, because she is unwilling! And I have no power in my prayer if the sick do not pray with me — that is, if they can pray. And so I wrote to our children to come. And last night, when I had them go to bed so early, I told them why, because they should get thoroughly rested, and then help me to-day, at seven o'clock, to pray at their mother's bedside!

CLARA. My dear, my dear!

SANG. We will surround you with a chain of prayer! One shall stand at your feet, one at your head, and I right in front of you! And then we shall not stop until you fall asleep! Not before! No, not before! And then we are going to repeat our prayers until you arise and walk among us! Yes, that is what we shall do.

CLARA. Ah, my dear!

HANNAH. And what did the children say?

SANG. Oh, you ought to have seen them! They became so moved. I assure you they became as white as that sheet. And then they looked at one another.

Then I understood they must be left alone.

I see you, too, are moved. You are closing your eyes. Perhaps you also would prefer to be by yourself, now? — Yes, we shall be visited to-day. By an exalted guest! It is fitting that we should be prepared! — What o'clock is it now?

HANNAH. It is past seven.

SANG. No, it can't be so late; for in that case they would be here. — You forgot to set your watch by our time.

HANNAH. No, I have n't.

SANG. Then, you did not set it right, my dear. Do you think it's possible that grown-up children who are to pray by their mother's bedside would oversleep?

HANNAH. I will go up to them.

SANG. No, no, no! These last moments they must have to themselves! I know how that is.

HANNAH. They shan't hear me. I just want to peep in.   [She goes out.]

SANG. But softly, softly!

It is fine to see her so enthusiastic.

CLARA. Ah, my dear!

SANG. There is something so troubled in your voice.

Oh, do have hope, now! I tell you, I have never felt more sure.

And you know from Whom this feeling comes.

Clara! — My beloved Clara!

[He kneels by her bedside.]

Before we come together for our great prayer, you must let me thank you! I have thanked God for you to-day. In all this glory of spring I have thanked Him. So infinitely great was the rejoicing all about me and in me. I went over in the main lines all that we have lived through together. Do you know, I believe I love you all the more because you do not entirely share my belief; — for that reason you are still more continually in my thoughts. Your devotion to me is wholly

a matter of your nature, your will — comes from nothing else. And that you remain steadfast in your own belief, even by my side; I am proud of that, too.

And then, when I remember that you — without the faith I have — that you have sacrificed your life for me —

CLARA. Adolf!

SANG. I will put my hand over your mouth, if you speak. Now it is my turn! — Ah, it is a noble thing that you have done. We others, we gave our faith; but you gave your life. What great confidence you must have in me! How I love you!

Every time my zeal for the faith caused you anxiety, and you trembled for me or for the future of our children, and then perhaps at such times did not consider what you did, . . . I know that you had not strength left to do it better.

CLARA. No, I had n't.

SANG. I am to blame. I did not know how to be careful of you, either.

CLARA. Adolf!

SANG. I know it is so. You have sacrificed yourself bit by bit. And not from faith, not from a hope of reward, in this life or the next; — from love alone. How I love you!

I wanted to tell you this to-day. If Hannah had not left the room, I should have asked her to leave us alone for a little while.

Thanks! To-day is your great day. Now the children will soon be here.

Ah, let me kiss you as I kissed you on the very first day of all!

[HANNAH comes in.]

SANG. Well?

HANNAH. It is past seven.

CLARA. I knew it.

SANG. Is it past seven? — And the children?

HANNAH. They were asleep.

SANG. They were asleep?

CLARA. I knew it.

HANNAH. Elias was sreepmg in his clothes. He had thrown himself on the bed as if he had not meant to sleep, but merely to rest, but nevertheless had fallen asleep. Rachel was sleeping with her hands folded over the bedclothes. She heard nothing.

SANG. I have asked too much of the children. — I always make the same mistake.

HANNAH. Yes, they had hardly slept these two days ; in fact, not since we met.

SANG. But what was God's purpose, then, in giving me such power just to-day? And in making me so certain? — I must try to find out. Pardon me a moment, dear! — Why just to-day? — [*Walks out.*]

CLARA. Did you wake them?

HANNAH. Of course. — Do you know what I believe is the matter?

CLARA. Good Heavens, yes! Oh, I am beginning to tremble so.

HANNAH. Is there anything I can do for you?

CLARA. No; but I myself must try to subdue it. — Ah! — There was something about their eyes, yesterday. Now I understand it.

HANNAH. They have no longer their father's faith.

CLARA. They have no longer their father's faith. — How they must have fought and suffered, the poor dears! For they love and honor him above everything in the world!

HANNAH. That was why they were so quiet yesterday.

CLARA. That was why they were so much moved by the least thing! — Ah, and that, too, is why Rachel wrote asking you to come. Some one *had* to be here — and she did not dare to come herself.

HANNAH. Doubtless you are right. — How they must have struggled over this!

CLARA. Oh, the poor things! The poor things!

HANNAH. Here comes Elias!

CLARA. Is he here?

ELIAS [*sinking on his knees before his mother's bed, with his face buried in his hands*]. Oh, mother!

CLARA. Yes, yes — I know!

ELIAS. You know? It could not be worse!

CLARA. No, it could not be worse.

ELIAS. When he said last night that to-day, at seven o'clock —

CLARA. Hush! I can't bear it.

HANNAH. Your mother can't bear it.

ELIAS. No, no! I knew, though, it had to come. In one way or another. It had to come, sometime.

HANNAH. Can you bear to hear it?

CLARA. I must find out. — Tell me — ?

HANNAH. What is it?

CLARA. Elias — are n't you there?

ELIAS. Here I am, mother.

CLARA. Rachel?

ELIAS. What do you mean, mother?

CLARA. Where is Rachel?

ELIAS. She is getting up now. She sat up with me until twelve o'clock last night. And then she was n't able any longer.

CLARA. How, my child — oh, how — did this happen?

ELIAS. That we lost our father's faith?

CLARA. That you lost your father's faith, my children?

[SANG *comes in.*]

SANG. You have lost your faith? — My son? — Have *you* lost your faith?

HANNAH. Look at Clara! Clara!

SANG. [*Hastens to her. He lays his hand upon her.*] It stops. It did not come. — Thank God!

CLARA. It is — passing away. — But hold me, dear!

SANG. I will hold you.

CLARA. And don't let me cry! Oh!

SANG. No, no! Don't cry! [*He leans over her and kisses her.*] Be strong now! — Clara! — That 's it! You must not be distressed. You must remember how distressed *they* have been. In all their conflict and pain they have tried to spare us. And shall we not spare them?

CLARA. Yes.

SANG. See, that is why you had this attack. We were to have time to consider matters. Else, perhaps, we should have become bitter against them. Especially I in my zeal. Where is Rachel?

HANNAH. She will be here presently. She sat up with Elias until twelve o'clock last night.

SANG. Those children! Oh, those children! — How could you — ? — No, no! I don't want to know it.

You were always honest. If you have done this — then you *had* to do it.

ELIAS. I had to. But it has been terrible.

SANG. You came by your faith too easily here with me. For I am altogether a man of the emotions. Perhaps this is but the beginning of a faith which cannot be lost.

ELIAS. I feel like a criminal; — but I am not!

SANG. Do you think I doubt you for a

moment, my son? Don't misunderstand me
in that way, because I can't quite control
myself! That comes from my having built
so firmly on your faith. — So it will take
time, before I — No, no, no! Forgive me,
Elias! It is surely not your fault.

[RACHEL *comes in, steps timidly a few paces
into the background. He sees her.*]

Rachel! — Oh, Rachel, dear! [*She comes
to him and falls on her knees.*] From your
early childhood you have taught me more
faith than all books. —

How can this be possible? No, if they
have won her over — still I must know
how! — For that any one could take you
away from me —

RACHEL. Not from *you*, father!

SANG. Forgive me! Oh! I did not wish
to hurt your feelings. — Come to me, child!
[*She throws her arms about his neck.*] I
promise you, children, that from now on
I shall not mention it again. — But first
I must get to know — and you surely will
not wonder at that? — how this has come
to pass.

ELIAS. If you were to talk with me
about it for days on end, father, — I surely
could not tell you all.

SANG. No, that is not my way. I cannot
discuss my faith. I don't know how to at all.

ELIAS. But you will certainly listen to
me — ?

SANG. If it will comfort you, — that is
quite another matter. Then you know I
will listen.

But can't you tell it quite briefly — ?
Quite briefly?

What was it that made you — that, —
well, that determined you, children?

ELIAS. I can tell you in a very few
words. Rachel and I did not find Christians
to be as you had taught us.

SANG. But, child — ?

ELIAS. You had sent us to the best men
you knew. And they undoubtedly were the
best. But Rachel and I agreed, and she
was the one who said it first : — "There is
only one Christian, and that is father."

SANG. But child, child!

ELIAS. If the others had been but a little more or a little less of what you are, a
part of it, — in *that* case we should certainly
not have felt disappointed. But they are
something else ; — entirely different.

SANG. What do you mean?

ELIAS. Their Christianity is a *compromise.*

In their life and teaching they submit
to the established order of things — that
which is established in their place and
their time. To institutions, to customs, to
prejudices, to economic conditions, and to
all other conditions.

They have found ways and means to make
their doctrine tally with conditions as they
are.

SANG. Are n't you a little too severe?

ELIAS. *You* seek out the most ideal in
it, and follow that. That makes the difference.

SANG. But how does this difference concern *you*, my child?

ELIAS. It started us thinking, father. —
Can you wonder at that?

SANG. Think as much as you will! If
only you do not judge.

RACHEL. I don't think we did. And do
you know why? Because we saw that their
doctrine was as natural for them as yours
is for you.

SANG. Well?

ELIAS. But what, then, is Christianity?
It is certainly not their kind?

SANG. Supposing it is n't. What harm is
there in it? If they practice it as they understand it?

RACHEL. Is Christianity, then, something
only one in a million can attain to, father
dear?

ELIAS. Must all the others remain bun-
glers in it?

SANG. What do you mean by a Christian?

ELIAS. Him alone do I call a Christian
who has learned from Jesus the secret of
perfection, and who strives after it in *all*
things.

SANG. Ah, that is a lovely definition!
You have something of your mother's fine
perception. — Ah, it has always been my
great dream that sometime you should —
No, no, no! — I promised you, children,
and I shall hold to it. You said — ? That
is very true : excellent!

But, my son, may not every one be permitted to *try* to become a Christian, without
necessarily being called a bungler? What?
Is it not right here that faith pieces out our
imperfection? And one man's merit atones
for the infirmity of millions.

ELIAS. There you have it! When we strive with all our hearts — then it is that faith helps out.

SANG. Well, then — ?

ELIAS. That is the practice of only one man, — and that man is you. The others — No, don't be afraid! I don't say it in order to accuse them. What right have I to do that? The others — either, they reduce so much the demands of Christianity that they can accept things quietly ; — it suits them well enough to do that ; — or, they really try — and overreach themselves! Yes, that's the word!

RACHEL. Yes, that's the word.

And so it was, dear father, that I said to Elias : "But if these ideals agree so little with people's conditions and abilities, even in these days, they cannot come from a Being who knows everything."

SANG. Was it *you*, who said that? —

ELIAS. We could no longer get rid of Rachel's doubts. And so we began to study. We followed these ideals backwards through history — and went *beyond* our era.

RACHEL. They are — all of them — much older than Christianity, father!

SANG. I know it, my child.

ELIAS. They were preached ages ago by religious enthusiasts . . .

SANG. . . . By religious enthusiasts among Orientals and Greeks, in an age of despair ; an age, in which the best of men only longed to depart, to depart this life for a land of new life! I know this, my children.

Was it here that you stumbled? Oh, you poor dears!

As if the land of new life, the millennium, were not just as true, even if it is an old, an age-old Oriental dream?

And if it has been so long in coming to pass that weak souls are beginning to call it an impossible dream — and the yearnings that lead to it, impossible ideals, . . . what does that prove?

Nothing about the teaching, but much about the teachers. Yes, alas! — much about the teachers.

Without talking about them, I will only tell what happened to myself. I saw that Christianity was crawling on its belly — and even then avoided all difficult places. Why does it do that? I asked myself. Is it because, if it should rise to its full stature, it would raise all things off their hinges?

Is it Christianity which is impossible? Or is it men who do not dare?

If only *one* dared — would there not be thousands who would dare? Then I felt that I ought to try to be this one. And that, I think, every one ought to try. In fact, if he does not, he has no faith. Because to have faith is to know that all things are possible to him that believeth — and then to show that faith!

Am I saying this in order to boast? On the contrary, I say it in order to accuse myself. For although I have now built so high and have received such grace, even I, for all that, fall again and again from God.

Have n't I been thinking all this time that it was *impossible* to save her there alone? Have n't I doubted, and waited for others to help?

Therefore God has taken His help from me. Therefore did He permit that you also should fall before "the impossible," and come to tell me of it. For thus His hour was to be prepared. *Now* He will show to all of us what is possible.

Ah — I went about and did not understand. Now I understand. I am to do it *alone!* Now I have received the command ; now I can do it.

Therefore came the great grace of preparation on this very day. All signs point that way.

Clara, do you hear? It is no longer I who speak ; it is the great certainty within me, — and you know from Whom that always comes. [*He kneels down by her.*]

Clara, my sweet beloved, why should you not be as dear to God as one who believes entirely? As if God were not the Father of all!

God's love is no privilege of the believers. It is the privilege of those who have faith that they *feel* His love and rejoice in it — and in its name make the impossible possible.

You patient one, you faithful one! Now I leave you to make trial of it. [*He rises.*]

Yes! In order to make trial of it! I shall go into the church, children ; for I want to be alone. And I shall not come from there until I have procured from God's hands sleep for your mother, and after sleep, health ; so that she may arise and walk among us.

Do not be afraid! I feel He will! He will

not grant it to me straightway; for this time I have doubted. But I shall stay and wait patiently for the austere, merciful Lord. — Farewell.

[*He kneels over her in a short prayer.*]
Farewell!

[*He kisses her. She lies motionless. He arises.*]

Thank you, my children! Now you have helped me, indeed. More than I could have hoped.

Now I myself will ring the bell for my prayer. So with the first stroke of the bell you will know that I have begun to pray for mother. Peace be with you!

HANNAH. [*Has mechanically opened the door for him.* SANG *goes out.*] This is . . . This is . . . [*She bursts into tears.*]

ELIAS. I must see . . . I must see him go in. [*He goes out.*]

RACHEL [*coming forward*]. Mother! Mother!

HANNAH. Don't speak to her. She is looking at you; but don't speak to her!

RACHEL. I am afraid.

HANNAH. Where I stand, I can see your father. Now he has almost reached the church. — Come! •

RACHEL. No! . . . No, I can't stand this! I am so afraid! — Mother! She looks at me; but she does not answer me. — Mother!

HANNAH. Hush, Rachel!

[*The bell begins to ring.*]

RACHEL. [*Sinks upon her knees. After a while, she starts up with a suppressed cry.*] For God's sake, Hannah!

HANNAH. What is it?

RACHEL. Mother is asleep!

HANNAH. Asleep?

RACHEL. Mother is asleep!

HANNAH. Really and truly?

RACHEL. I must find Elias. I must tell Elias! [*She goes out.*]

HANNAH. She sleeps like a child. Oh, God!

[*She kneels down. A rumbling sound is heard, growing louder and louder; rising to terrible power. There are shrieks without. The house trembles. The roar increases to thunder.*]

RACHEL [*outside*]. The mountain is falling! [*She shrieks, then comes rushing into the room.*] The mountain is falling upon the church! Upon us! Right over the church!

Upon us! On father, on us! That rushing and roaring! — it is getting dark, — Oh!

[*She cowers down, turning her face away.*]

ELIAS [*outside*]. Father! — Father! — Oh!

HANNAH [*bending over her sister's bed*]. It is coming! It is coming!

[*The uproar has reached its height. Then gradually it abates. Afterwards the church bell can be heard again, above the din.*]

HANNAH [*jumping up*]. It is still ringing! He is alive.

RACHEL. He lives!

ELIAS [*outside*]. Father is alive! [*Nearer.*] The church is standing. [*Comes into the room.*] The church is standing. Father is alive. Right by the church the slide turned aside — went toward the left. Father is alive, he is ringing the bell. Oh, God!

[*He throws himself over his mother's bed.*]

RACHEL. [*Comes forward.*] Elias! Mother — ?

HANNAH. She is asleep!

ELIAS. [*Jumps up.*] She is asleep?

RACHEL. Yes, she is asleep —

[*The church bell continues to ring.*]

HANNAH. She is sleeping as quietly as before.

ACT II

A small timbered room. In the background a door leading to an outer porch. The door is wide open. Through it one looks out over a narrow landscape, closed by bare mountains. On the right is a door. On the left, a large window. Over the door leading to the balcony hangs a gilded crucifix, set within a cross, over which is a sheet of glass.

In the background to the left stands a sofa; before it is a table upon which lie some books. Chairs stand against the walls.

ELIAS *enters hurriedly from the balcony. He is restless. In linen trousers and light shoes. He wears only a shirt on his upper body and has no hat. He stops, goes to the window and listens. Far away one hears quite distinctly a psalm sung by a man's voice.* ELIAS *shows strong emotion.*

RACHEL *enters softly through the door at the right, which had been closed. She closes it again after her. Her brother makes signs to her to stop and listen.*

RACHEL. [*Also strongly moved, says softly:*] Let me open the door into mother's room !

ELIAS [*softly*]. Is mother awake, then ?

RACHEL. No; but she will hear father, just the same. [*She disappears into the room on the right; then comes in again, leaving the door open behind her; says softly:*] She smiled.

ELIAS [*softly*]. O Rachel !

RACHEL [*moved*]. Elias ! — Don't speak ; — I can't bear it !

ELIAS. Look out of the window, Rachel ! — Could there be anything more beautiful ? Hundreds of people in *silence*, oh, such silence, about the church ; and he within, in prayer and song, without any idea that any one is outside. The windows are open, but they are too high for him to see them. And they don't dare for anything in the world to make a sound and disturb him !

See ! He spoke of a chain of prayer. All those people around the church — *that* is a chain of prayer !

RACHEL. Yes.

[*They listen to the singing. It stops.*] He is singing often to-day.

ELIAS. Close the doors, now ! I have so much to tell you. I have been here twice to look for you.

RACHEL. [*Goes out on tip-toe to the right ; returns, closing the door behind her. She says in a louder tone of voice:*] Still more people have come this afternoon.

ELIAS. And more are coming, all the time — from miles around ! You can't see all of them ; for many of them have gone to the grove to listen to the lay-preachers. Out there they will not disturb father. And then there are people going back and forth — between the grove and the church — — But just look down there by the shore —

RACHEL. Dear me, what 's that ? The fields are black with people. What is that ?

ELIAS. It 's the mission-ship that has arrived.

RACHEL. The mission-ship ?

ELIAS. Don't you know that all the people from the east of here have rented a steamboat to bring them to the missionary meeting in the town ? It is here in the fjord now.

RACHEL. Here ?

ELIAS. Yes, here !

RACHEL. But why did it come here ?

ELIAS. For the miracle ! When our delegates — Pastor Kroyer and some other pastor — went aboard at the stopping-place outside by the sea . . .

RACHEL. Well . . . ?

ELIAS. . . . And told what had happened here yesterday, and that father was still in the church, praying . . .

RACHEL. . . . Ah, I understand, now !

ELIAS. . . . Not one of them wanted to go on ! All wanted to come here ! The Bishop and the pastors begged them to keep their promise and stick to their agreement ; but no, they wanted to come here ! So the others had to give in. And now they are here.

RACHEL. The pastors also ?

ELIAS. The bishop and the pastors — of course !

RACHEL. They won't come in here, will they ? — You should be dressed a little differently, Elias.

ELIAS. I can't stand wearing clothes.

RACHEL. You can't stand — ?

ELIAS. They burn me. And then I have a longing — as if I wanted to walk on air. I can't describe it to you; but now and then I think I ought to be able to do it.

RACHEL. But Elias — !

ELIAS. There he is! There he is, walking!

RACHEL. Who ? — That one there ?

ELIAS. It is certainly the same man. Yes, it is ! That man they carried here this morning, and he was sick, oh, so sick ; and now he is walking about ; there you see him !

It was to-day, when father sang for the first time. No one had expected that he would sing ; we started to weep, all of us. Then the sick man rose up of himself. We did not notice it till he walked among us. —

Mother will also rise up, Rachel ! I can see it now before my eyes.

RACHEL. She will rise up. I expect it at any moment ; but it makes me afraid. Why are you looking at me, Elias ?

ELIAS. Because — at times, when you speak, it seems like verse. When others speak, too.

RACHEL. But, Elias — ?

ELIAS. And, at times, again, — now, for instance, — I hear only the sound of the words; not their sense. Because I hear at the same time something — something that is *not* spoken.

RACHEL. That is *not* spoken?

ELIAS. Most often, as if father was calling; — calling me by name — as he did yesterday morning. [*Agitated.*] He must have had some meaning when he gave me that name. It sounds in my ears and accuses me — and with his voice.

At times it pursues me without ceasing! And then I feel a desire to plunge into the greatest danger. I am certain to escape from it unharmed. No, don't be afraid! There is no one here.

RACHEL. Elias, come and sit down with me in mother's room! There is peace in there with mother.

ELIAS. I cannot. — Rachel, answer me before God, — try your final, most penetrating doubt, and answer me: *Is* this a miracle, that we saw here?

RACHEL Oh, God, Elias, — why do you always come back to that?

ELIAS. But is it not terrible that the only two who perhaps still doubt, — that they are his own children?

I would gladly give my life to be sure now.

RACHEL. No more, Elias! I beg you!

ELIAS. Only tell me what *you* believe! How about this mountain-slide? It was too great to be a mere *accident*. Is n't that so? And mother's sleep? Sleep — the moment he began ringing? And sleep despite the mountain-slide? Sleep, as long as *he* is praying?

Is not this, indeed, a miracle? And why, then, is not the other thing a miracle, too, a great miracle?

RACHEL. I almost believe it is, Elias.

ELIAS. You do?

RACHEL. But I am afraid of it, all the same!

ELIAS. Afraid of it, if it is a miracle? But then you cannot believe that it is a miracle?

RACHEL. Oh, yes.

ELIAS. For it *cannot* surely be his magnetic power of healing alone? Or the influence of his personality? No, it is more! Is it a miracle? Do you feel sure about it?

RACHEL. I cannot speak about this now. It is just to escape from it that I seek shelter in mother's room. It is as if mother's truthfulness fills all the room and drowns such questions.

Now the question is a different one, Elias!

ELIAS. A different one?

RACHEL. After this! What will come after this — when she has risen up? For that will not be the end. In the end —

ELIAS. In the end — ?

RACHEL. In the end it will be a question of our lives! [*She bursts into tears.*]

ELIAS. Rachel — ? My God!

RACHEL. Mother no longer has any strength left to resist. And he will urge her on — now all the more!

ELIAS. To what?

RACHEL. To this — whatever it is!

ELIAS. But suppose now it is a miracle, Rachel? Why be afraid, then?

RACHEL. I cannot foresee all the consequences for father and mother, for all of us. Ah, don't you understand me at all?

ELIAS. No.

RACHEL. No! It is all the same to me, what it is; but it will destroy us. It will kill us, finally!

ELIAS. The miracle?

RACHEL. Yes, yes. It is no blessing; it is a curse; — Elias!

[*She pulls him further back into the room.*]

ELIAS. What is it?

RACHEL. There is a man standing right underneath the window and staring in. — A strange man, so pale.

ELIAS. . . . In a coat buttoned all the way up — ?

RACHEL. Yes. — [*With a low cry.*] Why, there he is standing in the room!

[*She walks backwards, as if retreating before a vision, and seeks refuge in her mother's room.*]

ELIAS. In the room? — Here!

[*At this moment, a* STRANGER *appears on the balcony, from the left, crosses the threshold, stops, and looks about.*]

ELIAS [*as the* STRANGER *appears*]. There he is!

THE STRANGER. Will you permit me — ?

ELIAS. Who are you?

THE STRANGER. Does that make any difference?

ELIAS. I have seen you about here since yesterday.

THE STRANGER. Yes. I came here over the mountains.

ELIAS. Over the mountains?

THE STRANGER. I stood up there and saw the avalanche descend.

ELIAS. Indeed!

THE STRANGER. And heard the ringing of the bell. And to-day I beheld the sick man who rose up, when your father sang. — And now I ask you: Is it there, in that room, that your mother is sleeping?

ELIAS. Yes. But not in the next room; in the one behind it.

THE STRANGER. But if she rises up, — she will come in here — ? She will go towards the church, where he is — ? Am I right? She will come? This way?

ELIAS. Now that you mention it — ?

THE STRANGER. And therefore I ask you — I pray you — : May I stay here? — Wait here? Behold it? I have longed for it so ardently. And I can resist it no longer.

I shall not come in before I feel impelled to. I am not going to sit here and trouble you — be in the way. But when I feel *irresistibly impelled* to come in and wait here and see — May I?

ELIAS. Yes.

THE STRANGER. Thank you!

Let me tell you: this day decides my life.
[*He goes out by the balcony to the right.*]

ELIAS. This day decides my life! [KROYER *enters by the balcony from the left.*] Kroyer did you see the man there? The one to the right?

KROYER. Yes. Who was it?

ELIAS. Don't you know him?

KROYER. No.

ELIAS. A remarkable person, certainly. — This day decides my life! My God! That is the word I needed!

KROYER. I expected, Elias, that this would be an important day for you.

Indeed, who could resist what is happening here?

The fact alone of these hundreds kneeling in prayer about the church, and he inside, and knowing nothing about it! I cannot think of anything more beautiful!

ELIAS. Yes, yes! — Oh, I will cast aside fear and doubt; — this day will have to decide! Oh, the happy word!

I struggled and suffered without getting anywhere. And suddenly it is *given* to me! And straightway peace has come with it. — Let us talk together!

KROYER. No — not now. I have a message for you.

ELIAS. For me? — From whom?

KROYER. I came back here with the mission-ship.

ELIAS. I know it.

KROYER. And now the Bishop and the pastors wish to ask whether they may have this room for an hour?

ELIAS. What for?

KROYER. They feel the need of considering what attitude they are to take toward what is happening here. And we do not know any other place where we can be alone. — Well, now, don't be so astonished. We professionals, we of the preaching business, must of course try to look at such matters a little more judiciously, you know, than others.

ELIAS. But that would produce a note of discord in here, would n't it?

KROYER. Which may be transformed into harmony! For who can resist the miracle?

ELIAS. You are right! But in here? Wedge themselves in, as it were, between father and mother? And supposing father begins to sing again? Why, then we could n't open the door in to mother?

KROYER. What answer, do you think, your mother or your father would have given them?

ELIAS. Undoubtedly, yes! You are right! They shall have the room. — But let me be spared the — ?

KROYER. *I* will manage it. Both doors in to your mother are closed?

ELIAS. Yes.

KROYER. Then I will close the window here, and the door also, when the rest have come in.

ELIAS. Let *them* lock themselves in! I will go out and seek sympathy with the people out there. *They* trustingly expect something great to happen to-day, — and surely they will not wait long in vain.
[*He goes out.*]

KROYER. [*Follows him.*] Shall we pray for that, Elias?

ELIAS. Yes. Now I am going to try.
[*Both go out to the left.*]

KROYER. [*Comes in again from the left.*] Come in, please!
[*He goes to the window and closes it. Meanwhile the BISHOP and the PASTORS enter. KROYER goes back and closes the door.*]

BLANK.[1] Those who are acquainted in this ha-ouse, couldn't they get us something to ee-at?

THE BISHOP. We are cutting rather a comical figure — I know. But the fact is, we were terribly sea-sick.

BREI. We couldn't keep a-anything on our stomachs.

THE BISHOP. And when we finally got into smooth water, and we were to get a square meal —

BREI. Then came the mi-iracle!

FALK. I am so *awfully* hungry.

KROYER. I am afraid no one here has thought anything about food to-day, either; but I will go and see.   [*He goes out.*]

JENSEN. I've got downright hallucinations about eating. I've read about such things; but one reads so much one can't believe.

It's especially grouse I am seeing.

FALK. Grouse!

JENSEN. I even smell it; roast grouse!

BLANK. Gra-ouse?

SEVERAL. Are we going to have grouse?

KROYER. [*Returns and says while still in the doorway:*] I am very sorry. I was in both kitchen and pantry; both empty. And no one there.

BREI. Not a single soul?

FALK. I am so *awfully* hungry.

THE BISHOP. Now, my friends, don't let us cut too comical a figure.

We shall have to put up with the inevitable. Let us begin. Be so kind as to be seated!

[*He himself sits down on the sofa ; the others take chairs.*]

In brief, then, and as quietly as possible — for there is a sick person in the house, as you know, — we must arrive at an agreement about what attitude we shall take in this matter.

It has always been my opinion that, at the inception of such a movement, the clergy should, as a rule, remain neutral. Neither agree nor disagree, until the movement has subsided sufficiently *to be judged.*

To-day, therefore, I would have been profoundly grateful, if we had been permitted to journey on. But they would not let us journey on.

_____
[1] Blank and Brei talk in dialect of the Southwest of Norway, characterized by diphthongization of long vowels and high *a*'s.

THE PASTORS [*muttering to each other*]. They would not let us journey on. No, they would not let us journey on.

THE BISHOP. They all wanted to come here, here where the miraculous power, as it were, was thought to reside. And I do not reproach them for it.

But if we are among them, on the same ship, they will demand to hear our opinion. When we arrive at the meeting, people will want to hear our opinion there also. — Now, what is our opinion?

KROYER. Permit me to say, in all respect: either, we *believe* in the miracle, and shall act accordingly; or, we do not believe in it, and shall act according to *that.*

THE BISHOP. Hm? — There is a third possibility, my young friend.

THE PASTORS [*muttering to each other*]. There is a third possibility! Assuredly, there is a third possibility!

THE BISHOP. The older one grows, and the more experience one gets, the more difficult it becomes to form a conviction — especially, where supernatural matters are concerned. — In this case, time and conditions would scarcely permit of an investigation. And, supposing we arrive at different conclusions? In these times of skepticism, what kind of impression would be made by a disagreement among the clergy on the matter of miracles? About whether or no miracles are being wrought, these days, somewhere up North?

I see that old Blank wants the floor.

BLANK. If I understand Your Reverence correctly, it is not our business to deci-ide, once for all, whether we have to deal here with a mi-iracle or noa. Let God our Father deci-ide about that!

THE BISHOP. Yes, let Him decide! That is quite right! Thank you, dear old Blank!

BLANK. I hold that mi-iracles are subject to laws ju-ust as much as all other things, although we cannot perceive those laws. I hold the sa-ame as does Professor Petersen.

FALK. In that book he never publishes?

BLANK. But which he expects to publish in some years.

But if that is the case — what importance attaches to the individual miracle—whether we of little insight can see it or noa?

If the people believe they see it, let us praise God together with them.

THE BISHOP. So it is your opinion, after all, that we are to approve of the miracle?

BLANK. Neither approve nor disapprove. We simply praise God together with the people.

THE BISHOP. No, dear Blank, we shan't be able to get around this difficulty by singing hymns of praise.

THE PASTORS [*muttering among themselves*]. We shan't be able to get around this with hymns of praise. No, we shan't be able to get around this with hymns of praise.

THE BISHOP. The Reverend Brei has the floor.

BREI. I really don't understand what objections there are to acknowledging the miracle at once. Are miracles so rare, then? I am *always* seeing miracles. We are so used to them in my parish that it would be the unusual thing *not* to see them.

FALK. Wouldn't Brei be kind enough to tell us something about those miracles in his parish?

THE BISHOP. No, because that would tend to make us digress. — [*To* JENSEN.] You stood up? Do you want the floor?

JENSEN. Yes. All depends in this case on the fact that confronts us. Is it a miracle — perhaps several — or is it not a miracle?

KROYER. Precisely.

JENSEN. Every single miracle ought to be investigated. But then we ought to consult expert opinion, have a good medical authority, and perhaps have testimony taken by an efficient lawyer. All this done — then and only then, can we pastors with any safety hand down our spiritual verdict.

By "spiritual" I do not mean what we see and hear in the case of the lay-preachers and others who are filled by, or upon whom has descended, the spirit, as they say.

I mean, now as always, an unpretentious, solid, and matter-of-fact truth — all the more "spiritual" the more unpretentious, solid, and matter-of-fact it is.

FALK. Hear!

JENSEN. In this way it would probably appear that miracles never come to pass like this. Never!

It does not come, expected by hundreds and thousands, ready to do homage, and inflamed with ecstasy and curiosity.

Yes, I mean curiosity!

No, the miracle happens in a plain, quiet, unpretentious, matter-of-fact way, and to plain, quiet, unpretentious, matter-of-fact people.

FALK. As if spoken from my own heart.

KROYER. If Falk will permit me, may I make this remark. Ever since I have been up here in the North as pastor, I have noticed that it is just the most matter-of-fact people who often most easily fall a prey to superstition.

BLANK. Quite my experience! Quite true!

KROYER. In their skepticism they often deny what is plain to every one. But in return, they are attacked in the rear, as it were, by some inexplicable fear, and are thus influenced by things that are clean beyond our vision.

I have come to think that the supernatural has become so much of an inherited craving, that if we expel it one way . . .

BLANK. . . . It will return the other! Just what I have thought!

FALK. Well, now, whether it comes from the matter-of-fact or the visionary, I just want to inquire point-blank: Am I to understand that it is your intention to give up what clearness and order we have won in the church, and begin to flit about again like so many ordained *night-owls?*

BREI. Are you referring to me?

[*The* PASTORS *roar with laughter.*]

THE BISHOP. Hushshsh! Let us remember that there is a sick person in there!

FALK. The longing for miracles is an excrescence on faith, in the same manner as this lay-preaching business is on preaching — a derangement, a disease, in fact an atavism, an eructation.

[*In suppressing their laughter, the* PASTORS *begin to cough.*]

THE BISHOP. Hushshsh!

FALK. The miracle which is not sanctioned by the priests, and which is not, so to speak, appointed and installed by the supreme ecclesiastical council, presided over by His Majesty the King, that miracle is in my estimation like a vagabond, a tramp, a *burglar.*

[*The* BISHOP *laughs softly; the* PASTORS *likewise, with their eyes on him.*]

FALK. It is all right to be simple-minded. I, too, have been simple-minded. But if as a pastor in a large city one is to be sorrowful with the sorrowing at the grave at one o'clock, — and to be glad with the glad wedding-guests at three o'clock, — and perhaps be at a pauper's death-bed at four o'clock, — and then dine at the castle at five, — one soon learns to know the weakness of humankind. And one learns, not to depend upon individuals, but upon institutions.

Wherever the miracle appears, all institutions perish in a storm of sentiments and emotions !

For this reason the Catholic Church has tried to institutionalize miracles. But in so doing it has lost the respect of the intelligent, and has left to it only the simple-minded and the self-seeking.

I was once in a society of ladies, where I was alone with something like twenty ladies. [*Mirth.*] One of these ladies had a spasm. At once, a second. Then one after another, until there were six. [*The mirth increases.*] So I dashed water, first at those six, one at a time [*he imitates the action with his hands*] ; then on several of the others ; for such things are contagious.

[*Loud laughter.*]

THE BISHOP. [*The first to recover himself.*] Hushshsh !

[*He bursts out laughing again; finally, regains his composure.*]

Hushshsh !

FALK. That is good for them, I think. Dash water at them !

[*Laughter and coughing into handkerchiefs continues. Some of the PASTORS thank him heartily.*]

KROYER. Of course we know Falk and that he is a good man, — in spite of his odd ways. I believe that if, for example, he saw the old pastor's widow here — she is now almost a hundred years old — *he* would be the last one to dash water at her — although she goes about among us like a living miracle and infects all with her belief. The same is true of that young girl, Agatha Florvaagen, who tends the old woman. The miracle which brought her back to life, I saw *myself*, and many with me. To *our* eyes, to *our* hands, she was cold and dead. And he prayed over her, and raised her to life ! You must believe a man's testimony ! [*Astonishment.*]

They are here now.

SEVERAL. Are they here ?

KROYER. Perhaps they will come into this room. They are coming toward the house, though very slowly. The old woman wants to see. She wants to see her whom the avalanche could not awaken.

But now look at the old woman! Speak to her! Speak to the girl who is with her ! And you will get answers as clear, as trustworthy, as her own face.

This will help us more than all our abstract discussions.

I do not say this to find fault. I myself thought as you do, up until I became pastor up here. No one has felt more painfully than I what retractions the Church has been forced to make in this matter, and what paltry doctrines, what evasions are now left to us.

We are poor, without the power of miracles, — and without the courage to pray for miracles, — and we are forced to pretend either that we can do without it, or that we have the power and glory in its possession.

I know each one of you well enough to be sure that if you *dared* — yes, if you were absolutely certain that here you would see performed a miracle so great, that all the immortal conditions of the Bible were fulfilled : " *all those who saw believed* ": — ah, however frail you might be otherwise, you would become as children, you would surrender yourself altogether, you would devote all the days left to you to make it known!

[*Emotion, especially among the older men.*]

I dare make these avowals on your behalf, my brethren, because I stand within the circles of the spirit — whereof it is said you must be either within or without ! Once within, all the pitiful evasions vanish of themselves, and we dare at last confess the truth !

What is there left of Christianity, now the Church has lost the power of the miracle ?

ELIAS [*coming in from outside*]. Excuse me ! — Here is some one who wishes to see my mother. It is the old pastor's widow.

[*All arise. In the doorway they see the PASTOR'S WIDOW and AGATHA. ELIAS opens the door leading to the right, and goes in himself. The PASTORS have taken their chairs and respectfully make room.*]

THE PASTOR'S WIDOW [*who has come in as far as the threshold*].

Leave me now, Agatha! — Now I wish to be alone. — Alone. — For here where the Lord has been, — here is holy ground. — Here is holy ground.— Here one is "face to face." — And then it is best to be alone.

[*She stands now so that she can see into* CLARA'S *room. Then she makes an obeisance. She stretches both her hands aloft in great ecstasy. She looks in again and makes an obeisance. Then she turns to go.*]

She was white — shining white. — I might have known it. — Shining white. — And slept like a child. — Now I have seen it. — That throws light on all. — Oh, how that throws light on all! — Thank you for letting me be alone.

AGATHA. But *were* you alone?

THE PASTOR'S WIDOW. Quite alone.— No one but I. — She was shining white.

[*They are now outside the room.*]

ELIAS. [*Comes in from the right.*] Both doors are closed again. And now I shall close this one, too.

[*Goes out. The* PASTORS *stand silent.*]

KROYER. You did not speak to her?

THE BISHOP. No.

KROYER. There is a gleam of sunshine on the faces of all of you. — I will tell you why : — Those upon whose faces the supernatural has shone reflect its light.

Let us talk about this!

[*They assemble again and sit down.*]

JENSEN. May I put a question? — Don't you consider conversion to be a miracle?

KROYER. That which we call the miracle of conversion may be traced step by step by psychology ; therefore it is not a miracle.

It has its equivalent in other great religions, and in the purely moral conversion, although that is a secret one.

But a Christianity which is founded on miracles and in the course of time has lost the power to perform miracles — what is that?

Moral precepts, nothing more.

FALK. The essential of Christianity is not the miraculous, but the belief in a resurrection.

KROYER. . . . Which is possessed by *all* the great religions? Which all men of religious feeling have?

THE BISHOP. What, then, do *you* think Christianity is?

KROYER. To my feeling, Christianity is infinitely more than a moral precept.

We find precepts more full and more subtle in other places than the New Testament. To me, it is infinitely more than the power of sacrifice ; if that were not the case, then many another belief would stand as high as it.

Either, then, Christianity is a life in God, *beyond* and above the world and all its precepts ; or it is not. Either, it is more than fidelity to any creed whatsoever, a new world, that is, a miracle ; or it is not.

[*He sits down trembling with emotion.*]

There was so much, . . . I wanted to say; . . . but . . . I cannot.

THE BISHOP. As soon as you came aboard to-day, dear Kroyer, I noticed that you had over-exerted yourself and were sick. But they all become so who follow Pastor Sang.

THE STRANGER. [*Has opened the door from the balcony without closing it again. He has approached step by step.*] May I say a word? [*All turn around ; some get up.*]

THE BISHOP. Is that you, Bratt?

OTHERS. Pastor Bratt?

STILL OTHERS. Is *that* Bratt?

THE BISHOP. You did not come with us? How did you come here?

BRATT. Over the mountains.

THE BISHOP. Over the mountains? — You are not bound for the missionary meeting, then?

BRATT. No, I wanted to come here.

THE BISHOP. I understand you.

BRATT. I wanted to come to the miracle. — And so I came yesterday just as the mountain-slide descended. I was standing on the mountain, and saw it, not far away. And I heard the sound of the bell. — And I have been here since. — And this forenoon I saw a sick man carried to the church, and, during the pastor's song of psalms in there, arise, thank God and depart. May I say a word?

THE BISHOP. Of course.

BRATT. For I am a man in need, brethren, who come to you to beg you for help!

THE BISHOP. Speak, dear Bratt!

BRATT. I say to myself : "*Here*, at last, I stand before the miracle." And in the next moment : "Is it really a miracle?"

For this is not the first place I have visited, seeking to look upon it. I have turned back a disappointed man from all the places in Europe where miracles are wrought. Here, certainly, people's faith is simpler and greater ; and this is a great man. What I have seen here has taken possession of me with supernatural power. And in the next moment again, doubt ! That is my curse ! And I have drawn it down upon myself by promising the miracle to the faithful ones, these seven years I have been priest. Promising it to them, because it was so written — although I myself doubted ; for I have never yet seen it granted to one of the believing ! For seven years I have taught what I did not myself believe.

For seven years, therefore, have I prayed, every time the dark days came — and they came often, like the sleepless nights ! — prayed fervently : " Where is that power to perform miracles which Thou didst promise to those that believed in Thee ? "

[*He bursts into tears.*]

THE BISHOP. Ah, *you* speak frankly, dear Bratt ! You have always done so.

BRATT. He has proclaimed in binding words, each one stronger than the last, that the believer has this power. Power, indeed, to do even greater things than did the Son of Man. And what has become of it ?

After eighteen hundred years of infinite laboring in the faith, there is among us as yet not one of faith sufficient to work a miracle ! God's own promise is still unfulfilled !

The power of faith cannot have been weakened. That power cannot have gone contrary to all other powers of the race — have diminished by constant use. No !

After more than eighteen hundred years of preaching in many, many races, it must now form the inheritance of a thousand years, multiplied by education.

And still it is not strong enough to give us the miracle ? The yearning of all the faithful together still cannot bring forth one individual who has the power to work miracles, so that all that see believe ? For this condition stated in the Bible is indispensable ! Again and again we read : " *All those who saw believed.*" — A miracle, then, which will make all that see it believe. — And thousands upon thousands fall away ; because, although promised, it is not given us.

A man with a modern education, an enlightened woman of our times, will not be satisfied with those things which a man or a woman of an earlier time accepted as a matter of course. Not because their power of faith is less ; but because it is more *guarded*. Their conversion is so much more profound, and so much more deeply felt, that it is natural, even just, that they should be harder to win over. Indeed, he who accomplishes this wins the greatest prize that can fall to any one's lot in this life !

Therefore : stake a corresponding amount on your side ! Or else you will never win them over.

[*Subdued talking among the* PASTORS.]

Religion is no longer man's only ideal. If it is to be the highest, then you must prove it to be so ! Men can live and die for what they love — for their fatherland, their family, their convictions. And, since this is the highest that can be found within the bounds of natural law, and you must show them something still higher — very well, then, go *beyond* these bounds ! Show them the miraculous power !

[*Great agitation among the* PASTORS.]

FALK [*standing up*]. There is, somewhere in Scripture, a word of wrath concerning the generation that believes not excepting they see signs.

BRATT. And do you know what that generation answers ?

" We ask only for the signs God himself has promised — promised to those that believe ! Or, have you still not a single one with faith among you ? — Then what do you demand of us ? "

Yes, thus will this generation make answer.

But give this same generation a miracle — one which the very sharpest instruments of doubt cannot dissect — one about which it can be said, " all those who saw believed " ; then you may live to see that it is not the power of faith that is lacking ; but the miracle.

[*The* PASTORS *betray agitation.*]

The teachings need not set a premium on credulity. Even in the acutest of skeptics the elements of faith are the strongest and most numerous ! Is there any one who knows civilized man and is ignorant of that ? Is there a pastor who has not had the experience that, for the most part, the danger is precisely the opposite : that in default of the true, they lapse into a belief in false gods.

SEVERAL [*in subdued tones*]. That is true.

BRATT. Supposing a miracle did appear among us — one so great that "all who saw believed " — ?

First would come the millions rushing to it — those who live in need of it and long for it — the disappointed, the oppressed, the suffering, those who thirst after righteousness.

If it came to their ears that the kingdom of God, in the ancient meaning of the word, had descended to earth again, — no matter where, — weeping, rejoicing, aye, even if most of them knew they were in danger of dying on the way, — rather die on that way than live on any other ! — they would creep forth, each from his village, his cottage, his bed, the sick leading the way, and start out toward the revelation of God.

But they would not come alone. All those who seek for truth on earth would follow them. First would come those whose desire for truth is the greatest; the deep, earnest investigators, the exalted minds. *Their* fervor would be the most beautiful, their belief the most weighty. It is not the desire for truth they lack, not the power to believe ; it is the miracle.

All men desire certainty and peace on the greatest question in the world. Even the frivolous, those who have laid it aside as useless and impossible ! They are, all of them, without exception, so brought up as to long for more than they know, that is, to have faith. But you must give them the pledge !

The pledge that the teachings of the gospel are true ! And once they see *that*, they will believe in what they do *not* see.

Thus it was from the beginning.

Those who *now* rest satisfied with less, — with their personal experience, — they do like the Mohammedans, the Jews, the Buddhists. *They* also appeal to their personal experience, *all* of them !

The pledge that this personal experience is universal truth, that is what is lacking.

And that is what I seek ! For it is promised !

Oh, God, my God ! I am standing here before my last test.

THE BISHOP. Bratt ! Bratt !

BRATT. Before my *last* test. For the struggle exceeds my powers. I shall hand in my resignation as pastor — leave the church, leave my faith — if, if, if — !

[*He bursts into tears.*]

THE BISHOP. My dear son ! You must not —

BRATT. No, do not speak to me ! — I beg you ! — No, aid me to pray ! For it the miracle is not here it does not exist ! Indeed, this man is more than other men ; he is the noblest man living on earth ! A faith such as his no one has seen before. Nor has any man seen such faith *in* his faith.

ALL. That is true !

BRATT. And is it not easy to understand ? He had a large fortune when he came here. He gave away all. There is no counting the number of times he jeopardized his life in helping others. And there is no counting the miracles they believe he has performed. Just because there were so many of them, I had no faith in them.

PASTORS [*in low tones*]. That was the way with me, too.

BRATT. But perhaps we ought to have thought just the opposite ? — namely, that here we see what is meant by "faith " ? The existence of faith is the miracle ! It must work miracles ! Perhaps we ought to have thought thus ?

But whatever we ought to have thought, — we should not have cast glances of professional doubt at him, as *I* did myself, alas ! His love and his faith ought to have humbled me. I accuse myself, and in the depths of my heart beg him for forgiveness !

ALL THE PASTORS [*without exception*]. I too ! I too !

BRATT. He is the best man we know ; he has the greatest faith that exists, — what if the miracle were here ? [*Agitation.*]

JENSEN [*whispering*]. Look at the cross over the door there ! Is it the evening sun — or what is it ?

BRATT. I do not know. But you may rest assured that if the miracle does happen, then thousands will be present whom we do not see.

Ah, if only *we* too were allowed to be there ! If only we too were allowed to be there ! Think ! To witness something so great that "all who saw believed " !

And that *we* should be witnesses — you,

and you, and I? It is too much; it cannot be possible! —

But if it is possible, — then, brethren, there do not live together with us—with us of frail spirit, of little faith, and all uncharitableness! . . .

ALL. . . . Yes, yes! —

BRATT. . . . There do not live in our times others, as highly blessed as we; it is *we* unworthy ones who have been called!

[*Profound agitation.*]

And when I look out into this narrow landscape of bare, rocky fjord, under the cries of the sea-gulls, and think: The kingdom of God began in a luxuriant land, by the beaten roads of the world, in the sunny South, — how great a testimony would it be, if it were to come again in all its glory here, in a poor, secluded village close by the everlasting ice —

FALK. [*Arises, pale as death, and whispers:*] Yes, yes!

SEVERAL. Yes, yes!

BRATT. . . . Then it seems to me as if all signs point to it, and the miracle *must* come! [*All have arisen.*]

BISHOP [*softly*]. Would that it might come, so that I, an old man, might behold it!

BLANK. Yes, if we were but now gathered up into this great faith!

Not because we deserve it; but because we sorely need it.

[OLD BLANK *drops upon his knees; then others do the same.*]

BRATT. Because all the people need it sorely! More and more the longer they wait. Because it is promised. Because it *must* be here, if it *exists*. [*He kneels down.*]

His faith must accomplish it! His is the greatest faith in the world! And faith is able! Oh, it is!

ALL. It is, it is!

BRATT. If it were not able, — then all would be impossible.

Then the other things are not true, either. Then there would be in all this, something excessive — ?

Something beyond human power — ?

RACHEL. [*Calls from within in terror.*] Elias! [*She rushes in from the right, directly toward the window; she opens it, calling with all her might:*] Elias!

[*Then she throws herself backwards and would have fallen but for*

KROYER *catching her. She bursts into tears, but arises quickly, pointing toward the room:*]

There! There! She is no longer alone! Look — look!

[*All are standing. At that moment, ELIAS appears on the balcony. RACHEL at once tears herself away and hurries toward him.*]

Mother! Mother!

ELIAS. Has she risen up?

RACHEL. Yes, yes!

ELIAS. And walks?

RACHEL. Yes! — But she is not alone!

ELIAS. All must hear that!

RACHEL. No, don't go to father!

ELIAS. No; up on the house-top, up in the bell-tower, to ring it out to all the world!

RACHEL. But you have no ladder?

[*She gets no answer; in terror:*]

But there is no ladder!

KROYER [*with a movement of his hand, softly:*] Hush!

THE BISHOP. [*Whispers:*] Listen, ah, listen!

[*From the church is heard:*]

Hallelujah, hallelujah!
Hallelujah, hallelujah!

ALL. [*Drop on their knees and whisper:*] He knows it! He knows it!

[*Then enters CLARA in her white linen gown. Her eyes are fixed on the church; she stops and extends her hands toward the song.*]

ALL THE PASTORS. [*Respond in a low chorus:*]

Hallelujah, hallelujah!
Hallelujah, hallelujah!

RACHEL. [*On the threshold.*] Now father stands in the door.

[*He is now heard singing clear and strong:*]

Hallelujah, hallelujah!
Hallelujah, hallelujah!

[*Then the church bell and all the people join in. There is such jubilant strength in the song, that it sounds as if thousands were singing. It increases as the people in the groves come hurrying toward the scene. At one time it seems as if these "Hallelujahs" were lifting up the house.*

SANG *appears in the doorway; the evening sun rests upon his face. All arise and make way for him.*

He extends both his hands toward
CLARA, *who stands in the middle of
the room. She extends hers toward
him; he advances and embraces
her.*

*The song is pealing about them.
The room is full of people; likewise
the balcony; they climb up to look
over those in front; some stand in
the window.*

*Then she sinks slowly down on his
shoulder. The song stops; only the
bell keeps on ringing.*

*She makes an effort to collect her
strength and arise. She succeeds
only partly; then lifts her head and
looks at him.*]

CLARA. Oh, glorious, — when you came
— my beloved !

[*Her head sinks down again, her
arms drop, and her whole body re-
laxes.*]

SANG. [*Stands and holds her ; lays his
hand upon her heart ; then he bends over her
in astonishment. He looks up toward Heaven,
and says in a childlike way :*]
But this was not my intention — ?

[*He bends his knee and lays her head
upon it; examines her; lays her
down tenderly and rises, looking
again toward Heaven :*]
But this was not my intention — ?
Or ? — or ?
[*Clutches at his heart and falls.*]
[RACHEL *has stood like one petrified,
looking on. Now she screams aloud
and drops on her knees before her
parents.*]

KROYER. What did he mean — by that
" Or " ?

BRATT. I do not know for sure.— But
he died because of it.

RACHEL. Died ? — That is impossible !
[*The bell continues ringing.*]

Reference is made to : —
Leçons sur le système nerveux, faites par J. M. Charcot. Recueillies et publiées par le Dr. Bourne-
ville. 3e édition. 2 vols. Paris, 1881, chez A. Delahaye et E. Lecrosnier.
Études cliniques sur l'hystéro-épilepsie ou grande hystérie, par le Dr. Richer. 1 vol. Paris, 1881,
chez A. Delahaye et E. Lecrosnier.

THE FATHER

By AUGUST STRINDBERG

Translated by N. ERICHSEN

PERSONS

A CAVALRY CAPTAIN
LAURA, *his wife*
BERTHA, *their daughter*
DR. ÖSTERMARK
THE PASTOR
THE NURSE
NÖJD
THE ORDERLY

THE FATHER

ACT I

A sitting-room at the CAPTAIN'S. *A door in the background to the right. In the middle of the room a large round table strewn with newspapers and magazines. To the right a leather-covered sofa and table. In the right-hand corner a private door. To the left a bureau with a clock on it, and a door to the inner rooms. Arms on the wall, also guns and gamebags. Clothes-pegs by the door on which hang uniform coats. A lighted lamp on the large table.*

The CAPTAIN *and the* PASTOR *on the sofa. The* CAPTAIN *in undress uniform and riding-boots with spurs. The* PASTOR *in black with a white neckcloth, but without his clerical ruff; he is smoking a pipe. The* CAPTAIN *rings.*

[*Enter* ORDERLY.]

ORDERLY. Yes, sir.

CAPTAIN. Is Nöjd out there?

ORDERLY. Nöjd is waiting for orders in the kitchen.

CAPTAIN. Is he in the kitchen again! Fetch him in at once.

ORDERLY. Yes, sir. [*Goes.*]

THE PASTOR. What is wrong now?

CAPTAIN. Oh, the rascal has got the girl into trouble again; he is a thoroughly bad lot.

PASTOR. Nöjd, do you say? Why, he was to the fore in the spring, was n't he?

CAPTAIN. Yes, don't you remember? But won't you be kind enough to say a few friendly words to him, and perhaps you may make some impression on him. I 've sworn at him, and I 've flogged him too, but it has n't the least effect.

PASTOR. And now you want me to lecture him. What impression do you suppose the Word of God will make on a trooper?

CAPTAIN. Well, it certainly has no effect on me, you know.

PASTOR. I know that well enough.

CAPTAIN. But on him! Try at all events.

[*Enter* NÖJD.]

CAPTAIN. What have you been doing now Nöjd?

NÖJD. Begging your pardon, Captain, I can't possibly say while the Pastor is here.

PASTOR. Don't be bashful, my lad.

CAPTAIN. You had better confess, or you know how it will be.

NÖJD. Well, then, it was like this; we were at a dance at Gabriel's, and then — and then Ludwig said . . .

CAPTAIN. What has Ludwig to do with the story. Stick to the truth.

NÖJD. Yes, and then Emma said that we should go into the barn.

CAPTAIN. Ah, I suppose it was Emma who led you astray?

NÖJD. Well, that's about it. And I must say that unless the girl is willing nothing ever comes of it.

CAPTAIN. Once for all: are you the child's father or not?

NÖJD. How should I know?

CAPTAIN. What do you mean? Can't you tell that?

NÖJD. Why, no, one can never be quite sure.

CAPTAIN. Were you not the only one, then?

NÖJD. Yes, that time, but I can't be sure that I was the only one for all that.

CAPTAIN. Do you lay the blame on Ludwig, then? Is that what you mean?

NOJD. It is n't easy to know who to lay the blame on.

CAPTAIN. Yes, but you told Emma that you would marry her.

NÖJD. Oh, one always has to say that . . .

CAPTAIN. [*To* PASTOR.] This is really dreadful.

PASTOR. These are old stories! But listen, Nöjd, you are surely man enough to know whether you are the father or not.

NÖJD. Well, certainly, I and the girl — but you know yourself, Pastor, that it need n't come to anything for all that.

PASTOR. Look here, my lad, we are talking about you now. You will surely not leave the girl alone with the child. I suppose we can't compel you to marry her, but you shall provide for the child! that you *shall* do.

NÖJD. Well, then, Ludwig must, too.

CAPTAIN. Then the case must go to the courts. I can't disentangle all this, and after all it does n't concern me. So now, be off.

PASTOR. Nöjd, one word! Don't you think it is dishonorable to leave a girl like that in absolute destitution with her child? Don't you think so? Heigh? Don't you see that such a mode of action . . . h'm . . . h'm.

NÖJD. Yes, if only I knew for certain that I was father to the child, but one can never be sure of that, Pastor, and to slave all one's life for another man's child is not pleasant. Surely you, Pastor, and the Captain, can understand that for yourselves.

CAPTAIN. Be off.

NÖJD. God keep you, Captain.

CAPTAIN. But don't you go into the kitchen again, you rascal!   [NÖJD *goes*.]

CAPTAIN. Now, why did n't you come down upon him?

PASTOR. What do you mean? Did n't I give it him?

CAPTAIN. Why, you only sat and muttered to yourself.

PASTOR. To tell the truth, I really don't know what to say. It is a pity about the girl, certainly, but it is a pity about the lad, too. For just think if he were not the father. The girl can nurse the child for four months at the orphanage, and then it will be permanently provided for, but the lad can do no such thing. The girl will get a good place afterwards in some respectable house, but the lad's future may be ruined if he is dismissed from the regiment.

CAPTAIN. Upon my soul, I should like to be in the magistrate's shoes and judge this case. The lad is probably not quite innocent, — one can't be sure, — but the one thing one can be sure of is that the girl is guilty if there is any guilt in the matter.

PASTOR. Well, well, I judge no man! But what were we talking about when this tiresome story interrupted us? It was about Bertha and the confirmation, was n't it?

CAPTAIN. Yes, but it was surely not about the confirmation particularly, but the whole of her education. This house is full of women who all want to educate my child. My mother-in-law wants to make a spiritualist of her; Laura insists on her being an artist; the governess wants to make her a Methodist; old Margret a Baptist; and the servant-girls a Salvationist. It won't do to try and make a soul in patches like that: especially when I, who have the chief right to form her character, have all *my* efforts opposed. I am determined to get her out of this house.

PASTOR. There are too many women here governing the house.

CAPTAIN. Yes, are n't there? It is like going into a cage full of tigers, and if I did not hold red-hot irons under their noses they might tear me to pieces at any moment! And you, you laugh, you villain. Was it not enough that I took your sister for my wife, without your palming off your old stepmother on me?

PASTOR. Well, but, good Heavens, one cannot have stepmothers in one's house.

CAPTAIN. No, you think it better to have mothers-in-law instead — in other people's houses, that is to say.

PASTOR. Ah, well, every one of us has his burden in this life.

CAPTAIN. Yes, but I have certainly too heavy a one. I have even my old nurse in addition, who treats me as if I ought to wear bibs still. She is a good old soul, Heaven knows, but she is not in the right place here.

PASTOR. You must keep order among the women folk, Adolf. You let them dictate to you far too much.

CAPTAIN. Now, look here, will you enlighten me as to how to keep order among the women folk?

PASTOR. Laura was treated with a firm hand, but, then, although she is my own sister, I must admit she really *was* a little troublesome.

CAPTAIN. Laura has certainly her weak points, but with her they don't amount to much.

PASTOR. Pray speak quite plainly, I know her.

CAPTAIN. She has been brought up with romantic ideas and finds it a little difficult to accommodate herself to circumstances but in any case she is my wife . . .

PASTOR. And because she is your wife she is the best of them. No, my dear fellow, it is really she who oppresses you most.

CAPTAIN. In the mean time the whole house is turned upside down. Laura won't let Bertha leave her, and I can't let her remain in this bedlam.

PASTOR. Oh, Laura won't. Well, then, do you know, I'm afraid there will be difficulties. If she set her mind on anything when she was a child, she used to lie like a corpse till she got it, and then as likely as not she would give it back, explaining that she didn't care about the thing, whatever it was, but about getting her own way.

CAPTAIN. So she was like that even then? H'm — She really sometimes gets into such passions that I am quite anxious about her and fear that she is ill.

PASTOR. But what do you wish to do with Bertha that is so unpardonable? Is no compromise possible?

CAPTAIN. You mustn't think that I wish to make a prodigy of her, or a copy of myself. — I will not play the pander to my daughter and educate her exclusively for matrimony, for in that case she would have bitter days if she remained unmarried. But I will not, on the other hand, persuade her into a masculine career that requires a long course of training, which would be entirely thrown away in case she should wish to marry.

PASTOR. What do you intend, then?

CAPTAIN. I intend her to be a teacher. If she remains unmarried, she will be able to support herself, and at any rate be in no worse position than the poor schoolmasters who have to share their salaries with a family. If she marries, she can apply her knowledge to the education of her children. Don't you think I'm right?

PASTOR. Perfectly right. But hasn't she, on the other hand, shown such talents for painting that it would outrage nature to suppress them?

CAPTAIN. No! I have shown her performances to an eminent painter, and he says that they are only the kind of thing that can be learned in schools. But then a young fellow came here in the summer who, of course, understood the matter much better, and declared that she had a remarkable talent, and so it was settled to Laura's satisfaction.

PASTOR. Was he in love with the girl?

CAPTAIN. I take that entirely for granted.

PASTOR. Then, God be with you, old fellow, for in that case I see no help. But all this is very tiresome, and, of course, Laura has her supporters . . . in there.

CAPTAIN. Yes, that you may depend on! The whole house is already up in arms, and, between ourselves, it is not exactly a noble conflict which is waged from that quarter.

PASTOR. [Gets up.] Do you think I don't know that?

CAPTAIN. You also?

PASTOR. Also?

CAPTAIN. But the worst of it is that it seems to me as if Bertha's career was being determined by most objectionable motives, in there. They drop hints about man having to see that woman can do this and can do that. It is Man and Woman against one another, incessantly, all day long. Must you go now? Do stay for supper. I have certainly nothing to offer you, but, still. . . . You know that I am expecting the new doctor. Have you seen him?

PASTOR. I caught a glimpse of him as I passed by. He looked pleasant and trustworthy.

CAPTAIN. I'm glad of that. Do you think it possible he may side with me?

PASTOR. Who knows? It depends on how much he has been accustomed to women.

CAPTAIN. Oh! but won't you stay?

PASTOR. No, thanks, my dear fellow; I promised to come home to supper, and the old lady gets so uneasy if I am late.

CAPTAIN. Uneasy? Angry, you should say. Well, as you will. Let me help you with your overcoat.

PASTOR. It seems to be very cold this evening. Thanks. You must take care of your health, Adolf, you look so nervous.

CAPTAIN. Do I look nervous?

PASTOR. Yes, you are not really well.

CAPTAIN. Has Laura put that into your head? She has treated me these twenty years as if I were at the point of death.

PASTOR. Laura? No; but — but I'm really uneasy about you. Take care of yourself. That's my advice! Good-bye, dear old man; but didn't you want to talk about the confirmation?

CAPTAIN. Not at all! I assure you that

matter will proceed in the ordinary course at the expense of the official conscience, for I have no intention of being either a confessor or a martyr. We have put all that behind us. Good-bye. Remember me at home.

PASTOR. Good-bye, Adolf. Love to Laura. [*Goes.*]

[*The* CAPTAIN *opens his desk, and seats himself at it with his accounts.*]

CAPTAIN. Thirty-four . . . nine, forty-three . . . seven, eight, fifty-six.

[LAURA *enters from the inner rooms.*]

LAURA. Will you be so kind as to . . .

CAPTAIN. In a moment! Fifty-six . . . seventy-one, eighty-four, eighty-nine, ninety-two, a hundred. What is it?

LAURA. Am I disturbing you?

CAPTAIN. Not at all. Housekeeping money, I suppose?

LAURA. Yes, housekeeping money.

CAPTAIN. Put the accounts down there and I will go through them.

LAURA. The accounts?

CAPTAIN. Yes.

LAURA. Am I to keep accounts now?

CAPTAIN. Of course you are to keep accounts now. Our affairs are in a precarious condition, and in case of a liquidation there must be accounts or one may be punished as a fraudulent debtor.

LAURA. It is not my fault that our affairs are in a precarious condition.

CAPTAIN. That is exactly what will be shown by the accounts.

LAURA. It is not my fault that the bailiff doesn't pay.

CAPTAIN. Who recommended the bailiff so warmly? You! Why did you recommend a — shall we say — a fool?

LAURA. And why did you take the fool, then?

CAPTAIN. Because I was not allowed to eat in peace, nor to sleep in peace, nor to work in peace, till you got the man here. You wanted him so that your brother might be rid of him; your mother wanted him because I didn't want him; the governess wanted him because he was a Scripture-reader; and old Margret because she had known his mother from her childhood. That's why I took him, and if I hadn't taken him I should be shut up in a madhouse now, or lying in the family grave. Meantime, here is the housekeeping money

and your allowance. You can give me the accounts presently.

LAURA. [*Curtesies.*] Thanks so much. Do you also keep accounts of what you spend besides the housekeeping money?

CAPTAIN. That does not concern you.

LAURA. No, that is true, just as little as my child's education concerns me. Have my lords made up their minds after the conference of this evening?

CAPTAIN. I had made up my mind beforehand, and it therefore only remained for me to announce my intention to the one friend I and the family have in common. Bertha is to board in town and starts in a fortnight.

LAURA. Where is she to board, if I may venture to ask?

CAPTAIN. At Auditor Säfberg's.

LAURA. That free-thinker!

CAPTAIN. The law declares that children are to be brought up in their father's faith.

LAURA. And the mother is to have no voice in the matter?

CAPTAIN. None whatever. She has sold her birthright by a legal transaction, and surrendered her rights in return for the man's undertaking to care for her and her children.

LAURA. Therefore she has no power over her child.

CAPTAIN. No, none whatever. When one has once sold one's goods, one cannot have them back and yet keep the money.

LAURA. But if both father and mother agree . . .

CAPTAIN. How could that happen? I wish her to live in town, you wish her to live at home. The arithmetical result would be that she remained at the railway station, midway between town and home. This is a knot that cannot be untied. Do you see?

LAURA. Then it must be broken! What was Nöjd doing here?

CAPTAIN. That is a professional secret.

LAURA. Which the whole kitchen knows.

CAPTAIN. Good; then you must know it.

LAURA. I do know it!

CAPTAIN. And have your judgment ready beforehand.

LAURA. My judgment is the law's judgment.

CAPTAIN. It is not written in "the judgment of the law" who the child's father is.

LAURA. No, but one can usually find that out.

CAPTAIN. Wise people say that one never can tell those things.

LAURA. That is remarkable. Can one never tell who is the father of a child ?

CAPTAIN. No; so it is maintained.

LAURA. That is remarkable. How, then, can the father have such rights over the child ?

CAPTAIN. He only has them when he has assumed the responsibility, or has had the responsibility thrust on him. And in marriage there is, of course, no doubt about paternity.

LAURA. No doubt ?

CAPTAIN. No, I should hope not.

LAURA. And in case the wife has been unfaithful ?

CAPTAIN. This is no such case ! Have you anything further to ask about ?

LAURA. Nothing whatever.

CAPTAIN. Then I shall go up to my room, and perhaps you will be good enough to inform me when the Doctor comes.

[Shuts the bureau and gets up.]

LAURA. Certainly.

CAPTAIN. And as soon as he comes. For I don't wish to be rude to him. You understand.

[CAPTAIN goes through the private door to right.]

LAURA. I understand.

[LAURA gazes at the bank notes she holds in her hand.]

MOTHER-IN-LAW'S VOICE [within]. Laura!

LAURA. Yes.

MOTHER-IN-LAW'S VOICE. Is my tea ready ?

LAURA [in the doorway to the inner rooms]. You shall have it directly.

[LAURA goes toward the hall door in the background, as the ORDERLY opens it and announces — DOCTOR OSTERMARK.]

DOCTOR. [Enters.] Madam !

LAURA. [Goes toward him and gives him her hand.] Good-evening, Doctor ? We are all very glad to see you here. The Captain is out, but he will be back directly.

DOCTOR. I beg your pardon for coming so late, but I have had to pay some professional visits already.

LAURA. Won't you sit down ? Do !

DOCTOR. Thank you.

LAURA. Yes, there is a great deal of illness in the neighborhood just now, but I hope that you will settle down comfortably all the same. It is so very important for lonely country people like us to find a doctor who is interested in his patients. And I hear so much good of you, Doctor, that I hope the happiest relations will prevail between us.

DOCTOR. You are much too kind, but I hope, on the other hand, that my visits to you may not too frequently be caused by necessity. Your family, I believe, is usually in good health . . .

LAURA. We have fortunately not had any acute illness, but still things are not entirely as they ought to be.

DOCTOR. Indeed ?

LAURA. They are, Heaven knows, not so satisfactory as we might wish.

DOCTOR. You really alarm me.

LAURA. There are circumstances in a family, which one is bound in honor and conscience to conceal from the whole world . . .

DOCTOR. Excepting from the doctor.

LAURA. Exactly. It is, therefore, my painful duty to tell you the whole truth immediately.

DOCTOR. Can we not postpone this conference until I have had the honor of being introduced to the Captain ?

LAURA. No ! You must hear me before seeing him.

DOCTOR. It relates to him, then ?

LAURA. Yes — to him, my poor, dear husband.

DOCTOR. You make me uneasy, madam, and believe me, I sympathize with your misfortune.

LAURA [taking out her handkerchief]. My husband's mind is affected. Now you know all, and must judge for yourself when you see him.

DOCTOR. Is it possible ! I have read the Captain's excellent treatises on mineralogy with great admiration, and have always found them display a clear and powerful intellect.

LAURA. Really? I should be delighted if his whole family should prove to be mistaken.

DOCTOR. But of course it is possible that his mind is disturbed in other directions. Let me hear.

LAURA. That is what we also fear. You see, he has sometimes the most extraordinary ideas, which of course one would expect in a learned man if they did not exercise a disastrous influence on the welfare of his whole family. For instance, he has a fancy for buying all manner of things.

DOCTOR. That is serious; but what does he buy?

LAURA. Whole boxes of books that he never reads.

DOCTOR. Oh, it is nothing out of the way for a scholar to buy books.

LAURA. You don't believe what I say?

DOCTOR. Yes, madam, I am convinced that you believe what you say.

LAURA. Then, is it reasonable to think that one can see, by looking in a microscope, what is going on in another planet?

DOCTOR. Does he say he can do that?

LAURA. Yes, he says so.

DOCTOR. In a microscope?

LAURA. In a microscope, yes.

DOCTOR. This is serious, if it is so.

LAURA. If it is so. Then you have no belief in me, Doctor, and I am sitting here and confiding the family secret in you . . .

DOCTOR. Indeed, madam, your confidence honors me, but as a physician I must investigate and observe before I can judge. Has the Captain ever shown any symptoms of uncertainty of temper, or instability of will?

LAURA. Has he ever? We have been married for twenty years and he has never yet made a decision without abandoning it afterwards.

DOCTOR. Is he obstinate?

LAURA. He always insists on having his own way, but when he has got it, he drops the whole thing and asks me to decide.

DOCTOR. This is serious and requires close observation. The will, you see, is the mainspring of the mind, and if it is injured the whole mind collapses.

LAURA. And God knows that I have had to teach myself to meet his wishes halfway all through these long years of trial. Ah, if you only knew what a life I have endured with him — if you only knew?

DOCTOR. Your misfortune touches me deeply, and I promise you to see what can be done. I pity you with my whole heart, and I beg you to trust me absolutely. But after what I have heard I must impress one thing on you. Avoid suggesting any ideas that make a strong impression on the sufferer, for in a weak brain they are rapidly developed and readily turn to monomania or "idées fixes." Do you understand?

LAURA. You mean, avoid rousing his suspicions?

DOCTOR. Exactly so. One can make the insane believe anything just because they are receptive to everything.

LAURA. Indeed. Then I understand. Yes — yes. [*Ringing heard within.*] Excuse me, my mother has something to say to me. One moment. . . . Ah, there is Adolf.   [*Goes.*]

[CAPTAIN *enters the private door.*]

CAPTAIN. Ah, you are here already, Doctor. You are very welcome.

DOCTOR. Captain! It is a very great pleasure to me to make the acquaintance of so celebrated a man of science.

CAPTAIN. You are very good. My professional duties don't allow me to make any profound investigations, but I believe myself to be really on the track of a discovery.

DOCTOR. Really.

CAPTAIN. You see, I have submitted meteoric stones to spectrum analysis, with the result that I have found coal, that is to say, a clear trace of organic life. What do you think of that?

DOCTOR. Can you see that in the microscope?

CAPTAIN. No, deuce take it, in the spectroscope.

DOCTOR. The spectroscope! Pardon: Well, then, you will soon be able to tell us what is happening in Jupiter.

CAPTAIN. Not what is happening, but what has happened. If only the confounded booksellers in Paris would send me the books; but I believe that all the booksellers in the universe have conspired against me. Just imagine that for the last two months not a single one has even answered my communications, either letters or abusive telegrams. I shall go frantic over it, and I can't imagine what it all means.

DOCTOR. Oh, they are generally unbusinesslike fellows; you mustn't take it so much to heart.

CAPTAIN. No, but the deuce is that I shall not get my treatise done in time, and I know that they are working on the same lines in Berlin. But that's not what we ought to be talking about. . . . What about you? If you care to live here we have a small apartment at your disposal in the wing, or perhaps you would rather live in the old doctor's quarters.

DOCTOR. Just as you like.

CAPTAIN. No, as you like. Which is it to be?

DOCTOR. You must decide that, Captain.

CAPTAIN. No, I shall decide nothing. You must say what you wish. I wish nothing, nothing whatever.

DOCTOR. Oh, but I really cannot decide. . . .

CAPTAIN. For God's sake, do say, Doctor, what you would like. I have no will in this matter, no opinion, no wishes. Are you so utterly feeble that you don't know what you wish? Answer me or I shall get angry.

DOCTOR. As it rests with me, I choose to live here.

CAPTAIN. Good! Thank you. . . . Ah, forgive me, Doctor, but nothing annoys me so much as to hear people profess indifference about anything. [Rings.]

[Enter NURSE.]

CAPTAIN. Oh, there you are, Margret. Do you happen to know if the wing is in order for the Doctor?

NURSE. Yes, sir, it is.

CAPTAIN. All right. Then I won't detain you, Doctor; you must be tired. Good-bye and welcome again; we shall meet to-morrow, I hope.

DOCTOR. Good-evening, Captain.

CAPTAIN. I presume that my wife explained our circumstances to you a little, so that you have some idea how the land lies.

DOCTOR. Your excellent wife has given me a few hints about one thing and another such as were necessary to a stranger. Good-evening, Captain. [Goes.]

CAPTAIN. What do you want, you old dear! Is anything the matter?

NURSE. Now, my dear Mr. Adolf, you must just listen.

CAPTAIN. Yes, old Margret. Talk away, you are the only one I can listen to without getting into a rage.

NURSE. Now, just listen, Mr. Adolf. Don't you think you should go halfway and come to an agreement with mistress about this fuss over the child. Just think of a mother . . .

CAPTAIN. Think of a father, Margret.

NURSE. There, there, there! A father has something besides his child, but a mother has nothing but her child.

CAPTAIN. Just so, old lady. She has only one burden, but I have three, and I bear her burden, too. Don't you think that I should have had a better position in the world than a poor soldier's if I had not had her and her child?

NURSE. Yes, but it was n't that I wanted to say.

CAPTAIN. No, I believe that, for you wanted to make me confess I was in the wrong.

NURSE. Don't you believe, Mr. Adolf, that I wish you well?

CAPTAIN. Yes, dear friend, I do believe it, but you don't know what is for my good. You see, it is n't enough for me to have given the child life, I want to give her my soul too.

NURSE. I don't understand anything about that. But I do think that you ought to be able to agree.

CAPTAIN. You are not my friend, Margret!

NURSE. I? Ah, God! How can you say that, Mr. Adolf. Do you think I can forget that you were my child when you were little.

CAPTAIN. No, you dear; have I forgotten it? You have been like a mother to me, and have supported me hitherto when I had everybody against me, but now, when I really need you, you desert me and go over to the enemy.

NURSE. The enemy!

CAPTAIN. Yes, the enemy! You know well enough how things are in this house; you have seen everything from beginning to end.

NURSE. I have seen well enough! but, my God, why should two people torment the life out of one another; two people who are otherwise so good and wish all others well. Mistress is never like that to me or to any one else . . .

CAPTAIN. Only to me; I know it. But let me tell you, Margret, that if you desert me now, you will do wrong. For they have begun to plot against me, and that doctor is not my friend.

NURSE. Ah, Mr. Adolf, you believe evil about everybody; but, you see, it's because you have n't the true faith, that's just what it is.

CAPTAIN. But you and the Baptists have found the only true faith. You are, indeed, happy!

NURSE. At any rate, I am not so unhappy as you, Mr. Adolf. Humble your proud heart and you will see that God will make you happy in love to your neighbor.

CAPTAIN. It is a strange thing that you no sooner speak of God and love than your voice becomes hard and your eyes evil. No, Margret, you have certainly not the true faith.

NURSE. Yes, you're proud and hard enough in your learning, but it does n't amount to much when it comes to the pinch.

CAPTAIN. How arrogantly you talk, humble heart. I know well enough learning is of no use with such creatures as you.

NURSE. You should be ashamed of yourself! But in spite of everything, old Margret loves her great big boy best, and he will come back again, you'll see, like a good child, in the day of trouble.

CAPTAIN. Margret! Forgive me, but believe me there is no one here who wishes me well but you. Help me, for I am sure that something is going to happen. What it is I don't know, but some evil thing is on its way. [Scream from within.] What is it? Who is screaming?

[BERTHA enters from inner rooms.]

BERTHA. Father! Father! help me, save me!

CAPTAIN. What is it, my darling child? Speak!

BERTHA. Help me. She is going to hurt me!

CAPTAIN. Who is going to hurt you? Speak! Speak!

BERTHA. Grandmother! But it's my fault, for I deceived her!

CAPTAIN. Go on.

BERTHA. Yes, but you must n't say anything about it! Do you hear? Promise!

CAPTAIN. Well, but tell me what it is.
[NURSE goes.]

BERTHA. In the evening she generally turns down the lamp, and then she makes me sit at a table holding a pen over a piece of paper. And then she says that the spirits are to write.

CAPTAIN. What do you say? And you have never told me this?

BERTHA. Forgive me, but I dared not. For grandmother says that the spirits take revenge if one speaks about them. And then the pen writes, but I don't know if it is I. And sometimes it goes beautifully, but sometimes it can't do anything at all. And when I am tired nothing comes, but she wants it to come all the same. And this evening I thought I was writing beautifully, but then grandmother said it was all out of Stagnelius,[1] and that I was deceiving her, and then she got so fearfully angry.

CAPTAIN. Do you believe that there are spirits?

BERTHA. I don't know.

CAPTAIN. But I know that there are none.

BERTHA. But grandmother says that you don't understand, papa, and that you have much worse things that can see to other planets.

CAPTAIN. Does she say that? Does she say that? What else does she say?

BERTHA. She says that you can't work wonders.

CAPTAIN. I never said I could. You know what meteoric stones are,— stones that fall down from other heavenly bodies. I can examine them and say whether they contain the same elements as our world. That is all that I can see.

BERTHA. But grandmother says there are things that she can see, but that you cannot see.

CAPTAIN. Then she lies!

BERTHA. Grandmother does n't tell lies.

CAPTAIN. Why not?

BERTHA. Then mother tells lies, too.

CAPTAIN. H'm.

BERTHA. If you say that mother tells lies, I will never believe you again.

CAPTAIN. I have not said so, and therefore you must believe me when I tell you that your future welfare requires that you should leave your home. Will you? Will you go to town and learn something useful?

BERTHA. Ah, yes, I should love to go to town, away from here, anywhere! Only let me see you sometimes, often. Oh, it is always so gloomy and sad in there, as if it

[1] Erik Johan Stagnelius, poet and dramatist, 1793–1823.

were a winter's night, but when you come, father, it is like some spring morning when they take out the inner windows.

CAPTAIN. My beloved child. My dear child.

BERTHA. But, father, you must be good to mother, do you hear? She cries so often.

CAPTAIN. H'm. Then you will go to town?

BERTHA. Yes, yes.

CAPTAIN. But suppose mother will not let you go?

BERTHA. But she must let me.

CAPTAIN. But what if she won't?

BERTHA. Well, then, I don't know what will happen. But she must! She must!

CAPTAIN. Will you ask her?

BERTHA. You must ask her very nicely, for she does n't care about me.

CAPTAIN. H'm! Now if you wish it, and I wish it, and she does n't wish it, what shall we do then?

BERTHA. Ah, then, it will be all in a muddle again! Why can't you ask. . . .

[*Enter* LAURA.]

LAURA. Ah, so Bertha is here! Then perhaps we may hear her own opinion, as the question of her future has to be decided.

CAPTAIN. The child can hardly have any well-founded opinion as to how a young girl's life is likely to shape itself, while we, on the contrary, can easily make an approximate calculation, for we have seen a great number of young girls' lives unfold themselves.

LAURA. But as we are of different opinions, Bertha's must be the determining one.

CAPTAIN. No, I let no one usurp my rights, neither women nor children. Bertha, leave us. [BERTHA *goes out.*]

LAURA. You were afraid of hearing her opinion, because you thought it would be to my advantage.

CAPTAIN. I know that she wishes to go away from home, but I know also that you possess the power of changing her mind according to your pleasure.

LAURA. Am I really so powerful?

CAPTAIN. Yes, you have a fiendish power of getting your own way, but people who are not ashamed of interfering always have. How did you get Dr. Nordling away, for instance, and how did you get the new man here?

LAURA. Yes, how did I manage that?

CAPTAIN. You insulted the first, until he went, and made your brother scrape votes together for the other.

LAURA. Well, that was quite simple and perfectly legitimate. Is Bertha to leave home?

CAPTAIN. Yes, she is to start in a fortnight.

LAURA. Is that your determination?

CAPTAIN. Yes.

LAURA. Have you spoken to Bertha about it?

CAPTAIN. Yes.

LAURA. Then I must try to prevent it.

CAPTAIN. You cannot.

LAURA. Can't I? Do you really think I would trust my daughter to these wicked people to be told that everything her mother has taught her is mere foolishness? Why, she would despise me for the rest of her life!

CAPTAIN. Do you think that a father will allow ignorant and conceited women to teach his daughter that her father is a charlatan?

LAURA. It ought to mean less to the father.

CAPTAIN. Why so?

LAURA. Because the mother is nearer to the child, since it has been discovered that no one can tell for certain who is the father of a child.

CAPTAIN. What is the application in this case?

LAURA. That you do not know whether you are Bertha's father.

CAPTAIN. Do I not know?

LAURA. No; what no one can know, you surely cannot know.

CAPTAIN. Are you joking?

LAURA. No; I am only making use of your own teaching. Besides, how can you tell that I have not been unfaithful to you?

CAPTAIN. I believe a great deal of you, but not that, nor that you would talk about it if it were true.

LAURA. Assume that I was prepared to bear anything, even scorn and rejection, for the sake of being allowed to keep and dispose of my child, and that I was truthful just now when I declared that Bertha is my child, but not yours. Assume . . .

CAPTAIN. Stop!

LAURA. Only assume this : In that case your power would be at an end.

CAPTAIN. Yes, when you had proved that I was not the father.

LAURA. That would not be so difficult ! Should you like me to do that ?

CAPTAIN. Stop !

LAURA. I should, of course, only need to declare the name of the real father, give all details of place and time ; for instance — when was Bertha born? In the third year of our marriage.

CAPTAIN. Stop, or . . .

LAURA. Or what ? I am to stop now. Just think for a moment of all you do and decide, and whatever you do, don't make yourself ridiculous.

CAPTAIN. I consider all this most lamentable.

LAURA. Which is more ridiculous than ever.

CAPTAIN. And what of you ?

LAURA. Oh, I have managed too cleverly.

CAPTAIN. That is why one cannot contend with you.

LAURA. Then, why do you provoke contests with a superior enemy ?

CAPTAIN. Superior ?

LAURA. Yes, it is singular, but I have never looked at a man without knowing myself his superior.

CAPTAIN. Well, you shall be made to see your superior for once, so that you never shall forget it.

LAURA. That will be interesting.

[*Enter* NURSE.]

NURSE. Supper is ready. Will you come in, ma'am ?

LAURA. Yes, directly.

[CAPTAIN *lingers ; sits down in an arm-chair by the table.*]

LAURA. Won't you come in to supper ?

CAPTAIN. No, thanks, I don't want anything.

LAURA. What ! Are you annoyed ?

CAPTAIN. No, but I am not hungry.

LAURA. Come, or they will question me in a way that is — unnecessary. . . . Be good now. . . . You won't ; then stay there.

[*Goes.*]

NURSE. Mr. Adolf ! What is all this about ?

CAPTAIN. I don't know what it is. Can you explain to me how it is that a grown man can be treated as if he were a child ?

NURSE. I don't understand it, but it must be because you are all women's children, every man of you, great and small. . . .

CAPTAIN. But no women are born of men. Yes, but I am Bertha's father. Tell me, Margret, don't you believe it? Don't you ?

NURSE. Lord, how childish you are. Of course you are your own child's father. Come and eat now, and don't sit there and brood. There, there, come now.

CAPTAIN. Get out, woman. To hell with the witches. [*Goes to the private door.*] Svärd, Svärd !

[*Enter* ORDERLY.]

ORDERLY. Yes, Captain.

CAPTAIN. Let them put the horses in the covered sleigh at once.

NURSE. Captain, just listen !

CAPTAIN. Out, woman ! At once !

NURSE. Lord preserve us, what will come of all this !

[CAPTAIN *puts on his cap and prepares to go out.*]

CAPTAIN. Don't expect me home before midnight.

NURSE. Jesus help us, what will be the end of this !

ACT II

The same scene as in the previous Act. A lighted lamp on the table ; it is night. The DOCTOR. LAURA.

DOCTOR. From what I could find in the course of our conversation, the case is not yet clearly proved to me. To begin with, you had made one mistake in saying that he had arrived at these astonishing results about other celestial bodies by means of a microscope. Now that I hear it was a spectroscope, he is not only entirely cleared of any suspicion of insanity, but is shown to have done a great service to science.

LAURA. Yes, but I never said that.

DOCTOR. Madam, I made careful notes of our conversation, and I remember that I asked about this very point because I thought that I could not have heard aright. One must be scrupulous in making such assertions when a certificate of insanity is in question.

LAURA. A certificate of insanity ?

DOCTOR. Yes; you must surely know that an insane person loses his civil and family rights.

LAURA. No, I did not know that.

DOCTOR. There was a further point that seems to me suspicious. He spoke of his communications to his booksellers having remained unanswered. Permit me to ask if you intercepted them from motives of mistaken kindness.

LAURA. Yes, I did. It was my duty to watch over the interests of the household and I could not let him ruin us all without intervention.

DOCTOR. Pardon me, but I think that you cannot have considered the consequences of such an act. If he discovers your secret interference with his affairs, his suspicions will be aroused and will grow with the rapidity of an avalanche. But, besides this, you have raised obstacles to his will and consequently still further provoked irritability. You must know how maddening it is to have your most ardent desires thwarted and your will restrained.

LAURA. As if I did n't know that!

DOCTOR. Then consider what he must have gone through.

LAURA [getting up]. It is midnight and he has n't come home. We may fear the worst now.

DOCTOR. But tell me what actually happened this evening after I left. I must know everything.

LAURA. He talked in the wildest way about the most extraordinary things. Such fancies, for instance, as that he is not the father of his child.

DOCTOR. That is strange. How did such an idea come into his head.

LAURA. I really can't imagine, unless it was that he had to examine one of the men in a child maintenance case, and when I took the girl's part, he got excited and said that no one could tell who was father to a child. God knows that I did everything to calm him, but I fear that nothing can help him now.   [Cries.]

DOCTOR. This really cannot be allowed to go on. Something must be done, without, of course, rousing his suspicions. Tell me, has the Captain ever had such delusions before?

LAURA. Six years ago we had the same state of things and then he actually confessed, in his own letter to the doctor, that he feared for his reason.

DOCTOR. Ah, yes, this is of course a story that has deep roots, and the sanctity of family life — and so on — prevents . . . I cannot ask about everything, but must keep to the surface. What is done can't be undone, alas, and yet the remedy should have some application to the past. — Where do you think he is now ?

LAURA. I have no idea. He has such wild fancies now.

DOCTOR. Should you like me to stay till he returns ? I could say, to avoid suspicion, that I had come to see your mother, who is unwell.

LAURA. Yes, that will do admirably. And do not leave us, Doctor ; I can't tell you how anxious I am ! But would n't it be better to tell him right out what you think of his condition ?

DOCTOR. We never do that unless the patient speaks of the subject himself, and very rarely even then. It depends entirely on the direction the case takes. But we must n't stay here ; perhaps I had better go into the next room, it will look more natural.

LAURA. Yes, it will be better, and then Margret can sit here. She is accustomed to sit up when he is out, and she is the only one, too, who has any power over him. [Goes to the door on the left.] Margret, Margret !

[Enter the NURSE.]

NURSE. Yes, ma'am. Is the master home?

LAURA. No, but you are to sit here and wait for him, and when he comes you are to say that my mother is ill and that the Doctor is here because of that.

NURSE. Yes, ma'am. I'll see that it is all right.

LAURA. [Opens door to inner rooms.] Will you come in here, Doctor ?

DOCTOR. Thanks.

> [The NURSE sits at the table and takes up a hymn-book and spectacles.]

NURSE. Ah, yes, ah, yes !
                              [Reads half aloud.]

Ah, woe is me, how sad a thing
Is life within this vale of tears,
Death's angel triumphs like a king
And calls aloud to all the spheres —
'T is vanity, all vanity.

Yes, yes ! yes, yes !

All that on earth hath life and breath
Falls stricken down before his spear,
And sorrow, saved alone from death,
Inscribes above the mighty bier —
'T is vanity, all vanity.

Yes, yes.

[BERTHA *enters with a coffee-pot and some needle-work; she speaks low.*]

BERTHA. Margret, may I sit with you? it is so lonely up there.

NURSE. Oh! Good gracious, are you still up, Bertha?

BERTHA. I must work at papa's Christmas present, you see. And I 've got something good for you here.

NURSE. Yes, but, dear heart, it won't do. You have to get up in the morning and it is past twelve o'clock.

BERTHA. Well, what does that matter? I dare not sit up there alone; I believe it 's haunted.

NURSE. There, now, did n't I say so! Yes, mark my words, this house is no good place. What did you hear?

BERTHA. Oh, just fancy, I heard some one singing up in the garret.

NURSE. In the garret? At this time of night!

BERTHA. And it was a very, very sad song, such as I never heard. And it seemed as if it came from the lumber-room, where the cradle stands, you know, on the left. . . .

NURSE. Oh, dear, oh, dear; and it 's such fearful weather to-night! I believe the chimneys will blow down.

Ah, what is then this earthly life
But grief, affliction, trouble, strife?
E'en when fairest it has seemed
Vanity it must be deemed.

Yes, dear child, God send us a happy Christmas!

BERTHA. Margret, is it true that papa is ill?

NURSE. Yes; he is, indeed.

BERTHA. Then we shan't be able to keep Christmas Eve. But how can he be up if he is ill?

NURSE. You see, my child, the kind of illness that he has does n't prevent him from being up. Hush, there 's some one out in the hall. Go to bed now and take the coffee-pot away, or the master will be angry.

BERTHA [*going out with the tray*]. Good-night, Margret!

NURSE. Good-night, my child. God bless you!   [BERTHA *goes.*]

[*Enter* CAPTAIN. *He takes off his overcoat.*]

CAPTAIN. Are you still up? Go to bed.

NURSE. I was only waiting till . . .

[CAPTAIN *lights a candle, opens his desk, sits down at it, and takes letters and newspapers out of his pocket.*]

NURSE. Mr. Adolf.

CAPTAIN. What do you want?

NURSE. Old mistress is ill, and the Doctor is here.

CAPTAIN. Is it anything dangerous?

NURSE. No, I don't think so. It is only a cold.

CAPTAIN. [*Gets up.*] Who was the father of your child, Margret?

NURSE. Oh, I have told you that many and many a time; it was that scamp Johansson.

CAPTAIN. Are you sure that it was he?

NURSE. How childish you are; of course I am sure of it, since he was the only one.

CAPTAIN. Yes; but was he sure that he was the only one? No; he could not be, but you could be sure of it. You see that 's the difference.

NURSE. I can't see any difference.

CAPTAIN. No; you cannot see it, but the difference is there all the same. [*Turns over the pages of a photograph album that is on the table.*] Do you think Bertha is like me?   [*Looks at a portrait in the album.*]

NURSE. Why, yes; you are as like as two peas.

CAPTAIN. Did Johansson confess that he was the father?

NURSE. He had no choice.

CAPTAIN. How dreadful! There is the Doctor.

[*Enter* DOCTOR.]

CAPTAIN. Good-evening, Doctor. How is my mother-in-law?

DOCTOR. Oh, it is not at all serious; it is merely a slight sprain of the left foot. .

CAPTAIN. I thought Margret said that it was a cold. There seem to be different interpretations of the same case. Go to bed, Margret.   [NURSE *goes.*]

[*A pause.*]

CAPTAIN. Do sit down, Doctor Östermark.

DOCTOR. [*Sits down.*] Thanks.

CAPTAIN. Is it true that you obtain striped foals if you cross a zebra and a mare ?

DOCTOR [*astonished*]. Perfectly true.

CAPTAIN. Is it true that the foals continue to be striped if the breed is carried on with a stallion ?

DOCTOR. Yes, that is also true.

CAPTAIN. Therefore, under certain conditions, a stallion can be sire to striped foals ?

DOCTOR. Yes, so it appears.

CAPTAIN. That is to say: the offspring's likeness to the father proves nothing.

DOCTOR. Well . . .

CAPTAIN. That is to say, paternity cannot be proved.

DOCTOR. H'm . . . Well !

CAPTAIN. You are a widower and have had children ?

DOCTOR. Ye-es.

CAPTAIN. Did you never see how ridiculous you were as a father ? I know nothing so comical as to see a father leading his child about the streets, or to hear a father talk of his children. "My wife's children," he ought to say. Did you never realize how false your position was ? Were you never troubled by doubts, I won't say suspicions, for I assume, as a gentleman, that your wife was above suspicion ?

DOCTOR. No, really, I never was, and, indeed, Captain, a man must take his children on trust as Goethe, I think, says.

CAPTAIN. On trust when there is a woman in the case ? That is risky.

DOCTOR. Oh ! there are so many kinds of women.

CAPTAIN. Modern investigation has pronounced that there is only one kind ! . . . When I was young I was strong and — if I may boast — handsome. I can only remember two momentary impressions that in recalling them have caused me to doubt this. I was once on board a steamer sitting with a few friends in the fore-saloon. The young stewardess came and flung herself down by me, burst into tears, and told us that her sweetheart was drowned. We pitied her, and I ordered some champagne. After the second glass, I touched her foot, after the fourth her knee, and before morning I had consoled her.

DOCTOR. One swallow does not make a summer.

CAPTAIN. Now comes the second, and that was really a summer swallow. I was at Lysekil. A young woman was staying there. She had her children with her, but her husband was in town. She was religious, had extremely severe principles, preached morality to me, and was, I believe, entirely virtuous. I lent her some books, and when she was leaving she unexpectedly enough returned them. Three months later I found a visiting card in those very books with a fairly plain declaration. It was innocent, as innocent, that is to say, as a declaration of love from a married woman to a strange man who never made any advances can be. Now comes the moral. Whatever you do, don't believe too much.

DOCTOR. But don't believe too little either.

CAPTAIN. No. Not that either. But don't you see, Doctor Östermark, the woman was so unconsciously dishonest that she spoke of her infatuation for me to her husband. This very unconsciousness of their instinctive duplicity is what is so dangerous. It is, I grant you, an extenuating circumstance, but it cannot make me reverse my judgment ; only soften it.

DOCTOR. Captain, your thoughts are taking a morbid direction, and you ought to control them.

CAPTAIN. You must not use the word morbid. All steam boilers, as you know, explode when the pressure gauge registers 100, but the scale is not the same for all boilers ; do you understand ? In the mean time you are here to watch me. If I only were not a man I should have the right of making accusations, or complaints as they are so cleverly called, and, perhaps, I should be able to give you the whole diagnosis, and what is more, the history of my disease ; but I am unfortunately a man, and there is nothing for me but to fold my arms across my breast like the Roman, and hold my breath till I die. Good-night.

DOCTOR. Captain, if you are ill, it will not offend your dignity as a man to tell me all. Indeed, I am bound to hear the other side.

CAPTAIN. It is enough that you have heard the one, I imagine.

DOCTOR. No, Captain. And do you know when I heard Mrs. Alving eulogize her dead husband, I thought to myself it was a confounded pity the fellow was dead.

CAPTAIN. Do you suppose that he would have spoken if he had been alive? And do you suppose that any dead husbands would be believed if they were to come to life? Good-night, Doctor. You hear that I am calm, and you can safely go to bed.

DOCTOR. Good-night, then, Captain. I can take no further part in this affair.

CAPTAIN. Are we enemies?

DOCTOR. Far from it! Only it is a pity that we cannot be friends. Good-night.

[*Goes.*]

[*The* CAPTAIN *follows the* DOCTOR *to the door in the background, and then goes to the door at the left and opens it slightly.*]

CAPTAIN. Come in, I want to talk to you! I heard you standing out there listening.

[*Enter* LAURA *embarrassed.* CAPTAIN *sits down at the bureau.*]

CAPTAIN. It is late, but we must talk things out. Sit down. [*A pause.*] I have been at the post-office this evening to fetch the letters. From these it appears that you have kept back my letters, both on their departure and arrival. The direct consequence of this is that the delay has entirely frustrated the results I hoped for from my work.

LAURA. It was an act of kindness on my part, since you neglected your professional duties for this other work.

CAPTAIN. It surely cannot have been kindness, for you knew quite well that I should one day win more renown from that than from the service; but you were particularly anxious that I should not distinguish myself, lest your own insignificance should be eclipsed. In consequence of this I have intercepted letters addressed to you.

LAURA. That is very noble of you.

CAPTAIN. I see you have a high opinion of me. — It appears from these letters that for some time past you have been arraying my former friends against me by spreading reports about my mental condition. And you have succeeded in your efforts, for now there is not more than one person from the Colonel down to the cook who believes me to be sane. Now the facts about my illness are these: my reason is unaffected, as you know, so that I can discharge both my duties to the service and my duties as a father; my nerves are still more or less under my control, and will continue so as long as my will remains fairly intact. You have, however, so thoroughly undermined it that it will soon be ready to fly off the cog-wheel, and then the whole mechanism will go to smash. I will not appeal to your feelings, for you have none, that is your strength; but I will appeal to your interests.

LAURA. Let me hear.

CAPTAIN. You have succeeded by this conduct in arousing my suspicions to such an extent that my judgment is nearly destroyed, and my thoughts begin to wander. This is that approaching insanity you are waiting for, and that may come now at any time. The question then arises for you: Is it more to your interest that I should be sane or insane? Consider! If I succumb I shall have to leave the service, and you will be in a very awkward position. If I die, my life insurance will fall to you. But if I take my own life, you will get nothing. It is therefore to your interest that I should live out my life.

LAURA. Is this a trap?

CAPTAIN. Of course! But it rests with you to avoid it or to run your head into it.

LAURA. You say that you will kill yourself? You shall not do it!

CAPTAIN. Don't be sure. Do you think a man can live when he has nothing and nobody to live for?

LAURA. You surrender, then?

CAPTAIN. No, I offer you peace.

LAURA. The conditions?

CAPTAIN. That I may keep my reason. Deliver me from my suspicions and I throw up the struggle.

LAURA. What suspicions?

CAPTAIN. About Bertha's origin.

LAURA. Is there any doubt about that?

CAPTAIN. Yes, I have doubts, and you have awakened them.

LAURA. I?

CAPTAIN. Yes, you have dropped them like henbane in my ears, and circumstances have given them growth. Deliver me from uncertainty, tell me outright that my suspicions are justified, and I will forgive you in advance.

LAURA. You really can't expect me to

take upon myself a sin that I have not committed.

CAPTAIN. What can it matter when you are certain that I shall not betray you.? Do you think that a man would be likely to blazon his own shame abroad.

LAURA. If I say it is not true, you won't be convinced ; but if I say it is true, you will be convinced. You seem to hope it is true ?

CAPTAIN. Yes, strangely enough ; no doubt because the first supposition can't be proved ; only the last.

LAURA. Have you any reasons for your suspicions ?

CAPTAIN. Yes, and no.

LAURA. I believe that you want to prove me guilty, so that you can get rid of me and have absolute control over the child. But you won't lure me into any such snare.

CAPTAIN. You surely don't think that I would adopt another man's child, if I were convinced of your guilt ?

LAURA. No, I'm sure you would n't, and that convinces me that you lied just now when you said that you forgave me in advance.

CAPTAIN. [Gets up.] Laura, save me and my reason. You don't seem to understand what I say. If the child is not mine, I have no control over it, and don't want to have any; and that is precisely what you want, is n't it ? You will have the power over the child, and I shall be left to maintain you both.

LAURA. The power, yes. Has this whole life-and-death struggle been fought for anything but the power ?

CAPTAIN. You know I do not believe in a future life. The child was my future life. She was my conception of immortality, and perhaps the only one that has any analogy in reality. If you deprive me of that, you cut short my existence.

LAURA. Why did we not separate in time ?

CAPTAIN. Because the child bound us together ; but the bond became a chain. And how did it happen — how ? I have never thought of this, but now the memory of it rises up in accusation, perhaps in condemnation. We had been married two years, and had no child, you best know why. I fell ill and lay at the point of death. In an interval of the fever I heard voices outside in the drawing-room. You and the solicitor were talking about the fortune that I then still possessed. He explained that you could not inherit anything, because we had no children, and asked you if you were *enceinte*. What you answered I did not hear. I recovered, and we had a child. Who is its father ?

LAURA. You.

CAPTAIN. No, it is not I. There is a buried crime here which begins to give off poisonous exhalations ; and what a hellish crime. You have been tender enough about freeing black slaves, but you have kept white ones yourself. I have worked and slaved for you, your child, your mother, your servants ; I have sacrificed career and promotion, I have endured torture, flagellation, sleeplessness, unrest for your sake, until my hair has grown gray ; and all in order that you might enjoy a life without care, and when you grew old, enjoy it over again in your child. I have borne it all without complaint, because I thought myself the father of the child. This is the crudest form of theft, the most brutal slavery. I have had seventeen years of penal servitude and have been innocent. What can you give me in return for this ?

LAURA. Now you are quite mad !

CAPTAIN. [Sits.] That is your hope ! . . . And I have seen how you have labored to conceal your sin. I have had sympathy with you because I did not understand your grief ; I have often lulled your evil conscience to rest, because I thought I was chasing away a morbid thought ; I have heard you cry out in your sleep without allowing myself to listen. Now I remember the night before last, — Bertha's birthday, — I was sitting up reading between two and three in the morning. You screamed as if some one were strangling you, "Don't, don't !" I knocked on the wall because I wished to hear no more. I have long had my suspicions, but I did not dare to hear them confirmed. I have suffered this for you; what will you do for me ?

LAURA. What can I do ? I can swear by God and all that I hold sacred that you are Bertha's father.

CAPTAIN. Of what use is that, as you have said before that a mother can and ought to commit any crime for her child ? I implore you by the memory of the past, I implore you as a wounded man begs for a death-blow, to tell me all. Don't you see that I am as helpless as a child ; don't you hear that I am complaining as to a mother; won't you forget that I am a man, that I am a soldier who with a word can tame men and beasts ? I simply implore pity like a sick man ; I lay down the tokens of my power and pray for mercy on my life.

LAURA. [*Approaches him and lays her hand on his brow.*] What ! You are crying, man !

CAPTAIN. Yes, I am crying, although I am a man. But has not a man eyes ? Has not a man hands, limbs, senses, opinions, passions ? Is he not fed with the same food, hurt with the same weapons, warmed and cooled by the same summer and winter as a woman is ? If you prick us, do we not bleed ? If you tickle us, do we not laugh ? If you poison us, do we not die ? Why should not a man complain, a soldier cry ? Because it is unmanly ? Why is it unmanly ?

LAURA. Cry, then, my child, and you will have your mother with you again. Do you remember that it was as your second mother I first entered your life ? Your great strong body was without nerve. You were a giant child that had either come too early into the world, or perhaps was not wanted.

CAPTAIN. Yes, that's just how it was. My father and mother did not want me, and consequently I was born without a will. I naturally enough thought that I was completing myself when you and I became one, and therefore you got the upper hand ; and I, the commander in barracks and before the troops, became obedient to you, grew by you, looked up to you as a highly gifted being, listened to you as if I had been your ignorant child.

LAURA. Yes, so it was, and therefore I loved you as my child. But you know, you must have seen, when the nature of your feelings changed and you appeared as my lover, I blushed and the joy of your embraces turned to remorse as if my blood were ashamed. The mother became the mistress. Ugh !

CAPTAIN. I saw, but did not understand it. And when I imagined that you despised me for my unmanliness, I wanted to win you as a woman by being a man.

LAURA. Yes, but there was your mistake. The mother was your friend, you see, but the woman was your enemy, and love between the sexes is strife. Do not believe either that I gave myself ; I did not give, but I took — what I wanted. You had one advantage, however ; that I realized and wanted you to realize.

CAPTAIN. You always had the advantage. You could hypnotize me when I was wide awake, so that I neither saw nor heard, but merely obeyed ; you could give me a raw potato and make me imagine it was a peach ; you could force me to admire your foolish ideas as if they were strokes of genius ; you could lead me into crime, yes, even into dishonorable actions. For you were without understanding, and instead of carrying out my ideas, you acted on your own initiative. But when at last I awoke to reflection and realized that my honor was outraged, I wanted to blot out the memory by a great deed, an achievement, a discovery, or an honorable suicide. I wanted to go to the wars, but was not permitted. It was then that I threw myself into science. And now, when I was about to stretch out my hand and gather in its fruits, you suddenly cut off my arm. Now I am dishonored and can live no longer, for a man cannot live without honor.

LAURA. But a woman ?

CAPTAIN. Yes, for she has her children, which he has not. But we and the rest of mankind lived our lives, unconscious as children, full of imaginations, ideals, and illusions, and then we awoke ; it was all over. But we awoke with our feet on the pillow, and he who waked us was himself a sleep-walker. When women grow old and cease to be women, they get beards on their chin ; I wonder what men get who grow old and cease to be men. Those who crowed were no longer cocks but capons, and the pullets answered the call, so that when we thought the sun was about to rise, we found ourselves in the bright moonlight amidst ruins, just as in the good old times. It had only been a little morning slumber with wild dreams, and there was no awakening.

LAURA. Do you know, you should have been a poet!

CAPTAIN. Very possibly.

LAURA. Now I am sleepy, so if you have any more fancies, keep them till to-morrow.

CAPTAIN. A word more first about realities. Do you hate me ?

LAURA. Yes, sometimes, when you are a man.

CAPTAIN. This is race-hatred. If it is true that we are descended from monkeys, it must at least be from two separate species. We are not like one another, are we?

LAURA. What do you mean by all this?

CAPTAIN. I realize that one of us must go under in this struggle.

LAURA. Which?

CAPTAIN. The weaker, of course.

LAURA. And the stronger will be in the right.

CAPTAIN. Certainly, since he has the power.

LAURA. Then I am right.

CAPTAIN. Have you the power already, then?

LAURA. Yes; the power of the law, by means of which I shall put you under control to-morrow.

CAPTAIN. Under control!

LAURA. And then I shall educate my child myself without listening to your visions.

CAPTAIN. And who will pay for the education when I am not there?

LAURA. Your pension.

CAPTAIN. [*Goes menacingly towards her.*] How can you have me put under control?

LAURA. [*Takes out a letter.*] By means of this letter of which an attested copy is lying before the Commissioners in Lunacy.

CAPTAIN. What letter?

LAURA. [*Moves backwards toward the door on the left.*] Yours! Your declaration to the doctor that you are insane. [CAPTAIN *looks at her in silence.*] Now you have fulfilled your function as an unfortunately necessary father and breadwinner. You are not needed any longer and you must go. You must go since you have realized that my intellect is as strong as my will, and since you will not stay and acknowledge it.

[*The* CAPTAIN *goes to the table, takes the lighted lamp and throws it at* LAURA, *who escapes backwards through the door.*]

ACT III

Same scene as in former acts. Another lamp — the private door is barricaded with a chair.
LAURA. NURSE.

LAURA. Did he give you the keys?

NURSE. Give them to me, no, Heaven help us, but I took them from the things that Nöjd had out to brush.

LAURA. Then it is Nöjd who is on duty to-day.

NURSE. Yes, it is Nöjd.

LAURA. Give me the keys.

NURSE. Yes, but it seems like downright stealing. Do you hear his footsteps up there, ma'am? Backwards and forwards, backwards and forwards.

LAURA. Is the door safely fastened?

NURSE. Oh, yes, it's fastened safely enough.

LAURA. [*Opens the desk and sits down at it.*] Control your feelings, Margret. Nothing but calm can save us all. [*Knock.*] Who is it?

NURSE. [*Opens passage door.*] It is Nöjd.

LAURA. Let him come in.

NÖJD. [*Comes in.*] A note from the Colonel.

LAURA. Bring it here. [*Reads.*] Ah! — Nöjd, have you taken all the cartridges out of the guns and pouches?

NÖJD. I have done what you ordered, ma'am.

LAURA. Then wait outside while I answer the Colonel's letter.

[NÖJD *goes.* LAURA *writes.*]

NURSE. Listen, ma'am. Whatever is he doing up there now?

LAURA. Be silent while I write.

[*The sound of sawing is heard.*]

NURSE [*half aloud to herself*]. Oh, may God in His mercy help us all! Where will this end!

LAURA. There; give this to Nöjd. And my mother is to know nothing of all this. Do you hear?

[NURSE *goes to door.* LAURA *opens drawers in top of bureau and takes out papers.*]

[*Enter* PASTOR. *He takes a chair and sits by* LAURA *at the bureau.*]

PASTOR. Good-evening, sister. I have been away all day as you heard, and have only just got back. Distressing things have happened here.

LAURA. Yes, brother, never before have I gone through such a night and such a day.

PASTOR. Ah; but at all events I see that you are none the worse.

LAURA. No, God be thanked, but think what might have happened!

PASTOR. Do tell me how it all began. I have heard so many different accounts.

LAURA. It began with his wild fancy that he was not Bertha's father, and ended with his throwing the lighted lamp in my face.

PASTOR. But that is dreadful! It is fully developed insanity. And what is to be done now?

LAURA. We must try to prevent further violence, and the Doctor has sent to the hospital for a strait-waistcoat. In the mean time I have written to the Colonel, and am now trying to acquaint myself with the affairs of the household, which he has conducted in a most reprehensible manner.

PASTOR. It is a sad story, but I have always expected something of the sort. Fire and water must end in exploding! What have you got there in the drawers.

LAURA. [Opens a drawer in the bureau.] Look, he seems to have kept everything here.

PASTOR [looking through the drawer]. Good Heavens, he has your doll here, and there is your christening-cap and Bertha's rattle; and your letters; and the locket. [Dries his eyes.] He must, after all, have loved you very dearly, Laura. I never kept such things as these!

LAURA. I believe that he used to love me, but time — time changes so many things.

PASTOR. What is this great paper? The receipt for a grave! Yes, better the grave than the lunatic asylum! Laura, tell me, are you blameless in all this?

LAURA. I? Why should I be to blame because a man goes out of his mind?

PASTOR. Ah, well! I shall say nothing! Blood is thicker than water, after all!

LAURA. What do you dare to mean?

PASTOR [gazing at her]. Listen!

LAURA. What?

PASTOR. Listen. You surely cannot deny that it is in conformity with your wishes that you will be able to educate your child yourself?

LAURA. I don't understand.

PASTOR. How I admire you!

LAURA. Me? H'm!

PASTOR. And I shall become the guardian of that free-thinker up there. Do you know I have always considered him as a weed in our garden.

LAURA. [Gives a short suppressed laugh, and then becomes suddenly grave.] And you dare to say that to me — his wife?

PASTOR. You are strong, Laura, incredibly strong! Like a trapped fox, you would rather bite off your own leg than let yourself be caught! Like a master thief — no accomplice, not even your own conscience! Look at yourself in the glass! You dare not!

LAURA. I never use a looking-glass!

PASTOR. No, you dare not! Let me look at your hand. Not a treacherous blood-stain, not a trace of cunning poison! A little innocent murder that cannot be reached by the law; an unconscious sin; unconscious! That is a splendid invention! Do you hear how he is working up there? Beware! if the man gets out he will make short work of you.

LAURA. You talk as much as if you had a bad conscience. Accuse me if you can!

PASTOR. I cannot.

LAURA. You see! You cannot, and therefore I am innocent. You take care of your ward, and I will look after mine! There's the Doctor.

[Enter DOCTOR.]

LAURA [getting up]. Good-evening, Doctor. You at least will help me, will you not? But unfortunately there is not much to be done. Do you hear how he is going on up there? Are you convinced now?

DOCTOR. I am convinced that an act of violence has been committed, but the question is whether that act of violence is to be considered as an outbreak of anger or of madness.

PASTOR. But apart from the actual outbreak you must acknowledge that his ideas are those of a monomaniac.

DOCTOR. I think that your ideas, Pastor, are much more those of a monomaniac.

PASTOR. My firmly rooted convictions about the highest things —

DOCTOR. We will put convictions on one side. Madam, it rests with you to decide whether your husband has made himself liable to imprisonment and fine or to detention in an asylum! What do you think of the behavior?

LAURA. I will not answer for it now.

DOCTOR. Then you have no firmly rooted convictions as to what is most advantageous in the interests of the family? What do you say, Pastor?

PASTOR. Well, there will be a scandal in either case. It is not easy to say.

LAURA. But if he is only sentenced to a fine for violence, he will be able to repeat the violence.

DOCTOR. And if he is sent to prison, he will soon be out again. Therefore, we consider it most advantageous for all parties that he should immediately be treated as insane. Where is the Nurse?

LAURA. Why?

DOCTOR. She must put the strait-waist-coat on the patient when I have talked to him and given the order! But not before. I have — the — the garment out here. [*Goes out into the hall and comes in with a large parcel.*] Please ask the Nurse to come in.
[LAURA *rings.*]

PASTOR. Shocking! Shocking!

[*Enter* NURSE.]

DOCTOR. [*Takes out the strait-waistcoat.*] Please pay attention! I wish you to slip this strait-waistcoat on to the Captain from behind when I consider that circumstances require it to prevent outbreaks of violence. As you see, it has excessively long sleeves with the object of hindering his movements. They are to be tied at the back. There are two straps here that go through buckles, which are afterwards made fast to the arm of the chair or the sofa or whatever is convenient. Will you do this?

NURSE. No, sir, I can't do that; I can't, indeed!

LAURA. Why don't you do it yourself, Doctor?

DOCTOR. Because the patient distrusts me. You, madam, would appear the most obvious person, but I fear that he distrusts even you.
[LAURA *makes an involuntary movement.*]

DOCTOR. Perhaps you, Pastor.

PASTOR. No, I must decline.

[*Enter* NÖJD.]

LAURA. Have you delivered the note already?

NÖJD. Yes, ma'am.

DOCTOR. Is that you, Nöjd? You know the circumstances here; you know that the Captain is out of his mind, and you must help us to look after him.

NÖJD. If there is anything I can do for the Captain, you may be sure I will do it.

DOCTOR. You are to put this jacket on him . . .

NURSE. No, he shan't touch him. Nöjd shall not hurt him. I would rather do it myself, very, very gently. But Nöjd can stand outside and help me if necessary. He may do that.
[*Loud knocking at the private door.*]

DOCTOR. Here he is! Put the jacket under your shawl on that chair, and if you will all go out for the present, the Pastor and I will receive him, for that door will not hold out many minutes. Now, go.

NURSE. [*Goes out to left.*] Lord Jesus help us!

[LAURA *locks bureau, and goes out to left.* NÖJD *goes out at back.*]

[*The private door is forced open, so that the chair is thrown forward on the floor and the lock is broken.*]

[*The* CAPTAIN *comes in with a pile of books under his arm. Puts them on the table.*]

CAPTAIN. The whole thing is to be read here, and in every book. So I was not out of my mind! Here it is in the Odyssey, canto one, verse 215, page 6 of the Upsala translation. It is Telemakos who speaks to Athene. "My mother indeed maintains that he, Odysseus, is my father, but I myself know it not, for no man yet hath known his own origin." And this suspicion is harbored by Telemakos of Penelope, the most virtuous of women! It is beautiful! Is it not? And here we have the prophet Ezekiel: "The fool saith; see here is my father, but who can tell whose loins have engendered him." It is quite clear. What have I got here? Mersläkow's History of Russian Literature. "Alexander Pushkin, Russia's greatest poet, was tortured to death by the reports that were circulated about his wife's unfaithfulness rather than by the ball he received in his breast in a duel. On his deathbed he swore that she was innocent." Ass, ass! How could he answer for it? In the mean time you hear that I read my books — Ah, Jonas, are you there? And the Doctor, of course? Have you heard how I answered an English lady, when she complained of an Irishman who used to throw lighted lamps in his wife's face? "God, what women," I cried. — "Women," she lisped. — "Yes, of course," I answered

"When things go to such a length that a man, a man who loved and worshiped a woman, takes a lighted lamp and throws it in her face, then one can tell."

PASTOR. What can one tell?

CAPTAIN. Nothing. One never knows anything. One only believes. Is not that true, Jonas? One believes, and then one is saved! Yes; so one would be. No, I know that one may be lost by one's faith. I know that.

DOCTOR. Captain!

CAPTAIN. Hush! I will not speak to you; I will not hear you repeating the chatter in there like a telephone! In there! You know!—Listen, Jonas; do you believe that you are the father of your children? I remember that you had a tutor in the house who was good-looking, and who was a great deal gossiped about.

PASTOR. Adolf, beware!

CAPTAIN. Grope about under your wig, and feel if there are not two knobs there. By my soul, I believe he turns pale! Yes, yes; they only talk; but, good Lord, there is so much talk. Still, we are nothing but ridiculous dupes for all that, we married men. Don't you think so, Doctor? How was it with your marriage bed? Had you not a lieutenant in the house, too? Wait, and I will guess? His name is ——. [Whispers in DOCTOR's ear.] You see he turns pale, too! Don't be unhappy now. She is dead and buried, and what is done can't be undone! I knew him well, by the by, and he is now . . . look at me, Doctor . . . no, right into my eyes . . . a major of dragoons! By God, if I don't believe he has horns, too.

DOCTOR [annoyed]. Captain, won't you talk of something else?

CAPTAIN. Do you see? He immediately wants to talk of something else when I mention horns.

PASTOR. Do you know, Adolf, that you are insane?

CAPTAIN. Yes; I know that well enough. But if I only had the management of your crowned brains awhile, I should soon have you shut up, too! I am mad, but how did I become so? That does not matter to you, and it does not matter to any one! Will you talk of something else now? [Takes photograph album from the table.] Lord Jesus, is that my child! Mine! We cannot

tell that. Do you know what would have to be done to make sure? First, one would have to marry to get a position in society, then immediately be divorced and become lovers, and finally adopt the children. Then one would at least be sure that they were one's adopted children. That is right enough. But how does all this help me now? What can help me now that you have taken my conception of immortality from me; what do science and philosophy avail me when I have nothing to live for; what can I do with life when I have no honor? I grafted my right arm, half my brain, half my marrow on to another stem, for I thought they would grow up together and knit themselves into a more perfect tree, and then some one came with a knife and cut them asunder below the graft, and now I am only half a tree. As for the other half, it goes on growing with my arm and half my brain, while I pine and die, for they were the best parts I gave away. Now I will die. Do what you like with me. I shall not be found any more.

[The DOCTOR whispers to the PASTOR, and they go into the inner rooms on the left. Immediately afterwards BERTHA comes out.]

[The CAPTAIN sinks into a chair by the table.]

BERTHA. [Goes up to him.] Are you ill, father?

CAPTAIN. [Looks up offended.] I?

BERTHA. Do you know what you have done? Do you know that you threw the lamp at mother?

CAPTAIN. Did I?

BERTHA. Yes, you did. Just think if she had been hurt.

CAPTAIN. What would that have mattered?

BERTHA. You are not my father if you can talk like that.

CAPTAIN. What do you say? Am I not your father? How do you know that? Who told you that? And who is your father, then? Who?

BERTHA. Not you, at any rate.

CAPTAIN. Still not I! Who, then? Who? You seem to be well informed! Who told you? That I should live to see my child come and tell me straight in the face that I am not her father! But do you not know that you disgrace your mother when you say that? Do you not know that it is her shame if it is so?

BERTHA. Say nothing bad about mother; do you hear?

CAPTAIN. No; you all hold together against me! And so you have done all the time.

BERTHA. Father!

CAPTAIN. Do not say that word again!

BERTHA. Father, father!

CAPTAIN [drawing her to him]. Bertha, dearly beloved child, you are my child, are you not? Yes, yes; it cannot be otherwise. It is so. The rest was only morbid thoughts which come on the wind like pestilence and fevers. Look at me, and then I shall see my soul in your eyes! — But I see her soul, too! You have two souls, and you love me with one of them and hate me with the other. But you must only love me! You must only have one soul, or you will never have peace, nor I either. You must only have one thought, which is the child of my thought; you must only have one will, which is mine.

BERTHA. But I will not. I want to be myself.

CAPTAIN. You must not. You see, I am a cannibal, and I will eat you. Your mother wanted to eat me, but she could not. I am Saturn who ate his children because it had been prophesied that they would eat him. To eat or be eaten! That is the question. If I do not eat you, you will eat me, and you have already showed me your teeth! But don't be frightened, my darling child; I won't do you any harm.

[Goes to the trophy of weapons and takes down a revolver.]

BERTHA [trying to escape]. Help, mother, help, he's going to murder me!

NURSE [coming in]. Mr. Adolf, what is it?

CAPTAIN. [Examines revolver.] Have you taken the cartridges out?

NURSE. Yes, I just tidied them away, but sit down and be quiet, and I'll get them out again!

[She takes the CAPTAIN by the arm and puts him in a chair, into which he sinks feebly. Then she takes out the strait-waistcoat and places herself behind the chair. BERTHA slips out on the left.]

NURSE. Mr. Adolf, do you remember when you were my darling little child and I tucked you in of nights, and said "Gentle Jesus" to you, and do you remember how I got up in the night and gave you a drink; do you remember how I lighted the candle and talked about pretty things when you had bad dreams and could n't sleep? Do you remember?

CAPTAIN. Go on talking, Margret, it soothes my head so: go on talking again.

NURSE. Oh, yes, but you must listen to me! Do you remember when you once took the great kitchen knife and wanted to cut out boats with it, and how I came in and had to get the knife away by tricking you? You were a little foolish child so I had to trick you, for you did n't believe that we meant well by you. "Give me that ugly snake," I said, "or it will bite you!" and then you gave up the knife. [Takes the revolver out of the CAPTAIN's hand.] And then when you had to dress yourself and did n't want to. Then I had to coax you and say that you should have a golden coat and be dressed like a prince. And then I took your little vest that was only made of green worsted, and held it up in front of you, and said, "In with both arms," and then I said, "Sit nice and still while I button it down the back." [She gets the jacket on.] And then I said, "Get up now, and walk across the floor like a good boy so that I can see whether it's straight. [She leads him to the sofa.] And then I said, "Now you must go to bed."

CAPTAIN. What did you say? Was I to go to bed when I was dressed? . . . Damnation! What have you done with me? [Tries to free himself.] Ah! You infernally cunning woman! Who would have thought that you had so much wit. [Lies down on the sofa.] Trapped, shorn, outwitted, forbidden to die.

NURSE. Forgive me, Mr. Adolf, forgive me, but I wanted to hinder you from killing your child.

CAPTAIN. Why did n't you let me kill the child? For life is a hell and death a heaven, and children belong to heaven.

NURSE. How do you know what comes after death?

CAPTAIN. That is the only thing we do know, but of life we know nothing! Oh, if one had only known from the beginning.

NURSE. Mr. Adolf, humble your hard heart and cry to God for mercy; it is not yet too late. It was not too late for the thief on the cross when the Saviour said, "To-day shalt thou be with Me in Paradise."

CAPTAIN. Are you croaking for a corpse already, old crow?

[NURSE *takes a hymn book out of her pocket.*]

CAPTAIN. [*Calls.*] Nöjd, is Nöjd there?

[*Enter* NÖJD.]

CAPTAIN. Fling that woman out! She is trying to strangle me with her hymn book. Throw her out of the window, or up the chimney or anywhere.

NÖJD. [*Looks at* NURSE.] Heaven help you, Captain, but I can't do that, I simply can't. If only it were six men; but a woman!

CAPTAIN. Have you never got the better of a woman, heigh?

NÖJD. Of course I have, but it is a very different thing to lay hands on a woman.

CAPTAIN. Why is it so different? Have they not laid hands on me?

NÖJD. Yes, but I can't, Captain. It is downright as if you were to ask me to strike the Pastor. It's against nature! I can't!

[*Enter* LAURA. *She signs to* NÖJD *to go.*]

CAPTAIN. Omphale, Omphale! Now you play with the club while Hercules spins the wool. [LAURA *comes forward to the sofa.*]

LAURA. Adolf. Look at me. Do you think that I am your enemy?

CAPTAIN. Yes, I do think so. I believe that you are all my enemies! My mother, who did not want to bring me into the world because I was to be born with pain, was my enemy when she deprived my embryonic life of its nourishment and made a weakling of me. My sister was my enemy when she taught me that I was to be obedient to her. The first woman I embraced was my enemy, for she gave me ten years of illness in payment for the love I gave her. My daughter became my enemy when she had to choose between me and you. And you, my wife, you have been my arch-enemy, because you have never left me till I lay here lifeless.

LAURA. I don't know that I ever thought or intended what you think I did. It may be that an obscure desire to get rid of you as something troublesome may have existed within me, and if you see any plan in my conduct, it is possible that it was to be found there, although I was unconscious of it. I have never reflected about my actions, but they have proceeded on the lines that you yourself laid down, and before God and my conscience I consider myself innocent, even if I am not. Your existence has lain like a stone on my heart, which weighed so heavily that the heart sought to shake off the oppressive burden. These are the facts, and if I have wounded you to the death, I ask your forgiveness.

CAPTAIN. All that sounds plausible. But of what help is it to me? And whose is the fault? Perhaps that of a spiritual marriage! Formerly one married a wife, now one enters into partnership with a business woman, or goes to live with a friend. . . . And then one cheats the partner, and outrages the friend! What becomes of love, healthy physical love? It dies in the mean time. And what is the result of this love in shares, payable to the bearer without joint liability? Who is the bearer when the crash comes? Who is the fleshly father to the spiritual child?

LAURA. And with regard to your suspicions about the child, they are quite without foundation.

CAPTAIN. That is just what is so appalling! If at least there was any foundation for them, it would be something to take hold of, to cling to. Now there are only shadows that hide themselves in the bushes, and stick out their heads to grin; it is like fighting with the air, or firing blank cartridges at a sham-fight. A fatal reality would have called forth resistance, nerved life and soul to action; but now my thoughts dissolve into thin air, and my brain grinds a void until it is on fire. Put a pillow under my head, and throw something over me, I am so terribly cold!

[LAURA *takes her shawl and spreads it over him.* NURSE *goes to fetch a pillow.*]

LAURA. Give me your hand, friend.

CAPTAIN. My hand! The hand that you have bound! Omphale! Omphale! . . . But I can feel your shawl against my mouth; it is as warm and soft as your arm, and it smells of vanilla, like your hair when you were young! Laura, when you were young, and we walked in the birchwoods, with the oxlips and the thrushes . . . glorious, glorious! Think how beautiful life was, and what it is now. You did not wish to have it so, and neither did I, and yet it happened. Who, then, rules over life? . . .

LAURA. God alone rules . . .

CAPTAIN. The God of strife, then! Or perhaps the goddess nowadays. Take away the cat that is lying on me! Take it away!

[NURSE brings in a pillow and takes away the shawl.]

CAPTAIN. Give me my uniform coat! Throw it over me! [NURSE takes the coat from the clothes-pegs and lays it over him.] Ah, my rough lion-skin that you wanted to take away from me! Omphale! Omphale! Thou cunning woman who wast the lover of peace and the deviser of disarmaments! Wake, Hercules, before they take thy club from thee! You will wile our armor off us, too, and make believe that it is tinsel. No, it was iron, do you hear, before it became tinsel. In olden days the smith made the cuirass; now it is the needlewoman. Omphale! Omphale! Rude strength has fallen before treacherous weakness. — Out on you, infernal woman, and damnation on your sex! [He raises himself to spit at her, but falls back onto the sofa.] What sort of a pillow have you given me, Margret? It is so hard, and so cold, so cold! Come and sit here by me on the chair. There now! May I lay my head on your lap? Ah, that is warm! Bend over me so that I can feel your breast! Oh, it is sweet to sleep on a woman's breast, a mother's or a mistress's, but the mother's is best.

LAURA. Would you like to see your child, Adolf?

CAPTAIN. My child? A man has no children; it is only women who have children; and therefore the future is theirs, when we die childless. Oh, God! who lovest children!

NURSE. Listen, he is praying to God.

CAPTAIN. No, to you to put me to sleep, for I am tired, so tired. Good-night, Margret, and blessed be you among women.

[He raises himself but falls back on the NURSE's lap with a cry.]

[LAURA goes to the left and calls in the DOCTOR who enters with the PASTOR.]

LAURA. Help, Doctor! if it is not too late. Look, he has ceased to breathe!

DOCTOR. [Feels the patient's pulse.] It is a fit.

PASTOR. Is he dead?

DOCTOR. No; he may still come back to life, but to what an awakening we do not know.

PASTOR. "First death, and then the judgment."

DOCTOR. No judgment, and no accusations. You who believe that a God overrules the fortunes of men must ask of Him concerning this matter.

NURSE. Ah, Pastor, he prayed to God in his last moments.

PASTOR. [To LAURA.] Is that true?

LAURA. It is true.

DOCTOR. In that case, of which I can judge just as little as of the origin of the illness, my science is at an end. You try now, Pastor.

LAURA. Is this all that you have to say by this deathbed, Doctor?

DOCTOR. This is all! I know no more. Let him speak that knows more!

[BERTHA enters on the left and runs forward to her mother.]

BERTHA. Mother! Mother!

LAURA. My child, my own child!

PASTOR. Amen.

THE CHERRY ORCHARD

By ANTON TCHEKHOV

Translated, with text notes, by GEORGE CALDERON

LIST OF PERSONS

MADAME RANÉVSKY, *a landowner*

ÁNYA, *her daughter, aged seventeen*

BARBARA, *her adopted daughter, aged twenty-seven*

LEONÍD GÁYEF, *brother of Madame Ranévsky*

LOPÁKHIN, *a merchant*

PETER TROPHÍMOF, *a student*

SIMEÓNOF-PÍSHTCHIK, *a landowner*

CHARLOTTE, *a governess*

EPHIKHÓDOF, *a clerk*

DUNYÁSHA, *a housemaid*

FIRS, *man-servant, aged eighty-seven*

YÁSHA, *a young man-servant*

TRAMP

Stationmaster, Post-Office Official, Guests, Servants, etc.

The action takes place on Madame Ranévsky's property.

THE CHERRY ORCHARD

ACT I

A room which is still called the nursery. One door leads to ÁNYA's *room. Dawn; the sun will soon rise. It is already May; the cherry trees are in blossom, but it is cold in the garden and there is a morning frost. The windows are closed.*

[*Enter* DUNYÁSHA *with a candle, and* LOPÁKHIN *with a book in his hand.*]

LOPÁKHIN. So the train has come in, thank Heaven. What is the time?

DUNYÁSHA. Nearly two. [*Putting the candle out.*] It is light already.

LOPÁKHIN. How late is the train? A couple of hours at least. [*Yawning and stretching.*] What do you think of me? A fine fool I have made of myself. I came on purpose to meet them at the station and then I went and fell asleep, fell asleep as I sat in my chair. What a nuisance it is! You might have woke me up anyway.

DUNYÁSHA. I thought that you had gone. [*She listens.*] That sounds like them driving up.

LOPÁKHIN [*listening*]. No; they have got to get the luggage out and all that. [*A pause.*] Madame Ranévsky has been five years abroad. I wonder what she has become like. What a splendid creature she is! So easy and simple in her ways. I remember when I was a youngster of fifteen my old father (he used to keep the shop here in the village then) struck me in the face with his fist and set my nose bleeding. We had come, for some reason or other, I forget what, into the courtyard, and he had been drinking. Madame Ranévsky — I remember it like yesterday, still a young girl, and oh, so slender — brought me to the wash-hand stand, here, in this very room, in the nursery. "Don't cry, little peasant," she said, "it 'll mend by your wedding."[1] [*A pause.*] "Little peasant"! . . . My father, it is true, was a peasant, and here am I in

¹ *It 'll mend by your wedding:* a proverbial phrase.

a white waistcoat and brown boots; a silk purse out of a sow's ear, as you might say; just turned rich, with heaps of money, but when you come to look at it, still a peasant of the peasants. [*Turning over the pages of the book.*] Here 's this book that I was reading and did n't understand a word of it; I just sat reading and fell asleep.

DUNYÁSHA. The dogs never slept all night; they knew that their master and mistress were coming.

LOPÁKHIN. What 's the matter with you, Dunyásha? You 're all . . .

DUNYÁSHA. My hands are trembling; I feel quite faint.

LOPÁKHIN. You are too refined, Dunyásha; that 's what it is. You dress yourself like a young lady; and look at your hair! You ought not to do it; you ought to remember your place.

[*Enter* EPHIKHÓDOF *with a nosegay. He is dressed in a short jacket and brightly polished boots which squeak noisily. As he comes in he drops the nosegay.*]

EPHIKHÓDOF [*picking it up*]. The gardener has sent this; he says it is to go in the dining-room. [*Handing it to* DUNYÁSHA.]

LOPÁKHIN. And bring me some quass.

DUNYÁSHA. Yes, sir. [*Exit* DUNYÁSHA.]

EPHIKHÓDOF. There 's a frost this morning, three degrees, and the cherry trees all in blossom. I can't say I think much of our climate; [*sighing*] that is impossible. Our climate is not adapted to contribute; and I should like to add, with your permission, that only two days ago I bought myself a new pair of boots, and I venture to assure you they do squeak beyond all bearing. What am I to grease them with?

LOPÁKHIN. Get out; I 'm tired of you.

EPHIKHÓDOF. Every day some misfortune happens to me; but do I grumble? No; I am used to it; I can afford to smile.

[*Enter* DUNYÁSHA, *and hands a glass of quass to* LOPÁKHIN.]

EPHIKHÓDOF. I must be going. [*He knocks against a chair, which falls to the ground.*] There you are! [*In a voice of triumph.*] You see, if I may venture on the expression, the sort of incidents *inter alia.* It really is astonishing!

[*Exit* EPHIKHÓDOF.]

DUNYÁSHA. To tell you the truth, Yermolái Alexéyitch, Ephikhódof has made me a proposal.

LOPÁKHIN. Hmph!

DUNYÁSHA. I hardly know what to do. He is such a well-behaved young man, only so often when he talks one does n't know what he means. It is all so nice and full of good feeling, but you can't make out what it means. I fancy I am rather fond of him. He adores me passionately. He is a most unfortunate man ; every day something seems to happen to him. They call him "Twenty-two misfortunes," that 's his nickname.

LOPÁKHIN [*listening*]. There, surely that is them coming!

DUNYÁSHA. They 're coming! Oh, what is the matter with me? I am all turning cold.

LOPÁKHIN. Yes, there they are, and no mistake. Let 's go and meet them. Will she know me again, I wonder? It is five years since we met.

DUNYÁSHA. I am going to faint! . . . I am going to faint!

[*Two carriages are heard driving up to the house.* LOPÁKHIN *and* DUNYÁSHA *exeunt quickly. The stage remains empty. A hubbub begins in the neighboring rooms.* FIRS *walks hastily across the stage, leaning on a walking-stick. He has been to meet them at the station. He is wearing an old-fashioned livery and a tall hat ; he mumbles something to himself, but not a word is audible. The noise behind the scenes grows louder and louder. A voice says: "Let 's go this way." Enter* MADAME RANÉVSKY, ÁNYA, CHARLOTTE, *leading a little dog on a chain, all dressed in traveling-dresses ;* BARBARA *in greatcoat, with a kerchief over her head,* GÁYEF, SIMEÓNOF-PÍSHTCHIK, LOPÁKHIN, DUNYÁSHA, *carrying parcel and umbrella, servants with luggage, all cross the stage.*]

ÁNYA. Come through this way. Do you remember what room this is, mamma?

MADAME RANÉVSKY [*joyfully, through her tears*]. The nursery.

BARBARA. How cold it is. My hands are simply frozen. [*To* MADAME RANÉVSKY.] Your two rooms, the white room and the violet room, are just the same as they were, mamma.

MADAME RANÉVSKY. My nursery, my dear, beautiful nursery! This is where I used to sleep when I was a little girl. [*Crying.*] I am like a little girl still. [*Kissing* GÁYEF *and* BARBARA *and then* GÁYEF *again.*] Barbara has not altered a bit ; she is just like a nun; and I knew Dunyásha at once. [*Kissing* DUNYÁSHA.]

GÁYEF. Your train was two hours late. What do you think of that? There 's punctuality for you!

CHARLOTTE. [*To* SIMEÓNOF-PÍSHTCHIK.] My little dog eats nuts.

PÍSHTCHIK [*astonished*]. You don't say so! Well, I never!

[*Exeunt all but* ÁNYA *and* DUNYÁSHA.]

DUNYÁSHA. At last you 've come!

[*She takes off* ÁNYA's *overcoat and hat.*]

ÁNYA. I have not slept for four nights on the journey. I am frozen to death.

DUNYÁSHA. It was Lent when you went away. There was snow on the ground ; it was freezing ; but now! Oh, my dear! [*Laughing and kissing her.*] How I have waited for you, my joy, my light! Oh, I must tell you something at once, I cannot wait another minute.

ÁNYA [*without interest*]. What, again?

DUNYÁSHA. Ephikhódof, the clerk, proposed to me in Easter Week.

ÁNYA. Same old story. . . . [*Putting her hair straight.*] All my hairpins have dropped out.

[*She is very tired, staggering with fatigue.*]

DUNYÁSHA. I hardly know what to think of it. He loves me! Oh, how he loves me!

ÁNYA [*looking into her bedroom, affectionately*]. My room, my windows, just as if I had never gone away! I am at home again! When I wake up in the morning I shall run out into the garden. . . . Oh, if only I could get to sleep! I have not slept the whole journey from Paris, I was so nervous and anxious.

DUNYÁSHA. Monsieur Trophímof arrived the day before yesterday.

ÁNYA [*joyfully*]. Peter?

DUNYÁSHA. He is sleeping outside in the bath-house; he is living there. He was afraid he might be in the way. [*Looking at her watch.*] I'd like to go and wake him, only Mamzelle Barbara told me not to. "Mind you don't wake him," she said.

[*Enter* BARBARA *with bunch of keys hanging from her girdle.*]

BARBARA. Dunyásha, go and get some coffee, quick. Mamma wants some coffee.

DUNYÁSHA. In a minute!

[*Exit* DUNYÁSHA.]

BARBARA. Well, thank Heaven, you have come. Here you are at home again. [*Caressing her.*] My little darling is back! My pretty one is back!

ÁNYA. What I've had to go through!

BARBARA. I can believe you.

ÁNYA. I left here in Holy Week. How cold it was! Charlotte would talk the whole way and keep doing conjuring tricks. What on earth made you tie Charlotte round my neck?

BARBARA. Well, you could n't travel alone, my pet. At seventeen!

ÁNYA. When we got to Paris, it was so cold! There was snow on the ground. I can't talk French a bit. Mamma was on the fifth floor of a big house. When I arrived there were a lot of Frenchmen with her, and ladies, and an old Catholic priest with a book, and it was very uncomfortable and full of tobacco smoke. I suddenly felt so sorry for mamma, oh, so sorry! I took her head in my arms and squeezed it and could not let it go, and then mamma kept kissing me and crying.

BARBARA [*crying*]. Don't go on; don't go on!

ÁNYA. She's sold her villa near Mentone already. She's nothing left, absolutely nothing; and I had n't a farthing either. We only just managed to get home. And mamma won't understand! We get out at a station to have some dinner, and she asks for all the most expensive things and gives the waiters a florin each for a tip; and Charlotte does the same. And Yásha wanted his portion, too. It was too awful! Yásha

is mamma's new manservant. We have brought him back with us.

BARBARA. I've seen the rascal.

ÁNYA. Come, tell me all about everything! Has the interest on the mortgage been paid?

BARBARA. How could it be?

ÁNYA. Oh, dear! Oh, dear!

BARBARA. The property will be sold in August.

ÁNYA. Oh, dear! Oh, dear!

LOPÁKHIN [*looking in at the door and mooing like a cow*]. Moo-oo!

[*He goes away again.*]

BARBARA [*laughing through her tears, and shaking her fist at the door*]. Oh, I should like to give him one!

ÁNYA [*embracing* BARBARA *softly*]. Barbara, has he proposed to you?

[BARBARA *shakes her head.*]

ÁNYA. And yet I am sure he loves you. Why don't you come to an understanding? What are you waiting for?

BARBARA. I don't think anything will come of it. He has so much to do; he can't be bothered with me; he hardly takes any notice. Confound the man, I can't bear to see him! Every one talks about our marriage; every one congratulates me; but, as a matter of fact, there is nothing in it; it's all a dream. [*Changing her tone.*] You've got on a brooch like a bee.

ÁNYA [*sadly*]. Mamma bought it me. [*Going into her room, talking gayly, like a child.*] When I was in Paris, I went up in a balloon!

BARBARA. How glad I am you are back, my little pet! my pretty one!

[DUNYÁSHA *has already returned with a coffee-pot and begins to prepare the coffee.*]

BARBARA [*standing by the door*]. I trudge about all day looking after things, and I think and think. What are we to do? If only we could marry you to some rich man it would be a load off my mind. I would go into a retreat, and then to Kief, to Moscow; I would tramp about from one holy place to another, always tramping and tramping. What bliss!

ÁNYA. The birds are singing in the garden. What time is it now?

BARBARA. It must be past two. It is time to go to bed, my darling. [*Following* ÁNYA *into her room.*] What bliss!

[ENTER YÁSHA *with a shawl and a traveling-bag.*]

YÁSHA [*crossing the stage, delicately*]. May I pass this way, mademoiselle?

DUNYÁSHA. One would hardly know you, Yásha. How you 've changed abroad!

YÁSHA. Ahem! And who may you be?

DUNYÁSHA. When you left here I was a little thing like that [*indicating with her hand*]. My name is Dunyásha, Theodore Kozoyédof's daughter. Don't you remember me?

YÁSHA. Ahem! You little cucumber! [*He looks round cautiously, then embraces her. She screams and drops a saucer. Exit YÁSHA hastily.*]

BARBARA [*in the doorway, crossly*]. What 's all this?

DUNYÁSHA [*crying*]. I 've broken a saucer.

BARBARA. Well, it brings luck.

[*Enter ÁNYA from her room.*]

ÁNYA. We must tell mamma that Peter 's here.

BARBARA. I 've told them not to wake him.

ÁNYA [*thoughtfully*]. It 's just six years since papa died. And only a month afterwards poor little Grisha was drowned in the river; my pretty little brother, only seven years old! It was too much for mamma; she ran away, ran away without looking back. [*Shuddering.*] How well I can understand her, if only she knew! [*A pause.*] Peter Trophímof was Grisha's tutor; he might remind her.

[*Enter FIRS in long coat and white waistcoat.*]

FIRS [*going over to the coffee-pot, anxiously*]. My mistress is going to take coffee here. [*Putting on white gloves.*] Is the coffee ready? [*Sternly, to DUNYÁSHA.*] Here, girl, where 's the cream?

DUNYÁSHA. Oh, dear! oh, dear! [*Exit DUNYÁSHA hastily.*]

FIRS [*bustling about the coffee-pot*]. Ah, you . . . job-lot![1] [*Mumbling to himself.*] She 's come back from Paris. The master went to Paris once in a post-chaise. [*Laughing.*]

BARBARA. What is it, Firs?

[1] *Job-lot.* In the original, *nedotëpa*, a word invented by Tchekhov, and now established as classical. Derived from *ne*, not, and *dotyápat*, to finish chopping.

FIRS. I beg your pardon? [*Joyfully.*] My mistress has come home; at last I 've seen her. Now I 'm ready to die. [*He cries with joy. Enter MADAME RANÉVSKY, LOPÁKHIN, GÁYEF, and PÍSHTCHIK; PÍSHTCHIK in Russian breeches and coat of fine cloth. GÁYEF as he enters makes gestures as if playing billiards.*]

MADAME RANÉVSKY. What was the expression? Let me see. " I 'll put the red in the corner pocket; double into the middle — "

GÁYEF. I 'll chip the red in the right-hand top. Once upon a time, Lyuba, when we were children, we used to sleep here side by side in two little cots, and now I 'm fifty-one, and can't bring myself to believe it.

LOPÁKHIN. Yes; time flies.

GÁYEF. Who 's that?

LOPÁKHIN. Time flies, I say.

GÁYEF. There 's a smell of patchouli!

ÁNYA. I am going to bed. Good-night, mamma. [*Kissing her mother.*]

MADAME RANÉVSKY. My beloved little girl! [*Kissing her hands.*] Are you glad you 're home again? I can't come to my right senses.

ÁNYA. Good-night, uncle.

GÁYEF [*kissing her face and hands*]. God bless you, little Ánya. How like your mother you are! [*To MADAME RANÉVSKY.*] You were just such another girl at her age, Lyuba.

[*ÁNYA shakes hands with LOPÁKHIN and SIMEÓNOF-PÍSHTCHIK, and exit, shutting her bedroom door behind her.*]

MADAME RANÉVSKY. She 's very, very tired.

PÍSHTCHIK. It must have been a long journey.

BARBARA. [*To LOPÁKHIN and PÍSHTCHIK.*] Well, gentlemen, it 's past two, time you were off.

MADAME RANÉVSKY [*laughing*]. You have n't changed a bit, Barbara! [*Drawing her to herself and kissing her.*] I 'll just finish my coffee, then we 'll all go. [*FIRS puts a footstool under her feet.*] Thank you, friend. I 'm used to my coffee. I drink it day and night. Thank you, you dear old man. [*Kissing FIRS.*]

BARBARA. I 'll go and see if they 've got all the luggage. [*Exit BARBARA.*]

MADAME RANÉVSKY. Can it be me that's sitting here? [*Laughing.*] I want to jump and wave my arms about. [*Pausing and covering her face.*] Surely I must be dreaming! God knows I love my country. I love it tenderly. I could n't see out of the window from the train, I was crying so. [*Crying.*] However, I must drink my coffee. Thank you, Firs; thank you, you dear old man. I 'm so glad to find you still alive.

FIRS. The day before yesterday.

GÁYEF. He 's hard of hearing.

LOPÁKHIN. I 've got to be off for Kharkof by the five-o'clock train. Such a nuisance! I wanted to stay and look at you and talk to you. You 're as splendid as you always were.

PÍSHTCHIK [*sighing heavily*]. Handsomer than ever and dressed like a Parisian . . . Perish my wagon and all its wheels!

LOPÁKHIN. Your brother, Leoníd Andréyitch, says I 'm a snob, a money-grubber. He can say what he likes. I don't care a hang. Only I want you to believe in me as you used to; I want your wonderful, touching eyes to look at me as they used to. Merciful God in heaven! My father was your father's serf, and your grandfather's serf before him; but you, you did so much for me in the old days that I 've forgotten everything, and I love you like a sister — more than a sister.

MADAME RANÉVSKY. I can't sit still! I can't do it! [*Jumping up and walking about in great agitation.*] This happiness is more than I can bear. Laugh at me! I am a fool! [*Kissing a cupboard.*] My darling old cupboard! [*Caressing a table.*] My dear little table!

GÁYEF. Nurse is dead since you went away.

MADAME RANÉVSKY [*sitting down and drinking coffee*]. Yes, Heaven rest her soul. They wrote and told me.

GÁYEF. And Anastási is dead. Squint-eyed Peter has left us and works in the town at the Police Inspector's now.

[GÁYEF *takes out a box of sugar candy from his pocket, and begins to eat it.*]

PÍSHTCHIK. My daughter Dáshenka sent her compliments.

LOPÁKHIN. I long to say something charming and delightful to you. [*Looking at his watch.*] I 'm just off; there 's no time to talk. Well, yes, I 'll put it in two or three words. You know that your cherry orchard is going to be sold to pay the mortgage: the sale is fixed for the 22d of August; but don't you be uneasy, my dear lady; sleep peacefully; there 's a way out of it. This is my plan. Listen to me carefully. Your property is only fifteen miles from the town; the railway runs close beside it; and if only you will cut up the cherry orchard and the land along the river into building lots and let it off on lease for villas, you will get at least two thousand five hundred pounds a year out of it.

GÁYEF. Come, Come! What rubbish you 're talking!

MADAME RANÉVSKY. I don't quite understand what you mean, Yermolái Alexéyitch.

LOPÁKHIN. You will get a pound a year at least for every acre from the tenants, and if you advertise the thing at once, I am ready to bet whatever you like, by the autumn you won't have a clod of that earth left on your hands. It 'll all be snapped up. In two words, I congratulate you; you are saved. It 's a first-class site, with a good deep river. Only, of course you will have to put it in order and clear the ground; you will have to pull down all the old buildings — this house, for instance, which is no longer fit for anything; you 'll have to cut down the cherry orchard. . . .

MADAME RANÉVSKY. Cut down the cherry orchard! Excuse me, but you don't know what you are talking about. If there is one thing that 's interesting, remarkable in fact, in the whole province, it 's our cherry orchard.

LOPÁKHIN. There 's nothing remarkable about the orchard except that it 's a very big one. It only bears once every two years, and then you don't know what to do with the fruit. Nobody wants to buy it.

GÁYEF. Our cherry orchard is mentioned in Andréyevsky's Encyclopædia.

LOPÁKHIN [*looking at his watch*]. If we don't make up our minds or think of any way, on the 22d of August the cherry orchard and the whole property will be sold by auction. Come, make up your mind! There 's no other way out of it, I swear — absolutely none.

FIRS. In the old days, forty or fifty years ago, they used to dry the cherries and soak 'em and pickle 'em, and make jam of 'em; and the dried cherries . . .

GÁYEF. Shut up, Firs.

FIRS. The dried cherries used to be sent in wagons to Moscow and Khɐrkof. A heap of money ! The dried cherries were soft and juicy and sweet and sweet-smelling then. They knew some way in those days.

MADAME RANÉVSKY. And why don't they do it now ?

FIRS. They 've forgotten. Nobody remembers how to do it.

PÍSHTCHIK. [To MADAME RANÉVSKY.] What about Paris ? How did you get on ? Did you eat frogs ?

MADAME RANÉVSKY. Crocodiles.

PÍSHTCHIK. You don't say so ! Well, I never !

LOPÁKHIN. Until a little while ago there was nothing but gentry and peasants in the villages ; but now villa residents have made their appearance. All the towns, even the little ones, are surrounded by villas now. In another twenty years the villa resident will have multiplied like anything. At present he only sits and drinks tea on his veranda, but it is quite likely that he will soon take to cultivating his three acres of land, and then your old cherry orchard will become fruitful, rich and happy. . . .

GÁYEF [angry]. What gibberish !

[Enter BARBARA and YÁSHA.]

BARBARA [taking out a key and noisily unlocking an old-fashioned cupboard]. There are two telegrams for you, mamma. Here they are.

MADAME RANÉVSKY [tearing them up without reading them]. They 're from Paris. I 've done with Paris.

GÁYEF. Do you know how old this cupboard is, Lyuba ? A week ago I pulled out the bottom drawer and saw a date burnt in it. That cupboard was made exactly a hundred years ago. What do you think of that, eh ? We might celebrate its jubilee. It 's only an inanimate thing, but for all that it 's a historic cupboard.

PÍSHTCHIK [astonished]. A hundred years ? Well, I never !

GÁYEF [touching the cupboard]. Yes, it 's a wonderful thing. . . . Beloved and venerable cupboard ; honor and glory to your existence, which for more than a hundred years has been directed to the noble ideals of justice and virtue. Your silent summons to profitable labor has never weakened in all these hundred years. [Crying.] You have upheld the courage of succeeding generations of our humankind ; you have upheld faith in a better future and cherished in us ideals of goodness and social consciousness. [A pause.]

LOPÁKHIN. Yes. . . .

MADAME RANÉVSKY. You have n't changed, Leoníd.

GÁYEF [embarrassed]. Off the white in the corner, chip the red in the middle pocket !

LOPÁKHIN [looking at his watch]. Well, I must be off.

YÁSHA [handing a box to MADAME RANÉVSKY]. Perhaps you 'll take your pills now.

PÍSHTCHIK. You ought n't to take medicine, dear lady. It does you neither good nor harm. Give them here, my friend. [He empties all the pills into the palm of his hand, blows on them, puts them in his mouth, and swallows them down with a draught of quass.] There !

MADAME RANÉVSKY [alarmed]. Have you gone off your head ?

PÍSHTCHIK. I 've taken all the pills.

LOPÁKHIN. Greedy feller !

[Every one laughs.]

FIRS [mumbling]. They were here in Easter Week and finished off a gallon of pickled gherkins.

MADAME RANÉVSKY. What 's he talking about ?

BARBARA. He 's been mumbling like that these three years. We 've got used to it.

YÁSHA. Advancing age.

[CHARLOTTE crosses in a white frock, very thin, tightly laced, with a lorgnette at her waist.]

LOPÁKHIN. Excuse me, Charlotte Ivánovna, I 've not paid my respects to you yet. [He prepares to kiss her hand.]

CHARLOTTE [drawing her hand away]. If one allows you to kiss one's hand, you will want to kiss one's elbow next, and then one's shoulder.

LOPÁKHIN. I 'm having no luck to-day. [All laugh.] Charlotte Ivánovna, do us a conjuring trick.

MADAME RANÉVSKY. Charlotte, do do us a conjuring trick.

CHARLOTTE. No, thank you. I 'm going to bed. [Exit CHARLOTTE.]

LOPÁKHIN. We shall meet again in three weeks. [Kissing MADAME RANÉVSKY'S hand.] Meanwhile, good-bye. I must be off.

[*To* GÁYEF.] So-long. [*Kissing* PÍSHTCHIK.] Ta-ta. [*Shaking hands with* BARBARA, *then with* FIRS *and* YÁSHA.] I hate having to go. [*To* MADAME RANÉVSKY.] If you make up your mind about the villas, let me know, and I 'll raise you five thousand pounds at once. Think it over seriously.

BARBABA [*angrily*]. For Heaven's sake, do go!

LOPÁKHIN. I 'm going, I 'm going.

[*Exit* LOPÁKHIN.]

GÁYEF. Snob! . . . However, *pardon!* Barbara 's going to marry him; he 's Barbara's young man.

BARBARA. You talk too much, uncle.

MADAME RANÉVSKY. Why, Barbara, I shall be very glad. He 's a nice man.

PÍSHTCHIK. Not a doubt of it. . . . A most worthy individual. My Dáshenka, she says . . . oh, she says . . . lots of things. [*Snoring and waking up again at once.*] By the by, dear lady, can you lend me twenty-five pounds? I 've got to pay the interest on my mortgage to-morrow.

BARBARA [*alarmed*]. We can't! We can't!

MADAME RANÉVSKY. It really is a fact that I have n't any money.

PÍSHTCHIK. I 'll find it somewhere. [*Laughing.*] I never lose hope. Last time I thought, "Now I really am done for, I 'm a ruined man," when behold, they ran a railway over my land and paid me compensation. And so it 'll be again; something will happen, if not to-day, then to-morrow. Dáshenka may win the twenty-thousand-pound prize; she 's got a ticket in the lottery.

MADAME RANÉVSKY. The coffee 's finished. Let 's go to bed.

FIRS [*brushing* GÁYEF'S *clothes, admonishingly*]. You 've put on the wrong trousers again. Whatever am I to do with you?

BARBARA [*softly*]. Ánya is asleep. [*She opens the window quietly.*] The sun 's up already; it is n't cold now. Look, mamma, how lovely the trees are. Heavens! what a sweet air! The starlings are singing!

GÁYEF [*opening the other window*]. The orchard is all white. You 've not forgotten it, Lyuba? This long avenue going straight on, straight on, like a ribbon between the trees? It shines like silver on moonlight nights. Do you remember? You 've not forgotten?

MADAME RANÉVSKY [*looking out into the garden*]. Oh, my childhood, my pure and happy childhood! I used to sleep in this nursery. I used to look out from here into the garden. Happiness awoke with me every morning; and the orchard was just the same then as it is now; nothing is altered. [*Laughing with joy.*] It is all white, all white! Oh, my cherry orchard! After the dark and stormy autumn and the frosts of winter you are young again and full of happiness; the angels of heaven have not abandoned you. Oh! if only I could free my neck and shoulders from the stone that weighs them down! If only I could forget my past!

GÁYEF. Yes; and this orchard will be sold to pay our debts, however impossible it may seem. . . .

MADAME RANÉVSKY. Look! There 's mamma walking in the orchard . . . in a white frock! [*Laughing with joy.*] There she is!

GÁYEF. Where?

BARBARA. Heaven help you!

MADAME RANÉVSKY. There 's no one there really. It only looked like it; there on the right where the path turns down to the summer-house; there 's a white tree that leans over and looks like a woman.

[*Enter* TROPHÍMOF *in a shabby student uniform and spectacles.*]

MADAME RANÉVSKY. What a wonderful orchard, with its white masses of blossom and the blue sky above!

TROPHÍMOF. Lyubóf Andréyevna! [*She looks round at him.*] I only want to say, "How do you do," and go away at once. [*Kissing her hand eagerly.*] I was told to wait till the morning, but I had n't the patience.

[MADAME RANÉVSKY *looks at him in astonishment.*]

BARBARA [*crying*]. This is Peter Trophímof.

TROPHÍMOF. Peter Trophímof; I was Grisha's tutor, you know. Have I really altered so much?

[MADAME RANÉVSKY *embraces him and cries softly.*]

GÁYEF. Come, come, that 's enough, Lyuba!

BARBARA [*crying*]. I told you to wait till to-morrow, you know, Peter.

MADAME RANÉVSKY. My little Grisha! My little boy! Grisha . . . my son. . . .

BARBARA. It can't be helped, mamma. It was the will of God.

TROPHÍMOF [gently, crying]. There, there!

MADAME RANÉVSKY [crying]. He was drowned. My little boy was drowned. Why? What was the use of that, my dear? [In a softer voice.] Ánya's asleep in there, and I am speaking so loud, and making a noise. . . . But tell me, Peter, why have you grown so ugly? Why have you grown so old?

TROPHÍMOF. An old woman in the train called me a "mouldy gentleman."

MADAME RANÉVSKY. You were quite a boy then, a dear little student, and now your hair's going and you wear spectacles. Are you really still a student?

[Going toward the door.]

TROPHÍMOF. Yes, I expect I shall be a perpetual student.

MADAME RANÉVSKY [kissing her brother and then BARBARA]. Well, go to bed. You've grown old too, Leoníd.

PÍSHTCHIK [following her]. Yes, yes; time for bed. Oh, oh, my gout! I'll stay the night here. Don't forget, Lyubóf Andréyevna, my angel, to-morrow morning . . . twenty-five.

GÁYEF. He's still on the same string.

PÍSHTCHIK. Twenty-five . . . to pay the interest on my mortgage.

MADAME RANÉVSKY. I haven't any money, my friend.

PÍSHTCHIK. I'll pay you back, dear lady. It's a trifling sum.

MADAME RANÉVSKY. Well, well, Leoníd will give it you. Let him have it, Leoníd.

GÁYEF [ironical]. I'll give it him right enough! Hold your pocket wide![1]

MADAME RANÉVSKY. It can't be helped. . . . He needs it. He'll pay it back.

[Exeunt MADAME RANÉVSKY, TROPHÍMOF, PÍSHTCHIK, and FIRS. GÁYEF, BARBARA, AND YÁSHA remain.]

GÁYEF. My sister hasn't lost her old habit of scattering the money. [To YÁSHA.] Go away, my lad! You smell of chicken.

YÁSHA [laughing]. You're just the same as you always were, Leoníd Andréyevitch!

GÁYEF. Who's that? [To BARBARA.] What does he say?

[1] Hold your pocket wide: a proverbial piece of irony.

BARBARA [To YÁSHA.] Your mother's come up from the village. She's been waiting for you since yesterday in the servants' hall. She wants to see you.

YÁSHA. What a nuisance she is!

BARBARA. You wicked, unnatural son!

YÁSHA. Well, what do I want with her? She might just as well have waited till to-morrow. [Exit YÁSHA.]

BARBARA. Mamma is just like she used to be; she hasn't changed a bit. If she had her way, she'd give away everything she has.

GÁYEF. Yes. [A pause.] If people recommend very many cures for an illness, that means that the illness is incurable. I think and think, I batter my brains; I know of many remedies, very many, and that means really that there is none. How nice it would be to get a fortune left one by somebody! How nice it would be if Ánya could marry a very rich man! How nice it would be to go to Yaroslav and try my luck with my aunt the Countess. My aunt is very, very rich, you know.

BARBARA [crying softly]. If only God would help us!

GÁYEF. Don't howl! My aunt is very rich, but she does not like us. In the first place, my sister married a solicitor, not a nobleman. [ÁNYA appears in the doorway.] She married a man who was not a nobleman, and it's no good pretending that she has led a virtuous life. She's a dear, kind, charming creature, and I love her very much, but whatever mitigating circumstances one may find for her, there's no getting round it that she's a sinful woman. You can see it in her every gesture.

BARBARA [whispering]. Ánya is standing in the door!

GÁYEF. Who's that? [A pause.] It's very odd, something's got into my right eye. I can't see properly out of it. Last Thursday when I was down at the District Court . . . [ÁNYA comes down.]

BARBARA. Why aren't you asleep, Ánya?

ÁNYA. I can't sleep. It's no good trying.

GÁYEF. My little pet! [Kissing ÁNYA's hands and face.] My little girl! [Crying.] You're not my niece; you're my angel; you're my everything. Trust me, trust me. . . .

ÁNYA. I do trust you, uncle. Every one

loves you, every one respects you; but dear, dear uncle, you ought to hold your tongue, only to hold your tongue. What were you saying just now about mamma?—about your own sister? What was the good of saying that?

GÁYEF. Yes, yes. [*Covering his face with her hand.*] You 're quite right; it was awful of me! Lord, Lord! Save me from myself! And a little while ago I made a speech over a cupboard. What a stupid thing to do! As soon as I had done it, I knew it was stupid.

BARBARA. Yes, really, uncle. You ought to hold your tongue. Say nothing; that 's all that 's wanted.

ÁNYA. If only you would hold your tongue, you 'd be so much happier!

GÁYEF. I will! I will! [*Kissing* ÁNYA's *and* BARBARA's *hands.*] I 'll hold my tongue. But there 's one thing I must say; it 's business. Last Thursday, when I was down at the District Court, a lot of us were there together, we began to talk about this and that, one thing and another, and it seems I could arrange a loan on note of hand to pay the interest into the bank.

BARBARA. If only Heaven would help us!

GÁYEF. I 'll go in on Tuesday and talk it over again. [*To* BARBARA.] Don't howl! [*To* ÁNYA.] Your mamma shall have a talk with Lopákhin. Of course he won't refuse her. And as soon as you are rested you must go to see your grandmother, the Countess, at Yaroslav. We 'll operate from three points, and the trick is done. We 'll pay the interest, I 'm certain of it. [*Taking sugar candy.*] I swear on my honor, or whatever you will, the property shall not be sold. [*Excitedly.*] I swear by my hope of eternal happiness! There 's my hand on it. Call me a base, dishonorable man if I let it go to auction. I swear by my whole being!

ÁNYA [*calm again and happy*]. What a dear you are, uncle, and how clever! [*Embraces him.*] Now I 'm easy again. I 'm easy again! I 'm happy!

[*Enter* FIRS.]

FIRS [*reproachfully*]. Leoníd Andréyevitch, have you no fear of God? When are you going to bed?

GÁYEF. I 'm just off—just off. You get along, Firs. I 'll undress myself all right. Come, children, by-bye! Details to-mor-row, but now let 's go to bed. [*Kissing* ÁNYA *and* BARBARA.] I 'm a good Liberal, a man of the eighties. People abuse the eighties, but I think that I may say I 've suffered something for my convictions in my time. It 's not for nothing that the peasants love me. We ought to know the peasants; we ought to know with what . . .

ÁNYA. You 're at it again, uncle!

BARBARA. Why don't you hold your tongue, uncle?

FIRS [*angrily*]. Leoníd Andréyevitch!

GÁYEF. I 'm coming; I 'm coming. Now go to bed. Off two cushions in the middle pocket! I start another life! . . .

[*Exit, with* FIRS *hobbling after him.*]

ÁNYA. Now my mind is at rest. I don't want to go to Yaroslav; I don't like grandmamma; but my mind is at rest, thanks to Uncle Leoníd. [*She sits down.*]

BARBARA. Time for bed. I 'm off. Whilst you were away there 's been a scandal. You know that nobody lives in the old servants' quarters except the old people, Ephim, Pauline, Evstignéy, and old Karp. Well, they took to having in all sorts of queer fish to sleep there with them. I did n't say a word. But at last I heard they had spread a report that I had given orders that they were to have nothing but peas to eat; out of stinginess, you understand? It was all Evstignéy's doing. "Very well," I said to myself, "you wait a bit." So I sent for Evstignéy. [*Yawning.*] He comes. "Now then, Evstignéy," I said, "you old imbecile, how do you dare . . ."[*Looking at* ÁNYA.] Ánya, Ánya! [*A pause.*] She 's asleep. [*Taking* ÁNYA's *arm.*] Let 's go to bed. Come along. [*Leading her away.*] Sleep on, my little one! Come along; come along! [*They go towards* ÁNYA's *room. In the distance beyond the orchard a shepherd plays his pipe.* TROPHÍMOF *crosses the stage and, seeing* BARBARA *and* ÁNYA, *stops.*] 'Sh! She 's asleep, she 's asleep! Come along, my love.

ÁNYA [*drowsily*]. I 'm so tired! Listen to the bells! Uncle, dear uncle! Mamma! Uncle!

BARBARA. Come along, my love! Come along.

[*Exeunt* BARBARA *and* ÁNYA *to the bedroom.*]

TROPHÍMOF [*with emotion*]. My sunshine! My spring!

ACT II

In the open fields; an old crooked half-ruined shrine. Near it a well; big stones, apparently old tombstones; an old bench. Road to the estate beyond. On one side rise dark poplar trees. Beyond them begins the cherry orchard. In the distance a row of telegraph poles, and, far away on the horizon, the dim outlines of a big town, visible only in fine, clear weather. It is near sunset.

CHARLOTTE, YÁSHA, *and* DUNYÁSHA *sit on the bench.* EPHIKHÓDOF *stands by them and plays on a guitar; they meditate.* CHARLOTTE *wears an old peaked cap.[1] She has taken a gun from off her shoulders and is mending the buckle of the strap.*

CHARLOTTE [*thoughtfully*]. I have no proper passport. I don't know how old I am ; I always feel I am still young. When I was a little girl my father and mother used to go about from one country fair to another, giving performances, and very good ones, too. I used to do the *salto mortale* and all sorts of tricks. When papa and mamma died, an old German lady adopted me and educated me. Good ! When I grew up I became a governess. But where I come from and who I am, I haven't a notion. Who my parents were — very likely they weren't married — I don't know. [*Taking a cucumber from her pocket and beginning to eat.*] I don't know anything about it. [*A pause.*] I long to talk so, and I have no one to talk to, I have no friends or relations.

EPHIKHÓDOF [*playing on the guitar and singing*].

"What is the noisy world to me ?
Oh, what are friends and foes ? "

How sweet it is to play upon a mandolin !

DUNYÁSHA. That's a guitar, not a mandolin.

[*She looks at herself in a hand-glass and powders her face.*]

EPHIKHÓDOF. For the madman who loves, it is a mandolin. [*Singing.*]

"Oh, that my heart were cheered
By the warmth of requited love."

[YÁSHA *joins in.*]

CHARLOTTE. How badly these people do sing ! Foo ! Like jackals howling !

DUNYÁSHA. [*To* YÁSHA.] What happiness it must be to live abroad !

YÁSHA. Of course it is ; I quite agree with you. [*He yawns and lights a cigar.*]

EPHIKHÓDOF. It stands to reason. Everything abroad has attained a certain culmination.[1]

YÁSHA. That's right.

EPHIKHÓDOF. I am a man of cultivation; I have studied various remarkable books, but I cannot fathom the direction of my preferences ; do I want to live or do I want to shoot myself, so to speak ? But in order to be ready for all contingencies, I always carry a revolver in my pocket. Here it is. [*Showing revolver.*]

CHARLOTTE. That's done. I'm off. [*Slinging the rifle over her shoulder.*] You're a clever fellow, Ephikhódof, and very alarming. Women must fall madly in love with you. Brrr ! [*Going.*] These clever people are all so stupid ; I have no one to talk to. I am always alone, always alone ; I have no friends or relations, and who I am, or why I exist, is a mystery. [*Exit slowly.*]

EPHIKHÓDOF. Strictly speaking, without touching upon other matters, I must protest *inter alia* that destiny treats me with the utmost rigor, as a tempest might treat a small ship. If I labor under a misapprehension, how is it that when I woke up this morning, behold, so to speak, I perceived sitting on my chest a spider of preternatural dimensions, like that ? [*Indicating with both hands.*] And if I go to take a draught of quass, I am sure to find something of the most indelicate character, in the nature of a cockroach. [*A pause.*] Have you read Buckle ? [*A pause. — To* DUNYÁSHA.] I should like to trouble you, Avdotya Fëdorovna,[2] for a momentary interview.

DUNYÁSHA. Talk away.

EPHIKHÓDOF. I should prefer to conduct it *tête-à-tête.* [*Sighing.*]

DUNYÁSHA [*confused*]. Very well, only first please fetch me my cloak.[3] It's by the cupboard. It's rather damp here.

EPHIKHÓDOF. Very well, mademoiselle. I will go and fetch it, mademoiselle. Now I know what to do with my revolver.

[*Takes his guitar and exit, playing.*]

---

[1] *Furázhka*, the commonest men's headgear in Russia, shaped like a yachting cap.

[1] *Culmination.* This represents a similar blunder of Ephikhódof's in the original.

[2] *Avdotya Fëdorovna* (the ë is to be pronounced like the *yach* in *yacht*.) Dunya (diminutive Dunyásha), stands for Avdotya, formally Evdokiya, representing the Greek Eudoxia.

[3] *Cloak.* Talmotchka, a diminutive of *talma,* a sort of big cape, named after the tragedian.

YÁSHA. Twenty-two misfortunes! Between you and me, he's a stupid fellow. [*Yawning.*]

DUNYÁSHA. Heaven help him, he'll shoot himself! [*A pause.*] I have grown so nervous, I am always in a twitter. I was quite a little girl when they took me into the household, and now I have got quite disused to common life, and my hands are as white as white, like a lady's. I have grown so refined, so delicate and genteel, I am afraid of everything. I'm always frightened. And if you deceive me, Yásha, I don't know what will happen to my nerves.

YÁSHA [*kissing her*]. You little cucumber! Of course every girl ought to behave herself properly; there's nothing I dislike as much as when girls aren't proper in their behavior.

DUNYÁSHA. I've fallen dreadfully in love with you. You're so educated; you can talk about anything! [*A pause.*]

YÁSHA [*yawning*]. Yes. . . . The way I look at it is this; if a girl falls in love with anybody, then I call her immoral. [*A pause.*] How pleasant it is to smoke one's cigar in the open air. [*Listening.*] There's some one coming. It's the missis and the rest of 'em. . . . [DUNYÁSHA *embraces him hastily.*] Go towards the house as if you'd just been for a bathe. Go by this path or else they'll meet you and think that I've been walking out with you. I can't stand that sort of thing.

DUNYÁSHA [*coughing softly*]. Your cigar has given me a headache.

[*Exit* DUNYÁSHA. YÁSHA *remains sitting by the shrine.*]

[*Enter* MADAME RANÉVSKY, GÁYEF, *and* LOPÁKHIN.]

LOPÁKHIN. You must make up your minds once and for all. Time waits for no man. The question is perfectly simple. Are you going to let off the land for villas or not? Answer in one way; yes or no? Only one word!

MADAME RANÉVSKY. Who's smoking horrible cigars here? [*She sits down.*]

GÁYEF. How handy it is now they've built that railway. [*Sitting.*] We've been into town for lunch and back again. . . . Red in the middle! I must just go up to the house and have a game.

MADAME RANÉVSKY. There's no hurry.

LOPÁKHIN. Only one word — yes or no! [*Entreatingly.*] Come, answer the question!

GÁYEF [*yawning*]. Who's that?

MADAME RANÉVSKY [*looking into her purse*]. I had a lot of money yesterday, but there's hardly any left now. Poor Barbara tries to save money by feeding us all on milk soup; the old people in the kitchen get nothing but peas, and yet I go squandering aimlessly. . . . [*Dropping her purse and scattering gold coins; vexed.*] There, I've dropped it all!

YÁSHA. Allow me, I'll pick it up. [*Collecting the coins.*]

MADAME RANÉVSKY. Yes, please do, Yásha! Whatever made me go into town for lunch? I hate your horrid restaurant with the organ, and the tablecloths all smelling of soap. Why do you drink so much, Leoníd? Why do you eat so much? Why do you talk so much? You talked too much at the restaurant again, and most unsuitably, about the seventies, and the decadents. And to whom? Fancy talking about decadents to the waiters!

LOPÁKHIN. Quite true.

GÁYEF [*with a gesture*]. I'm incorrigible, that's plain. [*Irritably to* YÁSHA.] What do you keep dodging about in front of me for?

YÁSHA [*laughing*]. I can't hear your voice without laughing.

GÁYEF. [*To* MADAME RANÉVSKY.] Either he or I . . .

MADAME RANÉVSKY. Go away, Yásha; run along.

YÁSHA [*handing* MADAME RANÉVSKY *her purse*]. I'll go at once. [*Restraining his laughter with difficulty.*] This very minute. [*Exit* YÁSHA.]

LOPÁKHIN. Deriganof, the millionaire, wants to buy your property. They say he'll come to the auction himself.

MADAME RANÉVSKY. How did you hear?

LOPÁKHIN. I was told so in town.

GÁYEF. Our aunt at Yaroslav has promised to send something; but I don't know when, or how much.

LOPÁKHIN. How much will she send? Ten thousand pounds? Twenty thousand pounds?

MADAME RANÉVSKY. Oh, come. . . . A thousand or fifteen hundred at the most.

LOPÁKHIN. Excuse me, but in all my life I never met anybody so frivolous as you two, so crazy and unbusiness-like! I tell you in plain Russian your property is going to be sold, and you don't seem to understand what I say.

MADAME RANÉVSKY. Well, what are we to do? Tell us what you want us to do.

LOPÁKHIN. Don't I tell you every day? Every day I say the same thing over and over again. You must lease off the cherry orchard and the rest of the estate for villas; you must do it at once, this very moment; the auction will be on you in two twos! Try and understand. Once you make up your mind there are to be villas, you can get all the money you want, and you're saved.

MADAME RANÉVSKY. Villas and villa residents, oh, please, . . . it's so vulgar!

GÁYEF. I quite agree with you.

LOPÁKHIN. I shall either cry, or scream, or faint. I can't stand it! You'll be the death of me. [*To* GÁYEF.] You're an old woman!

GÁYEF. Who's that?

LOPÁKHIN. You're an old woman!
[*Going.*]

MADAME RANÉVSKY [*frightened*]. No, don't go. Stay here, there's a dear! Perhaps we shall think of some way.

LOPÁKHIN. What's the good of thinking!

MADAME RANÉVSKY. Please don't go; I want you. At any rate, it's gayer when you're here. [*A pause.*] I keep expecting something to happen, as if the house were going to tumble down about our ears.

GÁYEF [*in deep abstraction*]. Off the cushion on the corner; double into the middle pocket . . .

MADAME RANÉVSKY. We have been very, very sinful!

LOPÁKHIN. You! What sins have you committed?

GÁYEF [*eating candy*]. They say I've devoured all my substance in sugar candy.
[*Laughing.*]

MADAME RANÉVSKY. Oh, the sins that I have committed . . . I've always squandered money at random like a mad-woman; I married a man who made nothing but debts. My husband drank himself to death on champagne; he was a fearful drinker. Then for my sins I fell in love and went off with another man; and immediately — that was my first punishment — a blow full on the head . . . here, in this very river . . . my little boy was drowned; and I went abroad, right,

right away, never to come back any more, never to see this river again. . . . I shut my eyes and ran, like a mad thing, and *he* came after me, pitiless and cruel. I bought a villa at Mentone, because he fell ill there, and for three years I knew no rest day or night; the sick man tormented and wore down my soul. Then, last year, when my villa was sold to pay my debts, I went off to Paris, and he came and robbed me of everything, left me and took up with another woman, and I tried to poison myself. . . . It was all so stupid, so humiliating. . . . Then suddenly I longed to be back in Russia, in my own country, with my little girl. . . . [*Wiping away her tears.*] Lord, Lord, be merciful to me; forgive my sins! Do not punish me any more! [*Taking a telegram from her pocket.*] I got this to-day from Paris. . . . He asks to be forgiven, begs me to go back. . . . [*Tearing up the telegram.*] Isn't that music that I hear? [*Listening.*]

GÁYEF. That's our famous Jewish band. You remember? Four fiddles, a flute, and a double bass.

MADAME RANÉVSKY. Does it still exist? We must make them come up sometime; we'll have a dance.

LOPÁKHIN [*listening*]. I don't hear anything. [*Singing softly.*]
"The Germans for a fee will turn
A Russ into a Frenchman."
[*Laughing.*] I saw a very funny piece at the theater last night; awfully funny!

MADAME RANÉVSKY. It probably wasn't a bit funny. You people ought n't to go and see plays; you ought to try to see yourselves; to see what a dull life you lead, and how much too much you talk.

LOPÁKHIN. Quite right. To tell the honest truth, our life's an imbecile affair. [*A pause.*] My papa was a peasant, an idiot; he understood nothing; he taught me nothing; all he did was to beat me, when he was drunk, with a walking-stick. As a matter of fact I'm just as big a blockhead and idiot as he was. I never did any lessons; my handwriting's abominable; I write so badly I'm ashamed before people; like a pig.

MADAME RANÉVSKY. You ought to get married.

LOPÁKHIN. Yes, that's true.

MADAME RANÉVSKY. Why not marry Barbara? She's a nice girl.

LOPÁKHIN. Yes.

MADAME RANÉVSKY. She's a nice straight-forward creature ; works all day ; and what's most important, she loves you. You've been fond of her for a long time.

LOPÁKHIN. Well, why not ? I'm quite willing. She's a very nice girl. [*A pause.*]

GÁYEF. I've been offered a place in a bank. Six hundred pounds a year. Do you hear ?

MADAME RANÉVSKY. You in a bank ! Stay where you are.

[*Enter FIRS, carrying an overcoat.*]

FIRS. [*To GÁYEF.*] Put this on, please, master ; it's getting damp.

GÁYEF [*putting on the coat*]. What a plague you are, Firs !

FIRS. What's the use. . . . You went off and never told me. [*Examining his clothes.*]

MADAME RANÉVSKY. How old you've got, Firs !

FIRS. I beg your pardon ?

LOPÁKHIN. She says how old you've got !

FIRS. I've been alive a long time. When they found me a wife, your father was n't even born yet. [*Laughing.*] And when the Liberation came I was already chief valet. But I would n't have any Liberation then ; I stayed with the master. [*A pause.*] I remember how happy everybody was, but why they were happy they did n't know themselves.

LOPÁKHIN. It was fine before then. Anyway they used to flog 'em.

FIRS [*mishearing him*]. I should think so ! The peasants minded the masters, and the masters minded the peasants, but now it's all higgledy-piggledy ; you can't make head or tail of it.

GÁYEF. Shut up, Firs. I must go into town again to-morrow. I've been promised an introduction to a general who'll lend money on a bill.

LOPÁKHIN. You'll do no good. You won't even pay the interest ; set your mind at ease about that.

MADAME RANÉVSKY. [*To LOPÁKHIN.*] He's only talking nonsense. There's no such general at all.

[*Enter TROPHÍMOF, ÁNYA and BARBARA.*]

GÁYEF. Here come the others.

ÁNYA. Here's mamma.

MADAME RANÉVSKY [*tenderly*]. Come along, come along . . . my little ones. . . . [*Embracing ÁNYA and BARBARA.*] If only you knew how much I love you both ! Sit beside me . . . there, like that.

[*Every one sits.*]

LOPÁKHIN. The Perpetual Student's always among the girls.

TROPHÍMOF. It's no affair of yours.

LOPÁKHIN. He's nearly fifty and still a student.

TROPHÍMOF. Stop your idiotic jokes !

LOPÁKHIN. What are you losing your temper for, silly ?

TROPHÍMOF. Why can't you leave me alone ?

LOPÁKHIN [*laughing*]. I should like to know what your opinion is of me.

TROPHÍMOF. My opinion of you, Yermolái Alexéyitch, is this. You're a rich man ; you'll soon be a millionaire. Just as a beast of prey which devours everything that comes in its way is necessary for the conversion of matter, so you are necessary, too. [*All laugh.*]

BARBARA. Tell us something about the planets, Peter, instead.

MADAME RANÉVSKY. No. Let's go on with the conversation we were having yesterday.

TROPHÍMOF. What about ?

GÁYEF. About the proud man.

TROPHÍMOF. We had a long talk yesterday, but we did n't come to any conclusion. There is something mystical in the proud man in the sense in which you use the words. You may be right from your point of view, but, if we look at it simple-mindedly, what room is there for pride ? Is there any sense in it, when man is so poorly constructed from the physiological point of view, when the vast majority of us are so gross and stupid and profoundly unhappy ? We must give up admiring ourselves. The only thing to do is to work.

GÁYEF. We shall die all the same.

TROPHÍMOF. Who knows ? And what does it mean, to die ? Perhaps man has a hundred senses, and when he dies only the five senses that we know perish with him, and the other ninety-five remain alive.

MADAME RANÉVSKY. How clever you are, Peter !

LOPÁKHIN [*ironically*]. Oh, extraordinary !

TROPHÍMOF. Mankind marches forward, perfecting its strength. Everything that is unattainable for us now will one day be near and clear; but we must work; we must help with all our force those who seek for truth. At present only a few men work in Russia. The vast majority of the educated people that I know seek after nothing, do nothing, and are as yet incapable of work. They call themselves the "Intelligentsia," they say "thou" and "thee" to the servants, they treat the peasants like animals, learn nothing, read nothing serious, do absolutely nothing, only talk about science, and understand little or nothing about art. They are all serious; they all have solemn faces; they only discuss important subjects; they philosophize; but meanwhile the vast majority of us, ninety-nine per cent, live like savages; at the least thing they curse and punch people's heads; they eat like beasts and sleep in dirt and bad air; there are bugs everywhere, evil smells, damp and moral degradation. . . . It's plain that all our clever conversations are only meant to distract our own attention and other people's. Show me where those crèches are, that they're always talking so much about; or those reading-rooms. They are only things people write about in novels; they don't really exist at all. Nothing exists but dirt, vulgarity, and Asiatic ways. I am afraid of solemn faces; I dislike them; I am afraid of solemn conversations. Let us rather hold our tongues.

LOPÁKHIN. Do you know, I get up at five every morning; I work from morning till night; I am always handling my own money or other people's, and I see the sort of men there are about me. One only has to begin to do anything to see how few honest and decent people there are. Sometimes, as I lie awake in bed, I think: "O Lord, you have given us mighty forests, boundless fields and immeasurable horizons, and, we living in their midst, ought really to be giants."

MADAME RANÉVSKY. Oh, dear, you want giants! They are all very well in fairy stories; but in real life they are rather alarming.

[EPHIKHÓDOF *passes at the back of the scene, playing on his guitar.*]

MADAME RANÉVSKY [*pensively*]. There goes Ephikhódof.

ÁNYA [*pensively*]. There goes Ephikhódof.

GÁYEF. The sun has set.

TROPHÍMOF. Yes.

GÁYEF [*as if declaiming, but not loud*]. O Nature, wonderful Nature, you glow with eternal light; beautiful and indifferent, you whom we call our mother, uniting in yourself both life and death, you animate and you destroy . . .

BARBARA [*entreatingly*]. Uncle!

ÁNYA. You're at it again, uncle.

TROPHÍMOF. You'd far better double the red into the middle pocket.

GÁYEF. I'll hold my tongue! I'll hold my tongue!

[*They all sit pensively. Silence reigns, broken only by the mumbling of old* FIRS. *Suddenly a distant sound is heard as if from the sky, the sound of a string breaking, dying away, melancholy.*]

MADAME RANÉVSKY. What's that?

LOPÁKHIN. I don't know. It's a lifting-tub given way somewhere away in the mines. It must be a long way off.

GÁYEF. Perhaps it's some sort of bird . . . a heron, or something.

TROPHÍMOF. Or an owl. . . .

MADAME RANÉVSKY [*shuddering*]. There is something uncanny about it!

FIRS. The same thing happened before the great misfortune: the owl screeched and the samovar kept humming.

GÁYEF. What great misfortune?

FIRS. The Liberation.   [*A pause.*]

MADAME RANÉVSKY. Come, every one, let's go in; it's getting late. [*To* ÁNYA.] You've tears in your eyes. What is it, little one?   [*Embracing her.*]

ÁNYA. Nothing, mamma. I'm all right.

TROPHÍMOF. There's some one coming.

[*A* TRAMP *appears in a torn white peaked cap and overcoat. He is slightly drunk.*]

TRAMP. Excuse me, but can I go through this way straight to the station?

GÁYEF. Certainly. Follow this path.

TRAMP. I am uncommonly obliged to you, sir. [*Coughing.*] We're having lovely weather. [*Declaiming.*] "Brother, my suffering brother" . . . "Come forth to the Volga. Who moans?" . . . [*To* BARBARA.] Mademoiselle, please spare a sixpence for a hungry fellow-countryman.

[BARBARA, *frightened, screams.*]

LOPÁKHIN [angrily]. There's a decency for every indecency to observe!

MADAME RANÉVSKY. Take this; here you are. [Fumbling in her purse.] I have n't any silver. . . . Never mind, take this sovereign.

TRAMP. I am uncommonly obliged to you, madam. [Exit TRAMP. Laughter.]

BARBARA [frightened]. I 'm going! I 'm going! Oh, mamma, there's nothing for the servants to eat at home, and you 've gone and given this man a sovereign.

MADAME RANÉVSKY. What 's to be done with your stupid old mother? I 'll give you up everything I have when I get back. Yermolái Alexéyitch, lend me some more money.

LOPÁKHIN. Very good.

MADAME RANÉVSKY. Come along, every one; it 's time to go in. We 've settled all about your marriage between us, Barbara. I wish you joy.

BARBARA [through her tears]. You must n't joke about such things, mamma.

LOPÁKHIN. Amelia, get thee to a nunnery, go!

GÁYEF. My hands are all trembling; it 's ages since I had a game of billiards.

LOPÁKHIN. Amelia, nymphlet, in thine orisons remember me.[1]

MADAME RANÉVSKY. Come along. It 's nearly supper-time.

BARBARA. How he frightened me! My heart is simply throbbing.

LOPÁKHIN. Allow me to remind you, the cherry orchard is to be sold on the 22d of August. Bear that in mind; bear that in mind!

[Exeunt OMNES except TROPHÍMOF and ÁNYA.]

ÁNYA [laughing]. Many thanks to the Tramp for frightening Barbara; at last we are alone.

TROPHÍMOF. Barbara's afraid we shall go and fall in love with each other. Day after day she never leaves us alone. With her narrow mind she cannot understand that we are above love. To avoid everything petty, everything illusory, everything that prevents one from being free and happy, that is the whole meaning and purpose of our life. Forward! We march on irresistibly towards that bright star which burns

[1] There is a wretched pun in the original: Ophelia is called Okhmelia (from okhmelét, to get drunk).

far, far before us! Forward! Don't tarry, comrades!

ÁNYA [clasping her hands]. What beautiful things you say! [A pause.] Is n't it enchanting here to-day!

TROPHÍMOF. Yes, it 's wonderful weather.

ÁNYA. What have you done to me, Peter? Why is it that I no longer love the cherry orchard as I did? I used to love it so tenderly; I thought there was no better place on earth than our garden.

TROPHÍMOF. All Russia is our garden. The earth is great and beautiful; it is full of wonderful places. [A pause.] Think, Ánya, your grandfather, your great-grandfather and all your ancestors were serf owners, owners of living souls. Do not human spirits look out at you from every tree in the orchard, from every leaf and every stem? Do you not hear human voices? . . . Oh! it is terrible. Your orchard frightens me. When I walk through it in the evening or at night, the rugged bark on the trees glows with a dim light, and the cherry trees seem to see all that happened a hundred and two hundred years ago in painful and oppressive dreams. Well, well, we have fallen at least two hundred years behind the times. We have achieved nothing at all as yet; we have not made up our minds how we stand with the past; we only philosophize, complain of boredom, or drink vodka. It is so plain that, before we can live in the present, we must first redeem the past, and have done with it; and it is only by suffering that we can redeem it, only by strenuous, unremitting toil. Understand that, Ánya.

ÁNYA. The house we live in has long since ceased to be our house; and I shall go away, I give you my word.

TROPHÍMOF. If you have the household keys, throw them in the well and go away. Be free, be free as the wind.

ÁNYA [enthusiastically]. How beautifully you put it!

TROPHÍMOF. Believe what I say, Ánya; believe what I say. I 'm not thirty yet; I am still young, still a student; but what I have been through! I am hungry as the winter; I am sick, anxious, poor as a beggar. Fate has tossed me hither and thither; I have been everywhere, everywhere. But wherever I have been, every minute, day and night, my soul has been full of mysterious anticipations. I feel the approach of happiness, Ánya ; I see it coming. . . .

ÁNYA [*pensively*]. The moon is rising.

[EPHIKHÓDOF *is heard still playing the same sad tune on his guitar. The moon rises. Somewhere beyond the poplar trees,* BARBARA *is heard calling for* ÁNYA: "*Ánya, where are you?*"]

TROPHÍMOF. Yes, the moon is rising. [*A pause.*] There it is, there is happiness ; it is coming towards us, nearer and nearer ; I can hear the sound of its footsteps. . . . And if we do not see it, if we do not know it, what does it matter? Others will see it.

BARBARA [*without*]. Ánya? Where are you?

TROPHÍMOF. There 's Barbara again! [*Angrily.*] It really is too bad!

ÁNYA. Never mind. Let us go down to the river. It 's lovely there.

TROPHÍMOF. Come on!

[*Exeunt* ÁNYA *and* TROPHÍMOF.]

BARBARA [*without*]. Ánya! Ánya!

ACT III

A sitting-room separated by an arch from a big drawing-room behind. Chandelier lighted. The Jewish band mentioned in Act II is heard playing on the landing. Evening. In the drawing-room they are dancing the grand rond. SIMEÓNOF-PÍSHTCHIK *is heard crying, "Promenade à une paire!"*

The dancers come down into the sitting-room. The first pair consists of PÍSHTCHIK *and* CHARLOTTE; *the second of* TROPHÍMOF *and* MADAME RANÉVSKY ; *the third of* ÁNYA *and the* POST-OFFICE OFFICIAL; *the fourth of* BARBARA *and the* STATIONMASTER, *etc., etc.* BARBARA *is crying softly and wipes away the tears as she dances. In the last pair comes* DUNYÁSHA. *They cross the sitting-room.*

PÍSHTCHIK. "Grand rond, balancez . . . Les cavaliers à genou et remerciez vos dames."

[FIRS *in evening dress carries seltzer water across on a tray.* PÍSHTCHIK *and* TROPHÍMOF *come down into the sitting-room.*]

PÍSHTCHIK. I am a full-blooded man ; I 've had two strokes already ; it 's hard work dancing, but, as the saying goes, "If you run with the pack, bark or no, but anyway wag your tail." I 'm as strong as a horse. My old father, who was fond of his

joke, rest his soul, used to say, talking of our pedigree, that the ancient stock of the Simeónof-Píshtchiks was descended from that very horse that Caligula made a senator. . . . [*Sitting.*] But the worst of it is, I 've got no money. A hungry dog believes in nothing but meat. [*Snoring and waking up again at once.*] I 'm just the same . . . It 's nothing but money, money, with me.

TROPHÍMOF. Yes, it 's quite true, there is something horse-like about your build.

PÍSHTCHIK. Well, well . . . a horse is a jolly creature . . . you can sell a horse.

[*A sound of billiards being played in the next room.* BARBARA *appears in the drawing-room beyond the arch.*]

TROPHÍMOF [*teasing her*]. Madame Lopákhin! Madame Lopákhin.

BARBARA [*angrily*]. Mouldy gentleman!

TROPHÍMOF. Yes, I 'm a mouldy gentleman, and I 'm proud of it.

BARBARA [*bitterly*]. We 've hired the band, but where 's the money to pay for it?

[*Exit* BARBARA.]

TROPHÍMOF. [*To* PÍSHTCHIK.] If the energy which you have spent in the course of your whole life in looking for money to pay the interest on your loans had been diverted to some other purpose, you would have had enough of it, I dare say, to turn the world upside down.

PÍSHTCHIK. Nietzsche the philosopher, a very remarkable man, very famous, a man of gigantic intellect, says in his works that it 's quite right to forge bank notes.

TROPHÍMOF. What, have you read Nietzsche?

PÍSHTCHIK. Well . . . Dáshenka told me. . . . But I 'm in such a hole, I 'd forge 'em for twopence. I 've got to pay thirty-one pounds the day after to-morrow. . . . I 've got thirteen pounds already. [*Feeling his pockets ; alarmed.*] My money 's gone! I 've lost my money! [*Crying.*] Where 's my money got to? [*Joyfully.*] Here it is, inside the lining. . . . It 's thrown me all in a perspiration.

[*Enter* MADAME RANÉVSKY *and* CHARLOTTE.]

MADAME RANÉVSKY [*humming a lezginka* [1]]. Why is Leoníd so long? What

---

[1] *Lezginka.* A lively Caucasian dance in two-four time, popularized by Glinka, and by Rubinstein in his opera, *Demon.*

can he be doing in the town? [*To* DUNYÁSHA.] Dunyásha, ask the musicians if they'll have some tea.

TROPHÍMOF. The sale did not come off, in all probability.

MADAME RANÉVSKY. It was a stupid day for the musicians to come; it was a stupid day to have this dance. . . . Well, well, it doesn't matter. . . .

[*She sits down and sings softly to herself.*]

CHARLOTTE [*giving* PÍSHTCHIK *a pack of cards*]. Here is a pack of cards. Think of any card you like.

PÍSHTCHIK. I've thought of one.

CHARLOTTE. Now shuffle the pack. That's all right. Give them here, oh, most worthy Mr. Píshtchik. Ein, zwei, drei! Now look and you'll find it in your side pocket.

PÍSHTCHIK [*taking a card from his side pocket*]. The Eight of Spades! You're perfectly right. [*Astonished.*] Well, I never!

CHARLOTTE [*holding the pack on the palm of her hand, to* TROPHÍMOF]. Say quickly, what's the top card?

TROPHÍMOF. Well, say the Queen of Spades.

CHARLOTTE. Right! [*To* PÍSHTCHIK.] Now, then, what's the top card?

PÍSHTCHIK. Ace of Hearts.

CHARLOTTE. Right! [*She claps her hands; the pack of cards disappears.*] What a beautiful day we've been having.

[*A mysterious female* VOICE *answers her as if from under the floor:* "*Yes, indeed, a charming day, mademoiselle.*"]

CHARLOTTE. You are my beautiful ideal.

THE VOICE. "*I think you also ferry peautiful, mademoiselle.*"

STATIONMASTER [*applauding*]. Bravo, Miss Ventriloquist!

PÍSHTCHIK [*astonished*]. Well, I never! Bewitching Charlotte Ivánovna, I'm head over ears in love with you.

CHARLOTTE. In love! [*Shrugging her shoulders.*] Are you capable of love? Guter Mensch, aber schlechter Musikant!

TROPHÍMOF [*slapping* PÍSHTCHIK *on the shoulder*]. You old horse!

CHARLOTTE. Now, attention, please; one more trick. [*Taking a shawl from a chair.*] Now here's a shawl, and a very pretty shawl; I'm going to sell this very pretty shawl. [*Shaking it.*] Who'll buy? who'll buy?

PÍSHTCHIK [*astonished*]. Well, I never!

CHARLOTTE. Ein, zwei, drei!

[*She lifts the shawl quickly; behind it stands* ÁNYA, *who drops a curtsy, runs to her mother, kisses her, then runs up into the drawing-room amid general applause.*]

MADAME RANÉVSKY [*applauding*]. Bravo! bravo!

CHARLOTTE. Once more. Ein, zwei, drei!

[*She lifts up the shawl; behind it stands* BARBARA, *bowing.*]

PÍSHTCHIK [*astonished*]. Well, I never!

CHARLOTTE. That's all.

[*She throws the shawl over* PÍSHTCHIK, *makes a curtsy and runs up into the drawing-room.*]

PÍSHTCHIK [*hurrying after her*]. You little rascal . . . there's a girl for you, there's a girl. . . . [*Exit.*]

MADAME RANÉVSKY. And still no sign of Leoníd. What he's doing in the town so long, I can't understand. It must be all over by now; the property's sold; or the auction never came off; why does he keep me in suspense so long?

BARBARA [*trying to soothe her*]. Uncle has bought it, I am sure of that.

TROPHÍMOF [*mockingly*]. Of course he has.

BARBARA. Grannie sent him a power of attorney to buy it in her name and transfer the mortgage. She's done it for Ánya's sake. I'm perfectly sure that Heaven will help us and uncle will buy it.

MADAME RANÉVSKY. Your Yaroslav grannie sent fifteen hundred pounds to buy the property in her name — she doesn't trust us — but it wouldn't be enough even to pay the interest. [*Covering her face with her hands.*] My fate is being decided to-day, my fate. . . .

TROPHÍMOF [*teasing* BARBARA]. Madame Lopákhin!

BARBARA [*angrily*]. Perpetual Student! He's been sent down twice from the University.

MADAME RANÉVSKY. Why do you get angry, Barbara? He calls you Madame Lopákhin for fun. Why not? You can marry Lopákhin if you like; he's a nice, interesting man; you needn't if you don't; nobody wants to force you, my pet.

BARBARA. I take it very seriously, mamma, I must confess. He's a nice man and I like him.

MADAME RANÉVSKY. Then marry him. There's no good putting it off that I can see.

BARBARA. But, mamma, I can't propose to him myself. For two whole years everybody's been talking about him to me, every one ; but he either says nothing or makes a joke of it. I quite understand. He's making money ; he's always busy ; he can't be bothered with me. If I only had some money, even a little, even ten pounds, I would give everything up and go right away. I would go into a nunnery.

TROPHÍMOF [mocking]. What bliss !

BARBARA. [To TROPHÍMOF.] A student ought to be intelligent. [In a gentler voice, crying.] How ugly you've grown, Peter ; how old you've grown ! [She stops crying ; to MADAME RANÉVSKY.] But I can't live without work, mamma. I must have something to do every minute of the day.

[Enter YÁSHA.]

YÁSHA [trying not to laugh]. Ephikhódof has broken a billiard cue. [Exit YÁSHA.]

BARBARA. What's Ephikhódof doing here ? Who gave him leave to play billiards ? I don't understand these people.

[Exit BARBARA.]

MADAME RANÉVSKY. Don't tease her, Peter. Don't you see that she's unhappy enough already.

TROPHÍMOF. I wish she wouldn't be so fussy, always meddling in other people's affairs. The whole summer she's given me and Ánya no peace ; she is afraid we'll work up a romance between us. What business is it of hers ? I'm sure I never gave her any grounds ; I'm not likely to be so commonplace. We are above love !

MADAME RANÉVSKY. Then I suppose I must be beneath love. [Deeply agitated.] Why does n't Leoníd come ? Oh, if only I knew whether the property's sold or not ! It seems such an impossible disaster, that I don't know what to think. . . . I'm bewildered . . . I shall burst out screaming, I shall do something idiotic. Save me, Peter ; say something to me, say something. . . .

TROPHÍMOF. Whether the property is sold to-day or whether it's not sold, surely it's all one ? It's all over with it long ago ; there's no turning back ; the path is overgrown. Be calm, dear Lyubóf Andréyevna. You mustn't deceive yourself any longer ;

for once you must look the truth straight in the face.

MADAME RANÉVSKY. What truth ? You can see what's truth, and what's untruth, but I seem to have lost the power of vision ; I see nothing. You settle every important question so boldly ; but tell me, Peter, is n't that because you're young, because you have never solved any question of your own as yet by suffering ? You look boldly ahead ; is n't it only that you don't see or divine anything terrible in the future ; because life is still hidden from your young eyes ? You are bolder, honester, deeper than we are, but reflect, show me just a finger's breadth of consideration, take pity on me. Don't you see ? I was born here, my father and mother lived here, and my grandfather ; I love this house ; without the cherry orchard my life has no meaning for me, and if it must be sold, then for Heaven's sake, sell me too ! [Embracing TROPHÍMOF and kissing him on the forehead.] My little boy was drowned here. [Crying.] Be gentle with me, dear, kind Peter.

TROPHÍMOF. You know I sympathize with all my heart.

MADAME RANÉVSKY. Yes, yes, but you ought to say it somehow differently. [Taking out her handkerchief and dropping a telegram.] I am so wretched to-day, you can't imagine ! All this noise jars on me, my heart jumps at every sound. I tremble all over ; but I can't shut myself up ; I am afraid of the silence when I'm alone. Don't be hard on me, Peter ; I love you like a son. I would gladly let Ánya marry you, I swear it ; but you must work, Peter ; you must get your degree. You do nothing ; Fate tosses you about from place to place ; and that's not right. It's true what I say, is n't it ? And you must do something to your beard to make it grow better. [Laughing.] I can't help laughing at you.

TROPHÍMOF [picking up the telegram]. I don't wish to be an Adonis.

MADAME RANÉVSKY. It's a telegram from Paris. I get them every day. One came yesterday, another to-day. That savage is ill again ; he's in a bad way. . . . He asks me to forgive him, he begs me to come ; and I really ought to go to Paris and be with him. You look at me sternly ; but what am I to do, Peter ? What am I to do ? He's ill, he's lonely, he's unhappy. Who is to look after him ? Who is to keep him from doing stupid things ? Who is to give him his medicine when it's time ? After all, why should I be ashamed to say it ? I love him, that's plain. I love him, I love him. . . . My love is like a stone tied round my neck ; it's dragging me down to the bottom ; but I love my stone. I can't live without it. [*Squeezing* TROPHÍMOF's *hand.*] Don't think ill of me, Peter ; don't say anything ! Don't say anything !

TROPHÍMOF [*crying*]. Forgive my bluntness, for Heaven's sake ; but the man has simply robbed you.

MADAME RANÉVSKY. No, no, no ! [*Stopping her ears.*] You mustn't say that !

TROPHÍMOF. He's a rascal ; everybody sees it but yourself ; he's a petty rascal, a ne'er-do-weel . . .

MADAME RANÉVSKY [*angry but restrained*]. You're twenty-six or twenty-seven, and you're still a Lower School boy ![1]

TROPHÍMOF. Who cares ?

MADAME RANÉVSKY. You ought to be a man by now ; at your age you ought to understand people who love. You ought to love some one yourself, you ought to be in love ! [*Angrily.*] Yes, yes ! It's not purity with you ; it's simply you're a smug, a figure of fun, a freak. . . .

TROPHÍMOF [*horrified*]. What does she say ?

MADAME RANÉVSKY. "I am above love" ! You're not above love ; you're simply what Firs calls a "job-lot." At your age you ought to be ashamed not to have a mistress !

TROPHÍMOF [*aghast*]. This is awful ! What does she say ? [*Going quickly up into the drawing-room, clasping his head with his hands.*] This is something awful ! I can't stand it ; I'm off . . . [*Exit, but returns at once.*] All is over between us !

[*Exit to landing.*]

MADAME RANÉVSKY [*calling after him*]. Stop, Peter ! Don't be ridiculous ; I was only joking ! Peter !

[TROPHÍMOF *is heard on the landing going quickly down the stairs, and suddenly falling down them with a crash.* ANYA *and* BARBARA *scream. A moment later the sound of laughter.*]

[1] Literally, a gymnasist of the second form (from the bottom).

MADAME RANÉVSKY. What has happened ?

[ÁNYA *runs in.*]

ÁNYA [*laughing*]. Peter's tumbled downstairs.   [*She runs out again.*]

MADAME RANÉVSKY. What a ridiculous fellow he is !

[*The* STATIONMASTER *stands in the middle of the drawing-room beyond the arch and recites Alexey Tolstoy's poem, "The Sinner." Everybody stops to listen, but after a few lines the sound of a waltz is heard from the landing and he breaks off. All dance.* TROPHÍMOF, ÁNYA, BARBARA, *and* MADAME RANÉVSKY *enter from the landing.*]

MADAME RANÉVSKY. Come, Peter, come, you pure spirit. . . . I beg your pardon. Let's have a dance.

[*She dances with* TROPHÍMOF. ÁNYA *and* BARBARA *dance.*]

[*Enter* FIRS, *and stands his walking-stick by the side door. Enter* YÁSHA *by the drawing-room ; he stands looking at the dancers.*]

YÁSHA. Well, grandfather ?

FIRS. I'm not feeling well. In the old days it was generals and barons and admirals that danced at our dances, but now we send for the Postmaster and the Stationmaster, and even they make a favor of coming. I'm sort of weak all over. The old master, their grandfather, used to give us all sealing wax, when we had anything the matter. I've taken sealing wax every day for twenty years and more. Perhaps that's why I'm still alive.

YÁSHA. I'm sick of you, grandfather. [*Yawning.*] I wish you'd die and have done with it.

FIRS. Ah ! you . . . job-lot.

[*He mumbles to himself.*]

[TROPHÍMOF *and* MADAME RANÉVSKY *dance beyond the arch and down into the sitting-room.*]

MADAME RANÉVSKY. *Merci.* I'll sit down. [*Sitting.*] I'm tired.

[*Enter* ÁNYA.]

ÁNYA [*agitated*]. There was somebody in the kitchen just now saying that the cherry orchard was sold to-day.

MADAME RANÉVSKY. Sold ? Who to ?

ÁNYA. He didn't say who to. He's gone.

[*She dances with* TROPHÍMOF. *Both dance up into the drawing-room.*]

YÁSHA. It was some old fellow chattering ; a stranger.

FIRS. And still Leoníd Andréyitch does n't come. He's wearing his light overcoat, *demi-saison ;* he 'll catch cold as like as not. Ah, young wood, green wood !

MADAME RANÉVSKY. This is killing me. Yásha, go and find out who it was sold to.

YÁSHA. Why, he's gone long ago, the old man. [*Laughs.*]

MADAME RANÉVSKY [*vexed*]. What are you laughing at ? What are you glad about ?

YÁSHA. He's a ridiculous fellow is Ephikhódof. Nothing in him. Twenty-two misfortunes !

MADAME RANÉVSKY. Firs, if the property is sold, where will you go to ?

FIRS. Wherever you tell me, there I 'll go.

MADAME RANÉVSKY. Why do you look like that ? Are you ill ? You ought to be in bed.

FIRS [*ironically*]. Oh, yes, I 'll go to bed, and who 'll hand the things round, who 'll give orders ? I 've the whole house on my hands.

YÁSHA. Lyubóf Andréyevna ! Let me ask a favor of you ; be so kind ; if you go to Paris again, take me with you, I beseech you. It 's absolutely impossible for me to stay here. [*Looking about ; sotto voce.*] What 's the use of talking ? You can see for yourself this is a barbarous country ; the people have no morals ; and the boredom ! The food in the kitchen is something shocking, and on the top of it old Firs going about mumbling irrelevant nonsense. Take me back with you ; be so kind !

[*Enter* PÍSHTCHIK.]

PÍSHTCHIK. May I have the pleasure . . . a bit of a waltz, charming lady ? [MADAME RANÉVSKY *takes his arm.*] All the same, enchanting lady, you must let me have eighteen pounds. [*Dancing.*] Let me have . . . eighteen pounds.

[*Exeunt dancing through the arch.*]

YÁSHA [*singing to himself*].

"Oh, wilt thou understand
The turmoil of my soul ?"

[*Beyond the arch appears a figure in gray tall hat and check trousers, jumping and waving its arms. Cries of "Bravo, Charlotte Ivánovna."*]

DUNYÁSHA [*stopping to powder her face*]. Mamselle Ánya tells me I 'm to dance ; there are so many gentlemen and so few ladies. But dancing makes me giddy and makes my heart beat, Firs Nikoláyevitch ; and just now the gentleman from the post-office said something so nice to me, oh, so nice ! It quite took my breath away.

[*The music stops.*]

FIRS. What did he say to you ?

DUNYÁSHA. He said, "You are like a flower."

YÁSHA [*yawning*]. Cad ! [*Exit* YÁSHA.]

DUNYÁSHA. Like a flower ! I am so ladylike and refined, I dote on compliments.

FIRS. You 'll come to a bad end.

[*Enter* EPHIKHÓDOF.]

EPHIKHÓDOF. You are not pleased to see me, Avdótya Fyódorovna, no more than if I were some sort of insect. [*Sighing.*] Ah ! Life ! Life !

DUNYÁSHA. What do you want ?

EPHIKHÓDOF. Undoubtedly perhaps you are right. [*Sighing.*] But of course, if one regards it, so to speak, from the point of view, if I may allow myself the expression, and with apologies for my frankness, you have finally reduced me to a state of mind. I quite appreciate my destiny ; every day some misfortune happens to me, and I have long since grown accustomed to it, and face my fortune with a smile. You have passed your word to me, and although I . . .

DUNYÁSHA. Let us talk of this another time, if you please ; but now leave me in peace. I am busy meditating.

[*Playing with her fan.*]

EPHIKHÓDOF. Every day some misfortune befalls me, and yet if I may venture to say so, I meet them with smiles and even laughter.

[*Enter* BARBARA *from the drawing-room.*]

BARBARA. [*To* EPHIKHÓDOF.] Have n't you gone yet, Simeon ? You seem to pay no attention to what you 're told. [*To* DUNYÁSHA.] You get out of here, Dunyásha. [*To* EPHIKHÓDOF.] First you play billiards and break a cue, and then you march about the drawing-room as if you were a guest !

EPHIKHÓDOF. Allow me to inform you that it 's not your place to call me to account.

BARBARA. I 'm not calling you to account ; I 'm merely talking to you. All you can do is to walk about from one place to another, without ever doing a stroke of work ; and why on earth we keep a clerk at all Heaven only knows.

EPHIKHÓDOF [*offended*]. Whether I work, or whether I walk, or whether I eat, or whether I play billiards is a question to be decided only by my elders and people who understand.

BARBARA [*furious*]. How dare you talk to me like that ! How dare you ! I don't understand things, don't I ? You clear out of here this minute ? Do you hear me ? This minute !

EPHIKHÓDOF [*flinching*]. I must beg you to express yourself in genteeler language.

BARBARA [*beside herself*]. Out you go ! [*Following him as he retreats towards the door.*] Twenty-two misfortunes ! Make yourself scarce ! Get out of my sight !

[*Exit EPHIKHÓDOF.*]

EPHIKHÓDOF [*without*]. I shall lodge a complaint against you.

BARBARA. What ! You 're coming back, are you ? [*Seizing the walking-stick left at the door by FIRS.*] Come on ! Come on ! Come on ! I 'll teach you ! Are you coming ? Are you coming ? Then take that. [*She slashes with the stick.*]

[*Enter LOPÁKHIN.*]

LOPÁKHIN. Many thanks; much obliged.

BARBARA [*still angry, but ironical*]. Sorry !

LOPÁKHIN. Don't mention it. I 'm very grateful for your warm reception.

BARBARA. It 's not worth thanking me for. [*She walks away, then looks round and asks in a gentle voice :*] I did n't hurt you ?

LOPÁKHIN. Oh, no, nothing to matter. I shall have a bump like a goose's egg, that 's all.

[*Voices from the drawing-room : "Lo-pákhin has arrived ! Yermolái Alexéyitch !"*]

PÍSHTCHIK. Let my eyes see him, let my ears hear him ! [*He and LOPÁKHIN kiss.*] You smell of brandy, old man. We 're having a high time, too.

[*Enter MADAME RANÉVSKY.*]

MADAME RANÉVSKY. Is it you, Yermo-lái Alexéyitch ? Why have you been so long ? Where is Leoníd ?

LOPÁKHIN. Leoníd Andréyitch came back with me. He 's just coming.

MADAME RANÉVSKY [*agitated*]. What happened ? Did the sale come off ? Tell me, tell me !

LOPÁKHIN [*embarrassed, afraid of showing his pleasure*]. The sale was all over by four o'clock. We missed the train and had to wait till half-past eight. [*Sighing heavily.*] Ouf ! I 'm rather giddy. . . .

[*Enter GÁYEF. In one hand he carries parcels ; with the other he wipes away his tears.*]

MADAME RANÉVSKY. What happened, Lénya ? Come, Lénya ? [*Impatiently, crying.*] Be quick, be quick, for Heaven's sake !

GÁYEF [*answering her only with an up-and-down gesture of the hand ; to FIRS, crying*]. Here, take these. . . . Here are some anchovies and Black Sea herrings. I 've had nothing to eat all day. Lord, what I 've been through ! [*Through the open door of the billiard-room comes the click of the billiard balls and YÁSHA's voice : "Seven, eighteen !" GÁYEF's expression changes ; he stops crying.*] I 'm frightfully tired. Come and help me change, Firs.

[*He goes up through the drawing-room, FIRS following.*]

PÍSHTCHIK. What about the sale ? Come on, tell us all about it.

MADAME RANÉVSKY. Was the cherry orchard sold ?

LOPÁKHIN. Yes.

MADAME RANÉVSKY. Who bought it ?

LOPÁKHIN. I did. [*A pause. MADAME RANÉVSKY is overwhelmed at the news. She would fall to the ground but for the chair and table by her. BARBARA takes the keys from her belt, throws them on the floor in the middle of the sitting-room, and exit.*] I bought it. Wait a bit; don't hurry me; my head 's in a whirl; I can't speak. . . . [*Laughing.*] When we got to the sale, Derigánof was there already. Leoníd Andréyitch had only fifteen hundred pounds, and Derigánof bid three thousand more than the mortgage right away. When I saw how things stood, I went for him and bid four thousand. He said four thousand five hundred. I said five thousand five hundred. He went up by five hundreds, you see, and I went up by thousands. . . . Well, it was soon over. I bid nine thousand more than the mort-gage, and got it; and now the cherry orchard is mine! Mine! [*Laughing.*] Heavens alive! Just think of it! The cherry orchard is mine! Tell me that I'm drunk; tell me that I'm off my head; tell me that it's all a dream! . . . [*Stamping his feet.*] Don't laugh at me! If only my father and my grandfather could rise from their graves and see the whole affair, how their Yermolái, their flogged and ignorant Yermolái, who used to run about barefooted in the winter, how this same Yermolái had bought a property that has n't its equal for beauty anywhere in the whole world! I have bought the property where my father and grandfather were slaves, where they were n't even allowed into the kitchen. I'm asleep, it's only a vision, it is n't real. . . . 'T is the fruit of imagination, wrapped in the mists of ignorance. [*Picking up the keys and smiling affectionately.*] She's thrown down her keys; she wants to show that she's no longer mistress here. . . . [*Jingling them together.*] Well, well, what's the odds? [*The musicians are heard tuning up.*] Hey, musicians, play! I want to hear you. Come, every one, and see Yermolái Lopákhin lay his axe to the cherry orchard, come and see the trees fall down! We'll fill the place with villas; our grandsons and great-grandsons shall see a new life here. . . . Strike up, music!

       [*The band plays.* MADAME RANÉVSKY *sinks into a chair and weeps bitterly.*]

LOPÁKHIN [*reproachfully*]. Oh, why, why did n't you listen to me? You can't put the clock back now, poor dear. [*Crying.*] Oh, that all this were past and over! Oh, that our unhappy topsy-turvy life were changed!

PÍSHTCHIK [*taking him by the arm, sotto voce*]. She's crying. Let's go into the drawing-room and leave her alone to . . . Come on.

       [*Taking him by the arm, and going up toward the drawing-room.*]

LOPÁKHIN. What's up? Play your best, musicians! Let everything be as I want. [*Ironically.*] Here comes the new squire, the owner of the cherry orchard! [*Knocking up by accident against a table and nearly throwing down the candelabra.*] Never mind, I can pay for everything!

       [*Exit with* PÍSHTCHIK. *Nobody remains in the drawing-room or sitting-room except* MADAME RANÉVSKY, *who sits huddled together, weeping bitterly. The band play softly.*]

[*Enter* ÁNYA *and* TROPHÍMOF *quickly.* ÁNYA *goes to her mother and kneels before her.* TROPHÍMOF *stands in the entry to the drawing room.*]

ÁNYA. Mamma! Are you crying, mamma? My dear, good, sweet mamma! Darling, I love you! I bless you! The cherry orchard is sold; it's gone; it's quite true, it's quite true. But don't cry, mamma, you've still got life before you, you've still got your pure and lovely soul. Come with me, darling; come away from here. We'll plant a new garden, still lovelier than this. You will see it and understand, and happiness, deep, tranquil happiness will sink down on your soul, like the sun at eventide, and you'll smile, mamma. Come, darling, come with me!

ACT IV

Same scene as Act I. There are no window curtains, no pictures. The little furniture left is stacked in a corner, as if for sale. A feeling of emptiness. By the door to the hall and at the back of the scene are piled portmanteaux, bundles, etc. The door is open and the voices of BARBARA *and* ÁNYA *are audible.*

LOPÁKHIN *stands waiting.* YÁSHA *holds a tray with small tumblers full of champagne.* EPHIKHÓDOF *is tying up a box in the hall. A distant murmur of voices behind the scene; the* PEASANTS *have come to say good-bye.*

GÁYEF [*without*]. Thank you, my lads, thank you.

YÁSHA. The common people have come to say good-bye. I'll tell you what I think, Yermolái Alexéyitch; they're good fellows but rather stupid.

       [*The murmur of voices dies away.*]

[*Enter* MADAME RANÉVSKY *and* GÁYEF *from the hall. She is not crying, but she is pale, her face twitches, she cannot speak.*]

GÁYEF. You gave them your purse, Lyuba. That was wrong, very wrong!

MADAME RANÉVSKY. I could n't help it, I could n't help it!   [*Exeunt both.*]

LOPÁKHIN [*calling after them through the doorway*]. Please come here! Won't you come here? Just a glass to say good-bye. I forgot to bring any from the town, and could only raise one bottle at the station. Come along. [*A pause.*] What, won't you have any? [*Returning from the door.*] If I'd known, I would n't have bought it. I shan't have any either. [YÁSHA *sets the tray down carefully on a chair.*] Drink it yourself, Yásha.

YÁSHA. Here's to our departure! Good luck to them that stay! [*Drinking.*] This is n't real champagne, you take my word for it.

LOPÁKHIN. Sixteen shillings a bottle. [*A pause.*] It's devilish cold in here.

YÁSHA. The fires were n't lighted to-day; we're all going away. [*He laughs.*]

LOPÁKHIN. What are you laughing for?

YÁSHA. Just pleasure.

LOPÁKHIN. Here we are in October, but it's as calm and sunny as summer. Good building weather. [*Looking at his watch and speaking off.*] Don't forget that there's only forty-seven minutes before the train goes. You must start for the station in twenty minutes. Make haste.

[*Enter* TROPHÍMOF *in an overcoat, from out of doors.*]

TROPHÍMOF. I think it's time we were off. The carriages are round. What the deuce has become of my goloshes? I've lost 'em. [*Calling off.*] Ánya, my goloshes have disappeared. I can't find them anywhere!

LOPÁKHIN. I've got to go to Kharkof. I'll start in the same train with you. I'm going to spend the winter at Kharkof. I've been loafing about all this time with you people, eating my head off for want of work. I can't live without work, I don't know what to do with my hands; they dangle about as if they did n't belong to me.

TROPHÍMOF. Well, we're going now, and you'll be able to get back to your beneficent labors.

LOPÁKHIN. Have a glass.

TROPHÍMOF. Not for me.

LOPÁKHIN. Well, so you're off to Moscow?

TROPHÍMOF. Yes, I'll see them into the town, and go on to Moscow to-morrow.

LOPÁKHIN. Well, well, . . . I suppose the professors have n't started their lectures yet; they're waiting till you arrive.

TROPHÍMOF. It's no affair of yours.

LOPÁKHIN. How many years have you been up at the University?

TROPHÍMOF. Try and think of some new joke; this one's getting a bit flat. [*Looking for his goloshes.*] Look here, I dare say we shan't meet again, so let me give you a bit of advice as a keepsake: Don't flap your hands about! Get out of the habit of flapping. Building villas, prophesying that villa residents will turn into small freeholders, all that sort of thing is flapping, too. Well, when all's said and done, I like you. You have thin, delicate, artist fingers; you have a delicate artist soul.

LOPÁKHIN [*embracing him*]. Good-bye, old chap. Thank you for everything. Take some money off me for the journey if you want it.

TROPHÍMOF. What for? I don't want it.

LOPÁKHIN. But you have n't got any.

TROPHÍMOF. Yes, I have. Many thanks. I got some for a translation. Here it is, in my pocket. [*Anxiously.*] I can't find my goloshes anywhere!

BARBARA [*from the next room*]. Here, take your garbage away!

[*She throws a pair of goloshes on the stage.*]

TROPHÍMOF. What are you so cross about, Barbara? Humph! . . . But those are n't my goloshes!

LOPÁKHIN. In the spring I sowed three thousand acres of poppy and I have cleared four thousand pounds net profit. When my poppies were in flower, what a picture they made! So you see, I cleared four thousand pounds; and I wanted to lend you a bit because I've got it to spare. What's the good of being stuck up? I'm a peasant. . . . As man to man . . .

TROPHÍMOF. Your father was a peasant; mine was a chemist; it does n't prove anything. [LOPÁKHIN *takes out his pocket-book with paper money.*] Shut up, shut up. . . . If you offered me twenty thousand pounds I would not take it. I am a free man; nothing that you value so highly, all of you, rich and poor, has the smallest power over me; it's like thistledown floating on the wind. I can do without you; I can go past you; I'm strong and proud. Mankind marches forward to the highest truth, to the highest happiness possible on earth, and I march in the foremost ranks.

LOPÁKHIN. Will you get there?

TROPHÍMOF. Yes. [*A pause.*] I will get there myself, or I will show others the way.

[*The sound of axes hewing is heard in the distance.*]

LOPÁKHIN. Well, good-bye, old chap; it is time to start. Here we stand swaggering to each other, and life goes by all the time without heeding us. When I work for hours without getting tired, I get easy in my mind and I seem to know why I exist. But God alone knows what most of the people in Russia were born for. . . . Well, who cares? It does n't affect the circulation of work. They say Leoníd Andréyitch has got a place; he 's going to be in a bank and get six hundred pounds a year. . . . He won't sit it out, he 's too lazy.

ÁNYA [*in the doorway*]. Mamma says, will you stop them cutting down the orchard till she has gone?

TROPHÍMOF. Really, have n't you got tact enough for that?

[*Exit* TROPHÍMOF *by the hall.*]

LOPÁKHIN. Of course, I 'll stop them at once. — What fools they are!

[*Exit after* TROPHÍMOF.]

ÁNYA. Has Firs been sent to the hospital?

YÁSHA. I told 'em this morning. They 're sure to have sent him.

ÁNYA. [*To* EPHIKHÓDOF, *who crosses.*] Simeon Panteléyitch, please find out if Firs has been sent to the hospital.

YÁSHA [*offended*]. I told George this morning. What 's the good of asking a dozen times?

EPHIKHÓDOF. Our centenarian friend, in my conclusive opinion, is hardly worth tinkering; it 's time he was despatched to his forefathers. I can only say I envy him. [*Putting down a portmanteau on a bandbox and crushing it flat.*] There you are! I knew how it would be! [*Exit.*]

YÁSHA [*jeering*]. Twenty-two misfortunes!

BARBARA [*without*]. Has Firs been sent to the hospital?

ÁNYA. Yes.

BARBARA. Why did n't they take the note to the doctor?

ÁNYA. We must send it after them.

[*Exit* ÁNYA.]

BARBARA [*from the next room*]. Where 's Yásha? Tell him his mother is here. She wants to say good-bye to him.

YÁSHA [*with a gesture of impatience*]. It 's enough to try the patience of a saint!

[DUNYÁSHA *has been busying herself with the luggage. Seeing* YÁSHA *alone, she approaches him.*]

DUNYÁSHA. You might just look once at me, Yásha. You are going away, you are leaving me.

[*Crying and throwing her arms round his neck.*]

YÁSHA. What 's the good of crying? [*Drinking champagne.*] In six days I shall be back in Paris. To-morrow we take the express, off we go, and that 's the last of us! I can hardly believe it 's true. *Vive la France!* This place don't suit me. I can't bear it . . . it can't be helped. I have had enough barbarism; I 'm fed up. [*Drinking champagne.*] What 's the good of crying? You be a good girl, and you 'll have no call to cry.

DUNYÁSHA [*powdering her face and looking into a glass*]. Write me a letter from Paris. I 've been so fond of you, Yásha, ever so fond! I am a delicate creature, Yásha.

YÁSHA. Here 's somebody coming.

[*He busies himself with the luggage singing under his breath.*]

[*Enter* MADAME RANÉVSKY, GÁYEF, ÁNYA, *and* CHARLOTTE.]

GÁYEF. We 'll have to be off; it 's nearly time. [*Looking at* YÁSHA.] Who is it smells of red herring?

MADAME RANÉVSKY. We must take our seats in ten minutes. [*Looking round the room.*] Good-bye, dear old house; good-bye, grandpapa! When winter is past and spring comes again, you will be here no more; they will have pulled you down. Oh, think of all these walls have seen! [*Kissing* ÁNYA *passionately.*] My treasure, you look radiant, your eyes flash like two diamonds. Are you happy? — very happy?

ÁNYA. Very, very happy. We 're beginning a new life, mamma.

GÁYEF [*gayly*]. She 's quite right; everything.'s all right now. Till the cherry orchard was sold we were all agitated and miserable; but once the thing was settled finally and irrevocably, we all calmed down and got jolly again. I 'm a bank clerk now; I 'm a financier . . . red in the middle! And you, Lyuba, whatever you may say, you 're looking ever so much better, not a doubt about it.

MADAME RANÉVSKY. Yes, my nerves are better; it's quite true. [*She is helped on with her hat and coat.*] I sleep well now. Take my things out, Yásha. We must be off. [*To* ÁNYA.] We shall soon meet again, darling. . . . I'm off to Paris; I shall live on the money your grandmother sent from Yaroslav to buy the property. God bless your grandmother! I'm afraid it won't last long.

ÁNYA. You'll come back very, very soon, won't you, mamma? I'm going to work and pass the examination at the Gymnase and get a place and help you. We'll read all sorts of books together, won't we, mamma? [*Kissing her mother's hands.*] We'll read in the long autumn evenings, we'll read heaps of books, and a new, wonderful world will open up before us. [*Meditating.*] . . . Come back, mamma!

MADAME RANÉVSKY. I'll come back, my angel. [*Embracing her.*]

[*Enter* LOPÁKHIN. CHARLOTTE *sings softly.*]

GÁYEF. Happy Charlotte, she's singing.

CHARLOTTE [*taking a bundle of rags, like a swaddled baby*]. Hush-a-bye, baby, on the tree-top . . . [*The baby answers, "Wah, wah."*] Hush, my little one, hush, my pretty one! ["*Wah, wah.*"] You'll break your mother's heart. [*She throws the bundle down on the floor again.*] Don't forget to find me a new place, please. I can't do without it.

LOPÁKHIN. We'll find you a place, Charlotte Ivánovna, don't be afraid.

GÁYEF. Everybody's deserting us. Barbara's going. Nobody seems to want us.

CHARLOTTE. There's nowhere for me to live in the town. I'm obliged to go. [*Hums a tune.*] What's the odds?

[*Enter* PÍSHTCHIK.]

LOPÁKHIN. Nature's masterpiece!

PÍSHTCHIK [*panting*]. Oy, oy, let me get my breath again! . . . I'm done up! . . . My noble friends! . . . Give me some water.

GÁYEF. Wants some money, I suppose. No, thank you; I'll keep out of harm's way. [*Exit.*]

PÍSHTCHIK. It's ages since I have been here, fairest lady. [*To* LOPÁKHIN.] You here? Glad to see you, you man of gigantic intellect. Take this; it's for you. [*Giving* LOPÁKHIN *money.*] Forty pounds! I still owe you eighty-four.

LOPÁKHIN [*amazed, shrugging his shoulders*]. It's like a thing in a dream! Where did you get it from?

PÍSHTCHIK. Wait a bit. . . . I'm hot. . . . A most remarkable thing! Some Englishmen came and found some sort of white clay on my land. [*To* MADAME RANÉVSKY.] And here's forty pounds for you, lovely, wonderful lady. [*Giving her money.*] The rest another time. [*Drinking water.*] Only just now a young man in the train was saying that some . . . some great philosopher advises us all to jump off roofs. . . . Jump, he says, and there's an end of it. [*With an astonished air.*] Just think of that! More water!

LOPÁKHIN. Who were the Englishmen?

PÍSHTCHIK. I leased them the plot with the clay on it for twenty-four years. But I haven't any time now . . . I must be getting on. I must go to Znoikof's, to Kardamónof's. . . . I owe everybody money. [*Drinking.*] Good-bye to every one; I'll look in on Thursday.

MADAME RANÉVSKY. We're just moving into town, and to-morrow I go abroad.

PÍSHTCHIK. What! [*Alarmed.*] What are you going into town for? Why, what's happened to the furniture? . . . Trunks? . . . Oh, it's all right. [*Crying.*] It's all right. People of powerful intellect . . . those Englishmen. It's all right. Be happy . . . God be with you . . . it's all right. Everything in this world has to come to an end. [*Kissing* MADAME RANÉVSKY'S *hand.*] If ever the news reaches you that *I* have come to an end, give a thought to the old . . . horse, and say, "Once there lived a certain Simeónof-Píshtchik, Heaven rest his soul." . . . Remarkable weather we're having. . . . Yes. . . . [*Goes out deeply moved. Returns at once and says from the doorway:*] Dáshenka sent her compliments. [*Exit.*]

MADAME RANÉVSKY. Now we can go. I have only two things on my mind. One is poor old Firs. [*Looking at her watch.*] We can still stay five minutes.

ÁNYA. Firs has been sent to the hospital already, mamma. Yásha sent him off this morning.

MADAME RANÉVSKY. My second anxiety is Barbara. She's used to getting up early and working, and now that she has no work to do she's like a fish out of water. She has grown thin and pale and taken to crying, poor dear. . . . [*A pause.*] You know very well, Yermolái Alexéyitch, I always hoped . . . to see her married to you, and as far as I can see, you 're looking out for a wife. [*She whispers to* ÁNYA, *who nods to* CHARLOTTE, *and both exeunt.*] She loves you ; you like her ; and I can't make out why you seem to fight shy of each other. I don't understand it.

LOPÁKHIN. I don't understand it either, to tell you the truth. It all seems so odd. If there 's still time I 'll do it this moment. Let 's get it over and have done with it; without you there, I feel as if I should never propose to her.

MADAME RANÉVSKY. A capital idea ! After all, it does n't take more than a minute. I 'll call her at once.

LOPÁKHIN. And here 's the champagne all ready. [*Looking at the glasses.*] Empty ; some one 's drunk it. [YÁSHA *coughs.*] That 's what they call lapping it up and no mistake !

MADAME RANÉVSKY [*animated*]. Capital ! We 'll all go away. . . . *Allez,* Yásha. I 'll call her. [*At the door.*] Barbara, leave all that and come here. Come along !

[*Exeunt Madame* RANÉVSKY *and* YÁSHA.]

LOPÁKHIN [*looking at his watch*]. Yes.

[*A pause. A stifled laugh behind the door ; whispering ; at last enter* BARBARA.]

BARBARA [*examining the luggage*]. Very odd; I can't find it anywhere . . .

LOPÁKHIN. What are you looking for ?

BARBARA. I packed it myself, and can't remember. [*A pause.*]

LOPÁKHIN. Where are you going to-day, Varvára Mikháilovna ?

BARBARA. Me ? I 'm going to the Ragulins. I 'm engaged to go and keep house for them, to be housekeeper or whatever it is.

LOPÁKHIN. Oh, at Yáshnevo ? That 's about fifty miles from here. [*A pause.*] Well, so life in this house is over now.

BARBARA [*looking at the luggage*]. Wherever can it be ? Perhaps I put it in the trunk. . . . Yes, life here is over now ; there won't be any more . . .

LOPÁKHIN. And I 'm off to Kharkof at once . . . by the same train. A lot of business to do. I 'm leaving Ephikhódof to look after this place. I 've taken him on.

BARBARA. Have you ?

LOPÁKHIN. At this time last year snow was falling already, if you remember; but now it 's fine and sunny. Still, it 's cold for all that. Three degrees of frost.

BARBARA. Were there ? I did n't look. [*A pause.*] Besides, the thermometer 's broken. [*A pause.*]

A VOICE [*at the outer door*]. Yermolái Alexéyitch !

LOPÁKHIN [*as if he had only been waiting to be called*]. I 'm just coming !

[*Exit* LOPÁKHIN *quickly.*]

[BARBARA *sits on the floor, puts her head on a bundle and sobs softly. The door opens and* MADAME RANÉVSKY *comes in cautiously.*]

MADAME RANÉVSKY. Well ? [*A pause.*] We must be off.

BARBARA [*no longer crying, wiping her eyes*]. Yes, it 's time, mamma. I shall get to the Ragulins all right to-day, so long as I don't miss the train.

MADAME RANÉVSKY [*calling off*]. Put on your things, Ánya.

[*Enter* ÁNYA, *then* GÁYEF *and* CHARLOTTE. GÁYEF *wears a warm overcoat with a hood. The servants and drivers come in.* EPHI-KHÓDOF *busies himself about the luggage.*]

MADAME RANÉVSKY. Now we can start on our journey.

ÁNYA [*delighted*]. We can start on our journey !

GÁYEF. My friends, my dear, beloved friends ! Now that I am leaving this house forever, can I keep silence ? Can I refrain from expressing those emotions which fill my whole being at such a moment ?

ÁNYA [*pleadingly*]. Uncle !

BARBARA. Uncle, what 's the good ?

GÁYEF [*sadly*]. Double the red in the middle pocket. I 'll hold my tongue.

[*Enter* TROPHÍMOF, *then* LOPÁKHIN.]

TROPHÍMOF. Come along, it 's time to start.

LOPÁKHIN. Ephikhódof, my coat.

MADAME RANÉVSKY. I must sit here another minute. It 's just as if I had never noticed before what the walls and ceilings of the house were like. I look at them hungrily, with such tender love . . .

GÁYEF. I remember, when I was six years old, how I sat in this window on Trinity Sunday, and watched father starting out for church.

MADAME RANÉVSKY. Has everything been cleared out?

LOPÁKHIN. Apparently everything. [*To* EPHIKHÓDOF, *putting on his overcoat.*] See that everything's in order, Ephikhódof.

EPHIKHÓDOF [*in a hoarse voice*]. You trust me, Yermolái Alexéyitch.

LOPÁKHIN. What's up with your voice?

EPHIKHÓDOF. I was just having a drink of water. I swallowed something.

YÁSHA [*contemptuously*]. Cad!

MADAME RANÉVSKY. We're going, and not a soul will be left here.

LOPÁKHIN. Until the spring.

[BARBARA *pulls an umbrella out of a bundle of rugs, as if she were brandishing it to strike.* LOPÁKHIN *pretends to be frightened.*]

BARBARA. Don't be so silly! I never thought of such a thing.

TROPHÍMOF. Come, we'd better go and get in. It's time to start. The train will be in immediately.

BARBARA. There are your goloshes, Peter, by that portmanteau. [*Crying.*] What dirty old things they are!

TROPHÍMOF [*putting on his goloshes*]. Come along.

GÁYEF [*much moved, afraid of crying*]. The train . . . the station . . . double the red in the middle; doublette to pot the white in the corner.[1] . . .

MADAME RANÉVSKY. Come on!

LOPÁKHIN. Is every one here? No one left in there? [*Locking the door.*] There are things stacked in there; I must lock them up. Come on!

ÁNYA. Good-bye, house! Good-bye, old life!

TROPHÍMOF. Welcome, new life!

[*Exit with* ÁNYA. BARBARA *looks round the room, and exit slowly. Exeunt* YÁSHA, *and* CHARLOTTE *with her dog.*]

LOPÁKHIN. Till the spring, then. Go on, everybody. So-long! ·[*Exit.*]

[1] If you make your ball hit the cushion and run across into a pocket, it is a double; if I hit the cushion myself and pot you on the rebound, it is a doublette.

[MADAME RANÉVSKY *and* GÁYEF *remain alone. They seem to have been waiting for this, throw their arms round each other's necks and sob restrainedly and gently, afraid of being overheard.*]

GÁYEF [*in despair*]. My sister! my sister!

MADAME RANÉVSKY. Oh, my dear, sweet, lovely orchard! My life, my youth, my happiness, farewell! Farewell!

ÁNYA [*calling gayly, without*]. Mamma!

TROPHÍMOF [*gay and excited*]. Aoo!

MADAME RANÉVSKY. One last look at the walls and the windows. . . . Our dear mother used to love to walk up and down this room.

GÁYEF. My sister! my sister!

ÁNYA [*without*]. Mamma!

TROPHÍMOF [*without*]. Aoo!

MADAME RANÉVSKY. We're coming.

[*Exeunt. The stage is empty. One hears all the doors being locked, and the carriages driving away. All is quiet. Amid the silence the thud of the axes on the trees echoes sad and lonely. The sound of footsteps.* FIRS *appears in the doorway, right. He is dressed, as always, in his long coat and white waistcoat; he wears slippers. He is ill.*]

FIRS [*going to the door, left, and trying the handle*]. Locked. They've gone. [*Sitting on the sofa.*] They've forgotten me. Never mind! I'll sit here. Leoníd Andréyitch is sure to put on his cloth coat instead of his fur. [*He sighs anxiously.*] He had n't me to see. Young wood, green wood! [*He mumbles something incomprehensible.*] Life has gone by as if I'd never lived. [*Lying down.*] I'll lie down. There's no strength left in you; there's nothing, nothing. Ah, you . . . job-lot!

[*He lies motionless. A distant sound is heard, as if from the sky, the sound of a string breaking, dying away, melancholy. Silence ensues, broken only by the stroke of the axe on the trees far away in the cherry orchard.*]

APPENDIX

APPENDIX

I. AUTHORS AND PLAYS

WHEN numbers are in italics the reference is to the date of production; when in roman type to the date of publication. A foreign title followed by an English title signifies that the play has been translated under the latter title.

OSCAR FINGALL O'FLAHERTIE WILLS WILDE. Born Dublin, 1856. Lecturer, novelist, essayist, editor, and playwright. Died November 30, 1900, in Paris. PLAYS: Vera, or The Nihilists (produced in America); The Duchess of Padua, *1891;* Lady Windermere's Fan, *1892;* A Woman of No Importance, *1893;* Salome (first produced in French by Mlle. Sarah Bernhardt), *1894;* The Importance of Being Earnest, *1895;* An Ideal Husband, *1895.*

SIR ARTHUR WING PINERO. Born May 24, 1855, in London. Educated in private schools. Actor from June, 1874, to July, 1881. Knighted 1909. PLAYS: Two Hundred a Year (one act), 1877; Two Can Play at That Game, 1877; Daisy's Escape, 1879; Hester's Mystery (one act), 1880; Bygones (one act), 1880; The Money Spinner, 1880; Imprudence, 1881; The Squire, 1881; Boys and Girls, 1882; The Rector, 1883; Lords and Commons, 1883; The Rocket, 1883; Low Water, 1884; The Iron-Master (after Le Maître de Forges, by Georges Ohnet), 1884; In Chancery, 1884; The Magistrate, *1885;* Mayfair (adapted from Maison Neuve of Sardou), 1885; The Schoolmistress, *1886;* The Hobby-Horse, *1886;* Dandy Dick, *1887;* Sweet Lavender, *1888;* The Weaker Sex, *1888* (written 1884); The Profligate, *1889;* The Cabinet Minister, *1890;* Lady Bountiful, *1891;* The Times, *1891;* The Amazons, *1893;* The Second Mrs. Tanqueray, *1893;* The Notorious Mrs. Ebbsmith, *1895;* The Benefit of the Doubt, *1895;* The Princess and the Butterfly, *1897;* Trelawney of the Wells, *1898;* The Gay Lord Quex, *1899;* Iris, *1901;* Letty, *1903;* A Wife Without a Smile, *1904;* His House in Order, *1906;* The Thunderbolt, *1908;* Midchannel, *1909;* Preserving Mr. Panmure, *1911;* The Mind the Paint Girl, *1912;* The Widow of Wasdale Head, *1912;* Playgoers, *1913.*

HENRY ARTHUR JONES. Born September 20, 1851, at Grandborough, Bucks. Educated at Winslow, Bucks. Hon. M.A. Harvard, 1907. Author of The Renascence of the English Drama, 1896; Foundations of a National Drama, 1913; and many essays on drama in the reviews. PLAYS: A Clerical Error, *1879;* The Silver King, *1882;* Saints and Sinners, *1884;* Breaking a Butterfly (adaptation of Ibsen's A Doll's House), *1884;* The Middleman, *1889;* Judah, *1890;* The Dancing Girl, *1891;* The Crusaders, *1891;* The Bauble Shop, *1893;* The Tempter, *1893;* The Masqueraders, *1894;* The Case of Rebellious Susan, *1894;* The Triumph of the Philistines, *1895;* Michael and his Lost Angel, *1896;* The Rogue's Comedy, *1896;* The Physician, *1897;* The Liars, *1897;* The Manœuvres of Jane, *1898;* Carnac Sahib, *1899;* The Lackey's Carnival, *1900;* Mrs. Dane's Defence, *1900;* The Princess's Nose, *1902;* Chance, the Idol, *1902;* Whitewashing Julia, *1903;* Joseph Entangled, *1904;* The Chevaleer, 1904; The Heroic Stubbs, *1906;* The Hypocrites, *1906;* The Evangelist, *1907;* Dolly Reforming Herself, *1908;* The Knife, *1909;* We Can't be as Bad as All That, *1910;* Fall in Rookies, *1910;* The Ogre, *1911;* The Divine Gift, 1913; Mary Goes First, *1913.*

JOHN GALSWORTHY. Born in 1867. Educated at Harrow and New College, Oxford. Read law. Wrote stories under name of John Sinjohn. Novelist, critic, playwright. PLAYS: The Silver Box, 1906; Joy, 1907; Strife, 1909; The Eldest Son, 1909, *1912;* The Little Dream, 1910, *1911;* Justice, *1910;* The Pigeon, 1912; The Fugitive, 1913; The Mob, 1914.

GRANVILLE BARKER. Born London, 1877. Made his first appearance on the stage in 1891. In 1904 joined J. E. Vedrenne in the managership of the Court Theatre. In 1909 was manager of Charles Frohman's Repertory Theatre, The Duke of York's. Author with William Archer of Scheme and Estimates for a National Theatre, 1907. PLAYS: The Marrying of Ann Leete, *1901;* The Voysey Inheritance, *1905;* Waste, *1907;* The Madras House, *1910;* Prunella (with Laurence Housman), *1904;* Anatol (paraphrase from the German of Arthur Schnitzler), *1911.*

WILLIAM BUTLER YEATS. Born June 13, 1865, at Dublin, Ireland. Educated for art. Critic, poet, dramatist, organizer of the Irish National Theatre. Author of The Celtic Twilight, 1902; Ideas of Good and Evil, 1903; J. M. Synge and the Ireland of his Time, 1913. PLAYS: The Land of Heart's Desire; *1894;* The Countess Cathleen, *1899;* The Shadowy Waters, 1900; Cathleen ni Hoolihan, *1902;* The Hour-Glass, *1903;* On Baile's Strand, *1904;* The Pot of Broth, *1902;* The King's Threshold, 1904; Deirdre, 1907; Where There is Nothing, 1905 (rewritten with Lady Gregory as The Unicorn from the Stars. 1908).

JOHN MILLINGTON SYNGE. Born April 16, 1871, Rathfarnham, County Dublin, Ireland. Educated Trinity College, Dublin. Further educated himself by reading and travel on foot in France, Bavaria, and Italy. At the suggestion of W. B. Yeats returned to Ireland. Lived in Aran Islands. Newspaper writer and dramatist. Died March 24, 1909. Author of The Aran Islands, 1907; In Wicklow, In West Kerry, etc., 1906, 1907. PLAYS: In the Shadow of the Glen, 1903; Riders to the Sea, 1904; The Well of the Saints, 1905; The Playboy of the Western World, 1907; The Tinker's Wedding, 1909; Deirdre of the Sorrows, 1910.

LADY AUGUSTA GREGORY. Born Isabella Augusta Persse, of Roxborough County, Galway; was married in 1881 to Sir William Gregory, M.P. for Galway and Dublin, and Governor of Ceylon. Her husband died in 1892. She first became known through her researches in Celtic mythology. The chief published results of these were: Cuchulain of Muirthemne, 1902; Gods and Fighting Men, 1904; The Book of Saints and Wonders, 1908. The following plays have been written for the Irish National Theatre: Twenty-Five, 1903; Spreading the News, 1904; Kincora, 1905; The White Cockade, 1905; The Canavans, 1906; Hyacinth Halvey, 1906; The Gaol Gate, 1906; Devorgilla, 1907; The Rising of the Moon, 1907; The Jackdaw, 1907; The Workhouse Ward, 1908; The Image, 1909; The Travelling Man, 1910; Coats, 1910; The Full Moon, 1910; The Deliverer, 1911. Lady Gregory has also written other unproduced plays in Irish Folk History Plays, 1912; and in New Comedies, 1912; has translated for production plays by Molière, Goldoni, Sudermann, and Douglas Hyde; and has collaborated with Douglas Hyde in The Poorhouse, 1907; and with W. B. Yeats in The Unicorn from the Stars, 1907.

SIR JAMES MATTHEW BARRIE. Born Kirriemuir, N.B., May 9, 1860. Educated Edinburgh University. M.A.; LL.D.; Baronet, 1913. Novelist and dramatist. Has financially supported repertory movements. PLAYS: The Professor's Love Story, 1895; The Little Minister, 1897; The Wedding Guest, 1900; Quality Street, The Admirable Crichton, Little Mary, 1903; Peter Pan, 1904; Alice Sit by the Fire, 1905; What Every Woman Knows, 1908; Old Friends; The Twelve Pound Look, 1910; The Legend of Leonora; The Will; The Adored One, 1913.

GEORGE BERNARD SHAW. Born Dublin, July 26, 1856. Novelist, Fabian Socialist, critic, playwright. Author of The Quintessence of Ibsenism, 1891, 1913; Dramatic Opinions and Essays, 1907. PLAYS: Plays Pleasant and Unpleasant, 1898 (containing Widowers' Houses, The Philanderer, Mrs. Warren's Profession, Arms and the Man, Candida, The Man of Destiny, You Never Can Tell); Three Plays for Puritans, 1900 (containing The Devil's Disciple; Cæsar and Cleopatra, Captain Brassbound's Conversion); Man and Superman, 1903, 1905; The Admirable Bashville, 1903; John Bull's Other Island, How He Lied to her Husband, 1904; Major Barbara, 1905; The Doctor's Dilemma, 1906; Getting Married, 1908; The Shewing-Up of Blanco Posnet, 1909; Press Cuttings, 1909; Misalliance, 1910; The Dark Lady of the Sonnets, 1910; Fanny's First Play, 1911; Overruled, 1912; Androcles and the Lion, 1914; Pygmalion, 1914.

CLYDE FITCH. Born at Elmira, New York, May 2, 1865. Educated at Amherst. Died September 4, 1909, at Chalôns-sur-Marne, France. PLAYS: Beau Brummel, 1890, 1905; Betty's Finish, 1890; Frédéric Lemaître, 1890; A Modern Match, 1891 (subsequently played as Marriage); Pamela's Prodigy, 1891, 1893; The Masked Ball (from the French), 1892; The Harvest, 1893 (one-act play with plot afterwards used in The Moth and the Flame); A Shattered Idol, 1893 (from the French); The American Duchess, 1893 (from the French); The Social Swim, 1893; Mrs. Grundy, Junior, 1894 (from the French); His Grace De Grammont, 1894; April Weather, 1894; Mistress Betty, 1895 (subsequently revised and produced 1905 as The Toast of the Town); Gossip, 1895 (with Leo Ditrichstein); Bohemia, 1896 (from the French); The Liar, 1896 (from the French); A Superfluous Husband, 1897 (with Leo Ditrichstein); Nathan Hale, 1898, 1899; The Moth and the Flame, 1898; The Head of the Family, 1898 (from the German with Leo Ditrichstein); The Cowboy and the Lady, 1899; Barbara Frietschie, 1899, 1900; Sapho, 1900 (from the French); The Climbers, 1900, 1906; Captain Jinks of the Horse Marines, 1901, 1902; Lover's Lane, 1901; The Last of the Dandies, 1901; The Way of the World, 1901; The Girl and the Judge, 1901; The Marriage Game, 1901 (from the French); The Stubbornness of Geraldine, 1902, 1906; The Girl with the Green Eyes 1902, 1905; The Frisky Mrs. Johnson, 1903 (from the French); The Bird in the Cage, 1903; Algy, 1903; Her Own Way, 1903, 1907; Glad of It, 1903; Major André, 1903; The Coronet of a Duchess, 1904; Granny, 1904; Cousin Billy, 1904; The Woman in the Case, 1904; Her Great Match, 1905; Wolfville, 1905; The Girl who has Everything, 1906; Toddles, 1906 (from the French); The House of Mirth, 1906 (with Mrs. Wharton); The Truth, 1906, 1907; The Straight Road, 1906; Her Sister, 1907; The Blue Mouse, 1908 (adapted from the German); Girls, 1908; A Happy Marriage, 1909; The Bachelor, 1909, The City, 1910.

WILLIAM VAUGHN MOODY. Born July 8, 1869. Died October 17, 1910. Poet, dramatist, professor in the University of Chicago. Author of Ode in the Time of Hesitation; The Fire Bringer; The Masque of Judgment. PLAYS: The Great Divide, 1906; The Faith Healer, 1909.

AUGUSTUS THOMAS. Born St. Louis, Missouri, January 8, 1859. First writing done as a special newspaper writer. CHIEF PLAYS: Alabama, 1891; In Mizzoura, 1893; Arizona, 1900; Oliver Goldsmith, 1900; The Earl of Pawtucket, 1903; Mrs. Leffingwell's Boots, 1905; The Witching Hour, 1907; As a Man Thinks, 1911.

PERCY MACKAYE. Born New York, March 16, 1875. Educated at Harvard and Leipzig. Poet, dramatist, critic. Author of The Playhouse and the Play, 1909; The Civic Theatre, 1913. PLAYS: The Canterbury Pilgrims, 1903, *1909;* Fenris the Wolf, 1905; Sappho and Phaon, 1907, *1908;* The Scarecrow, 1908, *1910;* Mater, 1908, *1910;* Anti-Matrimony, 1910; Yankee Fantasies (one-act plays), 1911; To-morrow, 1913; A Thousand Years Ago, *1914.*

GERHART HAUPTMANN. Born November 15, 1862, at Obersalzbrunn. From 1874 to 1878 at the Breslau Realschule. At Jena, 1882, 1883. First interested in sculpture. His first work in literature, Promethidenlos, a poem, published in 1885. Has written novels. PLAYS: Vor Sonnenaufgang, *1889* (Before Dawn); Das Friedensfest, *1890* (The Coming of Peace); Einsame Menschen, *1891* (Lonely Lives); College Crampton, *1892* (Colleague Crampton); Die Weber, *1893* (The Weavers); Der Biberpelz, *1893* (The Beaver Coat); Hanneles Himmelfahrt, *1893* (Hannele); Florian Geyer, *1896* (Florian Geyer); Die versunkene Glocke, *1896* (The Sunken Bell); Fuhrmann Henschel, *1898* (Drayman Henschel); Schluck und Jau, *1900;* Michael Kramer, *1900* (Michael Kramer); Der rote Hahn, *1901* (The Conflagration); Der arme Heinrich, *1902* (Henry of Auë); Rose Bernd, *1903* (Rose Bernd); Elga, *1905* (Elga); Und Pippa tanzt! *1906* (And Pippa Dances); Die Jungfern vom Bischofsberg, *1907;* Kaiser Karls Geisel, 1908; Griselda, 1909; Die Ratten, *1911* (The Rats); Gabriel Schilling's Flucht, *1912.* Masque: In Commemoration of the War of Liberation, *1913.*

HERMANN SUDERMANN. Born September 30, 1857, at Matzicken, Heydekrug, East Prussia. Educated at Elbing, and Tilsit, University of Königsberg, and Berlin. For a time editor of the *Deutsches Reichsblatt.* First publication, Im Zwielicht (stories), and Frau Sorge (novel). PLAYS: Die Ehre, *1889;* Sodoms Ende, *1891;* Heimat, *1893* (Magda); Schmetterlingsschlacht, *1895;* Das Glück im Winkel, *1896* (The Vale of Content); Morituri (Teja, Fritzchen, Das Ewigmännliche), 1896 (translated); Johannes, *1898* (John the Baptist); Die drei Reiherfedern (The Three Heron's Feathers) *1899;* Johannisfeuer, *1900* (St. John's Eve; St. John's Fire); Es lebe das Leben, *1902* (The Joy of Living); Sturmgeselle Sokrates, *1903;* Stein unter Steinen, *1905;* Das Blumenboot, *1905;* Rosen (Die Lichtbänder, Margot, Der letzte Besuch, Die ferne Princessin), 1907 (translated); Strandkinder, *1909,* Der Bettler von Syrakus, *1911;* Der gute Ruf, *1913.*

EUGÈNE BRIEUX. Born Paris, January 19, 1858. Journalist. First production at Théâtre Libre, 1890. Officer of the Legion of Honor. Elected to the chair of Halévy in the French Academy, 1909. PLAYS: Bernard Palissy, *1879,* in collaboration with M. Gaston Salandri; Ménages d'Artistes, *1890;* Blanchette, *1892* (translated); M. de Réboval, *1892;* La Couvée, *1893;* L'Engrenage, *1894;* L'Évasion, *1896* (The Escape); Les Bienfaiteurs, *1896;* Le Berceau, *1898;* L'École des Belles-Mères, *1898* (School for Mothers-in-Law); Résultat des Courses, *1898;* Les Trois Filles de M. Dupont, *1899* (The Three Daughters of M. Dupont); La Robe Rouge, *1900* (The Red Robe); Les Remplaçantes, *1901;* La Petite Amie, *1902;* Les Avariés, *1902* (Damaged Goods); Maternité, *1903* (Maternity); L'Armature, *1905* (dramatized from a novel by Paul Hervieu); Les Hannetons *1906* (played by the London Stage Society and by Lawrence Irving but not printed in English); La Française, *1907;* Simone, *1908;* La Foi, *1909* (played as False Gods at Her Majesty's Theatre, *1909*); Suzette, *1910;* La Femme Seule, *1912.*

PAUL HERVIEU. Born Neuilly, September 2, 1857. Member of the bar. Member of the French Academy. Earliest work done in the novel. Many of his plays are in the repertory of the Comédie Française. PLAYS: Les Paroles restent, *1892;* Les Tenailles, *1895* (In Chains); La Loi de l'Homme, *1895;* L'Énigme, *1901;* La Course du Flambeau, *1901;* Théroigne de Méricourt, *1902;* Le Dédale, *1903* (The Labyrinth); Le Réveil, *1905;* Connais-Toi, *1909* (Know Thyself); Bagatelle, *1912.*

MAURICE MAETERLINCK. Born August 29, 1862, at Brussels, Belgium. Poet, philosopher, naturalist, playwright. Author of The Treasure of the Humble, 1896; Wisdom and Destiny, 1898; etc. PLAYS: La Princesse Maleine, 1889, *1890;* Les Aveugles, 1890, *1891;* L'Intruse, 1890, *1891;* Les Sept Princesses 1891, *1893;* Pélléas et Mélisande, 1892, *1893;* Alladine et Palomides, 1894, *1896;* L'Intérieur, 1894, *1895;* La Mort de Tintagiles,1894, *1899;* Annabella, 1895 (adapted from John Ford's 'T is Pity She's a Whore); Aglavaine et Sélysette, *1894,* 1896; Ariane et Barbe Bleue, 1901, *1907;* Soeur Béatrice, 1901, *1910;* Monna Vanna, 1902, *1902;* Joyzelle, 1903, *1903;* L'Oiseau Bleu, 1908, *1908;* Marie Madeleine, 1910, *1910.* All are translated into English.

BJÖRNSTJERNE BJÖRNSON. Born December 8, 1832, in a mountain town of northern Norway. Died 1910. Field of activity wide; novelist, poet, playwright, and political leader. PLAYS: Mellem Slagene, 1856; Halte-Hulda, 1858; Kong Sverre, 1861; Sigurd Slembe, 1862 (Sigurd the Bad); Maria Stuart i Skotland, 1864 (Mary Queen of Scots); D Nygifte, 1865 (The Newly Married Couple); Sigurd Jorsalfar, *1872;* Redaktören, *1874;* En Fallit, *1874;* Kongen, 1877; Leonarda, 1879 (Leonarda); Det Ny System, *1879* (The New System); En Hanske, *1883* (The Gauntlet); Over Ævne, I, 1883 (Beyond Our Power; Beyond Human Power); Geografi og Kjaerlighed, *1885* (Love and Geography); Over Ævne, II, 1895 (Beyond Our Might); Paul Lange og Tora Parsberg, *1898;* Laboremus, 1901 (Laboremus); Paa Storhove, *1902;* Daglannet, *1904;* Naar den ny Vin Blomstrer, *1909* (When the New Wine Blooms).

AUGUST STRINDBERG. Born Stockholm, Sweden, January 22, 1849. Died May 14, 1912. A voluminous writer of autobiography, essays, novels, plays, and scientific works. CHIEF TRANSLATED PLAYS: (Names in English) The Journey of Lucky Peter, *1883;* The Father, *1887;* Miss Julia, *1888;* Comrades, *1888;* Creditors, *1890;* Pariah, *1890;* Simoom, *1890;* The Stronger, *1890;* Debit and Credit, *1893;* Mother-Love, *1893;* Facing Death, *1893;* The Link, *1897;* Playing with Fire, *1897;* There are Crimes and Crimes, *1899;* Easter, *1901;* The Dance of Death, I and II, *1901;* Swanwhite, *1902;* The Dream Play, *1902;* Storm, *1907.*

ANTON TCHEKHOV. Born at Taganrog on the Black Sea, Russia, January 17, 1860. He was educated at the University of Moscow, and became Doctor of Medicine in 1884. Meanwhile he had been publishing stories, and soon became known as a story writer and dramatist. He wrote over three hundred short stories. He died in 1904 in a village of the Black Forest where he had gone to recover his health. PLAYS: The Swan Song, *1889;* The Proposal, *1889;* Ivanoff, *1889;* The Boor, *1890;* The Sea Gull, *1896;* The Tragedian in Spite of Himself, *1899;* The Three Sisters, *1901;* Uncle Vanya, *1902;* The Cherry Orchard, *1904.*

II. NOTES ON THE PRODUCTION OF PLAYS

OSCAR WILDE'S LADY WINDERMERE'S FAN had its first performance in the St. James Theatre, London, February 22, 1892. At this performance the part of Lord Windermere was taken by George Alexander; Lady Windermere, by Miss Lily Hanbury; Mrs. Erlynne, by Miss Marion Terry. For the first two nights the identity of Mrs. Erlynne was kept from the audience until the dénoument. At this time the play was rewritten to eliminate the mystery. The first American performances were at the Columbia Theatre, Boston, January 23, 1893, and at Palmer's Theatre, New York, February 5, 1893, with E. M. Bell, Julia Arthur, and May Brookyn in the parts mentioned above. The play has been often given in England, America, and on the Continent.

ARTHUR WING PINERO'S THE SECOND MRS. TANQUERAY was first performed at the St. James Theatre, London, Saturday, May 27, 1893, with Mrs. Patrick Campbell in the part of Paula, and George Alexander playing Aubrey Tanqueray. The play held the stage of this theatre until July 28 of the same year, when it was transferred to the provinces with Mr. Kendal as Tanqueray, and Mrs. Kendal as Paula. These players headed the company that first produced the play in New York at the Star Theatre, October 9, 1893. Mrs. Patrick Campbell's first American appearance in the part of Paula took place at the Powers Theatre, Chicago, December 30, 1901. The play has been often repeated in England and America, other Paulas having been Miss Charlotte Granville, Miss Evelyn Millard, Miss Cynthia Brooke, and Miss Olga Nethersole. Mme. Eleanora Duse has acted the part in an Italian version.

HENRY ARTHUR JONES'S MICHAEL AND HIS LOST ANGEL was produced simultaneously in London, at the Lyceum Theatre, and in New York, at the Empire Theatre, January 15, 1896. In the London production the part of Michael Feversham was assumed by Mr. Johnston Forbes-Robertson, and that of Audrie Lesden by Miss Marion Terry. In New York these parts were taken respectively by Henry Miller and Viola Allen. In both cities the run of the play came to an end within two weeks. No attempt has been made to repeat the play, though in the Preface to the reprint of 1909 Mr. Jones promises to produce it again, and shows that, though considered a financial failure, the receipts were higher in the ten nights of the London production than they had been for The Middleman, his greatest financial success, in a like period of its early production. The author considers that this play contains his best serious work, and selects this play for use in this book.

JOHN GALSWORTHY'S STRIFE was first performed for a series of matinées at the Duke of York's Theatre, London, beginning March 9, 1909. Thence it was transferred for evening and matinée performances to the Haymarket and Adelphi Theatres. The part of John Anthony was taken by Norman McKinnell; David Roberts, by J. Fisher White; Madge Thomas, by Miss Lillah McCarthy. The first performance in America took place at the New Theatre, New York, Wednesday, November 17, 1909. For this production the author shifted the scene of the play from Trenartha in Wales to southeastern Ohio, without, however, modifying the play in lines or characters. For this production Louis Calvert played the part of John Anthony; Albert Bruning, that of David Roberts, and Miss Thais Lawton, that of Madge Thomas.

GRANVILLE BARKER'S THE MADRAS HOUSE was first performed at Charles Frohman's Repertory Theatre, The Duke of York's, then under direction of the author, March 9, 1910. During three weeks it was performed in repertory ten times. The part of Eustace Perrin State was played by Arthur Whitby; Constantine Madras, by Sydney Valentine; Philip Madras, by Dennis Eadie; Jessica Madras, by Miss Fay Davis; Marion Yates, by Miss Mary Jerrold. This play is the author's selection from his works for use in this book.
    List of Persons; not printed with the play: — Philip Madras. — Jessica Madras, his wife. — Major Hippisley Thomas. — Constantine Madras. — Mrs. Madras, his wife. — Mr. Harry Huxtable. — Mrs. Katherine Huxtable, his wife. — Laura, Minnie, Clara, Julia, Emma, Jane, Daughters of Mr. and Mrs. Huxtable. — Eustace Perrin State. — Mr. Windlesham. — Mrs. Brigstock. — Mr. Brigstock. — Miss Chancellor. — Miss Yates. — Belhaven. — Costume Models Numero un to Numero dix.

WILLIAM BUTLER YEATS'S modern morality THE HOUR–GLASS was first produced by the Irish National Theatre Society, March 14, 1903, in Molesworth Hall, Dublin, where the performances of the Society were held before the Abbey Theatre was secured. The play is based on a story found in Lady Wilde's Ancient Legends of Ireland, 1887, of a wise man saved from eternal punishment by the faith of a child.

JOHN MILLINGTON SYNGE'S RIDERS TO THE SEA was first performed in Molesworth Hall, Dublin, February 25, 1904, by the players of the Irish National Theatre Society, with Miss Honor Lavelle in the part of Maurya; W. G. Fay playing her son Bartley; and Sarah Allgood, Cathleen. Subsequent performances have been at the Abbey Theatre, Dublin, 1909; the Court Theatre, London, 1911; and on tour by the Irish Players in England and America.

LADY GREGORY'S THE RISING OF THE MOON was written early in the author's active association with the Irish National Theatre. It was first printed in *Samhain*, the annual organ of the movement, in 1904, though its first production did not take place until three years later, March 9, 1907, at the Abbey Theatre. The first production in America was by Mr. and Mrs. W. G. Fay, who had at this time separated from the National Theatre Society. It has subsequently been frequently performed by the Irish Players in the Abbey Theatre and on tour in Great Britain and America.

CLYDE FITCH'S THE TRUTH opened at Cleveland, Ohio, in October, 1906, and was played beginning Monday, January 7, 1907, at the Criterion and Lyceum Theatres in New York, with William J. Kelly in the part of Warder; J. E. Dodson (in New York, William B. Mack) in the part of Roland; and Clara Bloodgood as Becky Warder. In the production at the Comedy Theatre, London, April 6, 1907, these parts were taken by Allan Aynesworth, Dion Boucicault, and Marie Tempest.

WILLIAM VAUGHN MOODY'S THE GREAT DIVIDE was given its first metropolitan production, Wednesday, October 3, 1906, at the Princess Theatre in New York, with Henry Miller in the part of Stephen Ghent, and Miss Margaret Anglin as Ruth Jordan. When produced at the Adelphi Theatre, London, September 25, 1909, Miss Edith Wynne Matthison played the part of Ruth Jordan.

AUGUSTUS THOMAS'S THE WITCHING HOUR was first performed at the Hackett Theatre, New York, November 18, 1907, (Providence, R. I., Nov. 16) with John Mason in the rôle of Jack Brookfield, Russ Whytal playing Judge Prentice.

PERCY MACKAYE'S "tragedy of the ludicrous," THE SCARECROW, was first performed by the Harvard Dramatic Club at Cambridge in 1910. Its professional production opened January 17, 1911, at the Garrick Theatre, New York, with Alice Fischer in the part of Blacksmith Bess; Edmund Breese in the part of Dickon; and Frank Reicher in the part of Lord Ravensbane (The Scarecrow).

GERHART HAUPTMANN'S THE WEAVERS was first performed, without government sanction, by the Society of the Freie Bühne, in Berlin, February 26, 1893. Subsequently, beginning September 25, 1894, it was performed 107 times at the Deutsches Theater in Berlin. The play was performed in translation by the Paris Théâtre Libre under M. Antoine, May 29, 1893. As early as April, 1895, it was performed in German at the Irving Place Theatre in New York.

HERMANN SUDERMANN'S THE VALE OF CONTENT (DAS GLÜCK IM WINKEL) was first presented April 4, 1896, at the Lessing Theater in Berlin. Its only known English performance has been at Miss Horniman's Gaiety Theatre in Manchester. The play has not before been published in translation.

EUGÈNE BRIEUX'S THE RED ROBE (LA ROBE ROUGE). The first performance took place at the Théâtre du Vaudeville, Paris, March 15, 1900, with M. Huguenet in the part of Mouzon; M. Grand in the part of Etchepare; and Mme. Réjane in the part of Yanetta. It was performed in Berlin in March, 1901, with Irene Triesch in the part of Yanetta. A subsequent performance was at the Comédie Française, September 23, 1909, with Mme. Delvair playing Yanetta. The play is newly translated.

PAUL HERVIEU'S KNOW THYSELF (CONNAIS–TOI) was first performed at the Comédie Française, March 29, 1909. The part of General de Sibéran was taken by M. Le Bargy; Pavail, by Georges Grand; Clarisse, by Mme. J. Bartet. The play has not before been printed in English, though produced in another translation by Arnold Daly in New York in 1910. It is the author's choice from among his works.

MAURICE MAETERLINCK'S PÉLLÉAS AND MÉLISANDE was first performed at the Théâtre des Bouffes, during the week of May 22, 1893. It was subsequently performed in French during the spring of 1895, under the auspices of the Independent Theatre in London, by M. Lugné-Poë and his company. The part of Mélisande was for a time in the repertory of Mrs. Patrick Campbell. The play was presented at the Kleines Theater in Berlin, May, 1903. The most noteworthy performance took place August 29, 1910, in the open air, at the Abbey of St. Wandrille, Normandy, with Mme. Georgette Leblanc as director and in the part of Mélisande. An opera founded on this play has been written by C. Debussy. The author names this play, Home, Monna Vanna, and The Blue Bird for choice among his works.

BJÖRNSTJERNE BJÖRNSON'S BEYOND HUMAN POWER (OVER ÆVNE, I). This is the first of two plays of the same title by Björnson. The present play was published in 1883 and deals with the problems of faith. The second part, published in 1895, deals with problems of capital and labor. The present play was performed in French at the Théâtre Libre in Paris, May 29, 1893. It was first given in Germany by the Berliner Theater under the direction of Paul Lindau, March 24, 1900. It was presented at the Republic Theatre, New York, January 18, 1902. by Mrs. Patrick Campbell.

List of Persons; not printed with the play: — Pastor Sang. — Clara Sang, his wife. — Elias, their son. — Rachel, their daughter. — Mrs. Hannah Roberts, Clara's sister. — Kroyer, Blank, Brei, Falk, Jenson, Bratt, Pastors. — The Bishop. — A Stranger. — A Pastor's Widow.

AUGUST STRINDBERG'S THE FATHER was published in September, 1887. It was first performed in Paris in the same year, as one of the early productions of M. Antoine's Théâtre Libre. In 1889 it was performed in Copenhagen, and the following year, October 12, 1890, formed one of the productions for the second year of the German Freie Bühne of Berlin. It was next given at the Théâtre L'Œuvre, in honor of Strindberg's visit to Paris, December 17, 1894, under the direction of M. Lugné-Poe. It was not performed in Stockholm until 1901. Productions in English were at the Rehearsal Theatre, London, by Warner and Edith Oland, July 23, 1911, and at the Berkeley Theatre, New York, April, 1912.

ANTON TCHEKHOV'S last play THE CHERRY ORCHARD was presented by the Art Theater at Moscow in 1904 under the direction of M. Stanislavsky. To this theater Tchekhov had contributed most of his plays. It was later very elaborately performed at the Theater Kommisarzhevsky, in St. Petersburg, established by the celebrated actress of that name. Another translation of this play under the title of The Cherry Garden, was made by M. S. Mandell for the Dramatic Department of the Yale Courant.

III. A READING LIST IN CONTEMPORARY DRAMATISTS

No attempt has been made to provide an exhaustive bibliography. Books are cited for availability and general usefulness. Only those magazine articles are noted that seem to be standing contributions to their subject.

OSCAR WILDE

Laurent, R. *Études anglaises.* Paris, 1910.
Ransome, A. *The Life of Oscar Wilde; a Critical Study.* London, 1912.
Sherard, R. H. *Oscar Wilde.* New York, 1906.
See Wilde's *The Soul of Man under Socialism*, 1891; *The Truth of Masks*, in *Intentions*, 1891.

SIR ARTHUR WING PINERO

Borsa, M. *The English Stage of To-day.* London, 1908.
Filon, A. *The English Stage.* London, 1897.
Fyfe, H. H. *Arthur Wing Pinero, Playwright.* London, 1902.
Hale, E. E. Jr. *Dramatists of To-day.* New York, 1911.
Wedmore, Sir F. "Literature and the Theater." *Nineteenth Century and After*, April, 1902.
See Pinero's lecture-essay on "Robert Louis Stevenson, the Dramatist," *Blackwood's Magazine* and *The Critic*, April, 1903.

HENRY ARTHUR JONES

Borsa, M. *The English Stage To-day.* London, 1908.
Howells, W. D. "The Plays of Henry Arthur Jones," *North American Review*, 1907.
See Jones's *The Renascence of the English Drama*, 1895; *Foundations of a National Drama*, 1912; Introductions to published plays, including prefatory letter to *The Divine Gift*, 1913.

JOHN GALSWORTHY

Dukes, A. *Modern Dramatists*, Chicago, 1912.
Herford, C. H. "The Plays of Mr. John Galsworthy" in *Essays and Studies.* Oxford, 1914.
See Galsworthy's "Some Platitudes Concerning Drama," in *The Inn of Tranquillity*, 1913.

GRANVILLE BARKER

Dukes, A. *Modern Dramatists.* Chicago, 1912.
Howe, P. P. *The Repertory Theatre: a Record and a Criticism.* London, 1911.
McCarthy, D. *The Court Theatre, 1904–07.* London, 1907.
See Archer, W., and Barker, G., *Scheme and Estimates for a National Theatre.* London, 1908. *See* Barker, G., "The Theatre: the Next Phase," *Forum*, August, 1910; "Two German Theatres," *Fortnightly Review*, January, 1911.

WILLIAM BUTLER YEATS

Gregory, Lady A. *Our Irish Theatre.* New York, 1913.
Krans, H. S. *William Butler Yeats and the Irish Literary Revival.* New York, 1904.
Moore, G. *Hail and Farewell.* 3 vols. London, 1911–1914.
Weygandt, C. *Irish Plays and Playwrights.* Boston, 1913.
See Yeats's *Ideas of Good and Evil*, 1903; *The Irish Dramatic Movement*, vol. IV, Collected Works, 1908; *J. M. Synge and the Ireland of his Time*, 1913.

JOHN MILLINGTON SYNGE

Bickley, F. *J. M. Synge and the Irish Dramatic Movement.* New York, 1912.
Bourgeois, M. *John M. Synge and the Irish Theatre.* London, 1914.
Gregory, Lady A. *Our Irish Theater.* New York, 1913.

Howe, P. P. *J. M. Synge: a Critical Study.* London, 1912.
Masefield, J. "J. M. Synge," *Contemporary Review,* April, 1911.
Moore, G. *Hail and Farewell.* London, 1911–1914.
Weygandt, C. *Irish Plays and Playwrights.* Boston, 1913.
Yeats, W. B. *Synge and the Ireland of his Time.* Dublin, 1911.
See Synge's Prefaces to *The Playboy of the Western World, The Tinker's Wedding,* and *Poems.*

LADY AUGUSTA GREGORY

Gregory, Lady A. *Our Irish Theatre.* New York, 1913.
Moore, G. *Hail and Farewell.* London, 1911–1914.
Weygandt, C. *Irish Plays and Playwrights.* Boston, 1913.
Yeats, W. B. Collected Works, vol. IV, 1908, including *The Irish Dramatic Movement; Samhain.*

SIR JAMES MATTHEW BARRIE

Browne, E. A. "Barrie's Dramatic and Social Outlook." *Fortnightly,* May, 1906.
Walkley, A. B. *Drama and Life.* London, 1908.
Williams, J. D. "The Charm that is Barrie." *Century Magazine,* Oct., 1914.

GEORGE BERNARD SHAW

Bab, J. *Bernard Shaw.* Berlin, 1910.
Chesterton, G. K. *George Bernard Shaw.* London, 1910.
Hale, E. E., Jr. *Dramatists of To-day.* New York, 1911.
Hamon, A. F. *The Technique of Bernard Shaw's Plays.* London, 1912.
Henderson, A. *George Bernard Shaw, his Life and Works.* Cincinnati, 1911.
Huneker, J. *Iconoclasts: A Book of Dramatists.* New York, 1905.
Jackson, H. *Bernard Shaw: a Study and an Appreciation.* London, 1907.
McCabe, J. *George Bernard Shaw.* London, 1914.
Walkley, A. B. *Drama and Life.* London, 1908.
See Shaw's *Dramatic Opinions and Essays,* 1907; *The Quintessence of Ibsenism,* 1891, 1913; Introductions
   to published plays; and Introduction to the English edition of *Three Plays by Brieux,* 1911.

CLYDE FITCH

Bell, A. *The Clyde Fitch I Knew.* New York, 1909.
Eaton, W. P. *At the New Theater and Others.* Boston, 1910.
Moses, M. J. *The American Dramatist.* New York, 1911.
Ruhl, A. *Second Nights.* New York, 1913.

WILLIAM VAUGHN MOODY

Barr, N. O., and Caffin, C. H. "William Vaughn Moody," *The Drama,* May, 1911.
Manly, J. M. Introduction to *Poems and Plays of William Vaughn Moody.* Boston, 1913.
Ruhl, A. *Second Nights.* New York, 1913.

AUGUSTUS THOMAS

Moses, M. J. *The American Dramatist.* New York, 1911.
Ruhl, A. *Second Nights.* New York, 1913.
Winter, W. *The Wallet of Time,* vol. II. New York, 1913.

PERCY MACKAYE

Moses, M. J. *The American Dramatist.* New York, 1911.
See MacKaye's *The Playhouse and the Play,* 1909; *The Civic Theatre,* 1913; Introduction to *The Scarecrow,*
   Macmillan edition.

GERHART HAUPTMANN

Bartels, A. *Gerhart Hauptmann.* Weimar, 1897.
Dukes, A. *Modern Dramatists.* Chicago, 1912.
Friedmann, S. *Das deutsche Drama des 19 Jahrhunderts.* Leipzig, 1903.
Hale, E. E., Jr. *Dramatists of To-day.* New York, 1911.
Holl, K. *Gerhart Hauptmann, his Life and Work.* London, 1913.
Huneker, J. *Iconoclasts: A Book of Dramatists.* New York, 1905.
Lessing, O. E. *Masters of Modern German Literature.* New York, 1912.
Lewisohn, L. Introductions to *Hauptmann's Dramatic Works.* New York, 1912–15.

Muret, M. *La Littérature Allemande d'Aujourd'hui.* Paris, 1909.
Röhr, J. *Gerhart Hauptmann's dramatisches Schaffen.* Dresden, 1912.
Schlenther, P. *Gerhart Hauptmann.* Berlin, 1898.
Steiger, E. *Das Werden des neuen Dramas.* Berlin, 1898.
Sternberg, K. *Gerhart Hauptmann.* Berlin, 1910.
Stoeckius, A. *Naturalism in Recent German Drama.* New York, 1903.
Spiero, H. *Gerhart Hauptmann.* Bielefeld, 1913.
Witkowski, G. *The German Drama of the Nineteenth Century.* New York, 1909.
Woerner, U. C. *Gerhart Hauptmann.* Berlin, 1901.
See Garnett Smith, "Contemporary German Drama," *Quarterly Review,* 1914.

HERMANN SUDERMANN

Axelrod, I. *Hermann Sudermann; eine Studie.* Stuttgart, 1907.
Bulthaupt, H. A. *Dramaturgie des Schauspiels.* Oldenburg, 1902–05.
Friedmann, S. *Das deutsche Drama des 19 Jahrhunderts.* Leipzig, 1903.
Hale, E. E., Jr. *Dramatists of To-day.* New York, 1911.
Huneker, J. *Iconoclasts; A Book of Dramatists.* New York, 1905.
Kawerau, W. *Hermann Sudermann; eine Kritische Studie.* Leipzig, 1897.
Litzmann, B. *Das deutsche Drama.* Hamburg, 1894.
Schoen, H. *Hermann Sudermann, Poete dramatique et Romancier.* Paris, 1905.
Witkowski, G. *The German Drama of the Nineteenth Century.* New York, 1909.
See Sudermann's *Verrohung in der Theaterkritik.* Berlin, 1902.

EUGÈNE BRIEUX

Baker, G. P. "The Plays of Eugène Brieux," *Atlantic Monthly,* July, 1902.
Benoist, A. *Le Théâtre d'Aujourd'hui.* Paris, 1911, 1912.
Bertrand, A. *E. Brieux.* Paris, 1910.
Doumic, R. *Le Théâtre nouveau.* Paris, 1908.
Dukes, A. *Modern Dramatists.* Chicago, 1912.
Sarcey, F. *Quarante Ans de Théâtre,* vol. VII. Paris, 1902.
Shaw, G. B. Preface to *Three Plays by Brieux.* New York, 1911.
Sorel, H. E. *Essais de Psychologie dramatique.* Paris, 1910.

PAUL HERVIEU

Benoist, A. *Le Théâtre d'Aujourd'hui.* Paris, 1911, 1912.
Binet, A. *L'Année psychologique,* vol. x. Paris, 1904.
Doumic, R. *Les Jeunes.* Paris, 1913.
     Le Théâtre nouveau. Paris, 1908.
Gregh, F. *La Fenêtre ouverte.* Paris, 1901.
Huneker, J. *Iconoclasts: A Book of Dramatists.* New York, 1905.
Sarcey, F. *Quarante Ans de Théâtre,* vol. VII. Paris, 1902.

MAURICE MAETERLINCK

Beaunier, A. *La Poésie nouvelle.* Paris, 1902.
Benoist, A. *Le Théâtre d'Aujourd'hui.* Paris, 1912.
Buschmann, J. *Maurice Maeterlinck, eine Studie.* Leipzig, 1908.
Doumic, R. *Les Jeunes.* Paris, 1913.
Hale, E. E., Jr. *Dramatists of To-day.* New York, 1911.
Harry, G. *Maurice Maeterlinck.* Brussels, 1909.
Huneker, J. *Iconoclasts: A Book of Dramatists.* New York, 1905.
Leneveu, G. *Ibsen et Maeterlinck.* Paris, 1902.
Sehring, L. *Maeterlinck als Philosoph und Dichter.* Berlin, 1908.
Symons, A. *The Symbolist Movement in Literature.* New York, 1908.
Thomas, E. *Maurice Maeterlinck.* New York, 1911.
Van Bever, A. *Maurice Maeterlinck.* Paris, 1904.
See Maeterlinck's essays in *The Treasure of the Humble; The Double Garden; Wisdom and Destiny; On Emerson and Other Essays.* Introduction to *Pélléas and Mélisande.*

BJÖRNSTJERNE BJÖRNSON

Bernardini, L. *La Littérature Scandinave.* Paris, 1894.
Boyeson, H. H. *Essays on Scandinavian Literature.* New York, 1905.
Brandes, G. *Ibsen-Björnson Studies.* London, 1899.

Collin, Chr. *Björnstjerne Björnson.* German ed. Leipzig, 1903.
Kahle, B. *Henrik Ibsen, B. Björnson und ihre Zeitgenossen.* Leipzig, 1908.
Payne, W. M. *Björnstjerne Björnson.* Chicago, 1910.
See essay on *Beyond Human Power* by L. M. Hollander in *The Drama*, February, 1914.

AUGUST STRINDBERG

Babillotte, A. *August Strindberg.* Leipzig, 1910.
Bernardini, L. *La Littérature Scandinave.* Paris, 1894.
Esswein, H. *August Strindberg.* Munich, 1909.
Huneker, J. *Iconoclasts: A Book of Dramatists.* New York, 1905.
Lind-af-Hageby, L. *August Strindberg: the Spirit of Revolt.* London, 1913.
See Björkman, E. "August Strindberg," *The Forum*, February, March, 1912. Introductions to English translations of *Plays*. New York, 1912 ff. See McCarthy, J. H., "August Strindberg," *Fortnightly Review*, 1892.
See Strindberg's autobiographical *Son of a Servant, Confessions of a Fool, Inferno*, and *Legends.* New York, 1913. *See* his Preface to *Miss Julia. See* his *Dramaturgie;* German edition translated by Emil Schering. Munich, 1911.

ANTON TCHEKHOV

Baring, M. *Landmarks in Russian Literature.* London, 1910.
Brückner, A. *A Literary History of Russia.* New York, 1908.
Dukes, A. *Modern Dramatists*, Chicago, 1912.
Phelps, W. L. *Essays on Russian Novelists.* New York, 1911.
See Introductions to Calderon's Translation of *Two Plays by Tchekhov*, London, 1912; *The Kiss and Other Stories*, translated by R. E. C. Long, New York, 1912; *Plays*, translated by Marian Fell, New York, 1912; *The Cherry Garden*, translated by M. S. Mandell, New Haven, 1908.

IV. A WORKING BOOK LIST IN CONTEMPORARY DRAMA

BIBLIOGRAPHIES

Adams, W. D. *A Dictionary of the Drama, A–G.* Philadelphia, 1904.
Arnold, R. F. "Bibliographie der Deut. Bühnen seit 1830," in *Das. moderne Drama.* Strassburg, 1908.
Chandler, F. W. *Aspects of Modern Drama,* Appendix. New York, 1914.
Clapp, J. B., and Edgett, E. F. *Plays of the Present.* Dunlap Society Publications, 1902.
Clarence, R. *The Stage Cyclopedia.* London, 1909.
Faxon, F. W. *Dramatic Index.* Boston, 1909 ff.
Pence, J. H. *The Magazine and the Drama: an Index.* Dunlap Society Publications, vol. XVII. New York, 1896.
Scott, C. *The Drama of Yesterday and To-day,* Appendix. London, 1899.

THEORY AND TECHNIQUE OF DRAMA AND THEATER

Archer, W. *Playmaking, A Manual of Craftsmanship.* Boston, 1912.
Avonianus (R. Hessen). *Dramatische Handwerkslehre.* Berlin, 1902.
Baker, G. P. *Technique of the Drama.* Boston, 1915.
Brisson, A. *Le Théâtre et les Mœurs.* Paris, 1906 ff.
Bulthaupt, H. A. *Dramaturgie des Schauspiels.* Oldenburg, 1898.
Burton, R. *How to See a Play.* New York, 1914.
Caffin, C. H. *The Appreciation of the Drama.* New York, 1908.
Carter, H. *The New Spirit in Drama and Art.* New York, 1913.
    The Theatre of Max Reinhardt. New York, 1914.
Craig, E. G. *On the Art of the Theatre.* Chicago, 1911.
    Towards a New Theatre. London, 1913.
Faguet, E. *Drame ancien; Drame moderne* Paris, 1898.
Hamilton, C. M. *The Theory of the Theatre.* New York, 1910.
    Studies in Stagecraft. New York, 1914.
Matthews, B. *A Study of the Drama.* Boston, 1910.
Moderwell, H. K. *The Theatre To-day.* New York, 1914.
Palmer, J. *The Future of the Theatre.* London, 1913.
Price, W. T. *Technique of the Drama.* New York, 1897.
    Analysis of Play Construction and Dramatic Principle. New York, 1908.
Rolland, R. *Le Théâtre du Peuple, Essai d'esthétique.* Paris, 1913.
Savits, J. *Von der Absicht des Dramas.* Munich, 1908.
Schlag, H. *Das Drama, Wesen, Theorie. und Technic.* Essen, 1909.
Shaw, G. B. *Dramatic Opinions and Essays.* 1907.
Strindberg, A. *Dramaturgie.* Translated into German by E. Schering. Munich, 1911.
Symons, A. *Plays, Acting, and Music.* 1909.
Walkley, A. B. *Drama and Life.* London, 1907.
Zabel, E. *Zur modernen Dramaturgie.* Oldenburg, 1903.

AUTHORS AND DRAMATIC MOVEMENTS

Archer, W. *English Dramatists of To-day.* London, 1882.
Arnold, R. F. *Das moderne Drama.* Strassburg, 1908.
Benoist, A. *Le Théâtre d'Aujourd'hui.* Paris, 1911.
Benoist-Hanappier, L. *Le Drame naturaliste en Allemagne.* Paris, 1905.
Bernardini, L. *La Littérature Scandinave.* Paris, 1894.
Besson, P. *Études sur le Théâtre contemporain en Allemagne.* Paris, 1900.
Björkman, E. *Voices of To-morrow.* New York, 1913.
Burton, R. *The New American Drama.* New York, 1913.
Chandler, F. W. *Aspects of Modern Drama.* New York, 1914.
Cheney, S. *The New Movement in the Theatre.* New York, 1914.
Clark, B. *Continental Dramatists of To-day.* New York, 1914.
Doumic, R. *De Scribe à Ibsen.* Paris, 1893.
    Essais sur le Théâtre contemporain. Paris, 1896.
    Le Théâtre nouveau. Paris, 1908.
    Les Jeunes. Paris, 1913.

Dukes, A. *Modern Dramatists*. Chicago, 1912.
Filon, A. *The English Stage*. London, 1897.
Fowell, F., and Palmer, F. *Censorship in England*. 1913.
Friedmann, S. *Das deutsche Drama des 19 Jahrhunderts*. Leipzig, 1903.
Gregory, Lady A. *Our Irish Theatre*. 1913.
Hale, E. E., Jr. *Dramatists of To-day*. 1911.
Henderson, A. *European Dramatists*. New York, 1911.
    The Changing Drama. New York, 1914.
Huneker, J. *Iconoclasts: A Book of Dramatists*. New York, 1905.
Kahn, A. *Le Théâtre social en France de 1870 à nos Jours*. Paris, 1907.
Keinzl, H. *Dramen der Gegenwart*. Graz, 1905.
Kerr, A. *Das Neue Drama*. Berlin, 1905.
Krans, H. S. *William Butler Yeats and the Irish Literary Revival*. New York, 1904.
Lemaître, J. *Impressions de Théâtre*. Paris, 1888–1901. 10 vols.
Litzmann, B. *Das deutsche Drama*. Hamburg, 1897.
Moore, G. *Hail and Farewell*. 3 vols. London, 1911 ff.
Moses, M. J. *The American Dramatist*. New York, 1911.
Pollard, P. *Masks and Minstrels of New Germany*. Boston, 1911.
Sarcey, F. *Quarante Ans de Théâtre*. Paris, 1900. Vols. VII, VIII.
Scott, C. *Drama of Yesterday and To-day*. London, 1899.
Séché, A. *L'Évolution du Théâtre contemporain*. Paris, 1908.
Steiger, E. *Das Werden des neuen Dramas*. Berlin, 1898.
Stoeckius, A. *Naturalism in Recent German Drama*. New York, 1903.
Weitbrecht, C. *Das deutsche Drama*. Berlin, 1900.
Weygandt, C. *Irish Plays and Playwrights*. Boston, 1913.
Winter, W. *The Wallet of Time*. New York, 1913.
Witkowski, G. *German Drama of the Nineteenth Century*. New York, 1909.
Zola, E. *Le Naturalisme au Théâtre, les Théories et les Exemples*. Paris, 1912.

ORGANIZATION AND THE THEATER

Archer, W., and Barker, H. G. *Scheme and Estimates for a National Theatre*. London, 1908.
Howe, P. P. *The Repertory Theatre: A Record and a Criticism*. London, 1911.
Jones, H. A. *The Renascence of the English Drama*. London, 1895.
    Foundations of a National Drama. London, 1912.
McCarthy, D. *The Court Theatre, 1904–07*. London, 1907.
MacKaye, P. *The Playhouse and the Play*. New York, 1909.
    The Civic Theatre. New York, 1913.
Thalasso, A. *Le Théâtre libre; essai critique, historique et documentaire*. Paris, 1909.

V. INDEX OF CHARACTERS

Andrew Gibbard. *Michael and his Lost Angel.*
Rose Gibbard. *Michael and his Lost Angel.*
Fräulein Göhre. **Woman** Teacher. *The Vale of Content.*
Golaud. Grandson of Arkël. Husband of Mélisande. *Pélléas and Mélisande.*
Mr. Cecil Graham. *Lady Windermere's Fan.*
James Green. A Trenartha workman. *Strife.*

Simon Harness. A Trades-Union official. *Strife.*
Heiber. A weaver. *The Weavers.*
Heide. A Police Superintendent. *The Weavers.*
Mrs. Heinrich. A weaver. *The Weavers.*
Gottlieb Hilse. A weaver. *The Weavers.*
Luise Hilse. A weaver. Wife of Gottlieb Hilse. *The Weavers.*
Mother Hilse. A weaver. *The Weavers.*
Old Hilse. A weaver. *The Weavers.*
Mr. Hopper. *Lady Windermere's Fan.*
Hornig. A rag-dealer. *The Weavers.*
Catherine Huxtable. *The Madras House.*
Clara Huxtable. *The Madras House.*
Emma Huxtable. *The Madras House.*
Henry Huxtable. *The Madras House.*
Jane Huxtable. *The Madras House.*
Julia Huxtable. *The Madras House.*
Laura Huxtable. *The Madras House.*
Minnie Huxtable. *The Madras House.*

Moritz Jaeger. A weaver. *The Weavers.*
Jago. A Trenartha workman. *Strife.*
Jan. A boy of ten. Madge Underwood's brother. Trenartha. *Strife.*
Janitor of the Court. *The Red Robe.*
Gordon Jayne, M.D. *The Second Mrs. Tanqueray.*
Lady Jedburgh. *Lady Windermere's Fan.*
Jensen. A minister. *Beyond Human Power.*
John. Coachman in Dreissiger's employ. *The Weavers.*
Philip Jordan. *The Great Divide.*
Polly Jordan. Wife of Philip. *The Great Divide.*
Mrs. Jordan. Mother of Philip Jordan. *The Great Divide.*
Judge of the Assizes. *The Red Robe.*

Pastor Kittelhaus. *The Weavers.*
Mrs. Kittelhaus. *The Weavers.*
Kroyer. A minister. *Beyond Human Power.*
Kutsche. A policeman. *The Weavers.*

Edward Lashmar. (Father Hilary.) *Michael and his Lost Angel.*
Laura. Wife of the Cavalry Captain. *The Father.*
Audrie Lesden. *Michael and his Lost Angel.*
Lewis. A Trenartha workman. *Strife.*
Lindon. *The Truth.*
Eve Lindon. *The Truth.*
Lopákhin. A merchant. *The Cherry Orchard.*
Lord Augustus Lorton. *Lady Windermere's Fan.*

Amelia Madras. *The Madras House.*
Constantine Madras. *The Madras House.*
Jessica Madras. *The Madras House.*
Philip Madras. *The Madras House.*
Maid. In Dreissiger's employ. *The Weavers.*
Maurya. An old woman. *Riders to the Sea.*
Mélisande. *Pélléas and Mélisande.*

Mistress Cynthia Merton. Sister of Justice Merton. *The Scarecrow.*
Justice Gilead Merton. *The Scarecrow.*
Rachel Merton. Niece of Justice Merton. *The Scarecrow.*
A Mexican. *The Great Divide.*
Micah. A servant of Justice Merton. *The Scarecrow.*
Mielchen. Daughter of Gottlieb and Luise Hilse. Six years old. A weaver. *The Weavers.*
Frank Misquith, Q.C., M.P. *The Second Mrs. Tanqueray.*
Mondoubleau. A Deputy. *The Red Robe.*
Morse. A Servant. *The Second Mrs. Tanqueray.*
Mouzon. Examining Magistrate. *The Red Robe.*

Neumann. Cashier in the employment of Dreissiger. *The Weavers.*
Dr. Newberry. Father of Winthrop Newberry. *The Great Divide.*
Winthrop Newberry. *The Great Divide.*
Nora. Younger daughter of Maurya. *Riders to the Sea.*
Nöjd. *The Father.*
The Nurse. *The Father.*

Dr. Orb. School Inspector. *The Vale of Content.*
Frau Orb. *The Vale of Content.*
An Orderly. *The Father.*
Sir George Orreyed, Bart. *The Second Mrs. Tanqueray.*
Lady Orreyed. *The Second Mrs. Tanqueray.*
Dr. Östermark. *The Father.*

Parker. A Butler. *Lady Windermere's Fan.*
Parlormaid at Underwood's. Trenartha. *Strife.*
The Pastor. *The Father.*
Paula. Second wife of Aubrey Tanqueray. *The Second Mrs. Tanqueray.*
Pavail. *Know Thyself.*
A Peasant. *The Weavers.*
Pélléas. Grandson of Arkël. Brother of Golaud. *Pélléas and Mélisande.*
Pfeifer. Manager in the employ of Dreissiger. *The Weavers.*
A Physician. *Pélléas and Mélisande.*
Placet. Counsel for the Defense. *The Red Robe.*
Lady Plymdale. *Lady Windermere's Fan.*
Policeman B. *The Rising of the Moon.*
Policeman X. *The Rising of the Moon.*
Police Officer. *The Red Robe.*
The Porter. *Pélléas and Mélisande.*
Some Pupils. *The Hour-Glass.*

Rachel. Daughter of Pastor Sang; twin sister of Elias. *Beyond Human Power.*
A Ragged Man. *The Rising of the Moon.*
Reverend Master Rand of Harvard College. *The Scarecrow.*
Madame Ranévsky. A landowner. *The Cherry Orchard.*
Lord Ravensbane. ("Marquis of Oxford, Baron of Wittenberg, Elector of Worms, and Count of Cordova.") Hypothetical son of Justice Merton. *The Scarecrow.*
A Red-haired youth. A workman. Trenartha. *Strife.*

Amelia Reddington. Daughter of Sir Charles Reddington. *The Scarecrow.*

Sir Charles Reddington. Lieutenant-Governor of the Colony of Massachusetts. *The Scarecrow.*

Mistress Reddington. Elder daughter of Sir Charles Reddington. *The Scarecrow.*

Goody Rickby. ("Blacksmith Bess.") *The Scarecrow.*

Riemann. A weaver. *The Weavers.*

Annie Roberts. Wife of David Roberts. Trenartha. *Strife.*

David Roberts. Member of the workmen's committee, Trenartha Tin Plate Works. *Strife.*

Mrs. Hannah Roberts. Sister of Mrs. Sang. *Beyond Human Power.*

Bettina von Röcknitz. *The Vale of Content.*

Freiherr von Röcknitz of Witzlingen. *The Vale of Content.*

Roland. *The Truth.*

Rosa. Maid at Wiedemann's. *The Vale of Content.*

Rosalie. A Maid. *Lady Windermere's Fan.*

George Rous. Member of the workmen's committee, Trenartha Tin Plate Works. *Strife.*

Henry Rous. A workman. *Strife.*

Mrs. Rous. Mother of George and Henry Rous. *Strife.*

Captain Rugby. Secretary of Sir Charles Reddington. *The Scarecrow.*

Pastor Adolph Sang. *Beyond Human Power.*

Clara Sang. Wife of Pastor Sang. *Beyond Human Power.*

William Scantlebury. Director of Trenartha Tin Plate Works. *Strife.*

Schmidt. A surgeon. *The Weavers.*

Sergeant. *The Rising of the Moon.*

Clarisse de Sibéran. *Know Thyself.*

General de Sibéran. *Know Thyself.*

Jean, son of General de Sibéran. *Know Thyself.*

Simeónof-Píshtchik. A landowner. *The Cherry Orchard.*

Eustace Perrin State. *The Madras House.*

Lady Stutfield. *Lady Windermere's Fan.*

Richard Talbot, Esquire. Betrothed to Rachel Merton. *The Scarecrow.*

Aubrey Tanqueray. *The Second Mrs. Tanqueray.*

Henry Tench. Secretary of Trenartha Tin Plate Works. *Strife.*

Henry Thomas. Member of the workmen's committee, Trenartha Tin Plate Works. *Strife.*

Major Hippesley Thomas. *The Madras House.*

Madge Thomas. Daughter of Henry Thomas. Trenartha. *Strife.*

Reverend Master Todd of Harvard College. *The Scarecrow.*

Tramp. *The Cherry Orchard.*

Peter Trophímof. A student. *The Cherry Orchard.*

Enid Underwood. Wife of Francis Underwood. Daughter of John Anthony. Trenartha. *Strife.*

Francis Underwood, C.E. Manager of Trenartha Tin Plate Works. *Strife.*

Vagret. Public Prosecutor, Court of the Third Class. *The Red Robe.*

Bertha Vagret. Daughter of Public Prosecutor Vagret. *The Red Robe.*

Madame Vagret. Wife of Public Prosecutor Vagret. *The Red Robe.*

Oliver Wanklin. Director of Trenartha Tin Plate Works. *Strife.*

Warder. *The Truth.*

Becky Warder. *The Truth.*

Weigand. A joiner. *The Weavers.*

Weinhold. Tutor to Dreissiger's sons. *The Weavers.*

Welzel. A publican. *The Weavers.*

Mrs. Welzel. *The Weavers.*

Anna Welzel. Their daughter. *The Weavers.*

The Old Widow. *Beyond Human Power.*

Wiedemann. Principal of Intermediate School. *The Vale of Content.*

Elizabeth Wiedemann. His second wife. *The Vale of Content.*

Helene, Fritz, Emil Wiedemann. Children of Wiedemann by his first wife. *The Vale of Content.*

Frederic H. Wilder. Director of Trenartha Tin Plate Works. *Strife.*

Burt Williams. *The Great Divide.*

Lady Windermere. *Lady Windermere's Fan.*

Lord Windermere. *Lady Windermere's Fan.*

Mr. Windlesham. *The Madras House.*

A Wise Man. *The Hour-Glass.*

The Wise Man's Wife and Two Children. *The Hour-Glass.*

Withycombe. *Michael and his Lost Angel.*

Wittig. A Smith. *The Weavers.*

Yásha. A young manservant. *The Cherry Orchard.*

Marion Yates. *The Madras House.*

Mrs. Yeo. Wife of a workman, Trenartha Tin Plate Works. *Strife.*

Little Yniold. Son of Golaud by a former marriage. *Pélléas and Mélisande.*